Dari-English Dictionary
First Edition

Mustafa Ajan Sayd

Dari-English Dictionary
First Edition

Mustafa Ajan Sayd

2009

Dari-English Dictionary, First Edition
Copyright © 2009 McNeil Technologies, Inc.

All rights reserved.

No part of this work may be reproduced or transmitted in any form or by any means, electronic or mechanical, including photocopying and recording, or by any information storage and retrieval system, without the prior written permission of McNeil Technologies, Inc.

All inquiries should be directed to:

Dunwoody Press
6525 Belcrest Rd, Suite 460
Hyattsville, MD 20782
USA

ISBN: 978-1-931546-69-0
Library of Congress Catalog Card Number: 2009937482
Printed and bound in the United States of America

Table of Contents

Preface i
Sample Entry ii
Pronunciation Guide iii
Labels
   Domains iv
   Grammar and Usage iv
The Dictionary
   ا, آ 1
   ب 27
   پ 51
   ت 71
   ٹ 91
   ج 91
   چ 107
   ح 119
   خ 125
   د 138
   ذ 159
   ر 161
   ز 172
   ژ 177
   س 177
   ش 193
   ص 203
   ض 206
   ط 207
   ظ 210
   ع 210
   غ 217
   ف 219
   ق 226
   ک 234
   گ 246
   ل 252
   م 256
   ن 279
   و 294
   ہ 298
   ی 302

Preface

This Dari-English Dictionary (First Edition) is based primarily on the *Dari-Russkiĭ slovar* (L. N. Kiseleva and Mikolaĭchik, V. I., 1978, 744 pages, Russian Language Publishing House, Moscow). The dictionary has been adapted and updated for an English-speaking audience. It is best used in combination with the *Dari-English Dictionary* (Qāmūs-i Darī-Inglīsī, Mohammad Nasim Neghat, principal investigator, University of Nebraska at Omaha, Center for Afghanistan Studies, xxv, 807 p, 1993).

This dictionary is intended for professional Dari-to-English translators. Explanations of Dari grammar, syntax, regional usages, and the like are not treated exhaustively in this dictionary. *Dari for Foreigners* (Center for Afghanistan Studies, University of Nebraska at Omaha) and the forthcoming Dunwoody Press publication *A Basic Dari Grammar* are recommended to students of Dari as supplements to this dictionary.

This dictionary will form the basis of revised editions to be published in the near future. New editions will feature neologisms, slang, and technical vocabularies. As part of the ongoing revisions, we welcome any comments, corrections, and additions to make this dictionary even more useful.

The Publisher
Dunwoody Press
Hyattsville, MD 20782
September 2009

Sample Entry

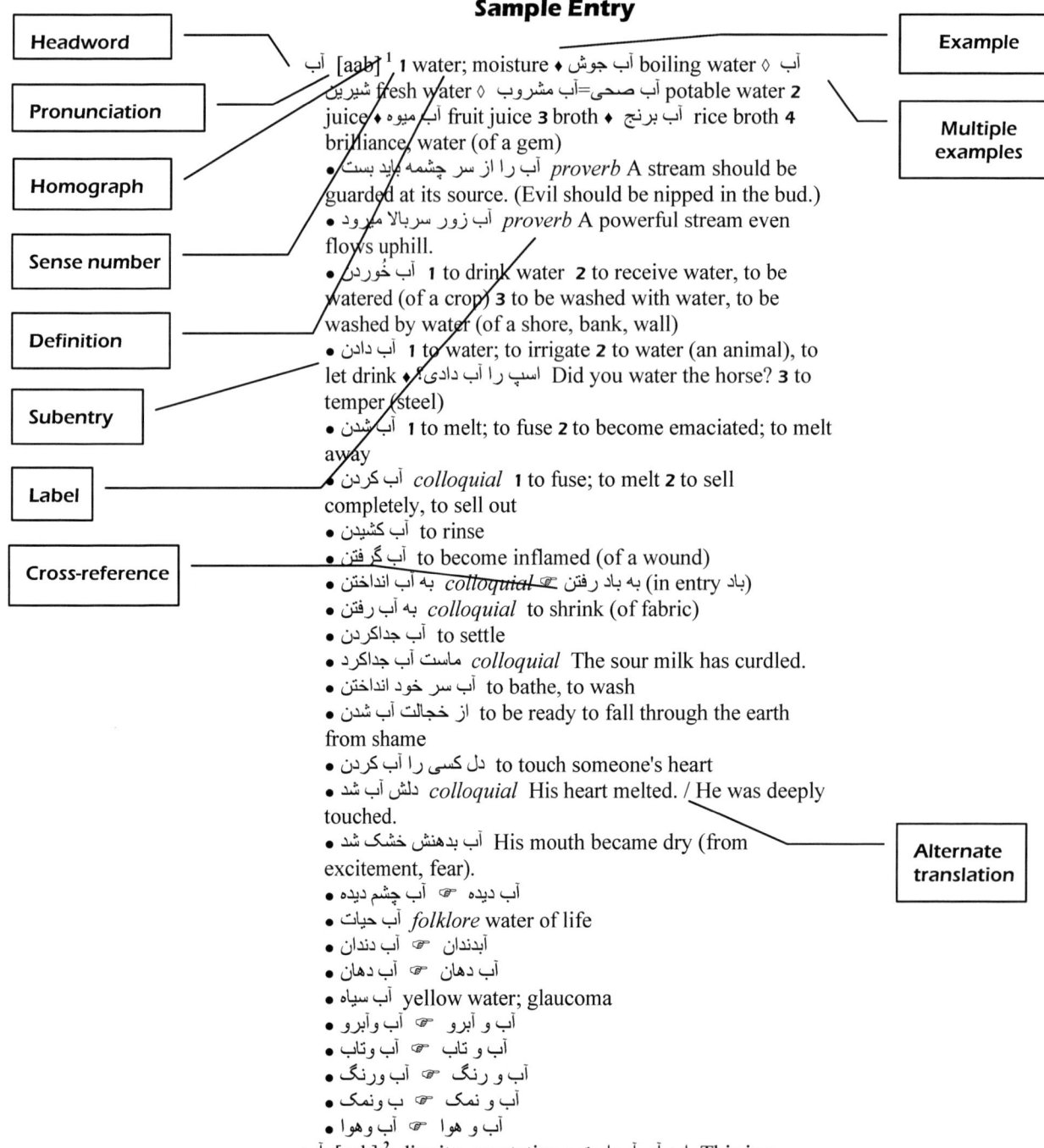

Dari-English Dictionary
First Edition

Mustafa Ajan Sayd

2009

Dari-English Dictionary, First Edition
Copyright © 2009 McNeil Technologies, Inc.

All rights reserved.

No part of this work may be reproduced or transmitted in any form or by any means, electronic or mechanical, including photocopying and recording, or by any information storage and retrieval system, without the prior written permission of McNeil Technologies, Inc.

All inquiries should be directed to:

Dunwoody Press
6525 Belcrest Rd, Suite 460
Hyattsville, MD 20782
USA

ISBN: 978-1-931546-69-0
Library of Congress Catalog Card Number: 2009937482
Printed and bound in the United States of America

Pronunciation Guide

Letter	Phonetic
ا, آ	a, aa
ب	b
پ	p
ت	t
ث	s
ج	j
چ	ch
ح	h
خ	kh
د	d
ذ	z
ر	r
ز	z
ژ	zh
س	s
ش	sh
ص	s
ض	z
ط	t
ظ	z
ع	a, o, e,
غ	gh
ف	f
ق	q
ک	k
گ	g
ل	l
م	m
ن	n
و	u, o, w, oo
ه	a, h
ی	i, y, ee

Labels

Domains	Grammar and Usage
agriculture	*abbreviation*
anatomy	*adjective*
astronomy	*adverb*
biology	*conjunction*
botany	*colloquial*
chemistry	*denominative*
diplomacy	*epistolary*
economics	*feminine*
electronics	*interjection*
finance/banking	*intransitive*
geography	*masculine*
geology	*obscure*
grammar	*opposite*
history	*plural*
law	*preposition*
literature/literary	*proverb*
linguistics	*slang*
mathematics	*suffix*
medicine	*transitive*
military	
music	
philosophy	
physics	
politics	
religion	
technical/technology	

آ, ا
1st letter of the Dari alphabet

آ [aa] ¹ ☞ آی

آ [aa] ² *colloquial* ☞ ها

اً [an] tanwin (*adverb suffix*) ♦ رسماً officially

آب [aab] ¹ **1** water; moisture ♦ آب جوش boiling water ◊ آب شیرین fresh water ♦ آب صحی=آب مشروب potable water **2** juice ♦ آب میوه fruit juice **3** broth ♦ آب برنج rice broth **4** brilliance, water (of a gem)

• آب را از سر چشمه باید بست *proverb* A stream should be guarded at its source. (Evil should be nipped in the bud.)

• آب زور سربالا میرود *proverb* A powerful stream even flows uphill.

• آب خُوردن **1** to drink water **2** to receive water, to be watered (of a crop) **3** to be washed with water, to be washed by water (of a shore, bank, wall)

• آب دادن **1** to water; to irrigate **2** to water (an animal), to let drink ♦ اسپ را آب دادی؟ Did you water the horse? **3** to temper (steel)

• آب شدن **1** to melt; to fuse **2** to become emaciated; to melt away

• آب کردن *colloquial* **1** to fuse; to melt **2** to sell completely, to sell out

• آب کشیدن to rinse

• آب گرفتن to become inflamed (of a wound)

• به آب انداختن ☞ به باد رفتن (in entry باد) *colloquial*

• به آب رفتن *colloquial* to shrink (of fabric)

• آب جداکردن to settle

• ماست آب جداکرد *colloquial* The sour milk has curdled.

• آب سر خود انداختن to bathe, to wash

• از خجالت آب شدن to be ready to fall through the earth from shame

• دل کسی را آب کردن to touch someone's heart

• دلش آب شد *colloquial* His heart melted. / He was deeply touched.

• آب دهنش خشک شد His mouth became dry (from excitement, fear).

• آب دیده ☞ چشم دیده

• آب حیات *folklore* water of life

• آب دندان ☞ آبدندان

• آب دهان ☞ آب دندان

• آب سیاه yellow water; glaucoma

• آب و آبرو ☞ آب وآبرو

• آب و تاب ☞ آب وتاب

• آب و رنگ ☞ آب ورنگ

• آب و نمک ☞ آب ونمک

• آب و هوا ☞ آب وهوا

آب [aab] ² dignity, reputation ♦ این آدم آب است This is a worthy man. / This is a man of honor.

اب [ab] (*plural* آبا [aabaa]) father ♦ آبا و اجداد fathers and grandfathers, ancestors

آبا [aabaa] *plural of* اب

اباء [ebaa] *literary* refusal (ورزیدن)
• اباء کردن (از) to refuse

آباد [aabaad] **1** settled in; well appointed ♦ شهر آباد well planned city or town ◊ مملکت آباد prosperous country **2** cultivated, tilled ♦ زمین آباد cultivated land **3** fat, fattened (of livestock) **4** (*opposite of* پاره پاره) *colloquial* whole (e.g., of clothing) **5** solvent, well-to-do

• آباد کردن **1** to settle, to populate; to build up **2** to cultivate, to till (land) **3** to build, to erect (a building, etc.)

• خانه آباد! Happiness and prosperity to this house! (greeting)

آبادی [aabaadi] **1** construction; development (of land) **2** fatness (of livestock) **3** inhabited place; village

ابایی [abaayi] fatherly
• وطن ابایی father's homeland, fatherland

آب باز [aabbaaz] swimmer

آب بازک [aabbaazak] *technical* float

آب بازی [aabbaazi] **1** bathing; swimming ♦ حوض آب بازی swimming pool **2** water sport, water sports
• آب بازی کردن to bathe; to swim

آب بره [aabbora] gully

آب پاش [aabpaash] **1** sprinkler **2** (*also* موتر آب پاش) sprinkler truck, watering truck

آب پاشی [aabpaashi] sprinkling or watering (of streets)

ابتداء [ebtedaa] **1.1** beginning; initial stage **1.2** *literary* the first foot of the second measure of a stanza (☞ رکن) **2** (*also* در ابتدا) at first, initially

ابتدائی [ebtedaayi] **1** initial, original ♦ مکتب ابتدائی primary school (up to seventh grade) **2** primitive, elementary **3** junior; lower; inferior (in rank or standing) **4** *chemistry* primary
• در یک کار ابتدائی بودن *colloquial* to barely understand, to poorly understand (something)

ابتر [abtar] wretched, hopeless; miserable
• ابتر شدن *colloquial* to live in poverty, to be in need

آبترازو [aabtaraazu] level (device), (surveyor's) leveling instrument

ابتکار [ebtekaar] **1** understanding; initiative **2** innovation
• ابتکار کردن to show initiative, to manifest initiative

ابتکاری [ebtekaari]
• عمل ابتکاری and کار ابتکاری understanding initiative *adjective*

ابجد [abjad] (*also* حساب ابجد) abjad (system of counting based on the numerical value of letters arranged in a definite order: ا. ب. ج.د)

آب جواز [aabjowaaz] water rice scourer, stamper

آب جاش [aabjaash] **1** abjush (kind of large light-colored raisin) **2** light-colored, small, seedless raisin, currants

آب جوش [aabejosh] boiling water

آب چرتک [aabchortak] squirter (child's toy)

آب چشم [aabecheshem] ☞ آب دیده

آبچکان [aabchakaan] moiré, watered velvet, plush

ابحار [abhaar] *plural of* بحر

آبخانه [aabkhaana] (*also* آبخانه آسیا) chute of a water mill
• آبخانه سلندر *technical* water jacket

آب خور [aabkhor] **1** feeding trough **2** ☞ آب خوره

آب خوره [aabkhora] **1** watering place **2** land irrigated from an irrigation ditch **3** abhura (amount of water needed to water a unit of area)

آب خوری [aabkhori] mug; (*also* ظرف آب خوری) ladle

آبخیز [aabkheez] *geology* water-bearing

آبخیزی [aabkheezi] high water, flood; overflow

ابد [abad] eternity ♦ باری ابد forever

آ, ١

ابداً [abadan] 1 (with negative predicate) never; by no means 2 *literary* eternally, constantly
آبدات [aabedaat] *plural of* آبده
آبدار [aabdaar] ¹ 1.1 watery, juicy 1.2 of the first water (of a gem) 1.3 tempered (of steel) 2 abdar (person in charge of irrigation)
• کلام آبدار a racy remark
آبدار [aabdaar] ² respected, worthy
آبداری [aabdaari] 1 tempering (of metal) 2 spreading of water during irrigation
ابداع [ebdaa] *literary* discovery, invention
ابدال [abdaal] 1 holy; hermit 2 *masculine proper name* Abdal
ابدالی [abdaali (and) awdaali] 1.1 Abdali (name of a group of Afghan tribes) 1.2 *historical* Eftalit *noun* 2 *historical* Eftalit *adjective*
آبدان [aabdaan] 1 tank, container for water 2 reservoir
• آبدان شیر دهن titanium
آب دست [aabedest (and) aabedast] *colloquial* ablution (ritualistic)
• آب دست کردن to perform ablution (ritualistic)
آب دندان [aabedandaan] lollipop, fruit-drop, sugar candy
آبده [aabeda] (*plural* آبدات [aabedaat]) 1 monument of antiquity 2 sanctuary; ancient temple
آب دهان [aabedahaan] saliva
ابدی [abadi] eternal
ابدیت [abadiyat] eternity
آبدیده [aabedida] tears
ابر [abr] 1 cloud; storm cloud ♦ ابر بارانی rain cloud 2 sponge (for washing)
ابراز [ebraaz] manifestation, revelation; expression ♦ ابراز قدردانی expression of acknowledgement
• ابراز کردن to manifest, to express
• ابراز مساعی کردن (در) to apply effort
آب رسانی [aabrasaani] delivery of water; water supply ♦ برج آب رسانی water tower ◊ موتر آب رسانی water truck ◊ نل آب رسانی water pipe, water main
آب رسیده [aabrasida]
• چونه آب رسیده slaked lime
آبرش [aabrash] 1 piebald (of horses) 2 multi-colored (of a bird, etc.)
ابرک [abrak] mica
• ابرک سفید muscovite, white mica
آب رو [aabraw] 1 (water) runoff; drainage ditch 2 aqueduct
• آب رو مستعمل = آب رو runoff channel ditch
آبرو [aabro] honor, reputation; prestige
• آبرو او ریخت He disgraced himself.
ابرو [abru] (*plural* ابروان [abrowaan]) brow; brows
• ابرو کشیدن *colloquial* to pencil one's eyebrows
• ابرو در هم کشیدن to frown
ابروکمان [abrukamaan] with arched eyebrows
ابروگک [abrugak]
• ابروگک زدن to signal with the eyebrows; to wink
آبرومند [aabomand] 1 honest 2 worthy, respected
آبرومندانه [aabromandaana] worthily, in a worthy manner
ابری [abri] *rare* cloudy
• کاغذ - marbleized paper (for binding books)
آبریز [aabreez] 1 drainage ditch, trench, gutter; runoff 2 leak (in a vessel, wall, etc.)

آبریزه [aabreeza] 1 *geography* basin, drainage area ♦ دریای کابل - basin or drainage area of the Kabul river 2 ☞ آبریز
ابریشم [abreeshom (and) abreeshem] silk; silk thread ♦ خام - raw silk
ابریشمی [abreeshomi] ☞ ابریشمین
ابریشمین [abreeshomin] silk *adjective*
ابزار [abzar] instruments; tools
آب زیر کاه [aabzeerekaah] 1 feigning demureness 2 crafty
آبستگی [aabestagi] pregnancy
آبستن [aabestan] pregnant
آبشار [aabshaar] waterfall
آبکش [aabkash] 1 cup (into which remnants of tea, etc., are poured) 2 dregs (of tea, etc.)
آبکشی [aabkashi] 1 rinsing (of laundry) 2 washing (of dishes)
آبکی [aabaki] liquid, watery ♦ ماست آبکی liquid sour milk
آب گردان [aabgardaan] 1 scoop, ladle 2 (also تونل آب گردان) drainage tunnel
آب گرمی [aabgarmi] electric boiler; water heater
آبگین [aabgin] 1 liquid, thin ♦ شیر آبگین watered milk 2 (*opposite* تبره) unbrewed, weak ♦ چای آبگین weak tea
ابلاغ [eblaagh]
• ابلاغ کردن to inform; to report
ابلاغیه [eblaaghiya] 1 notice, notification 2 official report; communique 3 appeal
ابلق [ablaq] 1 piebald (of a horse's coat) 2 variegated; two-colored 3 two-faced
آبله [aabela] 1 *medical* smallpox 2 pockmark 3 blister
• دستم آبله زد I got a blister on my hand.
• با آبله کف دست with a large amount of work, by the sweat of one's brow
ابله [ablah] 1 stupid 2 stupid person, simpleton
آبله کوبی [aabelakobi] smallpox vaccination
ابلیس [eblis] devil, Satan
آب میوه کشی [aabemeewakashi]
• ماشین آب میوه کشی juice extractor
ابن [ebn] (*plural* ابناء [abnaa] and بنی [bani]) *literary* son (in Arabic proper names) ♦ ابن سینا Ibn Sina: Avi Senna
ابنا [aabnaa] *geography* strait
ابناء [abnaa] (*plural of* ابن)
• ابناء بشر mankind, human kind
آب نارسیده [aabnaaresida]
• چونه آب نارسیده quick lime
ابن الوقت [ebnolwaqt] time-server, an unprincipled person who adroitly takes advantage of a situation
ابنیه [abniya] *plural of* بناء
ابو [abu] *literary* father (in Arabic proper names, nicknames, and titles) ♦ ابو بکر Abu Bakr
ابواب [abwaab] *plural of* باب ¹, 2
آب وآبرو [aaboaabro] honor, good name, reputation
ابو المعانی [abulma'aani] very wise, having achieved the essence [of being] (the title of a poet and philosopher in 17th-18th centuries, Bedil)
ابو الهول [abolhawl] sphinx
آب وتاب [aabotaab] brilliance; clarity, splendor
• با آب وتاب 1 brilliantly, with luster 2 grandiloquently
آب وخاک [aabokhaak] 1 land; country 2 homeland
آب ودانه [aabodaana] 1 subsistence; means of existence 2 *colloquial* fate

آب ورنگ [aaborang] 1 freshness, clarity 2 colorfulness, picturesqueness (of a picture or painting)
• آب ورنگ دادن to enliven, to impart colorfulness to
• آب ورنگ بخود گرفتن to become enlivened, to become brighter, more interesting ♦ اکنون زندگی او آب ورنگ بخود گرفته Now his life became more interesting.

ابوس [obus] *military* howitzer

آب ونمک [abonamak]
• -شدن: to be with one another, to become accociated (with), to mix with

آب وهوا [aabohawaa] climate

ابهام [ebhaam] *literary* vagueness, indefiniteness

ابهر [abhar] *anatomy* aorta

آبی [aabi] 1 light blue, blue 2 watery; water ♦ قوه آبی water power, hydraulic power 3 irrigated ♦ کشت آبی irrigated crops

ابیات [abyaat] *plural of* بیت¹

آبیاری [abyari] irrigation
• تحت آبیاری irrigated
• آبیاری کردن to irrigate

اپارتمان [apaartmaan] 1 apartment building (of the European type) ♦ اپارتمان مسکونی dwelling house 2 apartment

آپاندیسیت [aapandisit] appendicitis

آپاندیکس [aapandiks] *anatomy* appendix

آپه [aapa] *colloquial* 1 older sister 2 apa (polite salutation to a female stranger)

آتاشه [aataasha] attaché ♦ آتاشه نظامی military attaché

اتاق [otaaq] 1 room ♦ اتاق تجارت chamber of commerce ◊ اتاق خواب bedroom 2 cab (e.g., of a truck)

اتباع [atbaa] *plural of* تبعه

اتحاد [ettehaad] 1 unity; solidarity 2 union; association ♦ اتحاد شوروی Soviet Union

اتحادی [ettehaadi] 1 union *adjective* ♦ جمهوری اتحادی union republic 2 federative, federated, federal

اتحادیه [ettehaadiya] 1 association, union, league ♦ اتحادیه کارگران trade union 2 alliance, bloc ♦ اتحادیه تدافعی defensive alliance

اتخاذ [ettekhaaz] taking (steps), making (decisions, etc.)

آتش [aatesh (and) aatash] 1 fire, flame; campfire 2 burning coals, heat (in a furnace) 3 fire, firing (of a gun)
• *proverb* آتش که گرفت تر و خشکه میسوزاند When a fire flares up, it can't tell where it's dry and where it's wet. (In the face of misfortune, all are equal.)
• آتش دادن 1 to burn, to put to the fire 2 to roast (in fire), to bake (e.g., bricks)
• آتش در دادن to kindle (a fire, campfire)
• آتش زدن (را) to set on fire, to kindle
• آتش گرفتن 1 to catch on fire, to flare up, to burst into flames 2 to break out in anger, to flare up
• آتش برپا کردن to stir up discord, to incite hatred
• آتش گل کردن to extinguish a fire
• از آتش خاکستر ماندن *colloquial* to be a ne'er-do-well son of a famous father
• تمام بدنم آتش گرفتن I was thrown into a fever.

آتش افروز [aateshafroz] inciter; instigator

آتش بار [aateshbaar] fiery; sparkling

آتش باری [aateshbaari] artillery or mortar fire; artillery shelling

آتش بازی [aateshbaazi] fireworks

آتش پران [aateshparaan] 1 steel, flintstone (for kindling fire) 2 firing pin (of flintlock)

آتش پرچه [aateshparcha] *colloquial* pert, quick, dextrous

آتش خانه [aateshkhaana] 1 firebox ♦ آتش خانه بخاری firebox of a furnace 2 pan; primer (of a gun) 3 *obscure* artillery battery

آتش فشان [aateshfeshaan] (also کوه آتش فشان) volcano

آتش فشانی [aateshfeshaani] eruption of volcano

آتشک [aateshak] 1 *agriculture* anthracnose ♦ آتشک تاک anthracnose of grapes 2 syphilis

آتشکار [aateshkaar] furnace man, stoker

آتشکاو [aateshkaaw] poker (for fire)

آتش گل کن [aateshgolkon] (also آله آتش گل کن) *technical* fire extinguisher

آتش گیر [aateshgir] fire tongs

آتش میلیتار [aatashmilitar] military attaché

آتشی [aateshi] 1 bright red, fiery 2 *military* fire *adjective* ♦ پرده آتشی fire screen, curtain of fire

اتصال [ettesaal] 1 connection, communication; joining 2 *technical* connection; butt joint splice, mating 3 *electrical* contact; shorting

اتفاق [ettefaaq] 1 unity ♦ اتفاق نظر unity of views, unanimity ◊ به اتفاق together, in unison 2 incident; chance
• اتفاق افتادن to happen, to occur
• اتفاق کردن to unite

اتفاقی [ettefaaqi] accidental ♦ به صورت اتفاقی accidentally, by chance

اتکا [ettekaa] 1 reliance (on something) 2 hope
• اتکا کردن 1 to rely (on something) 2 to hope (به)

اتکل [atkal] *colloquial* 1 consideration, estimate 2 intuition, guess ♦ به اتکل intuitively, by guess

اتلس [atlas]¹ satin

اتلس [atlas]² ☞ اطلس ¹,²

اتم [aatom] ☞ اتوم

اتمام [etmaam] termination, completion
• به اتمام رساندن and اتمام بخشیدن to complete, to end, to bring to a conclusion

اتوتک [otutak] hoopoe (bird)

اتوم [atom] atom

اتومات [atumaat] 1 automatic device ♦ تیلفون اتومات automatic telephone 2 ☞ اتوماتیکی

اتوماتیکی [atumaatiki] automatic
• اتوماتیکی کردن to automate

اتومی [atomi] atomic ♦ وزن اتومی atomic weight

اتهام [ettehaam] suspicion, accusation ♦ به اتهام on suspicion, on accusation

آتی [aati] 1 future 2 next, as follows ♦ حسب قرار آتی است as follows below (further)

آثار [aasaar] *plural of* اثر

اثبات [esbaat] proof; confirmation
• به اثبات رساندن to prove, to confirm to substantiate

اثر [asar] (*plural* آثار) 1 trace, imprint ♦ Not از آن اثری نیست a trace remained of him. 2 action, effect 3 work, production (work of art), labor; monument (of art) ♦ اثر ادبی literary work 2 (در) به اثر as a result of, as a consequence of *denominal preposition*
• اثر کردن to act, to influence

اثنا [asnaa]
• در اثنای کار during worktime
• در این اثنا meanwhile; at that time

آ, ا

آثوری [aasuri] *historical* 1 Assyrian *adjective* 2 Assyrian *noun*

اجاره [ejaara] 1 rent; loan ♦ اجاره زمین land rent 2 contract ♦ اجاره دادن to rent out, to lend
• به اجاره کردن and اجاره کردن 1 to hire, to take on loan, to rent, to lease (from others) 2 to take a contract

اجاره دار [ejaaradaar] 1 renter, tenant 2 contractor

اجاره داری [ejaaradaari] possession (of something) on a rental basis

اجازت [ejaazat] and اجازه [ejaaza] permission, authorization
• اجازت دادن to give permission, to give authorization

اجاغ [ojgh] and اجاق [ojaaq] 1 hearth 2 hot plate 3 (also اجاغ فرنگی) brazier with a handle

اجانب [ajaaneb] *plural of* اجنبی 2

اجباری [ejbaari] 1 forced 2 necessary, mandatory
• قوت اجباری داشتن to be mandatory (concerning a court decision, etc.)

اجتماع [ejtemaa] 1 accumulation (of people); crowd 2 society
• اجتماع کردن to gather, to accumulate (of people, animals)

اجتماعی [ejtemaai'] public, social ♦ علوم اجتماعی social sciences ◊ آدم اجتماعی sociable person

اجتناب [ejtenaab] deviation (from something), avoidance (of something)
• اجتناب کردن (از) to deviate, to shun

اجداد [ajdaad] 1 *plural of* جد 2 ancestors

اجدادی [ajdaadi] 1 ancient, grandfatherly 2 hereditary, ancestral

اجرا [ejraa] 1 fulfillment, realization, execution, implementation 2 organization, conducting carrying out
• اجرا محاربه *military* wage battle
• کنسرت اجرا گردید. A concert was given.

اجراآت [ejraaaat] 1 measures, steps ♦ اجراآت ذیل به عمل آید It is necessary to take the following measures. 2 affairs, achievements 3 current work ♦ راپور- a report about work that has been done

اجرام [ajraam] *plural of* جرم [jerm]

اجرائیه [ejraaiya]
• قوه- executive authority
• کمیته- executive committee

اجرت [ojrat] lump-sum award, payment (for labor)

اجزاء [ajzaa] (*plural of* جزء [joz']) parts (of a whole), component parts ♦ کلام- *grammar* parts of speech
• -عروضی *literary* (types of the most typical combination of syllables in the metric foot: sabab, watad, and fasila)
• ☞ فاصله

اجسام [ajsaam] *plural of* جسم

اجل [ajal] death; ruination

اجل گرفته [ajal gerefta] doomed (*literally,* blindly going toward death)

اجمال [ejmaal] brief exposition; outline
• به صورت اجمال briefly, in (general) outline, roughly

اجمالی [ejmaali] abbreviated, brief
• نگاه اجمالی 1 passing glance 2 brief survey

اجناب [ajnaab] *plural of* جنب

اجناس [ajnaas] *plural of* جنس 4

اجنبی [ajnabi] 1.1 someone else's; alien, strange 1.2 foreign 1.3 unknown 2.1 (*plural* اجانب [ajaneb]) foreigner 2.2 stranger

اجنت [ajent] ☞ جاسوس

آجندا [aajanda] agenda, order of the day

اجنه [ajenna] *plural of* جن

اجوره [ojura] day's wages (for labor); daily earnings

اجوره کار [ojurakaar] hired worker, day laborer

آجیده [aajida] basted together; quickly sewn together
• آجیده کردن to baste; to sew quickly

اجیر [ajir] temporary; supernumerary (about employee)
• به قسم اجیر کار کردن to work as a supernumerary

آچار [aachaar] vegetable marinade (of eggplant, carrots, or tomatoes)
• آچار انداختن 1 to marinate 2 to prepare a marinade

احاطه [ehaata] 1 encirclement, envelopment 2 fence; enclosure ♦ احاطه باغ garden fence 3 girth, length along the circumference
• احاطه هریک درخت به ۵ مترمیر سد Each tree is five meters in girth.
• احاطه کردن 1 to envelop, to encircle, to surround 2 to fence off, to erect a fence

احتجاج [ehtejaaj] protest; objection
• احتجاج کردن to protest, to object

احتجاجیه [ehtejaajiya] note of protest

احتراز [ehteraaz] *literary* protection (of oneself against something); avoidance (of something); caution
• احتراز کردن to avoid (something); to beware, to be careful

احتراق [ehteraaq] burning; inflammation; combustion
• قابل احتراق combustible, flammable ♦ مایع قابل احتراق flammable liquid

احترام [ehteraam] respect, honor, esteem; honors
• احترام کردن to respect, to honor; to render honors

احتراماً [ehteraaman]
• احتراماً عرض میکنیم (epistolary style) I have the honor of informing you.

احتفال [ehtefaal] meeting (on the occasion of some important or ceremonious event)

احتکار [ehtekaar] speculation; profiteering
• احتکار کردن to speculate, to engage in speculation

احتکاکی [ehtekaaki]
• اصوات احتکاکی *grammar* slit or fricative consonants

احتکال [ehtekaal] *geology* erosion

احتمال [ehtemaal] 1 probability, possibility 2 assumption, supposition

احتمالی [ehtemaali] probable, permissible
• ماضی احتمالی *grammar* past subjunctive (tense)
• نظریات احتمالی theory of probability

احتیاج [ehtiyaaj] need, requirement
• اجناس (طرف) احتیاج عامه goods of mass consumption, consumer goods
• احتیاج داشتن (به) to need, to require

احتیاط [ehtiyaat] *military* 1 caution, circumspection 2 reserve
• ضابط احتیاط reserve officer
• احتیاط کردن to act cautiously, to show caution ♦ احتیاط کن که نیفتی Take care not to fall down! / Look out that you don't fall down!

احتیاطکار [ehtiyaatkaar] 1.1 cautious, prudent 1.2 thrifty 2 overly cautious person

احتیاطی [ehtiyaati] 1 left as a reserve; reserve *adjective* 2 emergency *adjective*
• قوای احتیاطی *military* reserve

احجار [ahjaar] 1 *plural of* حجر 2 *geology* rocks ♦ احجار رسوبی sedimentary rocks ◊ احجار سطحیه exogenous rocks

احد [ahad] 1 sole (epithet of Allah) 2 *masculine proper name* Ahad
- احدی 1 someone 2 no one (in negative sentences)
احداث [ehdaas] creation, erection, building ♦ احداث سرک ها laying or building of roads
احراز [ehraaz] acquisition, obtaining (of a job, position, etc.)
- احراز مقام assumption of a job, post, or position
- احراز کردن to obtain, to receive; to fill occupy (a place, job, post, etc.)
احزاب [ahzaab] *plural of* حزب
احساس [ehsaas] (*plural* احساسات [ehsasat]) sense, feeling
- احساس کردن to sense, to feel, to experience
احساسات [ehsaasaat] *plural of* احساس
احساساتی [ehsaasaati] sensitive, emotional (said of a person)
احسان [ehsaan] gift, favor; good deed
احسن [ahsan] *literary* best, prettiest, magnificent ♦ احسن اخلاق excellent character
احصائیات [ehsaaiyat] statistical information; numerical data
احصائیه [ehsaaiya] 1 account; calculation ♦ احصائیه نفوس population census 2 statistics ♦ رئیس احصائیه chief of the statistics department, directorate, administration
احضار [ehzaar] 1 summons (to court) 2 (*also* احضار عسکر) induction (into military service) 3 admission (of students) 4 recall (of a diplomatic representative)
احضارات [ehzaaraat] *military* (*also* حال احضارات) readiness ♦ احضارات محاربوی combat readiness
احکام [ahkaam] *plural of* حکم [hokom] 1
- احکام شریعت *religion* commandments; dogma; directions or instructions of the Sharia
احمر [ahmar] *literary* red ♦ لعل احمر ruby ♦ صلیب احمر the Red Cross
احمق [ahmaq] simpleton, fool
احوال [ahwal] *plural of* حال
- احوالتان خوب است؟ How are you? / How's your health?
- (از) احوال گرفتن to ask about (someone's) health
احوالات [ahwaalaat] *plural of* احوال
- ضبط احوالات criminal investigation department
احوالگیری [ahwaalgiri] notification or information about (someone's) health
- احوال گیری کردن to inquire about (someone's) health
احیاء [ehyaa] 1 return to life, rebirth 2 restoration, re-creation, renewal (از)
احیاناً [ahyaanan] 1 in case of, in the event of, if; even if 2 let us assume
آخ [aakh] Oh! / Oy! (when expressing pain, sympathy) *interjection*
- آخ کردن to say "oh," to sigh, to moan, to groan
اخ [ekh (exclamation with which one urges on a donkey or forces a camel to lie down)
اخبار [akhbaar] 1 *plural of* خبر 2 newspaper
اخباری [akhbaari] chronicle *adjective* ♦ فلم اخباری newsreel, documentary film
اخباری [ekhbari] *grammar* indicative ♦ وجه اخباری indicative mood
اختر [akhtar] 1 star 2 fate, luck
اختراع [ekhteraa] invention
- اختراع کردن to invent, to make a discovery
اختصار [ekhtesaar] abbreviation ♦ کسر اختصار reduction of a fraction *mathematical* ◊ به اختصار briefly, succinctly

اختصاص [ekhtesaas] 1 participation, connection 2 intention; predestination 3 peculiarity, specifics
- اختصاص دادن 1 to intend, to earmark, to devote, to dedicate (one's time to something) 2 to allocate (funds for something)
اختصاصی [ekhtesaasi] 1 especiál, special 2 specialized
اختلاط [ekhtelaat] 1 contact, acquaintance 2 discussion, conversation 3 mixing
- اختلاط کردن 1 to have contact with 2 to chat (with), to conduct a conversation (with) 3 to mingle
اختلاف [ekhtelaaf] 1 difference, discrepancy 2 (*also* اختلاف نظر) difference of opinion; contradiction 3 *mathematical* difference
اختلافات [ekhtelaafaat] contradictions
اختناق [ekhtenaaq] 1 asthma 2 suffocation
- دوره اختناق reaction period
اختیار [ekhtiyaar] 1 authority; right; powers 2 will; freedom of actions ♦ اختیار به شما است As you please! 3 jurisdiction, discretion 4 (opposite of جبر) *philosophical* freedom
- اختیار داشتن 1 to have the right, to possess powers or authority 2 to have freedom of actions, the right to choose
- اختیار کردن 1 to make a choice, to elect 2 to conduct, to carry out (a policy) 3 *polite* to deign (to do something) ♦ به این دیار مسافرت اختیار کردن They deigned to visit these parts / this area.
- اختیار خود را نداشتن not to be at one's own disposal, to be dependent
- به اختیار کسی گذاشتن to put at someone's disposal
- زیر اختیار نبودن not to depend on will, to be involuntary
- من در اختیار شما هستم I am at your disposal.
اختیاردار [ekhtiyaardaar] 1 responsible (for something) 2 *historical* sovereign
- اختیار دار بودن to be chief, senior (in some matter); to bear responsibility ♦ بعد از پدر پسر کلان اختیار دار خانواده است After the father, the oldest son is the head of the family.
اخذ [akhez] 1 levy, collection; receipt ♦ اخذ معاش receipt of wages ◊ اخذ مالیات levy, collection of taxes 2 ☞ اتخاذ
- اخذ کردن to take, to levy, to receive
- اخذ عسکر induction, draft, recruitment into the army
آخذه [aakheza]
- تونل آخذه آب (water) intake tunnel
- دستگاه آخذه radio receiver
آخر [aakher] 1 (*plural* اواخر [awakher]) end 2 last ♦ در روزهای آخر recently 3 in the last analysis, in the final analysis 4 you see, you know, after all, on the other hand
اخراج [ekhraaj] 1 removal; withdrawal 2 discharge, release; exclusion 3 evacuation, withdrawal (of troops)
آخرت [aakherat] *religion* the other world; life after death
آخرها [aakherhaa] *colloquial* last part, end (of something) ♦ در آخرهای امتحان at the end of the examination ◊ آخرهای خزان the last days of autumn 2 remnants, leftovers, small amount of something ♦ آخرهای برنج leftovers of rice
آخری [aakheri] and آخرین [akherin] last; final; concluding
اخطار [ekhtaar] warning (of danger); caution ♦ زنگ اخطار signal of alarm or alert
اخلاص [ekhlaas] 1 devotion, attachment 2 sincere attitude; trust
- اخلاص کردن 1 to be devoted, attached (بر، به) 2 to have a sincere attitude toward; to trust (بر، به)

اخلاط [akhlaat]
- اخلاط اربعه the four fluids of an organism: blood, black bile, yellow bile, and phlegm (according to ancient medicine)

اخلاف [akhlaaf] *plural of* خلف

اخلاق [akhlaaq] 1 character, temper; behavior 2 morality

اخوت [okhowwat] *literary* brotherhood

آخون [aakhun] and آخوند [akhund] 1 ahund (spiritual person) 2 teacher of a madrash (school at a mosque)

اخیافی [akhyaafi] (*also* برادر اخیافی) half-brother

اخیر [akhir] last, recent ◆ در پنجشنبه اخیر last Thursday

اخیراً [akhiran] recently

ادا [adaa] 1 completion, execution ◆ ادا نماز carrying out an annointment 2 payment ◆ ادا قرض payment of a debt ◊ ادامالیات payment of taxes 3 pronunciation
- کردن- 1 to complete, to execute, to carry out
- حق وطن کردن- to fulfull [one's] duty to the homeland 2 to pay 3 to pronounce, to utter (words, sounds)

آداب [aadaab] good manners, principles, proprieties
- معاشرت- etiquette

ادات [adaat] (*plural* ادوات [adawaat]) *grammar* auxiliary word; particle ◆ تاکید- emphatic particle ◊ نفی- negative particle

اداره [edaara] (*plural* ادارات [edaaraat]) 1 leadership, management, administration 2 department; institution; establishment 3 bureau, office ◆ اطلاعات- information bureau 4 editorial office (of a newspaper)
- کردن- to manage, to lead, to administer (را)

اداری [edaari] 1 administrative ◆ هیئت- administrative appartus 2 office *adjective* ◆ لوازم- office equipment

ادامه [edaama] 1 prolongation, duration 2 continuation, next part ◆ دارد- continued, continuation follows
- دادن- to continue
- یافتن- to last

ادب [adab] 1 breeding, culture; education 2 literature; philology ◆ اهل- men of letters; philologists

ادبا [odabaa] *plural of* ادیب

ادب پرور [adabparwar] encouraging the development of culture and literature (usually about a shah, government figure, etc.)

ادبی [adabi] literary; artistic ◆ انجمن- literary society

ادبیات [adabiyat] literature
- بدیعی- belles-lettres

ادرار [edraar] urination
- کردن- to urinate

ادراک [edraak] perception; understanding; comprehension

آدرس [aadras] address

ادعا [eddeaa] 1 claim, pretension 2 claim
- کردن- 1 to claim; to make a claim 2 to sue

آدم [aadam] 1 person 2 *colloquial* servant 3 *masculine proper name* Adam
- بابا (baba.) primogenitor
- برفی- snowman

ادمان [edmaan] gymnastics; calisthenics; physical exercises ◆ -و ورزش physical culture and sport

آدم چهره [aadamchehra]
- گل آدم چهره pansy

آدم خور [aadamkhor] cannibal; murderer

آدمیت [aadamiyat] humanity

آدمی زاد [aadamizaad] child; person

ادوات [adawaat] (*plural of* ادات 2) instruments; tools ◆ سنگی- stone implements

ادوار [adwaar] *plural of* دور

ادویه [adwiya] *plural of* دوا

ادویه پاشی [adwiyapashi] *agriculture* sprinkling
- کردن- to sprinkle (crops, trees)

ادویه فروشی [adwiyaforoshi] drugstore; a shop where they sell drugs

ادیان [adyaan] *plural of* دین

ادیب [adib] (*plural* ادبا [odaba]) expert in the field of literature; highly-educated philologist

ادیتوریم [aditoriam] auditorium ◆ تالار- lecture hall; conference room

اذان [azaan] 1 azan (muezzin's call to morning prayer) 2 *colloquial* (*also* خروس-) rooster's crowing (in the early morning)
- بی وقت- *colloquial* inappropriate request; inappropriate statement

اذواق [azwaaq] *plural of* ذوق

آذوقه [aazuqa] foodstuffs, provisions

اذیت [aziyat] 1 torture, oppression 2 anxiety, boredom
- کردن- 1 to torture, to oppress 2 to upset, to bore, to pester

آر [aar] ☞ آور

آراء [aaraa] *plural of* رأی
- اختلاف- difference (of opinion)
- به اکثریت- by or with a majority of the votes

ارابه [araaba] 1 wheel ◆ کراچی- cartwheel, wagon wheel 2 wagon, bullock-cart

ارادت [eraadat] *literary* disposition, inclination

ارادتمند [eraadatmand]
- شما- *epistolary* yours faithfully

اراده [eraada] 1 will; desire 2 intention
- چیزی کردن- *formal* to design to allow [someone] to do something

ارادی [eraadi] 1 conscious; volitional ◆ غیر- unconscious, instinctive 2 deliberate

آراستن [aaraastan] present tense stem آرای

آرای [aarraay] *literary* ☞ آرایش کردن

اراضی [araazi] land; locality, country; terrain; territory

اراکین [araakin] *plural of* ارکان

آرام [aaraam] 1 rest, calm 2 peaceful, quiet ◆ خواب- peaceful sleep 3 calmly, quietly ◆ -! Be quiet! Stop it! (prohibition)
- بشینید!- Sit still!
- شدن- 1 to find peace, to rest 2 to calm down, to become quiet ◆ درد پای-شد The pain in the foot / leg went away. ◊ طفل-شد The child quieted down.
- (-)کردن- شدن- to calm [someone] down; to pacify (یافتن)(گرفتن)
- اوهیچ-ندارد- نداشتن not to know rest, not to know peace ◆ He knows no rest / peace.

آرامش [aaraamesh] rest, peace; quiet ◆ آرامش بر قرار شد Peace reigned.

آرامگاه [aaraamgah] burial vault; mausoleum

آرامی [aaraami] 1 rest, peace 2 tranquility; well-being
- بارامی- به - ☞

آرامیدن [aaraamidan] 1 *literary* to recline, to rest 2 to lie, to repose (of the dead)

آرای [aaraay] *present tense stem* آراستن

آرایش [aaraayesh] adornment, decoration; apparel
- ‐دادن(کردن) to adorn, to decorate, to dress up

ارباب [arbaab] 1 *regional* elder of a village or clan; village elder or headman 2 *rare* boss, landlord, landowner 3 *plural* of رب [rab (b)]
- ارباب الانواع ☞ ‐انواع
- ‐فضل scientists, scholars, learned persons
- ‐قلم writers

ارباب الانواع [arbaabolanwaa'] *literary plural of* رب النوع

ارت [arat] *agriculture* water wheel (to lift water for irrigation) ♦ چرخ‐ well wheel

آرت [aart] art

ارت [art] *technical* (also ‐زمینی) ground ♦ لین‐زمینی *electrical* ground line
- ‐کردن to ground

ارتباط [ertebaat] 1 relations, contact, communication 2 communications ♦ بی سیم‐ wireless communications
- ‐داشتن 1 to have relations with, to have contact with 2 to communicate with
- ‐بر قرار کردن to establish communications
- ‐داخل‐شدن to get into communications with (ب), to establish contact

ارتباطچی [ertebaatchi] messenger

ارتباطی [ertebaati] communications *adjective* ♦ خطوط‐ communications

ارتجاع [ertejaa'] *political* reaction

ارتجاعی [ertejaayi] reactionary

ارتجاعیت [ertejaaiyat] *physics* resiliency, elasticity

ارتزاقی [ertezaaqi]
- مواد‐ foodstuffs, provisions

ارتعاش [erte'aash] oscillation, vibration

ارتفاع [ertefaa'] 1 height; altitude (also *mathematical, astronomy*) ♦ از سطح بحر‐ elevation above sea level 2 level (of a liquid in a container)

ارتقاء [erteqaa] *literary* rise; growth, upsurge ♦ صنایع‐ industrial growth

ارتکاب [ertekaab] perpetration (of misdemeanor, etc.)

آرتیزین [aarteezyan]
- چاه‐ artesian well

آرتیست [aartist] 1 actor, (performing) artist 2 painter (artist)

ارتینه [artina] *regional* 1 woman 2 wife

ارث [ers] inheritance
- به‐بردن to inherit
- به‐گذاشتن to bequeath, to leave as an inheritance

ارثی [ersi] hereditary, inherited

ارجل [arjal] *colloquial* 1 any, every, various; of any kind, of every kind 2 variegated

ارجمند [arjomand] nice, dear, treasured (of someone close to you)

ارجمندی [arjomandi] *colloquial* son; my son, dear son (salutation in a letter)

ارچق [archeq] crust, scab (on a wound)
- ‐بستن (گرفتن) to form new skin, to heal (of a wound) ♦ روی زخمهای اورا ‐ گرفته بود His wounds healed.

ارچه [archa] 1 archa, treelike juniper 2 coniferous tree

ارچه کاری [archakaari] 1 board sheathing, planking 2 carpentry

آرد [aard] meal
- ‐کردن to grind (meal), to mill

آرداب [aardaaba] and آردآوه [ardawa] cereal mash (food)

اردل [ardal] *historical* personal guard of an emir

اردلی [ardali] 1 attendant; orderly 2 ☞ اردلیان
- اردل bodyguards (of an emir)

اردو [ordu] ¹ forces, army

اردو [ordu] ² (also زبان ‐) Urdu language

اردوگاه [ordugaah] *military* camp, bivouac

ارزاق [arzaaq] *plural of* رزق

ارزان [arzaan] 1 inexpensive, cheap ♦ قیمت‐ at an inexpensive price 2 inexpensively, cheaply
- تمام شدن ‐ and افتادن‐ to manage, to make do, to get by cheaply
- خریدن‐ to buy cheaply

ارزان بیع [arzaanbay(a)] inexpensive; cheap

ارزش [arzesh] *economics* 1 price, cost; value ♦ اضافی‐ surplus value 2 value, importance
- ‐داشتن to cost, to be valued; importance

ارزن [arzan] millet

ارزنده [arzenda] important, significant; valuable ♦ زخمت‐ valuable efforts ◊ سهم‐ worthy contribution

آرزو [aarezo (and) aarezu] 1 desire, dream 2 wish ♦ کامیابی‐ a wish of success
- ‐داشتن to want, to desire; to dream (ر)

آرزومند [aarezomand (and) aarezumand]
- ‐بودن 1 to desire, to express a / the desire 2 to dream, to hope ♦ آرزو مندم که موفق باشید I wish you success! / I hope you succeed!

ارزیابی [arzyaabi] receipt of an evaluation, an evaluation
- ‐کردن to determine the price, to evaluate

ارزیدن [arzidan] 1 to cost, to have a price, to be valued 2 to be worthy, to deserve (به)

ارسال [ersaal] dispatching, sending
- ‐داشتن (کردن) to dispatch, to send (mail, a letter)

ارسالی [ersaali] dispatched, sent ♦ کتاب شماراگرفتم‐ I received the book sent by you.

ارسنیک [arsenik] arsenic

ارسی [orsi] 1 window 2 ursi (window without glass facing a terrace or another room)

ارشاد [ershaad] 1 *religion* admonition (to take the true path), sermon 2 giving of instructions, guidance
- امرو – میشود *obscure* I command and order (in edicts)

آرشیف [aarshif] archive

ارض [arz] earth ♦ کره ‐ the globe

ارضی [arzi] 1 land *adjective*, territorial 2 agrarian ♦ مسئله‐ the agrarian problem
- آفات‐ natural calamities (concerning earthquakes)

ارغمچی [arghamchi] *regional* rope, string

ارغوان [arghawaan] crimson, pink acacia

ارغوانی [arghawaani] crimson, of the color of a flowering acacia *adjective*

ارغوزک [arghuzak] variety of spinach

ارقام [arqaam] *plural of* رقم

ارکاره [arkaara] ¹ 1 iron bucket 2 small saucepan with a long handle (usually for melting butter)

ارکاره [arkaara] ² *historical* (also پهلوانی ‐) place for wrestling matches; athletic arena

ارکان [arkaan] ¹ *plural of* رکن
- دولت‐ highest officials; pillars of the state

-عسکری the highest command element, the generals
• جمله - *grammar* main parts of a sentence
ارکان [arkaan] **2** *military* (also حرب _) general staff ♦ رئیس- chief of the general staff
ارکسترا [aarkestraa] orchestra
ارکیولوجست [arkiolojest] archeologist
ارکیولوجی [arkioloji] archeologist
ارگ [arg] **1** fortress, citadel (within a city or town) **2** (also - شاهی) fortified residence of a king or shah **3** the Kabul arg (Kabul citadel fortress)
ارگان [orgaan] **1** organ (of power), administrative level, department level ♦ ارگان های مسؤول دولتی responsible state organs **2** (also نشراتی -) organ of the press
ارمان [armaan] and آرمان [aarmaan] **1** cherished dream, yearning **2** longing (for something) **3** *rarely* regret (over that which did not come true)
ارمبه [aramba] **1** support, prop **2** lever
ارمر [ormor] Ormurs (nationality in Afghanistan)
ارمونیه [armuniya] harmonium
ارمیچر [armeechar] *technical* armature (of a generator)
ارن [aran] ☞ هارن
ارنج [aaronj] **1** elbow **2** forearm **3** *technical* mandrel
ارواح [arwaa(h)] **1** *plural of* روح **2** spirit, apparition ♦ خبیثه evil spirits
• گشتن - *colloquial* to melt away (from grief, fear), to turn into a shadow
اروپایی [orupaayi] **1** European *adjective* **2** a European
اروغ [aarugh] and اروق [aaruq] belching
اره [arra] saw ♦ تسمه - band saw ◊ مدور circular saw
اره کشی [arrakaasi] sawing ♦ فابریکه- saw mill
اری [aaree] *regional* yes
اریا [aaryaa] Arya (chosen name of Indo-Iranian tribes who inhabited the area of Afghanistan in antiquity)
اریانا [aaryaanaa] *historical* Ariane (ancient Greek name for eastern part of Iranian plateau)
اریایی [aaryaayi] **1** Aryan *adjective* **2** an Aryan
اریان [aariyaan] ☞ آریایی
از [az] *preposition* **1** (indicates direction of movement) from, out of; away from; to (with an indication to the place of action) ♦ از خانه بر آمدند They went out of the house. ◊ گوشت را از بازار خریدی؟ Did you buy meat at the bazaar? **2** (indicates the initial moment of an action) from ♦ از چاشت تا عصر from noon until evening **3** (indicates the source of obtaining something) from ♦ از احمد قلم گرفتم I got a pen from Ahmad **4** across, through ♦ زورق از دریا تیر شد The ferry crossed the river. **5** because of, from ♦ از دیدن فرزند بسیار خوش شد He was delighted to see his son. ◊ درخت ها از گرمی خشک شد The trees dried out from the intense heat. **6** (designating the object onto which an action is directed; usually with the verb گرفتن) by ♦ از بند دستم گرفت He grabbed me by the wrist. **7** (when comparing) ♦ این شاگرد از آن شاگرد لایق تر است This student is better than that one. **8** (when indicating that something belongs to someone or something) ♦ این باغ از پدرم است This garden belongs to my father. **9** *colloquial* (second component of denominal prepositions) ♦ برای او for him, for it
• از سالها (است) it has been many years since; it has been a long time since ♦ از سالها رقیب بودند They have been rivals for a long time now.

زحاف [azaahif] *plural of* ازاحیف
آزاد [aazaad] free ♦ حرکات- natural manners ◊ هوای- fresh air, free air
آزادی [aazaadi] freedom; independence ♦ بیان - freedom of speech ◊ آزادی قلم (مطبوعات) freedom of the press
آزادی بخش [aazaadibakhsh] liberating, liberation *adjective* ♦ جنبش – ملی national liberation movement
آزادی خواه [aazaadikhah] **1** freedom-loving ♦ جوانان- freedom-loving youth. freedom-loving young people **2** liberal
آزار [aazaar] **1** present tense stem آزردن **2** offense, oppression **3** (second component of compound words with meaning of torturing, oppressing) ♦ مردم آزار oppressor, offender
• دادن- **1** to torture, to oppress **2** to bring down; to annoy
ازار [ezaar] *regional* trousers
ازاربند [ezaarband] belt; cord to tie up trousers
ازآنها [az-aanhaa] *colloquial* their, belonging to them ♦ خانه- their house
از او [az-o] *colloquial* his, belonging to him ♦ پدر - his father
از باد آمدن [azbaadaamadan] *slang* came out of the thin air, to get something for free (*literally*: coming from the air) ♦ از بادی آمد و بادی رفت easy come easy go
از باد هوا گفتن [azbaadehawaagoftan] *slang* empty claim (*literally*: talking from the air)
ازبر [azbar] by heart ♦ کردن- to learn by heart
ازبس (که) [azbas (ke)] so much ... that; so ... that, such ... that *compound conjunction* ♦ ازبس کار کردم دستهایم آبله کرد I worked so [hard] that calluses [appeared] on my hands.
از بست [azbast] asbestos ♦ تخته- sheet asbestos
ازبک [ozbak] **1** an Uzbek **2** Uzbek *adjective*
ازبکی [ozbaki] **1** Uzbek *adjective* **2** (also زبان-) the Uzbek language
ازبوسمنت [azbosement] asbestos cement
ازتو [az-tu] *colloquial* your, belonging to you ♦ کتاب -your book
از خود [az-xod] **1** *colloquial* one's, one's own ♦ فرزندی- نداشتند They did not have children of their own. **2** blood relative, blood sibling, close ♦ بجز یک خواهر دیگر کسی- ندارم Other than a sister, I don't have any blood relatives / siblings.
ازخودگذری [azkhodgozari] **1** humility, modesty **2** selflessness
از خودگی [azkhodegi] *colloquial* **1** relative, person who feels at home **2** kinship relations
• به طور - [to feel] at home, [to feel like] one of the family
• نکردن - not to accept as one's own, to shun
ازدواج [ezdewaaj] matrimony, marriage; wedding
• کردن - to enter into marriage
ازدیاد [ezdiyaad] multiplication, enlargement, increase
• کردن- to multiply, to increase
آزردگی [aazordagi] offence, grief, sadness
آزردن [aazordan] (*present tense stem* آزار [aazaar]) *rare* to offend, to grieve
آزرده [aazorda]
• کردن - to offend, to grieve
آزرده خاطر [aazordakhaater] and آزرده دل [azordadel] aggrieved; saddened
از شما [az-shomaa] *colloquial* your, belonging to you ♦ بچه- your son
از قصد [azqasd] **1** deliberately, on purpose **2** affectedly, hypocritically; pretending

از کار برآمده [azkaarbaraamada] *colloquial* out of commission; worn out; unsuitable, unfit

از کمر بالا [azkamarbaalaa] upper part of the torso; bust

از کمر پایان [azkamarpaayaan] lower part of the body; pelvis

ازل [azal] *literary* existence from the very beginning, state of being primordial or primeval

از ما [az-maa] *colloquial* our, belonging to us ♦ باغ - our garden

آزما(ی) [aazmaa(y)] *present tense stem* آزمودن

آزمایش [aazmaayesh] 1 trial, test ♦ آزمایشهای تحت الارضی underground tests 2 experiment

آزمایشگاه [aazmaayeshgaah] laboratory

از من [az-man] *colloquial* my, belonging to me ♦ بوت - my slippers

ازمنه [azmena] *plural of* زمان

آزمودن [aazmudan] (*present tense stem* آزما(ی) [aazmaa(y)]) to check, to verify, to test

آزمون [aazmun] *rare* trial; check, verification; test, sample

ازواج [azwaaj] *plural of* زوج

آژانس [aazhaans] agency (information, etc.) ♦ باختر - Bakhtar agency

اژدر [azhdar] and اژدها [azdaha] dragon

اساتذه [asaateza] *plural of* استاد

اسارت [asaarat] capturing, captivity; slavery, bondage

اساس [asaas] basis, foundation ♦ بر - on the basis of ♦ اساس چیزی را ماندن (گذاشتن) - to found something, to lay the foundation of something

اساس گذار [asaasgozaar] founder, initiator

اساسنامه [asaasnaama] regulations, charter ♦ حزب - party regulations, party charter

اساسی [asaasi] 1 basic, main ♦ قانون - constitution 2 fundamental, capital, cardinal ♦ تحولات - fundamental changes

اساطیری [asaatiri] mythical, legendary

اسامبله [asaambla] 1 assembly ♦ مؤسسه(عمومی)ملل متحد - UN General Assembly 2 meeting

اسامی [asaami] *plural of* اسم

آسان [aasaan] easy, not difficult; simple

آسانی [aasaani] ease, lack of complexity; simplicity ♦ به - easily, with ease

آسای [aasaay] *present tense stem* آسودن

آسایش [aasaayesh] peace, quiet, rest

اسباب [asbaab] 1 tools, instruments, implements ♦ بازی - toys 2 things, utensils

اسباب ساز [asbaabsaaz] intriguer, plotter

اسباب سازی [asbaabsaazi] machinations, intrigues

اسبست [asbast] ☞ ازبست

اسبق [asbaq] 1 past, preceding 2 former, ex ♦ رئیس جمهور - former president, ex-president

اسپ [asp] 1 horse 2 *chess* knight

اسپار [espaar] *agriculture* wooden plow with iron blade

اسپ دوانی [aspdawaani] (*also* مسابقه -) horse race

اسپرنگ [espreng] spring

اسپرنگ واشل [esprengwaashal] spring-loaded seal or gasket

اسپ سواری [aspsowaari (and) aspsawaari] horseback riding

اسپک [aspak] 1 rocking horse 2 (*also* اسپک چوبی) horse (on carousel)

است [ast] 1 (short form of predicative verb copula) ♦ هست to be 2 (verb copula of compound predicate, third person singular) ♦ او شاگرد - He is a student.

آستا [aastaa] *colloquial* 1 quietly, slowly, unhurriedly 2 softly, in a quiet voice 3 weakly, mildly

استا [ostaa] 1 ☞ استاد 2 *regional* barber, beard-cutter

استاد [ostaad] 1 instructor (at a college, university) 2 master 3 maestro (painter, artist, musician, etc.)

استادانه [ostaadaana] 1 masterful 2 masterfully, skillfully

استادن [estaadan] *colloquial* ☞ ایستادن

استادی [ostaadi] mastery, art; knowing one's business, knowledgeability

استادیوم [estaadiom] stadium

استاذ [ostaaz] (*plural* اساتذه [asaateza]) ☞ استاد

استاکار [ostaakaar] 1 master (usually of some trade) 2 *regional* construction worker; plasterer

آستان [aastaan] 1 threshold, entrance (of a house) 2 (آستان اولیا الله) saint's grave, sacred place

استانسه [estaansa] ☞ ایستگاه

آستانه [aastaana] ☞ آستان

استبداد [estebdaad] despotism; autocracy, tyranny ♦ رژیم - despotic regime

استثمار [estesmaar] exploitation

استثمارکننده [estesmaarkonenda] and استثمارگر [estesmargar] exploiter

استثنا [estesnaa] exclusion, exception ♦ به - with the exception of ♦ - کردن to exclude, to remove, to withdraw

استثنایی [estesnaayi] being an exception; exceptional

استحالوی [estehaalawi] ♦ احجار - *geology* metamorphic rocks

استحصال [estehsaal] 1 obtaining, procuring, extraction 2 production ♦ - کردن 1 to procure, to extract, to obtain 2 to produce

استحصالات [estehsaalaat] production; output; products of production

استحکام [estehkaam] strength, durability ♦ بخشیدن - to strengthen

استحکامات [estehkaamaat] *military* fortifications

استحمام [estehmaam] *literary* bathing, swimming

استخاره [estekhaara] fortunetelling (by means of the Koran or beads) about the outcome of a planned undertaking ♦ *proverb* در کار خیر حاجت نیست - When you intend to do good, don't guess how it will end.

استخبارات [estekhbaaraat] *military* 1 data, information from reconnaissance, intelligence information 2 intelligence (agent network); counterintelligence

استخدام [estekhdaam] hiring, hire ♦ کردن- to hire

استخراج [estekhraaj] 1 working, mining, extraction (of ore, etc.) 2 extraction, obtaining ♦ جذر - *mathematical* finding the root, extraction of root

استخوان [ostokhaan] bone; bones ♦ سر - *anatomy* skull ◊ کف پای - metatarsus ◊ فیل - ivory ◊ قدیم - strong bone (of a strong, hardy person)

استخوان بندی [ostokhaanbandi] 1 skeleton; carcass ♦ عمارت - framework of building 2 *technical* assembly of a framework ♦ - کردن to build a framework, to erect a framework

استخوانی [ostokhaani] bone *adjective*, made of bone ♦ شانه - comb made of bone 2 bony, skinny ♦ پنجه های - bony fingers

استدعاء [ested'aa] request, prayer

استر [astar] 1 lining (of clothing) 2 *technical* facing 3 *technical* layer, covering ♦ سمنت - cement covering, cement facing
• دادن - to sew on a lining

استراتیژی [estraateezhi] strategy

استراتیژیک [estraateezhik] and استراتژیکی [estrateziki] strategic

استراحت [esteraahat] 1 rest 2 peace, quiet, sleep
• کردن - 1 to rest 2 to sleep

استراحتگاه [esteraahatgaah] place of rest; resort; sanatorium

استرداد [esterdaad] 1 return (e.g., of that which was stolen) 2 restoration (e.g., of rights)

استردار [astardaar] lined ♦ کورتی - lined jacket

استرکاری [astarkaari] *technical* cementing; plastering

استرونومی [astronomi] astronomy

استشمام [esteshmaam] *literary* smelling, sense of smell
• کردن - to smell

استطاعت [estetaat] 1 resources; means; fortune 2 possibility, capability (to do something)

استعاره [esteaara] allegory; metaphor

استعاری [esteaari] allegorical; metaphorical

استعداد [este'daad] 1 capability; gift ♦ نطق - gift of speech 2 suitability, fitness ♦ زراعت - suitability for cultivation (about soil)

استعفاء [este'faa] retirement, going into retirement

استعمار [este'maar] 1 colonization 2 colonialism

استعمارگر [este'maargar] colonizer

استعمال [este'maal] 1 use, application 2 consumption, use (e.g., of narcotics) ♦ تریاک - opium addiction

استغاثه [esteghaasa] request, appeal; complaint
• کردن - to appeal; to submit a complaint

استفاده [estefaada] 1 utilization; use, usage ♦ از ثروتهای طبیعی - use of natural resources ◊ تجارتی - rental 2 extraction of benefit, advantage 3 benefit, advantage
• کردن - 1 to take advantage of; to use (از) 2 to derive benefit (از)

استفاده جو [estefaadaju] self-interested person

استفاده وی [estefaadawi] *economics*
• ارزش - consumer value

استفراغ [estefraagh] and استفراق [estefraaq] vomiting

استفسار [estefsaar] inquiry
• کردن - to ask (someone)

استفهامی [estefhaami] and استفهامیه [estefhaamiya] interrogative
♦ جمله - interrogative sentence

استقامت [esteqaamat] 1 steadfastness, fortitude, persistence, stubbornness 2 direction, side ♦ به - in the direction [of]

استقبال [esteqbaal] 1 reception, meeting; welcome 2 the future 3 *grammar* the future tense
• کردن - to meet, to meet halfway, to greet; to receive

استقرار [esteqraar] 1 establishment, confirmation, ratification
♦ صلح - the establishment of peace 2 consolidation (in positions) 3 settlement (somewhere)

استقراض [esteqraaz] loan; credit
• کردن - to get a loan; to obtain credit

استقلال [esteqlaal] independence, sovereignty ♦ جشن - independence day (in Afghanistan)

استلین [asetelin] acetylene

استماع [estemaa'] listening
• کردن - to listen

استمراری [estemraari] long, prolonged
• ماضی - *grammar* imperfect

استناد [estenaad] reference (to something) ♦ به - referring to
• کردن - to refer (به)

استنتاج [estentaaj] conclusion, finding; logical conclusion ♦ از کل به جزء - (logic) induction ◊ جزء به کل - (logic) deduction

استنطاق [estentaaq] interrogation, inquiry, investigation

استوا [ostowaa] (also خط -) equator

استوار [ostowaar] strong, persistent; firm

استوانه [ostowaana] 1 cylinder 2 (also موتر -) drum (of an automobile, a vehicle)

استوایی [ostowaayi] equatorial; tropical ♦ اقلیم - tropical climate

استوپه [ostupa] *archeology* stupa (memorial mound in India)

استودیو [estudio] studio

استهزا [estehzaa] mockery; sarcasm

استهزا آمیز [estehzaaaamiz] mocking; sarcastic

استهلاک [estehiaak] 1 consumption 2 amortization, depreciation; wear, wear and tear

استهلاکی [estehlaaki] consumer *adjective* ♦ تعاون - consumer cooperative ◊ مواد - consumer goods

استیشن [esteeshan] 1 *technical* station ♦ برق - electric power station ◊ فضایی - space station 2 (also ریل -) railroad station 3 ☞ ایستگاه

استیلا [estilaa] seizure, conquest; subjugation ♦ هند بدست انگلیس - conquest of India by the English

آستین [aastin] sleeve, sleeves
• برزدن - 1 to roll up [one's] sleeves 2 to undertake a job
• پوستین بابا کلان - *colloquial* second cousin twice removed, very distant relative

استیناف [estinaaf] *legal* appeal ♦ محکمه - court of appeal

آستینچه [aastincha] sleeve protectors (put on when baking bread in a tanur)

اسد [asad] 1 *astronomy* Leo 2 Asad (fifth month of the Muslim solar year; corresponds to July – August) 3 *masculine proper name* Asad

اسراء [osaraa] *plural of* اسیر

اسرار [asraar] *plural of* سر [ser(r)]

اسرائیل [esraayil]
• بنی - 1 Jews, Israelites, Israelis 2 an Israelite, Israeli

اسطرلاب [ostorlaab] *obscure* astrolabe

اسعار [as'aar] currency ♦ خارجه - foreign currency

آسغده [aasoghda] *rarely* charred log

اسفالت [esfaalt] 1 asphalt 2 bituminous lacquer
• کردن - to asphalt, to lay asphalt, to cover with asphalt

اسفالت کاری [esfaaltkaari] asphalting

اسفناک [asafnaak] sad, regrettable, deplorable

اسفنج [esfanj] sponge; sponge washrag, sponge mop
• پلاستیکی - plastic foam, foam rubber

اسقاط [esqaat]¹ 1 miscarriage, premature birth 2 abortion
• کردن - 1 to miscarry, to give birth prematurely 2 to abort

اسقاط [esqaat]² alms given at a funeral

اسقس [asqas] *colloquial* ☞ از قصد

اسکان [eskaan] changeover to settled way of life; settling, settling (of tribes in a new place)
اسکرنج [eskorenj] wrench
اسکرپر [eskrepar] *technical* scraper
اسکلیت [eskeleet] 1 skeleton, backbone 2 carcass
اسکنه [eskana (and) askana] chisel; cutter
اسکورنج [eskurenj] ☞ سکورنج
اسکی [eski] ☞ سکی
اسکیج [eskij] ☞ سکیج
اسلاف [aslaaf] *plural of* سلف [salaf]
اسلام [eslaam] Islam, Mohammedanism ♦ اهل - Muslims
اسلاو [eslaaw] 1 Slavic 2 Slav
اسلحه [asleha] weapon ♦ ناریه - firearm
اسلحه سازی [aslehasaazi] production of weapons, arms production
اسلوب [oslûb] 1 method, way 2 style, manner ♦ نوشتن - manner of writing, style
اسلیت [eslit] ☞ سلیت
اسلیپ [eslip] ☞ سلیپ
اسم [esem] 1 (*plural* اسامی [asaami]) first name, name 2 *grammar* (*plural* اسماء [asmaa]) noun ♦ ذات – noun, substantive ◊ فعل - noun of action; infinitive
• اسم تصغیر Diminutive noun
• اسم جمع Collective noun
• اسم خاص Proper noun
• اسم عام common noun
• اسم معنی abstract noun
3 invocation
♦ به - having assumed the name, in the guise of ♦ تاجر از - این قریه به آن قریه می رفت Under the guise of a merchant, he traveled from one village to another.
• - بردن - to mention, to name
• - گذاشتن (ماندن) to give a name [to], to name
• شب - *military* password
اسماء [asmaa] *plural of* اسم 2
اسماعیلی [esmaili] 1 an Ismaili 2 Ismaili *adjective*
آسمان [aasmaan] sky, heaven
• در ستاره و در زمین در خ‌تی(سایه یی)ندارد *proverb* He doesn't have a star in the sky or a shelter on earth. (He doesn't have house or home.)
• از - افتادن *colloquial* to get (something) easily, without any trouble
• از - تا زمین فرق داشتن to be strikingly different, to have nothing in common (in comparison)
• - وریسمان *colloquial* something said for no apparent reason, words spoken out of place
آسمانخراش [aasmaankharaash] tall building, skyscraper
آسمانی [aasmaani] 1 heavenly 2 light blue *adjective*, azure
• بلای – natural calamity
• سنگ – meteorite
اسمیه [esmiya] *grammar* nominal part (of a verb phrase) ♦ اسمیه ها *grammar* nominal parts of speech
اسناد [asnaad] *plural of* سند [sanad]
آسودگی [aasudagi] 1 rest, quiet, peace 2 prosperity, peaceful life
آسودن [aasudan] (*present tense stem* آسای [aasaay]) to calm down, to find peace, to find rest; to rest
آسوده حال [aasudahaal] having achieved prosperity; successful; well-to-do

آسوده دل [aasudadel] and آسوده خاطر [aasudakhaater] peaceful; appeased
اسهال [eshaal] diarrhea
اسهام [ashaam] *plural of* سهم 12
اسهامی [ashaami]
• شرکت - joint-stock company
آسیا [aasyaa] and آسیاب [aasyaab] 1 mill ♦ بادی - windmill 2 molars ♦ دندانهای - teeth; jaws; chewing apparatus
• آسیاسنگ ☞ سنگ –
• - کردن to grind
آسیابان [aasyaabaan] miller
آسیاسنگ [aasyaasang] millstone
آسیانه [aasyaana] grindstone
آسیاوان [aasyaawaan] ☞ آسیابان
آسیب [aasib] damage, loss; harm, injury
• - رساندن- to cause harm, to damage, to do harm; to inflict injury
اسید [asid] *chemistry* acid
اسیدبوریک [asidborik] boric acid
اسیر [asir] (*plural* اسراء [osaraa]) 1 prisoner ♦ حرب - prisoner of war 2 slave, captive, prisoner
• - کردن *literary* 1 to capture; to enslave 2 to captivate, to charm
اسیری [asiri] captivity
آش [aash]¹ 1 food; soup, broth 2 noodle soup
• همان آش همان کاسه است *proverb* old song
• آش بریدن to prepare noodle soup, to cook noodle soup
آش [aash]²
• آش دادن to tan (a hide)
اشارات [eshaaraat] *plural of* اشاره
• اعجامیه - *obscure* marks of punctuation
• ترافیکی - road signs
اشارت [eshaaraat] ☞ اشاره
اشاره [eshaara] 1 sign, signal 2 *grammar* demonstrative pronoun 3 hint
• - کردن 1 to indicate, to give a sign (به) 2 to hint (به)
اشاعه [eshaa'a] dissemination ♦ علم - dissemination of knowledge
آشامیدن [aasaamidan] *literary* to drink
آشپز [aashpaz] chef; cook
آشپزخانه [aashpazkhaana] kitchen
اشپلاق [eshpelaaq] 1 whistle 2 whistling
• - کردن to whistle
اشت [osht]
• - کردن *colloquial* to incite (to do something به)
اشتباه [esh tebaah] 1 doubt; suspicion ♦ قوی من بالای شما بود - I strongly suspected you 2 mistake, error
• - کردن 1 to doubt 2 to make a mistake, to err
اشتباهی [eshtebaahi] 1 dubious, doubtful 2 erroneous, misleading
اشتر [oshtor] camel
اشتراء [eshteraa] *literary* buying, purchase ♦ قوه - purchasing power (of money)
اشتراک [eshteraak] 1 participation (in something); membership; joint possession (of something) 2 general feature, common feature, common trait 3 subscription
• - داشتن 1 to have in common, to be similar (in some respect در) 2 to have a subscription

اشتراک - ۱ to participate (در) ۲ to subscribe (to a newspaper, magazine, etc.) (ورزیدن) کردن

اشتراک‌کننده [eshteraakkonenda] participant ♦ ممالک – در این کنفرانس the states (countries) participating in this conference, the participant states in this conference

اشتراکی [eshteraaki] and اشتراکیه [eshteraakiya] 1.1 collective, common 1.2 socialist adjective 2 obscure a socialist ♦ دوره - اولیه era of the primitive communal system

اشترنگ [eshtereng] helm, rudder; steering wheel

اشتعال [eshte'aal] ignition, explosion ♦ قابل - flammable, combustible

اشتغال [eshteghaal] occupation (in some job); exercise of duties

اشتق [ashtaq] dried apricots

اشتقاق [eshteqaaq] 1 grammar word-formation; formation of new forms 2 literary poetic figure involving the use, within the same line, of words having the same sound or the same roots (e.g., زمان and نظیر, and نظر and زمین)
♦ مصدر از ریشه فعل (از) یافتن - to be produced, to be formed • می یابد - The infinitive is formed from the verb root.

اشتقاقات [eshteqaaqaat] 1 derived words 2 derived forms (e.g., personal forms of a verb)

اشتک [oshtok] colloquial child

اشتکی [oshtoki] colloquial childhood

اشتوب [oshtub] primus stove ♦ لحیم کاری - technical blowtorch, soldering torch

اشتهاء [eshtehaa] appetite
♦ از – ماندن - to lose [one's] appetite

اشتهار [eshtehaar] 1 fame, popularity 2 dissemination of information (about someone)
♦ به – رسیدن - to become famous, popular

اشتهاری [eshtehaari]
♦ مجرم - wanted criminal

آشتی [aashti] peace, conciliation; peaceful settlement
♦ - دادن to reconcile
♦ - کردن to become reconciled; to come to an agreement

اشتیاق [eshtiyaaq] strong desire, aspiration; yearning; languor
♦ - کردن to desire passionately, to strive; to pine (for something, somebody)

آشتی‌ناپذیر [aashtinapaazir] 1 irreconcilable 2 incompatible

اشجار [ashjaar] plural of شجر

اشخاص [ashkhash] plural of شخص

اشرار [ashraar] plural of شریر ۲

اشرفی [ashrafi]
♦ گل - botany marigolds

اشعار [ashaar] plural of شعر

اشعه [ash'ea] plural of شعاع
♦ اکس ریز - x-rays

اشغال [eshghaal] 1 taking, seizure, occupation 2 (also وظیفه -) assumption of an office, position, or job

اشغالگر [eshghaalgar] usurper, occupier

اشغالی [eshghaali] occupation ♦ قوای - occupation forces

آشفتگی [aashoftagi] 1 anxiety, perturbation, anger, wrath 2 riot, mutiny, disturbance, sedition 3 disorder, confusion

آشفتن [aashoftan] (present tense stem آشوب [aashub]) 1 to be angry, to fall apart, to be put out [over] 2 to become indignant, to rebel 3 to fall into disorder, confusion

آشفته‌حال [aashoftahal] and آشفته خاطر [aashoftakhaater] agitated, perturbed, disordered

اشقار [eshqaar] 1 potash 2 alkali

آشک [aashak] dumplings (with a sharp onion or vegetable filling)

اشک [ashk] 1 tear; tears 2 colloquial tusk; tusks ♦ فیل - elephant tusks

آشکار [aashkaar] 1 evident, obvious 2 open, public
♦ - کردن to find out, to detect, to reveal, to bring to light; to divulge (e.g., a secret)

ایشک آقاسی [eshekaaqaasi] ☞ اشک آقاسی

اشکال [ashkaal] plural of شکل

اشکال [eshkaal] difficulty; obstacle

اشک‌پر [ashkpor] tearful, tear-stained ♦ چشمانش – شد Her eyes filled with tears.

آشکدو [aashkadu] squash

اشکم [eshkam] ☞ شکم

اشکمبه [eshkamba] colloquial 1 stomach, belly 2 entrails ♦ شوربای - soup with giblets

اشکنه [eshkana] soup made of dry apricots flavored with oil and egg

آشگر [aashgar] rolling pin (for rolling out dough)

آشنا [aashnaa] 1.1 friend 1.2 beloved 2.1 acquaintance (person); familiar, known 2.2 knowing (something), one who knows (something)

آشنایی [aashnaayi] 1 familiarity (with someone, something) 2 friendly relations 3 love

آشوب [aashob] 1 agitation, commotion 2 riot, mutiny, rebellion 3 calamity, misfortune

آشوب [aashub] present tense stem آشفتن

اشهاد [eshhaad] legal 1 establishment of a fact with the aid of witnesses 2 calling as a witness

اشیاء [aashya] plural of شیء
♦ لوازمه - household utensils

آشیانه [aashyaana] 1 nest (of a bird) 2 technical cell; socket 3 box; capsule

اصالت [asaalat] 1 authenticity 2 noble birth, noble origin 3 primacy
♦ حقیقت - philosophical realism
♦ ماده - philosophical materialism

اصحاب [ashaab] (plural of صاحب 1, 3) historical associates of Mohammed

اصرار [esraar] 1 insistence (upon something) 2 persistence, stubbornness
♦ - کردن to insist (در)

اصراف [esraaf] overexpenditure, squandering; prodigality extravagance

اصطلاح [estelaah] 1 expression, turn of speech, idiom 2 term ♦ تخنیکی - technical term

اصغری [asghari] minimal ♦ ارتفاع - minimal altitude

اصل [asel] (plural اصول [osul]) 1 basis, essence ♦ مطلب - the essence of the matter 2 article, section (of a law, etc.) 3 origin 4 original (version, copy) 5 grammar stem, root 6 economics fixed capital

اصلاً [áslan] 1 in essence 2 by birth ♦ هندی بود - By origin / birth / extraction he was an Indian.

اصلاح [eslaah] 1 correction 2 improvement ♦ نسل حیوانات - improving the bloodlines of livestock

اصلاحات [eslaahaat] reform; reforms

اصلاح طلب [eslaahtalab] proponent of reforms

اصل بست [aselbast] military personnel, cadre

اصل ونسب [aslonasab] 1 pedigree, origin 2 nobility, high birth
اصلی [asli] 1 basic, chief, essential 2 *grammar* root *adjective*, nonderivative 3 genuine 4 natural ♦ - ابریشم natural silk
اصلیت [asliyat] 1 nature, essence 2 authenticity
اصم [asam (m)] *grammar* voiceless, unvoiced (of a consonant)
اصناف [asnaaf] *plural of* صنف
اصوات [aswaat] 1 *plural of* صوت 2 *grammar* interjections
اصول [osul] 1 *plural of* اصل 2 principles, foundations ♦ اساسی - basic principles 3 system, order ♦ بندگی - slave-holding system
اصولاً [osulan] 1 according to regulations, by law 2 in principle
اصولنامه [osulnaama] 1 regulations charter; rules ♦ داخلی - *military* internal service regulations (garrison regulations) 2 order, routine; regulation
اصولی [osuli] 1 fundamental 2 methodological 3 based on legislation, legal
اصیل [asil] 1 noble, well-born 2 pureblooded, thoroughbred, pedigree 3 genuine; real
اضافت [ezaafat] 1 *grammar* (also - علامه) ezafeh (unstressed formant "e" affixed to the defined word and expressing an attributive relationship) 2 ☞ اضافه 1
اضافه [ezaafa] 1 addition, additive 2 additional, superfluous, spare ♦ تولید - *economics* surplus product
• بر - over, beyond, upwards of
• کردن - to add, to increase
اضافه کاری [ezaafakaari] overtime work
اضافگی [ezaafagi] 1 addition, raise 2 excess, remainder, balance
اضافی [ezaafi] 1 additional, supplemental ♦ ارزش - *economics* surplus value 2 *grammar* ezafeh *adjective*
• ترکیب – ezafeh word combination
اضحی [azhaa]
• عید – holiday of sacrifice, holiday of offering
اضداد [azdaad] *philosophical* opposites
• مبارزه – struggle of opposites, conflict of opposites
اضطراب [ezteraab] agitation, disorder, alarm
اضطراری [ezteraari]
• حالت - unusual situation, extraordinary situation
اضلاع [azlaa'] *plural of* ضلع
• متحده امریکا - United States of America
اطاعت [etaa'at] 1 obedience ♦ اوامر- execution of orders 2 subordination
• کردن - to obey, to show obedience
اطاق [otaaq] ☞ اتاق
اطراف [atraaf] 1 *plural of* طرف 2 environs, outskirts ♦ کابل - environs of Kabul ◊ جنگلهای - neighboring woods
• در - 1 around *denominal preposition* ♦ قلعه - around the farmstead 2 concerning, about ♦ در این موضوع خوب فکر کنید – Do a fair amount of thinking about this.
اطفال [atfaal] *plural of* طفل
اطفائیه [etfaaiya]
• عمله - firemen, fire-fighting squad
• موتر – fire truck
اطلاع [ettelaa'] piece of news, report, information
• دادن - to report; to inform
• حاصل کردن - to obtain information, to receive information
• به - رسانیده میشودکه It is brought to [your] attention that ...

اطلاع دهی [ettelaadehi] notification, informing
• فرمایید - *office* please inform / [I] request [you] inform
اطلاق [etlaaq] 1 reference (to something) 2 conferring (e.g., of a name), designation
• شدن - to be designated, to be named; to be employed, to be used (بر)
اطلس [atlas] ¹ atlas
• جغرافیایی - geographical atlas
اطلس [atlas] ² satin
اطلسی [atlasi] satin *adjective*
اطمینان [etminaan] 1 confidence; trust 2 reliability 3 assurance, confirmation
• دادن - to assure, to give hope to (به)
• داشتن - to be confident, to be certain, to be sure (در)
• کردن - to believe, to trust (به)، (بالای) ♦ به ما - نمی کنند They do not trust us.
اطمینانی [etminaani] 1 reliable, true, deserving of trust (about someone) 2 (also - شخص) proxy, agent, confidential agent
اظهار [ezhaar] expression; statement ♦ نظر - expression of one's opinion
• کردن - to express, to state
• نظر کردن - to express one's opinion, to speak
اظهارات [ezhaaraat] official statement, official declaration; delivery of a speech
اعاده [e'aada] 1 return; repayment (e.g., of a promissory note), payment (e.g., of a loan) 2 restoration, renovation ♦ اعتبار- restoration of solvency ◊ مناسبات - normalization of relations
اعاشه [eaasha] 1 provisions, foodstuffs ♦ حیوانی - forage, fodder 2 *literary* means of subsistence, livelihood
اعانت [eaanat] 1 material aid, material assistance 2 donation
• کردن - 1 to render material aid 2 to donate, to give as a gift
اعانه [eaana] grant, donation to give
• دادن - to pay a grant
اعتبار [e'tebaar] 1 authority, weight, influence 2 force, effectiveness (of a document) 3 *economics* credit
• قابل – 1 worthy of trust; authoritative, influential 2 having force, being in effect
• دادن - to open credit, to grant credit (به)
• داشتن - to have the force of law (about a document)
• از - ساقط بودن (شدن) to lose effect (about a document)
اعتبار نامه [e'tebaarnaama] *finance* letter of credit
اعتدال [e'tedaal] 1 balance, equilibrium 2 moderation ♦ آب و هوا - moderation of climate
اعتراض [e'teraaz] 1 objection, protest 2 *finance* protest (of a promissory note)
اعتراف [e'teraaf] 1 admission, acknowledgement ♦ به - گناه and گناه - admission of guilt 2 confession
• کردن - 1 to admit, to acknowledge (به) 2 to confess (را)
اعتصاب [e'tesaab] strike ♦ عمومی - general strike
اعتصاب شکن [e'tesaabshekan] strikebreaker
اعتصابی [e'tesaabi] 1 strike *adjective* ♦ جنبش - strike movement 2 striker
اعتقاد [e'teqaad] faith, conviction; religious belief
• کردن - 1 to believe (به) 2 to be convinced (به)
اعتماد [e'temaad] faith, trust ♦ متقابل mutual trust ◊ رای - a vote of confidence ◊ قابل - reliable, trustworthy
♦ داشتن - to believe, to trust (بر،به); to rely on (بر،به)

اعتماد [e'temaad] به وعده های آنها دیگر - نداریم We do not believe their promises anymore.

اعتمادنامه [e'temaadnaama] diplomatic credentials

اعتمادی [e'temaadi] ☞ اطمینانی

اعتنا [e'tenaa] attention, concern
• کردن - to pay attention, to direct attention; to show concern (به)

اعجاز [e'jaaz] performance of a miracle; miraculous deed ♦ پیغمبران - miraculous deeds of the prophets

اعجازی [e'jaazi] miraculous, connected with a miracle

اعجامیه [e'jaamiya]
• علامت and اشارات - obscure marks of punctuation

اعداد [a'daad] plural of عدد

اعدادی [e'daadi] secondary (concerning school) ♦ مکاتب - secondary schools

اعدادیه [e'daadiya] (also - مکتب) secondary school

اعدام [e'daam] execution ♦ حکم - death sentence
• کردن - to execute
• به - محکوم کردن to sentence to death, to give the death penalty

اعراب [a'raab] plural of عرب

اعزام [e'zaam] sending, dispatching (of an expedition); sending (of someone)

اعزامی [e'zaami] 1 sent, delegated ♦ حکومت - sent by the government 2 expeditionary ♦ اردوی - expeditionary forces

اعشاری [a'shaari] mathematical decimal ♦ کسر - decimal fraction

اعشاریه [a'shaariya] (also - علامه) decimal point

اعصاب [a'saab] plural of عصب

اعضاء [a'zaa] plural of عضو

اعطاء [e'ta] 1 gift, donation 2 award (of a decoration); bestowing (of a title, a rank)

اعظم [a'zam] great, most high, supreme ♦ امام - Imam Hanif (founder of Hanif doctrine)
• صدر اعظم ☞ صدر -
• وزیر - grand vizier

اعظمی [a'zami] maximum ♦ ارتفاع - maximum altitude

اعلا [a'laa] ☞ اعلی

اعلام [e'laam] 1 notification ♦ خطر هوایی - air alert 2 piece of news, report
• کردن - to notify, to inform, to report (به)

اعلامیه [e'laamiya] declaration, statement; communique

اعلان [e'laan] 1 promulgation, proclamation, announcement ♦ جنگ - declaration of war 2 announcement; poster; advertisement

اعلی [a'laa] 1 higher, superior, highest; royal, imperial ♦ حاکم - governor 2 best, outstanding, excellent ♦ پوستین - sheepskin coat of outstanding or excellent quality

اعلیحضرت [a'laahazrat] his majesty

اعمار [e'maar] construction, erection ♦ اپارتمانهای عصری - construction of modern dwellings or apartment buildings
• شدن - to build, to erect

اعماق [a'maaq] 1 plural of عمق 2 geology interior of the earth, mineral resources ♦ زمین - bowels of the earth

اعمال [a'maal] 1 plural of عمل 2 ironic deeds ♦ از اعمال تان خبر داریم We have heard a lot about your adventures.
• شاقه - penal servitude, hard labor

اعمال [e'maal] use, application

اعویه [a'wiya] anatomy vessels

اعیان [a'yaan] distinguished people, magnates ♦ اشراف - nobility, aristocracy ◊ مجلس - senate, upper house

اعیانی [a'yaani] 1 related by blood ♦ برادر - blood brother 2 noble, well-born ♦ زندگی - lordly life

اعیاد [ayad] plural of عید

آغا [aaghaa] 1 agha, lord, ruler 2 salutation mister, sir 3 head of a family, father 4 older brother, oldest brother

آغابلی [aaghaabalee] colloquial yes-man

آغاجان [aaghaajaan] affectionate daddy

آغاز [aaghaaz] beginning
• کردن - to begin (something)

آغالاله [aaghaa-laala] agha-lala (salutation to older brother, brother-in-law, husband of sister)

اغتشاش [eghteshaash] riot, mutiny, disturbance sedition, revolt ♦ طالبها - Taliban uprising

اغتنام [eghtenaam]
• فرصت - use of the moment convenient for the occasion

اغده [oghda] colloquial melancholy, sadness ♦ اغده اش ترقید He stopped grieving.

اغذیه [aghziya] plural of غذا

اغراض [aghraaz] plural of غرض

اغراق [eghraaq] 1 exaggeration 2 literary hyperbole

آغشته [aaghoshta] abundantly soaked, saturated (with something) ♦ درخون - stained with blood
• کردن - to soak, to saturate (with something), to stain (with something)

اغفال [eghfaal] literary leading astray, deception

آغل [aaghel] and اغل [aqal] livestock pen (in the steppe); yard; ranch

اغلاط [aghlaat] plural of غلط 2

اغلب [aghlab] for the most part; mainly, frequently

اغنیا [aghniyaa] plural of غنی

اغوا [eghwaa] 1 instigation, provocation 2 seduction, deception; leading astray

اغواگر [eghwaagar] troublemaker; instigator

آغوش [aaghosh] embrace
• به - کشیدن (گرفتن) to lock in an embrace, to embrace

اغیار [aghyaar] plural of غیر 2
• یارو - ours and theirs, one's own and someone else's

اف [of] Phew! / Ugh! / O! / Oh! interjection ♦ اف چطور درد میکند Boy, am I tired! ♦ اف چقدر مانده شدم Ouch, it hurts!

آفات [aafaat] 1 plural of آفت 2 (also - نباتات) agricultural pests

افاده [efaada] 1 expression (of an idea), exposition ♦ قدرت - the art of expounding on one's thoughts or ideas 2 turn of phrase, formulation 3 meaning; significance

افاده وی [efaadawi]
• قدرت - زبان expressiveness of language

افاعیل [afaa'il] 1 plural of فعل [fa'l (and) faal] 2 literary (also - عروضی) formulae of aruz (system of versification) in letters

افاغنه [afaaghena] plural of افغان

آفاق [aafaaq] 1 plural of افق 2 countries of the world; the world

آفاقی [aafaaqi] 1 world adjective, global ♦ سیاست - world policy 2 philosophical objective, real 3 (opposite انفسی) objective, impartial ♦ دید - objective view, approach

آ, ا

آفت [aafat] (*plural* آفات [afat]) 1 disease, illness 2 misfortune, trouble, disaster ♦ آسمانی - natural calamity 3 harm, damage (caused to crops or orchards by frost or pests)

آفتاب [aaftaab] sun ♦ بر آمد - The sun rose. ◊ نشست - The sun set. ◊ او را – زد - He had sunstroke. ◊ سر کوه - the sunset of life, extreme old age
• خوردن - 1 to become dried in the sun 2 to become sunburned
• دادن - 1 to dry [something] in the sun 2 to temper

آفتاب بارانک [aaftaabbaaraanak] sun and rain; blind rain (rain that falls while the sun is shining)

آفتاب برآمد [aaftaabbaraamad] 1 sunrise 2 east

آفتاب پرست [aaftaabparast] sunflower

آفتاب رخ [aaftaabrokh] sunny, facing the south (about a room)

آفتاب سوخته [aaftaabsokhta] heated by the sun, heated in the sun; sunburned

آفتاب گرفتگی [aaftaabgereftagi] eclipse of the sun

آفتاب گیر [aaftaabgir] 1 awning, sunshade 2 venetian blind ♦ - کلاه hat with a brim (for shade), sun hat

آفتاب نشست [aaftaabneshast] 1 sunset 2 west

آفتابه [aaftaaba] kumgan (narrow-necked pitcher with a spout used for ablution)

آفتابه لگن [aaftaabalagan] pitcher and basin (for washing hands before and after a meal)

آفتابی [aaftaabi] 1.1 sunny, illumined by the sun ♦ روز - sunny day 1.2 clear, obvious, evident 2 clearly, obviously, evidently
• شدن - to become clear, to clear up, to brighten up

افتادگی [aftaadagi] 1 unfortunate situation, pitiful condition; helplessness 2 shyness, modesty

افتادن [aftaadan] (*present tense stem* افت [aft]) 1 to fall (in various meanings) ♦ به پای کسی - دراز - to go sprawling ◊ to fall at someone's feet 2 to get [somewhere], to land [somewhere], to find oneself [someplace] ♦ به دست - to fall in the hands [of someone], to get caught 3 to be located, to be situated (on terrain) ♦ ده ما در مجاورت کوه بلند افتاده - Our village is situated close to a high mountain. 4 *colloquial* to lie; to loll 5 (component of compound verb) to lose significance
• از اهمیت - to go out of commission, to malfunction (about a machine)
• ازکار - to become unfit, to be unserviceable
• ازمود – to go out of style
• ارزان - *colloquial* to get away cheaply

افتاده [aftaada] 1 *past participle* افتادن 2.1 poor, unfortunate; humble 2.2 shy, modest

افتتاح [eftetaah] opening, beginning
• (یافتن) شدن - to be opened, to begin

افتخار [eftekhaar] pride; honor; glory, respect
• (به) کردن - to be proud

افتخاری [eftekhaari] honored, honorary ♦ ریاست - honorary presidium

افتضاح [eftezaah] shame, disgrace

افتو [aftaw] *colloquial* ☞ آفتاب
• سرکوه - ☞ آفتاب سرکوه in entry آفتاب

افتوز [aftoz] *medicine* 1 foot and mouth disease 2 ill with foot and mouth disease

افتوزدگی [aftawzadagi] *colloquial* sunstroke

افتوششه [aftawsheshta] *colloquial* ☞ آفتاب نشست

افتیدن [aftidan] ☞ افتادن
• در حرکت - 1 to start moving 2 to start on a trip

افراختن [afraakhtan] ☞ افراشتن

افراد [afraad] *plural of* فرد

افراز [afraaz] *present tense stem* افراشتن and افروختن

افراشتن [afraashtan] (*present tense stem* افراز [afraz]) to raise; to lift
• پرچم – to hoist a banner
• خیمه ها را - to pitch tents, to set up tents

افراط [efraat] overindulgence ♦ درخرج پول - acting like a spendthrift; acting like a squanderer ◊ درصرف غذا - lack of moderation in eating

افروختن [afrokhtan] (*present tense stem* افروز [afroz]) 1 to set on fire, to kindle 2 to illumine 3 to blaze up, to catch fire

افروز [afroz] 1 *present tense stem* افروختن 2 (second component of compound words meaning "igniting" / "illumining") ♦ جنگ افروز - warmonger, instigator of war

آفریدن [aafaridan] (*present tense stem* آفرین [afarin]) *literary* to create

آفریدگار [aafaridagaar] creator, author, the creator (epithet for God)

افریدی [afridi] Afridi (Pashtoon tribe)

آفرین [aafarin] ¹ 1 *present tense stem* آفریدن 2 (second component of compound words meaning "creating") ♦ شاهکار آفرین - a person creating masterpieces, brilliant artist

آفرین [aafarin] ² 1 Bravo! / Excellent! *interjection* 2 praise, cry of approval
• گفتن - to praise, to approve of (به)

آفرینش [aafarinesh] *literary* creation (of something)

افزار [afzaar] 1 instrument, tool ♦ جراحی - surgical instrument 2 tool of labor ♦ سنگی - stone tools

افزا (ی) [afzaa (y)] *present tense stem* افزودن

افزایش [afzaayesh] increase, addition, growth ♦ معاش - raise in wages
• نشانه – (grain.) ezafeh indicator ☞ اضافه

افزود [afzud]
• کردن - to increase, to add
• شدن (گردیدن) – to increase to grow *intransitive*

افزودن [afzudan] (*present tense stem* افزا (ی) [afzaay]) 1 to increase, to multiply (را به) 2 to increase *intransitive*, to multiply, to grow

افزودی [afzudi] ☞ افزایش

افزونی [afzuni] 1 excess, surplus 2 abundance 3 ☞ افزایش
2 ☞ افزودن یافتن

افسانوی [afsaanawi] fantastic ♦ سر زمین های عجیب و - wonderful, storybook lands

افسانه [afsaana] 1 story, tale ♦ افسانه ام به پایان رسید - My story is ended. 2 tradition, legend; fairy tale 3 invention, fiction, fabrication ♦ هر چه میگوید – است - Everything that he says is a fabrication.

افسر [afsar] officer ♦ افسران عالی رتبه - senior officers; the senior officers

افسردگی [afsordagi] 1 faded state 2 numbness 3 grief, dejection

افسرده [afsorda] 1 faded, withered (e.g., of a flower) 2 benumbed (e.g., from grief) 3 grief-stricken, despondent

افسوس [afsos] 1 Alas! / Pity! *interjection* 2 regret, pity
• کردن (خوردن) - to pity, to regret (something از)

15

افسون [afsun] 1 witchcraft, sorcery 2 slyness, deception
- کردن • 1 to practice witchcraft, to cast a spell, to conjure 2 to deceive, to delude

افسونگر [afsungar] 1 bewitching, magic 2.1 sorcerer, magician 2.2 cheat, deceiver

افسونگری [afsungari] witchcraft, sorcer

آفسیت [aafseet] *printing* offset

افشاء [efshaa] divulgence, publicity
- راز • divulging a secret

افشاندن [afshaandan] 1 to scatter, to strew ♦ گیسوان را افشانده می گریخت She was running with her braids flying out behind her. 2 to splash, to sprinkle 3 to shake off
- بینی • to blow one's nose

افضلیت [afzaliyat] *literary* superiority; advantage
- داشتن (از) • to surpass

افطار [eftaar] *religion* breaking of fast (after sunset during the month of Ramadan)
- کردن • to break a fast

افعال [af'aal] *plural of* فعل [fe'l]

افغان [afghaan] (*plural* افاغنه [afaaghena]) an Afghan ♦ ملت - Afghan people

افغانی [afghaani] 1 Afghan *adjective* 2 (*also* - زبان) the Afghan language, Pushtu/Pashto

افغانیت [afghaaniyat] state of belonging to the Afghan nation
- از - دور بودن • to be unfitting of an Afghan, to be incompatible with the code of honor of Afghans

افق [ofoq] (*plural* افاق [afaq]) 1 horizon; sky ♦ مرئی - visible horizon 2 mental outlook

افقی [ofoqi] horizontal

افکار [afkaar] *plural of* فکر
- فکر عامه • public opinion

افگار [afgaar (and) awgaar] injured, hurt
- شدن • to be injured, to be wounded; to be hurt; to be crippled, to be maimed, to be mutilated

افگندن [afgandan] 1 to throw 2 to overturn
- سایه • to cast a shadow
- نور • to give off light, to shine

افلاس [eflaas] 1 poverty, need 2 bankruptcy, failure; insolvency

افلاک [aflaak] *plural of* فلک

افواه [afwaah] hearing; rumors ♦ بی اساس - unfounded rumors

افیون [afyun] 1 opium ♦ نشه - state of intoxication (after taking opium) 2 poison, narcotic, dope

آقا [aaqaa] ☞ آغا

اقارب [aqaareb] relatives, close ones, kinfolk

اقامت [eqamat] 1 stay; residence 2 settlement, placement, deployment (somewhere)
- داشتن • to live, to stay
- کردن • to stop; to settle (somewhere)

اقامتگاه [eqaamatgaah] abode, place of residence; residence ♦ زمستانی - winter residence

اقامه [eqama] 1 ☞ اقامت 2 representation, bringing (of a suit, in court) 3 *literary* observance, commission, accomplishment
- نماز • anointment

اقبال [eqbaal] good fortune; success

اقتباس [eqtebaas] 1 borrowing ♦ لغات - *grammar* borrowing of words 2 extraction, extract; quotation

اقتباسی [eqtebaasi] and اقتباس شده [eqtebaasshoda]
- لغات • *grammar* borrowed words

اقتدار [eqtedaar] might, authority

اقتصاد [eqtesaad] 1 economic structure, economy ♦ ملی - national economy, national economic structure 2 (*also* - علم) economics (scientific discipline)
- مجله • the magazine lktisad

اقتصادی [eqtesaadi] 1.1 economic ♦ نقشه - economic plan 1.2 economically advantageous, profitable 2 (*plural* اقتصادیون [eqtasaadiyun]) economist

اقتصادیات [eqtesaadiyun] economic structure, economy

اقتضاء [eqtezaa] 1 necessity, need 2 demand, condition
- در اقتضاآت مختلف • 1 under different conditions 2 in different situations, in various situations

اقدام [eqdaam] 1 beginning; action 2 taking of steps or measures
- (به کار) کردن • to begin to act; to start, to undertake (a job)

اقدامات [eqdaamaat] 1 measures, steps 2 *military* operations

اقداماتی [eqdaamaati] executive (concerning authority)

اقرار [eqraar] 1 confirmation, certification (of something) 2 admission, acknowledgement (of something) 3 *legal* deposition
- کردن (را به) • 1 to confirm, to certify 2 to admit; to confess

اقرارخط [eqraarkhat] *historical* protocol, act (document, concerning the recognition of something or concerning some pledge, commitment, or obligation)
- شرعی • protocol, act (notarized in accordance with the norms of the sharia)
- عرفی • act, protocol (signed by witnesses but not notarized)

اقرار نامه [eqraarnaama] *legal* written obligation, pledge, or commitment; contract

اقساط [aqsaat] *plural of* قسط
- به – • in installments, in parts

اقسام [aqsaam] *plural of* قسم [qesem]

آقساقال [aaqsaaqal] 1 aksakal 2 elder (of a village)

اقصی [aqsaa] *and* اقصاء 1 extreme, far ♦ شرق - the Far East 2 remote region, remote land, outskirts ♦ در افغانستان – on the fringes of Afghanistan

اقگل [aqgol] akgul (variety of karakul)

اقل [aqal(l)] lesser, minimal ♦ حد - minimum

اقلاً [aqallan] at least; minimally

اقلام [aqlaam] *plural of* قلم²

اقلیت [aqaliyat] minority ♦ اقلیت های ملی - national minorities

اقلیم [eqlim] 1 climate ♦ بری - continental climate 2 *geography* belt, zone 3 country, territory 4 continent

اقلیمی [eqlimi] climatic ♦ شرایط - climatic conditions

اقوام [aqwaam] *plural of* قوم

اقه [eqa] *colloquial from* اینقدر

اقه گک [eqagak] *colloquial* so little, just barely

اکابر [akaaber] 1 adults ♦ تعلیم - instruction or training of adults, adult education 2 *literary* noblemen

آکادمی [aakaademi] academy ♦ علوم - academy of sciences

اکاردیون [akaardiun] accordian

اکبر [akbar] *literary* great, greatest (epithet of Allah)

اکت [akt]¹ actor's performance, acting (on the stage)
- صحنه دلچسپی را کردن • 1 to play (on the stage); to act ♦ They played an interesting scene. 2 to pretend, to feign ♦ پیش ما زیاد – نکو Don't pretend so much with us!

اکت [akt]² act (document)
- معاینه • act of inspection, inspection document

اکتساب [ektesaab] 1 acquisition by labor; earnings 2 obtaining of profit
- علم • acquisition of knowledge, mastery of science
اکتسابی [ektesaabi] acquired, earned; accumulated ♦ - تابعیت naturalization, transfer of citizenship
اکتشاف [ekteshaaf] 1 discovery 2 research, search 3 geology survey, prospecting
اکتشافات [ekteshaafaat]
- جغرافیایی • geographical discoveries
اکتفاء [ektefaa] contentment, satisfaction (with something)
- کردن • to be satisfied (به)
- نرود – باید • should not be limited
اکتبر [aktobar] October
اکتور [aktor] 1 actor; movie actor 2 colloquial pretender, performing artist
اکثر [aksar] 1 greater part, majority; many ♦ در - ممالک in many countries ◊ - حد maximum 2 ☞ اکثراً
اکثراً [aksaran] in most instances; mainly, frequently
اکثریت [aksariyat] majority ♦ - آراء the majority of votes ◊ مطلق - absolute majority
اکدیها [akadihaa] historical Akkadians
اکراه [ekraah] literary aversion; hatred
اکرم [akram] literary most generous, most lavish, most gracious (epithet of Allah)
اکزاز [ekzaaz] and اکزاس [ekzas]
- نل • technical exhaust pipe
اکس [aks] colloquial slight odor, slight smell (of something rotting)
- گرفتن – and برداشتن - • to begin to smell, to give off an odor (of meat, etc.)
اکسریز [eksreez] roentgen ♦ طبیب - roentgenologist (physician)
اکسل [aksal] technical axis, axle; shaft ♦ عقب- (aghab) rear axle (of motor vehicle) ◊ پیشروی - front axle (of motor vehicle)
اکسه [aksa] colloquial ☞ عطسه
آکسیژن [aaksijan] oxygen ♦ مایع - liquid oxygen
اکسیر [aksir] obscure 1 elixir ♦ حیات - elixir of life 2 (also اعظم -) philosopers' stone
اکسیلیتر [akseeleetar] technical accelerator; pedal
اکمال [ekmaal] 1 military replinshment of supplies, supply, rations ♦ البسه - clothing allowance, clothing ◊ - مالی monetary allowance 2 literary completion; execution, accomplishment
- کردن • literary 1 to supply, to place on subsistence 2 to complete; to execute, to accomplish
اکناف [aknaaf] (also خانه -) personal plot (of land)
- اطراف و مملکت • remote regions, periphery
اکنون [aknun] literary now, at present ♦ تا - until now
اک و پک [akopak] colloquial dumbfounded
- ماندن • to dumbfound
آکه [aaka] regional 1 older brother, oldest brother 2 aka (polite form of address to older person)
اکید [akid] urgent; categorical ♦ ممانعت - categorical prohibition
آگاه [aagaah] 1 knowing; informed 2 conscious
- بودن • to know, to be informed ♦ من خبر نداشتم ولی او - بود I didn't know [about this], but it was known to him.
- کردن • to inform (از)
آگاهانه [aagaahaana] consciously; knowingly

آگاهی [aagaahi] 1 knowledge (in some field); state of being informed 2 consciousness ♦ سطح - مردم level of consciousness of the masses
- یافتن • to become aware, to become informed (از)
اگر [agar] conjunction 1 if ♦ اگر تکت بیآبیم سینما میرویم If we get a ticket, we'll go to the movie. 2 if conditional ♦ وقت میداشتم باو کمک میکردم - If I had the time, I would help him.
اگرچه [agarche] conjunction although
اگریمان [agreemaan] diplomatic agrement (French)
اگست [agést] august
آگهی [aagahi] 2 ☞ آگاهی
آگین [aagin] (adjectival suffix) ♦ قهرآگین angry (about something)
آل [aal] colloquial 1 demon (who supposedly frightens women during childbirth) 2 witch
ال [al] wooden part of a plow
- زدن • to plow (land, soil)
الا [alaa] colloquial Hey! (indicates exultation) interjection
- یارجان • Hey, (female) friend! / Hey, sweetheart!
الا [ellaa] other than, besides, excluding
- و – • 1 if not, then … 2 otherwise
آلات [aalaat] plural of آله
- ادوات رادیو و • technical apparatus ♦ ادوات و - radio apparatus, radio equipment
- تجهیزات • military 1 equipment 2 armament (of an aircraft)
آلارم [aalaarm] military alarm, alert ♦ تعلیمی - training alert
الاستیک [elaastik] elastic adjective
الاستیکیت [elaastikiyat] elasticity
آلاشه [alaasha] jaw ♦ بالا - upper jaw ◊ پایین - lower jaw ◊ آلاشه اش گرم آمده He loves to talk.
الاغ [olaagh] literary donkey, ass
الاف [alaaf] flour seller
آلام [aalaam] plural of الم
آلایش [aalaayesh] literary 1 dirtiness 2 defiled state
الایی [elaayi] colloquial ☞ الهی
البته [albattá] of course, obviously
البسه [albesa] plural of لباس
البومین [albumin] chemistry albumin
آلپن [alpen] thumbtack
آلت [aalat] ☞ آله
التباس [eltebaas] literary confusion
- شدن • to be confused (با)
التزامی [eltezaami] grammar modal; subjunctive ♦ فعل - modal verb ◊ وجه - subjunctive mood
التصاق [eltesaaq] 1 adhesion, sticking 2 linguistics agglutination 3 medical adhesions (e.g., of the intestines)
التفات [eltefaat] 1 attention, respect 2 courtesy, good relationship
- کردن • to show attention, to render respect; to deal with courteously
التماس [eltemaas] request, entreaty
- کردن • to request, to entreat, to beseech
التهاب [eltehaab] medical inflammation ♦ معده - gastritis
اولتیماتوم [oltimaatom] ultimatum
التیام [eltiyaam] healing, closing, scabbing (of a wound)
الجبر [alshábér] algebra
الچه [alacha] alacha (hand-woven striped fabric)

الحاق [elhaaq] 1 connection, joining, joint 2 annexation ♦ - عدم سیاست policy of nonalignment

الحاقیه [elhaaquiya] addition (to a building), annex

الحال [alhaal] now, at present ♦ - تا until now, up to the present

الحان [alhaan] *plural of* لحن

الحمدلله [alhamdolellaa] *interjection* Glory to God! / Thank God!

الخ [elakh (*abbreviation of* الی آخر [elaaaakher]) and so forth

الاستیکی [elastiki] ☞ استیکی

السلام علیکم [assalaam - alaykom] Peace unto you! / Hello!

السنه [alsena] *plural of* لسان

الش [aalesh] 1 barter; substitution, replacement 2 exchange ♦ - کردن 1 to change, to replace ♦ او لباس خود را - کرد He changed his clothes. 2 to exchange, to barter

الطاف [altaaf] *plural of* لطف
♦ به - موفوره *epistolary* by our boundless mercy (from an emir's decree)

الف [alef] name of the first letter of Dari alphabet ♦ - ممدود alef with a long mark

الفاظ [alfaaz] *plural of* لفظ

الفبا [alefbaa] alphabet ♦ - به ترتیب in alphabetical order ◊ - مورس the Morse alphabet

الفت [olfat] *literary* attachment, affection, inclination, tendency; adherence, fidelity

القاب [alqaab] *plural of* لقب

الق بلق [alaqbalaq] *colloquial* motley, speckled; grayish - brownish - crimson

القصه [alqessa] in a word, putting it succinctly; so

القلی [alqali] *chemistry* 1 alkali 2 alkaline

القلیت [alqaliyat] *chemistry* 1 alkali 2 alkalinity

الک [elak] fine sieve, small sieve

الکترون [elektron] *physics* electron ♦ - آزاد free electron

الکتریکی [elektriki] electrical

الکل [alkol] ☞ الکول

الکل [alkol] alcohol, spirits

الکلی [alkoli] alcoholic

الکهول [alkhol] ☞ الکول

الله [allaa(h)] God, Allah

الله اکبر [allaaho-akbar] 1 Praise to Allah! / Glory to Allah! 2 Allah is greatest! (war cry during an attack) 3 God! My goodness! (when surprised, amazed)

الله التوفیق [allaah-attawfiq] *literary* May God help [you]!

الله توکلی [allaah-tawakkali] *colloquial* rashly; thoughtlessly

الم [alam] (*plural* آلام [alam]) 1 torture, pain, suffering 2 grief, sorrow, melancholy, depression

الماری [almari] cupboard, chest ♦ ادویه - medicine chest ◊ کتاب - bookcase

الماس [almaas] diamond

الماسک [almaasak] 1 lightning 2 *physics* electric arc

الماس گون [almaasgun] sparkling like a diamond ♦ - فواره a sparkling fountain, a fountain sparkling with spray

آلمانی [aalmaani] 1 German 2.1 a German 2.2 (*also* - زبان) the German language

المپیا [olampiyaa] the Olympic games, the Olympiad

المپیک [olampik] 1 Olympic 2 the Olympic Society (in Afghanistan)

المر [almar] obscure
♦ نشان - order of the sun, first degree
♦ نشان عالی - order of the sun, second degree

آل [aal] ☞ آل مستی

المناک [almanaak] 1 torturous, difficult 2 sad, deplorable ♦ - حادثه deplorable event

المونیم [almoniam] aluminum

النگه [alanga] *colloquial* flame, tongues of flame

آلو [aalu] plum, plum tree

الو [alaw] *regional* fire

الواح [alwaah] *plural of* لوح

الوان [alwaan] cotton fabric of an orange-red color

الوانی [alwaani] orange-red

آلوبالو [aalubaalu] cherry, cherry tree

آلوبخارا [aalubokhaaraa] Bukhara plum, prunes

آلوچه [aalucha] alycha (type of plum tree or fruit from such a tree)

آلود [aalud] (second component of compound words that mean:) 1 spotted, soiled ♦ خاک آلود spotted with dirt 2 moistened, wet (with something) ♦ عرق آلود sweaty, sweat-stained 3 full (of something) ♦ خشم آلود full of anger

آلودگی [aaludagi] 1 pollution (e.g., of air); contamination ♦ رادیو اکتیف - radioactive contamination 2 tainting (of a reputation)

آلودن [aaludan] (*present tense stem* آلای [aalaa (y)]) ☞ آلوده in entry آلوده کردن

آلوده [aaluda] 1 *past passive participle* آلودن 2 ♦ - کردن 1 to dirty, to soil 2 to sully (a reputation)

آلوده دامن [aaludadaaman] with sullied honor, with tainted reputation

آله [aala] (*plural* آلات [aalaat]) 1 instrument; tool ♦ موسیقی - musical instrument 2 device; unit; apparatus ♦ تسخین - heating unit, radiator

اله [ela (and) ella] ☞ هله

اله به اله [elabaela] *colloquial* (*also* - که) for ages and ages ♦ به خانه ما آمدید - It's been ages and ages since you have visited us.

اله [elaah] *literary* deity, god (pagan)

الهام [elhaam] 1 inspiration 2 *religion* revelation ♦ - بخشیدن to inspire

اله پتگی [alapatagi] *colloquial* state of great haste, bustle ♦ - به - از and hurriedly

اله پته [alapata] *colloquial*
♦ - بودن (شدن) to hurry very much, to rush, to bustle about

الهه [elaha] goddess ♦ حاصل خیزی - goddess of fertility

الهی (and) *colloquial* elaay] 1 Oh, God! *interjection* 2 *literary* divine

الهیات ☞ علم

الهیات [elahiyaat] theological sciences; theology

آلی [aalee] *colloquial of* حالا

الی [elaa] to (up to, as far as) *preposition* ♦ از غزنی الی کابل from Gazni to Kabul

الیف [alif] (*also* - تیل) drying oil

الیکین [alikain] hand-held kerosene lantern

اما [ammaa] but, however, nevertheless *conjunction*

اماج [omaaj] *and* اماچ [omaach] flour soup with greens (flavoured with sour milk)

آماده [aamaada] 1 ready, prepared (for something) ♦ - نبرد ready for battle 2 prepared, equipped
♦ - کردن (گردانیدن) to prepare
♦ - چیزی شدن / (برای) to get ready for something

آمادگی [aamaadagi] readiness; preparation training

امارت [emaarat] 1 emirate; principality 2 government, authority

آماس [aamaas] swelling; tumor
• کردن - to swell

اماکن [amaaken] *plural of* مکان
• متبر که - *literary* holy places

آمال [aamaal] *literary* desires; hopes

اماله [emaala] enema
• کردن - to give an enema

امام [emaam] 1 imam; high priest; spiritual head 2 (also مسجد -) religious attendant (leading prayers)

امامت [emaamat] 1 performing the duties of an imam 2 spiritual supremacy, imamate

امان [amaan] 1 safety, security, reliability, protection 2 mercy
• خواستن - 1 to ask for mercy, to beg for mercy; to surrender 2 to ask for salvation, to beg for salvation; to ask for asylum (از)
• دادن - 1 to spare, to grant mercy 2 to grant asylum
• بودن (در) به – 1 to be safe, to be unharmed 2 to be sheltered; to be saved (از) ♦ تا از باران به – باشم in order to be sheltered from the rain …

امانت [amaanat] 1 thing or article given for safekeeping or granted for temporary use 2 *finance* deposit
• دادن (به) - 1 to hand over for storage safekeeping 2 to give for temporary use 3 to deposit, to place as a deposit
• گرفتن (به) - 1 to accept for storage or safekeeping 2 to accept for temporary use 3 to accept a deposit, to accept as a deposit
• گذاشتن (به) - دادن •

امانت‌دار [amaanatdaar] honest; reliable; worthy of confidence

امانت‌کار [amaanatkaar] ☞ امانت دار

امانته [amaanta] snow with rain

امانتی [amaanati] 1 handed over in the form of a deposit, contribution 2 entrusted; handed over for storage or safekeeping, for temporary use

امبار [ambaar] ☞ انبار

امباق [ambaaq] co-wife, wives of the same husband (in relation to one another)

امباق‌دار [ambaaqdaar] having a co-wife (sharing one husband)

امبور [ambur] ☞ انبور

امبولانس [ambulaans]
• موتر - ambulance

امپراطور [emperaator] emperor

امپراطوری [emperaatori] empire

امپریالیزم [emparyaalizem] imperialism

امپیر [ampiar] *physics* ampere

امپیرمتر [ampiarmeeter] *physics* ammeter, ampere meter

امت [ommat] *literary* (also محمد -) followers of Mohammed (prophet)

امتحان [emtehaan] 1 verification, test 2 examination ♦ تحریری - written examination ◊ زبانی - oral examination
• دادن - to take an examination to pass an examination
• کردن - to verify, to test
• گرفتن - to give examinations

امتداد [emtedad] distance, length ♦ در - for the distance of; the length of

امتعه [amte'a] *plural of* متاع

امتناع [emtenaa] refusal, abstention
• کردن - to abstain, to refuse (از)

امتنان [emtenaan] *literary* 1 gratitude 2 satisfaction

امتیاز [emtiyaaz] 1 difference, distinction; peculiarity 2 privilege; advantage 3 concession ♦ صاحب - concessionaire
• دادن - 1 to make a distinction 2 to give privileges, advantages 3 to grant a concession

امتیازی [emtiyaazi] 1 distinctive, different 2 privileged, preferential ♦ معاش - personal rate 3 concessionary 4 *grammar* concessive

امثال [amsaal] *plural of* مثل

امداد [emdaad] help, support; cooperation ♦ تخنیکی - technical aid, technical assistance
• رساندن - to render aid, to help

امدادی [emdaadi] sent to help, sent to lend a helping hand; auxiliary ♦ فعل - *grammar* auxiliary verb ◊ قوای - *military* reinforcement

آمدآمد [aamadaamad] *colloquial* close approach (of something), eve ♦ بهار است - Spring is just around the corner.

آمدن [aamadan] (present tense stem (ی)آ [aa (y)]) 1 to come, to arrive 2 to begin 3 to be heard (of sounds, etc.)
• به هم - to close in; to come together; to close ♦ آن شب چشمش بهم نیامد That night he did not close his eyes. 2.1 (used in compound and gerundive verb phrases) ♦ دویده آمدن to run up 2.2 *obscure* (synonym of verb شدن in passive construction) ♦ در بالا گفته آمد که … it was previously mentioned that …

آمدورفت [aamadoraft] ☞ رفت و آمد

آمده [aamada] event; accomplishment; fact

آمر [aamer] 1 leader, manager, head; chief ♦ شعبه - chief of department or section 2 *literary* sovereign; leader
• آمر کار ☞ - کار

امر [ámer] [1] (*plural* اوامر [awaamer]) 1 order, command 2 official order, instruction, decree
• دادن - to order, to give an order, to issue an order ♦ آنچه – شود as will be decreed …
• فعل - *grammar* verb in the imperative

امر [ámer] [2] (*plural* امور [omur]) matter, business; circumstance, fact
• طبیعی است It is completely natural.

امرأ [omaraa] *plural of* امیر

امراض [amraaz] *plural of* مرض

آمران [aameraan] 1 *plural of* آمر [aamer] 2 senior officer complement, senior officers

امربر [amrbar] officer's attendant, orderly; messenger

آمرزش [aamorzesh] *religion* forgiveness, absolution of sins (by God)

آمرزگار [aamorzgaar] merciful, all-forgiving (about God)

آمرزیدن [aamorzidan] *religion* to forgive, to remit sins, to pardon (about God) ♦ خدا بیآمرزد! May God forgive [him]! (about the deceased)

آمرکار [aamerekaar] work superintendent

امروز [emroz] today
• و فردا کردن - to postpone from day to day

آمره [aamera] female chief, female manager, female head ♦ نارسینگ - woman in charge of obstetrical courses

امری [amri] *grammar* وجه - imperative mood

آمریت [aameriyat] 1 leadership, superintendance 2 *office* administration, management ♦ عمومی - main administration, main directorate

امسال [emsaal] 1 this year, the current year ♦ از - نه برآیی (curse) I hope you don't live through this year! 2 in this year

امشب [emshab] 1 tonight 2 this evening

امضا [emzaa] signature, signing
• کردن - to sign; to put [one's] signature

امعا [am'aa] (plural معا [me'aa]) intestines, bowels

امکان [emkaan] possibility, probability ♦ درصورت - if possible, if it is, will be possible ◊ از - بعید نیست it is not excluded, it is possible
• دادن - to provide the opportunity, to allow
• داشتن - to have the opportunity
♦ این امر – ندارد This is impossible. / This is difficult to carry out.

املا [emlaa] 1 spelling, orthography 2 dictation
• کردن - to dictate (a text for an exercise in spelling)

املاح [amlaah] plural of ملح

املاک [amlaak] (plural ملک [molk (and) melk]) 1 large land holding; estate 2 historical amlyak (administrative-fiscal unit)

املایی [emlaayi] orthographic

امن [amn] peace, calm; safety, security, reliability

امنیت [amniyat] 1 safety, security ♦ دراثنای کار safety measures ◊ - شورای security council 2 military security, protection ♦ قراول outpost, security detachment

امواج [amwaaj] plural of موج
• کوتاه – physics short waves

اموال [amwaal] plural of مال

آموختن [aamokhtan] present tense stem
آموز [aamoz]) 1 to study (something), to learn (something به; from somebody از) ♦ کودک باید ازبزرگان بیاموزد A child is supposed to learn from adults. 2 to teach (something به)

آموخته [aamokhta] 1 past participle of verb آموختن 2.1 accustomed, trained 2.2 domesticated
• کردن 1 to train 2 to domesticate, to tame

امور [omur] plural of امر

آموز [aamoz] 1 present tense stem آموختن 2 (second component of compound words with meaning of "trainee"
♦ نوآموز novice; newcomer

آموزش [aamozesh] rarely instruction, training; study

آموزشی [aamozeshi] instructive; cognitive
• فلم – documentary film

امی [ami] colloquial of همین

امیانی [amyaani] ☞ همیانی

آمیختن [aameekhtan] (present tense stem آمیز [aameez]) 1 ☞ آمیخته in entry آمیختن کردن 2 obscure to communicate [with], to maintain relations [with]

آمیخته [aameekhta] past participle آمیختن
• کردن - to mix, to intermingle, to combine

آمیختگی [aameekhtagi] 1 state of being mixed 2 mixture, combination

امید [omaid (and) omeed] hope
• دادن - to give hope, to instill hope
• داشتن - to hope, to put [one's] hopes (از); to set hopes [on]
♦ ... که - است I hope (we hope) that ... ◊ هیچ - نیست که ... There is absolutely no hope that ...

امیدبخش [omaidbakhsh] instilling hope; consoling, encouraging

امیدوار [omaidwaar]
• بودن - شدن to hope, to put hopes (on something)
• کردن - (را) to give hopes [to], to encourage

امیدواری [omaidwaari] hope; faith (in accomplishment of something)

امیر [amir] (plural امرا [omaraa]) 1 emir; prince 2 obscure military leader 3 masculine proper name Amir

آمیز [aameez] 1 present tense stem آمیختن 2 (second component of compound words with meaning of "mixed (with something)" / "containing (something)" ♦ پندآمیز instructive, edifying, didactic

آمیزش [aameezesh] 1 mixing, combining 2 contact

امیل [ameel] necklace (made of gold decorations, coins, etc.)
• کردن - to put on a string, to string

امین [amin] 1 1 faithful, reliable 2.1 (also شخص) authorized agent 2 historical (also مالیه -) official who collected taxes at the bazaar 3 masculine proper name Amin

امین [amin] 2 colloquial ☞ همین

آمین [aamin] Amen! / Truly! / So be it!

آمین گویک [aamingoyak] colloquial servile person, toady

آن [aan] 1 1 that, those ♦ آن کس that person ◊ آن درختها those trees ◊ آن چه that which, the fact that ◊ آن که he who, whoever
• آن وقت 1.1 that time 1.2 at that time 2 he; she

آن [aan] 2 colloquial ☞ هان
• آن ونی ☞ و نی

آن [aan] 3 (plural اوان [awaan]) instant, moment ♦ در یک آن in an instant ◊ هرآن all the time, every minute

انار [anaar] pomegranate ♦ درخت - pomegranate tree

انارپوست [anarpost] pomegranate peel (used as a dye)

آنان [aanaan] they (concerning people) ♦ را دعوت کنید - Invite them!

اناهید [anaahid] ☞ ناهید

انایی [an(n)aayi] colloquial none too clever, simple-minded

انبار [ambaar (and) anbaar] 1 sewage, manure 2 fertilizer 3 colloquial heap, pile (of something) ♦ انبار انبار in heaps, in a pile (concerning a large quantity of something) 4 storehouse, depository; warehouse
• دادن - to fertilize (land); to feed (crops)
• کردن - 1 to store, to lay in supplies 2 to collect manure; to prepare fertilizer

انبارخانه [ambaarxaana (and) anbaarxaana] 1 storeroom; warehouse 2 regional barn, granary

انبارکش [ambaarkash (and) anbaarkash] 1 person who collects manure (for fertilizing fields) 2 cesspool cleaner

انبان [ambaan] sack made of dressed hide (for pouring grain)

انبساط [enbesaat] 1 expansion; extension 2 expansion of the boundaries (of something), dissemination

انبر [ambur] tongs, pincers, wire cutters ♦ هموار - flat-nosed pliers

انبوه انبوه [amboh anboh] 1 dense, thick ♦ جنگل - thick forest ◊ ریش - thick beard 2 numerous, abundant ♦ گروه - a numerous (large) group

انبیاء [anbiyaa] plural of نبی

انتحار [entehaar] suicide
• کردن - to commit suicide

انتخاب [entekhaab] 1 election ♦ وکیل - election of a deputy 2 choice; selection ♦ طبیعی - biology natural selection
• کردن - 1 to choose, to elect 2 to select

انتخابات [entekhaabaat] elections ♦ اصولنامه - election statute ◊ انتخابات برای مجلس elections to the majlis

انتخاباتی [entekhaabaati]
• تبلیغات pre-election campaign
• دوره – convocation period (e.g., of parliament)

انتخاب کننده [entekhaabkonenda] elector; voter

انتخابی [entekhaabi] 1 (opposite of انتصابی) elective, electoral, elected 2 chosen, elected ♦ مجموع - شعر selection of poetry

انترکس [antraks] medicine anthrax

انترناسیونال [entarnaasionaal] international

انتروپولوژی [antropoloji] anthropology

انتساب [entesaab] literary 1 relationship, tie, connection; kinship 2 origin, genealogy

انتشار [enteshaar] 1 dissemination, transmittal (of news, etc.) ♦ مرض - spreading of a disease 2 announcement, publication; publishing ♦ نوت - finance issuance 3 physics (also شعاع -) radiation

انتصاب [entesaab] appointment, assignment (to a job)

انتصابی [entesaabi] 1 (opposite of انتخابی) appointed ♦ بصورت - by appointment 2 appointed, assigned (to a job)

انتظار [entezaar] expectation ♦ برخلاف - contrary to expectation, beyond expectation
• داشتن - 1 to await, to expect 2 to rely on, to put hopes (on someone از)
• کسی را کشیدن - to wait for, to expect someone

انتظام [entezaam] 1 order, system 2 discipline ♦ رامراعات کنید - maintain discipline! 3 putting into order
• بخشیدن (دادن) to put into order, to systematize; to organize

انتقاد [enteqaad] criticism ♦ ادبی - literary criticism

انتقال [enteqaal] 1 moving, transferring; shifting, transporting ♦ قابل - portable; transportable 2 transmittal, dissemination ♦ رسوم ازنسلی به نسلی - handing down of customs from generation to generation ◊ برق - transmission of electrical power ◊ قوه - technical drive shaft (in a motor vehicle) ◊ مرض - infection
• دادن - 1 to carry somewhere else, to transfer, to move; to throw over, to throw across 2 to transmit (electrical power, etc.)

انتقالی [enteqaali] 1 portable; mobile 2 transfer (point) 3 transitional (period)

انتقام [enteqaam] vengeance, revenge
• حالا می (از) - کشیدن (گرفتن) to get revenge (on someone) توانیم از او بگیریم پدرت را - Now we can get revenge on him for your father.

آنتن [aantan] antenna ♦ استقامت دار - directional antenna ◊ چهار کنج (چوکانی) - loop or coil antenna

انتها [entehaa] literary 1 end; edge ♦ راه - end of the road 2 ending (of a word)
• تا درجه – and تا درجه to the highest degree; extremely

انتهایی [entehaayi] final; extreme; ultimate ♦ کوشش - last effort, final effort

آنتی سیرم [antiseerom] medicine antidiptheria serum

انتیک [antik] 1 antique, ancient, old 2 antiquarian

آنتین [anteen] ☞ آنتن

آنجا [anjaa] 1 (also در -) there 2 (also به -) to there, thither 3 (also از -) from there, thence
• از آنجا (یی) که inasmuch as, in view of the fact that ... compound conjunction

انجام [anjaam] 1 ending, completion; finale ♦ محاربه - outcome of the battle 2 tip, end, extremity ♦ انجامهای انگشتان tips of the fingers 3 fulfillment, execution ♦ امر - execution of an order
• دادن – 1 to complete, to end, to finish 2 to fulfill, to carry out

انجماد [enjemaad] 1 congealing, freezing ♦ نقطه - and درجه - physics freezing point 2 hardening

انجمن [anjoman] 1 society, organization; association 2 literary meeting, session

انجن [enjen] motor, engine ♦ دیزلی - diesel engine
• راچاالان کردن - to start a motor

انجنیر [enjenyar (and) enjenir] engineer ♦ انجنیر معدن mining engineer

انجنیری [enjeniri] 1 engineering, engineer's adjective ♦ دستگاهای - پوهنحی engineering department or faculty ◊ - engineering works or structures (boiler room, sewer system, etc.) 2 engineering; technology

انجیر [anjir] ¹ fig ♦ درخت - fig tree

انجیر [anjir] ² medicine scrofula

انجیل [anjil] gospel

انجین [enjin] ☞ انجن

انچ [ench] inch

انحراف [enheraaf] 1 digression, deviation 2 political deviation 3 physics deviation, error
• کردن (از) - to digress, to deviate
• جایز - technical tolerance

انحراف ناپذیر [enheraafnaapazir] 1 undeviating, invariable 2 undeviatingly, invariably

انحصار [enhesaar] monopoly ♦ تجارت خارجی - monopoly of foreign trade

انحصارات [enhesaaraat] 1 plural of انحصار 2 (also - ریاست) administration of state monopolies

انحطاط [enhetaat] decline, depression

انحلال [enhelaal] 1 dissolving, melting; decomposition 2 liquidation (e.g., of an institution); dissolution (of parliament, etc.) ♦ حزب - disbanding of a party

انحنا [enhenaa] 1 curvature, curving ♦ قابل - flexible, bending 2 geology flexure (of the earth's crust)

• اند obscure (and) some, a small quantity
• و (اندی) - odd; a little over

انداخت [andaakht] firing, shooting, fire ♦ میدان - firing range
• کردن - to fire, to conduct fire; to shoot at, to shell

انداختن [andaakhtan] (present tense stem انداز [andaaz]) 1 to throw, to toss 2 to pour (a granular substance) 3 to pour (a liquid); to add seasoning (salt, oil) 4 to cover; to floor; to throw [something] down 5 colloquial to throw, to toss 6 (component of compound verbs) ♦ ازکار - to prevent [someone] from working, to keep [someone] from work

انداز [andaaz] 1 present tense stem انداختن 2 (second component of compound words with meaning of 2.1 "throwing" / "thrown" ♦ پای انداز carpet-covered walkway 2.2 "causing (something)" ♦ جنگ انداز trouble-maker, intriguer 3.1 mode, manner, style ♦ گفتار - manner of speech 3.2 colloquial pooling (of money); money collected as a

pool
- کردن • *colloquial* to arrange a pool, to set up a pool

انداز ه [andaaza] 1 size; magnitude, volume ♦ تخنیکی - technical data 2 measure, scale 3 degree, quantity ♦ تا اندازه یی to some degree, partly ◊ تا چه - how much, to what degree 4 *rarely* a measure (of poetry)
- کردن • to measure
- گرفتن • to measure, to cheat in measuring, to give false measure

اندازه گیری [andaazagiri] measurement ♦ مسافه - measurement of distance ◊ - آلات measuring devices or instruments

اندام [andaam] 1 build, figure 2 part of the body, organ

اندر [andar] (formant in terms of kinship with meaning "non-blood" / "step-") ♦ مادراندر stepmother ◊ برادراندر stepbrother

اندرآب [andaraab] Andarab (a quay in Kabul and also a section in Badakhshan)

اندرچو [andarchu] children's seesaw

اندرز [andarz] *literary* advice, admonition

اندک [andak] 1 little, few, not much; just barely ♦ اندکی صبرکو Wait a bit! 2 small, insignificant (concerning an interval of time) ♦ درمدت - and در- مدت within a short time

اندک رنج [andakranj] *colloquial* overly sensitive, quick to take offense

اندل [andal] *technical* starting lever; starting crank
- زدن • to turn a lever, crank; to start up

اندورو پایی [endooruparyi] Indo-European (concerning a family of languages)

اندوختن [andokhtan] (*present tense stem* اندوز [andoz]) 1 to gather, to store up, to accumulate ♦ مال - to accumulate wealth 2 to acquire ♦ علم - to acquire knowledge

اندودن [andudan] *rarely* to cover with a layer (of something) ♦ زر - and بازر- to gild

اندوه [andoh] sadness, grieving
- خوردن • to be sad, to grieve

اندوهگین [andohgin] 1 sad, grieving 2 depressed, doleful (about something)

اندیشناک [andeeshnaak] deep in thought, preoccupied

اندیشه [andesha] 1 thought, meditation 2 concern, fear
- داشتن • to be concerned, to be worried, to fear (از)
- کردن • to think (درباره)

اندیشیدن [andeeshidan] اندیشه کردن in entry اندیشه

اندیوال [andeewaal] *colloquial* 1 friend; companion (sharing one another's food) 2 partner, associate

اندیوالی [andeewaali] companionship; friendship, comradeship

انرجی [enarji] energy ♦ اتومی - atomic energy ◊ برق - electric power

انرژی [anarzhi] ☞ انرجی

انزجار [enzejar] 1 *literary* aversion 2 ☞ آزردگی
- یافتن • to feel aversion, to experience aversion

انزواء [enzewaa] *literary* solitude, reclusion ♦ سیاست - *political* isolationism

انس [ons] habit, fondness, attachment
- گرفتن • to be used to, attached to (someone) (با) ♦ این سگ با ما - گرفته است That dog took a liking to us.

انساج [ansaaj] *plural of* نسج

انسان [ensaan] person

انسانی [ensaani] human ♦ قوای - manpower ◊ عواطف human traits, humanity

انسانیت [ensaaniyat] 1 humanity, humaneness 2 pleasantness, kindness
- کردن • *colloquial* to deal (with someone) in a kind, humane way; to display kindness, humaneness

انستیتوت [enstitut] institute

انسجام [ensejaam] 1 state of being well-coordinated, well-organized, or in good repair; state of being in good adjustment 2 harmoniousness

انسدادی [ensedaadi] *grammar* plosive (of consonant)

انسولیتر [ensoleetar] *technical* insulator

انشاء [enshaa] 1 the art of expression (in words); epistolary art ♦ کتاب - collection of samples of epistolary style 2 composing, writing (documents, letters) 3 style ♦ عالی - high style 4 composition (in school)
- کردن • to write, to compose
- نوشتن • to write a composition

انشاءالله [enshaaalla(h)] God willing! / If God allows! / If God wills! / Perhaps! / Maybe! ♦ خوب میشود! - He will recover, God willing!

انشاپردازی [enshaapardaazi] 1 careful epistolary style 2 the art of writing, composing elegantly

انصاری [ansaari] Ansars (a group of sheiks in Afghanistan who consider themselves to be descendants of the first associates of Mohammed in Medina)

انصاف [ensaaf] justice ♦ ازروی - justifiably
- دادن • (کردن) 1 to give [someone his] due 2 to act on the basis of conscience, to act on the basis of justice ♦ اگر – بدهیم if one were to be fair …; speaking in all conscience …

انصراف [enseraaf] *literary* rejection, refusal (of something)
- کردن • to refuse (از)

انضباط [enzebaat] discipline

انضباطی [enzebaati] 1 strict, knowing how to put things in order ♦ معلم - strict teacher 2 disciplinary ♦ جزای - disciplinary punishment

انظار [anzaar] *plural of* نظر
- در مردم - in people's view, publicly

انعام [en'aam] 1 award, reward (including monetary); incentive award 2 tip, gratuity
- دادن • 1 to award, to reward, to endow 2 to give a tip or gratuity

انعقاد [en'eqaad] 1 convocation, opening (of a congress, meeting) 2 conclusion (of an agreement)
- یافتن • 1 to be convened, to take place (concerning a meeting) 2 to be concluded (concerning an agreement, etc.)

انعکاس [en'ekaas] 1 reflection, depiction (in various meanings) ♦ آواز - echo 2 reflex 3 reaction, response
- پیداکردن • 1 to be reflected (in various meanings) 2 to receive a response

انفاذ [enfaaz] *literary* realization, putting into practice, implementation, execution, fulfillment (of something) ♦ قانون - *legal* going into effect (of a law)

انفجار [enfejaar] ☞ انفلاق

انفرادی [enferaadi] 1 individual, personal; private ♦ زندگی - private life ◊ زراعت - individually owned farm 2 individual, separate ♦ حبس - individual conclusion

انفس [anfos] *plural of* نفس [nafs]

انفسی [anfosi] 1 subjective ♦ قضاوت - subjective opinion 2 *philosophical* subjective, existing only in person's consciousness (opposite of آفاقی)

انفصال [enfesaal] 1 *literary* separation, parting 2 *obscure* solution (of a problem); resolution (of a conflict)

انفلاق [enfelaaq] explosion ♦ هستوی - and ذروی - nuclear explosion ◊ قابل - explosive
• دادن - to explode *transitive*
• کردن - 1 to explode *intransitive* 2 to burst (of a balloon, bubble, etc.)

انفلاقی [enfelaaqi] and انفلاقیه [enfelaaqiya] explosive ♦ مواد - explosives ◊ وسایل - fireworks

انقباض [enqebaaz] 1 decrease in volume; reduction; narrowing, contraction 2 *technical* compression 3 *medicine* constipation 4 *physiological* (also قلب -) systole

انقسام [enqesaam] 1 *biology* division (of a cell) 2 *literary* division, dismemberment, fractionation into tiny parts

انقضأ [enqezaa] lapse, expiration (of period of time, of a deadline)
• یافتن - to end, expire (about a period of time)

انقطاع [enqetaa'] cessation; interruption, break
• بدون – 1 continuously 2 continuous

انقلاب [enqelaab] 1 revolution ♦ کبیر سوسیالیستی اکتوبر - great October socialist revolution 2 radical change, fundamental change, change, revolution, overturn, coup (in something) ♦ هوا - sharp change in the weather
• شمسی - *astronomy* solstice

انقلابی [enqelaabi] 1 revolutionary *adjective* 2 *plural* انقلابیات and انقلابیون [enqelaabiyun] revolutionary *noun*
انقلابیون [enqelaabiyun] *plural of* انقلابی 2

انکار [enkaar] 1 denial, negation ♦ خدا – denial of God, nonrecognition of God ◊ گناه - denial of guilt 2 refusal
• کردن - to deny; not to acknowledge, to reject

انکسار [enkesaar] *physics* fractionation ♦ نور - fractionation of light

انکشاف [enkeshaaf] development, growth, upsurge ♦ اقتصادی - economic development of a country ◊ زراعت - upsurge in agriculture ◊ ممالک در حال - developing countries
• دادن - 1 to develop, to promote an upsurge 2 to develop, to elaborate (a topic)
• کردن (یافتن) - to develop to progress *intransitive*

انکشاف نیافته [enkeshaafnayaafta]
• ممالک - poorly developed countries

انگاف [angaaf] joint (in stonework or brick masonry)

انگاف‌کاری [angaafkaari] *technical* mortaring of joints (in stonework or brick masonry) ♦ درز - cleaning of joints or seams (after welding)

انگشت [angesht] charcoal

انگشت [angosht] finger ♦ بی‌نام - fourth finger, ring finger ◊ خورد - little finger ◊ شهادت - index finger ◊ کلان - thumb ◊ میانه - middle finger
• ماندن - *colloquial* to object, to protest
• بدندان گرفتن - 1 to be greatly perplexed, surprised 2 to regret, to repent (something) (دراثر)
• در خانه کژدم کردن - 1 to risk, to play with fire 2 to tease, to annoy

انگشتانه [angoshtaana] thimble

انگشتر [angoshtar] ring, finger ring

انگشت‌نما [angoshtnomaa] renowned (for something); generally recognized attracting general attention to oneself

انگلیسی [englisi] 1 English *adjective* 2 (also زبان -) English language

انگور [angur] grapes ♦ قندهاری - kandagari (variety of black grapes that ripen very early) ◊ تاک - grapevine

انگورچینی [angurchini] harvesting of grapes

انگیختن [angeekhtan] (*present tense stem* انگیز [angeez]) 1 to incite (to something), to instigate (به) 2 to arouse, to inspire (به)

انگیز [angeez] 1 (*present tense stem of* انگیختن) 2 (second component of compound words with meaning "evoking something") ♦ هیجان انگیختن evoking alarm, alarming, disturbing

انگیزه [angiza] motivation, cause

انواع [anwaa'] *plural of* نوع
• ...-most varied ..., varied ... ♦ ترکاری - various green vegetables

آنوقت [aanwaqt] 1 then, at that time 2 afterwards, later, then

آنونی [aanonee] *colloquial* conversation; dialogue ♦ مه با او و نی نداریم We don't have anything to talk about with him.

انویس [enways] *communication* invoice

انه [aana] (adjectival and adverbial suffix) ♦ آزادانه - 1 free; relaxed 2 freely, in a relaxed manner ◊ روزانه - 1 daily 2 everyday *adjective*

آنها [aanhaa] 1 they 2 those (persons or objects) ♦ از - *colloquial* their, belonging to them ◊ کتاب (از) - their book

انهار [anhaar] *plural of* نهر

انهدام [enhedaam] annihilation; destruction

آنی [aani] 1 momentary, instantaneous 2 fleeting

انیس [anis] 1 close friend, someone close 2 (*male or female*) darling, sweetheart, beloved

انیسیاتیف [enisiaatif] initiative

او [aw] *colloquial* ☞ آب

او [o]¹ 1 he, she, it 2 that
• ازاو - *colloquial* his (her, hers); belonging to him (her) ♦ خانه (از) او - his (her) house
• درختها - those trees

او [o]² Oh! *interjection* ♦ او صمد Oh, Samad!

آوا [aawaa] ☞ آواز

اواخر [awaakher] *plural of* آخر
• تابستان بود - It was the end of summer.
• در - جون - during the last days of June
• دراین – recently; not long ago; the other day

آواره [aawaara] 1 vagrant, wanderer, roamer 2 homeless person, someone with no place to call home

آوارگی [aawaaragi] vagrancy, life of a wanderer; homelessness

آواز [aawaaz] 1 voice ♦ بلند - loud voice ◊ بم - bass ◊ به یک - in chorus; with one voice 2 noise, sound (of something) ♦ یاد - sound of the wind ◊ فیرتفنگ - sound of a rifle shot 3 cry, shout 4 *grammar* phoneme 5 song; melody, motif
• برآوردن - to give voice [to], to respond; to issue a sound, to make a sound

آوازخوان [aawaazkhaan] 1 (*male or female*) singer 2 singing *adjective* ♦ پرنده - songbird

آوازخوانی [aawaazkhaani] singing *noun*

آوازه [aawaaza] rumor, talk, fame
• رستم به از رستم - *proverb* Rustam's fame is greater than

Rustam [himself].
- شدن • - to become a subject of discussion, to be on everyone's lips (about a fact or piece of news)
- است که – • there is a rumor that, people / they say that

آوازه و دروازه [aawaazawdarwaaza] *colloquial* rumors, gossip, talk

اواسط [awaaset] *plural of* وسط
- در – زمستان • in the middle of winter

اوامر [awaamer] *plural of* امر

اوان [awaan] (*plural of* آن) time, period (of time) ♦ از همان - اوانیکه since …; ever since …

اوایل [awaayel] *plural of* اول
- خزان • 1 beginning of autumn 2 at the beginning of autumn

اوباز [awbaaz] ☞ آب باز

اوبازی [awbaazi] ☞ آب بازی

اوباش [awbaash] 1 riffraff, rabble; the rabble 2 hooligan, cut-throat

اوباشی [awbaashi] hooliganism, outrageous behavior; indecent conduct

اوتار [awtaar]
- صورتی - • vocal chords

اوتراق [otraaq] stopping place, bivouac
- کردن • - to make a stop (e.g., about tourists)

اوترایی [otraayi] descent, slope

اوتو [utu] (flat) iron
- کردن • - to press, to iron

اوتوماتیک [otomaatik] and اوتوماتیکی [otomaatiki] ☞ اتوماتیکی

اوج [awj] 1 *astronomy* apogee; zenith 2 summit, highest point; height (of a season, endeavor, activity, etc.) ♦ خلاقیت هنری - در at the prime of creative powers ◊ شهرت - در at the zenith or the height of fame 3 *aviation* ceiling 4 *military* vanguard; lead patrol
- گرفتن • - 1 to rise upwards, to gain altitude 2 to become intensified, to flare up ♦ میگرفت – آوازگریه طفل The child's crying became ever stronger.

اوج گیری [awjgiri] 1 gaining of altitude, take off 2 prime; rampant spread (e.g., of a reaction)

اوچکان [awchakaan] *colloquial* ☞ آب چکان

اوخور [awkhor] ☞ آب خور

اوخوره [awkhora] ☞ آب خوره

اوخوری [awkhori] ☞ آب خوری

اوخیزی [awkheezi] high water, flood, overflow

اودر [awdor] father's brother, uncle

اودربچه [awdorbacha] uncle's son, first cousin (on father's side)

اودرخسر [awdorkhosor] 1 brother of father-in-law (wife's father) 2 brother of father-in-law (husband's father)

اودرزادگی [awdorzaadagi] *colloquial* enmity hostility; rivalry

اودرزاده [awdorzaada] ☞ اودربچه

اودو [awdaw] *colloquial* fault-finding, nagging, excuses
- کشیدن • - to find fault; to excuse oneself, to think up excuses

اوده [uda] *colloquial* plot, conspiracy; oath, pledge

اوده شده [udashoda] *colloquial* charmed ♦ مار - charmed snake

اَور [aawar] 1 *present tense stem* آوردن 2 (second component of compound words with meaning of "causing" / "evoking") ♦ خنده آور ridiculous, laughable

اوراق [awraaq] 1 *plural of* ورق 2 *office* files, papers, documents
- شعبه – • 1 business office; registration office 2 archives
- قید – گردیدن • to be put into a file, to be filed

اورانیم [uraniyam] *chemistry* uranium

اوربند [orband] cessation of fire; armistice ♦ یکطرفه - unilateral cessation of fire

آوردن [aawardan and *colloquial* aawordan] (*present tense stem* آور [aawar] and *colloquial* آر [aar]) 1 to bring; to convey (here); to lead (someone) 2 to cite (e.g., arguments, reasons)
- پیش - • to take, to bring to, to present, to offer [to]
- عذر – • to offer excuses

اردو [ordu] ☞ اردو

اورسی [orsi] ☞ ارسی

ارگان [orgaan] 1 organ (organization) ♦ قضایی - judicial organ 2 (*also* نشراتی -) organ (of the press)

اورو [awraw] ☞ آب رو

اوزار [awzaar] ☞ ابزار and افزار

اوزان [awzan] *plural of* وزن

ازبک [ozbak] ☞ ازبک

اوستا [awesta] Avesta

اوسط [awsat] *literary* average ♦ بدرجه - and - به صورت on the average, moderately

اوش [osh] osh! (cry with which one stops a donkey, similar to "Whoa!")

اوشان [oshan] ☞ ایشان

اوصاف [awsaaf] *plural of* وصف and صفت

اوضاع [awzaa] *plural of* وضع 2

اوطان [awtaan] *plural of* وطن 2

اوف [of] 1 Oh! / Ah! / Ow! / Ouch! *interjection* 2 ☞ اف،گفتن and کشیدن - to sigh (to say "oh")
- نگفتن • - 1 to refrain from complaining, to suffer, to endure 2 not to dare to contradict, to remain silent

اوقات [awqaat] 1 *plural of* وقت 2 occasion, moment, circumstance ♦ در - ضرورت in necessary instances
- اوقاتش تلخ است • He is angry. / He is dissatisfied.

اوقات تلخی [awqaattalkhi] 1 indignation, anger 2 ruckus, quarrel
- کردن • - 1 to become indignant, to become angry 2 to be noisy, to cause a ruckus (همرای)

اوقاف [awqaaf] *plural of* وقف

اوقیانوس [oqiyaanus] ocean ♦ کبیر - Pacific Ocean

اوکش [awkash] *colloquial* 1 ☞ آبکش 2 ☞ اوکشی

اوکشی [awkashi] 1 *colloquial* rinsing (e.g., of laundry) 2 rinsing (of dishes, etc.)

اوگار [awgaar] ☞ افگار

اوگرایی [ograayi] *colloquial* 1 receiving money in installments (for goods that were sold) 2 payment, fee, dues; share

اوگردش [awgardesh] *colloquial* indisposition lethargy (caused by a change in climate)

اوگرمی [awgarmi] ☞ آب گرمی

اوگین [awgin] ☞ آبگین

اول [awwal] 1.1 first, initial ♦ مرحله - initial stage 1.2 first, main ♦- جایزه first prize ◊ نمره - highest (outstanding) rating 2 (*plural* اوایل [awayel]) beginning ♦ از - تا آخر from beginning to end ◊ در - جنگ at the beginning of the war 3 at first; earlier, previously

اول خویش دوم درویش *proverb* First to yourself and then to the dervish (beggar).

اولاً [awwálan] **1** firstly; first of all **2** at first

اولاد [awlaad] **1** *plural of* ولد **2** *colloquial* child ♦ شما چند – دارید؟ How many children do you have?

اولاددار [awlaaddaar] having children, with many children ♦ - زن woman having a child

اولاده [awlaada] posterity; descendants ♦ - بابر descendants of Babur

اول باری [awwalbaari] *colloquial* firstborn, first child

اولتر [awwaltar] first of all; firstly; chiefly

اولجه [ulja] *colloquial* trophy, spoils of war
• کردن - to seize as a trophy

اولچک [olchak] manacles, handcuffs

اول دستی [awwaldesti] *colloquial* first experience, first job (someone's)

اول نمره [awwalnomra] **1** first student **2** *sports* first-place winner (in a contest)

اولوس [olos] **1** family, tribe **2** people; population

اولوسی [olosi]
• جرگه - people's council

اوله [awla] *colloquial* ☞ آبله

اولی [awli] *colloquial of* حویلی

اولی [awwali] first (in sequence); the first-mentioned

اولیا [awliyaa] **1** *plural of* ولی **2, 3 2** (*also* امور -) leaders, rulers **3** parents; guardians of children

اولیاءالله [awliyaaollaah] holy fathers; ascetics, hermits; zealots

اولیت [awwaliyat] superiority; championship; priority; advantage

اولین [awwalin] ☞ اول **1**

اوموری [awmori] *colloquial* ditch, pit, hole (to let water run off a yard or courtyard)

اون [un] woolen yarn, wool ♦ لک - thick wool ◊ یک بسته - skein of wool

اونا [unaa] *colloquial* ☞ آنها

اونمو [onamu] *colloquial* that [person] over there; that [thing] over there

اونه [úna] *colloquial* There he is!

اوها [ohaa] *colloquial* they

اوهام [awhaam] **1** *plural of* وهم **2** superstition, prejudices

اوی [oy] ☞ او

آویختن [aaweekhtan] (present tense stem آویز [aaweez]) to hang, to suspend (on something بر)

آویز [aaweez]¹ *present tense stem* آویختن

آویز [aaweez]² *banking* letter of advisement, aviso

آویزان [aaweezaan] **1** hanging, hung **2** suspended, underslung
♦ چراغ - hanging lamp
• (شدن) بودن - to hang, to be suspended

آویزه [aaweeza] **1** earrings **2** pendants, ornaments
• گوش کردن - Put that in your pipe and smoke it.

آه [aah] **1** Ah! / Alas! *interjection* **2** deep breath, sigh
• آه کشیدن to sigh
• آه در جگر ندارد *colloquial* He doesn't have a penny to his name.

آها [aahaa] Oho! / Well done! / Nicely done! *interjection*

آهار [aahaar] **1** starch solution (for laundry) **2** *textiles* sizing
• دادن / زدن - **1** to starch (laundry) **2** *textiles* to size

اهالی [ahaali] population; inhabitants

اهانت [ehaanat] disregard, disdain, pejoration

اهتزاز [ehtezaaz] **1** oscillation, shaking **2** *technical* vibration
• در - بودن **1** to oscillate, to shake **2** to flutter (of a flag, etc.)
• کردن - *technical* to vibrate

اهتمام [ehtemaam] **1** diligence, zeal **2** concern, attention ♦ - به under the editorship

اهدا [ehdaa] **1** presentation of a gift **2** dedication (of a book)

اهرام [ahraam] pyramids (Egyptian)

آهسته [aahesta] **1** quietly, slowly, unhurriedly **2** softly, in a quiet voice **3** weakly, slightly

آهسته آهسته [aahesta-aahesta (and) aastaa-aastaa] **1** silently, cautiously **2** gradually

آهسته برو [aahestaberaw] "Don't Rush" (wedding song sung to a bride as she is being seen off on the way to her betrothed's home)

آهسته گی [aahestagi]
• به - **1** unhurriedly, slowly **2** softly **3** weakly, slightly

آهک [aahak] limestone

اهل [ahl] **1.1** resident, inhabitant ♦ قریه - village resident, villager **1.2** people ♦ خانه - family, household **2** *literary* kind; good ♦ فرزند - worthy son
• اهل و عیال ☞ - و عیال

اهل الله [ahollaa] righteous men

اهل تحقیق [ahletahqiq] researchers, scientists, scholars

اهل حدیث [ahlehadis] Wahhabites; mujtahids

اهل سنت [ahlesonnat] Sunnites

اهل قلم [ahleqalam] writers

اهل کار [ahlekar] capable; efficient; competent

اهل کسبه [ahlekasaba] artisans, craftsmen

اهل و عیال [ahloayaal] goods and chattels

اهلی [ahli] tame, domestic; domesticated ♦ حیوانات - domesticated animals

اهلیت [ahliyat] **1** capability (for business matters, affairs, pursuits) **2** dignity; merit, positive quality

اهمن و بهمن [ahmanobahman] first winter thaw (period from 10th through 30th of the month of Hut)

اهمیت [aham(m)iyat] importance, significance
• دادن (به) to attach significance; to consider important

آهن [aahan (and) aayen] *colloquial* iron ♦ گول - *technical* reinforcing iron ◊ سنگ - iron ore
• آهن چادر ☞ چادر -

آهن باب [aahanbaab] articles made of iron, hardware

آهن بری [aahanbori]
• قلم - *technical* cutter; chisel, gouge

آهن پوش [aahanposh] **1** iron roofing (of a building) ♦ زیر - attic **2** iron-bound

آهن تخته [aahantakhta] sheet iron

آهن جامه [aahanjaama] hardware

آهن چادر [ahanchaadar] roofing iron

آهن دار [aahandaar]
• کانکریت - reinforced concrete

آهن ربا [aahanrobaa] magnet

آهن کوب [aahankob] hammer (blacksmith's)

آهنگ [ahang] **1** melody, tune, motif **2** sound **3** *music* tone **4** *grammar* intonation

آهنگ دار [ahangdaar] melodic, melodious ♦ آواز - melodious voice

آهنگر [aahangar (and) *colloquial* aayengar] smith, blacksmith
• دکان - smithy, forge

آ, ا

آهنگری [aahangari (and) colloquial aayengari] 1 blacksmith's work or business; forging, working metal 2 smithy, forge

آهنگساز [aahangsaaz] composer

آهنی [aahani aayeni] colloquial iron, made of iron ♦ پل - iron bridge

آهنین [aahanin] literary 1 ☞ آهنی 2 hard, inflexible ♦ عزم - iron will

آهو [aahu] chamois, roe
• دشتی - (صحرایی) gazelle
• لچک - jayran, jairan; wild goat

آه و ثنا [aahosanaa] colloquial curse (usually directed at an offender) ♦ از مظلوم بترس - Beware of the curse of a person offended [by you]!

آهین [aaheen (and) ayeen] colloquial ☞ آهن

آهینگر [aaheengar (and) aayengar] colloquial ☞ آهنگر

آی [aay] present tense stem آمدن

آی [ay] Hey! interjection ♦ ای بچه - Hey, fellow!

آیا [aayaa] (interrogative particle) ♦ در این باره اطلاع دارید - Do you know about this?

آیات [aayaat] plural of آیت

ایالت [ayaalat (and) eyaalat] (plural ایالات [eyaalat]) region, district; province; state ♦ ایالات متحده امریکا United States of America

ایام [ayaam] plural of یوم

آیت [aayat] (plural آیات [ayat]) verse of the Koran

ایتالوی [itaalawi] 1 Italian adjective 2 an Italian

ایتالیایی [itaalyaayi] ☞ ایتالوی

ائتلاف [e'telaaf] entry into an alliance or a bloc; coalition
• کردن - to enter into an alliance, a bloc; to form a coalition

ائتلافی [e'telaafi] coalition adjective ♦ حکومت - coalition government

ائتلافیون [e'telaafiyun] political adherents of joining up, of a bloc; members of a bloc

ایثار [isaar] tribute, sacrifice, offering ♦ او به هر گونه - حاضر بود He was ready for any sacrifices.

ایجاب [ijaab] (plural ایجابات [ijaabaat]) requirement, demand; condition ♦ بنا به ایجابات فنی - according to specifications
• کردن - to require, to demand; to make necessary

ایجابی [ijaabi] positive, affirmative ♦ به طریق - in a positive sense, affirmatively

ایجاد [ijaad] 1 making, creation 2 establishment, founding (of something); formation

ایجادکاری [ijaadkaari] creativity, creative labor; creation

ایجادیات [ijaadiyaat] creation (as a result of action, work); works

ایجنت [eejant] agent, proxy

ایدآل [idaaal] ideal

ایراد [iraad] 1 pronouncing, reading ♦ کنفرنسها - giving or presentation of lectures ◊ نطق - making a speech, delivery of a speech 2 objection; reproach; fault-finding
• کردن - to deliver, to read (a speech, etc.)
• گرفتن - to object; to find fault; to reproach (از)

ایرانی [eeraani] 1 Iranian adjective 2 an Iranian

ایزار [eezaar] ☞ ازار

ایزد [izad] literary God, god

ایست [ist] present tense stem ایستادن

ایستاد [istaad]
• شدن - to stop (concerning a machine, etc.) intransitive
• کردن - to stop (a machine, etc.) transitive
• همینجا – کنید Stop here!

ایستادن [istaadan] (present tense stem ایست [ist]) 1 to be standing 2 to stand up, to rise 3 to stop intransitive; to stop running, operating, or working (concerning a motor, machine tool, etc.) 4 to stand firmly (on something) to hold on to, to adhere to (something) (سر)

ایستاده [istaada] 1 past participle ایستادن 2 standing, immobile, not moving ♦ آب - standing water, swamp
• شدن - 1 to stand ♦ آرام شوید Stand quietly! 2 to stand up, to assume a position or a pose 3 to get up (onto one's feet), to stand up
• کردن - 1 to put, to place, to set (about something) 2 to stand (someone on his feet), to lift (someone) 3 to install, to set up, to establish ♦ غژدی را - کردن They set up a tent. 4 ☞ ایستاد کردن in entry ایستاد
• به سر کسی - شدن colloquial to worry the life out of someone

ایستاده گی [istaadagi] 1 hardness, firmness, staunchness 2 persistence, stubbornness
• کردن - to be firm, steady; to display staunchness, persistence; to resist

ایستگاه [istgaah] 1 stop, stopping place; parking place; station ♦ ریل - railroad station ◊ سرویس - bus stop 2 technical station, unit ♦ برق - electric power station

ایشان [eeshaan] 1 polite he 2 rarely they

ایشیک آغاسی [eeshek-aaqaasi] and ایشیک آقاسی [eeshik-aaqaasi] historical 1 master of ceremonies (of an emir's court) 2 minister ♦ حضوری - minister of the court ◊ ملکی - minister of internal affairs

ایضاً [aayzan] literary also, as well as, too

ایضاح [eezaah] explanation, clarification; comentary

ایطالوی [itaalawi] ☞ ایتالوی

ایطو [ito] colloquial 1 that kind of, of that kind 2 so, thus

ایفا [ifaa] fulfillment, execution (of a duty, etc.) ♦ وظیفه - execution of duties
• کردن - to fulfill, to execute (duty, obligation, responsibility)

ایگاروبیگار [aygâaaro-bygaar] slang junk, stuff ♦ فلان کس ایگار و بیگار خود را از اینجا نقل داد he moved his junk from here

ایل [il] rarely year

آیل [aayel] oil

آیل پمپ [aayelpamp] technical oil pump, oil lubricating pump

آیل دانی [aayeldaani] technical oil cup (oil tank of an engine)

ایلچی [ilchi] 1 obscure ambassador 2 messenger, emissary; truce envoy, bearer of flag of truce

ایلدنگ [ailding] slang lazy, good for nothing ♦ ایلدنگ گشتن فایده ندارد being lazy would not serve any purpose

ایلک [eelak] sifter (for flour) ♦ میده بیزی - fine sieve ◊ کته بیزی - coarse sieve

ایله [eela] 1 free; released (to freedom); let go (from one's hands, etc.) 2.1 without cause, without reason; for no particular reason ♦ آمدم - I came for no particular reason 2.2 in vain; for naught
• دادن - 1 to release, to free; to leave ♦ تی - Stop that! 2 to give a divorce (to a wife) 3 to let down, to untie (hair)

ایله ← 4 about time, finally ♦ ایله بیله به گفت کدی it is about time you listened to me

ایله جاری [eelajaari] *colloquial* 1 militia, home guard 2 member of militia, home guardsman 3 ordinary folk, innocent people

ایله خرج [eelakharj] *colloquial* spendthrift, prodigal

ایله دهان [eeladahaan] *colloquial* windbag; one who shouts or sings at the top of his voice

ایله گرد [eelagard] *colloquial* idler; loafer

ایله گردی [eelagardi] *colloquial* loafing; idling

ایله یی [eelayi] *colloquial* 1 without cause; for no particular reason 2 for no reason at all

ایماق [aymaaq] Aymaks (nationality in Afghanistan)

ایمان [imaan] 1 faith, belief (in God); religion 2 faith, conviction

• آوردن - to turn into belief

• داشتن - 1 to believe (in someone به) 2 to be convinced (of something به)

ایمان دار [imaandaar] 1 devout, faithful 2 convinced, sure, positive

ایمان فروش [imaanferosh] *slang* traitor, sellout (*literally:* one who sells his fate)

ایمانی [imaani] *colloquial* honestly, honorably; according to one's honor, according to one's conscience

این [in] 1 this; these ♦ کتابها - these books ◊ بار - this time 2 he; she; it

• طریق – and رقم - 1 this kind, of this kind 2 so, thus

• است که - 1 so that …2 that's why, therefore

اینان [inaan] they (about people)

اینجا [injaa] 1 (also - در) here 2 (also -به) hither, to here

اینجانب [injaaneb] *epistolary* I ♦ معتقدم که - I assume that …

اینچنین [inchonin (and) inchenin] 1 so, thus, in this way 2 such, that kind of

آینده [aayenda] 1 future; coming ♦ سال- next year 2.1 the future ♦ در نزدیک - in the near future 2.2 *grammar* future tense

انسان [insaan] so, thus

اینسوتر [insotar] and انطرفتر [intaraftar] *colloquial* Come here! / Come closer!

ایطور [intawr] 1 such, that kind of, of this kind, of that kind 2 so, thus

اینقدر [inqadár] so much; thus much

اینک [inak] 1 and so, so 2 now

اینگونه [inguna] such, of that kind, that kind of

اینمی [eenami] *colloquial* that one, there he is; there it is

آینه [aayna] ← آینه

• کسی را به خود دیدن *colloquial* to measure by one's own yardstick

اینها [inha] *colloquial* they, those (about people and things)

ایوان [aywaan] *rarely* hall, palace, chamber

ایور [eewar] husband's brother

ایون [ayon] *physics* ion

آیونوسفر [aayonosfer] *physics* ionosphere

آیه [aaya] ← ایت

ایهام [inhaam] *literary* use of ambiguous expressions, use of double entendre; allegorical speech

آئیل [aayel] ← آیل

آیین [aayin] 1 system, procedure, custom, ceremonial *noun* 2 law, statute, rules ♦ نگارش - rules of stylistics 3 religion, faith, religious doctrine ♦ بودایی - Buddhism, the Buddhist religion

آینه [aayna] 1 mirror ♦ قدنما - cheval glass, pier glass 2 glass

آینه بر [aayinabor] *technical* glass cutter

آینه خانه [aayinakhaana] glass-enclosed veranda

آینه ساز [aayinasaaz] 1 mirror maker 2 glazier, glass cutter (person)

ب
2nd letter of the Dari alphabet

ب abbreviation of بسالت مند

ب [ba] 1 ← به 1 2 (prefix used to form) 2.1 (adjective designating the existence of some attribute or quality) ♦ بنام famous, known 2.2 (adverb) ♦ بدقت attentively, carefully, accurately

ب [be (and) bo] (verbal prefix, past tense, imperative mood and aorist) ♦ برو Go away! ◊ باید بکوشیم We must try. ◊ بیامد وبگفت He came and said …

با [baa] *preposition* 1.1 with, together with ♦ با او وداع کردیم We said goodbye to him. ◊ زلمی باتور پیکی میرود Zalmay is going / walking with Torpeky. 1.2 (when indicating the tool or instrument used in an action) ♦ با پنسل نوشتن to write with a pencil ◊ با چشم خود دیدن to see with one's own eyes 1.3 in, on ♦ با سرویس آمدند They arrived on a bus. 1.4 (indicates the precedence of one action in relation to another) ♦ باشنیدن این آواز بشدت تکان خورد After hearing that voice, he began to shake. 1.5 (indicates the recipient of the action with the verbs) ♦ گفتن to speak ◊ کمک کردن to help ◊ همسایه ها همیشه با ما کمک میکنند The neighbors always help us. 2.1 with, in spite of ♦ با این همه with all that, for all that, despite 2.2 (as part of compound conjunctions) ♦ باآنکه،باآنکه and باوجود آنکه in spite of the fact that; even though

با [ba] (adjectival prefix indicating the existence of some quality or attribute) ♦ باگذشت compliant; magnanimous ◊ باهنر skillful, able

باآبرو [baaaabro] 1 honest, respectable 2 worthy, respected; respectable

بااحتیاط [baaehtiyaat] 1 cautious, wary 2 cautiously, warily

باادب [baaadab] polite, courteous; well-bred

بااعتماد [baae'temaad] reliable, trustworthy; deserving of confidence ♦ منبع- a reliable source

باایمان [baaimaan] 1 believing, religious 2 convinced, confirmed ♦ انقلابی- a confirmed revolutionary

باب [baab]¹ *literary* (plural ابواب [abwaab]) 1 door, gate 2 chapter, section (of a book); paragraph 3 (numerative when counting buildings, structures, etc.) ♦ یک-حویلی one courtyard (with building, house)

• در- about, concerning, relative to *denominative prepostion* ♦ دراین- about this, in this regard

باب [baab]² *colloquial* 1 appropriate, suitable, corresponding 2 accepted; fashionable, in fashion 3 proper, fitting, decent

• بودن - to be accepted, to be fashionable, to be in fashion ♦ اینجا امروز لباس کوتاه-است Short clothing is in fashion now. ◊ مهمان نوازی – است Hospitality is the custom here.

• کردن - to make customary, to spread

• از-افتادن *colloquial* to go out of use, to become unstylish, to go out of style

• کسی (چیزی) یودن - 1 to be suitable, acceptable for

ب

someone or something 2 to be proper or fitting for someone or something ♦ این-من نیست This isn't suitable for me. / This isn't becoming to me

باب [baab] 3 (noun suffix, collective and plural) ♦ پوست باب furs ◊ نفت باب petroleum products

بابا [baabaa] 1 grandfather, granddad 2 father 3 baba (form of address for a murshid)

باباجان [babaaӡan] grandpa

بابایی [baabaayi] 1 paternity 2 colloquial aspiration to place oneself above others; claim to seniority

بابت [baabat] 1 (also-در) relative to, about, concerning, with regard to denominative preposition 2 (also- از) on account (of something), for (something) denominative preposition ♦ دادیم صد افغانی – پرداخت کرایه موتر دادیم We deposited 100 afghani in the payment account for rental of a vehicle.

بابونه [baabuna] camomile, daisy
• گل - a pampered weakling, a touchy person

بابه [baaba] 1 grandfather, granddad 2 father, papa, daddy 3 old man
• غورغوری - colloquial thunder

باپرده [baaparda] 1 honest, virtuous (woman); chaste (concerning a woman) 2 covertly, secretly ♦ این کار رابکو Do this secretly / inconspicuously.

باتجربه [baatajroba] experienced; knowledgeable

باتدبیر [baatadbir] resourceful; inventive

باتکلف [baatakallof] ceremonious, prim; ostentatious ♦ پیش - آمد prim manners ◊ سبک - refined style

باتلاق [baatlaaq] swamp, marsh

باتور [baatur (and) baator] 1 epic hero; hero; brave man 2 masculine proper name Batur

باج [baaj] historical tribute, duty; customs duty, customs tax

باجه [baaja] 1 brother-in-law

باجه [baaja] 2 colloquial 1 wind instrument 2 music

باجه خانه [baajakhaana] brass band

پرحرارت [baharaarat] ☞ پرحرارت

باحلاوت [baahalaawat] literary 1 tasty ♦ خوراک - tasty food, a tasty dish 2 pleasant, giving pleasure ♦ زندگی باحلاوت a life that is full of pleasures

باحوصله [baahawsela] 1 patient 2 able to bring (some job, some matter) to completion

باحیا [baahayaa] 1 respectable, modest, conscientious 2 bashful

باخبر [baakhabar] 1 versed (in), knowledgeable 2 informed

باخبری [baakhabari] knowledgeability

باخت [baakht] 1 loss, defeat (in a game, competition) 2 failure (of a policy, etc.)

باختر [baakhtar] 1 (also-آژانس) Bakhtar agency (Afghan telegraph agency) 2 historical Bactria

باختن [baakhtan] (present tense stem باز [baaz]) to lose (in a game, competition)

باد [baad] 1 1 wind ♦ سموم – simoom ◊ صبا - springtime wind; zephyr ◊ وباران - bad weather; rainy weather 2 air (e.g., in a ball) 3 gases (in the bowels, intestne) 4) tumor; swelling; inflammation 5 (also مفاصل -) rheumatic fever, arthritis 6 colloquial putting on airs
• باد فرنگ – فرنگ ☞
• وبروت – بروت ☞
• باد وبروت - to winnow (grain)

• دادن - to inflate, to blow up (a ball, a tire tube, etc.)
• بر دادن 1 to throw to the wind, to squander 2 to ruin, to annihilate, to destroy
• بر(به)-شدن and بر(به)-رفتن 1 to be thrown to the wind, to be squandered 2 to perish, to disappear
• پیمانه کردن - to beat the air, to engage in something useless
• از باد هوا بخشیدن to make empty promises; to promise more than one can do or more than one has the means to do
• از – هوا زندگی کردن and از – هوا زنده ماندن colloquial not knowing what to live on; to live on the "holy spirit"

باد [baad] 2 and بادا [bada] obscure may … (e.g., May you / he live to a hundred; long may it wave, etc.) ♦ زنده Long live (the king, etc.)! ◊ مبارک - I congratulate [you]! / Congratulations!

باد [baad] 3 colloquial ☞ ازای
• بعد - then, after that, after this

بادار [baadaar] 1 lord, your honor, gentleman, Mr. 2 master, boss, landlord

باداری [baadaari] 1 lordliness 2 status, position of a gentleman, lord
• کردن - 1 to command 2 to behave like a gentleman

بادام [baadaam] almonds; almond tree ♦ سنگی - almonds with hard shell ◊ کاغذی - almonds with thin shell

بادامچه [baadaamcha] 1 species of wild almond 2 pattern or design on fabric in the form of almonds 3 type of embroidery 4 necklace in the shape of almonds

بادامی [baadaami] 1 almond adjective ♦ حلوای - almond halvah 2 almond-shaped (e.g., of eyes) 3 beige, light-brown; almond-colored

بادباد [badbaad]
• شدن - to be scattered; to spill; to crumble

بادبان [baadbaan] sail
• افراشتن - to set a sail, to raise a sail

بادبر [baadbor] medicine carminative remedy

بادبرک [baadbarak] tumbleweed

بادپکه [baadpaka] ventilator, fan

بادخورک [baadkhorak] kestrel (bird)

بادخوره [baadkhora] tuberculosis of the skin, lupus

بادرنگ [baadrang (and) baadreng] cucumber; cucumbers

بادرو [baadraw] opening (for air); air hole

بادریزه [baadreeza] colloquial fallen fruit

بادسار [baadsaar] empty, empty-headed

بادفرنگ [baad(e)farang] 1 gangrene 2 syphilis

بادقت [baadeqqat] 1.1 attentive; fixed ♦ نگاه - fixed look, stare 1.2 careful, accurate 2 attentively; carefully, accurately

بادکویه [badkuia] colloquial 1 snowdrift 2 snowstorm, blizzard

بادنجان [baadenjan] (also سوسنی) eggplant
• رومی - tomato
• بد را بلا نمی زند - proverb A rotten eggplant isn't threatened by spoilage.
• بد - colloquial a mean and nasty, but tenacious old man

بادوام [baadawaam] 1 long, prolonged 2 long-lasting, stable

بادوبروت [baadobrut] colloquial 1 putting on airs 2 bragging
• کردن - to put on airs, to look down one's nose

بادی [baadi] 1 1 filled with air, inflated; air adjective ♦ توپ - inflated ball 2 wind adjective ♦ آسیاب - windmill 3 wind adjective, pneumatic ♦ تفنگ - air rifle

بادی [baadi] 2 1 body (of a truck) 2 hull (of a ship)

28

بادیان [baadiyaan] anise ♦ تخم - *botany* anise seed
بادیه [baadiya] desert, steppe
بار [baar] ¹ 1 load, freight; pack ♦ سفر - baggage ◊ گران - heavy burden 2 burden, yoke 3 fruit, a fruit ♦ درخت - fruit of a tree 4 (also شکم-) fetus 5 (also زبان-) coating on the tongue
• بارونه ☞ وبونه
• آمدن - 1 to grow up, to mature 2 to be grown, to be reared
• آوردن - 1 to raise, to rear 2 to involve, to entail, to be the result (of something) ♦ این حادثه مشکلات بزرگی را بار آورده • This event led to great complications.
• بستن - to pack up, to pack one's things
• دادن - to bear fruit
• کردن - to load, to pack, to burden
• کشیدن - to convey, to carry (cargo)
• دوش کسی بودن - to be a burden to someone
• بزیر کسی بودن - *colloquial* to be obligated to someone; to be in someone's debt
بارو بتک [baarobatak] *slang* (*literally:* load and luggage) belonging, excess baggage (family)
بار [baar] ² time ♦ اول - for the first time ◊ یک - one time, once
• دیگر- and دیگر 1 anew, again 2 next time; henceforth, in the future
• باربار ☞ باربار
بار [baar] ³ 1 *present tense stem* باریدن 2 (second component of compound words with meaning "spilling" / "carrying with itself / oneself") اشک بار pouring tears, weepy
بار [baar] ⁴ *literary* audience, reception (by a king, shah)
• دادن - to give an audience (usually about a king, shah)
• یافتن - to obtain an audience
بار [baar] ⁵ bar, restaurant
باران [baaraan] rain ♦ شدید - heavy rain ◊ میده - drizzle
• گیر آمدن-زیر to be caught in the rain
• از زیر – خیستن و بزیر ناوه نشستن - *proverb* Avoid the rain and get caught under a drainpipe. (i.e., Out of the frying pan and into the fire.)
بارانی [baaraani] 1 rain *adjective*, rainy ♦ هوای- rainy weather 2 waterproof coat, raincoat
باربار [baarbaar] many times, repeatedly; frequently, often
باربردار [baarbardaar] freight, cargo *adjective*, animal-drawn ♦ موتر -
truck
برباداری [baarbardaari] 1 conveyance of cargo or freight 2 animal-drawn transport; draft animals
باربند [baarband] rope, cord, string (for packing); straps
باربندی [baarbandi] 1 packing 2 loading, packing a load
بارپیچ [baarpeech] packing material, wrapping paper
بارجامه [baarjaama] 1 tare ♦ وزن با- gross weight 2 double sack (thrown across the back of a pack animal for carrying dry substances)
بارچالانی [baarchaalaani] authorization for sending off or exporting cargo
• بارنامه ☞ -موتر •
باردار [baardaar] 1 loaded, loaded down with 2 fruit-laden (of a tree) 3 pregnant 4 with calf, with foal
• زبان- tongue covered with coating (when a person is ill)
بارز [baarez] 1 outstanding, eminent ♦ ادبای - افغانی - prominent Afghan writers 2 obvious, evident
بارزده [baarzada] spoiled enroute (concerning a load, goods, etc.); damaged (concerning something)

بارش [baresh] 1 rain ♦ شروع شده است – and – است - It rained. / It started to rain. 2 precipitation
بارک الله [baarekallaa] Bravo! / Well done! (shout of approval, delight)
بارکش [baarkash] 1.1 cargo, freight *adjective* ♦ لاری (موتر) - truck 1.2 pack, cartage, dray (of an animal) 2 pack animal
بارکشی [baarkashi] conveying, transporting of cargo or freight
بارگیر [baargir] pack animal (camel, horse, donkey, etc.)
بارنامه [baarnaama] bill, invoice; receipt for cargo or freight ♦ نقلیه - bill of lading
بارو [baaru] *literary* fortress wall with towers; fortress rampart
باروبونه [baarobuna] traveling bags, belongings, goods and chattels
• بستن - to get ready for a trip, to pack one's baggage
باروت [baarut] powder, gunpowder
باروت دانی [baarutdaani] powder flask
باروت سازی [baarutsaazi] manufacture of gunpowder ♦ فابر - یکه gunpowder plant or factory
بارومتر [baaromeetar] barometer and بارومیتر [baaromeetar]
باره [baara] ¹
• دراین- in this respect
باره [baara] ² 1 inner part of a fortress wall with a broad track above (for moving about) 2 *literary* military camp; military fortress, military stronghold
باره [baara] *colloquial* (*literally*: profit, outcome) prosperous ♦ الهی باره اولاده نه بینی may your child not be prosperous
باری [baari] *adjective* cargo, freight; draft (of livestock) ♦ اسب pack horse; dray horse
باریاب [baaryaab]
• شدن- to obtain an audience, to be granted a reception (by a shah, king)
باریدن [baaridan] 1 to fall (of rain, snow) 2 to pour
باریک [baarik] 1 narrow, fine, not wide ♦ راه - narrow path 2 fine, slender, well-proportioned ♦ اندام slender or well-proportioned figure 3 fine, delicate ♦ موضوع- a delicate question
باریک بین [baarikbin] 1 perspicacious, acute, shrewd; keenly analytical (about something) 2 meticulous
باریک گیر [bârikgir] *colloquial* nitpicky, fault find
باز [baaz] ¹ 1 open, opened 2 untied
• کردن - 1 to open 2 to untie
باز [baaz] ² 1.1 again, anew, once more 1.2 then, later on; henceforth 2 (first component of compound verbs with the meanings) 2.1 reverse movement ♦ بازگشتن to return 2.2 cessation, ban ♦ باز ایستادن to stop, to cease doing [something] 2.3 complete opening of an action ♦ بازگفتن to speak, to say
• هم - nevertheless; besides; even more so
باز [baaz] ³ *present tense stem* باختن
باز [baaz] ⁴ 1 goshawk (usually female) 2 hunting bird
بازار [baazaar] bazaar, market ♦ خارجی - foreign market ◊ داخلی - domestic market
• بازارش گرم است *colloquial* Things are going well for him. / He is prospering.
• ما سرد شده است - *colloquial* Things are going so-so for us.
بازایستادن [baazistaadan] 1 to stop, to cease doing [something] ♦ هر دو طرف از جنگ باز ایستادند Both sides stopped the (از)

ب

battle. 2 to stop *intransitive*, to cease *intransitive* ♦ برف از بارش باز ایستاد The snow stopped falling.

بازخواست [baazkhaast] 1 inquiry, investigation (in regard to a complaint, claim) 2 bringing [someone] to responsibility or punishment (for infractions)
• عدم– 1 lack of responsibility 2 absence of control or supervision; connivance (with regard to abuses)
• – کردن 1 to make an inquiry (with regard to a complaint, claim) 2 to investigate (a case, a matter) 3 to bring to responsibility; to punish ♦ – روز judgement day

بازخواستگر [baazxaastgar] *colloquial* (*literally*: inquirer) big brother

بازدار [baazdaar] *present tense stem* بازداشتن

بازداشتن [baazdaashtan] (*present tense stem* بازدار [baazdaar]) to restrain, not to permit, to hold back

بازدید [baazdid] 1 visit, inspection (of a museum, etc.) 2 investigation; examination; monitoring
• – کردن 1 to visit, to inspect (از،را) 2 to investigate, to monitor (از،را)

بازگرد [baazgard] *present tense stem* بازگشتن

بازگشت [baazgasht] 1 return ♦ – به وطن return to the homeland 2 *banking* return, nonpayment (of a check, etc.)

بازگشتن [baazgashtan] (*present tense stem* بازگرد [baazgard]) to return, to come back *intransitive*

بازگفتن [baazgoftan] (present tense stem بازگو (ی) [baazgo (y)]) 1 to speak, to talk; to say, to express 2 to narrate, to expound, to set forth

بازگو (ی) [baazgoy] 1 *present tense stem* بازگفتن 2.1 narration, retelling 2.2 exposition, explanation (of something)
• – کردن 1 to speak, to talk; to say to express 2 to expound, to set forth

بازماندگان [baazmaandagaan] *plural of* بازمانده

بازماندن [baazmaandan] 1 not to allow, not to permit (to do something), to divert, to distract (from doing something); to hold back, to keep from (از) ♦ این وظیفه ما را از کار اصلی ما باز میماند This responsibility keeps us from performing our basic job. 2 ☞ بازیستادن 3 to survive, to pull through 4 to be left an orphan (after someone's death)

بازمانده [baazmaanda] 1 past participle بازماندن 2 having survived, having outlived (someone or something) 3 (*plural* بازماندگان [baazmaandagaan]) close relative of a deceased person

بازنگر [baazengar] 1 dancer 2 performing artist, actor 3 amusing person, comedian

بازو [baazu] 1 arm (from elbow to shoulder) 2 (*also* دروازه–) jamb (of a door) 3 armrest (of an armchair) 4 assistant ♦ این بچه بازوی من است This young man is my assistant.
• – دادن to help, to support (به)

بازودار [baazudaar]
• – چوکی armchair, easy chair

بازو [baazo] *idiom* (*literally:* arm) helping hand ♦ بازوی کسی را گرفتن helping someone

بازی [baazi] 1 game (of sports, etc.) ♦ فوتبال – football [soccer] game ◊ مبدان sports stadium 2 game, amusement ♦ اسباب – toys 3 fraud, deception; swindle, cheating 4 *colloquia* dance *noun*
• – خوردن to be deceived; to err
• – دادن 1 to play a practical joke; to trick 2 to deceive; to cheat, to swindle

to شطرنج–کردن *colloquial* 1 to play (something) ♦ کردندادن play chess 2 to play, to amuse oneself 3 به–درآمدن to start dancing; to dance, to spend the time dancing
• جان خود را به–نگیر (زا) ♦ به–گرفتن to take an unserious attitude Don't play with your life.

بازیچه [baazicha] toy

بازیگر [baazigar] 1 dancer 2 performing artist, actor 3 amusing person, comedian, jokester

بازیگوش [baazigosh] 1 sportive, playful; frolicsome 2.1 mischievous person, prankster 2.2 rake, good-for-nothing

بازیگوشی [baazigoshi] 1 sportiveness, playfulness 2 prank, mischief
• – کردن to be mischievous, to play pranks

باستانی [baastaani] antique, ancient ♦ – آثار monuments of antiquity

باسررشته [baasareshta] 1 thrifty, economical 2 meticulous, careful

باسواد [baasawaad] literate
• – کردن to teach [someone] to read and write

باسوادی [baasawaadi] literacy

باسی [baasi] 1 yesterday's ♦ غذاهای – yesterday's food 2 stale, not fresh ♦ نان – 1 stale bread 2 yesterday's dinner

باش [baash] 1 *present tense stem* بودن 2 Stay there! / Wait!

باشدکه [baashadke] 1 perhaps ♦ باشدکه ازاین بلاخلاص شویم Perhaps we will be delivered from this misfortune! 2 even if

باشرف [baasharaf] honest, noble

باشکوه [bashokuh] splendid, magnificent; solemn; gala

باشندگان [baashendagaan] 1 residents, inhabitants 2 population
• افغانستان – the population of Afghanistan

باشنده [baashenda] resident, inhabitant

باشه [baasha] hawk, gerfalcon (tamed for hunting)

باشی [baashi] 1 team leader (on a construction project) ♦ بسته کاران – leader of team of installation workers 2 (in compound words) senior, head ♦ موتروان باشی head of garage, garage manager

باصره [baasera] (*also* حس – and قوه–) vision

باصفا [baasafaa] 1 clean, clear ♦ صبح– a clear morning 2 *literary* beautiful, picturesque ♦ باغ– beautiful garden

باطل [baatel] 1 invalid, abolished, revoked 2 empty, vain ♦ – کار useless matter, empty matter

باطلاق [baatlaaq] ☞ باتلاق

باطله [baatela] ☞ باطل
• سند – invalid document

باعث [baa'es] cause, reason ♦ ازچه؟ For what reason? / Why?
• – شدن *colloquial* to insist on (something) to press for (something), to strive stubbornly for (something) ♦ هرچه–شدم قبول نکرد As much as insisted, he did not consent / agree.
• – چیزی شدن to be the cause of something, to serve as the reason for something

باغ [bagh] garden
• – بالا 1 garden situated on a high place 2 aagibala (palace and park in Kabul)
• – میوه orchard
• – وحش zoological gardens, zoo
• – سبزوسرخ نشان دادن *colloquial* to make extravagant promises

باغبان [baaghbaan] 1 gardener 2 garden watchman

باغبانی [baaghbaani] gardener's occupation; care of a garden, gardening

باغچه [baaghcaa] 1 small garden, front garden; lawn 2 kitchen garden, vegetable garden

باغداری [baaghdaari] gardening, horticulture

باغوان [baaghwaan] *colloquial* ☞ باغبان

باغیرت [baaghairat] 1 endowed with a sense of one's own dignity, zealously guarding one's honor 2 valorous, worthy of glory

بافت [baaft] 1 manufacture (of cloth, fabric), weaving ♦ هموار - smooth manufacture (of cloth) 2 plaiting, knitting 3 braiding (of a pigtail) 4 *anatomy* tissue ♦ استخوانی- bone tissue

بافتن [baaftan] 1 to weave (را) 2 to plait; to knit 3 to wind, to twist; to braid (a pigtail) 4 *colloquial* to lie, to fabricate ♦ کسی را - *colloquial* to get round someone (e.g., for the purpose of wheedling something or getting one's own way)

بافندگی [baafendagi] 1 weaving ♦ دستگاه- loom 2 knitting; plaiting

بافنده [baafenda] 1 weaver 2 knitter 3 braider, plaiter

باقی [baaqi] 1.1 continuing, existing 1.2 stable, immovable, eternal (epithet of a god) 1.3 remaining, the rest 2.1 remainder; continuation (e.g., of a story) 2.2 *mathematical* difference 2.3 *accounting* balance
• ماندن - 1 to remain stably, eternally; to be preserved 2 to leave behind ♦ چند اولاد از خود – ماند؟ How many children did he leave behind? 3 to be left behind (after someone's death)

باقیده [baaqideh] defaulter, one in arrears of payment, one who pays arrears

باقی مانده [baaqimeenda] 1 remaining, the rest 2.1 *mathematical* remainder (in division) 2.2 *mathematical* difference

باک [baak] fear, fright ♦ هیچ باکی نیست and باکی ندارد There's no need to be afraid! / It's nothing!

باکتریا [baakteriyaa] bacterium

باکتریالوژی [baakteriaalozhi] bacteriology

باکره [baakera] maid, virgin

باکفایت [baakefaayat] 1 capable, skillful; clever 2 skilled, qualified

باگذشت [baagozasht] 1 magnanimous, indulgent 2 complaint, obliging

بال [baal] 1 wing 2 feather, fin (of a fish)
• بالاوپر ☞ - وپر •

بالا [baalaa] 1.1 top, upper part (of something) 1.2 height ♦ متوسط - average height 2.1 upper, situated in the upper part (of something) 2.2 previously mentioned, previous, foregoing 3.1 (also-در) on top, from above, upstairs 3.2 (also-به) upward 4.1 (also-به and در-) on, above, on top of into *denominative preposition* ♦ سر زمین - on the ground ◊ بالای تقسیم حاصلات دست او - above his head 4.2 because of ♦ بگریبان هم انداختند They began to argue over the division of the harvest.
• از - from on top, from atop; along, on top of, through
• چرا-مه قار میکنید؟ *colloquial* Why are you angry at me?
• اوفیرکرده بودند - They were firing at him.
• هیچ گمانی بالایت نمی کنند No one will think of you.
• آمدن - to rise; to climb; to go up ♦ آب درچاه-آمد The water rose in the well.
• آوردن - to rise

• بودن - to be heard; to resound; to sound loudly ♦ خرخرخوابیدگان-بود The snoring of sleeping people was heard.
• زدن to pick up, to roll up ♦ آستین ها را – زد He rolled up his sleeves.
• شدن - 1 to rise, to climb, to ascend (a hill / mountain, etc.) 2 to climb up (onto something) ♦ سرخر-شد He got on the donkey.
• کردن - 1 to raise, to lift slightly 2 to lift, to lift up (one's head), to throw back (one's head)
• گرفتن - 1 to grow, to become stronger ♦ جنجال-گرفت A ruckus broke out. 2 to improve ♦ کارش-گرفت His business / affairs improved sharply.
• کسی - داشتن - to be in arrears to someone, to owe someone ♦ چندسیرگندم-یک دهقان داشت He was supposed to receive several sers of wheat from a certain peasant.
• کسی - شاندن - *colloquial* to force something on someone, to force someone to take (something)
• کسی را بالا بالا کردن *colloquial* to fuss over somebody
• گذشت دوروزچون دوسال بالای شان The two days dragged on like two years for them.

بالا زدن [baalaazadan] *colloquial* (*literally*: to left someone up) to honor someone, to introduce someone as an important person

بالازنی [baalaazani] *colloquial* to respect, to honor someone

بالاآب [baalaaaab] 1 upper reaches, upper course of a river; source (of a river, stream) 2 headwork of a canal

بالابلند [baalaabeland] tall, stalwart

بالابین [baalaabin] senior (in a group); leader; team leader

بالابینی [baalaabini]
• کردن- to oversee, to carry out supervision, to carry out leadership

بالاپوش [baalaaposh] overcoat

بالاتنه [baalaatana] 1 bodice (of two-piece dress) 2 woman's jacket, blouse

بالاجای [baalaajaay] *colloquial* the "upper crust," higher departments, upper (administrative) echelons

بالاحصار [baalaahesaar] Balahisar (a fortress in Kabul)

بالاخانه [baalaakhaana] balakhana room or enclosed terrace (on top of a house)

بالاخرجی [baalaakharji] over-expenditure (of money), spending in excess of the norm

بالاخره [belaakhera] finally, at last

بالادست [baalaadast] 1 higher 2 influential 3 superior, maintaining the upper position (in something)

بالاسر [baalaasar] 1 place of honor (at a meeting); front corner (in a home) 2 head (of a bed)

بالاوپایین [baalaawpaayin]
• شدن- to rise and fall; to waver, to vacillate

بالای و ظیفه [baalaayewazifa] without discontinuing work, without being away from the job

بالایی [baalaayi] upper, situated at the top ♦ درقسمت-عمارت in the upper part of building

بالبال کردن [baalbaalkardan] *colloquia l* 1 to unravel (of fabric), to pull out hair by hair 2 to tear somebody or something into pieces

بالت [baalet] ballet

بالتی [baalti] *electrical* small battery

بالش [baalesh] and بالشت [baalesht] pillow
- پوش بالش ☞ پوش
- روی بالش ☞ روی

بالشتک [baaleshtak] 1 small pillow; bolster (of a sofa) 2 *technical* cushion, lining; support

بالشویک [baalshewik] 1 Bolshevik 2 Bolshevist

بالعکس [belaks] on the contrary

بالغ [baalegh] 1 having achieved maturity, having achieved one's majority 2 an adult

بالک [baalak]
- زدن - *colloquial* to flap wings (about a bird)

بالکل [belkoll] completely; entirely fully; absolutely ♦ جورشده است He recovered completely.

بالوپر [baalopar] ☞ پروبال
- برآوردن - 1 to become fully fledged, to become independent, to be covered with plumage or feathers 2 to reach manhood, to become independent
- از-ماندن *colloquial* 1 to be left helpless 2 to be deprived of everything

بالون [baalun] 1 balloon ♦ گاز - gas balloon 2 air balloon 3 *chemistry* large retort

بالیدن [baalidan] to be proud [of] ♦ او به پسر خود میبالد He is proud of his son.
- به خود- to put on airs, to act pridefully

بام [baam] 1 roof, roofing ♦ سفالی - tile roof ◊ خسپوش - straw roof 2 top (of a carriage) 3 planking, overhead covering, ceiling

بامان خدایی [baamaanekhodaayi] farewell
- کردن - to bid farewell, to say good-bye

بامبوتی [baamboti] *colloquial* 1 awning; small roof (over something) 2 overhead covering, roof access room

بامداد [baamdaad] 1 early morning; sunrise 2 early in the morning; at sunrise

بامروت [baamorowwat] *literary* 1 manly, bold 2 magnanimous; humane

بامعلومات [baama'lumaat] knowledgeable; informed

باموفقیت [baamowaffaqiyat] 1 successful 2 successfully

بان [baan] (suffix designating agency) ♦ باغبان 1 gardener 2 garden watchman

بان [baan] *colloquial present tense stem* ماندن (in the meaning of) to leave, to put

بانت [baanat]
- موتر - fenders (of a motor vehicle)

بانجان [baanjaan] *colloquial* ☞ بادنجان

بانجانی [baanjaani] violet *adjective*

بانازاکت [baanazaakat] 1 fine, elegant 2 refined 3 delicate

بانس [baans] bamboo

بانک [baank] bank ♦ تجارتی - commercial bank ◊ زراعتی - agricultural bank

بانکداری [baankdaari] banking

بانکنوت [banknot] bank note

بانگ [baang] 1 shout, call 2 voice; sound 3 crowing (of a rooster) 4 call of muezzin to prayers
- زدن - 1 to make a sound; to shout 2 to crow (of a rooster) 3 to call to prayers (of a muezzin)

بانگ بی وقت [baangbaywakht] *slang* to speak out of turn

بانگس [baangs] ☞ بانس (also- چوب)

بانگی [baangi] yoke (for water buckets)

بانمک [baanamak] likable; charming

بانه [baana] *colloquial* 1 ☞ بهانه 2 lie, subterfuge (for the purpose of obtaining something)
- ساختن - to lie, to think up subterfuges, to employ a ruse

بانی [baani] *literary* founder

باوجدان [baawejdaan] conscientious; honest, decent, respectable

باوجود [baawojud] despite (something), in spite (of something)
- اینکه - despite the fact that; for all that ... *compound conjunction*

باور [baawar] faith, belief, trust
- کردن - to believe (usually someone's word, promise, etc.)
- (به) گپ شما - میکنم ♦ I trust your word. / I believe your words.

باوفا [baawafaa] faithful, true, devoted

باهم [baaham] jointly, together [with]

باهمی [baahami] 1 mutual, reciprocal 2 joint, collective
- زیست – ● coexistence

باهنر [baahonar] 1 clever, skillful 2 gifted, talented

باهوش [baahush] wise, quick (to catch on to something)

بای [baay]¹ 1 rich, propertied, wealthy 2 bai (rich landowner), rich person

بای [baay]²
- دادن - *colloquial* 1 to lose ♦ بازی راداده است He lost [the game]. 2 to lose (something)
- خودرا دادن *colloquial* to lose one's head, to get lost, to be flustered

باید [baayad] 1 should, must, it is necessary [to ...] ♦ چه- کرد؟ What to do? / What [should] be done? ◊ که بروم I must go. 2 perhaps, maybe, possibly ♦ طوریکه شاید و- as [one] is supposed to, as [one] should

بایر [baayer] and بایره [bayera] (also - زمین) 1 ground, soil that is not unfit for sowing 2 uncultivated land, idle land, long fallow land

بایسکل [baaysekel] bicycle

بایسکل سوار [baaysekelsawaar] bicyclist

بایلر [baaylar] 1 tank for boiling water, boiler 2 barrel

بایستن [baayestan] *obscure* to be obliged [to], to be intended [to]; to be needed, to be necessary

ببر [báber] lion (with a mane)

ببرلخی [babrelokhi] *slang* (literally: a loin that is made with bulrush) paper tiger *derogatory*

ببرک [babrak] *textile* castor (type of cloth with raised nap)

ببلیوگرفی [bebliografi] bibliography

ببو [babaw] *colloquial* witch, hag, bogey man (used to frighten children)

بت [bot] 1 idol, statue 2 a beauty, beautiful girl
- بت بر نجی - a ninny, a milksop, a frail person, a puny person

بت پرستی [botparasti] paganism, idolatry

بتر [batar] merging of adjacent vowels in بدتر

بترونو [betrono (and) botrono] a type of card game for gambling

بتنهایی [batanhaayi (and) batanaayi] independently, by one's own resources ♦ شما این کار را - کردید؟ Did you do this yourself? ◊ این کلمه بیکار نمی رود This word is not used independently / by itself.

بتون [beton] concrete
• بتون آرمه ☞ – آرمه
بتون آرمه [betonaarma] reinforced concrete
بته [batta] bata (dish made of boiled rice with meat gravy and vegetables) ◆ سبزی - bata with greens ◇ کرم - bata with cabbage
• بته بانجان ☞ – بانجان
• بته شلغم ☞ – شلغم
بته [bota] 1 bush, shrub; bushes, shrubbery 2 pattern, design, drawing 3 type of embroidery
بته بد [botebad] slang (literally: a bad bush) bad, rude, obscene, arrogant (person)
بته بانجان [batabaanjaan] bata with eggplant garnish ☞ بته
بته زار [botazaar] bushy thickets, undergrowth
بته شلغم [balashalgham] bata with stewed turnips ☞ بته
بجا [bajaa] 1 located or situated in its own place 2 not out of place, appropriate, proper 2 appropriately, opportunely, to the point
• کردن - to fulfill, to carry out, to realize
بجل [bojol] 1 anatomy astragalus, ankle bone, talus 2 knucklebone (for playing), alchik (a game)
بجل بازی [bojolbaazi] game of knucklebones, game of alchik
بجلک [bojolak] 1 (also -پای) ankle, anklebone 2 ☞ بجل 3 technical cam
بجه [baja] colloquial time; hour ◆ ساعت چند-است؟ What time is it?
بچشم [bachéshem] Yes, sir!, It will be done!
بچ کچا [bachkachaa] slang children and their mother
بچ کچه [bachkacha] slang kid
بچ کردن [bachkardan] colloquial to escape danger, to avoid
بچه گانه [bachagaana] ☞ بچگانه
بچه گی [bachagi] ☞ بچگی
بچه [bacha] 1 boy, son 2 young man, lad, fellow; (fam.) young fellow 3 child, infant
• ننه - colloquial pet, darling
• وطن –1 native resident 2 fellow countryman, fellow townsman
بچه اندر [bachaandar] stepson, natural son
بچه ترسانک [bachatarsaanak] and بچه ترسانی [bachatarsaani] (literally: to scare a child) colloquial 1 ridiculous threat; unsuccessful attempt 2 to making a show of one's power, flexing one's muscles frighten [someone]
بچه تورانک [bachatoraanak] colloquial 1 kids things (things that kids want to have) 2 something that gets one exited
بچه خور [bachakhor] colloquial 1 ☞ بچه مرده 2 tyrant, villain
بچه خورک [bachakhorak] 1 green, unripe fruit 2 ovary
بچه خیل [bachakhel] colloquial juvenile, young man
بچه گانه [bachagaana] 1 child's, children's ◆ لباس children's clothing ◇ بازی- child's game 2 in a childish manner
بچه گک [bachagak] colloquial 1 small child, infant 2 small boy, stripling
بچه گی [bachagi] 1 childhood, childhood years 2 childishness; naivete 3 gullibility
• کردن - to gape, to loaf ◆ نکو - Don't be a dunderhead! / Don't gape!

بچه مرده [bachamorda] colloquial abusive damned; ill-fated ◆ این – باز هم دزدی کرده است That damned guy stole [something] again.
بحار [behaar] plural of بحر
بحث [bahs] 1 argument; discussion; debate 2 discussion, consideration (of a matter or question)
• کردن 1- to argue (with someone) 2 to discuss, consider (بالای). در اطراف (what)
بحر [bahr] 1 (plural بحار [behar] and ابحار [abhar]) sea ◆ محیط - sea and ocean ◇ وبر - sea and land
بحر [bahr] 2 literary meter ◆ رمل - ramal meter
بحران [bohraan] crisis ◆ اقتصادی - economic crisis
بحرانی [bohraani] adjective crisis; critical (about a situation, etc.) ◆ حالت- critical condition
بحری [bahri] adjective sea, maritime, marine ◆ قوه- sea fleet
بحریه [bahriya] 1 ☞ بحری 2 sea fleet ◆ حربی - navy
بحل [behel] ☞ بهل
بحیره [bahira] inner sea; lake
بخار [bokhaar] 1 1 steam ◆ آب - water vapor 2 fumes, miasma 3 (also -زمین) low-lying fog
• دادن - to steam, to treat with steam
• شدن - to evaporate
بخار [bokhaar] 2 rash (on a person's body) ◆ در تمام وجود او بر آمده است - A rash broke out over his entire body.
بخار آلود [bokhaaraalud] and بخار دار [bokhardar] saturated with vapor ◆ هوای- vapor-saturated air
بخاری [bokhari] oven, stove; fireplace ◆ معمولی - iron stove, makeshift stove ◇ بخاری مرکز گرمی steam radiator, central-heating radiator
بخت [bakht] fate; happiness
• بخت-خود رفتن colloquial to find one's happiness (about a girl); to get married ◆ بختش بر گشت Good fortune changed him.
• بختش بسته است colloquial She doesn't have any luck. / She can't find a husband.
• خدا بختشه واز کنه colloquial May Allah arrange happiness for her! / May Allah send her a husband!
بخت آزمایی [bakhtaazmaayi] 1 test of fate; risk 2 daring
• کردن 1- to test fate 2 to dare
بختیار [bakhtiyaar] 1 happy; fortunate; joyous 2.1 masculine proper name Bakhtiyar 2.2 Bakhtiari (tribe)
بخچ [bakhch] colloquial ☞ بخش
بخدا [bakhodaa] By God! / I swear to God!
بخرد [bekhrad] literary 1 wise, wisest 2 sage, wise man
بخش [bakhsh] 1 literary 1 part, share 2 section; department; division 3 lot, destiny
بخش [bakhsh] 2 1 present tense stem بخشیدن 2 (second component of compound words with meaning "granting" / "giving") ◆ جان بخش life-giving, vivifying
بخشش [bakhshesh] 1 gift, present 2 tribute; tip
• کردن - 1 to give a present, to grant 2 to give a tribute; to give a tip
بخششی [bakhsheshi] 1 donated ◆ این قلم من -است This pen was given to me. 2 prize, bonus ◆ -معاش bonus 3 ☞ بخشش
بخشنده [bakhshenda] all-forgiving, magnanimous, merciful (epithet of God)
بخشودن [bakhshudan] (present tense stem بخشا(ی) [baxshaa(y)])

ب

literary **1** to forgive **2** to free (from payment of a tax or fine)

بخشیدن [bakhshidan] **1** to give, to present, to grant, to bestow **2** to forgive, to excuse

بخل [bókhol] *literary* **1** stinginess, greed **2** envy

بخمل [bakhmal] *colloquial* velvet

بخملی [bakhmali] *colloquial* velvet *adjective*

بخوبی [bakhubi] well; satisfactorily; excellently

بخور مریم [boxur(e)maryam] cyclamen

بخورونمیر [bokhoronamir] *colloquial* half-starving existence; meager ration ♦ یک بخورونمیری داشتیم We lived modestly, but didn't starve to death.

بخیل [bakhil] **1** stingy, greedy **2** envious

بخیلی [bakhili] ☞ بخل
- کردن • to be stingy, to be greedy
- نکن • Don't skimp.

بخیه [bakhya] **1** stitch, hand stitch **2** chain stitch
- (کردن) زدن • to do hand stitching; to sew a chain stitch

بد [bad] **1.1** poor, bad **1.2** evil; malicious **2.1** shortcoming; poor quality ♦ همسایه را همسایه داند - *proverb* [Only] a neighbor knows a neighbor's shortcomings. **2.2** evil, misfortune; unpleasantness **3** (first component of a compound words which designates an undesirable attribute or property) ♦ بدخلق angry; crude, coarse
- آمدن • to be displeasing, to be not to one's taste ♦ از بیکار نشستن بدش میآید *colloquial* He didn't like to sit idle.
- بردن • (از) *colloquial* to experience antipathy, aversion
- دیدن • را - to dislike, to be unfriendly toward ♦ من اوراز را بد میدیدم I couldn't stand Uraz.
- دیدن بد کسی طرف (به) • to look at someone with resentment, with animosity

بداخلاق [badakhlaaq] immoral, of poor or bad behavior

بداندیش [badaandeesh] **1** ill-intentioned, evil **2** malevolent ♦ جاهل-هر جای میزند نیش *proverb* Wherever an evil fool butts in, he does harm.

بدبخت [badbakht] **1** unhappy, unfortunate, ill-fated **2** *abusive* worthless, damned

بدبختی [badbakhti] misfortune; evil fate

بدبروت [badborut] *colloquial* **1** cantankerous, peevish **2** brawler, boor

بدبیار [badbiyaar] unfortunate, unlucky (in a game)

بدبین [badbin] **1.1** [one who is] looking disapprovingly (at something) **1.2** pessimistic **2** pessimist ♦ آنها نسبت به این کار خیلی-هستند They have a very negative attitude toward this.

بدبینی [badbini] pessimism; distrustfulness; negative attitude

بدترکیب [badtarkib] homely; ugly; deformed; ungainly ♦ الماری - poorly designed or unattractive cupboard or dresser

بدجنس [badjens] **1** unworthy, unfit **2** scoundrel, rascal, villain

بدجنسی [badjensi] meanness, baseness

بدچشم [badchashem] **1** harmful, noxious **2** impertinent

بدچشم [badchashm] *slang* (literally: to have bad eye) rude, abrasive

بدخشانی [badakhshaani] **1** Badakhshan *adjective* ♦ لهجه - the Badakhshan dialect **2** a Badakhshan, inhabitant of Badakhshan

بدخلق [badkholq] **1** angry, quarrelsome **2** impudent, crude, coarse

بدخواه [badx(w)aah] **1** malevolent; unfriendly **2** hostile person, enemy

بدخور [badkhor] **1** unpleasant to the taste, bitter (e.g., of medicine) **2** unfastidious about food

بدخوری [badkhori]
- کردن - to eat anything at hand, to be unfastidious about food

بددعا [baddoa] *colloquial* curse, evil wish

بدذات [badzaat] ☞ بدجنس

بدراه [badraah] ☞ گمراه
- کردن • **1** ☞ گمراه کردن **2** to dissuade (from taking a trip somewhere), to prevent from going somewhere

بدررفت [badarraft] drain, gutter (for water); sewer system ♦ آب های نلهای - sewage, runoff water ◊ -sewer pipes

بدرستی [badorosti] **1** correctly **2** well, as it should, properly ♦ چوب-نمیسوزد The firewood is not burning as it should / properly.

بدررفت [badaraft] ☞ بدررفت

بدرقه [badraqa] **1** send-off **2** accompaniment; escort; convoy **3** accompaniment (of something with or by something)
- کردن • **1** to see off **2** to escort, to convoy **3** to accompany (with something) ♦ با) حکایت خود را با شوخی هایشیرین-میکرد He accompanied his story with amusing jokes.

بدرنگ [badrang] ugly; homely ♦ زن - homely woman

بدرو [badaraw] spillway (of a mill, canal)

بدرود [bedrud (and) badrud] *literary* farewell, parting
- گفتن • to say good-bye, to part
- گفتن حیات • (به,را) to die, to say farewell to life

بدروی [badroy] **1** homely, ugly; deformed **2** sullen, gloomy

بدره [badra] **1** *obscure* bag, purse with money **2** *historical* 10,000 dirhem

بدری [badri]
- خوردن • *colloquial* to stumble, to stagger

بدزبان [badzobaan] **1** bitter, venomous to the tongue; abusive, foul-mouthed **2.1** foul-mouthed person **2.2** gossip

بدسته [badesta] *colloquial* on purpose, deliberately, intentionally

بدشگون [badshogun] and بدشگوم [badshogum] *colloquial* **1** serving as a bad omen, ominous **2** bringing misfortune

بدطالع [badtaale'] ☞ بدبخت

بددقت [badeqqat] ☞ بادقت

بدقسمت [badqesmat] ☞ بدبخت

بدکار [badkaar] **1** [one who] has done much that was bad; rotten **2** scoundrel, villain

بدکاری [badkari] sin; villainy

بدگذران [badgozaraan] and بدگذارا [badgozaara] **1** unsociable; discourteous; with bad manners **2** crude, coarse, impudent

بدگویی [badgoyi] malignant gossip, defamation; swearing

بدل [badal] **1.1** exchange, barter **1.2** replacement, substitution **1.3** compensation; equivalent **1.4** *grammar* opposition **2** substandard, of poor quality ♦ تکه - fabric of poor quality
- در • **1** in exchange for .. **2** in place (of something) ♦ در - پول نقد for cash
- کردن • **1** to exchange, to barter **2** to replace

بدمزه [badmaza] unsavory, unpleasant to the taste

بدمستی [badmasti] **1** strong intoxication **2** drunkenness; drunken brawl **3** hydrophobia (in a horse)
- کردن • to cause a ruckus (while drunk), to behave violently

بدمعاش [badma'aash (and) badm'as] 1 cut-throat, bandit 2 reveler; good-for-nothing

بدمعامله [badmo'aamela] 1 dishonest, unconscientious (in business, trade) 2 ☞ بدگذران

بدمعامله گی [badmo'aamelagi] dishonesty, unconscientiousness (in business, trade)

بدمنظر [badmanzar] unattractive, unpleasant in appearance (about something) ♦ شهر - unattractive town or city

بدن [badan] body, torso

بدنام [badnaam] having a poor reputation, having a bad name

بدنامی [badnaami] a poor reputation, a bad name

بدنفس [badnafs] person with bad inclinations; voluptuary; glutton

بدنه [badana] 1 body; skeleton; carcass ♦ طیاره - aircraft fuselage ◊ کشتی - hull of a ship 2 load-carrying beam in wall of house

بدنی [badani] bodily, corporal, physical ♦ تربیت - physical education, physical culture

بدنیت [badniyat] 1 ill-intentioned, being up to mischief 2 ☞ بدخواه

بدو [badw] beginning ♦ در امر - at the very beginning, at first

بدوبدو [bedawbedaw] colloquial 1 running about, bustle 2 trouble ♦ این کار - زیاد دارد This matter involves a lot of trouble.

بدوبلا [badobalaa] colloquial unnecessary things, worthless things; trash ♦ این - را از سر میز بردارید Get this trash off the table!

بدون [bedun] (also از -) except, apart from, with the exception of

بدوی [badawi] 1 primitive ♦ جامعه - primitive society 2 ☞ ابتدایی

بده زن [budazan] colloquial old woman, granny

بدهی [bedehi] accounting liabilities

بدی [badi] 1 evil, misfortune 2 spite, hatred
• کردن - to do evil; to inflict harm, to damage

بدیع [badi']
• علم - 1 theory of poetry 2 rhetoric

بدیعی [badi'i] artistic ♦ ادبیات - belles lettres / fiction

بدیهی [badihi] clear, obvious ♦ است - clearly, obviously

بذر [bazer] grain for sowing, seeds

بذری [bazri]
• تخم - seeds for sowing; grain for sowing

بذگر [bazgar] colloquial ☞ بزرگر

بذگری [bazgari] colloquial ☞ بزرگری

بر [bar] 1 present tense stem بردن 2 (second component of compound words with meanings) 2.1 "carrying" / "conveying" (something) 2.2 "leading" ♦ راهبر guide; leader

بر [bar] 2 1.1 chest, breast; side; upper part of body 1.2 embrace 2 dialect by, at, near denominal preposition ♦ برخانه by, at, or near home or the house
• دربرداشتن 1 to be dressed (in something را), to wear (clothing) ♦ لباس نو در بر داشت He was wearing new clothes. 2 to contain, to encompass, to include
• دربرکردن to put [something / clothing] on oneself
• در بر کشیدن to embrace, to draw to oneself
• دربرداشتن ☞ 1 دربرکشیدن ☞ 2 دربرگرفتن ☞

بر [bar] 3 1.1 (indicates the location, direction of an action) to; toward; against, upon; along preposition ♦ قلم برمیزاست The pen [is lying] on the table. ◊ برچوکی بنشستم I sat down on the chair. ◊ شیشه را برسنگ زدیم We shattered the glass against a rock. ◊ براو عاشق شدم I have fallen in love with her! 1.2 (used to designate division) by ♦ ده برشش Divide ten by six. 1.3 (becomes part of compound and denominal prepositions) ♦ برضد on (something or someone) ◊ برسر against (someone or something) 2 (verbal prefix) ♦ برآمدن 1 to go out 2 to climb, to rise ◊ برانگیختن to excite, to incite ♦ برشما است تا این کار رابکنید You must do this!

بر [bar] 4 width ♦ برودرازی زمین the width and length of a plot of land

بر [bar] 5 dry land, earth, or soil ♦ بحر و بر sea and land ♦ براعظم ☞ براعظم

بر [bar] 6 colloquial for (or it is translated by the dative case) denominal preposition ♦ برما for us

بر [bor] present tense stem بریدن

برابر [baraabar] 1.1 equal, identical; twin ♦ قد او باقد من - است He and I are the same height. 1.2 corresponding, appropriate 1.3 organized, well-arranged 2.1 equally, even; identical 2.2 according to, corresponding (with something) 3 (also در -) against, opposite denominal preposition ♦ در - آتش نشست He sat down [ekhactly] opposite the fire.
• از - past adverb
• - بودن 1 to be equal, identical, equivalent to 2 to correspond to, to suit (با); to meet (conditions, etc.) 3 to fit ♦ این کرتی بجانت – است This jacket fits you exactly.
• - شدن colloquial 1 to become equal; to become balanced; to come into conformity with 2 to happen, to occur ♦ همینطور - شد That is just what happened.
• - کردن colloquial 1 to equalize; to balance 2 to compare, to equalize / even (with someone or something) ♦ مرا با آن (با) - نکن Don't you compare me with him! 3 to measure, to try on (clothing, etc.) ♦ این لباس رابجانت - کن Try on this dress. 4 to bring into conformity (with dimensions, etc.); to adjust, to fit (to something به) 5 to arrange, to provide ♦ تا شما - میکنم فردا پنج هزار روپیه را برای By tomorrow I will raise 5,000 rupees for you.
• قد - کردن to measure height
• چند – several times (larger or more)
• دو - twice, double, two times (larger or more)
• در - چشم مردم in people's sight, before people's eyes

برابری [baraabari] 1 equality; equilibrium 2 comparing, equating 3 rivalry; opposition 4 accordance, correspondence; coincidence; agreement 5 chance ♦ این پول است از روی - بدست من آمده This money came to me by chance.
• - کردن 1 to measure one's strength against someone 2 to compete with someone, to oppose someone

برات [baraat] 1 promissory note, bill 2 order, document (for something) ♦ معاش - check, order to receive or obtain wages 3 colloquial written instruction, order
• عمر خو نیاوردیم - proverb No one has guaranteed us a long life! (We all walk under God.)

برات [baraat] 1 day of remembrance of the dead (15th of Shaban) ♦ شب - night before Barat (when illumination of the dead is arranged and a funeral repast is celebrated) 2 masculine proper name Barat

برادر [baraadar] brother ♦ سکه - and عینی - blood brother

برادراندر [baraadarandar] stepbrother

برادرخوانده [baradarkhanda] adopted brother

ب

برادری [baraadari] brotherhood
براده [boraada] sawdust ♦ آهن - iron filings ◊ چوب - wood shavings
برآر [baraar] برآور ☞
برآشفتن [baraashoftan] (present tense stem برآشوب [baraashob]) to be indignant, to be angry; to become indignant; to be upset
برآشفتگی [baraashoftagi] indignation, anger
براعظم [bareaa'zam] continent, mainland
برافتاد [baraftaad] 1 having gone out of use, out of style 2 obsolete, antiquated ♦ آن رسم دیگر شد - This custom is already antiquated / no longer followed.
برافتادن [baraftaadan] 1 to go out of use, to go out of style 2 to be antiquated, to be obsolete
برافراز [barafraaz] present tense stem برافراشتن
برافراشتن [barafraashtan] (present tense stem برافراز [barafraz]) to raise, to erect, to hoist ♦ پرچم - to hoist the banner
برافروختن [barafrokhtan] (present tense stem برافروز [barafroz]) to set fire to, to kindle, to rouse, to ignite, to inflame ♦ صورتش برافروخته شد His face flushed (with anger, etc.).
برافروز [barafroz] present tense stem برافروختن
براق [boraaq] embankment, rampart
براکت [braaket (and) baraaket] technical bracket
برآمدگی [baraamadagi] projection; protuberance ♦ کوه - prominence of a mountain
برآمدن [baraamadan] (present tense stem برآی [b (a) raay]) 1 to go out (of a room, of a building); to leave, to set off for (somewhere) 2 to mount, to ascend, to climb, to rise ♦ زن های همسایه به دیوار برآمدند The (female) neighbors climbed the duval. 3 to ascend, to rise (said of celestial bodies) ♦ آفتاب برآمد The sun rose. 4 to appear, to protrude, to stick out (from behind something or from under something) 5 to appear, to be detected; to break out (about a rash on the body) 6 to be obvious; to follow, to ensue (from something) ♦ (از سخن او برمی آید که ...) from his words it follows that ... 7 to sprout, to germinate (of seeds)
برانش [braansh] gills
برانگیختن [barangeekhtan] (present tense stem برانگیز barangeez) 1 to induce, to motivate, to inspire 2 to excite, to incite, to egg on (به)
برانگیز [barangeez] present tense stem برانگیختن
برآور [baraawar] present tense stem برآوردن
برآورد [baraaword (and) baraaward] 1 preliminary appraisal or evaluation, preliminary calculation or count 2 estimate ♦ لایحه-عمارت estimate for construction of a building 3 prices, rates
برآوردن [baraawardan (and) baraawordan] (present tense stem برآور [baraawar (and) baraawor] and برآر [baraar]) to take out, to take, to get, to extract
برآورده [baraawarda]
• ساختن (کردن) - to realize, to accomplish, to execute, to carry out ♦ آرزوی خودرا - ساخت He realized his dream.
• شدن - to be realized, to be carried out
براهمه [baraahema] plural of برهمن
براهین [baraahin] plural of برهان
برآی [b (a) raay] present tense stem برآمدن

برای [baraaye] 1 (also - از) for, for the sake of preposition 2 for, in the name (of something) preposition ♦ وطن - for the homeland 3 by (a specific time or deadline); as of (a certain time) preposition
• برای خدا - 1 for God's sake 2 ☞ خدا
• عید نوروز - commemorating the holiday of Nowruz
برائت [baraa'at] literary 1 remission of charge or accusation, acquittal 2 liberation, release (from obligation)
برای خدا [baraayekhodaa] colloquial alms, charity
برباد [barbaad]
• کردن - and دادن 1 to ruin, to destroy 2 to dissipate; to waste, to squander 3 to reduce to naught ♦ تمام زحمتهای مارا - کرده است He reduced all our efforts to naught.
• رفتن - and شدن 1 to perish, to die in vain 2 to be squandered, to be wasted ♦ دارایی پدر - شده است The father's fortune has been scattered to the winds.
بربالا [barbaalaa]
• گفتن - colloquial to overstate the price (of goods), to overcharge (of a vendor, seller)
بربریت [barbariyat] barbarianism; wildness, savagery ♦ دوره - period of barbarism
برپای [barpaay] (ی)
• کردن - 1 to raise, to erect, to build 2 to arrange, to organize ♦ جنگ – کردن to begin a war, to start a war
برتری [bartari] superiority; advantage
• داشتن - to surpass, to exceed, to have an advantage, to prevail, to predominate (بالای ، بر ، از)
برته [barta] barta (dish of stewed eggplant with sour milk)
برج [borj] 1 sentry tower, turret, fortification 2 tower ♦ برمه - derrick, drilling tower
برج [borj] (plural بروج [boruj]) 1 astronomy sign of the zodiac ♦ اسد - the constellation Leo 2 month of the solar year ♦ عقرب - the month Akrab
• زهرمار - boogeyman, sullen morose person
برجستگی [barjastagi] 1 protuberance; prominence 2 a height (hill) ♦ برجستگی های سطح زمین the relief of the terrain
برجسته [barjasta] 1 prominent; raised 2 prominent, eminent ♦ اثر هنری - a prominent artistic work
برحال [barhaal] existing, current (of a government, etc.); continuing to carry out one's responsibilities or duties
برخاست [barkhaast]¹ 1 ascent, lifting, rising, getting up 2 takeoff (of an aircraft)
برخاست [barkhaast]² 1 permission, authorization 2 document (releasing one from some obligation)
برخاستن [barkhaastan] (present tense stem برخیز [barkhez]) 1 to get up, to rise, to stand up 2 to rise up [against] (برمقابل)
برخلاف [barkhelaaf] 1 against, in spite of denominal preposition ♦ این - in defiance of this 2 enemy, opponent
برخورد [barkhord] 1 contiguity, contact 2 meeting, encounter (unexpected) 3 an encounter, collision, clash 4 approach ♦ یکطرفه - unilateral approach
• کردن - 1 to come in contact [with] 2 to meet, to come across (unexpectedly), to collide with, to run into 3 to treat, to regard, to appeal to, to address (به)
برخورد [barkhord] colloquial conflict, gunfight
برخوردار [barkhodaar] 1 enjoying (the fruits of something); having joined (something) 2 provided with (knowledge)

36

بـ ‏شدن (بودن از) - 1 to make use (of something); to join 2 to be provided (with something)

برخورداری [barkhordaari] 1 opportunity to enjoy (the fruits of something) 2 bringing (something) useful [to someone] (in contrast to محرومیت)
• از علم و دانش - bringing science and knowledge [to someone], accustoming [someone] to science and knowledge

برخوردن [barkhordan] 1 to collide with, to run into (به) ; to hit or strike against (به) 2 to meet, to run across (by accident) ♦ (به) دیروز به او برخوردم Yesterday I ran into him by accident.

برخی [barkhee] (also از -) some of …; a few of …; part

برخیز [barkheez] present tense stem برخاستن

برد [bord] prize, winnings, gain

برد و باخت ، برد و بای ☞ برد و باخت

برد و آورد [bord-o-aaward] colloquial (literally: to take away and bring) arguing

بردار [bardaar] ¹ present tense stem برداشتن

بردار [bardar] ² 1 wide, broad ♦ زنخ - broad chin 2 of double width (about fabric)

برداشت [bardaasht] 1 raising; holding, keeping (suspended) 2 patience, endurance 3 an advance 4 a debt; credit 5 demand (for goods) ♦ این مال – ندارد There is no demand for these goods.
• کردن - colloquial 1 to have patience; to sustain, to endure (از) ♦ کمی - کن Be patient a bit! 2 to receive an advance, to get an advance, to take on credit (products, goods)
• کسی را نداشتن - not to endure someone or something, to be impatient with someone or something ♦ من – پیش آمد او را ندارم I can't stand his tricks / pranks / escapades.

برداشتن [bardaashtan] (present tense stem بردار [bardar])
1 to lift, to raise 2 to lift, to raise (a little) 3 to take, to remove ♦ خرمن - to gather the harvest ◊ کاپی - to make a copy, to copy

بردبار [bordabaar] 1 patient, enduring 2 manifesting patience, endurance, or self-control

بردباری [bordabaari] 1 patience, endurance 2 tolerance, self-control

بردگی [bardagi] literary slavery ♦ دوره - era of slavery

بردن [bordan] (present tense stem بر [bar]) 1 to carry away; to haul away; to lead away 2 to conquer, to win (in a competition); cards to take a hand 3 colloquial to influence, to affect (someone از) strongly ♦ شراب او را برد The wine had a strong effect on him.

برد و باخت [bordobaakht] and بردوبای [bordobaay] 1 victory and defeat; a win and a loss 2 vicissitudes of fate ♦ زندگی – دارد In life [there are] successes and failures.

برده [barda] literary 1 slave 2 prisoner, captive

برزدن [barzadan] (present tense stem برزن [barzan]) to raise, to lift; to twist, to tuck in; to roll up
• آستین ها را - 1 to roll up one's sleeves 2 to get to work
• دامن – to tuck up a skirt

برزگاو [barzagaaw] 1 ox 2 colloquial blockhead, dummy

برزن [barzan] present tense stem برزدن

برس [bors] brush ♦ دندان - toothbrush ◊ بوت - shoe brush
• کردن - to clean with a brush
• دندان کردن - to clean one's teeth, to brush one's teeth

برساتی [barsaati] rain cloak; raincoat

برش [boresh] 1 a cut, a cut-out 2 pattern

برش [borsh] 1 ☞ برس 2 technical bushing ♦ رابری - rubber bushing
• دینمو – technical brush of a generator

برطرف [bartaraf]
• کردن - 1 to remove (from a post, job), to discharge, to fire 2 to abolish; to eliminate (obstacles, etc.)

برطرفی [bartarafi] 1 removal (from a post, job); dismissal 2 elimination; removal ♦ مشکلات - removal of obstacles

برعکس [bar'aks] on the contrary, opposite ♦ ما - contrary to, as opposed to us …

برغو (and برغو) [barghu (and borghu)] technical drill; countersink; reamer ♦ دستی - hand reamer
• کردن - to expand, to countersink

برف [barf] snow ♦ باران - snow with rain ◊ میبارد - It is snowing. ◊ پایش را برد - colloquial His foot became frostbitten.

برف انداز [barfandaaz] an opening in the parapet of a roof (for removal of snow)

برف باری [barfbaari] snowfall

برف پاک [barfpak] (also موتر -) windshield wiper, wipers

برف جنگی [barfjangi] playing with snowballs

برف خورک [barfkhorak] colloquial warm rain (promoting the thawing of snow)

برفدان [barfdaan] repository for snow; cellar

برفک [barfak] frost (on a window, etc.)

برف کوچ [barfkoch] snow avalanche; landslide; snow slip

برف گیر [barfgir] glacier; accumulation of snow and ice (on mountains)

برفی [barfi] colloquial person who is first to inform friends that snow has fallen (for which they are obliged to give him a gift or a treat)
• کردن - to inform [someone] about the first snow

برق [barq] 1 lightning; summer lightning 2 brilliance, sparkle, glare 3 electricity; electric current ♦ دستی - flashlight ◊ مسلسل - direct current
• زدن - 1 to flash (of lightning) 2 to shine, to sparkle, to glitter ♦ چشمانش - زد His eyes flashed.

برق [boroq] pipe (for passage of water under a road or highway)

برقرار [barqaraar]
• شدن - to be settled, to become firmly established ♦ آرمش - شده بود Quiet / Silence set in.
• کردن - to establish, to consolidate

برقراری [barqaraari] establishment; consolidation ♦ صلح - establishment of peace

برقک [barqak] lightning; summer lightning
• زدن - to flash (of lightning)

برقو [barghu] ☞ برغو

برقی [barqi] electrician; electrical installer
• کردن - to electrify

برک [barak] rough cloth made of pure wool

بریک [brek] ☞ بریک

برکات [barakaat] plural of برکت

برکت [barakat] (plural برکات [barakat]) 1 abundance; sufficient quantity 2 prosperity, happiness, good fortune 3 gain, profit, economy
• داشتن - to be profitable, economical (about something)

ب

این خانه - نداره colloquial In this house everything is going to rack and ruin.

برگ [barg] 1 leaf (of tree, plant) 2 slice 3 a rolled piece of dough (for patties)
- گل - and شکوفه - petal (of a flower)
- سبز - 1 green leaflet 2 frugal or modest gift ♦ تحفه سبزاست درویش proverb A dervish's gift is a frugal / modest one.
- برگ برگ کردن to cut in thin slices (meat)

برگد [berged] obscure colonel

برگرد [bargard] present tense stem برگشتن

برگرداندن [bargardaandan] 1 to turn, to send back; to return 2 to turn around, to turn over 3 to translate, to interpret (into another language)

برگریزان [bargreezaan] autumn, fall; the period when leaves fall ♦ برگ ریزی زیاداست و - Fall has set in, and many leaves are falling.

برگریزی [bargreezi] the falling of leaves; the shedding of leaves

برگزیدن [bargozidan] (present tense stem برگزین [bargozin]) literary 1 to select, to elect 2 to give preference (را)

برگزیده [bargozida] 1 elected; selected 2 elect (e.g., president-elect) ♦ مردم - elected representative of the people

برگزین [bargozin] present tense stem برگزیدن

برگشت [bargasht] 1 a return; a repayment, a restitution 2 a turn ♦ نقطه - a turning point 3 colloquial misfortune; bad luck ♦ سر این خانواده – آمده There is bad luck in this family.

برگشتاندن [bargashtaandan] ☞ برگرداندن

برگشتن [bargashtan] (present tense stem برگرد [bargard]) 1 ☞ بازگشتن 2 to turn, to make a turn, to turn around

برگشته [bargashta] 1 past participle برگشتن 2 bent or turned upward, bent, curved ♦ مژگان - curled eyelashes

برگ و نوا [bargonawaa] 1 (also زندگی -) means of livelihood; fortune ♦ زندگی او برگ ونوایی پیداکرده است His life began to return to normal. 2 outfit, gear; equipment; supplies

برمته [b(a)ramta] baranta (stealing livestock, seizing property, etc.)
- کردن - to steal livestock; to seize property

برمه [barma] technical drill; auger ♦ برقی - electric drill ◊ خال 1 ماشین – and دستگاه - ◊ نحاری - brace ◊ - center punch boring machine, drilling machine 2 drilling rig
- کردن - to drill, to bore; to perforate

برمه کار [barmakaar] 1 driller 2 borer

برمه کاری [barmakaari] 1 drilling 2 boring, drilling operations or work 3 cutting, digging (a tunnel)

برناحق [barnaahaq(q)] ☞ بناحق

برنامه [barnaama] 1 program, plan 2 (also کار -) time table, schedule; order, sequence, procedure (of work)

برنج [berenj] ¹ 1 rice (cleaned) ♦ باریک - rice with thin, long grains (for pilaf, chelav, etc.) ◊ لک - rice with large oval grains (for soup, porridge, garnishes)
- باریک - ☞ مئین and - مهین
- به لغمان بردن - proverb to take rice to Laghman (To take your own samovar to Tula; i.e., Taking coals to Newcastle.)

برنج [berenj] ² 1 (also زرد -) brass 2 (also سرخ -) bronze

برنجک [berenjak] 1 frost (on a window); hoar-frost 2 (variety of small white mulberry tree) 3 hand knitting, crocheting with knobs or protuberances

برنجی [berenji] 1 bronze adjective, brass adjective 2 color of bronze, bronze adjective

برنده [baranda] veranda; terrace (of a home)

برنده [borenda] 1 curved shoemaker's knife 2 technical cutter, chisel 3 literary supreme judge, God

برنه [barna]
- ولدنگ - technical welding torch

بروبابا [borobaabaa] colloquial 1 Stop it! / Don't! / It can't be! 2 Oh sure! / What nonsense!; What next! / What more do we need!

بروت [borut] moustache

بروت چربک [borutcharbak] colloquial a small bribe, a present
- دادن - to give a bribe, to grease (someone's) palm

بروج [boruj] plural of برج 2

برودت [burudat] cold, hard frost; freezing weather

برودکاست [brodkaast] radio broadcast; transmission, relay
- کردن - to broadcast by radio, to transmit, to relay

بروز [boruz] 1 manifestation, display; appearance 2 exposure, revealing, discovery, detection
- کردن - 1 to be manifested, to become apparent; to appear 2 to come to light, to be revealed, to be detected, to be discovered

برومند [baromand] 1 fruit-bearing 2 abundant; rich 3 large, big; stately ♦ جوان - a stately youth

برومین [bromin] chemistry bromine

برونز [bronz] bronze ♦ دوره - historical the Bronze Age

برونشیت [bronshit] bronchitis

بره [barra] 1 lamb ♦ پوست - lambskin 2 (also برج -) astronomy Aries

برهان [borhan] (plural براهین [barahin]) reason, argument; proof, evidence; argument

برهم [barham]
- خوردن (شدن) - 1 to become entangled, to become confused 2 to be in disorder, to be in confusion, to be in a sad state 3 to be broken, to get broken 4 to fall into decay; to worsen ♦ وضع دهقانان – شد The status of the peasants worsened.
- زدن (کردن) - 1 to entangle, to confuse; to put into disorder, to disarrange 2 to break (the peace, quiet, etc.)

برهم خوردگی [barhamkhordagi] disorder; disarray ♦ حال - ill health, indisposition ◊ وضع - worsening of status or condition

برهمن [barahman] (plural براهمه [barahema]) Brahman

برهم ودرهم [barhamodarham] 1 sparse, scattered 2 confused, entangled ♦ موهای - disheveled or tousled hair 3 intricate, involved, complicated ♦ وضع - complicated condition or position

برهم و درهم [barham-o-darham] slang not organized, mess

برهنه [berahna] 1 naked, nude; bare ♦ باپای - barefoot ◊ شمشیر - unsheathed sword, naked sword 2 in an undisguised manner, in a barefaced manner, frankly, openly
- گفتن - to speak openly or frankly
- سر خودرا - کردن colloquial to ask humbly, to entreat, to implore (for something)

بری [bar(r)i] 1 land 2 continental adjective ♦ اقلیم - continental climate

بریان [beryaan] fried; roasted (of nuts, grains) ♦ پسته - roasted pistachio nuts ◊ نخود - roasted peas
- کردن - to fry, roast (grains); to roast (nuts)

برید جنرال [breedjanraal] brigadier general

بریدگی [boridagi]
- شیر - coagulation, curdling of milk

بریدمن [breedman] lieutenant

بریدن [boridan] 1 to cut, to cut off 2 to chop off, to sever ♦ - گپ کسی را to interrupt someone's speech or talk 3 to cut out (e.g., a dress) 4 to break off (ties, connections); to cease (relations) 5 *colloquial* to decide; to solve; to make a decision ♦ مسئله را بریدن They settled the matter / solved the problem.

بریده [borida] 1 *past participle* بریدن 2 coagulated, curdled (of milk)
- شدن - to coagulate, to become curdled (of milk)

بریده بریده [boridaborida] 1 curt, incoherent ♦ - سخنان curt, incoherent speeches 2 curtly, incoherently

بریک [breek] *technical* brake ♦ پای - foot brake ◊ هیدرولیکی - hydraulic brake
- کردن - to brake

بریکیت [brikeet] briquette (of coal dust)

بریکیت سازی [brikeetsaazi] making briquettes ♦ - فابریکه briquette factory

برین [barin] *literary* high above the earth, to be in the empyrean or the clouds ♦ بهشت - paradise ◊ علم - theology; theosophy

بز [boz] male goat, billy goat; female goat, nanny goat
- بز مرده شاخ زرین *proverb* A dead goat has golden horns (something lost always seems to be valuable).

بزاز [bazzaaz] dealer or trader of a factory

بزازی [bazzaazi] 1 manufacturing trade 2 (also دکان-) manufacturing shop

بزدل [bozdel] 1 shy, timid 2 faint-hearted, cowardly

بزدل [buzdel] *slang* (*literally:* goat-hearted) chicken hearted, faint-hearted

بزر [bázer] seed grain; seeds

بزرگ [bozorg] 1.1 larger, big (in size or quantity) 1.2 prominent, eminent, great 1.3 old; mature 1.4 respectable, venerable 2 holy; holy person (able to work wonders)
- داشتن - to respect, to revere
- شدن - 1 to grow, to increase 2 to grow up; to mature, to become an adult

بزرگان [bozorgaan] 1 distinguished persons; dignitaries, high officials; nobles, magnates 2 wise men, scientists, scholars 3 saints, holy persons

بزرگر [bazergar] farmer; plowman

بزرگری [bazergari] farming; plowing

بزرگی [bozorgi] 1 size, quantity, magnitude, dimensions 2 grandeur 3 generosity, nobility 4 holiness, sanctity
- کردن - to manifest generosity, nobility

بزرو [buzraw] *colloquial* (*literally:* goat trail) a narrow trail in the mountain

بزری [bazri]
- تخم - seeds for sowing; seed grain

بزغاله [bozghaala] kid (goat)

بزق [bozoq] seedling; sapling

بزک [bozak] type of ibis (bird)

بزکان [bozakaan] rash (on the body of child sick with measles)

بزکشی [bozkashi] bulldogging a goat (game on horseback)

بزگر [bazgar] *colloquial* ☞ بزرگر

بزگری [bazgari] *colloquial* ☞

بزم [bázem] *literary* feast, banquet, a magnificent feast, banquet

بزنم [bezanom] *colloquial* 1 bellicose, brave 2 a brave man; daredevil

بزودی [bazudi] soon [after], shortly after

بزور [bazur] 1 forcible; forced ♦ خنده - forced laughter 2 by force, under compulsion ♦ - مقبول a painted beauty (overly made up)

بس [bas] enough, sufficient ♦ بس است Enough! / That's enough! / Quit it!
- ازبس *colloquial* strongly; very; much
- ازبس (که) ☞ ازبس (که)
- بس آمدن ☞ بس آمدن
- بس کردن to cease, to stop; to finish

بسا [basaa] 1 much, many; very much, very many; quite a few ♦ - ای How many! / So many! 2 many *adjective*
- از - جهات 1 for many reasons 2 in many respects

بساط [besaat]
- چیزی راجمع کردن (چیدن) - to cease, to put an end to (a matter); to wind up, to close down (an activity)
- بساط چیزی راهموار کردن to begin, to undertake something; to arrange something ♦ عروسی راهموار کردند - They arranged a wedding.

بس آمدن [basaamadan] 1 to cope with, to manage, to overcome (همراه ، کتی ، با) 2 to vie; to resist (با)

بست [bast] 1 *technical* joint, coupling, cramp, cramp iron, shackle 2 form, system; structure ♦ مالیات - tax system 3 cadre, personnel; tables of organization ♦ اضافه – کردن to reduce the tables of organization

بست [bast] 2 bast; inviolable sanctuary

بستان [bastaan] 1 orchard 2 flower garden; flower bed

بستر [bestar] 1 (also خواب -) couch, bed 2 (also دریا -) bed of river, channel

بستره [bestara] roadbed

بستری [bestari] recumbent, lying, confined to bed (of a sick person)
- کردن - to hospitalize

بستگی [bastagi] 1 1 obstacle, impediment, difficulty 2 strained circumstances; need

بستگی [bastagi] 2 thickening, clotting

بستگی [bastagi] 3 1 tie, bond, relation 2 dependence 3 kinship
- داشتن 1 to have ties [with], to bear a relation to (به ، با) 2 to depend on (به ، با) 3 to be related to (با)

بستن [bastan] (*present tense stem* بند [band]) 1 to lock, to shut, to close; to bar, to block 2 to tie [up] 3 to conclude (an agreement, contract)
- بار - to pack [up]
- دستمال به سر - to tie a kerchief on one's head, to cover one's head with a kerchief
- خون بسته شد The blood coagulated.

بستنی [bastani] (also نان -) a collection of food items on a tray (for a bride)

بست وبندها [bastobandhaa] *technical* hardware; fastenings (bolts and nuts)

بسته [basta] 1 *past participle* بستن 2.1 package; bundle; sheaf; bunch 2.2 pack or deck (of cards) 2.3 briefcase, small leather bag (for books and writing materials) 2.4 cramp iron, shackle, bolt

ب

- شدن ♦ - to stop (of bleeding)
- کردن - 1 ☞ بستن 2 to collect, to stack (weapons) 3 to assemble, to erect (a plant, a unit)

بسته بندی [bastabandi] 1 packing, baling (of cargo, etc.) 2 *technical* assembly

بسته کار [bastakaar] assembler; an installer of equipment

بسته کاری [bastakaari] *technical* assembly, installing, erecting; installation, erection work, operations
- سیم - ♦ binding or wrapping of wire, sheathing, insulation
- شدن ♦ - to be assembled, to be installed, to be erected

بسته یی [bastayi]
- حوزه - ♦ *geology* basin (of commercial minerals)

بسختی [basakhti] strongly; very; intensively

بسرعت [basor'at] quickly, rapidly; hurriedly, hastily, in a hurry

بسط [bast] *literary* dissemination; spread ♦ - آیین بودایی the spread of Buddhism

بسکتبال [basketaal] basketball

بسکه [baske] ☞ (ازبس (که

بسمل [besmel] 1 brought for sacrifice, slaughtered (about animals) 2 *livestock* slaughtered (by having the throat cut), slaughtered (by strangling) 3 half dead, breathing one's last breath, being at death's door
- کردن - ♦ 1 to bring for sacrifice, to sacrifice, to give up for slaughter 2 *livestock* to slaughter (by cutting the throat), to slaughter (by strangling)

بسم الله [besmellaa] 1 *abbreviation of* بسم الله الرحمن الرحیم 2 God be with you! (said before the beginning of an undertaking)
- کردن(گفتن) - ♦ 1 to say: "God be with you!" 2 to begin an undertaking

بسم الله الرحمن الرحیم [besmellaaharrahmanarrahim] in the name of Allah all-gracious, merciful

بسمه [basma] ☞ وسمه

بسنده [basenda] 1 sufficient 2 sufficiently, enough ♦ این – انیست That's not enough. / There's not enough of this.
- کردن - ♦ to be limited, to limit oneself to, to be satisfied, to content oneself with (به)

بسواسه [beswaasa] biswasa (a measure of area equal to 4.88 square meters)

بسوه [beswa] biswa (a measure of area equal to 97.5 square meters)

بسیار [besyaar] 1 numerous; abundant 2.1 much, many; in a large amount or quantity 2.2 very, highly, greatly ♦ خوب است - very good, very well

بسیج [basij]
- کردن - ♦ 1 to prepare, to get ready, to ready 2 to equip, to outfit 3 *military* to mobilize

بسیط [basit] 1 simple, uncomplicated; elementary ♦ سوال - a simple question; - موضوع a simple or uncomplicated subject 2 *grammar* simple, nonderivative (of a word) 3 *literary* vast, spacious

بشارت [bashaarat] happy news, good news

بشاش [bashshaash] happy; smiling; satisfied

بشپل بنداز [beshpelbendaz] *slang* (*literally:* smash and throw) unorganized work, lousy

بشدت [basheddat] strongly, with force; intensively ♦ باران – میبارد It is raining hard.

بشر [bashar] 1 person 2 (also - نوع) the human race, mankind

بشری [bashari] 1 human *adjective* 2 humanitarian ♦ علوم - the humanities

بشریت [bashariyat] mankind

بشقاب [beshqaab] dish, plate

بصراحت [basaraahat] evidently, obviously

بصیرت [basirat] *literary* 1 sight 2 perspicacity, insight; sagacity 3 knowledge, knowledgeability; competence; wisdom

بضاعت [bazaaat] 1 property, belongings, fortune 2 riches, wealth, prosperity

بطری [betri] *electrical* battery; storage battery ♦ آفتابی - solar battery

بطلان [botlaan]
- خط - کشیدن (بر) 1 to declare invalid; to refute, to disprove 2 to cross out, to strike out, to expunge; to abolish, to eliminate

بطن [báten] (*plural* بطون [botun]) 1 stomach, belly; abdominal cavity 2 *anatomy* ventrical (of the heart) 3 womb, uterus 4 *literary* secret meaning, hidden meaning, secret side, covert side (of something)

بطنین [batnain] *anatomy* ventricles (of the heart)

بطون [botun] *plural of* بطن

بعد [ba'd (and) baad] 1 after, later, afterward ♦ چه شد؟ - What happened later? 2 further, future, subsequent, following, next ♦ روز - the next day 3 after; following *denominal preposition*
- از - ♦ 1 after; beyond, following *compound preposition* ♦ از جنگ - after the war ◊ از شما - after you, following you 2 in, later, after *compound preposition* ♦ از دو سال - in two years, two years later, after two years

بعداً [ba'dan] 1 afterward, then, thereupon, subsequently; later 2 later on, subsequently

بعض [ba'z] part (of something); some ♦ مردم - part of the people ◊ وقت ها - sometimes, ◊ در - موارد in some cases at times

بعضا [ba'zan] 1 partly 2 sometimes

بعضی [ba'zee] 1 some, some people, somebody ♦ میگویند که - some people say that … 2 ☞ بعض

بعلاوه [ba'elaawa] additionally; in addition, as well ♦ این - in addition to this

بعید [ba'id] distant, far, remote ♦ شرق - the Far East ◊ ماضی - *grammar* past perfect (tense), pluperfect (tense) ◊ از امکان - نیست که it is not ruled out that …

بغاوت [baghawat] *literary* mutiny, revolt, riot

بغ بغ [baghbagh] bray of a camel

بغبغه [baghbagha] *colloquial* double chin

بغض [boghz] 1 hatred; malice 2 offense, wrong, feeling of resentment 3 lump in the throat

بغل [baghal] 1 side; bosom ♦ بغلم درد میکند My side hurts. ◊ در - in [one's] bosom 2 edge; side ♦ در - سرک on the side of the road 3 embrace 4 armful ♦ یک - علف a bundle of hay
- زیر ♦ 1 armpit 2 (also در زیر -) under [one's] armpit
- زدن - (کردن) ♦ to embrace, to clasp
- به – گرفتن 1 to draw to oneself, to embrace 2 to take in one's arms 3 to take (a child) into one's arms 4 to guard, to defend, to protect
- کردن - به ♦ to reconcile (someone with someone)
- کسی را گرم کردن ♦ *colloquial* to marry off someone, to find a husband for someone

بغل ـ یک ‌ ‌‌به *colloquial* to be obstinate, to persist, to rest (against), to set (against)

بغلجیب [baghaljeb] inner pocket

بغلک [baghalak] *colloquial* ☞ سینه بغل

بغل‌کشی [baghalkashi] embrace; enclosing in an embrace
• ‌ ‌- کردن to embrace, to hug one another, to enclose (one another) in an embrace

بغلی [baghali]
• ‌- بچه small child, baby, infant

بغیر [baghyr] (also ‌- از) besides, apart from; without

بقآ [baqaa] 1 being, existence 2 duration; eternity
• ‌- داشتن 1 to live, to exist, to be 2 to last, to continue; to be eternal, to be everlasting

بقال [baqqaal] 1 tradesman in groceries, grocer 2 greengrocer, vegetable seller

بقالی [baqqaali] trade in groceries ♦ دکان ‌- a grocery, grocery shop, grocery store

بقایا [baqaayaa] 1 *plural of* بقیه 2 vestiges ♦ فیودالیسم ‌- vestiges of feudalism

بق بق [beqbeq]
• ‌- خندیدن to laugh (quietly, with mouth closed)

بقچه [boqcha] 1 a bundle with [one's] things; a parcel, a package 2 bag (with sewing accessories)

بقلاوه [baqlawa] baklava (variety of pastry: small tube of dough with sweet filling)

بقه [baqa] frog
• ‌- کلان ☞ کوربقه

بقه [boqqa] breeding bull, sire, pedigree bull

بقه بازی [baqabaazi]
• ‌- کردن to swim like a frog

بقه بینی [baqabeni] *slang* (*literally:* frog like nose) pug nose *derogatory*

بقیه [baqiya] (*plural* بقایا [baqaya]) 1.1 remainder, remaining portion, remaining part 1.2 continuation; conclusion ♦ مطلب ‌- continuation of a subject 1.3 unpaid amount of a tax, arrears 2 remaining, the rest of ♦ مردم ‌- the rest of the people, the others

بکار [bakaar] needed, necessary; suited, fit
• ‌- بودن 1 to be needed, to be required ♦ چند دیگر ‌- است که صد شود؟ How much more is needed / needs to be added to make 100? 2 to be suited, to fit (a job, an undertaking), to be of use

‌- داشتن to have a need [for something], to need (something)

بکارت [bakaarat] virginity, chastity

بکالوریا [bakaaloryaa] degree, bachelor's degree, baccalaureate

بکر [béker] 1 virgin, chaste 2 fresh; original

بکس [baks] 1 bag ♦ جیبی ‌- purse ◊ خریطه ‌- map case 2 chest; box 3 suitcase 4 (also ‌- دستی) briefcase, portfolio

بگ [beg] ☞ بیگ

بگی [bagi] two-wheeled cart; small cart; carriage ♦ ‌- پایکی *obscure* bicycle

بگی [begi] *merging of* بگیر 1 Grab! / Seize! / Catch! / Hold! 2 Fetch! (command to a dog)

بگیربگیر [begirbegir] 1 round-up (during a hunt), cordon 2 bustle, turmoil; panic

بگی‌وان [bagiwaan] driver (of carriage, cart)

بل [bal] ¹
• چراغ را بل کن Light the lamp! ♦ بل کردن to turn on a light

بل [bal] ² *literary*
• بلکه این مرد تنها عالم نیست بل عارف هم است This person is not only a scientist / scholar, but also a wise man.

بل [bel] bill; invoice

بل [bal] *colloquial* very fast, hard, smack ♦ برویش بل سیلی زد He slapped him in the face hard

بل کردن [bal-kardan] ² *colloquial* to get ready to attack ♦ بجانش بل کرد e started on him

بلا [balaa] ¹ 1 grief, sorrow, misfortune, trouble; calamity, disaster 2 unfit thing, rotten thing ♦ این چه ‌- است که تو خریدی؟ What kind of rubbish did you buy?
• ‌- (ای) *colloquial* Woe of mine! (a form of address, usually to children) ♦ ای ‌- را چه میکنی؟ Oh, woe of mine, what are you doing?
• ‌- جان *colloquial* causing grief or sorrow ♦ دوستی او ‌- جان من شده است His friendship annoys me.
• چه ‌- What a shame!
• ‌- کجا است ؟ زیر پایت *proverb colloquial* Where is trouble? - It's under your feet (No sooner do you call for trouble and it's here.).
• ‌- دیدن ☞ به ‌- افتادن
• ‌- کردن to perform wonders, to perform miracles, to make amazing things, to make wonderful things
• ‌- جان کسی شدن to be a burden to someone
• ‌- جان خود را به ‌- دادن *colloquial* to bring misfortune or trouble on oneself; to put oneself in danger
• ‌- (به) پش It [really] doesn't matter! / To hell with him!
• ‌- به سرش and ‌- در جانش *colloquial* May the goblins take him.

بلا [balaa] ² *colloquial* 1 adroit, sly, cunning 2 desperate ♦ او ‌- آدم است He is a desperate / hopeless person.
• ‌- بد *colloquial* and بیدرمان ‌- a complete scoundrel, an out-and-out scoundrel

بلا [belaa] (negative prefix) ♦ بلا توقف without delay ◊ بلا فاصله immediately; at once; without delay

بلا استثنی [belaaestesnaa] and بلا استثنا 1 without exception 2 not having exceptions

بلا خور کسی شدن [balaakhor-kasay-shudan] *idiom* to love someone to death

بلا را بجان خریدن [balaa-ra-bajan-kharidan] *idiom* (*literally:* to buy oneself a monster) to buy trouble

بلا خور [balaakhor] and بلا خوار [balaakhaar] 1 sponger, parasite ♦ ‌- های چوچه children-spongers; children for whose sake it is necessary to obtain subsistence by hook or by crook 2 rich peasant, exploiter (one who lives on others' toil)

بلاد [belaad] *plural of* بلد

بلازده [balaazada] 1 *ironic, contemptuous* unfortunate, unlucky, good-for-nothing 2 unfortunate creature, poor devil; oaf, awkward person, clumsy person

بلا شرط [belaashart] 1 absolute, undoubted unconditional, unreserved, unqualified ♦ ‌- تسلیم unconditional surrender 2 absolutely, undoubtedly, unconditionally

بلاغت [balaaghat] 1 perfection of speech, perfection of style; eloquence 2 majority, maturity, coming of age

بلافاصله [belaafaasela] immediately; at once; without delay

بلاک [blaak] 1 *technical* (cylinder) block (of an engine) 2 block, unit, section (in house-building)

بلاگردان [balaagardaan] repelling misfortune, repelling bad luck (usually of an amulet or talisman)
• شوم - *colloquial* May all your troubles fall on me! (in expressing love and sympathy or interest)

بلاگک [balaagak] *colloquial* troublemaker ♦ ای - چه میکنی؟ Hey, troublemaker, what are you doing?

بلاگک [balaagak] *slang* (*literally:* a little monster) sly dog

بلاگی [balaagee] *slang* 1 thingamajig ♦ همو بلاگی چه شد where is the thingamajig 2 genitals (male or female)

بلا و بتر [balaa-o-batar] *slang* (*literally:* bad and good) junk, stuff

بلاوقفه [belaawaqfa] 1 continuously 2 continuous

بلبل [bolbol] 1 nightingale ♦ هزار داستان - singing nightingale 2 bulbul (general name for a number of birds that sing beautifully)

بل بل کردن [belbel-kardan] *colloquial* blinking of light from far

بلد [balad] ¹ (*plural* بلاد [belad] and بلدان [boldan]) *literary* city, town; region, district; country

بلد [balad] ² 1.1 knowing, versed (in something); acquainted (with something) 1.2 accustomed (to something), familiar (with something) 2 *rarely* guide, conductor
♦ (به)– این راه و - بودن 1 to know, to know how ◊ نیست He doesn't know this road. ◊ شمابه طبابت بلدید؟ Do you know how to be a doctor? / Do you know how to treat an illness? 2 to get accustomed to, to make oneself familiar with

بلدان [boldaan] *plural of* بلد

بلدیت [baladiyat] knowledge (of something), knowledgeability (in something); competence; familiarity (with something)

بلدیه [baladiya] town council, city council, municipality ♦ رئیس - chairman of town or city council

بلست [belest] span, 7-9 inches ♦ بلست بلست span by span; each span

بلستی [belesti] gnome; Lilliputian

بلشویک [bolshewik] ☞ بالشویک

بلع [bála]
• کردن – ☞ بلعیدن

بلعیدن [bal'idan] to swallow

بلغار [bolghaar] (also - چرم) yuft, Russian leather ♦ کفش - shoe or boot of colored yuft

بلغاری [bolghaari] 1 Bulgarian ♦ زبان - the Bulgarian language 2 made of yuft, made of Russian leather

بلغم [balgham] 1 phlegm, mucus 2 a lump (in the throat); hoarseness

بلقوه [belqowa] 1 potential 2 potentially

بلکس [balakas] *colloquial* flames

بلکه [bálke] 1 but also …, and ♦ نه فقط - … not only, but also … 2 *colloquial* maybe, perhaps

بلگ [balg] *colloquial* ☞ برگ

بلند [beland] 1.1 high ♦ مقام - high post 1.2 loud, ringing, clear ♦ گپ - loud conversation ◊ نام - celebrated name, famous name 2.1 highly 2.2 loudly, clearly, ringingly
• گپ زدن - to talk loudly
• بردن - to heighten, to raise ♦ سویه زندگی مردم را - بردن to raise the living standard of the people
• رفتن - 1 to be raised aloft, to ascend 2 *colloquial* to be raised (of prices)
• شدن - 1 ☞ رفتن - 2 to ring out, to sound loudly ♦ غرش - شدن – رعد The thunder roared.
• خودرا - گرفتن *colloquial* to put on airs, to fancy oneself ♦ خوده بسیار – نگی Don't put on such airs!

بلنداب [belandaab] and بلندآو [belandaaw] situated above water level in an irrigation canal (about a piece of land)

بلندآوازه [belandaawaaza] 1 celebrated, famous 2 having received much response, having received broad publicity

بلندبالا [belandbaalaa] high, tall; stately; well-porportioned, slender

بلندپردازی [belandpardaazi] 1 pomposity 2 discussions about something lofty or exalted; love for something lofty or exalted

بلندپرواز [belandparwaaz] 1 high-flying (of a bird) 2 with great pretensions; presumptuous overbearing

بلندپروازی [belandparwaazi] great unfounded pretensions; presumptuousness, arrogance

بلندقامت [belandqaamat] and بلندقد [belandqad (d)] high, strapping, tall

بلندمرتبه [belandmartaba] 1 high-ranking 2 eminent, prominent, uncommon

بلندی [belandi] 1 height, altitude 2 height (a hill), rise

بلوچی [baluchi] 1 Baluchi *adjective* 2.1 a Baluchi 2.2 (also - زبان) the Baluchi language

بلور [belawr] 1 cut glass ♦ کوهی - [rock] crystal 2 crystal

بلوری [belawri] and بلورین [belawrin] 1 crystal ♦ گلدان - crystal vase 2 crystalline; crystal-clear

بلوغ [bolugh] maturity; coming of age

بلوک [boluk] *military* platoon ♦ استحکام - sapper platoon

بلوک‌مشر [bolukmésher] ☞ بریدمن

بلول [bolol] (also سمنتی -) pipe, cement pipe (for sewer, etc.)

بلهوس [bolhawas] 1 inconstant, changeable (in one's opinion or taste), changeable 2 succumbing to moods, moody; capricious

بلی [bálee] Yes / So / Of course

بلی بلی [baleebalee] Really? / Indeed? / Is that so? / Well, well!

بلیارد [belyaard] billiards

بلیغ [baligh] 1 eloquent, achieving perfection (in style, letter writing) ♦ او آدم بسیار - است He has a beautiful style. 2 perfect (about style, letter writing) ♦ سخن - beautiful speech

بلیه [baliya] *literary* misfortune, trouble ♦ آسمانی - trial or test sent by God

بم [bam] ¹ 1.1 low note, low tone 1.2 low voice, deep voice, bass 1.3 bass string (of rubab, etc.) 2 bass *adjective*, low (of a voice, tone)

بم [bam] ² bomb ♦ بم اتومی atomic bomb ◊ بم دستی hand grenade, grenade

بم‌افگن [bamafgan] and بم‌انداز [bamandaz] (also بم طیاره) bomber

بم‌اندازی [bamandazi] dropping bombs, bombing
• کردن - to drop bombs

بمبارد [bambaard] and بمباردمان [bambaardmaan] bombardment ♦ طیاره - bomber
• کردن - to bomb, to bombard

بمبه [bamba] pump

بمبه‌دار [bambadaar] equipped with a pump ♦ تیل دانی - thumb-pressure oil can

بمبه‌یی [bambayi] piston *adjective*, sucker *adjective* ♦ قلم - fountain pen

بمبیرک [bambirak] dragonfly

بمبیرک [bambirak] *slang* (*literally:* dragonfly) helicopter

بم کفاندن [bam-kafandan] *slang* (*literally:* to explode a bomb) to make a big splash

بموقع [bamawqe'] **1.1** promptly, on time **1.2** it is appropriate; to the point; opportunely **2** prompt, appropriate; opportune

بن [bon] (also بن درخت) lower part of a tree trunk
- ازبیخ و بن کندن - to tear out (something) with its roots, to root out
- بن چاه the bottom of a well
- بن گوش ☞ بن گوش
- بن موی root of a hair

بنأ [benaa] (*plural* ابنیه [abniya]) **1** building, structure **2** base; foundation
- بر(به) - on the basis of, in accordance with; according to *compound preposition* ♦ به گفته شما - in accordance with what you said
- شدن - **1** to be built, to be erected; to be based [on] **2** to begin *intransitive* ♦ جنگ – شد The war began.
- چیزی راگذاشتن - **1** to lay the foundations of something **2** to begin something, to start something

بنا [bannaa] stone mason; builder

بنابران [benaabaraan] and بنابراین [benaabarin] therefore, consequently, on the basis of this, based on this *conjunction*

بناچاری [banaachaari] involuntarily, against one's will, by compulsion

بناحق [banaahaq(q)] **1** illegally, unjustly **2** undeservedly, in vain, to no purpose

بنادر [banaader] *plural of* بندر

بناق [banaaq] *colloquial* ☞ بناحق

بناکاری [benaakaari] **1** construction, construction project **2** architecture

بنام [banaam] celebrated, famous; eminent

بنجاره [banjaara] tradesman in haberdashery, a haberdasher

بنجاره گی [banjaaragi] **1** haberdashery trade **2** (also - دکان) haberdasher's shop **3** (also - سامان) haberdasher's goods, haberdashery مزار

بند [band] **1** present tense stem of verb بستن **2.1** bonds, fetters, hobble **2.2** confinement, imprisonment, captivity **2.3** dam, dike, weir; (also برق -) dam of electric power station **2.4** obstruction, jam, barrier ♦ راه - obstruction (in a road) **2.5** *anatomy* ligament, joint ♦ انگشت - phalanx of a finger **2.6** node (on the stalk of a plant) ♦ نی - section of a reed (between two nodes) **2.7** rope, cord, string, twine ♦ زیارت - cord, thread (tied by pilgrims "for luck" to the pole or fence of a mazar; ☞ مزار) ◊ ساعت - watch band ◊ کفش - shoelace **2.8** mountain ridge, mountain range
- شدن - **1** ☞ افتادن
- انداختن - to build a weir; to build a dam or dike
- بستن - **1** to shut off the water (in an irrigation ditch), to dam **2** to tie a cord, thread to the pole of a mazar "for luck" (about pilgrims)
- شدن - **1** to stop *intransitive*, to cease ♦ رفت و آمد – شده بود Movement ceased. **2** to be caught **3** *technical* to jam, to become wedged **4** *colloquial* to be nonplussed
- کردن - **1** to shut, to block (a road) **2** to discontinue, to stop

- ماندن - to stick, to get stuck
- از - آزاد کردن to free from captivity
- به پای کسی - انداختن **1** to put in chains **2** *figuratively* to tie someone's hands and feet
- پول را - کردن to lend money on interest
- ریگی - **1** groundless, unsubstantiated proposal, suggestion **2** plan built on sand
- دل من کنده شد - My heart stopped (from fear, alarm, etc.).
- آوازش – شد His voice weakened.
- بینی اش همیشه - بود His nose was constantly stuffed.
- دلش – است He is in love.
- کارش – است Things are not going well for him. / Things are going poorly for him.

بنداژ [bandaazh] and بندج [bandej] **1** belt **2** bandage
- بستن - to bandage; to apply a bandage

بندستی [bandedasti]
- ساعت - wristwatch

بندر [bandar] **1** customs point or post, border (where they collect customs duties) **2** pass (in mountains) **3** port

بندش [bandesh] **1** obstacle, obstruction **2** *technical* malfunction (e.g., in operation of a machine)

بندشدگی [bandshodagi] *technical* jamming, sticking

بندک [bandak] gold or silver loop (soldered to a rupee so that it can be strung on a necklace)

بندگی [bandagi] **1** slavery, bondage **2** *religion* the fate of a slave of God, the destiny of a man
- کردن - to bear one's cross, to submit to fate

بندل [bandal] **1** package, bale; sheaf bunch; bundle, parcel ♦ یک - چوب a bundle of firewood **2** skein (of thread)

بندوبازو [bandobaazu] *colloquial* build (i.e., of someone's body), figure ♦ - قوی دارد He has a strong build.

بند و واز [ban-o-waaz] *colloquial* relying, depending ♦ به آمدنش چندان بند و واز نیستم I do not rely on he is coming (I do not cares if he comes or not)

بندوبست [bandobast] **1** understanding, agreement, contract **2** compact, deal
- داشتن - to have an understanding, agreement; to have a compact
- داشتن ☞ **1** - کردن **2** to enter into a compact, a secret deal ♦ به قتل او – کردند They made a deal to kill him.

بند و بغل شدن [band-o-baghal] *colloquial* physically fighting, wrestling

بنده [banda] **1** slave **2** (also خدا -) slave of God **3** I (polite equivalent of personal pronoun, first person singular)

بندی [bandi] **1** captive **2** prisoner
- کردن - **1** to take captive, to capture **2** to arrest, to imprison

بندی خانه [bandikhaana] place of confinement, prison, jail

بندی دار [bandydaar] *colloquial* a person whose family member is in prison

بنزین [benzin] gasoline ♦ طیاره وی - aviation gas or gasoline

بنفش [benafsh] violet, lilac ♦ ماورا - *physics* ultraviolet

بنفشه [benafsha] violet (flower)

بنگ [bang] **1** Indian hemp, jute **2** bang, anasha (narcotic beverage made of Indian hemp)
- از سرش پرید - *colloquial* He is amazed. / He is dumbfounded.

بن گوش [bonegosh] ear lobe

ب

بنگی [bangi] dope addict (who uses bang); person who uses or is addicted to anasha

بنه [bona] 1 (also سفر -) traveling things, traveling supplies; baggage 2 *literary* string of carts
- بارو - ☞ باروبنه
- بستن – سفربستن and - to set off on a journey; to move, to migrate

بنی [bani] (*plural of* ابن) sons
- بنی آدم - ☞ آدم
- بنی اسرائیل - *historical* Israelites

بنیاد [bonyaad] 1 base, foundation 2 basis; grounds

بنیاد گذاری [bonyadgozaari] laying foundations (of anything)

بنی آدم [baniaadam] people; mankind; human race

بنیان [banyaan] 1 knit undershirt (man's) 2 vest; (striped) sailor's vest

بنیان بافی [banyaanbaafi] knitted goods

بنیه [bonya] 1 build (of a person) 2 endurance, strength

بو [baw] *rare present tense stem* بودن
- بوی ☞ بو

بواد [bowaad] *literary* May he …! / May you …!

بوبو [bobo] *colloquial* mama, momy

بوبین [bobin] *technical* induction coil, ignition coil, bobbin, reel, spool

بوت [but] boots; shoes; footwear

بوت پاک [butpaak] 1 brush (to clean or shine shoes) 2 *colloquial* toady, shoe polisher

بوت دوز [butduz] shoemaker; worker in shoe industry

بوتل [botal] 1 bottle, small bottle; flagon 2 compressed gas cylinder or bottle ♦ اکسیجن - oxygen tank or bottle

بوت موزه [butmoza] high boots with laces

بوت والا [butwaalaa] 1 shoe salesman, tradesman dealing in shoes 2 ☞ بوت دوز

بوته [buta] ☞ بته

بوته [bota] crucible (for melting gold and silver)

بودا [budaa] Buddha

بودایی [budaayi] 1 Buddhist ♦ آیین - Buddhism 2 Buddhist

بودجه [budja] budget; estimate

بودن [budan] (present tense stem باش [baash] and *rarely* بو [baw]) 1 to be, to exist 2 to be present, to be located 3 to reside 4 to be found, to inhabit ♦ پلنگ درکوه می باشد The leopard is found in the mountains. 5 *colloquial* to wait ♦ تو باش که من بیایم You wait [and] I'll arrive. 6 (component of compound words) ♦ راهی - to go, to be on the way 7 (auxiliary verb to form the past tense) ♦ بابایم شهر رفته بود که من رسیدم [My] father had [already] departed for the city when I arrived.
- بود نبود - once upon a time

بودنه [bodana] quail; female quail
- صورتی - *colloquial* with a deceptive exterior or appearance

بودنه بگیل [bodnebaygal]² *slang* (literally: a quail that runaway during a quail fight) a shy, timid (person) *derogatory*

بودنه بازی [bodanabaazi] 1 keeping quail (for fighting or for their singing) 2 quail fight

بودنه چرنگی [bodanae-cheringi] *slang* (literally: singing quail) a person who whines and nags

بودوباش [budobaash] residence, residing; stay, sojourn
- داشتن - to be located, to stay
- کردن - to live, to reside ♦ هر دو خانواده در یک حویلی میکر Both families lived on the same courtyard. / Both families lived in the same household / farmstead.

بوده [buda]
- از - *colloquial* in view of; because of *denominal preposition* ♦ از این کار من بسیار زحمت دیدم I am all worn out because of this matter

بور [bor] 1 gray 2 skewbald 3 gray-brown, brownish

بورژوازی [borzhwaazi] 1 bourgeoisie 2 bourgeois

بورس [bors] 1 stipend (paid by the state to students studying abroad) 2 exchange (e.g., stock exchange)

بورکس [boraks] *chemistry* borax

بوره [bura] 1 granulated sugar 2 (also اره – and چوب -) sawdust

بوره [bora] long-fallow lands; virgin land

بوریا [boriyaa] mat made of reeds, reed mat; woven mat
- بافتن - to weave a mat

بوریاباف [boriyaabaaf] mat maker

بوریاکوبی [boriyaakobi] *colloquial* invitation; reception (upon the occasion of a housewarming)

بوریایی [boriyaayi] made of mats, made of matting; mat *adjective* ♦ کلاه - straw hat

بوریک [borik] *chemistry* boric, boracic

بوریک اسید [borik-asid] *chemistry* boric acid

بوزه [boza] 1 boza, bouza, home-brewed beer (intoxicating beverage made of millet or rice chaff 2 koumiss

بستان [bostan] ☞ بوستان

بوسه [bosa] a kiss
- کردن - ☞ بوسیدن

بوسیدن [bosidan] to kiss

بوشارت [bushaart] man's outer shirt (worn over the trousers)

بوطل [botal] ☞ بوتل

بوغ [bugh] and بوق [buq] 1 trumpet; horn; bugle 2 trumpet's blare or blaring sound, toot; siren
- زدن - to blow the trumpet, to sound a horn, to give a signal (by sound)

بوغ بند [boghband] *slang* (literally: bed sheet used as a bag for storing pillows and comforters during the day) old bag (a fat woman) *derogatory*

بوکسنگ [bokseng] boxing
- کردن - to be involved in boxing, to box

بول [bawl] urine
- کردن - to urinate

بولانی [bolaani] *slang* (literally: Afghan side dish prepared with either leeks, boiled potatoes and onions or with ground beef put on a round flat piece of dough then folded and pan fried or baked, usually served with yogurt) peach (woman's part)

بولبرنگ [bolbereng] and بولبیرنگ [bolbereng] *technical* ball bearing ♦ رولک دار - roller bearing

بولت [bolt] 1 *technical* bolt; screw ♦ آنکری - anchor bolt 2 bolt (e.g., door bolt, to lock door)

بولدازر [buldaazar] ☞ بولدوزر

بول دانی [bawldaani] *medicine* bedpan

بولدوزر [boldozar] bulldozer

بولدوزرچی [boldozarchi] bulldozer operator

بالشویک [bolshawik] ☞ بولشویک

بولک [bolak]¹ 1 *colloquial* part of a load; a party of goods, a consignment of goods 2 a plot (of land), a parcel, a strip (of land)

بولک [bolak] ² *historical* financial administration or directorate; division or department of tax collection

بولی پران [bolyparaan] *colloquial* bully (someone who makes fun of others)

بولی گوی [bolygoy] *colloquial* bully (someone who makes fun of others)

بوم [bum] ¹ 1 *literary* country, land; region 2 ☞ بومی

بوم [bum] ² owl; eagle-owl

بومی [bumi] 1 local, native, indigenous 2 a native, aborigine

بونه [buna] ☞ بنه

بوی [buy] odor, scent, smell; fragrance, perfume ♦ - بد bad smell, stink, stench
- مشک پنهان نمی ماند *proverb* You can't hide the smell of musk. (Murder will out.)
- بردن - to have a feeling (about something), to suspect (something); to get wind (of something) (از) ♦ کسی به کارش – نمیبرد Nobody even suspects his activities / pursuits / employment.
- دادن - to smell (of), to give off an odor or smell
- کردن - to take a smell of, to sniff at
- گرفتن - to spoil, to become rotten, to acquire a musty or tainted smell
- چیزی را برداشتن - 1 to become permeated with the smell of something 2 to pick up the smell or odor of something; to pick up the track or scent (about a hunting dog)

بوی خون [boykhoon] *slang* (*literally*: the smell of blood) a sign of major danger ♦ از کار تو بوی خون میآید Your action leads to danger

بوی ناکی [boynaakee] *colloquial* stink (*literally*: bad smell)

بوی ناکی چیزی برآمدن [boynaakee-chizay-baraamdn] *idiom* to be disgraced, exposed
- بوی ناکی چیزی برآمدن [boynaakee-chizay-baraamdn] *idiom* to be disgraced, exposed

بویایی [buyaayi] 1 (sense of) smell 2 fragrance, perfume

بویبر [buybar]
- شدن - to smell, to feel (something); to smell, to get wind of (از)

بویدار [buydaar] ☞ بویناک

بویناک [buynaak] 1 smelling (of); odorous 2 fetid, stinking

بویدن [buyidan] to smell [something], to sniff at [something]

به [ba] ¹ *preposition* 1 (indicates direction of action) into, in, to, toward; on, onto ♦ شاگرد ها به مکتب آمدند The pupils came to school. 2 (indicates the place or time of action) in; at ♦ برادرش به فابریکه کار میکند His brother works in a factory / plant. ◊ به نیمروز at midday 3 (indicates the recipient of an action; usually with the verb دادن to give, گفتن to say, etc.) ♦ من به او کتاب دادم I gave him a / the book. ◊ پدرم به ما هیچ نگفت Father didn't say anything to us. 4 (indicates a goal, desire, etc.) for ♦ به دیدن من آمده بودند They came to meet me (*literally*: for a meeting with me). 5 (indicates the person or thing to whom / by which one swears or vows) ♦ (قسم) به خدا By God! / I swear to God. 6 (becomes part of compound denominal prepositions) ♦ به ذریعه by means of, through, via, with the aid of ◊ به همرای with, accompanied [by] 7 (becomes part of compound conjunctions) ♦ به نسبتی که because of the fact that …; in connection with the fact that …

به [ba] ² ☞ ب [ba]

به [be] ☞ ب [be]

به بلا انداختن [ba-balaa-andakhtan] *colloquial* to throw someone under a bus (to create a problem for someone)

بها [bahaa] 1 price, worth, cost, value ♦ تمام شد - net cost, prime cost ◊ به ناچیز - for next to nothing, for a trifle 2 estimation, estimate, appraisal
- دادن - to give an opinion, to give an appraisal (به) ; to assess, to characterize (به)

بهادر [bahaador] 1 brave, bold, courageous 2.1 a brave man, hero; *epic* hero, athlete 2.2 *masculine proper name* Bahadur

بهادری [bahaadori] a symbol of valor, a military award (e.g., order, medal)

بهار [bahaar] 1 spring ♦ شد - Spring has arrived! 2 during the spring, in the spring

بهاری [bahaari] 1 spring *adjective* ♦ گندم - spring wheat 2 springtime, vernal ♦ کشت - spring sowing

بهانه [bahaana] pretext, pretense, occasion, ground; excuse; subterfuge ♦ به – چیزی under the pretext of something
- جستن - to seek grounds (for something), to seek a pretext (for something), to make excuses
- کردن - 1 to plead (something) (را); to represent as a reason ♦ نیامدم ناجوری خود را - کرده به مکتب Alluding to indisposition, I did not go to school (*literally*: did not show up at or report to school). 2 to avoid (something under some pretext)

بهانه جویی [bahaanajoyi] 1 seeking causes, seeking pretexts 2 fault-finding, nagging 3 resorting to ruses or tricks or subterfuges

بهبود [behbud] and بهبودی [behbudi] 1 improvement of health, recovery 2 well-being, a state of flourishing
- یافتن - 1 to improve, to get better (about health) 2 to recover [one's health] 3 to achieve well-being, to achieve a state of flourishing

بهتر [behtar] 1 better ♦ هرچه - in the best manner possible 2 best
- دانستن - 1 to consider it right, to deem it right 2 to prefer (نسبت به)

بهتری [behtari] 1 improvement 2 advantage, supremacy
- داشتن - to have an advantage, to have supremacy (از)

بتنهایی [batanhaayi] ☞ به تنهایی

به جای رسیده [bajaayrasida] holy person, servant of God

به خدا [bakhoda] ☞ بخدا

بادقت [badeqqat] ☞ به دقت

بهر [bahr] 1 ☞ بهره 2 (also از) 2.1 for, for the sake of *denominal preposition* 2.2 because, because of *denominal preposition* ♦ چه ستمهایی از بهرت کشیدم How many wrongs I have endured because of you!

بهر در سر گردان [bahardarsargardaan] 1 one who runs hither and yon, one who runs about, one who fusses (about a matter), one who is troublesome 2 one who goes from house to house (for alms) 3 homeless, unsettled, one without shelter

بهره [bahra] 1 share, part; share (of stock) 2 use, benefit 3 profit, gain
- برداشتن - 1 to derive benefit, to benefit (از) 2 to obtain profit, to obtain income (از)
- داشتن - 1 to have part, to have a share (از) 2 to be endowed [with], to possess (از)

ب

از کاری – داشتن • to gain an understanding of some matter, to be competent

بهره برداری [bahrabardaari] deriving benefit, deriving use; obtaining profit ♦ از معادن - development of mineral deposit ◊ از خط آهن - operation of a railroad

بهره مند [bahramand]
• بودن (شدن) - 1 to be endowed [with], to possess; to join (از) 2 to enjoy; to take pleasure in (از)

بهره ور [bahrawar] ☞ بهره مند

باسرشته [basareshta] ☞ به سرشته

بهشت [behesht] paradise

بهشتی [beheshti] 1 heavenly 2 inhabitant of paradise

بکار [bakaar] ☞ به کار

بهل [behel] absolution of a sin, remission of a sin
• کردن - to forgive; not to reproach (about something را)
• من شیر خود را بتو - میکنم colloquial I bless you.

بهم [baham]
• آمدن - to draw closer, to coincide; to be joined, to be connected
• انداختن - to embroil, to urge on, to set one against another
• پیچیدن - to be intertwined, to be coiled up, to be rolled up, to become entangled
• پیوستن - to be fastened, to close; to be joined intransitive
• خوردن - to collide [with], to hit [against], to strike [against] ♦ دو موتر – خوردند Two vehicles collided.

به مشکل [bamoshkel] with difficulty, just barely

بناحق [banaahaq (q)] ☞ به ناحق

بنام [banaam] ☞ به نام

بهنگام [bahangaam] 1 promptly; opportunely 2 promptly; opportunely

بهی [behi] 1 ☞ بهبود

بهی [behi] 2 quince

بهی دانه [behidaana] quince seeds (used as a medicine for a cough)

بی [bee] 1 1 without, besides, with the exception [of]; outside preposition ♦ بی توقف without interruption ◊ بی رقیب beyond competition, hors concours ◊ بی شما without you, in your absence 2 (adjectival and adverbial prefix with meanings of "without" / "not") ♦ بی صبر impatient ◊ بی فایده useless

بی [bee] 2 colloquial ☞ بهی 2

بی آب [beeaab] 1 dry, arid ♦ دشت - arid steppe 2 not juicy (about fruit, etc.) 3 ☞ بی آبرو

بیابان [biyaabaan] desert; arid steppe

بیابان گرد [biyaabaangard] 1 one who roams about a desert; itinerant; nomadic 2 inhabitant of the steppe, nomad

بی آبرو [beeaabro] dishonest, without shame and conscience; having a poor reputation

بی احترامی [beeehteraami] disrespect, lack of respect; lack of tact, tactlessness ♦ با - disrespectfully
• کردن (نسبت به، با) - to show disrespect to act tactlessly

بی احتیاطی [beehtiyati] carelessness, imprudence; negligence
• کردن - to act carelessly, to act imprudently; to commit negligence

بی اختیار [beeekhtiyaar] 1 automatically, involuntarily; unconsciously, instinctively 2 automatic, involuntary; unconscious instinctive

بی ادب [beeadab] impolite, ill-bred; discourteous; rude ♦ ای - abusive You boor!

بی ادبی [beeadabi] impoliteness, state of being ill-bred; discourtesy; rudeness
• کردن - to behave discourteously, rudely

بیادر [biyaadar] colloquial ☞ برادر

بی اراده [beeeraada] 1 spineless, weak-willed; indecisive; without character 2 ☞ بی اختیار

بیاره [biyaara] vine, runner (of melon, watermelon, etc.)

بی استعداد [beeeste'daad] incompetent; untalented, mediocre

بی اشتهایی [beeeshtehaayi] lack of appetite

بی اعتدالی [beee'tedaali] unbalanced state; immoderation

بی اعتنایی [beee'tenaayi] 1 inattentiveness; indifference 2 neglect, disregard, contempt, scorn 3 carelessness, negligence

بی آلایش [beeaalaayesh] 1 irreproachably honest, irreproachably decent 2 unselfish, possessing pure thoughts or intentions

بی التفاتی [beeeltefaati] ungraciousness, discourtesy
• کردن - to treat ungraciously, to show discourtesy

بیادربخشی [byaadarbakhshi] slang (literally: dividing like brothers) to divide fair and square (equitably dividing things)

بیالوجست [biaaiojest] biologist

بیالوجی [biaaloji] biology

بیان [bayaan] (plural بیانات [bayaanaat]) account, description; explanation ♦ طرز - manner of expression; style ◊ علم - rhetoric; stylistics ◊ به - مطلب پرداخت He began to summarize the matter.
• داشتن (کردن) - to state, to set forth, to tell; to describe

بیانات [bayaanaat] 1 plural of بیان 2 statement, address; speech

بی اندازه [beeandaaza] 1 immeasurably, infinitely; very, extremely 2 immeasurable, infinite

بی انصاف [beeensaaf] 1 unfair, unjust 2 cruel, brutal, unscrupulous

بیانیه [bayaaniya] 1 declaration; statement 2 appeal 3 grammar apposition
• - جمله grammar expressive subordinate clause

بی آواز [beeaawaaz]
• صوت - obscure grammar voiceless consonant

بی اولاد [beeawlaad] childless

بی ایمان [beeimaan] 1 a non-Moslem, unbeliever, infidel 2 athiest 3 scoundrel; swindler

بی بازخواستی [beebaazkhaasti] 1 not making guilty persons answer [for something]; connivance (in regard to abuses) 2 injustice, lawlessness

بی بدل [beebadal] 1 irreplaceable, indispensable 2 uncompensated ♦ کار - unpaid labor

بی برگی [beebargi] poverty, need; state of being needy

بی بضاعت [beebezaa'at] 1 not having means, indigent 2 poor man

بی بها [beebahaa] priceless, precious, inestimable

بی بهره [beebahra] poor, unfortunate; deprived (of something), not obtaining benefit or use (from something) ♦ ازکاری – بودن to be incompetent in some matter

بی بی [bibi] colloquial 1 grandma, grandmother 2 mistress (of the house, form of address) 3 regional mama, mother
• بی بی کلان - ☞ کلان

بی بی [baybai] colloquial (literally: priceless)

بی بیخ [beebeekh colloquial not having heirs, childless

46

بی بی کلان [bibikalaan] greatgrandmother, greatgrandma

بی پار [baipaar] *colloquial* regular customer, a regular

بی پاس [beepaas] **1** not considering anyone [else], not respecting anyone [else] **2** not being able to appreicate kind treatment

بی پایان [beepaayaan] endless, limitless

بی پدر [beepadar] **1** orphan **2.1** of low birth, from a bad family; of unknown ancestry **2.2** *colloquial* rogue, rascal; an adroit person

بی پدرو مادر [beepadaromaadar] without kith or kin; orphan (who has lost both parents)

بی پرداخت [beepardaakht] **1** frivolous, light-hearted **2** inattentive, disrespectful

بی پرده [beeparda] **1.1** open, frank, direct **1.2** cynical **1.3** unmasked, exposed, shamed **2.1** openly, frankly, directly ♦ بگو - Tell [me] directly! / Tell [me] frankly! **2.2** cynically
- کردن - **1** to unmask, to expose **2** to shame (را)

بی پروا [beeparwaa] **1** carefree, light-hearted **2** negligent, careless

بی پروایی [beeparwaayi] **1** state of being carefree, light-heartedness **2** negligence, carelessness

بی پشت وپناه [beeposhtopanaah] defenseless, not having a defender, not having a patron

بی پیراهن تنبان [beeperaahantomban] and بی پرن تنبان [beperantomban] *colloquial* the poor

بیت [bayt]¹ (*plural* ابیات [abyaat]) *literary* **1.1** stanza **1.2** a strophe of two lines of poetry - a measure - completed intonationally and in meaning **1.3** the smallest form of lyric poetry **2** *colloquial* ☞ دوبیتی - خواندن *colloquial* to sing (a song)

بیت [bayt]² (*plural* بیوت [boyut]) *literary* **1** home, building **2** hearth, family

بی تاب [beetaab] **1** losing patience, rushing about fretting (from pain, love) **2** enfeebled, exhausted
- ساختن - to exhaust, to weaken ♦ تب او رابسیار – ساخت The fever exhausted him completely.

بی تابی [betabi] **1** loss of patience; anxiety, uneasiness, emotional experience **2** feebleness, exhaustion ♦ برای چه این گریه و -؟ Why the tears and agitation?

بیتار [baytaar] ☞ بطار

بیت الله [baytolla] (*also* شریف -) the temple at Mecca

بیت المال [baytolmaal] **1** state treasury; treasury **2** escheat; property in abeyance

بیت بافی [beetbaafi] manufacture of wicker furniture

بی تبلک [baytablak] *slang* person with no manners, uncouth person

بی تدبیر [betadbir] **1** unenterprising; passive **2** without foresight

بی تربیه [beetarbiya] ill-bred, unmannerly; impolite, rude
- ! - *abusive* Ignoramus! / Slob!

بی ترتیب [beetartib] **1** confused, disorderly **2** systemless, chaotic **3** irregular ♦ رفت وآمد سرویس - است The bus runs irregularly. **4** untidy (about clothing, etc.)

بی تعارف [beeta'aarof] **1** not observing etiquette, natural, unceremonious **2** without ceremony

بی تکلف [beetakallof] **1** simple, unpretentious ♦ - پذیرایی simple reception or welcome **2** free, free and easy **3** *literary* devoid of formal contrivances (about style)

بیتل کور [beetalkor] *slang* (*literally:* a blind mare) loser, bum, low-class person

بی تلخه [beetalkha] *colloquial* ☞ بی جگر

بی تناسب [beetanaasob] **1** unproportionate, asymmetrical **2** ungainly, awkward, clumsy ♦ - اندام ungainly figure

بی توقع [beetawaqqo] not having any confidence (in someone); not wishing (for anything for oneself)

بیتون [beeton] ☞ بتون

بیجا [beejaa] **1.1** inappropriate, unsuitable **1.2** vain, ungrounded, useless ♦ - خرج a useless expenditure **2.1** inappropriately; inopportunely; irrelevantly **2.2** in vain, for no purpose ♦ تو این کار را – کردی You did that in vain.
- گشتن - to go where one should not, to visit unseemly places
- نبودن - to be appropriate, to come opportunely / at an opportune time ♦ نخواهد بود که بگویم - It would be appropriate to say … / It is opportune to say …

بی جان [beejaan] **1** lifeless **2** *grammar* inanimate

بی جانی [beejaani] *grammar* inanimateness

بی جای [bejaay] ☞ بی جا

بی جایداد [beejaaidaad] not having fixed property (which can be taxed); indigent, poor

بیجک [bijak] bill, invoice; receipt

بی جگر [beejegar] cowardly, fainthearted

بی جلو [beejelaw] *colloquial* **1** obstinate, unbridled, unruly **2** willful, stubborn, disobedient
- شدن - to be disobedient, to behave obstinately, to be willful

بیچاره [beechaara] **1.1** poor, needy **1.2** unfortunate **1.3** helpless **2.1** a poor person (male) **2.2** a poor person (female)

بیچارگی [beechaaragi] **1** need, poverty **2** helplessness, hopeless or desperate situation

بی حال [beehaal] **1** weak, feeble, feeling bad **2** insensible, unconscious
- شدن - **1** to grow weak, to feel bad **2** to faint **3** to become numb, to be paralyzed (about extremities) ♦ دست وپایش وسردشد Her hands and feet were paralyzed and became cold.

بی حالی [beehaali] **1** weakness, faintness **2** fainting condition, loss of consciousness

بی حس [beehes(s)] **1** unconscious; insensible **2** numb, benumbed
- کردن - to make unconscious, to anesthetize

بی حسی [beehesi] **1** insensibility; numbness, torpidness **2** *medicine* anesthetizing; anesthesia

بی حوصله [beehawsela] **1** impetuous, impatient **2** downcast, apathetic; having lost interest (in something)

بی حیا [beehayaa] having lost [all] shame; impudent, shameless ♦ ای دختر - Oh, you shameless hussy!

بیخ [beekh] **1** root ♦ درخت - root of a tree **2** base; basis; foundation ♦ ستون - base of a column ◊ کوه - foot of a hill or mountain
- از – **1** under the root, down to the root **2** completely, absolutely, to the ground
- کسی (چیزی) را (بر) کندن- to destroy to the ground, to eradicate, to annihilate someone or something ♦ خدا بیخته بکنه

abusive May God strike you [dead]!

- از بیخ و بته [azbaykh-o-bota] *slang* (*literally:* from the bush) One who does not have relative *derogatory*
- بیخ چیزی پخته شدن *idiom* [baykh-chizay-pokhta-shudan] *colloquial* (*literally:* to have roots) to put down roots, to settle down
- بیخ گرفتن [baykh-gereftan] *slang* (*literally:* to have roots) to get rich, to become wealthy

بیخ بر [beekhbor]
- کردن - 1 to cut [something] down to the roots 2 to eradicate, to destroy

بی خبر [beekhabar] 1 ignorant [of something]; uninformed 2 without notice or warning, suddenly
- بودن (ماندن) - not to know, not to have information or news (از)

بی خبری [beekhabari] lack of knowledge, ignorance; lack of information

بیخ بوته [beexebut(t)a]
- ما هم از - نیامدیم *colloquial* We also can take care of ourselves.

بیختن [beekhtan] (*present tense stem* بیز [beez]) to sow, to sift

بی خدا [beekhodaa] atheist; infidel

بی خطر [beekhatar] 1 safe ♦ - راه safe road 2 provided in case of an accident or emergency, emergency *adjective*

بیخ کنی [beekhkani] destruction, eradication, annihilation

بیخواب [beekhaab] 1 suffering from insomnia, deprived of sleep ♦ طفل - restless baby, a baby that does not sleep well 2 awake, not sleeping

بی خوابی [beekhaabi] 1 insomnia, sleeplessness 2 being awake, staying awake

بی خود [beekhod] 1 being unconscious, being in an unconscious state 2 aloof, immersed in self-contemplation (about a wise man or mystic)

بی خودی [beekhodi] 1 unconsciousness, state of being in a faint 2 immersion in nonexistence, immersion in self-contemplation (by wise men or mystics)

بیخی [beekhi] *colloquial* 1 in a radical or fundamental manner; absolutely; completely ♦ سیاه شده بود - He turned completely black. 2 (with the negative form of a predicate) not at all …, not a bit, not in the least ♦ کار نمیکنند - They are not working at all.

بید [beed] willow
مجنون بید ☞ مجنون ●

بیداد [beedad] injustice; lawlessness

بیداد گر [beedaadgar] tyrant, despot; oppressor

بیداد گری [beedaadgari] tyranny, despotism; oppression

بیدار [beedaar] 1 not sleeping, awake 2 vigilant, indefatigable 3 awakened, aroused, conscious ♦ جوانان - conscientious young people
- کردن - 1 to awaken, to arouse, to rouse, to get [someone] out of bed 2 to arouse [someone] to activity

بیدار خوابی [beedaarkhaabi] 1 state of half sleep, drowsiness 2 state of being awake 3 ☞ بیخوابی
- کشیدن - 1 to be awake, to stay awake, not to sleep 2 to suffer insomnia
- دادن - not to permit [someone] to sleep, to deprive of sleep (form of torture)

بیداری [beedaari] 1 arousal from sleep, rising; *military* reveille 2 state of being awake; reality ♦ در - in one's waking hours 3 vigilance 4 consciousness ♦ ملت - the people's consciousness

بی دانه [beedaana] 1 seedless (e.g., of raisins), without pits 2 *colloquial* pits of the quince (used as medicine)

بی درد [beedard] 1 not grieving (for someone or something), indifferent; callous, ruthless 2 painless

بی دردسر [beedardesar] 1 easily, lightly, without care, without complications 2 easy, light, carefree

بی دردی [beedardi] 1 indifference; callousness, ruthlessness 2 painlessness

بیدگل [beedgol] *botany* oleander

بی دل [beedel] 1.1 despondent, sad, grieved 1.2 passionately in love 2 *literary* بیدل [bedil] (outstanding Persian-language poet and philosopher of the early 18th century)

بیدل شدن [baydel-shudan] *colloquia l*(*literally:* to be heartless) to lose confidence

بیدل خوانی [beedelkhaani] a literary party dedicated to the creative works and memory of the poet Bedil (☞ بیدل 2)

بیدل شناسی [beedelshenaasi] 1 study of the creative works of Bedil 2 a special course on Bedil (traditionally given at Kabul University)

بی دوام [beedawaam] short (in reference to time), short-lived; fragile

بیده [beeda] dried clover, hay

بیده خانه [beedakhaana] barn for storage of dry clover, hayloft

بی دین [beedin] unbeliever (in God), infidel; atheist

بیر [bir] beer ♦ یک بوتل - bottle of beer

بی راه [beeraah] 1 good-for-nothing, dissolute 2 having lost one's way
- شدن - 1 to take a bad or evil road; to become dissolute 2 to lose one's way, to stray

بی راهه [beeraaha] 1 unbeaten path; roundabout road 2 lack of good roads, impassability of roads

بیران [beeraan] *colloquial* ☞ ویرانه

بیرانه [beeraana] *colloquial* ☞ ویرانه

بی رخ [beerakh 1 smooth, without a groove (e.g., a screw, a shotgun) 2 smooth-bore (of a gun) *adjective*

بیرق [bayraq] banner, flag; *maritime* pendant, pennant

بیرقی [bayraqi] *colloquial* 1 famed for one's adventures; much-talked-of for bad deeds 2 inveterate scoundrel

بیرل [beeral] barrel (of iron)

بیرنگ [beerang] 1 drab, colorless, pale, faded 2 insipid, dull, inexpressive

بیرنگ [beereng] *technical* ☞ بولبرنگ

بیروبار [birobaar] *colloquial* 1 a gathering of people, a crowd 2 crush, dense crowd; commotion, hurly-burly ♦ میان بازار کمتر شده بود - The crush at the bazaar subsided.

بیرون [beerun] 1 outer, surface part (of something) ♦ شهر - suburb; outskirts of town or city 2.1 (also - در) outside, on the outside; out of doors; on the street 2.2 (also - به) outside, out ♦ از اندازه – excessively, immoderately 3 outside, beyond *denominal preposition* ♦ خانه - outside of the house, out of doors ◊ حصار - beyond the fortress wall
- شدن ☞ آمدن ●
- زدن - *colloquial* to break out (in a rash), to appear (of a rash, pimples)
- شدن - to go out
- کردن - to force to go, to drive out, to push or to chuck

48

آنان را – کنید Drive [someone or something] out the door!

بیرونی [beeruni] 1 outer, external ♦ نمود external appearance 2 Beruni Aburaykhan (outstanding central Asian scholar-encyclopedist of the 11th century)

بیره [bira] gum (of mouth)

بیره‌یی [birayi] *linguistics* alveolar (about sounds)

بیز [beez] *present tense stem* بیختن

بیزار [beezaar]
● (شدن) بودن - 1 to have no special liking for, to have an aversion for (از) 2 to suffer with difficulty, to endure with difficulty (از) ♦ من از تو بیزارم You bore me. ◊ این دختر از زندگی – شد This girl is sick of / tired of life.
● کردن - to bore, to annoy, to pester (someone را; with something از)
● کسی را از جان – کردن to poison life for someone, to spoil life for someone

بیزاری [beezaari] dissatisfaction, irritation, aversion, hatred

بی زمین [beezamin] landless ♦ دهقان - landless peasant

بژبلبم [bezhbelabam] *slang* (literally: the sound of bongos) hurry, yippy (the shout of happiness)

بی سابقه [beesaabeqa] unprecedented

بی ساخت [beesaakht] sincere, unsophisticated, simple ♦ پیش آمد - simple manners, plain manners

بیست [bist] twenty

بیستم [bistom] and بیستمین [bistomin] twentieth

بی سر [beesar] 1 neglected, homeless 2 disobedient, not acknowledging (anyone's) authority ♦ بچه من – شده My son has gotten completely out of hand.

بی سرشته [beesareshta] 1 uneconomical, negligent; not thrifty ♦ زن - poor housekeeper 2 untidy, sloppy ♦ بچه - untidy boy

بی سروته [beesarota(h)] incoherent, senseless, incomprehensible ♦ جواب - incomprehensible answer

بی سروسامان [beesarosaaman] 1 poor; unsettled in life, not provided with the necessities 2 disorderly, confused ♦ زندگی - an unsettled life, an irregular life

بی سکه [beesekka] 1 money without coinage 2.1 *colloquial* unattractive, homely 2.2 insignificant, imperceptible

بی سواد [beesawaad] illiterate

بی سیم [beesim] 1 wireless (of the telegraph) 2 radio telegraph ♦ تیلفون - radio telephone ◊ نفر - *military* radio operator ◊ نفر طیاره - onboard radio operator (on an aircraft)

بیش [beesh] many, much; more ♦ از آن - moreover ◊ ازپیش - more than before, worse than before

بی شبهه [beeshobha] ☞ بی شک

بی شرف [beesharaf] dishonorable, base ♦ بی شرف! *abusive* Scoundrel!

بی شک [beshak] 1 undoubtedly, indisputably 2 undoubted, indisputable
● ! - Of course! / Absolutely!

بیشه [beesha] grove, small wood

بی صدا [beesada] 1 soundless, noiseless 2 *linguistics* unvoiced ♦ کانسوننت - unvoiced consonant

بی صرفه [beesarfa] 1 uneconomical 2 uneconomically

بیضوی [bayzawi] 1 egg-shaped; oval; having the shape of an ellipse 2 an ellipse; an oval

بیضه [bayza] egg; testicle

بیطار [baytaar] veterinarian

بیطاری [baytaari] veterinary science, veterinary medicine ♦ مکتب - veterinary school

بی طاقت [beetaaqat] 1 not having the strength to endure (something); having lost patience 2 weak, exhausted
● کردن - to rob of strength, to exhaust, to wear out, to wear down ♦ سرمای شدید مرا – ساخت The severe cold exhausted me / wore me out.

بی طبقه [beetabaqa] classless ♦ جامعه - classless society

بی طرف [beetaraf] 1 neutral ♦ دول - neutral state, neutral country 2 objective

بی طرفی [beetarafi] 1 neutrality ♦ سیاست - policy of neutrality 2 objectivity

بیع [báy'a] 1 sale, selling 2 trade 3 *colloquial* price, cost
● کشیدن - *colloquial* to include in the price (about goods)
● از - افتادن *colloquial* to drop in price, to depreciate

بیعانه [bay'aana] deposit
● دادن - to give a deposit (when making a purchase)

بی عزت [beeezzat] 1 not enjoying respect; unprestigious 2 deprived of honor, deprived of dignity, humble
● شدن - to be deprived of respect, to lose prestige (نزد,پیش)
● او نزد من – شد He lost my respect.

بی عزتی [beezzati] 1 loss of respect, loss of prestige 2 loss of honor, loss of dignity 3 ☞ بی احترامی
● کردن - to show disrespect (با); to behave disrespectfully (بمقابل)

بیع زده [bay'zada] *colloquial* reduced in price, stale (about goods)

بی عقل [beeaql] reckless, foolish, unreasonable

بی علاقه [beealaaqa] not manifesting interest, desire, sympathy; indifferent
● شدن - to lose interest, to grow cold

بی علاقه گی [beealaaqagi] lack of interest, desire, sympathy; indifference

بی علت [beeellat] 1 motiveless, unfounded 2 ☞ بی عیت

بیع نامه [bay'naama] deed of purchase

بیع وبها [bay'obaha]
● کردن - *colloquial* to ask the price of (when making a purchase)

بی عیب [beeayb] and بی عیب وعلت [beeaybwoellat] devoid of shortcomings, devoid of flaws, irreproachable

بی غرض [begharaz] disinterested, impartial; uninterested, unconcerned

بیغم [beegham] 1 not knowing grief, without sorrow 2 carefree, lighthearted
● بودن - 1 not to know grief, not to know cares, to live in clover ♦ زمین هایت راکشت کن و – باش Work your land and live without knowing trouble! 2 not to be worried, not to be alarmed ♦ باشید - Don't worry!

بی غوری [beeghawri] not scrutinizing (a matter); an unserious attitude (toward a matter); carelessness ♦ مقمات مسئول - unserious attitude of responsible organs; carelessness of authorities

بی غیرت [beeghayrat] 1 not valuing honor, not valuing dignity 2 not possessing valor, not possessing courage

بی فروغ [beeforogh] 1 devoid of luster or brilliance, devoid of radiance 2 darkened, obscured, cloudy, melancholy
● سیمأی - 1 sad, melancholy face 2 inexpressive features (of a face) ♦ جنده - a weak smile

بی قاعده [beeqaa'eda] incorrect, contradicting rules, contradicting the norm ♦ فعل - *grammar* irregular verb

بی قدر [beeqaadr] 1 of no value, worthless, bad; insignificant 2 inestimable, incalculable (by someone) ♦ پیش کسی – بودن not to be appreciated by someone

بی قرار [beeqaraar] 1 restless, uneasy, fidgety ♦ بچه - a fidgety infant 2 perturbed, anxious, uneasy, agitated

بی قراری [beeqaraari] 1 anxiety, uneasiness, impatience 2 agitation
- کردن ● 1 to show impatience, to show anxiety 2 to be agitated or upset; to suffer

بیک [beek] 1 ☞ بیگ 2 (second component of compound personal names of Turkish origin) ♦ علی بیک Ali-Bek

بیکار [beekaar] 1.1 useless, unfit 1.2 unemployed, jobless 1.3 idle, not occupied in or with anything 2 idler, loafer ♦ از - بیزار خدا *proverb* God does not suffer loafers.
- افتادن ● to lie about without use, to be unused (about something)

بیکاره [beekaara] 1 not capable of anything; useless, unfit (about someone) 2 unnecessary, superfluous ♦ چیزهای - all sorts of trash or rubbish

بیکاره گی [beekaaragi] incapacity, inability (for a matter, of a job); uselessness, unfitness (of someone)

بیکاری [beekaari] 1 unemployment, joblessness 2 idleness, state of being unoccupied or free; loafing

بی کس [beekas] 1 not having close relatives, single 2 not having a breadwinner (about a family) 3 orphan; single person, bachelor

بی کسی [beekasi] state of being alone or single; state of being an orphan, orphanhood

بی کفایت [beekefaayat] 1 incapable; unqualified ♦ داکتر - unqualified physician 2 worthless, low

بیگ [beeg] Bey; Beg (title); Mister; head of a tribe

بیگار [beegaar] 1 labor conscription (of the population) 2 *historical* corvee

بیگاری [beegaari] 1 mobilized, sent for forced labor; serving (time) in forced labor 2 ☞ بیگار

بیگانه [beegaana] (*plural* بیگانگان [beegaanagaan]) 1.1 strange, foreign, outside, unknown, unfamiliar 1.2 foreign 2.1 stranger, outsider 2.2 foreigner
- شدن ● to avoid, to shun; to grow out, to fall out (of a habit of), to become strange or foreign (از)

بیگانه وار [beegaanawaar] 1 estranged, alienated; frightened, scared ♦ نگاه - alienated view, outrageous idea 2 in an alienated manner; in a frightened manner

بیگانگی [beegaanagi] 1 unfamiliarity (with associates) 2 lack of acquaintances, lack of friends 3 estrangement, alienation
- بیگانگی کردن ● [baygaanagi-kardan] (*literally:* being a stranger) being a stranger

بیگا(ه) [beegaa (h)] 1 evening; yesterday evening 2 in the evening; yesterday in the evening

بیگمان [beegomaan] 1 undoubtedly, unquestionably ♦ میآید – او He will come without fail. 2 undoubted, unquestioned

بی گنا(ه) [beegonaa (h)] innocent, guiltless, not guilty; sinless

بیل [beel] shovel, spade ♦ جوی کشی - small shovel for digging irrigation ditches
- زدن ● to dig, to dig the ground, to dig up the ground (for sowing)

بیلان [beelaan] and بیلانس [belans] *finance* balance ♦ سال - yearly balance
- ترتیبکردن ● to compile a balance

بی لب و لانجه [belabolaanja] *colloquial* silent, submissive, obedient, meek

بیلچه [belcha] small shovel; scoop; dustpan

بی لحاظ [beelehaaz] disrespectful; inattentive; impudent

بی لحاظی [beelehaazi] disrespectful attitude (toward someone); inattention, discourtesy
- کردن ● to show disrespect, to be inattentive
- به ، بمقابل ● to commit rudeness, to commit impudence

بیلداری [beeldaari] preparing the ground for sowing (digging, setting up irrigation ditches, etc.)

بیلر [beelar] large metal container, tank; iron barrel

بیلک [beelak] [1] oar
- زدن ● to row

بیلک [beelak] [2] *anatomy* shoulder blade ♦ بیلک های شانه shoulder blades

بیلنه [beelana] rolling pin (for dough)

بیم [bim] dread, fear, fright, misgiving, apprehension
- داشتن ● to dread, to fear, to be afraid [of], to be apprehensive (از)

بیمار [beemaar] *rarely* a sick person
- چشم ● languid eyes, languorous eyes

بیماردار [beemaardaar] one who takes care of a sick person

بیماری [beemaari] *rarely* sickness; indisposition; ailment

بی مانند [beemaanand] 1 matchless, peerless 2 splendidly, excellently

بی معنی [beema'naa (and) bema'ni] 1 empty, senseless; absurd ♦ حرف - empty words, foolish words ◊ کار - an empty, useless matter 2 *grammar* devoid of meaning, desemanticized

بی موجب [beemawjeb] 1 groundless, without cause 2 without a cause, appropos of nothing; groundlessly

بی مورد [beemawred] 1 inappropriate 2 inappropriately, inopportunely ♦ نباشد که بگویم - It is appropriate to say that …

بی موقع [beemawqe'] 1 inopportune; untimely, premature ♦ - مرگ untimely death 2 ☞ بی مورد

بیمه [bima] insurance ♦ حوادث - insurance against accidents ◊ صحیه مامورین - organization for insuring state employees ◊ مؤسسه - insurance company
- شدن ● to insure oneself, to be insured
- کردن ● to insure

بیمه کننده [bimakonenda] 1 insurer 2 insurant

بی میلی [beemaili] reluctance, unwillingness; displeasure ♦ با - reluctantly; with displeasure

بین [bayn] 1 (also در -) in, inside, within, in the middle of *denominal preposition* ♦ جنگل - in the forest, in the middle of the forest ◊ دبه - in a wineskin 2 between, among *denominal preposition* ♦ دو قشلاق - between two villages ◊ دو ستان - among friends
- از ● through *denominal preposition* ♦ راه از - جنگل میگذرد The road runs through the forest.

بین [bin] 1 *present tense stem* دیدن 2 (second component of compound words with meaning of "seeing") ♦ باریک بین perspicacious, subtly perceiving (something)

بینا [binaa] 1 seeing ♦ چشم - seeing eyes 2 vigilant
• شدن - (*literally* and *figuratively*) to recover one's sight, to begin to see clearly

بین الاقوام [bainolaqwaam] intertribal ♦ مناقشات - intertribal difference, intertribal discord

بین البین [bainolbain] intermediate; transition ♦ دوره - transition period

بین الملل [bainolmelal] 1 international 2 ☞ بین المللی

بین المللی [bainolmelali] international

بی نام [beenaam] 1 nameless, anonymous; unknown 2 unknown (i.e., not famous; unpopular)

بی نام [baynaam] (*literally:* nameless) kind of scorpion

بی نام ونشان [beenaamoneshaan] 1 unknown, obscure ♦ شاعر - unknown poet, anonymous poet 2 in obscurity, obscurely ♦ زندگی کرد - He lived in obscurity.

بینایی [binaayi] 1 vision 2 vigilance; insight, acumen, perspicacity

بین بین [bainbain] ☞ بین البین

بینش [binesh] 1 view, opinion 2 ☞ بینایی

بی نصیب [beenasib] 1 done out (of something), deprived (of something) 2 not honored (with something), not awarded (something)
• کردن - 1 to deprive (someone را) (of something از), to do (someone را) out (of something از) 2 not to honor (someone with something), not to award (something to someone)

بی نظیر [beenazir] not having an equal, peerless; unprecedented

بی نقص [beenoqs] without shortcomings, without flaw; of full value, full-fledged, irreproachable

بی نمک [beenamak] 1 not salted, fresh 2 *colloquial* uninteresting, boring (about something) 3 unattractive, devoid of charm or fascination (about someone)

بیننده [binenda] 1 *present tense stem* دیدن 2.1 spectator; observer 2.2 *literary* eye 3 far-sighted, sagacious

بی نوا [beenawaa] 1 poor, needy; unfortunate 2 poor person

بی نوایی [beenawaayi] poverty, need; state of being unfortunate, state of being deprived

بی نهایت [beenehaayat] 1 very; extremely; infinitely ♦ تابستان گرم - a very hot summer 2 endless, boundless ♦ راه - endless road ◊ عشق - boundless love

بینی [bini] nose
• به - رسیدن *colloquial* to be on the brink of exhaustion, to go to extremes
• به - گپ زدن *colloquial* to talk through the nose
• بینی خمیری – *colloquial* ☞ خمیری
• کوه - protuberance of a mountain; overhang of a cliff

بینی پراق [beniparaaq] *colloquial* (*literally:* wide nose) a person with big nose

بی نیاز [beeniyaaz] comfortable, not needy; well-to-do ♦ طبقه - well-to-do class

بی نیازی [beeniyaazi] material well-being, solvency; prosperity

بینی بریده [biniborida] *abusive* shameless; having neither shame nor conscience

بینی پچق [binipochok (and) binipecek] *colloquial* with a flat nose, with a nose like a pancake

بینیچه [binicha]
• دروازه - door plank (nailed to the door hinge so that it closes more tightly)

بینی خمیری [binikhamiri]
• برای خود - ساختن *colloquial* 1 to do (something) to clear the conscience, to do (something) for the sake of appearance or as a matter of form 2 to strive only outwardly to observe the rules of propriety

بیوت [boyut] and بیوتات [boyutat] *plural of* بیت

بی وجدان [beewejdan] dishonorable, unconscientious; not acting in accordance with [one's] conscience

بی وخت [beewakht] *colloquial* ☞ بی وقت

بی وزن [beewazn] 1 light, weightless 2 not having meter (about poetry)

بی وزنی [beewazni] lightness, weightlessness ♦ حالت - weightless state, weightless condition

بی وطن [beewatan] 1 not having a homeland; living far from [one's] homeland 2 wanderer; an exile

بی وطنی [beewatani] life far from [one's] homeland; emigration

بی وفا [beewafaa] 1.1 having betrayed [one's] duty, having violated an oath, disloyal ♦ دوست - disloyal friend 1.2 changing, fickle, inconstant (about fate, etc.) 2 traitor; traitress

بی وفایی [beewafaayi] 1 disloyalty, treason treachery; inconstancy 2 changeability, fickleness (of fate)

بی وقت [beewaqt] 1.1 untimely, not on time, at an inopportune time 1.2 not in time, late 2.1 inopportune 2.2 tardy, late

بیو گرافی [biograafi] biography

بیوگی [beewagi] widowhood, widowerhood

بیو لوجست [biolojest] biologist

بیولوجی [bioloji] and بیولوژی [biolozhi] biology

بیوه [beewa] (also - زن) widow

بیوه داری [baywadary] *colloquial* (*literally:* to have a widow) taking care of a widow and her children (by her dead husband's family)

بی همتا [beehamtaa] *literary* ☞ بی مانند

بیهوده [beehuda] 1 unavailing, useless, vain; senseless 2 uselessly; in vain; for naught

بیهوده گوی [beehudagoy] talker, windbag, idle talker

بی هوش [beehush] 1 insensible, unconscious 2 narcotized (i.e., to be under narcosis)
• شدن - 1 to faint (away), to lose consciousness 2 to fall asleep (under narcosis)
• کردن - to put under general narcosis

بی هوشی [beehushi] 1 unconscious state, fainting fit 2 state of insensibility, numbness (when under general narcosis)

پ
3rd letter of the Dari alphabet

پا [paa] ☞ پای

پابپا(ی) [paabapaa(y)] in step with …, together with …, side by side with … *denominal preposition* ♦ پا بپایش گام مینهاد He marched in step with him.
• بردن - 1 to lead by the hand 2 to teach (a child) to walk
• کردن – 1 to study carefully, to examine, to investigate (something) ♦ کو - *colloquial* study the how and why of

پ

things 2 *colloquial* to put in order, to arrange; to further, to advance (a cause or matter)

پابجای [paabajaay] and پابرجای [paabarjaay] ☞

پابند [paaband] ☞

پابیدی [pabandi] 1 attachment, adherence, fidelity 2 inclination, interest

• داشتن - 1 to be attached [to]; to be devoted [to] (به) 2 to show an inclination [for], to show an interest [in] (به) 3 to visit regularly, to visit punctually (e.g., school)

پاپای [paapaay] *colloquial* the first steps (of a child)

پاپای چینی [paapaaychini] and پاپای نینی [papaynini]

• کردن - *colloquial* to move one's feet carefully, to take uncertain steps (of a child)

پاپوش [paaposh] footwear; shoes; boots

پات [paat] chamber pot; vessel

پاتن [paatan] *tailoring* model; pattern

پاجامه [paajaama] ☞ پای جامه

پاچا [paachaa] *colloquial* 1 ☞ پادشاه 2 pacha (salutation to a sayyid) 3 *masculine proper name* Pacha 4 queen bee

پاچاگل [paachaagol] *botany* malcolmia

پاچاوزیری [paachaawaziri] children's game of shah and vizier

پاچه [paacha] 1 foot; shank (of an animal) 2 sheep or calve's feet (food) 3 trouser leg

• برزدن - *colloquial* 1 to take to a matter, to get to work 2 to get ready for battle, to get ready for a fight 3 to get ready to run

• ورمالیدن - *regional* to take to one's heels

پاچه سبک [paachasobok] *slang* (*literally: the bottom of someone's pants being light*) a disgraced person *derogatory*

پاچه کشال [paachakashaal] *slang* (*literally: the bottom of someone's pants being too long*) unkempt person *derogatory*

پاچه کنده [paachakanda] *slang* (*literally: the bottom of someone's pants being torn*) a dishonorable person, shameless

پاچه بلند [paachakanda] *slang* (*literally: someone who where short trouser*) tough-guy, bad ass *derogatory*

پاچه گیر [paachagir]

• سگ - *colloquial* 1 vicious dog, biting dog 2 malicious person

پاداش [paadaash] *literary* and پاداشت [paadaasht] 1 recompense, reward 2 penalty, punishment

پادشاه [paadshaah] 1 padishah, king; sovereign 2 *masculine proper name* Padishah

پادشاه گردشی [paadshaahgardeshi] replacement of a shah; accession of a new king

پادشاهی [paadshaahi] 1.1 power, authority of a padishah, king's reign 1.2 (also - دولت) kingdom, realm; monarchy 2 padishah's *adjective*, king's; royal, regal

پادشه [paadshah] *abbreviation of* پادشاه

پاده [paada] herd (of cattle) ♦ ماده گاوها - herd of cows

پاده وان [paadawaan] herdsman, drover

پاده وانی [paadaawaani] 1 occupation of herdsman, of drover 2 pay for protecting a herd; pay for a herdsman, for a drover

• کردن - to graze cattle, to graze a herd

پارت [paart] group (of people); company ♦ او از - ما است He is from our crowd. / He is one of our associates.

• پارت پارت شدن 1 to separate into groups 2 to disperse

پارتی [paarti] ¹ *historical* 1 Parthian 2 (also - زبان) Parthian language

پارتی [paarti] ² 1 party; evening party 2 entertainment, reception, banquet

پارتیزان [paartizaan] partisan

پارتیه [paartiya] batch, lot, consignment (of goods) ♦ یک – قالین batch of rugs

پارچاو [paarchaaw] 1 ☞ پارچاوه 2 ☞ پرچو

پارچه [paarcha] 1 piece; scrap; portion ♦ یک – سنگ *technical* splinter of stone, fragment of a rock ◊ یک – نان slice of bread 2 cloth, fabric, material 3 part; block; unit, component ♦ ربطیه - wedge, chock

• کردن - to disassemble, to take apart

پارچه باب [paarchabaab] fabrics, textiles

پارچه بافی [paarchabaafi] 1 weaving 2 textile production

پارچه کاری [paarchakaari] *technical* disassembly, overhaul (e.g., of an engine)

پارس [paars] ¹ Persia (ancient)

پارس [paars] ² (also - سنگ) philosophers' stone

پارسل [paarsal] parcel, package

پارسی بان [paarsibaan] ☞ پارسی وان

پارسی [paarsi] 1 Persian ♦ زبان - Persian language 2 *historical* ancient Persian 3 Zoroastrain

پارسی وان [paarsiwaan] Parsiwan (Tajiks and other Persian speakers population of Afghanistan)

پارکنگ [paarkeng] parking place or area (for motor vehicles)

• کردن - to park (a motor vehicle)

پارلمان [paarlamaan] parliament

پارو [paaru] ¹ manure, fertilizer

• دادن - to fertilize with manure

• کشیدن - to haul manure (to the fields)

پارو [paaru] ² 1 paddle, oar 2 *regional* wooden shovel (to shovel snow)

• زدن - 1 to paddle, to work with paddle 2 *regional* to shovel (snow)

پاروکشی [paarukashi] hauling manure (to the fields)

پاره [paara] 1.1 piece; fragment; segment ♦ تکه - scrap of material ◊ گوشت - piece of meat 1.2 portion, share ♦ پاره یی and از پاره یی some, a certain portion 2 torn, broken

• شدن - to be torn, to be broken

• کردن - to tear, to lacerate, to rend ♦ تو دلم را – کردی You broke my heart.

پاره پاره [paarapaara] 1 badly torn, torn to pieces 2 worn to shreds

پاره دوز [paaradoz] one who darns, one who mends

پاره گی [paaragi] torn place; hole, a tear, a slit

پارینه [paarina] 1 ancient, former, previous, old ♦ سوابق - این سرزمین the ancient past of this country 2 last year's, of last year

پاس [paas] 1 part (of a night, of a day) ♦ پاسی از شب گذشته بود Part of the night has passed. 2 attention; respect

• به - 1 for, in gratitude for *denominal preposition* ♦ خدمتی که کردید in gratitude for your services 2 in the name of, from *denominal preposition* ♦ به - خاطر in the name of; for the sake of, in deference to

پاسبان [paasbaan] watchman, guard; sentry, sentinel ♦ کاروان - guard of a caravan
- خاطر کسی را داشتن - to treat or deal with someone respectfully; to render someone his due
پاسبانی [paasbaani] guarding, protection; a guard
• کردن - to protect, to guard
پاسره [paasra] colloquial economy; economies
• کردن - to save, to preserve, to put aside
پاسره‌گر [paasragar] colloquial thrifty, economical
پاشان [paashaan] sparse, scattered ♦ افکار بسیار است - His thoughts are not collected. / He is absentminded.
پاشنه [paashna] 1 heel (of foot) 2 heel (of shoe) 3 butt (of a rifle) 4.1 (also دروازه -) pivot of a door 4.2 door hinge
• دادن - to give up, to surrender (firearms)
• زدن and کردن - to urge on to spur on a horse (by hitting with one's heels)
پاشی [paashi] (second component of compound words with meanings of "spilling"/"pouring") ♦ دواپاشی spraying with chemicals ◊ نورپاشی emission of light; illumination
پاشیدن [paashidan] 1 to pour, to strew ♦ نمک بر طعام - to put salt on food 2 to pour, to spill 3 to emit, to give off 4 to pour out, to run out intransitive 5 to flow, to pour intransitive 6 to emanate
• از هم – 1 to spill, to scatter intransitive, to tumble down, to go to pieces 2 to disperse intransitive, to disintegrate, to come apart, to fall to pieces ♦ سپاه از هم پاشید The [military] forces dispersed / scattered.
پاغنده [paghonda] lump, ball, clod; bunch, tuft ♦ پنبه - tuft of cotton batting ◊ برف - snow flakes
پافشاری [paafeshaari] persistence, insistence
• کردن (در) - to persist, to insist
پاک [paak] 1.1 (in various meanings) clean, pure ♦ دل - pure heart ◊ روی - clean face 1.2 honest, respectable 1.3 pure, chaste, holy (about someone) 2 completely; absolutely; decidedly ♦ دیوانه است - He is completely insane. ◊ مال احمد را خوردند - They robbed Ahmad of every speck. 3 (second component of compound words with meanings of "cleaning" / "wiping") ♦ روی پاک towel ◊ پنسل پاک eraser
• کردن - colloquial 1 to scrub, to clean; to wash clean of dirt 2 to brush off, to wipe (dust; spots; from something از) 3 to clean out, to rob
• حساب – کردن to settle accounts, to settle up, to settle monetary accounts
پاکت [paakat] envelope
پاکدامن [paakdaaman] 1 pure, chaste, virtuous 2 honest, respectable
پاک‌کاری [paakkaari] cleaning; clearing ♦ جوی - cleaning out irrigation ditches
پاک‌نویس [paaknawis] written cleanly; clean
• کردن - to make a clean copy
پاک‌وپاکیزه [paakopaakiza] 1 faultlessly clean, very neat, very tidy 2 beautiful, elegant (of clothing) ♦ کالای - پوشیده بود He was dressed immaculately.
پاکی [paaki]¹ 1 cleanliness, neatness, tidyness 2 moral purity; honesty; virtue
پاکی [paaki]² razor
• زدن - to make incisions with razor (to draw out blood by means of a horn)

پاکیزگی [paakizagi] 1 ☞ پاکی 2 irreproachability, faultlessness (of conduct, etc.)
پاکیزه [paakiza] 1 ☞ پاک 2 irreproachable, faultless (about conduct, etc.)
پالان [paalaan] pack saddle
پالان بر کسی ماندن [paalaan-barksay-maandan] idiom (literally: to put a saddle on someone) to insult someone, to fool someone, to make a fool of someone
پالش [paalesh] polishing; shining
• دادن - to polish; to shine; to clean until [something] shines ♦ بوت خود را – دادم I shined my shoes (until they shone).
پالک [paalak] spinach
پالوده [paaluda] ☞ فالوده
پالیدن [paalidan] 1 to search for, to rummage about (with one's hand) ♦ به جیب خود دست زد وپالید He stuck his hand in his pocket and rummaged about [in it]. 2 to conduct a search, to investigate
• سر کسی را - colloquial to search for (insects) on [someone's] head
پالیز [paaliz] melon field
پالیزبان [paalizbaan] 1 melon grower 2 watchman, guard in melon field
پالیزکاری [paalizkaari] melon-growing
پالیزوان [paalizwaan] ☞ پالیزبان
پالیسی [paalisi] policy
پالیگون [paaligon] polygon, firing range, practice are
پام [paam] colloquial from پهن
پامال [paamaal] ☞ پایمال
پان [paan] botany betel, pan
پاندول [paandol] pendulum (of clock)
پانزده [panzdah] fifteen
پانسمان [paansomaan] treatment of a wound and bandaging; applying a bandage
• کردن - to treat a wound and apply a bandage
پانسی [paansi] collquial capital punishment, death penalty
پاو [paw] 1 paw (an old measure of weight in Afghanistan, equal to ¼ of a charak); ☞ چارک 2 pound (measure of weight) ♦ دو - two pounds
پاورقی [paawaraqi] 1 comment in the margin; footnote, comment, note 2 special article (in a newspaper)
پاورهاوس [paawarhaaws] 1 electric power station 2 battery room
پای [paay] 1.1 leg, foot; poetry foot ♦ پیاده - on foot ◊ جای - track (of a foot, a footprint) ◊ کف - sole (of foot), foot 1.2 leg (of furniture) 2 at, by, near; below, under denominal preposition ♦ درخت ایستاد - He was standing under a tree. ◊ دیوار نشسته بودیم - We sat by the wall.
• انداختن - colloquial to rush [off] as fast as one can, to set out as fast as one's legs can carry one
پاپا(ی) – به - ☞
• بردار - برداشتن to go faster, to quicken one's step ♦ بردار - Go faster!
• بریدن (از) - to cease visiting
• زدن - colloquial to hamper, to harm
• کردن - to put on (one's feet)
• ماندن (به،در) - to start, to enter ♦ دخترم - بدو مانده My daughter has passed her second year.
• از – انداختن to exhaust; to weaken

پ

to fall off one's feet (from fatigue, etc.) افتادن - از and از - ماندن •
1 to recover, to begin to get up (out of bed, about a sick person) 2 to begin to walk (about a child) آمدن - به •
1 to trample, to crush 2 to break, to defy تحت - کردن and زیر - کردن • They broke the law. تحت را قانون کردند •
1 to walk, to stride زیر - گذاشتن • He strode through fields overgrown with grass. میگذاشت زیر علف پر های دشت 2 to defy, to disdain
to go beyond the limits, to cross the boundary of that which is permitted بیرون خود حد از - نهادن •
to be removed کشیدن میان از - •
1 to give up, to renounce (something) 2 to retreat, to retire, to withdraw, to go out of a game کشیدن پس - •
to interfere, to intervene, to get mixed up in, to get involved in نهادن میان در - •
to forbid someone to visit (something از); not to authorize someone to go (somewhere از) ابریدن را کسی - •
colloquial to get someone settled or placed; to help someone "catch on" کردن ابند را کسی - •
to squat نشستن (در) - دو بالای •
to be beyond comparison with someone or something نرسیدن (چیزی) کسی به - •
to be not fit to hold a candle to someone نرسیدن خاک به کسی - •
to reject, to refuse زدن پس - • زدم - راپس خود شخصی منافع I disdained my own personal interests.
colloquial to be set [against], to rest [against], to be obstinate کردن موزه یک رادر دو هر - • نماند پایم به - I am falling down from fatigue. ◊ رسیده گور بلب پایش He has one foot in the grave.

پای به خینه بودن [pay-ba-khina-boodan] idiom (literally: someone's foot being in henna) an excuse not to do something

پایاب [paayaab] 1 shoal; ford (across river, irrigation ditch) 2 shallow, not deep

پای افزار [paayafzaar] ☞ پیزار

پایان [paayaan] 1.1 lower, situated below • منزل - ground floor 1.2 following 2.1 bottom, lower part • بالا به - از from bottom to top 2.2 end, edge, limit • ندارد دشت این There is no end to this steppe 2.3 down, downward; below, at the bottom
to go down, to descend, to lose height, to sink, to fall - (شدن) رفتن •
to end, to complete - رساندن به •
to be finished, to end, to close, to be completed, to be concluded - رسیدن به •

پای انداز [paayandaaz] 1 door mat, rug carpet, runner 2 precious carpet or velvet (laid under the feet of an honored guest or betrothed)

پایاو [paayaaw] ☞ پایو

پای برجای [paaybarjaay] 1 strong, firm, steadfast, steady, staunch; unshakable unflagging, unflinching 2 solid, reliable (about a person)

پای برکاب [paaybarekaab] 1 ready for departure; intending to go on the road, intending to travel • است او - He is ready to depart. 2 not eternal, transient

پای برهنه [paayberahna] 1 bare, barefooted 2 barefoot adverb

پای بند [paayband] 1.1 hobble, trammels 1.2 leg manacles, shackles; fetters 2.1 tied, constrained; burdened 2.2 attached, devoted • خانواده - 1 burdened with a family 2 devoted to one's family
observing the law(s) absolutely - قانون •
honestly carrying out one's duty; zealous, diligent toward work - وظیفه •

پای بندی [paaybandi] ☞ پابندی

پای باپای [paaybapaay] ☞ (پابپای)

پای بیل [paaybeel]
to dig, to dig up earth (with a shovel) - کردن •

پایپ [paayp] pipe (for smoking) • تنباکوی - smoking tobacco, pipe tobacco

پای پاک [paaypaak] (also جالی -) a grating on the floor (for cleaning dirt or mud from one's shoes)

پای پاک [paaypaak] colloquial (literally: foot clean) cleaned out, completely • دزد برد پاک مارا دکان The thief cleaned out our store.

پای پچلک [paaypocholak] 1 sports hitting or striking with the foot, tripping, hooking 2 biting or caustic remark, cutting remark (in conversation)
1 to strike with the foot, to trip, to hook 2 to make cutting remarks, to bait, to tease - دادن •

پای پلاین [paayplaayn] conduit, pipeline • تیل - oil pipeline

پای پیچ [paaypeech] puttees

پای تابه [paaytaaba] foot-cloths

پای تخت [paaytakht] capital (e.g., a city) • است افغانستان - کابل Kabul is the capital of Afghanistan.

پای ترقیده [paaytarqida] slang (literally: cracked feet) destitute person, down and out

پای جامه [paayjaama] 1 trousers, sharovary (wide trousers) 2 drawers, undershorts

پایدار [paaydaar] durable, solid, steady, firm; inviolable, indissoluble • صلح - durable peace

پایداری [paavdaari] durability, solidity, steadiness, firmness; inviolability, indissolubility

پایدان [paaydaan] footboard, step (of vehicle, carriage)

پای درپای [paaydarpaay]
to put (shoes) on someone else's foot - پوشیدن •

بای درختی [paaydarakhti] windfall (about fruit)

پای درد [paaydard] pain in the feet or legs (e.g., from gout)

پای درهوا [paaydarhawaa] 1 suspended in the air, up in the air; indefinite, undecide • ماند - مسئله این That question remained undecided / That problem remained unsolved. 2 unfounded, empty, absurd • - های گپ senseless discourse or talk, nonsense

پایدل [paaydal] pedal (of bicycle)

پای دو [paaydaw] 1 servant; messenger; a boy on errands 2 bathhouse attendant

پای دوانک [paaydawaanak] a walker (for children beginning to walk)

پای دوی [paaydawi] 1 the job of messenger, of a boy on errands 2 the job of a bathhouse attendant

پای سنگ [paaysang] 1 a stone or small weight (which balances scales) 2 counterweight, makeweight

پایش [paayesh] colloquial perseverance, long lasting

پایشی [paayeshi] [1] colloquial durable, long lasting

پایشی [paayeshi] [2] colloquial long term guest

پای کسی را بند کردن [paay-kasay-raa-band-kardan] *idiom* (*literally:* to tie someone's foot) to get a man engaged or married

پای گشت [paaygasht] *colloquial* (*literally:* walking area) heavy pedestrian area, foot traffic

پای لچ کردن [paayluch] *idiom* (*literally:* to barefoot) mind set on, one who is determined to do a task ♦ خانه را خریده حالی پای لچ کرده باغ پشت He has bought the house; now he is planning to buy the garden.

پایگاو [paaygaaw] paygaw (measure of area equal to half a kulba; ☞ قلبه)

پایگاه [paaygah] base, bridgehead, beachhead ♦ راکت - missile base

پای لچ [paayloch] and *colloquial* پای لوچ [paayloch] 1 barefooted, without shoes, shoeless 2 barefoot *adverb* ♦ نگرد - Don't go barefoot!

پایمال [paaymaal] 1 crushed, trampled 2 demolished, trod upon 3 thrown down, destroyed, annihilated ♦ حقوق کسی را - کردن to tread upon someone's rights

پاینت [paaint] 1 point 2 *sports* point (in scoring) 3 one-tenth of a mark (in grading system of a university) 4 *technical* ignition point

پاینده [paayenda] 1.1 long-lived, lasting, eternal; permanent, constant ♦ باد - ... May [someone] live forever! / Long live …! 1.2 ☞ پایدار 2 *masculine proper name* Payenda ♦ ماندن - to remain firm, to remain long-lasting, to stand inviolable or indissoluble

پایه [paaya] 1.1 leg (of furniture); prop, support ♦ دیگدان - foot of a trivet 1.2 support, post, pole, pillar; mast ♦ پل - abutment of a bridge, pier ◊ پایه های لین ولتاژ بلند towers of high-voltage line 1.3 base, pedestal; foundation 1.4 *literary* rank, grade 1.5 degree, extent, level; step, stage ♦ ترقیات اجتماعی - stage of social development 1.6 (also - زینه) step (of stairs), rung (of ladder) 1.7 *literary* foot 2 (second component of compound words with meanings of "plot of land" / "field sown with something" ♦ پایه جواری plot of land planted in corn, cornfield
- طلا - gold equivalent
- گلون - almond; tonsil

پای مانده [paaymanda] 1 broken (by fatigue) 2 weak, helpless

پایو [paayaw]
- زمین - 1 plot of land situated far from an irrigation ditch 2 a plot of land which is last to receive water

پای وازی [paaywaazi] the first visit of young girl to her parents' home after her wedding

پایه دار [paayedaar] 1 on feet, on legs, on supports ♦ ماشیندار - machine gun (on legs) 2 durable, firm, solid, substantial

پایه دان [paayedaan] pedestal ♦ چراغ - pedestal for a lamp

پایه کی [paayaki] leg, foot *adjective*, put in motion by the foot or leg

پاییدن [paayidan] 1 to be long-lived; to live; to survive ♦ امید پاییدنش نیست There's no hope that he will survive. 2 to be, to stay, to remain, to linger ♦ از دو روز زیاتر نپایین *colloquial* Don't stay [there] more than two days. 3 to last, to keep *intransitive* ♦ گلهای بهار دیر نمیپاید Spring flowers don't bloom for long.

پایین [paayin] ☞ پایان 1, 2
- وبالاکردن - to shift, to turn (a sick person in bed)
- شو - *cards* You lead! / You play!

پایین سر [paayinsar] (opposite of بالا سر) foot (of a bed)

پایینی [paayini] lower, situated below ♦ قسمت – بخاری lower part of stove

پپای [papaay] ☞ پپای

پت [pat] 1 1 goat down 2 underfur 3 pile, nap, fleece ♦ پت قالین carpet pile, carpet nap

پت [pat] 2 *colloquial* flattened out

پت [pot] 1 hidden, concealed 2 covert, secret 3 *colloquial* dressed, covered (about the parts of the body) ♦ خود راپت کردن and پت شدن to hide oneself, to conceal oneself

پتاس [potaas] ☞ پوتاس

پتاسیم [potaasiam] ☞ پوتاسیم

پتاقی [pataaqi] *colloqial* cherry bomb

پتق [pataq] *slang* 1 a person with a flat nose, pug nose 2 Hazarah, Oriental *offensive*

پتاو [petaaw] *colloquial* 1 sunny, sun *adjective* 2 sunny side ♦ کردن - to warm oneself in a bit of sun, to bask in the sun

پت پت [potpot] secretly, surreptitiously, silently

پترول [petrol] gasoline; petroleum ♦ تانک - gasoline pump

پترول پمپ [petrolpamp] gasoline pump

پترول کشی [petrolkashi] extraction of oil

پتره [patra] 1 iron clamp 2 thin brass clamp (to repair broken ceramic dishware)

پتک [patak] *slang* (*literally:* canteen) shorty, short stuff

پتک [patak] insole, inner sole

پتلون [patlun] pants, trousers (of the European type)

پتنک [patanak] *colloquial* trembling, quivering, beating, throbbing, pulsation
- زدن - 1 to tremble, to quiver, to beat, to throb, to pulsate, to flutter 2 to endeavor, to try, to petition

پتنوس [patnus] tray

پتو [patu] woolen shawl, woolen rug

پتونی [patoni] *botany* (also - گل) petunia

پتوه [patwa]
- تسبیح - pompon of silk threads (which fastens beads)

پته طلب [patatalab] 1 check, draft 2 cash payment order (for receipt of an advance, etc.)

پته دادن [pata-daadan] *colloquial* to lie in ambush

پتی [pati] 1 1 made of goat down ♦ تکه - fabric [made] of goat down 2 (also - پشک) cat of longhaired breed

پتی [pati] 2 strip of fabric, ribbon, tape ♦ پتلون - stripe ◊ کلاه - band of a cap

پتی و کتی [pati-o-kati] *colloquial* whining complaining, carrying on

پچق [pecheq] (and) [pochoq] *colloquial* 1 compressed, flattened 2 rumpled, kneaded, flattened out, spread out
- کردن - 1 to crush, to squeeze, to push, to press 2 to rumple, to knead; to flatten ♦ بینی - flat nose

پچق [pochuq] *slang* 1 a person with a flat nose, pug nose 2 Hazarah, Oriental *offensive*

پچل پتن [pochulpatan] *slang* low-class person

پخ [pakh] 1 border, side 2 bevel, chamfer; *technical* fascia, flat

پخ [pekh] boo! (exclamation used to frighten or scare someone)
- به روی کسی پخ زدن to be impudent, to be insolent to someone; to snap at someone

پخ [pokh]
- پخ زدن *colloquial* to burst out (laughing)

پ

پخزدن [pekh-zadan] *slang* (*literally:* to snarl like a dog and a cat) to talk back

پخپلو [pakhpalow] *slang* unkempt, dull, dullard

پخت [pokht] cooking; baking (bread)

پختگی [pokhtagi] 1 *past participle* پختن 2.1 readiness (of food, etc.); maturity ripeness (of fruit, etc.) 2.2 wisdom; experience; mastery, skill 3 *colloquial* state of being hardened, tempered

پختن [pokhtan] (*present tense stem* پز [paz]) 1 to boil, to cook, to prepare (food); to bake 2 to be boiling; to be baking *intransitive*

• دیگ – to prepare dinner, to cook dinner

پختوپز [pokhtopaz] preparing, preparation (of food); cooking

پخته [pakhta] *botany* cotton, cotton plant ♦ خام – raw cotton

پخته [pokhta] [1] 1 *past participle* پختن 2.1 ripe, mature (of fruit) 2.2 wise from experience, worldly-wise; mature ♦ آدم – an experienced person, a worldly-wise person ◊ سخن – wise discourses 3 accomplished; perfect; absolute; skillful ♦ کار – a clever piece of work

• کردن – 1 to cook, to boil; to bake; to prepare (food) 2 to prepare (clay, mortar), to mix (clay, mortar) 3 to make wise by experience; to harden, to temper ♦ زندگی او را – کرد Life hardened him.

• کردن چیزی را سر کسی – to persuade someone into something, to try to persuade someone into something, to impose some decision on someone

پخته [pokhta] [2] paved with stone and gravel

• کردن – to pave with stone and gravel

پخته پران [pakhtaparaan] and [pakhtapaaranak] پخته پرانک • *colloquial*

• کردن – 1 to shake wadding or cotton vigorously 2 to scatter thoroughly, to destroy utterly, to give a thrashing [to], to scold strongly

پخته دار [pakhtadaar] wadded, quilted, made of wadding

پخته سال [pokhtasaal] 1 elderly; of mature age 2 old

پخته کار [pakhtakar] cotton grower

پخته کار [pokhtakar] experienced; skillful; wise

پخته کاری [pakhtakari] cotton growing, cultivation of cotton

پخته کاری [pokhtakari] 1 laying bricks or stone; masonry or brickwork; construction of a building made of calcined brick 2 a brick building 3 (*also* سرکها –) paving (of roads) with stone and gravel

• کردن – to pave a road

پخچ [pakhch] *colloquial* low, not high, short ♦ چت خانه – است The ceiling in the room is low. ◊ قد او آدم – است This person is short.

پخچک [pakhchak] *colloquial* 1 short 2 a short person, a dumpy person

پخسه [pakhsa] 1 a lump of clay (for clay or adobe constructions) 2 *colloquial* lump, little ball, lump (of something)

• زدن – to make a clay or adobe wall to erect a clay or adobe structure

• یک تف – spit, sputum

پخسه یی [pakhsayi] *adjective* clay, adobe

پخش [pakhsh] 1 spread, dissemination (of rumors, news, etc.) 2 transmission (by radio), broadcast (by radio) ♦ اخبار – broadcast of the latest news (by radio)

• کردن – 1 to disseminate, to spread (rumors, news, etc.) 2 to transmit (by radio), to broadcast (by radio)

پخل [pekhel] pus, matter (in the corners of the eyes)

پداگوژی [peedaagozhi] pedagogy ♦ مؤسسه – pedagogical institute

پدر [padar] father

پدرآزار ☞ – کلان

پدرخطا [padarkhataa] *colloquial* (*literally:* one whose father was bad) bastard *abusive*

پدر خانده [padar-khanda] *colloquial* (*literally:* claimed father) foster father (someone who is recognized as a father)

پدرآزار [padaraazaar] (*also* ومادرآزار –) good-for-nothing, one who has gotten out of hand (*literally*, one who causes grief for his parents) ♦ این بچه – ومادرآزار است This boy has gotten completely out of hand.

پدراندر [padarandar] stepfather

پدردار [padardaar] 1 of noble birth or extraction, from a good family 2 *rarely* company, firm *adjective*; of good quality

پدرزن [padarzan] father-in-law (wife's father)

پدرکلان [padarkalaan] grandfather, grandpa

پدرلعنت [padarla'nat] and پدرنالت [padarnalat] *abusive* villain, scoundrel

پدرومادر [padaromaadar] parents, father and mother

پدری [padari] 1.1 fatherly, paternal 1.2 hereditary ♦ زمین های – hereditary lands 2 fatherhood

پدید [padid] 1 visible 2 evident, clear, obvious

• آمدن – to appear, to arise; to occur

• آوردن – to promote the appearance (of something), to create, to originate

پدیدار [padidaar] ☞ پدید

• شدن – 1 to become visible, to come in sight, to show oneself 2 to become apparent, to be manifested, to be revealed, to come to light, to be discovered

• کردن – to show, to manifest, to discover, to detect, to reveal

پذیر [pazir] *present tense stem* پذیرفتن

پذیرایی [paziraayi] meeting, reception (of an official or guests)

• کردن (از، را) – to receive (at home)

پذیرفتن [paziroftan] (*present tense stem* پذیر [pazir]) 1 to take, to admit, to approve; to consent, to agree (را) 2 to receive (at home)

پر [par] 1 feather, feathers; down 2 wing, wings (of a bird) 3 fin (of a fish) 4 playing card 5 *technical* blade

• پر انداختن – 1 to lose plumage, to shed 2 to lose strength, to weaken, to become weak 3 (cards) to deal

• پر برآودن – 1 to become fully fledged 2 to reach manhood, to stand on [one's] feet

• پر زدن 1 and 2 ☞ پر انداختن • پر ریختاندن

• پر کردن and پر کندن – 1 to fly, to flit about 2 to flutter (about a bird in a cage)

• پرگرفتن cards to take

• پربه کلاه کسی زدن *colloquial* to persuade someone by flattery, to talk someone [into something]

پرکسی را خو دادن [parekasay-ra-khaw-daadan] *idiom* to calm someone down

پر [por] 1 full, filled ♦ ظرف پر ازآب a vessel full of water 2 much, many, very 3 (first or second component of compound words with meaning of "full of something" / "possessing some quality to a high degree") ♦ پرتوان

56

mighty, strong ◊ اشک پر full of tears (about eyes)
- پر کردن *colloquial* 1 to fill; to stuff; to pack 2 to set, to incite (against someone علیه)
- اشکم پر کردن *colloquial* 1 to stuff [one's] stomach, to overeat 2 *vulgar* to be pregnant

پرآب [porab] deep, having an abundance of water ♦ دریای - deep river ◊ چشمان - eyes full of tears

پرابلم [peraablem] problem

پرآب وتاب [poraabotaab] 1 grandiloquent, bombastic, high-flown 2 colorful, vivid, lively, picturesque ♦ حکایت - colorful tale or story

پراتا [paraata] puffs (variety of Afghan homemade pastry) ♦ روغنی - rich puffs made of flaky pastry

پراچی [parachi] Parachi (nationality of Afghanistan)

پراخوت [paraakhot] steamship

پراشوت [paraashut] parachute ♦ نجات - reserve parachute
- با – انداختن to drop by parachute
- با – جست کردن to jump by parachute

پراشوتی [paraashuti] parachute *adjective* ♦ نفر - parachutist

پراق [paraaq] *colloquial* wide, broad

پراگندن [paraagandan] 1 to disperse, to scatter, to diffuse ♦ نور - to disperse light, to shine 2 ☞ پراگنده کردن

پراگنده [paraaganda] 1 *past participle* پراگندن 2.1 dispersed, scattered, not collected 2.2 splintered, shattered; pulverized 3 uncoordinated; unsystematic
- کردن - to disperse (e.g., a crowd)

پراگندگی [paragaandagi] 1 dispersion, sparseness 2 state of being splintered, state of being scattered, state of being pulverized ♦ کارها - disorder of affairs, confusion in affairs

پرآمدوشد [poraamadoshod]
- سرک - a road with heavy traffic, a busy highway
- کوچه – crowded, noisy, public road

پران [par(r)aan] flying ♦ موش - bat

پراندن [par(r)aandan] 1 to scare off, to drive off (birds, etc.) 2 to throw with force, to cast, to hurl, to fling 3 *colloquial* to fling, to put in (a word, remark); to hurl (oaths, etc.)

پرانچه شدن [paraancha-shudan] *idiom* (*literally:* to fly away) to leave the nest

پراوج [poraawj] situated or located at the apogee; having achieved the highest point

پرباد [porbaad] 1 blown up tightly, filled with air 2 pompous; haughty ♦ گلوی - stentorian voice

پربازی [parbaazi] card game

پرپیروبار [porbirobaar] full of bustle, noisy ♦ کوچه - noisy street

پرپای [parpaay] shaggy-legged, with feathers on the feet or legs (about birds) ♦ کبوتر - feather-footed dove

پرپر [parpar]
- زدن - 1 to flit about, to fly 2 to flap [one's] wings desperately, to flutter (about a caught bird) 3 to flap about in hysterics; to sob
- کردن - 1 to tear, to tear off (petals, leaves, etc.) 2 to tear into small pieces

پرپخته [parepukhta]¹ *slang* (*literally:* an ace card) ace, a trusted friend

پرپخته [parepukhta]² *slang* a honorable opponent

پرپیچ [porpeech] and پرپیچ وخم [porpecokham] 1 twisting, winding, zigzag-shaped; spiral, spiral-shaped ♦ راه - winding road 2 intricate, complex, puzzling

پرت [part]¹ *present tense stem* پرتافتن
- میپرتم [mepartom] I am throwing. / I will throw.
- پرتو [parto] Stop! / Quit it!

پرت [part]² *colloquial* scratching, peeling ♦ جای – ناخن a scratch
- کشیدن - to scratch (e.g., with the fingernails); to peel ♦ پشک او را – کشید The cat scratched him.
- کشیدن ☞ کردن – and کندن –

پرتاب [partab] throwing, hurling, casting, flinging, tossing
- شدن - 1 to fall 2 to be abandoned, to be deserted, to be neglected 3 to be dropped (about an assault landing party)
- کردن - 1 to throw with force, to toss 2 to fling; to launch (a missile) 3 to drop (an assault landing party)
- خود را – کردن to throw oneself, to rush, to swoop down on (به)

پرتافتن [partaaftan] (*present tense stem* پرت [part]) to hurl, to cast, to fling; to throw

پرتگاه [partgaah] 1 steepness, steep slope; precipice 2 abyss, gulf

پرتو [partaw] *literary* 1 light; radiance, sparkling, twinkling, glitter ♦ مهتاب - light of the moon, moonlight 2 ray, beam; speck, patch of light; reflection, gleam

پرتوان [portawaan] strong, powerful, mighty ♦ اسپ - strong horse ◊ ماشین - powerful unit; powerful engine

پرجوش وخروش [porjoshokhorosh] 1 stormy, rough, seething ♦ دریای - rapid river 2 violent, boiling ♦ حیات - stormy life ◊ مجلس - noisy meeting

پرچاوه [parchaawa] 1 temporary wooden dam (to block an irrigation canal) 2 water drain, water runoff ♦ تونل - outlet canal, drain canal; overflow tunnel, discharge tunnel

پرچم [parcham] 1 banner, flag, colors 2 *historical* parcham (staff with horse's tail attached; ancient sign of authority) 3 *botany* stamen 4 *obscure* forelock, topknot

پرچو [parchaw] *colloquial* stopped (about a watermill)
- کردن - 1 to stop (a watermill); to close a chute (so that water flows freely into a river) 2 to suspend (something), to conserve (something)

پرچون [parchun] 1 small wares and notions (thread, needles, buttons) 2 (also طور) by retail; in trifles, on trifles

پرچون فروش [parchunforosh] a trader or dealer in small wares and notions

پرچه پرچه [parchaparcha] broken into parts, broken into pieces

پرچی [parchi] rivet ♦ گول - button-head rivet
- کردن - to rivet

پرچیکاری [parchikari] riveting

پرچین [parchin] ☞ پرچی

پرچین وچروک [porchinocharuk] wrinkled, puckered

پرحرارت [porharaarat] hot, hearty, torrid; ardent, fervent; passionate ♦ قلب - passionate heart ◊ نطق - fiery speech

پرخ [porkh
- زدن - *colloquial* 1 to burst out (laughing) 2 to break out (about a rash)

پرخاش [parkhaash] 1 quarrel, squabble 2 fight, scuffle

پرخام [parekhaam] *slang* (*literally:* a bad card) person one does not trust, unworthy opponent

پرخانه [parkhaana] 1 nostril ♦ بینی های پرخانه - wings of the nose, nostrils 2 slot, groove, hollow, depression on back end of arrow (into which feathers are placed)

پرخچه [parakhcha] (also چوب -) small wood chips, kindling, wood shaving

پرخور [porkhor] 1 voracious, gluttonous 2 glutton

پرخوری [porkhori] immoderation in food, gluttony

پرداخت [pardaakht] ¹ pay, payment ♦ قرض - payment of a loan ◊ کرایه - rent payment

پرداخت [pardaakht] ² *literary* 1 attention, consideration, respect 2 taking into consideration
• کردن - 1 to treat with consideration, to treat with respect 2 to take into consideration, to consider (به)

پرداختن [pardaakhtan] (*present tense stem* پرداز [pardaaz]) 1 to pay, to pay off 2 to start, to begin (به)

پرداز [pardaaz] ¹ *present tense stem* پرداختن

پرداز [pardaz] ² 1 finishing, trim, adorning, decoration; luster, gloss 2 polishing; grinding

پردل [pordel] 1 bold, courageous, brave valiant, venturesome 2 *masculine proper name* Purdil

پردم خوردن [pordam-khoordan] *colloquial* (*literally:* to eat as much as one could) to pig-out, gorge oneself

پرده [parda] 1 bed curtains, curtain, curtains; blind ♦ کلکین - window curtain 2 curtain, screen, veil, cover; shroud 3 *anatomy* film, pellicle; membrane ♦ گوش - eardrum 4 (also - سینما) motion picture screen 5 *theater* act, scene 6 layer, stratum 7 *music* tone 8 stops, frets (of a musical instrument)
• برداشتن - to raise a curtain to divulge a secret; (از روی)
• زدن - (روی، بر) 2 to (کشیدن) 1 to curtain off, to curtain cover, to hide, to conceal; (روی،بر)
• آوردن – روی 1 to stage, to put on the stage, to dramatize 2 to film, to make a movie

پرده باب [pardabaab] (also - تکه) fabric for portiere, door curtain

پرده پوشی [pardaposhi] 1 keeping (e.g., something secret, keeping to oneself, keeping a secret 2 concealment (of somebody's mistakes, delinquencies, etc.), shielding
• کردن - (از) to cover (e.g., mistakes, delinquencies), to shield

پرزحمت [porzahmat] heavy, difficult hard ♦ زندگی - hard life

پرزه [porza] ¹ *technical* part ♦ پرزه های فالتو spare parts ◊ های موتر parts, components of a motor vehicle

پرزه [porza] ² *colloquial* note, written communication; a short letter

پرزه جات [porzajaat] *plural of* پرزه

پرس [pres] *technical* pressing ♦ دستگاه - press ◊ ماشین – آهنگری forging press
• کردن - to press

پرسان [porsaan] 1.1 asking, inquiring; question 1.2 *colloquial* visiting a sick person 2 inquiring, interrogative ♦ با نگاه های – بهم دیدند They looked at one another inquisitively.
• کردن - to ask / to inquire, to ask a question
• رفتن بیمار به - to visit a sick person

پرست [parast] 1 *present tense stem* پرستیدن 2 (second component of compound words with meanings of "admirer" / "worshipper" / "adherent" / "follower") ♦ آتش پرست fire-worshipper

پرستار [parastaar] attendant, orderly, nurse (in a hospital)

پرستاری [parastaari] 1 care, tending (usually after a sick person) 2 occupation of a female attendant, nurse, duty of a female attendant, nurse (in a hospital) ♦ مکتب - courses for attendants orderlies (in Afghanistan)
• کردن - 1 to care for, to tend (usually a sick person) 2 to work as a female attendant, nurse (in hospital)

پرستیج [parastij] and پرستیژ [parastizh] prestige

پرستیدن [parastidan] to worship, to honor, to esteem, to respect, to revere

پرسروصدا [porsarosadaa] 1 noisy, bustling ♦ شب - fidgety night, troubled night 2 sensational, much-talked-about ♦ - سخنرانی sensational performance, sensational speech

پرسش [porsesh] question; asking, inquiring ♦ احمد دیگر پرسشی نداشت Ahmad had no more questions.

پرسشی [porseshi] interrogative ♦ جمله - *grammar* interrogative sentence

پرس و پال [porsopaal] 1 questions, making inquiries 2 inquest, investigation
• کردن - (از) to question, to make inquiries ♦ رفقا از من بسیار – کردند The comrades asked me and questioned me about everything.

پرسوناژ [parsonaazh] personage

پرسونال [parsonaal] and پرسنال [parsonal] personnel; staff ♦ فنی - technical personnel

پرسیدن [porsidan] to ask, to ask about

پرش [paresh] 1 flight; flying, soaring 2 beating, throbbing, trembling, quivering ♦ چشم - twitching of the eyelid ◊ قلب - *medicine* 1 beating of the heart throbbing of the heart 2 tachycardia (rapid heart action)

پرشاخ و برگ [porshaakhobarg] 1 thick, branchy (of a tree, etc.) 2 florid, flowery (of style) ♦ جملات - florid phrases; flowery expressions

پرطاوسی [paretaawosi] black tinged with blue, bluish; dove-colored

پرطوطایی [paretutaayi] golden-green (about color)

پرقیمت [porqimat] very expensive, precious; valuable ♦ - اثر a valuable work (of art) ◊ تجربه valuable experience

پرک [parak] 1 frill, flounce 2 *regional* churn, beater, whip

پرکار [parkaar] dividers, compass ♦ خارجی - *technical* calipers ◊ داخلی - *technical* inside caliper ◊ قطی - set or case of drawing instruments

پرکاری [porkaari] 1 stuffing (e.g., of a stuffed bird, animal), taxidermy 2 filling (of a tooth) 3 *technical* filling (with rubble)

پرگپ [porgap] ¹ *noun* (*literally:* full of talk) blabber-mouth, big mouth *derogatory colloquial*

پرگپ [porgap] ² *colloquial* someone who fabricate stories about another

پرگنه [pargana] 1 *historical* pargana, region, district (in India) 2 *historical* land laid under tribute

پرگیرودار [porgirodaar] rich with events, full of shocks, stormy ♦ عصر - troubled century, troubled era

پرما(ه) [parmaa(h)] ☞ پرمه

پرمشقت [pormoshaqqat] poignant; agonizing, hard, difficult; exhausting ♦ زندگی - a hard life ◊ کار - exhausting labor

پر منفعت [pormanfa'at] 1 profitable, lucrative ♦ سودای - profitable trade, lucrative trade 2 useful, helpful ♦ مصلحت - useful advice

پرموچ [parmuch] *colloquial* ☞ پژمرده

پرمه [parma] drill, auger; brace

پرند [parend] *colloquial* fragile, brittle; breaking easily

پرنده [parenda (and) paranda] 1.1 flying 1.2 feathered 2 bird ♦ پرندگان مهاجر and پرنده های کوچی migratory birds

پرنسیپ [p(e)ransip] principle
پروا [parwaa] 1 anxiety, trouble, care, fear, misgiving, concern, uneasiness, worry 2 taking (something) into consideration, considering (something)
• به - to take into consideration to consider (به) ♦ آنها به سخن من – نمیکنند They are not considering what I say.
• نداشتن - 1 to be unconcerned, to be untroubled / to be unworried ♦ او هیچ – ندارد He is not worried about anything. / Nothing touches him. / He doesn't care a rap. 2 not to attach importance [to something] ♦ من - پول راندارم I don't attach importance to money.
• داشتن - 1 to be afraid, to fear, to be frightened by something 2 to attach importance to something
پرواز [parwaaz] flying, soaring; flight
پروانگی [parwaanagi] colloquial 1 via, through; thanks to (somebody) 2 upon presentation (of a document, etc.)
پروانه [parwaana]¹ moth; butterfly
پروانه [parwaana]² 1 authorization permit, permission, order 2 pass
پروانه [parwaana]³ technical screw; blade wheel, impeller, propeller ♦ توربین - blade of turbine ◊ دوپره - two-blade propeller ◊ طیاره - propeller
پروبال [parobaal] feathers; wings
• زدن - 1 to flap wings, to flutter (about a caught bird) 2 to endeavor, to try, to take the trouble to; to fuss, to bustle ♦ خیلی – زد مگر کارش نشد No matter how he tried, the matter did not turn out well for him. / No matter how he tried, his business did not succeed.
پرابلم [poroblam] ☞ پروبلم
پروپاگاند [poropaagaand] propaganda
پراوپوست [paropost]
• کردن - to pluck (a bird)
پروتست [porotest] protest
• کردن - to protest, to make a protest
پروتوپلاسم [porotoplaasm] biology protoplasm
پروتوکول [porotokol] 1 protocol 2 agreement 3 protocol department
پرور [parwar] present tense stem پروردن
پروراندن [parwaraandan] ☞ پروردن
پروردگار [parward(e)gaar] creator, author, founder, originator; God, the Lord
پروردن [parwardan] 1 to educate, to bring up, to rear; to grow, to cultivate 2 to nurture, to cherish (a dream)
پرورده [parwarda] 1 past participle پروردن 2 (second component of compound words with meanings "educated"/ "reared") ♦ دست پرورده charge, pupil 3 preserved (in sugar)
• کردن - colloquial 1 to educate, to rear; to bring up 2 to preserve (in sugar), to keep, to put aside
پرورش [parwaresh] 1 education; rearing, raising, bringing up 2 breeding, cultivation ♦ حیوانات - raising livestock ◊ گل - cultivating flowers, floriculture
پروژکتر [porozhektar] and پروژهکتور [porozhektor] projector, searchlight
پروژه [porozha] (also ساختمانی -) 1 project (in construction) 2 construction site, construction project, a facility project under construction 3 rarely object of inspection, examination, sights

پروژهسازی [porozhasaazi] drawing up a construction project, designing, planning
پروف [poruf] 1 test, trial 2 model; rough copy, draft 3 printing proof
• دیدن - 1 to perform a check, to perform a test or a trial 2 printing to read proofs, to check proofs
• کردن - to try on, to try, to test
پروفیسر [porofaisar] professor
پروکساید [poroksaaid] chemistry peroxide
پروگرام [porograam] 1 program, plan ♦ کار - work plan, plan of operations 2 routine, order
پرولیتاری [poroleetaari] proletarian
پرولیتاریا [poroleetaaryaa] and پرولیتاریات [proleetaariaat] proletariat
پرولیتار [poroleetaar] proletarian
پره [para] 1 blade, wing ♦ دولاب - sail of a windmill ◊ paddle or blade of a hydraulic wheel 2 edge, border ♦ بیل - sharp blades 3 tooth, cog ♦ پره های چرخ teeth or cogs of gear wheel 4 architecture toothed or jagged fretwork, toothed or jagged frieze
پرهنگامه [porhangaama] noisy, stormy, troubled ♦ دوره - troubled century or era, stormy time
پرهیز [par(h)eez] 1 refusal to use [something] abstention; adherence to a diet 2 rarely avoidance, dismissal
• غیر قابل - mandatory, strict, absolute, inevitable, unavoidable
• کردن - 1 to refuse to use, to abstain; to maintain a diet, to adhere to a diet (از) 2 to avoid, to beware [of] (از)
پرهیزانه [par(h)eezaana] diet, dietetic nourishment
پرهیزگار [par(h)eezgaar] 1 abstemious, temperate, moderate (e.g., in eating) 2 leading an ascetic style of life 3 devout, pious
پرهیزگاری [par(h)eezgaari] 1 abstinence, abstemiousness, temperance, moderation (e.g., in eating) ♦ گربه دربرابر موش است - proverb This reminds one of the "abstemiousness" of a cat in regard to a mouse. (The wolf felt sorry for the mare and left the tail and mane.) 2 asceticism 3 piety, devotion
پری [pari] 1 fairy, peri 2 a beauty 3 masculine proper name Pari
پریدن [paridan] 1 to fly, to fly away; to take off, to fly up, to take wing; to fly up quickly, to rise easily 2 to jump, to hop; to jump up 3 to twitch, to tremble ♦ لبهایش میپرید His lips trembled. 4 to evaporate, to vaporize, to vanish (e.g., of a liquid) 5 colloquial to disappear 6 colloquial to break intransitive, to tear (e.g., about a taut rope or cord) intransitive
• خواب از چشمش پریدهبود His sleep was wasted.
پریروز [pariroz] the day before yesterday, two days ago
پریز [pareez] colloquial ☞ پرهیز
پریزانه [pareezana] colloquial ☞ پرهیزانه
پریشان [pereeshaan] 1 strewn; scattered ♦ موهای - loose flowing hair, tousled hair 2 sad, downcast, grieved, chagrinned 3 colloquial poor, needy
• کردن - 1 to strew; to scatter 2 to upset, to pain, to grieve ♦ حواس (خاطر) کسی را - کردن to upset, to pain, to grieve someone; to excite, to alarm someone
پریشانحال [pereeshaanhaal] 1 poor, needy 2 sad, downcast, depressed by grief; suffering

پریشان خاطر [pereeshaankhaater] perturbed, anxious, uneasy, worried, troubled

پریشان فکر [pereeshaanfeker] 1 absentminded, inattentive 2 depressed; confused, disturbed, troubled

پریشانی [pereeshaani] 1 state of being upset, grief, chagrin 2 melancholy, grief, sorrow 3 trouble, unpleasantness

پریشب [parishab] the evening before last, the night before last

پریفابریکت [p(e)rifaabriket] 1 ready-made; finished; made in a factory 2 prefabricated (about a home, building) ♦ - صورت by assembling finished panels; made of ready-made panels

پریکارد [perikaard] *anatomy* pericardium, the pouch around the heart

پز [paz] 1 *present tense stem* پختن 2 (second component of compound words with meanings "boiling" / "baking") ♦ صابون پز soap boiler

پزغند [pozghond] *botany* gall

پژمان [pazhmaan] 1 sad, cheerless, despondent, depressed, dispirited 2 drooped, withered

پژمردگی [pazhmordagi] 1 puniness, sickliness; exhaustion 2 dejection, depression, despondency

پژمردن [pazhmordan] 1 to wither, to droop, to get dry 2 to fall into dejection, to become depressed

پژمرده [pazmorda] 1 *past participle* پژمردن 2 ☞ پژمان

پژواک [pazhwaak] echo

پس [pas] 1 back side, rear part (of something), back, rear, backside 2.1 then, afterwards ♦ از این پس henceforth, from now on, in the future ◊ (اینکه) پس از آنکه after *compound conjunction* 2.2 thus, then, in such a case ♦ پس چرا نگفتی؟ Then why didn't you speak up? 2.3 consequently, so ♦ پس شما داکتر هستید So, you're a doctor? 3.1 (also درپس) beyond, outside of, behind; the other side [of] *denominative preposition* ♦ (در) پس درختان beyond or behind the trees 3.2 (also از پس) from behind *denominative preposition* ♦ (از) پس پرد from behind the curtain 3.3 after, following *denominative preposition* ♦ (از) پس آنها after them, following them

• بعد از پس ☞ in entry بعد از
• پس افتادن to be postponed, to be put off
• پس انداختن to postpone, to delay, to put off
• پس دادن to give back, to return
• پس رفتن to fall back, to retreat; to move aside
• پس زدن 1 to draw back, to throw back (e.g., a curtain) 2 to reject, to decline 3 *colloquial* not to break out, to break out mildly (about a rash on the body) 4 to subside, to rush back (e.g., about water)
• پس ماندن to fall behind, to be left behind, to be left far behind
• پس پس رفتن to move backwards, to go back, to go backwards
• پس کسی را ورداشتن and پس کسی را نماندن *proverb colloquial* to knock (criticize) somebody, to speak maliciously or caustically about somebody ♦ احمد پس محمود را نمی ماند When Mahmud is away, Ahmad starts knocking him at once.
• پس کلاه خود رفتن *colloquial* to be left with nothing; to be no better off than at the start
• پس گپ گشتن 1 to find fault with someone's words; to blame someone for every mistake, to nit-pick 2 to heed rumors, to heed talk; to collect gossip ♦ پس گپ مردم نگردید Don't pay attention to what people say!

• پس گوش انداختن (زدن) to put off, to delay, to drag out (a decision on a matter)
• پس نخود سیاه فرستادن *colloquial* to ravage, to ruin utterly

پس آب [pasaab] 1 (also صابون -) wash water, rinse water 2 leftovers diluted with water ♦ شربت - diluted sherbet

پسان [pasaan] then; afterwards; subsequently

پسانتر [pasaantar] later, in the future ♦ این موضوع - ذکر خواهد شد This will be discussed below.

پس انداز [pasandaaz] 1 savings, economies, accumulations, stock, supply 2 deposit (in a bank) ♦ حساب - current account of a depositor (in a bank)
• - کردن 1 to make economies, to make savings; to put aside, to accumulate 2 to make a deposit (in a bank)

پسانها [pasaanhaa] subsequently, in the future

پس آو [pasaaw] 1 *colloquial* ☞ پس آب 2 wood chip, litter (washed ashore)

پس آوردگی [pasaawardagi]
• (پسر) بچه - *colloquial* son of wife's first husband, stepson

پساوند [pasaawand] ☞ پسوند

پس آوه [pasaawa] remainder of water in an irrigation ditch (after the ditch is dammed)

پس پا(ی) [paspaa(y)]
• شدن 1 to give way (to others), to leave the scene, to remain out of work 2 to lose power, to lose authority; to lose meaning, to lose importance ♦ شاه شجاع در آن دروه - شده بود Shah Shojaa was already out of power at that time. 3 *historical* to be in disgrace or disfavor

پس پرده [pas(e)parda] secret, covert, hidden, behind the scenes ♦ گپ - secret talks, talks behind the scenes

پس پس [pospos] whispering, a whisper; talking (to one another) in whispers
• - کردن to whisper

پست [past] 1 low, not high, short 2 low-lying (about terrain) 3 low, contemptible, despicable 4 low, bass ♦ آهنگ - bass tone

پست [past] *colloquial* (*literally:* low) low class, amoral (person) *derogatory*

پستان [pestaan] 1 breast; nipple 2 udder

پستان بند [pestaanband] bag or tight binding (which is placed on a ewe's udder to wean lambs)

پستاندار [pestaandar]
• حیوانات - mammals

پستان داردی [pestaandardi] *medicine* mastitis

پستانک [pestaanak] 1 feeding bottle (for infants) 2 pacifier 3 cap, percussion cap (of cartridge of ammunition)

پستون [pestaan] *technical* piston

پستون دار [pestondaar] *technical* piston *adjective* ♦ انجن - piston engine

پسته [pesta] pistachio; pistachios ♦ درخت - pistachio tree

پسته یی [pestayi] pistachio *adjective*, light green (about color)

پستی [pasti] 1 low place, depression 2 meanness, baseness
• پستی و بلندی ☞ وبلندی

پستی وبندی [pastiwbeandi] 1 irregularities, roughness, ups and downs, pits and bumps (in a road) 2 outlines (of something) ♦ روزگار - vicissitudes of life or fate

پسخانه [paskhaana] 1 back room (in a house); auxiliary premises, utility building 2 storeroom, pantry 3 *historical* shah's train

• پس دکانی ☞ دکان - 3

پسخم [paskham] 1 rounded, curved from the back; having a slope, slant, or curve from the back 2 curve; bend; slope, slant

پس خورده [paskhorda] leftovers of food or water; leavings ♦ شیر ـ سگ نخورد proverb A lion doesn't eat a dog's leavings.

پس دکانی [pasdokaani] back part of dokan (a shop or store; this area serves as a utility building)

پس دوزی [pasdozi] overcasting seams
• ـ کردن to overcast seams

پسر [pesar] 1 son 2 boy

پسر اندر [pesarandar] stepson

پسر ایور [pesareewar] son of husband's brother, nephew

پسر خوانده [pesarkhaanda] adopted son

پس رو [pasraw]
• مرده شوی ـ abusive May you follow the deceased! / May you croak! / May you drop dead!

پس رو کردن [pasraw-kardan] colloquial (literally: to make someone go backward) to threaten, to scare someone (child)

پس سری [passari] slap in the back of the head

پس شام [paseshaam] last meal at night (at dawn) during the month of Ramadan

پس شوی [paseshawi (and) passhawi] colloquial ☞ پس شام

پس صبا [passabaa] colloquial ☞ پس فردا

پس فردا [pasfardaa] day after tomorrow

پس کوچه [paskocha] lane, alley; side street, impassable street

پسکه [poska] colloquial ☞ پوپنک

پسکی [pasaki] 1 counter (of a shoe) 2 backwards, back
• ـ رفتن to move backward, to go in reverse

پس گردنی [pasgardani] colloquial a blow to the neck, or to the back of the head; a slap on the back of the head

پس لگدی [paslogadi] colloquial 1 a backward kick, a blow with the heel, a kick 2 kicking

پسمان [pasmaan] being delayed (in doing something), being late (in doing something)
• ـ شدن 1 to remain indebted [to], to underpay ♦ در این معامله هزار افغانی ـ شدیم In this transaction we owe a thousand afghani. 2 to be in arrears

پسماندگی [pasmaandagi] backwardness, lag

پسمانده [pasmaanda] 1 backward, lagging 2 ☞ پس خورده

پسمانی [pasmaani] ☞ پسماندگی

پس منظر [pasmanzar] background ♦ تابلوی نقاشی ـ background of a picture or painting

پسند [pesand] 1 present tense stem پسندیدن 2 approval; choice; preference 3 (second component of compound words with meanings "approving" / "loving" / "liking" / "preferring" something) ♦ خودپسند self-satisfied
• داشتن (دیدن) ـ to approve, to find to one's taste
• ـ کردن to choose, to select

پسندیدن [pesandidan] to approve; to find to one's taste; to prefer ♦ دخترم این تکه را نپسندید My daughter didn't like this fabric.

پسندیده [pesandida] 1 past participle پسندیدن 2.1 having been found to one's liking, having been found to one's taste; pleasant, agreeable, welcome 2.2 suitable, acceptable 2.3 worthy of approval, praiseworthy, commendable ♦ حرکات ـ actions worthy of approval

پسوند [paswand] grammar affix; suffix ♦ پسوندهای تصریفی word-changing offices

پسینه [pasina] 1 grammar postposition ♦ مفعولی ـ a postposition forming a direct object ◊ پیشینه ها و پسینه ها prepositions and postpositions

پسینه [pasina] 2 late (about sowing) ♦ گندم ـ late wheat

پشت [posht] 1.1 back 1.2 reverse side, back side (of something) ♦ پیسه ـ the back side or reverse side of a coin 1.3 forefathers; generation ♦ بعد از پنج پشت through or after five generations ◊ لعنت به هفتاد و هفت پشتت abusive May your ancestors be cursed to the 77th generation! 2.1 (also- در) beyond, behind, from that side, from that direction denominative preposition ♦ حصار ـ outside the fence ◊ میز ـ at the table 2.2 for (to fetch) denominative preposition ♦ من کتاب آمدم ـ I came for the book. / I came to fetch the book.
• از ـ from behind ♦ از حصار ـ from behind the fence ◊ از ـ کوه from behind the mountains
• پشت پای ـ ☞ پای
• پشت چشم ـ ☞ چشم
• ـ کردن to take on (a load), to hoist (a load), to lift on one's back
• ـ گشتاندن 1.1 to turn one's back [upon], to turn aside, to avert (به) 1.2 to neglect (به)
• ـ نمودن literary to step back, to retreat, to run away
• گوش ـ انداختن to toss (one's braids) behind [one's] back
• کسی را به زمین آوردن ـ to overcome (in a struggle), to conquer. to vanquish
• کسی را دوتا کردن ـ to slay, to overcome someone; to plunge someone into grief ♦ مرگ فرزند ـ او را دوتا کرد He was overcome by his son's death.
• (چیزی) کسی ـ گشتن to try to see someone, to try to get something ♦ ما پیسه نمی گردیم We don't pursue money.
• گپ ـ گشتن 1 to attach importance to what people say; to heed gossip 2 to cavil at words
• گپ ـ نگرد 1 Don't listen to what they say! 2 Don't cavil at words!
• گوش ـ انداختن to neglect, to abandon, to give up; to leave motionless; to shelve (a matter)
• پشتش بکوه است colloquial He has powerful patrons (protectors). / It is as if he were behind a stone wall.

پشت [pesht] Shoo! / Get out of here! interjection

پشتاره [poshtaara] burden, load (carried on the back); package, bale, pack; bundle ♦ یک ـ خار bundle of thorns

پشت به پشت [poshtbapost] 1 continuously, continually, incessantly; in succession ♦ او سگرت میکشد ـ He smokes one cigarette after another. 2 from generation to generation

پشت پای [poshtepaay] lifting the foot or leg

پشت چشم [poshtecheeshm] eyelid
• ـ نازک کردن colloquial to express displeasure by one's expression (by half-shutting the eyes and pursing the lips)

پشت دست [poshtedast] the back of the hand

پشت زانو [poshtezaanu] popliteal fossa (pit or depression behind the knee joint)

پشت سر [poshtsar] 1 back of the head 2 behind somebody's back 3 ••• 1 after, following; denominative preposition ♦ من ـ راه میرفتند They followed after me / behind me. 2 in the absence (of somebody), behind (somebody's) back
• کسی ـ گپ زدن to talk behind (somebody's) back, to gossip about someone

پشت سر انداختن [peshte-sar-andaakhtan]¹ *colloquial* (*literally:* to throw behind) to put things off, to procrastinate

پشت سر گوی [poshtesargaay] *colloquial* a gossip, a person who loves to talk scandal

پشتک [poshtak] and پشتک پران [poshtakparaan] leapfrog (children's game)
• دادن - to offer [one's] back (to help [someone] climb somewhere)

پشتکی [poshtaki] *colloquial* ☞ پشتاره

پشت گوش کردن [peshte-goosh-kardan *colloquial*] (*literally:* to turn ears back) not listening, not carrying out an order

پشتن [peshton] *technical* ☞ پستون

پشتو [pashto] 1 Pashto *adjective* 2 (also -زبان) the Pashto or Pushtu language, the language of any of several Pashtoon tribes in Afghanistan and the NWFP of Pakistan

پشتوانه [poshtwaana] *finance* (also طلا -) guarantee, guaranty, payment, defrayment (in gold)

پشت و پناه [poshtopanaah] 1 support; stronghold, bulwark; defense, protection 2 patron, protector, defender

پشت و پهلو [poshtopahlu]
• کردن - 1 to turn over *transitive*, to shift from one side to the other (about a sick person) 2 to turn (a kabab on a spit)

پشت و رو(ی) [poshtoro(y)]
• کردن - to turn (clothes)
• پشت و رویش معلوم نیست It is not clear what he is (or represents). / You can't figure him out.
• پشت و روی نداشتن [pesht-o-rooy-nadaashtan] *idiom* (*literally:* not having back or front) opportunist, not a person of principle

پشتون [pashtun] a member of any several Pashto speaking tribe in Afghanistan and NWFP of Pakistan *adjective*
• قوم – any of several Pashto speaking tribes in Afghanistan and the NWFP of Pakistan

پشته [poshta] 1 hill, hillock, knoll, mound 2 heap, pile (of dirt); embankment; bank; knob 3 ☞ پشتاره

پشتی [poshti] 1 prop, support 2 sofa cushion; bolster; back (of furniture) 3 backing, encouragement, patronage; support; help 4 cover (of a book)
• دادن - to underlay masonry (to strengthen a wall)
• کردن - to bind (a book, magazines)

پشتیبان [poshtibaan] 1 patron, defender, protector 2 assistant, helper, defender, patron

پشتیبانی [poshtibaani] backing, support, help; patronage, protection
• کردن - 1 to support; to help, to patronize (از) 2 to protect (از)

پشتیوان [poshtiwaan] 1 *colloquial* ☞ پشتیبان 2 prop, support (for a wall, tree, etc.)

پشقاب [peshqaab] ☞ بشقاب

پشک [peshk] casting or drawing lots (in taking recruits into the army) ♦ او برآمده است - The lot fell upon him to go into the army.

پشک [peshak] cat

پشک جان [peshakjan] *slang* (*literally:* having the soul of a cat) a tough person

پشک هفت دم [peshake-haftdam] *slang* (*literally:* having the seven soul of a cat) a patient and tolerant person

پشکی [peshki] *colloquial* recruit, boot (in the military)

پشم [pash (e)m] wool ♦ بز - goat's hair ◊ ریسیده - woolen yarn, worsted ◊ چوب - *technical* excelsior ◊ شیشه یی - *technical* fiberglass, glass fiber

پشم آلود [pashmaalud] thickly covered with hair or wool, hairy; shaggy

پشمک [pashmak] pashmak (variety of halvah in the form of a bun of white filaments)

پشمی [pashmi] and پشمین [pashmin] woolen ♦ منسوجات - woolen fabric or cloth ◊ دستمال - woolen shawl

پشمینه [pashmina] 1 ☞ پشمی 2.1 woolen fabric, broadcloth 2.2 fine sheep's wool

پشمینه بافی [pashminabaafi] wool weaving, wool production ♦ - فابریکه cloth factory

پشو [pesho] *abbreviation of* پس شو

پشه [pashsha] 1 gnat ♦ خاکی – mosquito ◊ در هوا نعل میکند - He can shoe a gnat in flight! ◊ در سرتاسر باغ پشه یی پرنمی زد - Not a single gnat was flying in the garden. (Not a soul was in sight.) 2 *cards* clubs ♦ ماتکه - queen of clubs

پشه خانه [pash(sh)axaana] 1 bed curtains; mosquito netting 2 *botany* elm

پشه خورک [pash(sh)axorak] fly-catcher (bird)

پشه یی [pashayi] 1 Pashai (nationality and representative of the nationality) 2 the Pashai language

پشیمان [pesheemaan] regretting (a deed or action that has taken place), repenting
• شدن - to regret, to repent (از)

پشیمانی [pesheemaani] regret (about a deed or action that has taken place), repentance
• خوردن - to regret, to repent (از)

پطرول [petrol] ☞ پترول

پطره [patra] *technical* sheet (metal) patch

پطلون [patlun] ☞ پتلون

پطنوس [patnus] ☞ پتنوس

پف [pof] 1 Ugh! (noisy expiration) *interjection* 2 *colloquial* bragging, boasting
• پف کردن 1 to blow; to inflate 2 to blow out (e.g., a lamp) 3 to fan (a flame, etc.) 4 *colloquial* to boast, to brag
• به پف بند بودن and به پف ایستادن *colloquial* to hang by a thread, to be on the verge of downfall, death, ruin, etc.
• آب خود را پف پف کرده میخورد [aab-khudra-puf-puf-karda-maykhorad] *idiom* (*literally:* He blows water when drinking) He is being careful, He takes caution

پف آب [pofaab] and پف آو [pofaw] splashing, spattering, or spattering with water (from the mouth)
• کردن - to spatter, to spray with water (from the mouth)

پفک [pofok] air gun, air rifle
• زرگری - blowpipe (of a jeweller)

پکت [pakt] pact ♦ دفاعی - defensive pact

پکنیک [peknik] picnic

پکاورا [pakawra] pakawra (variety of potato dumplings fried in lard)

پکه [pak(k)a] 1 ventilator 2 fan, large fan 3 (also زغالی -) device for fanning coals 4 damper, stove damper, furnace damper
• (زدن) کردن - 1 to fan, to fan oneself 2 to fan coals (in a samovar, etc.)

پکه گوش [pakagosh] lop-eared

پکه یی [pakayi] *radio* fan (about an antenna) *adjective*

پگا (ه) [pagaa(h)] 1 morning 2 in the morning, during the morning

پل [pal] ¹ (also پلی) 1 foot 2 footprint; imprint
• پل گرفتن and پل زدن to follow [someone's] track, to pursue

پل [pal] ² 1 blade, point, edge ♦ پل چاقو the cutting edge of a knife ◊ پل ریش تراشی razor blade 2 *technical* cutter, chisel ♦ پل برمه hacksaw ◊ پل آهن بری drill bit, boring bit ◊ پل فریز cutter, milling cutter, cutting tool ◊ پل خراطی cutting tool ◊ پل نری screw plate, die; tap, screw tap

پل [pal] ³ millstone

پل [pol] bridge

پلاتفارم [pelaatfaarm] platform

پلاتین [palaatin] platinum

پلازما [palaazma] *biology physics* plasma

پلاس [palaas] pliers

پلاستر [palaastar] ☞ پلستر

پلاسترکاری [palaastarkaari] ☞ پلسترکاری

پلاستیک [pelaastik] plastic *noun*

پلاستیکی [pelaastiki] plastic *adjective*, made of plastic

پلاشترک [pelaashtarak] *dialect* swallow (bird)

پلان [pelaan] 1 plan ♦ پلانهای اقتصادی انکشافی economic plans ◊ پلان پنج ساله - five-year plan of development 2 diagram, scheme, sketch, plan ♦ پلان اداره کردن- management diagram management plan, management system, control diagram, control plan, control system ◊ پلان قریه - village plan

پلاو [palaaw] ☞ پلو

پلت [palet] 1 tablet, plate, small plate (on a door, e.g., for a number) 2 (also پلت نمبر -) number plate, license plate (on a motor vehicle)

پلتن [paltan] 1 infantry regiment 2 infantry *noun*

پلته [palta (and) pelta] *colloquial* 1 wick (of lamp) 2 cord

پلته دادن [palta-daadan] *slang* (to raise the wick of a hurricane lamp) to rekindle, to stir up trouble

پلته و چراغ کردن [palta-o-cheraagh-kardan] *idiom* (*literally*: to do the wick and the lamp) to be nosy, to be a busybody

پلخمان [palakhmaan] sling-shot

سنگ پلخمان شدن [sangepalakhmaan-shudan] *idiom* (*literally*: to become the sling-shot stone) to travel far away and not send news home

پلستر [palastar] 1 plaster, plastering 2 *medicine* plaster 3 *medicine* compress
• چسپاندن - 1 to apply a plaster 2 to make a compress
• کردن - to plaster, to do plastering plastering work

پلسترکاری [palastarkaari] plastering, plastering work

پلک [polak] 1 round gasket ♦ چرمی - *colloquial* leather gasket 2 small and flat earring (without a stone)

پلک [pelk] eyelid; eyelids
• زدن - to blink, to wink
• پلکها بهم فشردن to screw up one's eyes

پلکش [palkash] wooden shovel bound with iron (to lay irrigation furrows in a plowed field)

پلکی [palaki] *technical* gasket, washer ♦ فنر - 1 snap ring 2 washer

پلگ [palag] 1 *technical* spark plug (of engine) 2 plug, electric plug

پلگ وانه [palagwaana] *technical* spark-plug wrench

پل گیر [palgir] *technical*
• برمه - drill spindle

• ماشین خراطی - support, rest, carriage, saddle (of machine tool)

پلنگ [palang] ¹ leopard, snow leopard ♦ سال - year of the leopard (third year of 12-year animal cycle)

پلنگ [palang] ² large wooden bed (with painted legs)

پلنگپوش [palangposh] bedspread, coverlet

پلو [palaw] pilaf

پلوان [polwaan] polwan (bank or ridge encircling a plot of land)

پلوان شریک [polwaansharik] a neighbor on a plot of land (one who has a common polwan; ☞ پلوان)

پلورزیت [p(a)lawrezit] *medicine* pleurisy

پله [pal(l)a] 1 scale 2 door hinge 3 (also خورجین -) half of a saddle bag; compartment or section of a khorjin 4 step (of stairway), rung (of ladder) 5 brink, edge; end
• به - رساندن *colloquial* to rouse to a fury; to put [somebody] beside himself, to drive [someone] out of his wits

پله [pola] kernels of corn roasted in the sand
• زدن - *colloquial* to become inflamed, to be inflamed, to come to a head (about a boil), to be covered with a rash, with pimples
• یک - ارزش نداشتن not to be worth a farthing, not to be worth anything
• این ساعت خود را پله بخورید You can take your watch and throw it away!

پله بین [palabin] *colloquial* one who keeps his nose to the wind, a timeserver ♦ دوست - a mercenary friend

پله پز [polapaz] vendor of roasted kernels of corn

پله پله [pal(l)apal(l)a] *colloquial* ☞ پرچه پرچه

پله کش کردن [palakash-kardan] *colloquial* running, in a hurry, in a rush

پلی [pali] 1 pod (of peas, beans, etc.) 2 clove (of garlic)

پلی [poli] sodium bicarbonate

پلیت [paleet] ¹ 1 stripe (on uniform trousers) 2 pleat, crease (on clothing) ♦ دوخته - and بسته -stitched pleat, stitched crease ◊ واز - unstitched pleat, unstitched crease 3 tuck
• دادن - to make a pleat; to pleat
• گرفتن - 1 to take in (about clothing) 2 to make pleats 3 to make tucks

پلیت [palet] ² 1 *photography* plate 2 *technical* plate 3 *regional* dish, (dinner) plate
• بطری - storage battery jar

پلیته [palita] 1 wick (of lamp) 2 fuze lighter, igniter, primer (of a gun)

پلیس [polis] ☞ پولیس

پمپ [pamp] 1 pump ♦ ستیشن - pumping station 2 (also پترول -) gasoline pump

پن [pen] 1 pin; hairpin; brooch; clip ♦ نکتایی - *technical* tie pin 2 pin ♦ پن پستون - *technical* piston pin

پناه [panaah] 1 shelter, cover; refuge 2 defense, protection 3 safety catch
• به - پناه 1 to hide oneself, to take shelter, to conceal oneself (where بداخل،به) 2 to find refuge, to find shelter, to find asylum (with someone پیش) 3 to resort to protection (به)
• دادن - 1 to shelter, to give refuge (to someone را،به) 2 to take under protection
• - بردن ☞ - شدن
• پناه بخدا ☞ به خدا

پ

پناه بخدا [panaahbakhodaa] *colloquial* 1 God preserve! 2 God preserve me! / God save me!
- کردن (گفتن) - *colloquial* to entrust yourself to God (before beginning some matter)

پناه گاه [panaahgaah] 1 shelter, refuge ♦ بم - bomb shelter 2 dugout shelter

پناهگزین [panaahgozin] refugee; emigre

پنبه [pomba] 1 cotton; cotton plant ♦ خام - raw cotton 2 wadding

پنبه چینی [pombachini] picking cotton ♦ ماشین - cotton-picking machine

پنبه دانه [pombadana] cotton seed

پنبه کاری [pombakaari] ☞ پخته کاری

پنبه یی [pombayi] 1 cotton *adjective*; made of cotton, cotton *adjective* ♦ منسوجات - cotton fabric, cotton cloth 2 wadded, quilted ♦ لحاف - a quilt

پنج [panj] five

پنج پولی [panjpuli] panjpuli (Afghan coin equivalent to five puls)

پنجره [panjara] 1 lattice, grill (in a wall or door) 2 lattice door

پنجشنبه [panjshambe] Thursday

پنجصد [panjsad] five hundred

پنج کتاب [panjketaab] ☞ پنج گنج

پنج کلیان [panjkalyaan] horse with white legs and a white spot on the forehead ♦ مشکی - black horse with white legs and a white spot on the forehead

پنج گنج [panjganj] *obscure* panjganj (old school reader based on the work "Panjnama" by Farideddin Attar)

پنجه [panja] 1 hand; the five fingers 2 (also پای -) toes 3 paw (with claws); claws 4 fork
- انداختن - to measure swords [with somebody], to fight, to struggle
- انداختن - دادن - to start a fight, to enter into a fight, to come to blows, to fight
- صوتی - tuning fork

پنجه چنار [panjachenaar] plane tree with broad crown; spreading platan

پنجه کش [panjakash] (also- نان) variety of cookies (with furrows formed by fingers)

پنجگی [panjagi] *military* clip, magazine

پنجیک [panjyak] 1 one-fifth, a fifth part (of something) 2 one-fifth of a harvest (received by a peasant in the five-share system)

پنجیک کار [panjyakkaar] farm laborer or peasant who receives one-fifth of a harvest

پنجیک کاری [panjyakkaari] sharecropping system in which sharecropper receives one-fifth of a harvest

پنچر [panchar] puncture (of an automobile tire)
- شدن - to be punctured, to go flat (about an automobile tire)

پند [pand] advice; precept; moral admonition
- دادن - to advise; to preach [at], to admonish

پندار [pendaar] 1 *present tense stem* پنداشتن 2 opinion, supposition; assumption, guess

پنداشتن [pendaashtan] (present tense stem پندار [pendar]) to consider, to think, to suppose; to assume, to surmise

پندانه [pondaana] *colloquial* ☞ پنبه دانه

پندک [pandak] bundle, pack, small parcel, knapsack

پندک گل [pondoke-gul] *slang* (literally: flower bud) a beautiful child or young person (female)

پند نامه [pandnaama] 1 book of precepts 2 pandnama (genre of didactic prose)

پندیدگی [pondidagi] swelling; tumor

پندیدن [pondidan] 1 to be blown up, to be puffed up, to swell 2 to swell up, to bloat [with] 3 *colloquial* to be indignant, to lose one's temper, to fly into a rage

پنسل [pensel] (also- قلم) pencil

پنسل پاک [penselpaak] eraser

پنسلین [penselin] penicillin

پنگ پانگ [pengpaang] ping-pong, table tennis

پنهان [penhaan] 1 covert, secretive 2 secret
- داشتن - to keep secret, to hide, to conceal
- شدن - to hide oneself, to hide *intransitive*, to cover oneself, to seek shelter, to take cover
- از نظر - شدن - to disappear from view, to pass out of sight, to disappear

پنیر [paner] cheese ♦ پخته - unsalted cheese (which is eaten with currants) ◊ خام - brynza (cheese made of sheep's milk)

پنیرک [panerak] *botany* mallow, malva

پنیر مایه [panermaaya] ferment (for cheese)

پوپک [popak] tassel, pompom

پوپک دار [popakdaar] and پوپکی [popaki] with a pompom, with a tassel ♦ دم - bushy tail ◊ کلاه - cap with a tassel, with a pompom

پوپنک [popanak] mold ♦ نان را - زده است - The bread was covered with mold. / The bread became moldy.

پوتاس [potaas] 1 *chemistry* potash 2 *colloquial* potassium permanganate

پوتاسیم [potaasiam] and پوتاسیوم [potaasiom] *chemistry* potassium ♦ پرمنگنت - potassium permanganate

پوته [pota] a piece of fabric wrapped around the waist; broad sash

پوچ [puch] 1 empty on the inside, hollow ♦ بادام - empty almond nut 2 empty, dull, absurd, foolish 3 futile, vain, useless ♦ تلاش - vain efforts
- حرف - 1 empty words, foolish words 2 swearing, cursing
- گفتن - 1 to speak foolishness, to convey nonsense or rubbish 2 to swear, to use foul language

پوچاق [pochaaq] rind; husk; shell; peel ♦ خربوزه - melon rind

پوچک [puchak] 1 spent cartridge case 2 *colloquial* empty nut (walnut or almond)

پوچاق کسی را پراندن [pochaq-kasay-raa-paraandan] *idiom* (literally: to break someone's peal) to beat the daylights out of someone

پوچ گویی [puchgoyi] foul language

پود [pud]¹ *textiles* weft; wefting
- تاروپود ☞ تارو - پود

پود [pud]² pud (old measure of weight in afghanistan, equal to two sirs and one charak or 40 pounds)

پودر [podar] 1 powder ♦ دندان - tooth powder ◊ لحیم کاری - *technical* soldering powder 2 fine powder (e.g., face powder) 3 *technical* flux

پوده [puda] putrid; rotten, flabby; worm-eaten ♦ چوب - rotten tree
• آدم - *colloquial* dawdler, lout
پودین [pudin] and پودینگ [puding] pudding
پودینه [pudina] *botany* mint ♦ دشتی - wild mint
پورتریت [portreet] portrait
پوره [pura] **1.1** full, whole ♦ یکسال - whole year **1.2** exhaustive, comprehensive, sufficient **2.1** fully, in full **2.2** exhaustively, comprehensively, sufficiently; properly ♦ او را میشناسم - I know him very well. **3** precisely, exactly, just ♦ ده سال قبل - exactly 10 years ago
• شدن - to be finished, to be ended; to be completed; to be executed, to be accomplished ♦ وقتش شد – His time has run out. / His hour has come.
• کردن - to finish, to complete; to execute, to carry out
• این کار از ما ازتوان کسی – نبودن to be beyond one's powers ♦ (از دست ما) – نیست We are not up to this matter.
پوز [puz] **1** muzzle, snout (of an animal) **2** *coarse* mug, ugly face
• خوده دور دادن - *colloquial* to turn up the snout, to turn away; to take no heed of
• پوزش را بالا گرفت *colloquial* He doesn't care a hang.
• پوز کسی را پراندن [pooze-kasay-raa-paraandan] *idiom* (*literally:* to break someone's jaw) a threaten by saying "I will break your face"
پوز پیچ [poozpaych] *colloquial* scarf, muffler
پوزخند [puzhand] smile; grin, smirk
• زدن - to smile; to grin, to smirk
پوزش [pozesh] *literary* apology
• خواستن - to apologize
پوزوپکل [puzopakal] *coarse* ugly face; mug
پوز و چنه [pooz-o-chana] *slang* (*literally:* face and jaw) courage and ability *derogatory*
پوزه [puza] **1** protuberance; promontory, cape ♦ کوه - jut of a mountain **2** (also کشتی -) bow or prow of a ship
پوزیشن [pozeeshan] **1** position **2** situation, status **3** *colloquial* appearance, exterior
پوست [post] **1** skin; hide; fur ♦ آش داده - tanned hide ◊ گوسفند - tanned hide of sheep, sheepskin **2** crust; scab; pellicle; rind, peel, husk ♦ انار - pomegranate rind
• پیاز- **1** skin of an onion **2** anything thin, fragile, ephemeral
• (انداختن) افکندن - **1** to shed skin (about a snake, etc.) **2** to peel off, to skin off, to come off
• (کندن) کردن - **1** to peel off skin, to peel off a hide, to dress **2** to clean off a peel or a rind, to clean off a husk
• پشک (سگ) بروی کشیدن - *colloquial* to behave impudently, to behave defiantly; to behave like a cad or a boor
• واستخوان شده است - to become seriously emaciated, to become skeleton-like ♦ او واستخوان شده است He is just skin and bones.
• به - جای نشدن *colloquial* to be beside oneself with joy
• به - جای گرفتن به‌کسی *colloquial* and درآمدن به - کسی **1** to ingratiate oneself with, to worm oneself into somebody's confidence **2** to find an easy job, to settle in (with someone)
• پوست کسی را کاه پر کردن [pooste-kasay-raa-kaah-pur-kardan] *idiom* (*literally:* to stuff an animal) to punish harshly

پوست باب [postbaab] *collectively* furs
پوست کارد [postkaard] postcard
پوست مال [postmaal]
• شدن - to peel off, to exfoliate (about skin)
• کردن - to peel off, to skin (by friction or rubbing)
پوسته [posta] **1** mail ♦ هوایی- airmail ◊ بکس - post box ◊ تکس - stamp ◊ به ذریعه - by mail **2** *military* post, outpost ♦ ترصد - observation post ◊ رادار - radar post
پوسته خانه [postakhaana] post office
پوسته رسان [postarasaan] postman, mailman, letter carrier
پوستی [posti] postal, post office *adjective* ♦ تکت - stamp
پوستین [postin] sheepskin coat; coat of tanned hide, short coat of tanned hide ♦ گلدار - embroidered short coat of tanned hide
• پوستین را چپه پوشیدن [poostin-raa-chapa-poshidan] *idiom* (*literally:* to wear an animal's fur coat inside out) to get on one's bad side (threaten someone) ♦ اگر پوستینه چپه پوشیدم حقته میتم If I wear the fur coat inside out, I will beat you up.
پوستینچه [postincha] fur jacket; sheepskin coat, short fur coat
پوستین دوزی [postindozi] sewing articles made of sheepskin; fur business ♦ دکان - store and workshop (where articles made of sheepskin are made and sold)
پوسیدن [posidan] to rot, to decompose; to putrefy, to decay
پوش [posh] **1** *present tense stem* پوشیدن **2.1** edging, trim; case, covering; cover ♦ تکمه - covering [for] buttons ◊ کتاب - binding, book cover ◊ ماشیندار - *technical* machine-gun jacket **2.2** (also برای سیم) braiding of or for wiring, cable, or insulation **3** (second component of compound words with meanings "attired in something" / "covering, sheltering something" ♦ سیاه پوش dressed in black, being in mourning ◊ سر پوش lid, cover
• پوش بالش - بالشت ☞
• کردن - **1** to cover (a roof), to lay roofing **2** to wind, to wrap (wire or cable)
پوشاک [poshaak] and پوشاکه [poshaaka] clothes, clothing, attire
پوشاندن [poshaandan] **1** to cover, to shelter, to shield **2** to make a roof, to lay roofing (of a home) **3** to dress (someoneبه), to put on (something)
• عروس را لباس عروسی پوشاندن to put wedding clothes on the bride, to dress the bride in wedding clothes
پوش بالش [poshebaalees] pillowcase
پوشدار [poshdar]
• سیم – *technical* wire with insulation; cable
پوشش [poshesh] **1** roof, roofing ♦ تخته های کانکریتی - reinforced concrete ceilings, reinforced concrete floors **2** *technical* sheathing, planking; covering; pavement; roof
پوشیدن [poshidan] **1** to put on (oneself) **2** to wear (clothing, shoes, etc.) **3** to cover, to shelter, to protect
پوصله [pusala] and پوصوله [pusola] **1** surveying compass ♦ زاویه azimuth **2** compass
پوفک [pofak] **1** ☞ پفک **2** (also ز ن د ه -) shaving, shavings
پوقانه [poqaana] **1** urinary bladder of an animal (dried and inflated) **2** bubbles (e.g., in water) **3** an inflated ball, balloon
پوک [pok] **1** empty on the inside, hollow; inflated ♦ درون درخت است – This is a hollow tree. **2** friable, loose, flabby; rotten **3** empty, vapid, dull ♦ گپ - empty words, foolish words ◊

پ

آدم – dawdler, apathetic person; lout
• گپهای – زدن to talk nonsense, to convey nonsense
پوک گری [pokgaree] *slang* being obnoxious and showoff
پول [pul] 1 money, finances ♦ سیاه - small copper coins 2 pul (small Afghan coin equal to one-hundredth of an afghani) 3 riches, wealth, fortune
پولاد [polaad] 1 ☞ فولاد 2 *masculine proper name* Pulad, Pulat
پولادریزی [polaadreezi] ☞ فولادریزی
• فابریکه – steel foundry, steel mill
پولادی [polaadi] and پولادین [poladin] steel *adjective*; made of steel; made of damask steel, damask steel *adjective*
پولدار [puldaar] 1 having money, moneyed 2 rich, well-to-do
پولک [pulak] 1 sparkles, spangles, small shiny discs (for adornment) 2 *technical* small round gasket, washer
پولیپ [polip] *medicine* polyp
پولی تخنیک [politakhnik] 1 polytechnical 2 (also مؤسسه-) polytechnical institute
پولیس [polis] 1 police ♦ تهانه- police post ◊ سرمآمور - chief of police 2 policeman, police officer
پولیسی [polisi] 1 police *adjective* ♦ دریشی - police uniform 2 detective ♦ داستانهای - detective stories
پولی کلنیک [poliklenik] and پولی کلینیک [poliklinik] olyclinic, dispensary ♦ نسایی - maternity consultation center or clinic
پوند [paund] 1 pound sterling 2 pound (measure of weight)
پوهاند [pohand] pohand (high scholarly rank in Kabul University), professor
پوهنتون [pohantun] 1 university ♦ کابل - Kabul University 2 academy (educational institution) ♦ حربی - military academy
پوهندوی [pohandoy] pohandoy (scholarly rank in Kabul University that corresponds to senior instructor of a department)
پوهنزی [pohanzáy] faculty / department ♦ ادبیات - literary faculty or department
پوهنمل [pohanmal] pohanmal (scholarly rank in Kabul University that corresponds to docent)
پوهنوال [pohanwaal] pohanwal (scholarly rank in Kabul University; lower than a professor)
پوهنیار [pohanyaar] instructor (of higher educational institution); assistant, lecturer
پوهیالی [pohiaalay] junior instructor (rank)
په [pa (h)] *interjection* 1 Bah! / Well, well! ♦ په،عجب آدمی است Well, he is a strange person! 2 (also په په) Nice work! / Well done!
• په،چه لباس مقبولی است Oh, what a pretty / beautiful dress!
پهره [pahra (and) payra] 1 sentry, watch; guard 2 *obscure* eighth part of a day
• کردن - to guard, to make rounds (as a watch or patrol); to protect, to stand guard
پهره دار [pahradaar (and) payradaar] guard *adjective*; patrol *adjective*; sentry *adjective*
پهره دار خانه [pahradaarxaana (and) payradarxana] sentry box; guard post
پهره داری [pahradaari (and) payradaari] carrying out sentry duty, carrying out guard duty ♦ وظیفه - guard duty
پهلو [pahlu] 1.1 side ♦ راست - right side 1.2 lateral side, edge; wing (of a building) 1.3 *military* flank 1.4 side (of a problem), aspect 2.1 (also در-) at, near, by, beside, next to *denominative preposition* ♦ من نشست - He sat next to me. 2.2 (also از-) past, by ♦ از - آنها تیر شدیم We went past them. / We went by them.
• دادن - to give backing, support, or encouragement, to help
• زدن - to complete, to vie
• گرداندن/(با،به) - به - 1 to turn from side to side 2 to mill the wind; to discuss something for too long, to waste time in discussion
• غلتیدن – به - از to turn oneself from side to side, to be turned from side to side
خود را به یک پهلو انداختن [khud-raa-ba-yak-pahloo-andaakhtan] *idiom* (*literally*: to lie down on one's side) to be lazy (to make up excuses for not working)
پهلوان [pahlawaan] athlete; wrestler
پهلوانی [pahlawaani] wrestling
پهلوبندی [pahlubandi] support, backing, help
• کردن - to give support, backing, or help (به)
پهلودار [pahludaar] containing a hint; ambiguous (about speech, words)
پهلوداری [pahludaari] jamb (of door, window)
پهلوسبز [pahlusabz] *colloquial* a person from whom one can enrich himself (in something)
پهن [pah (a)n] 1 broad, spacious, roomy 2 flat; even, level, smooth ♦ زمین - level terrain ◊ طبق - shallow dish, dinner plate
• کردن - 1 to spread (e.g., influence) 2 to spread (rumors, etc.) 3 to make level, to make smooth; to flatten
پهناور [pahnaawar] broad; vast; immense, unbounded ♦ دریای - wide sea ◊ مملکت - vast country
پهناوری [pahnaawari] width, breadth; vastness; broad scale
پی [pay] ¹ 1 footprint, track 2.1 (also در پی) after, following, immediately after (behind) *denominative preposition* 2.2 for *denominative preposition* ♦ پی زغال رفت He went for coal.
• پی بردن to understand, to surmise; to notice
• پی کردن *regional* to measure the depth (of a river)
• در پی داشتن to have (something) as a consequence, to lead to ♦ این خشک سالی قحطی درپی دارد This drought will lead to hunger.
• پی کور کردن ☞ پی غلط کردن
• پی کسی (چیزی) رفتن 1 to go in someone's footsteps, to follow after someone or something 2 to be someone's follower
• پی کسی (چیزی) فرستادن to send for someone or something
• پی کور کردن to cover up tracks or traces, to confuse tracks or traces
• پی گم کردن to lose the track, to be thrown off the track
پی [pay] ² *anatomy* tendon, sinew; vein, nerve; ligament, chord
• پی کردن to cut down to the roots, to fell (a tree, etc.)
پی [pi] ☞ پیه
پیاپی [paiaapay] ☞ پی درپی
پیاده [piyada] 1.1 foot *adjective*, unmounted, going on foot 1.2 infantry *adjective* ♦ عسکر - the infantry, infantry *noun* 2.1 pedestrian 2.2 courier, messenger, errand boy 2.3 (also – عسکر and - قشون) infantry *noun* ♦ بحری - naval infantry, marines 2.4 (also - نفر) infantryman 2.5 *chess* pawn 3 on foot ♦ آمدیم - We came on foot.
• کردن - to land (an assault group or team)

پیاده رو [piyaadaraw] 1 footpath 2 sidewalk, pavement

پیادگی [piyaadagi] work of a messenger courier, of an errand boy
- کردن - to work as a messenger, courier, or errand boy

پیاز [piyaaz] 1 onion ♦ دشتی - wild onion ◊ موش - medicinal root 2 bulb (of plants)

پیاز کسی بیخ گرفتن [pyaaz-kasay-baykh-gereftan] idiom (literally: one's onion to have root) to become rich

پیازی [piyaazi] reddish-brown, of the color of an onion peel; reddish, rust-colored

پیاله [piyaala] 1 piyala, cup ♦ گلی - ceramic cup, piyala made of calcined clay 2 bowl

پیام [payaam] ☞ پیغام

پیانو [piaano] piano
- زدن (نواختن) - to play the piano

پیانونواز [piaanonawaaz] and پیانیست [pianist] pianist

پیاوه [pyaawa] vegetarian soup made of vegetables (seasoned with fried onions or garlic)

پی بر [paybor]
- شدن - colloquial to be cut down, to be cut off at the roots
- کردن - to cut down, to cut off at the roots

پیپ [pip] zinc container or can (for oil, gasoline); container, carboy; can, canister, tank

پایپ [paip] 1 rubber tube or tubing; flexible hose; hose ♦ حریق - fire hose ◊ کرمچی - canvas hose 2 ☞ پایپ

پیت [pit] peat

پیتاو [peetaaw] ☞ پتاو

پیچ [peech]¹ 1 present tense stem پیچیدن 2.1 curve; bend; turn; zigzag 2.2 coil, loop (of wire) 2.3 lock, curl (of hair) 2.4 threading, thread (of screw) 2.5 screw, wood screw, bolt ♦ چهار رخ - bolt with four-sided head ◊ سرگل - roundhead screw ◊ مخروطی - screw with conical head ◊ کانکریت - foundation bolt, holding-down bolt ◊ خشت و - bolts and nuts 2.6 move or hold (in wrestling)
- خوردن - 1 to curl, to meander, to coil, to be twisted 2 to loop, to turn, to swing (about a road, etc.)
- دادن - 1 to twist transitive, to spin transitive 2 to wind, to screw, to turn a screw 3 to wrap (something in paper, etc.) 4 colloquial to torment, to drive to exhaustion
- کردن - 1 to screw in, to turn, to turn tight, to tighten (bolt, etc.) 2 sports to execute a hold (in wrestling) 3 ☞ خوردن-
- کشیدن - to unscrew, to loosen

پیچ [peech]² 1 colic (in the intestines) 2 disorder or upset (of stomach)

پیچ در پیچ [pecapec] ☞ پیچ در پیچ

پیچاندن [peechaandan] 1 to roll, to wrap (in something در), to wrap up (with something در) 2 to bind; to wind (around); to turn (around)

پیچتاب [peechtaab] and پیچتو [pechtaw] technical screwdriver

پیچدرپیچ [peechdarpeech] 1 twisting, winding ♦ راه - winding road, meandering road 2 intertwined, confused 3 complex, complicated; tangled, intricate ♦ مسئله - complicated question, difficult problem
- کردن - to complicate; to confuse; to tangle

پیچش [peechesh]¹ medicine diarrhea; dysentery

پیچش [peechesh]² colloquial quarrel, conflict; argument

پیچک [peechak] 1 skein, ball (of thread, yarn) 2 reel; spool

پیچکاری [peechkaari] prick, injection
- کردن - to prick, to inject, to make an injection

پیچکش [peechkash] technical 1 die (for making threads on bolts, screws, etc.) 2 ☞ پیچ تاب

پیچوتاب [peechotaab] 1 curves, zigzags, turns 2 complexities, complications, difficulties 3 experiences, disturbances ♦ زندگی بسیار – دارد a life full of experiences
- خوردن - 1 to make a curve, to make a turn 2 to writhe (with pain, etc.)

پیچ وخم [peechokham] curve, zigzag

پیچه [picha] 1 bang, forelock 2 lock, curl, ringlet

پیچه پرک [pichaparak] lock, curl of hair (placed at the temples)

پیچه سفید [pichasafeed] colloquial 1 old woman, woman with gray at the temples 2 gray-haired, gray-headed feminine adjective

پیچیدگی [peechidagi] ☞ پیچیده گی

پیچیدن [peechidan] 1 to twist transitive intransitive, to wind transitive intransitive; to twirl transitive intransitive, to wind round transitive intransitive, to turn tight, to tighten; to coil transitive intransitive 2 to wrap, to be wrapped (in something در،میان) 3 to wrap around; to wind round (something بر،به) ♦ دستمال سرخی به کمر پیچیده بود He wound a red sash around his waist. 4 to turn, to make a turn ♦ موتر بطرف راست پیچید The vehicle turned to the right. 5 to delve deeply (into a matter), to go into detail ♦ دیگر به جزیات نمی پیچیم We won't go into details. 6 colloquial to have a quarrel, to have an argument, to get into an argument (because of something, over something سر)

پیچیده [peechida] 1 past participle پیچیدن 2 complex, complicated, confused, tangled; unclear

پیچیده گی [peechidagi] 1 difficulty, complication 2 confusion; intricacy ♦ این کار خیلی-دارد colloquial There is much that is not understood in this matter. 3 strained relations; quarrel, conflict ♦ بین آنها-پیدا شده است A conflict arose between them.

پیخ [pikh] spur (on a rooster)
- زدن - colloquial 1 to cut (someone) off rudely (in a conversation) 2 to make biting or caustic remarks

پیخال [pikhal] guano, bird droppings

پیدا [payda] 1 visible, noticeable 2 evident, clear, obvious 3 found, detected, discovered 4 extracted, procured, obtained; acquired
- شدن- 1 (also بودن-) to be clear, to be obvious; to appear, to follow ♦ طوریکه ازنامه اش-است as it appears from his letter 2 to appear, to manifest itself, to arise, to be detected, to be discovered 3 to be found, to turn up, to appear, to come up ♦ از این نمد حالا-نمیشود You won't find such thick felt nowadays. 4 to be found, to be obtained; to be acquired ♦ جلغوزه در کوههای افغانستان – میشود Pine nuts are found in the mountains of Afghanistan.
- کردن - 1 to find, to discover, to detect 2 to procure, to obtain, to get; to acquire
- اعتبار کردن to acquire authority or prestige

پیداگر [paydaagar] a person who earns money, one who has earnings; breadwinner ♦ این آدم خوب-است This person makes a good living. / This person makes good money.

پیداوار [paydaawaar] product produced; output, products ♦ اصلی افغانستان جوگندم ومیوه- است The main products of Afghanistan are wheat, barley and fruit.

پیدایش [paydaayesh] 1 appearance, origin, formation ♦ حیات - بروی زمین origin of life on earth 2 production, output; extraction
• داشتن - to be found; to be obtained ♦ این پرنده در ولایت کاپیسا زیاد – دارد In the province of Kapisa this bird is found in abundance.
پی درپی [paydarpay] 1 following one after the other, continuous ♦ باضربه های دشمن را مغلوبکرد He defeated the enemy / opponent striking him blow after blow. 2.1 one after the other, in a row ♦ سگرت میکشید - He smoked one cigarette after another. 2.2 continuously, continually, incessantly ♦ میخندیدند - They laughed incessantly.
پیر [pir] 1 old, elderly ♦ زن - old woman 2.1 old man, aged man, elder 2.2 sheikh, head of a religious sect 2.3 pir, spiritual mentor or tutor ♦ طریقت - pir, spiritual leader of Sufis
پیراهن [peeraahan] 1 shirt 2 dress ♦ خواب - (woman's) nightgown ◊ کمرچین - shirt with gathers in back
پیراهن وتنبان [peeraahanotomb an] shirt and trousers (men's as well as women's clothes worn at home consisting of roomy trousers that narrow toward the bottom and a long shirt)
پیراهن جان [peraahanejaan] slang (literally: one's own shirt) buddy, a close friend
پیراهن کهنه کردن [peraahan-kohna-kardan] idiom (to wear-out a shirt) to have experience
پیرایش [piraayesh] adorning, decoration (of somebody or something with something)
پیرایه [piraaya] literary decoration; attire, dress
پیرزن [pirzan] 1 old woman 2 metaphor universe
پیرمرد [pirmard] old person, old man
پیرن [peeran] colloquial ☞ پیراهن
پیرن وار [peeranwaar] dress length
پیرن وتنبان [peeranotombaan] colloquial ☞ پیراهن وتنبان
پیرو [pairaw] follower; adherent ♦ پیروان دین اسلام followers of Islam
پیروی بچه ادی [peroye-bache-aday] slang (literally: Pero the son of Aday) good time Charlie, happy-go-lucky
پیروز [peeroz] 1 victorious, triumphant; triumphal 2 successful
پیروزی [peerozi] victory, triumph
پیروی [pairawi] 1 following (after someone or something) 2 following, adhering to (something), observing (something), keeping (something) 3 following a course, carrying out (policy, etc.) 4 law conducting a case
• کردن - 1 to follow (after someone, something)(از،را) 2 to follow, to adhere to, to observe (از) 3 to follow a course, to carry out (a policy) ♦ از سیاست صلح جویانه – میکنند They are carrying out a peaceloving policy.
• (در); کسی را کردن - to be someone's follower (in something); to imitate someone (in something) (در) ♦ در شعر - بیدل را میکرده است In poetic works he imitated Bedil.
پیری [piri] old age; extreme old age
پیریزی [paireezi] 1 erecting, laying a foundation 2 foundation, creation
• کردن - 1 to erect, to lay a foundation 2 to found, to create
پیزار [paizaar] paizars (type of local Afghan shoes with turned up toes)
پیزاره [paizara] socle ♦ دیوار - socle of a wall

پیزن [paizan] obscure 1 going in track [of], searching 2 pursuer, persecutor
پیس [pees] 1.1 spots on the skin 1.2 eczema 2.1 having spots on the skin 2.2 suffering from eczema
پستون [piston] ☞ پستون
پیسه [paisa] 1 money 2 paisa (small copper coin)
• یک - شدن colloquial to disgrace oneself, to bring shame upon oneself
پیسه خود را کشیدن [paise-khud-raa-kashidan] idiom (literally: to bring the money back) to break even (in business)
پیسه خور [paisakhor] bribe-taker; usurer, extortioner
پیسه دار [paisadar] moneyed, well-to-do
پیسه سوزانک [paisasozaanak] colloquial 1 an expensive, but useless, thing 2 waste of money
پیسه گک [paisagak] technical gasket ♦ چرمی - leather gasket
پیش [peesh] ¹ 1 front, forepart, front part (of something) 2.1 front, frontal, situated ahead, located in front (of something) 2.2 former, past ♦ در زمان - in former times 3.1 (also به) forward ♦ بروید - Go forward! 3.2 (also از پیش) earlier, before, formerly, before this, up to this 4 denominative preposition 4.1 (also-در) at, near, next to; ahead of, in front of ♦ کلکین - in front of the window, at the window, by the window 4.2 in the presence of (someone), in the possession of (someone) ♦ قلم من - او است He has my pen. / My pen is with him / in his possession. 4.3 in the opinion of (someone); for (someone) ♦ من - in my opinion ◊ کورچه سرخ چه بور - proverb To a blind man it's all the same color. 5 (first component of compound words with meanings) 5.1 completed or taking place early ♦ پیش رس precocious; early-ripening 5.2 located or going ahead ♦ پیش جنگ military vanguard
• روی - ☞ پیشروی [peesheroy] 2
• از - before, ahead of, in front of compound preposition ♦ از این - before this, earlier, formerly
• از آن (این) که ... - until; before compound conjunction ♦ از وقت - prematurely, ahead of time
• آمدن colloquial 1 to approach, to draw near [to] 2 to protrude, to jut out 3 to begin to heal, to heal (about a wound)
• آوردن - 1 to move (something) up, to move (something) towards (oneself, something) 2 to push forward, to stick out; to thrust out
• بردن - 1 to push forward, to move forward, to promote, to develop 2 to accomplish, to realize, to put into practice
• رفتن - to be advanced, to be promoted, to be developed, to progress
• شدن - 1 to be nominated, to be proposed (e.g., about a matter, question) 2 to happen, to arise ♦ مشکلات - شد Difficulties arose.
• کردن - 1 to present, to deliver; to offer to give 2 to create (difficulties), to put obstacles in the way 3 to shut, to close (a door) 4 to make (a quotation), to quote
• گرفتن - 1 to begin, to start; to undertake 2 to carry out (a policy)
پیش [peesh] ² pesh (name of diacritical mark """, which signifies the short vowel "o")
پیشاب [peeshaab] urine
• کردن - to urinate
پیشاب دان [peeshaabdaan] anatomy urinary bladder

68

پیشاپیش [peeshaapeesh] in front of (someone), ahead of (someone) *denominative preposition*

پیش آمد [peeshaamad] 1 treatment; approach; conduct, behavior 2 incident, event
- کردن 1 to treat (someone, kindly, harshly, etc.); to have an approach, to have a point of view (با) 2 to occur, to happen, to take place

پیشانی [peeshani] 1 forehead, brow ♦ نان و پیاز - باز *proverb* He who is poor lives without care. (*Literally*, He who eats bread and onions doesn't frown.) 2 fate, fortune
- ترش کردن to frown, to knit one's brow

پیشانی باز [peeshaanibaaz] 1 happy, carefree 2 affable, friendly

پیشانی ترش [peeshaanitorsh] 1 gloomy, sullen; burdened with cares 2 unfriendly, ungracious

پیشانی ترش [payshani-tursh] *colloquial* (*literally:* sour forehead) sourpuss

پیشانی واز [peeshaaniwaaz] ☞ پیشانی باز

پیشاوند [peeshaawand] ☞ پیشوند

پیش آهنگ [peeshaahang] 1 forward *adjective*, leading, vanguard *adjective*; going ahead, going in front 2.1 leader 2.2 point, leader (of column) 2.3 initiator, pioneer; discoverer

پیش برآمدگی [peeshbaraamadagi] protuberance; prominence, bulge
- کلکین *construction* window frame

پیشبرد [peeshbord] 1 realization, implementation execution, fulfillment ♦ پروژه - realization of (construction) project ◊ پروگرام - fulfillment of a program 2 development, growth ♦ اقتصاد - development of the economic structure / of economics

پیش بند [peeshband] 1 apron; bib 2 breast belts (of horse's harness), martingale

پیشبین [peeshbin] 1 sagacious, perspicacious, acute, shrewd, astute 2 sensible, prudent

پیش بینی [peeshbini] 1 foresight, prevision; forecast, prognosis 2 sagacity, perspicacity, shrewdness, astuteness; foresight, prudence
- شدن to be foretold, to be forecasted, to be foreseen
- کردن to foresee; to foretell, to predict; to envisage; to expect

پیش پاافتاده [peeshepaaoftaada] banal; hackneyed, trite, ordinary, commonplace ♦ مطلب - trite subject

پیش پای بین [peeshepaaybin] 1 shortsighted, limited, having a narrow horizon or perspective ♦ مثل خر - مباش *proverb* Don't be like an ass that looks (only) under its limbs. 2 pursuing one's own goals, thinking only about personal gain

پیش پایی [peeshpaayi] a blow with the front of the foot; a kick
- زدن to strike with the foot, to kick

پیش پریروز [peeshpariroz] two days ago; the day before yesterday

پیش پزک [peeshpazak] *colloquial* 1 jumping forward (in a conversation), interrupting (someone) 2 *rarely* ☞ پیشرس

پیش پزکی [peeshpazaki]
- نکو *colloquial* Don't jump ahead! / Don't interrupt!

پیشتاز [peeshtaaz] going ahead, vanguard *adjective* ♦ توده ها - going at the forefront of the masses, leading the masses

پیشتر [peeshtar] 1 earlier, before, formerly 2 above, earlier ♦ گفته شد که - earlier it was said that …

پیش جنگ [peeshjang] *military* vanguard

پیش خانه [peeshkhaana] 1 front part of a home; anteroom 2 goods sent on ahead (during a migration) 3 *historical* main part of a shah's train or caravan

پیشخدمت [peeshkhedmat] waiter; servant; footman

پیشخور [peeshkhor] and پیشخوره [peeshkhora] living beyond one's means (at the expense of future income); taking products on loan, on credit
- شدن to spend on food, to spend (against future income), to take on credit

پیشخوری [peeshkhori] 1 life beyond one's means (at the expense of future income) 2 taking on loan, on credit (e.g., grain against a future harvest)

پیش خیمه [peeshkhaima] tent (sent on ahead of a military unit on the march)

پیشدست [peeshdast] 1 succeeding, progressing ahead of others, passing ahead of, outstripping, leaving behind 2 swift, prompt

پیشدستی [peeshdasti] 1 outstripping; superiority 2 adroitness; quickness, promptness
- کردن 1 to outstrip, to outrun (someone در،از in something) 2 to interrupt (someone), to jump ahead 3 to achieve superiority; to outdo

پیشدو [peeshdaw] *colloquial* servant for small errands; errand boy

پیشرس [peeshras] 1 early-ripening; precocious; fast-ripening 2 early, premature ♦ زمستان- early winter

پیشرفت [peeshraft] 1 movement forward advance; development, growth, progress 2 success, achievement 3 *military* offensive, advance
- کردن 1 to develop *intransitive*, to progress 2 to have successes 3 *military* to advance

پیشرفته [peeshrafta] forward, advance leading, progressive, developed ♦ ممالک - the developed countries

پیشرو [peeshraw] 1 going in front, leading, advance ♦ شاگرد - صنف the first or leading pupil in a class 2 leader

پیشروی [peeshrawi] 1 ☞ پیشرفت 2 march, tour, cruise, military campaign ♦ پیشرویهای اسکندر campaigns of Alexander the Great

پیشروی [peesheroy] 1.1 front ♦ دندان- front tooth ◊ شیشه پیشروی windshield of vehicle 1.2 situated opposite, vis-à-vis 2 *denominative preposition* 2.1 in front [of] ♦ کتاب-من است The book is in front of me 2.2 in front of one, in (someone's) presence
- نمود view from the front, full face ♦ رسم - sketch of a facade

پیش زبان [peeshzobaan] *colloquial* unduly familiar; unceremoniously interrupting others

پیش زبانی [peeshzobaani] *colloquial* undue familiarity in conversation; interruption of others

پیش طاق [peeshtaaq] *literary* portal; arch

پیش قبض [peeshqabz] knife carried on a belt; dagger

پیشقدم [peeshqadam] 1 surpassing (others), going in front 2 leader, frontrunner, foremost person; outstanding person
- ازکسی – بودن to be ahead of someone, to surpass someone, to outdo someone

پیش قراول [peeshqaraawol] advanced screen; patrol

پیشکار [peeshkaar] and پیشکاره [peeshkaara] 1 apprentice; assistant 2 steward; overseer (on an estate)

پ

پیش کش [peeshkash] gift; present
پیشکی [peeshaki] 1 an advance; a deposit 2 in advance, beforehand, as an advance
پیشکی [peeshki] called up into the army temporarily; draftee
پیشگاه [peeshgaah] literary
• در - in front [of], in the presence (of a high-ranking person); in front (of somebody) denominative preposition
پیش گفتار [peeshgoftaar] preface, foreword
پیشگویی [peeshgoyi] foretelling, prophecy, prediction; prophecy; prognosis, forecast
• کردن - 1 to prophesize, to predict 2 to make a forecast (of weather, etc.)
پیش گیری [peeshgiri] warning, prevention, suppression
• کردن - 1 to warn, to prevent; to suppress (از) 2 to hinder, to block (از)
پیش ناف [peeshnaaf] meat around the navel; peritoneum
پیشنهاد [peeshnehaad] offer, suggestion, proposal, idea; nomination
• کردن - to make a suggestion proposal; to present; to nominate
پیشوا [peeshwaa] 1 leader; head 2 (also اسلام- and دین-) head priest, imam
پیشواز [peeshwaaz]
• به‌کسی برآمدن (رفتن) to go out to meet someone, to meet someone
پیش وپس [peeshopas] moved (from its place), shifted; rearranged
• کردن - to move, to shift, to change places; to rearrange
پیشوند [peeshwand] grammar prefix ♦ فعل - preverb
پیشین [peeshin] 1 1 the time after noon (from 12 to 3 p.m.) ♦ - نماز afternoon namaz, afternoon worship 2 in the afternoon
پیشین [peeshin] 2 anatomy anus
پیشینانه [peeshinaana] colloquial at midday; in the afternoon; in the middle of the day
پیشینه [peeshina] grammar neologism preposition
پیشینیان [peeshiniyaan] literary ancestors forefathers; predecessors
پیغام [paighaam] 1 piece of news, news; report 2 message 3 appeal
• کردن - to pass on news, to report
• صادرکردن - to address by letter
پیغامبر [paighaambar] 1 bringing news; passing on a report 2.1 herald; messenger 2.2 ☞ پیغمبر
پیغله [peeghla] 1 girl, unmarried woman 2 salutation miss, mademoiselle
پیغمبر [paighambar] prophet; apostle ♦ گل- and بوته - arnebia (prophet flower)
پیک [paik] 1 herald; envoy; messenger ♦ آزادی - herald of freedom ◊ قاصدک بهار است The swallow is the herald of spring.
پیک [paik] 2 wine glass; goblet
پیک [peek] 1 awning 2 (also کلاه-) peak (of a cap)
پیکار [paikaar] literary battle
پیکال [paikaal] regional plot of land (planted in some kind of agricultural crop); a planted or sown field
پیکر [paikar] 1 figure; body ♦ بیجان - lifeless body, corpse 2 representation, depiction, portrayal; image; portrait 3 form; model 4 external appearance, look, aspect; character ♦ اقتصادی مملکت the character of the country's economic structure 5 obscure star, planet ♦ دو astronomy Gemini
پیکرتراشی [paikartaraashi] the art of sculpture (carving from stone)
پیکره [paikara] statue, sculpture
پیکنیک [peekneek] ☞ پکنیک
پیل [pil] 1 ☞ فیل
پیل [pil] 2 galvanic cell, primary cell; storage battery ♦ بطری - jar of storage battery ◊ خشک - dry cell
پیل [peel] colloquial from پهل
پیلبان [pilbaan] elephant keeper, kornak, elephant driver
پیلر [pilar] pillar ♦ سرحد - border post
پیل مرغ [pilmorgh] ☞ فیل مرغ
پیلوت [pilot] pilot; aviator ♦ اتوماتیکی - automatic pilot
پیله [pila] 1 (also کرم -) cocoon of silkworm 2 (also ابریشم -) silkworm
• پیله کشی ☞ تربیه-
پیله کشی [pilakashi] silkworm breeding
پیما [paimaa] 1 present tense stem پیمودن 2 (second component of compound words with meanings "going" / "moving" / "measuring off (distance)") ♦ بحرپیما mariner, seafarer
پیمان [paimaan] 1 promise; assertion 2 vow, oath 3 compact; agreement, contract, treaty 4 pact, accord ♦ عهدو - understanding; obligation
• بستن(کردن) - 1 to give [one's] word, to swear, to take an oath (با); to bet, to wager 2 to agree, to come to an agreement (با)
• باخود کردن to promise oneself; to take on an obligation
• عهدو کردن to conclude an alliance, to come to an agreement
پیمان شکن [paimaanshekan] not keeping one's word; violating an oath, breaking an agreement; perfidious, treacherous
پیمانه [paimaana] 1 measure, measuring vessel (container for measuring liquids and loose substances) ♦ باروت - measuring container for powder ◊ غله - measure for grain 2 degree, extent; size; scale ♦ به وسیع - on a broad scale 3 cup, bowl, goblet
• کردن - to measure, to measure off (by means of a measuring container) ♦ او پر شد - He has had his day. / His days are numbered.
پیمای [paimaay] ☞ پیما
پیمایش [paimaayesh] 1 gauging, measuring; measurement ♦ واحد - unit of measure ◊ وزن – واحد unit of weight, measure of weight 2 compiling an estimate, making an estimate; calculations, computations 3 an estimate
• کردن - a) to measure, to take a measurement b) to estimate the cost (of something); to compile an estimate (for construction, etc.)
پیمایشی [paimaayeshi] having to do with measuring, measurement ♦ واحد - unit of measure ◊ مرحله - کار عمارت preparatory stage of construction
پیمودن [paimudan] (present tense stem پیما [paimaa] and پیمای [paimay]) 1 to measure, to measure off (distance) 2 to go through, by, or across;, to drive through, by, or across; to swim through, by, or across
• مراتب چیزی را - to endure, to experience something
پین [peen] ☞ پن [pen]

پینکی [pinaki] *colloquial* drowsiness, somnolence
- رفتن - to doze, to be drowsy

پینکی [peenaki] *slang* cat-nap, power nap

پینه [pina] **1** a small patch, a patch **2** callus, corn
- بستن - to become calloused ♦ پایش - بسته است He got a corn on his foot.
- (کردن)زدن - to make patches, to patch up, to mend

پینه پینه [pinapina] all covered with patches, patched and repatched

پینه دوز [pinadoz] simple shoemaker

پینه سرزانو [penay-sare-zaano] *slang* (*literally:* knee patch) piece of crap, junk

پیوست [paiwast] **1.1** link, connection; fastening **1.2** joint; butt **2** joined, connected; fastened
- بودن - to be joined, to be connected; to abut, to adjoin
- شدن - **1** to associate [with]; to join [with]; (به،در) **2** to be joined, to be united, to unite ♦ (با) دوستانش با ما – شدند His friends joined us.
- باهم – شدن to be joined, to be linked; to be fastened
- کردن - to bind, to connect, to fasten; to couple; to join

پیوستگی [paiwastagi] **1** connection, cohesiveness, unity, togetherness **2** relation, dependence
- داشتن - **1** to be linked [with] (به), to be connected [with], to join **2** to have a relation [to], to depend [on] (به،با)

پیوستن [paiwastan] (*present tense stem* پیوند [paiwand]) **1** to be connected, to be joined; to close *intransitive*, to join **2** to connect; to join

پیوسته ابرو [paiwastaabru] with eyebrows that have grown together

پیوند [paiwand] **1** *present tense stem* پیوستن **2.1** tie, bond, connection ♦ ناگسستنی - indissoluble connection **2.2** connection, joint **2.3** grafting (of trees, plants) **2.4** *anatomy* joint; ligament **2.5** *grammar* copula
- داشتن ☞ in entry پیوستگی داشتن
- کردن - to graft (a plant), to make a graft
- گرفتن - to be grafted (about plants)
- باهم – دادن to join, to connect, to butt

پیوندی [paiwandi] **1** grafted (of plants) **2** *grammar neologism* agglutinative ♦ زبانهای - agglutinative languages

پیه [pih] grease; fat

پی هم [payeham] one after another; consecutively, continuously; in a row ♦ سالها - تیرمیشد The years passed one after the other.

ت
4th letter of the Dari alphabet

تا [taa]¹ (also تا به) to, up to; by *preposition* ♦ تا امروز up to today; by today ◊ از کابل تا هرات from Kabul to Herat

تا [taa]² **1** while; until *conjunction* ♦ تا زنده هستم با تو کمک خواهم کرد While I am alive, I will help you. **2.1** (also تا...که) that, so that; in order to ♦ آمدم تا(که)خبرتان رابگیرم I came [in order] to ask about your health. **2.2** as soon as, when ♦ تا که مرا دید خود را پنهان کرد As soon as he saw me, he did it himself [at once].
- تاآنجایکه and تاآنجاکه as far as, as much as *compound conjunction* ♦ تاآنجاکه من اطلاع دارم as far as I know…
- تاحدی که so that…; until, so *compound conjunction*
- تا وقتی(زمانی)که until *compound conjunction*

تا [taa]³ *colloquial* ☞ ته [tah] **2** down; downward; below
- تاوبالا ☞ تاوبالا
- تاشدن **1** to lower oneself down; to go down, to descend (from a roof, from a tree) **2** to alight from, to get out of (a vehicle, etc.) ♦ باش که تاشویم Stop, let us get out!
- تا کردن **1** to lower, to let down (a child from one's arms); to get (something) from above, to get (something) down ♦ تاکو Get [it]! (down from above) / Lower [it]! / Drop [it]! **2** to set down, to get (something) out (of a vehicle) **3** (also بارتاکردن) to unload (some kind of cargo, goods)

تا [taa]⁴ (a numerative in counting individual items) ♦ پنج تاتخم five eggs

تاب [taab]¹ **1** strength, force, steadfastness, staunchness **2** endurance, tenacity, staying power
- نیاوردن - not to endure, not to withstand; not to be in condition to resist or withstand (something) ♦ دشمن – حمله ما را ندارد The enemy did not withstand our attack.
- چیزی رانداشتن - not to stand (something) not to bear(something), not to endure (something) ♦ رفیق ما – مزاق را ندارد Our friend cannot take a joke.

تاب [taab]² **1** *present tense stem* تابیدن **2** light, radiance

تاب [taab]³
- تاب خوردن **1** to curl *intransitive*, to twine [about], to coil to roll up **2** to twist *intransitive*, to be twisted, to become twisted, to be screwed in **3** to wind *intransitive*, to be wound [around]
- دادن - **1** to curl, to spin, to twist *transitive* **2** to twist, to screw in *transitive* **3** to wind; to reel *transitive*

تابان [taabaan] giving off radiance, sparkling, twinkling, glittering; radiant, bright ♦ ماه - bright moon ◊ اشکهای - scalding tears

تابخانه [taabkhaana] ☞ اوه خانه

تابدار [taabdaar] curly (about hair)

تابستان [taabestaan] summer

تابش [taabesh] light; radiance, sparkling, sparkle, glitter, glare

تابع [taabe'] **1** subordinate, dependent; subject [to] **2** *mathematical* function
- جمله - *grammar* subordinate clause ♦ وقت – جمله temporal subordinate clause
- خود ساختن - to subdue, to subjugate

تابعیت [taabeiyat] **1** citizenship **2** dependence, subordination **3** *grammar* subordination
- قبول کردن - to become a citizen

تابلو [taablo] **1** picture, painting, canvas **2** sign, signboard, advertisement **3** table

تابلیت [taablet] table

تابناک [taabnak] ☞ تابان

تابوت [taabut] coffin; grave

تابه [taaba] large pan (for baking unleavened flatcakes)
- برک - brake drum

تابه خانه [taabakhaana] ☞ تاوه خانه

تابدان [taabadan] small window above a door (for ventilation, illumination)

تابه گی [taabagi]
- نان - unleavened flatcakes (baked on a large pan)

تابیدن [taabidan] ☞ تاب خوردن and تاب دادن in entry تاب³
- به خود - to stretch oneself

تاپه [taapa]¹ *colloquial* **1** mark, brand on a heap of threshed grain (placed there to prevent misappropriation) **2** seal,

71

ت

stamp **3** pattern, stencil (for tracing on fabric) **4** printed decorative fabric, kalamkar

تاپه [taapa] ² *colloquial* form, model (for casting, molding)

تات [taat] bast mat; bast matting; sackcloth, burlap

تأثّر [taassor] state of being moved or touched (emotionally); emotion; feeling

تأثیر [ta'sir] impression; effect, influence ♦ محیط بالای انسان - the effect of the environment on man or on a person

♦ (بالای،بر)(بخشیدن) کردن - **1** to make an impression, to touch **2** to have an effect, to influence

تاج [taaj] **1** crown **2** comb, crest (of a bird)

♦ تاج خروس ☞ **1** cock's comb **2** خروس -

تاج خروس [taj (e) xorus] *botany* amaranth, amaranthus

تاجدار [taajdaar] **1.1** crowned **1.2** crested, tufted, with a comb (of birds) **2** crowned head, monarach

تاجر [taajer] (*plural* تجار [tojjar]) dealer, merchant

تاجک [taajek] a Tajik

تاجکی [taajeki] **1** Tajik *adjective* **2** (also - زبان) Tajik language

تاخت [takht] gallop; galloping; hard run ♦ اسپ - horse's run, gallop ◊ سواران - race of riders, horse race

تاخت وتار و - تاراج ♦

♦ به - **1** at full gallop, at a gallop **2** at a run

♦ کردن - to set off at a gallop, to speed, to rush

تاختن [taakhtan] (*present tense stem* تاز [taaz]) **1** to set off at a gallop, to speed, to rush **2** to drive, to urge on (a horse) **3** to make a raid or foray, to attack, to assault **4** to criticze sharply, to attack (in an argument)

تاخت وتاز [taakhtotaaz] assault, raid; invasion, inroad

♦ کردن - to make an assault, to raid, to ravage

تاخرمنی [taakhermani] *colloquial* remainders of grain after threshing

تأخیر [ta'xir] delay, procrastination; postponement, deferment

♦ به - انداختن to put off, to postpone; to delay; to drag out

تادو [taadaw] *colloquial* ☞ تهداب

تأدیات [ta'diyaat] payments ♦ تجارتی - commercial payments

تأدیه [ta'diya (and) tadiya] payment, payment (of taxes); payment (of a check)

♦ کردن - to pay, to reimburse

تار [taar] ¹ **1** thread; string, twine ♦ خام - unbleached thread ◊ منجی - kenaf twine **2** string (of musical instrument) **3** (also -موی) hair, a hair **4** *textiles* warp

تاروپود ☞ وپود ♦

♦ دواندن - to spin a web (of a spider)

♦ کردن - to thread (a needle)

♦ گشتن - *colloquial* to become emaciated, to become withered or shriveled

♦ باکسی انداختن - *colloquial* to enter into secret or private relations with someone (friendly relations, intimate relations, etc.)

♦ جولا - spider's web

♦ قبرغه - rib

تار [taar] ² *literary* dark, gloomy; somber ♦ شب - dark night

تار [taar] ³ *music* tar

تار دواندن [taar-dawaandan] *idiom* (*literally*: to run string) to have an illegal connection or relationship

تاراج [taaraaj] pillage, plundering; robbery

♦ کردن - to pillage, to plunder, to loot, to commit robbery, to sack

تارپیچ [taarpech] *technical* threading, thread

تارپین [taarpin] turpentine

تارتابی [taartaabi]

♦ ماشین - spinning machine

تارتار [taartaar]

♦ شدن - to unravel (of fabric)

♦ کندن - to pull out hair by hair

تارتن [taartan] and ترتنک [taartanak] spider ♦ تار - spider's web, cobweb

تارریشی [taarreshi] spinning

تارک الدنیا [taarekoddonyaa] *literary* hermit, recluse

تارکش [taarkash] piece of fabric (usually an old piece from which they pull out the threads, twist them, and use them for sewing or embroidering)

تارکشی [taarkashi] hem stitch, openwork

تارکول [taarkol] asphalt, tar ♦ کاغذ - waterproof paper

تارو [taaru] francolin, partridge (bird)

تاروپود [taaropud] **1** *textiles* warp and woof **2** foundation, essence

تاروپیچ [taaropech] ☞ تارپیچ

تاروسوزن [taarosozan]

♦ دادن - *colloquial* to give consent to matchmaking for or the courting of one's daughter

تارومار [taaromaar]

♦ شدن - to be crushed, to be routed, to be destroyed

♦ کردن - to crush, to rout, to destroy

تارونار [taaronaar]

♦ شدن *colloquial* to waste away, to grow sickly (from yearning, grief, or sorrow)

تاری [taari] *regional* ☞ نخی

تاریخ [taarix (and) tarikh] **1** date ♦ نگارش مقاله - date an article was written **2** system of chronology **3** history ♦ افغانستان - history of Afghanistan **4** historical work; annals, chronicle

♦ بیهقی - "History" by Baihaqi

تاریخ دان [taarikhdaan] historian, expert in history

تاریخی [taarikhi] historical

تاریک [taarik] dark; gloomy; somber ♦ شب - dark night ◊ هوای - dust; twilight

تاریک ماه [taarikmaah]

♦ شب - dark night, moonless night

تاریکی [taariki] darkness, gloom

تاریکی خانه [taarikikhaana] darkroom (for developing film); photo laboratory

تاز [taaz] *present tense stem* تاختن

تازگی [taazagi] ☞ تازه گی

تازنی و بالازنی [tazanee-o-baalaazanee] *slang* (*literally*: lifting up and bringing down) insulting and praising (at the same time)

تازه [taaza] **1.1** fresh ♦ هوای - fresh air ◊ گل - fresh (unfaded) flower **1.2** recent, new ♦ خبر - news **2** just, quite recently

♦ بیرون آمده بود که ... - just, barely *compound conjunction* ♦ تازه که باران شروع شد He had barely left when the rain began.

♦ کردن - **1** to renovate, to refresh ♦ چلم را - to change the water for the water chestnut ◊ دل - *colloquial* to unburden one's soul **2** to fan (coals, the flame in a samovar, in a brazier, etc.) ♦ زغال را - کن Fan the coals!

ت

تازه دم [taazadam] not weary, not tired; fresh ♦ نیروی - *military* fresh forces

تازه کار [taazakaar] newcomer novice; beginner (in some matter or affair), inexperienced person

تازه گی [taazagi] freshness, novelty ♦ این کار - ندارد This is not new. / This is not original.

♦ به - و این در and - recently, the other day; just

تازه گیها [taazagihaa]

♦ در این- quite recently, a day or so ago

تازی [taazi] ¹ (also-سگ) hunting dog; borzoi, Russian wolfhound

تازی [taazi] ² *rarely* 1 Arab, Arabian *adjective* ♦ اسپ- Arabian horse 2 an Arab, an Arabian

تازیانه [taaziyaana] lash, whip, scourge

♦ زدن - to flog; to whip

تاس [taas] ¹ ☞ طاس

تاس [taas] ² bald ♦ سرش - است He has a bald head.

تاس [taas] ³ TASS (telegraph agency of the Soviet Union, news service)

تاسف [taassof] regret, feeling of sorrow or grief ♦ باکمال - with great regret, with sorrow

♦ خوردن - to regret; to grieve

تاسف انگیز [taassofangeez] and تأسف آور [taassofawar] evoking regret; sad, sorrowful

تأسیس [ta'sis] founding, creation, establishment

♦ کردن - to found, to create, to establish

تافتن [taaftan] (*present tense stem* تاب [taab]) 1 to heat, to make red hot 2 to shine, to beam

تاق [taaq] ¹ 1.1 odd, unpaired 1.2 unique; the only one of its kind ♦ احمد در پهلوانی - است Ahmad has no equal in wrestling. 2 odd number ♦ جفت است - "even-odd" (children's game)

تاق [taaq] ² ☞ طاق

تاقین [taaqin] *regional* type of hat or cap of gold fabric with decorations

تاک [taak] grapevine ♦ کوهی - wild grapes ◊ انگور میکند - The vine produced bunches of grapes.

تاک باغ [taakbaagh] vineyard, grape plantation

تاکتیک [taaktik] tactic, tactics

تاکداری [taakdaari] viticulture

تاکستان [taakestaan] *literary* vineyard

تاکوی [taakawi] basement, cellar

تأکید [ta'kid] 1 insistent assertion 2 confirmation, stress, emphasis 3 logical stress

♦ با (به) - insistently, urgently, categorically

♦ کردن - 1 to assert 2 to emphasize, to stress, to accent (را)

تأکیدی [ta'kidi] final, categorical, allowing no appeal ♦ حکم - categorical decision

♦ پیشوند – *grammar* imphatic prefix ♦ بگفت he said

تال [taal] ¹

♦ دادن - *colloquial* 1 to dawdle, to be slow; not to hurry ♦ چرا - میتی؟ Why are you dawdling? 2 to delay, to drag out (some matter)

تال [taal] ² a percussion musical instrument in the form of two copper bowls on which the rhythm is beaten

تالاب [taalaab] natural reservoir, pond

تالار [taalaar] large room (for receiving guests); hall, ballroom

تالاق [taalaaq] 1 (also سر-) crown (of the head) 2 top, summit, apex ♦ کوه - top of a mountain

♦ کسی رادر - خود نشاندن to burden yourself with someone, to put someone on your own neck

تالانه [taalaana] nectarine (variety of peach)

تالچی [taalchi] musician who plays the tal (☞ تال 2)

تالقداری [taaluqdaaree] *colloquial* (*literally:* belonging) wife

تالکار [taalkaar] *colloquial* (*literally:* a person who dawdle at work) lazy worker *derogatory*

تاله [taala]

♦ کردن - *colloquial* 1 to strew, to scatter, to throw about, to spread 2 to spread out, to lay, to lay out ♦ دسترخوان را - کو Spread the tablecloth! ◊ برگهای چای را در آفتاب - میکنند They spread tea leaves in the sun (to dry).

تألیف [ta'lif] 1 writing, composing (some kind of work) ♦ کتاب - writing a book 2 (*plural* تألیفات [ta'lifaat]) literary work

♦ کردن - to write, to compose

تام [taam(m)] full, absolute; perfect ♦ استقلال - complete independence, full sovereignty ◊ اکثریت - absolute majority ◊ عدد - *mathematical* whole number

تأمل [taammol] *literary* 1 considering, thinking over, reflection, meditation 2 hesitation, indecision

♦ کردن - 1 to reflect, to meditate, to think over, to consider 2 to hesitate, to waver, to vacillate

تأمین [ta'min] ensuring, providing, guaranteeing; satisfaction (of needs in something)

♦ احتیاجات کسی را - کردن to satisfy somebody's needs, to provide someone (with something از لحاظ …)

تان [taan] 1 (gen./acc.) you (dat. plural), to you *affixal pronoun, second person plural* ♦ گفتمتان I told you. 2 your *affixal pronoun, second person plural* ♦ کتابتان your book

تانستن [taanestan] *colloquial* ☞ توانستن

تانسل [taansol] *anatomy* tonsil

تانک [taank] ¹ *military* tank ♦ ثقیل - heavy tank ◊ خفیف - light tank ◊ نفر - tank crew member

تانک [tank] ² cistern; tank; reservoir, vessel ♦ آب - reservoir for water

♦ پترول - and تیل - gasoline pump; filling station, refueling station

♦ موتر – tank truck, gasoline tanker

تانکر [taankar] tanker ♦ تانکرهای تیل oil tankers (ships)

تانکه [taanka] *regional* two-wheel cab

تانکی [taanki] gas tank (in motor vehicle)

تانه [taana] 1 *colloquial* ☞ تهانه 2 *colloquial* ☞ طعنه

تأنی [taanni] *literary* absence of hurry, lack of hurry; sluggishness

♦ با - کار کردن to work slowly, without hurrying

تأنیث [ta'nis]

♦ علامه - *grammar* indicator of female gender

تاو [taaw] *colloquial* ☞ تاب 1, 2, 3

تاوان [taawaan] 1 compensation, recovery of a loss, reimbursement of a loss 2 (also جنگ-) contribution 3 damage, loss, losses ♦ مالی- material loss, pecuniary 4 *colloquial* (also گردن-) 4.1 burden, burdening 4.2 unprofitable business; waste (of something)

♦ دادن - to reimburse the cost (of something), to pay, to compensate

♦ شدن - *colloquial* to be unprofitable (for someone سر) ♦ این مال سر ما - شد These goods were unprofitable for us.

73

ت

- کردن (کشیدن) to incur damage, to suffer a loss
- چیزی را گرفتن to receive reimbursement, compensation for something
- به گردن کسی شدن and گردن کسی شدن- 1 to be unprofitable for someone 2 to become a burden to someone, to burden someone

تاواندار [taawaandaar] having suffered damage, having incurred a loss

تا و بالا [taa-o-baalaa] slang (literally: up and down) good and bad ♦ تا و بالا گفتن to exchange insults

تاوانی [taawaani] colloquial 1 ☞ تاواندار 2 unprofitable

تاور [taawar] technical tower, derrick

تاوه [taawa] colloquial ☞
- به – نشستن to suffer very much, to find no solace (from grief)

تاوه خانه [taawakhaana] obscure 1 device under the floor to heat living quarters 2 living quarters (heated from under the floor), room (heated from under the floor)

تاوه دان [tawadaan] colloquial ☞ تانه دان

تاوه گی [taawagi] colloquial ☞ تابه گی

تاویز [taawiz] colloquial ☞ تعویذ

تاویل [ta'wil] literary explanation, interpretation (e.g., of a dream); commentary

تأهل [taahhol] literary marriage, family life

تای [taay] colloquial ☞ ته

تایپ [tayp] typing (on a typewriter)
- کردن to type (on a typewriter)

تایپست [taaypest] typist; a person typing on a typewriter

تای دیگی [taaydeegi] colloquial ☞ ته دیگی

تایر [taayr] motor vehicle tire

تایرکش [taayrkash] jack

تأیید [ta'yid] 1 confirmation 2 corroboration, backing, encouragement
- کردن 1 to confirm 2 to give backing, to give encouragement

تب [tab] 1 heat; high temperature 2 fever ♦ تب محرقه typhus ◊ تب نوبتی intermittent fever; malaria
- داشتن 1 to have a fever, to have a high temperature 2 to be sick with a fever

تبادل [tabaadol] تبادله

تبادلوی [tabaadolawi] exchange ♦ ارزش - economics exchange value

تبادله [tabaadola] exchange, interchange ♦ افکار - exchange of opinions ◊ جنسی - economics barter
- کردن to exchange, to swap

تبار [tabaar] literary 1 family, kin, tribe 2 relationship, kinship 3 relatives; family

تباشیر [tabaashir] 1 white clay, chalk 2 pith of bamboo or reed (used as medicine)

تباشیری [tabaashiri]
- گروپ frosted lightbulb

تباه [tabaah]
- شدن to perish, to die ♦ در نتیجه خشکی باغ شد The garden died as a result of a / the drought.
- کردن to ruin, to spoil; to destroy

تباهکار [tabaahkaar] villain, scoundrel, undoer; destroyer, wrecker

تباهی [tabaahi] death, destruction, loss, wreck, ruin; annihilation, destruction, demolition

تباین [tabaayon] contradiction; difference ♦ افکار - opposition of views

تبتی [tebati] 1 Tibetan adjective 2.1 a Tibetan 2.2 (also- زبان) the Tibetan language 3 (also- اسپ) Tibetan (breed of horse distinguished by short stature and reduced speed and endurance)

تبحر [tabahhor] literary profound knowledge (of something); erudition

تبخال [tabkhaal] and تبخاله [tabkhaala] rash (on the lips), fever blister

تبخیر [tabkhir] evaporation

تبدل [tabaddol] transformation, conversion, change

تبدیل [tabdil] 1 change, transformation 2 ☞ شدن
- تبدیلی 1 to be changed, to be transformed 2 to be replaced [by]
- کردن 1 to change, to transform 2 to replace

تبدیلی [tabdili] 1 substitution replacement, change 2 transfer, job transfer ♦ پرسونل - replacement of personnel

تبر [tabar] ax

تبراق [tabraaq] 1 bag, rucksack (with laces) 2 soldier's knapsack

تبرزین [tabarzin] rarely saddle hatchet used in combat or battle; poleax; dervish's hatchet

تبرغان [tabarghaan] marmot

تبریک [tabrik] congratulation
- گفتن to congratulate (someone)(را) (on something) ♦ به مناسبت عید نوروز به شما – میگویم I congratulate you on nowruz.

تبریکی [tabriki] and تبریکیه [tabrikiya] congratulatory, salutatory ♦ تلگرام - congratulatory telegram

تبسم [tabassom] smile
- کردن to smile

تبشکن [tabshekan] and تبگردان [tabgardaan] 1 febrifugal, antipyretic 2 febrifuge, antipyretic

تبصره [tabsera] comment, explanation, commentary

تبعه [taba'] (plural اتباع [atbaa]) subject, citizen ♦ افغانستان - citizen of Afghanistan

تبعید [tab'id] banishment, deportation; exile
- کردن to banish, to deport; to exile

تبعیدگاه [tab'idgaah] place of banishment, place of exile

تبعیض [tab'iz] discrimination ♦ نژادی - racial discrimination

تبق [tabaq] and تبک [tabak] veterinary foot-and-mouth disease

تب لرزه [tabelarza] malaria

تبلور [tabalwor] chemistry crystallization

تبلیغ [tabligh] (plural تبلیغات [tabliqat]) propagandizing, propaganda ♦ تبلیغات انتخاباتی pre-election campaign
- کردن to propagandize

تبنگ [tabang] 1 tray (of hawker, peddler) 2 counter (in store, shop)
- کلکین construction window frame

تبنگ والا [tabangwaalaa] colloquial hawker, peddler

تبه [tabah] ☞ تباه

تبیله [tabila] colloquial ☞ طویله

تپ [tap]¹ roof, top (of a carriage, vehicle)

تپ [tap]² 1 clap; clapping 2 knock, tap; footfall, patter of feet ♦ تپ تپ ☞ تپ تپ

تپ [tap]³ 1 (also تپ دست شویی) bowl for washing, sink 2 (also تپ غسل) bath

تپ [tap] *colloquial* losses; loss (in trade)
- تپ خوردن to suffer a loss, to lose in trading, to be ruined in trade
- تپ زدن to swindle, to swindle (a certain sum of money)
- چیزی را به گردن کسی تپ کردن to foist something off on someone at an exorbitant price

تپاک گرفتن [tapaak-gereftan] *idiom* to become antsy, can't wait

تپاکی [tapaaki] *colloquial* a naughty child

تپانچه [tapaancha] *rarely* 1 slap on the ear, slap in the face 2 revolver, pistol

تپاندن [tapaandan] *colloquial* to tire (someone) out, to wear (someone) out, to drive (someone) to exhaustion

تپ تپ [taptap] *colloquial* 1 clap-clap, slap-slap, bang-bang (sound of two thngs striking each other) 2 tramp-tramp, tap-tap, pitter-patter (sound of feet walking, striding, etc.)
- پای - threat (usually empty); attempt to intimidate or scare
- کردن - 1 to lull, to rock a baby to sleep (by patting him) 2 to try to imtimidate or scare

تپش [tapesh] 1 beating (of the heart); pulsation 2 fluttering, quivering
- کردن - 1 to beat (concerning the heart); to pulsate 2 to try with all one's might, to strive desperately (for something) 3 to flutter, to quiver

تپک [tapak] iron shovel (for leveling soil)
- ماشین – کنکریت vibrator (for tamping or compacting wet concrete)

تپ و تاریک [tapotaarik] *colloquial* very dark, pitch dark

تپ و تلاش [tapotalaash] *colloquial* efforts, endeavors, cares, troubles
- افتادن به – to begin trouble or cares

تپه [tepa] hill, knoll; barrow

تپه [tapa]
- کردن - 1 to spread, to smear (with grease paint) 2 to botch (something) (concerning an artist) ♦ رنگها را - کرده است He applied the paints [helter-skelter].

تپه تویی [tapatuyi] and تپه تولی [tapatuli] *colloquial* by sense of touch, to the touch; blindly
- کردن - 1 to search (for something) by sense of touch, to fumble about, to rummage about 2 to go blindly

تپه گل [tapagol] *colloquial* with flowers, with a flowery design (about fabric) ♦ پیراهن - flowery dress

تپیدن [tapidan] 1 to beat (concerning the heart); to pulsate; to tremble to quiver 2 ☞ پش کردن in entry تپش

تتبع [tatabbo'] (*plural* تتبعات [tatabbo'at]) investigation research, analysis

تتر پاره [tatarpaara] *slang* riffraff

تتله [totla] *colloquial* stutterer, stammerer ♦ زبان - having a thick tongue ◊ او – است He stutters / stammers.
- شدن - to stutter, to stammer (about a person)

تتله گی [totlagi] *colloquial* stuttering stammering

تتو [toto] *colloquial children's speech* doggie, little dog

تثبیت [tasbit] 1 strengthening; fastening, attachment (to something) 2 consolidation, establishment; stabilization
- شدن - 1 to be fastened, to be attached (to something), to be secured 2 to become firmly established, to be stabilized

تثنیه [tasniya] 1 doubling 2 *grammar* dual number

تجار [tojjar] *plural of* تاجر

تجارت [tejaarat (and) tojaarat] trade, commerce ♦ خارجی - foreign trade
- کردن - to trade, to conduct trade

تجارت خانه [tejaaratkhaana] 1 trading firm, commercial firm 2 trade delegation

تجارتی [tejaarati] trade, trading, commercial ♦ معامله - trade transaction, trading operation

تجاوز [tajaawoz] 1 going beyond limits; exceeding (authority, etc.) 2 invasion, incursion, aggression 3 encroachment
- کردن - 1 to go beyond the limits (از); to exceed (authority, etc.) 2 to invade; to commit aggression
- به حقوق کسی – کردن to encroach on someone's rights

تجاوزکار [tajaawozkaar] aggressor

تجاویز [tajaawiz] *plural of* تجویز

تجاهل [tajaahol]
- کردن - *literary* to pretend to be an ignoramus, to feign ignorance, to feign to be ignorant

تجدد [tajaddod] 1 new ideas, new trends 2 innovation, novelty

تجدد پسند [tajaddodpesand] advocate of everything new; innovator

تجدید [tajdid] 1 renovation, renewal (of something) 2 resumption, repetition 3 rehabilitation, restoration
- انتخابات - election
- ساختمان - and بنا - rebuilding, reconstruction (of a building)
- نظر - change in a point of view, reconsideration (of something)
- کردن - 1 to renovate, to renew, to refresh 2 to resume, to repeat
- نظر کردن - (در ، در مورد); to change a point of view

تجربه [tajreba] 1 test, trial, experiment 2 experience, habit; practice
- داشتن - to have experience, to be experienced
- کردن - 1 to check, to test 2 to conduct a test, to conduct an experiment

تجربه کار [tajrebakaar] experienced; well versed (in something)

تجربه وی [tajrebawi] test *adjective*, experimental ♦ علوم - applied sciences

تجرد [tajarrod] *literary* 1 seclusion, solitariness; asceticism, life of a hermit 2 celibacy, unmarried life, single life

تجرید [tajrid] *literary* 1 separation, isolation 2 abstracting; abstraction

تجزیه [tajziya] analysis (in various meanings) ♦ جمله - *grammar* parsing of a sentence ◊ خون - analysis of blood ◊ کیمیاوی - chemical analysis
- کردن - to make an analysis; to break down, to dismember; to analyze

تجسس [tajassos] 1 search; investigation, inquiry 2 intelligence (from agents)
- کردن - 1 to seach for, to conduct a search, to investigate 2 to carry on intelligence activity (by agents)

ت

تجسم [tajassom] 1 embodiment, personification 2 idea, notion; imagination
• پیداکردن and یافتن - to be embodied, to be personified

تجلی [tajalli] literary 1 brilliant manifestation (of something) 2 appearance in all one's glory 3 exultation, apotheosis ♦ عقل - triumph of the mind, triumph of reason
• کردن - 1 to be manifested brilliantly 2 to shine, to be manifested in all [one's, its] glory, in all [one's, its] magnificence or splendor

تجلیل [tajlil] literary exaltation, exalting, extolling; doing honor, rendering homage ♦ عید - celebration
• کردن - 1 to extol, to exalt 2 to mark, to celebrate (a date, event)

تجمع [tajammo'] gathering, accumulation, concentration (also military) ♦ مردم - gathering of people

تجمل [tajammol] 1 ostentatious beauty; outer luster 2 luxury, splendor

تجنیس [tajnis] literary 1 likening, assimilation 2 tajnis (poetic figure consisting of the use of homonyms) 3 play on words; pun

تجویز [tajwiz] (plural تجاویز [tajaawiz]) permission; sanction ♦ خطا technical tolerance

تجهیز [tajhiz] supplying (with everything necessary); outfitting (e.g., for a journey)
• کردن - 1 to supply (with everything necessary); to outfit (e.g., for a journey) 2 to fit out, to equip

تجهیزات [tajhizat] 1 outfit, equipment, equipage ♦ سفری - field kit ◊ کشتی - military rigging of a ship 2 armament; accoutrements ♦ کارخانه - munition factory 3 equipment, apparatus ♦ اطفائیه - firefighting equipment

تحت [taht] 1 (also در) under denominative preposition ♦ آب - under water ◊ عنوان - headed [by], under the heading or title ◊ کنترول - under the supervision or control [of] 2 (first component of ezafeh word combinations with meanings "being the object of something" / "being subject to something") ♦ ساختمان - under construction ◊ کار - under development ◊ مراقبت - under surveillance (about somebody)

تحت الارضی [tahtolarzi] underground ♦ آب های - underground waters, subterranean waters

تحت البحری [tahtolbahri] 1 underwater 2 submarine (ship)
• ضد – دافع - and antisubmarine (about a ship, mine)

تحت الحمایگی [tahtolhemayagi] protectorate

تحت الحمایه [tehtolhemaaya] being under a protectorate; mandated

تحت الفاظ [tahtol (I) afz] (also تحت الفظی tahtol [I]afzi) word for word, literally

تحتانی [tahtaani] lower, located or situated below ♦ قسمت — عمارت lower part of a building

تحدید [tahdid] limitation, restriction; establishment of a limit

تحریر [tahrir] writing, spelling; writing down, jotting down
• صوت – آواز and - 1 sound recording 2 producing with sound / scoring (a film)
• کردن - to write; to write down, to jot down

تحریرات [tahriraat] 1 official papers; correspondence, mail 2 business correspondence ♦ مدیر - office manager, head of business office ◊ مدیریت - office, business office

تحریری [tahriri] 1 written, being stated (having been stated) in writing ♦ امتحان - written examination 2 in writing, in written form ♦ شکایتش - عرض شد His complaint was submitted in written form / in writing.

تحریف [tahrif] change, distortion (of text, of words)

تحریک [tahrik] inducing (someone to do something), instigation, incitement, provocation ♦ به - under instigation, by instigation
• کردن - to induce, to instigate (به); to provoke (into some kind of action)

تحریم [tahrim] 1 imposing a ban, imposing a prohibition; religion prohibition 2 embargo 3 boycott

تحسیب [tahsib] accounting extra charge

تحسین [tahsin] approval; praise
• کردن - to approve, to praise (را،از)

تحصیل [tahsil] 1 obtaining, acquiring ♦ اطلاعات - obtaining information 2 collection, levy (of a tax, etc.) 3 learning, teaching, studies, training; education ♦ سامان - training aids, teaching aids 4 mastering (something), mastery (of something), study, studying ♦ زبان پشتو - studying the Pashto language
• کردن - 1 to collect, to levy (a tax, etc.); to obtain, to receive, to recover (a debt) 2 to learn, to study, to get an education

تحصیلدار [tahsildaar] tahsildar, tax collector

تحصیلداری [tahsildaari] 1 the job of a tahsildar, job of a tax collector 2 collection of taxes

تحفظ [tahaffoz] military protection, defense ♦ بمقابل اسلحه اتومی - antinuclear defense

تحفه [tohfa] 1 gift, present; a gift sent or brought from somewhere else 2 literary rarity, curiosity, curio, wonder
• دادن - to give a present, to present a gift

تحقق [tahaqqoq] realization (of goals); fulfillment, realization (of dreams, etc.)
• بخشیدن - to realize, to carry out, to fullfill (به)
• یافتن - 1 to be realized; to come true 2 to be found to be true, to turn out to be true, to be confirmed

تحقیر [tahqir] humiliation, insult; contempt, scorn

تحقیق [tahqiq] 1 research, analysis, study (of a matter, a problem) ♦ اهل - scientists, scholars, researchers 2 law investigation, inquiry, inquest 3 examination (by experts)
• کردن - 1 to investigate, to research, to analyze, to study 2 law to conduct an investigation, to make an inquiry, to conduct an inquest 3 to conduct an examination (by experts)

تحقیقاً [tahqiqan] for certain for sure, exactly, precisely

تحقیقات [tahqiqat] plural of تحقیق
• علمی - scientific research, scholarly research, scientific work, scholarly work

تحقیقاتی [tahqiqaati] and تحقیقی [tahqiqi] research adjective ♦ کار علمی - scientific research, scientific research work

تحکیم [tahkim] strengthening, consolidation ♦ دوستی - strengthening or consolidation of a friendship

تحلیل [tahlil] 1 analysis (also mathematical); investigation, research 2 dissolving, solution 3 recooking, reheating (of food)

• کردن - 1 to analyze; to investigate, to research, to study 2 to dissolve

تحلیلی [tahlili] analytic

تحمل [tahammol] 1 enduring (difficulties, etc.) 2 patience; endurance

• کردن - to bear, to endure (difficulties, etc.); to suffer

تحمل ناپذیر [tahammolnaapazir] unbearable, intolerable

تحمیل [tahmil] 1 imposing, thrusting, foisting (something on someone) 2 entrusting (someone with duties, responsibilities)

تحمیلی [tahmili] imposed ♦ معاهده - agreement or treaty imposed by force

تحول [tahawwol] change, transformation; reorganization

• دادن - to change, to transform; to reorganize
• یافتن - to be changed, to be transformed; to be reorganized

تحویل [tahwil] surrendering, turning in, transfer (of material assets)

• دادن - to surrender, to turn in, to transfer
• شدن - to be transferred, to be turned in
• گرفتن - to take, to accept, to get, to receive, to obtain

تحویلخانه [tahwilkhaana] warehouse; depot, storehouse; storeroom

تحویلدار [tahwildaar] 1 custodian (of valuables); warehouse man, storekeeper; military quartermaster 2 (also نقدی -) cashier

تحویلدهی [tahwildehi] handing over ♦ پروژه - handing over of a construction project ◊ وتویلگیری - handing over and acceptance

تحویلگیری [tahwilgiri] acceptance, receipt, receiving ♦ سامان - acceptance of equipment, receipt of equipment

تحویلی [tahwili] ☞ تحویل
• محصول - payment of a tax

تخت [takht] 1.1 throne ♦ پادشاهی - czar's throne ◊ یا - است یا تابوت proverb Either throne or coffin. (All or nothing at all.) 1.2 (also حمام -) shelf (in steam bath), bench 1.3 throne, seat of honor of bride and groom at a wedding 2 flat, level, even, smooth

• خینه - wooden dish (with articles needed by a bride-henna, etc.)
• تخت روان ☞ روان
• کردن - to make level, to make even, to make smooth, to level

تخت بام [takhtbaam] takhtbaam (part of the roof onto which the balakhana opens; ☞ بالا خانه)

تخت جمعی [taxtjami'] and colloquial تخت جمعی [takhtjaami] party, reception in the home of the groom after a wedding

تخت روان [takhterawaan] palanquin (on riding animal) ♦ مثل - است as in a palanquin (about easy and smooth movement)

تخته [takhta] 1.1 board, plank; small board, small plank ♦ آشپزی - kitchen cutting board ◊ آلات - instrument panel ◊ سیاه - technical blackboard 1.2 shield, panel; screen 1.3 slab (of marble, of concrete, etc.) 1.4 piece, item; leaf, sheet; bale, package (numerative in counting rugs, skins, blankets, as well as papers, cards, diagrams, drawings) ♦ ده نمد colloquial ten pieces of felt 2 full to the brim, crammed full ♦ جوال ازکاه – است The bag is crammed full with straw.

• شدن - 1 to be stuffed full, to be crammed full (about a bag, sack) 2 to be closed (about a shop, store) ♦ دکان ها - شده

بودند All the shops were [already] closed.
• کردن - 1 to fill to overflowing, to stuff, to cram 2 to close (a shop, store) 3 to drive (nails)
• سینه - colloquial thorax
• به - شوی! abusive May the grave take you!

تخته کسی را شستن [takhtae-kasay-raa-shustan] idiom (literally: wash his preparation table) to write off, to forget about someone or something ♦ تخته اش را بشوید Forget about him.

تخته بند [takhtaband] medicine splint

تخته به پشت [takhtabaposht] backwards, onto the back

تخته پاک [takhtapak] rag (for wiping blackboard)

تخته پیچ [takhtapeech] technical 1 threading die 2 die ♦ نری - die for forming thread

تخته چوب [takhtachob] board, small board; board of picket fence ♦ احاطه wooden fence; picket fence

تخته سنگ [takhtasang] 1 flagstone (of slate) 2 large flat rock, stone slab (of a building foundation, tombstone, etc.)

تخته قالب [takhtaqaaleb] technical wooden decking, wooden casing

تخته نرد [takhtanard] board for playing nards

تخته ی [takhtayi] board, made of boards, planks, wooden, made of wood ♦ دیوار - wall of boards or planks, wooden wall

تخریب [takhrib] 1 demolition, destruction ♦ بم - high-explosive bomb, demolition bomb 2 sabotage, subversive activity

تخریبی [takhribi] 1 destructive ♦ نیروی - destructive force 2 sabotage adjective, subversive ♦ فعالیت - subversive activity

تخصص [takhassos] 1 specialization 2 speciality
• داشتن - to be a specialist, to have a specialty

تخصصی [takhassosi] special, specialized

تخصیص [takhsis] 1 assigning, assignment, appointing, appointment; allotting, setting aside (for something) 2 appropriation, allocation

• دادن - 1 to assign, to appoint, to earmark; to allot, to set aside (for something) 2 to appropriate, to allocate

تخفیف [takhfif] 1 softening, weakening ♦ تشنجات بین المللی - easing of international tension 2 rebate, reduction; lowering (e.g., of price) 3 reduction (e.g., of armaments)

• دادن - 1 to soften, to ease 2 to give a rebate; to reduce (a price)
• واگذار کردن - to grant a rebate

تخلص [takhallos] 1 takhallus, literary pseudonym 2 second name taken by choice

تخلف [takhallof] not keeping (a promise), nonfulfillment (of a promise); violating, violation (of a law, etc.)

تخلیقی [takhliqi] creative; constructive ♦ کار - creative work

تخلیه [takhliya] military 1 emptying (of a container, vessel, etc.) 2 unloading 3 evacuation

• کردن - military 1 to empty 2 to unload 3 to evacuate

تخم [tókhom] 1 grain 2 seed, seed (of fruit) 3 egg (of a bird) 4 (also مرغ -) chicken's egg 5 breed (of livestock) 6 parentage, extraction, lineage, family ♦ تخمش اصلیت ندارد He is not of noble lineage.

• خربوزه - 1 melon seed 2 type of earrings
• انداختن - 1 to lay eggs 2 to spawn
• پاشیدن - to sow (land)
• انداختن ☞ 1 colloquial ماندن - 2 to sit at home, not to go anywhere

ت

بد - حرام زاده *colloquial* and چشم - حرام *anatomy* eyeball
تخم پاشی [tokhompaashi] sowing
تخم پاکی [tokhompaaki] cleaning of grain ♦ ماشین - screening machine, grain cleaner
تخم دان [tokhomdaan] 1 *anatomy* ovary; testicle 2 *botany* ovary
تخم دانی [tokhomdaani] vessel, box (for eggs)
تخم ریزی [tokhomreezi] ☞ تخم پاشی
تخم گذاری [tokhomgozaari] laying eggs
تخمی [tokhmi] seed *adjective*, left for seed ♦ بادرنگ - seed cucumber ◊ ماکیان - laying hen
تخمیر [takhmir] 1 leavening (of dough) 2 fermentation
تخمین [takhmin] 1 estimating, approximate determination (of something) ♦ از روی - according to approximate calculations 2 ☞ تخمینا
• شدن - to determine approximately; to size up roughly, to figure roughly
• کردن - to estimate, to determine approximately
تخمیناً [takhminan] approximately, as a guide; roughly
تخمینی [takhmini] approximate; tentative; rough (approximate)
تخنیک [takhnik] technology; engineering; mechanics ♦ علم و - science and technolgy
تخنیکدان [takhnikdaan] technician engineer
تخنیکر [takhnikar] technician, engineer
تخنیکی [takhniki] technical ♦ برق - electrical engineering
تخیل [takhayol] imagination, dream; fiction, fancy, falsehood; fantasy
تخیلی [takhayoli] imaginary, supposed; invented, imaginary, fictitious
تدابیر [tadaabir] *plural of* تدبیر
• امنی - *military* safety measures security measures
تدارک [tadaarok] 1 preparation (of some matter, of some undertaking); preparing, preparation (for something) 2 ☞ تدارکات
• کردن - 1 to prepare, to ready (some measure, activity, or step) 2 to supply, to lay in, to store up, to stock
تدارکات [tadaarokaat] 1 *plural of* تدارک ♦ جنگی - military preparations 2 supply; stores, stocks
تدافعی [tadaafe'i] defense *adjective*, defensive ♦ توان - defense capability defensive power
تداوی [tadaawi] treatment, therapy ♦ بالضد - and بضد – allopathy ◊ بالمثل - and بمثل - homeopathy
تدبیر [tadbir] (*plural* تدابیر [tadabir]) 1 instruction, direction, measure (action) ♦ منزل - domestic science (as subject of instruction) 2 way, method, means; way out 3 resourcefulness; good management
• اندیشیدن - to think of a means, to think of a method; to find a way out
• کردن - to deal wisely (with something); to take measures, to take action
تدخین [tadkhin] *literary* smoking; incense
تدریج [tadrij] 1 gradualness 2 gradation, arrangement in order
• به - ☞ تدریجاً
تدریجاً [tadrijan] gradually
تدریجی [tadriji] gradual

تدریس [tadris] 1 instruction, teaching 2 teaching (as a field, activity); pedagogy
• کردن - to instruct, to teach
تدریسات [tadrisaat] *plural of* تدریس
تدقیق [tadqiq] 1 careful study, investigation, research 2 verification
تدمیر [tadmir] *law* ruining, destroying, killing
تدویر [tadwir] 1 starting (in motion, in action) ♦ فابریکه - start-up of a factory 2 operation, functioning
• کردن - to put (in motion, in action into operation), to make function
تدویری [tadwiri]
• مصارف - expenditures to maintain a government apparatus
تدوین [tadwin] 1 *literary* work; composition ♦ رساله - writing a composition 2 codification
• کردن - 1 to write, to compose 2 to compile a code, to codify
تذکار [tazkar] 1 mention, mentioning; reminder, reminding 2 statement, report
• دادن - 1 to mention, to remind 2 to state, to report
تذکر [tazakkor] mention, mentioning; underlining, emphasis
• دادن (کردن) - to mention; to note, to underline, emphasize (از)
تذکره [tazkera]¹ 1 (also مرور -) document for right of departure, of passage 2 passport, identification card
تذکره [tazkera]² (also اشعار -) tazkera (biography of poets with examples of their work), anthology
تذهیب [tazhib] 1 gilding, gilt 2 painting, decorating with gold (the borders of manuscripts and bindings of books)
تر [tar] 1 wet, moist, damp, humid 2 fresh (about fruit)
ترو تازه ☞ تروتازه
ترو خشک ☞ تروخشک
• تر شدن *colloquial* 1 to grow or to become damp, to become moist or wet 2 to be ashamed
• تر ساختن [tar-saakhtan] *slang* (*literally:* to make someone wet) to embarrass someone
ترات [taraat] *colloquial* run, trot, rapid or quick movement ♦ به یک - at a run, at a trot
• کردن - to run, to start running
ترج [toraj] *zoology* partridge
تراخوم [taraakhom] trachoma
تراز [taraaz] 1 *technical* ☞ آب ترازه 2 *finance* balance
• بستن - to balance; to balance accounts
ترازو [taraazu] scales, balance ♦ مشقالی - jeweler's scales
• به زمین زدن - *colloquial* to show disinterest (in a matter); to try to evade, to get out of (something)
تراژدی [teraazhedi] tragedy
تراژیک [teraazhik] tragic, tragical
تراش [taraash] *present tense stem* تراشیدن
• خوردن - *colloquial* to fall from the body, to grow very thin
تراشیدن ☞ – کردن •
تراشه [taraasha] shaving; shavings; scraps ♦ چرم - scraps of leather ◊ چوب - shavings
تراشه تخته [taraashatakhta] slab wood
تراشیدن [taraashidan] 1 to shave, to plane; to repair, to mend; to square, to rough-hew 2 to hew, to cut (out of stone), to

facet 3 to scrape, to plane 4 to shave (hair or a beard])
- برای خود دشمن • *colloquial* to make enemies for oneself

ترافیک [teraafik] traffic (on street, road)

ترافیکی [terafiki]
- علامات • road signs

تراق [taraaq] crash, noise, knock; thunder

تراک [taraak] 1 crack, split, chink, slit, slot 2 ☞ تراق

تراکتور [taraaktor] tractor ♦ راننده - tractor operator or driver

تراکم [taraakom] 1 gathering, accumulation ♦ اولیه - *economics* primary accumulation 2 concentration ♦ جمعیت - density of population ◊ سرمایه - concentration of capital 3 conglomeration

ترام [teraam] ☞ تراموی

ترام ریل [teraamrel] *historical* horse tramway (which went from Dar-ul-aman (a suburb) to the center of Kabul during the time of Amanullah Khan)

تراموی [teramwey] tram, streetcar

ترانسپورت [taraansport] transport

ترانسفارمر [taraansformar]
- ترانسفارمر • transformer

ترانسمیتر [taraansmeetar] (radio) transmitter

ترانسمیشن [taraansmeeshan] *technical* transmission

ترانه [taraana] 1 melody; tune; song ♦ ملی - folk song 2 *literary* tarana (a quatrain which rhymes in all four lines)

ترایی [toraayi] *botany* luffa

ترب [torob] mild green horseradish

ترباب [tarbab] fresh fruit

تربت [torbat] *literary* grave; tomb; vault, crypt

تربرف [tarbarf] wet snow; snow and rain ♦ می بارد - Wet snow is falling.

تربم [tarbam] *colloquial* (also صدای -) a low, pleasant voice; rich bass

تربند [tarband] wet bandage, a bandage with lotion (for the injured spot)

تربوز [tarbuz] watermelon ♦ ابو جهل - colocynth ◊ دو – بیکدست گرفته نمی شود *proverb* You can't pick up two watermelons [at once] with one hand.

تربیه [tarbiya] 1 education, upbringing ♦ اطفال – education or upbringing of children ◊ عقلی - development of mental abilities 2 breeding, cultivation (of livestock, plants) ♦ حیوانات - livestock breeding
- کردن • 1 to rear, to educate, to train, to teach 2 to breed, to cultivate (livestock, plants)

تربیوی [tarbiyawi] 1 educational, pedagogical 2 related to training (of personnel, etc.)

ترپال [tarpaal] 1 canvas top (of a vehicle) 2 tent, tarpaulin (thrown over a vehicle during rain)
- انداختن • to set up a canvas tent, to throw a tarpaulin (over a vehicle)

ترت [tort] *colloquial* 1.1 brittle, fragile ♦ چوب - fragile wood 1.2 honest, straightforward 2 straightforwardly, frankly, openly
- گفتن • to speak frankly

ترت گوی [tortgoy] *colloquial* speaking frankly to one's face; [always] speaking the truth

ترتیب [tartib] (*plural* ترتیبات [tartibaat]) 1 order, routine 2 *military* battle formation 3 order; arrangement; organization 4 drawing up, working up ♦ پروژه - drawing up a project

- دادن • 1 to regulate, to put in good order 2 to arrange, to organize, to put right, to adjust

ترتیبات [tartibaat] 1 *plural of* ترتیب 2 measures; activities, actions; training 3 *technical* equipment, device; mechanism ♦ ماشه - *military* trigger mechanism release mechanism
- گرفتن • to take measures; to get ready

ترتیب وار [tartibwaar] 1 one after another, in succession 2 regularly, methodically, successively

ترجمان [tarjomaan] 1 translator, interpreter, dragoman 2 spokesman (of views, opinions)

ترجمانی [tarjomaani] 1 work of a translator, interpreter, or dragoman 2 expression, statement (of views, opinions)

ترجمه [tarjoma] translation (from one language into another)
- لفظی • literal or word-for-word translation
- کردن • to translate, to interpret (from one language into another)

ترجیح [tarjih] preference
- دادن • to prefer, to show preference (for someone به)
- داشتن • to have preference; to excel to surpass (بر)

ترجیع بند [tarjiband] *literary* tarjiband (poetic genre characterized by the repetition after each stanza of the very same couplet-refrain)

ترحم [tarahhom] mercy, charity; pity, compassion

ترخشکی [tarkhoshki]
- انداختن • *colloquial* to toss or flip a stone with one wet side (to settle something by lot)

ترخیص [tarkhis] 1 release, liberation, setting free; dismissal 2 *military* release into the reserve

تردد [taraddod] 1 movement, traffic, circulation, plying ♦ موتر - runs or trips of vehicles ◊ امروز - زیاد است Today there is heavy traffic (on the street). 2 hesitation; indecisiveness

تردید [tardid] 1 declining (something) refusal (of something); denial, refutation 2 indecisiveness, vacillation, wavering; doubt ♦ جای – نیست undoubtedly, indisputably
- کردن • to decline, to refuse, to reject; to refute, to disprove

ترزبان [tarzobaan] talkative, glib of tongue

ترس [tars] fear, dread; fright, scare

ترسا [tarsaa] 1 heathen, pagan 2 fire worshiper, a Parsi

ترساندن [tarsaandan] to frighten, to intimidate, to scare

ترسب [tarassob] settling (of alluvia) ♦ دوره - *geology* alluvium, alluvion

ترسناک [tarsnaak] 1 frightful, dreadful, fearful, terrible, formidable, ferocious 2 ☞ ترسندوک

ترسندوک [tarsendok] *colloquial* 1 cowardly, fainthearted, timid 2 little coward

ترسو [tarso] *colloquial* cowardly, fearful

ترسیب [tarsib] *geology* sedimentation (of rock)

ترسیبی [tarsibi] *geology* sedimentary (about rock)

ترسیدن [tarsidan] to fear, to dread, to be afraid; to be timid

ترسیم [tarsim] drawing, portraying painting; tracing; inscription
- کردن • to draw, to portray, to paint; to plot, to sketch, to trace ♦ دایره – کردن to draw a circle

ترش [tors] 1 sour (to the taste) 2 turned sour, soured 3 dissatisfied, downcast
- شدن • 1 to turn sour (about milk, etc.) 2 to become sullen

ت

or morose, to be angry
- کردن • - to turn sour, to ferment
- روی – کردن • to take on a gloomy or sullen appearance, to take on a stern appearance; to frown

ترشک [torshak] 1 sorrel 2 *colloquial* very sour to the taste (e.g., about an unripe or green apple)

ترشی [torshi] 1 marinade; pickled vegetables; vegetables in vinegar (eggplant, onions, etc.) 2 *chemistry* acid 3 acidity
- انداختن • - to marinate, to pickle; to prepare a marinade

ترشیش [tarshish] beryl (gem)

ترصد [tarassed] observation; waiting; shadowing ♦ هوایی - *military* air observation, aerial observation ◊ محل - observation point or post

ترصیع [tarsi'] 1 *literary* introduction into verses of inner rhyme throughout 2 *literary* decoration with gems or precious stones

ترفیع [tarfi'] promotion (at work) ♦ رتبه - promotion in rank

ترق [taraq] 1 *onomatopoeia* Bang! 2 a clap; a knock, a tap; a crash, a noise
- کردن • - to clap; to knock, to tap; to crack
- افتو • - *colloquial* unbearable heat, scorching heat

ترق [tarq] chink, slit, slot, crack, split; cleft, fissure

ترق [taraq] *slang* Suddenly, unexpectedly, out of the blue ♦ ترق به خانه درآمد Suddenly he came home.

ترق زمستان [taraqe-zamestaan] *colloquial* dead of winter

ترقاندن [tarqandan] to chop, to split (firewood, etc.); to split, to splinter; to form or to make cracks or splits (in something)

ترقدم [tarqadam] *colloquial* bringing good luck or happiness, happy, lucky

ترق زدنی [taraqzadani] *colloquial* in a flash, in a twinkling of the eye ♦ به کابل هستیم - A wink and we're in Kabul.

ترق وتروق [taraqotoroq] 1 rumble, rumbling, crashing, rolling, crash, thunder, roar ♦ تفنگ - crackle of gunfire

ترقوه [tarqowa] *anatomy* clavicle

ترقی [taraqqi] 1 progress; growth, development 2 rise, increase, growth
- دادن • - to develop, to raise
- کردن(یافتن) • - to grow, to progress

ترقیدن [tarqidan] 1 to crack *intransitive*; to break (e.g., about a glass) 2 to burst, to explode ♦ الهی یک روز بترقی *abusive* May you break / crack!

ترک [tark] 1 leaving, quitting, abandoning, deserting 2 giving up, rejection; stopping, cessation ♦ ترک عادت breaking a habit
- ترک کردن • to stop, to cease, to quit
- ترک عادت کردن • to grow out of a habit, to break a habit
- ترک گفتن • to leave, to quit, to abandon, to desert

ترک [tork] 1.1 Turk [inhabitant of Turkey] 1.2 Turk (member of peoples speaking Turkic languages) 1.3 *obscure poetic* a handson youth 2 Turkish; Turkic

ترکاری [tarkari] greens, vegetables

ترکه [taraka] 1 property of deceased person, inheritance, legacy 2 division of an inheritance or legacy (according to the laws of the sharia)
- ترکه کردن • to divide an inheritance or legacy

ترکه خط [tarakakhat] statement about the division of the property of a deceased person; document about the right to an inheritance

ترکی [torki] 1.1 Turkish 1.2 Turkic 2 (also زبان ترکی) Turkish language

ترکیب [tarkib] 1 compiling, forming 2 composition, structure ♦ ترکیب جمله *grammar* composition of sentence or clause 3 (also ترکیب کیمیاوی) *chemistry* composition, compound 4 *philosophical* synthesis (opposite of تخلیل) 5 *grammar* formation of compound words 6 *grammar* combination of words ♦ ترکیب اضافی ezafeh combination of words
- ترکیب شدن • 1 to consist [of], to be constituted [of] (از) 2 to be combined (about words, etc.)
- ترکیب دادن • to put together, to compose, to compile, to constitute, to join, to combine

ترکیب بند [tarkibband] *literary* tarkibband (poem in which each strophe is accompanied by a special refrain of two rhyming lines)

ترم [torom] copper tube in the form of a horn (musical instrument)

ترمچی [toromchi] trumpeter; bugler

ترمیده [tarmayda] (also آردترمیده) specially ground wheat flour, fine flour

ترمیم [tarmim] repairing, mending, repair ♦ ترمیم اساسی major repair, major overhaul ◊ ترمیم خفیف minor repair ◊ فابریکه (کادخانه) ترمیم موتر motor vehicle repair plant (in Kabul)

ترمیم خانه [termimkhaana] repair shop, (locomotive) depot

ترمینل [tarminal] airport terminal; airport

ترنگ [tarang] clatter (of crockery); twanging (string of muscial instrument, etc.)

ترنگاندن [tarangaandan] 1 to extract or to elicit a peal, ringing, or tinkling, to make to ring or a sound 2 to strum, to saw, to bang (on a muscial instrument)

ترنگوترنگ [tarangotorong] banging, sawing (on a musical instrument); strumming; ringing, clanging, tinkling

ترنم [tarannom] *literary* 1 singing (verses, songs); playing melody (on a muscial instrument) 2 melody; trill; tune, motif

تروپ [torup] (also تروپهای نظامی) troops, military formations or units ♦ تروپ هنری *rarely* troupe

تروتازه [tarotaaza] 1 fresh, blooming, blossoming 2 healthy, looking well (about a person)

تروخشک [tarokhoshk] 1 some food; everything edible that is available ♦ صاحب خانه تروخشکی که داشتربرای مهمان آورد The master of the house brought out everything edible he could find for the guest. 2 everything without exception, everyone indiscriminately; both the innocent and the quilty ♦ در این ماجراتروخشک سوخت In this mess everyone suffered, both the innocent and the guilty.

تره [tara] serpentine melon, tara ♦ تره تخمی *colloquial* good-for-nothing, shallow person

تری تری دیدن [teray-teray-didan] *idiom* to stare desperately, to stare

تریاک [taryaak] opium

تریاکی [taryaaki] one who smokes opium, drug addict

تریسایکل [terisaaykal] wheelchair for invalids

تریشه [terisha] rag, shred; scrap; strip (of fabric, leather, paper) ♦ تریشه چوب a long, thin strip of wood

تریلر [tereelár] trailer

تزریق [tazriq] injection; infusion
- تزریق کردن • to give an injection; to perform an infusion

تزویر [tazwir] *literary* 1 fraud 2 pretense, sham, falsity, hypocrisy

تزیین [tazyin] decorating, decoration, adorning
• تزیین کردن to adorn, to beautify, to decorate, to tidy up

تزیینی [tazyini] and تزییناتی [tazyinaati] 1 decorative 2 finishing, trimming ♦ کارهای تزیینی finishing work, trimming work

تساوی [tasaawi] equality ♦ تساوی حقوق equality of rights

تسبیح [tasbih] prayer beads
• تسبیح کردن to count prayer beads, to finger prayer beads (while saying a prayer)

تستر [tastar] indicator

تسخین [taskhin] heating ♦ تسخین مرکزی central heating
• تسخین کردن to heat

تسریع [tasri] accelerating, acceleration, forcing, speeding up

تسطیح [tastih] smoothing; leveling ♦ تسطیح زمین - *technical* planning or laying out land, planning or laying out a plot of ground

تسکین [taskin] 1 calming, smoothing 2 fading away, lessening (of pain, agitation, etc.)
• تسکین دادن to calm, to soothe; to lessen (pain, etc.)

تسلسل [tasalsosl] succession, repetition; continuity ♦ تسلسل وقعات chain of events

تسلط [tasallot] 1 supremacy, rule 2 ownership (of something)
• تسلط داشتن 1 to have dominion [over], to rule (بر) 2 to own (بر)

تسلی [tasalli] comfort, consolation, calming, soothing
• تسلی یافتن to be calmed, to be soothed, to find comfort, to find consolation

تسلیت [tasliyat] comfort, consolation, expression of sympathy
• تسلیت دادن to comfort, to console, to express sympathy (را)(به)(گفتن)

تسلیحات [taslihaat] armament, arms, weapon, weapons

تسلیحاتی [taslihaati]
• مسابقه arms race

تسلیمی [taslim] ☞ تسلیمی
• تسلیم دادن to hand over, to transfer
• تسلیم داده شدن to be handed over, to be transferred (about something)
• تسلیم شدن 1 to surrender (to an enemy), to capitulate 2 to get, to receive, to accept, to take ♦ مبلغ ده هزار افغانی را تسلیم شدم the sum of 10,000 afghani received (a receipt)
• تسلیم دادن ☞ تسلیم کردن 1 2 *literary* to resign oneself, to submit (to something)

تسلیمی [taslimi] 1 surrender, capitulation ♦ تسلیمی قوا capitulation of troops ◊ تسلیمی وقبولی handing over (e.g., equipment); handing over (acceptance) 3 receiving, receipt, acceptance ♦ دست خط تسلیمی receipt (for something)

تسمه [tasma] 1 braid, ribbon 2 belt ♦ تسمه چرمی small leather belt, leather strap; strip of leather ◊ تسمه کمر (waist) belt 3 garter (for stockings); small strap (of woman's blouse)

تسماره [tasmaarra] *technical* bandsaw

تسمه گردان [tasmagardaan]
• چرخ تسمه *technical* pulley

تسمیه [tasmiya] name, appellatan ♦ وجه تسمیه etymology of a word

تسوید [taswid] making a rough copy; sketch, rough copy; draft (e.g., of a decision)

تسهیلات [tashilaat] privileges, advantages; favorable conditions

تشبث [tashabbos] 1 initiative; endeavor, attempt 2 zeal, fervor

تشبیه [tashbih] 1 comparison, likening 2 *literary* allegory

تشت [tasht] basin, trough

تشخیص [tashkhis] 1 distinguishing discernment, recognition 2 establishing, establishment, determining, determination 3 *medicine* diagnosis
• تشخیص دادن(کردن) 1 to discern, to recognize 2 to establish, to determine 3 to make a diagnosis

تشدید [tashdid] 1 intensification; aggravation 2 *grammar* reduplication of a consonant (designated by the symbol; a tashdid)

تشریح [tashrih] 1 description; explanation, elucidation 2 dissection, autopsy
• علم تشریح anatomy
• تشریح کردن 1 to discribe, to explain, to elucidate 2 to dissect, to perform an autopsy

تشریحی [tashrihi] 1 descriptive ♦ دستور تشریحی descriptive grammar ◊ زبان شناسی تشریحی descriptive linguistics 2 anatomical

تشریف [tashrif] *polite* rendering honor, doing honor
• تشریف آوردن to visit (somewhere), to deign to come
• تشریف بردن to leave, to depart, to deign to go, to leave
• تشریف داشتن 1 to deign to be (with someone) 2 to deign to be present

تشریفات [tashrifot] 1 a ceremonial; etiquette; formalities ♦ رئیس تشریفات دربار *historical* chief master of ceremonies of a court or household 2 *diplomatic* protocol ♦ مدیریت تشریفات protocol department

تشریک [tashrik]
• تشریک مساعی 1 uniting of efforts, collaboration 2 coordination (e.g., of branches of the army)

تشکر [tashakkor] 1 gratitude, thanks 2 I thank [you]! / Thanks!
• تشکر کردن to thank (از)

تشکیل [tashkil] formation, creation; forming ♦ تشکیل کابینه forming a cabinet
• تشکیل دادن to form; to create

تشناب [tashnaab] 1 washstand 2 lavatory

تشنگی [tashnagi] thirst
• رفع تشنگی کردن to quench [one's] thirst

تشنه [tashna] 1 experiencing thirst 2 strongly wanting (something), thirsting

تشویش [tashwish] anxiety, uneasiness, alarm, agitation

تشویق [tashwiq] encouragement, inducement, incentive; approval
• تشویق کردن to encourage, to induce; to approve

تصاحب [tasaahob] seizing, taking possession; assuming possession (of property, equipment)

تصادف [tasaadof] 1 unexpected meeting; chance 2 coincidence
• تصادف کردن 1 to meet unexpectedly, to run across (با) 2 to happen 3 to coincide, to occur simultaneously

تصادفاً [tasaadofan] by chance, accidentally

تصادم [tasadom] collision; accident, crash
• تصادم کردن to collide, to bump into (با)

تصاویر [tasaawir] *plural of* تصویر

تصحیح [tashih] correction, amendment; correcting

تصدیق [tasdiq] 1 confirmation; witnessing (e.g., a signature) 2 ratification 3 ☞ تصدیق نامه

تصدیق کردن ♦ 1 to approve (a decision); to confirm; to witness (a signature) 2 to ratify

تصدیق نامه [tasdiqnaama] 1 certificate, certificate (of completion of an educational institution) 2 certification, reference 3 character reference, testimonial 4 instrument of ratification

تصرف [tasarrof] 1 ownership possession, use (of something); the right of disposal 2 seizure, possession

(را) تصرف کردن ♦ to sieze, to possess something

(در) به تصرف کسی بودن ♦ to be in possession of something, to have something for one's use

تصریف [tasrif] grammar 1 declension 2 conjugation

تصغیر [tasghir]

پسوند تصغیر ♦ grammar diminutive suffix; diminutive

تصفیه [tasfiya] 1 cleaning, refinement, purification ♦ تصفیه هوا ventilation 2 political purge 3 liquidation, elimination (e.g., of differences) ♦ تصفیه حساب accounting settlement

تصمیم [tasmim] decision

تصمیم گرفتن (کردن) ♦ to decide, to make a decision

تصنیف [tasnif] 1 composition, work 2 distribution, allotment (into or by sections); classification ♦ تصنیف عمومی common, general, or overall classification

تصنیف کردن ♦ to distribute, to allot (into or by section); to classify

تصنیفات پلان ♦ drawing up or compiling a plan (with indication of expenditure items)

تصنیفات [tasnifaat] 1 sections (of something) 2 articles (e.g., of expenditures)

تصور [tasawwor] 1 mental notion, imagining, imagination 2 supposition, assumption, idea

تصور کردن ♦ 1 to picture, to imagine 2 to suppose, to think, to assume, to presuppose

تصوری [tasawwori] 1 imagined; imaginary 2 philosophical subjective

تصوف [tasawof] Sufism; mysticism

تصویب [taswib] ratification, confirmation; approval; sanction

تصویب نامه [taswib naama] decision, resolution (of a legislative body); decree; edict

تصویر [taswir] (plural تصاویر [tasaawir]) picture; portrait; portrayal, illustration

تصویر کسی راکشیدن ♦ to draw a portrait of someone

تضاد [tazad (d)] 1 opposite 2 opposition, antagonism ♦ مبارزه تضادها philosophical struggle or conflict of opposites

تضمین [tazmin] guaranteeing, guaranty, warranty; securing, ensuring

تضمین کردن ♦ to guarantee; to ensure

تضییق [tazyiq] squeezing, pressing; pressure, head ♦ پیچ تضییق technical fastening screw, clamping screw

تطبیق [tatbiq] 1 application, use (in practice), applying, application ♦ تطبیق کلتور زراعتی introduction of an agricultural crop 2 implementation, realization ♦ تطبیق پلان fulfillment of a plan 3 bringing into line [with], bringing into conformity [with]; collation

تطبیق کردن ♦ 1 to use, to employ, to apply (به یر) ♦ همین روش راتطبیق کنید! Use the same method! 2 to realize, to fulfill (a plan, project) 3 to collate 4 to match (surfaces, planes, pointers)

تطبیقات [tatbniqaat] 1 practical studies, classes, or activities; on-the-job training, production training, production practice 2 military training exercises

تطور [tatawwor] 1 change, displacement, change for the better 2 development, growth, evolution

تطهیر [tathir] literary cleaning ♦ تطهیر از (وجود) مین military mine clearing, mine sweeping

تظاهر [tazaahor] literary demonstrative display (of something); putting up for show; showing off

تظاهری [tazaahori] for show, ostentatious; demonstrative

تعادل [taaadol] 1 proportionality, state of being balanced, state of being in balance 2 equilibrium ♦ تعادل قوا physics equilibrium of forces 3 balance ♦ تعادل تجارتی trade balance

تعارف [taaarof] 1 exchange of courtesies or compliments, polite formalities 2 entertainment, regalement (of a guest)

تعارف کردن ♦ to entertain, to regale (a guest); to offer, to present courteously

تعالی [taaala] The Most High (epithet of Allah)

تعاون [taaawon] 1 mutual aid or assistance; aid, assistance 2 cooperation

تعاونی [taaawoni] cooperative ♦ دیپوی تعاونی trade cooperative (which supplies goods to the populace at fixed or stable prices)

تعبیر [ta'bir] 1 interpretation 2 expression, turn (of speech) ♦ تعبیر غلط improper expression, incorrect expression

تعبیه [ta'biya] military tactics

تعجب [taajjob] surprise, astonishment, amazement, wonder

تعجب کردن ♦ to surprise, to astonish, to amaze

تعداد [ta'daad] quantity, number; numbers; strength ♦ تعداد کثیر a large amount or quantity (of something)

تعدیل [ta'dil] 1 regulation, adjustment, adjusting 2 aligning, equalizing, straightening, rectifying 3 correction, correcting

تعدیلات [ta'dilaat] political balance, equilibrium; normalization

تعرض [taarroz] assault; attack; advance, offensive noun

تعرضی [taarrozi] 1 offensive adjective 2 aggressive

تعرفه [ta'refa] 1 tariff, statutory price; rate ♦ تعرفه بارگیری و بارانداری اموال tariff for loading-unloading operations 2 list; enumeration 3 schedule, timetable, roster

تعریف [ta'rif] 1 description, definition, testimonial, reference 2 literary praise, laudatory testimonial, reference

تعریف کردن ♦ 1 to describe; to define; to characterize 2 literary to praise, to lavish praise on

کلمه تعریف ♦ grammar article

تعریف نامه [ta'rifnaama] (also تعریف نامه استعمال) guide, manual, instructions, directions

تعصب [taassob] 1 fanaticism; intolerance 2 prejudice

تعطیل [ta'til] 1 time free from work; break 2 cessation, suspension (of work) 3 closing (of an enterprise)

تعظیم [ta'zim] literary 1 compliments, greeting 2 rendering of honors; expression of respect or esteem ♦ تعظیمات مرا بپزیرید Accept my greetings!

تعقیب [ta'qib] 1 following (something) ♦ تعقیب سیاست pursuing a policy 2 pursuing, pursuit

تعقیب کردن ♦ 1 to follow (something), to pursue (a policy), to carry out (a policy) 2 to monitor (the execution), to supervise ♦ این کار راتعقیب کنید! Look after this matter! 3 to pursue (someone), to chase

تعلق [taalloq] 1 relation, connection 2 tie, bond, belonging
- تعلق داشتن 1 to pertain, to have a relation [to], to have a connection [with] 2 to belong [to] (ب) ♦ این کار به شما تعلق دارد This pertains to you.
تعلقات [taalloqaat] 1 plural of تعلق; ♦ تعلقات خانوادگی ties of blood; family relations 2 questions relating to a matter 3 colloquial relatives, family members
تعلم [taallom] philosophical cognition
تعلیم [ta'lim] 1 instruction training, studies ♦ تعلیم وتربیه training and education; education 2 military (also تعلیم عسکری) drill training
- تعلیم دادن to instruct, to teach, to train
تعلیمات [ta'limaat] 1 plural of تعلیم ♦ تعلیمات ثانوی secondary education 2 instruction
- تعلیمات دادن to instruct
تعلیمات نامه [ta'limaat naama] regulations, charter; order, routine ♦ تعلیمات نامه یونیورستی university rules, university charter
تعلیم نامه [ta'lim naama] ☞ تعلیمات نامه
- تعلیمنامه عسکری military regulations
تعلیمی [ta'limi] 1 training school adjective; educational ♦ سال تعلیمی school year ◊ طیارات تعلیمی aviation training 2 instructive 3 didactic ♦ اشعار تعلیمی didactic poetry
تعلیم یافته [ta'lim yaafta] educated, cultured
تعمیر [ta'mir] 1 construction, construction project 2 building; edifice ♦ تعمیر بودوباش house, dwelling ◊ تعمیر نو new construction project, newly erected building, project ◊ سر تعمیر finance F.O.B. project
- تعمیر کردن to build, to erect
تعمیراتی [ta'miraati] construction adjective ♦ زمین تعمیراتی construction site
تعمیم [ta'mim] 1 spreading, dissemination ♦ تعمیم سواد spreading of literacy 2 introduction, inculcation ♦ تعمیم تعلیمات اجباری introduction of mandatory education
- تعمیم یافتن to receive dissemination; to be introduced
تعویذ [ta'wiz] amulet, talisman (in the form of a note with a prayer or exorcism worn on the neck or fastened to the arm)
تعین [tain] and تعیین [tayin] determination, determining, establishment, establishing; appointment, appointing, assignment, assigning
- تعین کردن to determine, to establish; to appoint, to assign
تغار [taghaar] 1 large clay vessel (for mixing dough or preparing kurut), kneading trough 2 clay trough (for washing clothes)
تغاره [taghaara] colloquial ☞ تغار
- تغاره بی بی feast of Bibi (arranged by the women in the month of Rajab in honor of the mystic patroness of birth)
تغذی [taghazzi] agriculture spreading fertilizer, feeding
- باکود کیمیاوی تغذی شدن to be fertilized (about soil)
تغذیه [taghziya] 1 nourishment, feeding 2 technical feeding, supplying (with electric current, etc.)
تغزل [taghazzol] 1 composing ghazels (type of poem) 2 lyric poetry
تغیر [taghayor] change ♦ تغیرات کمی philosophical quantitative changes ◊ تغیرات کیفی philosophical qualitative changes
تغییر [tagh'yir (and) taqir] changing; making changes
- تغییر دادن to make changes, to change
- تغییر کردن to change, to be transformed; to undergo changes intransitive
تف [tof] 1 spitting 2 spit 3 saliva ♦ تف به (در) دهنش خشک شد colloquial His mouth went dry (from fear, alarm).
- تف خود را با بالا انداختن saying (literally: to face up and spit in the air) dishonor or disgrace oneself
- تف کردن و گره کردن idiom (literally: to spit and make a knot) to be (stingy, tightwad, tightfisted)
تفاله [tofaala] 1 squeezings, husks, dregs (the leavings after juice has been squeezed out of fruit, etc.) 2 oil cake, concentrates (for livestock)
تفاوت [tafaawot] difference, distinction
- تفاوت داشتن to differ, to be distinguished
تفاهم [tafaahom]
- تفاهم نیک mutual understanding
تفت [taft] heat (issuing from something hot, burning); hot air; steam ♦ از کاسه به هواتفت برمی خاست Steam rose from the tureen.
- تفت دادن to steam, to prepare by steaming
- تفت نکردن colloquial to wear out quickly (about clothing) ♦ بوت پیش او تفت نمیکند On him shoes simply melt.
- به تفت رفتن colloquial to be quickly boiled soft (about vegetables, etc.)
- تفت نرسید جوش آمد idiom (literally: water boiled before it steamed) over eager, anxious, wants it now
تفتیش [taftish] 1 examination; inspection; check ♦ هیئت تفتیش inspection commission 2 customs inspection 3 check (of documents)
تفحص [tafahhos] (plural تفحصات [tafahhosaat]) search, survey, prospecting (geological, etc.)
- تفحص کردن to conduct a search, to prospect (for minerals)
تفدانی [tofdani] spittoon
تفرقه [tafreqa] 1 separation, division; split 2 discord, dissension, disagreement, difference
- تفرقه انداختن to sow discord; to make a split, to cause a split
تفریح [tafrih] 1 entertainment, amusement 2 rest, recreation 3 break, intermission, recess (between lessons)
- تفریح کردن to amuse oneself, to enjoy oneself, to have a good time; to rest
تفریق [tafriq] 1 distinguishing, discerning, differentiation 2 discrimination ♦ تفریق نژادی racial discrimination 3 mathematical subtraction
تفسیر [tafsir] 1 interpretation; commenting, comment 2 (also تفسیر قران) commentary on the Koran
تفصیل [tafsil] 1 detailed account 2 detail ♦ به تفصیل قصه کن! Tell [everything] in detail!
- تفصیل ☞ به تفصیل
تفکر [tafakkor] 1 reflection, meditation, consideration 2 thinking, thought
تفکیک [tafkik] 1 separation, breaking ♦ تفکیک اتوم physics splitting of the atom 2 separation, division, distinguishing
تفنگ [tofang] gun, rifle
- تفنگ زدن to fire
- با تفنگ زدن to fire a gun
تفنگچه [tofangcha] pistol, Nagant revolver; revolver ♦ تفنگچه ماشیندار machine gun
تفنگ دست [tofang dest] colloquial marksman, skilled shot

ت

تفوق [tafawwoq] superiority, dominance ♦ تفوق فضایی *military* superiority in the air, air superiority

تق [taq] knock, tap; clap; slap
- تق زدن to make a noise, to knock; to clap, to bang, to slam; to slap, to smack (به)

تقاضا [taqaazaa] 1 request, demand 2 demand (for goods) ♦ عرضه و تقاضا supply and demand

تقاعد [taqaa'od] retirement, retirement on pension

تق تق [taqtaq] ☞ تک تک

تقدم [taqaddom] 1 advancement moving ahead 2 preceding 3 superiority, championship, priority

تقدیر [taqdir] 1 rendering [someone his] due; approval 2 predetermination; fortune, destiny, fate
- تقدیر کردن to value, to appreciate, to render [someone his] due

تقدیر نامه [taqdir naama] school testimonial of good conduct and progress

تقدیم [taqdim] 1 handing in (an application, report) 2 presentation; presenting (a gift, etc.)
- تقدیم کردن 1 to hand in (an applicatlication, report) 2 to present, to deliver (a gift, etc.)

تقرر [taqarror] appointment (to a post, job)
- تقرر حاصل کردن and تقرر یافتن to receive an appointment, to be appointed (to a post, job)

تقریب [taqrib] coming, approach (of a holiday) ♦ به تقریب ... on the occasion [of] …, in connection [with] …

تقریباً [taqriban] approximately, about, almost

تقریر [taqrir] statement, address; utterance; speech

تقریری [taqriri] oral, spoken ♦ امتحان تقریری oral examination

تقریظ [taqriz] 1 opinion, review, critical essay, critique 2 review section, critic's section (in newspaper, magazine)

تقسیم [taqsim] *mathematical* division (also); separation, partition; distribution ♦ تقسیم آب distribution of water
- تقسیم شدن to divide *intransitive*, to be divided (also *mathematical*); to separate, to subdivide *intransitive*, to be separated, to be subdivided; to disintegrate, to come apart; to be distributed
- تقسیم کردن 1 to divide [(also *mathematical*) to separate, to subdivide; to distribute] 2 *cards* to deal

تقسیمات [taqsimaat] *plural of* تقسیم
- تقسیمات ملکیه administrative division
- شبکه تقسیمات آب water distribution system

تقصیر [taqsir] 1 fault, guilt 2 omission, error; mistake

تقطیر [taqtir] distillation

تقلب [taqallob] fraud, deception, swindle, cheating; counterfeit *noun*, forgery

تقلبی [taqallobi] false, counterfeit *adjective*, spurious

تقلص [taqallos] *medicine* pang, pangs

تقلید [taqlid] 1 imitation 2 mimicry, mimicking 3 following, taking after, adhering to (teachings, etc.)
- به تقلید ... 1 in imitation (of something) 2 following, adhering to (something)
- تقلید کسی را کردن 1 to imitate somebody 2 to mimic somebody 3 to take after somebody; to take an example from somebody

تقلیدی [taqlidi] imitative; imitation, false, counterfeit

تقنینیه [taqniniya] legislative ♦ قوه تقنینیه legislative power

تقویم [taqwim] 1 calendar 2 almanac

تقویه [taqwiya] 1 reinforcement, strengthening, consolidation 2 support, backing

تقویه کننده [taqwiya konenda] *technical* electrical amplifier or booster

تک [tak] *colloquial* Bang! (a shot from a gun)
- تک زدن (کردن) to fire (a gun once)
- تک به تک زدن to fire in succession

تکالیف [takaalif] 1 *plural of* تکلیف 2 *historical* duties, obligations (public works, etc.)

تکامل [takaamol] perfection improvement; growth, development, progress

تکان [takaan] 1 start, starting, flinching, unexpected movement (from fright, etc.) 2 jerk, jolt, shaking ♦ با یک تکان with one jerk
- تکان خوردن 1 to start, flinch, to recoil (from surprise) 2 to rock, to stagger, to shake 3 to receive a shock, a push, a jolt
- تکان دادن to push, to shove; to shake

تکاندن [takaandan] 1 ☞ تکان دادن in entry تکان 2 to shake out, to beat (a carpet, rug, etc.) ♦ پر تکاندن *colloquial* to shake out feathers, to shake itself out (concerning a bird) 3 to give a scolding, to dress down

تکان دهنده [takaan dehenda] staggering, startling, surprising, astonishing ♦ خبر تکان دهنده startling or staggering news

تکبر [takabbor] haughtiness, arrogance, superciliousness

تکت [teket] ticket; stamp ♦ تکت پوسته postage stamp ◊ تکت تیاتر theater ticket ◊ تکت رخصتی *military* leave papers; pass ◊ تکت لاتری lottery ticket

تکتانه [teketaana] ☞ تکت پولی

تکت پولی [teket puli] 1 tax, duty (paid when formalizing documents and indicated by affixing a stamp to the document) 2 dividend; interest (on a promissory note)

تکتفروشی [teketforoshi] selling of tickets ♦ غرفه تکتفروشی ticket office, ticket booth

تک تک [taktak] *interjection* 1.1 knock-knock, rat-tat 1.2 tick-tock (ticking of a clock) 2.1 knock (e.g., on a door) ♦ تک تک آسیا rumble, noise, beat of mill wheel 2.2 ticking (of a watch, clock)
- تک تک کردن 1 to knock *transitive*, to knock (at a door) 2 to tick (of a clock, watch)

تکتنها [taketanhaa] and تکوتنها [takotanhaa] *colloquial* 1 solitary, single, lone 2 by oneself, alone

تکتیک [taktik] tactic, tactics

تکثیر [taksir] increase (numerical), multiplication

تکر [takar] 1 collision, a hit, a punch (of one person on another) 2 a blow with the forehead, a blow with the head
- تکر خوردن to collide, to bump into, to hit against something; (به) ♦ دو موتربه هم تکر خوردن Two vehicles collided.
- تکرزدن 1 to strike [one's] head (against something) 2 to push, to shove with the head; to butt ♦ بز او را تکر زد The goat butted him.

تکر [tokor]¹ *colloquial* stumbling
- تکر خوردن to stumble (about horses, etc.)

تکر [tokor]² *colloquial* compress, lotion, wash
- تکر کردن to apply a compress, to wash, to apply a lotion

تکرار [takraar] repetition; resumption ♦ به تکرار again, anew

تکرگیر [takargir] *technical* shock absorber

تکری [tokri] wicker basket (for fruit)

تکس [taks] 1 tariff 2 duty, customs, tax

تکسی [taksi] (also موتر تکسی) taxi
تکلف [takallof] 1 ceremoniousness; stiffness 2 complicatedness (of style, form); pretentiousness
تکلم [takallom] conversation, talk
♦ تکلم کردن to talk, to converse
تکلیف [taklif] (plural تکالیف [takaalif]) 1 concern; difficulty ♦ اگر تکلیف نباشد! polite Would you be so kind? / If it's no trouble [for you]! ◊ کدام تکلیف دارید؟ What's troubling [you]? / What is your complaint? (question of physician) 2 care, trouble ♦ به تکلیف obscure with difficulty 3 obligation, duty
♦ تکلیف کشید به بخشید to cause trouble, to complicate ♦ تکلیف دادم polite Pardon me for the trouble!
♦ تکلیف کردن obscure 1 to appoint, assign (to a post, job) 2 to oblige (to do something)
تکله [takla] colloquial strong and healthy
تکمه [tokma] 1 button (e.g., of clothing) 2 push-button, button (of door bell) ♦ تکمه اداره کننده technical control button
تکمیل [takmil] 1 conclusion, completion; fulfillment ♦ تکمیل پروژه ها technical fulfillment of plans (for construction) 2 improvement 3 completing (a set), bringing up to strength
♦ تکمیل کردن 1 to conclude, to finish to complete; to fulfill 2 to improve, to perfect
تکنالوجست [teknaalojest] technologist production engineer
تکنالوجی [teknaaloji] and تکنالوژی [teknaalozhi] technology engineering
تکه [taka] 1 lead goat of a flock of sheep 2 male goat, sire
تکه [tekka] 1 fabric, cloth, material ♦ این تکه انگلیسی است This is English cloth / fabric. 2 a piece (of something) ♦ یک تکه نان a hunk of bread, a round of bread
تکه تکه [tekkatekka] 1 torn, broken up 2 broken down by fatigue or weariness, emaciated
تکه کار [tekkakaar] technical blank billet, intermediate product, half-finished article
تکیدن [takidan] 1 to fall, to fall off (about leaves, flowers) 2 to fall out (about hair) 3 to come off (about fingernails, etc.); to peel off, to scale off (about skin) 4 to become frayed, to become shabby (about clothing, fabric)
تکیه [takya] 1 support, bearing, rest, stop, lug 2 cushion (of sofa)
♦ تکیه کردن to lean on (به); to lean on one's elbows; to lean against
تکیه کلام [takyakalaam] comic expression, facetious saying
تگ [tag] colloquial 1 able to pretend or feign adroitly; sly, cunning ♦ روباه تگ است The fox is cunning. 2 pretender, cheat, fraud, impostor; a cunning person, a sly person
♦ خود را تگ انداختن to pretend, to feign
تگمار [tagmar] colloquial pretender
تل [tal] 1 of foot and shoe ♦ تل بوت sole of boots, sole of shoes 2 ☞ تلی
تلاش [talash] 1 trouble, fuss 2 endeavors, efforts 3 search, searching, seeking
♦ تلاش کردن 1 to go to [a lot of] trouble, to fuss 2 to endeavor, to try to achieve 3 to seek, to search, to look for
تلاشی [talaashi] a search
♦ تلاشی کردن to search, to conduct a search

تلافی [talaafi] 1 compensation, reimbursement, making up a loss, shortage, or deficiency 2 making up (for something lost, neglected)
تلبر [talbar] large wooden dish (for produce, foodstuffs)
تلخ [talkh 1.1 bitter; not sweet 1.2 unpleasant, objectionable ♦ سخنان تلخ bitter words; objectionable talk ◊ اوقات او تلخ است He is sad. / He is downcast. / He is saddened 2 bitterly ♦ تلخ گریستن to cry bitterly
تلخان [talkhan] talxan (ground mulberries sometimes mixed with crushed nuts)
تلخک [talkhak] with bitter pits or stones (about fruit) ♦ بادام تلخک bitter almond or almonds ◊ زردآلوی تلخک bitter apricot
تلخه [talkha] colloquial 1 gall bladder 2 self-respect, pride; a feeling of honor
♦ تلخه کسی به کار بودن idiom (literally: someone's gallbladder needed) to need the right person for the job
تلخه دار [talkhadar] 1 colloquial endowed with a feeling of honor, self-respect 2 courageous, brave, manly
تلخی [talkhi] 1 bitter taste 2 pain, bitterness, resentment
تلف [talaf]
♦ تلف شدن 1 to perish, to be killed, to be destroyed, to be ruined ♦ درختها از خنک تلف میشود The trees are dying from the cold. 2 to be squandered, to be wasted (about time, funds, resources)
♦ تلف کردن 1 to ruin, to destroy 2 to squander, to fritter away, to waste
تلفات [talafaat] losses; victims, sacrifices; losses (of life)
تلفظ [talaffoz] pronunciation
♦ تلفظ کردن to pronounce
تلقان [talqan] ☞ تلخان
تلقی [talaqqi] to greet, to receive (some kind of news, etc.)
تلقین [talqin] admonition, reproof; precept, lesson, sermon
تلک [talak] 1 mousetrap; trap 2 net (for catching birds) 3 figurative trap, snare, pitfall
♦ تلک ماندن 1 to set a trap 2 figurative to place snares, to arrange a trap (for somebody)
♦ تلک گردن colloquial burden, yoke on (somebody's) neck
تلگراف [telgeraaf] 1 telegraph 2 ☞
♦ تلگراف بی سیم 1 wireless telegraph 2 ironic gossip, tattler
تلگرام [telgeeraam] telegram ♦ مخابره تلگرام transmission of a telegram, telegraphing
♦ تلگرام دادن to send a telegram
تلم [telem] colloquial piece, slice (usually of a melon, watermellon)
♦ تلم کردن to cut into slices, to slice
تلم تلم [telemtelem] colloquial cut into pieces, into slices (usually of a watermelon, melon)
تلوار [talwaar] sword (with single-edge blade); saber
♦ تلوار چوبی 1 child's wooden sword 2 important in appearance, but shallow (about a person)
تلویزیون [telwizion] 1 television 2 (also دستگاه تلویزیون) television set
تلی [tali] (also تلی چای) sole of the foot, foot
تلی [teli] colloquial (literally: spleen) black and blue
تماس [tamaas] 1 contact, tie, bond, connection 2 establishing contact, ties (with someone)
♦ تماس داشتن 1 to be contiguous, to adjoin 2 to have contact,

ت

to associate, to be connected (with someone با)
- تماس گرفتن to come into contact (with someone با)
تماشا [tamaashaa] 1 inspection, survey (of something) 2 contemplation; admiration ♦ ما به تماشا گلزار آمدیم We came to admire the blossoming glade.
- تماشا کردن to look at; to admire, to contemplate
تماشابین [tamaashaabin] and تماشاچی [tamaashaachi] 1 spectator 2 (one who is) staring (at something), (one who is) admiring (something)
تمام [tamaam] 1 all, whole, full *adjective* ♦ تمام خلق all the people, the whole people ◊ بادقت تمام with full attention 2 end; conclusion
- تمام شدن 1 to end, to be ended; to conclude, to be concluded 2 to run out, to expire (about a deadline) 3 to cost, to come to (a certain price)
- گران تمام شدن to be expensive
- تمام کردن 1 to end, to conclude 2 to complete (an educational institution, i.e., to graduate)
تماما [tamaaman] entirely, wholly; fully, completely
تمام شد [tamaamshod]
- قیمت تمام شد prime cost, net cost
تمام نما [tamaamnomaa]
- آیینه تمام نما 1 true reflection, truthful representation (of something) 2 *mythological* magic mirror ♦ تابلوی تمام نما actual picture, real picture, true picture
تمامی [tamaami] *colloquial* ☞ تمام 1
- تمامی مردم all the people
تمامیت [tamaamiyat] integrity ♦ تمامیت ارضی territorial integrity
تمایل [tamaayol] leaning, inclination, aspiration, yearning; wish, desire, longing
- تمایل داشتن to be inclined (toward something); to have an inclination, to have a tendency; to aspire
تمباکو [tambaaku] tobacco
تمبان [tombaan] ☞ تنبان
تمبل [tambal] ☞ تنبل
تمبل تندوری [tambale-tandori] *slang* (*literally:* tandoori lazy) lazy kid, slacker
تمبر [tambar] ☞ تنبور
تمبه [tamba] ☞ تنبه
تمتراق [tamtaraaq] splendor; magnificence; pomp
تمثیل [tamsil] 1 staging, production, performance (in a theater) 2 imitation 3 *literary* comparison, assimilation
- تمثیل کردن 1 to put on, to produce (on the stage) 2 to imitate 3 *literary* to compare, to liken, to assimilate, to equate
تمثیلی [tamsili] intended for the stage; dramatic; a play in verse
تمجید [tamjid] praise, eulogy
تمدن [tamaddon] civilization, culture
تمدید [tamdid] extension (of the period of effectiveness, term of something), prolongation (of a contract or treaty)
تمرکز [tamarkoz] concentration
- تمرکز دادن 1 to concentrate 2 to gather, to draw up (troops)
تمرین [tamrin] and تمرینات [tamrinat] training session, drill exercise; rehearsal
تمسخر [tamaskhor] 1 mockery, gibe, taunt 2 satire, exposure
تمسق [tomsoq] tomsoq (variety of apricot of red color)

تمق [tomoq] special die for settling a bet (one of the bettors must keep the die with him at all times and present it on demand)
تمکین [tamkin] 1 importance, staidness, sedateness 2 restraint, reserve, the ability to bear up with dignity
تمنا [tamannaa] 1 wish, desire 2 request (about something) ♦ تمنا دارم I 1 to wish for 2 to request ♦ تمنا داشتن (کردن) request that you … / please … (in an application, written request)
تموز [tam (m)uz] the height of summer, the middle of summer; summer heat
تمویل [tamwil] *economics* financing
تمییز [tamiz] and
تمییز [tamyiz] 1 distinction, difference, distinguishing, discernment ♦ بدون تمییز مکان وزمان without regard to place and time 2 the ability to discern; comprehension, reasonableness, common sense 3 *legal* cassation
- تمییز داشتن to be reasonable, to sensible, to be quick [mentally]
- تمییز کردن to distinguish, to discern
تن [tan] body
- تن بتن ☞ تن به تن
- تن دادن 1 to give oneself up to, to give way to (something به) 2 to consent, to agree, to submit, to resign oneself, to shirk (به)
- به تن کردن to put on (clothing)
تن [ton] ton
تناژ [tonaazh] load capacity, tonnage
تن آسایی [tanaasaayi] 1 prosperity, materail well-being, easy life 2 effeminacy, sybaritism
تناسب [tanaasob] 1 correlation, ratio, proportion; symmetry ♦ تناسب اندام proportionality or symmetry of the figure ◊ همان تناسب *mathematical* in the same ratio 2 proportion
تناسل [tanaasol] procreation; propagation, multiplying, reproduction
تناسلی [tanasoli] sexual ♦ اعضای (آلات) تناسلی sexual organs
تنبان [tombaan] trousers worn around the house, wide trousers (men's and women's) ♦ تنبان شرعی wide trousers (worn by Muslims and covering the figure from the waist to the ankles) ◊ گیبی - trousers (with gathers and narrow about the hips)
تن بتن [tanbatan] one against one; one on one ♦ جنگ تن بتن single combat; duel
تنبل [tambal] loafer, lazy person
تنبور [tambur] tamboura (stringed musical instrument)
تنبورچی [tamburchi] and تنبورنواز [tamburnawazh] a person who plays the tamboura, tamboura player
تنبه [tamba] 1.1 wooden bolt, (door) lock 1.2 post, pillar, support (of a building) 2 pressed down, clamped down; leaned (against something)
تنخواه(ه) [tanxaa (h)] 1 salary, rate of salary; earnings 2 *historical* bestowing of land by an emir (for special services)
تند [tond] 1 sharp (about taste); pungent (about an odor) 2 strong, heavy (about wind, rain) 3 sharp, harsh, passionate, hot-tempered, quick-tempered, vehement (e.g., about a person's character) 4 quick, rapid, fast
تندباد [tondbaad] strong wind, hurricane, tornado, whirlwind

تندر [taandar] thunder ♦ تندرآسمانی misfortune sent down by heaven, God's punishment

تندزبان [tondzobaan] sharp, biting to the tongue, rough, coarse

تندور [tandor] colloquial ☞ تنور

تندور به دل کسی دردادن [tandoor-ba-dele-kasay-dardaadan] idiom expression (literally: to fire tandoor in someone's heart) to offend, to anger, to make someone's blood boil

تن ده [tandeh] colloquial 1 pliant, compliant, submissive, obedient 2 ready to shirk

تن دهی [tandehi] colloquial 1 pliancy, compliancy, submissiveness, obedience 2 readiness to shirk

تندی [tondi] 1 sharpness, pungence (of taste, of odor) 2 sharpness, abruptness, quickness, rapidity

تنزل [tanazzol] 1 lowering, dropping (e.g., of prices) 2 decline, collapse, retrogression
- تنزل دادن to lower, to reduce
- تنزل کردن to be lowered, to drop to fall

تنزیل [tanzil] 1 lowering, drop, fall, reduction; rebate 2 finance discount 3 religion sending down (about the Koran)

تنسته [tanesta] 1 fabric, cloth; weaving 2 textiles warp ♦ تنسته گلیم warp of a rug 3 cobweb

تنظیم [tanzim] 1 putting in order; organizing, regulating, adjusting ♦ مدیریت تنظیم organizing department, organization department 2 compiling (of a document)

تنفر [tanaffor] aversion, repugnance; antipathy; hatred
- تنفر داشتن (از) to feel aversion, to feel repugnance, to hate

تنفس [tanaffos] breathing, inhalation and exhalation ♦ جهاز تنفس respiratory organs
- تنفس کردن to breathe, to inhale, to breathe in

تنفسی [tanaffosi] linguistics aspirate adjective ♦ آواز تنفسی aspirate sound

تنقید [tanqid] criticism
- تنقید کردن (بالای،از) to criticize, to subject to criticism

تنک [tonok] 1 thin, fine ♦ کاغذ تنک thin paper 2 scanty, sparse (about hair)
- تنک کردن to roll (dough), to roll out (dough)

تنکار [tanakaar] technical borax

تنکیر [tankir]
- یای تنکیر grammar indefinite article, indicator of indefiniteness

تنگ [tang] 1 tight, narrow ♦ کوچه تنگ narrow street 2 straitened, strained, difficult ♦ نفس تنگ labored breathing, difficult breathing
- به کسی تنگ گرفتن to treat severely, to oppress (somebody)
- چاره کسی را تنگ کردن to put somebody in a hopeless situation

تنگ دست [tangdast] colloquial (literally: tight-handed) poor, brooke, needy (person)

تنگ کسی سست شدن [tange-kasay-sost-shudan] idiom (literally: one's waist belt get loose) to lose confidence

تنگ [tong] earthenware jug with narrow neck

تنگ چشم [tangchéshm] 1 stingy, miserly, greedy 2 envious

تنگ دستی [tangdasti] poverty, need

تنگ دل [tangdel] ☞ دل تنگ

تنگر [tongor] woman who looks after the bride (on the wedding night)

تنگه [tanga]¹ gorge, ravine

تنگه [tanga]² tanga (silver coin worth one-third of an afghani)

تنگی [tangi] 1 tightness, narrowness, scantiness ♦ تنگی نظر a narrowness of views, shortsightedness 2 ☞ تنگه¹

تنگی کوچه [tangikocha] colloquial alley

تنور [tanur] tanur (oven for baking flat cakes, usually set into the floor or the ground)

تنورپاک [tanurpak] wooden shovel (for raking coals from a tanur)

تنوری [tanuri]
- نان تنوری homemade flat cakes (baked in a tanur)

تنویر [tanwir] 1 illumination, lighting ♦ وسایل تنویر lighting fixtures 2 (also تنویر اذهان and تنویر افکار) enlightenment, education

تنه [tana] 1 body, trunk, torso 2 trunk (of a tree) 3 fuselage (of an aircraft); hull (of a ship)

تنها [tanhaa] 1 solitary, lone, single, alone 2 only, solely

تنها صورت [tanhaa-soorat] colloquial (literally: lonely) a person who does not have a helper at home (with no son or brother)

تنهایی [tanhaayi] solitude, loneliness, seclusion
- بتنهایی ☞ به تنهایی

تو [tu] 1 you (familiar form) 2 (in combination with the preposition از) your (familiar form) ♦ برادر ازتو your brother

تو [taw] colloquial ☞ تب

تو گرفتن [taw-gereftan] idiom (literally: to have a fever) to be eager, to be anxious derogatory saying

تو مرگ [tawe-marg] idiom (literally: struggle during dying) jealous, envious, eager derogatory

تو دادن [taw-daadan] colloquial (literally: to twist) to pocket ♦ از جمله دو صد افغانی را به خود تو داد Of the total, I kept two hundred Afghani for myself.

تواچی [tawaachi] assistant of a village elder (who usually informs the population of orders and instructions)

تواریخ [tawaarikh] plural of تاریخ

توازن [tawaazon] equilibrium, balance, stability ♦ توا - balance of forces

توافق [tawaafoq] unanimity; mutual assent, mutual consent, mutual agreement ♦ توافق نظر assent, agreement, consent, understanding
- توافق نظر کسی را حاصل کردن to obtain someone's assent or consent
- (درمورد) to come to an agreement with somebody

توان [tawaan] 1 present tense stem توانستن 2.1 might, power 2.2 capability, ability, means, resources ♦ توان مالی financial resources, financial means
- توان چیزی را داشتن solvency to be able, to be in a condition (to do something)
- توان چیزی رایافتن to find the strength (to do something)

توانا [tawaanaa] powerful, strong; mighty

توانایی [tawaanaayi] 1 strength, forces, might 2 authority, power; great influence

توانستن [tawaanestan] (present tense stem توان [tawaan]) 1 (with preceding past participles of a semantic verb) to be able, to be in condition; to know how ♦ خوانده نمی توانست He did not know how to read. ◊ گفته می توانیم که ۰۰۰ We can say that ... 2 (in independent use as a transitive verb) to cope (with something); to fulfill, to carry out, to accomplish, to perform ♦ تو آن کار را نتوانستی You did not cope with that matter. / You were not equal to that matter.

توانگر [tawaangar] *literary* rich, wealthy, well-to-do, prosperous

توبره [tobra] 1 bag or sack with laces, pouch 2 (also توبره اسپ) bag for oats (tied to a horse's muzzle, i.e., feedbag)

توبند [tawband] *colloquial* charm, prayer against fever (written on paper; worn on the neck)

توبه [tawba (and) toba] 1 repentence; confession 2 vow, promise, pledge

• توبه - ! I confess / I'm sorry! / I promise not to! / I won't any more! ♦ مرا از این کار توبه! May I do that sometime!

• توبه کردن 1 to repent, to confess, to be sorry (for something) (از) 2 to give a pledge, to promise not to, to renounce

توبه توبه [tawbatawba]

• توبه توبه! *colloquial* 1 God forbid! 2 One ought not sin! 3 Ugh, what filth / muck! / Ugh, what a dirty trick!

توپ [top]¹ 1 ball, small ball ♦ توپ برفی snowball 2 piece, roll (of material) ♦ یک توپ کرک one piece of cloth

• توپ برفی ساختن to play with snowballs

توپ [top]² 1 gun, cannon ♦ توپ دافع هوا antiaircraft gun 2 *colloquial* (also توپ چاشت) noon (the coming of which is heralded by a cannon shot in Kabul) ♦ بعد از توپ بیایید Come after 12!

• توپ زدن to fire, to fire a cannon

• به توپ پراندن to execute by cannon (by tying to the muzzle)

توپ بازی [topbaazi] a game played with a ball (similar to Russian game of lapta, which is like cricket or baseball)

توپچی [topchi] 1.1 artilleryman 1.2 (also عسکر توپچی) artillery *noun* 2 artillery *adjective* ♦ جبه خانه توپچی artillery depot

توپخانه [topkhaana] 1 battery (artillery) 2 artillery *noun*

توپکشی [topkashi] *colloquial* 1 heavy and unpleasant work 2 misfortune, trouble, disaster

توپوگرافی [topograafi] 1 topography 2 topographic ♦ نقشه توپو گرافی topographic map

توت [tut] 1 mulberry 2 (also درخت -) mulberry tree

توتا [totaa] ☞ طوطی

توت خورک [tutkhorak] variety of finch

توتو [toto] *children speech* doggie

توته [tuta] 1 *technical* pin, bobbin, spool 2 *colloquial* throat, gullet

توته [tota] 1 piece, hunk ♦ یک توته نان hunk of bread, round of bread 2 fragment, scrap ♦ نوته سنگ a fragment of stone or rock

• توته کردن to divide into parts, to break (e.g., a flat cake)

توته توته [totatota] broken into pieces; divided into parts

• توته توته کردن 1 to tear; to shred 2 to crush, to divide up, to split up, to pulverize, to make small

توتیا [totiyaa] 1.1 *chemistry* zinc suboxide; vitriol 1.2 eye ointment 2 *colloquial* uncommon, rare

توجه [tawajjo(h)] 1 paying attention (to somebody, something); directing attention (to somebody, something) 2 attentiveness, courtesy

• توجه کردن 1 to pay attention, to direct attention (به) 2 to show attention, to render courtesy, to do a favor (به)

توجیه [tawjih] orientation, directing ♦ زاویه توجیه field of fire

توده [toda] 1 heap, pile ♦ توده سنگ pile of rocks 2 knoll, mound, hillock, hill ♦ توده خاک mound of earth,

embankment; sand hills, sand dunes ♦ توده های ریگ 3 gathering (of people, livestock), crowd, throng

• توده کردن to pour (in a heap), to pour

تور [tawar] *colloquial* ☞ تبر

• تبرش دسته یافت *proverb* His words were confirmed. / His words were borne out.

تور [tor] 1 net, small net (for catching birds) 2 (also تور ماهیگیری) seine

• تور انداختن to cast a seine

• تور ماندن 1 to set nets, to spread nets 2 to set up intrigues, to machinate

تور خوردن [toor-khoordan] *colloquial* to get excited, to get worked up

توربوجت [turbojet] turbojet *adjective* ♦ انجین تور بوجت turbojet engine

توربین [turbin] turbine

توربین دار [turbindaar] turbine *adjective*, gas turbine *adjective* ♦ انجین توربین دار gas turbine engine

تورزم [torézem] tourism

توریست [turest] tourist

تورک [torak] hemorrhagic pox, purpura variolosa

تورن جنرال [turanjanraal] lieutenant general

توروبخیه [torobakhya] decorative stitch; figured or patterned stitch

تورید [tawrid] importation, import

توریه [tawriya] *literary* allegory ♦ شعر توریه allegorical poem

توزیع [tawzi'] 1 distribution 2 delivery

توس [tus] ☞ طوس

توسط [tawassot]

• به توسط 1 by means of, with the help of *denominative preposition* ♦ توسط تبر with an ax 2 on ♦ توسط طیاره on an aircraft, by aircraft 3 through, by way of ♦ توسط تیکه دار through a contractor

توسعه [tawse'a] broadening expansion; spreading, dissemination; development growth ♦ توسعه معلومات widening of knowledge ◊ توسعه نفوز spread of influence

• توسعه دادن to broaden, to expand; to spread, to disseminate; to develop

• توسعه یافتن to expand *intransitive*, to receive, dissemination, to grow, to develop *intransitive*

توشک [toshak] mattress; bedding

توشه [tosha] provisions (for the road); traveling provisions

توصیف [tawsif] 1 description; testimonial, reference 2 eulogy

• توصیف کردن 1 to describe, to define (از) 2 to paint, to draw a picture of, to lavish praise on (از)

توصیفی [tawsifi] *grammar* determinative, attributive ♦ عبارت توصیفی attributive combination

توصیه [tawsiya] 1 recommendation, advice 2 will, testament

• توصیه کردن 1 to recommend, to advise 2 to bequeath

توضیح [tawzih] explanation, elucidation

• توضیح دادن to explain, to elucidate

توطئه [tawte'a] intrigues, underhand plotting; plot, conspiracy

توغ [togh] 1 banner, staff with horse's tail attached 2 flag (attached to a pole at a sacred tomb)

توفان [tufaan] gale, hurricane, storm ♦ توفان بحری sea storm ◊ توفان ریگ sand storm

• توفان کردن 1 to rage (about the wind) 2 to flower or bloom wildly or unmanageably 3 to work wonders (at work, in sports, etc.)

توفانی [tufaani] stormy; storm *adjective*
♦ باران توفانی 1 wind with rain 2 driving rain, pouring rain ♦ شب توفانی cloudy night, rainy night

توفیق [tawfiq] *literary* help, assistance ♦ خداوند توفیق کند May God help [you]!

توقع [tawaqqo'] expectation; hopes, hope
♦ توقع کردن (از) to expect, to set hopes on, to hope

توقف [tawaqqof] stop, halt; delay

توقیف [tawqif] detention, arrest
♦ توقیف کردن to detain, to arrest

توکل [tawakkol] hope, hoping (to God)

تول [tol] weight ♦ تول اتومی atomic weight
♦ تول کردن to weigh
♦ تول ترازو *astronomy* Libra (constellation)

تولد [tawallod] birth
♦ تولد شدن (یافتن) to be born ♦ من در کابل تولد شدم I was born in Kabul.

تولدی [tawallodi]
♦ روز تولدی day of birth

تولدیافته [tawallodyaafta] native ♦ تولدیافته بلخ native of Balkh

توله [tola] 1 tola (variety of folk musical instrument in the form of a metal file or pipe) 2 tube 3 *anatomy* acoustic duct 4 *factory* whistle
♦ توله پای *anatomy* shin
♦ توله دست *anatomy* forearm

تولی [tolay] *military* detachment; group; team, flight

تولید [tawlid] production, manufacture ♦ تولید برق production of electric power ◊ قدرت تولید production capacity (of an enterprise, etc.) ◊ قوه تولید productivity, work, creation
♦ تولید آواز *linguistics* articulation (of sound)
♦ تولید کردن 1 to produce, to manufacture 2 to call into being, to give birth to ♦ رطوبت بعضی مرض ها را تولید می نماید Dampness causes certain illnesses.

تولیدات [tawlidaat] 1 *plural of* تولید 2 production, output, manufacture ♦ تولیدات زراعتی agricultural production or output ◊ تولیدات صنعتی industrial production or output

تولیداتی [tawlidaati] production *adjective* ♦ مؤسسات تولیداتی industrial enterprises

تولیدی [tawlidi] 1 productive ♦ حیوانات تولیدی productive livestock 2 ☞ روابط تولیدی production relations

تومت چی [tomat-chi] *colloquial* an accuser, finger pointer

تومت ناق [tomate-naaq] *slang* (*literally:* false accusation) troublemaker

تومور [tumur] *medicine* tumor; swelling

تونل [tonal] tunnel ♦ تونل اخذ آب پرچاوه water intake tunnel ◊ تونل tunnel for water run-off discharge

توهین [tawhin] insult; disgrace

توی [toy] wedding
♦ توی کردن to arrange a wedding, to celebrate a wedding

تویانه [toyaana] 1 wedding *adjective* ♦ لباس تویانه wedding dress, wedding attire 2 wedding gift

ته [tah] 1 bottom; bottom part, lower part ♦ ته کاسه bottom of a cup, bottom of a bowl 2 (first component of compound words with meanings) 2.1 bottom or lower part (of something) ♦ ته خانه basement, cellar 2.2 remainder ♦ ته دیگی burnt food (at the bottom of a pot)

تهاجم [tahaajom] attack, assault, invasion, inroad
♦ تهاجم کردن to attack; to invade, to encroach

تهانه [tahaana (and) tana] post ♦ تهانه سرحدی border post ◊ تهانه عسکری police post or station

تهانه دار [tahaanadaar (and) tanadar] 1 chief of a post 2 chief of a police station

ته خانه [tahkhaana] basement, cellar

تهداب [tahdaab] 1 foundation (of a building) 2 foundation, basis
♦ تهداب گذاشتن 1 to lay a foundation 2 to found, to base

تهداب گذار [tahdaabgozaar] founder; creator, initiator

تهداب گذاری [tahdaabgozaari] 1 laying of a foundation 2 founding, establishing, establishment
♦ تهداب گذاری شدن to be laid (of a foundation, etc.), to be founded, to be based

تهدید [tahdid] 1 threat 2 danger

ته دیگی [tahdeegi] remainder of soup or broth (at bottom of the pot); burnt food (stuck to bottom of pot)

تهذیب [tahzib] culture, standard of culture; politeness, courtesy; education, level of education

ته کاسه [tahkaasa] *geology* depression

تهمت [tohmat] unfounded charge or accusation; slander
♦ تهمت زدن to accuse without foundation; to slander, to make up tales

تهنشین [tahneshin] sediment, deposit; accumulation
♦ تهنشین شدن to fall, to be deposited, to settle

ته وبالا [tahobaalaa]
♦ ته وبالا کردن 1 to turn (things) over; to stir, to sort out (while making a choice) 2 to stir, to mix (food in a pot)

تهویه [tahwiya] ventilation; air conditioning ♦ دستگاه تهویه ventilation unit or system; air conditioner, air conditioning system

تهی [tehi] empty, hollow

تهی دست [tehidast (and) tehidest] 1 poor, beggarly, indigent 2 poor person

تهیه [tahiya] 1 preparation (e.g., of conditions) 2 laying in orprocurement (e.g., of foodstuffs) 3 making, manufacture
♦ تهیه کاغذ manufacture of paper

تیاتر [tiyaater (and) tayaatór] theater

تیار [tayaar (and) tiyaar] 1 ready, prepared ♦ نان تیار است Dinner is ready. 2 finished 3 willing, agreeable (to something) 4 *colloquial* fat, well-fed
♦ تیار - ! All right! / Agreed!
♦ تیار شدن *colloquial* 1 to prepare for, to get ready for 2 to be manufactured, to be made, to be produced 3 *colloquial* to put on weight, to grow fat
♦ تیار کردن *colloquial* 1 to ready, to prepare 2 to make, to manufacture 3 to fatten (livestock, cattle)

تیار خور [tayaarxor (and) tiyarxor] 1 a person provided with board and lodging 2 parasite, sponger 3 *obscure* servants, menials

تیپ [teep] 1 tape recording 2 recording tape
♦ تیپ کردن to record on tape; to make a recording on tape

تیپ [tip] model ♦ تیپ نو موتر new model of an automobile

تیپ ریکاردر [teeprecardar] tape recorder

تیت [tit] *colloquial* scattered
♦ تیت کردن to scatter, to strew

تی تی [ti-tit] *children speech* a car

ت

تیت وپرک [titoparak] *colloquial* 1 scattered, in disarray, in disorder ♦ لباسهای خودراتیت وپرک کرد He scattered his clothes [where they fell]. 2 scattered, dispersed ♦ اطفال تیت وپرک شدند The children scattered in all directions. ◊ افکار من بالکل تیت و پرک شده بود I got lost completely.

تیر [teer] ¹ 1 arrow 2 shot (from a bow) ♦ یک تیر ودو پاختک *proverb* [To kill] two turtle doves with one shot.
• تیر کاری *colloquial* 1 striking arrow 2 heavy loss, grief
• تیر انداختن to shoot (with a bow)
• تیر خوردن to be shot
• تیر زدن to shoot
• تیر کاری خوردن to be stricken with grief, to suffer a loss
• تیرش خطا رفت and تیرش به خاک خورد He didn't get away with it. / His trick didn't work.

تیر [teer] ² 1 log 2 (also تیر خانه) ceiling beam (of a house)
• تیر پشت *colloquial* and تیر کمر spine, backbone

تیر [tair] tire ♦ تیر موتر car tire

تیر فالتو [taire-faaltu] *slang* (*literally:* a spare tire) a jobless person, unemployed person

تیر [tayr]
• تیر شدن 1 to pass, to be over (about time) ♦ دوسال تیر شد Two years passed. 2 to cross, to walk (past), to drive (past) 3 to cross (از); to swim across, to sail across (از) ♦ سرحد تیر شدن از to cross a border 4 *colloquial* to give up, to renounce, to refuse, to decline
• تیر شو *colloquial* Go away! / Off with you! / Make yourself scarce! / Quit! / The deuce take you!
• از گناه کسی تیر شدن to forgive someone's fault or guilt
• تیر کردن 1 to spend (time) ♦ رخصتی را در دهات تیر کردیم We spent the holiday / leave in the country 2 to transfer, to convey (از) 3 to endure, to suffer, to undergo ♦ چه روز های بدی راتیر کرده است How much he had to endure! 4 to pass through (به،از) 5 *colloquial* to get [something] off one's hands 6 to pilfer, to steal, to walk away with
• از خود تیر کردن *colloquial* to get rid of somebody, to send somebody on his way
• از نظر تیر کردن to examine, to scrutinize
• ساعت کسی راتیر کردن to take somebody's time
• گپ راتیر کردن *colloquial* to avoid discussion (of something); to surpress conversation (about something), to change the subject of the conversation
• تیر آوردن [tayr-aawordan] *colloquial* (*literally:* to ignore) to ignore to turn a blind eye

تیر انداز [tirandaaz] archer
تیر اندازی [tirandaazi] archery, shooting with a bow
تیرک [tirak] ¹
• تیرک زدن *colloquial* to spray vigorously, to spurt
تیرک [tirak] ² axle (of a millstone)
تیرکش [tiraksh] embrosure; loophole gunport
تیرماه [tirmaah] *colloquial* fall, autumn ♦ تیرماه قاصد زمستان است *proverb* Autumn is the forerunner of winter.
تیروبیر [teerobeer]
• تیروبیر شدن *colloquial* to miss each other
• تیروبیر کردن *colloquial* to foist (something or somebody) by deception; to palm off one thing instead of another
تیره [tira] 1 dark (about a color) ♦ سبز تیره dark green 2 dull, dulled 3 somber, gloomy
• تیره وتار ☞ تیره وتار
• تیره شدن 1 to become dark, to grow dark; to become dull 2 to deteriorate, to go bad, to cloud over (about relationships, etc.)
• چای تیره strong tea
تیره بخت [tirabakht] ☞ سیاه بخت and بدبخت
تیره روز [tiraroz] ☞ سیاه روز
تیره گی [tiragi] 1 darkness, dark, gloom ♦ تیره گی هوا gloom, twilight, dusk 2 gloominess
• تیره گی اوضاع tenseness or tension of a situation.
تیره ماه [tiramaah] ☞ تیرماه
تیره وتار [tirawtaar] dark, black; submerged in gloom ♦ شب تیره وتار dark night
تیز [teez] 1.1 quick, rapid, speedy, swift, impetuous ♦ مرکب تیز از اسپ ایستاده بهتر است *proverb* A fast mule is better than a slow horse. 1.2 sharp, cutting ♦ شمشیر تیز sharp sword 1.3 sharp (about the mind, hearing, vision) 1.4 bright, vivid (about color, light); shrill (about a sound) 2 quickly, rapidly, swiftly, with great speed ♦ تیز رفته می توانی؟ Can you go quickly?
• تیز کردن 1 to sharpen 2 ☞ تیزتر in article
تیزاب [teezaab] 1 caustic solution; acid, pickle ♦ تیزاب لحیم *technical* soldering acid 2 *chemistry* acid ♦ تیزاب گوگرد sulfuric acid ◊ تیزاب نمک hydrochloric acid
تیزابی [teezaabi]
• اکمولاتور تیزابی lead-acid storage battery
تیزتر [teeztar]
• تیزتر کردن to accelerate, to expedite, to hasten, to quicken
تیزتیز [teezteez]
• تیزتیزدیدن to look fixedly or intently, to stare
• تیزتیز کردن to pierce with a look
تیزدو [teezdaw] 1 quick, rapid, fast; swift-footed, nimble 2 (also اسپ تیزدو) runner, fast horse
تیزرفتار [teezraftaar] speedy, fast
• موتر تیزرفتار automobile (passenger car)
تیزفهم [teezfahm] quick-thinking; sharp, keen-witted
تیزکاری [teezkaari] sharpening, stropping, whetting, grinding [to sharpen]
• چرخ تیزکاری *technical* abrasive disk or wheel
• مواد تیزکاری *technical* abrasives
تیشه [teesa] implement for hewing and felling (in the form of an ax, but with a narrow blade set perpendicularly to the plane of the handle) ♦ تیشه نجاری adz
• تیشه به پای خود زدن to hit oneself in the leg with one's own sword; to put obstacles in one's own way (to cut the bough on which one is sitting)
• تیشه به ریشه خود زدن *idiom* (*literally:* to hit one's root with an ax) to shoot oneself in the foot, to be one's own undoing
تیغ [teegh] 1 curved saber, saber, sword; blade (of saber or sword) 2 blade (of a knife, etc.) 3 razor
• تیغ کشیدن and تیغ زدن to fell, to kill (e.g., with a saber)
تیغ بندی [taygh-bandi] *colloquial* spell (a kind of witchcraft that saves someone's life from a knife or gun attack)
تیغه [teegha] 1 (also کوه تیغه) crest of mountain or hill; pointed summit, peak 2 sprout, shoot
• تیغه زدن to sprout, to give off shoots
تیکت [teeket] ☞ تکت
تیکر [tikar] shard, fragment, splinter (of earthenware) ♦ کلال به تیکر شکسته آب میخورد *proverb* The potter drinks water from a shard of crockery.

تیکه [teeka] agreement on the delivery (of something); contract
- به تیکه گرفتن to conclude an agreement on the delivery (of something), to make a contract

تیکه دار [teekadaar] supplier; contractor

تیگر [taygár] (also سگ تیگری) bulldog

تیگر [taygar] slang (literally: tiger) loafer

تیل [tail] 1 butter ♦ تیل خاک vegetable oil 2 (also مخزن تیل) fuel; kerosene 3 gasoline ♦ مخزن تیل gasoline tank
- تیل دادن to smear or to grease with butter or oil
- تیل کشیدن to squeeze or to press oil from seeds

تیلپک [teelpak] telpak (leather cap trimmed with sheep's wool)

تیل خاک [teelekhaak] kerosene

تیلدار [teeldaar] oil-bearing (about a well)

تیل دانی [teeldaani] technical oil can ♦ بمیه دار تیل دانی spraying oil can

تیلسکوپ [teeleskop] telescope

تیلفون [teelfun] telephone ♦ دستگاه تیلفون اتومات dial telephone exchange

تیل کشی [teelkashi] extraction of oil; production of vegetable oil

تلگراف [teelgeraaf] ☞

تلگرام [teelgeraam] ☞

تیل گیری [teelgiri] refueling

تیله [teela] colloquial push; pushing
- تیله کردن (دادن) to push, to shove

تیلی [teeli] colloquial spleen

تیمارداری [timaardaari] 1 care (usually of sick persons) 2 care, tending (of a horse)
- تیمارداری کردن 1 to care for, to nurse (sick persons) 2 to tend (a horse) (از)

تیم دادن [taym-daadan] colloquial flirting of boys with girls, showoff

تینچر أیدین [tinchar] ☞

تینچر أیدین [tinchaaaydin] and تینچر آیودین [tincharaayodin] tincture of iodine, iodine

تینس [teenes] tennis

تیوب [toyūb] and تیوپ [toyup] 1 tube; test tube; flask, retort 2 (also تیوب موتر) inner tube of automobile tire 3 tube (e.g., for toothpaste) 4 anatomy tube (of an ovary)

تیول [toyul] historical estate (bestowed for use for life); fief

ث
5th letter of the Dari alphabet

ثابت (sabet) 1 steady, solid, firm, durable 2 established, proven 3 (opposite of سیار) stable; stationary 4 grammar uninflected
- ثابت شدن 1 to gain strength, to become consolidated 2 to be established, to be proved or proven ♦ این فرضیه ثابت شده است This hypothesis was confirmed. 3 to ensure, to follow ♦ از آن ثابت می شود که ... From this it follows that ... 4 to turn out, to prove to be ♦ نتایج اطمینان بخش ثابت شدهاست The results turned out to be encouraging.
- ثابت کردن 1 to strengthen, to consolidate 2 to establish, to prove 3 to stabilize 4 to make stationary, to fix

ثابت قدم [saabetqadam] 1 staunch, steadfast, solid, unshakable ♦ مبارز ثابت قدم staunch champion 2 consistent

ثالث [saales] literary 1 third 2 (also ثالث بالخیر) arbitrator

ثالثاً [saalesan] literary in the third place, thirdly

ثانوی [saanawi] 1 second; secondary ♦ اهمیت ثانوی secondary significance ◊ تعلیمات ثانوی secondary education ◊ دوره ثانوی upper classes of secondary school (grades 10-12) 2 ☞ ثانی 1

ثانی [saani] 1 second 2 colloquial thereupon, later on, then

ثانیاً [saaniyan] secondly in the second place

ثانیه [saaniya] second (of time)

ثانیه گرد [saaniyagard] second hand (of a watch, clock)

ثبت [sabt] 1 entering on a list, registration, entry, record 2 record (on magnetic tape) ♦ ثبت آواز sound recording
- ثبت کردن 1 to enter on a list, to record, to register 2 to record (on magnetic tape)

ثبوت [sobut] 1 proof, evidence, establishment of a fact; confirmation 2 (legal term) 3 solidity, staunchness, stability
- به ثبوت رساندن to prove, to establish as fact, to confirm

ثروت [sarwat] 1 riches, wealth, fortune 2 abundance, plenty 3 natural resources

ثروت خیز [sarwatkheez] rich (in natural resources), abundant; copious, plentiful

ثروتمند [sarwatmand] rich, wealthy, well-to-do

ثریا [sorayaa] 1 astronomy Pleiades 2 feminine proper name Soraya

ثقافت [saqaafat] culture

ثقافتی [saqaafati] cultural ♦ روابط - cultural ties

ثقل [séqel] gravity, weight; load ♦ مرکز ثقل physics center of gravity

ثقیل [saqil] 1 heavy, weighty 2 grave, terrible, difficult, hard, arduous 3 hard-to-digest, heavy (about food) ♦ ماشیندار ثقیل heavy machine gun

ثلاث [salaas] literary three

ثلث [sols] a one-third part or portion, one-third

ثمر [samar] 1 fruit 2 product; result 3 benefit, gain, profit

ثمربخش [samarbakhsh] useful beneficial, advantageous, profitable; result-producing, successful ♦ کار ثمربخش fruitful labor or toil

ثمردار [samardaar] 1 fruit, fruit-bearing ♦ درختهای ثمردار fruit trees 2 productive

ثمره [samara] (plural ثمرات [samaraat]) 1 ☞ ثمر 2 posterity

ثنا [sanaa] literary praise, praising, laudation, eulogy (of God)
- ثنا گفتن to praise, to eulogize, to extol (usually God)

ثواب [sawab] retribution, reward (for a good deed) ♦ کار ثواب good deed, good
- ثواب داشتن to deserve reward, to be praiseworthy (about a good deed)
- کار ثواب کردن to do good, to be a benefactor

ثور [sawr] 1 astronomy Taurus 2 Saur (the second month of the Afghan calendar; corresponds to April-May)

ثی [see] name of the letter ث

ج
6th letter of the Dari alphabet

جا [jaa] ☞ جای

جابجا [jaabajaa] ☞ جای بجای

جادو [jaadu] witchcraft, sorcery; magic; incantation
- جادو کردن to practice witchcraft; to conjure

جادوسار [jaadusaar] bewitched, charmed
- جادوسار کردن to bewitch, to charm

جادوکش [jaadukash] removing sorcery, undoing witchcraft

جادوگر [jaadugar] 1 magician; sorcerer 2 conjurer, illusionist

جادوگری [jaadugari] magic, witchcraft; sorcery
- جادوگری کردن to practice witchcraft; to practice sorcery

جاده [jaadda] 1 main road, main street; avenue 2 highway

جاذب [jaazeb] 1.1 attracting (to oneself) 1.2 ☞ جذاب 1.3 absorbing (moisture), absorbent 2 (also کاغذ جاذب) blotting paper

جاذبه [jaazeba] 1 ☞ جاذب 2 (plural جواذب [jaawaazeb]) attraction, gravity, gravitation ♦ جاذبه زمین gravity, earth's gravity ◊ قوه جاذبه force of gravity, gravitational force

جار [jaar]¹ 1 loud cry, call (of a street vendor, hustler, etc.) 2 historical notification, public proclamation (by means of a crier)
- جار زدن 1 to shout, to yell, to call in (about a street vendor, etc.) 2 historical to notify, to proclaim publicly (through a crier)

جار [jaar]² colloquial ☞ جهر

جارجار [jaarjaar] colloquial 1 divulging, blab out, give away (e.g., a secret) 2 yell, shout, noise, hubbub
- جار جار کردن 1 to divulge, to blab out, to give away (a secret) 2 to raise a shout, to make noise, to raise a hubbub, to raise a din

جارچی [jaarchi] 1 hustler (at a shop, store, i.e., one who tries to get customers to come in) 2 street crier

جارو [jaaru] and جاروب [jorob] broom, besom (broom made of twigs), whisk broom
- جاروبرقی vacuum cleaner
- خاک جارو sweepings, dust
- جارو زدن (کردن) colloquial 1 to sweep; to clean 2 to clean out, to rob

جاروبته [jaarubota] bush with long branches (used to make brooms)

جاروجنجال [jaarojanjaal] shout, noise, din; loud quarrel, noisy quarrel
- جاروجنجال برپا نمودن to raise a shout, to make noise; to quarrel loudly or noisily

جاروکش [jaarukash] sweeper, cleaning attendant; trash man, garbage man

جاری [jaari] 1 current, running, elapsing 2 present ♦ سال جاری this year, the current year 3 occurring, resulting 4 being in circulation (about money) 5 current, effective (about a law, etc.)
- جاری بودن (شدن) 1 to flow, to run, to elapse 2 to occur, to result ♦ مطالعات جاری است Research / studies investigations are being conducted. 3 to be in circulation (about money) 4 to go into effect; to be in force, to function, to operate (about a law, etc.)
- حساب جاری accounting current account

جاسوس [jaasus] spy, scout

جاسوسی کردن [jaasusi] espionage; agent intelligence, undercover intelligence
- جاسوسی کردن to spy; to be involved in espionage, to be involved in intelligence

جاغر [jaaghor] 1 crop, craw (of a bird) 2 goiter (both the swelling and the disease) 3 excrescence (on the bark of a walnut tree)
- جاغر انداختن colloquial to accumulate fat, to grow a paunch
- جاغر خود را پر کردن colloquial and جاغر پر کردن to fill one's purse, to fill one's pockets (by dishonest means)

جاغر دار [jaaghordaar] 1 having a goiter, suffering from goiter 2 having money in the till, having a full purse

جاغور [jaaghur] 1 store, shop, magazine (of a gun) 2 breech of a gun

جاغوردار [jaaghur-daar]¹ slang (literally: a person with goiter) a greedy person

جاغوردار [jaaghur-daar]² slang a patient person, a stoic person

جاغوردار [jaaghur-daar]³ slang the ability to get a task done

جافری [jaafari] ☞ جعفری

جاکت [jaakat] 1 jacket 2 woman's jacket (knitted), jumper ♦ جاکت پشمی woman's wool jacket ◊ جاکت سلندر technical cylinder jacket

جاکت دامن [jaakatdaaman] woman's suit, skirt and jacket

جای گزین [jaagozin] ☞ جاگزین

جاگیر [jaagir] historical jagir (a strip of land given to a feudal lord on condition of performance of military service) 2 ☞ جای گزین

جاگیرداری [jaagirdaari] historical jagir system (a form of feudal land ownership; ☞ جاگیر)

جال [jaal] 1 seine, fishing net 2 net for catching birds, a noose, snare 3 dirty trick, intrigues; intrigue
- جال انداختن to cast a net, to cast a seine
- جال ماندن 1 to lay nets, to spread nets 2 to set up a dirty trick, to arrange intrigues
- جال والی بال volleyball net

جالب [jaaleb] attracting attention to oneself, interesting; distinctive ♦ جالب دقت and جالب توجه worthy of attention, interesting, important

جال ساز [jaalsaaz] colloquial plotter, intriguer

جال سازی [jaalsaazi] colloquial intrigues

جالق [jaaloq] 1 embroidered rug made of felt 2 horse blanket of embroidered felt 3 pillow placed under a saddle

جاله [jaala]¹ (also جاله طنابی) float, raft (made of boards or logs on wineskins)

جاله [jaala]² 1 colloquial ☞ ژاله 2 sludge, ice floes (floating down a river during the time the ice breaks up)

جاله [jaala]³ type of sweet dish made of small pieces of jelly-like starchy mass covered with fruit syrup

جاله وان [jaalawaan] boatman; ferryman, raftsman

جالی [jaali] ¹ 1 gauze; cheesecloth; tulle ♦ جالی موی hair net 2 (also جالی سیمی) metal netting, metal screen, grid, grating ♦ جالی پای پاک grating for wiping one's feet ♦ جالی (بالای) گرفتن to enclose with a net, to stretch a net

جالی [jaali] ² a large sheet or tent (onto which berries are shaken from a mulberry tree)

جالیز [jaaliz] *colloquial* melon field

جام [jaam] ¹ 1 metal cup or bowl for water 2 *obscure* goblet ♦ جام دعا and جام چهل کلی cup of forty keys or springs / cup of prayers (Sunnis believe that being sprinkled with water from this cup on the last Wednesday of the month of Safar brings good fortune.)

جام [jaam] ² 1 *obscure* glass, mirror 2 unit of measure of the thickness of mirrors ♦ جام دو آیینه mirror with two glasses, double mirror ♦ جام جمشید and جام جم the magic mirror of King Jamshid (which supposedly showed everything that could be desired)

جام [jaam] ³ jam

جامد [jaamed] 1 having stood stock-still, having become hard, having hardened 2 hard; solid ♦ جسم جامد solid, solid body 3 *chemistry* inorganic ♦ مواد جامد inorganic matter 4 *grammar* simple; nonderivative

جامدانی [jaamdaani] muslin (with flowers or some other decorative design woven into it)

جامع [jaame'] 1.1 full, comprehensive, all-embracing ♦ تعریف جامع full description 1.2 interesting, significant ♦ نطق مختصر ولی جامع a short, but interesting speech 1.3 main, large (about a mosque) ♦ مسجد جامع main or large mosque 2 main or large mosque

جامعه [jaame'a] 1 society; collective body, collective (noun) 2 league; concord, cooperation, collaboration ♦ جامعه ملل *historical* League of Nations

جامک [jaamak] shaving cup

جامن [jaaman] clothes for male or female dancers (broad skirt on one-piece robe)

جامنک [jaamanak] *botany* (also جامنک بقه) duckweed

جامه [jaama] 1 *literary* clothes, dress; garment, attire 2 *colloquial* smart holiday gown or robe 3 coat (e.g., of a horse) ♦ جامه بدل کردن 1 to shed a coat (e.g., about a horse) 2 to be changed, to be transformed 3 *literary* to die

جامه باب [jaamabaab] *colloquial* clothing, dress (about cloth, fabric) *adjective*, suitable for a dress, suitable for clothing

جامه دانی [jaamadaani] chest, trunk (for storage of clothing)

جامه کن [jaamakan] dressing room (at bath house)

جامه کوب [jaamakob] bat (for washing clothes)

جان [jaan] 1 soul, spirit ♦ جان است بادنجان که نیست! *proverb* To you, after all, this is a living soul, and not an eggplant! 2 *colloquial* body; organism; [one's] whole being, the entire essence ♦ تمام جانم درد میکرد My whole body ached. 3 (endearing form of address) dear; my dear, sweetheart, darling

♦ جان لچ *colloquial* 1 naked body, nude body 2 in naked form, nude, without clothes
♦ جان من and جانم my dear
♦ جان مادر and جان پدر dear child
♦ جان باختن 1 to play with [one's] life, to risk one's life, to stake one's life 2 to sacrifice one's life
♦ جان بخشیدن 1 to revive, to bring back to life 2 to inspire
♦ جان کندن 1 to be in agony, to be in the throes of death, to die 2 to overstrain oneself at work
♦ جان گرفتن 1 to come to life; to be revived 2 to become strong, to get well, to recover; to put on weight 3 to better one's fortune, to grow rich
♦ به جان رسیدن and به جان آمدن to lose patience, to lose one's temper
♦ به جان رساندن 1 to drive to exhaustion; to carry to extremes 2 to pester [somebody را] badly
♦ جان به سلامت بردن to save oneself, to save one's own life
♦ جان خود را شستن to wash oneself, to take a shower
♦ جان کسی راتازه کردن to give somebody a good lesson, to give somebody a scolding
♦ جان کسی راکشیدن to drag out a person's [whole] soul, to vex, to exasperate
♦ جان نثار کردن to give up [one's] life, to sacrifice [one's] life
♦ به جان خود شاخک شاندن to subject oneself to torture or torment without need (*literally*: to give [oneself] a good bloodletting)
♦ جانش برآمد 1 He breathed his last. / He passed away. 2 He strained himself to the utmost. / He is exhausted.
♦ این پول رابه جان خود مصرف کردیم *colloquial* We spent that money on ourselves.
♦ لباسی که در جانش بود ترشد The clothes that were on him got drenched.
♦ جان صاحب 1 (an endearing form of address to a horse or other animal) 2 *ironic, familiar* knave, rogue
♦ احوال جان؟ *colloquial* How are you? / How do you feel?

جان آقا [jaanaaqaa] janaga (form of address to an older brother or of a wife to her husband)

جانانه [jaanaana] 1.1 dear, beloved ♦ فرزند جانانه dear child, beloved child 1.2 favorite, pet, preferred ♦ خوردنی های جانانه favorite dishes 2.1 darling, sweetheart (female) ♦ جانانه من my darling! (female) 2.2 pet, favorite *noun* (masculine)

جانب [jaaneb] (*plural* جوانب [jaawaaneb]) side, direction ♦ جانب مقابل opposite side
♦ جانب ۰۰۰ in the direction
♦ ازجانب ۰۰۰ 1 from the direction 2 in the name of
♦ این جانب (epistolary style)

جانباز [jaanbaaz] 1 brave, courageous; risking [one's] life 2 brave man, daredevil

جانبازی [jaanbaazi] courage, bravery, daring
♦ جانبازی کردن to show or display courage, bravery, daring; to risk [one's] life

جانبداری [jaanebdaari] 1 support, patronage, protection 2 devotion, fidelity
♦ جانبداری کردن to support, to be a supporter, adherent, or advocate; to act as a patron, to protect (از)

جان بسر [jaanbasar] 1 being in a state of agony, dying 2 driven to exhaustion 3 exasperated
• جان in entry به جان آمدن ☞ جان بسر بودن •

جان بکن [jaanbakan]
• proverb تا جان بتن است جان بکن است While we live, we worry.

جانبی [jaanebi] side adjective, situated on or at the side ♦ دیوار جانبی عمارت the side wall of a building

جان جان [jaanjaan] colloquial 1 Good lad! / Good girl! / Bravo! (cry exclamation of praise, approval) 2 Dear! / Darling! / Please / would you be so kind! (during a supplication, request, apology, etc.)

جانجوری [jaanjori] health, strength of an organism ♦ جانجوری پادشاهی است proverb Health is the whole world.

جانخانی [jaankhaani] large sack (of coarse wool for storing or transporting grain)

جان خشکان [jaankhoshkaan] a large bath sheet

جاندار [jaandaar] 1 living being, living soul; animal ♦ خدا جاندار God's creature 2.1 live 2.2 grammar animate 2.3 vital, thrilling, stirring, exciting ♦ موضوع جاندار an exciting subject

جانستان [jaansetaan] literary 1 killer, murderer, monster (of cruelty) 2 disposing of the souls of the dead (about God)

جان شویی [jaanshoyi] washing the body (in a bath, etc.); washing; bathing ♦ صابون جان شویی toilet soap

جانشین [jaaneshin] successor; deputy, assistant
• جانشین امیر 1 viceroy, vice-regent, kaem-makam 2 heir to the throne

جانفشانی [jaanfeshaani] 1 selfless bravery, courage; selflessness 2 devotion 3 zeal, diligence

جانکندن [jaankandan] agony

جانکنی [jaankani] 1 heavy labor, exhausting labor 2 excessive zeal

جان نثار [jaannesaar] 1 sacrificing one's life; ready to give up one's life 2 selflessly devoted 3 epistolary [your] humble servant

جانور [jaanawar (and) jaanwar] 1 animal; living being, creature 2 abusive fool, idiot, dummy

جانه مرگ [jaanamarg] ☞ جوان مرگ
• خداته جانه مرگ کنه abusive May God take you while you're young!

جانی [jaani] 1 1 mortally dangerous, entailing sacrifices ♦ حادثه جانی unfortunate incident or accident 2 cordial, hearty, sincere ♦ یار جانی bosom friend ◊ دشمن جانی sworn enemy, mortal enemy

جانی [jaani] 2 1 criminal, sinful; villainous 2 criminal; villain, scoundrel

جاود [jaawed] and جاودان [jaawedaan] ☞ جاویدان

جاویدان [jaawidaan] 1 eternal, immortal 2 eternally, for all ages ♦ جاویدان باد May he live forever!

جاویدانی [jaawidaani] eternal, not transient

جاهل [jaahel] 1.1 ignorant, unenlightened 1.2 stupid 2.1 ignoramus, unenlightened person 2.2 dolt, fool ♦ از جاهل کلان خورد هوشیار بهتر است proverb Better to be small and smart than big and dumb.

جاهلی [jaaheli] 1 ignorance, darkness 2 stupidity, folly

جاهلیت [jaaheliyat] and جاهلیه [jaaheliya] 1 pre-Islamic period of Arab history 2 ☞ جاهلی

جای [jaay] 1.1 place; country, locality ♦ پغمان بسیار جای خوب است Paghman is a very fine place. ◊ جای است و جولا نیست proverb Here is [his] place, but the weaver [himself] is not here. (The bird has flown.) 1.2 lodging, apartment; dwelling, quarters 1.3 position; post; job 1.4 vacant position, vacancy 1.5 colloquial place for sleeping, bed 2 (also به جای) instead of, in exchange for denominative preposition
• جایی که there, where compound conjunction ♦ جایی که سنگ است در پای لنگ است There, where there are rocks, the lame leg will stumble on them [without fail]. (The chain is no stronger than its weakest link.)
• جای انداختن colloquial to make a bed ♦ جای انداخته گی است The bed has been made.
• جای دادن 1 to give way to (about sensations, feelings); to give refuge, to give shelter 2 to set [somebody] up (in an apartment, for the night); to quarter, to billet
• جای داشتن 1 to fit, to correspond; to be appropriate 2 to be justified, to be well-founded
• جای زدن jargon to filch, to swipe, to pinch (i.e., to steal)
• جای شدن 1 to be lodged, to be housed, to have room, to find room (somewhere, in something) (در , به) ♦ این اسباب در بکس جای نمیشود These things don't fit in the briefcase. 2 to take a position, to get settled 3 to set (about a joint or bone)
• جای کردن 1 to lodge, to house, to accommodate; to stow, to pack, to shove in 2 to place, to mount 3 to set (a joint) 4 to arrange a job, to appoint to a position
• جای گرفتن 1 to occupy a place or position, to settle down 2 to take root 3 ☞ جای شدن 1
• به جای آوردن 1 to recognize ♦ من شما را به جای نیاوردم I didn't recognize you 2 to fulfill; to carry out, to accomplish ♦ امر مرا به جای آوردید؟ Did you carry out my instructions?
• به جای خوردن to hit the target (about a bullet, an arrow, etc.)
• جای به جای کردن 1 to shift, to move 2 to accomodate, to place, to set up (somewhere), to quarter, to billet 3 to place, to sort out (things)
• جای خالی کردن colloquial 1 to vacate, to clear out, to give way to 2 to dodge, to evade, to avoid, to shun 3 to run away; to disappear, to vanish
• جای نشستن کسی رانیافتن not to know where to sit somebody (as a sign of respect, deference)
• جای و جاگه نداشتن not to have a home of one's own
• یکجای in article یکجایی شدن ☞ یک جای شدن
• جایش سبز باشد and جایش خالی نباشد May his place not be empty for long! / May he prosper and flourish! (traditional polite formulation when visiting the relatives of somebody who has gone away)
• جای ضرور toilet, bathroom, water closet
• به جای بود (شد) It serves [somebody] right! and به جای است
• به جای آنکه (آینکه) instead of compound conjunction

تاجاییکه جای [jaayajaay] and جای برجای [jaaybarjaay] so far as *compound conjunction* ♦ تاجاییکه معلوم است so far as [it is] known
- جای بجای [jaayajaay] and جای برجای [jaaybarjaay] right here, on the spot, not moving from place
- جای بجای شدن to be killed on the spot, to die on the spot, to die right away
- جای بجای کردن to kill on the spot; to kill with one blow
- جای بجای ماندن to stay in place, not to move from place

جای بند [jaayband] 1 being fattened for slaughter (about cattle) 2 having stood too long, having become restless (about a horse)

جای جای [jaayjaay] here and there, in places

جای خالی [jaaykhaali] 1 post-wedding visit (of young people to the parents of the bride) 2 ☞ جای سبزی

جایداد [jaaydaad] 1 immovable property, real estate 2 landed property, estate

جایداددار [jaaydaaddaar] 1 well-to-do, propertied 2 owner of landed property, owner of an estate, landowner

جای رسیده [jaayrasida] having achieved a high position, having achieved prosperity; flourishing ♦ او آدم جای رسیده است He is a person of position. / He has achieved a high position.

جایز [jaaez (and) jaayez] 1 permitted, authorized, permissible 2 right, legal
- جایز کردن 1 to adjudge, to award 2 to permit, to allow

جائزه [jaaeza] and جایزه [jaayeza] (*plural* جوایز [jaawaayez]) 1 award; prize ♦ جوایز نوبل Nobel Prize ◊ دارنده جوایز laureate, winner of an award 2 winnings (in a lottery, etc.)

جای سبزی [jaaysabzi] traditional visit of women to the parents of a person who has gone away for a long time (at which time they usually say: جایش سبز ☞ *entry* جای)

جای گزین [jaaygozin] and جای گیر [jaaygir]
- جای گیر شدن 1 to settle down, to take a place; to settle; to take up residence 2 to take root
- جای گزین کردن 1 to settle; to arrange, to accommodate, to find a place (for somebody) 2 to implant

جایمانده [jaaymaanda] *colloquial* 1 lying, recumbent, confined to bed (about a sick person) 2 weak, feeble, sickly, puny

جای نشین [jaayneshin] ☞ جانشین

جای نماز [jaaynamaaz] prayer rug, mat for performing the namay (prayer)

جای نمازوردار [jaaynamaazwardaar] *colloquial* 1 attendant in a mosque who lays down and picks up prayer rugs 2 noble's servant who carries noble's prayer rug

جایی [jaayi] *colloquial* 1 solid, reliable; enjoying trust (about a person) 2 local, coming from a given locate or a given region

جبار [jaabbaar] 1 ravisher, oppressor; tyrant, despot 2 tyrannical, despotic

جبال [jebaal (and) jaabaal] *plural of* جبل
- جبال هندو کش Hindu Kush mountains

جبر [jaabr (and) jáber] ¹ 1 compulsion, coercion, oppression ♦ به جبر by force, forcibly 2 injustice, offense 3 *philosophical* necessity (opposite of اختیار) 4 *physics* inertia
- جبر دیدن 1 to undergo coercion, oppression (از) 2 to suffer injustice, offense (از)

جبر [jaabr] ² algebra

جبراً [jaabran] forcibly, by force, by compulsion

جبران [jaabraan] 1 reimbursement, compensation ♦ جبران خساره reimbursement of losses 2 forfeit
- جبران کردن to reimburse, to make up, to compensate

جبری [jaabri] 1 forcible, compulsory 2 forced, emergency, obligatory, mandatory ♦ توقف جبری emergency situation 3 inevitable; fatal

جبل [jaabal] ¹ (*plural* جبال [jebal]) mountain

جبل [jaabal] ² crowbar

جبلت [jebellat] natural property, innate, inborn quality; character, nature

جبلی [jebelli] natural, innate, inborn

جبه [jaba] ¹ *colloquial* 1 swamp 2 small meadow

جبه [jaba] ² 1 ☞ جبه خانه 2 *colloquial* gold and silver ornaments suspended from a bracelet

جبه [joba] joba (broad outer clothing with long sleeves)

جبه خانه [jaabakhaana] 1 ammunition 2 ammunition depot 3 arsenal

جبه زار [jaabazaar] swampy terrain, marsh, swamp

جبهه [jabha] (*plural* جبهات [jabhat]) 1 (in various meanings) front ♦ جبهه آزادی ملی national liberation front 2 forehead, brow
- پشت جبهه *literary* 1 rear area, rear services 2 behind the front line, in the rear

جبه یی [jabayi] swamp (about a wild animal, bird) *adjective* ♦ کبک جبه یی swamp partridge

جبیره [jabira] reimbursement, making up (a shortage, lack, etc.), compensation
- جبیره کردن to reimburse, to make up, to compensate ♦ این مفاد خساره مارا جبیره نمیکند This profit does not cover our losses.

جبین [jabin] forehead, brow ♦ با جبین گشاده affably, sincerely; amiably
- عرق جبین ریختن to work in the sweat of one's brow, to work without sparing effort

جپ [jap] *colloquial* 1 pushing, shoving, swaying, reeling 2 heaving, splash, lapping (of water in a river, etc.)
- جپ خوردن 1 *intransitive* to rock, to swing, to stagger, to reel ♦ کاسه جپ خورد آب ریخت The cup was tipped and the water spilled. 2 to heave, to splash, to lap (about waves, water) 3 *intransitive* to splash out, to spill
- جپ دادن *transitive* 1 to rock, to swing, to sway, to shake 2 to make a crush (of people) 3 to spill (water, etc.) ♦ جپ نتی *colloquial* Don't spill!
- جپ زدن 1 to push one another (in a crowd) 2 to splash water on one's own face by handfuls ♦ یک جپ آب handful of water (splashed on the face when washing)

جپان [japaan] sedan chair, palanquin

جپه [japa] 1 wave 2 (also جپه قایق) pole (for propelling a boat); oar

جوپه [jopa] ☞ جپه

جت [jat] gypsy; gypsies

جت زن [jat-zadan] idiom (literally: gypsy) bitch, witch (a woman with a very bad attitude)

جت [jet] 1 jet adjective 2 (also طیاره جت) jet airplane

جتکه [jetka] abrupt movement, start, starting (from surprise, fright)
• جتکه خوردن to make an abrupt movement, to start (from surprise, from fright)
• جتکه دادن to make [somebody] flinch or start; to frighten, to scare

جته [jota] ¹ colloquial 1 remainder of water (after something); leftover water 2 abusive abandoned woman

جته [jota] ² colloquial pure, natural, unalloyed ♦ مروارید جته genuine pearl; pure pearl

جتی [joti] shoes (of local domestic industry)

جثه [jossa] 1 figure, body (of person, of an animal) 2 (body) build, frame ♦ جثه قوی sturdy build

ججق [jejeq] 1 fried sheep's fat; cracklings 2 colloquial of very dark complexion; black from sunburn or tanning
• ججق کردن colloquial to torment, to torture; to cause torment, to cause suffering; to rouse to a fury

ججوی [jajoy] botany anemone

جد [jad (d)] (plural داد [ajdad]) 1 grandfather, great-grandfather 2 ancestor, forefather

جد [jed (d)] effort
• جدوجهد ☞ جد و جهد

جدا [jodaa (and) jedaa] 1.1 detached, solitary; separated 1.2 separate, special, another ♦ این مسئله جدا است That's another question. 2.1 separately, apart, by oneself, in isolation 2.2 disjointedly, not together
• جداکردن 1 to separate, to isolate (از) 2 to disjoin, to disconnect, to take apart 3 to sever; to excommunicate (از) ♦ طفل راازشیر جداکردن to wean a child 4 to single out, to distinguish

جداً [jeddan] 1 zealously, with ardor; actively, energetically 2 seriously, in earnest

جداجدا [jodaajodaa] separately, one-by-one

جدار [jadaar] wall, side, side wall, partition ♦ جدار قوطی side of a box

جداگانه [jedaagaana] special, separate

جدال [jad (d) aal] colloquial bullying, pugnacious

جدایی [jodaayi] 1 separateness, disconnection, dissociation, isolation ♦ گوشت از ناخن جدایی ندارد proverb One won't tear the fingernail away from the flesh. 2 separation

جدل [jadal] 1 argument, quarrel 2 rarely battle ♦ جنگ و جدل discord, strife, fight, ruckus ♦ آنها دارند همیشه با هم جنگ و جدل They are always quarrelling. / They are always in conflict with each other.

جدوجهد [jeddojahd] zeal, diligence

جدول [jadwal] 1 line; column; rubric, heading 2 sheet ruled in columns or squares, graph paper; graph; table; scale ♦ جدول روزانه military schedule of the day ◊ جدول ضرب multiplication table ◊ جدول مندلیف Mendeleev's table 3 rarely irrigation ditch; brook, stream
• جدول کشیدن 1 to rule, to draw lines 2 to compile a graph, to compile a table

جدول دار [jadwaaldaar] lined, ruled in columns, squares

جدولکش [jadwalkash] 1 composite graph; list, register, log, journal 2 drawing pencil

جدولکشی [jadwalkashi] 1 ruling, drawing lines 2 compiling a graph, compiling a table

جدولی [jadwali] ☞ جدول دار

جدی [jádi] 1 astronomy Capricorn 2 Jadi (tenth month of the Afghan calendar; corresponds to December-January)

جدی [jeddi] 1 jealous, energetic, assiduous, diligent (about a person) ♦ طرفدار جدی active supporter 2 serious, important ♦ سوال جدی serious matter, important question

جدیت [jeddiyat] 1 zeal; activism, state of being active, quality of being active; quality or state of being energetic 2 seriousness, importance (of a matter or problem)
• به جدیت ☞ جداً

جدید [jadid] 1.1 new ♦ خانه جدید new house 1.2 recent, latest ♦ این اخبار جدید است This is the latest news. ◊ واقعه جدید a recent event 2 poetry jadid (Persian meter)

جدیداً [jadidan] recently ♦ برادر من جدیداً آمد My brother recently arrived.

جدیدالتشکیل [jadidottashkil] new, newly created, recently formed ♦ انجمن جدیدالتشکیل newly-formed society ◊ کشورهای جدیدالتشکیل آسیا وافریقا the new or young countries or states of Asia and Africa

جدیدالشمول [jadidoshshomul] 1 newly entered, newly enrolled (in school, in an institute) 2 newcomer, novice

جدیدی [jadidi] jadidi (the name given to the infidel inhabitants of Nuristan after their conversion to Islam)

جذاب [jazzaab] fascinating, absorbing; captivating, charming, delightful, ravishing ♦ قصه جذاب a fascinating story ◊ منظره جذاب captivating appearance

جذب [jazb] 1 attraction; inclination 2 suction, absorption 3 physics gravity, gravitation
• جذب کردن 1 to atract; to draw 2 to suck in, to soak in, to absorb

جذبه [jazba (and) jazaba] (plural جذبات [jazbaat]) 1 inclination, enthusiasm, passion 2 ardor; mood, spirits; feeling ♦ جذبات ملی national feeling 3 rarely severity; sternness

جذر [jaz (e) r] mathematical root ♦ جذر تربیعی square root
• جذر گرفتن to find the square root

جذوه [jazwa] jazwa, coffee maker, coffeepot

جر [jar] ¹ 1 small ditch to drain water, small irrigation ditch 2 deep ditch; ravine ♦ جر و جوی ruts, potholes 3 crack, slit, cleft, fissure 4 precipice, steep slope
• جرزدن to dig a ditch (to drain a swamp, etc.)

جر [jar] ² 1 tangled, entangled, awry ♦ موی جر tousled hair 2 intricate, complicated
- جر انداختن colloquial to muddle to make a muddle of (a matter, etc.); to cause turmoil, to cause confusion (در)
- جر کردن 1 to tangle, to entangle (threads, etc.) 2 to fluff up (hair), to raise a nap
- صدای جر hoarse voice

جر [jer] colloquial squeal, screech, cry, shout
- جر زدن to screech, to cry out loudly, to squeal (usually about children)

جراب [jeraab (and) jorab] 1 socks 2 (also جراب ساق دار) stockings

جراب بند [jeraabband] garter belt (to hold up stockings)

جرأت [jor'at] boldness, courage, resoluteness, daring ♦ به جرأت boldly, resolutely, daringly
- جرأت دادن to make bold, to embolden
- جرأت کردن، جرأت گپ زدن to dare, to venture; to resolve ♦ جرأت نداشت He didn't dare talk.

جراثیم [jaraasim] plural of جرثوم

جراح [jarraah] surgeon

جراحت [jaraahat] wound; ulcer; sore

جراحی [jarraahi] 1 surgical; operation adjective ♦ آلات جراحی surgical tools 2.1 surgery 2.2 (also عمل جراحی) surgical operation

جراسک [jaraasak] cricket

جرائد [jaraa'ed] and جراید [jaraayed] 1 plural of جریده 2 the press, print

جرایم [jaraayem] plural of جریمه

جرت [jert] colloquial Jert! (a cry of mockery and censure usually accompanied by a characteristic gesture: sticking out one's thumb and drawing it to the side)

جرثقیل [jar (e) saqil] winch, hoist; hoisting crane ♦ جرثقیل ثابت tower crane ◊ موتر جرثقیل and جرثقیل سیار truck-mounted winch or hoist; truck-mounted crane

جرثوم [jorsum] (plural جراثیم [jaraasim]) literary ☞ مکروب

جرح [jarh] 1 injury, wound, trauma, mutilation 2 inflicting wounds, inflicting mutilation ♦ قتل و جرح mutilation and murder

جرس [jarras] onomatopoeia crackle (of gunfire); roll (of a drum); rip, snap (of cloth tearing, of a tree breaking, etc.)

جرس [jaras] small bell, cymbol

جرعه [jor'a] mouthful, gulp (of water, etc.)
- جرعه جرعه خوردن to drink in gulps, to sip

جرغات [jorghaat] ☞ جغرات

جرغه [jaragha] ☞ جرقه

جرقه [jaraqa] spark ♦ جرقه برق electric spark

جرق و برق [jaraq-o-baraq] colloquial nice and shiny, sharp

جرکنی [jarkani] digging of trenches, digging of ditches (to drain a swamp)

جرگه [jerga (and) jarga] 1 jirga, council of elders, council of tribe or family (among the Afghans) ♦ لویه جرگه The Great Assembly (highest representative organ of Afghanistan; it is convened to decide important questions.) 2 gathering, circle; congress 3 house (of parliament)

جرم [jerm] (plural اجرام [ajraam]) physics body; mass ♦ اجرام آسمانی celestial bodies

جرم [jorm] fault, guilt, sin, misdemeanor; crime, offense ♦ به جرم خیانت for treason, on a charge of treason
- مرتکب جرم شدن to commit a crime

جرمن [jarman] 1 a German 2 colloquial ☞ جرمنی

جرمنی [jarmani] 1 German adjective 2 (also زبان جرمنی) the German language

جرند [jerand] golden red, bay (of a horse's coat)

جرنگ [jarang] ringing, peal, tinkling; clanging ♦ جرنگ ساعت striking of a clock

جرنگ و برنگ [jering-o-bering] slang poof, lost, vanish

جرنگس [jerengas] ring, ringing (of bells on the neck of camel, donkey, etc.)

جرنیل [jarnayl] colloquial general ♦ جرنیل ملکی chief or head of tribal militia

جره [jara] colloquial 1.1 single, unmarried 1.2 rarely hollow, empty 2 bachelor 3 rarely empty, without a load

جره [jor (r) a] male hunting hawk

جری [jari] 1 cut, depression, slot, groove 2 thread, threading جری و جوک ☞ جری و جوک

جری [jar (r) i] grammar inflected ♦ حالت جری indirect form (of a noun)

جریان [jaryaan (and) jarayaan] 1 current, movement; circulation ♦ جریان آب current of water ◊ جریان هوا air circulation; draft 2 course, flow, process ♦ جریان انکشاف process of development 3 current, movement (political, social); trend (in science, etc.) 4 (also جریان برق) electric current ♦ جریان متناوب alternating current ◊ جریان مستقیم direct current
- جریان داشتن 1 to flow, to run 2 to occur, to take place
- جریان کردن to flow, to stream
- (در)جریان بودن 2 داشتن جریان ☞

جریانات [jaryaanaat] 1 plural of جریان 2 events ♦ جریانات سیاسی political events 3 processes ♦ جریانات اجتماعی social processes

جریب [jerib] jerib (measure of land area, equivalent to 1,952 square meters or 19.52 acres; in old Afghan measures, corresponds to 20 beswa.)
- جریب کردن to measure an area of land in jeribs

جریبان [jeriban] botany geranium

جریب کش [jeribkash] land surveyor

جریدار [jeridaar] technical having a slot, with a slot, slotted ♦ خشت جری دار slotted nut

جریده [jarida] (plural جرایده [jaraiyed]) newspaper (not daily); magazine; periodical

جریده نویس [jaridanawis] journalist

جریکش [jarikash] technical grooving chisel, gouge

ج

جری کشی [jarikashi] *technical* milling ♦ قلم جری کشی cut-off tool ◊ ماشین جری کشی milling machine

جریمه [jarima] 1 (*plural* جرایم [jaraayem]) punishment, penalty, fine 2 *literary* ☞ جرم [jorm]
• جرایم کردن to impose a fine, to fine

جری و جوک [jariwojawak] aiming device, sight (on a rifle, etc.)

جزء [joz] (*plural* اجزاء [ajzaa]) 1 part, portion, share, fraction ♦ جزء جمله *grammar* part of a sentence ◊ جزء کلام *grammar* part of speech 2 part, section (of a book); installment 3 *grammar* particle 4 (*also* جزءعروضی) foot (poetry)

جز [jez] 1 burning, acute pain (from a bite, sting, burn, etc.) 2 ☞ جزجز
• جزکردن 1 to sizzle (about fat on a frying pan) 2 to burn, to sting, to itch (from an acute pain)

جزاء [jazaa] 1 punishment, penalty, retribution ♦ جزاء ضرب *literary* corporal punishment ◊ جزاء مرگ capital punishment 2 penalty, fine ♦ دفتر جزاء *military* book of commendations and punishments 3 *rarely* recompense, reward 4 (*also* جزاء شرط) *grammar* principal clause (when there is a conditional subordinate clause)
• جزاء دادن to punish, to inflict a penalty
• جزاء دیدن to be punished, to bear punishment; to pay

جزایر [jazaayer] *plural of* جزیره

جزایری [jazaayeri] 1 Algerian *adjective* 2 an Algerian

جزایل چی [jazaayelchi] *historical* musketeer; rifleman (in Ahmad Shah's army)

جزایی [jazaayi] 1 punitive 2 criminal, penal ♦ قانون جزایی penal code

جزبازی [jozbaazi] classes (children's game)

جزبندی [jozbandi] stitching, binding (of a book)
• جزبندی کردن to stitch; to bind

جزجز [jezjez] *onomatopoeia* the gurgling of boiling water in a kettle or the sizzling of fat or oil in a frying pan

جزدان [jozdaan] portfolio, briefcase; bag for textbooks

جزر [jáz (e) r] ebb, low tide ♦ مدوجزر flow and ebb, high tide and low tide

جزغاله [jezghaala] *colloquial* cracklings, residue left after frying sheep fat

جزو [jozw] ☞ جزء

جز و بو [jax-o-baw] *idiom* nagging, pestering ♦ بچیم جز و بو محکم گرفته که برش پوفانه بخرم My son is pestering me to buy him a balloon.

جز و فز [jaz-o-faz] *slang* (*literally*: hot and sizzling) to bluster

جزوتام [jozotaam] [m] 1 full, complete, exhaustive, comprehensive; thorough ♦ حسابهای جزوتام *military* full settlement 2 subunit; unit

جزیره [jazira] (*plural* جزایر [jazaayer]) island

جزیره نما [jaziranomaa] peninsula

جزیه [jazya] *historical* jazya, tax (on the heterodox in Muslim countries)

جزئی [joz'i] 1 small; insignificant, trifling, trivial ♦ خدمت جزئی a small service 2 partial, incomplete ♦ کسوف جزئی partial solar eclipse

جزئیات [joz'iyaat] particulars, details, trifles

جسارت [jasaarat] 1 courage, bravery, daring 2 audacity, boldness

جست[1] [jast] jump ♦ بایک جست with one jump
• جست زدن to jump, to skip

جست[2] [jast] 1 (*also* فلز جست) zinc 2 *pharmacy* zinc powder, powder (for the eyes)

جستجو [jostojo] search
• جستجوکردن to search, to look for, to try to find

جستن [jastan] (*present tense stem* جه [jah (and) jeh]) 1 to jump, to skip 2 *regional* to run away, to go away ♦ بجی Go! / Go away!

جستن [jostan] (*present tense stem* جوی [joy]) to search, to look for

جسته وگریخته [jastawgoreekhta] *colloquial* 1 by fits and starts, irregularly; in a slipshod manner 2 confusingly, inconsistently, anyhow

جسد [jasad] 1 body (of person, of an animal) 2 (*also* جسد مرده) dead body, corpse

جسر [jaser (and) jéser] wooden bridge on wineskins
• جسر بسته کردن to build a bridge

جسم [jesem] (*plural* اجسام [ajsaam]) 1 *physics mathematical* body, solid; object ♦ جسم جامد solid 2 body, flesh ♦ جسم زنده living flesh, living organism

جسمانی [jesmani] 1 corporal, physical; carnal 2 material ♦ عالم جسمانی material world

جسمی [jesmi] ☞ جسمانی
• ضعف جسمی physical weakness
• کار جسمی manual labor

جسور [jasur] 1 courageous, brave, decisive, resolute 2 daring bold

جشن [jásen] holiday, festival; anniversary; birthday; jubilee ♦ جشن سالگرد
• جشن گرفتن to celebrate, to mark

جعبه [ja'ba] 1 chest; box; case ♦ جعبه میز table drawer 2 bellows

جعفری [ja'fari] fur blanket (of lambskin with a lining)

جعل [ja'l] forgery, falsification
• جعل کردن to forge; to shuffle unfairly; to falsify

جعل کاری [ja'lkaari] swindle, fraud, deception; falsification (of documents, etc.), forgery

جعلی [ja'li] false, counterfeit, spurious

جغاره [joghaara] jogara (cereal)

جغد [joghd] owl

جغرات [joghrat] sour milk, mast (yogurt)

جغرافی [joghrafi] 1 ☞ جغرافیا 2 ☞ جغرافیایی

جغرافیا [joghraafiyaa] geography

جغرافیایی [joghraafiyaayi] geographic, geographical

جغرافیه [joghraafiyaa] ☞ جغرافیا

جغز [jaghz] crack, split; breakage damage; trace, sign of a blow ♦ الماس جغز دارد There are scratches on the diamond.
- جغز شدن to crack *transitive* and *intransitive*; to break *intransitive* ♦ استخوانش جغز شد He has a broken bone.

جغزی جغزی [jaqzijaqzi] *colloquial* cracked all over, scratched all over; shattered or smashed to pieces

جغل [joqol] threshing (with the aid of oxen)
- جغل کردن to thresh (with the aid of oxen)

جغل [jogholmaal] ☞ جغلمال
- جغلمال کردن 1 to beat unmercifully, to thrash soundly [somebody] 2 to wear out, to shred (e.g., clothes)

جغل پغل [chaghal-o-paghal] *slang* kids, tiny tyke ♦ فلان جغل پغل زیاد دارد He has many children.

جغله [jaghala] ¹ 1 small, crushed, fragmented ♦ قند جغله finely broken loaf-sugar 2.1 splinters, fragments, small pieces (of something) ♦ جغله میده and جغله خورد chip (marble chip) 2.2 gravel, crushed rock ♦ جغله دریایی river pebbles
- جغله انداختن to cover (a road) with gravel
- جغله کردن to crush (stone)

جغله [jaghala] ² *colloquial* kiddies, small fry (about children) ♦ جغله هارا ببرید Take the children away!

جغله پاشی [jaghalapaashi] strewing crushed rock, to cover with crushed rock
- جغله پاشی کردن to strew crushed rock

جغله سنگ [jaghalasang] ☞ جغله 1, 2.2

جغه [jeqa (and) joqa] *colloquial* ☞ جیغه

جغه دار [jeghadaar] ☞ جیغه دار

جفاء [jafaa] 1 cruelty, ruthlessness 2 offense, injury, oppression
- جفاء دیدن (کشیدن) 1 to worry, to suffer 2 to suffer offense or injury; to undergo oppression (از)
- جفاء کردن 1 to torment, to make suffer 2 to cause offense or injury; to oppress

جفاکار [jafaakaar] 1 tormentor, torturer, oppressor; offender 2 cruel, ruthless

جفاکاری [jafaakaari] 1 tyranny; oppression 2 cruelty, ruthlessness

جفاکش [jafaakash] 1 worrying, suffering 2 offended, wronged, oppressed

جفت [joft] 1.1 pair (numerative in counting pairs of objects) ♦ یک جفت موزه pair of shoes 1.2 pair, couple 1.3 even number ♦ جفت است تاق even-odd (game) 1.4 (also جفت جنین) *anatomy* placenta, afterbirth 1.5 adding a stitch (in knitting) 2.1 twin, duplicate 2.2 even ♦ اعداد جفت even numbers 2.3 pushed tightly or closely together, well fitted ♦ دروازه خوب جفت است The doors close tightly, the doors are fitted well.
- جفت کردن 1 to unite in a pair; to double; to combine 2 to push together, to adjust, to fit (something to something else)

جفت [juft] *interjection* B.S (it is said to someone who talks out of the ordinary)

جفتک [joftak] 1 jump (with both feet at once) 2 kicking
- جفتک زدن 1 to jump (with both feet at once) 2 to kick

جفت و تاق [joftotaaq] even-odd (game)

جفتی [jofti] coupling, pairing
- جفتی کردن to couple, to pair

جق [joq]
- جق خوردن *colloquial* to stir, to move, to budge ♦ هیچ از جای خود جق نمی خورد He won't budge. / He won't stir.
- جق زدن to teem; to swarm (about insects, worms, etc.)

جقیدن [joqidan] *colloquial* 1 to swarm, to toss and turn 2 to fuss, to bustle

جک [jak] ¹ 1 large earthenware jug with handles (for making sour milk) 2 animal skin (for churning butter)
- جک زدن 1 to churn butter in an animal skin 2 to babble, to beat the air

جک [jak] ² *technical* jack

جوک [jok] ☞ جک

جگ [jag] jug (of glass, of porcelain); decanter, carafe

جگر [jegar] 1 liver 2 boldness, courage, bravery, valor 3 generosity, magnanimity
- جگر داشتن to be bold, to have courage, to dare, to venture (to do something)
- جگر کردن to show generosity, to show magnanimity; to have a bit of generosity ♦ دو هزار افغانی برای خیرات جگر کرد He generously gave 2,000 afghanis for charitable purposes.
- جگرم Dear! / Beloved! / Heart of mine!
- جگر جگر است دیگر دیگر *proverb* One's own [people] are [always] one's own, but a stranger is [always] a stranger.

جگربند [jegarband] pluck; liver

جگرخراش [jegarkharaash] harrowing, piercing ♦ چیغ های جگر خراش heart-rending wails or howls

جگرخور [jegarkhor] witch (according to legend, flies astride a block of wood and eats people's livers at night)

جگرخون [jegarkhun] shaken with grief, suffering

جگرخونی [jegarkhuni] 1 emotional experience; torment, agony 2 difficulties; heavy labor, excruciating work

جگردار [jegardaar] *colloquial* manly, courageous, bold (opposite of بی جگر)

جگرگوشه [jegargosha] 1 child; dear child 2 ced, close; [one's] own

جگره [jagra] 1 agrument, bargaining (at the time of a purchase, sale) 2 quarrel, fight
- جگره کردن 1 to bargain, to haggle 2 to quarrel, to fight

جگری [jegari] wine-colored, crimson, dark-red

جل [jal] 1 sunstroke; fainting spell, swoon (from a heat stroke) ♦ محمود رادر صحرا جل زده است Mahmud suffered a sunstroke on the steppe. 2 hot wind, samum, simoom

جل [jel] *colloquial* 1 agitation, anxiety, uneasiness, alarm 2 moan, groan, weeping, crying, sobbing
- جل زدن 1 to be agitated, to be worried, to be anxious; to toss [in bed] 2 to moan, to groan, to weep, to cry, to sob

ج

جل [jol] a warm horse-blanket of coarse pile ♦ جل و پوستک belongings, things
• جل کردن to cover with a horse blanket, to throw on a horse blanket
• جل نهادن (بر) to break to the saddle
• جل خود را از آب کشیدن to cope with one's affairs, to carry out an assigned task to the extent of one's abilities

جل و جنده [jul-o-janda] *slang* junk, stuff (used and useless clothes and households goods)

جل ماده [jale-maada] *slang* (*literally:* a female lark (bird)) chatterbox

جلا [jalaa] 1 luster, brilliance, sparkling, twinkling, radiance ♦ جلا منرال the luster of mineral 2 polish, gloss; polishing
• جلا دادن to polish, to shine

جلاب [jallaab] 1.1 secondhand dealer, speculator, horse dealer 1.2 herdsman, drover 2 (second component of compound words with meaning of "involved in resale" / "dealing in something") ♦ پوست جلاب dealer in hides or leather ◊ اسپ جلاب horse dealer

جلاب [jolab] laxative
• جلاب کردن (خوردن) to take a laxative

جلاد [jallad] executioner

جلال [jalal] and جلالت [jalaalat] 1 grandeur, glory 2 splendor, magnificence

جلالت ماب [jalaalatmaāb] *obscure* excellency (as a title)

جلالی [jalaali] 1 *historical* relating to the era of Jalalud-din (Malik Shah) 2 Jalali (popular person of Afghan folklore)

جلب [jalb] 1 drawing in; attracting 2 (also جلب افراد and عساکر) call-up for military service, mobilization
• جلب کردن 1 to attract, to draw in 2 to call up (for military service)
• به خود جلب کردن to attract, to draw to oneself

جلبی [jalbi] draftee

جلبی [jelabi] jelabi (sweet dish in the form of a thin pastry straw fried in butter and covered with syrup)

جلت [jalt] *colloquial* 1.1 swift, nimble; quick, fast ♦ یورغه جلت a fast trot 1.2 fast, hasty, hurried; swift, impetuous 2 swiftly, nimbly; quickly, speedily ♦ این اسب جلت میرود This horse runs fast.

جلتی [jalti] *colloquial* 1 swiftness, nimbleness 2 speed, quickness; impetuosity ♦ به جلتی swiftly, quickly, impetuously

جلجل [joljol]
• جلجل کردن *colloquial* to creep / to crawl, to swarm (about insects)

جلد [jald] ☞ جلت

جلد [jold (and) jeld] 1 skin, hide 2 piece, item (numerative in counting skins, hides) ♦ هزار جلد پوست قره قل a thousand karakul skins 3 binding, cover (of a book) 4 volume; copy ♦ هفت جلد کتاب seven books
• جلد شیر 1 lion's skin 2 *ironic* clothing of a soldier, military uniform

جلدی [jaldi] ☞ جلتی

جلدی [joldi (abd) jeldi] skin *adjective* ♦ امراض جلدی skin diseases

جل زده گی [jalzadagi] fainting (from heat stroke), affected by sunstroke

جلسه [jalsa (and) jalasa] 1 meeting, conference ♦ جلسه علنی open meeting 2 session 3 commission, committee; assembly
• جلسه کردن to sit, to meet, to conduct a meeting

جلغوزه [jalghoza] 1 pine which gives edible nuts; mountain cedar 2 pine nut (fruit of the mountain cedar)

جلف [jalaf] *colloquial* 1 profligate (about a woman) 2 prostitute

جلک [jelak] *colloquial* 1 basket (for carrying watermelons, etc.; it is packed on riding animals) 2 ☞ جیلک

جلگه [jelga] 1 plain, low place 2 glade, clearing; small meadow; water meadow, flood plain

جلنگ [jolong] 1 vine (of a melon, watermelon, etc.) 2 narrow gore, gusset (in clothing)

جلو [jelaw] 1 bridle, rein; reins 2 the first pair of strings on a rabab
• جلو دادن 1 to relax the reins, to trot (a horse) 2 to give vent, to loosen discipline, to relax supervision
• جلو کسی (چیزی) راگرفتن 1 to hold, to restrain somebody, something ♦ جلو اورا بگیرید Hold him! / Stop him! 2 to hamper, to hinder somebody, something
• زیر جلو کسی دویدن to be subordinate to somebody; to attend somebody, to wait on somebody

جل وپوستک [jolopostak] *colloquial ironic* belongings, things
• جل و پوستک کسی را کندن to drive somebody away from a long-occupied place; to evict somebody ♦ جل وپوستک ره بکن وبرو Gather your things and scram!

جلوگیری [jelawgiri] 1 stopping, holding 2 preventing, averting, banning, barring
• جلو گیری کردن (از) 1 to stop, to hold, to detain, to delay 2 (از) to avert, to prevent, to ban, to stop, to suppress

جلوه [jelwa] 1 show, showing oneself, showing off 2 external appearance
• جلوه کردن to shine (with beauty, grace) to be in full luster; to stand in splendor or beauty

جلوه گر [jelwagar]
• جلوه گر بودن(شدن) - 1 to be seen, to show oneself, to come into sight 2 to appear in brilliance or radiance 3 to stand in splendor or beauty ♦ از دو طرف راه باغهاو گلستانها جلوه گربودند On both sides of the road, gardens and flowerbeds could be seen.

جلی [jali] 1 evident, clear, obvious ♦ این مسئله بر همه حلی شده است It became obvious to everyone. 2 clear, legible, distinct ♦ خط جلی legible handwriting

جلیل [jalil] 1 great, glorious, renowned, famous ♦ خا ند ان جلیل famed, illustrious family 2 *epistolary* dear, most honorable

جم [jam]¹ *colloquial from* جمع

جم و غند [jam-o-ghend] *colloquial* straighten up, organizing (house or office)

جم [jam]² (☞ جام جم (جمشید in entry جم

100

جماد [jamad] (*plural* جمادات [jamaadaat]) 1 solid 2 inorganic substance; stone; mineral

جمادار [jamaadaar] ☞ جمدار

جمادی [jamaadi] hardness (physical state)

جماعت [jamaa'at] 1 crowd, throng 2 society, the public 3 meeting, gathering 4 *obscure* class (in school)

جمال [jamaal] beauty ♦ حسن وجمال charm, fascination; prettiness

جمامه [jamaama] cruca (oil-bearing plant)

جماهیر [jamaahir] *plural of* جمهور and جمهوری ♦ اتحاد جماهیر شوروی Soviet Union

جنب [jomb] ☞ جنبه

جنباندن [jombaandan] ☞ جنباندن

جمبه [jamba] ☞ جمپ

جمپ [jamp] 1 push 2 shaking, jolting, tossing

جمپر [jampar] knitted jacket (for woman); jumper; sweater

جمپن [jampen] *technical* (also جمین موتر) shock absorber ♦ جمپن سلندری cylindrical shock absorber

جمپن خوری [jampenkhori] *technical* shock absorbing, damping

جمجمه [jomjoma] skull, cranium

جمدر [jamdar] wild oats

جمشید [jamsheed] Jamshid (ancient Iranian mythical king from the Pashdadiyan dynasty)

جمع [jam' (and) jáma] 1.1 aggregate, sum total; total; sum ♦ جمع معلومات totality, aggregate of information, of knowledge 1.2 meeting, assemblage, gathering; concentration 1.3 shortening, abbreviation, contraction (e.g., of muscles) 1.4 addition ♦ اجزای جمع items, terms, components 1.5 group (of people) ♦ جمعی some people; several people ◊ از جمعی شاگردان part of the pupils or students 1.6 *grammar* plural, plural number 2 in sum, all together ♦ جمعش چند میشود؟ How much will it be all together? 3 all, everything, everyone, everybody ♦ جمع اهالی the whole population
● جمع کل 1 total sum, overall total 2 in sum, all together
● جمع وخرج ☞ جمع خرج
● جمع بودن 1 to total, to sum up 2 *grammar* to form the plural
● جمع شدن 2 ☞ جمع شدن
● 1 to be assembled, to be concentrated 2 ☞ جمع شدن
● جمع زدن *mathematical* to add
● جمع شدن 1 to gather together, to concentrate *intransitive*; to crowd 2 to contract, to be strained (e.g., about muscles) 3 to shrink (about cloth, fabric) 4 *mathematical* to be added, to increase 5 *colloquial* to die, to go to the next world
● جمع کردن 1 to gather; to concentrate; to accumulate 2 to gather, to put together (things) ♦ کالارا جمع میکردیم We packed up. 3 to tuck up, to press to oneself ♦ پاهایش راجمع کردن to tuck one's legs under oneself 4 to add
● خودرا جمع کردن *intransitive* 1 to collect one's thoughts, to concentrate 2 to shrivel, to shrink
● کسی راجمع کردن to nurse, to tend, to look after somebody; to be guardian of somebody
● یک سر صد سر را جمع میکند، صد سر یک سر رانی *proverb* One head is capable of coping with hundreds of [other] heads, but a hundred heads [sometimes] cannot look after one.
● خدا اورا جمع کند *colloquial* May God take him!

جمع آوری [jam'aawari] collection, gathering; accumulation, laying-in
● جمع آوری انگور vintage

جمع بست [jam'bast (and) jamabast] 1 summary, combined, total *adjective* 2 total, balance

جمع بندی [jam'basti] 1 ☞ جمع بست 2 جمع بستی

جمع بندی [jam'bandi] 1 adding up the total, summing up 2 sum subject to taxation 3 journal or record of income derived from rent

جمع خرج [jamakharj] *accounting* income and expenditure; debit and credit

جمع دار [jam'daar (and) jamadaar] *obscure* 1 jamadar (lowest officer rank) 2 senior policeman

جم گل [jamgol] and جمع گل [jamgol] jamagol (variety of karakul with tight curl)

جم و جوش [jamojosh] ☞ جم وجوش

جمعه [jom'a] (also روز جمعه) Friday
● مسجد جمعه main or principle mosque

جمعه رات [jom'araat] the evening before Friday, Thursday before the holiday

جمعیت [jam'iyaat] 1 society; company; collective *noun*; meeting ♦ جمعیت صلیب احمر The Red Cross ◊ جمعیت علما the council of ulema alims (scholars) 2 environment, surroundings

جملات [jomalaat] *plural of* جمله 1.2

جمله [jomla] 1.1 totality, aggregate; sum; total ♦ جمله (این) از آن including ◊ از جمله شگردان from among the pupils or students 1.2 (*plural* جملات [jomalaat]) *grammar* sentence, clause ♦ جمله تابع (and) جمله اصلی main clause ◊ جمله فرعی subordinate clause ◊ جمله مرکب compound sentence ◊ جمله مفرده simple sentence 2 all, everybody; everything ♦ جمله نمایندگان all the delegates
● جمله ساختن to form a sentence, to construct a sentence
● جملات اصلی Kernel sentence
● جمله امری Imperative sentence
● جمله پرسشی Interrogative sentence
● جمله تعجبی Exclamatory sentence
● جمله خبری declarative sentence
● جمله ساده Simple Sentence
● جمله مختلط (هسته یی) Complex Sentence

جمنازیم [jamnaaziam] and جمنازیوم [jamnaazium] 1 gymnasium 2 stadium

جمناستک [jamnaastek] gymnastics

جم وجوش [jamojosh] *colloquial* 1 crowd, gathering (of people) ♦ در باغ جم وجوش است It is very crowded (with people) in the garden. 2 agitation, animation (of a crowd); livelines, briskness (of a bazaar) ♦ امروز بازار جم وجوش است Business is brisk at the bazaar today.

جمود [jomud] 1 freezing, congealing, thickening, stiffening, hardening 2 state of ossification, state of numbness or stiffness ♦ جمود مفصل ossification of a joint, stiffness of a joint 3 intertness; immobility ♦ جمود تجارت depression in trade, low level of trade ◊ جمود فکری sluggishness of the mind

جمه دار [jamadaar] colloquial ☞ جمدار

جمهور [jamhur]
● رئیس جمهور president of a republic

جمهوری [jamhuri] republican ♦ سیستم جمهوری republican system of government, a republic

جمهوریت [jamhuriyat] republic

جن [jenn] (plural اجنه [ajenna]) evil spirit, demon, jinni ♦ اور اجن گرفته A demon has possessed him. / A demon has implanted itself in him.
● جن گرفتن to be possessed by evil spirits

جناب [janaab (and) jenaab] 1 excellency (title of a high-ranking person) 2 Mister (with respect, for a collocutor) ♦ جناب شما you, Mr … ◊ جناب معلم صاحب Dear Mr. teacher!

جناح [janaah (and) jenaah] 1 side; side of the road, curb ♦ بوجناح سرک military along both sides of the road 2 wing, flank ♦ از جناح چپ from the left flank, on the left flank

جنازه [janaaza (and) jenaaza] 1 dead body, corpse 2 a stretcher or litter with a deceased person; a coffin with a corpse 3 (also مراسم جنازه) funeral, burial ♦ تشییع جنازه funeral procession

جناور [jenaawar] colloquial 1 living being, creature 2 animal, beast 3 bird of prey 4 humorous, crude insect; louse ♦ جناور خدا swine, pig ◊ جناور fool of the heavenly father

جنایت [jenaayat] crime; villainy
● مرتکب جنایت‌شدن and جنایت کردن to commit a crime, to commit villainy

جنایتکار [jenaayatkaar] criminal, villain; scoundrel

جنب [janb] (plural اجناب [ajnaab]) side; edge
● در جنب beside, next to, by, near denominative preposition

جنب [jonb] present tense stem جنبیدن

جنباندن [jonbaandan] to move; to rock; to shake ♦ رحیم چوکی مرا جنباند Rahim moved my chair

جنبش [jonbesh] 1 movement; rocking; heaving, swaying; shaking 2 movement (in society) ♦ جنبش آزادی بخش ملی national liberation movement
● جنبش کردن ☞ جنبیدن

جنبنده [jonbenda] colloquial living soul ♦ در تمام باغ جنبنده یی به نظر نمیخورد In the entire garden not a [single] living soul was [to be] seen.

جنبه [jamba] 1 side, aspect; point of view 2 character, nature, trait, feature, property 3 grammar category 4 colloquial group of supporters or adherents, group of followers (of somebody)

جنبه باز [jambabaaz] colloquial squabbler, troublemaker, plotter, intriguer

جنبه بازی [jambabaazi] colloquial 1 clannishness, cliquishness 2 squabble

جنبه وپره [jambawpara] 1 group, grouping; clique; bloc 2 ☞ جنبه بازی

جنبیدن [jonbidan] 1 intransitive to move, to stir, to putter about 2 intransitive to rock, to heave, to sway; to shape

جنت [jannat] religion paradise, garden of paradise, Eden

جنتری [jantari] calendar ♦ ساعت با جنتری watch or clock with a calendar

جنت مکان [jannatmakaan] one who has been awarded paradise, one who has settled in paradise (with respect, about a deceased person) ♦ جنت مکان پدر شما … your father, may he be in paradise …

جنجال [janjaal] 1 complication, difficulty; trouble, unpleasantness; conflict ♦ جنجالهای سیاسی political complications ◊ زندگی ما پر از جنجال است Our life is full of troubles / cares. 2 noise, hubbub, ruckus, quarrel
● جنجال کردن colloquial 1 to create complications, to create difficulties; to cause trouble, to cause unpleasantness 2 to twist, to obsure, to confuse, to muddle (some matter) 3 to make a hubbub, to raise a ruckus, to quarrel

جنجر [janjar] and جنجرک [janjarak] botany sisymbrium

جند [jend] colloquial ☞ جن
● جند گرفتن ☞ جن گرفتن in entry جن

جنده [janda]¹ colloquial 1 old, torn, frayed, worn out ♦ کفشهای جنده tattered shoes 2.1 old dress, torn or tattered dress 2.2 rags, tatters (of a dervish, of a Sufi) 2.3 variety of striped homespun cloth

جنده [janda]² (also جنده زیارت) flag on a pole (above the tomb of a holy person, etc.)

جنده پوش [jandaposh] 1 person dressed in rags, a raggedly dressed person 2 dervish, Sufi

جنرال [janraal] general

جنرال قونسل [janraalqonsol] consul general

جنریتر [jenereetar] generator ♦ جنریتر گروپ دار electron tube generator, vacuum-tube oscillator

جنس [jens] 1 nature 2 species; genus, kind; class; variety; breed, strain ♦ جنس آدم people, human race 3 sex 4 (plural اجناس [ajnaas]) goods 5 grade, quality 6 grammar gender
● اسم جنس grammar collective noun

جنسی [jensi] 1 natural, inherent in nature 2 goods adjective, commodity (payable in kind) adjective 3 material adjective ♦ تحویلدار جنسی manager of a warehouse 4 sexual ♦ امراض جنسی venereal diseases

جنسیت [jensiyat] 1 grade, quality ♦ جنسیت اموال را بلند بردن to raise the quality of goods 2 (purity of) breed (of livestock) 3 belonging to a specific sex ♦ جنسیت انها یکی است They are of the same sex.

جنگ [jang] 1 war; struggle; battle ♦ جنگ تن به تن duel, single combat ◊ جنگ جهانی world war ◊ جنگ زرگری colloquial a quarrel to distract attention ◊ جنگ وطنی patriotic war, war in defense of a homeland 2 quarrel, conflict; fight ♦ جنگ

شدیار سر شدیار *proverb* An argument over a field is settled right there on the field. ◊ جنگ را به پیسه میخرد *colloquial* If only he would fight.
- جنگ انداختن 1 to incite to war 2 to sow discord, to cause conflict 3 ☞ به جنگ انداختن
- جنگ داشتن *colloquial* to be in a quarrel
- جنگ کردن 1 to fight, to be at war, to struggle, to battle 2 to quarrel, to be in conflict, to fight, to scuffle
- به جنگ انداختن to throw into battle, to set on (each other) to fight (e.g., cocks, quail)

جنگ [jong] ¹ collection; reader, reading book; album ♦ جنگ خطی album for poetry

جنگ [jong] ² *colloquial* baby camel, small camel

جنگ ماندن [jing-maandn] *colloquial* taken a-back, to be shocked, speechless, dumbstruck

جنگ اندازی [jangandaazi] kindling war, stirring up war; incitement, setting on (of one person against another)

جنگجوی [jangjoy] 1.1 martial, warlike, bellicose, battle, fighting *adjective* 1.2 *colloquial* bullying, pugnacious 2 *colloquial* a bully, a brawler

جنگروک [jangarok] *colloquial* pugnacious person, bully

جنگره [jangara] 1.1 bullying *adjective*, pugnacious 2 quarrelsome, loud 3 brawling, cantankerous

جنگ طلبانه [jangtalabaana] aggressive (e.g., course, policy)

جنگل [jangal] woods, forest ♦ جنگل انبوه thick woods, thicket ◊ جنگل بودنه camouflage, decoys made from twigs (to catch quail)

جنگل [jangal] *colloquial* unorganized, mess ♦ خانه جنگل است the house is a mess ◊ اشتک ها جنگلی کرده اند the kids have made a mess

جنگلبان [jangalbaan] forester, forest guard

جنگل داری [jangaldaari] forestry

جنگل دوزی [jangaldozi] embroidering a design on cloth or fabric with gold and silver threads

جنگلک [jangalak] Jangalak (a region in Kabul) ♦ فابریکه جنگلک the Jangalak (motor vehicle repair) plant

جنگله [jangala] 1 parapet; railing on a roof; skirting 2 baggage rack (on the roof of an automobile)

جنگله بالا [jangala-baalaa] *colloquial* (literally: to over load a truck) stuff, jam-packed, overloading

جنگلی [jangali] 1 forest *adjective*, wild 2 *colloquial* ignoramus; savage

جنگنامه [jangnaama] 1 chronicle of a war, epic poem of a war 2 "Jangnama" (epic poem about the first Anglo-Afghan war)

جنگ و جدل [jangojadal] discord, strife, struggle, fight; conflict, clash

جنگ و گریز [jangogoreez] raids, raids in the enemy's rear area (a partisan tactic in waging war)

جنگی [jangi] 1.1 battle, fighting *adjective*, martial, warlike, bellicose, brave, valiant; روحیه جنگی fighting spirit 1.2 battle, fighting *adjective*; military, war *adjective*; line, drill *adjective* ♦ مهمات جنگی ammunition 1.3 *colloquial* being involved in a quarrel (with somebody) 2 fighting man, warrior
- جنگی بودن(شدن) to be in a quarrel, to quarrel, to squabble

جنگیدن [jangidan] to fight, to be at war [with]; to struggle (with, against); to battle; to wage war

جنوب [janub] south ♦ جنوب شرق southeast ◊ جنوب غرب southwest

جنوب شرقی [janubesharqi] southeastern, southeast *adjective* ♦ به جنوب شرقی غزنی southeast of Ghazni

جنوب غربی [janubeqarbi] southwestern, southwest *adjective* ♦ به جنوب غربی کابل southwest of Kabul

جنوری [jenwari] January

جنون [jonun] insanity, madness

جنی [jenni] possessed, raging, raving; crazy, mad

جنین [janin] *biology* embryo

جو [jaw (w)] atmosphere, air

جو [jaw] barley, barleycorn ♦ نان جو barley flatcake ◊ جوبه جو ☞ جو به جو
- جو بکاری جو میورداری *proverb* Sow barley and you will reap barley. (You must reap what you have sown.)

جو دو خر را تقسیم نتوانستن [jawe-du-khar-raa-taqseem-natawaanistan] *idiom* (literally: a person who cannot divide barley between two donkeys) total loser, an irresponsible and lazy person

جواب [jawaab (and) jowaab] 1 answer, response ♦ جواب مکتوب answer to a letter ◊ در جواب ... in answer to ... 2 message, report, communication 3 refusal, declining 4 discharge (from work), dimissal
- جواب دادن 1 to answer, to respond 2 to answer with a refusal, to refuse, to decline 3 (also از کار جواب دادن) to discharge, to give a dismissal 4 *colloquial* to compensate, to reimburse ♦ پول راکه او تلف کرده بودجوابش رامن دادم I paid back the money that he had squandered.
- جواب گرفتن ☞ جواب دادن 2, 3
- جواب چای *colloquial* *euphemism* small need

جواب ده [jawaabdeh] responsible, bearing responsibility, answering (for something)

جواب دهی [jawaabdehi] responsibility

جواب سوال [jawaabsawaal] 1 answer to a problem 2 ☞ جواب و سوال

جواب و سوال [jawaabosawaal] conversation, dialogue, talk, discussion; mutual questioning

جوابی [jawaabi] and جوابیه [jawaabiya] answering, reciprocal ♦ اقدامات جوابی retaliatory measures

جواذب [jawaazeb] *plural of* جاذبه

جوار [jawaar] close vicinity, proximity
- در جوار near, in the vicinity *denominative preposition* ♦ جوار کابل near Kabul, in the environs of Kabul

جواری [jowaari] corn, maize ♦ نان جواری cornmeal ◊ آرد جواری cornmeal flatcake
- جواری بریان ☞ جواری بریان

جواری بریان [jowaariberyaan] *colloquial* roasted corn (ears of corn boiled in salted water and browned)

جواری پایه [jowaaripaaya] cornfield

جواز [jawaaz] 1 permission, authorization; admittance 2 pass, permit (for entry, passage, etc.) ♦ جواز سفر trip ticket 3 license 4 certification; written certificate; certificate ♦ جواز بودن to be authorized, to be allowed ♦ به هیچ صورت جواز نیست [This] is not permissible in any way. / [This] is in no way permissible.
♦ جواز استخدام 1 certificate (authorization) for entry on a job 2 recommendation (positive, favorable)

جواز [jowaaz] 1 press, squeezer ♦ جواز تیل کشی press for extracting oil; oil press (set in motion by an ox or horse) ◊ جواز نیشکر press for extracting sap from sugarcane 2 ☞ جهاز

جوازنامه [jawaaznaama] 1 document of authorization, document of admittance; license 2 patent

جوال [jawaal (and) jowaal] bag (of coarse wool for grain or flour)

جوالدوز [jawaaldoz] 1 large, thick needle (for sewing bags, rugs, etc.); awl ♦ *proverb* سوزن را بخود بزن جوالدوز را بدیگران Stick yourself with a needle, but another person with an awl. 2 a person who sews sacks

جوالی [jawaali] porter, carrier; loader

جوان [jawaan (and) *colloquial* jowan] 1.1 young, youthful ♦ دختر جوان young girl ◊ درخت جوان *colloquial* young tree 1.2 dashing, handsome 1.3 daring, bold 2 young man, youth
♦ جوان شدن to become mature, to achieve maturity ♦ دختر او جوان شده است His daughter became an adult. / His daughter grew up.

جوانب [jawaaneb] *plural of* جانب 1
♦ اطراف و جوانب environs

جوانمرد [jawaanmard] 1.1 noble, magnanimous, generous 1.2 manly, courageous, brave, valiant 2.1 fine fellow, daredevil 2.2 gentleman

جوانمردی [jawaanmardi] 1 nobility, magnanimity, generosity 2 fortitude, courage, bravery, valor

جوانمرگ [jawaanmarg] having died while still young, having died prematurely ♦ جوان مرگ شوی *abusive* May you die young!

جوانمرگی [jawaanmargi] early death, premature demise

جوانه [jowaana] and جوانه گاو [jowaanagaaw] *colloquial* young bull, bull-calf (through the third year)

جوانی [jawaani (and) *colloquial* jowaani] 1 youth ♦ دوره جوانی time of youth 2 ☞ جوانمردی 3 *colloquial* display of courage, foolhardiness, daring, boldness 4 *colloquial* dashing appearance 5 *colloquial* gift, present
♦ جوانی کردن to make a present of
♦ از جوانی نا امید شوم May I not see my own youth! (formula for an oath)

جوانی دانه [jawaanidāna] pimple, blackhead

جواهر [jawaaher] *plural of* جوهر 1

جوایز [jawaayez] *plural of* جایزه

جوبجو [jawbajaw] thoroughly; scrupulously

جوپه [jopa] *colloquial* 1 group, small group (e.g., of people) ♦ جوپه جوپه in groups; in a body 2 batch, lot (of goods)

جتی [juti] *colloquial* ☞ جتی

جو جو [jawjaw] 1 smashed into smithereens; shattered, splintered 2 exhausted, worn out
♦ جو جو کردن 1 to smash to smithereens; to shatter, splinter 2 to tire; to wear down 3 to beat unmercifully; to thrash soundly 4 to rout, to defeat completely

جوخوره [jawkhora] *colloquial* single portion of barley (given to a horse)

جودان [jawdaan] black spot on the teeth of a horse, donkey or mule (depending on the degree of the condition of which, the animal's age is determined)
♦ جودان رازدن to grow old, to grow decrepit (about a horse)

جودان زده [jawdaanzada] 1 old, decrepit (about a horse, donkey, etc.) 2 old grumbler, old and feeble (about a person)

جودر [jawdar] ryegrass, darnel

جودونیم [jawdonim]
♦ یک جو دونیم است *colloquial* like two halves of a grain of barley (like two drops of water)

جور [jor] 1 healthy, well ♦ جور استی؟ Are you well? / How are you? (greeting) ◊ جور باشی Good-bye! 2 whole, unharmed, in good repair 3 well fitted (about a dress, shoes), fitting well (on somebody) ♦ این بوت به پای شما جور است These shoes fit you. 4 *colloquial* not bad, middling, so-so ♦ جور است Pretty well! / Not bad!
جوروتیار ☞ جور و تیار
♦ جور آمدن 1 to come to an agreement (با) 2 to get on with, to reconcile with
♦ جور بودن 1 *colloquial* to be on good terms, to be friends (با) 2 to be close, to be on friendly terms
♦ جور آمدن 1 to get well, to recover 2 to get right, to be adjusted, to be repaired 3 *colloquial* to make friends; to become intimate, to take up with (about lovers) 4 ☞ جور آمدن 2
♦ جور کردن to adjust; to fix; to repair
♦ جودار کردن *colloquial* to put oneself in order, to preen oneself

جور [jawr] violence, coercion, oppression ♦ جور و جفا cruelty, tyranny
♦ جور دادن to coerce, to oppress; to torment, to harass, to offend, to hurt
♦ جور کشیدن and جور دیدن to suffer coercion, to suffer oppression; to suffer injury or wrong

جورپرسانی [jorporsaani] making inquiries about [somebody's] health, notifying [others] about how one feels
♦ جورپرسانی کردن to inquire about [somebody's] health, to inform [somebody] about how one feels (از)

جورس [jowras] 1 early, early ripening, fast-ripening (*literally*, being in time during the ripening of barley) 2 (also سیب جورس) jowras (the earliest variety of apples)

جوروتیار [jorotayaar] healthy, well, happy ♦ درهرات برادر شمارادیدم جوروتیاربود I saw your brother in Herat; he was in the best of health.

جوره [jora] 1 pair ♦ یک جوره زیر گوشی pair of earrings ◊ جوره موزه pair of boots 2 equal ♦ این دو پهلوان با هم جوره استند These two wrestlers are equal in strength. 3 partner (in a game); rival, opponent (in a fight, competition) 4 *cards* pack 5 *physiology* afterbirth, placenta 6 *masculine proper name* Jora
- جوره شدن 1 to mate (about animals); to take up [with], to become intimate [with] 2 to measure one's strength [against], to measure oneself [against]; to enter into single combat ♦ دو پهلوان جوره شدند Two athletes joined in single combat.
- جوره کردن 1 to couple, to pair; to bring together 2 to make [somebody] measure his strength (in the ring)
- جوره نداشتن to have no equals (in something)

جوری [jori] health

جوز [jowz] 1 nut tree; nut, nuts ♦ جوز هندی coconut 2 walnut 3 (also جوز قندی) nuts in sugar

جوزا [jowzaa] 1 *astronomy* Gemini 2 Jowza (third month of the Afghan calendar; corresponds to May-June)

جوزگره [jowzgereh] a small knot on the cord of prayer beads

جوزه [jowza] nutmeg

جوس [jus] juice (of fruit)

جوش [josh] 1 *present tense stem* جوشیدن 2.1 boiling, boiling up ♦ آب جوش boiling water 2.2 emotion, excitation; ardor, enthusiasm 2.3 the very height (of something); the highest degree, apogee ♦ جوش جوانی the bloom of youth ◊ جوش گرمی great heat, scorching heat ◊ در باغ جوش گل است In the garden everything is blooming lushly. 2.4 fermentation (of wine, yeast)
- (به)جوش آمدن 1 to boil, to begin to boil, to boil up 2 to become agitated 3 to get excited 4 to be seized with enthusiasm, to be filled with enthusiasm 5 to lose one's self control, to let oneself go, to run high (about feelings) 6 to ferment (about wine); to rise (about dough)
- (به)جوش آمدن ☞ جوش آمدن
- آمدن 1 to be welded; to be soldered (about metal) 2 to knit (about bones) ♦ دست من که شکسته بود حالا جوش خورده است My broken arm has already healed. 3 *colloquial* to get on [with], to be on good terms [with], to get along together; to get accustomed [to]
- جوش دادن 1 to boil 2 to weld; to solder
- جوش زدن 1 to boil, to seethe, to bubble 2 (in direct and figurative meanings) to spout, to jet, to be in full swing
- به جوش آوردن 1 to bring to a boil 2 to make agitated or excited, to make furious 3 to evoke enthusiasm, to fill with enthusiasm ♦ گپ او مرا به جوش آورد His words made me furious. / His words filled me with enthusiasm.

جوشاندن [joshaandan] to boil
- در آب جوشاندن to cook, to boil

جوشانده [joshanda] 1 *past participle* جوشاندن 2 medicinal broth made of herbs, a decoction

جوش و خروش [joshokhorosh] 1 seething, bubbling; raging 2 fervor, enthusiasm, spirit 3 excitement, hullabaloo

جوشی [joshi] variety of rice with large grains

جوشیدن [joshidan] 1 to boil, to begin to boil 2 to spout, to jet, to seethe (about water) 3 to sprout together (about plants)

جوغ [jugh] ☞ یوغ

جوقیدن [joqidan] *colloquial* ☞ جقیدن

جوک [jowak] 1 front sight (of a gun) 2 linnet (bird) 3 type of embroidery

جوک [jok] 1 leech 2 bloodsucker; vampire; usurer
- جوک چسپاندن to apply leeches

جوک دوزی [jowakdozi] type of embroidery

جوکوب [jowkob] coarsely ground, not very finely crushed ♦ نمک جوکوب not very fine salt
- جوکوب کردن to grind coarsely, to crush not very finely

جوگی [jogi] 1.1 yogi 1.2 gypsy 1.3 breed of doves of black color with white heads 2 black, dark-haired, dark-complexioned

جول [jol] *colloquial* shaking; tossing, rolling, pitching; bumping; swaying
- جول خوردن *intransitive* to shake, to roll, to toss, to pitch; to sway
- جول دادن *intransitive* to shake; to rock, to swing; to sway

جولا [jolaa] 1 weaver ♦ جولا تکه می بافد The weaver is weaving cloth. 2 spider ♦ خانه جولا spider web 3 disease of grapevines and fruit trees

جولاگری [jolaagari] *colloquial* the craft of a weaver; weaving

جولاگک [jolaagak] 1 spider 2 spider mite (pest of cotton plant and other crops) 3 ☞ خانه جولا in entry جولا

جولاه [jolaah] ☞ جولا

جولاهک [jolaahak] ☞ جولاگک

جولای [jolaay] July

جولی [joli] 1 double bag (in the form of a saddlebag in which manure is usually carried) 2 piece of tent material for carrying grass (the four corners are tied in a knot and the bag thus formed is thrown over the shoulder) 3 ☞ جالی²

جون [jun] June

جوهر [jawhar] (*plural* جواهر [jawaher]) 1 gem, precious stone, jewel 2 essence, main point 3 *philosophical* substance 4 extract, essence 5 *chemistry* alkaloid; acid; compound 6 luster, gloss, play of color on steel (e.g., of a blade)

جوهری [jawhari] jeweler ♦ قدر زر زرگر شناسد قدر جوهر را جوهری *proverb* The goldsmith is a good judge of gold, and, of gems, the jeweler.

جوی [jaw (w) i] 1 atmospheric; meteorological *adjective* ♦ اوضاع جوی meteorological conditions, weather conditions 2 air, traveling or going by air or through the air ♦ راههای جوی airways

جوی [joy] ¹ *present tense stem* جستن

جوی [joy] ² small irrigation ditch; brook, stream
- جوی کشیدن to lay an irrigation ditch
- جوی کندن to dig ditches for irrigation, to dig irrigation ditches
- جوی طلا و نقره *colloquial* profitable spot, goldmine; "lode"
- بالای جوی طلا و نقره نشستن to occupy a profitable spot
- کسی را از لب جوی تشنه پس بردن *proverb* to send somebody off with nothing for his pains

جویا [joyaa]
- جویا شدن 1 to seek, to look for, to search for 2 to ask, to make inquiries (of somebody از ; about somebody or something ماجرا را از ; را) ; to be interested (in something را) ♦ او جویا شدیم We began to ask him about what had happened.

جویبار [joybaar] 1 large irrigation ditch; brook, stream which branches into several arms 2 a place that abounds in brooks or streams, in irrigation ditches

جویدن [jawidan] 1 to chew, to masticate 2 *colloquial* to nag; to scold, to reprimand, to rebuke, to reprove (somebody)

جویده [jawida] *past participle* جویدن
- جویده جویده گفتن to speak indistinctly, to mumble, to mutter

جوی کشی [joykashi] 1 laying irrigation ditches 2 cleaning of irrigation ditches

جوی کنی [joykani] ☞ جوی کشی 1

جوین [jawin] barley *adjective* ♦ نان جوین (dark) barley flatcake

جویه [joya] deep furrows in field, in a melon field, etc. (for discharging water during irrigation) ♦ جویه تاک ditch for irrigating a vineyard

جویه کشی [joyakashi] laying deep furrows (for discharge of water) in a field, melon field, etc. ♦ بیل جویه کشی shovel for digging furrows (in a field or melon field)

جه [jah (and) jeh] *present tense stem* جستن

جهات [jahaat] *plural* جهت
- جهات اصلی *geography* countries of the world

جهاد [jahaad] 1 *religion* holy war, war against unjust-invaders 2 merciless struggle, merciless fight

جهاز [jehaaz (and) jahaaz] ¹ ship, vessel ♦ جهاز بحری ocean liner ◊ جهاز هوایی aircraft

جهاز [jehaaz (and) jahaaz] ² 1 *technical* tool, instrument, device, apparatus ♦ جهاز تلگراف telegraph apparatus, telegraph set 2 *anatomy* organs, organ ♦ جهاز دوران خون blood circulation system

جهازرانی [jehaazraani (and) jahazrani] *obscure* navigation

جهالت [jahaalat] 1 ignorance 2 (intellectual) darkness, lack of culture 3 wildness, savagery, barbarism, barbarity

جهان [jahaan] 1 world, universe 2 people; society 3 world of phenomena, realm of phenomena ♦ جهان اطفال children's world

جهان بینی [jahaanbini] 1 knowledge of life 2 world outlook, ideology ♦ جهان بینی علمی scientific world outlook

جهانداری [jahaandaari] possession, rulership of the world; control of the state; power of a monarch

جهان دیده [jahaandida] experienced, worldly-wise; grown wise through living, having seen much

جهان سوز [jahaansoz] 1 commit the whole world to flames (epithet of a conqueror) 2 devastating, destructive, incinerating ♦ جنگ جهان سوز war of devastation

جهان گرد [jahaangard] 1 traveler, tourist 2 wanderer

جهان گردی [jahaangardi] traveling about the world; tourism

جهان گیر [jahaangir] subjugator, conqueror

جهان وطنی [jahanwatani] 1 cosmopolitanism 2 cosmopolitan

جهانی [jahaani] world *adjective*, worldwide, universal ♦ جنگ جهانی world war ◊ صلح جهانی peace throughout the world

جهت [jahat] and جهة [jahata] (*plural* جهات [jahaat]) 1 side, direction ♦ باد از جهت های نامعین میوزید The wind blew from various directions. 2 trend, tendency ♦ جهت نو در ادب a / the new trend in literature 3 cause, reason, basis, grounds ♦ از این جهت in view of this, therefore ◊ بدان جهت که ۰۰۰ in view of the fact that …, because …, for the reason that …, on the basis of the fact that …

جهت یابی [jahaatyaabi] orientation (on the terrain), determination of the cardinal points ♦ جهت یابی در مسایل سیاسی orientation in political matters

جهد [jahd] endeavor, effort
- جهد و کوشش کردن to endeavor, to exert effort

جهر [jahr] *literary* raising the voice (in singing, etc.) ♦ به جهر loudly, for all to hear
- به جهر خواندن to read loudly, to read aloud

جهش [jahesh] (*literally* and *figuratively*) jump, leap

جهل [jahl] ☞ جهالت 1

جهنم [jahannam] hell, Hades, Gehenna

جهود [jahud] ☞ یهود

جهیدن [jahidan] to jump, to leap, to jump up

جهیز [jeheez (and) jeez] *colloquial* dowry (of a bride)

جهیزنمایی [jeheeznomaayi] display of a birde's dowry (before the wedding)

جهیل [jahil] lake ♦ جهیل آرال Aral Sea

جی [ji] *regional* sir, master (form of address) ♦ آقاجی Sir!

جیالوجست [jiaalojest] geologist

جیالوجی [jiaaloji] geology

جیب [jaib] collar (of dress, shirt)

جیب [jeeb] pocket ♦ جیبش را پوپنک زده *proverb* Mold grew in his pocket. (He doesn't have a cent.)

جیب خرج [jeebkharj] 1 pocket money 2 petty cash

جیبی [jeebi] pocket *adjective* ♦ بکس جیبی purse, wallet ◊ چراغ جیبی (pocket) flashlight

جیت [jeet] ☞ جت [jet]

جیر [jir] chamois, suede

جیره [jayra] porcupine

جیره [jaira] *slang* (*literally*: porcupine) a bitch, a woman with a bad attitude

جیره [jira] 1 ration; allowance 2 maintenance costs (of servants, etc.)

جیره بندی [jirabandi] 1 setting a ration 2 apportionment, rationing (of foodstuffs)

جیره خور [jirakhor] 1 receiving a ration; being on rations 2.1 hired servant 2.2 boarder; dependent 2.3 hireling, mercenary ♦ جیره خوران استعمار the hirelings of imperialism

جیز [jeez] colloquial ☞ جهیز

جیغ [jeegh] ☞ چیغ

جیغه [jeegha] 1 crown 2 plume (on a hat) 3 crest, comb (on birds)

جیغه دار [jeeghadaar] 1 decorated with a plume (about hats) 2 with a comb or crest on the head (of birds)

جیفل [jaifal] nutmeg

جیفه دنیا [jifae-donyaa] colloquial trifle

جیک [jik] colloquial unexpected push, jolt, or shock; starting, flinching (from surprise)
• جیک خوردن to start, to flinch; to rock, to swing
• جیک دادن to push, to shove; to make start, to make flinch (from surprise)

جیکر [jaikar] 1 cards joker 2 colloquial clown, buffon; jester 3 colloquial pushy person, sly person

جیل [jeel] colloquial string (of beads); garland (of flowers, etc.) ♦ دو جیل مهره two strings of beads ◊ پنج جیل سماروق five bunches of mushrooms (dried)
• جیل کردن to string; to tie into a garland

جیل [jayl] colloquial stubborn

جیلک [jeelak] a man's light, summer robe (without wadding and lining)

جیلی [jeeli] colloquial swelling of the glands (in the throat)

جیم [jim] ¹ name of the letter ج

جیم [jim] ² ticking; pique (cloth)

جیمی [jimi] beige; earthy; grayish; khaki (color) ♦ شلوار جیمی khaki-colored trousers

جین بکس [jainbaks] technical 1 junction box 2 connecting sleeve

جینجک [jinjak] steppe mimosa

جیوب [joyub]
• جیوب و جهی anatomy paranasal sinuses

جیو جیو [jiw-jiw] colloquial 1 chirp, peep (of nestlings, fledgelings) 2 flattery
• جیو جیو کردن 1 to cheep, to peep 2 to fawn [upon], to make over, to be obsequious (پیش)

جیو جیو کردن [jiw-jiw-kardan] slang to be a yes-man

جیوفزیکی [jiofeziki] geophysical

جیولوجست [jiolojest] ☞ جیالوجست

جیولوجی [jioloji] ☞ جیالوجی

چ
7th letter of the Dari alphabet

چابک [chaabok] 1 quick, swift; nimble 2 quickly, swiftly; nimbly

چابک دست [chaabokdast] 1 able, skillful ♦ او در کسب خود بسیار چابکدست است He is skillful in his business. 2 adroit, clever, cunning

چابک دستی [chaabokdasti] 1 ability, skill 2 swiftness, quickness; outstripping
• چابک دستی کردن 1 to display ability, to display skill 2 to outstrip (someone in something)

چابکسوار (and) چابکسوار [chaaboksowaar (and) chaaboksawaar] 1 skillful horseman, skillful rider; jockey 2 breaker of horses, horse trainer

چابکی [chaaboki] quickness, swiftness; nimbleness, adroitness

چاپ [chaap] 1 printing, print, press 2 issue, edition, publication ♦ چاپ اول first edition ◊ چاپ سنگی lithographic publication, lithography 3 impression, imprint ♦ چاپ پای footprint 4 stamping (of a design or pattern on cloth, etc.) 5 colloquial spot
• چاپ شدن to be printed, to be published
• چاپ کردن 1 to print, to publish 2 to make an impression or imprint; to stamp (a pattern, design on cloth, etc.)
• از چاپ برآمدن to come out, to be published
• زیر(تحت)چاپ بودن to be in the process of being printed

چاپار [chaapaar] messenger, express messenger, courier ♦ داک چاپار express mail

چاپار خانه [chaapaarkhaana] mail, post office

چاپ انداز [chaapandaaz] 1 participant in boz kesh, a game played on horseback that involves dragging a dead goat's body (☞ بزکشی) 2 clever horseman, clever rider

چاپ چاپ [chaapchaap]
• چاپ چاپ شدن colloquial 1 to cover oneself with spots 2 to dirty oneself

چاپخانه [chaapkhaana] printing house, printing press

چاپگر [chaapgar] printer, worker in a printing house

چاپلوس [chaapalus] flatterer, toady, lickspittle

چاپلوسی [chaapalusi] flattery, toadying

چاپوغ [chaapugh] gore, inset (under the arms of a garment)

چاپی [chaapi] ¹ printed, printed by the typographic method

چاپی [chaapi] ² colloquial massaging, massage
• چاپی کردن 1 to massage, to rub; to give a massage 2 colloquial to give a sound thrashing (to someone را)

چاپیدن [chaapidan] 1 colloquial to steal 2 to seize, to catch 3 to snatch the goat, to take possession of the goat (in the game of goat dragging playedon horseback; ☞ بزکشی)

چاپی گر [chaapigar] colloquial masseur

چات [chaat] anatomy perineum

چاتی [chaati] large earthenware jug (for keeping foodstuff)

چاتی [chaati] slang (literally: deg) fatso, a fat person

چاج [chaaj] and چچ [chach] winnowed grain

چادر [chaadar] 1 small shawl, veil (worn by women on the head); cap, chador 2 literary tent

چادرشب [chadaarshab] and چادرشو [chaadarshaw] tent in which bedding is rolled up for the day

چادری [chaadari] burka, chador (outerwear for Moslem women in Afghanistan; consists of a long shawl draped over the figure from head to ankles)

چار [chaar] ¹ *colloquial* ☞ چهار

چار [chaar] ² *rarely* ☞ چاره
- چار باید زیستن ناچار باید زیستن *proverb* Whether it's good or bad, one must live on.

چارابرو [chaarabru] young man with barely sprouting whiskers or moustache, a youth
- چارابروشدن to achieve the age of youth

چارېند [chaarband] *anatomy* sacrum

چاربیتی [chaarbaiti] 1 *literary* stanza of verse consisting of four couplets 2 *colloquial* (also چاربیت) quatrain, couplet (popular genre of oral folk poetry)

چارپاره [chaarpaara] *literary* stanza of four lines of verse of any length and free rhyming

چارپای [chaarpaay] quadruped, four-legged animal; animal ♦ چارپایان domestic livestock ◊ چارپای *abusive* Brute! / Beast! / Blockhead!

چارپایی [chaarpaayi] wooden cot; trestle bed with wicker in the middle ♦ چارپایی ات را بکشند *abusive* Let them carry you out feet first! (*literally*, Let them carry your cot out!)

چارتار [chaartaar] chartar (four-string musical instrument like a mandolin)

چارتراش [chaartaraash] 1 planed on four sides, tetrahedral 2.1 boards 2.2 beam; squared beams; lath

چارج [charj] *electrical* 1 charge ♦ چارج مثبت positive charge ◊ چارج منفی negative charge 2 charging (of a battery)
- چارج کردن 1 to charge (e.g., a battery) 2 *colloquial* to start up, to incite (a person)

چارچتا [charchatta] 1 rows of stalls or shops under one roof 2 charchatta (market row in Kabul)

چارچشم [chaarchashm] *colloquial* eye to eye; face to face
- چارچشم شدن to talk eye to eye, to have it out [with]

چارچشمه [chaarchashma] 1 amazed, stricken 2 devouring with one's eyes, coveting, looking enviously [at]
- چار چشمه شدن to be amazed, to be struck (by something), *idiom* to be taken unawares
- چار چشمه نگریستن 1 to look in amazement, to stare (at someone, something به) 2 to devour with one's eyes, to stare (به) 3 covet, to jones for, to have one's eye on something (greedily)

چارچوب [charchob] and چارچوبه [chaarchoba] 1 wooden frame (of door, of window) 2 limits, bounds, boundaries 3 stretcher, litter
- از چارچوب تجاوز کردن to go beyond the limits

چارخانه [chaarkhaana] 1 checked (about cloth) 2.1 box with four compartments (for tobacco) 2.2 type of stitch

چارخشتی [chaarkheshti] depression in the dirt floor of a room for hot coals over which a sandali (low table) is placed; ☞ صندلی

چاردانگ [chaardaang] four cardinal points ♦ چاردانگ عالم the entire world ◊ چاردانگ افغانستانه گشتیم *colloquial* traveled all over Afghanistan

چاردرد [chaardard] *colloquial* prenatal pains; pangs (of a woman in childbirth) ♦ زن او چار درد شتهه His wife is giving birth.

چاردیواری [chaardewaari] and چاردیوالی [cardewali] 1 roofless structure consisting of four walls 2 "four walls", shelter, dwelling 3 plot of land protected by a mud wall

چارراه [chaarraah] and چارراهی [chaarraahi] intersection (of roads, streets); crossroads

چارزانو [chaarzaanu]
- چارزانو نشستن to sit with one's feet tucked in under oneself and one's knees spread apart (the usual position for Afghans)

چارسو [chaarso] *colloquial* crossroads; square

چارسوق [chaarsawq (and) chaarsoq] 1 ☞ چهارسوق 2 charsawk (bazaar in the north of Herat)

چارسیره انداختن [chaar-sayra-andaakhtan] *idiom* (*literally:* to drop four *saire*) to live in someone else's house temporarily or permanently, to campout

چار شاخ [chaarshaakh and] چار شاخه [chaarshaakha] pitchfork with four prongs (for winnowing grain)
- چارشاخ زدن to winnow

چارشانه [chaarshaana] strong, powerful; hardy, of great endurance

چارشنبه [chaarshambe] ☞ چهارشنبه

چاراعیب [chaaraib]
- چار عیب شرعی *colloquial* all four mortal sins (murder, theft, deceit, depravity)

چارغوک [chaarghawak]
- چارغوک کردن *colloquial* to crawl (about a child who has not yet begun walking)

چارک [chaarak] charak (an old measure of weight in Kabul; equal to 4 pao and ¼ sir or 766.4 grams)

چار کلاه [chaar-kolahah] *slang* (*literally:* four hats) cornices, clique

چارکنج [chaarkonj] 1 charkonj (name of a variety of pastry) 2 چهارکنجه

چارکنجه [chaar-kunja] *slang* (*literally:* square) stocky person, fireplug

چارگل [chaargol] silver decoration in the form of a floweret worn by women (pierced through left nostril)

چار گوشه [chaargosha] ☞ چهار گوشه

چارمغز [chaarmaghz] walnut ♦ درخت چارمغز walnut tree

چارناچار [chaarnaachaar] *colloquial* 1 willy-nilly; against one's will 2 of necessity; without fail

چاروق [chaaruq] charuk (type of peasant shoe made of rawhide with the sole lined with nails)

چاروناچار [chaaronaachaar] ☞ چارناچار

چارنال کردن [chaar-naal-kardan] *colloquial* (*literally:* using four horse-shoes) to high-tail it, running away, escape

چاره [chara] 1 measure, means 2 remedy 3 way out (of a situation); means of deliverance (from something) ♦ چاره ای نیست There is no way out. 4 trick, ruse
- چاره اندیشیدن(جستن) 1 to think of a means (of deliverance, etc.), to seek a means (of deliverance, etc.) 2 to resort to tricks or ruses
- چاره کردن 1 to take measures 2 to solve (difficulties, problems) 3 to cure
- چاره کسی را کردن *colloquial* to have done with somebody, to be finished with somebody

چاره جویی [chaarajoyi] 1 seeking measures, means, methods (of deliverance from something or for accomplishing something) 2 zeal, fervor (in work)

چاره دار [chaaradaar] 1 possessing great ability 2 knowing what to do ♦ این آدم چاره دار است This person can do everything.

چاره ساز [chaarasaaz] 1.1 adjective taking measures, helping, assisting 1.2 curing; healing, curative 2 assistant; redeemer, deliverer
● چاره سازان در علاج کار خود بیچاره اند proverb He who helps others is [often] helpless in arranging his own affairs.

چاره سازی [chaarasaazi] taking measures; finding a way out, finding deliverance (from something)

چاری [chari] palkash (scraper or small shovel), a trowel used in arranging irrigation furrows and ridges to discharge water

چاریار [chaaryaar] colloquial ☞ چهاریار
● یاچاریار Let's go! (call to action)

چاریک [charyak] ☞ چهاریک

چاریکار [chaareekaar (and) chaarikaar] sharecropper who works for one-fourth of the harvest

چاریکاری [chaarekaari] sharecropping, work for one-fourth of a harvest

چاسکو [chaasku] eyedrops

چاشت [chaacht] noon ♦ ترق چاشت midday heat; hottest part of the day)

چاشتکی [chaachtaki] colloquial at noon, in the middle of the day, at 12 noon

چاشته [chaachta] obscure agricultural chashta (measure of water equal to the amount needed to water a plot during midday)

چاشنی [chaachni] ¹ seasoning (for a dish)

چاشنی [chaachni] ² detonator, fuze primer

چاغ [chaagh] colloquial from چاق

چاق [chaaq] 1 strong, of strong build; healthy 2 stout, corpulent

چاقو [chaaqu] folding knife, penknife ♦ چاقو هزار پیشه all-purpose knife (with blades for various purposes, corkscrew, etc.)
● چاقو زدن to strike with a knife, to stab
● چاقویش دسته یافت colloquial His suspicions were confirmed. / His anger was justified.

چاقو کش [chaaqo-kash] colloquial (literally: one who pulls out a knife) knife fighter, brawler

چاک [chaak] 1.1 chink, slit, cleft; crack, split, break, rupture 1.2 cut; tear, slit ♦ چاک دامن cutout in a skirt ◊ چاک پیراهن slit in a skirt 1.3 scar 2.1 broken, ruptured; torn, slit 2.2 thrown open, unfastened, undone ♦ یخن پیراهن او چاک بود The collar of his shirt was thrown open.
● چاک دادن(کردن) 1 to tear; to cut 2 to slit, to make an incision, to cut slightly
● گریبان چاک کردن to tear the collar off one's shirt (in grief, despair, etc.)

چاکبر [chaakbar] gussets inserted on the sides of a man's shirt

چاک چاک [chaakchaak] 1 badly cut up, shredded 2 cracked, chapped ♦ قلب چاک چاک tormented heart
● چاک چاک راه رفتن colloquial to walk with one's feet spread apart

چاکر [chaakar] 1 subordinate person, dependent person 2 rarely servant ♦ من چاکر شما هستم I am your obedient servant.

چاکری [chaakari] 1 subordinate position, dependence 2 rarely service

چاکلیت [chaaklet] chocolate; chocolate candies

چال [chaal] ¹ colloquial 1 ruse, deception; trick, maneuver ♦ چالت به جانم نمی خورد I won't succumb to / fall for your ruse. / Your trick won't work. 2 cards a play; chess a move
● چال رفتن 1 cards to make a bet, to bet 2 to wriggle out of some mess or kettle of fish adroitly

چال [chaal] ² 1 hole, pit; hollow, depression; cavity 2 anatomy cavity

چالاک [chaalaak] 1.1 smart, bright, agile, adroit 1.2 clever, experienced 1.3 dissipated, dissolute 2 dodger, cheat, swindler

چالان [chaalaan] operating, switched on; started ♦ موتر چالان است The engine has been started. ◊ ریل چالان است The train is ready for departure.
● چالان کردن to put into action, to switch on, to start, to launch
● کار ش چالان است colloquial His affairs are going swimmingly.

چالانی [chaalaani] start, putting in motion or operation, launch ♦ چالانی فابریکه start-up of an enterprise

چالباز [chaalbaaz] colloquial fraud; swindler; cheat

چامبیل [chaambeel] and چامبیلی [cambeli] white jasmine

چامپه [chaampa] champa (measure of length equal to the width of the palm)

چامه [chaama] poem; kasida; song

چاندنی [chaandani] 1 cover or case for a carpet 2 fabric, material (for upholstering ceilings and walls)

چانس [chaans] colloquial good luck; good fortune; chance ♦ اویک چانس گرفت He was in luck

چانواری [chaanwaari] colloquial execution (by shooting), shooting down
● چانواری کردن to shoot, to shoot down
● چانواری شدن to be executed (by shooting); to be shot down

چاوچاو [chaawchaaw] yelp (of a dog)
● چاوچو کردن to yelp

چاولی [chaawli] wattle hand; winnowing fan (in the form of a seive)

چاونی [chaawni] barracks, military post, cantonment

چاه [chaah] 1 well; deep hole, deep pit ♦ چاه آتشفشان crater of a volcano ◊ چاه غله pit for storing grain 2 bore hole; excavation, digging ♦ چاه نفت oil well ◊ چاه زنخدان dimple in the chin ◊ چاه غبغب fold or crease in a double chin

چاهکن [chaahkan] 1 worker who digs wells 2 one who weaves nets, one who spins intrigues, one who prepares dirty tricks ♦ چاه کن را چاه در پیش proverb A trap awaits him who lays a trap (for someone).

چای [chaay] tea ♦ چای فامل dark tea
● چای خوردن to drink tea

چایبر [chaaybar] a large vessel with a spout in which brewed tea is served (to guests)

چایجوش [chayjosh] 1 copper or cast iron kettle for boiling water (for tea) 2 large tea kettle for boiling water ♦ چای جوش برقی electric teapot

چایخانه [chaŷkhaana] chaikhana, tearoom
چای خور [chaaykhor] one who loves to drink tea; connoisseur of tea ♦ احمد بسیار چای خور است Ahmad is a great lover of tea.
چایخوری [chaaykhori]
• ظروف چایخوری tea things, tea service
چایدار [chaaydaar] *obscure* chaidar (person responsible for the ceremony of tea drinking at court)
چایدانی [chaaydaani] tea caddy
چای صاف [chaaysaaf] strainer (for tea)
چاینک [chaaynak] teapot (for brewing tea)
چپ [chap] 1 left 2 opposite, reverse 3 erroneous, wrong; false
• چپ افتادن *colloquial* to treat in an unfriendly manner; to have strained relations, to have no special liking for ♦ همسایه همرایش چپ افتاد (همرای/با) [His] neighbor disliked him.
• دست چپ 1 the left hand 2 at the left hand
• چپ دادن to delude, to deceive
• چپ شدن to slip away, to dodge, to evade, to avoid
• چپ چپ دیدن(نگریستن) to look askance, to peer at in an unfriendly manner, to look with an unfavorable eye
• از راه چپ شدن to stand aside, to move to the side
• چیزی (کسی) را از سر خود چپ کردن *colloquial* 1 to get out of something, to avoid something 2 to get rid of somebody by cunning

چپ [chop] 1 silent; quiet ♦ چپ باش Be quiet! 2 silently, quietly; inaudibly 3 silence ♦ چپ تو و چپ من *proverb* You be silent and I will be silent. (Let this be between us.)
چپات [chapaat] a blow with the palm, a slap
• چپات شدن *technical* to be rolled, to be milled
• چپات دهن کسی شدن [chapaate-dahan-kasay-shudan] *idiom* (*literally:* to slap someone in the mouth) to slap someone down, to hush, to shut someone down, to stop someone from saying something or expressing his opinion
چپاتی [chapeeti] thinly rolled bread, lavash (flat, unleavened bread)
چپاول [chapaawal] robbery, burglary
چپاوی [chapaawi] 1 special, extraordinary, urgent ♦ داک چپاوی *historical* express mail (delivered on horses in fast relays) 2 چپوی ☞
چپچپ [chapchap] 1 champing 2 smacking (when kissing) 3 slapping (of feet on clay)
چپخون [chapkhun] *regional* snowstorm
چپدر [chapdar] horse with a chestnut coat, white mane, and white tail
چپدست [chapdast] ☞ چپه دست
چپر [chapar]¹ 1 hut made of twigs and grass 2 *agricultural* threshing drag consisting of a wicker shield with a weight on it (pulled by oxen or horse around the threshing floor when threshing grain)
• چپر زدن to erect a hut made of twigs and grass
چپر [chapar]² ☞ چاپار
چپرست [chaprast] loop; bolt; hinge; hook, fitting (of door, window)
چپراسی [chapraasi] courier, messenger (in an institution, establishment) ♦ چپراسی مکتب school servant ◊ چپراسی هوتل hotel servant

چپرپیچ [chaparpeech]
• چپرپیچ کردن 1 to pack tightly, to strap tightly 2 to wrap tightly (a child)
چپرکت [chaparkat] bed
چپری [chapari] ☞ چپر
چپک [chapak] *colloquial* ☞ چپه دست
چپکوچه [chapkucha] narrow, crooked street, alley
چپ گردشی [chapgardeshi] sharp turn, zigzag (in a road)
چپلک [chaplak] 1 summer sandals 2 old crushed shoes (with broken-down counters)
چپلی [chapli] 1 chapli (men's sandals) 2 men's sandals
چپن [chapan] 1 chapan (men's outerwear in the form of a robe with quilted wadding) 2 medical robe
چپنکی [chapanakee] *slang* (*literally:* someone with Afghan cape) naive, simple (person) *derogatory*
چپاو [chapaw] *colloquial* ☞ چپاول
چوروچپو ☞ چور و چپو
چپوله [chapola] *colloquial* chatter, nonsense, empty words
چپه [chapa] 1.1 turned over, overturned, capsized 1.2 turned inside out ♦ چرم چپه reversed leather 2 upside down; head first; inside out ♦ چپه و راسته in disorder, anyhow; topsy-turvy
• چپه شدن 1 *intransitive* to overturn, to capsize; to nose over (about a vehicle) 2 to be turned inside out 3 to collapse, to cave in; to be demolished (about a house, a structure) ♦ دیوار چپه شد The wall caved in. 4 *intransitive* to spill ♦ آب از کاسه چپه شد Water spilled from the cup.
• چپه کردن 1 *transitive* to overturn, to capsize; to knock down (e.g., an aircraft); to derail (a train) 2 to turn inside out 3 to bring down, to knock down (a wall); to demolish (a house, structure) 4 to spill (water, etc.) 5 to draw or to allot for one's own plot of land, to intercept (water for irrigation)
• کار چپه است The matter is not getting on. / Everything is going topsy-turvy.
• کارهای چپه میکنی You are acting badly! / You are behaving badly.
• چپه انداختن [chapa-andaakhtan] *colloquial* (*literally:* to put upside down) to be on top of something ♦ خود را بر کاری چپه انداختن to work hard night and day to finish a task
• چپه راه گشتن [chapa-raah-gashtan] *idiom* (*literally:* to walk backward) to walk with false pride, to be over proud *saying derogatory*
چپه [chap (p) a] oar
چپه تراش [chaapataraash] *colloquial* cleanly scraped, shaved twice (about a beard)
چپه تو [chapataw] *colloquial* tied, wrapped in a dashing manner, tied in a devil-may-care manner (about a turban) ♦ دستار خود را چپه تو بسته کرده است He wrapped his turban as if he didn't give a damn.
چپه دست [chapadast] left-hander
چپه شاخ [chapashaakh *colloquial* 1 dashing; daring, bold 2 dashing person; daring person, bold person
چپه گردان [chapagardaan] turning (of clothing)
• چپه گردان کردن to turn (clothing)
چپه گردن [chapagardan] ☞ چپه یخن
چپه گی [chapagi] *colloquial* 1 downfall, fall, ruin 2 failure; misfortune
چپه یخن [chapazakhan] 1 turn-down collar 2 lapel (on a shirt, etc.)

چت [chat] ¹ roof; ceiling; shed; awning

چت [chat] ²
- چت کردن • *colloquial* to clip, to trim (hair, a beard)

چت [chat] ³ *colloquial* reveler, debauchee; daredevil, dissolute person

چت [chet]
- چت افتادن • *colloquial* 1 to lie on one's back 2 to fall flat on one's back
- چت کردن • *colloquial* to defeat (in boxing, wresting), to throw (in wrestling)

چتر [cháter] 1 overhang (of roof); shed 2 awning

چتری [chatri] umbrella

چتک [chatak] ☞ چست

چتکه [chetka] *colloquial* spray (of water, etc.)

چتکی [chotki] *colloquial* a small quantity, very little (e.g., of something); pinch (of salt, etc.)

چتل [chatal] 1 unclean, dirty, stained 2 dishonest, unscrupulous

چتلی [chatali] sewage; excrement

چتنی [chatni] piquant, spicy sauce (with coriander, pepper, and vinegar)

چته [chat (t) a] 1 roofing of a bazaar 2 covered bazaar
- از چته پریدن • *colloquial* 1 to put on airs 2 to violate all the rules (in swearing, in an argument)

چتی [chati] *colloquial* 1 senseless, not making sense; trifling, trivial 2 in vain, for no purpose, for nothing ♦ چتی به بلا رفت He suffered in vain.
- چتی گشتن • *regional* to wander, to roam, to loaf, to loiter

چتی برو [chati-bro] *colloquial* (*literally:* lousy going) lousy, no-good (perons) ♦ او آدم چتی برو است He is a lousy person. ◊ او کارهای چتی برو میکند He does lousy things.

چتی [cheti] *colloquial* document for receiving money, promissory note
- چتی اش مهر شده است He was very lucky.

چج [chaj] wicker tray for winnowing grain
- چج زدن(کردن) • to winnow

چجکار [chajkaar] worker who winnows grain; a winnower

چجو [chaju] and چجی [chaji] chaju and chaji (names of invocation given to a child in a family where children often die)

چجه [chaja] 1 overhang (of a roof) 2 *technical* projection, extension ♦ چجه بام projection of a roof 3 *medicine* splint
- چجه کردن • 1 to apply a splint (at the place of a break in a bone) 2 to spread a tail like a fan (about a peacock)

چخ [chakh Go away! / Git! (said when chasing away a dog)
- چخ کردن • 1 to chase away a dog 2 *rude* to fire from a job

چخماخ [chakhmaakh] and چخماق [chakhmaaq] ☞ چقماق

چخه [chokha] chokha (a loose-fitting quilted robe with long sleeves)

چدن [chodan] ☞ چودن

چر [cherr] 1 squeal, cry (e.g., of an infant) 2 ripping (sound of a cloth being torn)
- چر زدن • 1 to squeal, to cry (about an infant) 2 to make noise, to shout, to howl to wail, to screech

چرا [charaa] pasturage
- چرا کردن • to graze, to pasture
- به چرا کردن • to drive (livestock) to pasture

چرا [charaa (and) cheraa] Why? / What for?

چراکه ☞ چراکه

چراغ [charaagh] 1 lamp, lantern ♦ چراغ برق electric lamp ◊ چراغ ذغالی traffic light, signal light ◊ چراغ ترافیکی *technical* arc lamp ◊ چراغ موتر automobile headlight 2 (*literally* and *figuratively*) lamp, luminary ♦ چراغ علم lamp of science ♦ چراغ هیچکس تاصبح نمی سوزد *proverb* Nobody's lamp burns until morning. (Nobody's good fortune is long-lived.)

چراغان [charaaghaan] illumination

چراغپایه [charaaghpaaya] 1 lamppost 2 pedestal or support for a lamp

چراغدان [charaaghdaan] 1 pedestal or support for a lamp; candlestick, candelabra 2 small shelf or small niche where a wick lamp is placed

چراغدستی [charaghdesti] *colloquial* kerosene lamp

چراکه [charaake] because, since *compound conjunction*

چراگاه [charaagaah] pasture, common pasture

چراندن [charaandan] and چرانیدن [charaanidan] to graze, to pasture

چرب [charb] greasy, oily
- چرب کردن • to lubricate with grease, to grease, to oil
- او چربتر از من سخنرانی کرد He made a report better than I did.

چرب پهلو [charbpahlu] 1 a person on whom one can enrich oneself 2 well-to-do person, prosperous person

چرب دست [charbdast] 1 having superiority, surpassing, superior (to somebody in something) 2 adroit; energetic

چرب دستی [charbdasti] 1 superiority; advantage 2 adroitness, ability
- چرب دستی کردن • 1 to excel, to overcome (بالای) 2 to show adroitness, to show ability

چرب کاری [charbkaari] *technical* lubrication, lubricating, oiling, greasing ♦ مواد چرب کاری lubricating materials

چربو [charbu] internal fat, animal fat
- چربو کردن • to grow fat (about animals)
- چربوی سر شکمبه • *colloquial* 1 unexpected profit 2 fifth wheel

چربی [charbi] 1 greasiness, oiliness 2 fat, grease 3 superiority, predominance, preponderance
- چربی کردن • ☞ چربیدن

چربیدن [charbidan] to excel, to predominate, to have a preponderance (بر، بالای)

چرت [chort] 1 idea, thought; meditation; preoccupation, concern 2 drowsiness, somnolence
- چرت زدن • 1 to think, to meditate, to be preoccupied (سر) ♦ من به چرت کار خود رفتم I fell to thinking about my own affairs. 2 to doze, to slumber
- چرت زدن • ☞ به چرت رفتن
- چرت کسی را خراب کردن • 1 to frighten somebody (by a sudden shout, knock, etc.) 2 to disturb, to upset, to put in bad spirits ♦ چرت ات را خراب نکو Don't attach any importance! / Don't be upset!

چرتی [chorti] *colloquial* 1 meditating, immersed in thought 2 depressed, dispirited, despondent

چرچر [chorchor] 1 onomatopoeia of the babbling or murmuring of a spring, a brook, a stream 2 babbling, murmuring

چرچر [chercher] *colloquial* 1 cry, shout, noise, hubbub, din 2 twitter, chirp (of birds)

● چر چر کردن 1 to cry out, to shout, to make noise, to be noisy 2 to raise loud chirping, to raise a hubbub (about birds)

چرچرک [chercherak] 1 cricket ♦ چرچرک بامبیام خاموشک کار تمام proverb While [one] cricket chirps, jumping from roof to roof, another arranges all his affairs on the sly. 2 windbag

چرخ [charkh] 1 wheel, roller; flywheel ♦ چرخ آسیا mill wheel ◊ چرخ چاه reel (of a well) ◊ چرخ تیز کاری grinding wheel ◊ چرخ دوغ separator ◊ چرخ کلالگری potter's wheel 2 spinning wheel 3 revolution; rotation; spinning 4 skies 5 fate, fortune ♦ چرخ فلک 1 the vicissitudes of fate 2 whirligig, spinner (children's toy)

● چرخ دادن transitive to twirl, to turn round and round, to twist, to whirl; to wind up

● چرخ زدن intransitive to twirl, to turn round and round, to twist, to whirl; to describe circles

● چرخ کردن to grind, to sharpen

● چرخ کسی را چنبر کردن colloquial to give somebody a dressing down; to make life "merry" for someone

چرخاب [charkhaab] whirlpool

چرخاندن [charkhaandan] 1 transitive to twirl, to turn round and round, to twist, to whirl; to spin 2 to drive

چرخ تاب [charkhtaab] and چرخ تو [charkhtaw] silk winder

چرخک [charkhak] top (children's toy)

● چرخک زدن 1 intransitive to spin, to twirl, to whirl 2 to make a pirouette

چرخ کاری [charkhkaari] technical polishing or finishing of a shaft

چرخو [charkhaw] and چرخوی [charkhawi] colloquial ☞ چرخاب

چرخه [charkha] 1 wheel 2 spinning wheel 3 reel, spool

● چرخه کردن to spin; to twist

چرخه ریشک [charkhareesak] and چرخه ریسک [charkhareeshak] wagtail (bird)

چرخی [charkhi] 1.1 round, spherical ♦ گنبد چرخی spherical dome, cupola 1.2 able to spin or twirl, rotating ♦ میز چرخی table with revolving or rotating cap 2 inhabitant of Carkh (region of Afghanistan)

چرخیدن [charkhidan] 1 to describe circles intransitive, to twirl, to turn round and round, to twist, to whirl 2 to roll intransitive

چرده [charda] regional mountain turkey (tetraogallus)

چرس [chars] chars (variety of hashish)

● چرس کشیدن to smoke chars

چرسی [charsi] one who smokes chars (hashish), a drug addict

چرق چرق [chereqchereq (and) cheraqcheraq] 1 twittering, chirping (of sparrows, etc.) 2 crunch; crackle

چرک [cherk] 1 dirt 2 pus, excretion, discharge ♦ چرک دندان film or coating on the teeth ◊ چرک گوش earwax, cerumen

● چرک شدن to become dirty, to become covered with grime

● چرک کردن 1 to soil, to dirty 2 to rub oneself briskly, to wash oneself with a special mitten in the bath (in order to remove dirt from the skin)

● چرک گرفتن to gather a head, to fester; to discharge pus

چرکاب [cherkaab] and چرکاو [cherkaaw] flushing a street or courtyard (by spraying water on the ground)

● چرکاب کردن 1 to flush a street or courtyard (by spraying water on the ground) 2 to grovel before somebody (پیش)

چرک آلود [cherkaalud] 1 purulent, festering 2 ☞ چرکین

چرک بردار [cherkbardaar] not easily soiled, not showing dirt (about fabric)

چرکسوز [cherksoz] colloquial not washed off, unwashed (about clothing)

چریک و پریک [cherik-o-perik] slang kids, tykes derogatory

چرک و چتل [cherkochatal] colloquial extremely dirty; dirty-faced

چرکه [cherka (and) chorka] wild duck, teal

چرکین [cherkin] 1 dirty, soiled 2 unclean, foul, defiled

چرم [charm] leather

چرم باب [charmbaab] leather goods

چرمک [charmak] 1 (also چرمک دلاک) leather strop for shaving 2 (also چرمک دوکی and چرخه) leather ring (into which a spindle in placed)

چرم گر [charmgar] currier, tanner, master at dressing leather

چرم گری [charmgari] 1 tanning leather production. 2 tannery

چرمه [cherma] 1 cord of lace, metallic thread 2 gold braid (for decoration)

چرمه کاری [chermakaari] trimming or decorating with lace or metallic thread; edging or trimming with gold braid

چرمی [charmi] and چرمین [charmin] 1 leather, made of leather 2 tanning, leather-dressing

چرمینه [charmina] traces, belts

چرند [charand] 1 empty words, nonsense, rubbish 2 garrulous person, windbag

چرنگ زدن [chering-zadan] idiom bellyaching, whining, nagging, complaining (a kid or an adult)

چروپر [cheroper] colloquial squeal, screech, uproar, hubbub (raised by children) ♦ بچه ها در خانه چروپر انداخته بودند The small children in the house raised a din and uproar.

چروکیدن [charukidan] to become wrinkled, to wrinkle; to become or be crumpled, to become or be rumpled; to shrivel; to shrink

چره [char (r) a] shot (for a shotgun)

چره [chor (r) a] medicine rupture, hernia ♦ چره ناف umbilical hernia

چره یی [char (r) ayi] (also چره یی تفنگ) fowling piece or gun

چریدن [charidan] intransitive to graze, to pasture

چسان [cheshaan] 1 What kind? / Of what type? ♦ چسان کتاب؟ What kind of book? 2 How? / By what means?

چسپان [chaspaan] colloquial 1.1 quick, bright, smart 1.2 ☞ چسپناک 1.3 close-fitting 2 quickly, brightly; smartly

چسپاندن [chaspaandan] to glue, to stick; to fasten, to attach; to press (something) tightly (against something else) ♦ گوش خود را به تخته در چسپاند He pressed his ear tigthly against the door.

● به هم چسپاندن to glue together, to fasten together

چسپناک [chaspnaak] sticky ♦ مایع چسپناک viscous liquid

چسپندوک [chaspendok] and چسپوک [chaspok] colloquial ☞ چسپناک

چسپیدن [chaspidan] 1 to stick, to adhere (to something), to be stuck ♦ به هم چسپیدن to stick together 2 to snatch [at], to clutch [at] 3 to join, to attach oneself (to somebody) 4 colloquial to foist oneself on, to be a burden; to stay for a long time (about a quest) 5 colloquial to be to one's taste (about food); to give good results (about medicine)

چست [chost] lively, quick, ready ♦ چست و چالاک adroit, nimble, resourceful, keen-witted

چستان [chestaan] ☞ چیستان

چستی [chosti] speed, quickness; adroitness; resourcefulness
چشک [chashak] tasting, trying (food)
چشم [chashm (and) cheshem] 1 eye ♦ چشم بیمار languishing eyes ◊ چشم لق languorous eyes ◊ چشم خمار protruding or bulging eyes ◊ در پیش چشم before [one's] eyes, in [one's] sight 2 gaze
• چشم نیست کلوخ شدیار است proverb He doesn't have eyes, but clumps of dirt (about a shameless person).
• تا چشم کار میکند ۰۰۰ 1 while the eyes can see 2 as long as one has sight
• چشم افکندن(انداختن) to cast a glance, to look, to give a glance
• چشم برداشتن (از) 1 to lose hope; to stop counting (on somebody) 2 to cease being interested
• چشم برنداشتن (از) not to take one's eyes off
• چشم پوشی کردن ☞ چشم پوشیدن and چشم بستن in entry چشم • پوشی
• چشم دوختن (بر بالای) to stare (at somebody)
• چشم رساندن ☞ چشم کردن
• چشم زدن to blink, to wink
• چشم کردن to give the evil eye, to cast a spell
• چشم کشیدن to look angrily ♦ بسوی من چشم خود را نکش Don't look at me so angrily!
• چشم نرداشتن to fall in (somebody's) eyes
• از چشم افتادن to be deprived of (somebody's favor, faith, trust
• از چشم کشیدن colloquial to obtain (something from somebody) with difficulty; to extract; to snatch ♦ من این پیسه را چشمش کشیدم I extracted this money from him with difficulty.
• از چشم ماندن to cease to see, to be deprived of sight
• به چشم خوردن intransitive to be hit in the eyes (figuratively), to meet, to be observed
• چشم آب(او)دادن to delight [one's] sight by the appearance (of something), to enjoy the comtemplation (of something)
• چشم بازار را کشیدن ironic to make a riduculously unprofitable purchase, to buy (something) that would make a cat laugh
• چشم بد داشتن 1 to have the evil eye 2 to be shameless, to be brazen-faced
• چشم به راه داشتن to await (the arrival of somebody)
• چشم بهم آوردن 1 to close the eyes, to doze 2 to die
• چشم پوشی کردن colloquial ☞ چشم پت in entry چشم پوشی
• چشم چیزی را داشتن to expect something (from somebody از); to count on something, to hope for something ♦ من از او چشم دوستی داشتم I hoped for his friendship.
• چشم (بالای) خود (را) سرخ کردن to look greedily to covet ♦ او چشم خود را بالای این باغ سرخ کرده است He coveted this garden.
• چشم سیاه کردن 1 to pencil the eyes, to put make-up on the eyes 2 to be greedy, to envy
• چشم کسی راچپ کردن colloquial to distract somebody's attention; to escape, to slip away from somebody by desception
• چشم کسی رادور دیدن to make use of somebody's absence (to commit unseemly acts) ♦ اکرم چشم پدر خود را دور میبیند شوخی میکند Akram always frolics in his father's absence.
• چشم کسی را روشن کردن to inform somebody of joyous news (about the arrival of a relative, etc.) ♦ چشم شما روشن With joy to you! (said when informing somebody of the arrival of a dear guest)
• چشم خود را گرم کردن colloquial 1 to take a nap 2 ☞ سرخ کردن
• از (با) زیر چشم دیدن to look furtively, to look on the sly; to glance secretly
• بالای چشم خود نشاندن to spoil, to indulge, to pamper, to coddle, to carry in one's arms
• به چشم بد دیدن to treat poorly, to treat in an unfriendly manner, not to approve (به)
• به چشم خوب دیدن to treat well, to treat in a friendly manner, to look approvingly
• به چشم سردیدن to see with one's own eyes, to see for oneself
• در چشم کسی خاک زدن to pull the wool over somebody's eyes
• چشم بد 1 the evil eye, a spell 2 impure glance, lustful glance, lascivious glance
• چشم بلبل 1 a pattern of spots (in embroidery, on cloth or fabric) 2 speckled or spotted fabric or cloth
• چشم بی آب shameless eyes, insolent eyes
• چشم وچراغ ☞ چشم چراغ
• چشمهایش آلو بالو میچیند His eyes poke about so. / He rummages through everything around him with his eyes.
• چشمش برداشت (ورداشت) colloquial نمیکند که ۰۰۰ He cannot watch calmly as… / He cannot tolerate…
• چشمش به هوا است colloquial He doesn't care a rap. / He is devil-may-care.
• چشمهایش حلقه زده است His eyes have become hollow / have sunken in. (about sick person)
• به چشم At your service! / Willingly! / With pleasure!
• به او چشم رسیده است He was bewitched.
• چشم و دیده نداشتن [chashm-o-dida-ndaashtan] idiom (literally: not to have eye and sight) to be jealous of someone, to be envious
چشم‌انداز [chashmandaaz] 1 view, field of vision 2 glancing over, estimating by eye
چشم بچشم [chashmbachashm] eye to eye; face to face
• چشم بچشم شدن 1 to remain eye to eye 2 to meet face to face
چشم براه [chashmbaraah] expecting (the arrival of somebody)
• چشم براه کسی بودن to expect, to wait [for]
چشم بسته [chashmbasta] 1 not having seen life; naive, inexperienced 2 simpleton
چشم بلق [chashmbuluq] colloquial bug eyes
چشم بندی [chashmbandi] 1 hypnosis, mesmerism 2 sorcery, witchcraft, delusion 3 deception, eyewash, puffery
چشم بهم زدن [chashmbahamzadan] (also به یک چشم بهم زدن and) colloquial (تا چشم بهم زدن) in a flash, in a moment
چشم پاره [chashmpaara] colloquial 1 shameless, impudent, insolent 2 shameless person, impudent person, insolent person
چشم پت [chashmpot] 1 not glancing, with closed eyes 2 joking, with lightness or easiness 3 without hesitating, without arguing; without looking back
چشم پتکان [chasmpotakaan] hide and seek, blind man's bluff (children's games)
• چشم پتکان بازی کردن to play hide and seek, to play blind man's bluff

چشم پوشی [chashmposhi] connivance, indulgence
• چشم پوشی کردن (از،به) to connive, to indulge
• به کار کسی چشم پوشی کردن to decide somebody's matter or case injustly, to commit an injustice in regard to somebody
چشم تنگ [chashmtang] envious; miserly, stingy
چشم داشت [chashmdaasht] hope; expectation
چشم دید [chashmdid] seen with one's own eyes
چشم رق [chushom-riq] slang punk, naughty, arrogant
چشم روشنی [chashmroshani] 1 report of joyous news (usually about the arrival of a dear person, etc.); congratulations (in this regard) 2 a gift for good news 3 a gift to one who has returned from afar
چشم زخم [chashmzakhm] colloquial spell, bewitchment ♦ به او چشم زخم رسید He was bewitched. / A spell was cast over him.
چشم سفید [chashmsafeed] colloquial shameless, impudent, insolent
چشم سوخته [chashm-sookhta] idiom (literally: burned eye) burnt once, twice shy; someone who has a fear ♦ احمد چشم سوخته شده و در آینده قطعا حاضر به آمدن در اینجا نخواهد شد Ahmad is scared, he would never come in here again.
چشم سیر [chashmseer] not greedy; not envious (opposite of چشم گرسنه)
چشمک [chashmak] ¹ winking
• چشمک زدن (کردن) 1 to blink; to wink, to make eyes (at someone) 2 to twinkle, to flicker (about a flame, stars, etc.)
چشمک [chashmak] ² 1 small opening, peephole 2 netting or veil for the eyes (in a woman's chadra
چشم گرسنه [chashmgorosna] and چشم گشنه [chashmgoshna] colloquial greedy, avid, insatiable
چشم و چراغ [chashmocharaagh] luminary; salt of the earth ♦ چشم و چراغ مجلس the pride of a meeting, a society, or a club ◊ چشم و چراغ خانواده the hope of a family
چشمه [chashma] spring, source ♦ چشمه خضر source of the water of life, source of life
چشمه سار [chashmasaar] agricultural land irrigated from springs
چشیدن [chashidan] 1 to taste; to try 2 to test, to experience
چطور [chetawr (and) colloquial chetor] 1 What kind? / Of what kind? / Of what variety? / What? ♦ چطور زن؟ What kind of woman? 2 How? / By what means?
چغ [chegh] curtain woven of reed, curtain of rusk or cane (on doors)
چغت [cheghet] colloquial dirty, soiled ♦ چرب و چغت shiny from dirt, greasy
چغتایی [chaghataayi] 1 Chaqatay adjective ♦ قوم چغتایی the Chaqatay tribe 2 a Chaqatay
چغر [chegher] cheqer (wheel with scoops or buckets used to draw water from an irrigation ditch for irrigation)
چغل [choghol] colloquial 1 informer 2 gossip, taleteller, scandalmonger
چغل [cheghel] hand winnow (in the form of a large sieve)
چف [chof] onomatopoeia of the sound of air exhaled from the mouth with force
• چف کردن 1 to blow (on something); to blow out (a lamp, etc.) 2 to blow (on somebody) (while making an invocation, incantation, or exorcism)
چفت [cheft] ¹ loop on a door chain; latch; bolt
چفت [cheft] ² pole for supports in a vineyard

چفتی [chefti] plank, lath
چف و پف [chofopof] loud breathing; blowing, puffing
• چف و پف کردن to blow (on somebody) (while making an invocation, incantation, or exorcism)
• به چف و پف تیر کردن 1 to live in want, to live on prayers alone 2 to fuss over, to be indulgent (toward somebody)
• به چف و پف کلان شدن colloquial to grow up in clover, to grow up in comfort, to be spoiled
• چف و پف کرده with caution, with care
چق چق [choqchoq] colloquial 1 clucking the tongue 2 babble (of an infant)
• چق چق کردن 1 to cluck the tongue (with pity or with reproach) 2 to babble (about an infant)
چقدر [cheqadar] 1 How much? / How many? 2 how; how much ♦ چقدر خوش بودم How happy I was! / How pleasant it was for me!
چقزر [choqzar] regional ☞ چقدر
چقور [choqor] ☞ چقر
چقر و چقر [chaqarochoqor] uneven; with ruts, with pits ♦ دیوار چقر و چقر rough, uneven wall ◊ راه چقر و چقر pockmarked road; road with potholes
چقماق [chaqmaaq] 1 (also سنگ چقماق) steel (for striking fire) ♦ flint 2 (also نقنگ چقماق) firing pin of bolt of rifle
چقمق [chaqmaq] ☞ چقماق
چقمقی [chaqmaqi]
• تفنگ چقمقی a flintlock
چقور [choqur] deep ♦ چاه چقور deep well
• چقور شدن to settle, to sink (about soil)
چقوری [choquri] 1 depth ♦ چقوری چاه depth of a well 2 hole, pit; hollow, cavity; ravine 3 foundation pit ♦ کندن کاری چقوری digging a foundation
چک [chak] ¹ drop (of water) ♦ در چاه یک چک آب نیست There is not a drop of water in the well.
چک [chak] ² 1 framework of a well 2 technical chuck ♦ سه الاشه یی چک three-jawed chuck 3 honeycombs 4 jug, jar (for churning butter)
• چک زدن to churn butter in a jug or jar
چک [chak] ³ bite
• چک انداختن to plunge the teeth into, to bite
• چک زدن to take in one's teeth; to bite, to bite off
چک [chek] check, promissory note ♦ چک بانک bank check
چک [chok] colloquial bent, stooping, stooped, crooked, hunched
• چک شدن to bend, to bow down (from old age, sickness, etc.)
• چک کردن to bend (somebody) to one's will, to subjugate (somebody)
چکامه [chakaama] work of poetry; ode, qasida
چکان [chakaan] dripping, oozing, trickling ♦ چشمه چکان a barely trickling spring
چکاندن [chakaandan] to pour, to pour drop by drop, to put drops (in the eyes) ♦ بیست قطره بچکان Pour out 20 drops!
چک بست [chekbast] finance transfers
چکچک [chakchak] 1 onomatopoeia drip-drip, drop-drop (sound of something dripping) 2.1 dripping 2.2 applause
چکر [chakar] ¹ colloquial stroll, short leisurely trip; joyride; round, lap
• چکر زدن 1 to do a lap, to circle 2 to walk, to stroll, to take

چکر [chakar] ² gear wheel (of a bicycle) یک چکر میزنم وپس میایم I will [only] go there and back and I will return. a stroll, to take a joyride ♦

چکری [chokri] edible rhubarb

چکش [chakosh] sledge; hammer, mallet ♦ چکش دستی hand hammer ◊ چکش نری دار chasing hammer (of coppersmith)

چکش کاری [chokoshkaari] working parts with a hammer; forging parts

چکک [chakak] dripping; drip of thawing snow ♦ چکک دل شیر را آب میکند proverb Little by little one can even weary a lion to death. (Drop by drop eats away a stone.) ♦ بام خانه چکک میکند The roof of the house leaks. • چکک کردن to leak

چککی [chakaki] drops (medicine)

چکله [chakla] 1 drop, droplet ♦ یک چکله آب مابین کاسه نیست There is not a drop of water in the cup. 2 spray

چکله [chekla]
• موتر چکله flatbed truck (for hauling logs, etc.)

چکلیت [chakleet] chocolate

چکمن [chakman] frock coat, chakman

چکن [chakan] 1 chakan (designs, decorative patterns embroiderd on cloth with colored twisted silk) 2 ☞ چکن دوزی

چکنت [cheknat] technical lock nut

چکن دوزی [chakandozi] embroidering, sewing with colored twisted silk (on clothing, skull caps, etc.)
• چکن دوزی کردن to embroider (clothing, skull cap)

چکنی [chakani] colloquial embroidered with silk, embroidered with a solid or overall design ♦ توپ چکنی ball embroidered with silk

چکه [chak (k) a] non-fat sour milk, discard of sour milk; cottage cheese

چکه [choka] stick with a nail on the end (for urging on a donkey)

چکه پران [chaka-paraan] slang slick, slimy

چکه دانه [chakadaana] berry of the honeysuckle

چکیدن [chakidan] 1 to drip, to pour in drops 2 to ooze, to seep out, to leak

چکیدن [chokidan] colloquial to pound, to grind, to pulverize

چکیده [chakida] [chak (k)a] 1 (also چکیده نان and نان چکیده) a small piece of dough that has fallen off the side of the oven while baking flat cakes and is baked on the coals 2 ☞ چکه

چکیده [chokida] oat flour with mulberries and almonds

چگس [chagas] roast, perch (for a hunting bird); crossbeam, crossbar

چگونگی [chegunagi] 1 circumstances 2 quality, property; character, nature (of some phenomenon)

چگونه [cheguna] ☞ چطور

چل [chel] colloquial ☞ چهل

چلان [chalaan] ☞ چالان

چلاندن [chalaandan] 1 to start (e.g., a vehicle, a motor) 2 to put into circulation (e.g., money) 3 colloquial to treat, to get along with (با)

چلاو [chalaaw] ☞ چلو

چلباز [chalbaaz] 1 cunning person; cheat, fraud; swindler 2 sly, cunning, crafty, roguish

چلبازی [chalbaazi] 1 slyness, cunning; insidiousness, perfidy; dirty trick 2 swindle, intrigues, trickery

چلپ [chalap] and چلپاس ♦

چلپاس [chalapaas] 1 onomatopoeia squelch-squelch (e.g., sound of mud under suction from footsteps) 2.1 squelching (e.g., when walking through mud) 2.2 splash

چلپاسه [chalpaasa] lizard (which usually inhabits the roofing of a house)
• چلپاسه بی خون an uninteresting person, an unattractive person; neither fish nor fowl

چلپک [chalpak] thin flatcake fried in butter or oil (a memorial dish)

چلتار [cheltaar] head wrapping of dervishes (long band of woolen threads which is wrapped over a kerchief)

چل چراغ [chelcharaagh] 1 large ceramic candlestick with holes for candles (which are lit on the eve of Barat; ☞ برات) 2 candelabra, chandelier

چلچله باز [chalchalabaaz] (and) [chelchelabaaz] charlatan, cheat, swindler

چلر [cholar] slang 1 scaredy-cat derogatory 2 wimp, small potato, nobody

چلش [chalesh] ☞ چلند

چلغوزه [chalghoza] ☞ چلغوزه

چلفس [chalfas] colloquial sloppy person

چلک [chalak] (and) [chelak] ☞ چیلک

چلم [chelam] (and) [chelem] chelam, hookah, water pipe
• چلم بردن to inhale until one becomes giddy (from a water pipe); to take pleasure from smoking a water pipe
• چلم کشیدن to smoke a water pipe

چلم بردار [chelambardaar] a person who provides (for payment) a water pipe ready to smoke

چلمکش [chelamkash] a person who smokes a water pipe

چلمه [chalma]
• چلمه زدن to be dirty, to be bedraggled

چلمی [chelami] ☞ چلم کش

چلن [chalan] ☞ چلند

چلند [chaland] colloquial 1 circulation (of money, etc.); finance turnover 2 force, effect (e.g., of a law) 3 manners, treatment; conduct
• چلند داشتن 1 to have circulation, to be in circulation 2 to have force (about a law) 3 to have weight, significance, authority; to be quoted ♦ گپ او چلند ندارد His words have no weight.
• چلند کردن 1 to put into circulation (money, etc.) 2 to put into effect (e.g., a law) 3 to treat (somebody با)

چلنی [chalani] large skimmer; colander

چلنی چلنی [chalanichalani] colloquial full of holes; holey, riddled with holes

چلو [chelaw] (and) [chalaw] chelaw (rice that is boiled in water and lightly salted; used as a garnish for meat)

چلوس [chalus] colloquial 1 blockhead, dolt, fool 2 idler, loafer

چلوصاف [chelawsaaf] colander
• چلوصاف او از آب بر آمد His escapades were discovered. / It became clear what he represents.

چله [chella] ¹ 1 chella, 40-day period (time of greatest winter cold or summer heat) ♦ چله تابستان summer chella, 40-day period of summer (approximately from 25 June until the beginning of August) ◊ چله خورد (also چله خورد زمستان) minor winter chella (the 20 days of the end of winter from the beginning of February until the last 8/9days of February) ◊ چله کلان (also چله کلان زمستان) major winter chella (the 40 days of the beginning of winter from 25

چ

December until the beginning of February)**2** forty days (after a wedding, birth, funeral) **3** 40-day retreat for fasting and prayers by Sufi
- از چله چه گله *proverb* What's the use of complaining about the winter cold? (No matter how you curse the winter, it won't get any warmer.)
- درخت چله *regional* tree under which a woman who has recently given birth must walk upon the expiration of 40 days after the birth (as a sign of her cleansing)
- چله کشیدن to observe 40-day retreat for fasting and prayers

چله [chella] ² **1** wedding ring, ring **2** (also چله گوش) metal ring worn in the ear

چله [chella] ³ *textiles* warp (prepared for weaving a shawl)

چلی [chalee] *colloquial* (*literally:* a servant and a student of a Mullah) poseur

چلیپا [chalipaa] cross

چلیدن [chalidan] **1** to have circulation, to be in circulation (about money, etc.) **2** *colloquial* to have force, to be in effect (about a law, etc.) **3** to wear out, to wear through, to be wiped out (about clothing, etc.)
- دستش میچلد *colloquial* He is not in need.
- کارش چلیده است *colloquial* His affairs are moving along, his affairs are going well.

چلیک [chalik] can

چم [chem] turf, sod

چمبر [chambar] ☞ چنبر

چمبر خیار [chambarkhiyár] serpentie melon

چمبیل [chambeel] and چمبیلی [chambeeli] ☞ چامبیل

چمچه [chmcha] **1** soup ladle, ladle; **2** scoop, dipper
- چمچه زدن to mix with a ladle (soup)

چمچه مار [chamchamaa] cobra

چمچه مست [chamchamast] *colloquial* **1** a river during the spring flood **2** a person who becomes drunk quickly

چملک [chomlok] **1** wrinkled, puckered ♦ چملک چملک wrinkled; crumpled; all in wrinkles **2** rumpled, crumpled ♦ دستمال چملک a crumpled handkerchief

چملکی [chomloki] **1** state of being wrinkled **2** *technical* compression

چمن [chaman] **1** meadow, clearing, glade **2** blooming meadow, flower garden **3** lawn **4** *regional* willow grove

چمن زار [chamanzaar] meadows; flowering glades

چموس [chamus] shoes made of rawhide worn in the country (like boots)

چموش [chamushs] *colloquial* restive, kicking (about a horse, donkey)

چمیدن [chamidan] to move smoothly or gracefully; to march, to perform

چنار [chenaar] **1** poplar **2** chenar, eastern plane tree
- چنار نیله ☞ چنار نیله

چنار نیله [chenaarneela] silver poplar

چناری [chenaari] (also رنگ چناری) bluish gray (color of the trunk of the poplar)

چناق [chanaaq (and) chenaaq] **1** chin **2** breastbone (of a bird) **3** *colloquial* game of "take and remember"; a bet ♦ چناق دلخواه game or bet with the condition that the winner has the right to demand what he wants
- چناق شکستاندن to break a wishbone, to play "take and remember"; to make a bit

چنان [chonaan (and) chenaan] **1** such **2** so, thus ♦ چنان که... so …, that; in such a way that

چنانچه [chonaanche (and) chenaanche] **1** that is **2** ☞ چنانچه گفته آمد as [already] stated

چنانکه [chonaanke (and) chenaanke] as (at the beginning of introductory clauses) ♦ چنانکه دیدیم as we have seen …

چنبر [chambar] **1** hoop, rim; ring ♦ چنبردایره rim of a tambourine **2** fence (around a home, castle) **3** *anatomy* (also چنبر گردن) collar bone, clavicle

چنبیلی [chambeeli] *botany* white jasmine

چنته [chanta] bag on a belt (carried across the shoulders)

چند [chand] **1** How much? / How many? ♦ چند اولاد دارید؟ How many children do you have? ◊ چند خریدید؟ How much did you pay? **2** some, several ♦ چند روز گذشت Several days passed. ◊ دو چند double, twice ◊ هرچند (که) *compound conjunction* ☞ هرچند

چند [chond]
- چند نشستن *colloquial* to sit with both legs folded under oneself

چندان [chandaa] so much, thus much; so ♦ نه چندان not so much, not very, not especially

چند ماهه [chandmaaha]
- طفل چند ماهه baby, infant in arms; child less than one year old

چاندنی [chcandani] ☞ چاندنی

چاندین [chcandin] ☞ چند [chand] **2**

چندک کندن [chonduk-kandan] *colloquial* to pinch someone

چنگ [chang] ¹ **1.1** the hand, five fingers **1.2** claws, paw **1.3** hook, small hook **2** *colloquial* crooked, doubled up
- چنگ شدن to be doubled up, to be bent, to bend (e.g., from weakness)
- چنگ ماندن to double up convulsively (about extremities)
- از چنگ رفتن to slip out of [one's] hands; to be lost
- از چنگ گریختن to escape the clutches paws (of something), to save oneself
- به چنگ آمدن to fall into [somebody's] hands, to be caught
- به چنگ آوردن to secure for oneself, to get

چنگ [chang] ² chang (musical instrument in the form of a metal pipe or fife with apertures)
- چنگ نواختن and چنگ زدن to play the chang

چنگال [changal] **1** claws, paw (of beast of prey) ♦ در چنگال شیر in the claws of a lion **2** ☞ چنگ ¹ **3** hook; hook (of a well) **4** stick of elephant driver
- چنگال زدن (به) to claw, to grasp, to seize

چنگالی [changali] changali (ritual dish consisting of unleavened flat cakes broken into small pieces and eaten with butter and sugar)

چنگک [changak] hook (e.g., of a door, etc.) ♦ چنگک چاه (well) hook ◊ چنگک ماهی گیری fishhook ◊ چنگک نانوایی (also چنگک سیخ) long hook (for extracting flat cakes from a tanur [oven])

چنگک و ماده گی [changakomaadagi] hook (for fastening); hook and eye

چنه [chana] *colloquial* **1** lower jaw, chin **2** projection (of a building, etc.)
- چنه زدن to bargain, to haggle

چنین [chonin] **1** such **2** so, thus

چو [cho] ☞ چون **1.1, 2**

چو [chaw] yelp, howl (of dog that has been whipped or beaten)
- چو زدن to set up a howl, to yelp (of a dog)

چو [chew] *regional* rumor, hearsay
- چو انداختن to start a rumor, to spread hearsay

چو [choo] *interjection* geddy-up, is used to direct a horse or a caw

چوب [chob] 1 wood ♦ چوب سبک soft wood (from the juniper, willow, etc.) ◊ چوب سنگین hard wood (of the oak, etc.) ◊ چوب سوخت firewood 2 (also تعمیر چوب) construction lumber, boards ♦ چوب اره کشی timber, sawed lumber ◊ چوب گرد round timber, rough log 3 stick; lath; pole چوب دست drumstick 4 beam; squared beam; log ♦ چوب دول log
- چوب دست ☞ چوب دست
- چوب زدن 1 to beat with a stick, to punish with a stick 2 to make biting remarks; to hint, to allude maliciously (about something)
- زیر چوب انداختن to subject to punishment with sticks
- از آدم چوب تراشیدن to make nonsense; to undertake an impossible task

چوب بازی [chobbaazi] duel with long sticks and shields (form of sporting contest)

چوب پیچ [chopeech] screw

چوب تره [chobtara] an awning made of boards in garden; a summer house

چوب خانه [chobkhaana] lumberyard

چوب خط [chobxat (t)] 1 pointer for reading a book 2 stick, small board (used to keep accounts in a shop)

چوب دست [chobdast] cane; stick; staff

چوب سای [chobshay] wood file, rasp

چوب شکن [chobshkan] woodcutter

چوبک [chobak] 1 small stick; twig, small twig ♦ چوبک کشمش stem of a raisin ◊ چوبک گوگرد match (without a head) 2 (also چوبک طبل) drumstick
- چوبک زدن 1 *colloquial* to poke (into something) with a stick, to pick with a stick 2 to tease (somebody) 3 to put a spoke in [somebody's] wheel

چوب کاری [chobkaari] 1 wood work in construction 2 beating, punishing with sticks

چوب گز [chobgaz] *construction* straight-edge gauge, moon bar

چوب و سپر بازی [choboseparbaazi] type of sporting match (in which an attacker is armed with a long stick and the other participant defends himself with a shield)

چوبین [chobin] wood, wooden, made of wood ♦ پل چوبین wooden bridge

چوپان [chopan] herdsman, shepherd

چوپانی [chopani] 1 pasturage of sheep and goats 2 breeding of sheep and goats

چوت [chot] 1 abacus 2 *colloquial* calculations; approximate determination 3 opinion, assumption, supposition
- به چوت من *colloquial* 1 in my opinion 2 according to my calculations
- چوت زدن 1 to calculate; to estimate 2 to guess, to assume, to suppose
- چوت کردن to think, to suppose

چوته [chota] loincloth ♦ جز یک چوته و یک سوته دیگر چیزی ندارد *proverb* He is as naked as a jaybird. (*literally,* He doesn't have anything other than a loincloth and a staff.) 2 sport trunks or shorts, swimming trunks

چوتره [chawtara] small rise of ground in the form of a bench (usually in a garden or at the entrance of a house)

چوتی [choti] braided hair; braid; braids

چوچکان [chuchakaan] chuchakan (widespread children's game like tipcat)

چوچو [chawchaw] *colloquial* ☞ چو [chaw]

چوچه [chucha] 1.1 nestling, fledgeling, young one (of animals) 1.2 child, baby 1.3 child in mother's womb, fetus 1.4 *technical* rod, bar ♦ چوچه چودنی cast iron rod or bar 2 first component of compound words with meaning: "the young (of)" ♦ چوچه بز kid ◊ چوچه سگ puppy; cub
- چوچه دادن a) to have offspring; to breed to multiply b) to increase ♦ پیسه او چوچه میته *colloquial* His money multiplies like chicks.
- چوچه کشیدن 1 to hatch fledgelings 2 to sit at home without going anywhere (like a brood hen sitting on eggs)

چوچه بز [chuchabokh kid]

چوچه سگ [chuchasag] puppy

چوچه کشی [chuchakashi] production of fledglings, hatching fledglings ♦ ماشین چوچه کشی incubator

چوچه گرگ نشود بزرگ [chuchagorg] wolf, cub ♦ *proverb* You won't make a saint out of wolf cub. (The grave will cure a hunchback.)

چوچه گک [chuchagak] *endearment* 1 child, little child, my little baby 2 nestling; chick

چوچه گی [chuchagi] *colloquial* infancy, childhood

چوچه مرغ [chuchamorgh] chick, fledgeling

چوخه [choxa (and) chuxa] ☞ چوغه and

چودن [chawdan (and) chodan] *technical* cast iron ♦ چودن خام conversion iron

چور [chur] 1 robbery, burglary, pillage 2 *colloquial* completely, fully, wholly, decidedly ♦ از یادم رفت I completely forgot. / It fell completely out of my memory.
- چور و چپو ☞ چوروچپو
- چور انداختن 1 to give up for plunder 2 to throw to a throng (money, etc.)
- چور کردن 1 to loot, to rob 1 to take away, to take, to seize

چورت [churt] ☞ چرت

چورتی [churti] ☞ چرتی

چورس [chawras]
- چوب چورس four-sided beam

چوروچپو [churochapaw] foray, raid, robbery

چوره [chura] rupture, hernia

چوری [churi] [1] bracelet (worn on the wrist or forearm)

چوری [churi] [2] 1 groove, cut 2 thread
- چوری کشیدن to make a thread

چوری [chawri] fly swatter (usually made from the tail of a horse or yak)
- چوری زدن پیش *colloquial* to fawn on, to be obsequious to

چوری دار [charidaar] *technical* with thread, having a thread

چوری کشی [churikaasi] *technical* making a thread, cutting a thread

چوشک [choshak] 1 (baby's) pacifier 2 sucker

چوشیدن [choshidan] to suck

چش کردن [chush-kardan] [1] *colloquial* sucking, absorbing ♦ زمین آب را چش کرده است The water was absorbed by the ground

چش کردن [chush-kardan]² *colloquial* (*literally:* to suck) to suck down, drinking. او از بس تشنه بود دو گیلاس آبرا چش کرد He was so thirsty that he drunk two glasses of water.

چش کردن [chush-kardan]³ *colloquial* to rip someone off, to take someone's money in an illegal way
• خون کسی را چوش کردن *idiom* to suck someone's blood

چغه [chugha] and چقه [chuqa] *regional* 1 chuqa, caftan 2 jacket 3 type of overcoat

چوقت [chewaqt] ☞ چه وقت in entry چه [ce]

چوک [chawk] 1 crossroad, crossing 2 market square (where rows of commercial stalls meet) ♦ بازار چوک chauk bazaar (in Kabul) 3 landing (in front of the door of a home or shop) 4 place for public gatherings
• کارش چوک است *colloquial* His affairs are going well.

چوکات [chawkaat] 1 frame ♦ چوکات دروازه door jamb ◊ چوکات عکس frame of a portrait ◊ چوکات کلکین window frame 2 *technical* framework, skeleton ♦ چوکات برمه drilling frame 3 chassis 4 *military* cadre 5 bounds, limits ♦ در چوکات امکانات within the realm of the possible ◊ در چوکات پروگرام within the limits of the program
• از چوکات برآمدن to go beyond the limits (of something)

چوکره [chokra] boy attendant; servant, apprentice, assistant

چوکی [chawki] 1 chair, seat 2 post, guard detachment

چوکیدار [chawkidaar] guard, watchman

چوکیداری [chawkidaari] guarding protecting, patroling

چوگان [chawgaan] polo mallet

چوگان بازی [chawgaanbaazi] polo

چولی [chawli] ☞ چاولی

چومی [chumai] *medicine regional* lip infection

چون [chon] 1 *conjunction* 1.1 when, as soon as 1.2 since, so far as, so long as, because 1.3 *literary* if 2 *preposition* like, similar to 3 how, in what manner
• چونکه *compound conjunction* ☞ ···که

چون [chawan] ☞ چودن

چونکه [chonke] *compound conjunction* since; for; because

چون وچرا [chonocherā] 1 arguments 2 cavils, objections, wrangles, altercations

چونه [chona] lime, slaked lime ♦ آب نارسیده چونه unslaked lime, quick lime
• چونه کردن to whitewash

چونه گچ [chonagach] 1 alabaster 2.1 of rock masonry, of brick masonary (about a house) 2.2 whitewashed

چونه میده [chonamaida] slaked lime

چه [che] 1.1 What? ♦ چه گفت؟ What did he say? 1.2 What kind? / What? ♦ چه وقت؟ At what time? / When? ◊ این چه ادم است؟ What kind of person is he? 2 *conjunction* for, so long as, so far as, since ♦ چه واضح است که··· *proverb* since it is clear that…
• چه···چه 1 both… and ♦ چه علی خواجه چه خواجه علی it all comes to the same thing 2 either … or; whether … or

چهار [chahaar] four

چاربند [chahaarband] ☞ چار بند

چار پاره [chahaarpaara] ☞ چار پاره ¹,²

چارپای [chahaarpaay] ☞ چار پای

چارپایی [chahaarpaayi] ☞ چار پای

چارتار [chahaartaar] ☞ چار تار

چارتراش [chahaartarash] ☞ چار تراش

چارچوب [chahaarchob] and چهار چوبه [chahaarchoba] ☞ چار چوب

چار خشتی [chahaarkheshti] ☞ چهار خشتی

چهاردهن [chahaardahan (and) chaardahan] *technical* cross piece

چهاردیواری [chahaardewaari] ☞ چار دیواری

چهارراهی [chahaarraahi] ☞ چارراهی

چهارزانو [chahaarzaanu] ☞ چارزانو

چهار سوق [chahaarsawq] intersection of two rows of stalls at a bazaar

چهارسیمی [chahaarsimi (and) chaarsimi]
• لین چهار سیمی *technical* electric line of four wires

چهار شانه [chahaarshaana] ☞ چارشانه

چهارشنبه [chahaarshambe] Wednesday

چهارصد [chahaarsad] four hundred

چهاریک [chahaarak] 1 ☞ چارک 2 ☞ چهاریک

چهارکنجه [chahaarkonja] 1 quadrangular 2 quadrangle

چهار گوشه [chahaargosha] 1 quadrangular; square *adjective* 2 quadrangle; square *noun*

چارمغز [chahaarmaghz] ☞ چار مغز

چهار میخ [chahaarmeekh] *historical* form of torture or execution of nailing the hands and feet to four stakes

چهارنعل [chahaarna'l (and) chaarna'l] 1 gallop, full gallop 2 at a gallop, at full speed

چهار یار [chahaariaar] the four caliphs, the successors of Mohammed (Abu-Bakr, Omar, Othman, and Ali)

چهاریک [chahaaryak (and) charyak] one-fourth (of something), a quarter, a fourth

چهچهه [chahchaha (and) chehcheha] 1 chirping; twittering 2 warble, trill (of a nightingale)
• چهچهه زدن to chirp, to twitter

چهره [chehra] 1 face, physiognomy 2 look, appearance 3 ☞ چیره [cera]
• چهره شدن 1 to settle in (with somebody), to get a place, to get a position 2 *obscure* to be enrolled as a soldier, to be enrolled for military service
• چهره کردن 1 to settle [somebody] in (with somebody), to arrange patronage (for somebody) ♦ او خود رادر آن اداره چهره کرد He was able to get a job in this establishment. 2 *obscure* to enroll as a soldier, to enroll for military service

چهره خط [chehraxat (t)] distinctive marks

چهل [chehel] 1 forty 2 the fortieth day ♦ چهل زاچ and چهل طفل the fortieth day after birth (when woman becomes "clean") ◊ چهل مرده a donation or alms in memory of a deceased (on the fortieth day after demise)

چهل کلی [chehelkeli]
• جام چهل کلی silver or copper bowl with forty keys, to each of which is fastened a prayer (on the last Wednesday of the month of Safar, when the recovery of the prophet is celebrated, they sprinkle water from this bowl)

چی [chee] 1 *colloquial* ☞ چه 2 name of the letter چ

چیت [chit] calico, chintz ♦ چیت گلنار calico of scarlet color

چیچک [chechak] 1 smallpox 2 pockmark (on the face) 3 infestation of fruit trees by the scale insect

چیچکی [cheechaki] pockmarked ♦ چیچکی روی pockmarked face

چیدن [chidan] (present tense stem چین [chin]) 1 to lay, to spread, to place, to arrange 2 to pluck (grass, flowers); to gather (berries, fruit)
• خوراکها را روی میز چین to set the table with food

روی هم چین • to place one on top of the other, to lay in a pile, to pile up

چیره [chira] *colloquial* superior, conquering
• چیره شدن to gain the upper hand, to overcome, to overpower (بر،به)
• او به عزم خود چیره است *regional* He is firm in his decision.

چیره [chera] *regional* printed linen or canvas panel (depicting a beast of prey or dragon)

چیره چیره [chirachira] *colloquial* badly torn, torn to pieces ♦ کالای چیره چیره clothing torn to rags

چیره دست [chiradast] 1 skillful, able ♦ شاعر چیره دست talented poet 2 good (at something) 2 a resourceful person, past master, no fool (in some matter)

چیره دستی [chiradasti] 1 skill, skillfulness, ability, mastery 2 adroitness

چیز [chiz] thing, object

چیز فهم [chizfahm] 1 knowing, versed 2 conscientious [in]

چیزی [chizee] 1 something 2 a little, some, a few, a small quantity ♦ چیزی زمین خریداری کردم I bought a little land / some land. ◊ ما صاحب چیزی پول شدیم We came in possession of a small sum of money. 3 hardly, partly 4 nothing ♦ به او چیزی ندادند They didn't give him anything. / They gave him nothing. ◊ هیچ چیزی nothing ◊ چیزی کم a little less, almost

چیستان [chistaan] riddle

چیغ [cheegh] 1 loud weeping, crying; a cry, a shout, a wail, a howl 2 *regional* a call
• چیغ کشیدن and چیغ زدن 1 to weep loudly, to cry loudly, to shout, to wail, to howl 2 *regional* to give voice, to call loudly ♦ بچه چیغ زد The child began to cry.

چیلک [cheelak] 1 spindle 2 can, tank

چیله [chayla] wooden support, prop for vineyard

چیم [chim] name of the letter چ

چین [chin] 1 fold, pleat, gather 2 wrinkle, crease (on the face)
• چین شدن 1 to be gathered in folds, pleats, or gathers 2 to knit one's brow, to screw one's face into wrinkles, to frown
• چین دادن 1 to make folds or pleats, to make gathers, to gather into a pleat (e.g., a skirt) 2 to knit (one's brows)

چینایی [chinaayi] 1 Chinese *adjective* 2.1 inhabitant of China, a Chinese 2.2 (also زبان چینایی) the Chinese language

چینج [cheenj] exchange, barter, substitution, replacement
• چینج کردن to exchange, to replace, to substitute

چین خوردگی [chinkhordagi] 1 presence of folds or pleats, state of having gathers 2 state of being wrinkled 3 *geology* folding

چینل [cheenal] *technical* channel (television channel, etc.)

چینل سیستم [cheenalsistem] *technical* multichannel communications system

چینی [chini] 1.1 ☞ چینایی 1.2 china, porcelain *adjective* ♦ سامان چینی plates and dishes 2 china (ware), porcelain (ware)

چینی باب [chinibaab] 1 articles made of china or porcelain and faience, chinaware or faienceware 2 silicates

چ
8th letter of the Dari alphabet

ح *obscure* official abbreviation of حمیت مند

حاجات [haajaat] *plural of* حاجت

حاجت [haajaat] (*plural* حاجات [haajaat]) 1 want, necessity; need ♦ حاجت گفتن نیست There is no need to talk. 2 natural need

حاجتمند [haajatmand] 1 needy, poor 2 beggar, indigent, poor man

حاجی [haaji] haji (a Moslem who has made a pilgrimage to Mecca) ♦ حاجی برگشته *colloquial* false haji, "sham" haji (one who has not reached Mecca or who has turned back on the way)

حادثه [hadesha] (*plural* حوادث [havaades]) event; occurrence, incident; accident ♦ حوادث ترافیکی road accidents

حاشیه [hashiya] (*plural* حواشی [havaashi]) 1 edge; border, edging 2 margins (of a book, notebook) 3 note (in the margins of a book, of a notebook); comment, footnote
• حاشیه نوشتن to make notes, to write comments, to write footnotes (in the margins of books, of notebooks)

حاصل [haasel] (*plural* حاصلات [haaselaat] and حواصل [haavasel]) 1 harvest, crop 2 production; product 3 total, result
• حاصل جمع 1 the whole, overall total 2 *mathematical* sum
• حاصل ضرب *mathematical* product
• حاصل دادن 1 to bear fruit, to give a crop 2 to be of use or benefit, to bring results
• حاصل شدن to be received, to be obtained, to be acquired
• حاصل کردن to get, to receive, to acquire

حاصلات [haaselaat] *plural of* حاصل 1, 2

حاصلخیز [haaselkheez] fertile, fruitful

حاصلخیزی [haaselkheezi] fertility, fruitfulness (of soil)

حاضر [haazer] 1.1 present ♦ او حاضر است He is here. 1.2 present (about time) 1.3 ready ♦ حاضرم این کار را بکنم I am ready to do this. 2 (*plural* حاضرین [haazerin] and حضار [hozzaar]) person attending, participant (in a meeting, etc.)
• حاضر شدن 1 to appear; to make one's appearance 2 to ready oneself
• حاضر کردن 1 to ready, to prepare (برای) 2 to bring, to convey

حاضرباش [haazerbaash] *obscure* servant, orderly; officer's attendant

حاضرجواب [haazerjawaab] resourceful; witty

حاضری [haazeri] 1 appearance, presence; appearance at work 2 check, roll call
• حاضری گرفتن to note [somebody's] presence at work or on duty
• حاضری امضاء کردن to register oneself (at work, on duty)

حافظ [haafez] 1 keeper, custodian 2 a person who knows the Koran by heart 3 blind reciter of the Koran (i.e., recites the Koran without looking) 4 *polite* blind man 5 Hafiz (classic poet of 14th century)

حافظه [haafeza] memory ♦ او حافظه خوب دارد He has a good memory.

حاکم [haakem] 1.1 ruler; chief 1.2 *administrative* chief of a rural district 2 prevailing; ruling

حاکمیت [haakemiyat] sovereignty ♦ حاکمیت ملی national sovereignty 2 supremacy, dominion, authority

حال [haal] state of health ♦ حال بد poor condition, ill health ◊ چه حال داری؟ How do you feel? 2 the present situation
• از حال رفتن to lose consciousness; to become weak
• از حال کشیدن to tire, to exhaust, to make (somebody) faint

ح

به حال آمدن to come to one's senses, to regain consciousness
زمان حال *grammar* present tense of a verb

حالا [haalaa] now, right now, at present

حالت [haalat] 1 condition, state, status; situation; circumstances ♦ حالت طبیعی normal state, natural state ◊ حالت نزع agony 2 *grammar* case
• حالت (جمله) Case
• حالت اضافی Genitive case
• حالت فاعلی Nominative case
• حالت متممی Dative case
• حالت مفعولی Objective case (Accusative case)

حالی [haali (and) aali] *colloquial* right now, right away, at once, immediately

حامل [haamel] 1 transporting; carrying (something) (usually in combinations) ♦ حامل توریپدو torpedo-carrier (aircraft, ship) 2.1 the bearer 2.2 holder (of an obligation)

حامله [haamela] pregnant
• حامله شدن to become pregnant

حامله دار [haameladaar] *colloquial* pregnant ♦ زن حامله دار pregnant woman
• حامله دار شدن to become pregnant

حامله گی [haamelagi] pregnancy

حامی [haami] *literary* patron, protector; defender

حاوی [haavi] *literary* embracing, covering, containing
• حاوی بودن to embrace, to cover; to contain, to include (از) ♦ مقاله شما حاوی از چندین مطلباست Your article touches on several problems.

حب [hob (b)] love, affection; friendship ♦ حب مملکت love for the homeland, patriotism

حباب [hobaab] bubble ♦ حباب صابون soap bubble

حبس [habs] arrest, confinement, detention, imprisonment
• حبس کردن to arrest, to take under arrest ♦ حبس است He is under arrest. / He has been arrested.

حبسخانه [habskhaana] 1 place of confinement 2 *military* guardhouse

حبوبات [hobubaat] 1 leguminous plants 2 cereals; food grains, bread grains

حبیب [habib] 1 dear, beloved, darling 2 *masculine proper name* Habib

حبیبیه [habibiya] Habibia (lyceum in Kabul named in honor of Emir Habibulla)

حتماً [hátman] without fail, certainly

حتمی [hatmi] 1 obligatory, compulsory, indispensable, necessary, undoubted, indisputable 2 ☞ حتماً

حتمی الوقوع [hatmiolwoqu] unavoidable, inescapable, inevitable

حتی [ha(t)ta] even *conjunction*

حتی الامکان [hattalemkaan] and حتی المقدور [hattalmaqdur] as far as possible

حج [haj (j)] haj (pilgrimage to Mecca)

حجاب [hejaab] 1 coverlet, curtain; veil 2 modesty 3 membrane; partition ♦ حجاب حاجز *anatomy* diaphragm

حجاج [hajaaj] *plural of* حاجی

حجار [hajjaar] stone mason; lapidary, diamond cutter

حجاری [hajjari] lapidary business, diamond cutting

حجام [hajjam] barber (who performs bloodletting by means of a horn; ☞ شاخک

حجامت [hajaamat] bloodletting

حجت [hajjaat] 1 *literary* proof, evidence; argument 2 promissory note; loan receipt

حجر [hajar] 1 (*plural* احجار [ahjar]) rock 2 (numerative when counting mills) ♦ یک حجر آسیاب one mill

حجره [hojra] (*plural* حجرات [hojrat]) 1 small room; cell 2 cell (in prison) 3 cell (in a honeycomb) 4 *biology* cell 5 *regional* premises for gatherings and for meeting guests in a village

حجم [hójom] volume, size; capacity; thickness

حد [hadd] (*plural* حدود [hodud]) limit, bound ♦ حدود اعظم maximum ◊ حدود اصغر minimum

حدس [hads] supposition, guess, conjecture ♦ حدس و قیاس assumptions, hypotheses
• حدس زدن to suppose, to assume; to guess, to surmise; to make guesses

حدود [hodud] plural of حد
• در حدود within the limits, about ♦ در حدود پنج متر about 5 meters

حدیث [hadis] *literary* 1 *religion* hadith, legend, tradition about the affairs of the prophet Mohammed or his followers 2 story, legend; conversaton, discussion

حذف [hazf] 1 omission (e.g., of a letter, a prefix) 2 reduction, abbreviation, ejection, rejection
• حذف کردن 1 to eject, to reject, to omit 2 to reduce, to abbreviate

حرارت [haraarat] 1 temperature ♦ درجه حرارت هوا air temperature 2 heat, heightened temperature 3 ardor; enthusiasm

حراست [haraasat] 1 guarding, protection 2 care; concern, anxiety (about the safety of something) ♦ زیر حراست under supervision; under protection

حرام [haraam] unlawful, illicit, forbidden (by the laws of the sharia)
• مال مردم حرام است [to encroach on] somebody else's property is against the laws of the sharia 2 impure, profane 3) gained by dishonest means (about riches, money)

حرامخور [haraamkhor] 1.1 living on unearned income 1.2 living at somebody else's expense 2.1 parasite, sponger 2.2 scoundrel

حرام زاده [haraamzaada] cheat, swindler, scoundrel

حرام کار [haraamkaar] 1 encroaching on the honor of women or girls 2 debauchee, libertine

حرامغز [haraamaghz] and حراممغز [harammaqz] spinal cord

حرب [harb] war ♦ حرب دوم جهانی World War II ◊ حرب داخلی civil war

حربی [harbi] 1 military, war ♦ وسایط حربی military equipment 2 combat

حربیه [harbiya] ☞ حربی

حرص [hers] greed, greediness, avidity, self-interest

حرف [harf] 1 (*plural* حروف [huruf]) letter (of the alphabet) ♦ حرف کلان capital letter 2 word; speech 3 *grammar* particle ♦ حرف نفی negation 4 *grammar* preposition
• حرف به حرف 1 by the letters, letter by letter 2 literally
• حرف زدن to talk

حرفت [herfat] ☞ حرفه

حرفه [herfa] 1 trade, craft 2 occupation, employment, field of activity, profession

حرکات [harakaat] 1 *plural of* حرکت 2 *military* operations

حرکت [harakat] 1 movement, motion 2 departure 3 conduct, behavior; action; act, deed
- حرکت دادن to move; to put in motion
- حرکت کردن 1 to move *intransitive* 2 to set (out, off), to leave
- به حرکت آمدن and به حرکت افتادن to move *intransitive*, to go in motion

حرم [harm] 1 forbidden place, sacred place 2 harem

حرمت [hormat] 1 respect, esteem 2 honor, dignity, virture

حرم سرای [haramsaraay] 1 inner part of a house; women's quarters 2 *obscure* palace harem

حروف [horuf] *plural of* حرف 1
- حروف هجا alphabet
- حروف مطبعه print, type
- حروف اتصاف Connecting letters (adjective suffix)
- حروف اصوات Interjections
- حروف اضافت Preposition
- حروف ربط Conjunctive letter
- حروف علت Subject letter (subjective suffix

حروفچین [horufchin] compositor, typesetter

حروفی [horufi] typographical type, printing ♦ دستگاه حروفی printing press

حریت [horriyat] *literary* freedom, will

حریر [harir] silk, silk fabric

حریره [harira] liquid gelatin, starchy thin gruel (for sick persons)

حریص [haris] greedy, stingy ♦ دهن حریص دندان ندارد *proverb* A greedy mouth doesn't have teeth. (God doesn't give horns to a butting cow.)

حریف [harif] 1 rival, competitor, opponent 2 partner

حریق [hariq] 1 fire (e.g., a building on fire) 2 fire (generic term), flame, blaze

حریم [harim] *literary* 1 fence 2 external wall of the Kaaba (at the great Mosque in Mecca)

حزب [hezb] (*plural* احزاب [ahzab]) political party ♦ حزب کمونیستی communist party

حزبی [hezbi] 1 party *adjective* 2 party member

حس [hess] (*plural* حواس [hawas (s)]) feeling, sensation
- حس شدن to be felt; to make itself felt
- حس کردن to feel, to experience some kind of feeling; to sense, to become aware [of]

حساب [hesaab] bill, account; counting; calculation ♦ حساب جاری current account (in a bank) ◊ علم حساب arithmetic
- حساب شدن to be counted, to be computed
- حساب کردن to count, to compute
- به حساب رفتن to take into consideration, to be taken into consideration ♦ هر چیز به خود حساب دارد Each thing requires its own approach. / Each matter has its own procedure.

حسابی [hesaabi] 1 account *adjective*, calculating 2 account *adjective*, report *adjective*, fiscal 3 arithmetic *adjective*, 4 efficient, businesslike, serious, worthy ♦ آدم حسابی a worthy person ◊ کار حسابی a genuine matter, a serious matter ◊ سوال حسابی sensible question

حساس [hassaas] 1 sensitive; keen, delicate; impressionable 2 punctilious 3 sensitive (about an instrument, etc.)

حساسیت [hasaasiyat] 1 sensitivity; keenness, impressionability 2 punctiliousness 3 sensitivity (of an instrument, etc.)

حسب [hasb] according to, in accordance with, in conformity with *demonstrative preposition* ♦ حسب مقررات in accordance with instructions or directions ◊ حسب امکان as possible ◊ حسب دلخواه at the heart's command

حسب الامر [hasbolamr] in accordance with the order, according to the order, by order [of]

حسب الامکان [hasbolemkaan] as possible

حسب المعمول [hasbolma'mul] as usual, by habit

حسد [hasad] envy; malicious jealousy; malice, spite
- حسد خوردن and حسد بردن to envy (somebody به) maliciously; to be jealous [of]

حسد آمیز [hasadaameez] envious; covetous; wicked, malicious

حسرت [hasrat] 1 longing yearning (for something); a strong desire to have (something) 2 sorrow, grief
- حسرتکشیدن and حسرت خوردن 1 to long [for], to yearn [for] 2 to be sad, to grieve, to mourn

حسرت انگیز [hasratangeez] 1 evoking a longing or yearning, causing sorrow or grief 2 regrettable; unfortunate

حسرت بار [hasratbaar] sorrowful, sad

حسن [hasan] 1 *literary* beautiful, handsome 2 *masculine proper name* Hasan

حسن غمکش [Hassane-ghamkash] *slang* (*literally:* Hassan the griever) someone to turn to (a person who takes care of others while accepting any kinds of difficulties)

حسن [hosn] 1 beauty, charm; elegance, grace 2 good, blessing, boon 3 (first component of set expressions) ♦ حسن تفاهم mutual understanding ◊ حسن نیت good will, good intention

حسن تفاهم [hosnetafaahom] mutual understanding

حسن غمکش [Hassane-ghamkash] *slang* (*literally:* Hassan the griever) someone to turn to (a person who takes care of others while accepting any kinds of difficulties)

حسن معامله [hosnemo'aamela] 1 good treatment 2 honesty (in transactions)

حسن نیت [hosneneyat] good will, good intention

حسن همجواری [hosnehamjawaari] good-neighborliness, neighborly relations

حسنه [hasana] good deal

حسود [hasud] 1 envious 2 envious person

حسی [hessi] material *adjective*, tangible; perceptible by the organs of sense

حسیات [hessiyaat] 1 feelings, sensations 2 spirit; emotions; mood, frame of mind

حسینی [hosayni] 1 (also انگور حسینی) hosayni, "lady fingers" (variety of grape) 2 rosy, rose (in the names of plants or birds) ♦ قاز حسینی flamingo

حشر [háshar] [1] *literary* gathering, assemblage, crowd (of people) ♦ روز حشر *religion* judgement day, day of resurrection from the dead

حشر [hashar] [2] hashar (community help in rural areas during gathering of the harvest, building roads, etc.)

حشره [hashara] 1 insect; small insect 2 reptile

حشره شناس [hasharashenaas] entomologist

حشمت [hashmat] *literary* splendor, magnificence, grandeur

حشمت ماب [hashmatmaab] *obscure* [his] excellency (title of presidents of the republic)

ح

حصار [hesaar] 1 stronghold, fortress, fort, fortification 2 fence, wall 3 encirclement, siege
• حصار کردن 1 to encircle with a wall, to guard, to protect, to fence in 2 to lay sieze [to], to blockade

حصص [hesas] *plural of* حصه

حصول [hosul] getting, obtaining, acquiring; achievement, attainment (of something)

حصه [hessa] (*plural* حصص [hesas]) share, part, portion
• حصه حصه *and colloquial* حصه حصه کردن to divide into parts, to disassemble
• حصه گرفتن 1 to receive a share (در) 2 to take part (در)

حصه دار [hessadaar] participant; companion, partner; shareholder

حضار [hozzaar] 1 *plural of* حاضر 2 audience, the public

حضرت [hazrat] 1 majesty, highness ♦ علیا حضرت her majesty (the queen) 2 holiness ♦ حضرت امام صاحب his holiness the imam

حضور [hozur] presence ♦ در حضور کسی *polite* in the presence of somebody
• حضور داشتن *polite* to design to be present, to honor with one's presence
• به حضور پذیرفتن to give an audience
• به حضورتان عرض میکنم *epistolary* I bring to your attention. / I inform you.
• به حضور محترم مدیر صاحب to the attention of the manager

حفاظت [hefaazat] guarding, defense, protection; safeguarding
♦ تحت حفاظت under the protection
• حفاظت کردن to guard, to protect, to defend

حفر [hafr] digging, excavating
• حفر کردن to dig, to excavate

حفره [hafra] hole, pit, hollow, depression; crater

حفریات [hafriyaat] earth-moving operations, excavation; excavations (archeological)

حفظ [hefz] 1 guarding, protection, defense; custody, storage, protecting ♦ حفظ ماتقدم *medicine* prophylaxis 2 memorizing, learning by heart
• حفظ و مراقبت ☞ حفظ و حراست
• حفظ داشتن to know by heart, to remember by heart
• حفظ کردن 1 to keep, to preserve, to save, to guard, to protect 2 to memorize, to learn by heart

حفظ الصحه [hefzossehha] 1 hygiene; sanitation ♦ حفظ الصحه شخصی personal hygiene ◊ قوانین حفظ الصحه sanitation standards 2 care of public health

حفظ و مراقبت [hefzomoraaqebat] safekeeping; care ♦ حفظ و مراقبت سرک ها maintenance of roads in good condition

حق [haq (q)] 1 truth; rightness, fairness, justice ♦ حق با شما است you are right ◊ بر خلاف حق *and* به جانب شما حق unjustly, illegally 2 (*plural* حقوق [hoquq]) legal right (to something) ♦ حق مالکیت right of property ◊ حق کار right to work 3 pay (for labor), remuneration; payment 4 something belonging by right; a share ♦ این خانه حق او است This house belongs to him by right. 5 *literary* God, Allah ♦ حق تعالی the most high Allah
• حق الاجاره ☞ حق اجاره
• حق الزحمت ☞ حق زحمت
• در حق relative to, concerning; in regard to, with respect to *denominative preposition* ♦ حق داشتن to have the right
• حق کسی را ادا کردن *colloquial* 1 to give somebody his due, to pay somebody according to his deserts 2 to thrash somebody, to force somebody to pay

حقاً [haqqan] 1 truly 2 justly; by right

حقابه *and* حقآبه [haqqoba] right to water; share of water (for irrigation)

حقارت [haqaarat] 1 humiliation, humbleness, pitiful condition 2 contempt, scorn, disdain, neglect, disregard

حق الاجاره [haqqolejaara] rent payment

حق الزحمت [haqqozzahmat] remuneration for labor; wages; fee

حق الله [haqqollaa] part of a harvest or income that is given to a mullah (*literally*, God's; that which is due God)

حق آوه [haqaawa] *colloquial* ☞ حق آبه

حقایق [haqaayeq] *plural of* حقیقت

حق بطرف [haqbataraf] right, correct ♦ او حق بطرف است He is right. / Truth is on his side.

حقدار [haqdar] 1 having the right (to something) 2.1 owner 2.2 a person to whom we are obligated (for something) (e.g., father, mother)

حق داری [haq (q) daai] giving [one's] due, requital in all fairness; acknowledgement (of somebody's) right (to something)
• حق داری کردن 1 to render what is due, to act in all fairness 2 to share (something) fairly (e.g., an inheritance)

حق شناس [haq (q) shenas] respecting the rights (of others), just, fair; giving (people their) due

حق ناحق [haqqnaahaqq] willy-nilly

حق ناشناس [haq (q) naashenaas] ungrateful, thankless

حق وحلال [haq (q)ohalaal] legal, obtained by honest means ♦ این پول حق وحلال است This is honestly earned money.

حقوق [hoquq] 1 *plural of* حق 2 2 the aggregate of juridical norms and laws, the law ♦ علم حقوق jurisprudence

حقوق شناسی [hoquqshenaasi] science of law, jurisprudence

حقوقی [hoquqi] juridical, law *adjective*, lawful ♦ مشاور حقوقی legal adviser, jurist

حقه [haq(q)a] 1 legal, just ♦ حقوق حقه legal rights 2 undoubted

حقیر [haqir] 1 low, contemptible, despicable, pitiful 2 humble, meek, submissive

حقیرانه [haqirana] 1 pitiful, insignificant (about something) 2 poor, humble, meek

حقیقت [haqiqat] (*plural* حقایق [haqayeq]) 1 truth ♦ حقیقت مطاق *philosophical* absolute truth ◊ حقیقت نسبی *philosophical* relative truth ◊ حقیقت است correct; right, true 2 actuality, reality, fact ♦ در حقیقت actually, in fact
• حقیقت داشتن to correspond to actuality ♦ حقیقت ندارد [This] does not correspond to reality. / It is not true.

حقیقتاً [haqiqatan] 1 really, truly 2 actually, in fact

حقیقت بین [haqiqatbin] realist

حقیقی [haqiqi] 1 actual, real 2 genuine, true, authentic, natural

حکام [hokkaam] *plural of* حاکم 1

حکایت [hekaayat] story; short story; tale
• حکایت کردن to tell, to narrate

حکایه [hekaaya] ☞ حکایت

حکم [hakam] arbiter; mediator, intermediary, arbitrator

حکم [hekam] *plural of* حکمت 4

حکم [hókom] (*plural* احکام [ahkam]) 1 order, direction; instructions ♦ حکم طاس *colloquial* categorical order ◊ به حکم طاس *colloquial* without fail, certainly ◊ حکم نیست It is not allowed, there is no order! (e.g., to admit [someone]

somewhere) **2** sentence, verdict (of a court)
- به حکم ۰۰۰ owing to, in consequence of, on account of, because *denominative preposition* ♦ به حکم ضرورت by virtue of necessity
- حکم دادن **1** to issue an order, to issue an instruction **2** to pass sentence
- حکم کردن **1** to order, to command; to govern, to rule **2** to sentence, to condemn
- حکم چیزی را داشتن to be tantamount to something, to signify something

حکماً [hókman] without fail, certainly, undoubtedly, absolutely

حکم بردار [hokmbordaar] industrious, painstaking, obedient, dutiful, submissive

حکمت [hekmat] **1** wisdom, knowledge **2** *literary* teaching, philosophy ♦ اهل حکمت wise men, philosophers **3** *obscure* doctoring (by the methods of eastern medicine) **4** wise saying, aphorism

حکمران [hokmraan] **1** lord, master, sovereign, ruler **2** *obscure* chief, head (of a region, of a district)

حکمرانی [hokmraani] power, authority, government

حکم فرما [hokmfarmaa] ruling, reigning
- حکم فرما بودن to rule, to reign

حکم فرمایی [hokmfarmaayi] supremacy, rule, sway

حکمیت [hakamiyat] arbitration, mediation; court of arbitration; - تجارتی

حکومت [hokumat] **1** government, cabinet **2** power, authority, government **3** *obscure* small rural district, region
- حکومت کردن to govern, to rule [over] (somebody or something بر،به)

حکومتی [hokumati] **1.1** governmental **1.2** state *adjective* **2.1** *obscure* administration of a region, of a small rural district **2.2** *obscure* region, district, small rural district, governorship

حکیم [hakim] **1** (also حکیم جی) sorcerer, doctor **2** *literary* wise man; philosopher **3** physician (using the methods of eastern medicine)

حکیم جی [hakeemji] *colloquial* medicine man (a person who makes homemade medicine)

حکیمانه [hakimaana] **1** wisely, judiciously, reasonably **2** wise, reasonable ♦ نصایح حکیمانه wise pieces of advice, sensible pieces of advice

حل [hal (I)] **1** solution ♦ حل مسایل solution of problems ◊ حل معما unraveling a riddle or a rebus ◊ راه حل way of solving (something) **2** dissolving, dissolution (of sugar and salt in water, etc.)
- حل شدن **1** to be solved **2** to be dissolved
- حل کردن **1** to solve; to unravel **2** to dissolve

حلاجی [hallaji] **1** trade or occupation of a scutcher, of a carder of cotton **2** carding, scutching or ginning cotton **3** (also ماشین حلاجی) tool for separating cotton seeds from the fiber
- حلاجی کردن **1** to scutch cotton, to card cotton **2** *slang* to squeeze someone, to put the screws to someone

حلال [halaal] **1** permitted, authorized (by the shariya) **2** clean, pure, suitable for food ♦ آب حلال pure water, drinking water ◊ گوشت حلال edible meat; sanctioned meat **3** legal, acquired by honest means ♦ پول حلال honestly earned money
- حلال شدن **1** to be permitted, authorized (by the shariya) **2** to be slaughtered (according to the laws of the shariya; about birds, livestock)
- حلال کردن **1** to authorize, to permit **2** to slaughter (according to the laws of the shariya)

حلال گوشت [halaalgosht] edible (about a bird, animal, or meat which is permitted to be used as food according to the shariya)

حلاوت [halaawat] *literary* sweetness, delight; enjoyment, pleasure

حلبی [halabi] **1.1** tin **1.2** sheet metal **2** tin *adjective*

حلبی سازی [halabisaazi] **1** trade or occupation of a tinsmith **2** (also دکان حلبی سازی) shop of a tinsmith

حلق [halq] larynx, throat; gullet
- از حلق کسی کشیدن *colloquial* to take from somebody by force, to tear out of [somebody's] throat, to extract from somebody

حلقه [halqa] **1** ring; circle **2** circle, club ♦ حلقه های هنری artistic circles ◊ حلقه چشم eye socket **3** *technical* eye, ring, loop **4** (numerative in counting tires, recording cassettes, etc.) ♦ پنج حلقه تیپ five cassettes ◊ چهار حلقه تایر four tires
- حلقه زدن and حلقه بستن to encircle, to surround (somebody, something); to wind round (somebody, something دور)
- حلقه کردن **1** to make a ring; to link with rings **2** to twist **3** *colloquial* ☞ حلقه زدن
- حلقه محاصره *military* encircling ring

حلقه به گوش [halqabagush] **1** slavishly devoted, submissive ♦ غلام حلقه به گوش devoted slave **2** slave, servant

حلقه حلقه [halqahalqa] **1** in rings, in a ring-shaped manner, in curls **2** ring-shaped
- حلقه حلقه شدن to curl, to be twined round
- حلقه حلقه کردن **1** to twist **2** to curl in rings

حلوا [halwaa] halvah ♦ حلوا مغزی halvah with nuts

حلوایی [halwayi] **1.1** confectioner, pastry chef **1.2** *colloquial* vendor of halvah **2** pale yellow, cream (about a color)

حل و فصل [hallofasel] solution, examination (of a question, problem)
- حل و فصل شدن to be solved, to decide [on]
- حل و فصل کردن to solve

حلویات [halwiyaat (and) halawiyaat] sweets; confectionaries

حلماست [halmaasat] **1** epic, epic work **2** *literary* military valor, heroism

حماسه [hamaasa] ☞ حلماست

حماسی [hamaasi] epic *adjective*; heroic ♦ اشعار حماسی epic poetry, an epic

حماقت [hamaaqat] stupidity, obtuseness

حمال [hammaal] loader, stevedore, porter, carrier

حمام [hammaam] bath, bathhouse
- حمام گرفتن(کردن/رفتن) to wash (oneself, in a bathhouse); to bathe (in a bathroom)

حمامی [hammaami] bathhouse attendant

حمایت [hemaayat] ☞ حمایه

حمایتی [hemaayati] ☞ حمایوی

حمایل [hemaayel] *plural of* حمیل
- حمایل کردن to hang on the neck (medal, necklace)

حمایوی [hemaayawi] protective, protectionist ♦ حصولات گمرکی حمایوی protective duties

حمایه [hemaaya] **1** defense protection, guarding **2** support, patronage **3** *military* coverage, cover, support

ح

حمایه کردن • 1 to defend, to protect; to guard 2 to give support; to patronize 3 *military* to cover, to support

حمل [hámel] 1 transference, conveyance, transport, transportation 2 cargo, load, burden 3 pregnancy
- حمل برداشتن • to become pregnant
- حمل شدن • to be conveyed, to be hauled, to be transported
- حمل کردن • to convey, to haul, to transport

حمل [hamal] 1 *astronomy* Aries 2 Hamal (first month of Afghan solar year; corresponds to March-April)

حملات [hamalaat] *plural of* حمله

حمل ونقل [hamlonaqel] 1 transport, transportation ♦ قابل حمل ونقل transportable 2 (also وسایل حمل ونقل) transport; means of transport
- حمل ونقل کردن • to convey, to transport

حمله [hamla] (*plural* حملات [hamalat]) 1 assault; attack; storm ♦ حمله متقابله counterattack ◊ حمله هوایی air attack, air assault 2 attack, fit, bout (of a disease) ♦ حمله قلبی heart attack
- حمله بردن / آوردن / کردن • to assault, to attack

حملهور [hamlawar]
- حمله ور شدن (به،بر) • to assault, to attack, to storm

حمیت [hamiyat] 1 feeling of honor, feeling of self-respect; pride 2 fervor, zeal

حمیت مند [hamiyatmand] *obscure* title of a colonel

حمیل [hameel] (*plural* حمایل [hamayel]) necklace (of gold decorations, coins, etc.)

حنا [hen (n) aa] henna ♦ حنابیارید "Put on the henna!" (the name of a ritual wedding song sung on the eve of the wedding night)
- حنابندان ☞ شب حنا •
- حنا بستن • to paint with henna (the hair, fingernails, etc.)

حنابندان [henaabandaan] festivities; party on the occasion of painting with henna (the hair and fingernails of a bride before the wedding)

حنایی [hen (n) aayi] of the color of henna; reddish-yellow

حنجره [hanjara] 1 voice ♦ او حنجره خوبی دارد She has a good voice. 2 larynx, windpipe

حنفی [hanafi] 1 Hanafi (about a Moslem sect) 2 a Hanafi Moslem, a follower of the Hanafi sect of Islam

حوا [hawwaa] 1 *biblical* Eve 2 *feminine proper name* Hawwa

حوارث [hawaades] *plural of* حادثه

حواس [hawaas (s)] *plural of* حس
- حواس جمع کردن • to concentrate *intransitive*; to collect one's thoughts

حواشی [hawaashi] 1 *plural of* حاشیه 2 *literary* menials, servants; retinue

حوالدار [hawaaldaar] 1 noncommissioned officer, sergeant (of infantry) 2 ☞ حواله دار

حواله [hawala] 1 handing over, delivery (of a package, baggage) 2 transfer of property or of the rights to property 3 *commerce, finance* transfer of payment; money order; bill of exchange
- حواله دادن(کردن) • 1 to hand over, to deliver (a package, baggage, etc.) 2 to transfer, to turn over (property, etc.) 3 to remit, to send, to transfer (money and payments)
- حواله شدن • 1 to be delivered, to be handed over (about a package, baggage, etc.) 2 to be transferred, to be turned over (about property) 3 to be sent, to be transferred (about money, payments)

حواله سرکاری • a share of a peasant's crop (which is to be turned over to the state)

حواله دار [hawaaladaar] *obscure* person authorized to collect arrears from peasants (usually from one of the lower military or police ranks)

حواله نامه [hawaalanaama] bill of exchange

حوالی [hawaali] 1 environs; neighborhood 2 *denominative preposition* (also در حوالی) 2.1 near, near by, close by ♦ در حوالی زمستان near or close to the city ◊ در حوالی شهر not long before winter, on the threshold of winter 2.2 around, in the environs of

حوایج [hawaayej] *plural of* حاجت

حوت [hut] 1 *astronomy* Pisces 2 Hut (twelfth month of the Afghan solar year; corresponds to February-March) ♦ وت اگر حوتی کند موشها را در قطی کند *proverb* If the month of Hut shows itself, then mice will be hiding in the box.

حوری [huri] and حوریه [huriya] houri ♦ حوری جنت maid of paradise; houri

حوزه [hawza] 1 distinct, region 2 *geography geology* basin ♦ حوزه آمودریا basin of the Amu Darya ◊ حوزه بسته *geology* closed basin, inland basin

حوصله [hawsela] 1 patience; self-control; fortitude, determination ♦ حوصله اش سر رفت His patience ended. 2 mood, frame of mind 3 ability (to do something)
- حوصله داشتن • 1 to possess patience, to possess self-control 2 to be disposed [to], to be staunch; to be in condition (to do something) ♦ من حوصله این کار راندارم I am not disposed to do that. / I cannot cope with this matter.
- حوصله کردن • to endure; to control oneself

حوصله دار [hawseladaar] 1 patient; self-possessed, self-restrained 2 ready to undertake (something); capable of carrying a matter through to completion

حوض [hawz] basin; reservoir ♦ حوض شنا swimming pool

حولی [hawli] and حویلی [hawili] enclosed courtyard (with dwellings); house (with an encircling courtyard, farmstead) ♦ میان حولی in the courtyard

حیاء [hayaa] shame; shyness, bashfulness; timidity
- حیاء کردن • to be ashamed; to be shy

حیات [hayaat] life, existence
- (در)حیات بودن • to be alive ♦ آیا پدر شما (در) حیات است؟ Is your father still alive?
- بدرود حیات گفتن • to die

حیاتی [hayaati] vital, burning ♦ مسئله - a vitally important matter

حیادار [hayaadaar] ashamed; bashful, shy, timid

حیث [hays]
- به حیث • as *denominative preposition* ♦ به حیث ترجمان as a translator, as an interpreter
- از حیث • in relation [to], from the point of view [of] ♦ از هر حیث in every respect

حیثیت [haysiyat] 1 prestige, reputation, authority 2 characteristic, quality
- به حیثیت • as, in the role of ♦ به حیث دیپلومات as a diplomat
- حیثیت چیزی را داشتن to acquire the characteristics (of something); to become like (something), to become similar (to something); to play the role of (somebody or something) ♦ از هر حیثیت in every respect

حیران [hayraan] amazed, surprised
- حیران شدن • to be amazed, to be surprised, to be astonished

124

حیرت [hayrat] surprise, amazement
- به حیرت آمدن and به(در)حیرت افتادن (از)ماندن) to be surprised, to be amazed (at somebody, at something
- به حیرت افتادن
- به حیرت آوردن to surprise, to amaze, to astonish

حیرت زده [hayratzada] 1 amazed, astonished 2 amazedly, in an astonished manner

حیض [hayz] menstruation, menses
- حیض داشتن to menstruate

حیف [hayf] 1 regret, repentance 2 What a pity! / Alas! *interjection*

حیله [hila] ruse, trick, subterfuge
- حیله کردن to use cunning, to cheat, to swindle, to machinate

حیله باز [hilabaaz] and حیله ساز [hilasaaz] ☞ حیله گر

حیله گر [hilagar] 1 cunning, crafty 2 cheat, swindler, fraud, trickster, sly person

حیله گری [hilagari] trickery, fraud, deception; guile, craft

حین [hin] time, period
- در حین during *denominative preposition* ♦ در حین باز گشت when returning

حیوان [haywaan] 1 animal; brute, beast ♦ حیوان اهلی domestic animal 2 *rude* rude fellow, boor, cad

حیوان داری [haywaandaari] stock raising; cattle breeding

حیوان رو [haywaanraw] pack trail ♦ راه حیوان رو pack road

حیوان شناس [haywaanshenas] zoologist

حیوان شناسی [haywaanshenaasi] (*also* علم حیوان شناسی) zoology

حیوانی [haywani] 1 animal (relating to livestock) ♦ اعاشه حیوانی forage, fodder ◊ آفات حیوانی diseases of domestic livestock 2 coarse, rude, low, base, brutal, bestial

حیوی [hayawi] *literary* vital, burning

خ
9th letter of the Dari alphabet

خا [kha] ☞ خات

خات [khat] *colloquial* ☞ خواهد
- صبا به کابل خات رفتم Tomorrow I will go to Kabul.
- خات بیایه perhaps, possibly, probably ♦ فاطمه به خانه خات باشه Possibly, he will come. ◊ Fatima should be at home. / Fatima is probably at home.

خاتونک [khatoonak] *colloquial* tiny female

خاتمه [khaatema] end; ending, completion
- خاتمه دادن to end, to finish, to complete
- خاتمه یافتن to end *intransitive*; to be ended, to finish *intransitive*; to be finished, to be completed

خاد [khad] *colloquial* ☞ خواهد

خادم [khaadem] servant, attendant

خادمه [khaadema] maidservant, housemaid, maid, charwoman

خاده [khaada] 1 pole 2 squared beam

خار [khaar] burr, thorn
- در چشم کسی خار شدن to interfere [with], to harm (somebody); to be a thorn in (someone's) flesh

خار پشت [khaarposht] (and) خار پشتک [khaarposhtak] hedgehog

خارج [khaarej] 1.1 external, exterior, situated outside (of something) 1.2 foreign 2 foreign countries
- از خارج from abroad
- خارج شدن 1 to go out (from somewhere); to advance (beyond the bounds of something) 2 to be excluded, to be dismissed; to be transferred
- خارج کردن(ساختن) 1 to take out, to lead out; to carry out (beyond the bounds of something) 2 to exclude; to dismiss

خارج رحمی [khaarejerahami]
- حمل خارج رحمی extrauterine pregnancy

خارجه [khaareja] 1 ☞ خارجی 3 ♦ دول خارجه foreign states ◊ وزارت(امور)خارجه ministry of foreign affairs 2 foreign countries

خارجی [khaareji] 1 external, exterior ♦ سطح خارجی exterior surface 2 strange, alien 3 foreign ♦ سیاست خارجی foreign policy

خارچنگ [khaarchang] crawfish; lobster

خارخانه [khaarkhaana] hut of camel burr, alhagi, and grasses

خاردار [khaardaar] prickly, covered with thorns
- سیم خاردار barbed wire

خارش [khaaresh] 1 scab 2 itch
- خارش دادن to scratch; to scrape
- خارش کردن to scratch oneself, to itch

خارق العاده [khaareqolaada] extraordinary, exceptional, unusual

خارکش [khaarkash] gather and seller of brushwood

خاریدن [khaaridan] to scratch

خاشاک [khaashaak] small chips, kindling; straw; brushwood

خشخاش [khashkhash] ☞ خشخاش

خیاشنه [khashna] ☞ خیاشنه

خاشه [khasha] 1 ☞ خاشاک 2 خس و خاشاک

خاص [khas (s)] 1 special, separate 2 private, own 3 special, exclusive 4 selected
- اسم خاص proper name; noun
- خاص وعام the aristocracy and the common people, the upper strata and the lower strata

خاصتاً [khaassatan] especially

خاصمانه [khaasemaana] hostile, unfriendly ♦ حرکت خامانه hostile act

خاصه [khaassa] 1.1 ☞ خاص 1.2 magnificent, excellent; perfect; choice, select 2 (*plural* خواص [khawaas]) characteristic, peculiarity; distinguishing feature

خاصه دار [khaassadaar] *historical* mercenary solider from Afghan tribes (who protected roads and mountain passes)

خاصیت [khaas (s) iyat] (*plural* خصایص [khasaayes]) 1 peculiarity, characteristic feature, characteristic 2 nature 3 influence, effect (e.g., of medicine)

خاستن [khaastan] (*present tense stem* خیز [khez]) to stand, to rise

خاطر [khaater] به(از) 1.1 memory 1.2 consciousness; emotional state 2 for the sake of, because of *denominative preposition*
- از خاطر بردن to forget
- به خاطر آوردن 1 to remember, to recall 2 to remind
- (به)خاطر داشتن to remember
- خاطرم جمع نبود My soul was uneasy, I was worried / anxious / uneasy.

خاطر خواه [khaatir-khwah] *colloquial* protector, supporter (someone's parents, boss teacher)

خ

خاطرات [khaateraat] *plural of* خاطره
- خاطرات شما از این سفر چیست؟ What are your impressions of the trip?

خاطرپریشان [khaaterpareeshaan] pained; grieved, sad; downcast; having lost [one's] peace of mind

خاطرجمع [khaaterjam'] 1 calm; confident 2 cool; composed
- خاطر جمع باشید Be calm! / Don't worry!

خاطرجمعی [khaaterjam'i] calm *noun*; tranquility; confidence; presence of mind

خاطره [khaatera] 1 recollection 2 impression 3 idea, thought

خاک [khaak] 1 ground, soil, earth ♦ خاک آبدار water-bearing soil ◊ خاک های نرم pool soil 2 country; territory 3 dust, ashes 4 *colloquial* grave
- به خاک سپردن to commit to the earth, to bury
- خاک خوردن *colloquial* to pass away, to die
- خاک و دود شدن to go to rack and ruin; to be cast to the winds
- خاک در چشم کسی انداختن(زدن) to dupe, to pull the wool over someone's eyes

خاک آلود [khakaalud] dusty, covered with dust; soiled, dirty

خاکباد [khaakbaad] dust storm

خاک برداری [khaakbardaari] excavation, excavation of earth ♦ خاک برداری و پرکاری earth-moving operations

خاک بسر [khaakbasar] 1 unfortunate; poor 2 contemptible, pitiful
- خاک بسر شدن 1 to get into trouble, to suffer grief 2 to perish, to die

خاکپای [khaak (e) pay] *colloquial* nothing; nonentity, nobody (*literally*, dust under the feet)
- خاکپای شما *obscure polite* your most insignificant servant

خاک پر [khaakpor] dusty, covered with dust

خاک توده [khaaktuda] pile of earth, pile of soil

خاکروب [khaakrob] sweeper of trash, litter, or debris

خاکروبه [khaakroba] 1 trash can 2 trash, litter

خاکریز [khaakreez] embankment, bank

خاکستر [khaakestar] ashes

خاکستردانی [khaakestardaani] 1 ashtray 2 *technical* ashpit

خاکستری [khaakestari] gray, ash-colored

خاکنا [khaaknaa] *geography* cape, spit

خاکه [khaaka] 1 dust; powder ♦ خاکه ذغال سنگ coal dust 2 draft, outline; rough sketch

خاکی [khaaki] 1 grayish-green, khaki-colored; gray-brown 2 dusty
- تخم خاکی unfertilized chicken egg

خاگینه [khaagina] omelette

خال [khaal] 1 birthmark, mole 2 beauty spot, beauty mark, patch (on the face) 3 speck, speckle, spot
- خال زدن 1 to vaccinate 2 to speckle, to place a spot 3 to make a pinprick (when tattooing)

خال خالی [khaalkhaali] in specks, in spots; spotted, spotty, motley

خالدار [khaaidaar] 1 with a birthmark or mole, with birthmarks or moles 2 in specks; spotted, spotty
- ماهی خالدار trout

خال سنبه [khaalsomba] *technical* punch; center punch

خالص [khaales] 1 pure; genuine, real; natural ♦ پطرول خالص uncontaminated gasoline 2 sincere, candid, frank
- وزن خالص net weight

خالصه [khaalesa] 1 state property 2 virgin lands, long-fallow lands (state lands)

خالصه چی [khaalesachi] *historical* overseer of a shah's personal lands

خالق [khaaleq] 1 creator (epithet of God) 2 *masculine proper name* Khalik

خال کوبی [khaalkubi] tattooing
- خال کوبی چیچک *colloquial* vaccination

خالگذاری [khaalguzaari] *technical* prick; indentation; mark, marking

خاله [khaala] aunt (mother's sister)

خاله بازی [khalabaazi] khalabazi (playing "house," i.e., a popular children's game in which the children play the roles of grown-up members of the family and relatives)

خاله خشو [khaalakhoshu] sister-in-law; aunt of wife (or husband)

خاله زاده [khaalazaada] first cousin (male or female on the mother's side)

خاله خوبرده [khaale-khaw-burdah] *slang* (*literally*: a sleepy ant) lazybones, dullard, dolt, dimwit *derogatory*

خاله کمپیرک [khaala-kampirak] *slang* (*literally*: old lady) granny, old bag, old hag *derogatory*

خالی [khaali] 1 empty; free; vacant, unoccupied ♦ ستل خالی empty bucket ◊ جای خالی unoccupied place or seat 2 unseasoned, unspiced (about food)
- نان خالی (just) bread alone
- خالی کردن to empty, to vacate

خالیگاه [khaaligaah] 1 gap, blank, omission 2 break (e.g., in supply of electricity) 3 *technical* clearance; clear space 4 cavity, emptiness

خام [khaam] 1 raw, unripe, green ♦ مواد خام raw material ◊ خشت خام raw brick, unfired brick 2 clay, adobe, of raw-brick 3 rash, thoughtless, ill-considered, empty ♦ گپ های خام empty words, rash words 4 immature, inexperienced (about a person)
- خام و ختل [khaam-o-khatal] *colloquial* raw, unripe food, uncooked food

خامک [khaamak] 1 ☞ خامک دوزی 2 shoots of a vine

خام کار [khaamkaar] unskilled, unskillful; inexperienced

خام کاری [khaamkaari] lack of ability, lack of skill; lack of experience

خامک دوزی [khaamakdozi] embroidering; sewing with unspun thread

خاموش [khaamaash] 1 quiet, taciturn; silent, speechless 2 having fallen silent, having lapsed into silence, having died away 3 having subsided; dead (about an engine) ♦ خاموش Be silent! / Quiet!
- خاموش شدن 1 to fall silent, to lapse into silence; to die away, to fade away, to calm down *intransitive* 2 to die out; to be extinguished 3 *technical* to be switched off, to be stopped, to stop, to die (about an engine or a unit)
- خاموش کردن 1 to force to be silent; to calm down *transitive*; to placate 2 to put out, to extinguish 3 *technical* to switch off, to stop *transitive*, to throttle down (an engine, a unit)

خاموشک [khaamoshak] *colloquial* to look as if butter would not melt in one's mouth

خاموشی [khaamoshi] silence; quiet, calm, peace
- رو به خاموشی رفتن to fall silent, to lapse into silence; to die away, to fade away, to calm down *intransitive*

خامه [khaama]¹ dirt *adjective* (unpaved) ♦ سرک خامه dirt road

خامه [khaama]² 1 feather, pen 2 *botany* pistil

خامه کاری [khaamakaari] 1 earth-moving work (in building roads) 2 construction (e.g., a building of raw brick and clay) 3 building, erecting (something made of raw brick and clay); adobe construction

خامی [khaami] 1 immaturity, unripeness 2 lack of experience, inexperience 3 imperfection; shortcoming

خان [khan] 1 khan (leader of a tribe or family) 2 landowner, fuedal lord; prince 3 Khan (honorary title affixed to proper names) ♦ احمد خان Ahmad-Khan

خانچه [khaancha] ☞ خوانچه

خانچه پوش [khaanchapush] ☞ خنچه پوش

خاندان [khaanedan] *biology* family

خاندان [khaan (a) daan] 1 family, home, hearth 2 dynasty

خاندانی [khaan (a) daani] 1 family *adjective* 2 dynastic, ancestral

خان زاده [khaanzada] 1 son of a khan 2 noble, of noble birth, origin, or descent

خانقه [khaanaqa (and) xaanqa] monastery (of Sufi, ascetics); home of a dervish

خانگی [khaanagi] 1 home *adjective*, relating to home 2 at home, under home conditions

خانم [khaanom] 1 Mrs.; lady 2 wife

خانواده [khaan (e) waada] family, kin

خانه [khaana] 1 house, home, dwelling ♦ خانه آباد happy, prosperous house ◊ خانه گرگ بی استخوان نیست *proverb* There's no wolf's lair without bones. 2 section (of a cupboard, dresser, or table) 3 cell (of a beehive) 4 column, square 5 (second component of compound words that have the meaning "building" / "premises")
- کتابخانه 1 library 2 bookstore ♦ خانه بندی *colloquial* place of confinement; jail, prison 3 خانه به *colloquial* within the limits [of], of the size [of], of the dimensions [of] ♦ به خانه دو هزار افغانی no more than 2,000 Afghanis
- خانه آباد I wish [you] success! (*literally*, May your home prosper!)
- خانه خدا 1 mosque 2 Mecca, Kaaba

خانه بدوش [khaanabadush] 1.1 tramp, grant, wanderer 1.2 nomad 2 nomadic
- قبایل خانه بدوش nomadic tribes

خانه پر [khaanapori] filling in, entering (into a column, into a blank)
- خانه پری کردن to fill in, to make an entry (in a column, in a blank)

خانه تکانی [khaantakaani] *colloquial* general tidying up of the home (before a holiday, etc.)

خانه جنگی [khaanajangi] internecine war, civil war

خانه خانه [khaanakhaana] consisting of sections (compartments of cupboard, dresser, table, etc.)

خانه خراب [khaanakharaab] *colloquial* completely destroyed; having lost [one's] hearth (about a man whose wife died); The deuce take you! / May you rot in hell! God damn!

خانه دار [khaanadar] 1.1 married; domestic, family *adjective* 1.2 settled (as opposed to کوچی) 2 master of the house, head of the family

خانه داری [khaanadaari] keeping household; housekeeping
- خانه داری کردن to keep house

خانه داماد [khaanadaamaad] son-in-law (living with his wife's relatives)

خانه زاد [khaanazaad] home *adjective*; homegrown, raised at home ♦ اسب خانه زاد a horse raised on one's own farm

خانه سازی [khaanasaazi] home building ♦ فابریکه خانه سازی home-building combine

خانه سامان [khaanasaamaan] a person who manages finances or property; manager (in an establishment); superintendant (of a building)

خانه گشتک [khaana-gashtak] *colloquial* (*literally*: to go to houses) taking turns inviting friends to dinner or lunch

خانه نشین [khaananeshin] 1 sitting at home, not working 2 retired

خاور [khaawar] east; the East ♦ خاور میانه the Middle East

خاوک [khaawok] *colloquial* 1 sleepyhead 2 sleepy, drowsy

خاویار [khaawyaar] (fish) roe, caviar

خائن [khaa;yen] betrayer, traitor

خایه [khaaya] *anatomy* testicle

خاییدن [khaayidan] ☞ جویدن

خباز [khabbaaz] baker

خبازی [khabbaazi] 1 bread baking, occupation of a baker 2 bakery
- خبازی کردن to be occupied in baking bread, to bake bread

خبر [khabar] (*plural* اخبار [akhbaar]) piece of news, news, report; information ♦ خبر تازه news; novelty آخرین خبرها latest news
- خبر داشتن *colloquial* to know, to be conversant [with] ♦ او خبر داردکه... he knows that...
- خبر دادن to inform, to notify
- خبر شدن *colloquial* to find out, to be notified, to obtain news about …
- خبر دادن ☞ خبر کردن
- خبر گرفتن 1 to find out, to obtain information (از) 2 to visit (somebody) (از) (at a time of illness)

خبردار [khabardaar] knowing, conversant; informed
- خبر دار شدن 1 to be informed 2 to find out, to obtain news, to receive news
- خبر دار کردن 1 to inform; to notify 2 to warn
- خبر دار باش Take care! / Careful! / Stand aside!

خبر داری [khabardaari] 1 care, caution 2 knowledge, conversance

خبر رسان [khabarrassaan] 1 informer, informant 2 *military* officer's attendant 3 *rarely* herald, messenger

خبر رسانی [khabarrassaani] information ♦ آژانس خبر رسانی information agency

خبر کش [khabarkash] informer, sneak

خبر گذاری [khabargozaari] 1 information *adjective* ♦ آژانس خبر گذاری باختر Bakhtar News Agency 2 agency (information agency) ♦ خبرگذاری تاس Tass, Telegraph Agency of the Soviet Union

خبرگیرایی [khabargiraayi] *colloquial* obtaining information, making inquiries; finding out
- خبر گیر ایی کردن (از کسی) to ask [about]; to find out (e.g., about someone's health)

خبر نشان [khabarneshaan] *technical* sensor, sensing device; data unit

خبل [khabl] *literary* (one of the permissible ways of changing the foot of a meter, basically replacing two long syllables with two short ones)

خبن [khabn] *literary* (one of the permissible ways of truncating the foot of a meter: replacing a long syllable with a short one)

خبیثه [khabisa]
• ارواح خبیثه evil spirits, evil spirit

خپ [khap] 1 quiet, silent 2 covert, secret ♦ خپ خپ *colloquial* secretly surreptitiously, on the shy, noiselessly, silently
• خپ شدن to fall silent, to lapse into silence; to die away, to fade away
• خپ گرفتن to lurk, to hide, to conceal oneself

خپک [khapak] *colloquial* reticent, secretive, shy ♦ زیر خپک بوریا still waters, quiet pool

خت [khet] *colloquial* 1 sludge, slime, dirt 2 turbid, dirty ♦ آب خت turbid water
• آب راخت کردن ماهی گرفتن *proverb* to fish in troubled waters

ختک [khatak] 1 Khattaki (tribe) 2 a Khatak

ختم [khatm] end, termination; completion; conclusion
• ختم شدن to end *intransitive*, to be completed
• ختم کردن to end, to terminate; to complete; to conclude

خجالت [khajaalat] shame, embarrassment
• خجالت دادن to shame, to embarrass
• خجالت کشیدن to be ashamed, to feel shy, to be embarrassed

خجسته [khojasta (and) xojasta] happy, fortunate; blessed

خجور [khajur] (type of pastry or biscuit fried in butter or oil)

خدا [khoda] god, deity ♦ خدا تعالی the most high God
• خدا کردن (گفتن) to pray to God, to call on God
• خدابیامرزد May he live in paradise! / May God forgive him!
• خدا را شکر Praise be to God! / Thank God!; God forbid! / God preserve!
• به خدا I swear to God! / Really and truly!
• ترابه خدا (and) از برای خدا for God's sake / for the sake of God
• به امان خدا good-bye

خدا داد [khudaa-daad] *colloquial* (literally: God-given) out of the sky, lucked out (plenty of something obtained for free)

خدازده [khudaa-zada] curse (*literally:* God damned) an unfortunate and God-damned (person)

خدازدگی [khudaa-zadagee] *idiom* God damned (someone who harms him/herself) to be one's own worst enemy ♦ اگر خدازدگی خودش نمی بود باین روز دچار نمی شد If he was not his own worst enemy, he would not be in this bad situation.

خداشر مانده [khodaasharmaanda] *abusive* scoundrel; blasphemer; God-shamed) God damned (person)

خداناترس [khodaanaatars] 1 cruel, merciless, ruthless 2 a non-Moslem; monster (of cruelty)

خداوند [khodaawand] ☞ خدا

خدای [khodaay] ☞ خدا

خدایا [khodaayaa] *interjection* Oh, God! / Oh, Lord!

خدایی [khodaayi] 1 Godly, sent by God 2 charity, alms (in the name of God)

خدمات [khadamaat] *plural of* خدمت
• خدمات عامه social services

خدمت [khedmat] (*plural* خدمات [khadamaat]) 1 service ♦ خدمت دولتی civilian service (not military) ◊ خدمت ملکی state service ◊ خدمت عسکری military service 2 waiting; attendance, service ♦ نفر خدمت servant, servants, service personnel
• خدمت کردن 1 to work, to be at work 2 to serve (somebody به)
• به خدمت شما 1 at your service 2 for you

خدمتچی [khedmatchi] ☞ نفر خدمت *military*

خدمتگار [khedmatgaar] 1 servant, attendant ♦ خدمتگار وطن servant of the fatherland 2 *epistolary* yours faithfully

خدمتگاری [khedmatgaari] 1 ☞ خدمت گذاری 2 readiness for services, obligingness

خدمتگذاری [khedmatgozaari] work, service

خدمتی [khedmati] official ♦ خدمتی رفتن to go on a trip; TDY (temporary duty); on official business

خدمه [khadama] *plural of* خادم

خر [khar] 1 donkey, ass ♦ خرماده female donkey, female ass 2 *abusive* ass, fool, blockhead
• از خر جیل پایان شدن [az-khare-jayl-paayaan-shudan] *idiom* (*literally:* to come down of a mad donkey) to come down off of one's high horse, to give up on a false argument, to calm down

خر [khar] *slang* (*literally:* donkey) jackass, dumbass, stupid

خر [khor] (☞ خرخر) 1 bad ♦ هوای خراب bad weather 2 destroyed, broken 3 spoiled, unfit
• خراب شدن 1 to spoil *intransitive*, to become unfit 2 to be destroyed, to break; to be broken

خرابات [kharaabaat] 1 *plural of* خرابه 2 *poetical* wine shop, public house, pub

خراباتی [kharaabaati] *poetical* 1 habitué of wine shops, of pubs 2 (*also* رند خراباتی) reveler

خرابکار [kharaabkaar] 1 violator; wrecker; saboteur 2 *colloquial* libertine, dissolute person

خرابکاری [kharaabkaari] 1 destruction; ruin, devastation 2 sabotage; blasting or demolition work; subversive activity, diversion

خرابه [kharaaba] (*plural* خرابات [kharaabat]) 1 ruins 2 a neglected, deserted place

خرابی [kharaabi] unfitness, bad condition, spoiling; damage, defect
• خرابی هوا 1 foul weather 2 ruin, devastation
• خرابی وضع اقتصادی 1 difficult economic position 2 depravity, corruptness

خراته [kharaata] 1 overalls 2 (women's) slip (apparel)

خراد [kharraad] turner, lathe operator

خرادی [kharraadi] 1 turning; lathe *adjective* ♦ ماشین خرادی lathe ◊ ماشین خرادی چوب wood lathe 2 lathe work
• خرادی کردن 1 to work on a lathe, to operate a lathe, to be occupied with lathe work 2 to sharpen, to grind, to turn on a lathe

خراش [kharaash] 1 *present tense stem* خراشیدن 2.1 scratch, abrasion; irritation of the skin 2.2 planing, shaving; scraping

خراشیدن [kharaashidan] 1 to scratch *transitive* and *intransitive*, to itch 2 to plane, to shave; to scrape; to scratch

خرافات [khoraafaat] superstition, prejudice; fanaticism

خرافاتی [khoraafaati] superstitious; prejudiced ♦ شخص خرافاتی superstitious person; fanatic

خربوزه [kharbuza] melon

خرج [kharj] 1 expenditure, expense, expenses ♦ خرج سفر 2 consumption (e.g., of energy) 3 *military* allowance
- خرج شدن to be expended, to be spent
- خرج کردن to expend, to spend; to consume
- به خرج دادن گوش to show diligence, to endeavor, to try

خرجی [kharji] *colloquial* 1 grub, provisions (for the road) 2 pocket money

خرچ [kharch] ☞ خرج

خرخر [khorkhor] 1 snore; snoring 2 wheeze 3 purring (of a cat)
- خرخر زدن 1 to snore 2 to wheeze

خرد [kherad] mind, intellect, intelligence, reason; wisdom

خرد [khord] ☞ خورد²

خرد جال [kharedajjaal] ☞ دجال in entry خرد جال

خردجال¹ [khardajall] *slang* (*literally*: impostor, antichrist) radio, TV

خردجال² [khardajall] *slang* unorganized, slob, messy (person) *derogatory*

خردسال [khordsaal] 1 small, young 2 infant, child

خردوانی [khar-dawaani] *slang* (*literally*: racing donkey) hurry and haste; haste makes waste

خرده [khorda] ☞ خورده

خرده فروش [khurda-froosh] *colloquial* building material wholesaler

خرده گیر [khurda-geer] *colloquial* (*literally*: to take small things) nitpicker, fault finder

خرده بورژوازی [khordaburzwazi] petty bourgeoisie

خرده فروش [khordaforos] ☞ خورده فروش

خرس [khers] bear

خرسک [khersak] *colloquial* creepers, crawlers (children's clothing)

خرسند [khorsand] 1 satisfied, happy, content 2 glad, joyful, merry, jolly

خرسندی [khorsandi] 1 satisfaction, contentment 2 gladness, joy; rejoicing; triumph

خرسنگ [kharsang] boulder, large rock (usually in a river)

خرسنگ دار [kharsangdaar] rocky ♦ اراضی خرسنگ دار rocky terrain

خرطوم [khortum] 1 trunk, proboscis 2 hose

خرقه [kherqa] rags, tatters; hair shirt (of an ascetic, of a dervish)
- خرقه مبارکه sanctuary (where the clothing of the prophet Mohammed is located)

خرقه پوش [kherqaposh] 1.1 dressed in rags or tatters 1.2 dressed in torn clothing 2.1 a dervish, a wandering monk 2.2 an ascetic, a Sufi

خرک [kharak] *colloquial* support; trestle

خرکار [kharkaar] 1 a drayman who hauls goods on a donkey 2 a hired hand appointed to look after donkeys

خرکاری [kharkaari] 1 hauling goods on a donkey 2 *colloquial* heavy work, hard work
- خرکاری کردن 1 to be engaged in hauling goods on a donkey 2 *colloquial* to work like a convict, to do hard work

خرگاه [khergaah] 1 nomad's tent; felt tent (in which Uzbeks and Turkmen people live in Afghanistan) 2 *rarely* (large) tent, marquee

خرگری [khargari] *colloquial* utter stupidity, utter foolishness, stupidity, obtuse obstinacy

خرگوش [khargosh] 1 hare 2 rabbit

خرم [khorram] 1.1 fresh, pleasing, gladdening to the eye 1.2 joyful, glad, merry, jolly, content 2 *masculine proper name* Horram

خرما [khormaa] 1 date (fruit) 2 (also درخت خرما) date palm

خرمایی [khormaayi] 1 date *adjective* 2 light brown, chestnut-colored

خر مجم [khare-majam] *colloquial* (*literally*: absolutely donkey) ass, dumbass

خرمستی [kharmasti] drunken revelry, a brawl, a drinking spree, carousing

خرمگس [kharmagas] horsefly; gadfly

خرمن [kherman] heap of grain; grain gathered at the threshing floor

خرمن گاه [khermangaah] threshing floor

خرمن گل [kharmane-gul] *slang* (*literally*: a heap of flowers) a beautiful female

خرمهره [kharmohra] 1 large, coarse beads or shells (suspended from the neck of animals) 2 cheap item; coarsely-made item of low value

خرمی [khorrami] 1 joy, mirth, gaiety 2 freshness; brightness, brilliance (of a garden, of greenery, of flowers, etc.)

خروار [kharwaar] kharwar (unit of weight equal to 10 mana); ☞ من

مشت نمونه خروار [musht-namoonae-kharwaar] *idiom* (*literally*: one full hand is the sample of a ton) what you see is what you get, representative sample

خروج [khoruj] 1 going out; exit; departure 2 banishment, exile 3 appearance (e.g., of a messiah)

خروس [khorus] cock, rooster

خروسک [khorusak] *military* cotter pin, linchpin; flag; cocking piece

خروسک [khorosak] *medicine* croup

خروشان [khorushaan] stormy; impetuous ♦ دریای خروشان a swift rivulet

خره و شره [khara-o-shara] *colloquial* plenty of things, abundance of things ♦ از همه چیز خره و شره افتاده بود There were plenty of everything.

خرید [kharid] purchase, buying, purchasing ♦ او برای خرید رفت He went to make some purchases.
- خرید کردن 1 to buy, to purchase, to acquire 2 *colloquial* to make purchases for a wedding

خریدار [kharidaar] buyer, purchaser
- این جنس خریدار ندارد There is no demand for these goods.

خریداری [kharidaari] a purchase, a buy
- خریداری کردن to make purchases, to buy, to acquire

خریدن [kharidan] to buy; to purchase; to buy up, to corner

خریدوفروش [kharidoforosh] huckstering; trade, bargaining

خریده خور [kharidakhor] living on purchased products (about people who don't have land, about inhabitants of towns and cities)

خریطه [kharita] 1 map; chart 2 ☞ خلطه

خز [khaz(z)] fur

خ

خزان [khazaan] 1.1 autumn 1.2 fading; withering; old age 2.1 faded, withered 2.2 wasted away, aged
- خزان دین 1 to fade, to yellow, to wither (about leaves)
- خزان شدن 1 to fade, to wither, to grow dark or dim 2 to age

خزانه [khazaana] 1 treasury, finances 2 storehouse 3 (also خزانه تفنگ) breech of a gun

خزانه چی [khazaanachi] (and) خزانه دار [khazaanadaar] treasurer

خزانی [khazaani] autumn adjective, autumnal

خزند [khazand] 1.1 protuberance, projection on the wall of a house under a window 1.2 window sill 2 placed one on top of the other (about stones, bricks, firewood, etc.)
- خزند کردن 1 to place one on top of another (about bricks, stones, firewood) 2 to lay (bricks, etc.)

خزنده [khazanda] 1.1 reptile 1.2 insect 2 reptile adjective; crawling, creeping ♦ حیوانات خزنده reptiles

خزه [khaza] ambush; hunting blind

خزیدن [khazidan] to creep, to crawl

خزینه [khazina] ☞ خزانه

خس [khas] 1 brushwood, windfallen trees and branches 2 dry grass, hay 3 dry blade of grass, a straw

خسارات [khasaaraat] plural of خساره

خساره [khasaara] (and) خسارت [khasaarat] (plural خسارات [khasarat]) loss; losses; harm, hurt, damage
- خساره دیدن 1 to suffer damage, to suffer losses 2 to suffer, to receive injury
- خساره رساندن to inflict damage, to harm, to hurt
- خساره پوره کردن to compensate for a loss

خساره مند [khasaaramand] having suffered a loss, having suffered harm

خس پوش [khasposh] 1 hunting wolf hole; trap, pit; snare 2 done in an off-hand manner, haphazardly; not durable, fragile ♦ خانه خس پوش shanty, hovel

خسپیدن [khospidan] to lie, to lie down; to rest; to sleep

خستگی [khastagi] 1 tiredness, weariness, fatigue 2 lethargy; indisposition

خسته [khasta] 1 tired, weary, fatigued 2 physically exhausted, ill

خسته [khesta] colloquial pit, stone (of fruit)

خسته کن [khastakon] 1 weakening, physically exhausting, fatiguing ♦ کار خسته کن exhausting work, hard work 2 tedious

خس دزد [khasdozd] colloquial petty thief, pilferer

خسر [khosor] 1 father-in-law (wife's father) 2 father-in-law (husband's father)

خسران [khosran] 1 wife's relatives 2 husband's relatives

خسربره [khosorbora] wife's brother, brother-in-law

خسرخیل [khosorkheel] older relatives on wife's side; father-in-law's relatives

خسرونی [khosruni] regional matchmaking

خسک [khasak] 1 bug; bedbug 2 ☞ خسکی

خسکی [khasaki] uncultivated (about a tree) ♦ درخت خسکی an uncultivated tree, wild tree, tree growing in the wild

خس و خاشاک [khasokhaashaak] 1 litter, rubbish, trash 2 colloquial riffraff, any unneeded items or things

خسیس [khasis] 1 stingy, greedy 2 mean, base, low

خشت [khesht]¹ 1 brick ♦ خشت خام calcined brick ◊ خشت پخته adobe ◊ خشت کاشی سفیده ceramic (floor) tile ◊ خشت کاشی glazed tile 2 (large) nut (of a bolt) 3 bolt (of a weapon)

خشت [khesht]² cards diamonds

خشتک [kheshtak] inset (in inseam of pants)

خشت کاری [kheshtkaari] 1 bricklaying 2 conducting or performing bricklaying
- خشت کاری کردن 1 to put up (a wall, a building), to build, to brick 2 to perform bricklaying, to lay bricks

خشتمال [kheshtmaal] molder of bricks

خشتمالی [kheshtmaali] molding of bricks

خشتی [kheshti] 1 brick adjective, made of adobe 2 having the shape of a brick; square, quadrangular ♦ قند خشتی lump sugar

خشخاش [khashkhaash] 1 botany opium poppy 2 poppyseed

خش خش [kheshkhesh] rustle; rustling
- خش خش کردن to make a rustle; to rustle

خشره [khashra] colloquial (literally: rotten) bottom of the barrel

خشک [khoshk] 1 dry, dead, withered, dried-up ♦ درخت خشک withered tree ◊ میوه خشک dried fruits
- نان خشک 1 dry bread 1.2 bread alone, plain bread 2 arid; waterless ♦ تابستان خشک an arid summer 3 dry, stale; not interested in anything (about a person) 4 (also خشک وخالی) empty; insipid, dull
- خشک شدن 1 to dry, to get dry, to grow dry; to dry up, to wither 2 to grow stale (literally and figuratively) 3 to cease giving milk (about a cow) 4 to become insensible, to lose feeling, to become paralyzed (about an arm, leg, etc.)
- خشک کردن 1 to try transitive 2 to drain
- به (بر) جای خشک شدن to freeze on the spot, to become rigid (from surprise, amazement, etc.)

خشک ابی [khoshkaabi] drought

خشکاوه [khoshkaawa] dry valley, waterless valley

خشک آوی [khoshkaawi] colloquial ☞ خشک آبی

خشک آی [khoshkaay] dried fruits

خشک پای [khoshkpaay] bringing misfortune or bad luck (about a person)

خشک دماغ [khoshkdomaagh] crazy

خشک سالی [khoshksaali] drought, arid year

خشک قدم [khushk-qadam] colloquial (literally: dry footstep) jinx (person)

خشکه [khoshka] 1 land; dry land
- ممالک محاط به خشکه 1 states; countries that do not have outlets to the sea 2 dry, dried ♦ توت خشکه dried mulberry

خشکه شویی [khoshkashoyi] dry cleaning

خشکی [khoshki]¹ 1 dryness, aridity 2 drought

خشکی [khoshki]² colloquial mad, crazy, insane; abnormal

خشکی [khoshki]³ colloquial lichen; herpes
- خشکی زدن to become weather-beaten; to coarsen; to become rough

خشم [khá;sem] anger, wrath, fury, rage; malice; irritation
- خشم کردن 1 to be angry (at somebody بر, به) 2 colloquial to torment, to terrorize
- به خشم امدن to become angry, to go into a rage

خشم آگین [khashmaagin] (and) خشم الود [khasmelud] angry, incensed, cross ♦ اواز خشم آگین angry voice, cross voice

خ

خشمگین [khashmgin] angered, angry, in a rage (about somebody)
• خشمگین شدن to be angry, to be cross, to go into a rage
خشن [khashen (and) xashan] coarse, rude (about a person, an act)
خشنود [khoshnud] 1 content, satisfied 2 glad, joyful
خشنودی [khoshnudi] 1 contentment, satisfaction 2 gladness, joy
خشو [khoshu] 1 mother-in-law (wife's mother) 2 mother-in-law (husband's mother)
• زبان خشو colloquial cactus
خشونت [khoshunat] coarseness, roughness; sharpness; abruptness; rudeness
خصایص [khasaayes] (and) خصائص plural of خاصیت
خصلت [khaslat] disposition, character, nature (of a person)
خصمانه [khasmaana] 1 hostile, unfriendly 2 in a hostile manner, in an unfriendly manner
خصوص [khosus] 1 از این خصوص in this regard, in regard to this or that 2 در خصوص relative to, in regard to denominative preposition
• خصوص که ... the moreso that…
خصوصاً [khosúsan] 1 especially, in particular 2 privately, unofficially
خصوصی [khosusi] special ♦ قطعات خصوصی military special troops, special forces
خصوصیت [khosusiyat] 1 detail 2 peculiarity; characteristic, typical feature; specific noun; distinctiveness
خضر [khézr] 1 Khizr (prophet who, according to Moslem tradition, drank from the source of the water of life) 2 the prophet Elijah ♦ آب خضر the water of life
خط [khat (t)] (plural خطوط [khotut]) 1 letter (epistle); writing, script 2 handwriting 3 line ♦ خط استوا equator ◊ خط مستقیم straight line ◊ خط منحنی curve, curved line ◊ خط منکسر broken line 4 way, track, path, route 5 colloquial down (above the lip's)
• خط طعه colloquial little letter
• خط ریل (and) خط أهن rarely railroad journey
• خط آوردن colloquial to be covered with down
• خط زدن to strike out, to cross out
• خط کشیدن to draw a line; to line, to rule
• خط زدن ☞ خط گرفتن
• خط نوشتن to write a letter
• زیر چیزی خط کشیدن to underline something
خطا [khataa] mistake, error; inadvertance; miss, slip, blunder, oversight
• خطا دادن 1 to drop (something) inadvertently 2 to shoot (an arrow)
• خطا خوردن 1 to fall out of, to break away from (something) inadvertently 2 to become unraveled (about stitches) 3 to weaken, to break (about a string)
• خطا کردن 1 to err, to make a mistake, to commit a blunder; to be mistaken 2 to act poorly, badly, or incorrectly
خطاب [khetaab] address (speech)
• خطاب بر آنها گفت addressing him, he said
• خطاب کردن to make an address (speech), to make an appeal
خطابه [khetaaba] speech, sermon ♦ میز خطابه platform, rostrum

خطاط [khat (t) aat] calligraphist
خطاطی [khat (t) aati] calligraphy
خطاکار [khataakaar] 1 mistaken, committing an error 2 sinful, having committed an offence 3 sinner
خطاکاری [khataakaari] 1 mistake, error; miss, slip, blunder 2 offence, fault; sin
خط السیر [khat (t) ossayr] ☞ خط سیر in entry خط
خط آهن [khat (t) eaahan] rarely railroad
خطبر [khatbar] 1 messenger, courier 2 pointer for reading a book (so as not to confuse the lines)
خطبه [khotba] religion khotba (holiday sermon with a mention of the ruling sovereign)
خط بینی [khatebini] colloquial vow, pledge, promise
• خط بینی کشیدن to renounce, to make a promise
خطخطی [khatkhati] colloquial striped ♦ بالاتنه خطخطی woman's striped jacket
خطر [khatar] (plural اخطار [akhtaar]) danger; threat; risk; alarm ♦ خطر مرگ mortal danger ◊ زنگ خطر danger signal, alarm signal; alarm system ◊ زنگ خطر حریق fire signal, fire alarm; fire alarm system
• خطر داشتن to be dangerous
• به (در) خطر انداختن to be subject to danger, to be subject to risk
خط رجه [khat (t) eraja] marking line, marking
• سیر خط رجه technical adjustment; alignment, sighting
خطرناک [khatarnaak] dangerous, risky ♦ وضع خطرناک dangerous situation, critical position
خط سبز [khat (t) esabz] just barely emerging mustache or beard
خط کش [khat (t)kaas] ruler ♦ خط کش لوگاریتمی slide rule ◊ خط کش مقیاس scale; measuring rule
خط کشی [khat (t) kaasi] lining, ruling
• خطکشی کردن to line, to rule, to make parallel lines
خط مشی [khat (t) emashy] political line, policy, course
خطمی [khatmi] (also گل خطمی) mallow, hollyhock
خط وبروت [khat (t) oborut]
• سر خط وبروت آمدن colloquial to reach maturity
خط وخال [khat (t) oxaal] beauty (e.g., of the face)
خطور [khotur]
• به خاطر کسی خطور کردن to come to mind, to cross [one's] mind
• به خاطرم خطور کرد it occured to me, an idea came to my mind
خطوط [khotut] 1 plural of خط 2, 3, 4, 5
• خطوط مواصلاتی communications (transportation)
• خطوط زیرزمینی ایجینیری underground engineering services
خفا [khefaa] literary secret ♦ در خفا secretly, in secret
خفتن [khoftan] (present tense stem خواب [khaab]) ☞ خوابیدن
خفک [khafak] colloquial asthma
• خفک شدن to pant, to gasp, to experience an attack of asthma
خفگی [khafagi] grief; chagrin; disorder
خفه [khafa] 1 disturbed, upset, grieved 2 angry, resentful (of somebody) 3 experiencing an attack of asthma
• خفه شدن 1 to be disturbed, to be upset, to be grieved 2 to be angry, to be resentful (of somebody) 3 to gasp, to pant 4 to fall silent, to lapse into silence; to fade away, to die away
• خفه کردن 1 to upset, to grieve 2 to anger, to annoy, to

irritate 3 to choke, to strangle, to suffocate; to press, to squeeze 4 to force to keep silent

خفه کن [khafakon] *technical* ☞ سلنسر

خفیف [khafif] 1 light ♦ سلاح خفیف light armament ♦ تانک خفیف light tank 2 weak, feeble ♦ صدای خفیف weak voice, weak sound ♦ حرکت خفیف easy movement, slight movement 3 soft (about a sound)

خلا [khalaa] 1 emptiness, void 2 *physics* airless space, vacuum 3 *anatomy* cavity

خلاص [khalaas] 1 finished, completed 2 having run short; ended 3 free; unemployed (with work, with business) 4 freed; saved; delivered

• خلاص شدن 1 to be finished, to finish *intransitive*, to be completed 2 to run short, to be coming to an end 3 to be fired, to be released (from work, from business) ♦ ماز کار خلاص شدیم We were released from work. / We were let go from work. 4 ☞ خلاصی یافتن

• خلاص کردن 1 to finish, to complete 2 to release, to discharge (from work) 3 ☞ خلاصی دادن 4 in entry *colloquial* to dismantle, to disassemble (a unit, a part)

• خلاص *colloquial* Done! / Finished! / The deed is done! / Enough!

خلاص گیر [khalaasgir] one who separates people who are fighting

خلاصه [kholaasa] 1.1 resume, review, brief content ♦ خلاصه اطلاعات information summary ♦ خلاصه اوضاع جوی weather summary 1.2 essence, main point, quintessence ♦ خلاصه امر the essence of a matter 2 in general, in brief

• خلاصه کردن 1.1 to sum up the results; to generalize, to summarize 1.2 to reduce; to abbreviate; to make short, brief, or concise

خلاصی [khalaasi] deliverance, freedom

• خلاصی دادن to save; to deliver, to free, to save (somebody را, به)

• خلاصی یافتن to be delivered, to be freed, to be saved

خلاف [khelaaf] contradicting

• خلاف قانون 1 contradicting the law 2 illegal 3 خلاف contrary to ♦ خلاف انتضار contrary to expectations

• خلاف کردن to violate (rules, etc.)

خلافت [khelaafat] 1 *historical* caliphate 2 title of a caliph 3 *obscure* vicegerency

• خلافت کردن to rule as a caliph

خلاف رفتاری [khelaafraftaari] violation, breach, infringement

♦ خلاف رفتاری کردن an action against the rules, against the law; to commit offenses

خلاق [khallaaq] creator, founder; originator

خلاقه [khallaaqa] creative ♦ قدرت خلاقه creative powers

خلاقیت [khallaaqiyat] creativity ♦ خلاقیت هنری artistic creativity

خلال [khelaal]¹ *literary* span; intermission; break, interval 2 در خلال at the time [of], during, in the course [of] *denominative preposition* ♦ در خلال این مدت during this time

خلال [khelaal]²

• خلال کردن 1 to tousle; to stroke; to comb a beard with one's fingers 2 to cut or slice into small pieces (e.g., vegetables)

خلاندن [khalaandan] 1 to prick, to sting 2 to stick [into]; to stab; to pierce

خلته [khalta] ☞ خلطه

خلش [khalesh] stitch (e.g., pain in the side) ♦ خلش قلب stabbing pain in the heart

خلط [khalt] 1 mixture, admixture 2 mixing; combination; combining

• خلط شدن to be mixed; to be joined; to be combined

• خلط کردن to be mix; to join; to combine

خلط [khelt] *medicine* phlegm

خلطه [khalta] sack, bag

خلطه موی [khaltamóy] hairnet

خلع [khal' (and) xal'a] *literary* 1 moving away; moving off 2 abolition; revocation ♦ خلع سلاح disarmament

خلعت [khal'at] *historical* granted robe (robe granted as a mask of distinction)

خلف [khalaf] (*plural* اخلاف [akhlaf]) 1 descendant, offspring; son 2 successor, follower; deputy, assistant

خلفاء [kholafaa] *plural of* خلیفه 5

خلق [khalq]¹ 1 *collective* people, the people 2 people *plural*; inhabitants

خلق [khalq]² creation

خلق [kholq] (*plural* اخلاق [akhlaaq]) disposition; character; nature

خلقت [khelqat] *literary* 1 creation 2 world; people 3 disposition, nature (of a person)

خلقی [khalqi] people's, national

خلل [khalal] 1 damage, loss; harm, injury 2 interference, impediment

• خلل رساندن (and) خلل دادن 1 to inflict damage, to cause harm 2 to meddle, to interfere, to impede

خلل ناپذیر [khalalnaapazir] steadfast; unshakable, inviolable

خلم [khalem] snivel *noun*

خلموک [khelmok] *colloquial* snotty

خلوت [khalwat] 1.1 *literary* solitude, seclusion 1.2 secluded place 1.3 *obscure* privy council, secret conference 2 desert, uninhabited, secluded ♦ کوچه خموت deserted street

• خلوت شدن to become empty, to become deserted, to become uninhabited, to become sparsely inhabited, to become uncrowded

• خلوت کردن 1 to go into seclusion, to retire (for discussions) 2 to clear [out] (e.g., a room of outsiders)

خلوت خانه [khalwatkhaana] secluded place, cozy spot; secret place, secret spot

خلوت نشین [khalwatneshin] 1.1 secluded 1.2 loving seclusion 2 recluse, hermit

خله [khala] 1 stitch (e.g., in the side); colic 2 *colloquial* harp-pointed stick (for prodding pack animals)

• خله کردن to feel a stitch (e.g., in the side), to feel a stabbing pain

خلیته [khalita] ☞ خریطه

خلیج [khalij] gulf ♦ خلیج فارسی Persian Gulf

خلیفه [khalifa] 1 master, craftsman 2 khalifa (polite form of address for craftsmen, masters, chauffeurs, etc.) 3 khalifa (class monitor in a village school) 4 spiritual leader of Sufis (in contemporary rural area) 5 (*plural* خلفاء [kholafa]) *historical* caliph, deputy (of a prophet, of an imam) 6 *obscure* pakhlavan (who had disciples)

خلیل [khalil] 1 *religion* true friend (epithet of Abraham) 2 Khalils (name of a tribe) 3 *masculine proper name* Khalil

خلیلی [khalili] 1 Khalili (variety of fast-ripening grape) 2 Khalils (tribe)

خم [kham] 1.1 bent, curved, crooked 1.2 stooped; hunched, crooked 2 bend, curve, curvature
• خم شدن *intransitive* to bend, to bow, to stoop 2 to sag, to be bowed, to be bent; to be distorted
• خم کردن *transitive* 1 to bend, to bow, to tilt 2 to fold, to distort, to curve
خم [khom] large earthenware jug (for keeping water, wine, oil, etc.)
خمار [khomaar] 1 drunkenness, intoxication, hangover 2 intoxication (from love)
خمارآلود [khomaaraalud] (and) خمارآلوده [khmaraluda] intoxicating ♦ چشم خمارآلود drunken eyes, intoxicated eyes
خمبه [khamba] large wicker basket (for storing grain); grain bin, granary
خمچه [khemcha] 1 delicate sprout, shoot, a blade of grass 2 a blade of grass (about a frail person)
خمره [khomra] earthenware vessel for milk (used only as a milk pail)
خمس [khoms] a fifth part, one-fifth
خمسه [khamsa] 1 khamse, quintet (five poems combined into one whole, e.g., by Nizami, Navoi) 2 the five senses (sight, hearing, smell, touch, taste)
خم و چم [kham-o-cham] *colloquial* (*literally:* to bow down) to bow down before someone to toady
خمندک [khamendok] (and) خمندوک [khamendok] *zoology* tick
خمیازه [khamyaaza] 1 stretching 2 yawning
• خمیازه کشیدن 1 to stretch oneself 2 to yawn
خمیدن [khamidan] ☞ خم شدن in entry خم [kham]
خمیده [khamida] 1 *past participle* خمیدن 2.1 bent, folded, curved, crooked 2.2 hunched, round-shouldered, stooping
خمیر [khamir] 1 dough 2 nature (of man)
خمیر تراش [khamirtaraas] *colloquial* metal scraper (for cleaning dough from the sides of a kneading trough)
خمیرترش [khamirtorsh] ☞ خمیرمایه
خمیر ترش [khameer-turah] *slang* (*literally:* starter dough) a mean and unhappy person *derogatory*
خمیرگر [khamirgar] kneader of dough
خمیرمایه [khamirmaaya] yeast, leaven
خنشا [khonshaa] ☞ خنشی
خنشی [khonsaa] 1.1 fruitless, useless 1.2 *chemistry* neutral 2 hermaphrodite
• خنشی شدن 1 to turn out to be unsuccessful or futile; to come to naught; to be paralyzed 2 *chemistry* to be neutralized
• خنشی کردن 1 to make unsuccessful, to reduce to naught 2 to stifle, to suppress (a riot, etc.) 3 *chemistry* to neutralize
خنجر [khanjar] dagger
خنجک [khenjak] *botany* pistachio tree
خنچه [khoncha] *colloquial* ☞ خوانچه
خنچه پوش [khonchaposh] *colloquial* ☞ خوانچه پوش
خندان [khandaan] 1 laughing, smiling 2 while laughing, while smiling; while grinning
خنداندن [khandaandan] to make laugh, to amuse, to force to laugh, to entertain
خندق [khandaq] 1 ditch, gutter with sewage 2 ditch, trench ♦ خندق ضد تانک antitank ditch
خنده [khanda] laugh, smile, grin ♦ به خنده (با) while laughing, with a laugh, while chuckling

• خنده کردن to laugh, to laugh aloud; to chuckle, to grin, to smile
خنده آور [khandaaawar] funny, comical; ridiculous, laughable
خندیدن [khandidan] to laugh, to laugh aloud; to smile; to chuckle
خنصر [khensar] the little finger
خنظل [khanzal] *botany* colocynth
خنک [khonok (and) xonak] 1 cold; cool; fresh; chilly 2 cold *noun*, hard frost, cool *noun*
• خنک خوردن to freeze, to be frozen; to catch cold, to catch a chill
• خنک زدن 1 to nip with frost (a crop, trees) 2 to freeze *transitive*; to freeze together
• خنک کردن *transitive* to cool, to chill
• خنک گرفتن to freeze *intransitive*; to feel cold, to shiver, to suffer from cold ♦ گوشم را خنک برده است My ear is frostbitten.
خنک خور [khonokkhor] frozen turf
خنک زدگی [khonokzadagi] cold (i.e., a head cold)
خنک زده [khonokzada] 1 frozen, frozen together ♦ نهال خنک رده a sprout nipped by frost 2 frozen, chilled, having caught a cold or a chill
خنکی [khonoki] cold *noun*, chill
خو [khaw] *colloquial* ☞ خواب
خو [kho] *colloquial* 1 ☞ خوب 2, 3 2 you see / you know / is it not? / after all (*particle adding emphasis*)
• تو خو رفتی You'd better have gone!
• خوب خو هستی؟ Everything is all right with you, isn't it?
خواب [khaab] 1 *present tense stem* خوابیدن *and* خفتن 2.1 sleep ♦ خواب سمور sound and prolonged sleep ◊ اطاق خواب bedroom 2.2 dream ♦ خواب پریشان bad dream
• این کتاب خواب آوردن to lull to sleep, to evoke sleep ♦ این کتاب خوابم میاورد This book lulls me to sleep
• (در)خواب بودن to sleep
• خواب دادن 1 to lull to sleep, to put to sleep 2 to bring down, to put down (in wrestling match)
• خواب دیدن 1 to have a dream 2 to dream
• به خواب رفتن (and) خواب رفتن to lie down to sleep, to go to sleep
• از خواب پریدن to jump up half awake
• در خواب دیدن to see in a dream
• اورا خواب برد He fell asleep. / He was overcome by sleep.
• پایش را خواب برد His foot / leg fell asleep.
• او را خواب برد ☞ خوابش برد
• خوابش پرید His dream vanished.
• خوابش میبرد He is nodding off. / He is dozing off.
• خوابم نمیاید I can't sleep.
• خواب سنگین داشتن to be untroubled, to be carefree
خواب آلود [khaabaalud] sleeping, sleepy ♦ چشم خواب آلود sleepy eyes
خواباندن [khaabaandan] 1 to lull to sleep, to make (somebody) sleep 2 to make (somebody) lie down, to lay down, to put [to bed]; to throw down
خواب آور [khaabaawar] lulling to sleep, evoking sleep ♦ سکوت خواب آور a lulling quiet
خواب بردگی [khaabbordagi] numbing (of the extremities)
خواب پر [khaabpor] sleepy, sleeping

خوابگاه [khabgoh] place or room for sleeping
• خوابگاه کارتوس *military* [cartridge] chamber
خواب نامه [khaabnaama] *obscure* dream book, interpreter of dreams
خوابوخور [khaabokhor]
• خواب و خور او همانجا است He sleeps and eats there. / He lives there.
خوابیدن [khaabidan] (*present tense stem* خواب [khab]) 1 to sleep; to fall asleep 2 *colloquial* to lie; to lie down 3 to be knocked off one's feet, to be thrown to the ground (in wrestling, in a fight)
خواجه [khaaja] 1 master, owner; haja (rich merchant or landowner) 2 eunuch
خوار [khwaar]¹ 1 poor, indigent 2 weak, feeble, infirm 3 unfortunate, humble
• خوار کردن to offend; to treat badly; to humble
خوار [khwaar]² *colloquial* ☞ خواهر
خوارو زار [khwaarozar] poor, pitiful, contemptible
خواری [khwaari] 1 need, poverty 2 heavy toil, suffering 3 misfortune, a bitter lot
خواری کش [khwaarikash] *colloquial* toiler, a person who lives by the sweat of his brow
خوازه [khawaaza] construction scaffolding
خوازه کار [khawaazakaar] worker who erects scaffolding
خواست [khaast] 1 will, desire 2 request, petition
• بنا به خواست شما 1 at your wish, in accordance with your desire 2 in accordance with your request 3 *colloquial* request for alms
خواستگار [khaastgaar] wooing (somebody), claimant for (somebody's) hand
• او خواستگار دختر وزیر است He is wooing the minister's daughter.
خواستگاری [khaastgaari] matchmaking; courting; proposal of marriage
• به خواستگاری رفتن to go courting
• خواستگاری کردن (را) to court, to woo (somebody)
خواستن [khaastan] (*present tense stem* خواه [khaah]) 1 to want, to desire, to wish 2 to request, to demand 3 to summon, to invite
خواسته [khaasta]
• بنا به خواسته های ملت according to the people's will
خواص [khawaas] 1 *plural of* خاصه (and) خاصیت ♦ خواص فزیکی physical properties 2 aristocracy, nobility
خوانچه [khaancha] wooden tray (for serving food)
خوانچه پوش [khaanchaposh] embroidered table napkin (for covering a tray)
خواندن [khaandan] 1 to read 2 *colloquial* to teach, to learn 3 to sing
• آواز خواندن to sing a song
• درس خواندن to study, to learn ♦ برادرم در پوهنتون کابل درس میخواند My brother is studying at Kabul University.
خواندنی [khaandani] deserving of attention, interesting (about a book, magazine, etc.) ♦ کتاب خواندنی an interesting book ◊ خواندنیها cognitive literature
خوانندگی [khaanendagi]
• خوانندگی و نویسندگی literacy; ability to read and write
خواننده [khaanenda] 1.1 reader; reciter 1.2 singer 2.1 reading 2.2 singing ♦ مرغان خواننده singing birds, songbirds 3 knowing how to read, literate ♦ شخص خواننده و دانسته a

literate, educated person ♦ بابای پیرش خواننده ونویسنده بود His old grandfather knew how to read and write.
• خواننده کردن to teach reading and writing
خواه [khaah] 1 *present tense stem* خواستن 2.1 (second component of compound words with meanings of "wishing, desiring" / "asking, requesting" / "supporter, advocate") ♦ خیرخواه well-wisher 2.2 benevolent, well-wishing 3 خواه...خواه either... or...; whether... or... *conjunction* ♦ خواه بد خواه خوب whether bad or good
خواهان [khaahaan] 1 to want, to desire, to wish [for]; to long (for somebody or something) ♦ موفقیت شمارا خواهانیم We wish you success. 2 to ask (somebody) (از); to demand
خواهد [khaahad] 1 *aoristic form of third person singular of verb* خواستن 2 (invariable component of analytic forms of the future tense and dubitative mood) ♦ خواهد رفتم (possibly) will go
خواهر [khaahar] sister
خواهر اندر [khaaharaandar] stepsister
خواهر خوانده [khaaharkhaanda] adopted sister
خواهرزاده [khaaharzaada] nephew; niece (on sister's side)
خواهش [khaahesh] desire, wish; request ♦ بر طبق خواهش خود at one's own wish, according to one's own desire
• بمانید خواهش میشود همه بر جای خود Everyone stay in his seat / at his place, please.
• خواهش داشتن to have a request
• خواهش دارم بیایید I ask you to come. / Please come.
• خواهش کردن (از) to ask (somebody)
خواهشمند [khaaheshmand]
• خواهشمند بودن to desire, to wish; to ask, to request
خواه مخواه [khaahmakhaah] willy-nilly; against one's will
خوب [khub] 1.1 good, kind ♦ آدم خوب good person 1.2 fine, high-quality, of good quality ♦ تکه خوب fine material 1.3 appropriate, suitable, proper ♦ این دریشی برای کار خوب است This clothing is appropriate for work. 1.4 handsome, beautiful ♦ صورت خوب handsome or beautiful face 2.1 well ♦ خوب است که آمدی It's good that you came. 2.2 very, magnificently ♦ خوب گرسنه است He grew very hungry. 2.3 very well, all right ♦ خوب بروید Very well, go.
خوبان [khubaan] *literary poetry* beauties
خوبروی [khubroy] 1 handsome, beautiful 2 handsome man
خوبی [khubi] 1.1 beauty 1.2 advantage, superiority 1.3 something pleasant 1.4 blessing, boon 2 به خوبی ☞ بخوبی
• برویت خوبی بیاید Good luck! / May you be lucky! (friendly parting words)
خوجه یین [khojayin] 1 well-to-do person, bourgeois 2 owner; boss; master
خود [khod] 1.1 myself, himself, oneself, herself, itself, themselves ♦ من خودم I, myself 1.2 one's own, my own, his own, her own, its own, their own ♦ کتاب خودش رآورد He brought his own book. 2 باخود to oneself ♦ افسوس که گفتم باخود I said to myself: pity!
3 (first component of compound words with meaning "self-") ♦ خود ساخت homemade (self-made) ◊ خودبینی self-love, egoism
• از خود رفتن to lose consciousness, to faint
• به خود آمدن to come to oneself, to regain consciousness
• به خود آوردن to bring to [one's] senses, to make [one] conscious
• به خود خوردن to be ashamed

- به خود گرفتن (and) به خود کش کردن to take (something) as referring to oneself, to admit, to acknowledge
- به خود نرسیدن not to have the opportunity to take care of oneself (because of being very busy)

بخود گرفتن [ba-khud-gereftan] *colloquial* (*literally:* to take to oneself) to take things personaly
- از خود one's own; own, native; relation, relative

خوداختیار [khodekhtiyaar] independent; free (about a person)
خودآموز [khodaamoz] self-instructor
خود بخود [khodbákhod] 1 spontaneously, by itself 2 spontaneous ♦ انفلاق خود بخود spontaneous explosion
خودبین [khodbin] 1 egoist, self-lover 2 egoistic, proud, presumptuous
خودبینی [khodbini] egoism, self-love; presumptuousness
خودپرست [khodparast] ☞ خودبین
خودپرستی [khodparasti] ☞ خوربینی
خودپسند [khodpesand] self-satisfied
خودپسندی [khodpesandi] self-satisfaction, self-admiration
خودداری [khoddaari] 1 self-control, self-restraint 2 abstention; evasion; shunning
- خودداری کردن 1 to control oneself, to manifest self-restraint or self-control 2 to abstain (از)

خودرفتار [khodraftaar] self-propelled
خودرنگ [khodrang] fountain pen
خودروی [khodroy] wild, growing wild (about plants) ♦ بته خودروی wild bushes
خودساخت [khodsaakht] homemade, handmade
خودساز [khodsaaz] ☞ خودنما
خودستای [khodsetaay] 1 occupied with self praise 2 boaster, braggart
خودستایی [khodsetaayi] self-praise, boasting
خودسر [khodsar] willful, self-willed, obstinate
خودسری [khodsari] 1 self-will, willfulness 2 arbitrariness
خودفروش [khodforosh] 1 haughty, vain; conceited 2 boaster, braggart
خودکار [khodkaar] 1 automatic 2 (*also* قلم خودکار) ball-point pen
خودگی [khodgi]
- ازخودگی نکردن *colloquial* not to consider as one's own; to avoid, to shun

خودمختار [khodmakhtaar] independent; self-governing; autonomous
خودنما [khodnamaa] vain; showing off; posing, fancying oneself [as]
خودنمایی [khodnamaayi] vanity, showing oneself off, self-admiration
- خودنمایی کردن to show off, to pose

خودنویس [khodnawis] registering, (self) recording
- دستگاه خودنمویس automatic recording apparatus

خودی [khodi]¹ individuality, peculiarity
خودی [khodi]²
- به خودی خود 1 by himself 2 by itself; unintentional; spontaneous

خور [khor] 1 *present tense stem* خوردن 2 (second component of compound words with mean of "eating" / "devouring" / "drinking") ♦ آدم خور cannibal, man-eater ◊ رشوت خور bribe-taker

خوراک [khoraak] 1 food, nourishment 2 portion, helping, serving (of food) ♦ دو خور اک کباب two helpings of shashlik
- مواد خوراکه food products, foodstuffs

خوراکه باب [khoraakabaab] foodstuffs; provisions, victuals; food
خوراندن [khoraandan] 1 to feed; to give drink [to], to water [livestock] 2 to make eat, to make drink
خورجین [khorjin] khorjin, saddlebag
خورد [khord]¹ khord (measure of weight equal to a quarter of a pound or 110 grams)
خورد [khord]² small, little; insignificant ♦ بچه خورد a little child
- خورد کردن(ساختن) 1 to diminish; to decrease; to reduce; to make small; to pulverize, to crumble; to chop 2 to smash, to shatter 3 *rarely* to change (money)

خورد [khord]³
- به خورد کسی دادن to feed somebody, to feed (something) to somebody

خوردترک [khordtarak] *colloquial* 1 young; younger ♦ برادر خوردترک younger brother 2 undersized, short, very short
خوردضابط [khordzaabet] *obscure* noncommissioned officer, sergeant
خوردن [khordan] 1 to eat 2 to drink 3 to dash against, to strike against (به) ♦ پایم به سنگ خورد I struck my foot against a rock. 4.1 to hit the target, to destroy the target (about a bullet, about a shell) 4.2 (component of compound verbal combinations) ♦ to suffer defeat
- قابل خوردن 1 eatable, edible 2 suitable for drinking, potable
- شکست خوردن to mourn, to grieve
- غصه خوردن to be sad

خوردنی [khordani] 1 edible, suitable for food and drinking 2 food
- خوردنیها foodstuffs, provisions

خوردوبرد [khordobord] *colloquial* misuse; misappropriation
خوردوبزرگ [khordobozorg] old and young ♦ خاندانی the entire household; goods and chattel
خورده [khorda]
- خورده گرفتن 1to find fault, to cavil 2 to object (to بر)

خورده بین [khordabin] petty, small-minded; fault-finding; nagging; pedantic, punctilious
خورده بینی [khordabini] pettiness, small-mindedness; cautiousness; pedantry, punctiliousness
خورده فروش [khordaforosh] 1 merchant, dealer in small goods, retail merchant 2 hawker; shopkeeper
خورده فروشی [khordaforoshi] 1 trade in small goods, retail trade 2 occupation of a hawker, of a shopkeeper
خورده گیری [khordagiri] ☞ خورده بینی
خورده مالک [khordamaalek] *rarely* petty landowner
خورشید [khorshid] *literary* 1 sun 2 *feminine proper name* Khorshid
خوش [khosh] 1.1 pleasant, good ♦ بوی خوش pleasant scent 1.2 joyful, happy; good ♦ خبر خوش good news 2 well, excellently 3 (first component of compound words with meanings "good" / "pleasant"/ "joyful") ♦ خوش اخلاق of good disposition ◊ خوشحال joyful, happy, content
- خوش بودن to be content, to be joyful ♦ از دیدن شما بسیار خوش بودیم We were happy to see you.
- خوش داشتن to love ♦ اوگلهارا خوش دارد She loves flowers.

خ از) خوش شدن to rejoice (in somebody, in something)
• خوش کردن to prefer; to choose ♦ از این فلم خوشم آمد I liked that film.
• خوش آمدید Welcome! / You are always welcome!
• خوش باشید Good luck and joy! (response of a guest to a host's greeting)
خوشا [khoshaa]
• خوش بحالش How lucky he is! / How good for him!
خوش اخلاق [khoshakhlaaq] 1 of good disposition 2 virtuous; moral
خوش الحان [khoshelhaan] singing sweetly, singing well (about birds) ♦ مرغان خوش الحان songbirds, birds that sing well
خوش آمد [khoshaamad] 1 flattery, a compliment 2 toadyism, fawning
• خوش آمد زدن(گفتن) 1 to flatter; to give compliments 2 to fawn [upon]; to curry favor [with]; to please; to oblige
خوش آمدگر [khoshaamadgar] (and) خوش آمدگوی [khoshaamadgoy] flatterer, toady
خوش اندام [khoshandaam] slender, well built, of fine physique; graceful
خوش آهنگ [khoshaahang] 1 sweet, mellifluous; melodious; melodic, tuneful 2 harmonious
خوش آیند [khoshaayand] 1 pleasant, nice ♦ بوی خوش آیند pleasant scent 2 suitable, right, proper, favorable ♦ هوای خوش آیند favorable weather
خوش باور [khoshbaawar] gullible; simple-minded; open-hearted
خوشبخت [khoshbakht] happy; fortunate; lucky; successful
• خوشبخت کردن to make happy
خوشبختانه [khoshbakhtaana] fortunately, luckily
خوشبختی [khoshbakhti] (good) luck, well-being; prosperity, success
خوش بیان [khoshbayaan] sweet-talking; eloquent
خوشبین [khoshbin] 1 optimist 2 regarding (something) well, thinking well (of something), looking (at something) with approval ♦ آنها به کار ما خوشبین نیستند They do not approve of our work.
خوشتر [khoshtar]
• خوشتر داشتن to prefer, to choose; to select, to show preference
خوش ترکیب [khoshtarkib] 1 comely, handsome, nice-looking 2 well built
خوش جلو [khoshjelaw] (opposite of شخ جلو) quiet; gentle (about a horse, etc.); easily led (in harness)
خوشحال [khoshhaal] joyful; merry; content; satisfied
خوشحالی [khoshhaali] joy, gaiety; pleasure; amusement
خوش خبری [khoshkhabari] good news, joyful news
• خوشخبری دادن (and) خوشخبری آوردن to report good news, to report joyful news
خوش خلق [khoshkholq] ☞ خوش خوی
خوش خوان [khoshkhaan] possessing a pleasant voice, singing well (about a person, a bird)
خوش خور [khoshkhor] 1 pleasing to the taste 2 of good quality (about food, about medicine)
خوش خوی [khoshkhoy] merry, jolly; affable, friendly; of good disposition
خوشدار [khoshdaar] colloquial loving, sympathizing ♦ خوشدار این شخص است He sympathizes with this man.

خوش روی [khoshroy] 1 affable, friendly, cordial 2 ☞ خوش سیما
خوش زبانی [khush-zabaani] colloquial (literally: sweet talk) buttering up to talk derogatory
خوش سیما [khoshsimaa] handsome, beautiful, attractive
خوش صحبت [khoshsohbat] pleasant, agreeable, sociable ♦ مرد خوش صحبت good company, pleasant company
خوش طبع [khoshtab'] 1 cheerful, merry, witty, humorous 2 talented, gifted ♦ شاعر خوش طبع talented poet, gifted poet
خوش قدم [khoshqadam] bringing good luck, bearing good luck
خوش گذران [khoshgozaraan] enjoying one's life
خوش گذرانی [khoshgozaraani] 1 prosperous life, prosperity 2 merry pastime
• جای خوش گذرانی a place of pleasure, a place of entertainment
خوش مزه [khoshmaza] 1 tasty, pleasing to the taste 2 interesting; piquant; amusing
خوشنما [khoshnomaa] beautiful to the eye; picturesque ♦ باغ خوشنما picturesque garden ◊ شهر خوشنما beautiful city
خوشنودی [khoshnudi] pleasure
• این تکلیف نیست خوشنودی است polite It's not trouble, but a pleasure.
خوشنویس [khoshnawis] 1 having good handwriting 2 a calligraphist
خوشنویسی [khoshnawisi] calligraphy
خوش وقت [khoshwaqt] ☞ خوش بخت
خوشه [khusha] 1 ear ♦ خوشه گندم ear of wheat 2 cluster, bunch ♦ خوشه انگور bunch of grapes
• خوشه چیدن 1 to glean ears of wheat (after reaping) 2 to glean grapes (after the harvest)
• خوشه کردن to ear, to form ears
خوشه چین [khushachin] 1 person who gleans ears of wheat (after reaping) 2 gleaning crumbs, living on crumbs (about poor people) ♦ خوشه چینان عرفان those who toil in the cornfield of enlightenment
خوشی [khoshi] contentment; satisfaction; gladness, joy
• خوشی کردن to be content, to be satisfied, to be glad, to be happy, to rejoice
• اظهار خوشی کردن to express satisfaction
خوف [khawf] fear, fright, dread
خوفناک [khawfnaak] terrible, frightful, dreadful, horrible, dangerous
خوک [khok] pig, swine, hog, boar, wild boar
خوگیانی [khogyani] Khogiani (tribe)
خول [khul] cartridge case; tube; case; socket ♦ خول کارتوس cartridge case of a bullet ◊ خول مرمی case of a shell
خو مرغی [khawe-moorghi] slang (literally: chicken sleep) to nod off, napping while sitting up
خون [khun] blood
• فشار خون 1 blood pressure 2 colloquial hypertension, hypertonia, high blood pressure
• خون خوردن to feel keenly, to get in a bad mood, to get upset (e.g., because of envy); to feel unhappy; to torment oneself (because of spite, envy)
• خون گرفتن 1 medicine to bleed, to phlebotomize 2 to avenge, to pay for blood with blood
• خون جگر خوردن 1 to feel keenly; to grieve, to mourn; to eat one's heart out 2 not to spare oneself (for the sake of

achieving something)
- خون گریه کردن *colloquial* to cry bloody tears, to grieve strongly, to mourn strongly
- خون را به خون شستن to spill blood for blood, to avenge evil with evil
- خون از چشمش پرید Everything went dark before him. / Everything went dark before his eyes. (from a powerful shock, etc.)

خوناب [khunaab] *poetry* bloody tears

خون آلود [khunaalud] 1 blood-stained; stained in blood 2 bloodshot (about eyes)

خون بار [khunbaar] bloody; bleeding ♦ اشک خون بار bloody tears

خون بها [khunbahaa] 1 achieved through bloodshed ♦ آزادی خون بها freedom won by bloodshed 2 a fine for murder, a ransom paid to avoid a blood feud, a payment for blood

خون پر [khunpor] bloodstained

خونخوار [khunkhaar] 1 bloodthirsty, cruel, brutal, savage, fierce, ferocious 2 bloodsucker, parasite; extortioner

خون خواری [khunkhaari] bloodthirstiness, cruelty, ferocity

خونخور [khunkhor] ☞ خون خوار

خوندار [khundaar] 1.1 having committed murder, having spilled somebody's blood 1.2 expecting retribution in blood 2 the object of a blood fued

خونریزی [khunreezi] 1 bloodshed; (mass) murder 2 hemorrhage ♦ خونریزی مغز brain hemorrhage 3 bleeding, hemorrhage
- خونریزی کردن to shed blood, to commit bloodshed, to commit murder

خونسرد [khunsard] cool, composed; calm

خونسردی [khunsardi] coolness, composure; calmness, calm

خونگرم [khungarm] fervent, passionate, ardent

خونگرمی [khungarmi] fervor, passion, ardor

خونی [khuni] 1 bloody (about a battle, etc.) 2 a killer, a murderer

خونین [khunin] ☞ خونی 1

خوی [khoy] disposition, character

خویش [khesh] 1 ☞ خود 2 relation, relative

خویشاوند [kheeshaawand] relation, relative ♦ آنها خویشاوند ندان یکدیگراند They are relatives.

خویشاوندی [kheeshaawandi] ☞ خویشی

خویش خوری [kheeshkhori] *colloquial* a party among the relatives of the bride and groom (a day before the wedding)

خویشی [kheeshi] relationship, kinship
- خویشی داشتن to be related

خیابان [khiyaabaan] 1 walk, path (in a garden) 2 Khiaban (name of a highway through the city of Herat)

خیار [khiyaar] ☞ بادرنگ

خیاشنه [khyaashna] sister-in-law (wife's sister)

خیاط [khayaat] tailor; cutter

خیاطه [khayaata] 1 *medicine* catgut 2 thread for a sewing machine

خیاطی [khayaati] tailoring
- خیاطی کردن to engage in tailoring

خیال [khiyaal] thought; assumption, supposition; notion ♦ به خیال in my opinion
- خیال کردن 1 to think, to consider, to suppose 2 to imagine; to assume; to surmise

- خیال چیزی را داشتن to intend (to do something), to make up one's mind (to do something) ♦ احمد خیال رفتن دارد Ahmad intends to leave.
- خیال پلو *colloquial* ☞ خیال پلو

خیال پرست [khiyaalparast] visionary, dreamer

خیال پرستی [khiyaalparasti] inclination toward fantasy, toward fantasizing

خیال پلو [khiyaalpalaw] *colloquial* wild illusions, delirious illusions, ravings
- خیال پلو زدن to nourish wild illusions, to dream in vain, to hope in vain

خیالی [khiyaali] 1 made-up, concocted; fabricated; imaginary 2 fantastic ♦ دنیای خیالی world of fancy, world of dreams 3 *colloquial* imagining much about oneself

خیام [khayyaam] *obscure literary* 1 master tentmaker 2 Omar Khayam (pseudonym of a poet)

خیانت [khiyaanat] treachery; betrayal; treason; faithlessness, perfidy
- خیانت کردن (به) to betray
- به وطن خیانت کردن to betray one's native land

خیر [khayr] good; blessing, boon; good deed
- خیر خواستن to beg for alms
- خیر مقدم گفتن to greet (somebody) on [his] arrival, to say "welcome"
- خیر 1 All right! / Okay! / Things will settle down! 2 Well, it had better be all right! (threat)
- خیر ببینید 1 The best to you! / May you be happy! 2 Well done! / That's right! (exclamation of approval, encouragement or praise)
- خیر سرت Would you be so kind! (when making a request)
- خیر نبینید *abusive* May no good come to you!
- کار خیر marriage, wedding

خیر [khir] *colloquial* obstinate, stubborn, willful, disobedient

خیرات [khayraat] 1 deeds pleasing to God; charity 2 alms (usually dispensed at a funeral)
- خیرات کردن 1 to perform deeds pleasing to God; to engage in charity or philanthropy 2 to dispense alms (usually at a funeral)
- خیرات شدن 1 to be brought for sacrifice (about a sheep, ox, etc.) 2 to be dispensed in the form of alms (usually at a funeral)

خیرات خانه [khayraatkhaana] *obscure* asylum, almshouse

خیراتی [khayraati] intended for distribution in the form of alms ♦ نان خیراتی bread being distributed as alms

خیراتی [khairatee] *colloquial* (*literally:* charity) free, getting something because of someone else's hard work

خیراندیشی [khayraandishi] benevolence, friendliness

خیرچشم [khirchashm (and) xircesem] 1.1 tiresome, disobedient (about a child) 1.2 stubborn, obstinate; impudent, insolent, impertinent 2 scamp, mischievous child

خیر خواه [khayrkhaah] 1.1 benevolent, kindly; well-disposed 2 friendly, amicable 2 well-wisher

خیره [khira] 1 dim, dull ♦ آیینه خیره dull mirror ◊ عینک خیره dark glasses, protective glasses (against the sun) 2 gloomy, dark, poorly illuminated 3 dark (about a color)
- رنگ خیره 1 dark color 2 dark paint or dye
- چشم من خیره شده است My eyes began to see poorly.

137

خیره خیره [khira-xira] **1** fixedly, intently ♦ خیره به او نگریست [He / I] looked intently at him. **2** thoughtfully, pensively

خیره سر [khirasar] **1** capricious; wild; extravagent; whimsical **2** a madcap

خیره کننده [khirakonenda] blinding, dazzling

خیریت [khayriyat] **1** good; blessing, boon **2** well-being
● خیریت (است)؟ Well now, is everything in order? / Is everything all right? (question during a salutation)
● خیر خیریت است Everything is perfectly fine.

خیریه [khayriya] charitable, philanthropic ♦ مؤسسات خیریه charitable institutions

خیز [kheez] **1** *present tense stem* خیستن **2** jumping, leaping; a jump, leap **3** (second component of compound words with meaning of "abounding in something") ♦ ثمر خیز fertile, fecund, fruit-bearing
● خیز زدن to jump, to leap; to make a jump, to make leap; to skip
● خیز کردن to dash, to rush; to throw oneself into

خیزاندن [kheezaandan] **1** to make jump, leap, or skip **2** to make stand, to make get up

خیزک [kheezak] *colloquial* skip, jump, leap
● خیزک زدن to skip, to jump up, to jump (e.g., from joy)

خیستن [kheestan] (*present tense stem* خیز [khez]) **1** to jump up, to get up, to stand up **2** takeoff (e.g., of an aircraft)

خیشاوه [kheeshaawa] weeding
● خیشاوه کردن to weed

خیک [khik] (and) خیگ [khig] **1** wineskin (for making brynza, a sheep's milk cheese) **2** large sack (wineskin for crossing a river)

خیل [kheel] **1.1** kin; family; tribe **1.2** khel (subdivision of a tribe), clan; family; (becomes part of tribal names) ♦ سلیمان خیل Sulemankheli **1.3** flock (of birds) ♦ خیل کبوتر flock of doves **2** (second component of compound words with meanings of "family" / "kin" / "relatives" ♦ دامادخیل bridegroom's relatives

خیل خیل [kheel-xeel] *colloquial* in large groups, in detachments; in crowds; in flocks

خیل و ختک [khayl-o-khatak] *slang* kinfolk, relatives *derogatory*

خیله [kheela] *colloquial* ridiculous; funny; foolish, stupid

خیله خند [kheelakhand] *colloquial* object or subject of mockery; common laughingstock
● از دست تو خیله خند شدم to be made a laughingstock ♦ از دست تو خیله خند شدم Because of you I became a laughingstock / an object of ridicule.

خیمه [khayma] tent; marquee

خینه [khina] *colloquial from* خنا
● خینه ماندن *colloquial* to smear with henna (e.g., the hair)
● خینه در پای ماندن *colloquial* to sit at home, not to show oneself on the street (like a bride who has applied henna to her feet or legs)

د
10th letter of the Dari alphabet

داخل [daakhel] **1** located in…, inside (of something) ♦ اشخاص داخل اطاق the people located in the room
● داخل (در) به inside; in, into *denominative preposition*
● داخل (در) په **1** in the premises, in a room **2** into the premises, into a room
● داخل شدن **1** to enter; to drive into (ezafeh, در) **2** to be included; to contain *intransitive*, to be a member, to be a part (of something)
● داخل کردن **1** to introduce, to bring [into], to put [into] (ezafeh, در) **2** to include; to enter; to make an entry (in a log, diary, etc.)

داخل رحمی [daakhelerahami] intrauterine ♦ حیات داخل رحمی intrauterine development (of a fetus)

داخله [daakhela] **1** ☞ داخل **2** ☞ داخل
● داکتر داخله physician-therapist, doctor-therapist
● سرویس داخله therapeutic ward (in a polyclinic)

داخلی [daakheli] **1** internal, interior, inner ♦ تجارت داخلی internal trade, domestic trade **2** *opposite of* خارجی native inhabitant of a country

داد [daad]¹ **1** cry, shout for help **2** justice, equity, fairness
● داد (وای) ای **1** Help! **2** Woe is me!
● داد وبیداد ☞ داد وبیداد
● به داد کسی رسیدن to come to somebody's assistance, to intercede for someone, to stand up for someone

داد [daad]² *literary* **1** gift, present **2** favor; grace, mercy ♦ داد خدا God's mercy
● داد کردن **1** to grant, to give a present, to make a present **2** to do a favor

دادا [daadaa] *colloquial* **1** sister dear (form of address to an older sister) **2** Dad, Papa

دادخواه [daadkhaah] petitioner; plaintiff

دادخواهی [daadkhaahi] **1** prosecuting, suing, lodging a complaint **2** demanding justice

دادرس [daadras] defender, protector, intercessor, patron

دادرسی [daadrasi] rendering assistance, intercession; justice

دادگر [daadgar] **1** judge **2** ☞ دادرس

دادگری [daadgari] **1** administering justice **2** post of judge

دادن [daadan] (*present tense stem* د [deh]) **1** to give, to give up, to give back **2** (component of compound verbs and verb combinations) ♦ نشاندادن to show
● تشکیل دادن to form, to organize, to create

دادوبیداد [daadobeedaad] cry; shout; weeping, crying; scene, scandal
● دادوبیداد کردن to shout out, to cry out; to cry, to weep; to make a scene, to cause a row

دادوگرفت [daadogereft] barter, exchange; trade

داده [daada] **1** tutor (a servant who rears or educates a child) **2** *regional* dad, papa

دار [daar]¹ **1** *present tense stem* داشتن **2** (second component of compound words with meanings "possessing (something)" / "protecting (something)" / "guarding (something)") ♦ اولاددار having children, having a family ◊ خزانه دار keeper of the treasury, treasurer ◊ زره دار reserved

دار [daar]² **1** gallows **2** pillar; pole **3** a structure of poles and a stretched rope (for a rope-walker)
● به دار کشیدن to hang (on a gallows)

دار [daar]³ *literary* **1** house, place, abode **2** edge, bound, limit

دارا [daaraa] rich, propertied, well-off, wealthy ♦ شخص دارا rich person, wealthy person
● دارا چیزی بودن to have; to possess (something)

دارالامان [daarolamaan] **1** *literary* place of peace and quiet **2** Darolaman (region of Kabul)

دارالانشاء [daarolenshaa] secretariat (e.g., of the UN)

دارالحکومه گی [daarolhokumagi] *obscure* provincial government

دارالسلطنه [daarossaltana] residence of a monarch; king's palace, emir's palace

دارالعلوم [daarololum] academy ◆ دارالعلوم عربی ecclesiastical academy (in Kabul)

دارالفناء [daarolfanaa] *religion* earthly life, transitory world, temporal world

دارالفنون [daarolfonun] 1 institute, higher education institution 2 academy (special) 3 Darolfonun (region of Kabul)

دارالمجانین [daarolmajaanin] lunatic asylum

دارالمعلمین [daarolmo'allemin] pedagogical school

دارالوکاله [daarolwekaala] legal advice office, legal consultation office

دارایی [daaraayi] *finance* 1 property, belongings 2 fortune, riches, wealth 3 assets

دارباز [daarbaaz] 1 rope-walker; acrobat 2 *colloquial* juggler, conjurer; trickster, cheat

دارچینی [daarchini] ☞ دالچینی

دار دار [daardaar] *colloquial* bustle, turmoil, commotion, rumpus

دارداری [daardaaree] *colloquial* loud mouth, obnoxious (person)

دارکش [daarkash] executioner, hangman

دارو [daaru] medicine; drug

داروغه [daarugha] *obscure* 1 chief of a district 2 official in the countryside (watching over the withholding of part of the crop for the use of the emir's officials)

دارومدار [daaromadaar] *colloquial* tie, bond, contact, (social) intercourse
● دارومدار داشتن to maintain relations, to associate with

داره [daara] armed gang, band

داریوش [daariush] *historical* Darius (ruler of the Achaemenid dynasty)

داس [daas] sickle
● داس ودرو *colloquial* peasant's toil
● داس بقلخ تیز کردن to do something unwillingly (*literally*, to sharpen a sickle with a lump of earth)

داستان [daastaan] 1 narration, narrative, story, tale 2 dastan, poem; narrative, tale, story 3 tradition, legend
● استان زندگی history of life

داستان پردازی [daastaanpardaazi] 1 writing of stories or tales, writing of narratives 2 *ironic* profuse talk, loquacity, verbosity

داستان سرای [daastaansaraay] *literary* 1 elocutionist, reciter, singer of dastans (poems) 2 storyteller, narrator (of folk tales)

داسکله [daaskala] pruning knife (shaped like a sickle)

داش [daash] 1 oven for brick, brick kiln ◆ داش آب داری crucible furnace ◊ داش کلالی kiln 2 stove, range, oven ◆ داش برقی electric stove

داشت [daasht] durability (e.g., of clothing)

داشتن [daashtan] (*present tense stem* دار [daar]) 1 to have, to possess ◆ پدر ومادر ندارد He doesn't have a father or mother. 2 to hold *intransitive*, to keep 3 to hold [on], to hold (by something) 4 *component of compound verbs and verb combinations* ◆ نگهداشتن to keep
◊ اظهار داشتن to declare, to express (an opinion, etc.)

داشتی [daashti] *colloquial* strong, durable

داشی [daashi] 1 baked in an oven (about bread) 2 person who kindles the fire in ovens (in a bakery)

داعی [daa'i] *literary* 1 praying (for somebody) 2 a missionary; a preacher

داغ [daagh] 1.1 spot, patch; blot; track; footprint; scar 1.2 bald spot (on the head) 1.3 stamp, brand 1.4 cauterization (of a wound); a prick with a hot needle (form of treatment) 1.5 (*also* داغ دل (and) داغ جگر) pain, grief of the soul 2 hot
● داغ زدن to stamp, to brand
● داغ کردن to make hot, to make burning hot; to bring to a great heat
● داغ شاندن to cauterize (a wound); to prick with a hot needle (treatment)
● دل کسی را داغ کردن to pain; to grieve; to anger somebody

داغدار [daaqghaar] 1 soiled with spots or stains 2 branded 3 deformed; discredited, disgraced

داغدیده [daaghdida] mourning (for the deceased) ◆ مادر داغدیده a mother mourning over [her] child

داغسر [daaghsar] 1 with a bald spot, balding 2 field sparrow

داغلی [daagholi] *colloquial* scoundrel, rogue, rascal

داغمه [daaghma] 1 worn out, old ◆ لباس داغمه shabby or threadbare clothing 2 utility waste, usable scrap ◆ سامان داغمه scrap or scrap material

داغی [daaghi] 1 branded 2 suspected (or) accused (of something bad)

دافع [daafe'] (first component of fixed phrase ezafeh combinations with meanings of: "repulsing" / "preventing")
◆ دافع تانک antitank

دافع تانک [daafe'etaank] antitank ◆ توپ دافع تانک antitank gun

دافع هوا [daafe'ehawaa] antiaircraft ◆ توپ دافع هوا antiaircraft gun

داک [daak] mail, post

داک [daak] *slang* waste land, empty desert (of life) ◆ امروز جاده ها بکلی داک بود Market streets are completely empty today

داکتر [daaktar] 1 doctor, physician ◆ داکتر نسایی gynecologist ◊ داکتر نوکریوال doctor on duty 2 (*also* داکتر علوم) doctor (scholarly degree)
● در خانه که افتاب نمی اید داکتر میاید *proverb* The doctor [often] comes to the home where the sun does not peep in.

داکتری [daaktari] 1 occupation of a doctor or of a physician; doctoring 2 doctor's degree, diploma

داکخانه [daakkhaana] post office, post

داکه [daaka] muslin; gauze

داکی [daaki] mailman, mail carrier; courier

دال [daal]¹ name of the letter د

دال [daal]² thick soup (of legumes in meat broth) ◆ دال ماش lentil soup ◊ دال نخود pea soup

دالان [daalaan] *obscure* hall, salon

دالچینی [daalchini] cinnamon (spice)

دالر [daalar] dollar

دالفین [daalfin] dolphin

دام [daam] net; snare, trap
● دام انداختن (نهادن) to spread nets; to set a trap or snare
● به دام افتادن to fall into a net, into a trap or snare
● به دام انداختن to lure into nets

داماد [daamaad] 1 fiancé, betrothed; bridegroom 2 son-in-law; brother-in-law

د

دامادخیل [daamadkheel] 1 family of son-in-law or of brother-in-law 2 relatives of betrothed or of bridegroom

دامان [daamaan] ☞ دامن

• در دامان طبیعت in the lap of nature

دامترک [daamtarak] (also موتر دامترک) dump truck

داملا [daamollaa] 1 *obscure* teacher in ecclesiastical school 2 damolla (polite form of address to persons known for their erudition and piety)

دامن [daaman] 1 flap; hem 2 skirt 3 edge; bottom; extremity (of something) ♦ دامن آسمان the sky ◊ دامن کوه gentle slope of a mountain

• دامن برزدن *colloquial* 1 to take up hem on clothing 2 to set to a task, to take to a task

دامن جمع کردن ☞ دامن چیدن

• دامن زدن to fan (a flame, hostility)

• دامن خمع کردن 1 to stop associating [with], to cease an acquaintanceship (از) 2 to keep [from], to avoid, to shun (از)

• در دامن کسی افتادن to resort to someone's patronage, to someone's protection

• دست به دامن کسی زدن 1 to implore, to beg somebody (for something) 2 to seek patronage, to seek protection from somebody

• کسی نگفت که دامنشان تاست یا بالا *colloquial* Nobody had anything bad to say about them.

دامن آلوده [daamanaaluda] 1 with damaged reputation, defamed, discredited 2 dissipated, dissolute; lewd, debauched

دامن دار [daamandaar] (and) دامن دراز [damandaraz] long-skirted

دامنگیر [daamangir]

• دامنگیر کسی شدن 1 to ask or to beg somebody (for something); to seek support from somebody 2 to happen, to occur with somebody (about illness, etc.) ♦ مرض سخت دامنگیر او شد He became seriously ill. ◊ مصیبت دامنگیر آنها شد Misfortune befell them

دامنه [daamana]¹ 1 (also دامنه کوه) edge, slope (of a mountain) 2 range, scope 3 *physics* amplitude

• دامنه چیزی راکوتاه کردن to cease something, to wrap up, to close down something; to limit, to restrict (e.g., actions)

• دامنه چیزی راهموار کردن to promote the development of something; to make way for something

دامنه [daamana]² *colloquial* typhus, spotted fever

دامنه دار [daamanadaar] 1 wide, broad, with great scope 2 long-winded, long (about a story, etc.)

دان [daan]¹ 1 *present tense stem* دانستن 2 (second component of compound words with meaning "knowing something") ♦ پشتودان expert in Pashto language

دان [daan]² *colloquial* ☞ دهان

دان [daan] ☞ دانی

• گلدان pot for flowers

دانا [daanaa] 1 *literary* knowing; scholarly, learned 2 wise person

داناندن [daanaandan] 1 to give to understand 2 to teach, to make understand

دانایی [daanaayi] *literary* knowledge, erudition; wisdom

• دانایی توانایی است *proverb* Knowledge is power.

دانس [daans] dance

• دانس کردن to dance

دانستگی [daanestagi] understanding, judgement; discretion ♦ به دانستگی knowing in advance (about something); consciously, willingly

دانستن [daanestan] (*present tense stem* دان [dan]) 1 to know, to have knowledge ♦ دانستن توانستن است *proverb* To know means to be able. 2 to understand, to comprehend 3 to consider; to think; to recognize

دانسته [daanesta] 1 *past participle* دانستن 2 knowledge (of something); information 3 learned, wise ♦ آدم دانسته learned person

• دانسته شدن to take into consideration, to count on, to rely on

• باید دانسته شودکه ••• It should be kept in view that…

• دانسته کردن to give to understand; to bring to (someone's) notice, to explain (به) ♦ به او دانسته کنید Explain [it] to him!

دانش [daanesh] science; knowledge

دانش آموز [daaneshaamoz] pupil, student ♦ دانش آموزان پوهنتون university students

دانشمند [daaneshmand] 1 learned, erudite 2 scholar; scientist; erudite *noun*

دانگ [daang] *colloquial* 1 shepherd's stick, herdsman's stick 2 bludgeon, club; cudgel 3 pole, staff

دانگه یی [daangayi] *colloquial* knave, rogue, good-for-nothing, loafer

دانه [daana]¹ 1 grain, seed; nut or pit (of a fruit) ♦ دانه انار pomegranate seed ◊ دانه برنج grain of rice 2 particle ♦ دانه ریگ grain of sand ◊ دانه برف snowflake 3 ball, bead (in abacus, etc.) ♦ دانه تسبیح bead of prayer beads 4 blackhead, pimple 5 piece, item (numerative in counting pieces or objects) ♦ ده دانه تخم ten eggs 6 bird feed (grain)

• دانه کردن 1 to thresh; to clean grain (from the husk) 2 to peel (e.g., a pomegrante); to husk (e.g., ears of corn)

دانه [daana]² *colloquial regional* window, ursi (☞ ارسی) ♦ خانه ما سه دانه دارد In our house there are three windows.

دانه باب [daanabaab] piece goods

دانه خوره [daanakhora] feeding trough (for birds)

دانه دار [daanadaar] friable, crumbly, grain by grain (about well prepared pilaf)

دانه دانه [daanadaana] 1 rare, thin, sparse ♦ باران دانه دانه occasional rain ◊ ریش دانه دانه sparse beard 1.2 by the grain, by the drop 2 rarely, sparsely

• دانه دانه باریدن to drizzle (about rain)

دانه کش [daanakash] 1 gathering grains (about an ant) 2 *poetic* toiler, a painstakingly working person

دانه گک [daanagak] grain; kernel; pea ♦ دانه گک های ریگ grains of sand

دانی [daani] (noun suffix with meanings "receptacle" / "vessel") ♦ چایدانی tea caddy, tea canister ◊ گلدانی vase for flowers

داو [daaw] 1 move, lead, turn 2 stake (in a game)

داودی [daawodi]

• گل - chrysanthemum

داو طلب [daawtalab] 1 wishing to participate in bargaining, haggling, or an auction 2 volunteering (for something), voluntarily applying oneself (to something)

داو طلبی [daawtalabi] 1 auction 2 voluntary participation (in something)

داهی [dahi] *literary* 1 skillful, capable 2 talented, able (about somebody)

داير [daayer] (and) دائر [daeer] 1 started; fixed, adjusted, aligned; set up 2 operating, functioning 3 established, founded
• داير شدن 1 to be started, to be fixed, to be adjusted, to be aligned, to be set up; to begin to function 2 to take place, to be convened ♦ جلسه داير شده نتوانست The meeting / conference could not take place.

دايركت [daayrakt] directory, production (of a film)
• داير کت کردن to produce (a film)

داير کتر [daayraktar] movie director, producer (of a film)

دايروى [daayerawi] 1 round, spherical 2 circular; cyclical ♦ حالت دايروى (cyclic) recurrence

دايره [daayera] [dawayer] 1 circumference, circle ♦ دايره استوا equator ◊ دايره ساعت dial, face ◊ دايره طول geography degree of longitude ◊ دايره عرض geography degree of latitude ◊ دايره نصف النهار Arctic Circle ◊ دايره قطبى geography meridian 2 lap, round, cycle 3 sphere, field ♦ دايره نظر horizon ◊ دايره وسعت range; scope; band 4 (plural دواير) establishment; institution ♦ دواير مملکتى state establishment; state institution
• دايره کشيدن to draw a circumference

دايره [daay (e) ra] tambourine, tambourin
• دايره زدن to beat a tambourine, to beat a tambourin, to beat time

دايروى [daayerawi] ☞ دايروى

دايره زن [daay (e) razan] playing the tambourine, playing the tambourin

دائرة المعارف [daaeratolma'aaref] encyclopedia

دايم [daayem] 1 ☞ دايمى 2 ☞ دايماً

دايماً [daayeman] constantly, always; eternally

دايمى [daayemi] 1 constant; permanent; regular; eternal; long; protracted, prolonged 2 continuous, indefinite ♦ اعضاى دايمى permanent members

داين [daayen] literary creditor, lender

داينمک [daaynamok] moving, dynamic

داينمو [daaynamo] (also ماشين داينمو) technical dynamo

دايه [daaya] wet nurse; nurse; nanny

دايى [daayi] colloquial 1 ☞ دايه 2 midwife

دباغ [daabbaagh] tanner of leather; currier, leather dresser

دباغى [daabbaaghi] 1 tanning leather, dressing or currying leather 2 the trade or craft of a tanner

دبل [dabal] 1 thick, compact, dense 2 double (about cloth or fabric, food etc.)
• گل دبل variety of karakul with a large curl
• نان دبل loaf of bread

دبنگ [dabang] colloquial 1 dolt, blockhead 2 gawk, dawdler

دبه [daba] vessel for keeping oil (made of wood or rawhide)

دبير [dabir] 1 clerk; secretary 2 secretary (leader of an organization) ♦ دبير کل general secretary (e.g., of a party)

دپ بودن هوا [dap-boodane-hawaa] colloquial hazy weather ♦ امروز هوا بسيار دپ است The weather is very hazy today.

دپلوم [deplom] diploma

دپ و دپ [dap-o-dup] slang flaunt, magnificent splendor, to showoff derogatory

دجال [dajjaal] false messiah, false prophet (who is supposed to appear mounted on a donkey before the end of the world)

دچار [dochar] ☞ دوچار

دخالت [dakhaalat] 1 interference; intervention, meddling ♦ دخالت در امور مملکت interference or meddling in the affairs of a country 2 connection [with], participation [in] (something)
• دخالت داشتن to be concerned, to be involved
• دخالت کردن to interfere; to intervene; to meddle (در ، به)

دخانيات [dokhaaniyaat] tobacco goods ♦ استعمال دخانيات incense

دخت [dokht] literary daughter; girl (usually in compound titles and proper names) ♦ شاه دخت princess ◊ توران دخت feminine proper name Turandokht (literally, Turan's daughter)

دختر [dokhtar] 1.1 girl 2.1 marriageable girl 2.2 daughter
• دختر خانه adult girl (not yet married and keeping house)
• دختر برادر (and) دختر خواهر niece
• دختر ماما (and) دختر کاکا first cousin (daughter of an uncle)
• دختر عمه (and) دختر خاله first cousin (daughter of an aunt)
• دختر رز poetic wine, juice of grapes
• دختر صوفى ☞ دختر صوفى

دختر اندر [dokhtarandar] stepdaughter

دختر خوانده [dokhtarxaanda] adopted daughter, foster daughter

دختر صوفى [dokhtaresofi] oriole

دخترى [dokhtari] 1 girlhood; childhood (of a girl) 2 virginity

دختر فروشى [dukhtar-feroshee] colloquial (literally: Daughter seller) the act of accepting money and wealth from someone who wants to marry one's daughter derogatory

دخل [dákhel] 1 income, profit ♦ دخل و خرج income and expenditure 2 cash box, till (where a merchant places his daily receipts) 3 connection, relationship
• دخل داشتن 1 to have a connection, to have a relationship ♦ اين کار به شما دخل ندارد (به) This doesn't concern you. 2 to participate, to play a role (in something) 3 to have access (to something)

دخمه [dakhma] crypt, vault; grave

دخول [dokhul] 1 entrance, place of entry ♦ اجازه دخول نيست Do not enter. / Entry forbidden. 2 entry (into some place or somewhere) 3 military incursion, invasion 4 receipt (of money, of deposits) ♦ دخول اين زمين سالى هزار افغانى است This land brings in a thousand afghani yearly.

دخيل [dakhil] 1 participating, involved, having direct relationship (to something) 2 versed, experienced, competent (in something)
• کلمات دخيل loanwords

در [dad] literary beast, wild beast, beast of prey

دره [dada] regional 1 Papa, Dad 2 uncle

در [dar]¹ door ♦ در باغ (wicket) gate of a garden ◊ در الماري door of a cupboard
• در به در گشتن 1 haunt somebody's threshold (while achieving or obtaining something) 2 to loiter one's time away
• از هر در صحبت کردن to talk about this and that; to chatter, to jabber

در [dar]² 1 (indicates the direction of action) to; in; into; on; onto preposition ♦ امروز آيها در تياتر ميروند Today they are going to the theater. 2 (indicates the place of an action) in; at; on ♦ برادرم در پوهنتون درس ميخواند My brother is studying at the university. 3 (indicates the time of an action) in; at; during ♦ در يک هفته کار را in recent years ◊ در اين سالهاى اخير

د

They finished the work / job in one week. خلاص کردند **4** (indicates the circumstances, situation, etc.) in; at; during; under ◊ در غریبی و تنگدستی in poverty and need **5** (becomes part of compound ezafeh *preposition*)
- در باره and **1** about, concerning, relative to **2** (verbal prefix) ♦ درآمدن to enter
- در گرفتن to catch fire, to ignite, to blaze up

در [dor (r)] pearls; pearl

درآر [daraar] *present tense stem* درآوردن

دراز [daraaz] **1.1** long ♦ گردن دراز long neck **1.2** long, prolonged ♦ عمر دراز long life **1.3** stretched; long-winded; extensive; verbose ♦ داستان دراز long story **2** (first or second component of compound words with meaning "long") ♦ دراز عمر long-standing, of many years
- زبان دراز garrulous; saucy-tongued
- دراز افتادن to lie down, to sprawl (بر); to lie down for a while, to rest
- دراز کردن **1** to lengthen; to prolong; to elongate **2** to stretch **3** to prolong; to extend, to drag out (a story, etc.) **4** *colloquial* to bring down (an opponent), to knock (an opponent) off his feet
- دراز کشیدن to lie, to rest

درازپای [daraazpaay] long-legged

درازچوکی [daraazchawki] bench; sofa

درازعمر [daraazómor] long lived; perennial (about plants)

درازقد [daraazqad (d)] of great height, tall

درازگوش [daraazgosh] **1.1** long-eared **1.2** *colloquial* curious **2** donkey

درازمدت [daraazmoddat] **1** long-term ♦ قرض درازمدت long-term credit **2** long, prolonged

درازی [daraazi] **1** length; extent **2** duration ♦
- به این درازی so long, of such length

درآمد [daraamad] **1** profit, income; *accounting* receipts **2** entrance, entry ♦ دروازه درآمد entrance door **3** *colloquial* treatment, manners; approach
- درآمد کرد *colloquial* to treat (somebody) (با); to have an approach

درآمدن [daraamadan] (*present tense stem* درای [daray]) **1** to go in, to enter; to drive into or in **2** to go into, to fit into (something) (به)
- به شکل کسی(چیزی)درآمدن to be changed into somebody or something, to be turned by somebody or something

دراموی [deraamawi] dramatic

درامه [deraama] drama, play ♦ درامه منظومه a play in verse

درامه نویس [deraamanawis] playwright, dramatist

درامه نویسی [deraamanawisi] the drama, dramatic art

درآمیختن [daraameekhtan] (*present tense stem* درآمیز [daramez]) *intransitive* to mix, to join, to unite, to combine [with]
- با هم در آمیختن to associate [with]

درانی [doraani] Durani (Afghan tribe)

درآوردن [daraawardan] (*present tense stem* درآور [daraawar] (and) درآر [daraar]) **1** to bring in; to enter; to insert; to introduce **2** to plunge [into]; to pull; to draw **3** *colloquial* to derive (benefit); to obtain (profit) ♦ او از این معامله دو هزار افغانی درآورد He obtained 2,000 afghani from this transaction.
- به خنده درآوردن to make laugh
- به گریه درآوردن to make cry or weep
- به شکل کسی(چیزی)درآوردن to be changed into somebody or something; to shape somebody or something
- به نظم درآوردن to set to verse

درآویختن [daraaweekhtan] (*present tense stem* درآویز [darawez]) to get into a quarrel, into a fight; to grapple [with], to come to blows [with]

درآی [daraay] *present tense stem* درآمدن

درایور [deraaywar] driver, chauffeur ♦ درایور لاری truck driver

درایوری [deraaywari] driving (a motor vehicle); occupation of chauffeur or driver
- درایوری کردن to drive (a vehicle); to be a chauffeur or driver

درب [darb] *literary* entry, entrance; gate, gates

دربار [darbaar] **1** court (of a monarch) **2** place, palace (where a monarch gives and holds audiences) **3** reception, audience (by a monarch) ♦ امروز دربار تجار است Today the sovereign is receiving merchants.
- دربار کردن to give an audience, to receive (about a monarch)

درباره [darbaara] about, concerning, relative to *denominative preposition* ♦ درباره این about this

درباری [darbaari] courtier

دربان [darbaan] doorkeeper; hall porter; watchman; janitor; porter

دریچه [darbacha] ☞ دریچه

دربدر [darbadar] **1.1** homeless, shelterless **1.2** impoverished, ruined **1.3** idler, lounger **2.1** poor man, wanderer **2.2** loafer, idler

دربدری [darbadari] **1** homelessness; wandering about the world **2** loafing, idling about

دربدیوار [darbadeewaar] (also همسایه دربدیوار) close neighbor, living door to door, living opposite one another

دربند [darband] (numerative in counting structures, courtyards, dwellings) ♦ سه دربنت حویلی three courtyards ◊ یک دربند باغ one garden

درپرده [darparda] **1** wooden partition in old houses (separates the entrance door from the living area) **2** portable partition, screen

درپرده یی [darpardayi]
- پانل های درپرده یی interior wall panel

درج [darj] **1** entry, entering (in a list, etc.) **2** inclusion; including, insertion (e.g., of an article in a newspaper)
- درج کردن **1** to note, to jot down, to enter (in a list) **2** to include, to insert (e.g., an article in a newspaper or magazine)

درجن [darjan] (also درجن کلان) dozen ♦ درجن خورد half a dozen, six items ◊ یک درجن پیاله a dozen cups

درجن کردن [darjan-kardan] *slang* (*literally*: to make it a dozen) hoarding, stockpiling, saving, collecting (a stingy person who does not spend)

درجه [daraja] (*plural* درجات [darajaat]) **1** degree; level; stage; step ♦ تا این درجه to such a degree ◊ درجه رطوبت degree of humidity **2** degree ♦ درجه صفر freezing point ◊ گرمی تا چهل درجه میر سید The temperature (heat) reached 40 degrees (C). **3** rank; degree; title ♦ درجه علمی scholar's degree **4** category; rank, rating; class ♦ درجه اول of the first category, of first class

درجه اعلی ٪ highest quality or grade, of the highest quality or grade

درجه‌بندی [darajabandi] 1 classification; sorting 2 grading

درحال [darhal] right now, immediately

درخت [darakht] tree ♦ درخت باردار fruit tree

درخت‌زار [darakhtzaar] grove

درخشان [dorokhshaan] shining, sparkling, twinkling, flashing, radiant ♦ چهره درخشان a radiant face, a joyful face ◊ ستاره درخشان a twinkling star ◊ عقل درخشان a brilliant mind

درخشیدن [dorokhshidan] to shine, to beam, to sparkle, to twinkle, to flash

درخواست [darkhaast] 1 request, application, petition 2 inquiry; claim; order
- درخواست کردن 1 to request, to petition 2 to make an inquiry; to make a claim; to place an order

درخواستی [darkhaasti] 1 demand, condition; term, rule, regulation 2 ☞ درخواست

درخور [darkhor] literary 1 deserving, worthy (of something) 2 meeting the rules of decency or decorum, befitting

درد [dard] 1 pain; illness, disease ♦ درد گلون sore throat ◊ درد مفاصل sore joints, rheumatism 2 suffering, torment, pangs, torture
- درد بی دوا (and) درد بی درمان 1 incurable ailment 2 inconsolable grief
- درد بدار دوای بد proverb An unpleasant ailment is treated with unpleasant medicine. (Fight fire with fire.)
- درد دل 1 pain in the heart, sickness of the heart 2 emotional pain, sorrow, grief, chagrin
- درد سر ☞ درد سر
- درد و علم misfortunes and sorrows, trials and tribulations
- درد کردن to ache, to give rise to a feeling of pain
- پایم درد میکند my leg / foot hurts
- درد کشیدن to worry, to suffer
- درد دل کردن(گفتن) to share (one's) sorrows, to unburden one's heart / soul (با،به)
- به درد کسی خوردن to be useful; to be fit, to be suited [for], to fit, to suit ♦ به دردت میخورم I will [still] be useful to you.

دردادن [dardaadan] (present tense stem دره [dardeh]) 1 to set fire [to]; to light, to kindle (a flame), to ignite 2 colloquial to vex, to irritate, to infuriate; to drive [somebody] out of [his] mind
- پول رادادن colloquial to spend money (to buy useless things)
- دختر خودرادادن colloquial to marry off [one's] daughter unhappily (i.e., to make a bad marriage)

دردآلود [dardaalud] full of torment, full of suffering ♦ نگاه دردآلود a look full of suffering

دردانه [dor (r) daana] 1.1 pearl 1.2 a favorite, a pet (about the only child in a family) 2 (also عزیز دردانه) infinitely dear, unique, only

نازدانه و دردانه [naazdaana-o-durdaana] colloquial sweetie pie, lovely and dear (child)

درد رسیده [dard-rasida] colloquial (literally: one who had pain) victim, a person who has been suffered and victimized

دردسر [dardesar] concern, trouble, anxiety
- دردسر دادن (را،به) to bother, to bore, to pester ♦ شمارچه دردسر بدهم I won't bother you.
- باعث دردسر کسی شدن to give somebody a lot of trouble

دردمند [dardmand] 1 ill (with something), suffering (from something) ♦ دردمند عشق in love 2 compassionate, sympathetic

دردناک [dardnaak] 1 ailing, aching (about organs and parts of the body) ♦ دندان دردناک aching tooth 2 painful, agonizing ♦ عملیات دردناک painful operation

دررفتن [darraftan] 1 literary to leave, to go away, to depart; to go out 2 to go off, to be discharged (about a gun) ♦ تفنگ دررفت The gun went off.

درز [darz] 1 slit, narrow crack; clearance 2 seam
- درز کردن 1 to get a crack 2 to part at the seams
- درز گرفتن to take in, to make tucks
- بین آنها درز افتاد colloquial Their friendship is showing signs of discord.

درزکشا [darzkoshaa] technical wedge

درزگیری [darzgiri] 1 caulking (of walls); puttying, filling in (cracks, joints) 2 sewing together 3 taking in (clothing) (i.e., making smaller by sewing)

درزمایه [darzmaaya]
- درز مایه گرفتن to take in with a double seam; to hem with a double seam; to make a double seam (when sewing clothing)

درزی [darzi] regional tailor

درس [dars] (plural دروس [dorus]) 1 lesson, lessons, studies 2 (also درس عبرت) lesson, edifying example
- درس خواندن to learn; to study
- درس دادن (را،به) 1 to teach, to instruct 2 to teach; to give a lesson
- درس گرفتن 1 to take lessons 2 to learn a lesson (from something)
- درس تیار کردن to prepare a lesson

درست [dorost] 1.1 right, correct 1.2 decent, respectable, honest (about somebody) 1.3 in good repair, whole 2.1 correctly ♦ این درست است That is correct. 2.2 well, thoroughly, properly, as one should ♦ درست فکر کن Think carefully!
- درست کردن 1 to correct; to put right; to adjust, to arrange, to organize 2 to manufacture, to make, to produce

درست‌کار [dorostkaar] conscientious, honest, decent, respectable

درستی [dorosti] بدرستی ☞ به درستی

درس‌خانه [darskhana] room for studies, auditorium

درسی [darsi] educational; school; pupil adjective ♦ سامان درسی school supplies ◊ کتاب درسی textbook

درشت [dorosht] 1 hard, firm; strong; rough, rugged 2 coarse, poorly processed or made, rough (e.g., rough draft) ♦ آرد درشت coarse-ground flour 3 rude, coarse; sharp, harsh ♦ گپ درشت rude words, impudence, rudenesses

درشته [doroshta] green crushed grain (fodder)

درشتی [doroshti] 1 hardness; roughness 2 coarseness, crudeness; impudence, rudeness
- درشتی کردن to act rudely, to talk rudely; to be impudent or impertinent

درفش [darafsh] shoemaker's awl with bent tip

درک [darak]¹ 1 piece of news, rumor, news (about somebody) ♦ هیچ درکش نیست There is no news of him. 2 conducting inquiries, making inquiries (about somebody)
- درک زدن to investigate, to make inquiries (about somebody)

د

درک کردن • to get, to obtain; to obtain with difficulty
• رفت تا پیسه درک کند He went to get some money.
• درک یافتن to find out, to get news
• درک نداشتن (از) not to give news about oneself; to disappear completely, to vanish completely ♦ شما هیچ درک ندارید You have vanished completely.
• من درک اورا یافتم I determined his coordinates
درک [darak]² point of view; consideration ♦ از این درک from this point of view
• از هر درک 1 from all points of view, in all respects 2 about everything, about various things
• از درک ۰۰۰ 1 from the point of view [of] …, in respect to … 2 because of ♦ من از درک وفاداری او دوست دارم I love him for his loyalty. 3 at the expense [of]; by ♦ این خساره از درک صادرات جبران شده می تواند This loss can be made up by export.
درک [dark] 1 understanding, realization 2 knowledge, comprehension
• درک کردن 1 to understand, to realize 2 to comprehend, to get to know
درکار [darkar] necessary, needed
• درکار است one should, it is necessary
درگاه [dargah]
• به درگاه خداوند (grandiloquent) before the most high, when addressing the most high
درگذر [dargozar] 1 present tense stem درگذشتن 1.2 rejection (of a claim, of a suit) 2 generosity, magnanimity; foregiveness, pardon
• درگذر کردن 1 to reject (a claim, a suit) 2 to show generosity, magnanimity; to forgive, to pardon
درگذشت [dargozasht] literary death, decease, demise
درگذشتن [dargozashtan] present tense stem درگذر [dargozar] 1 to pass by, to pay no attention (از) 2 literary to leave this world, to die
• ازگناه کسی درگذشدن to forgive someone for a fault
• از دعوی خود در گذشتن to reject a suit, to reject a claim
درگرفتن [dargereftan] (present tense stem درگیر [dargir]) 1 to catch fire, to break out (about a fire) 2 to start intransitive (about an argument), to become animated (about a discussion, etc.)
• جنگ درگرفت War broke out.
درگیر [dargir] present tense stem درگرفتن
درگیران [dargiraan] kindling (for starting a fire, lighting a hearth)
درم [derám] technical drum ♦ درم برک brake drum
درمان [darmaan] treatment
• درمان کردن to treat, to doctor
درماندگی [darmaandagi] 1 infirmity; feebleness, helplessness 2 need, misfortune
درماندن [darmaandan] 1 to become feeble; to become helpless; to turn out to be incapable (to do something) ♦ این مردم به نان شب وروز خود درمانده اند These people are not [even] capable of earning their daily subsistence. 2 to suffer need
درمانده [darmaanda] 1 poor, unfortunate 2 poor person
درنده [darenda] 1 predatory ♦ حیوانات درنده predatory animals 2 (plural درندگان [darendagan]) beast, predator
درنگ [darang] peal, ringing, tinkling, clang
• درنگ کردن to peal, to ring, to tinkle

درنگاندن [darangaandan] to jingle, to set to ringing
درو [daraw] 1 present tense stem درویدن 2 reaping, mowing
• درو کردن to reap, to mow, to cut
دروازه [darwaaza] 1 door; gate, (wicket) gate ♦ دروازه اطاق door of a room ◊ دروازه درآمد entrance door, front door ◊ دروازه شهر gate of a city, city gates 2 technical sluice, lock
دروازه وان [darwazawan] 1 (and) دروازه بان [darwazabaan] doorkeeper, guard 2 ☞ دربان
دروان [darwaan] ☞ دربان
درود [dorud] literary greeting, salute, salutation; blessing, benediction
• درود برشهدای وطن Glory to those who fell for the homeland!
• درود گفتن 1 to greet, to congratulate 2 to bless, to give one's blessing, to glorify, to sing the praises of
درودگر [dorudgar] (and) [darudgar] joiner; carpenter
دروس [dorus] plural of درس
دروسل [dorosal] technical throttle
دروش [dorawsh] ☞ درفش
دروغ [dorogh] untruth, lie ♦ دروغ مصلحت آمیز a lie for salvation ◊ وعده دروغ a false promise
• به دروغ by means of a lie, by fraud, by deceit
• دروغ گفتن to lie, to cheat
دروغ شاخدار [drooghe-shaakhdaar] colloquial (literally: a lie that has horns) a lie that grows horns, a big lie
دروغین [doroghin] false; dummy; deceptive, delusive; feigned ♦ عشق دروغین feigned love
دروگر [darawgar] reaper, mower
درون [darun] 1.1 interior, inner part, interior part 1.2 [one's] inside, soul 2.1 (also به درون (and) در درون) inside, inside of denominative preposition 2 از درون out of, from within
• درون شدن to go inside, to penetrate
درویدن [darawidan] to reap, to mow, to cut
درویزه [darweeza] obscure 1.1 beggarly 1.2 beggarlines 2 charity, alms
درویش [darwesh] 1 dervish, wandering monk 2 beggar, poor person
درویشی [darweshi] 1 dervishism, life of a dervish 2 beggarliness; itinerant life; life of poverty
دره [dara] 1 gorge, ravine, canyon; mountain pass ♦ دره خیبر Khyber Pass 2 valley ♦ دره کابل valley of Kabul River
دره [dorra] a leather lash on a wooden handle (which serves to exact punishment)
درهم [darham] ☞ درهم برهم
درهمبرهم [darhambarham] (and) درهم وبرهم [darhamobarham] 1 put into disorder; confused 2 complicated, complex, intricate ♦ مسئله درهم برهم a complicated question, an intricate question
• درهم برهم کردن 1 to put into disorder or disarray, to confuse; to mix up 2 to complicate; to confuse
دری [dari] (also زبان دری) the Dari language (name of the second state language of Afghanistan- along with Pashto; it is also called Farsi or Farsi - Kabuli)
دریا [daryaa] river ♦ دریا کابل Kabul River
• دریا رابکوزه جای دادن colloquial to try to do the impossible; to perform an empty, senseless deed
دریاب [daryaab] present tense stem دریافتن
دریاچه [daryaacha] lake

دریافت [daryaaft] 1 receipt; levy; collection 2 income, earnings 3 comprehension; guess, conjecture; surmise ♦ دریافت کردن ☞ دریافتن 1, 3

دریافتن [daryaaftan] (*present tense stem* دریاب [daryab]) 1 to receive; to obtain; to get 2 to find again, to find 3 to understand, to comprehend; to guess, to surmise

دریافتی [daryaafti] 1 receipt, receipts 2 received, transferred [to], received [into] (a till); entered as receipts ♦ مبلغ دریافتی money received

دریایی [daryaayi] 1 river *adjective*, riverine, fluvial 2 *rarely* sea, maritime, marine

دریچه [daricha] 1 door, small window 2 hatch; manhole

دریدن [daridan] 1 to tear, to tear up 2 to tear *intransitive*, to be torn, to be torn up

دریشی [dereeshi] clothing, (man's) suit ♦ دریشی پیلوت flight uniform ◊ دریشی عسکری military full-dress uniform, military uniform

دریشی خواب ☞ دریشی خواب ♦

دریشی کار ☞ دریشی کار ♦

دریشی خواب [dereeshikhaab] pajamas

دریشی کار [dereeshi (ye) kaar] protective clothing; working clothes; overalls

دریغ [dareegh] 1 pity, regret 2 What a pity! / Alas! *interjection*

♦ دریغ کردن to begrudge (something for somebody); to refuse or deny (something)

♦ دریغ نکردن not to spare (something for somebody), not to refuse or deny (something) ♦ از هیچ گونه مساعدت دریغ نخواهند کرد They will not refuse to help in any way.

درایور [deraiwar] ☞ درایور

درایوری [deraiwari] ☞ درایوری

درویزه [daryuza] ☞ درویزه

دز [daz (and) dez] sound of a shot (from a gun) ♦ تفنگ دز کرد a shot rang out

دزد [dozd] thief, robber; brigand ♦ دزد خانه house burglar

♦ دزد به سر خود پر دارد *proverb* A thief gives himself away. / An uneasy conscience betrays itself. (*literally,* a thief has feathers on his head.)

دزدانه [dozdaana] (and) دزدکی [dozdaki] 1 by stealth; stealthily, furtively, quietly; on the sly; thievishly; in an underhand way 2 secret, covert

دزدی [dozdi] stealing, theft; robbery

دزدیدن [dozdidan] to steal, to pilfer

دزدیده [dozdida] *past participle* of دزدیدن ♦ نگاه دزدیده a glance cast stealthily

دساتیر [dasaatir] *plural of* دستور ♦ دساتیر حفظ الصحه rules of sanitation and hygiene

دسانت [desaant] assault landing ♦ دسانت بحری amphibious landing ♦ دسانت را پیاده کردن to land an assault force

دسایس [dasaayes] *plural of* دسیسه

دسپلین [deseplin] discipline

دسپیچر [despichar] dispatcher

دست [dast (and) dest] 1 arm, hand 2 front leg, front paw (of an animal) 3 a game, a set (of chess, etc.); one game, one hand ♦ یک دست بازی نرد one hand or one round of the game of nards 4 (numerative when counting clothing) ♦ شش دست یک دست دریشی six pairs of pajamas ◊ یک دست دریشی خواب one suit 5 یک دست قطعه pack of cards 6 to seize, to catch hold of, to grab (by something) ♦ دست به یخن او انداخت (به) He grabbed him by the collar. 7 to infringe, to encroach

♦ از دست because of (somebody); from; through the fault (of somebody) *denominative preposition* ♦ از دست این کو دکان آرام نبودم I knew no rest because of these children

♦ زیر دست (در زیر دست also) under the command [of], under the leadership [of]; under the guidance [of] دست انداختن

♦ دست چپ 1 left hand, left arm 2 at the left hand; from the left; on the left; to the left

♦ دست راست 1 right hand, right arm 2 at the right hand; from the right; on the right; to the right

♦ دست خالی ☞ دست خالی

♦ دست به دست hand in hand

♦ پیش دست at hand, within easy reach of one's hand

♦ دست شکسته تاوان گردن *proverb* to pay for a broken arm with [one's] neck

♦ دست برداشتن to leave in peace; to give up, to renounce, to relinquish

♦ دست بردن (از) to extend [one's] hand (toward something); to thrust [one's] hand (به) ♦ او دستش را به جیبش برد He thrust [his] hand in [his] pocket.

♦ دست دادن 1 to shake hands [with] 2 to happen [to], to occur [to] (را) 3 to seize, to grip (about a feeling of fear, etc.)

♦ دست داشتن 1 to know how (to do something) well, to be skillful (در) 2 to be mixed up [in], to be involved [in] (به) ♦ آنها در این بی نظمی دست داشتن They were mixed up in these disorders.

♦ دست زدن 1 to touch, to seize with the hand, to grab with the hand 2 to interfere, to butt in, to poke one's nose in ♦ او به هر چیز دست میزند He pokes his nose in everywhere. 3 to take to (a task, etc.), to set down (e.g., to work); to begin ♦ حکومت به اقدامات وسیعی دست زده است The government began [to carry out] broad measures.

♦ دست شستن to give up (something) as lost or hopeless; to leave, to abandon, to foresake; to decline, to refuse, to renounce, to relinquish (از)

♦ دست کشیدن (بالای) 1 to stroke, to pet, to caress 2 to cease, to quit; to give-up (از)

♦ دست گذاشتن to lay a hand [on]; to seize, to capture, to take possession [of] (بر,به)

♦ دست یافتن to obtain, to secure, to take possession [of] (به); to take into [one's] hands, to appropriate (بالای)

♦ از دست دادن to let escape, to lose

♦ از دست رفتن to be missed; to be overlooked; to be lost, to disappear, to vanish ♦ فرصت از دست رفت The incident was overlooked.

♦ به دست آمدن 1 to be received; to be obtained; to be achieved 2 to come [from], to be extracted [from] ♦ ابریشم از کرم پیله به دست میاید Silk comes from a cocoon.

♦ به دست آوردن to get; to obtain; to secure for oneself; to acquire

♦ به (در) دست بودن to have available, to be on hand

♦ معلوماتی که به (در) دست است ... according to available information ...

♦ روی دست بودن to be in the process of execution, to be in production ♦ پروژه های بزرگ اقتصادی روی دست است Great economic plans are being carried out.

145

- دست از پای خطا نکردن not to lose one's presence of mind, not to be confused ♦ دست از پای خطا نکو colloquial Don't become flustered!
- دست از جان شستن not to spare [one's] life, to act selflessly
- دست از سر کسی برنداشتن not to leave in peace, to stick like a leech
- دست به دست زدن to throw up one's hands in grief or in distress; to regret
- دست به گردن انداختن to embrace intransitive, to embrace (somebody)
- دست دراز کردن 1 to extend [one's] hand (literally and figuratively) 2 (also دست گدایی دراز کردن) to beg for alms 3 to infringe, to encroach (به)
- دست داشتن ☞ دست قوی داشتن
- پدرم در خطاطی دست قوی داشت My father was very skillful in calligraphy.
- دست و روی شستن to wash oneself
- دست تو بالا است colloquial You gained! You are the winner! (e.g., in a sale or purchase)
- دستش نمیرسد 1 He won't touch (with his hand). / He won't reach. 2 He has no time.
- دستش کو تاه است colloquial He is not up to it. / He is not in condition (to do something). / He can't (do something).
- هرچه از دستم بیاید ... everything that depends on me ...; everything that I can do ...
- دست آخر in the last place or instance
- دست اول as a beginning, as a handsel (in trade)
- دست غیب literary providence, the finger of fate
- دستت کم ☞ دست کم
- روی دست in effect; in force; being in the stage of realization or execution
- دست سبک داشتن idiom (literally: to have a light hand) bully, someone who beats up kids for no particular reason
- دست زیر سنگ بودن idiom (literally: someone's hand being under a rock) to depend on someone else; one's hands are tied

دستادست [dastaadast] 1 directly, from hand to hand 2 for cash 3 ☞ دست بدست 1

دستار [dastaar] turban
- دستار بستن to wind a turban, to don a turban

دستاس [dastaas] handmill (to grind salt, grains, etc.)

دست افزار [dastafzaar] hand implement, hand tools

دست آموز [dastaamoz] hand adjective; tamed, domesticated

دست انداز [dastaandaaz] 1 oppressor, tyrant 2 ☞ دست دراز 1

دست اندازی [dastandazi] 1 using one's fists, taking the law into one's own hands 2 ☞ دست درازی 1
- دست اندازی کردن to be involved in using one's fists, to be free with one's hands ♦ دست اندازی نکو Don't be free with your hands!

دستاویز [dastaaweez] paper, document

دست بازی [dastbaazi] 1 roguery, swindle, cheating, foul play 2 colloquial playful brawl, scuffle, row
- دست بازی کردن 1 to swindle, to cheat 2 colloquial to pommel one another (playfully)

دست بافت [dastbaaft] woven by hand, homemade

دست بالا [dastbaalaa]
- دست بالا بودن(شدن) colloquial 1 to gain the upper hand; to triumph; to overshadow, to eclipse (به) 2 to buy or sell profitably, to be the gainer or winner

دست بدامان [dastbadaaman]
- دست بدامان بردن(شدن) to entreat, to implore (for something); to resort to, to fall back on (somebody's) help or protection

دست بدست [dastbadast] 1 hand in hand, in a friendly manner, amicably 2 jointly, together ♦ کارا را دست بدست کردیم We did this job together. / We carried out this work together. 3 ☞ دستادست

دست برد [dastbord] theft, abduction, appropriation
- خانه دستبرد آتش شد The house fell prey to fire.

دست بردار [dastbardaar]
- دست بردار نبودن not to lag behind, not to budge, not to fall back, to achieve persistently (از)
- از سر کل کسی دست بردار شدن colloquial to leave in peace, to leave alone ♦ دیگر از سر کل مه دست بردار می شوی؟ Will you leave me alone at last?

دست بسینه [dastbasina] 1 obliging, respectful, deferential; ready to obey 2 obligingly, respectfully, deferentially; while obeying

دست بگردن [dastbagardan]
- دست بگردن شدن 1 to embrace intransitive; to embrace (somebody) 2 to be reconciled, to make up with

دست بگریبان [dastbagareebaan] (and) [dastbageraibaan]

دست بند [dastband] 1 bracelet 2 colloquial experiencing need, needy ♦ او دست بند شد He is poor.
- دست بند بودن to be needy, to be hard up

دست بوسی [dastbusi] obscure 1 kissing of hands 2 visit, call (usually to a high-ranking person)

دست و گریبان [dastbayakhan] ☞ دست به یخن

دست و پاچه [dastpaacha] ☞ دست وپاچه

دست پاک [dastpaak] towel (for drying the hands); table napkin
- ما دست پاک شما نشدیم colloquial We do not intend to whitewash you / to shield you.

دست پالک [dastpalak] colloquial 1 feeling; groping; rummaging 2 by the sense of touch; gropingly; to the touch
- دست پالک کردن to rummage [in / about]; to feel, to touch

دست پخت [dastpokht] baked at home, homemade ♦ این دست پخت خود من است I made this myself.

دست پرورده [dastparwarda] pupil ♦ این بچه دست پرورده من است This boy is my pupil.

دستت خلاص [dastat-khalaas] idiom (literally: your hands are free) show me what you've got ♦ دستت خلاص هر چه میکنی Go ahead do whatever you are able to. (a sentence used to accept someone's challenge or threatening)

دست چینی [dastejam'i] ☞ دست چین

دست چین [dastchin] 1 picked by hand (about fruit) 2 select, selected
- دست چین کردن 1 to pick (fruit from a tree) 2 to select

دست خالی [dast (e) xaali] with nothing, without result, in vain; with empty hands

دست خط [dastxa(t)t] signature; painting
- دست خط کردن to sign, to place one's signature

دست خورده [dastkhorda] colloquial not new, used, slightly marred

دست خوش [dastkhosh] 1 sacrifice, victim; booty, loot, plunder; prey, catch 2 prize, winnings
- دستخوش کسی(چیزی)شدن to fall prey to somebody or something

دست دراز [dastdaraaz] 1 rudely interfering (in somebody's affairs); encroaching (on something) 2 ☞ دست انداز 1

دست درازی [dastdaraazi] 1 rude interference (in somebody's affairs), encroachment 2 ☞ دست اندازی

دسترخوان [dastarkhaan] 1 dastarkhan (a tablecloth spread on the floor and then covered with food and refreshments) 2 covered table

دسترس [dastras] access (to something); opportunity to have or to get (something)
- دسترس داشتن to have access (to something), to have the opportunity to use (something)
- به دسترس کسی بودن (شدن) to be accessible; to be at (somebody's) disposal ♦ به دسترس کسی گذاشتن to place at somebody's disposal

دست رنج [dastranj] 1 labor, work 2 earnings

دست زده [dastzada] soiled by hands; rumpled, crumpled; stale ♦ این نان دست زده است Somebody touched this flatcake.

دست شانده [dastshaanda] colloquial ☞ دست نشانده 3

دست شوی [dastshoy] 1 washstand 2 sink, washbowl; dishwashing machine

دست فروش [dastforosh] vendor who sells (something) out of hand

دستک [destak] (also چوب دستک) beam, girder; rafter, truss

دستکاری [dastkaari] 1.1 repairing, mending, repair 2 small odd jobs 3 handwork 2 handmade ♦ این تاقین دستکاری است This cap is handmade.

دست کش [dastkash] glove, mitten; gloves, mittens ♦ دست کش رابری rubber gloves

دست کشاده [dastkoshaada] generous, kind

دست کم [dast (e) kam] at least, no less than

دستکول [dastkawl] woman's handbag, reticule (woman's drawstring bag)

دستکی [dastaki] 1 technical lever; grip; handle 2 colloquial hand; manual; made by hand

دستگاه [dastgaah] 1 rig; plant; machine tool; machine ♦ دستگاه برق electric motor ◊ دستگاه برمه drilling rig 2 enterprises; plant, factory; shop ♦ دستگاه خشت سازی brick factory, brickworks 3 apparatus, device; instrument ♦ دستگاه رادیو radio receiver ◊ دستگاه دولتی state apparatus

دست گذاری [dastgozaari] feeble impulse, encroachment
- دست گذاری کردن 1 to have a feeble impulse in regard to (somebody or something به) 2 to lay hands (on something بالای)

دست گردان [dastgardan] 1 bought or sold out of hand ♦ من این لباس را دست گردان خریدم I bought these clothes out of hand 2 ☞ دست فروش

دست گل داشتن [daste-gul-daashtan] slang (literally: to have a flowery hand) to be handy

دستگیر [dastgir]¹ 1 handle; bracket ♦ دستگیر دروازه door handle 2 literary caught; detained, arrested

دستگیر [dastgir]² 1 assisting, helping, protecting; patronizing (somebody) 2 assistant; patron

دستگیری [dastgiri] 1 rendering assistance or help; patronage protection; care 2 receiving into [one's] hands, attainment ♦ اگر دهقان کار نکند نان دستگیری او نخواهد کرد colloquial If a peasant doesn't work, he won't obtain bread.
- دستگیری کردن to render help or assistance; to protect, to patronize

دست لاف [dastlaaf] colloquial handsel (in trade, in bargaining)
- دست لاف کردن to give a handsel (in trade, in bargaining)

دستمال [dastmaal] ☞ دسمال

دست مایه [dastmaaya] small amount of capital (for starting a business)

دستمبو [dastambo] (and) دستمبول [dastambo] shamam (fragrant small melon)

دست مزد [dastmozd] remuneration for labor; earnings, wages

دست ناخورده [dastnaakhorda] 1 untouched 2 whole, undamaged

دست نارس [dastnaaras] unkind, unsympathetic; not helping anybody

دست نشانده [dastneshaanda] 1 henchman ♦ حکومت دست نشانده satellite state 2 protege 3 seedling, sapling (about a tree)

دست نویس [dastnawis] 1 written by hand, manuscript adjective 2 manuscript noun
- دست نویس شدن to be written, to be copied ♦ این نسخه به خط نستعلیق دست نویس شده است This manuscript is written in nastaliq script.

دست وبال [dastobaal]
- دست وبال جمع کردن colloquial to prepare (for something); to make ready (for a journey)
- دست وبال کسی را باز کردن colloquial to untie somebody's hands, to give somebody freedom of action

دست وبالک [dastobaalak]
- دست وبالک زدن colloquial to move freely, to work the arms and legs (about a child)

دست وپاچگی [dastopaachagi] colloquial perplexity; confusion; embarrassment ♦ با دست وپاچگی in confusion; in embarrassment; in panic

دست وپاچه [dastopaacha] colloquial perplexed; confused; embarrassed

دست وپاشکسته [dastopaashekasta] colloquial lout, nincompoop, dunderhead

دست وپای [dastopaay] colloquial
- دست وپای زدن (کردن) 1 to be zealous; to endeavor, to try 2 to fuss, to bustle [about]
- از دست وپای ماندن to weaken, to become weak, to lose one's strength; to grow decrepit
- دست وپای شور دادن to stir intransitive, to turn intransitive, to swing intransitive
- دست وپای کسی بودن to be a support to somebody, to encourage somebody
- دست وپای گم کردن to become flustered, to be shy

دست ودان [dastodaan]
- دست ودان بودن colloquial to spend one's entire earnings on food (without putting anything aside) ♦ ما مردم دست ودان استیم پاسره نداریم We spend all our earnings [and] we don't put anything aside.

دستور [dastur] (plural دساتیر [dasātir]) 1 procedure, rule; custom ♦ به دستور پشتونها according to the customs of the Pathan people 2 instructions, directions; order, decree 3 (also دستور زبان) grammar 4 enema
- دستور تشریحی Descriptive grammar
- دستور مقایسی Comparative grammar
- دستورسنتی Traditional grammar
- دستور دادن to give instructions, to give an order, to decree
- دستور کردن to give an enema

دستور العمل [dasturolamal] guide for action, instructions; directions; directive

دست وردار [dastwardaar] *colloquial* ☞ دست بردار

دستور نویس [dasturnawis] author of book on grammar; grammarian ♦ دستور نویسان عربی Arab grammarians

دست وگریبان [dastogereebaan] (and) دست ویخن [dastoyakhan] ♦ *colloquial* 1 to grapple in a fight, to come to blows in hand-to-hand fighting (با) 2 to badger (somebody) into a fight or argument, to pester

دست و یخن شدن [dast-o-yakhan-shudan] *idiom* (*literally:* grabbing by the shirt collar) grab by the neck, physically fighting

دسته [dasta] 1.1 group, detachment ♦ دسته عسکر detachment of soldiers ◊ دسته دسته in groups 1.2 gang, band ♦ دسته دزد gang of thieves 1.3 (also دسته موسیقی) orchestra; ensemble 1.4 sheaf, bunch, bundle; batch; ream ♦ دسته کاغذ batch of paper ◊ دسته گل bouqet of flowers 2.1 (in combination with numbers is used as a numerative) ♦ دو دسته کاغذ two batches of paper ◊ یک دسته کلید one bunch of keys 2.2 دسته کردن to assign by groups, to group

دسته [desta] ¹ 1 handle; grip ♦ دسته کارد knife handle 2 *technical* starting handle, lever

دسته [desta] ² ☞ به دسته بدسته

دسته یی [dastayi] group *adjective*; mass *adjective*; collective ♦ رقص دسته یی group dance

دسته بندی [dastabandi] dividing (into categories, groups), grouping; classification

دسته جمعی [dastajam'i] 1 together, collectively; in chorus 2 joint; group *adjective*, collective ♦ میله های دسته جمعی collective outings into the countryside; picnics

دستی [dasti] 1 done by hand; made with one's own hands ♦ کار دستی handwork 2 hand, intended/ or designed for the hands ♦ بکس دستی small hand-luggage

دستی [desti] *colloquial* right now, immediately, this minute ♦ دستی میاید He will arrive right away

دست یاب [dastyaab]
• دست یاب کردن 1 to find 2 to get, to obtain, to procure

دست یار [dastyaar] assistant, helper (in work); apprentice ♦ دختر دست یار مادر شده است The daughter became [her] mother's helper.

دستیاری [dastyaari] help, assistance

دست یافت [dastyaaft] ☞ دست یاب

دسک [desk] 1 desk, table, (school) desk 2 *technical* disk ♦ دسک کلچ clutch plate

دسمال [desmaal] 1 shawl; kerchief ♦ دسمال بینی handkerchief ◊ دسمال سر head scarf, kerchief ◊ دسمال دست table napkin ◊ دسمال کمر kerchief tied around the waist (of men) 2 (also دسمال روی) towel

دسیسه [dasisa] (*plural* دسایس [dasayes]) intrigue; intrigues; underhand plotting ♦ حتماً دسیسه ای در کار است There is something behind that without fail.

دش [dash] dash

دشت [dasht] 1 steppe; plain 2 semidesert ♦ دشت ودریا vast, spacious, wide; boundless

دشتی [dashti] 1 steppe *adjective*, plain *adjective* 2 wild, field *adjective* (about plants, animals)

دشلمه [deshlama] *colloquial* drinking coffee or tea while sucking small bits of sugar

• چای دشلمه خوردن to drink unsweetened tea while sucking small bits of sugar

دشمن [doshman] enemy, foe ♦ دشمن جانی mortal enemy; deadly enemy

دشمن دار [doshmandaar] being in a state of mortal enmity
• دشمن دار بودن to have mortal enemies, to be the object of a blood fued

دشمن داری [doshmandaari] state of mortal enmity

دشمنی [doshmani] enmity, animosity; hostility; hatred

دشنام [dashnaam] swearing, bad language; curse, oath
• دشنام دادن to rail [at], to scold, to abuse, to reprove, to rebuke, to swear, to curse, to use bad language (به را)

دشوار [doshwaar] *literary* hard, difficult, arduous, laborious, strenuous

دشوار گذر [doshwaargozar] almost impenetrable, almost impassable; inacessible ♦ نقاط دشوار گذر almost impenetrable areas

دعا [doaa] praise, praising, laudation (of God); prayer
• دعا بد calling down misfortunes and disasters (on somebody); curse
• دعا خیر (and) دعا نیک blessing, benediction; prayer about granting good and prosperity
• دعا خواندن to say a prayer, to pray
• دعا گفتن to call down blessings, to pray (for somebody)

دعا گوی [doaagoy] 1 blessing, praying (for somebody) 2 well-wisher

دعا گویی [doaagoyi] praying (for somebody's well-being); wishing (somebody) well

دعاوی [da'aawi] *plural of* دعوا [da'wa] (and) دعوی [da'wi]

دعوا [da'waa] (*plural* دعاوی [da'aawi]) 1 claim, pretension 2 action; suit, lawsuit 3 assertion
• دعوا داشتن to have a claim, to lay claim [to] (به)
• دعوا کردن 1 to bring a suit [against], to bring an action, to announce a claim, to make a claim; to go to court 2 to assert, to declare

دعواجلب [da'waajalab] *colloquial* litigious person

دعواگر [da'waagar] pretender, claimant, plaintiff

دعوت [da'wat] 1 invitation (e.g., to be a guest) 2 reception, banquet, dinner (given in honor of somebody or something)
• دعوت دادن to arrange a reception; to give a dinner (in honor of somebody)
• دعوت کردن 1 to invite (as a guest, etc.) 2 to summon (to something)
• دعوت شدن to be invited (as a guest, to a banquet, etc.)

دعوت نامه [da'watnaama] invitation card

دعوی [da'wi] ☞ دعوا

دغدغه [daghdagha] (also دغدغه خاطر) alarm; anxiety, uneasiness; agitation; commotion, perturbation
• دغدغه خاطر doubt, hesitation; vacillation

دغل [daghal] 1 cheat, swindler, rogue 2 *colloquial* cardsharp (who does not pay gambling debts)

دغلی [daghali] 1 cheating, swindling, roguery 2 *colloquial* cheating (in card games)

دفاتر [dafaater] *literary plural of* دفتر

دفاع [defaa] 1 defense, protection ♦ وزارت دفاع ملی ministry of defense 2 defense (of a dissertation) 3 *legal* defense
• دفاع کردن 1 to protect, to defend (somebody-something) (از) 2 to defend (a dissertation) 3 *legal* to act in (somebody's)

defense
- از جان خود دفاع کردن to protect oneself, to defend oneself
دفاعی [defaa'i] 1 defense *adjective*, defensive ♦ استقامات دفاعی defensive works, fortifications ◊ توان دفاعی defensive might 2 protective; guard; guarding; warning
دفتانگ [deftaang] *grammar* diphthong
دفتر [daftar] (*plural* دفاتر [dafaater]) 1 book (account book, ledger) ♦ دفتر های تجارتی commerical ledgers trade ledgers ◊ دفتر جمیع (and) دفتر کل ledger 2 register, list, roll, inventory 3 office, bureau
دفتردار [daftardaar] office worker, clerk
دفتری [defteri] *medicine* diphtheria
دفع [dáf(a)] 1 repulse of a blow or an attack, rebuff ♦ دفع دشمن repulse of the enemy 2 removal, elimination, overcoming, prevention 3 *legal* defense
- دفع آتش extinguishing a flame or fire, prevention of a fire
- دفع گرسنگی a / the struggle against hunger
- دفع کردن 1 to beat off, to repulse (a blow, an attack); to rebuff, to give a rebuff 2 to remove, to eliminate, to liquidate; to overcome, to prevent
دفعتاً (and) دفعته [daf'atan] suddenly, all of a sudden
دفعه [daf'a (and) dafa'] (*plural* دفعات [dafaat]) time ♦ این دفعه for this once, for this time, this time ◊ برای اولین دفعه for the first time, first
دفن [dáfen] burial, interment ♦ مراسم دفن funeral
- دفن کردن to bury, to inter, to commit to the earth
دفه [dafa] (*also* ن) (د فه سوز ن) eye (of a needle)
دق [deq] 1 sad, melancholy; missing, longing for 2 sadness, melancholy *noun*; boredom, tedium
- دق آوردن (شدن) to be sad, to be melancholy; to be bored ♦ من اینجا دق آوردم I am bored here. ◊ برای اینکه دق نشوید ... so that you won't be bored ...
- ما پشت پدر دق شدیم We miss our father.
- از کسی دق شدن to bear a grudge, to be angry at somebody
دق [daq] 1 ☞ دک 2 ☞ دکه
دقایق [daqaayeq] *plural of* دقیقه
دقت [deqqat] 1 attention ♦ در این مسئله باید دقت تام بعمل آید The most intent attention should be given to this problem. 2 attentiveness; exactness, precision; carefulness, thoroughness, care
- عدم دقت inattentiveness, carelessness
- دقت داشتن (کردن) 1 to be attentive 2 to keep an eye [on]; to look [after]; to watch [over] (something); to investigate, to examine, to scrutinize (در)
- باید دقت کرده شودکه ... it is necessary to see to it that…
دقیت [deqiyat] 1 sadness; melancholy 2 offence, injury, wrong, resentment, grief, chagrin
دقیق [daqiq] 1 exact, precise, accurate, correct 2 careful, thorough 3 fine, delicate
دقیقه [daqiqa] (*plural* دقایق [daqaeq]) minute
دقیقه شماری [daqiqashomaari]
- دقیقه شماری کردن to wait impatiently, to count the minutes
دقیقه گرد [daqiqagard] minute hand
دک [dak]¹
- دک خوردن *colloquial* to knock, bang, or bump against accidently, to run into
- دک ماندن *colloquial* to be stupefied, to be paralyzed on the spot (from surprise, etc.); to be struck dumb, to be dumbfounded, to be taken aback

دک [dak]² charged
- دک کردن to charge
دکاکین [dakaakin] *plural of* دکان
دکان [dokaan] 1 store, shop; stall ♦ دکان نانوایی bakery, baker's shop 2 workshop of a craftsman (who sells his articles on the spot) ♦ دکان مسگر workshop (shop) of a coppersmith
دکانچه [dokaancha] 1 counter 2 bench, shop 3 sleeping platform, bunk; planking
دکاندار [dokaandaar] shopkeeper, merchant
دکانداری [donkaandaari] 1 occupation of a shopkeeper or a merchant 2 *colloquial* ability to sell profitably (by deceiving the purchaser)
- دکانداری کردن 1 to keep shop, to be occupied in trading or vending 2 to fool, to make a fool of (in trading)
دکتاتوری [dektaatori] dictatorship
دکتر [doktor] ☞ داکتر
دکتورا [dokotoraa] ☞ داکتری
دک دک [dokdok]
- دک دک کردن *colloquial* to beat strongly, to thump (about the heart)
دکشنری [dekshenari] dictionary
دکمه [dokma] ☞ تکمه
دکه [daka] *colloquial* instant, moment; twinkling ♦ یک دکه خو نکدم I didn't get a minute's sleep.
دگر [degar] ☞ دیگر
دگرجنرال [degarjanraal] *military* general
دگرمن [dagarman] lieutenant colonel
دگروال [dagarwaal] colonel
دل [del] 1 *anatomy* heart 2 heart, soul 3 stomach, belly; womb ♦ دل و جگر pluck; liver ◊ دلم درد میکند My stomach hurts. 4 strength of spirit; courage, boldness
- دل تان ☞ دل تان
- دل ناخواه(ه) unwillingly, without any special desire
- دل ناخواه عذر بسیار *proverb* When one's heart is not in something, there are many excuses.
- دل و نادل *colloquial* willy-nilly; like it or not
- از دل بیرون not enjoying favor, not being liked [by somebody]
- از دل وجان with one's whole heart, from the bottom of one's soul
- به دل خود (and) به دل to oneself; by oneself
- درزیر دل in the depth of one's soul
- دل پر و چاغر خالی *proverb* The heart is full, but the craw is empty. (i.e., There are many wishes, but no opportunities to realize them.)
- دل مادر به بچه از بچه به کوچه *proverb* A mother's heart [reaches out] to a son, but a son's [heart] [reaches out] to the streets.
- یک دل نه صد دل عاشق شد *colloquial* He has fallen madly in love.
- دل انداختن to lose one's presence of mind; to be timid, to quail, to be frightened
- دل باختن to be carried away, to be enamored; to be fascinated, to be captivated (به)
- دل بستن to become romantically attached (to somebody); to fall in love with; to grow fond of (به)
- دل دادن to fall in love (به)
- دل زدن to doubt, to hesitate; to vacillate ♦ من دل میزنم I am vacillating

149

- دل کردن to show courage or boldness, to venture (at something); to dare
- دل کندن (از) to grow cold, to lose interest, to stop loving;
- دل گرفتن to cheer up *intransitive*, to recover one's spirits, to get confidence (in one's own powers)
- از دل انداختن to forget, to cast out of one's head
- از دل بر آمدن (رفتن) to be forgotten, to be cast out of [somebody's] head
- به دل نشستن (and) به دل چسپیدن *colloquial* to be retained in one's memory, to be engraved in one's memory
- دل خالی کردن to confide (in somebody); to talk heart-to-heart ♦ بیاکه دلی خالی کنیم Let's talk heart-to-heart!
- دل خود را یخ کردن to vent [one's] malice, to vent [one's] anger (on somebody); to get even (with somebody)
- دل کسی را آب کردن 1 to touch somebody's heart, to touch deeply; to move somebody (emotionally) 2 to torment somebody with prolonged waiting
- دل کسی را بدست آوردن *literary* to return somebody's love, to satisfy somebody's desires
- دل کسی را خوش کردن 1 to entertain, to amuse somebody 2 to make somebody happy
- دل کسی آمدن *colloquial* to share somebody's pain or grief; to put oneself in somebody's place; to sympathize with somebody
- سیر از دل گرسنه نمی آید *proverb* A satiated person cannot understand a hungry person.
- به دل جای دادن to harbor (spite, hatred) in [one's heart
- به دل خود گفتن to think to oneself
- به دل کسی نبودن *colloquial* not to depend on anybody's wishes, not to be under anybody's will ♦ این کار به دل من و تو نیست This matter does not depend on my wish or yours.
- دل او بدبد میشود He feels sick. / He feels bad.
- دلم (آب)خورد *colloquial* My heart jumped / thumped (with joy).
- دلم به حالتت میسوزد *colloquial* I pity you. / I am sorry for you.
- دلم تنگ شد *colloquial* I was bored. / I was pining. (برای)
- دلش سیاه شد *colloquial* He is bored. / He is sick [to death] of everything. (از)
- دلم نشد که... *colloquial* I didn't want to.
- دلش از دلخانه برآمد (and) دلش بیجاشد *colloquial* His heart sank. / His heart skipped a beat.
- دل از دلخانه رفتن *idiom* (*literally:* one's heart to go out of the cage) to be sad, to lose hope
- دلش نمیخواهد He has no liking [for].
- (در)دل شب late at night; at midnight
- جائیکه دل می ره پای می ره *saying* (*literally:* where heart goes, foot goes) Home is where the heart is.
- دل به دریا زدن *idiom* (*literally:* to put one's heart in the river) looking for an easy way out, (to get away from difficulties)

دل پری [delpuree] *colloquial* (*literally:* full heart), complete trust, full confidence

دلادل [delaadel] ☞ دلدل [deldel]

دلار [dalaar] dollar

دل آزار [delaazaar] 1.1 sad, grievous; distressing 1.2 cruel (about a sweetheart or a loved one) 2 tormentor; offender

دل آزرده [delaazorda] offended; grieved ♦ شاید از من دل آزرده است Perhaps I have hurt his feelings?

دلاک [dallaak] 1 barber 2 barber at a bathhouse (who performs bloodletting) 3 bathhouse attendant

دلال [dallaal] 1 middleman (in commercial transaction); broker, agent ♦ دلال بورس stockbroker 2 *colloquial* procuress; procurer; pimp

دلالت [dalaalat] 1 advancing arguments, proof, evidence 2 instructions; setting (somebody on a path, etc.)
- دلالت کردن 1 to testify, to prove, to demonstrate (بر) 2 to be confirmed; to be corroborated 3 to set (somebody on a path); to persuade; to incite (به) ♦ تو مارا به این راه دلالت کردی You set us on this path.

دلالی [dallaali] 1 negotiation (in trade or bargaining); broking; brokerage 2 (also اجرت دلالی) commission; brokerage

دل آور [delaawar] 1 brave, bold, daring, courageous 2.1 brave man, courageous man; bold spirit, daredevil 2.2 *masculine proper name* Delawar

دل آوری [delaawari] bravery, boldness, daring; courage, valor

دلاویز [delaaweez] delightful; ravishing; exquisite; captivating; fascinating; charming, pleasing, pleasant

دلایل [dalaayel] *plural of* دلیل

دلباخته [delbaakhta] 1 ☞ دلداده 2 having lost one's head, having become frightened

دلباز [delbaaz] ☞ دل واز

دل بد [delbad]
- من دل بد هستم 1to feel sick ♦ بد بودن (شدن) I feel sick. 2 to be hurt, to be offended, to be angry (از) ♦ او از شما دل بد است He is angry at you. / He was hurt by you.

دل بدک [delbadak] ☞ دل بدی 1

دل بدی [delbadi] 1 sickness, nausea, faintness 2 offence; injury; wrong; feeling of resentment (toward somebody)
- دل بدی آوردن (به) to make (somebody) sick

دلبر [delbar] 1 beloved (female), sweetheart (female) 2 fascinating, bewitching, captivating, charming (about a female) 3 *feminine proper name* Delbar

دلبستگی [delbastagi] affection; love

دلبند [delband] 1 close to the heart, dear ♦ فرزند دلبند dear child 2 liver; pluck

دل پاک [delpaak] sincere, tender, loving; simple-hearted; artless

دلپذیر [delpazir] ☞ دلپسند

دلپر [delpor] 1 assured, sure, confident, trusting (in somebody or something) 2 relying (on somebody-something)
- دلپر بودن 1 to be confident (in somebody), to trust (از) 2 to rely (از)

دلپری [delpori] confidence (in something)
- به دلپری کسی with somebody's support; relying on somebody

دلپسند [delpesand] 1 attractive, alluring; inviting; charming, delightful 2 nice, sweet; desired

دلتا [deltaa] *geography* delta ♦ دلتا دریا river delta

دلتان [deletaan] *colloquial*
- دلتان As you please! / As you wish!

دل تنگ [deltang] 1 depressed, despondent; sad, cheerless, doleful 2 bored

دل تنگی [deltangi] 1 depression, despondency, dejection 2 boredom, tedium

دلجگر [deljegar] ☞ دلبند 2

150

دلجوش [deljosh] *colloquial* heartburn

دلجویی [deljoyi] comfort, consolation, kindness; sympathy
- دلجویی کردن 1 to comfort, to console; to show much kindness 2 to express sympathy

دل چرکی [delchirkee] *colloquial* (*literally:* dirty heart) being upset with someone

دلچسپ [delchasp] 1 interesting, fascinating; absorbing ♦ فلم دلچسپ an interesting film 2 pleasing, pleasant, attractive (about something)

دلچسپی [delchaspi] interest (in something); enthusiasm or passion (for something)
- دلچسپی گرفتن and داشتن to be interested [in]; to be carried away [by]; to be keen [on]; to show the liveliest interest (به،در)

دل خانه [delkhaana] *colloquial* thorax

دلخراش [delkharaash] 1 touching one's soul or heart; startling, staggering, rending, heartrending 2 harsh, sharp, unpleasant

دلخسته [delkhasta] 1 grieving, suffering 2 despondent, depressed

دلخوا(ه) [delxaa (h)] 1.1 desirable, welcome ♦ خواب دلخوا desirable answer 1.2 dear to the heart, desired
- زن دلخوا beloved wife 2.1 will, wish, desire ♦ به دلخوا خود at one's own pleasure, at one's own discretion 2.2 wish (carried out according to the conditions of a game)
- چناغ دلخوا bet (according to which the loser must carry out any wish of the winner)

دلخوری [delkhori] *colloquial* irritation, vexation, annoyance; emotional experience
- دلخوری کردن to be vexed, to be annoyed; to deplore; to regret (something); to suffer

دلخوش [delkhoj] satisfied with everything; glad, joyful, good-humored
- خودرا دلخوش کردن to enjoy oneself, to make merry

دلخوشی [delkhoji] happy mood, good-humored mood; serene state of mind
- دلخوشی دادن to entertain (hopes); to comfort, to console; to calm, to quiet, to soothe

دل خون [delkhun] seized by sorrow or by grief; suffering deeply

دلداده [deldaada] having given one's heart; in love, enamored [of] ♦ داستان دو دلداده tale of two lovers

دلداری [deldaari] ☞ دلجویی

دلدرد [deldard] (and) دلدردی [deldardi] pain in the stomach, colic

دلدل [daldal] swamp, marsh

دلدل [deldel]
- دلدل کردن *colloquial* not to make up one's mind, to vacillate, to manifest indecisiveness

دلدلزار [daldalzaar] swampy terrain, marshes, swamps

دلدلک [deldelak] *colloquial* vacillating, not making up one's mind (to do something)

دلده [dalda] 1 groats (made of wheat) 2 porridge or thick soup (made of coarse-ground wheat grains)
- کور هم میداندکه دلده شور است *proverb* If the porridge is salty, even a blind person will notice.

دل ربا [delrabaa] 1 charming, delightful, fascinating, bewitching 2.1 a beauty, a charmer (female) 2.2 sweetheart, beloved (female)

دل ربایی [delrabaayi] charm; fascination; beauty
- دل ربایی کردن to captivate, to charm, to bewitch

دلزده [delzada]
- من از این کار دلزده شدم I am sick to death of this work.

دلستان [delsetaan] *literary* ☞ د ل ر با

دل سرد [delsard] grown cold (toward something); disappointed; having lost interest ♦ او از این کار دل سرد شد He lost interest in this work / job / matter / business.

دل سردی [delsardi] 1 coldness; disappointment 2 indifference

دل سوخته [delsokhta] 1 suffering 2 *colloquial* in love, enamored ♦ من دل سوخته او هستم I am burning with love for her.

دلسوز [delsoz] 1 tenderhearted, compassionate; sympathetic 2 solicitous 3 sorrowful, mournful; touching; pathetic ♦ آهنگ دلسوز a melancholy tune

دلسوزی [delsozi] 1 pity; sympathy 2 solicitous attitude; concern

دل سیاه [delsiyaah] *colloquial* 1 experiencing aversion, repugnance, loathing (toward something) 2 vexing; bearing a grudge

دل سیاهی [delsiyahi] *colloquial* 1 aversion, repugnance, loathing 2 offense, injury, wrong; vexation, annoyance; grief, chagrin

دلفریب [delfereeb] 1 seductive; deceptive, delusive 2 charming, bewitching

دلک [delak]
- دلک گوش *colloquial* lobe of the ear

دلکش [delkaj] charming, fascinating, likable; attractive

دلکشا [delkojaa] gladdening the heart, enrapturing, delighting
- کاخ دلکشا (and) قصر دلکشا Dilkusha (former royal palace in Kabul)

دل کشالی [delkashaalee] *colloquial* anxiety, apprehension, worry

دل کلان کردن [del-kalaan-kardan] *colloquial* (*literally:* to make one's heart bigger) to be big-hearted, to be generous

دل گرفتن [del-gereftan] *colloquial* (*literally:* to gain heart) to gain confidence, to get the courage

دل گیر [delgeer] *colloquial* 1 sad, depress 2 boring

دلکو [delko] *technical* breaker, interrupter

دلگرم [delgram] (*opposite of* دلسرد) 1 full of ardor, full of zeal; zealous 2 keenly interested (by something), fascinated, enthralled ♦ او بکار خود دلگرم است He is fascinated by his work.

دلگرمی [delgarmi] (*opposite of* دل سردی) zeal, inclination (for something); fascination

دلگیر [delgir] 1 depressing, sad, cheerless 2 angry, hurt; grieved, chagrined

دلگی مشر [delgaymejeer] *military* commander of a section

دل مرده [delmorda] 1 insensible, torpid (e.g., from grief) 2 languid, apathetic

دل نواز [delnawaaz] pleasant, sweet; delightful
- آهنگ دل نواز bewitching, enchanting, or fascinating melody

دلو [dalw] 1 *astronomy* Aquarius 2 Dalu (11th month of the Afghan solar year; corresponds to January-February)

دل واز [delwaaz] *colloquial* pictorial, picturesque

دلوگرده [delogorda] *colloquial* 1 patience, self-control 2 zeal, fervor, ardor; courage

دله [dala] *colloquial* procurer, procuress; pimp
دلگی [dalagi] *colloquial* pandering, pimping
دلیر [daleer (and) delèr] ☞ دل آور
دلیری [daleeri (and) deleeri] ☞ دل آوری
دلیل [daleel] (*plural* دلایل [dalaayel]) 1 reason, foundation, basis; argument, proof, evidence ♦ به این دلیل که... on the basis that... 2 sign, indication; criterion
• دلیل آوردن to cite reasons, to argue; to prove; to demonstrate
دم [dam]¹ 1 breathing, respiration, heavy breath; sigh ♦ دم سرد a heavy sigh 2 steam, fumes ♦ دم دیگ steam from a kettle 3 (also دم شکم) gas (in the intestines, bowels) 4 bellows
• دم انداختن to inflate, to fill with air
• دم خوردن 1 to be deceived, to labor under a delusion, to be tempted or enticed 2 ☞ دم کشیدن
• دم دادن 1 *colloquial* to deceive, to seduce; to delude 2 ☞ دم کردن
• دم کردن 1 to brew (tea); to steep (herbs, etc.) 2 to steam; to stew, to braise ♦ پلو دم کردن to let pilaf stew 3 *colloquial* to charm away an illness (by blowing in the patient's face)
• دم کشیدن 1 to breathe 2 to be brewing, to be brewed (about tea) 3 to be ready (after cooking) on steam; to be stewed
• دم گرفتن 1 ☞ دم راست کردن 2 ☞ دم کشیدن b, c
• دم نبر آوردن not to utter a word, not to breathe a word
• دم راست کردن to take a breath, to take a short rest
• دم فرو بردن to grow silent, to fall silent, to lapse into silence
• به دم آمدن *colloquial* to gather one's strength (after an illness), to get better, to recover; to convalesce
• چه دم داری؟ *colloquial* How are you?
دم [dam]² moment, instant ♦ به یک دم instantly, in a moment; immediately, at once, right away
• دم به دم ☞ دم بدم
• دم را غنیمت شمردن to make use of the moment, to enjoy the moment, not to miss the opportunity, not to lose the chance
• دم غنیمت است Take the opportunity! / Seize the moment!
• دم کسی چاق بودن[dame-kasay-chaq-boodan] *idiom* (*literally:* someone's heart beign fat) fat and happy, to be lucky and fortunate
دم [dam]³ 1.1 blade, point (of a knife, of a sword) 1.2 edge (of something), boundary, border 2.1 دم by; at; near *denominative preposition* ♦ دم راه by the road 2.2 before, on the eve [of]
• دم مرگ 1 near death, on the verge of death 2 death's hour, the hour of death
• دم راه کسی برآمدن *colloquial* to go out to meet somebody, to meet somebody
• دم راه کسی را گرفتن to stand in somebody's way threateningly, to block somebody's way
دم [dom] tail ♦ دم طاوس peacock's tail
• دم به دم in a line, in a row, in file; in single file
• دم جنباندن *colloquial* 1 to wag a tail 2 to be obsequious, to fawn; to cringe
• دم کسی را بریدن not to let somebody (go somewhere), to scare away, to drive off (از)
• دمت سیخ باشد *colloquial* Never set foot [here] anymore!
• دم گاو *botany* mullein
دمبدم [damaadam] ☞ دمبدم

دماغ [damaagh] 1 (also سر دماغ) brain, cerebrum ♦ دماغ کو چک cerebellum 2 *colloquial* nose 3 presumption, arrogance, haughtiness
• دماغ کردن to turn up one's nose, to put on airs
• از دماغ خود کشیدن *colloquial* 1 to cast (something) out of [one's] head, to stop thinking about something (را) 2 to concoct, to fabricate
• سر دماغ بودن to be cheerful, to be in good spirits
• دماغش سوخت He became angry. / He is infuriated.
دماغسوز [damaaghsoz] nervous; angry, cross
• دماغ سوز کردن to anger, to make angry, to upset, to ruffle
دماغه [damaagha] 1 *geography* cape 2 jut (e.g., of a mountain)
دماغی [damaghi] 1 cerebral, brain *adjective*; mental; intellectual ♦ کار دماغی mental work 2 *colloquial* arrogant, haughty
دمب [domb] *colloquial* ☞ دم [dom]
• دمب کسی را سیخ کردن *colloquial* to drive away, to send away, to send somebody packing
دمبال [dombaal] ☞ دنبال
دمباله [dombaala] ☞ دنباله
دم بدم [dambadan] 1 continuously; frequently, often 2 continuous; frequent
دمبدولی [dambaduli] swinging by the hands and feet (children's game)
دمبک [dambak] tambourine, tambourin
• دمبک زدن to beat a tambourine or tambourin
دمبک [dombak] *colloquial* [small] tail
• دمبک زدن *colloquial* 1 to wag a tail (about a dog) 2 to flatter, to fawn, to adulate
دمبل [dombal] (and) دمبل دانه [dombaldana] boil, carbuncle
دمبوره [dambura] dambura (musical instrument similar to mandolin)
دمبه [domba] ☞ دنبه
دمپخت [dampokht] prepared in steam ♦ برنج دمپخت rice for pilaf (prepared in steam)
• دمپخت شدن *colloquial* to sweat, to perspire, to be covered with sweat (from the heat)
دمپخت [dampuskht] *slang* (*literally:* steamed rice) spinster, old maid (a woman has remained single beyond the conventional age for marring) *offensive*
دمپنگ [dempeng] (and) دمپینگ [demping] dumping
دمترک [damtarak] ☞ دامترک
دم چاشت [dame-chaasht] *colloquial* high noon, noon-time
دمچی [domchi] breeching (part of harness)
دمدار [damdaar] elastic
دم درحال [damdarhaal] *colloquial* right away, right now; in an instant, in a moment
دمدم [damdam]¹ sound of a drum or of a tambourine; drumbeat
دمدم [damdam]²
• دمدم صبح *colloquial* dawn, daybreak; the hour before dawn or before daybreak; at dawn, at daybreak
دمدمی مزاج [damdami-mazaaj] *colloquial* wishy-washy, capricious, unstable (person) ♦ آدم دمدمی مزاج کاری را انجام داده نمیتواند A capricious person cannot accomplish anything
دم راستی [damraasti] a short rest, a short respite

دم ساز [damsaaz] 1.1 agreeable, friendly, amicable 1.2 harmonious 2 (also رفیق دم ساز) bosom friend

دمش [damesh] 1 appearance of shoots, sprouting of shoots 2 swelling (of the bowels or intestine), flatulence

دمغازه [domghaaza] *anatomy* (also استخوان دمغازه) coccyx, sacrum

دم غچی [domeghochi]
- سوهان دم غچی *technical* rhombic file

دمک [damak]¹ manual iron roller (for leveling roads)

دمک [damak]² 1 loop stitch 2 overstitching loops

دمگر [damgar]¹ worker at the forge (in blacksmith's shop)

دمگر [damgar]² *colloquial* sorcerer who charms away illness; exorcist; charmer (e.g., of snakes)

دمگری [damgari]¹ blowing with bellows; blacksmithing

دمگری [damgari]² *colloquial* sorcery, charming away illness, exorcising illness

دمگیری [damgiri] break (in work), rest; respite

دموکراتیک [demokraatik] democratic ♦ مرام دموکراتیک democratic program

دموکراسی [demokraasi] democracy ♦ دموکراسی ملی national democracy

دمه [dama] 1 haze; fog 2 swelling, rising (e.g., of a river)
- آب دمه کرد و از سر بند گذشت to swell (about a river) ♦ The water rose and gushed through the dam.

دمیدن [damidan] 1 to break, to glimmer (about dawn, daybreak) 2 to sprout, to send out shoots or sprouts ♦ سبزه دمید The grass sprouted. 3 to show, to sprout (about mustache, a beard)

دنبال [dombaal] 1.1 back part (of something) 1.2 tail
- دنبال (also ازدنبال (and) به دنبال) 1 behind; immediately after; following closely *denominative preposition* 2 (also به دنبال) for; to fetch (with verbs to go for …, to bring, etc.)
- دنبال کسی [following] after somebody, in pursuit of somebody
- در را به دنبال خود بست He closed the door behind himself.
- دنبال کردن to follow after somebody, to pursue somebody
- دنبال کسی(چیزی)گشتن to seek; to look for, to search for somebody or something

دنباله [dombaala] 1.1 sequel; continuation; consequences ♦ این مقاله دنباله دارد This article has a continuation / sequel. 1.2 ☞ دنبال 1 2 to include a secret or hidden meaning within itself ♦ حرف او دنباله داشت Something was hidden behind his words.
- دنباله داشتن to have a sequel; to have consequences

دنباله دار [dombaaladaar] 1 continuing; long; prolonged 2 entailing consequences

دنبل [dambal (and) danbal] dumbbells

دنبوره [dambura] ☞ دمبوره

دنبه [domba] 1 (also دنبه گوسفند) fat tail (of a sheep) 2 sheep fat
- دنبه کردن to grow fat or plump; to grow a fat tail

دنبه دار [dombadaar] fat-tailed (of a sheep)

دند [dand]¹ 1 natural reservoir; lake 2 stagnant water; puddle
- دند شدن to become stale or stagnant (about water); to form a lake or puddle

دند [dand]² fertile green plain

دندان [dandaan] tooth; teeth ♦ دندان پیشین front tooth, incisor ◊ دندان کرسی molar
- دندان خاییدن *colloquial* to gnash [one's] teeth; to threaten, to menace
- دندان کشیدن 1 to pull out a tooth, to extract a tooth 2 to cut, to erupt (about a child's teeth)♦ این طفل دندان کشید The child cut his teeth.
- دندان کندن to sink [one's] teeth; to bite, to be in the habit of biting (about animals)
- دندان گرفتن to grasp with the teeth, to bite
- دندان بر جگر گذاشتن to endure by clenching the teeth; to do (something) reluctantly or grudgingly
- دندان تیز کردن بالای to covet something, to have one's eye on (something), to solicit (something)
- دندان چیزی راکشیدن to stop soliciting something, to give up, to renounce something
- دندان سفید کردن to show [one's] teeth; to snap [at]; to bare [one's] teeth

دندان قرچک [dandaan-qarchak] *slang* (*literally:* gnashing of teeth) to bare the teeth, to threaten one's getting revenge

دندان ساز [dandaansaaz] dentist; specialist in making dentures

دندان سازی [dandaansaazi] dentist's office, dental laboratory or workshop

دندان شکن [dandaanshekan] 1.1 crushing, tooth-shattering (blow, answer, etc.) 2 almost impassable, dangerous (about a road, a pass) 2 dandanshekan (name of a gorge and a pass)

دندان قرچک [dandaanqerechak] *colloquial* gnashing of teeth
- دندان قرچک کردن to grit one's teeth, to gnash one's teeth

دندان قرچک [dandaan-qarchak] *slang* (*literally:* gnashing of teeth) to bare the teeth, to threaten one's getting revenge

دندانک [dandaanak]
- دندانک زدن *colloquial* to set [one's] teeth to chattering (from the cold)

دندانه [dandaana] 1 tooth; cog, lug; denticle, serration ♦ دندانه اره teeth of a saw ◊ دندانه سوهان cut of a file 2 step; steps (of a staircase, etc.)
- دندانه تاک cutting or graft of a grapevine

دندانه دار [dandaanadaar] 1 toothed, cogged, having teeth or cogs ♦ چرخ دندانه دار cog wheel 1.2 gear, pinion 2 jagged, notched, serrated 3 broken, jagged, meandering (about a coastline)

دندانه کشی [dandaanakashi] *technical* milling, cutting ♦ ماشین دندانه کشی milling machine

دندانی [dandaani] *grammar* dental (about consonants)

دندوره [dandora] *colloquial* to make a big deal out of something, to ballyhoo

دنده [danda] 1 club, stick (for games played with a ball); (tennis) racket 2 (machine-) turned plank or strip (of a door, mirror, etc.) 3 stem, stalk; cutting; graft

دنده پنج [dandapanj] *technical* 1 stop 2 shoe

دنده کلک [dandakelak] tipcat (children's game)

دنگ [dang]¹ 1 peal, ringing, clanging; clank, clang; noise, tap (e.g., of metal) 2 ☞ دنگ دنگ
- دنگ Boom! / Bang! / Ding!
- دیوانه رادنگی *proverb* For a madman it is enough to hear any kind of ringing (to set him off).

دنگ [dang]² *colloquial* 1 unbalanced; whimsical; crazy, mad 2 dumbfounded, flabbergasted; stricken, staggered

دنگ دنگ [dangdang] 1 sound of a tambourine or a kettledrum; sound of a bell or a handbell ♦ دنگ دنگ Ding-dong! 2 *colloquial* racket, ballyhoo; conversations, talk (around something)

دنی [dani] *literary* low, contemptible, mean, base

دنیا [donyaa] 1 world, universe ♦ دنیا حیوانی animal world 2 (*opposite of* آخرت) this world, earthly world, earthly affairs ♦ دنیا است Such is this world! 3 riches, wealth, worldly blessings

• از دنیا رفتن to die
• به دنیا آمدن to appear in the world, to be born
• چشم از دنیا پوشیدن (and) از دنیا تیر شدن to abandon this world, to die

دنیاپرستی [donyaaparasti] love for riches or wealth; attachment to worldly goods or blessings

دنیادار [donyaadaar] 1 rich, wealthy 2 a rich man

دنیاوی [donyaawi] ☞ دنیوی

دنیایی [donyaayi] 1 world *adjective*, worldwide; universal 2 ☞ دنیوی

دنیوی [donyawi] 1 mundane, everyday; worldly 2 secular; temporal; worldly (not spiritual)

دو [du] two ♦ هر دو both ◊ هر دوی آنها both of them

• دو دو [dudu]
• دو به دو [dubadu]
• از دو یکی کردن *colloquial* to settle (a quarrel); to find a compromise

دو [daw]¹ 1 *present tense stem* دویدن 2.1 run, running ♦ دو اسپ run of a horse 2.2 *aviation* run ♦ دو نشست ◊ طول landing run دو بیجا ♦ length of run 3 running about, bustle useless bustle

• دو دو [dawadaw] ☞ دوادو
دو [daw]² 1 raising, doubling the rate or stake (when purchasing); auction 2 stake (in a game)
• دو زدن to bet on something (in a game of chance)
• دو بالا کردن 1 to give more (at an auction) 2 to double the stake (in a game)

دو [daw]³ *colloquial* swearing, bad language or abuse; scolding, reprimand
• دو زدن to abuse, to rail [at], to scold, to reprimand
• دو شدن to be ashamed

دوا [dawaa] (*plural* ادویه [adwiya]) 1 medicine, medicinal remedy 2 chemical; chemicals
• دوادرد دندان کندن است *proverb* The (best) medicine for a toothache is to pull (the tooth).
• دوا شدن to be cured
• دوا کردن to treat (medically)

دوا و درمان [dawaa-o-darmaan] *idiom* (*literally:* medicine and treatment) medical treatment ♦ برادرش دوا و درمانش را میکند His brother takes care of his medical treatment.

دوآبه [duaaba] place or point of confluence of two rivers

دواپاشی [dawaapaashi] spraying with chemicals ♦ دواپاشی کردن to spray (crops) with chemicals

دوات [dawaat] inkwell

دواخانه [dawaakhaana] pharmacy, drugstore

دوادو [dawaadaw] 1 running about; fuss, bustle; hurry, haste 2 on the run
• دوادو کردن to run back and forth, to rush about (in search of something), to fuss, to bustle

دوازده [dawaazda(h)] twelve

دواساز [dawaasaaz] apothecary, pharmacist

دواسازی [dawaasaazi] manufacture of medicines or pharmaceutics

دوافروشی [dawaaforoshi] pharmacy, drugstore; sale or selling of medicines

دوام [dawaam] 1 duration 2 durability ♦ دوام دادن to continue
• دوام داشتن 1 to be long-lived; lasting, to keep a long time 2 to be durable, to serve for a long time (about things)
• دوام نداشتن to be short-lived, to be fragile; not to keep for long ♦ آتش آن چوب دیر دوام نمی کند This firewood burns for a short time.
• دوام کردن ☞ دوام داشتن a

دوام دار [dawaamdaar] long, prolonged; durable ♦ صلح دوام دار durable peace

دوان [dawaan] 1 running 2 (*also* دوان دوان) at a run, at full speed 3 (second component of compound words with meanings "laying" / "installing") ♦ نل دوان pipe fitter; plumber; sanitary engineering specialist (i.e., layer of sewer pipes)

دواندن [dawaandan] 1 to drive, to urge on; to set at full gallop (a horse, etc.) 2 to wind (e.g., threads) 3 to lay (pipes, cable) 4 to crush and drive off (an enemy)

دوایر [dawaayer] *plural of* دایره 4

دوباره [dubaara] 1 anew, again 2 repeated; begun anew ♦ کار دوباره repeated work

دوبالا [dubaalaa] ☞ دوچند

دوباله [dubaala] (*also* طیاره دوباله) biplane

دوبدو [dubadu] eye to eye; in private, privately; face to face

دوبدو [dawbadaw]
• دوبدو شدن *colloquial* to have words (with somebody), to quarrel; to swear at one another,

دوبرابر [dubarabar] ☞ دوچند (and) دوچندان

دوبرا [dubara] broad, double (about cloth or fabric)

دوبلاژ [dublaazh] dubbing (of a film)
• دوبلاژ شدن to be dubbed (about a film)
• دوبلاژ کردن to dub (a film)

دو بندی [dubandi] place or point of confluence of two mountain rivers (flowing out of gorges)

دوبوره [dubura] land which is sown and provides a harvest the year after next

دوبی [dobi] laundryman; laundress

دوبیتی [dubaiti] *literary* 1 a stanza of two couplets (four lines of verse) 2 a quatrain; stanza

دوبی خانه [dobikhaana] laundry

دو پاره شدن [dupaara-shudan] *colloquial* (*literally:* to split into two piece) blow up any minute, someone about to explode due to anger ♦ به حدی قهر است که کم مانده دو تکه یا دو پاره شود He is so angry that he could explode anytime.

دوپره [dupara] *technical* two-bladed ♦ پروانه دوپره two-bladed propeller

دوپشته [duposhta]
• دوپشته سوار بودن to ride double, to ride two together (on a horse, bicycle, etc.)

دوپله یی [dupallayi] folding, two-leafed, two-section ♦ الماری دوپله یی two section cupboard

دو پلیته [dupalita]
• دامن دوپلیته skirt with counterfolds, in a counterfold

دوپوسته [duposhta] *colloquial* 1 having two envelopes 2 pretender, dissembler; plotter, intriguer

دوپ [dopa] *colloquial* a gross fraud; deceiver; charlatan
* دوپه کردن to wheedle or extort money from somebody by deceit

دوپیازه [dupiyaaza] meat broth with onion and vinegar

دوتا [dutaa] 1 two pieces, two items; a pair 2.1 divided in two; cut or broken into two halves 2.2 bent double, bent in two
* دوتا دوتا in twos; two by two
* دوتا دوتا بیایید Come in two by two!
* دوتا کردن 1 to divide into two parts, to cut in two 2 *colloquial* to run away, to disappear, to vanish

دوتار [dutaar] dutar (two-string musical instrument)

دوتایی [dutaayi] *cards* two, deuce ♦ دوتایی خشت deuce of diamonds

دوچار [duchar] to undergo something, to encounter something
* به چیزی دو چار شدن to subject somebody to something
* کسی را به چیزی دو چار کردن to bring something down on somebody

دوچند [duchand] (and) دوچندان [ducandan] 1 twice as much, doubly 2 twice as large; double
* دوچند کردن to double, to increase by double

دوخت [dokht] embroidering, sewing; cut, style; cutting out (a dress)

دوختن [dokhtan]¹ (*present tense stem* دوز [doz]) to sew, to embroider, to sew on or to; to sew up, to mend
* چشم دوختن 1 to stare [at], to direct one's fixed stare [at] (بر،به) 2 to covet; to have one's eye on (بر،به)

دوختن [dokhtan]² (*present tense stem* دوش) to milk, to milk dry ♦ کارش دوختن گلو بود Her responsibility was to milk the cows.

دوخت و برش [dokhtoboresh]
* کورسهای دوخت وبرش courses in cutting and sewing

دود [dud] smoke, fumes; soot; lampblack
* دود انداختن to smoke, to fill with smoke
* دود دادن to cure in smoke, to fumigate
* دود کردن to give off smoke, to smoke, to burn (e.g., of a cigar)
* به دود کسی کور شدن to suffer for nothing or for no purpose (*literally*, to lose one's sight because of somebody else's smoke)
* دود کسی برآمدن [dood-kasay-baraamadan] *idiom* (*literally*: smoke is coming out of someone) somebody who has lost everything, down and out, someone's life has been destroyed
* دود دل deep grief, deep sorrow, mental suffering

دودآلود [dudaalud] 1 shrouded, blanketed in smoke, smoky 2 smoke-blackened, all covered with soot

دودبوی [dudboy] permeated with the smell of smoke (about food, etc.)

دودپر [dudpor] ☞ دودآلود
* چای جوش دودپر smoke-blackened boiler or kettle

دودرو [dudraw] 1 aperture for exit of smoke; an opening in wall into which a stovepipe is placed 2 *technical* flue, chimney, chimney block ♦ گلدرهای کانکریتی دودرو concrete chimney blocks

دودزده [dudzada] 1 smoked ♦ ماهی دودزده smoked fish 2 smoke-blackened, covered with soot

دودسته [dudasta] (and) dudesta 1 with both hands, by two hands 2 with two handles, two-handed

دودکردن [dood-kardan]¹ *slang* (*literally*: to smoke) angry, smoke is coming out of one's ears *derogatory*

دودکردن [dood-kardan]² *slang* (*literally*: to smoke) to light up (cigarette, hash etc)
* چیزی را دوستـه گرفتن to take something with both hands

دودکش [dudkash] chimney, smokestack; exhaust pipe; flue

دودل [dudel] (and) دودلک [dudelak] (and) دودله [dudela] vacillating, indecisive
* دودل بودن to vacillate, not to make up one's mind (to do something)

دودلی [dudeli] vacillation, indecisiveness; uncertainty; lack of confidence ♦ بادودلی indecisively, uncertainly

دودمان [dud (e) maan] *literary* 1 hearth, home 2 family, kin, tribe

دودو [dudu] in twos, in pairs, two by two ♦ دودو تقسیم کن Divide (give out) in twos!

دودو [dawdaw]¹ ☞ دوادو [dawaadaw]
* به دودو at a run; on the run

دودو [dawdaw]² ☞ دوبدو [dawbodaw]

دوده [doda] *colloquial* flatcake (made of corn or millet flour)

دودی [dudi] smoky (about a color)
* عینک دودی sunglasses

دور [dawr] 1.1 *plural* ادوار [adwaar] 1.2 movement in a circle, going round, whirling, spinning, rotation, revolution 2 time; epoch, age, era 3.1 *colloquial* sequence (in a game) 3.2 دور (also به دور) around, round *denominative prepositions* ♦ دور وپیش surroundings; environs; neighborhood ◊ دور خانه around the house
* دور خوردن to go round, to spin, to whirl, to revolve, to rotate, to turn (e.g., around an axis or axle)
* دور دادن to turn, to whirl, to spin, to revolve, to rotate *transitive*
* دور زدن to go around, to bypass, to skirt, to describe a circle
* دور کسی (چیزی) گرفتن to surround; to encircle, to form a ring around somebody or something; to gather around somebody or something

دور [dur] 1 distant, faraway, remote ♦ راه دور distant journey, long way 2 far off, far away; in the distance ♦ دور ودراز lengthy; prolonged; protracted; long ◊ از دور from a distance, from far away, from afar
* دور افکندن (انداختن) to throw away; to throw out
* از خود دور کردن to drive off, to drive away from oneself
* دور از حالی که ... *colloquial* God keep it away! / May this / it not be repeated! ♦ دور از حالی که شما مریض بودید May the time when you were sick not come again!

دورادور [dawraadawr] 1 everywhere, all round, on all sides; from all sides ♦ دور ادور او را عسکر گرفت Soldiers surrounded him on all sides. 2 دور ادور around, round *denominative preposition* ♦ دور ادور باغ دیوار است There is a wall around the garden.

دوران [dawraan]¹ 1 rotation, revolution, going round, whirling, spinning ♦ دوران سر giddiness, dizziness 2 circulation; turnover ♦ دوران خون blood circulation ◊ دوران سرمایه circulation of capital

دوران [dawraan]² 1 era, epoch, age ♦ دوران حجر stone age 2 time; period, term ♦ دوران امتحانی trial period

د

دوراندیش [durandeesh] forseeing; prudent; far-sighted, far-seeing

دورانی [dawraani]
- زینه دورانی winding staircase, spiral staircase
- سرمایه دورانی *economics* operating funds

دوراهه [duraaha] (and) دوراهی [duraahi] fork (at junction) of two roads

دوربین [durbin] 1.1 far-sighted, long-sighted 1.2 ☞ دور اندیش 2 binocular, binoculars; spyglass; telescope

دوربین دار [durbindaar] *military* equipped with an optical sight or a telescopic sight

دوردست [durdast] distant, far off, faraway, remote

دوردستها [durdasthaa] distance long way off; distant places, remote place

دورگ [durag] (and) دورگه [duraga] 1 not pure blood, of mixed breed 2 hybrid *noun*, a crossbreed

دورمنزل [durmanzel] *military* long-range

دورنگی [durangi] duplicity, double-dealing; hypocrisy

دورنما [durnomaa] perspective; vista, view; panorama

دوروزه [duroza] 1 two-day 2 swiftly-flying; fleeting, short-lived ♦ جوانی دوروزه fleeting youth

دوروی [duroy] two-faced person; hypocrite, dissembler

دورویه [duroya] two-sided (about cloth or fabric)
- دورویه ودوپشته *colloquial* double dealer; plotter, intriguer

دورویی [duroyi] duplicity, double-dealing, sham; hypocrisy

دوره [dawra] 1 circle, circumference 2 set, series ♦ دوره جامه set of clothing 3 epoch, age, era ♦ دوره سنگ stone age ◊ دوره امپریالیزم era of imperialism 4 cycle, phase, stage 5 (*also* دوره اجلاسیه) convocation (of a legislative body); session 6 inspection trip ♦ برای دوره این ولایت عزیمت کردند He went on an inspection trip around the provinces.
- دوره کردن 1 to circle, to go round, to make circles 2 to form a circle, to stand in a circle 3 to look over again, to study (material already covered), to repeat
- دوره تسلیم دادن (office term) to turn over one's duties

دوره گرد [dawragard] wandering merchant, vendor, hawker, peddler ♦ عطار دوره گرد a drysalter who sells by peddling

دوری [duri] distance, long way off; distance, remoteness
- دوری جستن 1 to evade, to avoid; to shun (از) 2 to abstain, to refrain; to beware, to be careful, to be on one's guard (از)

دوریه [dawriya] *military* turning movement; patrol ♦ دوریه شب night patrol

دوزانو [duzanu]
- دوزانو نشستن to kneel on both knees; to sit with one's legs folded under oneself

دوزبانه [duzabana] 1 bilingual 2 giving contradictory evidence or readings; contradicting itself or oneself 3 insincere, hypocritical

دوزنه [dozaana]
- مرد دوزنه bigamist, man having two wives

دوس [dawos] *offensive* procurer, wife-seller (about a husband who sells his own wife)

دوساختن [daw-saakhtan] *idiom* (*literally*: to place a bet) to disgrace and embarrass (someone) ♦ او ما را پیش رقیبهای ما دو ساخت He embarrassed us before our rivals *saying*

دوست [dost] 1.1 friend ♦ دوست نزدیک close friend 1.2 *masculine proper name* Dost 2 (second component of compound words with meanings "loving something" / "a follower of something") ♦ بشردوست philanthrophic, humanist
- دوست داشتن to love

دوستدار [dostdaar] friend, well-wisher
- دوستدار شما your devoted friend (at the end of a letter)

دوست داشتنی [dostdaashtina] 1 nice, sweet, likable; attractive 2 dear; worthy of love

دوستی [dosti] friendship, favor, liking; inclination; friendly relations

دوش [dosh]¹ shoulder ♦ دوش بر دوش shoulder to shoulder

دوش [dosh]² *present tense stem* دوختن and دوشیدن

دوشاب [doshaab] thick syrup made of boiled grapes, grape must

دوشاخه [dushaakha] 1 *technical* fork, yoke ♦ دوشاخه کلچ clutch fork 2 stick with forked end (for gathering brushwood) 3 (*also* دوشاخه خرمن) wooden pitchfork (for pitching straw)

دوشش آمدن [dushash-aanadan] *idiom* (*literally*: to have boxcar in dice) to have good luck, to have a run of good luck, to have a lucky streak.

دوشنبه [dushambe] (*also* روز دو شنبه) Monday

دوشیدن [doshidan] to milk

دوشیزه [doshiza] girl, unmarried woman; young lady, miss

دوشینه [doshina] *literary* yesterday's

دوصد [dusad] two hundred

دو طبقوی [dutabaqawi] *technical* two-stage, two-step, two-phase ♦ انجن راکتی دو طبقوی two-stage rocket engine

دو طرفه [dutarafa] two-sided ♦ معاهده دو طرفه bilateral agreement, contract, or treaty
- چوب دوطرفه *technical* I-beam, H-beam

دوغ [dogh] 1 dugh (refreshing drink made of sour milk mixed with water and spices) 2 buttermilk
- دوغ زدن to churn butter (while separating the buttermilk)

دو غولی [dughuli] *colloquial* twins

دو فصله [dufasla] (*also* زمین دو فصله) land which gives two crops per year

دوقات [duqaat] 1 made double; folded; bent in half 2 double up, crooked, bent, hunched
- دوقات شدن 1 to fold in half 2 to bend, to bow [down], to lean over

دوک [duk] 1 spindle 2 spoke; knitting needle

دوکان [dukaan] ☞ دکان

دوکمه [dukma] 1 button (on clothing) 2 (push) button

دوکمه گک [dukmagak] *technical* (push) button or knob

دوگانگی [dugaanagi] *colloquial* twins

دوگانه [dugaana] 1 double; twofold 2 two ♦ دول دوگانه two powers 3.1 *colloquial* female friend 3.2 one of twins, a twin

دوگپه [dugapa] *colloquial* (*literally*: a two words person) to talk out of both sides of the mouth, not a straight shooter

دوگره [dogra] *regional* 1 poor, indigent 2 beggar, poor person

دول [dawl] *colloquial* 1 kind, sort; way, method 2 external appearance; luster, gloss 3 posing, showing off, putting on airs; dandyism
- دول کردن to put on airs, to assume airs

دول [dowal] *plural of* دولت

دول [dol]¹ 1 bucket, pail; tub 2 (*also* دول آسیا) filling funnel, feeding hopper (of a mill), mill box or bin 3 (*also* دول چا) leather bag (for drawing water from a well)

دول [dol]² ☞ دهل

دولا [dulaa] 1 double, doubled 2 ☞ دوقات

دولابچه [dolaabcha] small wall cupboard; recess, niche (with shelves)

دولانه [dolaana] hawthorn, haw

دولت [duwlat] 1 (plural دول [dowal]) state, power ♦ دولت شوروی Soviet state 2 authority; power, might 3 riches, wealth, fortune; status ♦ دولت سر دولت می آید Wealth goes to wealth. 4 *masculine proper name* Dawlyat

دولتمند [dawlatmand] 1 rich, wealthy, prosperous 2 a rich or wealthy person

دولچه [dolcha] 1 a small pail, small bucket; a small tub 2 small basin (for washing clothes or washing oneself) 3 *technical* box, container (for mortar) 4 (also ارطدولچه) cup or small bucket of a water-lifting wheel

دولچی [dolchi] *colloquial* drummer

دول زدن [dool-zadan] *idiom* (*literally:* to beat the drum) to spread rumors ♦ برادرش قصه را به همه جا دول زده است His brother spread the news everywhere.

دولق [dulaq] women's broad trousers for wearing on the street (visible under the chador)

دولکی [doolakee] *slang* (*literally:* drummer) bum

دولمه [dolma] 1 dolma (variety of stuffed cabbage roll) ♦ دولمه تاک برگ stuffed grape leaves; دولمه کرم stuffed cabbage 2 a dish with meat stuffing ♦ دولمه آش کدو squash stuffed with meat

دولی [dawli] *colloquial* frivolous dandy, a fop

دولی [duli] *obscure* an enclosed one-person palanquin or litter (in which women, usually brides, were carried in the olden days)

دوم [dowwom] ☞ دویم

دوند [dawend] (and) دونده [dawenda] 1 race, racing ♦ اسپ دوند racehorse, fast horse 2 moving, shifting ♦ تپه های دوند shifting sand hills

دونیم [dunim]
• دونیم کردن to divide into two parts, to divide in half

دووقته [duwaqta] 1 two-shift, double-shift 2 in two shifts ♦ به دووقته کار کردن to work in two shifts

دویدن [dawidan] 1 to run, to rush along, to speed along 2 *colloquial* to run about, to bustle; to endeavor 3 *colloquial* to make up the eyes (with antimony)

دویم [doyom (and) duyum] second (ordinal number)

دویم وفول [dimoful] main light switch (in a motor vehicle)

ده [dah (and) daa] ten

ده [deh]¹ 1 *present tense stem* دادن 2 (second component of compound words with meanings of "paying" / "giving") ♦ مالیه ده taxpayer

ده [de (h)]² 1 village 2 (first component of compound geographical names) ♦ ده مزنگ Deh Mazang (region in Kabul)

دده یی [dadayee] *noun* (*literally:* dog with no owner) loafer, vagabond, a person who wanders around

دهات [dehaat (and) diyaat] 1 *plural of* ده² 2 *colloquial* country place, countryside

دهاتی [dehaati] 1 country *adjective*, rural, farm *adjective* 2 villager, peasant; farmer; rural inhabitant, farm inhabitant

دهاقین [dahaaqin] *plural of* دهقان

دهان [dahaan] 1 mouth; jaws; pharynx 2 inlet, outlet; opening, orifice, aperture; mouth, neck (of a vessel or bottle) ♦ دهان آتش خانه mouth of a stove ◊ دهان بوطل neck of a bottle ◊ دهان جوال edge, rim; opening of a bag or sack

• دهان انداختن 1 to bite *intransitive* 2 to unleash abuse (on somebody); to fall [on]; to fly [at]

• دهان بستن *colloquial* 1 to stop talking [about], not to refer to or mention (something) (از) ♦ مه دیگه از ای گپ دهان بستم I won't say another word about this 2 to not take into the mouth, to abstain (from food)

• دهان جوال گرفتن to hold a sack (when someone is filling it with something)

• دهان کسی را بستن to force to be silent (by giving hush money or a bribe)

• دهان کسی را شیرین کردن *colloquial* to whet somebody's appetite (for something)

• از دهان افتیدن *colloquial* to be forgotten, not to be mentioned

• از دهان انداختن to forget, not to mention

• یک دهان a single portion, serving, or helping (of something); one gulp, sip, or mouthful; one piece

• یک دهان نصوار نصور a single pinch of snuff, a single chew of chewing tobacco

دهان بسته [dahaanbasta] 1 closed, tied up; knotted ♦ خلطه دهان بسته a sack tied closed 2 taciturn, reticent of tongue, restrained in speech 3 forced into silence

دهان بند [dahaanband] 1 muzzle 2 rope, cord, string, braided cord (for tying up a bag, wineskin, etc.)

دهان پاره [dahaanpaara] 1 not reticent of tongue; unduly familiar; garrulous, talkative, indiscreet 2 windbag, chatterbox, gossip

دهان پتک [dahaanpotak] cork, plug; spigot

دهان پر [dahaanpor] loaded from the muzzle, muzzle-loading, muzzle-loaded (about a gun)

دهان پراو [dahaanparaw] *colloquial* 1 not saying a word, like one who has a mouthful of water, forced into silence 2 ashamed (and therefore silent)

دهان پتی [dahaanputee] *colloquial* (*literally:* mouth covering) silence, mum

دهان دریده [dahaandarida] ☞ دهان پاره

دهانگی [dahaanagi] bit

دهانه [dahaana] 1 ☞ دهنه 2 ☞ دهانگی

ده باشی [dahbaashi] 1 foreman 2 (also ده باشی پوسته خانه) a junior rank of the postal department (under whom there are 10 subordinates)

ده تابره [dahtaayra] *technical* three-axle (about a motor vehicle)

ده تایی [dahtaayi] 1 *cards* ten ♦ ده تایی قره ten of spades 2 in twos, two by two

دهر [dahr] *literary* world, universe

دهری [dahri] *literary* atheist

دهشت [dahshat] fear; terror, horror

ده صومه [dahsoma] *colloquial* ten rubles, a ten

دهقان [dehqaan] (*plural* دهاقین [dahaaqin]) 1 a dehqan, a farmer, a peasant 2 hired farm worker; sharecropper

دهقانی [dehqaani] 1 peasant *adjective*, farmer *adjective* 2.1 occupation of a peasant 2.2 sharecropping 2.3 a portion of a crop (for a peasant sharecropper)

• دهقانی کردن 1 to work as a peasant 2 to be a sharecropper

دهل [dóhol] large drum ♦ دهل و سرنا(ی) drum and zourna (sort of lute)

• دهل زدن to beat a drum

دهلیز [dahleez] 1 gallery, corridor 2 (also دهلیز قلب) *anatomy* auricle (of the heart)

دهن [dahan (and) daan] 1 ☞ دهن 2.1 by; at; near; by the side of *denominative preposition* ♦ در دهن at [the very] door, in the doorway 2.2 به دهن to; toward ♦ ده دهن دروازه رسید He approached to [the very] door.

دهنشین [dehneshin] 1 settled (as opposed to nomadic) 2 a rural inhabitant, one who lives in the countryside or in a village

دهنه [dahana] 1 mouth (of a river); entry (into a gorge, valley) 2 (place where water leaves the main irrigation ditch and enters lateral ditches) 3 ☞ دهنگی 4 ☞ دهان

ده [daha] 1 ten, a bunch or group of ten 2 *religion* (محرم) the first ten days of mourning of the month of Muhharam; ten days after the death (of someone) 3 (also دهه گران) the first ten days of fasting (in the month of Ramadan) 4 *historical* a detachment of ten infantrymen

دیار [diyaar] *literary* country; land

دیالکتیک [di (y) aalektik] 1 dialectics 2 dialectical

دیالوگ [di (y) aalog] dialogue

دیانت [diyaanat] *literary* 1 devotion, piety, religiousness 2 honesty; decency

دیبت [deebet] *accounting* debit

دیپارتمنت [deepaartment] 1 department (in an establishment) 2 department, chair (in a university) ♦ دیپارتمنت زبان دری the Dari language department

دیپلوم [diplom] diploma, degree

دیپلومات [diplomaat] diplomat

دیپلوماتی [diplomaati] diplomatic ♦ پاسپورت دیپلوماسی diplomatic passport

دیپو [deepo] 1 depot, warehouse ♦ دیپو ادویه storehouse of medicines or medical supplies 2 fire station
• دیپو کردن to stockpile, to accumulate

دیپوزیت [deepozit] 1 *finance* depost 2 *geology*

دید [did] 1 vision, sight; contemplation; inspection, survey, examination, review ♦ قابل دید noteworthy, interesting 2 (also قابلیت دید) *military* visibility 3 view, opinion, point of view ♦ دید واقع بینانه realistic view, realistic approach

دیدار [didaar] 1 appointment; rendezvous; meeting 2 visit, inspection, survey 3 look, aspect, appearance

دیدن [didan] (*present tense stem* بین [bin]) 1 to look; to see ♦ بهم دیدن to look at one another, to exchange glances 2.1 inspection, survey, examination, review 2.2 visit, visitation 2.3 (component of compound verb combinations of intransitive sematic sense) ♦ بدی دیدن to suffer harm (from somebody)

دیدنی [didani] 1.1 notable; remarkable; interesting 2 obvious; apparent; visible 2 *colloquial* that which has been endured; trials, ordeals, hardships, privations, misfortunes, troubles

دیدنی دار [didanidaar] having suffered much, having seen grief

دیدوبازدید [didobazdid] visit of friends; exchange of visits

دیده [dida] 1 *past participle* دیدن 2 eye, eyes
• دیده و دانسته ☞ دیده و دانسته
• دیده نداشتن (and) دیده نتوانستن 1 to envy 2 not to bear, not to endure (somebody or something)
• قدم شما بالای دیده (and) دیده بالای دیده *colloquial* You are always welcome! / For goodness' sake!

دیده گی [didagi] 1 *past participle* دیدن 2 seen with one's own eyes; fact, facts
• دیده گی و شنیده گی seen and heard

دیده دانسته [didwdaanesta] *colloquial* consciously; intentionally; deliberately

دیر [dayr] house of prayer, temple

دیر [deer] 1.1 for a long time, a long time 1.2 late *adverb* 2 long, lengthy; protracted; prolonged
• دیر آید درست آید *proverb* Better slowly, but properly.
• تا دیر for a long time; over a period of a long time ♦ حرارت ذغال سنگ تا دیر دوام مینماید The heat [from burning] coal lasts a long time.
• دیر وقت a long time
• دیر پاییدن to last a long time; to exist a long time
• دیر شدن to be detained, to be delayed; to linger; to be late; to be slow
• دیر کردن to delay; to detain; to drag out (with something)
• دیر ماندن 1 to be dragged out, to be delayed; to be detained 2 ☞ پاییدن

دیر پای [deerpaay] 1 long, prolonged; lasting, durable 2 solid, firm, strong

دیر دیر [deerdeer] rarely; now and then; from time to time; infrequently ♦ من او رادیردیر می بینم I rarely see him.

دیررس [deerras] ripening late, late

دیرک [deerak] 1 (also دیرک خیمه) post, pole (serving as a support of a tent); upright, stanchion 2 (also دیرک کشتی) mast 3 beam, girder; rafter, truss

دیر مانده [deermaanda] not fresh, stale, having lain about for a long time (about produce, etc.), old (about goods)

دیروز [diroz] 1 yesterday *adverb* 2 the whole of yesterday

دیره [deera] *colloquial* dwelling, abode; stop; temporary quarters, camp 2 village, settlement

دیرین [deerin] (and) دیرینه [deerina] old; bygone; antique; ancient ♦ دوست دیرین old friend

دیزانتری [dizaantari] dysentery

دیزاین [dizaayn] drawing, design; outline, sketch
• دیزاین کردن to draw; to point to, to depict; to make an outline, to sketch

دیزل [dizal] diesel ♦ انجین دیزل diesel engine

دیزل آیل [dizalaayl] diesel oil

دیزلی [dizali] diesel *adjective* ♦ جنریتر دیزلی diesel generator

دیز نفکشن [deezenfekshan] disinfection

دیسی [disee] *colloquial* (*literally:* hometown) not original, not good quality, rebuilt, knock-off (machines, guns, etc.)

دیسی [disee] *slang* (*literally:* not original) fake (person)

دیش [deesh] small bath (for washing photographic film)

دیشب [dishab] 1 yesterday in the evening, during last night 2 yesterday's evening; the past night

دیکته [dikta] dictation

دیکلیمی [dikleemee] recitation; declamation

دیکور [deekor] decoration; scenery

دیگ [deeg] cauldron, boiler (for cooking pilaf); pan ♦ دیگ حمام bath kettle ◊ دیگ چودنی cast iron kettle
• دیگ دلده واری میجوشد *colloquial* He is just like a pot with boiling porridge (about a person who loses his temper easily).

دیگان [deegaan] *regional* Degan (name of Tajiks living in the south of Afghanistan)

دیاگنی [deegaani] (also زبان دیگانی) Degani (name of the language of Tajiks living in the south of Afghanistan)

دیگچه [deegcha] 1 small pan, small kettle 2 degcha (sweet ceremonial dish made of rice and milk prepared to be distribluted to the poor on the last Wednesday of the month of Safar - in honor of the recovery of the prophet Mohammed after his serious illness)

دیگچه پزانی [deegchapazaani] 1 simple refreshments, a dish, food (prepared in an off-hand manner) 2 children's game (in which the children pretend to prepare food)

دیگدان [deegdaan] hearth (for a kettle), trivet

دیگر [digar] 1.1 other another, different ♦ دیگر آدم a different person, another person; این گپ دیگر است This is another matter. 1.2 next, following ♦ دیگر بار the next time, at the next time 2 anew, once more, again ♦ روز دیگر the next day 2.2 still; yet; some more, more; already ♦ دیگر چه گفت؟ What else / more did he say? ◊ دیگر هیچ نگفت He didn't say anything else / more. 3 well, you see after all *intensifying particle* ♦ حالا دیگر زمستان نیست It's not winter now, you see. / After all it's not winter now.

• دیگر شدن 1 to change, to exchange *intransitive* 2 to be replaced ♦ پاسبانان ساعت به ساعت دیگر میشد The sentries were replaced every hour.

دیگر [deegar] the time after noon; the hours after noon ♦ نماز دیگر afternoon namaz (prayer)

دیگرگون [digargun] (and) دیگر گونه [digarguna]

• دیگر گون شدن 1 to change *intransitive* 2 to become worse (about the weather, etc.)

دیگرگونی [digarguni] change

دیگی [deegi] 1 cooked (in a kettle or pot) 2 cleaned for cooking (about grain)

دموکراتیک [deemokraatik] ☞ دموکراتیک

دموکراسی [deemokrashi] ☞ دموکراسی

دین [dayn] (*plural* دیون [doyun]) 1 monetary debt 2 indebtedness, debts 3 debt, obligation

• دین خود را ادا کردن 1 to pay a debt 2 to fulfill an obligation or a debt

دین [din] (*plural* ادیان [adyaan]) religion; belief, faith ♦ دین اسلام Islam, Moslem belief, Moslem faith

دینار [dinaar] 1 dinar (Indian coin equal to one-tenth of a paise) 2 *historical* gold coin, gold piece

دینامیت [dinaamit] dynamite

دین دار [dayndaar] 1 debtor 2.1 having debt, being in debt 2.2 under obligation, indebted (to somebody for something)

دیندار [dindaar] 1 devout, pious 2 just; righteous; virtuous

دینداری [dindaari] 1 devotion, piety 2 honesty; virtuousness

دینمو [daynamo] *technical* dynamo

دینه [dina] (and) دینه روز [dinaroz] *colloquial* yesterday (during the day)

دینه پریروز [dinapareeroz] *colloquial* 1 the day before yesterday 2 recently, just; before now ♦ احمد دینه پریروز کابل بود Ahmad was in Kabul recently.

دینی [dini] referring to religion; spiritual ♦ علوم دینی theological sciences

دینیات [diniyaat] God's law; theology (as a subject of teaching)

دیو [deew] 1 demon; evil spirit; genie 2 fairy tale giant; demon 3 *colloquial* "fiend" (about an evil person)

تورا دیو زده است؟ *colloquial* Has a spell been cast over you? (to someone sitting doing nothing)

دیوار [deewaar] 1 wall (of house, etc.) ♦ دیوار به دیوار in the neighborhood, side by side, wall to wall 2 wall, adobe wall ♦ دیوار باغ wall of a garden, fence of a garden 3 *anatomy* paries

• دیوار بینی septum of the nose

• دیوار کشیدن (and) دیوار کردن to build a wall, to lay a wall; to enclose with a wall

دیوار نمکش [diware-namkash] *slang* (*literally:* clay wall that absorb moisture) one who takes things personaly

دیواره [dewaara] 1 ☞ دیوار 2 brim; brink, edge; parapet

دیواری [deewaari] wall *adjective* ♦ ساعت دیواری wall clock

دیوال [deewaal] *colloquial* ☞ دیوار

• دیوال گرفتن to enclose with a wall; to fence in

دیوال مسجد [daywaale-masjid] *slang* (*literally:* the wall of a mosque) a lazy person

دیوالی [deewaali] *colloquial* 1 an insolvent; a ruined person; a bankrupt 2 having fallen into difficulties

دیوان [diwaan]¹ 1 court, tribunal ♦ دیوان حرب military tribunal 2 *historical* divan, state council (under an emir) ♦ دیوان انشاء an emir's office, a department in charge of official correspondence (under an emir)

دیوان [diwaan]² divan (a collection of a poet's verse)

دیوان [diwaan]³ couch, sofa

دیوان بیگی [diwaanbegi] *historical* 1 (the person who manages the finances and provisions at an emir's court) 2 the chief of an emir's office

دیوانگی [deewaanagi] insanity, madness; wild behavior; recklessness; possession (by devils, etc.)

• دیوانگی کردن to behave like a madman, to rave, to behave recklessly or rashly; to rage, to storm, to be possessed (i.e., by devils, etc.)

دیوانه [deewaana] 1.1 insane, mad 1.2 furious; violent; frantic; possessed 1.3 (also دیوانه عشق) madly in love 2 madman; madcap

دیوانه وار [deewaanawaar] 1 madly; furiously; violently; like an insane person, like a madman ♦ دیوانه وار فریاد میکشد He yelled like a madman. 2 insane; furious; violent (about something) ♦ وزش دیوانه وار بادها violent gusts of wind

دیوتی [dyuti] 1 duty, watch, standing at a post 2 duty of service, duty

دیوث [dayus] 1 procurer; pimp 2 villain, scoundrel (usually about a husband who sells his own wife)

دیوزده [deewzada] 1 possessed; raging, raving; frenzied; foolish; cracked 2 *colloquial* loafer, lazy person, idler

دیوسرشت [deewseresht] (and) دیوسیرت [dewsirat] evil, ill-tempered; harmful, pernicious

دیون [doyun] *plural of* دین [dayn]

دیویزیون [diwiziyon] division; battalion *artillery*

ذ

11th letter of the Dari alphabet

ذات [zaat] (*plural* ذوات [zawaat]) 1 person ♦ ذات شهریاری sovereign, sir 2 essence; crux, main point; nature, character, substance

• به ذات خود 1 by its / his / her / etc. nature, in essence 2 in itself / by himself / by herself

ذ

ذاتاً [zaatan] 1 as a matter of fact; strictly speaking 2 in its essence, in its nature 3 by birth; by origin (from somewhere)

ذات الحركه [zaatolharaka] technical self-propelled ♦ ابوس ذات military self-propelled howitzer

ذات الریه [zaatorriya] medicine pneumonia, inflammation of the lungs

داتی [zaati] (opposite of کسبی) 1 innate; native; inborn; natural 2 from time immemorial; inherent; inalienable 3 military relating to personnel, relating to cadres

ذال [zaal] name of the letter ذ

ذایقه [zaayeqa] taste, sense of taste ♦ به ذایقه من to my taste

ذبح [zábh] (and) zába 1 immolation, sacrificing (an animal) 2 slaughter of livestock
● ذبح کردن to kill, to slaughter (livestock)

ذخایر [zakhaayer] 1 plural of ذخیره 2 reserve capital

ذخیره [zakhira] (plural ذخایر [zakhayer]) 1 stock, supply, reserve 2 fund ♦ ذخیره تیل storehouse
● ذخیره کردن to store, to put aside, to make or build a reserve or a supply

ذرات [zarraat] plural of ذره

ذرایع [zaraaye'] plural of ذریعه
● ذرایع حمل ونقل means of transportation

ذرع [zar] (and) zára obscure zar (measure of length, roughly equivalent to 110 cm.)
● ذرع شرعی cubit (measure of length)

ذروه [zorwa] literary summit, highest point; apogee, acme
● به ذروه عروج رسیدن to achieve the summit
● به ذروه قدرت رسیدن to achieve the highest authority or power

ذروی [zarrawi] atomic, nuclear ♦ بم ذروی atomic bomb ◊ نیروی ذروی atomic energy, nuclear energy

ذره [zarra] (plural ذرات [zarraat]) 1 atom 2 physics molecule; corpuscle 3 smallest particle, grain; grain of sand ♦ ذره طلا a grain of gold
● یک ذره (and) ذره یی colloquial a little bit, very little

ذره بین [zarrabin] magnifying glass, loupe; microscope

ذره ذره [zarra-zarra] colloquial 1 by the drop, by the grain, little by little 2 in detail; scrupulously

ذره وی [zarrawi] ☞ ذروی

ذریعه [zari'a] (and) zariya (plural ذرایع [zaraye']) means, method ♦ به ذریعه پوسته by mail
● (به)ذریعه with the aid of, by means of ♦ تسخین به ذریعه بخاراب heating by means of steam, steam heating

ذغال [zoghaal] coal, carbon

ذغال سنگ [zoghaal e sang] (hard) coal

ذغالی [zoghaali] 1 coal adjective 2 coal miner
● چراغ ذغالی technical arc lamp

ذکاوت [zakaawat] 1 mind, intellect; abilities, faculties 2 cleverness, brightness, comprehension

ذکر [zéker] 1 mention ♦ در این کتاب ذکری از آن رفته است There is mention of him / it in this book. 2 remark; statement; utterance 3 religion repetition of the epithets of Allah (part of the prayer ritual)
● ذکر کردن to mention; to note

ذکی [zaki] 1 intelligent; able, capable 2 quick, clever, bright

ذلت [zellat] literary baseness, contemptibility; humility, humbleness

ذلیل [zalil] literary 1 low, contemptible 2 pitiful, unfortunate

ذمت [zemmat] (and) ذمه [zemma] obligation; responsibility, duty; debt
● به ذمت خود گرفتن to be obliged (to do something), to take responsibility on oneself

ذمه بردار [zemmabardaar] obliged, having taken responsibility on oneself

ذمی [zemmi] historical non-Moslem subject

ذو [zu] ☞ ذی

ذوات [zawaat] plural of ذات

ذوالجلال [zoljalaal] literary great, powerful, mighty (epithet of Allah)

ذو الحجه [zelhejja] ☞ ذی الحجه

ذو القرنین [zolqarnain] "two-horned" (nickname of Alexander the Great)

ذو القعده [zolq'ada] ☞ ذی القعده

ذوب [zawb] (and) ذوبان [zawbaan] 1 melting ♦ ذوب آهن smelting of iron ◊ نقطه ذوب melting point 2 thawing; melting ♦ ذوب برف thawing of snow
● ذوب شدن 1 to melt intransitive 2 to thaw intransitive

ذوجنسین [zujensayn] botany bisexual flowers

ذوحیاتین [zuhayaatayn] amphibian

ذوق [zawq] (plural اذواق [azwaaq]) 1 a sense of the elegant, taste ♦ اهل ذوق connoisseurs (of the beautiful) 2 interest, enthusiasm; passion ♦ باذوق و شوق enthusiastically, with enthusiasm 3 gladness; joy; pleasure
● ذوق داشتن to show interest (به), to be keen [on], to take a fancy [to] ♦ او ذوق مفرط به موسیقی داشت He had a passion for music.
● ذوق کردن 1 to be glad or happy, to rejoice 2 to anticipate pleasure; to take pleasure, to delight, to obtain pleasure

ذوقمند [zawqmand] 1 interested, showing interest (in something) 2.1 fan or lover of something, admirer 2.2 connoisseur of art

ذوقی [zawqi] 1 corresponding to [one's] inclinations; fascinating, interesting ♦ کار ذوقی hobby 2 amateur adjective 3 artistic, esthetic ♦ آثار ذوقی artistic works 4 ☞ ذوقمند

ذوی العقول [zawiloqul] 1 reasoning beings, people (as distinguished from animals) 2 grammar nouns designating persons

ذهن [zehn] mind, consciousness, intellect
● به ذهن سپردن to engrave in [one's] memory, to memorize
● دور از ذهن بودن to be incredible, to be hard to believe

ذهن نشین [zehnneshin] 1 retained in memory 1 engraved in [one's] conciousness; understood, mastered

ذهنی [zehni] mental, intellectual; spiritual ♦ آزادی ذهنی freedom of thought ◊ مدنیت ذهنی spiritual culture

ذهنیت [zehniyat] (and) ذهنیات [zehniyat] 1 way of thinking, cast of mind 2 psychology; psychics

ذی [zi] (first component of compound words with meanings "having something" / "possessing some virtue or quality") ♦ ذیروح animated, lively; live, living

ذی الحجه [zelhejja] Dhu'l-hijja (12th month of Moslem lunar year, when pilgrimages are made)

ذی القعده [zelga'da] dhu'l-qa'da (11th month of Moslem lunar year)

ذیحق [zihaq (q)] 1 having the right; competent 2 right, just; deserving of something

ذی حیات [zihayaat] 1 living, existing 2 a living being

ذی دخل [zidákhel] 1 included, entered into the composition (of something) 2 participating, involved, having relation [to]
• ذی دخل کردن to include, to inculcate, to introduce, to make part (of something)
ذی روح [ziroh] *grammar* animate ♦ اسم ذی روح animate noun
• غیر ذی روح inanimate
ذی صلاحیت [zisalaahyat] competent ♦ هیئت ذی صلاحیت competent commission
ذی علاقه [zialaaqa] having relation [to]; interested
ذیل [zayl] following ♦ به قرار ذیل in the following manner
• در ذیل below; further; at the bottom
ذیلا [zaylan] 1 below 2 at the bottom 3 herewith
ذی نفع [zináf (and) zináfa] 1 materially or pecuniarily interested 2 having a share, participating in the profits

ر
12th letter of the Dari alphabet

را [raa] [1] name of letter ر
را [raa] [2] *suffix* 1 (forms a direct object expressed by a singular noun or a noun meaning a person) ♦ او کتاب را خواند He read [this] book. ◊ من بچه را سرزنش کردم I scolded the child. 2 (forms an indirect object signifying) 2.1 (the addressee of an action) ♦ استاد ما را کاغذ داد The teacher gave us paper. 2.2 (the person or thing about which one is thinking or speaking) ♦ آینده را فکر نمی کرد He didn't think about the future.
• مرا چه؟ *colloquial* What is it to me? / What does it matter to me?
رابر [raabar] elastic, eraser; rubber
• درخت رابر 1 rubber tree 2 ficus
را برتیپ [raabarteep] insulating tape
رابری [raabari] elastic *adjective*; rubber *adjective*
رابطه [raabeta] (*plural* روابط [rawaabet]) tie; link; bond; relation
• رابطه داشتن to be linked, to have connection [with]
• با کسی رابطه پیدا کردن to establish ties or relations with somebody
• رابطهء نحوی Syntactic linkage
• رابطهء متقابل Interdependence
رابیا [raabiyaa] large wineskin (used to carry water for horses or oxen)
رابیل [raabeel] (and) رابیلی [raabeeli] yellow jasmine
راپوت [raapot] *colloquial* ☞ راپور
راپور [raapor] (and) راپورت [raaport] 1 report, message ♦ این راپورت تصدیق نشد This report was not confirmed. 2 report; account ♦ راپورت اجرآت report about work accomplished
راجا [raajaa] 1 prince; rajah 2 *colloquial* generous, magnanimous; unselfish
راجستری [raajestari] 1 registered 2 (also مکتوب راجستری) registered letter
• راجستری کردن 1 to register 2 to send (a letter) registered
راجع [raaje] 1 applicable, relevant, pertinent 2 راجع به about, concerning, regarding, relating [to] *compound preposition*
• راجع شدن to concern, to have to do with; to apply [to], to pertain [to] (به)
• راجع کردن to direct, to send; to address (به)

راحت [raahat] 1.1 peace; rest 1.2 calm; quiet; relief 2 quiet; calm; tranquil; comfortable, cozy ♦ این بستر بسیار راحت است This bed is very comfortable. 3 quietly; calmly; comfortably ♦ راحت خواب کنید Sleep well!
• راحت شدن 1 to calm [oneself] down, to find peace, to find quiet ♦ دوا را بخور راحت میشوی Take the medicine [and] you'll feel better. 2 to put oneself at rest (forever), to die
راحت طلب [raahattalab] a pampered weakling; an effeminate man; a spoiled person 2 a lazy person
راحتی [raahati] calm; quiet; cozy, comfortable
رادار [raadaar] radar ♦ دستگاه های رادار radar installations
رادیو [raadio] 1 radio ♦ نشریات رادیو radio transmission, radio broadcast 2 radio receiver
• به رادیو اعلان کردن to announce over the radio
رادیو تخنیکی [raadiotakhniki] *adjective* radio engineering
رادیو گرافی [raadiograafi] 1 roentgenography (i.e., taking x-rays) 2 x-ray photograph ♦ رادیو گرافی ریتین photograph of the lungs
• رادیو گرافی کردن to take an x-ray photograph
راز [raaz] secret
• راز دل گفتن (به) to entrust a secret
راز و نیاز [raazoniyaaz] 1 frank discussion; heart-to-heart talk 2 talk or conversation of people in love
• راز و نیاز کردن (با) to pour out one's heart
رأس [raa's] (*plural* رؤس [rous]) 1 head, leader 2 head (numerative when counting livestock) ♦ صد رأس است one hundred horses 3 در رأس headed [by]
راسبری [raasbaari] raspberry, raspberries
راست [raast] 1.1 straight, even 1.2 right ♦ دست راست right arm 1.3 true; right, correct ♦ گپ راست true words ◊ از طریق راست truly, correctly 2 truth ♦ راستش اینست که ۰۰۰ the problem is that … 3.1 directly 3.2 truly, correctly
• راست شدن 1 to straighten itself / oneself, to smooth itself out 2 to stand on end (about hair)
• راست کردن 1 to straighten up or out, to smooth out 2 to correct, to fix, to set right 3 *colloquial* to manufacture; to make 4 *colloquial* to adorn, to decorate, to dress up, to array
راستان [raastaan] *colloquial* overturned, on [its] back; backwards; flat, prone
راستکار [raastkaar] honest, decent
راست گوی [raastgoy] straightforward, truthful (about somebody)
راسته [raasta] (*opposite of* چپه) 1 right-side (about clothing, cloth) ♦ بافت راسته right-side knitting 2.1 on or from the face side 2.2 *colloquial* ☞ راستان راسته افتادن *colloquial* to fall backwards, to fall on [one's / its] back
راسته بافی [raastabaafi] knitting of socks
راستی [raasti] 1.1 straightforwardness, truthfulness, honesty 2.1 truth (also به راستی) 2.2 actually, in fact, really ♦ تو راستی امروز می روی؟ Are you really leaving today? 2.3 راستی! *colloquial* Honestly! / Upon my word!
• به راستی و درستی directly, frankly, honestly; in an honest way
• راستی کردن 1 to act honestly, to act according to one's conscience 2 *colloquial* to vow, to swear
راستین [raastin] real, true ♦ عشق راستین true love
راسخ [raasekh] *literary* 1 strong; firm, solid; steadfast ♦ عزم راسخ firm resolve 2 resolute, determined

راش [raash] 1 threshed grain (on threshing floor) 2 *colloquial* heap, pile

راشبیل [raashbeel] wooden shovel

راشبیلک [raashbeelak] *colloquial* shoulder blade

راشدین [raashedin] the first four religious caliphs (Abu-Bakr, Omar, Osman, and Ali)

راشه درشه [raasha-darsha] *idiom* (*literally:* come and go) visiting each other

راصد [raased]
- چراغ راصد searchlight

راضی [raazi] 1 satisfied, content 2 agreeable
- راضی کردن(ساختن) 1 to make satisfied, to satisfy 2 to win over, to covince

راضی نامه [raazinaama] peaceful settlement; amicable agreement

راغ [raagh] 1 foothills; mountain slope 2 meadow, field (on a mountain slope) 3 Ragh (area in Badakhshan)

راکب [raakeb] (*plural* راکبین [raakebin]) 1 going, riding (in a train, carriage, etc.) 2.1 fare; passenger 2 rider (on horseback)

راکت [raaket] rocket ♦ راکت بالیستکی ballistic rocket, ballistic missile ◊ حامل راکت missile carrier

راکت انداز [raaketandaaz] 1 grenade launcher 2 (also نفر راکت انداز) grenade launcher operator

راکتانس [raaktaans] *electrical* reactance, reactive resistance

راکتچی [raaketchi] flare signaler

راکتی [raaketi] rocket, missile *adjective* ♦ عسکر راکتی missile troops, rocket forces

راکد [raaked] *literary* stationary, fixed, immoveable; stagnant ♦ سرمایه راکد frozen capital

راکول [raakol] rakol (harrow, i.e., wooden frame with iron teeth drawn by a horse or ox that smooths out the surface of an arable field)

رام [raam]¹ 1 quiet; mild; obedient, dutiful; manual, hand 2 tamed, subdued
- رام کردن(به خود) 1 to subordinate to oneself; to subdue 2 to tame, to domesticate

رام [raam]² *colloquial* ☞ رحم [raahm]

رامت [raamat] *colloquial* ☞ رحمت

رامشگر [raameshgar] *literary* singer; musician

ران [raan]¹ 1 thigh; hip; leg, haunch 2 ham

ران [raan]² 1 *present tense stem* راندن 2 (second component of compound words with meaning "name of the doer") ♦ گاوران ox driver ◊ طیاره ران pilot

راندن [raandan] 1 to drive away, to expel; to banish 2 to drive, to urge on (a horse, etc.) 3 to drive (about means of transportation)

رانده [raanda] *past participle* راندن
- رانده خدا damned by God

رانکی [raanaki] breeching (part of a harness)

راننده [raanenda] 1 *present participle* راندن 2 driver (of motor vehicle, etc.) ◊ راننده تراکتور tractor operator

راه [raah] 1.1 road, way ♦ راه اسفالت شده (and) راه پخته asphalt road 1.2 راه پیاده رو footpath 1.3 pavement, sidewalk 2 way, means; way out ♦ راه دیگری نیست There is no other way out. 3 row, row of loops (in knitting) 4 (also راه اسپ) pace, gait 5.1 راه by means [of], with the aid [of], by the use of *denominative preposition* ♦ از راه مزاکره by means of negotiations 5.2 via, through ♦ از راه هرات via Herat 5.3 درراه for, for the sake [of], in the name [of] ♦ درراه استقلال for independence

راه آهن ☞ راه آهن

راه حل ☞ راه حل

- راه بردن to comprehend, to understand
- راه پیمودن to walk, to ride ♦ مدتی دیگر راه پیمود He rode [on] a little more.
- راه دادن 1 to make way [for], to let pass 2 *colloquial* to give way [to], to indulge, to humor 3 *colloquial* to presage good, to promise success (about fortune telling, omens, etc.) ♦ فالش راه داد a good card fell to him
- راه داشتن 1 to have entry, to have access; to be connected or linked (by a stairway, by a gallery) ♦ بام راه دارد there is a passage to the roof 2 to be possible, to be feasible
- راه رفتن to walk, to go
- راه زدن to commit robbery, to rob
- از راه گشتاندن *colloquial* 1 to turn back from the road, to talk out of the intention to go (somewhere) 2 to lead astray, to seduce
- از راه گشتن *colloquial* to be led astray (also *figuratively*)
- از راه خود گشتن to renounce one's views, to renounce one's beliefs, etc.
- راه انداختن (به) 1 to see (somebody) off, to send (somebody) off 2 to begin; to unleash; to put right
- به راه آوردن 1 to help (somebody) find his way (about someone who is lost) 2 to set on the true path, to direct
- راه خود را کج کردن to turn to the side, to make a detour
- راه کسی را گرفتن 1 to intercept somebody on the road (for the purpose of a meeting) 2 to stop somebody (for the purpose of robbery)
- سر راه افتادن to be obtained without labor
- پول سر راه نیفتیده *colloquial* Money isn't scattered about on the road.
- سر کسی راه یافتن to twist somebody around one's little finger, to order somebody about
- چشمش راه کشید *colloquial* He was lost in contemplation.

راه آهن [raah (e) aahan] railroad

راهب [raaheb] (*plural* راهبین [raahebin]) monk; hermit

راهبر [raahbar] ☞ رهبر

راه بلد [raahbalad] 1 knowing the road *adjective* 2 guide

راه بلدی [raahbaladi] knowledge of the road; showing the way
- راه بلدی کردن to show, indicate, or point out the road, to guide ♦ مراه بلدی کنید Show me the road!

راه حل [raahehal] (I) way, means of solving; deciding (something)

راهدار [raahdaar] striped, in stripes

راهداری [raahdaari] 1 road toll, transit duty 2 pass; permit

راه رو [raahraw]¹ 1 road, path 2 passer-by, traveler, wayfarer
- راه رو بودن to go, to move, to proceed

راه رو [raahraw]² covered passageway; corridor
- راه رو اطراف تعمیر *construction* structure surrounding or alongside a passageway

راهزن [raahzan] robber, bandit

راهزنی [raahzani] robbery, banditry

راهسپار [raahrepaar]
- راهسپار شدن *literary* to set out (on a trip, journey, etc.)

راهگذر [raahgozar] ☞ رهگذر

راهنما(ی) [raahnomaa (y)] 1 guide, textbook; handbook 2 guidebook ♦ راهنمای کابل guidebook on Kabul 3 guide (person) 4 manual, instructions (on the use of something)

راهنمایی [raahnomaayi] 1 indication of the way, showing the way, showing the road 2 guiding (somebody); familiarizing somebody) (with a matter, route, etc.)

• راهنمایی کردن 1 to show the road, to lead, to direct 2 to guide (somebody); to acquaint (در)

راهنمون [raahnomun] ☞ راهنما(ی)

راهنمونی [raahnomuni] ☞ راهنمایی

راه نورد [raahnaward] 1 traveler, wayfarer, wanderer; tourist 2 messenger, courier

راهوار [raahwaar] pacer (horse)

راه وبیراهه [raahobeeraaha]

• از راه وبیراهه رفتن to go straight, to go through an area without roads by cutting a path

راه ورسم [raahoraasem] custom; usage; system

راهی [raahi]

• راهی بودن to go, to be on the way

• راهی شدن to start on a journey, to set out on a journey

• راهی کردن to send off on a journey; to send

رأی [ra'y] (and) رای [raay] (plural آرا [aaraa]) 1 opinion ♦ رأی تجویز the determining opinion 2 vote ♦ حق رأی suffrage, the right to vote 3 vote ♦ رأی اعتماد vote of confidence

• رأی دادن (در باره) 1 to express an opinion, to judge 2 (برای) to give one's vote, to vote

• رأی زدن to consult, to talk things over, to exchange opinions

• رأی گرفتن to put to a vote

رایج [raayej] (and) رائج [raaej] 1 being in circulation (about money); current, popular (about goods) 2 prevalent, widespread; generally accepted, conventional, usual

رأی دهی [raa'ydehi] voting

رایگان [raayegaan] 1 free (of charge), gratis; gratuitous 2 without charge, for nothing

رایی [raayi] colloquial ☞ راهی

• رایی بودن (a modifying verb which gives an action a meaning of duration) ♦ گفته رایی است He continues to talk.

رب [rab (b)] God, Lord (form of address to God) ♦ یا رب O, God!

ربا [rabaa] present tense stem ربودن

رباب [rabaab (and) robab] rabab (musical string instrument)

ربابی [rabaabi] musician who plays the rabab

رباط [rabaat] 1 rabat, inn, caravansary 2 colloquial march, stage (from one stop to the next)

رباعی [rabaa'i] (plural رباعیات [robaaiyaat]) 1 rubaiyat stanza (poem consisting of four lines with a special rhyme scheme) 2 quatrain, couplet

رباعیات [robaa'iyaat] 1 plural of رباعی 2 collection of quatrains, collection of rubaiyat stanzas ♦ رباعیات عمر خیام rubaiyat stanza of Omar Khayyam

رب النوع [rabbonnaaw (and) rabbanaawa] god; duty; idol (heathen)

ربط [rabt] 1 connection, tie, bond, link 2 relation, connection ♦ این کار با من چه ربط دارد؟ What connection does that have with me?

• فعل ربط grammar linking verb

• کلمه ربط grammar conjunction

ربع [rob' (and) róba] one-fourth, one-quarter, a fourth part of something, a quarter of something ♦ سه ربع three-fourths ◊ یک متر و ربع one and one-quarter meters

ربودن [rabudan] (present tense stem ربای [raba (y)]) 1 to steal; to take, to take away; to snatch, to snatch out (e.g., of somebody's hands) 2 to attract; to draw

• دل کسی را ربودن to captivate, to charm, to fascinate somebody

رب‌ةالنوع [rabbatonnaw] goddess (heathen)

رپوت [rapot] colloquial ☞ راپور

رپوتچی [rapotchi] (and) رپوتی [rapoti] colloquial spy; informant, informer

رتبوی [rotbawi] depending on rank, befitting [one's] rank (about salary, etc.)

رتبه [rotba] 1 rank, grade; title (i.e., of rank) ♦ عسکری - military rank, military title ◊ به - سفیر کبیر in the rank of ambassador 2 degree ♦ علمی - scholar's degree

رجال [rejhaal] plural of رجل

رجحان [rojhaan] literary 1 advantage; preference; superiority 2 legal preferential right of acquisition (of something)

• - داشتن (بر) to have an advantage; to excel; to surpass

رجز [rajaz] literary rajaz (poetic meter)

راجستری [rajestari] ☞ رجستری

رجعت [raj'at] 1 return; relapse ♦ مرض - relapse of an illness 2 military retreat, withdrawal, falling back

رجل [rajol] (plural رجال [rajal]) 1 husband; man 2 figure, person ♦ دولت - statesman

رجوع [roju'] 1 returning, return 2 recourse (to somebody with something) 3 reference (to something)

• - کردن 1 to return (to something) ♦ به سر مطلب - کنیم Let's return to the matter / to the business at hand! 2 to take recourse (to somebody or something) 3 to refer; to make a reference

رجه [raj (j) a] string, cord (for leveling or aligning lines)

رحل [rahl (and) rehl]

• - اقامت انداختن to select as a place of residence; to take up residence, to make one's home, to settle

رحلت [rahlat] literary 1 departure; migration, emigration; transmigration 2 decease, demise, death

• - کردن 1 to depart; to migrate; to emigrate; to transmigrate 2 to move to another world, to die

رحم [rahm] pity, compassion

• (به،بر) - آوردن(کردن) to show compassion, to pity

• نیکان بر بدان ستم است بر - آوردن proverb To spare scoundrels is to offend good people

• - کنید Have pity! / Have mercy!

رحم [rahem] 1 anatomy uterus, womb ♦ سر - cervix of the uterus 2 relatives, relations; ties of blood

رحمان [rahmaan] 1 gracious, merciful (epithet of Allah) 2.1 masculine proper name Rahman 2.2 Rahman (pseudonym of Afghan poet Abdur Rahman of 17th century)

رحمت [rahmat] 1 mercy, grace (of God); forgiveness, pardon; blessing, benediction ♦ او(به)بر - God's mercy on him! 2 masculine proper name Rahmat

• - کردن (بر) to show mercy, to forgive; to pardon

163

رحمة الله علیه (and) رحمت الله علیه [rahmatollahalayh] May God have mercy on him! (upon mention of the name of a deceased)

رحم دل [rahmdel] 1 merciful; charitable 2 *masculine proper name* Rahmdel

رحیم [rahim] 1 kind, good, gracious (epithet of Allah) 2 *masculine proper name* Rahim

رخ [rakh]¹ 1 side, edge, facet 2 *technical* thread; notch; cut

رخ [rokh]² 1 face; features of the face 2 look, appearance 3 *colloquial* side, direction

- رخ آوردن 1 to turn one's face (in some direction) 2 to make one's way [to / toward], to set off or out (in some direction)
- رخ کردن *colloquial* to check, to collate cards (at the beginning of a game)
- رخ دادن to happen, to occur, to take place
- رخ دادن [rukh-dadan] *colloquial* (*literally:* happening) happening, booming, things go right ♦ کار دکان احمد خوب رخ داده Ahmad's store's business is booming
- رخ گرفتن [rukh-gereftan] *colloquial* (*literally:* to face) to face, to engage ♦ او از شرمندگی با مه رخ گرفته نمیتانه He cannot face me because he is embarrassed

رخ [rokh]³ *chess* rook, castle

رخبین [rakhpin] *regional* soup made of buttermilk

رخت [rakht] 1 clothing; linens ♦ آلشی - *colloquial* spare clothing; a change of linens ◊ پوشیدنی - underthings 2 household utensils; belongings, things ♦ سفر - traveling things, goods and chattel 3 fabric, cloth; textiles 4 silk matt or matte

- بدر بردن (and) (بر)بستن - to move, to migrate, to leave, to go away (از)
- از جهان بر بستن (بدر بردن) *literary* to move to the other world, to die

رخت باب [rakhtbaab] textiles, fabrics; textile fabrics

رخت برانی [rakhtboraani] (also - محفل) gathering of the relatives of a bride or newborn (in regard to the preparation of a dowry, trousseau, layette)

رخت خواب [rakhtexaab] bed, bedding

رخدار [rakhdaar] 1 threaded, sifted, having a thread, having ruffling ♦ تفنگ - ruffle 2 cut, faceted, having facets ♦ الماس - faceted diamond

- سیخ - *technical* twisted ribbed bar (for concrete)

رخسار [rokhsaar] (and) رخساره [rokhsaara] *literary poetic* cheeks

رخصت [rokhsat] 1 permission to go away; liberation (from something) 2 *colloquial* free, freed, released ♦ مه - استم؟ Am I free? (i.e., to go)

- خواستن - to ask permission to leave
- شدن - 1 to obtain permission to go or to leave 2.1 to be freed, to be released 2.2 to be released on furlough or holiday 3 to be discharged, to retire
- کردن - 1 to permit to leave, to free, to release 2 to dismiss (for holidays or vacation); to grant leave or furlough 3 to discharge
- از - گرفتن - 1 to ask somebody for permission to go or leave, to get permission from somebody to leave 2 *polite* to part with somebody, to leave somebody

رخصت نامه [rokhsatnaama] 1 pass 2 furlough papers

رخصتی [rokhsati] 1 termination of lessons or studies; leaving work, departure from work (at the end of the work day) 2 leave; vacation, holiday 3 departure

- ورقه - *military* pass
- رفتن - to go on leave
- گرفتن - to take (to obtain) leave

رخنمود [rokhnomud] event; occurrence; incident

- شدن - to happen, to occur, to take place

رخنه [rakhna] 1 breach, break, gap, hole (e.g., in a wall) 2 aperture, slot, crack, slit

- کردن - 1 to make a breach, to make a hole 2 to break through, to force one's way through (در،به) 3 to penetrate; to find a way (در،به)

رد [rad(d)] 1 refusal, rejection; repudiation ♦ رد پیشنهاد rejection of a proposal or suggestion 2 repulse, rebuff 3 track, trace ♦ رد پای footprint ◊ رد عراده rut

- رد کردن - 1 to decline, to reject 2 to repulse, to rebuff
- از پهلوی کسی(چیزی) - شدن to pass by somebody or something

ردالعمل [rad (d) olamal] reaction; reacting

ردو بدل [rad (d) obadal] 1 exchange (of words, of opinions) 2 exchange, barter (in trade)

رده [rada] row, line; rank 2 layer, stratum (of an adobe wall)

ردی [raddi] defective, unfit worthless

- کاغذ - mackle; paper litter

ردیتر [reditar] *automotive* radiator

ردیف [radif] 1 row; series; rank, category 2 order; succession; sequence 3 *literary* radif (word or combination of words which follow the rhyme and do not change throughout a stanza)

رذالت [razaalat] (and) رذاله [razaala] meanness, baseness

رز [raz] 1 grapevine 2 vineyard

- دختر رز *poetic* wine

رزق [razq] (*plural* ارزاق [arzaq]) 1 food; provisions 2 daily bread

- وروزی - subsistence; means of subsistence or livelihood

رزگی [razgi] *colloquial* 1.1 tiny, wee; diminutive 1.2 small 1.3 crumbs ♦ نان - bread crumbs 2 cracked grain (groats)

رزم [rázem] *literary* battle

رزمی [razmi] 1 *literary* epic *adjective* ♦ ادبیات - epic literature 2 *rarely* combat, battle, connected with the waging of battle *adjective*

رژیسور [razhisor] producer (theatrical)

رژیم [rezhim] 1 regime, system order ♦ استبداد - despotic regime 2 order of things, routine of life 3 diet

رس [ras] 1 foodstuffs, provisions 2.1 (also رس عساکر) ammunition 2 allowance

رسا [rasaa] *literary* 1 suitable, proper; appropriate; satisfying; close to the norm 2 mature; perfect; complete ♦ عقل - mature intellect

- در یک کاری دست - داشتن *colloquial* to be a master in some pursuit

رسالت [resaalat] 1 ministry; mission of a prophet 2 mission, role ♦ تاریخی - historic mission

رساله [resaala]¹ (*plural* رسایل [rasayel]) 1 brochure, booklet 2 treatise, composition, work ♦ علمی - thesis, dissertation

رساله [resaala]² *historical* cavalry troop, squadron, the cavalry

رساله دار [resaladaar] *historical* commander of a troop or squadron

رسام [rassaam] artist, graphic artist

رساندن [rasaandan] to lead, to accompany, to convey
- خود را - ۱ to run up [to], to come up [to]; to approach (به) 2 to catch up [with], to overtake (به) **2** to tell, to inform; to communicate ♦ سلام - to pass on greetings, to give greetings ♦ خبر - to report a piece of news **3** to witness, to testify; to mean, to indicate **4** (component of compound verbs with meanings "to cause" / "to inflict") ♦ ضرر - to cause harm

رسایل [rasaayel] *plural of* رساله

رستم [rostam] Rostam (legendary epic hero)
- نام - به از - *proverb* A celebrated name, but not much to look at.

رستن [rostan] (*present tense stem* روی [ruy]) ☞ روییدن

رستوران [restoraan] restaurant

رسته [rasta] **1** commercial row; passageway at a bazaar (between rows of stalls) ♦ مسگری - row of coppersmiths **2** row, line ♦ در ختان - row of trees

رسخت [roskhat] *colloquial* ☞ رخصت

رسد [rasad] part, portion, share ♦ این - من است This is my share.
- کردن - to divide into parts or portions, to share

رسل [rosol] *plural of* رسول

رسم [raasem] [1] (*plural* رسوم [rosum]) **1** custom; rule ♦ وآیین - (and) ورواج - generally accepted rules; traditions **2** rite; ceremony
- بودن (شدن) - to be accepted, to be a custom
- کردن - to make it a rule, to make it a custom
- رسم الخظ ☞ – خط ♦

رسم [raasem] [2] **1** drawing picture, sketch **2** draft; rough drawing
- بالایی - view from above (in a draft)
- پیشروی - view from the front (in a draft)
- کردن - **1** to draw; to make rough sketch, to make a rough copy **2** to draft, to sketch, to design

رسمآ [raasman] officially

رسم الخط [rasmolrat (t)] **1** calligraphy **2** orthography, spelling; the rules of orthography or spelling **3** written language; print, type

رسم ورواج [rasmorewaj] customs, traditions

رسمی [rasmi] official *adjective* ♦ امور - affairs of state ◊ جریده - official printing organ, semiofficial organ ◊ لباس - uniform ◊ غیر - unofficial

رسمیت [rasmiyat] state of being official; formality
- پیداکردن (یافتن) - to take on an official character; to acquire force (about a law, etc.)
- به - شناختن to recognize officially (e.g., a state, a country)

رسوا [roswaa] disgraced; shamed
- شدن - to disgrace oneself; to bring shame upon oneself

رسوایی [roswaayi] disgrace; shame

رسوب [rosub] **1** deposit, sediment **2** *geology* alluvium, sediment

رسوبات [rosubaat] *geology* deposits ♦ بحری - marine deposits

رسوبی [rosubi] *geology* alluvial; sedimentary ♦ احجار - sedimentary rocks

رسوخ [rosukh] influence, authority ♦ صاحب - respected person, influential person
- تحت - کسی افتادن (درآمدن) **1** to fall under somebody's influence **2** to be subject to somebody, to submit to somebody (about territory, about a region)

رسول [rasul] (*plural* رسل [rosol]) **1** envoy, prophet; messiah **2** *obscure* messenger, herald **3** *masculine proper name* Rasul

رسوم [rosum] *plural of* رسم

رسومات [rosumaat] duty, customs; excise taxes

رسید [rasid] **1** receipt; receiving; arrival; delivery **2** receipt
- کردن - to sign (for something)

رسیدات [rasidaat] *plural of* رسید

رسیدگی [rasidagi] **1** maturity, ripeness **2** scrutiny, examination; check
- کردن - to scrutinize; to examine, to investigate; to check, to monitor, to inspect

رسیدن [rasidan] **1** to attain, to reach ♦ به سن بلاغت - to reach a mature age ◊ به مقصد - to attain goals **2** to arrive, to come ♦ به وقت - to arrive in time, to be in time **3** to fall; to set in; to come ♦ نوبت شما رسیده است Your turn has come. **4** to ripen, to mature **5** to rise (about dough) **6** to suffice, to be enough
- تاچه رسد not to mention… / to say nothing of

رسیده [rasida] **1** *past participle* رسیدن **2** sprouted ♦ گندم - wheat that has given off shoots ◊ ریش - a beard that has sprouted
- ادم - mature person, adult

رشادت [rashaadat] valor, bravery, courage

رشتک و بافتک [reshtak-o-baaftak] [1] *colloquial* (*literally:* roots and weaving) pull, connections (among people)

رشتک و بافتک [reshtak-o-baaftak] [2] *slang* (*literally:* roots and weaving) relatives

رشتن [reshtan] ☞ ریشتن

رشته [reshta] [1] **1** thread, string ♦ مرو ارید - string of pearls **2** *anatomy* chord, ligament ♦ رشته های صوتی - vocal chords **3** *biology* hair, fiber; antennae, feelers **4** bonds, tie ♦ دوستی - bonds of friendship **5** *colloquial* relatives, kin, family
- سخن - thread of the conversation
- حیات او قطع شد - His life ended suddenly.

رشته [reshta] [2] nematode, worm (living parasitically under the skin)

رشته داری [reshtadaari] maintaining ties of relationship; blood relationships

رشد [roshd] development, growth ♦ سر مایه - growth of capital ◊ غیر - noncapitalist path of development
- سر مایه داری - the developing countries

رشدی [roshdi] (and) رشدیه [roshdiyaa] *obscure* middle, of the second stage (about school) ♦ مکتب - secondary school

رشک [rashk] envy; jealousy; ambitious striving (for something)

رشک [reshk] nit

رشکی [reshki] (and) رشکیگک [reshkigak] *colloquial* diminutive, wee; small

رشمه [reshma] **1** cord; string, rope (e.g., for laundry) **2** (also پشمی -) thick woolen thread, coarse woolen yarn

رشمه رشمه [reshmareshma]
- باران - میبارد *colloquial* There is frequent rain. / It rains frequently.

رشوت [reshwat] bribe
- دادن - to give a bribe, to bribe (به)
- گرفتن - to take a bribe

رشوت خور [reshwatkhor] bribe-taker, grafter, extortioner

رشوت خوری [reshwatkhori] bribery, graft, extortion

رشوه [reshwa] ☞ رشوت

رشه [rasha] heap of grain, threshed grain (on the threshing floor) ♦ گندم - threshed wheat

رصد [rasad] astronomical observation

رصدخانه [rasadkhaana] observatory

رضاء [razaa] 1 will; consent, assent, approval ♦ به - خود at one's own pleasure ◊ خاطر با - with consent, voluntarily 2 satisfaction, contentment 3 *masculine proper name* Reza

رضاعی [razaa'i]
● - برادر foster brother

رضاکار [razaakaar] volunteer

رضا کارانه [razaakaaraana] 1 voluntary; accomplished of one's own free will 2 voluntarily, of one's own free will

رضامند [razaamand] 1 satisfied, content 2 agreeable [to]; concordant [with] 3 grateful, thankful ♦ استم - خیلی او از من I am very grateful to him.

رضامندی [razaamandi] satisfaction; consent, assent; gratitude, thankfulness

رضانامه [razaanaama] laudatory reference, testimonial, positive recommendation 2 written consent; agreement or understanding about a voluntary admission or confession (of something)

رضایت [razaayat] ☞ رضاء
● - عدم difference of opinion; dissent
● - بهم رساندن to come to an understanding, to come to an agreement (در)

رطوبت [rotubat] 1 moisture, dampness 2 humidity ♦ هوا - air humidity

رعایا [raaayaa] *plural of* رعیت

رعایت [re'aayat] (and) رعایه [re'aaya] 1 observance; taking into consideration, heeding ♦ انتظام- maintaining order ◊ حقوق - respecting the rights [of] respect for the rights [of] ◊ مقررات - fulfillment of the rules compliance with the rules ◊ عدم - noncompliance (with the law, rules, etc.) 2 consideration, respect
● کسی - به out of respect for somebody; taking somebody into consideration
● - کردن 1 to observe, to adhere [to], to take into consideration 2 to take (somebody) into consideration, to respect

رعد [ra'd] (and) raad thunder ♦ وبرق - thunderstorm, thunder and lighting

رعنا [ra'na] 1 pretty, comely; refined, elegant (about a woman) 2.1 (also - گل) yellow sweetbrier 2 *feminine proper name* Rana

رعیت [ra'iyat] (and) rayat (*plural* رعایا [raaayaa]) 1 peasant; subject 2 subjects, people

رعیت پرور [ra'iyatparwar] *literary* just, concerned about the people (about a ruler)

رعیتی [ra'iyati] 1 citizenship 2.1 civil 2.2 *opposite of* سرکاری private

رغبت [raghbat] desire; aspiration; yearning; interest
● - کردن(داشتن) to desire, to aspire [to], to strive [for] (به)

رف [raf] niche, shelf in a wall below the ceiling (for dishware, also a decorative shelf)

رفاقت [rafaaqat] 1 comradeship, friendship 2 *military* escorting, convoying, accompanying ♦ طیاره شکاری - *military* escort fighter

رفاه [rafaah] (and) رفاهت [rafaahat] 1 *literary* prosperity, peace 2 well-being, welfare
● وزرات - عامه ministry of public works (in Afghanistan)

رفتار [raftaar] 1 movement, motion; walking ♦ اسپ - pace or gait of a horse ◊ تیز - fast speed 2 *military* march, field march 3 mode of action; manners, treatment
● - کردن 1 to go, to move 2 to conduct oneself, to act 3 to treat (با)

رفتن [raftan] (*present tense stem* رو [raw]) 1 to go (on foot or in a vehicle; to depart, to go away) 2 (used in aspectual constructions expressing the progressive nature of an action) ♦ تپه های اطراف کابل آباد شده رفته است The hills around Kabul were settled gradually. 3 (component of compound verb combinations) ♦ از بین - to disappear, to vanish
● فرو - to plunge into, to penetrate deep into
● توگفته برو ما گوش میکنیم *colloquial* You talk; we are listening.

روفتن [roftan] ☞ رفتن

رفت وآمد [raftoaamad] 1 walking (to and fro, there and back); movement (of a crowd) ♦ در که چه - زیاد است There is much movement / traffic on the street. 2 plying 3 intercourse; contact; visiting (somebody)
● کردن (داشتن) - 1 to go (on foot or by vehicle) (to and fro, there and back); to have contact (with somebody) 2 to make trips, to ply

رفت وآمد رو [raftoraw] *colloquial* ☞ رفت وآمد

رفته رفته [raftarafta] little by little, a little at a time

رفع [ráf'a] removal, elimination ♦ احتیاجات - satisfaction of needs ◊ کسالت - recovery (of health) ◊ حاجت - satisfaction of a natural necessity

رفقا [rofaqaa] *plural of* رفیق

رفو [rofo] (and) rafo darning, mending (of clothing)
● - کردن to darn, to mend

رفورم [reform] reform

رفوگر [rofogar] darner, mender

رفوگری [rofogari] 1 workshop where clothes are mended 2 رفو

رفیده [rafida] rafida (cloth pad used to attach flat cakes to the hot sides of a tanur or oven for baking)

رفیق [rafiq] (*plural* رفقا [rofaqa]) 1.1 comrade, friend 2 *masculine proper name* Rafiq
● سفر - (and) راه - companion, fellow traveler

رفیقه [rafiqa] comrade (about a woman); friend (female)

رقابت [raqaabat] rivalry; competition

رقاص [raqqaas] 1 dancer 2 pendulum (of a clock)

رقبه [raqaba] area, territory; zone ♦ جنگلها- forest zone ◊ مملکت - state's area

رقت [reqqat] 1 pity, compassion 2 delicacy (of feelings); tenderness, sensitivity
● آوردن - کردن)) to feel pity, to feel compassion; to be moved, to be touched (بر،به)

رقت بار [reqqatbaar] 1 pitiful, lamentable, deplorable ♦ حال - pitiful state 2 evoking sympathy, touching

رقص [raqs] dance
● - کردن to dance

رقصاندن [raqsaandan] *idiom* (*literally:* to make someone dance) to send someone on a wild goose chase ♦ یک هفته بدنبال همین کار رقصاندمش I wasted his time for one week.

رقعات [roq'aaat] *literary* **1** memoirs; notes **2** collection of letters, collection of epistles

رقعه [roq'a] note, short letter ♦ عذریه - note of apology

رقم [raqam] (*plural* ارقام [arqam]) **1** kind; sort **2** way, method, mode, manner ♦ چه؟ - How? / In what manner? / What kind [of]? / Of what kind? **3** cipher, number **4** *literary* a written edict or decree, a rescript ♦ پادشاهی - king's edict
• کردن - *literary* to write

رقم رقم [raqamraqam] various, of different kinds, all sorts of

رقوم [roqum] siyaq (a special numbering system used formerly in the countries of the east)

رقیب [raqib] rival, competitor; opponent (in a contest or game)

رقیق [raqiq] **1** watery, diluted ♦ چای - weak tea **2** rarified (about air)

رقیمه [raqima] *epistolary polite* letter, epistle ♦ شریفه رسید - Your letter was received.

رکاب [rekaab] **1** stirrup, stirrups **2** *technical* clamp, cramp, yoke, collar, strap **3** pedal (of a bicycle)
• در - کسی بودن (رفتن) to escort somebody, to accompany somebody; to be in somebody's retinue

رکاب باشی [rekaabbaashi] *historical* chief of a detachment of a shah's guard (Under Emir Habibullah Khan, the guard was recruited from the people of Nuristan.)

رکاب دار [rekaabdar] *obscure* groom

رکابی [rekaabi]¹ *historical* shah's guard (under Emir Habibullah Khan, usually recruited from the people of Nuristan)

رکابی [rekaabi]² small plate, saucer

رکتیفایر [rektifaayr] ☞ ریکتنفایر

رکعت [rak'at (and) rakat] *religion* rakat (a low bow from the waist during prayer so that the hands touch the knees)

رکن [rókon] (*plural* ارکان [arkaan]) **1** *literary* support, pillar **2** *literary* supporting part of a couplet; foot
• چهار - beginning and end of each of two lines in a couplet

رکود [rokud] **1** depression, decline; collapse **2** deadlock (e.g., in talks)

رکوع [roku'] *religion* part of the Moslem prayer ceremony which consists of performing bows (☞ رکعت)

رکیک [rakik] indecent, improper, coarse (about words)
• سخنان - coarseness, swearing, bad language

رگ [rag] **1** blood vessel; vein; artery **2** tendon, sinew; nerve; vein ♦ رگهای برگ veins of a leaf **3** *geology* vein **4** breed, species; race
• رگ زدن **1** to let blood (by opening a vein) **2** *colloquial* to urinate

بد رگ • [badrag] *colloquial* (*literally:* bad vein) SOB, bastard

رگ خواب ☞ رگ خو

رگ خو [ragekhaw] *colloquial* tender place, sore spot; vulnerable side, weak spot (of some person)
• کسی را پیدا کردن - to find somebody's weak spot; to cut somebody to the quick

رگ خواب [ragekhaab] **1** carotid artery **2** tender place, sore spot; vulnerable side, weak spot

رگ زن [ragzan] barber (who performs bloodletting)

رگ و رگبست [rag-o-ragbast] *colloquial* (*literally:* vein and vein connection) blood (relatives) roots and background (person)

رم [ram] **1** *present tense stem* رمیدن **2** fright, scare
• رم کردن **1** to be frightened to recoil, to jump aside in fright(از) **2** to be shy

رمال [rammaal] *literary* fortuneteller; soothsayer

رماندن [ramaandan] to frighten, to scare away (birds, animals)

رمبه [ramba] *agriculture* hoe, chopper

رمز [ramz] (*plural* رموز [romuz]) **1** secret; riddle; enigma **2** conventional sign, symbol; code; cipher ♦ کلید - key to a cipher
• کردن - to encipher

رمزنویسی [ramznowisi] **1** enciphering, cryptography **2** stenography; shorthand

رمضان [ramazaan] **1** Ramadan (ninth month of the Moslem lunar year; month of fasting) ♦ عید - holiday after fasting, holiday of Ramadan **2** *masculine proper name* Ramazan

رمضانی [ramazani] Ramadani (a custom according to which a group of children makes the rounds of houses singing and dancing to collect money to celebrate the month of Ramadan)

رمل [ramal] *literary* ramal (one of the basic meters of Arab-Persian versification)

رمل [rámel] *literary* fortunetelling (usually with dice)

رمنده [ramenda] **1** easily frightened, fearful ♦ آهوی - shy deer, shy doe **2** avoiding encounters, reserved

رموز [romuz] *plural of* رمز

رموک [ramuk] *colloquial* ☞ رمنده
• اسپ - shy horse

رمه [rama] flock, herd (of sheep, of goats); drove

رمیدن [ramidan] ☞ رم کردن in entry

رنج [ranj] **1** burdens, difficulties **2** pain, suffering, ailment **3** *colloquial* consumption
• بردن (کشیدن) - **1** to toil, to labor, to endure burdens **2** to suffer, to experience pain
• دادن- **1** to create difficulties; to hamper, to impede(به) **2** ☞ رنجانیدن
• چیزی رابر خود گوار ساختن - *literary polite* to take the trouble to do something

رنج [renj] *technical* wrench ♦ دهن بسته - box wrench

رنجانیدن [ranjaanidan] **1** to offend, to anger **2** to torment; to harass; to cause pain

رنجش [ranjesh] offense; vexation, annoyance; grief; chagrin

رنجور [ranjur] **1** sick; infirm, feeble **2** sufferer, martyr

رنجوری [ranjuri] **1** illness, disease, ill health; indisposition **2** grief, sorrow; depression, low spirits

رنجیدن [ranjidan] to take offense, to be angry [with]; to be pained; to be grieved (از)

رند [rend] **1.1** adroit, resourceful **1.2** dissipated, dissolute; licentious, reckless **2.1** cunning person, resourceful person **2** debauchee, featherbrain

رنده [randa] plane (tool); draw knife; gear shaper-cutter, mortising cutter ♦ دستگاه - planer

رنده کاری [randakaari] planing, rough-hewing

رنگ [rang]¹ **1** color; coloration, coloring ♦ تیره - dark color **2** (*also* روی -) color of the face ♦ با پریده - with a face gone pale **3** *cards* suit; trumps ♦ پشه است - Spades are trumps. **4** paint; dye ♦ خشک - paste paint, oil paste **5** (*also* قلم -) ink

ر

- رنگ بوت ☞ بوت •
- رنگارنگ ☞ رنگ به- (and) رنگ رنگ •
- آوردن - 1 to become juicy; to redden (about ripening fruit) 2 to recover, to get well, to become strong or stronger (about a person)
- باختن - *colloquial* 1 to be frightened; to blanch (from fear) 2 to be confused, to be embarrassed
- (کردن) زدن - 1 to color, to paint, to dye 2 to shine, to polish or clean (shoes) with cream or polish
- خود را زرد کردن - to disgrace oneself, to cover oneself with shame (before somebody پیش) ♦ رنگش پرید He became pale. / He paled. / He is embarrassed.
- رنگش زرد شد *colloquial* He disgraced himself. / He was disgraced.

رنگ [rang]² 1 type, kind, sort; method, manner ♦ ؟- چه What kind [of]? / Of what kind? ◊ ؟- به چه In what manner? / How?

- به همین - است 1 That's the way. / Here's how. / Here's the way. 2 *colloquial* ruse, trick, subterfuge
- ریختن - *colloquial* to think up tricks, to devise ruses, to use cunning
- (گرفتن) دیگر پیدا کردن - *intransitive* 1 to change, to be transformed 2 to take another turn

رنگ [reng] *technical* ring ♦ پستون - piston ring
رنگارنگ [rangaarang] of every kind, various, all sorts of ♦ میوه های - the most diverse vegetables
رنگ باز [rangbaaz] *colloquial* sly person, swindler, cheat, fraud
رنگ بوت [rangebut] cream for boots, (shoe) polish
رنگ به رنگ [rangbarang] ☞ رنگارنگ
رنگ پریده [rangparida] 1 pale, blanched 2 ☞ رنگ رفته
رنگ رفته [rangrafta] faded, discolored; peeled, having lost the brilliance of coloring
رنگ رو [rangraw] *colloquial* fading; rapidly becoming discolored
رنگ ریز [rangrez] dyer of fabrics
رنگ ریزی [rangrezi] 1 the craft business of dyeing (fabrics) 2 a dye house
رنگ زرد [ranzard] 1 pale, pallid; emaciated 2 ☞ روی زرد
رنگ مال [rangmaal] (house) painter, paperhanger
رنگ مالی [rangmali] dyeing; (house) painting
رنگ و روی [rangeroy] *literary* 1 external view, exterior view, look, appearance 2 beauty, attractiveness
رنگه [ranga] color, colored; painted, dyed ♦ فلم - color film
رنگه باب [rangabab] colored fabrics, colored cloth
رنگین [rangin] 1 colorful, bright; flowery, florid 2 ☞ رنگه
رنوی [ranwey] (also خط) runway
رو [raw] [raftan]¹ 1 *present tense stem* رفتن 2.1 motion, movement 2.2 flow, current (of water in a river, etc) ♦ روهای بحری sea currents 3 roundabout road, crossing, ford
رو [raw]² *colloquial* quickly, rapidly, swiftly ♦ رو بیا Go quickly!
رو [ro] 1.1 face ♦ روی زیبا beautiful face 1.2 the front side; surface ♦ روی زمین earth's surface 1.3 cause, reason, basis, grounds ♦ از این رو for this reason; therefore 2.1 روی(به) on *denominative preposition* ♦ روی میز on the table
- پیش روی ... before somebody's eyes; in front of somebody
- روی(به) شانه 1 on the shoulders, onto the shoulders, shoulder 2 over; on ♦ سه ماه روی این تصویر کار کرده است He worked on this painting for three months. 2.2 از روی by; through; because of, out of ♦ از روی مجبوریت by compulsion
- (نهادن) رو گذاشتن 1 to go, to set out [for] (به) 2 to begin to develop (in a direction) ♦ شهر رو به آبادی گذاشت The city began to develop conveniences and amenities.
- روی کار آمدن 1 to enter the scene (of action); to come to power 2 to come to light, to reveal itself (about facts)
- روی کسی را شستن *colloquial* to catch somebody (e.g., in a lie), to expose somebody's machinations
- از روی کسی نفتادن *colloquial* not to fall in somebody's estimation; not to let somebody down ♦ مه که از روی او افتاده نمی توانم I can't let him down.
- به روی خود نیاوردن not to give a sign, not to react
- به روی کسی آوردن to point out (a blunder, etc.) to someone, to give someone to understand (an error, etc.)
- روی کسی رانمی بیند He doesn't consider anybody.
- رویش سیاه *colloquial* Shame on him!
- روی غریبی سیاه *colloquial* Damn this poverty!
- روبرو ☞ روبه رو •

روا [rawaa] 1 permitted; authorized; legal 2 proper, fitting; acceptable
- داشتن - 1 to approve, to permit 2 to consider acceptable, to consider permissible

روابط [rawaabet] *plural of* رابطه
رواج [rawaaj (and) rewaaj] 1 circulation (of money, of goods) 2 custom
- داشتن - 1 to be in circulation (about money, goods) 2 to be accepted; to be in use

روادار [rawaadaar]
- (شدن)بودن - 1 to treat tolerantly; to allow 2 not to be against, to consent; to concur ♦ او-است که این خانه از من باشد He is not against having this house belong to me. ◊ من-نیستم که... I do not consent ... / I will not permit ...

رواداری [rawaadaari] good attitude, good relation; approval
رواش [rawaash] *botany* edible rhubarb
روان [rawaan] 1.1 going, moving 2 flowing; fluent (about words, speech) 2 smoothly, fluently (about speech) ♦ روسی - He spoke Russian fluently. 3 soul, spirit
- بودن - to go, to move; to flow
- شدن - to start off, to set out [for] (somewhere) ♦ بچه ها طرف مکتب - شدند The children went off to school.
- کردن - *colloquial* 1 to send, to send off 2 to learn (a lesson) by heart

روان شناسی [rawaanshenaasi] psychology
روانه [rawana] ☞ شدن- روان شدن in entry روان
- کردن ☞ روان کردن a in entry روان •

روایت [rewaayat] 1 narration, narrative, story, tale 2 tradition, legend
- ... است - 1 legend says ... 2 the story goes that ... 3 oral tradition, oral version

روب [rob]¹ *present tense stem* رفتن [roftan] (and) روفتن
روب [rob]² *military* aiguillette
روبا [robaa] ☞ روباه
روبانکشاف [robaenkeshaaf] developing, progressing ♦ ممالک - developing countries
روباه [robaah] fox, vixen

ر

روباه خانه [robaahkhaana] 1 ventilation vent, hole (in a foundation) 2 duct (in wall of a boiler room)

روبراه [robaaraah] 1 put right; adjusted; arranged, organized ♦ همه کارها - بود Everything was put right. 2 colloquial ready for departure, prepared for a journey
- ♦ کردن - 1 to put right, to arrange, to organize 2 to send off (on the road)

روبرو(ی) [robaro (y)] 1.1 face to face 1.2 facing; opposite 1.3 (opposite of نیم رخ) full face 2 opposite, in front [of] denominative preposition
- ♦ شدن - to meet face to face, to run into (به)

روبروشدن [robaroshudan] colloquial to get in someone's face

روبنا [robenaa] 1 above ground part of a building 2 superstructure 3 philosophy superstructure

روبه آفتاب [robaaftaab] sunny, turned with its face to the sun (about a building, a room)

روبه افزایش [robaafzaayesh] growing, intensifying, increasing ♦ - بادقت with ever increasing attention

روپوش [roposh] case, cover; covering, casing, housing, jacket
- ♦ موتور - technical cowling or hood of an engine

روپه [rupa] colloquial 1 rupa (popular coin equal to 100 puls) 2 money, coins 3 ☞ روپیه

روپیه [rupiya] rupee (monetary unit of Afghanistan that has gone out of use)

روت [rot] ceremonial rich flatcake (baked for the 40th day after childbirth)

روجایی [rojaayi] ☞ روی جایی

روح [roh] (plural ارواح [arwaah]) 1 spirit, soul ♦ ارواح مردگان - souls of the dead 2 spirit, emotional state
- ♦ بخشیدن - to fill with enthusiasm, to inspire; to enliven
- ♦ و روان - endearment darling, sweetheart

روحاً [rohan] 1 spiritually; morally, ethically ♦ جسماً و - physically and mentally 2 mentally, in spirit

روحانی [rohaani] (plural روحانیان [rohaaniyaan] (and) روحانیون [rohaaniyun]) 1 priest, spiritual person 2 ecclesiastical (pertaining to the church, religion)

روح پرور [rohparwar] (and) روح نواز [rohnawaaz] delightful; charming; bewitching ♦ آهنگ - delightful melody, a melody that delights the ear

روحی [rohi] 1 spiritual 2 moral, ethical; psychic, emotional ♦ - حالت emotional state

روحیات [rohiyaat] 1 plural of روحیه 2 psychology

روحیاتی [rohiyaati] 1 psychological ♦ داستانهای - psychological short stories 2 ☞ روحی

روحیه [rohiya] (plural روحیات [rohiyaat]) spirit, emotional mood; morale

رود [rod]¹ river, small river

رود [rod]² rud (old stringed instrument)

روداد [rodad] ☞ روی داد

رودبار [rodbaar] 1 floodplain of a river 2 agriculture land irrigated by a river (by means of diversion ditches)

رودخانه [rodkhaana] river channel, riverbed

روده [roda] 1 anatomy intestine; intestines ♦ کلان - large intestine ◊ خرد - کلان راخورد - colloquial The intestines are cramped from hunger. 2 pipe; tube, hose

رو رو [raw-raw] colloquial (literally: go go) on the go, fast, quickly ♦ او کار خود را رورو خلاص میکند He finishes his work quickly

روز [roz] 1 day; daytime ♦ شب - day and night; 24 hours 2 day, date ♦ تولدی – birthday ◊ رخصتی - day off
- ♦ دیگر - 1 the next day 2 on the next day ♦ به - - with every (passing) day 3 time
- ♦ سیاه(بد) – black day, adversity, misfortune
- ♦ چلیدن - colloquial to struggle to make a living, to barely make ends meet
- ♦ روز آمدن بر سر کسی idiom (literally: a day to come on someone) having a bad time in life, facing hardship ♦ سرش روز آمده He is having a hard time with life.

روزانه [rozaana] 1 day adjective, daily 2 by day 3 pay by the day

روز بسته [rooze-basta] colloquial (literally: complete day) live-long day, a whole day

روزپر [rozpor] full day, full work shift
- ♦ قرارداد شدن - to contract for a whole day, to contract for a full shift

روز چلانی [rozchalaani] colloquial a life of poverty, a pitiful existence

روز چپه کردن [rooz-chapa-kardan] colloquial (literally: flipping over a day) to be a time server (to get paid for the day whether or not one works)

روزگار [rozgaar] 1 time, era, epoch ♦ در روزگاران پیشین in olden times 2 life, living conditions; circumstances

روز گذرانی [rooz-guzaraani] colloquial (literally: to go through the day) wasting a day, wasting a day without accomplishing something ♦ او را آوردم که کار کند اما او روز گذرانی می کند I hired him to work, but he is not doing anything derogatory

روز گشته [rooz-gashta] colloquial (literally: having backward day) unfortunate, unlucky (person)

روزمره [rozmara] 1 daily, everyday adjective 2 daily, every day adverb

روزن [rawzan] ☞ روزنه

روزنامه [roznaama] rarely newspaper

روزنه [rawzan (and) rozana] 1 opening; hole; aperture (in a wall or ceiling) 2 small window
- ♦ امید - a ray of hope

روزه [roza] 1 fast (by Moslems in the month of Ramadan) 2 ☞ رمضان
- ♦ داشتن(گرفتن) - to maintain a fast, to fast

روزه داری [rozadaari] maintaining a fast; fasting

روزی [rozi] 1 ☞ رزق 2 share, portion, lot
- ♦ روز نو-نو proverb If day comes, there will be bread.

روزی خور [rozikhor] literary person, God's slave who lives on daily bread

روزی رسان [rozirasaan] providing subsistence (about God)
- ♦ میرساند - proverb God will provide. / God will not abandon [one].

روس [rus] Russian (about person) noun ♦ زن او - است His wife is a Russian.

روساء [roasaa] plural of رئیس

روستا [rustaa] literary village

روستایی [rustaayi] literary 1 rural, country; village adjective 2 villager, peasant

روسی [rusi] 1 Russian adjective 2 (also زبان -) the Russian language

ر

روش [rawesh] 1 conduct, behavior, mode of action 2 way, method; methods, methodology ♦ تحقیق - method of research

روش [rosh] colloquial clearly, directly, in plain terms, without beating around the bush
- گفتن • - to speak directly or frankly, to speak without beating around the bush, to speak plainly

روشن [roshan] 1.1 bright, light, clear ♦ شب - clear night ◊ عقل - lucid mind 1.2 illuminated, aflame 1.3 clear; apparent, obvious ♦ جواب - a clear answer 2 *feminine proper name* Roshan
- کردن • - 1 to illuminate; to light up 2 to light (a lamp, an electric light) 3 to ascertain; to explain, to elucidate, to make clear (را)
- باکسی – کردن • *colloquial* to end dealings with somebody; to settle up with somebody once and for all

روشناس [roshenaas] 1 familiar 2 known, well-known

روشنایی [roshnaayi] 1 light, illumination ♦ خفیف - weak light 2 radiance, brilliance ♦ مهتاب - radiance of the moon
- دادن • - to give off light, to shine; to sparkle, to glitter
- کردن • - to light (an electric light), to illuminate

روشندان [roshandaan] window, small window

روشن فکر [roshanféker] 1 enlightened, intellectual, educated 2 intellectual *noun*

روشنی [roshani] 1 ☞ روشنایی 2 clearness; clarity; distinctness; intelligibility 3 *colloquial* easing, relief; joy, gladness
- در • - in the light [of] ♦ در معلومات تازه - in the light of new data
- افکندن • بر - to shed light [on], to make clear

روشنی انداز [roshaniandaaz] projector

روغتون [roghtun] hospital, clinic

روغتیا [roghtiyaa]
- وزارت • - Ministry of Public Health (in Afghanistan)

روغن [roqan (and) rawqan] 1 oil; fat, lard, suet, grease ♦ دنبه - fat of (sheep) tail ◊ زرد - boiled butter ◊ نباتی - vegetable oil 2 grease, ointment ♦ موتر - lubricating oil
- کردن(دادن،زدن) • - to lubricate (with oil, grease, etc.)
- کشیدن • - to press oil, to squeeze oil (from seeds)
- سر آمدن • to thicken, to congeal (about soup or broth); to begin to boil away

روغنداغ [roghandaagh] vessel with a handle (for melting butter)

روغن کشی [roghankashi] pressing of oil (from seeds)

روغنی [roghani] oil; oily ♦ رنگ - oil paint 2 oil-bearing (about agricultural crops)

روغنیات [roghaniyaat] *technical* oils; lubricants

روفتن [roftan] (*present tense stem* روب [rob]) to sweep

روک [rawak] 1 sliding drawer (of a table or desk) 2 roller, caster (of an easy chair, bed)

روکر [rokar] *technical* rocker arm, connecting rod

روکش [rokash] ☞ روی کش

روگردانی [rogardaani] 1 deviation; evasion; refusal 2 dissent, resistance
- کردن • ازقانون - to circumvent a law, to violate a law

رول [rol]¹ role
- ادا کردن • - to act, to perform, to play a role

رول [rol]² 1 *technical* road roller 2 roll (of paper, etc.)

رولر [rolar] *technical* roller; runner, traveling roller

روم [rum] *historical* 1 Byzantium 2 Turkey ♦ بحیره - Mediterranean Sea 3 rum sultanate of the seljuks

روماتیزم [rumaatizem] rheumatism ♦ مفصلی - rheumatic fever

رومال [romal] ☞ روی مال

رومان [romaan] novel

رومی [rumi] *historical* 1 Byzantine 2 Latin, Roman ♦ حروف - Roman alphabet

رومیزی [romeezi] ☞ روی میزی

رون [rawn] 1 series 2 turn; round, lap ♦ امروز - من است Today is my turn.

رونتگن [rontgan] roentgen, x-rays

رونده [rawenda] 1 going 2 flowing
- بودن(شدن) • - to make ready for a journey, to depart ♦ او است He is departing.

رونق [rawnaq] 1 bloom, blossoming; flourishing; reanimation; rise, upsurge 2 *literary* magnificence, splendor
- گرفتن • - to reach (full) bloom; to achieve an upsurge; to flourish

روی [rawi] *literary* base syllable or sound of a word (serving as the foundation for rhyming)

روی [ro] (^oy)¹ ☞ رو
- انداختن • - *colloquial* to ask (for something), to beg (for something), to supplicate, to implore
- دادن • - 1 to happen, to occur, to take place 2 *colloquial* to encourage, to cheer up
- گرفتن • - to cover [one's] face, to cover oneself up (about Moslem women)
- گشتاندن • *colloquial* to turn away [from somebody]; to refuse scornfully; to turn up (از)
- به...رفتن • - to have a tendency for …
- به خوابیدن • to lie face down
- روی برایش نمانده که باز آمده بتواند • *colloquial* He is ashamed to come again.

روی [roy]² *present tense stem* رستن [rostan] (and) روییدن [royidan]

روی [roy]³ 1 zinc 2 tin 3 bronze, brass

رویاروی [royaaroy] ☞ روبرو(ی)
- کردن • - to turn over

رویاندن [royaandan] to raise, to cultivate, to grow

روی بالش [roybaalesh] pillowcase

روی بند [royband] veil for the face (on Moslem women)

روی پاک [roypaak] (face) towel

روی جایی [royjoyi] sheet, bedsheet

روی داد [roydaad] 1 event, incident 2 condition; state, status

روی دار [roydaar] 1 intercessor, patron 2 respectable person, important person

روی داری [roydaari] 1 patronage, intercession 2 respectability, decency

روی رفت [royraft] face stitch; stitch

روی زرد [royzard] ashamed, disgraced
- ساختن(کردن) • - to shame, to put to shame

روی زمینی [royezamini] ground *adjective*

روی سیاه [roysiyaah] disgraced ♦ شدن - to disgrace oneself

روی سیاهی [roysiyaahi] shame, disgrace; dishonor

رویکار [roykaar] facade (of a building)

رویکاری [roykaari] facing a facade; trimming or finishing a facade

ر

روی کش [roykash] 1 shawl, light blanket 2 cover; cloak ♦ زیر - under a cover of snow 3 *technical* facing ♦ سنگ - از برف facing stone 4 *technical* covering, patch
روی گردان [roygardaan] turning (of clothing)
• کردن - to turn (clothing)
رویگری [roygari] coating with zinc, galvanizing; tinning
روی مال [roymaal] towel
روی میزی [roymeezi] tablecloth
روی نماگی [roynomaagi] *colloquial* a present to the bride from the groom's relatives (on the day of her unveiling)
روی نویس [roynawis] 1 copied (from something) 2 a copy
• کردن - to copy, to make a copy (of something)
روی نویسی [roynawisi] copying, making a copy
رویه [roya] 1 the right side (of clothing), the outer side, the face side ♦ استرو - the lining and face 2 upostery (of a chair, of an easy chair) 3 covering (with glazing, etc.) ♦ کاشی - glazing (for tiles)
رویه [rawiya] 1 mode of action, conduct, behavior; treatment 2 custom, habit 3 tactic; tactics
روییدن [royidan] to grow
ره [ra] *colloquial variant of postposition* را ♦ تکسی ره ایستاد کرد He stopped the taxi.
ره [rah] ☞ راه
رها [rahaa]
• کردن - 1 to free; to set free 2 to let out (e.g., of one's hands)
رهانیدن [rahaanidan] ☞ رها کردن in entry رها ♦ از چنگ مرگ - to save from death
ره آورد [rahaaward] present, gift (brought from a trip)
رهایش [rahaayesh] stay; sojourn
• قابل - living *adjective*, habitable
• مساحت عمومی قابل - total dwelling space, total floor space
• داشدن(کردن) - 1 to stay, to be located (somewhere) 2 to live, to reside ♦ او در این خانه دارد He lives in this house.
رهایشگاه [rahaayeshgaah] residence, abode, place of settlement
رهایی [rahaayi] liberation, deliverance
• دادن - to liberate, to save
رهبر [rahbar] 1 guide 2 leader
رهبری [rahbari] 1 duties of a guide 2 leadership
رهبری شده [rahbarishoda]
• اقتصاد - controlled economy, controlled economic system
راهرو [rahraw] ☞ راهرو
• ریخت - *technical* gate, runner
راهزن [rahzan] ☞ راهزن
رهگذر [rahgozar] 1 traveler, wayfarer; passer-by, one who drives or rides by 2 attitude; aspect, point of view
• از ... - 1 in relation [to], from the point of view [of] 2 because of, in connection with ...
• از این - in this regard
• از هر - in all respects, from all points of view
رهگم [rahgom] 1 having lost the way, lost 2 having strayed from the true path, gone astray; mistaken
رهن [rahn] guarantee, pledge
راهنما(ی) [rahnomaa (y)] ☞ راهنما(ی)
رهنمایی [rahnomaayi] ☞ راهنمایی
رهنورد [rahnaward] ☞ راهنورد
ری [ray] *colloquial* ☞ رأی 1
• سر کسی ری زدن to fear somebody
• مه سر او ری نمیزنم I am not afraid of him at all.
• ری دادن to promise profit, to be profitable ♦ این مال ری میته یانی؟ Are these goods profitable or not?
ریا [riyaa] hypocrisy, sham, pretense; sanctimony
ریاحین [riyaahin] *plural of* ریحان
ریاست [riyaasat] 1 chairmanship; leadership ♦ تحت - under the chairmanship, under the leadership [of] ... 2 department, directorate, administration ♦ مستقل - chief directorate, main administration, department ♦ مستقل مطبوعات - press department
ریاضی [riyaazi] mathematical
• علوم - the exact sciences
ریاضیات [riyaaziyaat] mathematics; the mathematical sciences
ریاکار [riyaakaar] hypocrite; bigot
ریالزم [riyaalézem] (and) ریالیزم [riyaalizem] realism
ریایی [riyaayi] hypocritical, affected; bigoted, sanctimonious; false; insincere
ریتین [riyatayn] *anatomy* lungs; both lungs
ریحان [rayhaan] (*plural* ریاحین [riyaahin]) 1 *botany* basil 2 an aromatic plant
ریخت [reekht] 1 appearance, look ♦ ریختش بد است He has a repulsive appearance. 2 form 3 casts, moldings
• جای - *technical* runner
ریختاندن [reekhtaandan] (*present tense stem* ریزان [reezan]) 1 to pour, to pour out, to spill 2 to pour; to strew; to spill 3 to pour, to unload (e.g., from a vehicle) 4 to lose (e.g., teeth) ♦ او هنوز دندانهای شیری خودرا نریختانده بود His baby teeth haven't fallen out yet.
ریختن [reekhtan] (*present tense stem* ریز [reez]) 1 to pour, to flow; to run out, to pour *intransitive* ♦ فرو - to pour out, to stream down; to run out 2 to fall (about leaves) 3 to fall out (about teeth, hair) 4 ☞ ریختاندن 1, 2 ♦ آب راریخت He poured out the water.
ریخته [reekhta] 1 *past participle* ریختن 2.1 cast, whole, cast in one piece 2.2 sturdily cut out, compact, dense, stocky
ریخته گر [reekhtagar] foundry hand; founder, smelter; molder
ریخته گری [reekhtagari] smelting, founding, casting; founding, foundry work
• عینک - protective glasses (for a foundry hand)
ریخته گی [reekhtagi] 1 founding, casting 2 *past participle* ریختن
ریز [reez]¹ *present tense stem* ریختن
ریز [reez]² 1 trill, warble (of a nightingale, etc.) 2 ☞ ریزه 2
• کردن - 1 to break out (in song, tears, etc.), to sing (about song birds) 2 *colloquial ironic* to talk much and rapidly; to sing like a nightingale
ریزان [reezaan] 1 *present tense stem* ریختاندن (and) 2 (second component of compound words with meanings of "scattering" / "spilling" / "pouring out") ♦ برگ ریزان shedding of leaves
ریزاندن [reezaandan] ☞ ریختاندن
• آب رانریزان Don't spill the water!
ریزرف [rizarf]
• کردن - to reserve, to order in advance (a place on a steamship, at a hotel, etc.)
ریزرویشن [rizarweeshan] 1 reservation (of places on a steamship, at a hotel, etc.) 2 ticket department

ریزش [reezesh] 1 head cold, cold; chill; flu 2 *colloquial* spread, distribution (of something)

ریزشگاه [reezeshgaah] *geology* runoff (of water), overflow

ریزگی [reezgi] *colloquial* 1 small fragments, splinters; crumbs ♦ ریزگی های نان crumbs of bread 2 scraps, pieces

ریز وپاش [reezopaash] *colloquial* small household goods; all sorts of trifles

ریزه [reeza] 1 crumb; grain; little bit ♦ ریزه های خوان crumbs from the table 2 little, small

ریزه کاری [reezakaari] 1 small work, fine work 2 fine jewelry; delicate carving by hand

ریزه گک [reezagak] *colloquial* tiny, diminutive, wee

ریزه گی [reezagi] childhold, infancy

ریسپان [reespaan] *colloquial* 1 ☞ ریسمان 2 snake, serpent

ریسمان [reesmaan] rope, cord; string, twine ♦ باربندی - cord or rope for tying up baggage

ریسیدن [reesidan] ☞ ریشتن

ریش [rish] beard
- زیر • chin
- کردن - • to tear the hair from one's own beard (as a sign of grief)
- او از زیر - من خر سوار تیر شد • He wound me around his little finger.

ریش [rees]¹ *present tense stem* ریشتن (and) ریشیدن

ریش [rees]² wound

ریشتن [reeshtan] (*present tense stem* ریش [reesh]) to spin yarn, to spin threads

ریشخند [rishkhand] mockery, sneer, gibe, taunt

ریش سفید [rishsafeed] 1 gray-bearded, old; venerable 2 an elder an aksakal

ریشه [reesha] 1 root, roots 2 threads, fringe 3 corn stigmas 4 *grammar* root, stem ♦ فعل - root (stem) of a verb
- دواندن • 1 to take root 2 to become stronger
- سنگ - • asbestos

ریشه دار [reeshadaar] with a fringe

ریشه ریشه [reeshareesha] *colloquial* frayed, shabby, threadbare; worn to shreds

ریشیدن [reeshidan] ☞ ریشتن

ریفارم [reeform] reform

ریکارد [rikaard] 1 *phonograph* record 2 recording (on a record or tape)
- پرکردن - • to record (on a record or tape)

ریکارد گیری [rikaardgiri] (and) ریکارد دنگ [rikaardeng] sound recording

ریکتیفایر [reektifaayr] 1 *electrical* rectifier 2 *radio* detector

ریگ [reeg] sand ♦ روان - moving sands; sand hills
- از - روغن کشیدن • *colloquial* to be extremely practical, to be extremely prudent; to extract use from everything

ریگزار [reegzaar] 1 sandy terrain 2 sands; dunes

ریگستان [reegestaan] 1 rocky desert 2 the region of Registan or Rigestan

ریگمال [reegmaal] (also کاغذ-) emory paper

ریگی [reegi] sand, sandy ♦ توفان - sandstorm ◊ طلای - gold dust

ریل [reel] 1 railroad 2 train

ریم [rim] pus (from a wound)

رینوس [rous] *plural of* رأس

ریوی [riyawi] pulmonary ♦ امراض - pulmonary diseases

ریه [riya] *anatomy* lung

رئیس [rais] (*plural* رؤساء [roasaa]) 1 head, chief, leader, chairman ♦ شرکت - head of a company 2 manager, director ♦ پوهنتون - rector of a university 3 فاکولته - dean of a faculty ◊ (also مستقل -) chief of a department; chief of a chief directorate, main administration

ز
13th letter of the Dari alphabet

زا [zaa] name of the letter ز

زابلستان [zaabolestaan] *historical* Zabolestan (ancient country of the territory of modern Afghanistan; homeland of the legendary Rostam)

زاچ [zaach] childbearing woman (from the first through the fortieth days after childbirth)

زاد [zaad]¹ ☞ زاده 1

زاد [zaad]² *literary* road supplies, stores, supplies, provisions

زادن [zaadan] ☞ زاییدن

زاده [zaada] 1 *past participle* زادن 2 child, offspring; son

زار [zaar] 1 pitiful; mournful, sad 2 lamentable; deplorable, sorrowful; regrettable
- وزبون - • weak, sickly
- زار زار گریه کردن • to cry bitterly

زار [zaar] affix with meanings of "abundance" / "focus" (of something) ♦ ریگ زار sands, dunes

زارع [zaare'] (*plural* زارعین [zare'in]) farmer; peasant

زاری [zari] 1 entreaty, supplication 2 weeping, crying, sobbing
- کردن - • 1 to entreat, to implore, to supplicate, to ask (for something) tearfully 2 to weep, to cry, to sob

زاغ [zaagh] 1.1 raven, crow ♦ گرگی - an old, shabby raven 1.2 *abusive* an old grumbler, an old hag 2 *colloquial* old fox, cheat, swindler, sly person
- زبان - را - میداند • *proverb* To understand a raven, you must be a raven.
- او خیلی – است • He is a slick customer.

زاغابی [zaaghaabi] (and) زاغاوی [zaaqaawi] cormorant (bird)

زاغچه [zaaghcha] jackdaw

زاغ نول [zaaghnol] *technical* 1 round-nose pliers 2 pickax, hoe

زاک [zaak] 1 vitriol 2 (also سفید -) alum

زانو [zaanu] knee ♦ کاس – *anatomy* kneecap
- زدن - • *colloquial* 1 to kneel (on one or both knees) 2 to sit on one's heels (with one's knees resting on the floor) 3 to get ready (for resolute actions)
- بالای دو - نشستن ☞ زدن •

زانوخم [zaanukham] *technical* 1 elbow of a pipe, pipe elbow 2 bracket, support

زاویه [zaawiya] 1 *mathematical* angle ♦ قایمه - right angle ◊ به - 40 درجه at an angle of 40 degrees 2 try square 3 *surveying* compass 4 *literary* solitary place, secluded place; cell

زاویه سنج [zaawiyasanj] (and) زاویه گر [zawiyagar] protractor, angle gage, goniometer

زاویه نشین [zaawiyaneshin] ☞ گوشه نشین

زاه [zaa (h)] moisture, dampness
- زدن - • 1 to percolate; to leak; to ooze, to seep out (about water) 2 to grow damp, to become damp

زاه آب [zaa (h) aab] 1 water (percolating or seeping through the soil or a filter) 2 water diverted along drainage canals

زاه بر [zaa (h) bor] 1 drain 2 drainage ditch

زاهد [zaahed] monk, hermit; ascetic

زاه کش [zaa (h) kash] ☞ زاه بر

زاهکشی [zaa (h) kashi] drainage

زای [zaay] *present tense stem* زادن (and) زاییدن

زاید [zaayed] 1 added, appended; augmented 2 superfluous, unnecessary

زایر [zaayer] (and) زائر [zaaer] pilgrim

زایل [zaayel] (and) زائل [zaael]
- شدن - 1 declining; tending toward sunset, to set (about heavenly bodies) 2 to diminish, to wane; to disappear 3 to perish, to lose one's life, to die
- کردن - to bring to naught; to destroy, to ruin

زاییدن [zaayidan] (*present tense stem* زای [zay]) 1 to give birth, to bear, to bring into the world 2 to be born, to come into the world

زبان [zobaan (and) zabaan] language, tongue; speech ♦ تحریری - written language ◊ تکلمی - spoken language; colloquial language
- تحریری - ☞ نگارش *colloquial*
- گشتاندن - to deny one's words, to tell a lie
- از - افتادن(ماندن) to be deprived of the gift of speech, to lose the gift of speech
- به - درآمدن to begin to speak, to find the gift of speech
- زیر - گفتن to speak indistinctly; to mutter under one's breath
- بدل کردن - *colloquial* to contradict, to be impudent, to be impertinent
- به - شدن - *colloquial* to quarrel [with], to bicker [with]
- یکی کردن - to come to an agreement with, to come to an understanding [with], to get along well (with somebody)
- زبانش بریده شد He fell silent. / He didn't dare speak.
- مردمی - soft, tender, or sweet words, endearing speeches
- یا نان گندمی یا - مردمی by bread or kindness (to achieve one's goal)

زبان بازی [zaabanbaazi] seduction by words; flattery, deception

زبان بریده [zobaanborida] not daring to speak; forced to be silent

زبانچه [zobaancha] *technical* lug; pin, peg

زبان دراز [zobaandaraaz] 1 unrestrained in speech, impudent, insolent 2 garrulous, talkative

زبان درازی [zobaandaraazi] lack of restraint in speech
- کردن - 1 to be impudent, to be insolent, to be rude 2 to talk at random

زبان زد [zobaanzad]
- بودن(شدن) - to be on everyone's lips, to be the subject of conversation

زبان شناس [zobaanshenaas] linguist

زبان شناسی [zobaanshenasi] science of language, linguistics

زبانه [zobaana] 1 (also آتش -) language (of a tribe) 2 pointer of a scale (for weighing)

زبانی [zobaani] 1 oral, verbal 2 orally, in words

زبر [zabar] 1 zabar (diacritical mark designating the short vowel "a") 2 *literary* upper, above, over ♦ - آدم است very best person, excellent chap

زبردست [zabardast] strong, powerful; superior
♦ او در پهلوانی – است He is very strong in a fight.

زبر دستی [zabardasti] strength, might; superiority

زبون [zabun] 1 weak, sickly, puny, helpless 2 unfortunate, pitiful, miserable

زپ [zep] zipper

زپورت [zoport] *technical* support

زجر [zájer] 1 torment, torture 2 yoke, oppression
- کشیدن - to experience torment or torture; to suffer oppression

زچگی [zachagi]
- روزهای - *colloquial* the period after childbirth (lasting forty days)

زچه [zacha] *colloquial* ☞ زاچ

زچه خانه [zachakhaana] 1 house in which a child was born 2 room or place for women in childbirth

زحاف [zehaaf] (*plural* ازاحیف [azaahif] (and) زحافات [zehaafaat]) zehaf (derivative variant of a metric foot obtained as a result of the contraction of the foot)

زحمت [zahmat] 1 toil, effort 2 trouble
- دادن - to trouble, to burden, to cause trouble
- کشیدن (را،به) - to toil, to labor; to endure difficulties

زحمت قرین [zahmatqarin] entailed with difficulties; laborious; difficult

زحمت کش [zahmatkash] 1 worker, toiler 2 industrious; hard-working; diligent

زخ [zakh] (and) زخه [zakha] 1 wart 2 knot (in wood) 3 bump, lump, growth

زخم [zákhem] 1 wound, injury 2 ulcer; sore
- کاری - 1 mortal wound 2 irreparable grief, terrible bereavement
- سر رحم - *medicine* erosion of the cervix of the uterus
- خوردن - to receive an injury, to be wounded
- سر - کسی نمک پاشیدن to rub salt on somebody's wound

زخم پیچ [zakhempeech] bandage

زخمی [zakhmi] wounded
- شدن - to be wounded

زخیره [zakhira] ☞ ذخیره

زدا(ی) [zadaa (y)] *present tense stem* زدودن

زدگی [zadagi] 1 chafe; chafing; abrasion 2 flaw, defect (in clothing); damage, hole (made by a moth)

زدن [zadan] (*present tense stem* زن [zan]) 1 to hit, to beat; to strike, to knock (را،به) 2 to kill, to defeat, to rout 3 to hit (about a blow, strike, etc.) ♦ آفتاب زدش He suffered sunstroke. 4 to fell (trees) 5 component of verbal combinations ♦ گپ – to talk, to converse
- زیر – گرفتن to subject to beatings, to beat unmercifully

زدودن [zodudan] (*present tense stem* زدا(ی) [zoda (y)]) to clear off, to wipe off, to clean

زده [zada] (*past participle* زدن) 1 brought down, slain, struck down 2 having lost consciousness, barely alive 3 having been dealt a blow, having been poisoned by carbon monoxide
- شدن - 1 to be beaten, to be beaten unmercifully (until one loses consciousness) 2 to be struck down (by a bullet, by illness, disease, etc.) 3 to die (from a blow, from a rupture of the heart) 4 to be poisoned by carbon monoxide

زده و کنده [zadawkanda] *colloquial* just barely; hardly; with one's last efforts ♦ خود را به خانه رساند - He just barely made it home.

زر [zar] 1 gold ♦ زر سرخ pure gold 2 (*also* زر سفید) silver 3 money; riches, wealth
• زر پیش زر رود *proverb* Money goes to money.

زراعت [zeraaat] 1 agriculture, farming ♦ عملی - agricultural training (in educational institutions) ◊ متخصص - agronimist 2 crop ♦ زغ - crop of flax
• کردن - 1 to be occupied in agriculture or farming 2 to raise (an agricultural crop)

زراعت باب [zeraaatbaab]
• اراضی - lands suitable for agriculture

زراعت کار [zeraaatkaar] farmer, peasant

زراعتی [zeraaati] agricultural, agrarian ♦ مملکت – agrarian country

زراندود [zaraandud] gilded, gilt; inlaid with gold

زربافت [zarbaaft] 1 woven with gold 2 brocade

زربفت [zarbaft] ☞ زربافت

زرچوبه [zarchoba] *botany* yellowroot, turmeric, ginger, (in powder form, it is used as a spice)

زرخیز [zarkheez] fertile; rich (about land)

زرد [zard] yellow, of yellow color ♦ شیری - cream (-colored) ◊ کاهی - straw yellow

زردآلو [zardaalu] apricot; dried apricot[s] ♦ تلحک - apricot with a bitter pit ◊ شیرینک - sweet apricot of the highest grade

زردچوبه [zardchoba] ☞ زرچوبه

زردزرد [zardzard]
• دیدن - to look with envy, to look with yearning (at something unattainable)

زردک [zardak] carrot

زردنبوک [zardambok] *colloquial* 1 yellow; sickly, puny; emaciated, weak 2 a puny person

زردوزار [zardozaar] 1 having turned yellow (from illness), jaundiced; enfeebled 2 depressed by grief
• شدن - to wither; to pine

زرده [zarda] *medicine* 1 bile, gall 2 jaundice (disease) 3 sweet pilaf (with fruit and saffron)

زردی [zardi] 1 yellow color; yellowness 2 egg yolk 3 ☞ زرده
• گرفتن - to turn yellow (in color)

زردینه [zardina] 1 light, light-colored; blond, fair-haired 2 (*opposite of* سبزینه) pale-skinned, white-skinned

زرزری [zarzari] 1 dress with gold embroidery 2 golden, gilded, gilt

زرشک [zereshk] barberries ♦ درخت - barberry bush

زرشوی [zarshoy] prospector

زرشویی [zarshoyi] prospecting

زرع [zaar'a] 1 cultivation; tilling; working the soil 2 sowing ♦ اراضی تحت - sowing area

زرک [zerk] (*and*) زرکه [zerka] rock partridge, alectoris kakelik

زرکوب [zarkob] stamped with gold, inlaid with gold

زرگر [zargar] goldsmith, jeweler

زرگری [zargari] jewelry business or trade; profession of a goldsmith
•- زبان jargon, argot

زرگل [zargol] *botany* marigold

زرگون [zargun] golden, gold (in color)

زرنباد [zorombaad] zedoary (fragrant East Indian drug)

زرنگ [zerang] *colloquial* adroit, clever, sprightly

زرنگار [zarnegaar] painted with gold

زرورق [zarwaraq] 1 thin disks (with which women decorate their hair) 2 foil

زره [zereh] 1 armor 2 chainmail; coat of mail

زره دار [zere (h) daar] armored ♦ کشتی - ironclad battleship ◊ موتر - armored car

زری [zari] 1 woven of gold threads; brocaded 2 ☞ زرین

زرین [zar (r) in] 1 gold, made of gold 2 golden, of the color of gold

زشت [zesht] 1 bad 2 homely 3 crude; rough; unpleasant

زعفران [za'faraan] saffron

زعماء [zoamaa] *plural of* زعیم

زعیم [zaim] (*plural* زعماء [zoamaa]) 1 head, chief, leader 2 responsible person (person in charge)

زغاره [zajghra] millet bread; flatcake made from millet

زغال [zoghaal] coal
• زغال سنگ ☞ - سنگ

زغال خانه [zoghaalkhaana] 1 coal bin 2 coal yard

زغال سنگ [zoqaal (e) sang] coal, hard coal

زغالکن [zoghaalkan] coal miner

زغالی [zoghaali] coal vendor, charcoal dealer

زغر [zegher] 1 flax 2 flax seed, linseed

زق [zeq] ☞ زک

زقطو [zaqataw] *colloquial* very salty, oversalted

زقوم [zoqum] 1 cactus 2 upas tree 3 bitter taste, poison (about something bitter, about something unpleasant)

زک [zek] leather bag, wineskin (used to cross a river)

زکات [zakaat] *religion* zakat tithe (tax paid by Moslems for the benifit of the poor)

زکام [zokaam] cold; inflammation of upper respiratory tract

زکاوت [zakaawat] *literary* purity, chastity; righteousness

زکی [zaki] *literary* pure, righteous, pious, devout

زلزله [zelzela] earthquake ♦ ضد - aseismic, earthquake proof

زلف [zolf] lock, curl, hair ♦ پریشان - loose flowing curls

زلفی [zolfi] 1 ring for door chain 2 door chain. 3 *military* sword knot

زلو [zalu] (*and*) زلوک [zalok] leech

زمام [zemaam] 1 the reins of government; authority, power 2 *rarely literary* reins

زمامدار [zemaamdaar] ruler

زمان [zamaan] (*plural* ازمنه [azmena]) 1 time; period; era, epoch ♦ در قدیم - in olden times ◊ نادیر - for a long time 2 *grammar* tense (of a verb)

زمانه [zamaana] 1 time, times ♦ خراب شده - *colloquial* Well, the time has come! 2 world; fate, destiny

زمانه ساز [zamanasaz] 1 to be able to adjust, to be able to adapt 2 time-server

زمبور [zambur] ☞ زنبور

زمبیل [zambeel] ☞ زنبیل

زمخت [zamokht] 1 gloomy; sullen; somber; dreary, dismal 2 astringent (to the taste)

زمرد [zomorrod] emerald

زمره [zomra] category, class, rank; sort

زمزم [zamzam] Zamzam (name of a sacred spring in Mecca)

زمزمه [zamzama] 1 rumor, common talk; talk 2 quiet singing; tune 3 babble, murmur

زمستان [zemestaan] winter
- مرگ غریبان - *proverb* Winter is the ruination of poor people.

زمهریر [zamharir] 1 severe cold, hard frost ♦ مثل - است It's cold as hell! / [It's] terrible cold! 2 hoarfrost

زمبق [zambaq (and) zamboq] *botany* 1 iris 2 (also هراتی -) white lily

زمین [zamin] 1 earth (the planet) ♦ کره - the (terrestrial) globe 2 land, soil ♦ آباد شده - cultivated land 3 country, locality 4 domain, territory ♦ زمین های کوچایان the domains of nomadic tribes

زمیندار [zamindaar] 1 farm owner; farmer 2 landowner ♦ کوچک - small landowner

زمینداری [zamindaari] 1 farming; occupation of a farm owner 2 landownership

زمینگیر [zamingir] 1 helpless, rooted to the spot 2 cripple; paralytic

زمین کن [zaminkan] (and) زمین کاو [zaminkaw] unskilled laborer, ditch digger

زمینه [zamina] 1 foundation, ground, base ♦ مساعد - favorable grounds (for something) ◊ در این - on these grounds 2 as regards this 2 condition; precondition, prerequisite 3 background, ground

زمینی [zamini] ground ♦ هدف - *military* ground target

زن [zan] 1 woman ♦ زن شوهردار married woman 2 wife
- زن و شوی ☞ زن و شو
- زن گرفتن to get married (about a man), to take a wife

زناشویی [zanaashoyi] marriage, matrimony; family life, married life

زناق [zenaaq] chin

زن ایور [zaneewar] husband's brother's wife; wife of a brother-in-law (husband's brother)

زمبق ☞ زمیق

زنبور [zambur] 1 wasp 2 (also عسل -) bee

زنبور خانه [zamburkhaana] beehive

زنبور عسل [zambur (e) asal] bee

زنبورک [zamburak] *historical* small cannon, falconet (muzzle loaded and carried on a camel)

زنبیل [zambel] 1 hardbarrow made of boards or woven twigs (for carrying bricks, clay, etc.) 2 basket, bag

زنجبیل [zanjabil] (and) زنجفیل [zanjafil] *botany* ginger ♦ پرورده - ginger in sugar

زنجیر [zanjir] 1 chain, (small) chain (for a door, a watch, etc.) 2 fetters, shackles 3 *technical* (caterpillar) track, tracks (of a tractor) 4 *obscure* (numerative in counting elephants) ♦ دو – فیل two elephants
- کردن to close with a chain (a door)

زنجیر دار [zanjirdaar] track, tracked, caterpillar, with tracks

زنجیری [zanjiri] 1 shackled, clad in chains 2 chain, chained [up]
- سگ watchdog (also - دیوانه); violent, raving, mad, crazy

زنچه [zancha] *colloquial* henpecked *derogatory*

زنخ [zanakh] 1 chin 2 lower jaw

زندان [zendaan] *literary* jail; dungeon

زندگانی [zendagaani] (and) زندگی [zendagi] life; way of life, mode of life
- کردن to live, to exist

- صاحب شدن to begin to live well, to begin to live prosperously; to grow rich

زنده [zenda] 1 live, living 2 animated, lively ♦ باد - Long live!
- باشی - *colloquial* 1 Well done! 2 Good-bye! / Bless you!

زنده جان [zendajan] 1 living being, living creature ♦ بقه هم - است A frog is also a living thing. 2 Zendehjan or Zindajan (a section in the city of Kabul)

زنده دل [zendadel] merry, gay, lively; cheerful; joyous

زنکه باز [zanakabaz] ladies' man; philanderer

زنگ [zang]¹ 1 tinkling, ringing (of a small bell, etc.); striking (of a clock), chime; signal 2 handbell; bell
- زدن 1 to peal, to ring, to chime 2 to signal
- اخطار(خطر) - signaling, signal

زنگ [zang]² rust; corrosion ♦ اثر - signs of corrosion ◊ ضد - anti-corrosion
- زدن to rust, to be covered with rust
- (and) دل - grief; sorrow
- خاطر -

زنگ دار [zangdaar] 1 with a peal, with a chime, with a bell ♦ ساعت - clock with a chime 2 ringing; clear; sonorous; resounding 3 *grammar* voiced (about a consonant)

زنگوله [zangola] 1 handbell; bell; cymbal 2 (also یخ-) icicle
- بستن to be covered with icicles

زنند [zanend] (and) زنندە [zanenda] 1 strong, capable of fighting ♦ سگ های - fighting dogs 2 biting, poisonous (about snakes) 3 biting, caustic (about words)

زن وشوی [zanoshoy] a married couple, a couple; husband and wife

زوال [zowaal] *literary* 1 setting (of a heavenly body) 2 decline; decay; atrophy; dying off 3 disappearance; death; loss; downfall

زواله [zawaala (and) zowaala] piece of dough in round shape (needed for rolling out and baking one flatcake)

زوج [zawj] (*plural* ازواج [azwaaj]) 1.1 husband 1.2 pair 2 twin, double; even

زوجات [zawjat] *plural of* زوجه

زوجه [zawja] (*plural* زوجات [zawjaat]) wife

زود [zud] 1 quickly, rapidly 2 (second component of compound words with meanings "quickly performed" / "easily yielding") زود گذر fleeting; transient

زودزود [zudzud] frequently, often; after a brief interval of time ♦ من او را می بینم I see him frequently.

زودگذر [zudgozar] fleeting, transient

زودی [zudi] ☞ بزودی
- به این - به so quickly, so soon; so early

زور [zor] 1.1 strength, power might; effort ♦ به - with effort ◊ بیجا - vain effort 1.2 by force 2.1 pressure, coercion 2.2 strong, powerful, violent, furious ♦ سیلاب - violent current, powerful mud flow 3 strongly, powerfully
- زورت در کمرت *colloquial* If you want to show your strength, then show it! / I am not afraid of you.
- من نمی رسد - I am not up to it.
- دادن 1 to exert pressure, to press, to squeeze 2 to cut, to prick (with words) ♦ حرف او مرابسیار - داد His words offended me very much.
- زدن to exert effort, to try, to strive
- طوس است - *cards* The ace wins!
- به زور کسی نازیدن [ba-zoor-kasay- nazydan] *idiom* (*literally*: to be proud because of someone else) to mistreat

175

other people because one has a connection with powerful people *derogatory*

زورآور [zoraawar] 1.1 strong, possessing remarkable strength 1.2 *colloquial* obstinate, stubborn, willful 2 *colloquial* an obstinate person, a stubborn person, a willful person

زورآوری [zoraawari] *colloquial* 1 strength, might; athletic ability, athletic prowess 2 obstinacy, stubbornness, willfulness

زورق [zawraq] 1 launch, long boat, skiff 2 gondola (of a hot-air balloon)

زوزه [zuza] 1 hum, buzz, drone; honking; buzzing; light tinkling 2 peep, chirp; squeal, screech (of an animal)

زولانه [zawlaana] 1 shackles, fetters, chains 2 (also-اسپکی) horse hobble
- زدن - to chain (a prisoner), to put (a prisoner) in chains

زوولوجست [zoolojest] zoologist

زوولوجی [zooloji] zoology

زه [zah] ☞ زاه

زه [zeh] 1 string (from gut, intestines) 2 catgut 3 (زه تابیده also زه کمان) bowstring

زهاب [zahaab] ☞ زاه آب

زهد [zohd] *religion* renunciation of the world; mode of life of a hermit; asceticism

زهر [zahr] poison
زهرمار ☞ مار -

زهراگین [zahraagin] (and) زهرآلود [zahraalud] poisonous

زهرخند [zahrkhand] taunting laugh, malicious laugh 2 malice; malicious joy

زهرمار [zahremaar] 1 snake poison 2 loathsome, muck (about food)
- کردن - *colloquial* to flinch in disgust (when rejecting something unpalatable)
- زهرمارت شوه *abusive* May you choke!
- برج – - boogeyman; a sullen person, a surly person; an unfriendly person

زهرموره [zahrmora] (and) زهرمهره [zahrmohra] black pebble used as an antidote (supposedly obtained from the skull of a snake)

زهرناک [zahrnaak] ☞ زهرآگین

زهروی [zohrawi]
- امراض - venereal diseases

زهره [zahra] 1 bile, gall; gall bladder 2 courage, fortitude; self-control
- زهره اش او شد *colloquial* He became frightened. / His heart sank into his boots.

زهره [zohra] 1 *astronomy* Venus 2 *feminine proper name* Zohra

زهرکفک [zahrakafak] *colloquial* scared to death, barely alive from fright or fear

زهگیر [zehgir] 1 notch or groove in a bow (for fastening the bowstring) 2 neck (of a stringed instrument)

زی [zi] *present tense stem* زیستن

زیات [ziyaat] ☞ زیاد

زیاد [ziyaad] 1 in large numbers; numerous; large ♦ به مقدار - in a large amount, in a large number 2.1 many ♦ بسیار - very many 2.2 strongly, to a great degree ♦ پریشان مباش - Don't grieve [so] strongly. 3 شدن - *intransitive* to increase, to multiply; to become stronger, to intensify

زیادت [ziyaadat] 1 great number, large amount 2 increase, addition

زیادتی [ziyaadati] surplus, excess ♦ وزن - excess in weight, overweight

زیاده [ziyaada] 1 greater *adjective*, superfluous, unnecessary 2 more ♦ از حد - excessively; too
2.1 ☞ زیاد ●

زیادهتر [ziyaadatar] 1 mainly, chiefly 2 ☞ زیاده ●
- (نسبت به) بودن - to exceed, to surpass

زیادی [ziyaadi] 1 ☞ زیادتی 2 superfluous, unnecessary

زیارت [ziyaarat] 1 pilgrimage, visitation of holy places 2 *polite* visiting (somebody); calling on (somebody)
- کردن - 1 to visit holy places 2 *polite* to call upon (somebody)

زیارتگاه [ziyaaratgaah] place of a pilgrimage; sacred thing

زیان [ziyaan] harm, damage, loss
- کردن(رساندن) - to cause harm, to inflict damage
- دیدن - to suffer damage, to bear a loss

زیان آور [ziyaanoawar] 1 harmful, injurious 2 unprofitable; disadvantageous

زیب [zeeb] 1.1 *literary* ornamentation, decoration 1.2 beauty 2 proper, appropriate; worthwhile

زیبا [zeebaa] 1 beautiful, fine 2 *feminine proper name* Zeba

زیبایی [zeebayi] beauty; charm ♦ زیباییهای طبعیت the beauties of nature

زیتون [zaytun] olive ♦ درخت - olive tree
- روغن ◊ olive oil

زیر [zeer] 1.1 bottom, lower part (of something) *preposition* 1.2 zer, kasreh (sublineal mark indicating the vowel "e") 1.3 *music* high note, high tone 1.4 thin string, fine string 2 also-در (and)-به - under *denominative preposition* ♦ درخت - under the tree ◊ ازـدرخت out from under the tree
- دست کسی، - لب - under somebody's command; under somebody's subordination
- زیرلب ☞ لب ●
- زیرلب - لب *colloquial* to filch, to swipe
- گرفتن - to put down (in a fight), to overcome
- اختیار نبودن - not to be subject to will; to be random (about movement, an impulse)
- موتر شدن - to be run over by a vehicle, to be hit by a vehicle
- نظر گرفتن - to take under [one's] control, to take under [one's] care

زیرا [zeeraa] (also-که) since, because, for

زیر آبی [zeereaabi] submarine; underwater

زیر بغل [zeer (e) baghal] armpit

زیر بغلی [zeer (e) baghali] small drum (in the shape of a tambourine, without sticks, usually carried under the arm)

زیربنا [zeerbenaa] 1 foundation; base 2 *philosophical* basis

زیرپیراهنی [zeerperaahani] (and) زیر پیرنی [zerperani] 1 undershirt 2 woman's slip

زیر جامن [zeerjaaman] *colloquial* ☞ زیر جامه

زیر جامه [zeerjama] pants; shorts

زیرجلو [zeerjelaw] 1 *historical* groom 2 foot servant (who leads the master's horse by the bridle)

زیر خانه [zeerkhaana] 1 basement; cellar 2 lower floor, ground floor

زیردار گریخته [zeeredaargoreekhtagi] (and) زیر دار گریخته [zeredargorekhta] 1 *colloquial* inveterate scoundrel, cutthroat 2 old fox, rogue, rascal

زیر دست [zeerdast] 1 subordinate *adjective* 2 subject, dependent

زیرزمینی [zeerezamini] 1 underground ♦ آب های - *geology* subsoil waters 2 cave; cellar

زیرک [zirak] keen-witted, resourceful

زیرکی [ziraki] keen-wittedness, resourcefulness

زیرگاو [zeeregaaw]
● - شیر fresh milk

زیر گوشی [zeergoshi] 1 earrings; earring 2 small pillow

زیر لب [zeerelab] in an undertone, in a low voice, under one's breath; indistinctly
● - گفتن 1 to speak in a low voice, to talk under one's breath 2 to mutter indistinctly

زیروبالا [zeerobaalaa]
● - کردن to turn upside down; to stir

زیروبم [zeerobam] high and low notes; strummings; series of notes; modulations (of a melody)

زیره [zira] caraway, caraway seeds

زیست [zist] life, existence; living, residing ♦ باهمی - coexistence ◊ کردن - to live, to exist

زیستن [zistan] (*present tense stem* زی [zi]) to live, to exist.

زین [zin] saddle
● (بستن)کردن - to saddle

زینت [zinat] decoration, ornament

زینه [zina] 1 ladder; stairs ♦ سطحی - *technical* ramp 2 step; rung 3 stage

زینه خانه [zinakhaana] staircase landing

زیور [zeewar] precious attire

ژ
14th letter of the Dari alphabet

ژاله [zhaala] hail

ژاندارم [zhaandarm] gendarme

ژرف [zharf] *literary* 1 deep 2 profound; serious

ژرفا [zharfaa] *literary* depth ♦ در - تیره گی in deep gloom

ژنده [zhanda] ☞ جنده

ژنده پوش [zhandaposh] 1 ragamuffin 2 *obscure* dervish; sheikh

ژورنالیست [zhurnaalist] journalist

ژورنالیسم [zhurnaalism] journalism

ژیکلور [zhiklor] jet, nozzle

ژیگولو [zhigolo] dandy, gigolo

ژیولوژی [zhiolozhi] geology

ژیولوژیکی [zhiolozhiki] geological

س
15th letter of the Dari alphabet

سابر [saabar] 1 velour or suede leather, chrome chamois ♦ بالاپوش - velour coat, suede leather coat 2 piece of chamois, small rag (for wiping lenses, eyeglasses, etc.)

سابق [saabeq] 1 previous, past; former, late, one-time 2 (also- در) formerly; earlier, before

سابقه [saabeqa] (*plural* سوابق [sawaabeq]) 1 the past (e.g., of a person); past history (of a matter) 2 antiquity; tradition ♦ دوستی - antiquity of a friendship or an acquaintanceship ◊ عرفانی مشترک - common cultural traditions 3 (also- خدمت) length of service on a job; service record 4 precedent 5 *grammar* prefix
● - داشتن 1 to be ancient or old; to last a long time 2 to have length of service; to have experience 3 to have precedent

سابقه دار [saabeqadaar] 1 experienced; with long service 2 having precedent

سات [saat] *colloquial* ☞ ساعت -

سات وگری ☞ -وگری ●

سات تیری [saatteeri] *colloquial* ☞ ساعت تیری

سات وگری [saatogari] *colloquial* every minute, incessantly ♦ او - نان میخوره He eats incessantly.

ساتول [saatul] large knife, cleaver (for chopping meat)

ساجق [saajeq] chewing resin; chewing gum

ساچ [saach] *zoology* pink starling, rose-colored starling

ساچمه [sachma] shot (for firing from a gun)

ساحری [saaheri] witchcraft, sorcery, magic

ساحل [saahel] (*plural* سواحل [sawaahel]) shore; coast

ساحه [saaha] 1 territory; area; zone ♦ دید - field of vision or sight ◊ زراعت - sowing area 2 arena, sphere ♦ عملیات - sphere of activity

ساخت [sakht] 1 system, structure 2 article; manufacture ♦ جاپان - of Japanese production

ساختگی [saakhtagi] 1 made, manufactured; ready-made ♦ - اشیا و اجناس finished products and semifinished products ◊ لباس - ready-made dress 2 artificial, imitation; forged, false

ساختمان [saakhteman] 1 construction, design; arrangement, structure ♦ جمله - *grammar* sentence structure 2 construction project, construction

ساختن [saakhtan] (*present tense stem* ساز [saaz]) 1 to construct, to build, to erect 2 to make, to manufacture 3 to get along [with]; to be reconciled (with somebody, to something ♦ با) - هم to come to an arragement, to enter into a secret deal or arrangement 4 *colloquial* to make oneself out to be (somebody) 5 (component of compound words) ♦ سربلند - to confer (honor)

ساخته کار [saakhtakaar] 1 falsifier, forger; cheat, fraud 2 pretender

ساخته کاری [sakhtakari] 1 falsification, forgery; deception, fraud 2 pretense, sham

سادو [saadu] 1 *historical* performer of religious songs extolling the deeds of the prophet 2 flatterer, adulator, glorifier

سادو گری [saadugari] flattery, obsequious praise (of somebody); glorification ♦ مکن - Stop singing (somebody's) praises!

ساده [saada] 1 simple, uncomplicated ♦ چاره - simple means 2 simple, nonderivative 3 smooth, plain, unfigured, without a design (about cloth) 4 dim-witted, silly, doltish ♦ خدا - simple-hearted, naive; other-worldly

ساده کار [saadakaar] master workman who performs preliminary delicate work (before it is trimmed or decorated); a master workman who makes semifinished products

ساده کاری [sadakari] 1 plain work (without trim, paintings, etc.) 2 manufacture of semifinished products

ساده گی [saadagi] 1 simplicity 2 dimwittedness; naivete

ساده لوح [saadalawh] simpleton, ninny, fool

س

سار [saar] starling; buzzard
سار [saar] (substantive suffix with meaning "place abounding" (with something)) ♦ نمکسار salt marsh
ساربان [saarbaan] ☞ ساروان
سارنگ [saarang] sarang (Indian bow instrument with up to 100 strings)
ساروان [saarwaan] leader of caravan, caravan driver; camel driver
ساری [saari]¹ infectious, contagious
ساری [saari]² sari (women's garment made of an unfitted piece of cloth) ♦ امراض ساری
ساز [saaz]¹ 1 *present tense stem* ساختن 2 (second component of compound words with meanings "making something" / "performing something") ♦ ساعت ساز watchmaker ◊ اسباب ساز plotter, intriguer
ساز [saaz]² 1.1 saz (musical instrument) 1.2 melody, motif, tune ♦ پران - sazeparan (melody and rhythm of native Badakhshan music) 2 coordinated; agreed; fixed; adjusted
• آمدن - 1 *colloquial* to come to terms, to come to an agreement, to come to an understanding 2 to become intimate (about a man and a woman)
• (نواختن)کردن - to play (a musical instrument)
• کسی را گرفتن *colloquial* to mimic somebody; to caricature somebody
ساز [saaz]³ 1 equipment, outfit ♦ سفر - traveling outfit, accoutrements 2 harness, gear accoutrements
• سازوسامان - سامان ☞
سازش [saazesh] 1 understanding, arrangement, agreement 2 collusion, secret compact; deal
سازشکار [saazeshkaar] 1 double-dealer 2 *rarely* compliant person, person who is easy to live with or to get on with
سازگار [saazgaar] suitable, proper, appropriate; favorable
• سازگاری ☞ (شدن)بودن -
• سازگاری کردن in entry
سازگاری [saazgaari]
• کردن - زمانه کرد The situation was favorable. -to favor
• بامحیط – کردن *intransitive* to adapt oneself to conditions, to adapt
سازمان [saazmaan] organization, enterprise; institution, establishment
سازنده [saazenda] musician
سازوسامان [saazosaamaan] equipment; outfit, accountrements
ساطور [saatur] large knife (for cutting meat)
ساعت [saaat] 1 time, hour ♦ چند بجه است؟ - What time is it? ◊ سه(بجه)است بند دستی – It's three o'clock 2 clock, watch ♦ – wristwatch ◊ جیبی – pocket watch
• خود را تیر کردن - to spend one's time, to amuse oneself
• کسی را تیر کردن - to entertain somebody, to occupy somebody (with something), to keep somebody busy (with something)
ساعت تیری [saaatteeri] 1 passing time; pastime 2 entertainment amusement, diversion
• کردن - 1 to waste time, to kill time 2 to amuse oneself; to have a good time
ساعت ساز [saaatsaaz] watchmaker
ساعد [saaed] *anatomy* forearm
ساعی [saa'i] diligent, industrious, zealous, assiduous, painstaking

ساغری [saaghari (and) saaghri] hindquarters, croup, rump (of horse or donkey)
ساق [saaq] 1 (*also* پای -) shin, shank 2 (*also* موزه -) top (of a boot) 3 (*also* درخت -) trunk of a tree
ساقدار [saaqdaar]
• جوراب – long socks, stockings
• بوت – (high) shoes
ساقط [saaqet] 1 fallen (about authority or power, about a regime); overthrown, toppled 2 having lost force, annulled
ساقه [saaqa] stem, stalk; cutting, graft
ساکت [saaket]¹ 1 having lapsed into silence, silent 2 quiet; calm; peaceful
• شدن - to fall silent; to calm down, to settle down
ساکت [saaket]² ☞ وال ساکت
ساکن [saaken] 1.1 motionless, still; placid, calm; *physics* static 1.2 living *grammar*, dwelling, inhabiting ♦ کابل - residing in Kabul 1.3 quiescent, not having a vowel in the phoneme (about a letter) 2 (*plural* سکنه [sakana] (and) ساکنین [saakenin]) resident, inhabitant
سال [saal] 1 year ♦ گذشته - the past year, last year 1.2 during the past year, during the last year ♦ ازنه بر آمدن *colloquial* not to live even a year, not to last a year ◊ از - نه برآیی *abusive* May you die this year! 2 year (in system of chronology) ♦ شمسی - solar year ◊ قمری - lunar year 3 years, age ♦ چند – داری؟ How old are you? 4 remembrance of the deceased (one year after death, by distributing alms)
سالبر [saalbar] bearing fruit after a year, bearing fruit in a year (about a tree)
سالخورده [saalkhorda] elderly, aged, advanced in years; of (extreme) old age
سالگره [saalgera] anniversary, date (of some event)
سالگشت [saalgasht] *agriculture* follow
سالم [saalem] *literary* 1 healthy; strong, sound ♦ آدم - healthy person ◊ عقل - sound mind 2 whole, intact, safe, unharmed 3 full, untruncated (about a poetic meter)
سالن [saalan] ☞ سالند
سالنامه [saalnaama] yearbook; annual; almanac; anthology
سالند [saaland] 1 seasoning condiment for pilaf or for rice (a vegetable or meat condiment) 2 ragout ♦ کدو - ragout made of pumpkin with meat ◊ کچالو - stewed potatoes
سامان [saamaan] 1 (*also* حیاتی -) necessary things, household articles ♦ خانه - household utensils, furniture ◊ قرطاسیه - stationery 2 property; equipment; material ♦ جنگ - *military* accoutrements 3 equipment; stock, inventory ♦ برق - electrical equipment 4 state of order (of everyday life, of a household)
• فالتو - *technical* 1 spare tools and accessories 2 spare parts
• کار - tool
• خانه او – ندارد There is no order in his house. / There is disorder in his house
سامانه [saamaana] *colloquial* pomp, ostentatious splendor, show
سامعه [saame'a] (*also* -قوه) hearing, ability to hear
سامعین [saame'in] listeners; audience
سامی [saami]¹ Semitic ♦ زبانهای - Semitic languages
سامی [saami]² *technical* sleeve; bushing
سان [saan]¹ manner, method ♦ آن - thus, in this manner
• همانسان چسان چه the same way as, in this same manner
• یکسان یک به - like, not unlike

178

سان [saan] ² *colloquial* madapollam (type of cotton named after a city in India); calico ♦ سفید - bleached coarse calico ◊ کوره - unbleached coarse calico

سانتی [saanti] (and) سانتی متر [saantimeter] centimeter

سانتی گراد [saantigraad] Celsius thermometer, thermometer

سانحه [saaneha] (*plural* سوانح [sawaaneh]) incident, accident

سانقه [saanaqa] sanaqa (round wooden playing-marbel, the size of a golf ball)

• سانقه بازی ☞ •

سانقه بازی [saanaqabaazi] children's game consisting of hitting a round, wooden playing-marble ☞ سانقه

سای [saay] ¹ *present tense stem* ساییدن

سای [saay] ² say; dry riverbed; ravine, gorge, gully

سایر [saayer] 1 ordinary, common 2 other; the rest, the rest of

سایره [saayra] 1 goldfinch; sayra ♦ جته - a goldfinch that has not been taught to sing 2 *feminine proper name* Sayra

سایز [saayz] size, measure; stature ♦ بوت - shoe size ◊ بالاپوش - overcoat size

سایز گیری [saayzgiri] measurement; measuring; taking measurements

سایکالوجست [saaykaalojest] psychologist

سایکالوجی [saaykaaloji] psychology

سایکل [saaykal] cycle, bicycle

سایگی [saayagi] a variety of currants that are green in color (they are dried in the shade and therefore retain their sourness)

ساینس [saayans] 1 science 2 natural sciences

• فاکولته – 1 physical and mathematical faculty or department 2 faculty or department of natural sciences

ساینسدان [saayansdaan] 1 scientist 2 naturalist 3 physicist; mathematician

سایه [saaya] 1 shade, shadow; canopy ♦ (در)زیر - درخت - in the shade of a tree 2 *literary* protection; patronage 3 *colloquial* demon, evil spirit 4 *colloquial* hysterical state, hysterics

• انداختن - to cast a shadow, to shade (بالای)

• زیر – گرفتن *literary* to take under [one's] protection, to protect; to patronize

• میگیرد - آدمه ای *colloquial* He is possessed.

سایه بان [saayabaan] ☞ سایه وان

سایه رخ [saayarokh (and) سایه روی [saayaroy] facing north, not sunny, shady (about a room, about a building)

سایه وان [saayawaan] 1 awning 2 canopy

ساییدگی [saayidagi] *technical* rubbing, wearing away; wear and tear

ساییدن [saayidan] (*present tense stem* سای [saay]) 1 to rub ♦ - دندانها را به هم to grit one's teeth 2 to wear away, to wear out, to wear (a hole) through 3 to demolish; to shatter; to crush (rock)

سبابه [sabbaaba] (also- انگشت) index finger

سبب [sabab] reason, cause *preposition* ♦ از این - therefore, for this reason

• به - because of, owing to, on account of, in view of *denominative* ♦ به ناجوری - because of illness

• شدن - to be the reason, to lead (to something)(را); to give rise to

سبحان الله [sobhaanallaa] *religion* 1 Good heavens! / My God! (in great astonishment, surprise) 2 Bravo! / Splendid!

سبد [sabad] wicker basket (made of cane or reed)

سبز [sabz] 1.1 green; young ♦ رشقه یی - rich green, bright green 1.2 blooming, blossoming, flowering ♦ باغ - blooming garden 2 dark (about skin), dark-complexioned

• شدن - 1 to become green, to germinate, to sprout 2 *colloquial* to sprout (about whiskers)

سبز برگی [sabzbargi] *historical* a tax levied on melon fields

سبزه [sabza] 1 green grass, verdure; sprouts, shoots 2 dark-complexioned

• کردن(لغت)لگد - *colloquial* 1 to stroll on the first grass 2 to go out into a meadow or a field (on the first day of Nawruz)

سبزه خورک [sabzakhorak] field lark

سبزوخرم [sabzokhorram] turning green; blooming, blossoming, all in bloom

سبزه لغت [sabzalaghat] (and) سبزه لغتی [sabzalaghati] *colloquial* holiday outing into the fields; outdoor festivities with games in a meadow (on the first days of Nawruz)

سبزی [sabzi] 1 green color, verdure 2 green vegetables, greens 3 seasoning or condiment made of greens (for meat and rice)

سبزی باب [sabzibaab] ☞ سبزیجات

سبزی پالک [sabzipaalak] spinach

سبزیجات [sabzijaat] vegetables, greens

سبزی چلو [sabzichalaw] chelaw with vegetable or meat sauce or gravy

سبزی کاری [sabzikaari] 1 market gardening, vegetable growing 2 vegetable garden

سبزینه [sabzina] (*opposite of* زردینه) dark-complexioned, dark-skinned

سبق [sabaq] 1 lesson; studies; learning 2 lesson, example; edification

• خواندن - to study a lesson; to learn, to study

• گرفتن - to learn a lesson (from something), to take an example (from something)

سبک [sabk] style, school, trend (in art, in literature) ♦ هندی - the Indian style (in poetry, etc.)

سبک [sobok] 1 light, not heavy 2 weak, insignificant 3 not serious, frivolous, not sedate; insubstantial; worthless (about a person)

• کردن - دست کسی را to help, to come to somebody's aid

سبکدوش [sobokdosh]

• کردن – to free, to save; to deliver

• (از) کردن - از وظیفه to dismiss from a job or post

سبکی [soboki] 1 lightness 2 insubstantiality, frivolousness, worthlessness

سبوس [sabos] 1 bran 2 husk, husks, peel

سبوسک [sabosak] dandruff

سبیل [sabil] *obscure* 1 way, track, path, road 2 way, method, means

• بر - as *denominative preposition* ♦ مثال – بر - as an example

سپار [sepaar (and) sopaar] *present tense stem* سپردن

سپارش [sopaaresh] 1 errand, mission, task, assignment, job 2 recommendation, advice 3 request for somebody's sake, petition, intercession

• کردن - 1 to charge [with], to commission [with], to advise, to recommend 2 to ask for somebody's sake, to petition, to intercede

سپاه [sepaah] *literary* forces, army

سپاهی [sepaahi (and) sepaayi] 1 warrior, fighting man, soldier ♦ سپاهیان خاصه historical guard (of a king) 2 historical sepoy

سپتمبر [septambar] September

سپر [separ] 1 shield 2 technical shield, screen 3 military parapet, breastwork
• - افگندن (انداختن) to run; to shirk (before somebody); to surrender, to yield

سپردن [sopordan] (present tense stem سپار [separ]) 1 to give, to transfer, to hand over, to deliver 2 to instruct, to entrust (to somebody) 3 to commission, to order, to tell (somebody)
• به خدا سپردیم colloquial God be with you! / Good-bye!

سپل [sapal] hoof of a camel or elephant

سپند [sepand] botany wild rue, harmel (burned to ward off a spell)

سپورت [seport] sport ♦ سپورتهای پهلوانی athletic types of sports ◊ سامان – sports equipment
• کردن - to indulge in sports

سپید [sapeed] ☞ سفید

سپیده [sapeeda] colloquial 1 dawn, daybreak ♦ تا - until dawn, until daybreak 2 white (of an egg) 3 ☞ سفیده

سپیده دم [sapeedadam] 1 dawn, daybreak 2 at dawn, at daybreak

ستادیوم [setadium] (also سپورتی -) stadium ♦ غازی - Gazi Stadium (in Kabul)

ستاره [setaara] 1 star, planet ♦ دمدار – comet ◊ قطب - North Star 2 fortune, luck 3 white spot (on horse's forehead) 4 silver disks, spangles (sewn on clothing, on hats, etc.)

ستاره پیشانی [setaarapeesaani] with a white spot on the forehead (about a horse)

ستاژ [setaazh] probation, on-the-job training ♦ دور – period of probation, period of on-the-job training

ستاک [setaak] a young sprout or shoot (of a tree)

ستان [staan (and) estaan] (serves to form the names of places, countries, etc.) suffix ♦ گلستان garden, flower garden ◊ افغانستان Afghanistan, land of the Afghans

ستان [setaan] present tense stem ستاندن

ستاندارد [setaandaard] 1 standard noun 2 standard adjective
• غیر - technical nonstandard equipment, nonstandard stock or inventory

ستاندن [setaandan] 1 to take, to levy, to collect 2 to take away
• پس – پول هارا من پس می ستانم And I will take this money back. - to return, to take back

ستای [setaay] present tense stem ستودن

ستایش [setaayesh] praise, approval ♦ قابل - worthy of praising, deserving of approval

ستر [sater] 1 covering 2 military shelter, cover
• واخفاء – ستر واخفاء ☞
• ستره ☞ [satra]

ستراتژی [setraateji] (and) ستراتیژی [setraateezhi] strategic

سترجنرال [sterjanraal] military general

ستروخفاء [satroekhfaa] military camouflage

ستره [satra] shawl; veil

ستره [sotra] clean; neat, tidy ♦ لباس - clean clothes, neat clothing

ستره گی [sotragi] cleanliness ♦ پاکی و - cleanliness and neatness

ستقه [satqa] colloquial ☞ صدقه

ستل [saatel] pail, bucket ♦ حمام - small washtub ◊ نوله دار - watering can (for a garden)

ستم [setam] oppression, cruel treatment
• در حق کسی - کردن to oppress, to harm somebody; to treat somebody cruelly

ستمگار [setamgaar] (and) ستمگر [setamgar] 1 oppressor 2 offender; tyrant

ستمگری [setamgari] oppression, tyranny

ستودن [sotudan] (present tense stem ستای [setay]) to praise, to extol

ستودیو [setudio] studio ♦ رادیو - radio studio ◊ فلم گیری - movie studio

ستور [sotur] pack animal (horse, mule)

ستون [sotun] 1 column; pillar, support ♦ تیلگراف - telegraph pole ◊ فقرات - spinal column 2 column (of a newspaper, of figures, etc.)

ستیج [seteej] (and) ستیژ [seteezh] stage

ستیشن [seteeshan] 1 station ♦ برق - electric power station ◊ واترپمپ - water supply facility 2 (also ریل -) (railroad) station

سجاده [sajjaada] rug (on which prayers are said)

سجاف [sejaaf] border, edging ♦ پهن - broad trim, decoration (of a different fabric)

سجده [sajda] bowing to the ground (during prayer)

سجع [sája] literary rhymed prose

سجل [sejel] 1 card; list, roll; register 2 registration form; personal file

سجود [sojud] performing prostrations or low bows to the ground (during prayer)
• سجده ☞

سچه [sochcha] colloquial (opposite of جته) 1 pure; clean (in a ritualistic sense); untouched ♦ آب - pure water 2 pure, unalloyed ♦ مروارید - natural pearl

سحر [sahar] early morning, daybreak, dawn, sunrise

سحر [sehr] witchcraft; magic; sorcery
• کردن - to practice witchcraft, to perform magic, to practice sorcery

سحر گاهان [sahargaahaan] early in the morning, at dawn, at daybreak

سخاوت [sakhaawat] generosity, magnanimity

سخت [sakht] 1.1 difficult, heavy, hard ♦ روزهای - hard days ◊ زمستان - severe winter, hard winter ◊ مبارزه - cruel struggle, savage struggle 2 hard, tough ♦ چوب - hard wood 2.1 in a hard manner, severely 2 strongly, firmly, very
• بزمین خورد - He hit the ground hard. / He fell to the ground hard.
• کردن - to make thicker, to thicken, to condense
• گرفتن - to treat severely (بر), to show cruelty
• زندگی بروی - گرفته بود Life treated him cruelly.

سخت جان [sakhtjaan] of great endurance, tenacious

سخت جانی [sakhtjaani] endurance, tenacity

سخت دل [sakhtdel] hardhearted, heartless

سخت سر [sakhtsar] stern, with a stern temper

سخت جان ☞
•

سخت کاری [sakhtkaari] technical hardening; quenching

سخت گیر [sakhtgir] strict, demanding; severe, stern (about somebody)

سخت گیری [sakhtgiri] strictness, demandingness, exactingness; severe treatment, stern treatment

سختی [sakhti] 1 hardness, strength, solidity 2 difficult circumstances, need, want 3 trouble, misfortune, disaster 4 strictness, severity, sternness 5 *rarely* stinginess

بسختی ☞ به - ٠

سخن [sokhan] word, speech ♦ موزون - rhythmic speech, verses, or poetry

• گفتن - to speak, to make a speech
• به - درآمدن to begin to speak

سخن دان [sokhandaan] 1 expert on literature; man of letters; writer 2 poet

سخن رانی [sokhanraani] speech, report; lecture

سخنگوی [sokhangoy] 1 speaking, orating 2 an orator

سخنور [sokhanwar] 1 man of letters; writer 2 poet

سخی [sakhi] 1 generous, magnanimous 2 *masculine proper name* Sakhi

سد [sad] ☞ صد

سد [sa(d)d] (*plural* سدود [sodud]) 1 wall; bank; barrier 2 dam 3 obstacle

• راه - شدن to block somebody; to bar somebody's way

سدره [sádra] gift for sayyids (when visiting them)

سدس [sods] one-sixth

سدود [sodud] *plural of* سد

سدوزی [sadozi] Sodozai clan (a branch of the Durrani tribe, from which the rulers of Afghanistan in the 17th century were descended)

سدیگر [sedigar] (*abbreviation from* سه دیگر) *literary* 1 third 2 in thirds

سر [sar] 1.1 head ♦ از سر تاپای from head to toe 1.2 entirely, completely, as a whole, wholly 1.3 *numerative* head ♦ گوسفند ۱۰۰ سر 100 head of sheep 1.4 upper part, top (of something) ♦ میخواهی از اول شروع کنی؟ Do you want to start from the beginning? 1.6 end; edge; tip ♦ سر چادر border or edging of a chador ◊ سر موی the tip of a hair 1.7 *technical* head, tip, point, lid, cover 1.8 additional payment (in barter) 2 (first component of compound words with meanings "head" / "chief" and "covering" / "closing") ♦ سر طبیب chief physician ◊ سر میزی tablecloth

• سر بد در(به)بلای بد *proverb* An evil fate for a wicked head.
• سر زنده باشد کلاه بسیار است *proverb* If the head be whole a hat will be found.
• سراز from, beginning from, with *compound preposition* ♦ سر از امروز from today [on], beginning today
• س ۱.۱ at, during *denominative preposition* ♦ سرنان during a meal 1.2 (*also* به سر) on (something), on top [of], on the surface (of something) ♦ سرآب on the water ◊ سر پای on the feet; standing, upright 1.3 by; at; near ♦ سر راه by the road 1.4 about, concerning, relative to ♦ سر چیست؟ گپ What are you talking about? 1.5 (indicates the object of the action with various verbs) ♦ او سر این دختر عاشق شد He fell in love with this girl.
• به سر خود ☞ سر خود ٠
• سر برداشتن to hold up [one's] head, to rise [against]
• سرپیچیدن (and) سر تافتن to avoid; to shun (carrying something out); to disobey (از)

• سر خوردن 1 to meet accidentally, to run into; to collide [with] ♦ دیروز با معلم صاحب در پارک سر خوردم Yesterday I met [my] teacher in the park. 2 to concide, to tally ♦ حسابها(با) هم)سر خورد The accounts tallied.
• سر دادن 1 to let go, to release 2 to give way [to] (tears, etc.), to let out, to emit (a moan, a sigh, etc.) 3 to make an additional payment with money (during barter) ♦ چند افغانی سر میدهی؟ How many afghani will you give in addition? 4 to give up; to devote [one's] life (برای در ۰۰۰ راه)
• سر در نیاوردن to wallow [in], to entangle oneself, to be unable to gain an understanding [of] (از)
• سر رفتن 1 to overflow, to boil over (about milk) 2 to run low [of], to run short [of] (about patience, etc.) ♦ حوصله اش سر رفت His patience ran out.
• سر زدن 1 to appear, to arise (از) 2 to shoot, to show, to sprout (about young shoots) 3 to behead, to decapitate, to cut off the head 4 to cut, to prune (trees, branches)
• سر شدن to begin, to start *intransitive*
• سر کردن 1 to begin, to start, to set about, to make a beginning 2 to sharpen (a quill, a pencil) 3 *colloquial* to burst open, to break (about a boil, abscess) 4 ☞ به سر کردن
• سر ماندن 1 *colloquial* to lie down, to take a nap 2 to yield (to an opponent), to submit, to surrender
• سر نگرفتن not to get on well, not to come about; not to take place ♦ موافقه ماسر نگرفت Our agreement did not come about. / We did not come to an agreement.
• سر ماندن ☞ سر نهادن ٠
• از سر گذشتاندن 1 to get rid (of somebody), to send [somebody] on his way 2 to do (something) carelessly
• از سر گذشتن not to spare one's own life, to sacrifice oneself
• از سر گرفتن to begin anew, to do everything from the beginning
• به سر بردن to live, to exist
• به سر رسیدن to come to an end
• به سر کردن to wear on one's head, to put on one's head ♦ چادری اش را به سر کرده رفت Putting on [her] chador, she went out.
• سر از پای نشناختن 1 to lose one's presence of mind, to lose one's head 2 to display incompetence (in business)
• سر باز زدن 1 to refuse to do (something) (از), to disobey 2 to behave obstinately, to rebel, to revolt
• سر به گریبان کردن to retire into oneself, to be lost in thought; to be preoccupied
• سر خم کردن to bow one's head (before somebody پیش); to obey
• سر کسی را خوردن *colloquial* to spoil somebody's life; to send [somebody] to the grave
• سر واز کردن *colloquial* to burst, to break (about a boil or abscess)
• از سر گذشتن ☞ از سر تیر شدن ٠
• از سر گذ شنا ندن ☞ از سر تیرکردن ٠
• از سر کل کسی دست بردار نبودن *colloquial* to be a burden to somebody; to stick to somebody like a wet leaf
• کاری را سر کسی کردن 1 to force somebody to do something; to obtain something from somebody ♦ کار خود را سر ما کرد He got what he wanted from us and departed. 2 to do something through someone else
• کسی را از سر گرفتن *colloquial* to force somebody to divulge a secret, to force somebody to give himself away

181

سر

- سر بانی سرنه وردارى abusive May you lie down (in the evening) and not get up (in the morning)!
- سرت بوی قورمه میدهد It will cost you your head! / May you be killed!
- سرته بخوری abusive May you drop dead!
- سرت گردم colloquial endearment My dear! (literally, I will give my life for you!)
- سر خود را گرفت و رفت colloquial But he died suddenly.
- سرش از زدن است colloquial His head should be cut off!
- سرش به تنش بار شده Life is cheap / not dear to him.
- سرش پیش من خم است colloquial I have him [right] in my hands.
- مه سر شما پول دارم colloquial You owe a small debt.

سر [ser (r)] (plural اسرار [asraar]) secret ♦ سر عسکری(حربی) military secret
- سر شدن colloquial to be disclosed; to come to the surface (about a secret, etc.)
- سر کردن to reveal (somebody's secrets); to discover (something); to expose, to unmask

سر [sor] music note; key
- سر کردن to tune (a musical instrument)

سرا [saraa] ☞ سرای

سراب [saraab] ☞ سراو

سراپای [saraapaay] 1 from head to foot, from head to toe 2 all; the whole, as a whole ♦ سراپای او لرزید His whole body began to tremble. / His whole body trembled.

سراپرده [saraaparda] 1 literary bed curtains; curtain 2 historical shah's marquee; shah's palace

سراج [seraaj] 1 literary lamp 2 masculine proper name Seraj

سراج الاخبار [seraajolakhbaar] Siraj-ul-Akhbar (newspaper published at the beginning of the 20th century by the Afghan intellectual Mahmud-i-Tarzi)

سراچه [saraacha] room for receiving guests (separate from the wife's half of a home); husband's wing (of a home)

سراسر [saraasar] 1 wholly, as a whole, in full, fully 2 ☞ سرتاسر

سراسیمگی [saraaseemagi] confusion; embarrassment; perplexity ♦ - با in confusion, in panic

سراسیمه [saraaseema] 1 confused; embarrassed; perplexed 2 in confusion; in embarrassment ♦ به اطرافش نظر کرد - He looked around in embarrassment / confusion.

سرانداز [sarandaaz] 1 woman's shawl (thrown over the head and shoulders) 2 a light carpet or rug (spread on top of another carpet or rug in a place of honor in a room)

سراو [saraw] irrigated by a river or irrigation canal (about land)

سراوس [saraws (and) saros] historical detachment of bodyguards (during the reign of Habibullah Khan)

سرای [saraay]¹ 1 courtyard (with dwellings within) 2 (also تجارتی-) commercial house, trading base (with warehouses and places for transport facilities) 3 inn

سرای [saraay]² present tense stem سرودن

سرایت [seraayat] spread (of a disease)
- کردن - to spread, to be transmitted (about a disease) intransitive

سرایچه [saraaycha] ☞ سراچه

سرایدار [saraaydaar] (and) سرایوان [saraywan] 1 lease-holder or owner of a commercial house 2 owner of an inn

سرب [sórob] lead

سرباری [sarbaari] 1 small pack, bale (which is placed over a load) 2 an additional load, burden

سرباز [sarbaaz]¹ historical 1 selflessly brave, selfless 2.1 hero, daredevil 2.2 sarbaz, soldier

سرباز [sarbaaz]² ☞ سرکشاده
- ظروف -● open vessels
- مجرای – ● open drain, gutter, or sewer

سربازی [sarbaazi] 1 selfless bravery, heroism 2 military deeds, military valor ♦ در مردی و – مشهور بود He was well-known for heroism and valor.

سربالا [sarbaalaa] 1 up, uphill, upwards 2 ☞ سربلند

سربالایی [sarbaalaayi] 1 rise (in a road) 2 colloquial assigning an overstated price, overcharging 3 ☞ سربلندی

سربر [sarbor]
- کردن ● to trim, to prune (trees), to cut (grass)

سربراه [sarbaraah]
- کردن – ● 1 to send away, to send off, to send 2 to put right, to put in good order

سربسته [sarbasta] 1 closed, sealed 2 whole, untouched (about somebody)

سربسر [sarbasar] 1 equally; one for one, in equal proportion; a draw 2 one after the other, in succession 3 continuously, uninterruptedly, without break

سربفلک (کشیده) [sarbafalak (kashida)] high, up to the sky
- کوهای – ● high mountains, mountains that reach the skies

سربلند [sarbeland] 1 having deserved honor, glory; awarded honor 2 proud (of something) 3 glorious; famous, renowned
- ساختن - ● to award, to confer; to do honor(را)

سربلندی [sarbelandi] 1 honor, glory; fame; pride ♦ استقلال ما – ماست Our independence is our pride. 2 grandeur; high position

سربمهر [sarbamohr] 1 sealed 2 unopened, not unsealed (about a package, etc.)

سربند [sarband]¹ (also آب) 1 dam 2 main lock of an irrigation ditch (whence distribution of water begins)

سربند [sarband]² woman's head shawl, kerchief

سرپایان [sarpaayaan] 1 sloping, slanting ♦ این راه - است This road goes downhill. 2 down, downwards, downhill

سرپایانی [sarpaayaani] (downhill) slope

سرپایی [sarpayi] house slippers, bedroom slippers

سرپتنوسی [sarpatnusi] napkin for a tray

سرپرده [sarparda] cornice (above a door) for blinds or drapery

سرپرست [sarparast] 1 supervising (somebody or something) 2 manager, chief, senior person ♦ فابریکه - factory manager

سرپرستی [sarparasti] 1 care, looking after, supervision (of somebody or something) 2 leadership
- کردن - ● 1 to look after, to take care [of]; to watch [over] 2 to lead, to guide(را،از)

سرپناه [sarpanaah] roof over [one's] head; shelter ♦ آنها سرپناهی نداشتند They had no shelter.

سرپوش [sarposh] 1 lid, cover, covering 2 technical cap, mantle ♦ محافظه - safety cap, protective cap 3 colloquial patron, protector

سرپوشیده [sarposhida] 1 closed, with a closed top ♦ موتر - closed car or vehicle 2 hidden, concealed, covert, secret

سرپیچ [sarepeech] *technical* head of a screw; counterpropeller

سرپیچی [sarpeechi] **1** insubordination, disobedience **2** turn, bend, or curve in the road, zigzag
• کردن - to show insubordination or disobedience, to oppose, to resist (از)

سرتاسر [sartaasar] from end to end, from one edge to the other ♦ این باغ را دیدم - I examined this garden from beginning to end. ◊ - دنیا in all the world

سرتمبه [sartamba] *colloquial* self-willed; stubborn; obstinate

سرتیر [sarter] selflessly brave, desperate

سرتیری [sarteri] *colloquial* **1** selfless bravery **2** careless work, hackwork
• کردن - to work in a slipshod manner; to do hack work

سرج [sarj] cheviot, serge

سرجایی [sarjaayi] bedspread; pique bedspread

سرجم [sarjam] ☞ سرجمع

سرجمع [sarjám (a)] **1** sum, total **2** in total, in sum; in all

سرجه [sorja] hard snow, snow that has become covered with ice; frozen snow-crust
• خوردن - to slide along the snow crust (on a board)

سرچاینکی [sarchaaynaki] cloth cover (for a teapot with brewed tea)

سرچپه [sarchapa] *colloquial* **1** overturned, placed upside down **2.1** upside down ♦ کتابش را گرفته بود - He was holding the book upside down. **2** not as one should, backwards ♦ تمام کار های تو – است With you everything is topsy-turvy!

سرچرخی [sarcharkhi] *colloquial* dizziness

سرچوک [sarecawk] center of a bazaar, bazaar crossroad
• خبرهای - (and)- افواهات bazaar talk, bazaar gossip

سرحد [sarhad (d)] (*plural* سرحدات [sarhad (d) aat]) border; border zone, border region
• آزاد - region of the independent Pathan tribes

سرخ [sorkh] red, scarlet ♦ الونی - bright red ◊ جگری - wine-colored
• شدن - **1** to turn red, to flush; to blush (with shame) **2** to fry, to roast, to broil, to brown (on a fire)

سرخار [sarkhaar] spikes (cemented into the upper part of adobe walls)

سرخاکی [sarekhaaki] alms (distributed after the burial of a deceased)

سرخانه [sarkhaana] reservoir of a water pipe

سرخ باد [sorkhbaad] erysipelas

سرخ بید [sorkhbeed] sorkhbed (a variety of weeping willow that blooms with small red blossoms)

سرخچه [sorkhcha] sorkhcha (variety of wheat with reddish grains)

سرخط [sarxat (t)] **1** writing samples (in calligraphy) **2** contract, agreement (about hiring for a job)

سرخکان [sorkhakaan] measles

سرخم [sarkham] *colloquial* **1** ashamed, embarrassed **2** obedient, submissive **3** submerged (in a matter), occupied (with something)

سرخود [sarekhod] at one's own will; voluntarily
• خانه قاضی رفتن - *proverb* to put one's own head into the noose (*literally*, to go to [meet] fate voluntarily)

سرخ وزرد [sorkhozard]
• شدن - *colloquial* **1** to be embarrassed, to blush **2** to change countenance (out of anger, etc.)

سرخ وسفید [sorkhosafeed] brimming with health, fresh, rosy, ruddy

سرخوش [sarkhosh] **1** carefree; happy **2** slightly tight (from drinking), in one's cups

سرخی [sorkhi] **1** redness, red color **2** rouge **3** flesh (of meat) **4** grain rust (disease of cereals)

سرخیل [sarkheel] head of family, leader of a tribe

سرد [sard] **1** cold, very cold **2** dry, cold; reserved, unfriendly
♦ خنده سرد - a forced laugh ◊ سرد خندیدن - to laugh half-heartedly

سردآبه [sardaaba] ☞ سردآوه

سردار [sardaar] **1** sardar, prince (feudal title) **2** leader **3** *masculine proper name* Sardar

سردآوه [sardaawa] closed basin (for storing water)

سردخانه [sardkhaana] refrigerator, refrigerating plant

سردرختی [sardarakhti] fruit (s), fruit obtained from a tree (as opposed to melons)

سردرد [sardard] **1** suffering from a headache **2** preoccupied; worried, depressed, despondent (about something)

سردردی [sardardi] **1** headache **2** ☞ دردسر
• به - دچار بودن to suffer from a headache

سر در گم [sardargom] dark, obscure; complicated, intricate

سردست [saredast] at hand; at one's disposal ♦ این کتاب فعلاً – نیست We do not have this book at our disposal at present.

سرددل [sarddel] hardhearted, cold, indifferent

سردستی [saredasti] *colloquial* in a hurry, hurriedly
• چیزی را - برای خود پختن to make something for oneself hurriedly

سردسیر [sardseer] **1** severe, cold (about a climate) **2** (*also-* منطقه) frigid zone

سردوز [sardoz] thick threads or cord (for sewing bags or sacks)

سردی [sardi] **1** *rarely* cold *noun* **2** coldness; dryness; quality of reserve (in dealing with people)

سرراست [sarrast] directly, straight, at once ♦ شمارا - به خانه تان می رسانیم We'll take you straight home.

سرراهی [sarraahi] present, gift (brought from the road)

سررشته [sarreshta] ☞ سرشته

سرزمین [sarzamin] country; land, territory

سرزنش [sarzanesh] rebukes, reproaches; reproof, dressing down ♦ بنای – راگذاشت She began to scold me.

سرزور [sarzor] **1** stubborn, obstinate, self-willed **2** refractory, rebellious

سرسبد [saresabad]
• گل - **1.1** best part (of something) **1.2** the life of the party **2** best of all (about somebody)

سرسبیل [sarsabil] *colloquial* **1** neglected, left without protection, without support ♦ اولادش - ماند His children were left without supervision. **2** lounging about idly, loafing one's time away

سرستونی [sarsotuni] capital (of a column)

سرسخت [sarsakht] strong, stalwart; hardy

سرسر [sarsar]
• کردن- to sort; to select, to pick out (separating the large from the small) ♦ زغال را – کرد He sorted [the] coal.

183

سرسراوس [sarsaros (and) sararaws] *historical* chief of emir's bodyguards

سرسری [sarsari] (and) سرسرکی [sarsaraki] *colloquial* 1 superficial, careless; done hurriedly, done anyhow 2 superficially, hurriedly, anyhow

سرسفید [sarsafeed] old woman; little old lady

سرش [seresh] glue, paste
- کردن• - to glue, to paste, to glue together, to paste together

سرشام [sareshaam] 1 breaking the fast at the beginning of the evening (on fast days) 2 evening meal

سرشانه [sarshaana] shoulder straps; epaulets

سرشت [seresht] nature, nature (of man); character

سرشتن [sereshtan] 1.1 *literary* to knead, to mix (dough, mortar) 1.2 to make, to create 2 a creation (of man)

سرشته [saresshta] 1 knowing one's business; ability, skill, sense 2 order; arrangement, organization 3 accuracy; thrift, economy
- کردن • - 1 to prepare, to arrange, to put in good order ♦ نان کیید را - Prepare everything necessary for dinner! / Set the table for dinner! 2 to cope [with], to manage ♦ یک بتنهایی او عایله کلان را – میکند He supports a large family by himself.
- کسی را کار کردن • - 1 to manage, to arrange at somebody else's expense 2 to settle accounts with somebody

سرشته داری [sareshtadaari] *historical* tax department of a province or district

سرشته مند [sareshtamand] 1 being a good judge (of something in business); capable, efficient (in management) 2 accurate, thrifty

سرشخ [sarshakh] 1 willful, capricious 2 restive ♦ اسپ - a restive horse

سرشکن [sarshekan] difficult; puzzling ♦ کار - difficult work ◊ راه - dangerous road

سرشکنی [sarshekani] *colloquial* crush (of a crowd); bustle; turmoil

سرشماری [sarshomaari] 1 census (of the population) 2 count (of livestock)

سرشناس [sarshenaas] 1 well-known; eminent; respected; authoritative 2 an important person

سرشوخ [sarshokh] 1 mischievous, prankish 2 a mischievous child or person, a prankish child or person

سرشیر [sareshir] cream

سرطان [saratan] 1 *medicine* cancer 2 *astronomy* the constellation Cancer

سرطبیب [sartabib] chief physician

سرعت [sor'at] speed; tempo ♦ رفتار - speed of movement
- بسرعت ☞ به - •

سرغچ [sorghoch] (and) سرغوچ [sorghoch] sealing wax; seal
- کردن• - to affix a seal, to seal

سرفراز [sarfaraaz] ☞ سربلند

سرفه [sorfa] cough
- کردن • - to cough, to have a cough

سرقت [sarqat] theft, embezzlement

سرقوماندان [sarqumaandaan] commander in chief ♦ اعلی - supreme commander in chief

سرقو ماندانی [sarqumaandaani] (and) سرقو ماندانیت [sarqumandaniyat] the high command

سرقه [sarqa] ☞ سرقت

سرک [sarak] 1 thoroughfare ♦ پخته - roadway; highway 2 street 3 seam

- کردن• - to sew, to sew up, to mend, to sew together (something torn)

سرکاتب [sarkateeb] senior clerk ♦ اوراق - manager of correspondence; archivist

سرکار [sarkaar] *obscure* authorities; government; leadership

سرکاری [sarkaari] 1 state; official ♦ اخبار های - official newspapers 2 (opposite of رعیتی) public ♦ عمارت - public building
- شدن • - to go into the treasury or public coffers, to be confiscated (for use of the state)

سرکپ [sarkap] *technical* cover lid; head, cap

سرکرده [sarkarda] 1 leader (of a tribe); head 2 chief, senior person

سرکس [sarkas] circus

سرکسازی [saraksaazi] road construction

سرکشاده [sarkoshaada] open; not sealed
- مکتوب – • postcard

سرکش [sarkash] insubordination, disobedience; riot; meeting

سرکنده [sarkanda] *colloquial* madcap, daredevil

سرکوب [sarkob] 1 rising [above], towering [over], dominating (nearby terrain) 2 ☞ سرکوبی
- خانه تان نباید – حویلی ما باشد • Our inner courtyard should not be seen from your home (a mandatory condition in Moslem life).

سرکوبی [sarkobi] suppression, repression; destruction

سرکه [serka] vinegar

سرگذشت [sargozasht] 1 incident; event; adventure ♦ خودراگفت - He told what happened to him. 2 story (of one's life); narration (of one's experiences)

سرگردان [sargardaan] 1 moving, roaming, wandering 2 unsettled, drifting 3 confused; disarrayed

سرگردانی [sargardaani] 1 fruitless efforts, trouble, difficulties 2 misfortunes, sorrows

سرگرم [sargarm] absorbed; submerged (in a matter); carried away (by some pursuit)

سرگرمی [sargarmi] 1 pursuit; occupation; enthusiasm, passion 2 diversion, amusement, pastime ♦ برای - for amusement, for relaxation

سرگز [sar (e) gaz] a whole piece of cloth; a length (of cloth)

سرگنس [sargans]
- شدم • *colloquial* [I feel] as if my head is in a fog. / My head is spinning.

سرگنس [sargich] ☞ سر گیچ

سرگیری [sargiri]
- کردن • *colloquial* to keep from taking a rash action; to hold fast

سرگین [sargin] horse dung, donkey dung

سرلوحه [sarlawha] 1 sign, signboard 2 headpiece; vignette

سرمأمور [sarma 'mur]
- پولیس • chief of a police station (in a province)

سرماه وروز [saremaahoroz] *colloquial* woman in the last month of pregnancy

سرمایه [sarmaaya] capital ♦ اصلی - fixed capital ◊ دورانی - working capital, circulating capital

سرمایه دار [sarmaayadaar] 1 prosperous person, rich man 2 capitalist

سرمایه داری [sarmaayadaari] 1 capitalism 2 capitalist, capitalistic *adjective* ♦ غیر - noncapitalistic

سرمشق [sarmashq] **1** model (for imitation), example **2** samples of writing (in calligraphy)

سرمقاله [sarmaqaala] lead article, editorial

سرمنشاء [sarmansha] instigator ♦ او - این کار بود He was the instigator in this matter.

سر منشی [sarmonshi] **1** chief of a secretariat ♦ مؤسسه ملل متحد - General Secretary of the U. N. **2** *historical* chief of the personal secretariat of an emir

سرمنگسک [sarmangasak]
● افسانه - *colloquial* fairy tale about a white bull-calf

سرموی [saremoy] *colloquial* (also- سرمویی) (and) یک-)
1 a little bit, just barely **2** (with a negative predicate) not an iota, not a hair ♦ یک سرموی گناه نداریم We are not at all to blame.

سرمه [sorma] antimony (also used to paint eyebrows, eyelashes, hair) ♦ به چشم زدن(کشیدن) - to paint the eyes with antimony
● ناآزموده را به چشم مکش *proverb* Don't paint your eyes with untested antimony.

سرمه اندود [sormaandud] painted with antimony, made up with antimony (about the eyes)

سرمه یی [sormayi] dark blue

سرمیزی [sarmezi] **1** tablecloth **2** table, desk *adjective* ♦ چراغ - table lamp, desk lamp

سرنی(ی) [sorna (y)] ☞ سرنی

سرنگ [sorong] undermining (in explosive operations)
● پراندن - to blow up, to dynamite (rock)

سرنگ پرانی [sorongparaani] explosive operations

سرنگون [sarnegun] **1** overturned **2** overthrown
● کردن - **1** to overturn **2** to overthrow **3** to knock down (an aircraft)

سرنل [sarenal] *technical* **1** connecting sleeve **2** sleeve

سرنوشت [sarnawesht] fate

سرنی [sornay] zourna (type of lute); karnay

سرنی چی [sornaychi] musician who plays the zourna or the karnay

سرنیزه [sarneeza] **1** trihedral bayonet; dagger bayonet, short bayonet **2** point of a bayonet

سرو [sarw] cypress
● روان(خرامان) - *poetry* graceful, slender as a cypress (about a beautiful woman)

سروبر [sarobar] external appearance, exterior, appearance (from standpoint of clothing, outfit)
● سروبرش را درست کردیم We dressed him up.

سروجان [sarojan] **1** head and trunk; entire body **2** life; property; everything most dear ♦ سروجانم فدای آزادی I will give up everything for freedom.
● خود را شستن - to wash oneself, to bathe, to take a bath

سرود [sorud] **1** music, tune, melody **2** song, hymn

سرودن [sorudan] (*present tense stem* سرای [saray]) to compose or to sing (poetry)

سرور [sorur] *literary* joy; gladness; merriment, gaiety

سروسامان [sarosaamaan] property, belongings

سروسودا [sarosawdaa] *colloquial* troubles, cares; grief, sorrow; thoughts; fears; misgivings

سروصدا [sarosadaa]
● احمد معلوم نیست - *colloquial* Nothing has been heard about Ahmad. / There is no news about Ahmad.

سروصورت [sarosurat] **1** fine appearance; presentable appearance **2** state or quality of being in good order
● گرفتن - **1** to acquire [the proper] appearance **2** to be put in good order, to be put right

سروقت [sarewaqt] on time, in time, promptly ♦ او - به کار خود حاضر میشود He gets to work on time.

سروقت [sarwaqt]
● به - کسی رسیدن *colloquial* to come to somebody's assistance

سروکار [sarokaar] relation, connection
● با کسی – داشتن to be connected with somebody, to have business with somebody

سروی [sarwee] **1** surveying, exploration (of terrain); geodetic survey ♦ - وپروژه سازی surveying and planning operations or work **2** geological prospecting

سرویس [sarwis] **1** servicing, everyday services **2** service ♦ اطلاعات - communications service; information service **3** (- also هوایی) airline **4** (also شهری) city bus

سره [sara] **1** excellent, selected, choice, best ♦ خربوزه - melon of the highest grade **2** pure, unadulterated; of high standard (about gold and silver)
● کردن - to select (picking out the best)

سره میاشت [sramiaasht] Red Crescent Society

سری [sari]
● بوت - top, instep (of boots)

سری [ser(r) i] secret, covert; not to be divulged, not to be made public ♦ مکتوب - a secret letter

سریاور [saryaawar] *obscure* adjutant

سریع [sari'] quick, fast, rapid

سریع السیر [sariossair] high-speed, fast, rapid

سرین [sorin] buttocks; hips

سزا [sazaa] **1** recompense (for good) **2** punishment, penalty ♦ جسمانی - corporal punishment
● دادن - **1** to requite according to (somebody's) deserts **2** to punish, to inflict penalty on

سست [sost] **1** weak, feeble ♦ آدم - weak person **2** tired, weary **3** flabby, flaccid **4** soft, friable, crumbly; loose, pliant ♦ خاک - loose soil
● شدن - *intransitive* to weaken, to grow weak or feeble; to become soft or flabby ♦ باش - Relax! **2** *colloquial* to lose [one's] senses, to faint **3** to slacken, to slow down (about work, etc.) کار ما - شده است Our work slackened. **4** to calm down, to subside, to slacken (about noise, about the wind)

سطح [sath] **1** surface, plane ♦ اطاق - (and) خانه - floor of a room ◊ مرتفع - plateau **2** level ♦ بحر - sea level ◊ زندگی - standard of living

سطحی [sathi] *adjective* surface; superficial; cursory

سطر [sáter] line
● سر -**1** new paragraph **2** from the new paragraph, from the indentation

سطل [satel] ☞ ستل

سعادت [saaadat] **1** happiness; good fortune, prosperity, success **2** *masculine proper name* Saadat

سعی [sa'y] effort, endeavor
● کردن(نمودن) - to undertake efforts, to make efforts, to endeavor, to try

سعید [sa'id] **1** happy, promising success, favorable **2** *masculine proper name* Said

185

سغد [soghd] *historical* Sogdiana (ancient name of area around Samarkand)

سفارت [safaarat] 1 embassy, diplomatic mission 2 duties of an ambassador

سفارت خانه [safaaratkhaana] residence of an ambassador, an embassy

سفارش [sefaaresh] ☞ سپارش

سفال [sofaal] 1 pottery, ceramics 2 crock, crocks 3 *regional* chicken egg

سفالین [sofaalin] ceramic, made of calcined clay ♦ جام - a ceramic cup or bowl

سفت [seft] strong, solid; hard, rigid; tough

سفر [safar] 1 journey, trip ♦ به خیر - Bon voyage! / Have a good trip! 2 military campaign, march

● کردن - 1 to travel 2 to carry out a campaign or a march

● رسمی - official visit (by a political figure to some country)

سفرا [sofaraa] *plural of* سفیر

سفربری [safarbari] mobilization ♦ عمومی - general mobilization

سفرخرج [safarkharj] (and) سفرخرچ [safarkharch] 1 travel expenses 2 travelling allowance

سفرمینا [safarmainaa] sappers; sapper battalion

سفره [sofra] 1 tablecloth 2 tablecloth with refreshments or food; served dinner (on a tablecloth) 3 (also آردی -) sofra (a piece of leather on which dough is prepared)

● انداختن - to spread a tablecloth; to set a table for dinner, to set a table

سفلا [soflaa] 1 the lower reaches (of a river) 2 low (about terrain), located in a depression

سفید [safeed] 1 white, of white color 2 clean, not covered with writing ♦ کتابچه - a clean notebook

● کردن - 1 to whiten, to whitewash 2 to tin 3 *colloquial* to clear things up; to have it out (با); to fight ♦ بیاکه ما و تو – کنیم Come on, let's have it out!

سفیدار [safeedaar] silver poplar

سفیدبخت [safeedbakht] 1 happy (about a woman) 2 beloved wife, favorite wife

سفیدچونه [safeedchuna] whitewashing; alabaster (for coating walls)

سفیدچه [safeedcha] safedcha (variety of wheat with whitish grains)

سفیدکاری [safeedkaari] whitewashing; covering with alabaster

سفیده [safeeda] 1 ceruse (cosmetic) 2 whiting (paint) ♦ روغنی - white oil paint

● کردن - 1 to powder oneself, to put on make-up, to put ceruse (on one's face) 2 to cover, to paint white, to whitewash

سفیدی [safeedi] 1 whiteness; white color 2 white (of an egg), albumen 3 fat, grease, fat (on meat) 4 *colloquial* milk; milk products

سفیر [safir] (*plural* سفرا [sofaraa]) ambassador ♦ کبیر - Ambassador Extraordinary and Plenipotentiary

سفینه [safina] 1 ship, vessel ♦ فضایی - space ship 2 *literary* collection of poetry ♦ خطی - the manuscript of a collection of poetry

سقا [saqqaa] (and) سقاو [saqqaaw] hawker of drinking water, a water carrier

سقف [saqf] 1 ceiling; roofing 2 *technical* overhead covering between floors or of an attic

سقف پوشی [saqfposhi] laying roofing

سقوط [soqut] 1 fall; overthrow ♦ ستاره - the falling of a star ◊ استبداد - the downfall of despotism 2 decline, decay, collapse, disintegration ♦ دادن - to knock down (an aircraft)

● کردن - 1 to fall, to collapse, to be subverted 2 to be overthrown, to be deposed, to be dethroned

سقه [soqqa] 1 confirmed, established (about a fact, etc.) 2 truth; fact

سک [sek] siph

سکالرشپ [skaalarshep] (and) سکالرشیپ [skaalarship] 1 scholarship, allowance (paid by the state to students studying abroad) 2 studying abroad (at state expense)

سکته [sakta] 1 stop; hitch, hesitation, stutter; pause 2 *medicine* apoplectic stroke; a stroke

● قلب - 1 a heart attack 2 infarction

سکته گی [saktagi] *technical* malfunction; trouble, disruption; failure; damage

سکرتر [sekartar] secretary ♦ اول سفارت - first secretary of an embassy

سکشن [sekshan] 1 section 2 *technical* section, cross-section ♦ تعمیر - cross-section of a building

سکلاندن [soklaandan] *colloquial* 1 to tear, to tear off 2 to break off, to end relations (با،همرای) ♦ مه با محمود سکلاندم I broke off with Mahmud.

سکلیدن [soklidan] *colloquial* to burst, to break *intransitive*

سکنجبین [sekanjbin] sweet-and-sour syrup (made of sugar and vinegar, used as a medicine)

سکنه [sakana] *plural of* ساکن

سکو [saku] stone or wooden bench (in a garden or at the entrance to a home)

سکوت [sokut] silence; quiet calm; hush

● کردن - to be silent, to keep silent; to keep silence

سکورنچ [skurench] *technical* adjustable wrench

سکون [sokun] 1 calm tranquility, immobility 2 rest, quiet 3 *grammar* quiescence; absence of consonant

سکونت [sokunat] 1 residence; stay; residing 2 address (column in a questionnaire)

● داشتن(کردن) - to live, to reside to stay (در)

سکه [saka] own, blood (descended from the same parents) *adjective* ♦ شریف برادر سکه ام است Sharif is my own brother (from the same mother and father).

سکه [sek (k) a] 1 a minted coin 2 stamp; punch 3 *colloquial* appearance, exterior

● به نام کسی – زدن to mint a coin on somebody's behalf

سکه دار [sek (k) adaar] 1 with an impression; with a stamped coat of arms 2 *colloquial* visible, noticeable, having shape or form

سکی [seki] skis

● کردن - to ski

سکیچ [skeech] preliminary draft, outline; sketch, rough drawing

سگ [sag] dog

● سگ پاچه گیر 1 vicious dog 2 vicious like a dog (about somebody)

● مثل سگ و فقیر Like a dog and a beggar. (Like cats and dogs.)

● سگ هر سوار است *contemptuous* He is ready to serve anyone.

سگابی [sagabi] otter

سگ انگورک [sagangurak] *botany* nightshade

سگ جان [sagjaan] *contemptuous* tenacious as a dog

سگرت [segret] cigarettes

سگرت دانی [segretdaani] cigarette case, cigar case

سگرتی [segreti] a smoker

سگریت [segreet] ☞ سگرت

سگک [sagak] 1 buckle; clasp; fastener; hook ♦ کمربند - belt buckle 2 mole cricket (insect)

سگ گری [saggari] *colloquial* wickedness, maliciousness; caddishness, rudeness

سگ ماهی [sagmaahi] catfish; sturgeon

سل [sel] tuberculosis, consumption
• سل شدن 1 to be sick with consumption 2 *colloquial* to reach exhaustion, to exhaust oneself

سلاته [salaata] salad made of tomatoes

سلاح [selaah] weapon, arms; armament

سلاخ [sallaakh] animal slaughterer, butcher, flayer

سلاخی [sallaakhi] 1 slaughter of livestock 2 occupation of a butcher, of a flayer

سلاست [salaasat] *literary* fluency, facility (of verse, etc.); clarity, smoothness (of thought, speech)

سلاطین [salaatin] *plural of* سلطان

سلاله [solaala (and) salaala] *literary* 1 dynasty, house 2 geneology

سلام [salaam] 1.1 greeting, salutation, regards ♦ نظامی - saluting, rendering military salute 1.2 farewell 2.1 ! _ Hello! / Greetings! / Welcome! 2.2 Good-bye!
• شاهی - *historical* national anthem (of royal Afghanistan)

سلامت [salaamat] 1 healthy; unharmed, safe 2 safely, in an unharmed condition, intact
• باش - Good-bye! / Bless you!

سلامتی [salaamati] health, well-being ♦ شمارا میخواهم - I wish you health!

سلام علیکم [salaamalaýkom] ! _ 1 Hello! / Peace be with you! 2 Good-bye! / Greetings! / Regards!

سلام علیکی [salaamaleki] *colloquial* nodding acquaintance
• با کسی – داشتن to be slightly acquainted with somebody (only to exchange greetings)

سلام و علیک [salaamoalayk (and) salamoaleek]
• کردن - to exchange greetings, to say how do you do, to greet

سلامی [salaami] 1 salute (with cannons) 2 playing the national anthem
• کردن - to give a salute, to salute ♦ گرفت – باجه خانه The orchestra played the [national] anthem.

سلایی [salaayi] 1 small stick for applying antimony (cosmetic) 2 pencil for lining the eyes

سلب [salb] *literary* 1 taking away, deprivation ♦ اختیارات - removal of authority 2 negation; reversal (of a decision, etc.) 1 to take away, to deprive (- کردن) 2 to cancel, to reverse (a decision از)

سلتراج [selteraj] ☞ سلدراج

سلتی [selti] 1 Celtic 2 (also - زبان) Celtic language

سلجوقی [saljuqi] *historical* Seljuk, Seljukian

سلخ [salkh *literary* opposite of* غره [qorra]) last day of the lunar month

سلدراج [selderaj] 1 drawers (underwear) 2 tights; bloomers (women's undergarments)

سلسله [selsela] 1 chain, file, row, line ♦ کوه - mountain range 2 series ♦ جلسات - a series of meetings, a session ◊ اقدامات یک a series of measures 3 official hierarchy 4 house, dynasty; geneological line

سلسیوس [salsiyus] Celsius ♦ صدرجه - 100 degrees Celsius

سلطان [soltaan] (*plural* سلاطین [salaatin]) 1 sultan; sovereign, monarch 2 *masculine proper name* Sultan

سلطنت [saltanat] 1 kingdom, monarchy; sultanate 2 power, authority, rule, sway
• کردن - to rule, to wield power, to govern

سلطنتی [saltanati] king's, royal, regal, sultan's ♦ دربار - king's court

سلف [salaf] (*plural* اسلاف [aslaf]) ancestor, forefather, predecessor

سلف [salf] *technical* 1 starter 2 throttle

سلفر [solfor] sulfur

سلفریک [solforik] sulfuric ♦ اسید - sulfuric acid

سلمانی [salmaani] barber's shop

سلندر [salandar] 1 cylinder 2 tank (oxygen tank, tank of compressed air)
• آبخانه – *technical* water jacket

سلنسر [selensar] *technical* muffler, silencer

سلنگ روز [selengroz] egress for wiring (in a ceiling)

سلوک [soluk] 1 behavior, conduct, mode of life 2 treatment (of somebody) ♦ صاحب - polite, well-mannered 3 *obscure* asceticism

سلول [selul] *biology* cell

سله [salla] turban

سلیپ [slip]
• کردن - to skid

سلیپر [selipar] house slippers; slippers

سلیت [slit] 1 (also - سنگ) shale 2 slate 3 slate blackboard

سلیتر [selitar] *technical* 1 insulator, isolator 2 porcelain insulator (for electical wires)

سلیس [salis] *literary* fluent, smooth; well-rounded ♦ شعر - flowing, well-rounded verse

سلیقه [saliqa] 1 taste (as a sense of the elegant) 2 natural inclination, ability (for something)

سلیقه دار [saliqadar] 1 having good taste; knowing the particulars (of something); comprehending 2 capable

سلیکان [selikaan] *chemistry* silicon

سلیمان [soleemaan (and) solaymaan] 1 Solomon (biblical ruler) 2 *masculine proper name* Suleyman
• حضرت گنج - fantastic riches

سلیمان خیل [soleemaankheel] Suleymankheli (tribe)

سلیمانی [soleemaani] (also - مرغ) hoopoe (bird)

سم [sam (m)] poison, venom, bane

سم [som] hoof

سمارق [samaaroq] mushroom, fungus; mushrooms, fungi

سماعت [samaa'at] (and) سماعه [samaa'a] hearing case (in court)
• قابل – under or within the jurisdiction [of]
• کردن - to hear a case (in court)

سمال [samaal] *colloquial* Look out! / Careful! / Stand aside!
• کردن - to be careful, to keep one's eyes open
• کو - Be careful! Look out!

سماوات [samaawaat] *colloquial* ☞ سماوار

سماوار [samaawaar] 1 samovar 2 tearoom, chaykhana

سماواری [samaawaari] (and) سماوارچی [samaawaarchi] vendor of hot tea, worker or proprietor of a chaykhana

سمب [somb] colloquial ☞ سم [som]

سمبک [sombak] colloquial
• زدن - to hoof, to pick with the hoof, to trample with the hoof (about a horse)

سمبوسه [sambòsa] ☞ سنبوسه

سمت [samt] 1 side, direction ♦ سمت ها - directions of the world (north, south, etc.) 2 land, territory, province, region ♦ مشرقی - (formerly) eastern province of Afghanistan (according to an old administrative subdivision)

سمع [sám'] (and) sáma 1 hearing, ability to hear 2 (legal) hearing
• قابل - بودن to be subject to a hearing (in court)

سمنت [semant] cement

سمنک [semanak] samanak (ritual dish in the form of a sweet, thin gruel made from wheat sprouts during the days of Nawruz)

سمنک پزی [samanakpazi] preparing samanak

سمنک ☞ •

سموم [samum] simoom, hot wind; sandstorm

سموم زدگی [samumzadagi] faint, fainting (of a person who is caught in a simoom)

سمینار [seminaar] seminar

سمستر [semeestar] semester

سمی کولن [semikolon] grammar semicolon

سن [senn] age ♦ بلاغت - mature age ◊ وسال - age, years

سنا [senaa] (also - مجلس) senate

سناتوریم [sanaatoriam] sanatorium

سناچ [sanaach] 1 leather bag inflated with air (for crossing a river) 2 wineskin (for storing wine and other liquids)

سنبل [sonbol] 1 hyacinth 2 spikenard (plant) 3 poetic locks, ringlets, curls (of beautiful girl or woman)

سنبله [sonbola] 1 astronomy constellation Virgo 2 Sonbola (the sixth month of the calendar; corresponds to August-September)

سنبوسه [sanbosa] a patty with a piquant meat stuffing (of a triangular form)

سنبه [sonba] 1 technical chisel; knockout (tool) 2 technical center punch 3 ramrod; cleaning rod 4 (also توپ-) rammer, bore brush

سنت [sonnat] 1 religion Sunna ♦ اهل - Sunnites 2 (plural سنن [sonnan]) custom; law; rule; instruction 3 circumcision (rite)
• کردن - 1 to perform a prayer 2 to perform a circumcision

سنتره [santara] tangerine, tangerine tree; tangerines (of a large size)

سنتکس [santaks] syntax

سنج [senj] wall, parapet (surrounding a flat roof)

سنج [sanj] 1 present tense stem سنجدن ☞ 2 سنجش 3 (second component of compound words with meaning of "measuring") ♦ ارتفاع سنج - altimeter

سنجاق [sanjaaq] 1 pin; hairpin 2 paper clip

سنجد [sanjed] botany sorb, oleaster (fruits) ♦ درخت- sorb tree

سنجش [sanjesh] 1 measuring, measurement; calculation, counting; technical estimate ♦ مصارف برای ساختمان - estimate of expenditures for construction 2 considering, weighing 3 plans, computations; estimates

سنجیدن [sanjidan] 1 to weigh; to measure 2 to consider, to evaluate
• چاره – to try to find a remedy (for something); to take measures

سند [sanad] (plural اسناد [asnaad]) 1 document, paper; reference 2 diploma 3 official document; deed

سندان [sandaan] anvil

سندر [sondor] cinnabar (with which Indians adorn the part in their hair and place dots on their foreheads)

سندلی [sandali] ☞ صندلی

سنگ [sang] 1 rock, stone ♦ آسیا - millstone ◊ دوبی - smooth rock (on which to wash clothing) ◊ لخشان - a smooth rocky hillock (on which children slide) ◊ پنج و - game of pebbles ◊ پارس - philosopher's stone ◊ محک - touchstone 2 (also ترازو -) weight, set of weights; counterweight, counterpoise
• پیش پای کسی انداختن - to create obstacles; to poke a stick in (somebody's) wheel
• صبر بدل زدن - colloquial to resign oneself (to something), to refuse; to renounce; to relinquish (something) reluctantly
• آسمانی - unexpected trouble, unexpected misfortune
• دوره – historical the Stone Age
• میترقد - [Even] stones are splitting. (about a severe frost)

سنگ اندازی [sangandaazi] laying stone on a road, covering a road with stone

سنگ آهن [sangeaahan] minimum iron ore, ironstone

سنگباران [sangbaaraan]
• کردن - to hurlstones [at], to injure or to kill with stones

سنگ بازی [sangbazi]
• کردن - to throw stones at each other

سنگ بقه [sangbaqa] turtle, tortoise

سنگ پارچه [sangparcha] 1 stone block; fragment of stone 2 construction rubble stone

سنگ پای [sangepaay] (pumice) stone for cleaning the feet

سنگ پشت [sangposht] ☞ سنگ بقه

سنگ تراش [sangtaraash] stone mason, bricklayer

سنگدان [sangdaan] gizzard (of a bird)

سنگدل [sangdel] cruel, hardhearted

سنگر [sangar] breastwork, embankment; fortification; entrenchment; emplacement
• گرفتن - to dig in, to take a defensive position

سنگرکنی [sangarkani] digging emplacements; construction of fortifications, sapper operations

سنگریزه [sangreeza] gravel

سنگ ریشه [sang (e) reesha] asbestos

سنگسار [sangsaar] 1 historical stoning to death (a form of execution) 2 ☞ سنگلاخ

سنگ فرش [sangfarsh] paved with stone ♦ راه - paved roadway, cobblestone roadway

سنگک [sangak] colloquial taking a long time to become soft from boiling (about hard peas, beans, etc.)

سنگ کاری [sangkaari] masonry ♦ تهداب - masonry of a foundation

سنگ کن [sangkan] worker in a quarry

سنگکی [sangaki] (opposite of کاغذی) hard, tough (about a nut) ♦ بادام - an almond with very hard shell

سنگلاخ [sanglaakh] rocky bed of a mountain river

سنگ نمک [sang (e) namak] geology rock salt

سنگی [sangi] rock *adjective*, stone *adjective*, made of rock or stone ♦ - پل stone bridge

سنگین [sangin] 1 heavy, weighty 2 difficult, grave; terrible ♦ - وظیفه difficult task or assignment; heavy responsibility 3 *colloquial* reliable, staid, sedate (about a person) 4 ☞ سنگی ♦- دل a heart like a rock, cruel heart

سنگینی [sangini] 1 weight, gravity, heaviness; load 2 reliability, staidness, sedateness

سنن [sonan] *plural of* سنت 2

سنوات [sanawat] (*plural of* سنه) ♦ - در گذشته in past years, in days gone by, in bygone days

سنه [sana] (*plural* سنوات [sanawat]) 1 year; date ♦ - قمری lunar year 2 system of chronology ♦ - عیسوی system of chronology since the birth of Christ

سنی [sonni] 1 Sunni *adjective* 2 Sunni *noun*

سو [saw]
● کردن - to polish (an alabaster surface)

سو(ی) [so (y) (and) su (y)] 1 side, direction ♦ از هر سو from everywhere, from all sides or directions ◊ این سو بیا Come here! 2 (also به سوی) toward, to, in the direction toward *denominative preposition* ♦ بسوی غرب to the west ◊ بسوی آن دویدم I ran to him ◊ آن سوتر farther, further; above, over, beyond the limits (of something) ◊ به این سو up to now ◊ از یک هفته به این سو for a week now as much as a week ago

سوء [su'] (first component of compound words with meanings of "poor" / "bad" / "malicious") ♦ سوءاداره bad management, mismanagement, inability to organize, lack of administrative abilities

سوابق [sawaabeq] *plural of* سابقه

سوءاجرات [su'ejaaraat] 1 bad management, mismanagement 2 abuse, misuse

سواحل [sawaahel] *plural of* ساحل

سواد [sawaad (and) sewaad]¹ 1 literacy 2 copy, written copy ♦ - تصدیق شده certified copy 3 rough copy
● داشتن - to be literate (to know how to read and write)
● گرفتن - to make a copy, to copy

سواد [sawaad]² 1 black, niello (a chemical compound used to ornament silver with niello) 2 silhouette, contours, outlines (usually of a town or village seen from a distance) ♦ دهکده یی از دور پیدا شد - In the distance, the outlines of a village came in sight. 3 outskirts, suburb; environs (of a city)

سوءاداره [su'edaara] inability to organize, lack of administrative abilities; inability to manage

سوادکاری [sawaadkaari] 1 ornamenting or inlaying niello (or silver) 2 niello

سوار [sowaar (and) sawaar] 1 going on horseback, mounted, horse *adjective* 2.1 rider, horseman ♦ از دل پیاده نمی آید(نمی) داند *proverb* A rider cannot sympathize with a person on foot (a person with a full stomach cannot understand a hungry man). 2 *chess* knight; bishop
● شدن - 1 to mount (a horse, elephant, etc.) 2 to board, to get on (any type of transportation)

سوارکار [sowaarkaar] 1 skilled rider, skilled horseman; jockey 2 participant in a mounted game involving dragging a goat's body

سوارکاری [sowaarkaari] fancy riding, trick riding; sport on horseback

سواره [sowaara] 1 on horseback 2 ☞ سوار 3 *colloquial* stubble, stubble field
● رفتن - to go on horseback
● سواره را بگیر پیاده است *idiom* (*literally:* take on one who is riding, first, then the one on foot) take on the first thing first

سواری [sowari] 1.1 riding (about an animal) 1.2 passenger (about a vehicle, etc.) 1.3 horse, mounted, cavalry *adjective* ♦ - فرقه cavalry division 2 *colloquial* transport, transportation, means of conveyance 3 به-••• *colloquial* on, mounted on, by means of (*denominative preposition*) ♦ به – سرویس on a bus ◊ به – تانکه in a cab

سوءاستعمال [su'este'maal] 1 careless attitude, unskillful use 2 abuse, misuse (of something)

سوءاستفاده [su'estefaada] illegal use; wrongful use, malfeasance (on a job, etc.)

سؤال [sawaal] (*plural* سوالات [sawaalaat]) 1 question; asking, inquiring, questioning ♦ - علامه question mark 2 request
● کردن - 1 to ask, to question, to ask a question 2 to request, to ask for (از), to make a request

سوالیه [sawaaliya]
●- جمله interrogative sentence
● علامت – question mark

سوانح [sawaaneh] 1 *plural of* سانحه 2 biography
● کارت – service record, work record

سوب [sob] *colloquial* ☞ صبح [sobh]

سوپراوکساید [suparoksayd] peroxide

سوءتفاهم [su'tafaahom] misunderstanding; lack of understanding

سوته [sota] 1 a stout stick, a cudgel 2 cane, walking stick, staff (of a shepherd, of a dervish) 3 battledore (for beating clothes when doing laundry) 4 wooden pestle, pestle (for grinding medicine)

سوجی [suji]¹ semolina

سوجی [suji]² pelvis, hip; head of leg bone ♦ سوجی اش برآمد He has a dislocated hip.

سویچ [swech] ☞ سویچ

سوخت [sokht] 1 burning, combustion ♦ - قابل flammable, combustible 2 fuel ♦ - چوب firewood 3 burning, inflammation

سوختاندن [sokhtaandan] to burn, to burn up, to burn down

سوختگی [sokhtagi] 1 *past participle* سوختن 2.1 a burned place, a burn 2.2 a charred place or spot 2.3 a place or spot reduced to ashes, smoldering ruins, a site after a fire

سوختن [sokhtan] (*present tense stem* سوز [soz]) 1 to burn, to burn down, to be burned down 2 to burn; to sting; to ache; to hurt (about a painful spot) 3 to be tormented, to suffer 4 to go to rack and ruin, to go for naught 5 ☞ سوختاندن
●- ازعشق to burn with love
● پولش سوخت That's his money down the drain.
● احمد خانه خودرا سوخت Ahmad burned his house down.

سوخته [sokhta] 1 *past participle* 2 lost, not received (about money, etc.) ♦ - مالیات arrears 3 exhausted, worn out

سود [sud] 1 profit, gain; interest (on capital) 2 use, benefit
● بودن - to extract profit, to extract gain
● خوردن - to collect interest (on capital); to lend money on interest

سودا [sawdaa]¹ bargain, deal, commercial transaction; bargaining, haggling, huckstering; purchase and sale

189

س

• کردن - to trade, to deal, to sell
• او گاو خوده - colloquial He sold his cow.
• پشت – رفتن to go to make purchases, to make purchases

سودا [sawdaa]² 1 thought, concern; alarm, anxiety; uneasiness ♦ به همین - بودتا خواب شد This thought possessed him until he fell asleep. 2 grief, sorrow; chagrin
• (کردن)زدن - 1 to fall to thinking, to worry, to be alarmed (about something) 2 to grieve, to mourn, to be upset
• در سر پرورانیدن - to nurture a thought, to nurture an idea, to cherish a hope or dream

سودا [sodaa] 1 soda water 2 soda

سوداگر [sawdaagar] 1 merchant, businessman 2 tradesman; shopkeeper; huckster

سوداگری [sawdaagari] 1 commerce, trade 2 trade turnover
• کردن - to engage in trade, to engage in commerece
• داشتن - to have trade turnover

سودایی [sawdaayi] 1 possessed (by some thought), nervous 2 melancholy, sad

سودخور [sudkhor] moneylender, usurer

سودمند [sudmand] useful; advantageous, profitable

سودن [sudan] (present tense stem سای [saay]) to rub, to grind (into a powder)

سوده [suda] 1 past participle سودن 2 powder; rock dust

سودیم [sodiam] sodium ♦ کلوراید - sodium chloride

سور [sur] valuable variety of karakul (gray with luster)

سوراخ [soraakh] 1 opening; hole 2 burrow
• کردن - to make a hole [in], to pierce, to skewer, to poke through

سورت [ŝort] grade; sort; brand
• کردن - to sort; to trade

سورت [surat] sura, a section or chapter of the Koran

سورت بندی [sortbandi] (and) سورت کاری [sortkari] sorting grading

سورتی [suraati] maidservant (having children from her master)

سوره [sura] ☞ سورت

سوز [soz]¹ 1 present tense stem سوختن 2 pain, suffering ♦ سوزهای دل troubles of the heart ◊ وگداز - torture, torment, suffering

سوز [soz]²
• دادن - colloquial boasting (about something) (while flaunting it); to tease somebody (while showing him something) ♦ اطفال لباس جدید خودهارا بیکدیگر - میدادند The children boasted about their new clothing in front of each other.

سوز [sawz] colloquial ☞ سبز

سوزاک [sozaak] medicine gonorrhea

سوزان [sozaan] 1 burning, flaming ♦ شمع - burning candle 2 hot, ardent, burning; fiery ♦ اشک - scalding tears 3 sorrowful, mournful, poignant ♦ آه - painful sigh

سوزاندن [sozaandan] 1 to burn, to sting ♦ دود چشم را میسوزاند The smoke stings the eyes. 2 ☞ سوختاندن

سوزش [sozesh] 1 burning 2 itch 3 pain, torment
• کردن - to burn, to smart (about an injury or wound, about a burn)

سوزن [sozan] needle
• زدن - 1 to prick with a needle 2 to make an injection, to make injections

• جای - زدن نبود obscure There was no place to stick a needle (there was no place for an apple to drop).

سوزن دوزی [sozandozi] hand embroidery; sewing

سوزنک [sozanak]¹ 1 tingling (when the extremeties are numb) 2 bubbling or boiling of water
• زدن - 1 to tingle (when numb) 2 to begin to boil (about water)

سوزنک [sozanak]² military firing pin assembly; firing pin, striker

سوزنمایی [soznomaayi] colloquial bragging, boasting (about something), showing (something to somebody to tease him)

سوزنی [sozani] sozani (piece of colored fabric embroidered with silk and used as a bedspread)

سوزه [sawza] ☞ سبزه

سوژه [suzhe] subject, topic, plot ♦ فلم - plot of a film

سوسمار [susmaar] monitor (type of large lizards)

سوسن [sawsan] botany field iris

سوسنی [sawsani] dark lilac, dark violet ♦ بادنجان - variety of eggplant (with very dark, almost black skin)

سوسیالستی [sosiaalesti] socialist, socialistic

سوسیالیزم [sosiaalizem] socialism

سوشلست [soshalest] 1 socialistic, socialist adjective 2 a socialist

سوغات [sawghaat] gift (brought from a trip); present
• آوردن - to give presents, to bring presents

سوق [sawq]
• دادن - 1 to send, to transfer (troops) 2 to direct in a specific direction (a thought, efforts, etc.)

سوق [suq] literary market, bazaar
چهار سوق ☞ چهار –

سوءقصد [su' (e) qasd] attempt
• کردن - to make an attempt (on somebody's life)

سوکاری [sawkaari] polishing (a surface covered with whitewash or alabaster)

سوگند [sawgand] vow; oath
• خوردن - to swear, to make a vow; to take an oath
• دادن - to force to swear; to swear in

سوگوار [sogwaar] mourning; wearing mourning; having buried (somebody); mourning (for somebody) ♦ زن - a woman in mourning

سوگواری [saagwaari] 1 observing mourning, mourning (for somebody) 2 sorrow, grief (over somebody's death)

سوم [so(w)wom] third

سون [son] colloquial ☞ سو(ی)

سوند [sund] 1 kenaf (a plant) 2 artificial silk, rayon, viscose

سوندی [sundi] rayon, viscose adjective, made of artificial silk

سوهان [suhaan] file; rasp ♦ درشت - bastard file ◊ دقیق - barette file ◊ میده - smooth-cut file
• کردن - to cut with a file, to file off
• عمر - anxiety; trouble; grief, sorrow

سوهان ریز [suhaanreez] metal filings

سوهان کاری [suhaankaari] filing (metal); metalworking

سویتی [soweeti] Soviet adjective

سویچ [swich] 1 switch; button of a switch, switch button 2 knife-switch ♦ technical بازودار - tumber switch 3 [ignition] switch (in a motor vehicle)
• کردن - to switch on (a current, light

سویچ بورد [swichbord] 1 *electrical* switchboard, panel 2 (also تیلفون -) switchboard, commutator

سویه [sawiya] level stage ♦ کلتوری - cultural level ◊ به - عالی at a high level

سه [se] three

سهام [sehaam] *plural of* سهم

سهامی [sehami] joint-stock ♦ شرکت - joint-stock company

سه برگه [sebarga] clover, trefoil, shamrock

سه پای [sepaay] (and) سه پایه [sepaya] 1 tripod; tripod support 2 trivet

سه تار [setaar] sitar (Indian three-string musical instrument)

سه دانه [sedaana] *colloquial* room with three windows, orsi ☞ ارسی •

سه شاخه [seshakha] *agriculture* three-pronged pitchfork

سه شنبه [seshambe] Tuesday

سه صد [sesad] three hundred

سه فصله [sefasla] giving three crops a year

سه کنجه [sekonja] 1 triangular 2 triangle

سه کنجی [sekonji] corner (of a room, etc.)
♦ کسی را به - گیر کردن to drive somebody into a corner; to place somebody in a hopeless or desperate position

سه کوت [sekot] *agriculture* system of dividing a harvest (in which the leaseholder or tenant receives one-third)

سهل [sahl (and) sáhal] easy, simple, not difficult

سهل انگاری [sahlangaari] 1 unconcern, carelessness, laziness 2 indulgence

سهم [sahm] ¹ 1 part, portion, share; sharing (in something) ♦ بارز - notable contribution 2 (*plural* اسهام [asham] (and) سهام [seham]) share (of stock)
♦ - گرفتن to participate, to take part ♦ او در این فلم – میگیرد He has a part in this film.

سهم [sahm] ² *literary* fear, fright, terror

سهمدار [sahmdaar] shareholder, stockholder; partner ♦ شرکت - stockholder in a company

سهمگیری [sahmgiri] participation (in something); contribution (to something) ♦ جوانان در دفاع کشور - participation of young people in the defense of the fatherland

سهو [sahw (and) sáhwa] 1 unpremeditated error; blunder, slip 2 slip of the tongue, slip of the pen
♦ - کردن to err, to make mistake, to commit a blunder, to slip

سهواً [sahwan] mistakenly, by mistake; unintentionally

سهولت [sahulat] 1 easiness, simplicity, lack of difficulty 2 easing (of conditions); providing with something

سهیل [sohail] 1 *astronomy* Canopus (star) 2 *masculine proper name* Sokhail

سهیم [sahim] 1 participant; participating, involved (in something) 2 ☞ سهم دار

سی [si] thirty

سیاح [sayaah] (*plural* سیاحین [sayaahin]) traveler; tourist

سیاحت [sayaahat] 1 journey; traveling; wandering 2 trip, excursion
♦ - کردن to travel

سیادت [siyaadat] leadership; supremacy; domination; management; control ♦ او – قوم را دارد He is head of the tribe.

سیار [sayaar] 1 moving; wandering; traveling 2 mobile; field, march *adjective* ♦ شفاخانه - field hospital

سیارات [sayaaraat] *plural of* سیاره 1

سیاره [sayaara] (*plural* سیارات [sayaaraat]) 1 planet 2 ☞ سیار

سیاست [siyaasat] 1 policy; political line 2 governing (of a state); government (of a state) 3 diplomacy 4 *obscure* execution, punishment

سیاست مدار [siyaasatmadaar] political figure

سیاسی [siyaasi] 1.1 political ♦ اقتصاد - political economy 1.2 diplomatic 2 (*plural* سیاسیون) diplomat

سیاسیون [siyaasiyun] *plural of* سیاسی

سیاق [siyaq] 1 way, mode, manner, method, style ♦ عبارت – phrase, turn of speech; manner of expression 2 *obscure* siyaq (special method of accounting by means of conventional symbols)

سیال [siyaal] 1 equal, pair 2 rival, competitor

سیالداری [siyaaldaari] (and) سیالی [siyaali] 1 unwillingness to lag behind others, sense of competition 2 exchange of gifts (between the relatives of the bride and groom on the occasion of the wedding)

سیانتست [siaantest] 1 scientist 2 naturalist

سیانس [siyaans] 1 science 2 natural sciences

سیانه [siaana] *colloquial* 1 shy, cunning 2 pushy person; a cheat, swindler

سیاه [siyaah] 1 black, dark, somber, gloomy 2 dark-complexioned, tanned
♦ ساختن - to blacken, to slander, to defame, to discredit (somebody) (نزد)
♦ - کردن *colloquial* 1 to paint black, to dye black 2 to darken 3 to jot down in an offhand manner, to make rough notes
♦ - گرفتن to mark (attendance), to register *transitive*, to take stock

سیاه آیل [siyaahaayel] *technical* nigrol (lubricating oil)

سیاه بخت [siyaahbakht] 1 poor, unfortunate 2 person of ill-starred fate

سیاه بختی [siyaahbakhti] ill-starred fate, unhappy lot

سیاه پوست [siyaahpost] a black-skinned person

سیاه پوش [siyaahposh] 1 dressed in mourning; mourning (for somebody) 2 *historical* kafir-siyahposh (infidel, dressed in black)
♦ - بودن to wear mourning; to mourn somebody

سیاه جرده [siyaa (h) jarda] *colloquial* swarthy; black-haired ♦ - جوان کوتاه قد و short, black-haired lad

سیاه چاه [siyaahchaah] pit, hole; dungeon, jail

سیاه چوب [siyaahchob] *botany* cotoneaster

سیاه دانه [siyaahdaana] coriander seeds; fennel seeds (which are sprinkled on flat bread loaves)

سیاه دل [siyaahdel] evil, cruel, pitiless, merciless

سیاه روز [siyaahroz] 1 poor, needy, indigent 2 unfortunate creature, poor devil, poor person

سیاه روزی [siyaahrozi] adversity, trouble, misfortune
♦ - محک دوستان است Adversity is a touchstone for friends (a friend in need is a friend indeed).

سیاه روی [siyaahroy] disgraced, shamed; having a bad name or ill fame

سیاه زاغ [siyaahzaagh] 1 black raven 2 *colloquial* a person who does not turn gray with age

سیاه زبان [siyaahzobaan] *colloquial* a person whose curses or imprecations come true; evil-wisher

سیاه سر [siyaah (h) sar] *colloquial* woman, peasant woman, old woman

سیاه سرفه [siyaahsorfa] whooping cough

سیاه موی [siyaa (h) moy] 1 black-haired; dark-curled 2 siyamoy (name of Jalal's beloved, a popular personage in Afghan folklore)

سیاهه [siyaaha] list; inventory
- کردن - to make an inventory, to enter into an inventory, to inventory

سیاهی [siyaahi] 1 blackness; dark, darkness 2 ink, India ink 3 *colloquial* nightmarish sleep, nightmare ♦ پخې - مرا امشب Tonight I was tormented by nightmares. کرده بود

سیایل [siaayel] ☞ سیاه آیل

سیب [seeb] apple
- یک - ودو نیم like two halves of an apple (like two drops of water)

سیت [set] 1 set (of something); collection; suite [of furniture] ♦ چای خوری - tea service ◊ *technical* سامان فالتو set of spare parts ◊ نفشه کشی- set of drawing instruments 2 instrument, apparatus ♦ رادیو - radio set, radio receiver

سیت [sit] 1 place, seat, armchair; stall 2 (driver's) cab ♦ *technical* وال - valve seat

سیخ [sikh] 1.1 iron rod, spit (for roasting) ♦ *proverb* نه - سوزد و نه کباب In order to keep the spit from burning up, the meat wasn't burnt either. 1.2 (also بافت-) knitting needle 1.3 (also تفنگ-) ramrod, cleaning rod 1.4 (also تندور-) poker 1. 5 *technical* (also ولدنگ-) welding electrode 2.1 upright, standing, jutting, protruding 2.2 (زدن)کردن - to thrust, to stab, to stick 2.3 ☞ سیخک زدن in entry
- کردن - دم کسی را *colloquial* to drive out, to get rid [of], to send somebody on his way
- دمت – *colloquial* May you never set foot here! / Away with you! / Make yourself scarce!

سیخدم [sikhdom] pin-tailed duck

سیخ دوانی [sikhdawaani] *technical* laying a steel framework

سیخ سیخ [sikhsikh] standing erect, standing upright, standing on end; to bristle

سیخک [sikhak] 1 small spit, skewer 2 *technical* rod, spindle, pin 3 hairpin
- زدن - to thrust, to stab

سید [sayed] (*plural* سادات [saadaat]) 1 Sayyid (a descendant of the prophet Mohammed) 2 *masculine proper name* Sayyid

سیر [sayr] 1 pleasure trip; excursion, inspection (of something) ♦ علمی - trip for scientific purposes 2 an outdoor fete, recreation ♦ لاله - an outing into the fields in the spring (when the tulips are blooming) 3 run; process; movement, motion ♦ خط - route, course, orbit
- کردن- to take a pleasure trip, to make an excursion; to inspect (something)

سیر [seer]¹ 1.1 full, satisfied 1.2 satiated, saturated (with something) 2 in abundance, to one's heart's content ♦ *proverb* سیرت ندیدم سفرت پیش آمد I am not yet tired of looking at you and you are already leaving.
- شدن 1 to be satiated, to eat one's fill 2 (also -آمدن) to be saturated (از) - شدم من از این زندگی I have had enough of that / this life.

سیر [seer² (and) sir¹] ser (a measure of weight equal to four charaks, roughly 7.06 kg)

سیر [sir]² garlic

سیرآب [seeraab] 1 having quenched one's thirst, having had something to drink 2 watered, irrigated, rich with water ♦ - دریای دره deep river ◊ - well-irrigated, fertile valley
- کردن - to fill up, to saturate with moisture, to irrigate

سیرت [sirat] 1 character, nature, inner qualities (of a person) 2 way of life

سیر چشم [seerchashm] not greedy, not envious; kind, good

سیره [sayra] goldfinch
- کودی بیار - *colloquial* a person who strives to earn more for his family

سیزده [sizdah] thirteen

سیستم [sistam (and) sistem] system ♦ تعلیمی - educational system ◊ متریک - metric system
- به – درآوردن to systematize

سیستماتیک [sistemaatik] (and) سیستماتیکی [sistemaatiki] systematic, regular

سگرت [sigreet] ☞ سگرت

سیل [sayl] 1 *colloquial* sight, spectacle 2 inspection (of something) 3 ☞ سیر [sayr] 2
- کردن - to spy; to stare [at]; to be a spectator

سیل [seel] 1 sel, torrent, flow 2 flood; inundation, high water; avalanche
- پرندگان - *colloquial* flock of birds

سیل آب [seelaab] flood, inundation, high water

سیلاب [silaab] *grammar* syllable

سیلابه [seelaaba] wood chips, debris (brought by high water, by a sel)

سیلابی [seelaabi] 1 pertaining to sel, fed by mountain torrents or streams (about a river) 2 flooded, inundated (about land)

سیلان [saylaan] flow, outflow
- خون - hemmorhage (when blood does not coagulate)
- داشتن - to flow, to flow out (about a liquid); to run, to spill

سیلانی [saylaani] 1 traveling (for the purpose of inspecting something) 2 traveling on a pleasure trip or for recreation

سیل بین [saylbin] 1 spectator; visitor (of an exhibit, etc.) 2 idle loafer

سیلو [silo] 1 (grain) elevator 2 bread-baking plant, bakery (in Kabul)
- نان European-style bread

سیلی [sili] a slap in the face

سیلیسیم [silisyám] *chemistry* silicon

سیم [sin]¹ 1 wire ♦ اتصالی - fuse 2 conductor ♦ پوشدار - insulated conductor, insulated wire, cable 3 electrode ♦ ولدنگ - welding electrode

سیم [sim]² silver

سیم [seyom] ☞ سوم

سیم [siyom] thirtieth

سیما [simaa] 1 face; features (of the face; appearance) 2 *masculine proper name* Sima

سیماب [simaab] mercury

سیمبر [simbor] cutting pliers

سیم پیچان [simpeechaan]
- دستگاه *technical* winding machine, coiling machine

سیم تابی [simtaabi] manufacture of fittings or accessories

سیم دوزی [simdozi] embroidery with silver, embroidering with silver thread

سیمرغ [simorgh] *folklore* simorgh (a fantastic bird)

سیمسار [simsaar] dealer in small items; person who sells various petty goods

سیمگل [simgel] coating (for walls, a plaster made of clay with cattail fluff)
- کردن - to coat walls, to plaster, to cover with plaster

سیمنت [simant] cement

سیمی [simi] 1 wire *adjective* ♦ تار - metal string (for musical instrument) 2 ☞ سیمن

سیمیان [simiyaan] simiyan (dish of thin homemade noodles cooked with butter and sugar)

سیمین [simin] 1 silver *adjective*; silver-plated, silvered 2 bright, white, silvery

سین [sin] name of the letter س

سینتکس [seentaks] ☞ سنتکس

سیند [sind] 1 river 2 sea

سینما [sinemaa] movie, movie theater

سینماتوگرافی [sinemaatograafi] cinematography ♦ کمیته - committee on cinematography

سینه [sina] breast, chest, bosom
- پرده - *anatomy* diaphragm
- صندوق - (and) پنجره - thorax
- به - 1 face to face 2 hand to hand (to fight, etc.)

سینه بغل [sinabaghal] inflammation of the lungs, pneumonia

سینه بند [sinaband] 1 brassiere 2 breast collar (of horse's harness)

سینه چاک [sinachaak] *colloquial* crushed with grief, heartbroken

سینه دردی [sinadardi] a cold with a cough

سینه مال [sinamaal]
- پرواز - low-level flight, hedge-hopping

سینی [sini] 1 copper tray 2 large copper dish

سیه [siyah] 1 black; dark, gloomy; somber 2 dark-complexioned, dark from a tan

ش
16th letter of the Dari alphabet

ش *abbreviation of* 1 شجاعت مند 2 شجاعت همراه

شا [sha] ☞ شاه

شاباش [shaabaash] ! - Well done! / Bravo!

شابلون [shaablon] curve (instrument for drawing curves); officer's rule, officer's slide rule

شاپ [shaap] 1 shop; workshop 2 *colloquial* store, shop

شاخ [shaakh] 1 horn, horns ♦ حجامت - horn for drawing blood, blood-sucking tube 2 ☞ شاخه
- کشیدن - *colloquial* to be dumbfounded, to become rigid, to freeze (from fear, from surprise, from astonishment)
- جوانی ات بشکنه - *abusive* May you die young!

شاخشماری [shaakhshomaari] *historical* tax levied on trees and gardens

شاخص [shaakhes] 1.1 sign, criterion, indicator 1.2 *economics technical* index 1.3 landmark, stake 2 typical, characteristic, noticeable, visible, marked, distinguishing

شاخک [shaakhak] 1 ☞ شاخ حجامت in entry شاخ 2 antenna, feeler (of an insect)
- شاندن - to let blood, to suck out blood (by means of a blood-sucking tube made of a cow's horn)

شاخل [shaakhal] French lentil

شاخه [shaakha] 1 branch; bough 2 branching, offshoot, spur 3 branch (e.g., of industry) 4 *electrical* plug

شاخه بری [shaakhabori] trimming, pruning of trees
- کردن - to trim, to prune trees

شاخی [shaakhi] wooden pitchfork (to turn and winnow grain)

شاد [shaad] glad, joyous, joyful, merry, content

شاداب [shaadaab] 1 irrigated, drenched with water 2 green, blooming ♦ دره - blooming valley

شادابی [shaadaabi] planting of greenery, planting of trees and shrubs, organization of public services and amenities (of a city, etc.)

شادباش [shaadbaash] good wishes, congratulations
- گفتن - to congratulate; to greet, to welcome

شادی [shaadi]¹ 1 gladness, joy, merriment 2 feast, revelry, festival (on the occasion of a birth, circumcision) 3 wedding
- کردن - 1 to make merry, to have a good time, to enjoy oneself 2 to celebrate [one's] wedding

شادی [shaadi]² monkey, marmoset

شادی باز [shaadibaaz] 1 street juggler, gypsy with a monkey 2 cheat, swindler; rascal

شارت [shaart]
- کردن - *electrical* to have a short-circuit
- شدن - *electrical* to be short-circuited

شارتی [shaarti] *electrical* short circuit

شارژور [shaarzhor] *military* cartridge clip; magazine

شارلات [shaarlaat] gross fraud; charlatan, cheat, swindler

شارلاتی [shaarlaati] gross fraud; eyewash, puffery

شاروال [shaarwaal] city head, mayor ♦ کابل - mayor of Kabul

شاروالی [shaarwaali] city council, town council; municipal headquarters, mayor's office

شاریدگی [shaaridagi] 1 *past participle* شاریدن 2.1 shabbiness; worn spot 2 intertrigo (on a baby, a rash, diaper rash)

شاریدن [shaaridan] 1 to become quite thin, to become worn (from rubbing), to unravel (about threadbare cloth, etc.) 2 to peel *intransitive*, to peel off, to flake off, to chip (about skin, plaster, etc.) 3 to become limp (from moisture); to rot, to decay slightly 4 to tumble down, to crumble (with age)

شاریده [shaarida] 1 *past participle* شاریدن 2 rubbed sore
- پایم - بود I had a sore spot / blister on my foot.
- چشمان - eyes sore from trachoma (conjunctivitis)

شاعر [shaa'er] (*plural* شاعران [shaa'eraan] (and) شعراء [so'ara]) poet

شاعری [shaa'eri] 1 poetic creation; poetry 2 composing verses

شاغاسی [shaaghaasi] *historical* master of ceremonies

شافت [shaaft] *technical* shaft; axle ♦ کلی - universal shaft

شاق [shaaq (q)] *literary* serious, grave, painful, burdensome, onerous, agonizing

شاقول [shaaqul] *technical* plumb

شاقه [shaaq (q) a] ☞ شاق
- اعمال- penal servitude

شاگرد [shaagerd] 1 pupil, apprentice; assistant (in a shop or store) 2 student

شاگردانه [shaagerdana] a tip for a master's pupil or an apprentice

شاگردی [shaagerdi]
- کردن - to learn a trade; to work as an apprentice

193

شال [shaal] homespun woolen rug; shawl; kerchief ♦ کشمیری - cashmere shawl (knitted with designs or embroidered)

شال انگشتر [shaalangoshtar] presentation of a ring (to the fiancée from the fiancé during the first days of the betrothal)

شالباف [shaalbaaf] weaver who makes homespun blankets and rugs

شالگی [shaalaki] 1 homespun, made of coarse homespun wool 2 (also دستر خوان -) tablecloth of homespun wool

شاله [shaala] neglected, unhealed wound; ulcerated skin, sore, ulcer

شالی [shaali] unhusked rice, paddy

شام [shaam] evening ♦ گاو گم- twilight, dusk
• کردن - *colloquial* 1 to wait 2 to be late
• سر - ☞ سرشام

شامپین [shaampeen] champagne

شامپیون [shaampiyon] champion; victor, winner

شامت [shaamat] stroke of fate; grief, sorrow, trouble, misfortune

شام شام [shaamshaam] in the evenings

شامکی [shaamaki] *colloquial* in the evening, towards evening

شامل [shaamel] 1.1 containing within itself 1.2 entered, enrolled; being a member; participating 2 (*plural* شاملین [samelin]) participant
• شدن - 1 to be a member, to participate (در) 2 to be enrolled, to enter, to go [to] (work, school, etc.)
• کردن - 1 to make a participant, to enter (on a list) 2 (also ساختن-) to enroll [in], to appoint [to], to arrange (a job, etc.) ♦ این مسئله در بحث ما نیست This matter doesn't pertain to our argument.

شاملات [shaamelaat] communal land, communal property

شامه [shaamma] (also حس -) sense of smell; scent; flair

شامیانه [shaamiyana] large tent, awning of fine fabric (stretched over a courtyard for protection against the sun during festivals)

شأن [shan (and) shaan] (*plural* شئون [shoun]) 1 merit, virtue, honor, prestige 2 ☞ شأن وشوکت

شان [shaan] their, to them *enclitic pronoun, third person plural* ♦ کتاب شان their book ◊ گفتمشان I told them.

شان [shaan] honeycombs

شاندن [shaandan] 1 to plant, to make sit down 2 to seat, to set down ♦ درخت - to plant trees 3 to fit, to mount (e.g., a gem into the setting of a ring) 4 to put, to place, to install ♦ برای گرم کردن خانه ها بخاری می شانند They are installing stoves to heat the rooms. ◊ دکمه - to sew on a button

شانزده [shaanzda (h)] sixteen

شأن وشوکت [shaanoshawkat] magnificence, splendor

شانه [shaana] 1 shoulder ♦ -به- shoulder to shoulder 2 *anatomy* shoulder blade 3 comb 4 *textiles* reed (in a loom)
• دادن - to support, to help
• زدن - 1 to shoulder, to push with the shoulder, to push one's way through (when making a path for oneself) 2 - کردن ☞
• کردن - to comb (somebody's) hair, to comb
• بالا انداختن - to shrug one's shoulders (as a sign of indifference)
• خالی کردن - to get off, to get away (with something), to evade

شانه سرک [shaanasarak] hoopoe

شانه گک [shaanagak]
• زدن - *colloquial* to neglect, not to pay attention [to]

شاور [shaawar] shower, showers, shower room ♦ گرفتن - to take a shower

شاول [shaawol] *technical* plumb ♦ کردن - to check the straightness with a plumb (of walls, etc.)

شاه [shaah] 1.1 shah, sovereign, monarch 1.2 fiance, betrothed, bridegroom 1.3 *cards* king 1.4 *chess* ! - Check! 2 (first component of compound words with meanings "main" / "superior") ♦ شاه راه main road, highway ◊ شاه زور most powerful

شاه انداز [shaahandaaz] 1 loving to show off 2 a fop, a boaster, a braggart

شاه اندازی [shaahandaazi] foppery; showing off

شاهانه [shaahaana] shah's, king's ♦ ذات - his majesty the king ◊ دربار - royal court, king's court

شاهباز [shaahbaaz] 1 large hawk with white coloring 2 *music* pick

شاه بالا [shaahbaalaa] *colloquial* member of a wedding (boy who attends the groom during a wedding)

شاه بز [shaahboz] lead goat (that leads a herd or flock)

شاهتیر [shaahtir] *technical* supporting beam; truss, rafter

شاه خیل [shaahkheel] (and) شاه خیلی [shaahkheeli] relatives and friends of the bridegroom (who deliver the bride to the groom's home)

شاهد [shaahed]¹ 1 (*plural* شهود [shohud]) witness; eyewitness 2 *poetry* sweetheart, beloved (male or female)
• بودن - to witness; to be a witness (to something)

شاهد [shahed]² (*plural* شواهد [shawaahed]) evidence, proof ♦ قول - confirmation of (somebody's) words

شاهدانه [shahdaana] hemp

شاهدی [shaahedi] testifying, testimony ♦ دادن - to testify, to give testimony

شاه راه [shahraah] main road, highway ♦ موتررو- superhighway

شاهرگ [shaahrag] *anatomy* jugular vein

شاهزاده [shaahzaada] shah's son, prince; czar's son

شاه زور [shaahzur] person who has remarkable strength; strongman, athlete

شاه کار [shaahkaar] work; composition of great skill, masterpiece

شاه کاری [shaahkaari] 1 manifestation of great skill (in something) 2 demonstration of valor or prowess; great deeds, heroic deeds

شاه کاسه [shaahkaasa] large basin, tureen (for food)

شاهگری [shaahgari] (and) شاهگکانی [shaahgakaani] *colloquial* honoring of the bridegroom on the first day after the wedding (they name the bridegroom "shah" and select a vizier for him, and the two of them judge those present, giving one an award and another a punishment)

شاه مقصود [shaahmaqsud] jasper; carnelian, sard

شاهی [shaahi]¹ 1 shah's, royal ♦ دولت - kingdom, monarchy 2 *historical* king's bodyguard, household guard; troops

شاهی [shaahi]² 1 shai (small Afghan coin worth 1/6 of a kran or puls) 2 taffeta (variety of silk fabric)

شاهین [shaahin] red-headed peregrine falcon (hunting bird)

شایان [shaayaan] 1 deserving, worthy (of something) 2 remarkable, splendid, brilliant ♦ فتح - remarkable victory

شاید [shaayad] possibly, perhaps ♦ آمده باشد - Perhaps he has already arrived. ◊ طوریکه - و باید as [one] should, in the proper manner

شایسته [shaayesta] 1.1 ☞ شایان 1.2 praiseworthy, laudable, commendable

شایع [shaaye] promulgated; widespread
• کردن - 1 to promulgate, to spread (news, rumors) 2 to write (e.g., in a newspaper); to communicate, to inform
• طوریکه - شده است as we have learned, as they report

شایق [shaayeq] 1 strongly desiring, craving, yearning, thirsting (for something) 2.1 (plural شایقین [sayeqin]) lover (of something), amateur 2.2 adherent, follower, admirer, worshipper
• (چیزی)کسی-بودن 1 to desire strongly, to yearn (for somebody or something) 2 to desire to take part in something

شایقین [shaayeqin] plural of شایق 2
• تیاتر - theater-goers

شایی [shaayi] ☞ شاهی 2

شب [shab] 1 night; evening ♦ شب مهتاب moonlit night ◊ بخیر Good night! 2 at night, during the night; in the evening, during the evening
• شب گذراندن to spend the night, to stay overnight
• شب برات the night of the 14th of the month of Shaban (when a funeral repast is usually held)
• شب قدر ☞ قدر

شباشب [shabaashab] late at night, in the middle of the night ♦ نزد ما آمد - He came to our place in the middle of the night.

شبان وروزان [shabaanorozaan] day and night; around the clock ♦ ناراحت بود - He knew no peace neither day nor night.

شبانه روز [shabaanaron] day, 24 hours ♦ دریک - during a day, in the course of a day

شباهت [shabaahat] likeness, resemblance, similarity
• داشتن - (با،به) to resemble, to have similarity

شب باش [shabbaash] stopping for the night; overnight guest, one who stays overnight

شب بو(ی) [shabbo (y)] botany 1 cheiranthus 2 tuberose 3 stock [matthiola]

شب بینک [shabbinak] goatsucker (bird)

شب پرک [shabparak] (and) شب پره [shabpara] 1 bat (flying mammal) 2 moth

شب پوش [shabposh] 1 blanket, kerchief (thrown over the head during sleep) 2 nightcap

شبت [shebet] fennel; dill

شبح [shabah] (plural اشباح [ashbaah]) 1 outline, contour, silhouette 2 apparition, specter, ghost, phantom

شبخون [shabkhun] night sortie; night attack

شبدر [shabdar] (☞ شب زنده داری [shabzendadaari]) night watch, keeping a vigil at night

شبش [shebesh] louse (insect)

شب قدر [shab (e) qaadar] 21st night of the month of Ramadan (when, according to tradition, the last suras of the Koran were sent down)

شبکه [shabaka] 1 net; netting, gauze; veil 2 grating, lattice, grill (e.g., on a window) ♦ آهنی - iron grill 3 system of ways, system of lines, network ♦ شبکه آب رسانی water-supply system

شبکه دار [shabakadaar] retiform, reticulated, latticed; openworked

شبکه کاری [shabakakaari] carvings, fretwork, carving ♦ چوب - carving in wood

شب گرد [shabgard] (and) شب گشت [shabgasht] night patrol; night watch

شب گل [shabgol] party, evening party (in an intimate circle, in the lap of nature)

شب گیر [shabgir]
• (and) آه - ناله poetry predawn moan, sigh (of parting lovers)

شب نامه [shabnaama] 1 proclamation, leaflet 2 historical evening newspaper

شب نشینی [shabneshini] party, evening party

شبنم [shabnam] dew

شب وروز [shaboroz]
• گذشتاندن - to spend one's days, to live, to exist

شبه [shoba] doubt; suspicion ♦ شبه یی نیست که ۰۰۰ there is no doubt that…
• داشتن - (به) 1 to doubt, to be in doubt, to vacillate 2 to suspect, not to trust

شبه [shabh (and) shába] 1 literary similar subject, analog 2 (first component of compound words with meaning 'semi-')

شبه جزیره [shabhejazira] peninsula

شبه ناک [shobanaak] dubious, shady, suspicious

شبه واول [shabhewaawal] grammar semi-vowel

شبهه [shobha] ☞ شبه

شبینه [shabina] 1 night adjective; nighttime, evening adjective 2 yesterday's (about food), left over from yesterday's meal

شبیه [shabih] 1 resembling (somebody) 2 similar [to], like, analogous

شپ [shop]
• کردن - colloquial 1 to gulp, to drink noisily 2 to smack one's lips (while eating)

شت [shat]
• شت زدن colloquial to struggle; to flutter, to quiver ♦ مانند ماهی - زدن to struggle desperately to make both ends meet

شت [shot] with a paralyzed or crippled hand or arm

شتاب [shetaab] 1 present tense stem شتافتن 2 haste, hurry
• با - 1 hastily, hurriedly 2 liveliness, vivacity; quickness, rapidity
• کردن - to hurry, to be in a hurry

شتابی [shetaabi] ☞ شتاب 2

شتافتن [shetaaftan] (present tense stem شتاب [setab]) to hurry, to be in a hurry

شتر [shotor] camel ♦ آنوقت که - دم خود را می بیند proverb when a camel sees its tail; when a lobster whistles

شتربان [shotorbaan] camel driver

شترخار [shotorkhaar] camel's thorn

شترک [shotorak]¹ wave(s), ripple(s), whitecap(s) (on water)
• زدن - to splash, to lap; to move (about a wave)

شترک [shotorak]² bittern (bird)

شترکینه [shotorkina] wicked, malicious; vindictive, vengeful, rancorous

شترگاو [shotorgaaw] giraffe

شترگردن [shotorgardan] technical brace
• برمه - drill with oblique handle

شترمار [shotormaar] coluber (type of nonpoisonous snake)

شترمرغ [shotormorgh] 1 ostrich 2 vulture

شجاع [shoja'] 1 brave, bold, courageous 2 *masculine proper name* Shoja

شجاعت [shojaaat] 1 bravery, courage 2 act of heroism; feat, exploit

شجاعت مند [shojaaatmand] 1 ☞ شجاع 2 *obscure military* title of major

شجاعت همراه [shojaaathamraah] *obscure military* title of general

شجر [shajar] (*plural* اشجار [ashjaar]) *literary* tree

شجره [shajara] 1 genealogical tree, geneology 2 list of saints

شحم [shahm] fat, suet

شحمی [shahmi] fatty ♦ مواد - fatty matter

شحنه [shahna] chief of police

شخ [shakh] 1.1 hard, hardened 1.2 tight, tense 1.3 stiffened, having become stiffened; numbed, having become numb 4 sheer, steep 2 firmly, tightly; strongly
• شخ بسته کردن to tie tightly, to bind tightly; to tighten firmly, to fasten tightly
• شخ شدن 1 to become hard, to harden 2 to stretch *intransitive*, to strain oneself, to exert oneself 3 to become stiff, to become numb ♦ پایم شخ شده است My leg became stiff. 4 to get severely tired

شخ جلو [shakhjelaw] 1 requiring firm pressure on the bit, obstinate (about a horse) 2 stubborn, self-willed (about a person)

شخص [shakhs] (*plural* اشخاص [ashkhaas]) 1 person, individual ♦ مسؤول - responsible person 2 *grammar* person

شخصاً [shákhsan] personally ♦ او - مسؤول است He bears personal responsibility.

شخصی [shakhsi] 1 personal, own, self-; private 2 *grammar* personal ♦ ضمایر - personal pronouns

شخصیت [shakhsiyat] 1 personality, individuality 2 person, personage, character ♦ حقوقی - juridical person

شخی [shakhi] 1 hardness 2 stiffness, numbness (of the extremities) 3 steepness, steep rise ♦ به یک - بالا شدیم We climbed a steep slope. 4 *colloquial* tiredness, weariness, fatigue
• راست - کردن to take a breath, to take a short rest

شد [shod] *colloquial* possibility, feasibility, practicability
• شد نداره That is impossible! / That can't happen! / That doesn't happen!

شدت [sheddat] 1 strength, force, scope, great degree of something ♦ با - زیاد with great strength, force, or effort; strongly; intensively 2 acuity, keenness, aggravation ♦ مبارزه - the sharpness of the struggle, the intensity of the struggle 3 severity, sterness
• بشدت ☞ به-
• - یافتن 1 to become stronger, to intensify 2 to become aggravated, to become strained

شدگار [shodgaar] ☞ شدیار

شدن [shodan] (*present tense stem* شو [shaw]) 1 to become ♦ برادرم داکتر شد My brother became a doctor. 2 to come / to set in, to begin ♦ بهار شد Spring came. 3 to come, to make, to be, to turn out ♦ این کار میشود This matter is feasible. / This is possible. شد شد،نشد نشد *colloquial* If it works out-fine, but if it doesn't work out, we'll manage! 4 to occur, to take place, to happen ♦ چه شد؟ What happened? 5 *colloquial* to go; to elapse; to pass 6 (in the third person singular acts as a modal word) ♦ میشود It is possible. / One may. ◊ نمیشود It is impossible. / One may not. 7 (serves to form the passive voice) ♦ مکتوب شما فرستاده شد Your letter has been sent. 8 (forms an impersonal clause or sentence in combination with the past participle of a verb) ♦ هر قدر جلو رفته شود همانقدر هوا تبدیل به سردی میگردد The farther one goes, the colder it gets. 9 (acts as the forming component of verbal combinations) ♦ دق شدن to miss, to long for ◊ چه میشود که ۰۰۰ But can't one …? / But what if …? ◊ ۰۰۰شدکه دو سال It's already two years since … / It's already two years that …

شدنی [shodani] 1 possible, feasible, practicable; real; realistic 2 future; predestined, preordained by fate

شدیار [shodyaar] tilled field, arable land; fallow
• جنگ - سر - proverb An argument over a tilled field should be resolved right there in the field.
• - کردن to plow the land, to till a field

شدید [shadid] 1.1 powerful, strong, intensive ♦ باد - a strong wind 2 acute, sharp ♦ درد - acute pain 2 furious; violent; fierce; cruel; savage ♦ جنگ - fierce battle 3 ☞ شدیداً

شدیداً [shadidan] 1 strongly, powerfully, intensively 2 acutely, sharply 3 severely, sternly; furiously; violently; fiercely; cruelly; savagely

شر [shar] 1.1 evil; harm 1.2 evil machinations; villainy, villainous act 2 *colloquial* wild, untamed
• شر انداختن to sow evil, to cause discord, to cause dissension
• شر کسی را از سر خودم کردن 1 to luckily escape somebody's intrigues or machinations 2 to shake off somebody, to get rid of somebody
• من با او شر ماندم I have known much sorrow with him.

شراب [sharaab] (*plural* اشربه [ashreba]) wine; alcoholic beverage ♦ ارغوانی - red wine ◊ خوردن - to drink wine

شراب خوری [sharaabkhori] use of alcoholic beverages; drunkenness

شرابی [sharaabi] 1 drunk, drunken 2 a drunk, drunkard; an alcoholic

شرارت [sharaarat] 1 villainy, villainous act, evil deed 2 meanness, baseness; infamy, infamous act; lewdness, depravity, debauchery

شراره [sharaara] gleam (of a flame); flash, spark
• - کردن to blaze up, to break out, to flash

شرافت [sharaafat] 1 honor, self-respect 2 nobility

شرافت ماب [sharaafatmaab] reverend (form of address for a spiritual or ecclesiastical personage or a respected person)

شراکت [sheraakat] 1 membership, participation; complicity 2 association, amalgamation, company
• - کردن to amalgamate, to join a company

شرانداز [sharandaaz] 1 sowing discord, sowing dissension; instigator 2 pernicious person, troublemaker

شرایط [sharaayet] 1 *plural of* شرط 2 conditions; situation ♦ داخلی مملکت - the situation within the country

شراین [sheraayin] *plural of* شریان

شربت [sharbat] 1 sherbet (a cooling drink made with fruit syrup) 2 syrup ♦ انار - pomegranate syrup

شرح [sharh] description, explanation; interpretation; commentary
• شرح حال ☞ حال -

● کردن (دادن) - to explain, to elucidate; to interpret, to comment [on]

سرش [sheresh] ☞ شرش

شرشر [sharshar] 1 noise of falling water; babble, murmuring (of brook or stream) 2 rustle, rustling

شرشره [sharshara] small waterfall; overfall of water; river shoal

شرشف [sharshaf] *botany* rape, winter cress ♦ تیل - rapeseed oil

شرشم [sharsham] 1 ☞ شرشف 2 mustard

شرط [shart] (*plural* شرایط [sharaayet]) 1 condition, stipulation 2 bet, stake, wager

● به شرطی که ... / به‌آن (این) شرط که ... on condition that ..., with the condition that ... *compound conjunction*

● بستن - to bet, to make a wager

● کردن - 1 to set as a condition; to stipulate 2 to come to an agreement

● پوره کردن - to carry out the conditions of a bet

● به - کارد with the right to cut open or to cut a piece (about the sale of watermelons, melons, etc.)

شرط بندی [shartbandi] making a bet; stake, wager

شرطی [sharti] conditional; stipulated, agreed

شرطیه [shartiya] ☞ شرطی

● جمله شرطیه *grammar* conditional clause or sentence

شرع [shar'] (and) shára] (*also* انور (and) شریف (-) sharif, Moslem law

شرعآ [sharaan] as prescribed by the sharia, according to the sharia

شرعی [shara'i] 1 permitted by the sharia, legal, lawful ♦ دعوی - suit according to the sharia ◊ عذر - زن legal wife ◊ valid or good reason 2 ☞ شرعآ

شرف [sharaf] 1 honor; glory; respect, esteem ♦ قول - word of honor 2 *masculine proper name* Sharaf

شرفه [sharfa] *colloquial* 1 rustle 2 sound of footsteps

شرفیاب [sharafyaab]

● شدن - to be awarded honor (to be accepted by somebody)

شرفیابی [sharafyaabi] reception (by a highly-placed person), audience

شرق [sharq] 1 east ♦ از طرف - from the east, from the eastern side or direction 2 the East ♦ دور - اقصی the Far East

شرق شناس [sharqshenaas] orientalist

شرق شناسی [sharqshenaasi] oriental studies

شرقی [sharqi] 1 eastern, east ♦ سرحد - the eastern border 2 inhabitant of the East

شرکا [sorakaa] *plural of* شریک

شرکت [sherkat] 1 sherkat, company; firm ♦ تجارتی - commercial firm, trading firm ◊ سهامی - joint-stock company 2 participation

● داشتن - to be a member, to be a shareholder (of a company, etc.)

● کردن - to participate, to take part (در)

شرم [sharm] 1 shame, feeling of shame 2 modesty; bashfulness, timidity, shyness 3 (term of the adat) fine besides a ransom (paid for committing shameful actions in relation to a deceased person)

● کردن (داشتن) - 1 to be ashamed (از) 2 to be embarrassed

شرمسار [sharmsaar] ashamed; confounded, desconcerted; having gotten into an awkward situation

شرمساری [sharmsaari] shame; discomfiture, awkward situation

شرمگین [sharmgin] shy, timid, bashful

شرمندگی [sharmendagi] 1 ☞ شرمساری 2 bashfulness; shyness; modesty

شرموک [sharmok] (and) شرمندوک [sharmendok] *colloquial* shy; bashful, timid (about a child)

شرمیدن [sharmidan] to be ashamed; to feel shy ♦ من میشرمم I am ashamed.

شرنگ شرنگ [sharangsharang] clanging (of metal, of chains); tinkling, clanking

شروع [shoru'] beginning, commencement ♦ در - کار at the start of work, at the beginning of work ◊ کردن - to begin, to set about, to start (به)

شریان [sheryaan] (*plural* شراین [sherayin]) *anatomy* artery ♦ شش - pulmonary artery

شریر [sharir] 1.1 evil *adjective*, bad 2 vicious; depraved; nasty, naughty; vile, wicked ♦ مرد - villian; scoundrel 2 (*plural* اشرار [ashraar]) thug, bandit; criminal element

شریعت [shari'at] sharia (code of Moslem laws) ♦ ازهر - the sacred law of the sharia ◊ کردن - to decide in accordance with the sharia; to judge by the sharia

شریف [sharif] 1.1 honest; glorious; famous, renowned 2 holy, sacred; esteemed, revered ♦ بخارای - *historical* Holy Bukhara ◊ قرآن the sacred Koran 3 noble, distinguished 2 (*plural* اشراف [ashraaf]) representative of the aristocracy or nobility, aristocrat 3 *historical* sharif (title of the rulers of Mecca and descendants of Mohammed) 4 *masculine proper name* Sharif

شریک [sharik] (*plural* شرکاء [shoraka]) 1 partner; shareholder 2 participant, accomplice ♦ جرم - accomplice in a crime

● بودن (شدن) - 1 to be a member, to join, to join in 4 *technical* to be connected up (to an electrical circuit)

شریکی [shariki] 1 common, joint 2 together, jointly ♦ این مقاله را ما نوشتیم We wrote this article together. 3 membership, participation; complicity

شست [shast] 1 thumb, big toe 2 ☞ شستی

● سر دو - پای بودن *colloquial* 1 to be ready to rush into a fight; to run 2 to be in readiness

شستشو(ی) [shostosho(y)] 1 wash; laundering 2 washing

شستن [shostan] (*present tense stem* شوی [soy]) 1 to launder 2 to wash ♦ دست وروی - to wash oneself

◊ به - دادن to give (something) to be laundered

شستشو(ی) [shostoshoy] ☞ شستشو(ی)

شسته [shosta] 1 *past participle* شستن 2.1 clean; neat, tidy 2.2 clear; accurate; legible

شستی [shasti] a ring with a small mirror (that women wear on the thumb)

شش [shosh] *anatomy* lung; lungs

شش [shash] six

ششت وخیر [sheshtokheez] *colloquial* contact, mutual visiting

● داشتن - to maintain an acquaintanceship, to associate [with]

ششتن [sheshtan] (*present tense stem* شین [sin]) 1 to sit, to sit down, to take a seat ♦ جای - کسی رانیافتن بشینید Sit down! not to know where to seat (somebody, as a sign of respect) 2 to reside; to be found, to be located ♦ جانه - dwelling or living quarters 3 to have a beneficial effect, to help ♦ این دوا به جانش

197

شینه می *colloquial* This medicine will help him. 4 to suit someone, to become someone (about clothing)

ششتن [shoshtan] *colloquial* ☞ شستن

ششدر [shashdar] 1.1 position in the game of backgammon in which a six is rolled but there is no place to move because all six of the opponent's spaces are blocked 1.2 hopeless situation, position with no way out 2 astonished, surprised; not knowing what to do
- ماندن - 1 to be confused; not to know what to do 2 to put one's foot in it

ششصد [shashsad] six hundred

شصت [shast]¹ sixty

شصت [shast]² ☞ شست

شصت و شکست [shastoshekast] *colloquial* the last 10-day period of the month of Hut (☞ حوت), the change from winter to spring (before New Year's Day)

شطرنج [shatranj] chess ♦ تخته - chess board

شعار [she'aar] 1 slogan, motto 2 *literary* rule, custom; tradition

شعاع [sho'aa] (*plural* اشعه [ashe'a]) 1 ray, beam; light; reflected light (of the moon, of the sun) 2 radiance, luster, brilliance 3 *mathematical* radius
- افکندن - to emit light, to shine, to beam

شعایر [shaaayer] 1 rites, ceremonies, customs 2 rituals (of Islam)

شعبات [sho'abaat (and) sho'baat] *plural of* شعبه

شعبان [sha'ban] Sha'ban (the eighth month of the Afghan lunar year)

شعبه [sho'ba] (*plural* شعبان [sho'abat]) 1 department, sector; branch ♦ زبان دری - Dari Language Department (in Kabul University) ◊ شرکت - branch office of firm 2 branch, field 3 section (of a book) ♦ شعبه های دستور زبان branches of grammar

شعر [she'r] (*plural* اشعار [ash'ar]) 1 poem, rhyme, verses, poetry ♦ آزاد - free verse 2 two-line poem (complete in thought)
- گفتن - to compose verse, to write poetry

شعرا [sho'araa] *plural of* شاعر

شعله [sho'la (and) shola] fire, flame; flash (of fire)
- زدن - to burn, to flame, to blaze

شعله ور [sho'lawar]
- شدن - to burn brightly, to flame, to blaze

شعور [sho'ur] 1 mind, intellect, intelligence; understanding, comprehension 2 *philosophical* consciousness ♦ نفسی - self-consciousness 3 conscientiousness; honesty

شعوری [sho'uri] reasonable; wise; conscientious; conscious
- غیر - unconscious (not deliberate); instinctive; subconscious
- بصورت غیر - unconsciously; instinctively

شغال [shaghaal] jackal

شغل [shoghol] matter, business, affair; occupation, employment, pursuit

شغنی [shoghni] 1 shoqni *adjective* (pertaining to a people or a mountain range in the Pamirs) 2 a shoqni (people who inhabit a region of the Pamirs)

شف [shaf] free end of a turban (which hangs down on the shoulder)

شفا [shefaa] curing; recovery
- یافتن - to be cured; to recover

شفابخش [shefaabakhsh] healing, curative

شفاخانه [shefaakhaana] hospital; dispensary; outpatient clinic
- حیوانی - veterinary hospital
- عسکری - military hospital

شفاعت [shafaa'at] intercession
- کردن - to intercede [for] (از)

شفاف [shaffaaf] 1 transparent, clear ♦ آب - limpid water, pure water 2 very fine; thinnest; translucent

شفتالو [shaftaalu] peach ♦ درخت - peach tree

شفتل [shaftal] Persian clover, trifolium (variety of annual forage grass also used as fertilizer)

شفر [shéfer] cipher

شفری [shefri] enciphered ♦ تلگرام - enciphered telegram

شفشاهنگ [shafshaahang] *geology* stalagmite

شفق [shafaq] 1 sunset 2 twilight, dusk

شفقت [shafaqat] compassion, mercy; charity; kindness, goodness

شق [shaq (q)]¹ 1 hole, crack, split, fissure, breach, gap 2 cleaving, splitting; dividing

شق [shaq (q)]² (*plural* شقوق [shoquq]) branch; section

شق القمر [shaq(q)olqamar] a miracle (performed by a prophet)

شقایق [shaqaayeq] *botany* 1 wild poppy 2 variety of tulip

شقه [shaq (q) a] 1 half of the carcass of a sheep (cut lenthwise) 2 piece, part, half (of something)
- کردن - to cut into two parts

شقیقه [shaqiqa] temple (part of the head)

شک [shak] 1 doubt, uncertainty ♦ جای شک نیست که... there is no doubt that... 2 suspicion, apprehension, misgiving

شکار [shekar] 1 hunt; hunting; catching; snaring 2 game, the object of a hunt 3 catch, prey
- دیروز به - کردن - to hunt, to catch; to kill, to shoot (game) ♦ شکار رفته دو خرگوش را - کردم Yesterday, while hunting, I shot two hares.

شکار خلطه [shekaarkhalta] *colloquial* game bag

شکاری [shekaari] 1 hunter 2 hunting; fowling
- طیاره - fighter aircraft

شکاف [shekaaf] chink, crack, slit, fissure, breach; hole, opening, aperture; orifice

شکافتن [shekaaftan] 1 to cleave, to split, to chop, to break, to cut *transitive* 2 to split, to be split, to be cut; to crack, to break, to burst *intransitive*

شکافتگی [shekaaftagi] 1 ripped place, rent, tear, slit 2 break, chink; slit, crack

شکایت [shekaayat] 1 complaint, lamentation 2 making a complaint ♦ از تو - شده است A complaint was made about you. / They are complaining about you.
- کردن - 1 to complain, to lament (از) 2 to make a complaint, to lodge a complaint

شکر [shókor] 1 gratitude, thanks 2 !- Thanks! / I thank [you]!
- خدا را - Thank God!

شکر [shakar] granulated sugar

شکرانه [shokraana] gift to a wise man or mullah (for a prayer, amulet, etc.)

شکرپاره [shakarpaara] variety of sweet dried apricot

شکررنج [shakarranj] *colloquial* a minor quarrel, tiff (between lovers, comrades, or friends)

شکرگذار [shokrgozaar] thankful, grateful

شکر گذاری [shokrgozaari] expression of thanks, expression of gratitude

شکری [shakari] 1 sugar *adjective*, sugary, saccharine 2 cream-colored

شکست [shekast] 1 defeat, rout, downfall 2 brokenness (of spirit); despair; contrition; grief
• خوردن - to suffer defeat

شکستاندن [shekastaandan] 1 to break; to smash; to split ♦ اتم - to split the atom ◊ مقاومت دشمن را شکستاندند They broke the enemy's resistance. 2 to violate, to break (a treaty, the silence)

شکستگی [shekastagi] 1 break; breakage; fracture 2 *technical* disruption 3 debility; tiredness, weariness, fatigue; collapse, breakdown, loss of strength 4 *colloquial* timidity, state of being downtrodden
• شکستگی ها *geology* break, fault, displacement (of rock)

شکستن [shekastan] (*present tense stem* شکن [sekan]) 1 to break, to be smashed; to split, to be split *intransitive* 2 *colloquial* ☞ شکستاندن

شکسته [shekasta] 1 *past participle of* شکستن 2 broken (about a line) ♦ ساحل - meandering coastline 3 skekasta (a type of cursive writing)

شکسته نفس [shekastanafs] modest, unassuming

شکسته نفسی [shekastanafsi] modesty, lack of pretense, simplicity (of a person)

شکفتاندن [shokoftaandan]
• گل - *colloquial* to make a big deal (over a trifle); to raise a clamor (over something)

شکفتن [shokoftan] to bloom, to blossom, to blossom out (about fruit trees)

شکل [shákel] (*plural* اشکال [ashkaal]) 1 shape, form ♦ به - in the shape of, in the form of 2 manner, means 3 *mathematical* figure 4 illustration, figure, picture (in a book) 5 *literary* (one of the permissible means of changing the foot of a poetic meter: replacing two long syllables with two short ones)

شکم [shekam] stomach, belly, abdomen; womb
• انداختن - *colloquial* to grow stout, to put on weight, to develop a large belly
• کردن - *colloquial* to be pregnant, to become pregnant

شکم بند [shekamband] corset, girdle

شکمبو [shekambu] *colloquial* glutton

شکمبه [shekamba] entrails (of an animal)

شکم پروری [shekamparwari] gluttony

شکمدار [shekamdaar] 1 *colloquial* pregnant 2 pot-bellied (*e.g.*, about a vessel)

شکن [shekan] 1 *present tense stem* شکستن 2.1 bend, pleat, crease, wrinkle 2.2 lock, curl (of hair) 3 (second component of compound words with meanings "breaking" / "wrecking" / "destroying") ♦ دندان شکن shattering; crushing ◊ عهد شکن perfidious; treacherous

شکناندن [shekanaandan] *colloquial* to break, to smash

شکنجه [shekanja] 1 binding press, bookbinding press 2 *technical* clamp; vise 3 *historical* stocks (for shackling somebody) 4 torture
• کردن - to torture, to subject to torture, to put on the rack

شکنند [shekanend] fragile, brittle ♦ چوب - tree with soft wood

شکوفانی [shokufani] blossoming, flourishing ♦ ادب وهنر - the flourishing of literature and art

شکوفه [shokufa] bud, blossom (of a fruit tree)
• کردن - to bloom, to blossom, to blossom out (about fruit trees)

شکوه [shokoh] splendor, magnificence

شکوه [shekwa] complaint, grumble, lamentation
• کردن - to complain, to grumble, to lament

شگافتن [shegaaftan] ☞ شکافتن

شگوم [shogum] *colloquial* ☞ شگون

شگون [shogun] sign, omen ♦ نیک - good sign, good omen

شل [shal] 1 crippled, paralyzed 2 with a paralyzed leg (or legs); shuffling or dragging a foot (or feet)

شل [shol] 1 weak; friable; crumbly; soft (e.g., about the ground) 2 pliable; pliant; complaisant 3 slack (e.g., about a rope)

شلاق [shallaaq] whip, lash, scourge
• زدن - to whip, to flog, to lash

شلغم [shalgham] turnip; rutabaga

شلغم بته [shalghambata] condiment of turnip and meat (served with boiled rice)

شلغمی [shalghami] having the shape of a turnip

شلشل [sholshol]
• کردن - *colloquial* to swarm, to crawl (about insects)

شلک [shelek] salute, volley, salvo
• کردن - to salute, to fire a volley or a salvo (in honor of somebody or something)

شلند [shelend] mountain lizard

شلنگ [sheleng] shilling

شلوار [shalwaar] wide trousers

شل وشت [shaloshot] *colloquial* 1 with paralyzed arms and legs 2 a paralytic; a cripple

شله [shalla] *colloquial* 1 stubborn, importunate, irksome 2 a faultfinder; an irksome person; a pest

شله [shola] ☞ شوله

شما [shomaa] 1 you (polite form of address) 2 (also شمایان) you 3 (also از) (in an ezafeh construction) your ♦ برادر از - your brother

شماته [shamaata] 1 peal, ringing, striking (of a clock) ♦ این ساعت دارد - This clock strikes the hours / the time. 2 noise, uproar; rowdy scene

شمار [shomaar] 1 *present tense stem* شمردن 2 counting, calculation, tallying
• قابل - 1 countable, calculable, yielding to calculation 2 piece (about goods)
• شدن - 1 to be calculated, to come [to] 2 to be considered, to be reputed
• کردن - to count, to calculate
• از - برآمدن *colloquial* not to yield to calculation, to be countless, to be innumerable

شماره [shomaara] 1 number, amount 2 issue ♦ جریده - issue of a newspaper

شمال [shamal] wind

شمال [shemaa (and) shomaal] north ♦ شرق - northeast ◊ غرب - northwest

شمالی [shemaali] northern, north *adjective*

شمسی [shamsi] pertaining to the sun; sunny; solar ♦ سنه - solar year
• حروف - *grammar* solar letters (of the Arabic alphabet)

شمردن [shomordan] (*present tense stem* شمار [somar]) 1 to count, to calculate 2 to consider

199

شمرده [shomorda] 1 *present tense stem* شمردن 2 measured, accurate; precise ♦ کلمات - clear; lucid; distinct; precise; distinct words

شمس [shams] 1 *literary* sun 2 *masculine proper name* Shams

شمشاد [shamshad] *botany* box (tree), boxwood

شمشیر [shamsheer] sword, blade, saber
- کشیدن - 1 to draw a sword, to draw a saber 2 to assault, to attack, to take up arms (بر،روی)

شمشیربازی [shamsheerbaazi] dance with a saber or blade

شمشیری [shamsheeri] *colloquial* 1 battle; fighting; combat; bellicose; daring; bold 2 a bully, a pugnacious fellow

شمع [sham' (and) sháma] 1 candle ♦ مومی - wax candle ◊ در بزم کوران سوزاندن *proverb* to light candles at a feast for the blind (to cast pearls before swine) 2 *technical* electrical candlepower 3 prop, support
- بستن - to thicken, to congeal, to become hard, to harden

شمله [shamla] protruding end of a turban

شمول [shomul] 1 inclusion (in a number) ♦ به ··· - including 2 enrollment, entrance, admittance (into an educational institution, etc.) ♦ شاگردان به پوهنون - admittance of students into the university 3 participation (in something)

شمه [shamma] *colloquial* a grain, a particle, a small share or portion (of something) ♦ شمه ای a little bit, a little

شنا [shenaa] swimming
- کردن - to swim

شناخت [shenaakht] 1 acquaintance 2 knowledge, ability 3 recognition, study ♦ ادبیات - study of literature
- از - برآمدن *colloquial* to become unrecognizable (e.g., after an illness)

شناختن [shenaakhtan] (*present tense stem* شناس [senes]) 1 to know, to be acquainted [with] ♦ او را میشناسید؟ Do you know him? 2 to understand, to get to know, to become acquainted with; to recognize, to distinguish ♦ شب را از روز نشناختن to work both night and day (literally, not to distinguish night from day)

شناس [shenaas] 1 *present tense stem* شناختن 2 (second component of compound words with meanings "knowing", "versed" in something) ♦ شرقشناس orientalist, specialist in oriental subjects

شناور [shenaawar] 1 swimming, floating ♦ موتر - amphibious vehicle 2.1 swimmer 2.2 *technical* float (of a carburetor)

شناوری [shenaawari] swimming ♦ حوض - swimming pool

شنبه [shambe] Saturday

شنگرف [shangarf] 1 cinnabar (paint) 2 red ink

شنگری [shengari] *colloquial* a woman who has married without rites or a ceremony

شنو [shonaw (and) shenaw] *present tense stem* شنودن،شنیدن and

شنوا [shanawaa] able to hear, hearing *adjective* ♦ گوش من - است My ears hear.

شنوایی [sho(a)waayi] 1 hearing, ability to hear 2 audition; hearing, auscultation

شنودن [shonudan] ☞ شندن

شنیده گی [shonidagi] heard ♦ دیده گی - heard and seen

شنیدن [shonidan] (*present tense stem* شنو [sonaw (and) senaw]) 1 to hear 2 to listen [to], to hear out 3 to obey

شنیده [shonida] *past participle* شنیدن
- شنیده کی بود مانند دیده *proverb* What is heard doesn't match what is seen.

شو [shaw] 1 *present tense stem* شدن

شو [shaw] 2 *colloquial* ☞ شب

شوال [shawwaal] Shawwal (tenth month of the Moslem lunar year)

شواهد [shawaahed] data (serving as proof); evidence

شوپرک [shawparak] *colloquial* ☞ شب پرک

شوخ [shokh] 1.1 playful, frolicsome; mischievous, naughty ♦ بچه - a naughty little boy 1.2 pert, forward, impudent, bold 2.1 joker, jester 2.2 mischievous child or person

شوخچشم [shokhchashm] 1 with a sly look 2 bold, impudent, impertinent, insolent

شوخی [shokhi] 1 joke 2 prank; fun 3 mischievousness, mischief

شور [shor] 1 1 salt *adjective*, salty, salted; oversalted ♦ آب - salt water 2 saline; barren; sterile (about soil)
- کردن - to salt; to put too much salt [on / into]
- چشم - the evil eye

شور [shor] 2 1 uproar, hubbub, row 2 disturbance, commotion 3 ardor, fervor
- انداختن - to cause an uproar, to cause a commotion, to create a furor

شور [shor] 3
- خوردن - to make a motion, to stir ♦ نخورید - Don't move!
- دادن - 1 to shake ♦ سر خود را - دادن to nod [one's] head (as a sign of consent or assent) ◊ تایید کنان سرش را - داد He nodded [his] head affirmatively. 2 to shake, to mix, to stir (a liquid in a container, etc.)

شورا [shoraa] 1 council (administrative organ) ♦ امنیت - security council 2 consultation

شور انداز [shorandaaz] 1 a rowdy, a ruffian, a troublemaker; an instigator 2 disturbing, perturbing; exciting, stirring

شوربا [shorbaa] shurba; soup; soup with meat ♦ اشکنبه - soup with pluck or giblets ◊ کدو - shurba made of pumpkin (with cinnamon)

شوربابرنج [shorbaberenj] broth with rice

شوربخت [shorbakht] unhappy; unfortunate, unlucky

شورچشم [shorchashm] possessing the evil eye

شورش [shoresh] revolt, insurrection; riot; mutiny
- کردن - to revolt, to riot; to mutiny

شوروا [shorwaa] ☞ شوربا

شوروشر [shoroshar] (r) *colloquial* 1 noise, uproar, cry, shout, ruckus, brawl, quarrel 2 disturbance, bustle, turmoil

شوروشوق [shoroshawq] enthusiasm, ardor, fervor; enthusiastically, fervently, with enthusiasm

شوروی [shorawi] 1 Soviet ♦ اتحاد - Soviet Union 2.1 *colloquial* soviet union 2 (*plural* شورویان [shorawiyaan]) Soviet citizen

شوره [shora] 1 saltpeter, nitrate 2 salt crust (that appears on soil, on walls) 3 scab, scale, crust 4 ☞ شوره زار
- خوردن (زدن) - 1 to be covered with a crust, with salt (about the soil etc.) 2 to be covered with scabs, with crusts (about sores)

شوره زار [shorazaar] saline soil, salt marsh

شوری [shoraa] ☞ شورا

شوق [shawq] 1 strong desire, attraction 2 inclination, interest 3 fervor, ardor, zeal
- شوق وذوق ☞ وذوق
- داشتن - to desire strongly; to have an inclination [for], an interest [in] (به)
- کردن - to show ardor, to show zeal

ش

شوقمند [shawqmand] 1 ardently interested (in something), ardently fascinated (by something) 2 a lover (of something), an amateur enthusiast

شوق وذوق [shawqozawq] 1 fascination, ardor, enthusiasm 2 rapture; ecstasy; admiration; delight

شوقی [shawqi] (opposite of مسلکی) amateur; dilettante

شوکار [shawkaar] man on duty during the night shift ♦ - سرویس night bus

شوکت [shawkat] 1 literary grandeur, might 2.1 splendor, magnificence 2.2 masculine proper name Shawkat

شوگشت [shawgasht] colloquial ☞ شب گشت 2

شوله [shola] shola (thin rice pudding or gruel with onion or carrot seasoning) ♦ گوشتی - shola with meat ◊ ماش - shola with lentils

• شولی ته بخو پردی ته بکو colloquial Eat your own porridge and don't meddle in our lives!

• شولی ته پف کده بخو colloquial Blow on your porridge before you eat it! (i.e., Be on one's guard! / Look sharp!)

• شومانده - colloquial lout; bumpkin; nincompoop; dawdler

شوم [shum] 1 ill-fated, ill-starred, luckless 2 ominous; sinister; fatal

شوم قدم [shumqadam] bringing misfortune or bad luck

شوهر [shawhar] husband

• - کردن to marry (i.e., to take a husband)

شوهردار [shawhardaar] married (pertaining to a woman) ♦ - زن married woman

شوی [shuy] ☞ شوهر

شه [shah] ☞ شاه

شهادت [shahaadat] 1 evidence, testimony; proof ♦ - تأییدی confirming testimony 2 religion death for [one's] faith 3 heroic death (for high ideals)

• - دادن to give testimony, to testify, to confirm

• به - رسیدن religion 1 to accept death for [one's] faith 2 to lose one's life heroically (for high ideals)

شهادت نامه [shahaadatnaama] certificate (about completion of an educational institution); recommendation; diploma

شهامت [shahaamat] valor; courage, bravery; heroism

شهباز [shahbaaz] pick (for a rabab, a stringed musical instrument)

شهد [shahd] honey

شهدا [shahadaa] plural of شهید

شهر [shahr] city

شهر پناه [shahrpanaah] city walls; city fortifications

شهرت [shohrat] 1 fame, popularity; state of being generally known 2 (also خواب-) good fame, good reputation

• - پیدا کردن 1 to acquire fame, to acquire popularity 2 to win good fame, to gain prestige

شهرت طلبی [shohrattalabi] ambition; vanity; vainglory

شهر سازی [shahrsaazi] town building ♦ وعمرانات - building and making public inprovements in a town

شهر گشت [shahrgaast] march of the bride's procession through the city, town, or village (on the way to the groom's home)

شهری [shahri] 1 city, town adjective 2 city-dweller, town-dweller ♦ شهریان کابل inhabitants of Kabul, Kabulites

شهریار [shahriyaar] literary sovereign, monarch

شهزاده [shahzaada] ☞ شاهزاده

شهلا [shahlaa] 1 (also چشم-) large, expressive eyes 2 a person with large expressive eyes 3 feminine proper name Shahla

• نرگس - narcissus or daffodil with a large corolla

شهوت [shahwat] passion, lust; longing; sexual desire

شهود [shohud]¹ plural of شاهد

شهود [shohud]² literary 1 evidence, proof 2 phenomenon 3 world of phenomena; this world

شهید [shahid] (plural شهدا [shohadaa] (and) شاهدان [shahedaan]) 1 religion having died for [one's] faith 2 having died a hero's death (for high ideals)

• - شدن 1 to accept a martyr's death for [one's] faith 2 to die a hero's death

شهیر [shahir] well-known, famous; celebrated ♦ هرات - the famous city of Herat

شهین [shahin] 1 beam (of a scale) 2 balance wheel 3 ☞ شاهین

شی [shay] (plural اشیاء [ashyaa]) 1 thing, object 2 matter, question 3 goods (usually in the plural)

• از - بر آمدن colloquial to become unfit or worthless; to wear out

شیاطین [shayaatin] plural of شیطان

شیب [sheeb] slope (of a mountain)

شیت [sheet] ☞ شید

شیخ [shayx (and) sheekh] (plural شیوخ [shoyukh]) 1 head of a tribe, an elder 2 sheikh; spiritual teacher; head of a spiritual order 3 sheikh (honorary title of eminent theologians, of spiritual persons, etc.)

شیخ الاسلام [shaykholeslaam] Sheikh ul Islam (head of a Moslem community or an expert and theorist of Islam)

شیخ السفرا [shaykhossofaraa] dean of the diplomatic corps, doyen

شید [sheed] 1 blanket cover; slipcover 2 decorated ceiling, ceiling (light) fixture ♦ شیدهای تباشیری decorated ceiling of chalk, ceiling (light) fixtures of chalk

شیدا [shayda] ardently loving, madly in love

• (چیزی) کسی - بودن to love somebody or something ardently or passionately ♦ وطن خود بود - He loved his homeland passionately.

شیر [sheer] 1.1 tiger, lion 1.2 metaphor a bold person, a brave person, a hero ♦ خدای - the Lion of Allah (epithet of Ali) ◊ خانه روباه بیرون proverb a lion or tiger at home, but a fox away from home (brave before a lamb, but a lamb before the brave) 1.3 astronomy the constellation Leo 1.4 reverse side of a coin, heads 2 (first component of proper names) ♦ شیر محمد Sher-Mohammed

• آمدن - colloquial to have success, to succeed, to be successful, to return in victory

• - آمدی یا روبا؟ Did [he / you] win or lose?

• بادم - بازی کردن to undertake a dangerous game, to risk, to take a risk

• (برفین) برفی - 1 a lion or tiger fashioned from snow (children's game) 2 a person who seems frightful (but is in fact a coward)

• شیر وخط ☞ وخط

شیر [shir] milk ♦ مادر - mother's milk

• - دادن 1 to nurse, to suckle 2 to rear on milk

شیرآبی [shir (e) aabi] pale blue, light blue (about color)

شیرآور [shiraawar] ☞ شیری [shiri] 2

شیرازه [sheraaza] 1 a braid or tape fastening the leaves of a book (in the binding) 2 the binding of a book 3 stone lining

(of an adobe wall) 4 order, system; strong ties
- زدن - 1 to stitch 2 to edge with braid or tape, to sew braid or tape along an edge

شیرازه بندی [sheraazabandi] 1 stitching, binding 2 putting in order, putting (something) in good order

شیرآغا [sheraghaa] sher-agha (polite form of address from a sister to a brother or from a wife to a husband)

شیرببر [sheerbábar] African lion

شیربرنج [shirberenj] rice pudding (made with milk and sugar)

شیربها [shirbahaa] payment for a bride, bride money

شیرپاک [shirpaak] honest, decent; from a good family

شیرچای [shirchaay] tea brewed in boiling milk (in which they put sugar or salt as well as butter, etc.)

شیرچوشک [shirchoshak] 1 nipple (for milk); drinking bottle (from which children suck milk) 2 child's drinking cup with partially covered top

شیرخشت [shirkhesht] congealed sap on the cotoneaster (used as medicine)

شیرخوار [shirkhaar] (and) شیرخور [shirkhor]
- طفل - baby

شیردار [shirdaar] 1 nursing (about a woman) 2 ☞ شیری [shiri] 2

شیردان [shirdaan] 1 abomasum 2 ☞ شیردانی

شیردان [sherdaan] ☞ شیردهن

شیردانی [shirdaani] vessel for milk, cream pitcher

شیر دروازه [sherdarwaaza] Sherdarwaza (one of two mountain spurs that meet at Kabul)

شیردهان [sherdahaan] ☞ شیردهن

شیردهن [sheerdahan] faucet; valve ♦ آبی - hydrant

شیرگرم [shirgarm] tepid, lukewarm, somewhat warm (as milk fresh from the cow)

شیرمال [shirmaal] rich flatcakes (mixed with milk)

شیرمست [shirmast] 1 milk adjective, milky; lactic; reared on milk, milk-fed (about a lamb) 2 well-fed, well-nourished, plump (about a baby)

شیروار [shirwaar] agriculture seasonal women's cooperative to process milk (to prepare butter and cheese for the winter)

شیروانی [shirwaani] pyramidal roof; hipped roof, roof with gable

شیروخط [sheerokhat] colloquial heads or tails (game)

شیروشکر [shiroshakar] 1 embroidered with gold and silver 2 cloth with yellow flowers on a white field

شیره [shira] thick sap (of plants, of trees)
- چهار تخم - invigorating medicinal beverage or tonic

شیری [shiri] 1 milk adjective ♦ دندان - milk-tooth, baby-tooth 2 milk adjective, dairy, giving milk ♦ گاوهای - milk cows, dairy cows 3 milky white, of the color of milk

شیریخ [shiryakh] ice cream

شیرین [shirin] 1.1 sweet, tasty 1.2 fresh (about water) 1.3 pleasant, nice ♦ خواب pleasant dream, pleasant sleep 1.4 dear, beloved 2 pleasantly, nicely ♦ بسیار – گپ میزند He talks (chats) very nicely. 3 feminine proper name Shirin

شیرین بویه [shirinboya] licorice root, licorice (used as an expectorant)

شیرینچه [shirincha] pimple; pimples; rash

شیرینی [shirini] 1 sweets, candy, tidbits (fruit drops, candied nuts, halvah) 2 charm, attraction, attractiveness 3 reward; remuneration for a service; gift, entertainment (on making a good bargain)
- دادن - colloquial to arrange party on the occasion of a betrothal or engagement

شیرینی باب [shirinibaab] sweets, candy; confectionery

شیرینی خوری [shirinikhori] 1 engagement, betrothal 2 party (on the occasion of an engagement or betrothal)

شیشه [shisha] 1 glass; an article or item made of glass ♦ وسنگ باهم نسازد - Glass and stone cannot get along (about something incompatible). 2 bottle, vial ♦ عطر - bottle of perfume

شیشه بر [shishabor] glass cutter ♦ قلم - diamond (for cutting glass)

شیشه ساز [shishasaaz] glazier, glass cutter (person); glassblower

شیشه یی [shisheyi] glass adjective, made of glass ♦ مهره - glass beads

شیطان [shaytaan] (plural شیاطین [shayaatin]) 1 evil spirit, devil 2 a cunning person, a vile person, a master of tricks or pranks 3 mischievous child, mischievous person ♦ بچه - imp
- او سر – را خاریده colloquial He has an extremely independent attitude. / He is quite devil-may-care [about something].

شیطان چراغ [shaytancheraagh] wick lamp

شیطانک [shaytaanak] 1 (also آسیا -) a miller's pusher 2 ☞ شیطان چراغ

شیطانی [shaytaani] 1.1 devilish; diabolical; satanic 1.2 wicked, malicious, perfidious, insidious 2 mischief, naughtiness ♦ نکو - Don't be naughty!

شیطنت [shaytanat] 1 diabolical intrigues; devilry 2 evil, insidiousness; dirty trick

شیعه [shi'a] 1.1 (also- اهل) a Shiite; Shiites 1.2 the Shiite sect (followers of Ali) 2 Shiite adjective

شیفته [shifta] 1 captivated, fascinated, charmed 2 passionately loving (something) ♦ آزادی - passionately loving freedom, freedom-loving

شیله [sheela] 1 dry riverbed (of a mountain stream) 2 seasonal river (that dries up in the summer) ♦ شیله های موسمی seasonal rivers 3 hollow, depression

شیمه [shima] colloquial power, might, strength
- از - افتادن (ماندن) to lose [one's] strength, to grow weak
- سر - آمدن to get better, to convalesce, to restore one's energy
- این آرد - ندارد This flour is thin / weak (thick dough cannot be obtained from it).

شین [shin] the name of the letter ش

شیوخ [shoyukh] plural of شیخ

شیوع [shoyu'] dissemination; trumpeting, announcing
- دادن - to spread, to disseminate; to trumpet, to announce (by means of the press, the radio, etc.)

شیون [shewan] literary weeping, crying; moan, groan; complaint

شئون [sho'un] 1 plural of شأن 2 fields, spheres, limits

شیوه [sheewa] 1 mode, way, method, manner 2 conduct, behavior, habits 3 coquetry, affection

شیوه دار [shewadaar] well-mannered, civil, courteous

ص
17th letter of the Dari alphabet

ص *abbreviation of* صداقت همراه

صابون [saabun] soap ♦ کالاشویی - laundry soap
- زدن ♦ to soap, to rub with soap, to cover with soap; to wash (something) with soap

صابون پزی [saabunpazi] soap-boiling

صاحب [saaheb (and) saaeb] 1.1 owner, proprietor, holder 1.2 sahib, mister, sir (form of address) ♦ - معلم Mister teacher! 1.3 *literary* (*plural* اصحاب [ashaab]) friend; companion 2 *masculine proper name* Sahib

صاحب خانه [saaheb (e) xaana] owner of a house; landlord; head of a family

صاحب رسوخ [saahebrosukh 1 influential, having authority; having prestige 2 an influential person

صاحب صورت [saaheb (e) surat] beautiful, handsome

صاحب قران [saahebqeraan] *literary* lucky, fortunate, born under a fortunate combination of stars

صاحب منصب [saahebmansab] 1 officer 2 responsible person; official, functionary

صاحب نفس [saaheb (e) nafas] *colloquial* one whose prayers and incantations are effective

صاد [saad] the name of the letter ص

صادر [saader]
- کردن - 1 to issue (an order, etc.); to publish; to carry out; to pronounce (e.g., a decision or judgement) 2 to export

صادرات [saaderaat] expert

صادره [saadera] 1 outgoing (about a document) 2 [being] issued (about a decree, etc.) 3 [being] exported

صادق [saadeq] 1.1 truthful; upright; honest 1.2 faithful; loyal; devoted 2 *masculine proper name* Sadeq

صاعقه [saa'eqa] lightning

صاف [saaf] 1.1 clear, pure ♦ آب - pure water, limpid water 1.2 lucid, frank 2.1 clearly, distinctly 2.2 frankly, directly
- کردن - 1 to clean, to purify; to filter, to strain 2 to drain (boiled rice) 3 to settle matters (with somebody) (با)

صاف باطن [saafbaaten] (and) صاف دل [saafdel] 1 candid, frank, openhearted 2 good-natured, simple-hearted

صاف و ساده [saafosaada] (and) صاف و ستره [saafosotra] *colloquial* 1 directly, frankly 2 naively, simple-heartedly, openheartedly

صافه [saafa] 1 gauze, cheesecloth, netting (for straining) 2 strainer, filter
- از - کشیدن to strain, to filter

صافی [saafi]¹ 1 purity, transparency, limpidity 2 clarity, distinctness

صافی [saafi]² 1 dish towel, kitchen towel; dishrag 2 *technical* rag, waste 3 strainer

صالون [saalon] hall; salon ♦ کلان - large hall, great hall; grand ballroom

صامت [saamet] *grammar* consonant (about a sound)

صبا [sabaa] 1 morning 2 in the morning, tomorrow
- دیگر - (and) - پس *colloquial* the day after tomorrow
- باد - *poetic* spring wind, zephyr

صباح [sabaah] ☞ صبا

صبح [sobh] 1 morning ♦ دمید - The day began to dawn. 2 in the morning
- صادق - 1 early morning 2 in the early morning, at dawn

صبحانه [sobhaana] 1 in the morning 2 morning *adjective*

صبحکی [sabhaki] *colloquial* early, in the morning

صبر [sáber] 1 patience 2 meekness
- کردن - 1 to bear (something) patiently 2 to wait
- کنید - Be patient! Wait!

صبور [sabur] (and) صبر ناک [sabernaak] patient

صحاف [sahhaaf] 1 bookbinder 2 book vendor, bookseller

صحافی [sahhaafi] 1 bookbinding 2 bookbinding shop, bindery

صحبت [sohbat] 1 conversation, talk 2 *literary* company, gathering of friends
- کردن - to talk [about], to discuss (something)

صحبتی [sohbati] good company; a sociable person, good mixer

صحت [sahhat] 1 health, state of health ♦ عامه - care of public health 2 correctness, rightness
- داشتن - to be correct, to be right
- یافتن - to get better, to recover

صحت مند [sehhatmand] healthy, possessing good health

صحتمندی [sehhatmandi] good health

صحرا [sahra] 1 field; steppe 2 desert

صحرانشین [sahraaneshin] inhabitant of the steppes; nomad

صحرایی [sahraayi] 1 steppe *adjective*, field *adjective*; wild (about plants, about animals) 2 *military* توپخانه - field *adjective* 3 ☞ صحرانشین

صحن [sahn]¹ 1 area; surface 2 level ground; grounds, playing field 3 (also- حویلی) yard 4 (also- خانه) floor [in a house]

صحن [sahn]² (and) saan calico (cloth)

صحنه [sahna] stage
- تمثیل – 1.1 performance, play 1.2 theater 2 sight, spectacle, scene ♦ [This is] a very sad بسیار غمناک است spectacle 3 field, arena ♦ جنگ - field of battle

صحنه سازی [sahnasaazi] 1 staging, dramatization, performance 2 something concocted, something contrived, something performed deliberately

صحی [sehhi] 1 sanitary; medical; hygienic 2 healthy; hygienic ♦ آب - potable water, water fit to drink 3 medical ♦ - سرویس medical opinion

صحیح [sahih] 1 right, correct; exact, precise 2 correctly; exactly, precisely
- است - [That's] right!

صحیه [sehhya] ☞ صحی
- نفر - hospital attendant
- وزارت - Ministry of Health

صد [sad] one hundred; a hundred ♦ صد فی صد 100 percent

صدا [sadaa] 1 voice; tone ♦ بلند - loud voice ◊ بم - low tone, deep tone 2 cry; shout; call 3 sound; noise ♦ پای - sound of footsteps ◊ تفنگ - sound of a gunshot
- از یک دست صدا نمی خیزد *proverb* You can't clap with one hand (you can't conquer alone).
- براوردن - 1 to give out a sound; to make noise 2 to give tongue [to], to say a word ♦ صدایی نه براورد He didn't utter a word.
- کردن - to cry; to shout; to call
- از - افتادن *colloquial* to become hoarse from shouting

203

ص

صدادار [sadaadaar] 1 ringing, loud 2 *grammar* voiced ♦ کانسوننت - voiced consonant

صدارت [sadaarat] 1 chairmanship, leadership 2 post of prime minister

صداشناسی [sadaashenaasi] phonetics

صداقت [sadaaqat] 1 truthfulness; uprightness, sincerity 2 faithfulness; loyalty; fidelity; devotion

صداقتماب [sadaaqatmaab] *obscure official* your excellency (form of address to a deputy minister or adviser)

صدر [sadr (and) sádera] 1 head, chief, chairman ♦ مجلس - chairman of a meeting 2 place of honor (at a meeting) 3 *literary* sadr (initial rokn in couplet; ☞ رکن)

صدر اعظم [sadra'zam] 1 prime minister 2 *historical* Grand Vizier

صدف [sadaf] 1 shell ♦ مروارید - shell of a pearl oyster 2 mother-of-pearl

صدق [sedq] 1 truth 2 ☞ صداقت
 • با دل - in all sincerity

صدقه [sadqa (and) sadaqa] 1 charity, alms; donation (for religious purposes) 2 sacrifice; offering
 • دادن - to give alms, to make a donation
 • شوم - (and) تو شوم - [You are] my dear one! / I will give my life for you! (in supplication, when expressing devotion, fidelity, etc.)

صدمه [sadama] 1 blow, collision; wreck, crash, accident 2 damage; injury; harm
 • خوردن - to suffer damage, to be in a wreck, crash, or accident
 • دیدن - 1 to suffer injury 2 ☞ خوردن -
 • رساندن - to mar; to inflict harm, damage, or injury

صدور [sodur] 1 issue; publication; promulgation (of an order, etc.) 2 carrying out, making (e.g., a decision, a judgement) 3 giving (a reference, a promissory note) 4 export, exporting

صدری [sadi]¹ century

صدی [sadi]² a hundred (currency bill)

صراحت [saraahat] clarity, unambiguousness (e.g., of an utterance)
 • صراحتا به - ☞ •

صراحتاً [saraahatan] clearly, precisely, accurately

صراحی [soraahi] jug, pitcher (with high neck); carafe
 • خالی چه قلقل کند - *proverb* [Water] doesn't gurgle in an empty jug.

صراف [sarraaf] 1 moneychanger 2 appraiser of precious stones 3 banker

صرافی [sarrafi] 1 exchange of money, banking operations 2 *obscure* occupation of a moneychanger

صرف [sarf]¹ 1 expenditure ♦ وقت - expenditure of time, spending time 2 taking (food) ♦ چای - tea-drinking
 • کردن - 1 to spend 2 to take (food) 3 to show, to manifest (concern, etc.)

صرف [sarf]² 1 morphology 2 *grammar* declension; conjugation
 • کردن - to decline; to conjugate
 • صرف اسم Declension
 • صرف عام Inflection
 • صرف فعل Conjugation

صرف [serf] only; solely
 • دروغ - downright lie

صرفنظر [sarfenazar]
 • از- despite, in spite of
 • کردن - 1 to refuse; to decline; to renounce (از) 2 to ignore; to disregard

صرف ونحو [sarfonáhw] grammar; morphology and syntax

صرفه [sarfa]
 • کردن - to save, to economize

صرفه جویی [sarfajuyi] thrift; economy

صریح [sarih] definite, unambiguous

صغیر [saghir] 1 small, little 2 young 3 *colloquial* left without a father (about a child)

صف [saf] (*plural* صفوف [sofuf]) 1 row, line ♦ در صف اول - in the first row 2 *military* formation; rank
 • صف بستن - to form a line; to assume a formation

صفا [safaa] 1.1 purity, clarity 1.2 gladness, joy, pleasure 2 ☞ صاف
 • آوردید - Welcome! (*Literally,* You have brought joy with you!)

صفات [sefaat] *plural of* صفت

صفاکاری [safaakaari] finishing, trimming; polishing; finish or decoration work

صفایی [safaayi] 1 neatness, order 2 making neat, putting in order; tidying up
 • کردن - 1 to clean, to tidy up (a room) 2 to polish, to shine
 • محصول - payment, fees for utilities

صفایی والا [safaayiwaalaa] 1 person who collects payment for tidying up public places 2 worker of a municipal administration

صف بندی [safbandi] forming up, standing in formation ♦ کردن - to line up (in a rank)

صفت [sefat] (*plural* صفات [sefat]) 1 virtue; characteristic, quality 2 positive quality, virtue ♦ آن عیب است نه - This is not a virtue but a vice. 3 epithet 4 *grammar* adjective; attribute ♦ نسبتی(نسبی) - relative adjective

صفحه [safha] (*plural* صفحات [safahaat]) 1 page (of a book) 2 surface 3 area, territory ♦ صفحات شمال افغانستان The northern areas of Afghanistan 4 *astronomy* phase

صفر [safar] 1 Safar (second month of Afghan lunar year) 2 *masculine proper name* Safar

صفر [séfer] zero ♦ زیر - below zero

صفرا [safraa] bile, gall ♦ کیسه - gall bladder

صفراوی [safraawi] 1 bile, gall *adjective* ♦ طرق - bile ducts 2 excitable, choleric (about temperament)

صفوف [sofuf] *plural of* صف

صفوی [safawi] 1 *historical* Safavid, Safawid, or Safavi *adjective* 2 a member of the Safavid, Safawid, or Safavi dynasty

صفه [sofa] earth or brick platform or dais (in a courtyard or garden for sitting and sleeping)

صک [sak (k)] (*plural* صکوک [sokuk]) 1 document, receipt 2 (*also* صک بیع) bill of sale; deed of purchase

صکوک [sokuk] *plural of* صک

صکوکات [sokukaat] *historical* duty or payment to formalize transactions or fiscal papers; stamp-duties

صلا [salaa] 1 invitation 2 call, call-up, summons
 • زدن(کردن) - 1 to invite (to the table); to invite (to be a quest) 2 to call, to summon

صلاح [salaah] 1 advisability, expediency, usefulness 2 interests, needs ♦ مملکت - the interests of the state 3

204

ص

colloquial advice, opinion
- دادن - • to give advice
- شما چه می‌دهید؟ What do you advise?
- دیدن - • to consider (something) advisable or expedient, to consider (something) useful

صلاحیت [salaahiyat] 1 fitness, suitability; conformity 2 competence 3 authority
- داشتن - • 1 to be competent (در) 2 to fit, to suit; to conform, to be in keeping [with] (برای)

صلح [solh (and) sóla] peace; armistice; truce ♦ دنیا - peace throughout the world ◊ شورای جهانی - World Peace Council
- کردن - • to conclude peace

صلح آمیز [solhaameez] peace *adjective*, peaceful, peace-loving; conciliatory (about something)

صلح خواه [solhkhaah] 1 yearning for peace, peace-loving 2 an advocate of peace

صلح خواهی [solhkhaahi] a yearning for peace, peaceableness, peaceful disposition ♦ سیاست - peace-loving policy

صلح دوست [solhdost] ☞ صلح خواه

صلعم [sal'am] abbreviation of the literary expression: صلی الله علیه وسلم May Allah bless him and send him peace! (about Mohammed)

صلیب [salib] cross ♦ اهل - Christians

صمیم [samim]
- از - قلب • in all sincerity

صمیمی [samimi] sincere; tender; loving (about somebody) ♦ - دوست true friend

صمیمیت [samimiyat] sincerity; warmth; tenderness of feeling; cordiality

صناعت [sanaa'at] 1 art; skill, craftsmanship 2 ☞ صنعت

صنایع [sanaaye'] 1 *plural of* صنعت - مکتب vocational and technical school 2 industry ♦ سنگین - heavy industry

صندق [sandoq] ☞ صندوق

صندقه [sandoqa] delicate wall, parapet (surrounding the flat roof of a house)

صندله [sandala] sandala (mixture of crushed brick and lime usually used to coat walls)

صندلی [sandali] sandali (low table covered with a blanket under which a brazier with hot coals is placed to warm the feet and legs)
- ماندن - • to set up a sandali

صندف [sanduf] sateen

صندوق [sanduq] 1 trunk, box, chest ♦ ادویه - medicine chest, first aid kit 2 (ballot) box 3 cashbox, till ♦ پس انداز - savings bank 4 fund (of money)

صندوقدار [sanduqdaar] cashier; treasurer, paymaster, purser

صنعت [san'at] 1 trade, business 2 industry 3 ☞ صناعت

صنعتکار [san'atkaar] (and) صنعت گر [san'atgar] artisan, craftsman

صنعتی [san'ati] industrial

صنف [senf] (*plural* صنوف [sonuf] (and) اصناف [asnaf]) 1 kind, sort, category 2 class (in school) ♦ در - پنجم است He is (studying) in the fifth class. 3 *political* class; estate ♦ کار گر - the working class 4 branch of the army

صنف بندی [senfbandi] classification
- کردن - • to separate into classes, to divide into classes, to classify

صنفی [senfi] 1.1 guild *adjective*, class *adjective* 2 vocational 3 class *adjective* ♦ مبارزه - class struggle 2 classmate

صنم [sanam] *literary* 1 idol, object of worship 2 a beauty, beautiful girl; sweetheart, beloved

صنوبر [sanawbar] *botany* 1 stone pine 2 pine, pine tree

صنوف [sonuf] (*plural of* صواب [sawaab]) 1.1 correctness; rightness, righteousness 2 good 2 *opposite of* (خطا) right, just ♦ رأی - right opinion

صوابدید [sawaabdid] 1 approval, sanction 2 advice; discretion, judgement ♦ شما - at your discretion

صوب [sob] *colloquial* ☞ صبح

صوبایی [subaayi] provincial, regional

صوبجات [subajaat] *obscure plural of* صوبه

صوبکی [sobaki] *colloquial* ☞ صبحکی

صوبه [suba] (*plural* صوبجات [subajaat]) *obscure* district; province ♦ سرحد - Northwest Frontier Province

صوبه دار [subadaar] *obscure* 1 subadar (junior officer's rank in the infantry) 2 district chief, district head

صوت [sawt] (*plural* اصوات [aswaat]) sound; voice; tone
- مافوق - • 1 ultrasound, ultrasonics, supersonics 2 supersonic (e.g., aircraft)

صوتی [sawti] acoustic; sound
- واحد - • *grammar* phoneme

صور [sur] trumpet; horn; bugle

صورت [surat] 1 appearance; exterior 2 beautiful appearance, fine appearance 3 picture, image, portrait 4 form, mode ♦ به اجمال - briefly, in short, in brief 5 case, circumstance ♦ به ضرورت - in case of necessity ◊ درهر - in any case, in any event; in some way or other 6 list, register; record 7 *philosophical* form 8 (also -فعل) *grammar* mood
- صورت حال ☞ • حال -
- در صورتیکه... • *conjunction compound* 1 if by chance 2 while; whereas
- دادن - • 1 to impart the appearance [of], to fashion, to form [into] 2 to make beautiful
- گرفتن - • 1 to take place 2 to come true, to be realized ♦ دارد - [This is] possible / feasible.

صورت پذیر [suratpazir] feasible ♦ نیست - [This is] not feasible.

صورت حال [suratehaal] 1 official document 2 detailed account of a matter or case
- نوشتن - • 1 to draw up an official document 2 to give a detailed account of a matter or case

صورت دار [suratdaar] 1 beautiful, handsome; distinguished 2 having a beautiful or handsome form

صورت گر [suratgar] 1 artist; painter 2 sculptor

صورتی [surati] *colloquial* 1 ☞ 2 having a deceptive exterior; externally beautiful, but empty or shallow 3 ☞ صورت دار

صوری [sowari (and) suri] 1 external, outward, superficial 2 for show, ostentatious

صوف [suf] underground passage, tunnel
- زدن(تیار کردن) - • to dig a passage or a tunnel

صوفه [sufa (and) sofa] ☞ صفه

صوفی [sufi] a sufi; a dervish-mystic

صوفیانه [sufiyaana] 1 sufi *adjective* ♦ زندگی - the life of a sufi 2 *colloquial* frugal, poor, modest (i.e., not rich)

صوم [sawm] *literary* fast, abstention from food

صوم [som (and) sum] *colloquial* ruble

صیاد [sayaad] hunter

صید [sayd] 1 hunting, trapping 2 object of the hunt, bag (of game)
- کردن to hunt, to catch

صیغه [sigha] 1 form; method, way ♦ به این - in that way 2 form (for casting), casting box 3 formula (pronounced during the conclusion of some kind of agreement or contract) ♦ طلاق - divorce formula

صیف [sayf] *literary* summer

صیفیه [sayfiya] 1 summer cottage, country house 2 country place

صیقل [sayqal] 1 sharpening, pointing 2 polishing 3 *technical* grinding

صیقلگر [sayqalgar] 1 sharpener, grinder (person) 2 polisher (person)

صیهونیت [sayhuniyat] Zionism

ض
18th letter of the Dari alphabet

ضابط [zaabet] 1 intermediate officer's rank (in Afghan army), commissioned officer ♦ اعاشه - quartermaster ◊ امر - adjutant 2 *historical* ruler, steward, manager

ضابطه [zaabeta] (*plural* ضوابط [zawaabet]) 1 procedure, rule; law 2 strictness; severity; discipline

ضاد [zaad] name of the letter ض

ضامن [zaamen] 1 guarantor; person who makes a guarantee or pledge 2 *rarely* guarantee
- کسی بودن - to guarantee, to bear responsibility (for somebody) ♦ من - او هستم I'll vouch for him.

ضامنی [zaameni] ☞ ضمانت

ضایع [zaaye']
- خون زیادی - کرده است کردن 1 to expend, to waste, to lose ♦ He lost much blood 2 to ruin; to destroy

ضایعه [zaae'a] loss, losses

ضبط [zabt] 1 confiscation, attachment; seizure (of property) 2 booking, registration 3 learning by heart, cramming
- کردن 1 to confiscate, to seize; to attach (property) 2 to book, to register 3 to learn by heart, to cram
- احوالات - *obscure* criminal investigation, subversive investigation; criminal investigation department (of the police)

ضبطی [zabti] confiscated

ضخامت [zakhaamat] 1 thickness, density ♦ طبقه برف - thickness of the snow cover 2 unwieldiness, bulk, bulkiness

ضخیم [zakhim] 1 thick, stout; dense, solid 2 large, big, bulky, unwieldy

ضد [zed (d)] 1.1 opposite, contrary, opposed ♦ آنها با هم ضدند They differ sharply from one another. 1.2 hostile; antagonistic 2 *colloquial* malicious obstinacy; malice 3 ضد: (also برضد) *denominative preposition* 3.1 despite, in spite of, notwithstanding 3.2 against, opposite ♦ برضد دشمن against the enemy 4 ضد ... (prefix corresponding to English "anti-" / "counter-") ♦ ضدراکت antimissile

ضد امپریالیستی [zeddeamperiaalisti] anti-imperialistic

ضدانفلاق [zeddeenfelaaq]
- ماده - antiknock compound

ضدراکت [zedderaaket] antimissile

ضدزنگ [zeddezang] anticorrosive

ضدعفونی [zeddeofuni] antiseptic; disinfecting, disinfection

ضدهوایی [zeddehawaayi] antiaircraft

ضدی [zeddi] 1 hostile, inimical; opposite, contrary 2 *colloquial* wicked, malicious; stubborn, obstinate

ضدیت [zeddiyat] 1 contrast; opposition; contradiction 2 antagonism, hositility

ضدین [zeddayn] two opposites; antipodes

ضراب [zarraab] minter

ضرابخانه [zarraabkhaana] mint

ضرایب [zaraayeb] *plural of* ضریب

ضرب [zarb] (*plural* ضروب [zorub]) 1 blow, stroke; beating 2 *music* time; beating time (e.g., on a drum) 3 *colloquial* damage, injury; multilation; loss 4 *mathematical* multiplication ♦ جدول - multiplication table 5 *historical* minting (of coins) 6 one-sided drum (which is held under one's arm while time is beaten with the hand)
- خوردن - to receive a blow, to receive an injury
- زدن - 1 to beat, to strike, to hit 2 to beat time (on a drum, etc.)
- کردن - 1 to multiply 2 ☞ زدن
- به - رساندن to mint (coins)
- میل - competition of wrestlers or weightlifters in which they juggle heavy wooden beams; ☞ میل
- به-چوب - *colloquial* unwillingly, reluctantly, grudgingly

ضرب المثل [zarbolmasal] proverb; saying

ضربان [zarabaan] beating (of the heart); pulsation

ضربت [zarbat] ☞ ضربه

ضرب وجمع [zarbojam']
- ماشین - adding machine

ضربوی [zarbawi] shock *adjective* ♦ موج - *military* shock wave, blast wave

ضربه [zarba] 1 blow, strike; push; jolt ♦ سخت - powerful blow 2 *military* strike, attack 3 *military* burst (of machine gun fire, etc.) 4 *technical* incision, notch

ضرر [zarar] harm, hurt, injury; damage; loss
- به... - harmful, deleterious (to somebody)
- ندارد - [That is] not harmful! / No harm done! / No trouble!
- رساندن - 1 to harm, to spoil 2 to cause damage or loss
- دیدن - 1 to be harmed, injured, or damaged; to spoil, to go bad, to rot 2 to suffer damage or loss

ضرررسان [zararrasaan] (and) ضررناک [zararnaak] 1 harmful, injurious, bad, deleterious 2 bringing loss, disadvantageous, unprofitable

ضروب [zorub] *plural of* ضرب

ضرور [zarur] 1.1 necessary 1.2 important; pressing, urgent (about a matter, etc.) 2 it is necessary, without fail, certainly ♦ ... است که - it is necessary that ... 3 *colloquial* probably
- جای - *colloquial* bathroom, latrine, lavatory, outhouse

ضرورت [zarurat] 1 necessity, want, need ♦ به وقت - when required; as needed 2 importance, urgency ♦ این کار - دارد This matter is urgent.
- داشتن - to need, to want, to experience or feel a need (به)

ضرورتاً [zarúrtan] 1 because of need, on account of need, necessarily, perforce 2 without fail; inevitably, of necessity

ضروری [zaruri] 1 ☞ ضرور 1 2 inevitable; unavoidable; mandatory

ضروريات [zaruriyaat] 1 necessary matters, urgent matters; needs ♦ زندگى - vital needs 2 objects of primary necessity ♦ سفر - traveling gear

ضريب [zarib] (plural ضرايب [zarayeb]) coefficient ♦ كارمفيد - coefficient of efficiency, efficiency

ضعف [za'f (and) zof] 1 weakness, feebleness; collapse, breakdown ♦ قلب - heart insufficiency 2 faintness, fainting fit; nausea
• كردن - 1 to grow weak or feeble, to lose strength (because of sickness, etc.) 2 to fall in a faint

ضعيف [zaif] 1.1 weak, feeble 1.2 old, infirm 2 weak being, weak essence

ضعيف البنيه [zaifolbonya] of frail build, puny, undersized, frail

ضعيف العقل [zaifoláqel] imbecile, weak-minded

ضلع [zel' (and) zéla] (plural اضلاع [azlaa']) 1 mathematical side 2 region, district

ضم [zam (m)] literary addition, appendix, addendum

ضماد [zemaad] 1 medical plaster 2 bandage with ointment 3 compress

ضمانت [zamanaat] 1 pledge; deposit, security ♦ به - ... on pledge (of something) 2 guarantee, commitment; bail
• كردن - to guarantee; to vouch for
• گرفتن به - 1 to take on pledge or on guarantee 2 to bail, to go bail [for]

ضمانت نامه [zmaanatnaama] guarantee, bail; letter of guarantee

ضماير [zamaayer] plural of ضمير ²

ضمايم [zamaayem] plural of ضميمه

ضمن [zemn] (also - در) 1 in the course [of], during, at the time [of] denominative preposition ♦ فتگو در in the course of conversation 2 among, in the number [of] denominative preposition
• دراين - meanwhile

ضمناً [zémnan] besides, moreover; at the same time; by the way

ضمنى [zemni] 1 accessory; collateral; additional 2 indirect; implied

ضمه [zamma] zamma, pesh (vowel point: diacritical mark designating the short "o")

ضمير [zamir] ¹ 1 heart, soul 2 conscience; consciousness 3 masculine proper name Zamir

ضمير [zamir] ² (plural ضماير [zamaayer]) grammar pronoun
• متصل (پيوسته) - combining form of a pronoun, pronominal enclitic
• ضمير اشارى Demonstrative
• ضمير شخصى Personal pronoun
• ضمير مشترك Reflexive pronoun
• ضمير منفصل Independent pronoun

ضميران [zamiraan] botany basil

ضميمه [zamima] 1 (plural ضمايم [zamayem]) appendix, supplement (e.g., to a book) 2 appended, added, annexed, supplemented

ضوابط [zawaabet] plural of ضابطه

ضياء [ziyaa] literary 1 light, radiance ♦ الملت و الدين - historical light of the nation and religion (title of the Emir Abdurrahman) 2 masculine proper name Ziya

ضيافت [ziyaafat] banquet; dinner party

ضيق [ziq] 1 narrowness tightness; stricture, constriction 2 difficulty, straits
• نفس - short breath; asthma

ط
19th letter of the Dari alphabet

طا [taa] (also طاى مؤلف) name of the letter ط

طابع [taabe'] printer; publisher

طاس [taas] ¹ 1 copper bowl 2 (also حمام -) copper basin (for washing)

طاس [taas] ² ☞ تاس ²

طاعت [taaat] 1 honoring God 2 humility; meekness; submissiveness, obedience ♦ طاق pious or devout people, humble, meek, or submissive people

طاعون [ta'un] plague

طاق [taaq] ¹ 1 arch; vault 2 niche (in the upper part of a wall); shelf built into a wall
• نسيان گذاشتن به - to shelve, to pigeon-hole
• ابرو - curve of the eyebrows

طاق [taaq] ² ☞ تاق

طاقت [taaqat] 1 strength; staying power; endurance 2 physics power, energy 3 rarely electrical voltage, tension
• مافوق - 1 beyond one's strength 2 it is beyond one's power[s] or competence
• آوردن (به) - to endure, to bear

طاقت سوز [taaqatsoz] (and) طاقت فرسا [taqatfarsa] sapping [one's] strength, exhausting; wearing down

طاقچه [taaqcha] a small niche with a shelf

طاقه [taaqa] 1.1 solitary; individual 1.2 colloquial single, lone, quite alone 2 piece; item (numerative when counting shawls, kerchiefs) ♦ يك كشمير شال one cashmere shawl
• ماندن - colloquial to be left alone, to remain single

طالار [taalaar] ☞ تالار

طالب [taaleb] (plural طلاب [tollaab]) 1.1 student 1.2 colloquial pupil (of a school attached to a mosque) 2 seeking (something), striving [for], aspiring [to] (something) 3 masculine proper name Taleb
• بودن - to desire, to need, to ask [for]

طالب العلم [taalebol'elm] 1 student 2 student of an ecclesiastical school, taleb

طالع [taale'] 1 luck; success; fortune ♦ colloquial من درگور - My lot is a very unlucky one! 2 rising (about a heavenly body)
• داشتن - to be happy, to be lucky, to have success
• طالع كسى بر كردن idiom to have good luck, to succeed

طالع وبخت [taalewbakht] colloquial fate, destiny, lot

طاوس [taawus] peacock, peafowl

طاير [taayer] (plural طيور [toyur]) literary bird

طايفه [taayfa] (plural طوايف [tawayef]) 1 tribe, family; clan 2 group (of people); crowd

طب [tebb] medicine

طبابت [tabaabat] 1 physician's practice 2 ☞ طبيبى

طباخ [tabbaakh] cook; chef

طباخى [tabbaakhi]
• كتاب - cookbook

طباعت [tabaaat] printing; printing business

طبخ [tabkh] preparation of food

ط

طبراق [tabraaq] 1 canvas or leather bag or pouch 2 cartridge belt

طبع [tab' (and) tába]¹ 1 nature, substance 2 disposition, character 3 gift, talent

طبع [tab' (and) tá'ba]² printing; publication ♦ اول - first edition
- کردن • to print, to publish

طبعاً [táb'an] 1 by nature 2 naturally, of course

طبع آزمایی [tab'aazmaayi] 1 test of strength 2 examination, test; trial, experiment

طبق [tabaq] large plate, large dish ♦ چینی - china dish

طبقات [tabaqaat] plural of طبقه

طبقات العرض [tabaqaatolarz] (also علم -) geology

طبقات العرضی [tabaqaatolarzi] geological ♦ ادوار - geological periods

طبقاتی [tabaqaati] class ♦ اختلافات - class contradictions

طبقه [tabaqa] (plural طبقات [tabaqat]) 1 layer, stratum (e.g., of soil); seam 2 floor, tier 3 estate, class ♦ حاکمه - the ruling class 4 category, rank 5 stage (of a rocket, missile)

طبقه بندی [tabaqabandi] classification; systematization ♦ حیوانات - taxonomy of animals

طبقه دار [tabaqadaar] tiered, in tiers ♦ باغ - terraced garden

طبقی [tabaqi] colloquial viands, refreshments (sent by the groom's parents to the bride's home)

طبل [tabl (and) tábal] 1 large drum (a small barrel with one leather-covered end which one beats with sticks) 2 drumbeat
- زدن • to beat a drum

طبل زن [teblzan] drummer

طبله [tabla] 1 tabla (paired percussion instrument) 2 tambourine

طبی [tebbi] medicinal; medical
- مواد – medicines, drugs

طبیب [tabib] 1 tabib (a doctor who uses the methods of Eastern medicine) 2 physician, doctor

طبیبی [tabibi] 1 the profession of a doctor, of a tabib 2 doctoring

طبیعت [tabiat] 1 nature ♦ در دامن - in the lap of nature 2 disposition, temperament 3 mood, humor

طبیعی [tabi'i] 1 natural ♦ متابع - natural resources ◊ علوم - natural sciences 2 (plural طبیعیون [tabi'iyun]) natural historian, naturalist 3 naturally, of course ♦ است - It goes without saying.

طپیدن [tapidan] ☞ تپیدن

طحال [tehaal] anatomy spleen

طراح [tarraah] 1 draftsman; designer; planner 2 colloquial instigator; initiator

طراز [teraaz] 1 decoration, appointments 2 manner; way; form ♦ به نوین - in a new manner

طرح [tarh (and) tárha] 1 plan, sheme ♦ داستان - plot or outline of a story 2 sketch, outline; draft 3 project
- کردن • 1 to make a sketch, to draw 2 to put together (a plan, a draft, a project), to develop (a plan, a draft, a project) ♦ پروژه تعمیر بندرا نموده اند - They developed a plan for construction of a dam.

طرح ریزی [tarhrezi] 1 development of a plan; planning 2 founding, establishing, laying (e.g., of a foundation)

طرد [tard] 1 removal, elimination, abolition 2 rejection, repudiation 3 literary banishment, exile, sending away
- کردن • to eliminate, to abolish

طرز [tarz] form; condition; way, method, manner ♦ عبارت - manner of expression

طرز العمل [tarzolamal] mode of action, manner of action, conduct, behavior; practice

طرف [taraf] 1.1 side; from the right side 1.2 side, direction; ♦ به - راست در in a westerly direction 1.3 legal party (plaintiff or defendent) 1.4 (also مقابل-) opponent; rival 2 (in combinations it designates the object or subject of an action or feeling) ♦ اعتماد - enjoying trust, confidence, or faith 3 (also به-) to, onto, toward denominative preposition ♦ مکتب برو - Run to school!
- از - • from, from the direction [of], in the name [of]
- قرار گرفتن (چیزی) بودن • to be the object of something, to be subjected to something
- به این تا • up to now, up to the present
- ... از چند سال به این • It's already several years since…

طرفدار [tarafdaar] 1 supporter; advocate; adherent, follower 2 supporting (somebody or something); consenting, for (when voting)
- بودن (چیزی) کسی • to take somebody's side; to support somebody or something

طرفداری [tarafdaari] 1 support, sympathy 2 adherence

طرفین [tarafayn] (dual number of طرف) both sides, both parties ♦ متعاهدین - both contracting parties

طرق [toroq] plural of طریق 1
- تنفسی • respiratory passages

طرق پولی [toroqpuli] historical road duties

طره [torra] literary 1 the end of a turban that is turned up; plume 2 lock of hair, curl, ringlet

طریق [tariq] (plural طرق [toroq]) 1 mode, manner, way 2 figurative way, road, path
- از - • with the aid [of], by means [of] ♦ از- رادیو by radio

طریقت [tariqat] tariqat (path of spiritual perfection among sufis) ♦ اهل - a sufi

طریقه [tariqa] 1 ☞ طریق 2 doctrine; belief, conviction; path, way

طشت [tasht] 1 large copper basin; (wash) tub; bathtub 2 geography basin (of a river)

طعام [ta'aam] food
- صرف – taking food; a meal

طعمه [to'ma (and) tama] 1 food; forage, feed (for birds and animals) 2 catch, bag, prey; victim
- دادن • 1 to feed, to give additional food to 2 to give bait [to], to lure
- آتش شدن • to be a victim of fire, to burn down

طعنه [ta'na (and) taana] 1 reproach, reproof, rebuke 2 blame, censure; mockery
- دادن • to reproach, to reprove, to rebuke, to blame, to censure
- گفتن • to sting, to taunt, to offend, to hurt

طغرا [toghraa] historical monogram (on decrees of an emir)

طغیان [toghyaan] 1 overflowing the banks, overflow (of a river); flood 2 roughness, choppiness (at sea) 3 revolt, mutiny, riot
- کردن • 1 to go outside [its] banks, to overflow (about a

river) 2 to seethe, to be agitated, to be rough (about the sea) 3 to rise in mutiny, to riot

طغیانی [toghyaani] 1 ☞ طغیان 2 impetuous, rapid (about a flow, a current); rough, choppy (about the sea)

طفل [téfel] (plural اطفال [atfaal]) child
- شیر خوار (and) جند ما هه - infant in arms; baby

طفلانه [teflaana] 1 child's, children's ♦ بالاپوش - child's overcoat 2 childishly, like a child

طفلی [tefli] childhood; infancy ♦ از - since childhood

طفولیت [tofuliyat] ☞ طفلی

طفیلی [tofaili] 1 sponger, parasite, idler 2 biology parasite 3 (also - مهمان) uninvited guest

طفیل [tofail] 1 ☞ طفیلی 1, 2
- به (and) ··· از – denominative preposition 1 thanks to, with the aid [of] 2 because of, for

طلا [telaa] 1 gold ♦ احمر - pure gold ◊ ساعت - gold watch 2 colloquial gold coin

طلاب [tollaab] plural of طالب

طلاق [talaaq] divorce, dissolution of marriage
- دادن - to give a divorce (to a wife)
- کردن - to be divorced (from a husband)

طلاکاری [telaakaari] 1 guilding 2 gilt

طلایه [talaaya] 1 advance outpost, outpost 2 patrol, night patrol

طلایی [telaayi] 1 gold, of gold 2 golden

طلب [telab] military colloquial 1 search [for], searching [for]; quest; aspiration 2 request 3 call, summons, inquiry ♦ آتش - request for fire 4 debt (due from somebody); sum given as a loan 5 salary, pay
- داشتن - to demand payment of a debt from somebody ♦ دارم- من بالای شما You owe a small debt. / You owe. / You must pay.
- کردن - 1 to strive [for], to seek [after] 2 to ask [for], to request, to demand 3 to call, to summon, to invite

طلبات [talabaat] 1 demands 2 needs, requirements, interests

طلبدار [talabdaar] debtor

طلبگار [talabgaar] 1 demanding, soliciting 2.1 wooer, fiancé, betrothed 2.2 plaintiff, petitioner; creditor
- بودن (شدن) - 1 to demand, to solicit 2 to woo

طلبگاری [talabgaari] match-making

طلبی [talabi] taken for a certain time, borrowed (about something)

طلبیدن [talabidan] ☞ طلب کردن (in entry طلب)

طلسم [telésem] 1 talisman, amulet, charm (usually a metal or silver disk engraved with the names of angels; worn around the neck) 2 sorcery, witchcraft

طلسمی [telesmi] 1 magic, magical; bewitching 2 bewitched, spellbound

طلوع [tolu'] rising (of a heavenly body)
- کردن - to rise, to ascend (about heavenly bodies)

طمع [tam' (and) táma] 1 greed, avidity 2 yearning to possess (something)
- داشتن - 1 to yearn to possess, to solicit (something) 2 to look forward [to], to anticipate [with pleasure], to count on (something)
- کردن - 1 to show greed 2 ☞ داشتن

طمعکار [tamakaar] greedy, covetous, grasping, avid; soliciting (something)

طناب [tanaab] 1 string; rope; cord 2 tanab (measure of area that differs in different regions)
- کردن - to measure an area in tanabs

طناز [tannaan] ringing, sonorous, resounding

طنبور [tambur] ☞ تنبور

طنز [tanz] literary 1 joke, gibe; bantering 2 playfulness, coquetry

طنطنه [tantana] 1 noise; roll, beat (of a drum) 2 solemnity, pomp

طنین [tanin] 1 sound, sounding 2 hum, buzzing (of insects) 3 echo; resonance

طنین دار [tanindar] 1 resounding, sounding, vibrating 2 grammar voiced ♦ کانسو ننت - voiced consonant

طواف [tawaaf] literary 1 ritual walk around the Kaaba (or the grave of a saint) 2 pilgrimage

طواف [tawwaaf] 1 peddler (of fruit, of water) 2 hawker

طوایف [tawaayef] plural of طایفه

طور [tur] biblical Mount Sinai

طور [tawr] (plural اطوار [atwaar]) 1 manner, means, method 2 kind, sort
- دیگر - otherwise
- چطور ☞ چه –
- همینطور ☞ همین –
- به - in the form of, as
- به - قطعی - resolutely, decisively
- بطوریکه compound conjunction 1 as, like 2 so that

طوس [tus] cards ace

طوطا [totaa] colloquial ☞ طوطی

طوطی [toti (and) tuti] parrot (usually talking)

طوطیا [totiyaa] 1.1 blue vitriol 1.2 obscure eye ointment (of zinc oxide) 2 literary rare, uncommon

طوغ [tugh] banner; standard

طوفان [tufaan] ☞ توفان

طوق [tawq] 1 necklace (in the form of a loop cast in gold or silver) 2 collar; ring (on birds) 3 (also - زنجیر) hoop with chain (on the neck of a prisoner) 4 yoke

طوقک [tawqak] anatomy clavicle

طول [tul] 1 length ♦ وعرض - length and width, breadth 2 duration 3 geography longitude
- دادن - to drag out (a conversation, etc.)
- کشیدن - to last, to continue

طولا [tulaa]
- ید - داشتن literary to be an expert (in something), to know (something) to perfection (در)

طولا [tulan] in length, lengthwise

طو لابلد [tulalbalad] geography 1 meridian 2 longitude (in degrees)

طولیاف [tulalyaaf] long-staple (about cotton)

طولانی [tulaani] 1 lengthy; long ♦ عمر - long life 2 grammar extended (about a sentence)

طومار [tumaar] 1 scroll; parchment, manuscript (on a long paper scroll) 2 sacred text (e.g., the Talmud) 3 colloquial prayer against the evil eye (the prayer is written on paper that is rolled up and tied with a braided cord)

طوی [toy] name of the letter ط

طویل [tawil] 1.1 lengthy; long 1.2 drawn out, slow (about sound, about a tune) 2 (also - بحر) tavil (poetic meter)

طویل المدت [tawilolmoddat] long-term, lasting, of long duration, prolonged, protracted

طویله [tawila] stable; stall; hitching post, tether

طهارت [tahaarat] 1 *religion* ritualistic ablution 2 bathing, washing 3 keeping oneself neat, neatness

طی [tay] 1 going, traveling (along a path, on a journey), following (a course) 2 folding [up], rolling [up]
- مسافت (and) مراحل - covering a distance, crossing, passage, march
- کردن - 1 to go, to traverse, to travel, to overcome a distance 2 to fold [up], to roll [up]

طیار [tayaar] 1 flying 2 volatile

طیارات [tayaaraat] 1 *plural of* طیاره 2 aviation *noun* ♦ بحری - naval aviation

طیاروی [tayaarawi] aviation *adjective* ♦ محروقات - aviation fuel

طیاره [tayaara] (*plural* طیارات [tayarat]) aircraft; airplane ♦ جیت - jet aircraft ◊ سوپر سونیک - supersonic aircraft

طیاره بردار [tayaarabardaar] (*also*- کشتی) aircraft carrier

طیاره ران [tayaararaan] (*and*) طیاره ران [tayarawan] pilot

طیاری [tayari] theory and application of flying, aeronautics

طیر [tayr] *literary* 1 (*plural* طیور [toyur]) bird 2 *plural of* طایر

طینت [tinat] nature; character

طیور [toyur] *plural of* طیر

ظ
20th letter of the Dari alphabet

ظا [zaa] (*also* مؤاف-) name of letter ظ

ظالم [zaalem] 1.1 tyrant, despot 1.2 offender 2 cruel, unjust 3 cruelly, unjustly; despotically

ظاهر [zaaher] 1.1 evident, obvious, visible, apparent 1.2 outward, external 2 (*plural* ظواهر [zawaher]) external appearance, semblance ♦ در - outwardly, by appearance 3 *masculine proper name* Zaher
- شدن - to be revealed, to be discovered, to come to light, to become apparent, to show
- ساختن(کردن) - to show, to manifest, to display

ظاهراً [zaaheran] 1 outwardly, by appearance 2 evidently, obviously

ظاهربین [zaaherbin] 1 not probing into the essence of a matter 2 shallow person, superficial person

ظاهربینی [zaaherbini] superficiality (of judgements, etc.); shallowness, superficiality

ظاهر داری [zaaherdaari] 1 ostentatious courtesy; ceremoniousness 2 showing off; feigning 3 pretense, sham
- کردن - to use cunning, to be crafty; to feign, to sham, to pull the wool over [someone's] eyes

ظاهری [zaaheri] 1.1 outward, exernal 1.2 seeming, imagined 1.3 ostentatious 2 affected appearance, semblance

ظرافت [zaraafat] 1 elegance, grace 2 refinement (of style, of manners); courtesy 3 subtlety of mind; wit 4 joke, witty remark, witticism

ظرف [zarf] (*plural* ظروف [zoruf]) 1 vessel, bowl ♦ چای- tea set (cups, teapot) 2 *grammar* adverb ♦ مکان - adverbial modifier of place 3 *philosophical* form ♦ ومظروف - form and content

ظرفیت [zarfiyat] 1 capacity ♦ تانک - capacity of a tank ◊ مکتب به – هشصد شاگرد a school with a capacity of 800 students 2 cargo capacity, lifting capacity (of an aircraft), tonnage (of a ship) 3 load, capacity (of an enterprise)

ظروف [zoruf] 1 *plural of* ظرف 2 *collective* plates and dishes ♦ ظروف چینی china

ظریف [zarif] 1.1 elegant; refined 1.2 witty, subtle 1.3 humorous, playful 2 *masculine proper name* Zarif

ظریفه [zarifa] 1 ☞ ظریف 2 *feminine proper name* Zarifa
- صنایع – fine arts

ظرافت [zarifi] ☞ ظریف

ظفر [zafar] 1 victory, triumph 2 *masculine proper name* Zafar

ظل [zell] *literary* 1 shade, canopy 2 patronage, protection ♦ در ظل ··· under the canopy; under the patronage, protection

ظلم [zólm (and) zólom] 1 yoke; oppression 2 injustice, cruelty
- کردن - 1 to yoke, to oppress (بر) 2 to commit cruelty, to offend severely (بر)

ظلمانی [zolmaani] dark, gloomy ♦ شب سیاه - pitch-dark night

ظلمت [zolmat] pitch darkness, gloom, blackness

ظلمدیده [zolmdida] (*and*) ظلم رسیده [zolmrasida] oppressed; offended

ظن [zan (n)] (*plural* ظنون [zonun]) 1 opinion; thought, idea ♦ حسن ظن high opinion; confidence; faith ◊ سوء ظن low opinion; lack of confidence, lack of faith 2 guess; suspicion; supposition, assumption, conjecture

ظنون [zonun] 1 mental, supposed 2 doubtful, questionable, suspicious

ظواهر [zawaaher] 1 *plural of* ظاهر 2 phenomena, manifestations ♦ ظواهر طبیعت phenomena of nature

ظوی [zoy] name of the letter ظ

ظهر [zohr] noon, midday, middle part of the day, noontime hours

ظهور [zohur] 1 appearance, emergence, beginning, rise 2 manifestation, baring, revealing, displaying
- کردن - 1 to appear, to emerge, to arise 2 to become apparent, to show, to come to light, to be revealed

ع
21st letter of the Dari alphabet

عابد [aabed] 1 pious, devout 2 (*plural* عابدین [abedin]) praying, adoring, idolizing

عابر [aaber] (*plural* عابرین [aaberin]) *literary* passer-by

عاج [aaj] ivory

عاجز [aajez] 1 helpless; forlorn, pitiful 2 incapable (of something); incompetent (at something) 3 humble, meek, submissive
- ماندن(شدن) - to be not up to (doing something), to be not in a condition or position (to do something) (از)

عاجزانه [aajezaana] humbly, meekly, submissively ♦ عوض میکنم که ···· - I make bold to inform [you] that…

عاجزی [aajezi] 1 helplessness, defenselessness 2 humility, submissiveness

عاجل [aajel] urgent, pressing ♦ کمک - first aid (to a sick person)

عادت [aadat] 1 usual practice, custom 2 habit ♦ به گشیدن سگرت - smoking habit
- دادن - to train, to inculcate (به)
- کردن (گرفتن) to get accustomed [to], to accustom oneself to

عادتاً [aadatan] by custom; by habit, out of habit

210

عادل [aadel] 1 just (about somebody) 2 *masculine proper name* Adel

عادی [aadi] 1 accustomed (to something), inculcated (with, in something) 2 ordinary, simple ♦ مردم - simple people

عار [aar] shame, disgrace, dishonor
- داشتن - to be ashamed [of], to consider dishonorable, shameful (از)

عارض [aarez]¹ complainant, plaintiff; submitter of a petition
- شدن - to make a complaint, to complain (از)

عارض [aarez]²
- شدن - to happen, to take place, to occur (به)

عارضه [aareza] (*plural* عوارض [awaarez]) 1 occurrence, event, incident 2 *technical* difficulty, trouble, malfunction, fault, defect 3 falling ill; complication (after an illness)

عارضه دار [aarezadaar] *technical* faulty, malfunctioning, out-of-order, defective, inoperative

عرضی [aarezi] 1 non-permanent, temporary 2 accidental; casual; incidental ♦ به طور - 1 accidentally 2 temporarily

عارف [aaref] 1 having known [the] truth, grown wise 2 a mystic 3 *masculine proper name* Aref

عاری [aari]
- بودن - to be devoid [of], to not contain (از)

عاریت [aariyat] 1 temporary use (of a thing), borrowing 2 ☞ عاریتی 1
- گرفتن - به to borrow

عار یتا [aariyátan] for a time, as a loan

عاریتی [aariyati] 1 taken for temporary use 2 temporary, transient 3 false, artificial, unnatural, unreal

عازم [aazem]
- شدن - to set out [for], to depart (به) ♦ او - پیشاور شد He went to Peshawar.

عاشق [aasheq] (*plural* عاشقان [and] عشاق [oshshaaq]) in love, a lover ♦ ومعشوق - lovers, a couple in love
- شدن - to fall in love, to come to love, to grow fond (of) (به)

عاشقانه [aasheqaana] 1 amorous, loving (about something) 2) lyrical

عاشقی [aasheqi] amorousness, love, flirtation; amorous relations

عاصی [aasi] 1.1 a sinner 1.2 a disobedient person; a rebel; an insurgent 2 rebellious; mutinous; insubordinate; unruly

عاطفت [aatefat] (and) عاطفه [aatefa] (*plural* عواطف [awaatef]) feeling of sympathy; benevolence, goodwill

عاقبت [aaqebat] (*plural* عواقب [awaaqeb]) 1.1 consequence; outcome, upshot ♦ خیر - happy outcome, favorable outcome 1.2 the future 2 finally, as a result

عاقبت اندیش [aaqebataandeesh] thinking about the consequences, prudent, farsighted

عاقل [aaqel] clever, intelligent; judicious, wise, of sound mind

عالم [aalam] 1 world; universe ♦ حیوانات - animal world 2 people, the people ♦ بشریت - mankind 3 (also -یک) great number, countless number, incalculable amount

عالم [aalem] 1 knowing, versed [in]; learned, scholar, scientist 2 (*plural* علما [olama] (and) عالمان [aalemaan]) 2.1 learned man 2.2 alem (expert on Moslem law) 2.3 theologian 2.4 *masculine proper name* Alem

عالمگیر [aalamgir] 1 world *adjective*, worldwide, universal ♦ جنگ - world war 2 subjugator of the world

عالیان [aalamiyaan] people, the people; the population of the globe, the population of world

عالی [aali] 1 higher, highest, high ♦ تعلیمات - higher education ◊ رتبه - high rank 2 supreme, chief ♦ شورای - Supreme Soviet (USSR) 3 superior (of sort, of grade) excellent, first-rate ♦ جنس - excellent goods, first-rate goods

عالی رتبه [aalirotba] high-ranking ♦ مامورین - higher ranks (other than ministers) ◊ منصبداران - senior officers

عالی شأن [aalisha'n] *obscure* famous, renowned; glorious, splendid, magnificent; eminent, distinguished (in addressing generals)

عالیقدر [aaliqádar] *obscure* highly revered, highly esteemed (in addressing ministers)

عالی همت [aalihemmat] 1 magnanimous; generous 2 possessing high thoughts or designs

عام [aam (m)] general, common, universal; mass *adjective* ♦ اعتصاب - general strike ◊ قتل - mass annihilation

عام فهم [aamfahm] generally understood, popular

عامل [aamel] 1 (*plural* عمال [ommaal]) agent, authorized agent or representative; attorney 2 (*plural* عمله [amala]) worker 3 (*plural* عوامل [awaamel]) factor, cause 4 *medicine* pathogen

عاملی [aameli] 1 businesslike efficiency; industriousness 2 efficiency; promptness; quickness

عام وخاص [aammokhaass] the aristocracy and the common people; the upper classes and lower classes

عامه [aamma] 1 the people; the common people 2 *literary* all; everybody, everyone ♦ مردم - all the people, all people

عامی [aam (m) i] 1 illiterate person, ignorant person 2 common person

عامیانه [aamiyaana] 1 of the common people ♦ زبان - colloquialism, popular speech, common parlance; colloquial language 2 vulgar

عانه [aana] *anatomy* pubis

عاید [aayed]
- (شدن) بودن - 1 to bear a relation [to], to concern, to have to do [with] (به) ♦ مسئولیت به شما – نخواهد بود Responsibility doesn't fall on you. 2 to come in, to be received (about money, about income)

عایدات [aayedaat] income, receipts (of money) ♦ ملی - national income

عایق [aayeq] *technical* 1 nonconducting, insulating ♦ گاز - gastight, gas-proof 2.1 insulator, nonconductor ♦ برق - electrical insulator 2.2 insulation

عایق دار [aayeqdaar] *technical* insulated (about wire)

عایق کاری [aayeqkaari] *technical* 1 insulating, insulating operations 2 filling in joints, caulking joints (with concrete, with cement)

عایله [aayela] family; wife and children

عبادت [ebaadat] service (to God), worship (of God); saying prayers

عبارت [ebaarat] (and) عباره [ebaara] 1 a turn of speech; a phrase; an expression ♦ دیگر به - in other words 2 style 3 *grammar* word combination ♦ اضافی - ezafeh word combination
- عبارت استعاری Metaphorical phrase
- عبارت اضافی Attributive phrase
- عبارت بی مرکز (برون مرکز) Exocentric
- عبارت توصیفی Genitive phrase
- عبارت مرکز دار (درون مرکز) Endocentric

ع

عبارت معین شدهء ادبی Literary phrase
(از) بودن - to consist (of)
عباسی [abbaasi] *obscure* abbasi (silver coin worth one tanga; ☞ تنگه)
عبث [abas] 1 empty, useless; vain 2 for nothing, to no purpose; in vain
• کردن - to waste, to spoil, to spend [money] in vain
عبد [abd] 1 *literary* 1.1 slave 1.2 "God's slave," person 2 (becomes part of proper names) ♦ عبدالحق Abdulhak
عبرانی [ebraani] 1 Hebrew, Judaic 2 (also - زبان) Hebrew language, ancient Hebrew language
عبرت [ebrat] instructive example; edification, lesson
• گرفتن (از) - to learn a lesson; to learn by example
عبور [obur] passage, crossing; ford
• دادن - 1 to convey, to ferry, to transport, to carry across (از) 2 to authorize passage, to let go past
• کردن (از) - to pass, to go past, to cross, to ferry across
♦ هیرمند را ذریعهء ذورقها عبور کردند They crossed the Helmand on ferries.
عبورومرور [oburomurur] movement, traffic, plying
عتیق [atiq] ancient, antique
عتیقه [atiqa] antiquarian articles, antiquities
عتیقه شناس [antiqashenaas]
عثمانی [osmaani] Turkish, Ottoman ♦ امپراطوری - *historical* the Ottoman Empire
عجالتاً [ejaalatan] 1 urgently, hurriedly 2 for now, meanwhile
عجایب [ajaaeyeb] *plural of* عجیبه
عجب [ajab] 1 suprisingly, strangely, strickingly ♦ که ... اینست - It is surprising that... ◊ چاق استی *colloquial* My, you certainly are fat/stout! 2 ☞ عجیب
عجز [ajz] 1 ☞ عاجزی 2 humble request, entreaty, supplication
عجله [ajala] hurry, haste
عجم [ajam] *historical* 1 non-Arabs (from the viewpoint of the Arabs: Persians, Iranians, Tajiks) 2 Iran, Persia
عجوزه [ajuza] 1 old woman, witch, hag 2 (also - دنیا) *metaphysics* this world, transitory world, mortal world
عجیب [ajib] surprising, astonishing, amazing, unusual
عجیب و غریب [ajibo-gharib] strange, unusual; unlike anything else
عجیبه [ajiba] 1 (*plural* عجایب [ajaaeyeb]) miracle, wonder, marvel 2 ☞ عجیب
عدالت [adaalat] fairness; justice
عداوت [adaawat] enmity, hostility, animosity, hatred
عدت [eddat] term, period (during which a divorced woman or widow cannot remarry)
عدد [adad] (*plural* اعداد [a'daad]) 1 number, digit ♦ صحیح - whole number ◊ کسری - fraction, fractional number 2 item, piece (numerative) - شش تخم six eggs 3 *grammar* numeral ♦ ترتیبی - ordinal, ordinal number
• عدد اصلی Cardinal number
• عدد توصیفی Ordinal number
عدس [adas] lentil
عدسه [adasa] 1 lens, optical glass 2 *photography* objective, lens
عدسی [adasi] 1 lenticular, lens-shaped; biconvex, double convex 2 ☞ عدسه

عدل [ádel] rightness, legality; justice, fairness
عدلیه [adliya] organs of justice; justice ♦ وزارت - Ministry of Justice
عدم [adam] 1.1 lack (of something) 1.2 nonexistence 2 (fulfills the role of the negative prefixes un- / in- / non- / dis-) ♦ عدم تناسب disproportion ◊ عدم توجه inattention
عدم اعتماد [adam (e) eetemaad] distrust, mistrust
عدم انتشار [adam (e) enteshaar]
• سلاح ذروی - nonproliferation of nuclear weapons
عدم بلدیت [adam (e) baladiyat] lack of information; ignorance; lack of knowledge
عدم تعرض [adam (e) taarroz] nonaggression ♦ معاهده - nonagression pact
عدم تناسب [adam (e) tanaasob] disproportion
عدم توجه [adam (e) tawajjoh] inattention; ignoring; carelessness; unconcern
عدم مداخلت [adam (e) modaaxalat] noninterference, nonintervention ♦ سیاست - policy of nonintervention
عدم موفقیت [adam (e) mowaffaqiyat] failure, setback, lack of success; downfall
عدو [adow (w)] *literary* enemy, foe
عده [edda] 1 number, quantity 2 great number, multiplicity
• یک – (and) عده یی 1 some (about people) 2 a group (of people)
عذاب [azaab] 1 torture, torment 2 difficulty
عذر [ózor] 1 request for forgiveness, for pardon 2 pretext or grounds (for refusal); excuse ♦ شرعی - legitimate excuse (from the standpoint of the shariya)
• آوردن (برای) - to make excuses, to excuse oneself, to justify oneself
• خواستن - to ask forgiveness, to apologize
عذرخواهی [ozorkhaahi] request for [someone's] pardon
• کردن - to offer apologies, to apologize
عرابه [araaba] carriage, araba (kind of cart)
عرابه کش [araabakash] draft (about an animal)
عراده [araada] 1 wheel 2 (also - توپ) gun carriage 3 (numerative in counting vehicles, railroad cars, automobiles) ♦ چند گادی several carriages ◊ پنج موتر - five automobiles
عرایض [araayez] *plural of* عریضه
عرب [arab] (*plural* اعراب [a'raab]) Arab; Arabs
عربده [arbada] drunken spree, violent uproar, ruckus
عربی [arabi] 1 Arabic, Arabian 2 (also - زبان) Arabic language
عرصه [arsa] 1 area, arena; field (of battle, etc.) 2 field, sphere (of activity) 3 interval of time, period
عرض [arz]¹ 1 oral report, presentation (before a higher personage) ♦ مطلب - statement of the essence of a matter ◊ ورقه - a report 2 respectful request; respectful communication
• من یک - دارم *polite* 1 I have a most humble request [for you]. 2 I must say something [to you].
• کردن - 1 to report (to a higher personage) 2 *polite* to communicate, to say
• به کسی رساندن – *official* to inform somebody respectfully
عرض [arz]² 1 width, breadth ♦ وطول - width and length ◊ ۰۰۰ در- for a distance [of] ◊ در راه - on the road, during a journey 2 ☞ عرض البلد

عرض [araz] 1 symptom 2 (opposite of گوهر) *philosophical* external characteristic of an object, immaterial characteristic of an object, accidence

عرض البلد [arzolbalad] *geography* 1 latitude 2 parallel

عرض بیگی [arzbeegi] *historical* chief of an office for receiving complaints of the populace (attached to a court)

عرضحال [arzehaal] complaint; petition; application

عرضه [arza] 1 statement of a case or of a matter, report 2 *commercial* supply (of goods, of output)
- کردن - 1 to set forth (a case, a matter), to present (for review, for consideration) 2 *commercial* to offer (goods)

عرف [orf] 1 (opposite of شرع) common law, civil law 2 custom

عرفان [erfan] 1 knowledge; wisdom 2 enlightenment 3 *literary* mysticism, knowledge of God

عرفی [orfi] (opposite of شرعی) based on civil law; common, secular, lay

عرق [araq] 1 sweat; perspiration 2 product of distillation; extract ♦ گلاب - rose water
- کردن - *colloquial* 1 to sweat, to perspire, to be covered with sweat or with perspiration 2 to break out in a sweat in embarrassment, to turn a bright red (from shame)

عرق [erq] 1 blood vessel; vein 2 (also - ونژاد) family, kin, clan, tribe; lineage, extraction

عرق چین [araqchin] woman's light hat or skullcap

عرق گیر [araqgir] sweat cloth (laid under a saddle)

عروج [oruj] *literary* 1 ascension (to the pinnacle of something) 2 flourishing, heyday (e.g., of power, might); zenith (of fame, etc.)

عروس [arus] 1 fiancée; bride 2 daughter-in-law, sister-in-law
- هزار داماد - *metaphysical* this fickle world

عروس خیل [aruskheel] (and) عروس خیلی [aruskheli] 1 the persons who present the bride (at a wedding) 2 relatives of the bride

عروسی [arusi] 1 wedding banquet, wedding 2 marriage
- کردن - 1 to hold a wedding 2 to marry, to take a wife; to take a husband

عروض [aruz] *literary* 1 aruz (a system of Arabic-Persian versification) 2 (also - عام) prosody, metrics 3 final foot of the first line of verse (مصراع ☞)

عریان [oryaan] bared, exposed, stripped bare, naked, nude, bare

عریض [ariz] wide, broad; vast

عریضه [ariza] (*plural* عرایض [araayez]) 1 written application, application 2 *polite epistolary* [my] humble epistle, my humble letter

عز [azz] (and) ezz *literary* almighty, omnipotent, all-powerful (epithet of Allah) ♦ عز و جل - Allah, almighty and great

عزا [azaa] mourning; grieving for a deceased

عزاداری [azaadaari] observing [a period of] mourning; funeral ceremony

عزت [ezzat] 1 honor, dignity 2 esteem, respect ♦ جان - self-respect
- دادن - to do honor [to] to render homage [to], to extol, to exalt
- کردن - to respect, to esteem, to have a high opinion [of]

عزت النفس [ezzatonnafs] self-respect; feeling of honor

عزت مند [ezzatmand] (and) عزتناک [ezzatnak] worthy, respected, honorable, respectable, venerable

عزم [ázem] intention, plan; decision
- کردن - to intend, to plan, to contemplate (doing something); to make a decision ♦ سفر کردن - to intend to travel

عزیز [aziz] 1.1 dear ♦ برادر - dear brother 1.2 respected ♦ دوست - respected friend 2.1 close friend, relative 2.2 influential person, prestigious person; a notable

عزیز داری [azizdaari] relationship through marriage; kindred relationships

عزیمت [azimat] 1 departure 2 ☞ عزم
- کردن - to depart; to set out (for somewhere)

عساکر [asaaker] *plural of* عسکر

عسکر [askar] 1 army 2 (*plural* عساکر [asaker]) warrior, fighting man, soldier

عسکری [askari] 1 military, army 2.1 (also - خدمت) military service 2.2 serviceman
- به - رفتن to go off to military service

عسل [asal] honey

عسلی [asali]
- تخم – soft-boiled egg

عشاق [oshshaaq] *plural of* عاشق

عشرت [eshrat] pleasure, amusement, entertainment, diversion; merry pastime

عشق [eshq] 1 love, passion 2 bent, inclination; attraction, yearning (for something)

عشق پیچان [eshqpeechaan] *botany* (also - گل) bindweed, convolvulus

عشوه گری [eshwagari] coquetry, flirting

عصا [asaa] stick, cane, walking stick
- پیری - son, support in old age

عصاره [osaara] 1 squeezed out juice, extract 2 squeezings, husks (e.g., of grapes)
- معدوی - gastric juice

عصب [asab] (*plural* اعصاب [a'saab]) nerve ♦ عرق النسا - sciatic nerve

عصبانی [asabaani] 1 nervous, irritable 2 agitated; angry
- شدن - 1 to be nervous, to feel nervous; to be agitated, upset, uneasy 2 to be angry, to lose one's temper, to fly into a rage

عصبانیت [asabaaniyat] nervousness, irritability

عصبی [asabi] 1 nervous, neural, mental, psychological ♦ - مرضهای nervous diseases or illnesses 2 ☞ عصبانی

عصر [áser] 1 century, era, epoch 2 afternoon 3 afternoon prayer

عصری [asri] contemporary, modern ♦ هوتل - modern hotel
- نمودن - to modernize

عصمت [esmat] 1 chastity, purity 2 *feminine proper name* Esmat

عصیان [esyaan] 1 mutiny, revolt, riot; insubordination 2 sin, transgression

عضلات [azalaat (and) azolaat] 1 *plural of* عضله 2 musculature, muscles

عضله [azala (and) azola] (*plural* عضلات [azalat]) *anatomy* muscle

عضو [ózw] (*plural* اعضاء [a'zaa]) 1 *anatomy* part of the body, organ, member, limb; extremity 2 member, participant (in something)

عضوی [ozwi] organic ♦ مواد - organic matter, organic substances

ع

عضویت [ozwiyat] 1 organism, living organism 2 membership
• داشتن - to be a member (of an organization, of the party, etc.)

عطاء [ataa] gift giving; gift, present
• کردن - to give [as a gift], to make a present [of]

عطار [attaar] 1 chandler; vendor of spices and medicines 2 perfumer, vendor of perfumes

عطاری [attaari] (also-دکان) shop of spices and medicines; perfume shop or store

عطر [áter (and) éter] 1 aroma, fragrance 2 perfume

عطر کشی [aterkashi] perfumery

عطریات [atriyaat] aromatic substances; volatile oils; perfume

عطسه [atsa] sneezing, sneeze
• زدن (کردن) - to sneeze

عطف [atf]¹ 1 connecting, joining, linking (e.g., of words in a sentence)
• کلمه – grammar conjunction
• واو اول – grammar connecting novel

عطف [atf]² literary turning (of the attention); disposition, inclination
• کردن - to turn [one's] attention [toward]; to show a disposition [for]

عظمت [azamat] 1 grandeur; power, might 2 majesty; splendor, magnificence

عظمی [ozmaa]
• صدارت – 1 post of prime minister 2 office of the prime minister

عظیم [azim] 1 great; mighty, powerful ♦ دول - the great powers 2 majestic; grand, grandiose

عفت [effat] bashfulness, shyness, modesty

عفریت [efrit] genie, demon, evil spirit

عف عف [af-af]
• کردن - to bark, to yelp, to yap

عفو [áfw] 1 pardon, apology; excuse 2 pardon, forgiveness, amnesty ♦ کنید - Excuse [me]! [I am] sorry!

عفونیت [ofunat] 1 decay, rotting, decomposition 2 infection

عفونی [ofuni] infectious, contagious; infected, contaminated ♦ ادویه ضد - disinfectants

عقاب [aqaab] eagle

عقاید [aqaayed] plural of عقیده

عقب [aqab] 1 rear part (of something); military rear 2 back adjective, rear adjective, located behind 3 denominative preposition (also - (به) از) beyond, behind; after ♦ کاروان می رفت (از) - He walked [following] behind the caravan.
• ماندن - to fall behind, to lag, to be left behind
• نشاندن - to drive back, to hurl back
• نشستن - to step back, to retreat

عقب مانی [aqbmaani] backwardness, lag

عقب نشینی [aqbneshini] retreat, withdrawal
• کردن - to retreat, to withdraw

عقد [aqd] 1 concluding, conclusion (of a treaty, of a contract) 2 concluding a marriage, wedding ♦ نکاح - marriage contract
• کردن - to conclude (an agreement, a treaty, a contract, a marriage)
• نکاح درآمد به – to enter into a legal marriage

عقدات [aqadaat] anatomy radices of the lungs (literally, roots of the lungs; sing radix pulmonis)

عقده [oqda] 1 knot, node, junction 2 (also -عصبی) ganglion 3 difficulty, obstacle, impediment ♦ دل - melancholy, depression, weight or burden on the heart

عقرب [aqrab] 1 scorpion 2 astronomy scorpio (zodiacal constellation) 3 Aqrab (eighth month of the Afghan year; corresponds to October-November)

عقربک [aqrabak] 1 hand of a watch or clock 2 regional structure of branches and stones (to strengthen the banks of rivers)

عقل [áqel] mind; reason; intellect ♦ سلیم - sense, wisdom; common sense
• نی جان در عذاب - proverb When one does not have a mind, it is nothing but trouble for the body.
• از - برآمدن colloquial to take leave of one's senses
• خام - colloquial rash step, blunder

عقوبت [oqubat] 1 punishment, penalty 2 torture, torment

عقیدت [aqidat] (and) عقیده [aqida] (plural عقاید [aqaayed]) 1 belief, conviction 2 view, opinion ♦ من به – in my opinion
• داشتن (به) 1 to believe (in something) 2 to think, to suppose

عقیده مند [aqidamand] 1 believing (in something) 2 convinced, believing

عقیم [aqim] 1 barren, not providing offspring 2 futile, ineffectual, unsuccessful

عکاس [akkaas] photographer

عکاسی [akaasi] (also - عکاسی) acacia

عکاسی [akkaasi] 1 profession of a photographer, occupation of photographer 2 عکس گیری ☞

عکس [aks] 1 reflection ♦ صدا - echo 2 image, picture, photograph ♦ سیاه وسفید - black and white photograph 3 opposition, contrast; opposite (to something) ♦ به - on the contrary ◊ به –گفته شما in contrast to what you said
• گرفتن - to photograph

عکس العمل [aksolamal] 1 reaction, reacting 2 reflex 3 opposition, counteraction; resistance ♦ ملی - people's resistance, popular resistance

عکس گیری [aksgiri] photographing, shooting (a photograph)

عکه [akka] magpie

علاج [elaaj] 1 medicine, remedy 2 way out (of a situation)
• کردن - 1 to treat, to cure 2 to find a way out (of a situation)

علاقه [alaaqa (and) elaaqa]¹ (plural علایق [alayeq]) 1 tie, bond, ties, relations ♦ دوستی - friendly relations, bonds of friendship 2 interest, inclination, bent
• داشتن - to maintain ties (تا); to have a relationship
• (and)نشان دادن گرفتن - to show interest, to show an inclination

علاقه [alaaqa]² administrative region, district, rural district

علاقه دار [alaaqadar] alaqadar, head man of a district or of a rural district (who also carries out police functions)

علاقه داری [alaaqadaari] headquarters of a district or a rural district, police station of a district or rural district

علاقه مند [alaaqamand] 1.1 interested (in something) 1.2 attached, devoted 2.1 lover, fan, enthusiast 2.2 subscriber

علالت [alaalat] literary ill health, indisposition; ailment

علامت [alaamat] (and) علامه [alaama] (plural علامات [alaamat] (and) علایم [alaayem]) 1 sign, symbol ♦ تصنیف رتبه مشخصه – military badge of rank, insignia 2 signal, indicator ♦

214

- conventional sign 3 sign, indication, symbol; omen ♦ فارقه - *juridical* special criterion

علامه‌گزاری [alaamagozaari] placing marks or signs; marking out, marking

علانیه [alaaniya] ☞ علنی

علاوتاً [elaawatan] besides, moreover

علاوه [elaawa] addition, supplement ♦ ازاین- (and)براین- moreover, in addition to that ◊ ازمقدار معین above the required amount or quantity

• - کردن to add [to], to supplement

علایق [alaayeq] *plural of* علاقه

علایم [alaayem] (*plural of* علامت)

• - ترافیکی traffic signals; road signs

علت [ellat] (*plural* علل [elal]) 1 illness, ailment, malady, indisposition 2 flaw, defect 3 cause, grounds ♦ به -... because [of]

• - حروف *grammar* weak radicals (in Arabic grammar)

علف [alaf] 1 grass 2 forage, feed

علفچر [alafchar] 1 pasture, meadow 2 tax on pasturage

علف دروی [alafdarawi] mowing; hay mowing

علل [elal] *plural of* علت

علم [alam] banner, flag; standard

علم [élem] 1 (*plural* علوم [olum]) science, scientific discipline ♦ ادب - philology, history of literature 2 knowledge, information (about something)

علم و خبر - ☞ وخبر

• - آوردن to find out, to obtain information, to ascertain

• - داشتن *colloquial* to know, to have information (about something) ♦ ما از مریض بودن او – نداریم We didn't know that he was sick.

علماء [olamaa] *plural of* عالم 2

علم الاجتماع [elmolejtemaa'] social science, sociology

علم آوری [elmaawari] acquaintance (with something); ascertainment (of something)

علم بردار [alambardaar] standard-bearer

علم وخبر [elmokhabar] 1 customs declaration 2 *military* (also - ورق) efficiency

علمی [elmi] related to science; scientific ♦ - درجه scholarly degree ◊ فعالیت - scientific activity

علنی [alani] 1 open, public ♦ بصورت - publicly, openly 2 obvious, blunt

علوفه [olufa] *military* forage, fodder; provisions

علوم [olum] (*plural of* علم)

• پوهنحی – - physics-mathematics department or faculty

علی [ali] 1 *literary* high, notable, distinguished, noble 2.1 *masculine proper name* Ali 2.2 (also-حضرت) the Imam Ali

علیا [olyaa] 1 upper, located at the source of a river 2 (alsoدریا -) the upper reaches of a river

علی آباد [aliaabaad] Aliabad (region of Kabul where the university is located)

علیاحضرت [olyaahazrat] her majesty (about the wife of a shah, about a queen)

علی الترتیب [alattartib] one after another, in succession

علیت [elliyat] *philosophical* causality ♦ ارتباط - causal relationship

علیحده [alaa (h) edda] 1 separate 2 separately

علیکم السلام [alaykom-assalaam] Hello to you also! / Peace be with you also! (answer to a greeting)

علیل [alil] 1 sick; sickly, infirm, feeble 2 maimed, crippled

علیه 1 [aliya] ☞ علی

• دولت-افغانستان *diplomatic* the high Afghan state, the imperial Afghan state

علیه [alayh] (also-بر) against *denominative preposition* ♦ استبداد - against despotism

علیه الرحمه [alayhorrahma] *religion* May the grace of God be with him. (about a deceased saint)

علیه السلام [alayhossalaam] *religion* May he have peace and tranquility. (upon mention of the name of a caliph)

عمارت [emaarat] 1 building, structure 2 construction, organization of public services and amenities

• - کردن to build, to erect a building

عماری [emaari] covered seat (for riding on an elephant), palanquin

عمال [ommaal] *plural of* عامل 1

عمامه [ammaama] turban

عمداً [ámdan] intentionally, deliberately

عمده [omda] 1 chief *adjective*, main ♦ - جمله *grammar* main clause 2 essence, the main thing

عمده فروشی [omdaforoshi] wholesale trade

عمر [ómer] 1 life, human lifetime ♦ به - خود all one's life; in one's lifetime 2 age, years

• خدا - بدهد *colloquial* God grant [them] long life! (usually about children)

• کردن - to live (of a certain age)

• چند – کرده؟ How old is he?

• خودرا خورده - *colloquial* to have had one's day

• نوح - longevity (literally Noah's lifetime)

عمران [omraan] 1 amenities and comforts (of a city, of a country) the state of being well managed or well kept (of a city, of a country) 2 state of being well tilled (of land)

عمرانات [omraanaat] (*plural of* عمران)

• - و شهرسازی city construction and organization of public services and amenities

عمق [omq] (*plural* اعماق [a'maq]) 1 depth 2 bottom (of the sea, of a well)

عمل [amal] (*plural* اعمال [a'maal]) 1 deed; act, work 2 practice ♦ - ازروی according to practice 3 action; process ♦ احتراق - process of combustion ◊ جراحی - surgical operation 4 *mathematical* operation 5 *biology* function 6 use of narcotics, drug addiction

• - کردن 1 to work, to act; to function 2 *medicine* to operate 3 to function (about the stomach)

عملاً [a'malan] practically, in fact

عمل کرد [amalkard] *agriculture* actual yield or harvest (taken from a given sector) 2 actual income

عمل کردی [amalkardi] 1 *agriculture* established size of tax (ensuing from the actual harvest) 2 rate of income

عمله [amala] 1 *plural of* عامل 2 2 service personnel

• - کانکنی miners

عملی [amali] *military* 1.1 practical ♦ درس - practical training; field training 1.2 actual, actually feasible, feasible in fact 2 smoker (of opium), narcotic addict

• - کردن to realize, to accomplish, to implement, to put into practice

عملیات [amaliyat] (and) عملیه [amaliya] action; operation

• - کردن *medicine* to operate

عمو [amu] uncle (father's brother)

عمودی [amudi] 1 vertical; plumb 2 perpendicular

ع

عموم [omum] 1 all, everything; everyone, everybody ♦ - خلق all the people, the entire people 2 ☞ عمومی
• بصورت - in general outlines; in a geneal form
عموماً [omúman] generally, in general; on the whole
عمومی [omumi] 1 common, general ♦ کتب خانه - public library ◊ مجلس - general meeting 2 chief, general ♦ سامبله - the general assembly ◊ سرک - highway
عمومیات [omumiyaat] common attitudes or positions; public or common areas; general opinion; testimonial (about something)
عمومیت [omumiyat]
• داشتن - to be prevalent, to be widespread; to be generally accepted, to be practiced
عمه [amma] aunt (brother's sister)
عمیق [amiq] literally and figuratively deep
• شدن - 1 to become deep to deepen 2 to delve deeply [into]; to probe deeply (into something)
عناصر [anaaser] plural of عنصر
عنصر in entry چهار عنصر ☞ - اربعه •
عنان [enaan] 1 bridle, reins 2 the reins (of govenment, etc.)
• اختیار - 1 power, authority (over somebody or something) 2 self-control, self-mastery, liberty
عنان گسیخته [enaangoseekhta] 1 having become disobedient; having taken the bit between one's teeth 2 unrestrained, impetuous, unbridled
عناوین [anaawin] plural of عنوان
عنایت [enaayat] favor, attention; consideration; goodwill
عنبر [á'mbar] 1 ambergris fragrance or perfume 2 locks, curls, or tresses of a sweetheart
عنبر آگین [abraagin] sweet-smelling, fragrant, perfumed, aromatic
عندلیب [andaleeb] blackbird (songbird)
عنصر [onsor] (plural عناصر [anaaser]) 1 chemistry element 2 primary element, element [of nature] ♦ چهار - the four elements, the four primary elements of nature (water, land, wind, fire) 3 element, representative (about a person)
عنعنوی [an'anawi] traditional
عنعنه [an'ana] tradition
عنقریب [anqarib] soon, in the near future ♦ زمستان - است colloquial Winter is at hand. / Winter is just around the corner.
عنوان [onwan] (plural عناوین [anaawin]) 1 heading, headline; name, title ♦ تحت - under the name [of] 2 address
• به ... - under the guise [of]; under the pretext [of]
عوارض [awaarez] 1 plural of عارضه 2 hindrances, impediments, obstacles ♦ تخنیکی - technical malfunctions 3 (also طبیعی -) [natural] features (of the terrain); relief ♦ جوی - geology weathering (wind) erosion
عواطف [awaatef] plural of عاطفه
عواقب [awaaqeb] plural of عاقبت
عوام [awaam] people, the people, common people, the common people ♦ مجلس - the House of Commons
عوامل [awaamel] plural of عامل 3
عودت [awdat] literary 1 return, restitution 2 renewal, resumption
عوض [ewaz] barter, substitution; exchange ♦ به - in exchange for, instead of
• کردن - to substitute, to replace; to exchange, to barter

عوضی [ewazi] 1 substitution, replacement 2 colloquial deputy 3 historical person hired to undergo [someone else's] military service
عهد [ahd] 1 (plural عهود [ohud]) 1 promise, obligation 2 treaty, alliance
• عهد وپیمان ☞ - وپیمان
• کردن - to promise, to make a commitment
عهد [ahd] 2 (plural عهود [ohud]) time, period, epoch
عهد شکن [ahdshekan] violating an oath, breaking a vow; treacherous, perfidious
عهد شکنی [ahdshekani] nonfulfillment of an oath or a vow; treachery, perfidy
عهد وپیمان [ahdopaymaan] mutual commitment; vow of faithfulness or fidelity (from one person to another)
عهده [ohda] 1 duty, debt; responsibility 2 position, post; service, work
• از - بدر شدن to cope with one's duties, with one's business
عهده دار [ohdadaar] 1 official, employee; office worker; functionary; bureaucrat 2 obscure noncommissioned officer
• (از) بودن - to carry out the functions (of); to perform duties
عهده داری [ohdadaari] performing duties; service, work; government service
عهود [ohud] plural of عهد 1, 2
عیاش [ayaash] fast liver, debauchee; man who enjoys life
عیاشی [ayaashi] merry pastime; leading a fast or dissipated life
عیال [ayaal] 1 family (wife, children) 2 wife ♦ واطفال - wife and children
عیان [ayaan] 1 evident, clear; obvious 2 evidently, clearly; obviously
عیب [ayb] (plural عیوب [oyub]) deficiency, shortcoming, flaw; defect
عیب گویی [aybgoyi] malignant gossip, detraction; slander, aspersion
عید [id] (plural عیاد [ayaad]) holiday, festive occasion, festival
عیدالفطر [idolfeeter] ☞ عید رمضان in entry رمضان
عیدی [idi] 1 money and gifts (distributed on the occasion of a holiday) 2 written holiday greeting (usually in rhyme)
عیسوی [isawi] 1.1 Christian 1.2 of the Christian era, AD ♦ - سنه ۱۹۷۵ the year 1975 of the Christian era, 1975 AD 2 a Christian
عیسی [isaa] 1 (also مسیح -) Jesus Christ 2 masculine proper name Isa
عیش [aysh] merriment, gladness, joy; enjoyment of life ♦ وعشرت - a merry; dissipated life
عین [ayn] 1 name of the letter ع
عین [ayn] 2 literary 1 eye 2 source, spring 3 essence; main point
• در - زمان 1 at this very time 2 at the same time
عیناً [aynan] 1 exactly, precisely, accurately; just 2 really, genuinely
عینک [aynak] (eye) glasses
• زدن - to put on glasses; to wear glasses
• زانو - anatomy kneecap, patella
عینی [ayni] literary philosophical 1 own, of the same parents ♦ برادر - [one's] own brother 2 similar, identical 3 graphic; obvious; visible, apparent 4 objective ♦ حقیقت - objective reality
عیوب [oyub] plural of عیب

غ
22nd letter of the Dari alphabet

غار [ghaar] 1 cave, cavern, grotto 2 burrow, hole, den, lair 3 (also -مورچه) anthill 4 nest (of wasps, hornets)

غارت [ghaarat] robbery, pillage; brigandage ♦ وتاراج - destruction, devastation
- کردن - to rob, to sack, to plunder, to commit robbery, to destroy, to ravage, to ruin, to bring to ruin

غارتگر [ghaaratgar] thief, robber, brigand

غاز [ghaaz] goose; geese

غازدار [ghaazadaar] gas *adjective*; containing gas ♦ بم های - gas bombs

غازی [ghaazi] [1] *religion* participant in a holy war, fighter for Islam 2 hero; conqueror, victor 3 *historical* ghazi (honorary title bestowed for military services)

غازی [ghaazi] [2] *adjective* gas

غاصب [ghaaseb] aggressor, invader; usurper

غاصبانه [ghaasebana] predatory; aggressive; forcible, violent

غافل [ghaafel] 1 being in the dark, not noticing anything 2 happy-go-lucky, lighthearted, carefree
- از چیزی - بودن [1] not to know 2 not to notice; not to bear [something] in mind, to lose sight [of]

غافلانه [ghaafelaana] 1 not knowing, not suspecting 2 lightheartedly, in a carefree manner 3 through lack of knowledge, through ignorance

غافلی [ghaafeli] 1 lack of knowledge, ignorance 2 carelessness, lightheartedness 3 sluggishness, irresponsibility

غالب [ghaaleb]
- آمدن(شدن) - 1 to get the upper hand, to overcome, to overpower, to conquer 2 to surpass, to prevail [over]

غالباً [ghaaleban] 1 fully possible, very likely 2 mostly, for the most part, mainly

غالمغال [ghaalmaghaal] noise, din, racket, uproar; cry, shout
- کردن - to make noise, to cry, shout, to raise a ruckus

غرور [ghorur] pride, arrogance

غره [ghorra] 1 first day of the lunar month 2 new moon

غری [ghari] 1 libertinism, dissipation, lewdness, depravity 2 poor conduct, hooliganism

غریب [gharib] 1.1 poor, needy; indigent ♦ حلق - the poor, the poor people 1.2 without kith or kin, strange, foreign ♦ ما اینجا هستیم - We are strangers/foreigners here. 1.3 *literary* (also - عجیب و) astonishing, amazing; strange, unusual 2 (*plural* غربا [ghorabaa] (and) غریبان [gharibaan]) 2.1 a poor person, beggar 2.2 stranger, alien, foreigner

غریب خانه [gharibkhaana] *polite* my humble home, my miserable dwelling

غریب کار [gharibkaar] 1 peasant going off to seasonal work, seasonal migratory worker 2 *colloquial* artisan, craftsman

غریب کاری [gharibkaari] seasonal work, seasonal trade, seasonal business

غریبی [gharibi] 1 poverty, need 2 labor for hire 3 ☞ غریب 4 کاری wandering far from one's homeland

غریدن [ghor (r) idan] 1 to thunder, to rumble 2 to roar, to bellow, to howl (about an animal)

غریزه [ghariza] (*plural* غرایز [gharaayez]) 1 natural inclination 2 instinct

غریزی [gharizi] 1 natural, innate 2 instinctive

غزال [ghezaal (and) ghazaal] 1 gazelle, chamois; young she-goat 2 *poetic* a graceful, delicate girl 3 *feminine proper name* Ghezal

غزل [ghazal] 1 ghazal (a type of lyric poem) 2 lyric song
- سرودن(and) خواندن - 1 to recite ghazals, to compose ghazals 2 to sing

غزل خوان [ghazalkhaan] 1 poet who composes ghazals 2 singer who sings about love

غزلیات [ghazaliyaat] collection of ghazals (by some author)

غزنوی [ghaznawi] 1 *historical* Ghaznavid, pertaining to the dynasty of the Ghaznavids 2 ☞ غزنیچی

غزنیچی [ghaznichi] 1 Ghazni *adjective* ♦ پوستین - ghazni sheepskin coat 2 Ghazniite, inhabitant of Ghazni

غژدی [ghezhdi] ghejdi, marquee, tent of Afghan nomads (made of coarse woolen cloth of black color)

غژغژ [ghezhghezh] wheezing, speaking huskily or hoarsely, wheeze

غژگاو [ghazhgaaw] yak

غسل [ghósol] ablution (of the body), bathing, washing
- کردن - 1 to perform ablution 2 to bathe, to wash oneself

غسل خانه [ghosolkhaana] bathroom, bathhouse

غشو [ghashaw] currycomb (for currying horses)

غصب [ghasb] appropriation, seizure, capture, usurpation

غصه [ghossa] melancholy, depression, grief, sorrow
- خوردن - to be melancholy, to be sad, to mourn, to lament

غضب [ghazab] anger, wrath, malice, fury, rage ♦ با - angrily, with malice, irritatedly
- به آمدن - to get angry [at], to become furious, to go into a rage

غضبناک [ghazabnaak] angered, incensed; furious

غضروف [ghozrof] *anatomy* cartilage

غف غف [ghafghaf] ☞ غف غف

غفلت [ghaflat] 1 carelessness, negligence 2 unconcern, lightheartedness
- خواب – stagnation, backwardness

غلات [ghallaat] *plural of* غله

غلاف [ghelaaf] 1 scabbard sheath (of a saber, etc.) 2 case; cover ♦ ماشیندار – jacket, barrel jacket of a machine gun 3 blanket cover, quilt cover 4 envelope

غلام [gholaam] 1 slave 2 servant 3 *epistolary* [your] obedient servant 4 *cards* jack 5 *masculine proper name* Gholam

غلام گردش [gholaamgardesh] *obscure* 1 wall, partition (separating the inner part of a courtyard from the entrance) 2 servants' quarters

غلامی [gholaami] slavery, bondage

غلبه [ghalaba] victory
- کردن - to conquer, to defeat, to overcome

غلبیل [ghalbeel] 1 sieve 2 *technical* screen, sifter
- کردن - to sift
- آب کردن - *colloquial* to pass water through a sieve (to beat the air)

غلبیل غلبیل [ghalbeel-ghalbeel] holey, full of holes, riddled
- کردن - to riddle, to perforate, to cover with holes

غلت [ghalt] present tense stem of verb غلتیدن
- زدن - 1 to roll, to roll over 2 to run, to flow (about water)
- خود را دادن - *colloquial* to escape (somebody), to give (somebody) the slip; to shirk (something)

غلتاندن [ghaltaandan] 1 to demolish (e.g., a house); to pull down 2 to roll, to turn over

غلتک [ghaltak] 1 reel, bobbin spool; cylinder, roller (on which something is wound) 2 *colloquial* cradle

غلتیدن [ghaltidan] 1 *intransitive* to roll, to turn over 2 *intransitive* to crumble, to cave in, to collapse ♦ دیوار غلتید The wall collapsed.

• ز پهلو به پهلو to toss and turn from side to side (while sleeping)

غلجی [ghelji] Ghilzais; Ghilzai (tribe)

غلچه [ghalcha] *colloquial* 1 Galchas (general name of inhabitants of the Pamirs) 2 coarse person, uncultured person; country bumpkin

غلط [ghalat] (*plural* اغلاط [aghalaat]) 1 erroneous, incorrect, wrong; false 2.1 mistake; slip, blunder ♦ به - by mistake 2.2 untruth, falsehood, lie ♦ این - است It is not true.

• دادن - to lead into error, to delude, to deceive, to cheat, to trick, to swindle
• کردن - to err, to make a mistake, to commit a blunder
• به - رفتن to be mistaken, to err

غلط فهمی [ghalatfahmi] misunderstanding; lack of understanding; error; delusion

غلط نامه [ghalatnaama] list of misprints, errata (in a book)

غلطی [ghalati] 1 mistake, slip, blunder 2 slip of the pen, misprint

غله [ghalla] (*plural* غلات [ghallaat] (and) غله جات [ghallajaat]) 1 bread grain (wheat, rye) 2 grain of cereals (barley, millet, etc.) 3 cereals

غله باب [ghallabaab] 1 grains; grain 2 cereals

غله پاک [ghallapaak] (also - ماشین) winnowing machine, winnower

غله خانه [ghallakhaana] granary for storing grain; threshing barn

غله گی [ghallagi] *colloquial* 1 *adjective* grain, bread 2 *adverb* by means of grain, with grain, bread; in kind (about a tax)

غلیظ [ghaliz] 1 thick, dense; compact; glutinous; viscous 2 coarse, rough; unpleasant, disagreeable

غم [gham] *obscure* 1 grief, sorrow, anguish 2 thought, anxiety, concern, care ♦ غم اولاد concern for children ◊ غم وطن thought for the homeland ◊ غم نداری بز بخره *proverb* If you have no cares, buy a goat. 3 tax, duty

• غم خوردن to grieve, to sorrow ♦ غم مخور Don't grieve! / Don't sorrow!
• غم دادن *obscure* to pay a tax, to pay a duty
• غم کسی یا چیزی را خوردن 1 to grieve for somebody or something 2 to look (after somebody or something), to care (for somebody or something) ♦ برادرم غم شانرا خورده است My brother already took care of them.
• به غم خود بودن to think one's own thoughts; to be left with one's cares

غم آگین [ghamaagin] (and) غم انگیز [ghamangeez] sorrowful, sad ♦ آواز - mournful voice

غمبر [ghambor] cooing of a pigeon, dove)

• زدن - to coo

غمخوار [ghamkhaar] comforter, consoler; defender, intercessor, soul mate ♦ ما اینجا - نداریم We have no one to whom to tell of our grief.

غمخواری [ghamkhaari] 1 concern, care 2 sympathy, compassion

غمخور [ghamkhor] ☞ غمخوار ر

غمزده [ghamzada] crushed by grief, brokenhearted, unhappy, miserable

غمشریک [ghamsharik] 1 sharing (somebody's) grief, sympathizing 2 a friend who helps in time of trouble

غمغم [ghom ghom] 1 muttering, mumbling, indistinct grumbling 2 babble (of a baby beginning to talk)

• - کردن 1 to grumble, to mumble 2 to babble (about a baby)

غمکش [ghamkash] patiently bearing misfortune and adversity

• حسن - *colloquial* the good soul Hasan (about a person who, forgetting about himself, takes care of others)

غمگین [ghamgin] grieving, mourning, being sad, being melancholy; sad, dismal, despondent

غنایم [ghanaayem] *plural of* غنیمت

غنایی [ghenaayi] 1 song *adjective*, musical 2 lyric ♦ شعر - lyric poetry

غنچه [ghoncha] 1 *botany* bud, ovary ♦ گل - flower bud; 2 little mouth (of a woman, of a child)

• - ناشکفته 1 unopened bud 2 *poetic* girl; virgin
• - بستن کردن to give off buds, to bud

غندل [ghondal] 1 tarantula 2 solpugid (arachnid)

غندمشر [ghondmésher] *obscure* colonel ♦ دوم - lieutenant colonel

غندی [ghondi] small hill; knoll; hillock

غنگ [ghang (and) gheng] peal, ringing, clank, clang (usually of metal objects)

غنودن [ghonudan] *literary* 1 to take one's rest, to rest 2 to sleep, to doze, to slumber

غنی [ghani] 1.1 rich, well-to-do 1.2 possessing (something) in abundance 2.1 (*plural* اغنیاء [aghniyaa]) rich man 2.2 *masculine proper name* Ghani

غنیمت [ghanimat] (*plural* غنایم [ghanaayem]) 1 war booty, spoils of war, trophy 2 boon; advantage ♦ وقت - است Time is a great boon/blessing.

• فرصت (وقت) را – شمردن (داشتن) Don't miss the opportunity/chance. / Make use of the moment.

غواض [ghawwaas] 1 diver ♦ دریشی- diving suit 2 (bos.) pearl diver

غور [ghawr] 1 penetration (into the essence), attention 2 study, examination, scrutiny ♦ ومطالعه - consideration and study (of a matter, etc.)

• (در،به) - کردن 2 to go deep (into), to delve (into) to study, to examine, to scrutinize
• تحت - بودن to be studied, to be under consideration

غور [ghor] *historical* Ghor, Ghur (region in northern Afghanistan)

غوررسی [ghawrrasi] 1 elucidation, investigation examination (of a case) 2 study, consideration (of complaint, etc.)

غوره [ghora] unripe fruit, green fruit (used for seasoning meat dishes) ♦ آلوچه - green cherry plum ◊ آب - juice of unripe fruit; sour condiment

غوری [ghuri] large dish (for pilaf, fruit, etc.)

غوزه [ghoza] 1 pod (of cotton) 2 cocoon (of a silkworm) 3 head (of a poppy) 4 pinecone

• آب - water bubbles

218

غوطه [ghota]
- خوردن - to plunge [into], to be immersed [in]
- زدن - to dive
- کردن - to dip, to immerse

غوغا [ghawghaa] noise, din, uproar, hubbub, cry, shout, yell

غول [ghol] *colloquial* 1 demon, evil spirit 2 giant *noun* 3 uncouth person, coarse person, uncultured person, blockhead ♦ استی؟ - Are you blockheaded?, Don't you know how to behave yourself at all?

غول پیکر [gholpaykar] *adjective* gigantic, giant ♦ نباتات giant plants, gigantic plants

غولک [gholak] 1 bow; catapult, slingshot 2 *rarely* earthenware money pot

غولنگ [gholeng] dried apricot (with pit)

غولنگ آب [gholengaab] (and) غولنگ او [gholengaw] compote of dried apricots

غوله [ghola] short log, block ♦ چوب - wooden block

غیاب [ghiyaab]
- در کسی - *literary* in somebody's absence, by correspondence

غیب [ghayb] 1 *religion* secret, mysterious ♦ دست hand of providence 2 absence, disappearance
- کردن - *colloquial* 1 to hide; to conceal (something) 2 to annihilate, to do away with, to kill, to murder (somebody)

غیبت [ghaybat] malignant gossip, derogation, defamation; slander
- کردن - to defame [someone] in his absence; to slander

غیچک [ghechak] ghechak (musical instrument played with a bow)

غیچکی [ghechaki] musician (who plays a ghechak; ☞غیچک); street fiddler

غیر [ghayr] 1.1 different; other 1.2 strange, foreign, alien 2 (*plural* اغیار [aghyaar]) stranger, alien 3 [ghaire] (negative prefix) ♦ غیر اقتصادی uprofitable, uneconomical
- در - آن (این) 1 otherwise 2 moreover, besides
- از - (به) *preposition* besides; with the exception [of] ♦ این بچه دیگر اولاد دارید؟ —Do you have other children besides this boy?

غیر اتصال [ghayreettesaal]
- خط - dotted line

غیر اقتصادی [ghayreeqtesaadi] unprofitable, uneconomical

غیرت [ghayrat] 1 self-respect; pride; self-esteem; از - out of pride; out of self-respect 2 zeal, zealous attitude (toward something)

غیرتمند [ghayratmand] 1 endowed with a feeling of honor; proud 2 valiant, manly 3 *obscure* (form of address to an officer in the rank of captain)

غیر حاضر [ghayrehaazer] absent; not present (for class, for work, etc.)

غیر ذی روح [ghayreziruh] *grammar* inanimate

غیر صحی [ghayresehhi] unhealthy; unhygienic; unsanitary ♦ آب و هوای - unhealthy climate ◊ شرایط - unsanitary conditions

غیر عضوی [ghayreozwi] inorganic

غیر قانونی [ghayreqaanuni] unlawful; illegal ♦ بطور - unlawfully, illegally

غیر قصدی [ghayreqasdi] 1 unpremeditated, inadvertent, unintentional, accidental 2 inadvertently; accidentally

غیر مرضی [ghayremar'i] invisible, imperceptible; unobservable

غیر مستقیم [ghayremostaqim] indirect; roundabout

غیر معیاری [ghayreme'yaari] nonstandard

غیر ممکن [ghayremomken] 1 impossible; inconceivable 2 impracticable

غیر منتظر [ghayremontazer] unexpected; sudden

غیر منسلک [ghayremonsalek]
- ممالک - nonaligned countries

غیر منقولی [ghayremanquli] (and) غیر منقول [jayremanghuli] immovable (about property)

غیر نظامی [ghayrenezaami] 1 nonmilitary; noncombat 2 civilian, peaceful; civil
- کردن - to demilitarize

غیره [ghayra]
- و - and so on, and so forth, etc.

غین [ghayn] name of the letter غ

غیور [ghayur] 1 valiant, courageous, brave 2 zealous, ardent, fervent, very passionate

ف
23rd letter of the Dari alphabet

ف abbreviation of فضیلت ماب (and) فضیلت همراه

فابریکه [faabrika] 1 factory; plant ♦ برق - electric power station ◊ حربی - war plant 2 shop (of an enterprise)

فاتح [faateh] 1 winning; conquering 2 victor; conqueror 3 *masculine proper name* Fateh

فاتحانه [faatehaana] 1 triumphal, victorious, triumphant (about something) 2 victoriously, triumphantly

فاتحه [faateha] 1 the initial sura of the Koran, fateha (recited as a prayer for a deceased) 2 (also خیر -) prayer, blessing
- خواندن - to recite the fateha (for a deceased person)
- کردن - to give a blessing, to bless
- کسی را خواندن - *colloquial* to consider somebody dead; to hold a requiem for somebody

فاتحه خوانی [faatehakhaani] a requiem, a service in a mosque for a deceased person (after a funeral)

فاتیا [faatiyaa] *colloquial* ☞ فاتحه
- رفتن - to go (to somebody's place) for a funeral repast; to go to a requiem

فاجعه [faaje'a] catastrophe; tragic event

فاجه [faaja] yawning
- کشیدن - to yawn; to stretch oneself

فاحش [faahesh] gross; flagrant ♦ غلطی - grossest error

فاحشه [faahesha] profligate woman

فارس [faars]¹ 1 Fars (a region in the south of Iran) 2 *historical* Persia

فارس [faars]² ☞ پارس²

فارسی [faarsi] 1 Persian ♦ ادبیات - Persian literature 2 (also - زبان) the Persian language, the Farsi language

فارسی زبان [faarsizabaan] 1 Persian-language ♦ ادبیات - Persian-language literature, literature in the Persian language 2 speaking in the Persian language, Persian-speaking

فارغ [faaregh] 1 freed (from business, etc.); excused (from something) 2 unoccupied, having spare time 3 free of cares
- شدن - to finish (از); to become free, to be liberated, to get out [of] (از)
- کردن - to free, to liberate (از)

فارغ التحصیل [faareghottahsil] having completed an educational institution, a graduate

فارغ بال [faareghbaal] 1 happy-go-lucky, carefree, light-hearted 2 free 3 well-to-do

فارقه [faareqa] ¹
- علامات - special signs or marks; distinctive features, distinguishing features

فارقه [faareqa] ² dash

فارم [faarm] ¹ (also زراعتی -) agricultural farm
- دولتی (حکومتی) - 1 state farm 2 sovkhoz (Soviet state farm)
- تعاونی ♦ collective farm

فارم [faarm] ² form, questionnaire, blank form

فارمسی [faarmasi] medicine pharmacy

فارنیچر [faarnichar] ☞ فرنیچر

فاریدن [faaridan] colloquial 1 to have a positive effect, to provide good results; to do, to fit, to suit ♦ هوای جلال‌آباد به من میفارد The climate of Jalalabad suits me. 2 to please, to be to one's taste, to suit one's taste

فاژه [faazha] ☞ فاجه

فاسد [faased] 1 poor; spoiled, rotted, rotten, decayed ♦ هوای - stuffy air, stifling air 2 depraved, demoralized, corrupted
- کردن - transitive 1 to spoil; to soil; to pollute 2 to corrupt, to demoralize

فاسفورس [faasforas] (and) فاسفور [faasfor] chemistry phosphorus

فاسولیه [faasoliya] 1 bean, beans 2 stewed bean pods (seasoning for a meat dish)

فاش [faash]
- شدن - to be divulged; to be disclosed
- کردن - to divulge; to disclose

فاشزم [faashézem] fascism

فاشیست [fashist] a fascist

فاشیستی [fashisti] adjective fascistic, fascist

فاصل [faasel]
- حد - boundary
- خط – demarcation line

فاصله [faasela] ¹ technical 1 space, distance 2 period of time, interval 3 clearance
- داشتن - 1 to be remote [from], to be distant [from] (از) 2 to alternate; to have an interval

فاصله [faasela] ² literary fasela (one of the forms of combining syllables in an aruz)

فاصله دار [faaseladaar] 1 widely spaced, having spaces ♦ - دندانهای widely spaced teeth 2 intermittent, broken, interrupted

فاسولیه [faasoliya] ☞ فاسولیه

فاضل [faazel] (plural فضلا [fozalaa]) 1 learned man, erudite man, scholar 2.1 learned, erudite 2.2 worthy, honored (usually about a scholar)

فاعل [faa'el] 1 acting 2.1 agent; doer 2.2 grammar subject of an action; subject ♦ مفعول و - subject and object
- اسم - 1 doer 2 present participle

فاعلی [fa'eli] 1 active, operative 2 effective
- حالت – grammar nominative case
- صفت - grammar attribute expressed by a present participle

فاقد [faaqed] literary devoid (of something); forfeited, lost ♦ nuclear-free - اسلحه اتومی ◊ nuclear-free منطقه – اسلحه اتومی - nuclear-free zone

فاقه [faaqa] 1 poverty, need 2 hunger, starvation 3 fast; fasting, abstaining from food
- کردن - 1 to live in want, to starve 2 to fast

فاقه کش [faaqakash] 1 starving, hungry 2 poor, indigent

فاقه کشی [faaqakashi] 1 fasting, hunger strike 2 mortification of the flesh (among sufis)

فاکولته [faakulta] faculty, department (at a university) ♦ ادبیات - Department of Literature

فال [faal] omen; sign, token ♦ این – خوب است This is a good sign.
- دیدن - to tell [somebody's] fortune, to tell fortunes
- به - نیک گرفتن to consider [something] a good omen

فالبین [faalbin] fortune-teller, soothsayer

فال بینک [faalbinak] ladybug

فال بینی [faalbini] fortune-telling; foretelling (fate)

فالتو [faaltu] 1.1 superfluous, unnecessary 1.2 useless, good-for-nothing, unfit 2 (also - سامان) technical spare part; spare parts

فالج [faalej] 1 paralyzed 2 colloquial ☞ فلج
- شدن - to be paralyzed

فالوده [faaluda] cooling beverage (made of fruit juices, ice, and starch)

فالیز [faaleez] melonfield; (melon) garden requiring irrigation

فالیز کاری [faaleezkaari] melon-growing

فامل [faamel] ☞ فامیل
- چای- black tea, dark tea

فامیل [faamil] 1 family 2 (also -نام) surname 3 biology family

فاناتیک [faanaatik] 1 fanatical 2 a fanatic

فانوس [faanus] 1 lantern 2 magic lantern 3 lampshade; decorated ceiling

فانه [faana] 1 wedge (of wood or iron) 2 technical spline, shim, dowel 3 bolt (e.g., door bolt)

فانی [faani] impermanent, temporal, temporary, transient, transitory ♦ دنیای - [this] transitory world

فایده [faayeda] (plural فواید [fawaayed]) 1 benefit 2 profit, gain 3 interest, advantage ♦ مگر هیچ - نیست It is absolutely useless!
- داشتن - to be useful, to be advantageous
- کردن - 1 to be of benefit 2 to help, to have an effect (e.g., about medicine)
- گرفتن - 1 to obtain benefit, to profit 2 to make use [of], to make the most [of], to take advantage [of] ♦ ازوقت - بگیرید Make use of time!

فایده مند [faayedamand] 1 useful 2 beneficial; profitable

فایر [faayr] ☞ فیر

فایق [faayeq]
- شدن - to surpass, to exceed; to overcome, to surmount

فایقیت [faayeqiyat] superiority
- داشتن - to have superiority ♦ تیم ما - داشت Our team was ahead.

فتاح [fattaah] 1 winner, victor, conqueror 2 masculine proper name Fattah

فتادن [fetaadan] ☞ افتادن

فتبال [fotbal] football, soccer

فتح [fath (and) fateh] (plural فتوح [fotuh] (and) [fotuhat]) 1 victory 2 conquest 3 success, achievement, attainment 4 masculine proper name Fateh
- کردن - 1 to defeat, to win a victory 2 to conquer, to subdue

ف

فتحه [fatha] fatha (diacritical mark ' for the short vowel "a")
فتق [fátaq] *medicine* hernia ♦ ناف - umbilical hernia
فتنه [fetna] *colloquial* 1 discord, dissension, difference 2 sedition, mutiny 3 trouble-maker, seditionary, intriguer, plotter; squabbler
فتنه انگیز [fetnaangeez] 1 sowing sedition, sowing discord; instigating, inciting 2 ☞
فتنه گر [fetnagar] instigator; provocateur; trouble-maker, seditionary
فتوا [fatwaa] ☞ فتوی
فتوح [fotuh] (and) فتوحات [fotuhaat] *plural of* فتح
فتوی [fatwaa] *religion* fatwa (decision or verdict pronounced by a mufti on some matter in accordance with the laws of the sharia)
فتیر [fatir] 1 unleavened (about dough, about bread) 2 an unleavened flatcake
فتیله [fatila] wick
فحاش [fahhaash] a foul-mouthed man
فحاشی [fahhaashi] 1 ribaldry, foul language, swearing 2 lewdness, depravity, libertinism, debauchery
فحش [fohsh] coarse word, obscenity
• کردن - to swear, to curse; to use foul language
فخر [faxr (and) fáxer] 1 pride, object of pride 2 honor; glory, fame; respect, esteem
• کردن - to be proud [of], to take pride [in] (سرراز)
فخری [fakhri] 1 fakhri (variety of grapes with large pink berries) 2 honorable; famous; glorious
فخریه [fakhriya] *literary* fakhriya (poem or part of a poem in which the poet enumerates and evaluates his merits)
فدا [fedaa] 1 sacrifice 2 ransom (for a prisoner or captive) 3 *masculine proper name* Feda
• کردن - to sacrifice
فداکار [fedaakaar] selfless, selflessly brave; selflessly devoted
فداکاری [fedaakaari] selfless bravery; selfless devotion
فدایی [fedaayi] 1 sacrificing oneself, going to [one's] death (for one's homeland, etc.) 2 warrior-hero; selfless fighter (for the homeland)
فدراسیون [federaasioon] federation ♦ فتبال - football/soccer federation
فدرال [federaal] (and) فدرالی [federali] federal; federative ♦ جمهوریت - federal republic
فدریشن [federeeshan] ☞ فدراسیون
فر [far] (verbal prefix) ♦ فرآمدن to descend, to go down
فر [far (r)] *literary* 1 nimbus 2 luster, brilliance, radiance
فر [fer (r)] *colloquial* snorting (of a horse, etc.)
• زدن - to snort (about a horse)
فرا [faraa] (verbal prefix) ♦ فراخواندن to recall ◊ فراگرفتن to become proficient [in]; to master
فراخ [faraakh] 1 large, big, vast 2 broad, spacious
• کردن (ساختن) - 1 to broaden, to make spacious 2 to open, to throw or fling open
فراخ پیشانی [faraakhpeeshaani] 1 affable, friendly, cordial 2 hospitable
فراخدل [faraakhdel] 1 broad nature 2 magnanimous, noble; good, kind
فراخدلی [faraakhdeli] magnanimity, kindness, goodness
فراخواندن [faraakhaandan] to recall (e.g., an ambassador)
فراخی [faraakhi] *technical* 1 wide open space, spaciousness, scope 2 clearance

فرار [feraar (and) faraar] 1 flight, escape 2 banishment, exile
• کردن - 1 to escape, to take flight 2 to banish, to expel (beyond the boundaries of a state); to send away
فرارسیدن [faraarasidan] to come, to set in (about time, etc.) ♦ وقت جدایی فرارسید The time has come to part.
فراری [feraari (and) faraari] 1 fugitive; refugee 2 fugitive soldier, deserter
فراز [faraaz] 1.1 summit, height; eminence 1.2 rise (in a road, etc.) 2 *denominative preposition* 2.1 (also -به (and) بر-) on (something); above (something)
• از - ♦ آب از – بند 1 through (something), over (something) ♦ آب از – بند فرو میریخت Water flowed over the dam. 2 off, from above, from the top (of something)
فراست [feraasat] wit, intellect; acumen; quickness of wit
فراش [farraash] 1 *historical* servant who spreads carpets (in a shah's chambers) 2 servant, watchman, guard (at a mosque)
فراغت [faraaghat] 1 free time, rest, leisure 2 contentment; satisfaction; serenity, tranquility ♦ خاطر - peace of mind
فراق [feraq] parting, separation
فراگرفتن [faraagereftan] 1 to grip; to seize ♦ ترس اورافر اگرفت He was seized by fear. 2 to master (knowledge, etc.)
فرآمدن [faraamadan] (present tense stem) ♦ فرا (ی) 1 to descend, to go down 2 to get out (of a bus, etc.); to dismount
• از قهر - to calm down, to cease to be angry
فراموش [faraamosh] 1 having vanished from memory, forgotten 2 فراموشی ☞
• کردن - to forget, not to remember
فراموشکار [faraamoshkaar] forgetful, absentminded; not composed
فراموشی [faraamoshi] 1 oblivion 2 loss of memory
فرامین [faraamin] *plural of* فرمان
فرانسوی [faraansawi] 1 French 2.1 a Frenchman 2.2 (also زبان-) the French language
فراوان [faraawaan] 1 abundant, plentiful ♦ بارش - abundant precipitation 2 very much, in abundance ♦ امسال میوه – است There is much fruit this year.
فراوانی [faraawaani] 1 abundance; surplus 2 large amount, great number
فرآورده [faraawarda] product ♦ زراعتی - agricultural output, agricultural production ◊ زحمت - product of labor
فراویل [faraawil] flywheel (in an automobile)
فراهم [faraaham] (verbal prefix) ♦ شدن -آمدن) 1 (also آمدن-) to come together, to gather [together], to assemble (somewhere) 2 to be concentrated, to pile up 3 to be made ready, to be provided for (about conditions, etc.) ◊ کردن - 1 to collect, to accumulate 2 to ready, to provide (e.g., conditions)
فراهم آوری [faraahamaawari] 1 gathering, collecting; accumulation 2 preparation, providing for ♦ لازمه تسهیلات - preparation of the necessary conditions
فرآ (ی) [faraa (y)] *present tense stem of* فرآمدن
فرایض [faraayez] *plural of* فریضه
فربه [farbeh] fat, plump, stout; well-fed; obese, corpulent
فرتوت [fartut] 1 old, decrepit, dilapidated; worn out 2 senile ♦ پیر - senile old man
فرجام [farjaam] bit and bridle
فرح [farah] *literary* gladness, joy, merriment, gaiety
فرح بخش [farahbakhsh] glad, joyous, joyful, gratifying

ف

فرخنده [farkhonda] 1 happy, blissful 2 blessed; flourishing, thriving, prosperous

فرد [fard] (plural افراد [afraad]) 1.1 individual, person 1.2 military soldier; fighting man, warrior; private 1.3 biology individual 1.4 literary separate couplet (usually interspersed in prose) 2.1 individual, separate 2.2 unique 2.3 odd

فردا [fardaa] tomorrow

فردوس [ferdáws] paradise, Eden; canopies of paradise

فردی [fardi] 1 individual, personal 2 separate, isolated

فرزند [farzand] son, child; offspring; descendant

فرزندی [farzandi]
● به - گرفتن to adopt

فرزین [farzin] chess queen

فرس [faras] 1 literary horse, steed 2 chess knight 3 astronomy Pegasus

فرسا(ی) [farsaa (y)] present tense stem of فرسودن (It does not form personal forms.)

فرست [ferest] present tense stem of فرستادن

فرستادن [ferestaadan] to send, to dispatch; to forward

فرستاده [ferestaada] 1 past participle of فرستادن 2 (plural گان [ferestaadagaan]) 2.1 messenger, envoy 2.2 envoy, prophet

فرستاندن [ferestaandan] ☞ فرستادن

فرسودن [farsudan] (present tense stem فرسا(ی) [farsa (y)] to wear through, to wear out)

فرسوده خاطر [farsudakhaater] sad, downcast, dispirited, despondent

فرش [farsh] 1 carpet, reversible rug (everything that they lay on the floor) 2 floor (of a room) 3 flooring, planking, roofing 4 roadway
● کردن - 1 to cover (with carpets, etc.), to spread, to lay 2 to pave, to make flooring (out of stone, etc.)
● زمردین - poetic spring meadow, emerald carpet (of grass)

فرشته [fereshta] 1 angel 2 colloquial good person, kind person; inoffensive person

فرشی [farshi]
● نباتات - trailing plants, creeping plants

فرصت [forsat] 1 occasion, chance, opportunity, favorable moment 2 time, leisure, spare time
● یافتن - 1 to find a convenient occasion, to find a suitable moment 2 to find time (for something)
● از دست دادن - to lose the opportunity, to miss the moment
● از دست رفت - The moment has been lost.

فرض [farz] obscure 1.1 assumption, supposition 1.2 religious instructions 2 obligatory, compulsory, indispensable, necessary
● کردن - to assume, to suppose

فرضاً [fárzan] 1 supposedly, presumably 2 let us suppose, let us assume; for example

فرضی [farzi] 1 supposed, assumed 2 imaginary 3 obscure prescribed by religion or morals

فرضیه [farziya] 1 supposition, assumption, hypothesis ♦ این – ثابت گردیده است This hypothesis was confirmed. 2 obscure instruction, command (of a religion)

فرط [fart] surplus, excess; extreme degree (of something)
● از ٠٠٠ - from an excess [of]; with a high degree (of something)

فرع [far' (and) fára] (plural فروع [foru']) 1 (opposite of اصل) secondary; derived (from something) 2 offshoot, branch, appendage 3 interest (on capital)

فرعاً [fár'an] 1 partially 2 in the form of interest

فرعون [fer'awn] pharaoh ♦ مومیازده - pharaoh's mummy
● - مرغ guinea fowl

فرعی [fara'i] 1 secondary ♦ انتخابات - partial elections ◊ جمله grammar subordinate clause 2 subsidiary, auxiliary ♦ - کانال drain 3 derivative, accessory; collateral ♦ - شاخه subsection, subdivision ◊ اقسام - subspecies

فرفرک [ferferak] 1 paper pinwheel 2 top (a toy) 3 colloquial featherbrain; lazy-bones, loafer

فرق [farq]¹ distinction, difference; divergence, discrepancy
● داشتن - to differ, to be different (from something) ♦ (از) ندارد - There is no difference. It's all the same.
● دادن - to distinguish

فرق [farq]² 1 (also سر -) crown, top of the head 2 top of a mountain
● کسی را به - سر خود جای دادن (شاندن) to think highly of somebody, to respect, to esteem, to revere somebody

فرقوی [ferqawi] ☞ فرقه وی

فرقه [ferqa] 1 group; sect 2 party; faction 3 military division

فرقه [farqa] technical countersink, reamer

فرقه کاری [farqakaari] technical countersinking, reaming

فرقه مش [ferqamésh (e) r] obscure general of a division

فرقه وی [ferqawi] group adjective; sectarian; factional

فرم [farm (and) ferm] firm; commercial house

فرم [form] ☞ فورم

فرما(ی) [farma (y)] present tense stem of فرمودن

فرمان [farmaan] (plural فرامین [faraamin]) 1 firman, edict, decree 2 order, command ♦ مبارک - epistolary imperial order
● دادن - 1 to issue a firman, to issue an edict, to issue a decree 2 to order; to command

فرمان بردار [farmaanbardaar] 1.1 obedient, submissive; subordinate 1.2 faithful, dutiful 2 historical vassal

فرمان روایی [farmaanrawaayi] 1 government, power, authority 2 supremacy, dominion
● کردن - 1 to govern, to wield power [over] 2 to rule [over], to exercise dominion [over]

فرمایش [farmaayesh] (plural فرمایشات [farmaayeshaat]) 1 order, instruction 2 polite words, discourse (of a collocutor) 3 order; demand 4 technical order, requisition
● کردن (دادن) - to order; to make an order

فرمایشات [farmaayeshaat] 1 plural of فرمایش 2 technical task, assignment ♦ تنظیم - planning assignment, project requirement

فرمایش دهنده [farmaayeshdehanda] customer

فرمایشی [farmaayeshi] 1 ordered, required 2 made to order

فرمودن [farmudan] (present tense stem (فرما) ی [farma(y)]) 1 to order, to command 2 polite to deign to do (something); to deign to say (something) ♦ بفرمایید If you please! / If you would! / Please!

فرموده [farmuda] 1 past participle of فرمودن 2 order, instruction

فرنگی [farangi] 1 English; European 2 an Englishman; a European

فرنی [ferni] ferni (pudding made of ground rice with milk and sugar)

فرنیچر [farnichar] furniture

فرو [foro] (verbal prefix indicating movement downward or inward) ♦ فرورفتن to settle, to sink

فروبردن [forobordan] 1 to dip, to submerge, to immerse; to plunge a stick into, to thrust into 2 to take up, to absorb 3 to swallow, to gulp down

فروخت [forokht] sale, market
- فروخت کردن to sell, to market

فروختن [forokhtan] (present tense stem فروش [foros]) to sell; to market

فروروفتگی [fororaftagi] 1 excavation, hollow, depression 2 *geology* lowering (of the ground), hollow, depression

فرورفتن [fororaftan] 1 to penetrate (into something), to go into, to pierce 2 to sink 3 to settle, to sink 4 to sit down, to set (about heavenly bodies)
- به فکر - to give oneself up to thoughts

فروری [farwari] February

فروریختن [fororeekhtan] 1 to run out, to pour out; to flow down, to trickle down; to gush out, to spout 2 to crumble, to fall, to cave in

فروزان [forozaan] 1 blazing, flaming 2 shining, glittering, sparkling

فروش [forosh] 1 *present tense stem of* فروختن 2 sale, issue, distribution (of goods)
- شدن - to be sold, to be sold off, to be sold out

فروشدن [foroshodan] 1 to go down; to descend; to get down [from] (e.g., from a tree) 2 ☞ فرورفتن 1

فروشنده [foroshenda] vendor, merchant

فروع [foru'] *plural of* فرع

فروغ [forogh] *literary* 1 light; luster, brilliance; radiance 2 indulgence, concession

فرومآندن [foromaandan] 1 to stick, to get stuck 2 to be helpless, to be unable to do (something)

فرومایه [foromaaya] 1 low, base ♦ آدم - a base person 2 contemptible, despicable, miserable

فرونشاندن [foroneshaandan] 1 to put out, to extinguish (a fire) 2 to calm, to soothe; to curb, to subdue (somebody's anger, etc.)

فرهنگ [farhang] 1 dictionary, lexicon 2 knowledge; wisdom; culture

فرهنگی [farhangi] 1 cultured, cultural ♦ همکاری - collaboration in the field of culture 2 instructive, elucidative, educational

فریاد [faryaad] 1 cry for help, call 2 complaint; weeping, crying

فریادرس [faryaadras] 1 defender, protector, patron 2 savior, redeemer (about God)

فریب [fereeb (and) fareeb] 1 *present tense stem of* فریختن 2.1 fraud, deception, lie 2.2 temptation
- خوردن - to be deceived; to give in to deception, to yield to temptation
- دادن - to deceive; to seduce

فریبایی [fereebaayi] charm; fascination ♦ این دختر آنقدر - ندارد This girl is not so fascinating.

فریبکاری [fereebkaari] 1 fraud, deception, trickery 2 lie, hypocrisy

فریبنده [fereebenda] 1 deceptive, delusive, sly 2 charming, fascinating; seductive

فریبی [fereebi] 1.1 fraudulent, roguish, mischievous 1.2 sly, cunning; hypocritical 2 *colloquial* fraud, cheat, liar, a sly person

فریز [fereez]
- ماشین – *technical* milling machine

فریزکار [fereezkaar] milling-machine operator

فریضه [fariza] (*plural* فرایض [faraayez]) 1 religious rite (fast, prayer) 2 duty, responsibility ♦ این فریضه من بود It was my duty.

فریفتن [fereeftan (and) fareeftan] (present tense stem فریب) 1 to deceive, to cheat, to swindle 2 to entice; to seduce

فریفته [fereefta] 1 *past participle of* فریفت 2 in love, enamored, charmed, taken with ♦ من – این دختر بودم I was in love with that girl.

فریکونس [ferikwens] (and) فریکونسی [ferikwensi] *physics* frequency

فریم [fereem] 1 *technical* frame, casing, housing 2 skeleton, framework 3 rim (for eyeglasses) 4 embroidery frame, lace frame

فزون [fozun] (and) فزونتر [fozuntar] 1 increasing, growing 2 superfluous, unnecessary ♦ این گپ – است These words are superfluous.
- شدن - 1 to increase, to grow 2 to become stronger, to gain strength, to intensify

فزونی [fozuni] 1 abundance, great number 2 increase, augmentation, growth

فزیک [fezik] physics ♦ ذروی (هسته یی) - nuclear physics

فزیکی [feziki] 1 physical, physics *adjective* 2 material, natural ♦ محیط - physical-geographical environment

فزیولوژی [feziolozhi] 1 physiology 2 physiological

فساد [fasaad] *colloquial* 1 spoiling, rotting, decomposition 2 decay ♦ خون - poor composition of the blood ♦ اخلاق - moral decay; depravity 3 pus 4 disorder; disturbance, sedition; discord, dissension
- کردن - 1 to injure, to harm, to hurt; to spoil; to mar, to corrupt 2 (also برپا کردن -) to strew disorder, to incite mutiny or rebellion, to sow discord or dissension; to incite dissension

فسخ [faskh] 1 abolition, abrogation, cancellation, annulment ♦ قرارداد - abrogation or dissolution of a treaty 2 breaking off (relations)

فسون [fosun] ☞ افسون

فش [fesh] noisy breathing (through the nose); puffing, panting
- فش زدن to puff, to pant
- فش کردن to blow one's nose

فشار [feshaar] 1 *present tense stem of* فشردن 2.1 pressure, head ♦ خون - blood pressure ◊ تحت - (زیر) under pressure 2.2 pressure, oppression 2.3 *grammar* accent 2.4 *medicine* pangs (during childbirth)
- آوردن - 1 to crush, to squeeze, to press (بر،به) 2 to exert pressure 3 to exert pressure (بر،به) (during childbirth)
- دادن - to crush, to squeeze; to press

فشارسنج [feshaarsanj] *technical* manometer

فشردن [foshordan (and) feshordan] (present tense stem فشار [feshaar]) to squeeze, to crush, to press, to compress

فصاحت [fasaahat] strictness, severity, correctness, purity (of style) ♦ بیان - eloquence

فصحا [fosahaa] *plural of* فصیح 2

ف

فصل [fásel] (plural فصول [fosul]) 1 time, period ♦ سال - چهار four seasons of the year ۞ خزان - the fall season, fall, autumn 2 harvest 3 chapter (of a book), section, paragraph 4 linguistics pause

فصل بندی [faselbandi] division into chapters, division into paragraphs

فصلی [fasli] seasonal ♦ مزدوران - seasonal workers

فصول [fosul] plural of فصل

فصیح [fasih] 1.1 strict, correct, elegant, refined (about style) 1.2 (opposite of عامیانه) literary, standard (about language, pronunciation) ♦ زبان - literary language 2 (plural فصحا [fosahaa]) man of letters; writer

فصیح البیان [fasiholbayaan] (and) فصیح بیان [fasihbayaan] possessing the gift of oratory, eloquence

فیصل [fasil] breastwork, embankment, rampart

فضا [fazaa] 1 space, free space, empty space ♦ خارجی - [outer] space, the cosmos 2 air, the atmosphere ♦ تازه - pure air, fresh air ۞ زمین - earth's atmosphere 3 atmosphere, conditions, situation ♦ بین المللی در - international situation ۞ تفاهم - in an atmosphere of mutual understanding

فضانورد [fazaanaward] astronaut, cosmonaut

فضایل [fazaayel] plural of فضیلت

فضایل آگاه [fazaayelaagaah] omniscient, most wise; most worthy (form of address to a mufti or ghazi)

فضایی [fazayi] 1 air adjective, aerial ♦ پوسته- air mail 2 cosmic, space ♦ پرواز - space flight

فضل [fázel] literary 1 wisdom; learning, erudition 2 favor, grace; generosity, magnanimity; virtue

فضلا [fozalaa] plural of فاضل

فضلات [fozalaat] plural of فضله

فضل پروری [fazelparwari] propagation of culture and science; concern for the development of education, concern for the growth of enlightenment

فضل فروشی [fazelforoshi] ostentatious erudition; snobbery

فضله [fozla] (plural فضلات [fozalaat]) 1 waste, scrap, refuse, garbage 2 manure, dung, feces, excrement

فضول [fozul] 1 unnecessary, superfluous; excessive 2 excessively talkative; obtrusive, importunate

فضول خرج [fozulkharj] 1 extravagant; wasteful 2 a spendthrift, prodigal, squanderer

فضولی [fozuli] 1 needlessness, excessiveness 2 obtrusiveness, importunity; interference, meddling (in others' talk, business)

• نکو - 1 Don't be an impudent fellow! 2 Quit talking nonsense!

فضیح [fazeeh]

• ساختن - to disgrace, to defame

فضیلت [fazilat] (plural فضایل [fazaayel]) 1 merit, worth, superiority 2 virtue, nobility

فضیلت ماب [fazilatmaab] (and) فضیلت همراه [fazilathamraah] most worthy, most wise (in addressing a mufti, ghazi and other ecclesiastical person)

فطر [féter] (also- عید) holiday of the ending of the fast in the month of Ramadan; ☞ رمضان

فطرت [fetrat] 1 nature ♦ انسانی - human nature 2 innate characteristic; inclination, predisposition

فطره [fetra] alms (distributed in honor of the end of fasting in the month of Ramadan)

فطری [fetri] 1 natural, innate, inborn 2 typical by character, typical by nature

فطیر [fatir] ☞ فتیر

فعال [fa'aal] 1 active; aggressive; energetic 2 effective, efficacious

فعالیت [fa'aaliyat] 1 work, action, operation 2 activities, activity 3 (alsoحربی-) military operations

• کردن - 1 to work, to operate, to function (about an enterprise, a plant, a factory, etc.) 2 military to wage battle, to fight

فعل [fe'l] (plural افعال [af'aal]) 1 deed; action; act 2 grammar verb, verb form ♦ مجهول - verb in the passive voice ۞ معلوم - verb in the active voice

• فعل امر مطلق Definite imperative
• فعل حال استمراری Present Continuous
• فعل حال اقتداری Potential present
• فعل حال شرطی Conditional present
• فعل حال مطلق Perfective present
• فعل ربط Copulative verb
• فعل لازم Intransitive verb
• فعل ماضی استمراری Post continuous tense
• فعل ماضی اقتداری Potential past tense
• فعل ماضی بعید Remote past tense
• فعل ماضی شرطی Past conditional tense
• فعل ماضی قریب Near past tense
• فعل ماضی مطلق Past perfect tense
• فعل متعدی Transitive verb
• فعل مثبت Affirmative form
• فعل منفی Negative form
• فعل نهی Prohibitive
• فعلهای معاون Auxiliary verbs

فعل [fa'l] (plural افاعیل [afaa'il]) (alsoعروضی -) literary repeated part of the formula of a poetic meter (e.g., فاعلاتن in the ramal meter)

فعلاً [fé'lan] at the present moment, at present, now

فعلی [fe'li] 1 real; present; actual 2 grammar verbal ♦ جمله - verbal clause

فغان [feghaan] weeping, crying, moan, groan, cry, wail

فقدان [foghdaan] (and) feqdaan 1 absence, lack, shortage 2 loss

فقر [faqr] shortage, lack; poverty; need ♦ وناداری- poverty, destitution, absence of funds for [one's] keep

فقرا [foqaraa] plural of فقیر

فقرات [faqaraat (and) feqaraat] (plural of فقره [faqra]) ♦ ستون - anatomy spinal column, spine, backbone

فقرالدم [faqroddam] anemia

فقره [faqra] (plural فقرات [faqaraat]) anatomy vertebra

فقره [faqara (and) feqra] 1 article; section; paragraph 2 subject, theme, topic, question, problem 3 phrase; saying

• فقره Clause
• فقره (بند) Clause (Closed)
• فقره های معترضه Parenthetical Clauses

فقط [faqat] 1 merely, only, solely ♦ نه ... بلکه... - conjunction not only, but also... 2 obscure end, ending; That's all! / The end! (at the end of a letter, etc.)

فقه [feqh (and) féqa] 1 religion feqh (Moslem jurisprudence) 2 literary knowledge, understanding

فقید [faqid] 1 (official form of courtesy) deceased, the deceased (mainly about a monarch) 2 literary lost

فقیر [faqir] (*plural* فقراء [foqara]) 1 poor, indigent 2.1 a poor man 2.2 fakir, ascetic, wandering dervish

فقیری [faqiri] 1 ☞ فقر 2 life of a hermit, asceticism, life of a dervish
- کردن - to beg; to go begging

فقیه [faqih] expert in Moslem religious laws, Moslem theologian

فکاهت [fokaahat] wit; humor; wittiness

فکاهی [fokaahi] humorous, witty ♦ بطور - in jest, as a joke

فکر [féker] (*plural* افکار [afkaar]) 1 thought, idea 2 opinion ♦ غلط - erroneous opinion ◊ به - من - in my opinion
- کردن - 1 to think, to reflect, to ponder 2 to consider, to suppose 3 to worry, to be concerned [about]
- به - یک کاری بر آمدن to conceive, to think up, to undertake (something)
- به (در) - کسی (چیزی) بودن to think, to be concerned, to worry about somebody or something
- فکرتان شد؟ ● *colloquial* Did you catch [it]? (the essence) / Did you understand?

فکراً [fékran] mentally; in the mind

فکری [fekri] 1 lost in thoughts, sunk in reverie 2 mental, intellectual ♦ ارتقای - mental development 3 ideological ♦ - وحدت harmony of ideas conformity of ideas

فگندن [fegandan] ☞ افکندن

فل [fel] ☞ فیل

فلات [falaat] plateau

فلاح [fallaah] *literary* fallah, peasant

فلاحت [fallaahat] *literary* agriculture, farming

فلاسفر [falaasafar] philosopher

فلاسفه [falaasefa] *plural of* فیلسوف

فلاکت [falaakat] 1 poverty, need 2 trouble, misfortune
- به - دچار شدن 1 to be in need, to live in poverty 2 to get into trouble, to come to grief

فلاکس [falaakas] (also - گل) phlox

فلاوجی [felaaoji] philology

فلالوجیک [felalojik] philological

فلالین [falaalin] flannel; flannelette

فلان [folaan (and) felaan] 1 such-and-such, certain 2 some ♦ - کس - some person; someone ◊ چیز - something

فلانی [folaani (and) felaani] some person, a certain person

فلتر [faltar] filter ♦ دقیق - *technical* fine-particle filter ◊ هوا - air filter
- کردن - to filter, to perform filtering

فلج [falaj] a paralysis
- شدن - to be paralyzed

فلز [felez] (*plural* فلزات [felezaat]) metal; ore

فلزات [felezaat] 1 (*plural of* فلز) غیر آهن - nonmetals 2 ores, deposits

فلزکاری [felezkaari] working of metals, processing of metals; metal-working industry

فلسفه [falsafa] philosophy

فلسفی [falsafi] philosophical

فلفل [felfel] black pepper

فلک [falak] (*plural* افلاک [aflaak]) 1 sky, skies, heaven; celestial sphere, heavenly sphere 2 fate, destiny, lot

فلک زده [falakzada] unfortunate, punished by fate

فلم [félm] 1 film, motion picture film ♦ اخباری – newsreel ◊ هنری - feature film 2 *cinematography, photography* film ♦ نیگاتیف - negative

فلم بردار [felmbardaar] cameraman

فلم برداری [felmbardaari] ☞ فلم گیری

فلم دایرکتر [felmdaayraktar] film director, film producer

فلم سازی [felmsaazi] production of films, creation of films ♦ - صنعت motion picture industry

فلم شویی [felmshoyi] development of movie film or photographic film ♦ لابراتوار - dark room, photo laboratory

فلم گیری [felmgiri] filming or shooting a movie ♦ آز ادر هوای - shooting on location ◊ دستگاه - movie camera

فلوت [folut] *technical* float

فلولوجی [feloloji] philology

فلیته [falita] 1 ribbon, tape 2 wick

فن [fan (n)] (*plural* فنون [fonun]) 1 technique 2 profession, trade 3 art, craftsmanship ♦ فن حرب art of war 4 ruse, trick, move (in wrestling)

فنا [fanaa] nonexistence, decay, death
- شدن - to become obsolete, to have had one's day, to disappear, to die

فناناپذیر [fanaanaapazir] imperishable, eternal; unfading; never disappearing, never vanishing

فنانس [fenaans] finances

فندق [fondoq] 1 hazelnut, filbert 2 *poetic* lips of a beautiful woman

فنر [fanar] spring

فنری [fanari] springy, resilient; elastic

فنون [fonun] *plural of* فن

فنی [fanni] 1 technical, special ♦ اشخاص - specialists; technicians 2 artistic

فواره [fawwaara] fountain, spurting stream, spurting jet
- زدن - to gush, to spring forth

فواید [fawaayed] *plural of* فایده

فوت [fawt] 1 demise, decease, death 2 waste; loss ♦ وقت - waste of time
- شدن - to die; to pass away

فوتبال [futbaal] ☞ فتبال

فوتوگراف [fotograaf] photograph

فوتوگرافر [fotograafar] photographer

فوتوگرافی [fotograafi] 1 photographer's studio 2 photographic

فوته [fota] loincloth (worn by men at baths)

فوج [fawj] 1 forces; army 2 regiment; armed detachment ♦ محافظ - garrison (of city or stronghold)
- فوج فوج in throngs, in a throng

فوج دار [fawjdaar] military leader, commander

فوج کشی [fawjkaasi] military campaign; invasion, inroad, incursion

فوجی [fawji] 1 military, army *adjective* 2 soldier, serviceman

فوراً [fawran] urgently, immediately

فورم [form] 1 uniform 2 school bench, school desk

فورمه [forma] ☞ فارم²

فوری [fawri] 1 immediate, urgent ♦ بصورت - urgently 2 ☞ فوراً

فوسیل [fosil] fossil; mineral

فوسیل شناسی [fosilshenaasi] paleontology

فوصل [fosel] ☞ فوسیل

فوق [fawq] 1 top, highest point, summit, peak, apex ♦ در - above, earlier 2 (first component of compound words meaning super-, extra-) ♦ فوق العاده extraordinary; unusual

فوق العاده [fawqol'aada] 1 unusual, uncommon 2 extraordinary, special; urgent 2 special issue (of a newspaper, of a magazine)

فوقانی [fawqaani] located above; upper ♦ ورقه - upper layer, upper stratum

فوقیت [fawqiyat] ☞ فایقیت
♦ فضایی - air superiority

فولاد [folaad] steel ♦ پتی - sheet steel ♦ مخلوط - steel alloy

فولادریزی [folaadreezi] steel casting

فولادسازی [folaadsaazi] production of steel ♦ فابریکه - steel mill, steel foundry

فولادی [folaadi] 1 (literally and figuratively) steel adjective, of steel 2 of the color of steel, steel-colored

فونولوجی [fonoloji] phonology

فونیتیک [foneetik] phonetics

فونیم [foneem] grammar phoneme

فونیم شناسی [foneemshenaasi] 1 phonetics 2 phonology

فهم [fahm (and) faam] understanding; comprehension; reasonableness

فهماندن [fahmaandan] to make it clear [that]; to explain, to make [somebody] understand

فهمیدن [fahmidan] 1 to know; to understand ♦ (من) نمی فهمم I don't know. 2 to learn, to find out, to ascertain

فهمیده [fahmida] intelligent, knowing; conscious

فی [fi]¹ preposition per [person], for [each], from [each] ♦ فی روز during the day ◊ فی سال during the year ◊ فیصد for [each] hundred per hundred ◊ فی نفر for [each] person, per person, per capita ◊ فی ماه هزار افغانی a thousand afghanis per month

فی [fi]²
♦ فی گرفتن colloquial to find fault [with]; to reproach, to upbraid (on trivial grounds)

فی الجمله [filjomla] on the whole, in general; in sum

فی الحال [filhaal] for this time, for the present; at the present moment

فی الحقیقت [filhaqiqat] in actuality, actually; in fact

فی المثل [filmasal] for example, for instance

فیته [fita] 1 ribbon, tape, braid 2 recording tape 3 (also اندازه - گیری) tape measure

فیدرل [feederal] federal

فیدریشن [feedereeshan] ☞ فدریشن

فیر [fayr (and) fayer] 1 shot; fire, firing, volley ♦ تفنگ - rifle shot ◊ توپ - shell fire, gunfire 2 salute (by firing)
♦ با توپ استقبال کردن to greet with an artillery salute
♦ - کردن to fire, to fire [at, upon]; to conduct firing

فیروزه [firoza] turquoise

فیروزی [feerozi] ☞ پیروزی

فیس [fis] 1 payment, fee (e.g., to a physician) 2 (entrance) fee
♦ - دادن 1 to pay a fee 2 to make a payment

فیسوک [fisok] colloquial an arrogant person, a presumptuous person

فیشن [feeshan] 1 fashion, style, cut (of clothing) 2 vogue
♦ ودرشن - colloquial swagger, airs and graces

فیشنی [feeshani] 1 modish, stylish, fashionable ♦ کرتی - a stylish jacket 2 a dandy, fop

فیصد [fisad] (used in designating percentages) ♦ ۱۷۰ اهالی 70 percent of the population

فیصدی [fisadi] amount, quantity (of something) in percentages; percentage ratio ♦ بیکاری موسمی - percentage of seasonal unemployment ◊ به حساب - as a percentage

فیصله [faysala] 1 decision, resolution ♦ (and) - قطعی final decision 2 determination, decision, verdict, sentence (of a court)
♦ - کردن to make a decision, to resolve
♦ - صادر کردن to pronounce judgement, to pronounce a verdict or a sentence

فیض [fayz] literary 1 abundance, plenty, bounties; paradise 2 good, benefit 3 masculine proper name Fayz

فیض آثار [fayzaasaar] literary miraculous, beneficial; bringing healing or recovery ♦ درخت - sacred tree (touching which brings healing recovery) ◊ زیارت - miraculous shrine, sacred thing (which attracts pilgrims wishing to be healed)

فیکس [fiks] chemistry (photography) fixing agent

فیل [fil] 1 elephant 2 chess bishop
♦ بالای - مست سوار بودن colloquial to know no restraint (in something), to behave violently, to lose one's self-control completely

فیل [feel] failure (e.g., in an examination)
♦ - شدن to suffer failure, to fail (an examination)

فیلپایه [filpaaya] 1 post, upright; pedestal 2 pillar, column

فیلتر [filtar] ☞ فلتر

فیلسوف [failaasuf (and) filsuf] (plural فلاسفه [falaasefa]) philosopher

فیل مرغ [filmorgh] turkey cock; turkey hen

فیلو شپ [feeloshep] (and) فیلو شیب [feeloship] 1 fellowship abroad (for persons who have graduated from higher educational institutions) 2 allowance, grant, scholarship, stipend (for persons who are appointed to a fellowship abroad)

فین [fayn] of the highest quality, of superior quality (about fabrics)

فینانس [feenaans] ☞ فنانس

فینانسمان [feenaansmaan] financing; appropriation, allocation ♦ اسعاری - currency appropriations

فیودال [feeodaal] feudal lord

فیودالزم [feeodaalézem] feudalism

فیودالی [feeodaali] feudal

فیوز [fiuz] 1 electrical fuse 2 fuze

فیوزبکس [fiuzbaks] fuse box, box with safety fuse

ق
24th letter of the Dari alphabet

قاب [qaab] 1 deep dish (for pilaf) 2 case; holster 3 frame (for a photograph)

قابل [qaabel] 1.1 worthy, worth, worth doing 1.2 capable, able 2 (first component of set expressions with meanings "deserving of something" / "fit for something") ♦ استعمال - fit, usable ◊ قدر - worthy of high appraisal; estimable

قابل استعمال [qaabeleeste'maal] fit, usable

قابل غور [qaabeleghawr] subject to consideration, subject to discussion; deserving study

قابل غدر [qaabeleghadr] worthy of high appraisal; estimable

قابله [qaabela] midwife

قابله گی [qaabelagi] midwifery; obstetrics ♦ کورس - midwifery classes; obstetrics classes

قابلی [qaabeli] qabeli (a type of pilaf with spices)

قابلیت [qaabeliyat] 1 capability, ability, skill; qualification 2 fitness, suitability (for something) 3 property (of shrinking, of catching fire, etc.) ♦ احتراق -combustibility, flammability ◊ تحمل فشار - technical bearing capacity, carrying capacity

قابو [qaabu] 1
• کردن (دادن) - colloquial to get ready, to prepare for an attack)

قابو [qabu] 2 obscure gate, gates, door

قابوچی [qabuchi] 1 obscure doorkeeper 2 hall porter

قاپیدن [qaapidan] to snatch, to grab, to seize; to catch
• از هوا - to catch in the air, to grab on the wing

قات [qaat] 1.1 layer, stratum; bed, row 1.2 turned-in edge (of clothing); fold, pleat, crease 2 (also - در) denominative preposition colloquial between (something), in (the folds of something) ♦ کتاب - in a book
• کردن - 1 to shut (a book) 2 to fold, to roll up ♦ لحاف را – کو Fold the blanket! 3 to turn down, to turn under (the edge of something) 4 to hem (after turning down an edge)
• کمر تان را - کنید Bow! / Stoop! / Bend!

قاتر [qaater] mule

قاتکی [qaataki] folding, collapsible; portable

قاتل [qaatel] 1 killer, murderer 2 killing, murderous, mortal; fatal, lethal

قاتی [qaati] colloquial ☞ قحطی

قاج [qaaj] (also دگمه-) loop (for fastening)

قاچاق [qaachaaq] 1 smuggling 2 contraband, smuggled goods

قاچاقی [qaachaaqi] 1 contraband adjective, smuggled 2 smuggler

قادر [qaader]
• بودن شدن - to be able (به); to be in a condition or a position (to do something) ♦ آنها به حرکت نبودند – They were not able to move.

قار [qaar] colloquial ☞ قهر

قاری [qaari] (plural قارئین [qare'in]) 1 reader 2 reciter of the Koran, expert on the Koran

قاز [qaaz] 1 goose 2 swan ♦ حسینی - flamingo

قاش [qaash] 1 slice (usually of a watermelon, of a melon) 2 (also زین -) saddle pommel

قاشق [qaashoq] spoon ♦ چای - teaspoon
• پنجه - cover (i.e., tablecloth and other fittings)

قاصد [qaased] 1 messenger, envoy 2 herald ♦ است زمستان - تیرماه Autumn is the harbinger of winter.

قاضی [qaazi] (plural قاضیان [qaaziyaan] (and) قضات [qozzaat]) judge (who judges on the basis of the laws of the sharia)

قاضیی [qaaziyi] 1 judging; arbitration 2 post of judge, profession of judge

قاطع [qaate'] 1.1 literary cutting, intersecting 1.2 firm, categorical 2 mathematical secant

قاعده [qaa'eda] (plural قواعد [qawaa'ed]) 1 rule, law ♦ های صرف grammar rules of conjugation 2 custom, usage 3 norm

قاغمه [qaaghma] ☞ قاقمه

قاغوش [qaaghosh] soldier's barracks (dormitory)

قاف [qaaf] name of the letter ق

قافله [qaafela] 1 caravan; string of carts 2 train, troop train

قافله باشی [qaafelabaashi] historical 1 chief of a caravan, head of a caravan 2 chief of department for protection of commerce and roads

قافیه [qaafiya] rhyme
• بستن - to rhyme

قاق [qaaq] 1 dry, stale ♦ نان - stale flatcake; stale bread 2 dried

قاقمه [qaaqma] 1 peasant's outer garment (made of coarse woolen cloth) 2 cloth made of camel's wool

قالب [qaaleb] 1 form (for casting, molding, etc.) ♦ خشت - form for making bricks ◊ ریخته گری - technical casting form 2 last (e.g., shoemaker's last) 3 body (of a person) 4 matrix 5 technical adaptor, holder, cartridge, casette 6 stamp, punch, die, stencil, pattern (for printing fabrics)
• زدن - 1 to form, to cast 2 to stamp (a pattern or design on fabrics)

قالب بندی [qaalebbandi] technical sheathing, lining, planking, timbering, making a form

قالب ریزی [qaalebreezi] technical pouring into molds, forms; casting

قالب سازی [qaalebsaazi] ☞ قالب گیری

قالب گیری [qaalebgiri] technical molding ♦ مواد - molding material

قالین [qaalin] carpet with pile

قالین باب [qaalinbab] carpets, rugs

قامت [qaamat] height (of a person); stature

قاموس [qaamus] large dictionary; lexicon

قانع [qaane'] 1 satisfied with little, undemanding 2 satisfied; agreeable (to something)
• ساختن - 1 to satisfy 2 to try to win over (to something), to persuade, to talk into
• خود را ساختن - to reconcile oneself (to something)

قانغوز [qaanghuz] (and) قنغزک [qanquzak] dung beetle

قانقرتک [qaanqortak] colloquial Adam's apple

قانون [qaanun] (plural قوانین [qawaanin]) 1 law ♦ اساسی - basic law, constitution ◊ اوم - physics Ohm's Law 2 juridical law ♦ نظامی - martial law

قانونمندی [qaanunmandi] conformity with a law, regularity

قانونی [qaanuni] 1 lawful, legal 2 law adjective, juridical 3 legislative ♦ مجلس - legislative assembly

قانونیت [qaanuniyat] lawfulness; legality

قاه قاه [qaahqaah] 1 onomatopoeia ha-ha 2 burst of laughter, loud laugh
• خندیدن - to roar with laughter, to break out in a loud laugh

قاید [qaayed] leader

قایق [qaayeq] rowboat

قایل [qaayel]
• بودن - to declare (for something), to admit (something)

قایم [qaayem] 1.1 steady, firm, stable, durable, solid 1.2 founded, established 1.3 mathematical perpendicular; right ♦ زاویه - right angle 2 chess stalemate
• کردن – 1 to establish, to strengthen, to consolidate (relations, ties, etc.) 2 to attach, to fasten

قایم مقام [qaayemmaqaam] 1 acting; deputy 2 historical qayem-maqam, viceroy

ق

قبا [qabaa] qaba (loose-fitting male garment with long sleeves)
- برای کسی بریدن *colloquial* to set up a dirty trick on someone

قباحت [qabaahat] 1 indecent trick, ugly act 2 infamy; outrage

قجاله [qabaala] deed of purchase, document indicating ownership (of something)

قبایل [qabaayel] plural of قبیله
- آزاد - independent Pathan tribes
- علاقه آزاد - the zone of independent tribes

قبر [qáber] grave
- کسی را کندن *colloquial* to prepare a pitfall for somebody

قبرستان [qabrestaan] cemetery, graveyard

قبرغه [qaborgha] *anatomy* rib ♦ استخوان های - ribs

قبرکن [qaberkan] grave digger

قبض [qabz] (also معدہ-) *medicine* constipation
- کردن - *medicine* to constipate

قبضه [qabza] 1 handle, hilt (of a saber, of a sword) 2 (numerative in counting silent weapons) ♦ 10 ده - شمشیر sabers

قبضیت [qabziyat] *medicine* constipation

قبل [qábel] previous, former
- بر - *preposition* up to, before ♦ بر آن - before
- بر آنکه - *compound conjunction* before

قبلا [qáblan] 1 before 2 beforehand

قبل التاریخ [qablattaarikh] prehistoric ♦ دوره - prehistoric period

قبل المیلاد [qablalmilaad] pre-Christian, relating to the time before the appearance or introduction of Christianity

قبل الولاده [qablalwelaada] *medicine* prenatal ♦ معاینه خانه - maternity clinic

قبله [qebla] 1 qibla (the direction toward Mecca toward which Moslems face when praying) 2 Mecca ♦ رویم از - بگردد *colloquial* May I never face Mecca! (an oath) 3 *rarely* western side, west

قبله گاه [qeblagaah] 1 Mecca 2 place of worship 3 *epistolary* revered parent, precious father (form of address to a father)

قبله نما(ی) [qeblanomaa(y)] compass

قبول [qabul] 1 acceptance (of a condition, of an offer, a proposal); assent, accord 2 receiving (guests), reception (of guests)
- داشتن - to accept (conditions, offers, proposals); to consent, to agree, to assent ♦ دارم - I agree.
- کردن - 1 to receive (guests) 2 ☞ داشتن -

قبولاندن [qabulaandan] to force to accept, to force to agree, to force to consent
- نضریات خود را به کسی - to impose one's views on somebody

قبولدار [qabuldaar]
- بودن (شدن) - to agree (to something) (را); to accept (some condition)

قبولی [qabuli] 1 acceptance, receipt (of goods) 2 *finance* acceptance ♦ وتسلیمی - issue-receipt

قبیح [qabeeh] 1 indecent, shameful 2 nast, bad, outrageous

قبیله [qabila] (*plural* قبایل [qabaayel]) 1 tribe; family 2 *biology* order

قبیله وی [qabilawi] tribal; family *adjective*

قپان [qapaan] commercial scales

قت قت [qotqot] cackling (of a hen)
- کردن - to cackle

قت قتاس [qotqotaas] *colloquial* ☞ قت قت

قتقتک [qetqetak]
- دادن - to tickle

قاتل [qátel] murder
- عام - carnage, slaughter
- کردن - to kill, to murder

قطی [qoti] ☞ قتی

قحط [qaht] (and) قحطی [qahti] 1 bad harvest; crop failure; drought; famine 2 acute need, shortage (of something)

قد [qad(d)] 1 height (of a person) 2 stature, figure
- قد کشیدن - to grow, to shoot up, to grow up
- قد راست کردن - 1 to straighten [one's] back, to stand erect, to draw oneself up 2 *colloquial* to heal well
- یک قد پریدن - *colloquial* to jump, to jump up (e.g., in fright)
- قدش نمی رسد - *colloquial* He can't reach (something).

قدامت [qadaamat] 1 antiquity, olden times 2 remoteness (of an event); age (e.g., of rock)

قداندام [qadandaam] ☞ قدواندام

قدبرابری [qadbaraabari]
- کردن - *colloquial* to measure [one's] height (با)

قدبلند [qadbeland] tall, strapping, stalwart (about somebody)

قدبلندک [qadbelandak]
- کردن - to rise up on tiptoe (trying to see something)

قدپست [qadpast] short, undersized, dwarfish (about somebody)

قدر [qáder] 1 quantity, amount; measure, extent, degree ♦ به - امکان as far as possible, to the extent possible 2 price; value; importance
- چه قدر - ☞ چه -
- هر - که ••• - no matter how much, however much …
- هر - که لازم باشد - as much as [one] pleases, as much as necessary
- کردن - to value, to esteem, to respect
- کسی (چیزی) را داشتن - to know the worth of somebody (or something); to appreciate or to value somebody (or something)

قدر [qadar] fate, destiny, predestination

قدرت [qodrat] 1 strength; feasibility, possibility ♦ این از - من بالا (بیرون) است This is not within my power / abilities. 2 authority; power ♦ نظامی ◊ قدر تهای بزرگ - the great powers military power, military might 3 *electrical physics* capacity 4 legal force, effectiveness 5 *masculine proper name* Qodrat
- دارای - بودن (شدن) to retain [its] force, to retain [its] effectiveness; to come into force, to come into effect

قدردان [qaderdaan] 1.1 giving [somebody his] due, acknowledging the merits (of somebody) 1.2 grateful, thankful 2 connoisseur, expert

قدردانی [qaderdaani] 1 due appreciation, recognition of merits 2 gratitude, thanks ♦ ابراز - expression of gratitude, expression of thanks

قدری [qadree] a little, some, a small amount or quantity

قدس [qods] *literary* holy, sacred ♦ شهر - holy city, Jerusalem

قدسیت [qodsiyat] *literary* holiness, sacredness ♦ نور - nimbus of holiness

قدغن [qadaghan] prohibition, ban
- کردن - to forbid, to prohibit, to ban

قدم [qadam] (*plural* اقدام [aqdaam]) **1** step; stride; walk, gait
- به - **1** step by step **1.2** in step [with] **2** step (in a dance) **3** step, measure
- برداشتن - **1** to step, to stride, to walk **2** to take measures, to act
- ماندن (نهادن) (در، بر) - to enter, to go in or into
- اوخشک است *colloquial* He brings misfortune. / He doesn't bring good luck.

قدما [qodamaa] **1** ancient (people, peoples) **2** ancestors, forefathers **3** authors of antiquity

قدنما (ی) [qadnomaa (y)]
- آینه - full-length mirror, cheval glass
- عکس - full-length portrait

قدو [qadaw]
- کردن - *colloquial* **1** to test the depth of water (by getting into a river) **2** to make inquiries, to find out (about something); to test soil by feel

قد اندام [qad (d) oandaam] measurements, proportions (of a person's figure)
- گرفتن - to take (somebody's) measurements (about a tailor)

قدوبالا [qad (d) obaala] (and) قدوقامت [qad (d) oqaamat] build, frame, figure; height (of a person)

قدوم [qodum] *literary* **1** arrival **2** *religion* advent

قدیفه [qadifa] **1** cloak, cape, shawl (female or male) **2** (also حمام -) bath sheet

قدیم [qadim] **1** the ancient past, the olden times ♦ از - of yore, since olden days, long since **2** ☞ قدیمی
- در زمان - in former times

قدیمها [qadimhaa] in olden times, in antiquity, in ancient times

قدیمی [qadimi] old, ancient, antique

قراء [qoraa] *plural of* قریه

قرابت [qaraabat] **1** closeness, proximity, vicinity, neighborhood **2** relationship, kinship, kindred relationships
- داشتن - **1** to be close, to be in close proximity (به) **2** to be related

قرار [qaraar] **1.1** rest, peace, calm, quiet, tranquility **1.2** order; disposition, arrangement ♦ به ذیل - in the following order **1.3** decision, resolution **2** (also به -) in accordance [with], according [to] *denominative preposition*
- به امر - by order [of]
- دادن - to decide, to determine
- داشتن - to be located; to stay, to settle down
- شدن - to be established, to be decided, to be resolved
- بر این شدکه ... - It was agreed that ...
- کردن - **1** ☞ دادن **2** *colloquial* to quiet, to soothe, to calm, to placate, to pacify (e.g., a child)
- گرفتن - **1** to resolve, to make up one's mind [to], to be determined [to] **2** *colloquial* to compose oneself, to quiet down, to calm down

قرارداد [qaraardaad] **1** agreement **2** contract ♦ پروژه سازی - planning contract **3** *literary* establishing, establishment, determination

قراردادن [qaraardaadan] *auxiliary verb for formation of set verbal combinations* (*synonym of verbs* ساختن (and) کردن) ♦ ممنوع - to forbid, to prohibit

قراردادی [qaraardaadi] **1** having contracted, having concluded an agreement (for delivery, etc.); contracted **2** contractor; supplier

قرارگاه [qaraargaah] abode, residence; stop **2** general headquarters (of commander); headquarters

قراری [qaraari] **1** rest; calm, quiet; peace **2** established; agreed; coordinated

قرآن [qoraan (and) qor'aan] Koran ♦ شریف - the Sacred Koran

قران [qran (and) qeran] qran (ancient Afghan coin worth half an afghani or half a rupee)

قران [qeraan] *literary* the convergence of two celestial bodies (which is a happy omen)
- صاحب - happy, fortunate (about somebody born in the period of convergence of Jupiter and Venus)

قراول [qaraawol] **1** guard, watch, patrol **2** vanguard ♦ امنیت - sentry outpost **3** sight, rear sight (of a gun)
- کردن - **1** to guard, to keep watch **2** (also به گرفتن) to take aim

قرائت [qeraa'at] **1** reading the Koran (aloud, in singing voice) **2** reading
- کردن - **1** to read the Koran (aloud, in a singing voice) **2** to read; to study

قرائت خانه [qeraaatkhaana] reading room, reading hall

قرائتی [qeraa'ati]
- کتب - books for reading; readers, reading books

قراین [qaraayen] *plural of* قرینه
- از - معلوم میشود که ... the data indicate that ...

قرب [qorb] nearness, proximity; neighborhood, vicinity
- قرب و جوار ☞ وجوار

قربان [qorbaan] **1** sacrifice; something sacrificed, something offered as a sacrifice **2** *masculine proper name* Qorban
- عید - Qorban-Bayram (Moslem holiday of sacrifice)
- قربانت گردم *colloquial* I would give my life for you!

قربانی [qorbaani] **1** being offered or having been offered as a sacrifice; intended for immolation **2.1** (also گوسفند -) lamb (sent by the fiance to the home of the fiancee during the holiday of Qorban-Bayram) **2.2** sacrificing, offering as a sacrifice
- شدن - to be sacrificed, to be offered as a sacrifice, to perish as a sacrifice
- کردن - to sacrifice (somebody or something); to offer in sacrifice or as a sacrifice

قربت [qorbat] *literary* **1** (Sufism) nearness (to God) **2** proximity (to a shah, to highly placed person)

قرب و جوار [qorbojawaar] environs, adjoining, adjacent, contiguous regions ♦ در شهر - in the environs of a city or town

قرت [qort] swallowing; drink, mouthful, sip, gulp
- کردن - to swallow

قرتک [qortak]
- زدن - *colloquial* **1** to choke (something) down; to try to choke (something) down **2** to swallow saliva (in anticipation of food)

قرچ [qarch]
- زدن - *colloquial* to bite or crack (something) loudly or with a crunch

قرچ قرچ [qerchqerch] squeak, creak, crunch; gnashing or gritting of teeth

• کردن - to squeak, to creak, to crunch; to gnash [one's] teeth, to grit [one's] teeth
قرحه [qarha (and) qorha] (*plural* قرحات [qorhat]) ulcer, sore, wound
قرص [qors] 1 circle, disc 2 (*also* نان -) round loaf of bread, flatcake 3 (*also* تسمه -) *technical* pulley 3.2 wafer, tablet
قرض [qarz] (*plural* قروض [qoruz]) 1 debt, loan 2 advance money, credit
• به - دادن 1 to give as a loan 2 to lend, to loan
• کردن (گرفتن) - to borrow, to take on credit
قرضدار [qarzdaar] debtor
قرض داری [qarzdaari] debts, liabilities
قرضه [qarza] 1 state loan ♦ - سند obligation 2 ☞ قرض
قرطاس [qertaas] 1 paper; document 2 stamped paper
قرطاسیه [qertaasiya] (*also* - سامان) office supplies (paper, etc.)
• دفتر داری - *abbreviation* office supplies
قرعه [qor'a (and) qoraa] 1 lot 2 lottery ticket
• انداختن - to cast lots
• کشیدن - to draw lots; to draw a lottery ticket
قرعه کشی [qar'akashi] 1 casting of lots 2 drawing (in a lottery)
قرغز [qerghez] (and) قرغیز [qerghiz] Kirghiz
قرقره [qarqara] 1 crane (bird; *Anthropoides virgo*) 2 comb or crest of birds; plume
• دم خود را - کردن to spread its tail like a fan (about birds)
قرقی [qoroqi] forbidden
• زمین - preserve, reservation, reserve
قرمساق [qoromsaaq] *colloquial* procurer; pimp
قرن [qarn] (*plural* قرون [qorun]) century
قروت [qorut] qorut (dried sour milk preserved in the form of very hard pellets)
• سزای - آب گرم است The [one] way to cope with qorut is hot water. (i.e., One must take stern measures against a stern temper.)
قروض [qoruz] *plural of* قرض
قرون [qorun] *plural of* قرن
• اولی - the first centuries (of the history of mankind); ancient epoch
• وسطی - the Middle Ages
قره [qara] *colloquial* 1 black 2 *cards* spades
قره غاچ [qaraghaach] elm
قره قش [qaraqosh] black starling
قره قل [qaraqol] karakul fur
قره قلی [qaraqoli] 1 karakul *adjective* ♦ پوست - karakul hide 2 karakul fur
قریب [qarib] 1.1 near 1.2 like, similar 1.3 kindred, related 2.1 near *adverb*, nearly 2.2 approximately, about ♦ دیوانه شوم است - I am close to insanity. / I am almost mad or insane.
قریبی [qaribi] nearness, closeness; likeness, resemblance; relationship, kinship
قریحه [qariha] talent, gift ♦ ادبی - literary talent
قرینه [qarina] (*plural* قراین [qarayen]) sign, indication; symptom; token; evidence
قریه [qariya] (*plural* قراء [qoraa]) village, hamlet
قریه دار [qaryadaar] village elder
قزاق [qazaaq] 1 cossack 2 kazakh
قزلباش [qezelbaash] *historical* Ghezelbash (*singular* and *plural*) (descendants of Turkic warriors of the Iranian Shah Abbas who settled in Afghanistan starting in the 16th century)

قسط [qest] (*plural* اقساط [aqsaat]) 1 a payment on the installment plan 2 paying in installments
قسم [qasam] 1 vow 2 (*also* عسکری -) oath
• خوردن - to make a vow; to swear, to swear on oath
• دادن - 1 to compel (somebody) to swear, to compel (somebody) to make a vow 2 to swear (somebody) in, to administer the oath to (somebody)
قسم [qésem] (*plural* اقسام [aqsaam]) kind; sort; grade; category, rank
• این - this sort of, of this kind
• چه - what sort of, of what kind
• قسم قسم various, of all sorts or kinds
قسمت [qesmat] 1 part, portion, share 2 sector, subdivision 3 lot, destiny, fate
• شاید رفته باشد *colloquial* Perhaps it was fated thus.
قشتی [qoshti] *colloquial* ☞ کشتی [koshti]
قشتیگیر [qoshtigir] *colloquial* ☞ کشتی گیر [koshtigir]
قشر [qésher] 1 layer; stratum 2 stratum, group (of people) 3 rind, peel; skin, shell ♦ انار - rind of pomegranate
قشقه [qashqa] religious mark on the forehead (among Hindus)
• تازه - کردن to confirm one's adherence or fidelity (to something); to show one's faithfulness or loyalty
قشلاق [qeshlaaq] 1 wintering place, winter quarters (of nomads) 2 village, gheslagh
قشله [qeshla] (*also* عسکری -) 1 barracks for soldiers 2 cantonment, military post
قشون [qoshun] *obscure* army, forces ♦ اسکندر - the army of Alexander the Great ♦ قشون سرخ the red army
قصاب [qassaab] butcher
قصابه [qasaaba] a precious shawl (skillfully embroidered)
قصاص [qesaas] retribution; punishment; execution (for murder, treachery, etc.)
قصاید [qasaayed] *plural of* قصیده
قصب [qasab] fine linen (made by hand, usually with a design)
قصبه [qasaba] 1 large village, small town 2 regional center (including several villages)
قصد [qasd] 1 intention, purpose 2 plan, scheme; design
• از - ازقصد ☞
• به - for the purpose [of]; intending [to]
• داشتن (کردن) - 1 to intend (to do something) 2 to comtemplate (something), to infringe (on something)
• جان - کردن to make an attempt on [somebody's] life
قصر [qáser] (*plural* قصور [qosur]) palace
قصور [qosur] *plural of* قصر
قصوری [qosuri] *colloquial* repayment, vengeance
• خواندن - to threaten, to promise payment
• گرفتن - to repay, to take vengeance
قصه [qessa] 1 story, tale 2 fable 3 event, incident
• خواندن - *colloquial* 1 to tell a tale 2 to talk profusely
• کردن - to tell, to narrate ♦ به تفصیل - کنید Tell [me] in more detail!
• خلاص شد - 1 And that's the end of the tale! 2 The matter is ended!

230

قصه خوانی [qessakhaani] 1 telling of stories, tales, parables 2 (also بازار-) an area of printers in Peshawar (where cheap popular literature in Pashto and Farsi is published and sold)

قصیده [qasida] (*plural* قصاید [qasaayed]) *literary* qasida, ode, panegyric, eulogy

قضا [qazaa] fortune, chance
- وقدر - fate, predestination
- از - by the will of fate; accidentally, by chance
- کردن - 1 to miss the time (of prayer) 2 to die

قضات [qozaat] *plural of* قاضی

قضازده [qazaazada] 1 unhappy; unfortunate; poor 2 suffering a calamity; having fallen into trouble

قضاکورکی [qazaakuraki] *colloquial* completely by accident, as a result of blind chance

قضاوت [qazaawat] opinion, judgement ♦ خلق - the opinion of people; the people's verdict
- کردن - 1 to consider, to judge, to express an opinion 2 to pronounce judgement (about a court)

قضایا [qazaayaa] *plural of* قضیه

قضایی [qazaayi] 1 judicial ♦ قوه - judicial power, judicial authority 2 fat,mal (i.e., related to fate)

قضیه [qaziya] (*plural* قضایا [qazaayaa]) 1 case, lawsuit 2 event, incident 3 matter, problem, question ♦ کلان - serious matter, serious problem, serious question ◊ برعکس است - That's not how the matter stands at all. 4 premise, judgement (e.g., in logic)

قطار [qataar] 1 line, row, chain
- در - 1 among 2 side by side [with] ♦ در نویسندگان - among the writers 2 column, rank, formation (of troops)
- موترها - motor vehicle column, motor vehicle convoy
- شدن - to form up, to line up, to stand in a line or in a row
- نشستن - to sit down next to

قطاره [qataara] 1 fence (around a grave, around a flowerbed) 2 barrier; parapet, rail, railing ♦ قطاره های زینه - railing or banister of a staircase

قطاری [qataari] 1 set in rows, stretched out in ranks 2 ordinary, common, commonplace

قطب [qótob] pole (also an electrical term) ♦ شمالی - North Pole ◊ ستاره - the North Star

قطب نما [qotobnomaa] compass

قطبی [qotbi] polar, arctic ♦ مناطق شمالی - the Arctic

قطر [qótor] 1 diameter 2 caliber (of a gun) 3 *mathematical* diagonal

قطران [qatraan] resin, tar; asphalt

قطره [qatra] (*plural* قطرات [qatraat]) drop ♦ قطره قطره - by the drop, drop by drop ◊ قطره ای از دریا است [That is] a drop in the ocean.

قطره چکان [qatrachakaan] (and) قطره گیر [qatragir] pipette, medicine dropper

قطع [qat' (and) qáta] 1 cutting off; severance 2 ceasing, cessation 3 *mathematical* section 4 size of a book
- کردن - 1 to cut, to cut off, to sever 2 to interrupt (discourse, etc.), to break off (discourse, etc.) 3 to cease, to break, to break off (relations, etc.)
- همدیگررا کردن - to intersect, to cross *intransitive*
- منازل کردن - *literary* to traverse a path

قطعاً [qátaan] 1 finally 2 absolutely; entirely, totally

قطعات [qeta'aat] *plural of* قطعه

قطعه [qet'a] ¹ (*plural* قطعات [qeta'at]) 1 part, piece; segment 2 (also عسکری -) *military* subunit, unit 3 *technical* panel; block ♦ کانکریت - concrete panel 4 (playing) card
- بازی کردن - to play cards

قطعه [qet'a] ² *literary* qeta (a form of short poem usually of philosophical content)

قطعه بازی [qet'abaazi] game of cards; card game

قطعی [qata'i] decisive, final ♦ فیصله - final decision, firm decision

قطی [qo (t) ti] 1 small box; case 2 tin can ♦ خوارک - canned food ◊ شیر - canned milk

قعر [qa'r (and) qáar] 1 the deepest spot (of a river, of a sea); the deep 2 bottom
- در بحر - 1 deep in the sea 2 at the bottom of the sea

قف [qaf] ☞ کف [kaf] ¹,²

قفا [qafa]
- در - 1 behind 2 behind the back, in the absence (of somebody) *denominative preposition*
- در قفای کسی بد گفتن - to defame, to revile somebody behind his back

قفس [qafas] 1 cage (for birds, wild beasts) 2 captivity

قفسچه [qafascha] (also دکان -) counter

قفل [qófol] ☞ قلف

قفمال [qafmaal] ☞ کفمال

قلا [qalaa] qala (a home, usually with a farmstead, which is surrounded by a high adobe enclosure with towers on the corners)

قلابه [qolaaba] 1 fishhook 2 *colloquial* overstitching (e.g., seams, buttonholes)

قلاچ [qolaach] (measure of length equal to a handspan)

قلاغ [qolaagh]
- گرفتن - *colloquial* to mimic ♦ مرا نگیر - Don't mimic me!

قلایی [qalaayi] ☞ قلعی

قلب [qalb] ¹ (*plural* قلوب [qolub]) heart ♦ از صمیم - with all [one's] heart, from the bottom of [one's] heart

قلب [qalb] ² 1.1 counterfeit, spurious, false ♦ زر واپس میاید - *proverb* Counterfeit gold comes back [to the owner]. 1.2 dishonest, dishonorable ♦ آدم - dishonest man ◊ او دست دارد - He is a pilferer. 2 *grammar* inversion

قلبه [qolba] 1 wooden plow; plow 2 team of oxen 3 *technical* cultivator 4 *historical* a measure of arable land equal to 20-40 jeribs
- کردن - to plow, to till; to loosen soil, to break up soil

قلبه کشی [qolbakaasi] plowing, tillage

قلبه گاو [qolbagaaw] plow ox, ox

قلبی [qalbi] ¹ 1 pertaining to the heart, cardiac, heart *adjective* ♦ حمله - heart attack 2 sincere, heartfelt; cordial

قلبی [qalbi] ² counterfeit, false

قلت [gellat] 1 lack [of], deficiency [of], shortage 2 insignificant amount (of something)

قلعه [qal'a] 1 stronghold, fortress, fort
- ☞ قلا

قلعه بندی [qal'abandi] encirclement, siege (of a fortress)

قلعه بیگی [qal'abeegi] commandant of a fortress or of a fort; chief of a garrison

قلعی [qalai] tin; tinning

قلعی گر [qalaigar] tinsmith

قلف [qolf] lock; bolt ♦ کردن - to lock, to bolt

ق

قلفک [qolfak] 1 (door) bolt 2 latch, catch (of a door, of a window)
قلل [qolal] *plural of* قله
قلم [qalam]¹ 1 qalam (reed pen); penholder, pen ♦ به - written by so and so (about a story, about a book) 2 pencil ♦ ابرو - eyebrow pencil ◊ مشق - chalk, piece of chalk (for writing) 3 style; manner of writing 4 cutting tool, chasing tool, caulking tool 5 (also آهن بری) (and) (آهنگری -) chisel; gouge
• زدن - to cross out, to cross off, to touch up, to retouch
• کردن - to cut off, to cut, to clip, to trim
• از قلم انداختن - to omit (when writing down); not to enter (in a list)
• از - ماندن - to be omitted (when being written down); not to get (on a list)
• - مخصوص - secret control unit; special department
• - درسه - in three layers (about carving on stone, on wood)
قلم [qalam]² (*plural* اقلام [aqlaam]) 1 paragraph, point, section (of a document, prescription, etc.) 2 item (of export, of import)
قلم تراش [qalamtaraas] penknife; (pencil) sharpener
قلم خور [qalamkhor] *colloquial* retouched, forged (about text)
قلمداد [qalamdaad]
• کردن - to compile an inventory, to compile a list (of something)
قلمدادی [qalamdaadi] entered in a list, entered into a register; enumerated
قلمدان [qalamdaan] qalamdan (pencil case decorted with carving or painting)
قلمرو [qalamraw] 1 territory (of a state) ♦ در - هند - on or in India's territory 2 *historical* subject, territory, possessions
قلمه [qalama] cutting (of a non-fruit tree, of a bush) ♦ شاندن - to plant cuttings
قلمی [qalami] 1.1 manuscript *adjective*, written by hand ♦ - نسخه a manuscript 1.2 engrafted (about a tree) 2 qalami (higher grade of karakul with a clear design)
• آنتن- *technical* rod antenna
قلنج [qalenj] sharp shooting pain (of the scapular muscles)
قلندر [qalandar] 1 wandering dervish 2 gypsy (with a dancing bear)
قلوب [qolub] *plural of* قلب
قلوی [qalawi] (*plural* قلویات [qalawiat]) *chemistry* alkali
قله [qolla] (*plural* قلل [qolal]) top of a mountain
قلی [qoli] porter, carrier; loader, stevedore
قلیان [qalyaan] hookah, water pipe
قلیل [qalil] *literary* little; few; not numerous
قمار [qemaar] game of chance, gambling game (of dice, of cards)
قمار باز [qemaarbaaz] player of games of chance; gambler
قمچین [qamchin] whip, knot; lash
قمر [qamar] 1 moon 2 *astronomy* satellite
قمری [qamari] lunar (about a system of chronology)
قمری [qomri] turtledove
قمیص [qamis] shirt
قناد [qannaad] confectioner, vendor of sugar and sweets
قناعت [qanaa'at] 1 satisfaction with little; simple tastes 2 satisfaction; contentment 3 confidence; certitude, conviction
• کردن - to be content with little
• حاصل کردن - to be convinced (of something), to attain assurance (of something)
قناعت بخش [qanaaatbakhsh] 1 satisfying 2 convincing; persuasive
قند [qand] lump sugar
• خشتی - lump sugar
• به دل - شکستاندن *colloquial* to be secretly glad, to rejoice inwardly
قنداغ [qondaagh] (and) قنداق [qondaaq] 1 diaper, swaddling cloth ♦ - بند swaddling clothes 2 butt (of a rifle or shotgun) 3 carriage (of a gun)
قنددانی [qanddaani] sugar bowl
قندک [qandak] variety of sweet melon
قنغال [qenghaal] *colloquial* a girl engaged (to someone) or promised in marriage (to someone); fiancée
قنغال بازی [qenghaalbaazi] *colloquial* secret meetings (of the fiance and fiancee before the wedding)
قوا [qowaa] 1 (*plural of* قوه) (and) 2 armed forces, troops, forces ♦ بحری - naval forces
قوای کار - ☞ کار
قواعد [qawaa'ed] 1 *plural of* قاعده 2 (also زبان -) grammar
• ترافیکی - traffic rules
قواله [qawaala] *colloquial* ☞ قیاله
• او را کسی نمی خواند - He doesn't count. / Nobody takes him seriously.
قوام [qewaam] 1 thickness, density 2 thickening, condensation
• به - آوردن to thicken, to condensate
قوانین [qawaanin] *plural of* قانون
قوای کار [qowaayekaar] *obscure* construction battalion (under the Ministry of Public Works in Afghanistan)
قوت [qowwat] 1 strength, force, power, might ♦ بازو - one's own strengths ◊ جسمانی - physical strength ◊ به - by force, under compulsion 2 ability ♦ باصره - ability to see, sight, vision 3 power, state 4 ☞ قوه 1
• دادن - to strengthen, to reinforce
• یافتن - to become stronger, to intensify
قوت [qut] daily bread, subsistence
• ما – خود را از دهقانی مینماییم We make a living by peasant labor. / We eat by peasant labor.
قور [qor] hot ashes with smoldering coals; heat (of stone, of a fire)
قور [qur] dirt (on the body, on clothing)
• بستن (زدن) - to become dirty, to become soiled, to make oneself dirty, to soil oneself; to be covered with dirt ♦ دستهایش - زده است His hands were covered with dirt.
قورمه [qorma] qorma (meat stew with spices)
قورمه یی [qormayi]
• لحاف - blanket made of scraps
قوریه [qoriya] seedlings
قوس [qaws]¹ 1 bend, curve; curvature; arc 2 *mathematical* arc 3 *astronomy* Sagittarius 4 Ghaus (ninth month of Afghan solar year; corresponds to November - December)
• قزح - rainbow
قوس [qaws]² dual number
قوسین [qawsayn] bracket, parenthesis; brackets, parentheses ♦ کلان - parentheses ◊ کوچک - quotation marks
• داخل (and) - مابین in parentheses, in brackets
• داخل - گرفتن to place in brackets or parentheses

232

قول [qul] *technical* handle; grip; lever
- پستون - connecting rod

قول [qol] dry river bed, dry lake

قول [qawl] 1 word, expression, utterance 2 word, promise 3 *grammar* particle
- دادن - to give [one's] word

قولته [qulta] *colloquial* pockmark; pockmark (on the face)

قولنج [qulenð] ☞ قلنج

قوم [qawm] (*plural* اقوام [aqwaam]) 1 people, nationality ♦ پشتون - Afghan people 2 family, tribe; clan 3 relatives

قوماندان [qumaandaan] 1 commanding (general), commander ♦ اردو - army commander 2 chief 3 commandant

قوماندانی [qumaandaani] 1 command, headquarters ♦ اعلی عسکر - supreme command, high command 2 *obscure* police headquarters, police station

قومانده [qumaanda] command
- دادن - to command, to give a command

قومدار [qawmdaar] well-born, high-born, influential; carrying weight, being influential (in one's own tribe)

قومداری [qawmdaari] ties of relationship and tribe, family and tribal relationships; authority, prestige (among one's own tribe)

قومی [qawmi] 1 family-tribal; national 2 of the common people, pertaining to the common people
- مرد - 1 man of the tribe, man of the people 2 fellow tribesman
- قوای - militia, homeguard

قومیت [qawmiyat] 1 tribal or national affiliation 2 devotion or fidelity to one's family or to one's tribe; patriotism

قونسل [gonsal] (and) قنسل [qonsul] consul

قوه [gowa] (*plural* قوا [qowaa]) 1 power; energy; capacity; output ♦ اسپ - *physics* horsepower ◊ برق - electric power ◊ اجرائیه - executive authority, executive power
- تولید - 1 production capacity 2 ☞ قوت [qowwat] 3 authority, power 4 *mathematical* طاقت power

قوی [qawi] strong, powerful; firm, sturdy

قهر [qahr (and) qaar] 1 anger, ire, wrath, irritation 2 offense, resentment
- با - 1 angrily, in a fit of temper 2 with resentment, grudgingly
- بودن - to be at odds (with somebody), not to talk (to somebody) ♦ مه با او - استم - *colloquial* I am at odds with him.
- شدن - to become angry (at somebody); to take offense (at somebody) (بالای)
- کردن - to fall out (with somebody); to stop talking (to somebody) (با)

قهراً [qáhran] against [one's] will, reluctantly

قهرمان [qahramaan] 1 hero 2 champion

قهروک [qahrok (and) qaarok] *colloquial* angry, touchy

قی [qay] vomiting
- قی آوردن - to cause vomiting
- قی کردن - to throw up, to vomit; to belch

قیادت [qiyaadat] leadership; guidance, management
- به ... - under the leadership [of], under the guidance or management [of]

قیاس [qiyyaas] 1 measure, dimensions, size 2 measuring, measurement; comparison 3 conclusion, deduction; supposition, assumption

قیاسی [qiyaasi] 1 pertaining to measurement, measuring ♦ واحد - measure, scale ◊ وزن - measure of weight 2 comparable, analogous 3 speculative, hypothetical

قیافت [qiyaafat] (and) قیافه [qiyaafa] 1 physiognomy, face 2 exterior, appearance (of a person)

قیام [qiyaam] uprising, revolt; speech (against somebody) ♦ ملی - people's revolt, popular revolt

قیامت [qiyaamat] 1 resurection from the dead; the end of the world, doomsday 2 uproar, clamor; turmoil; alarm, commotion 3 astonishing deed, fantastic deed; wonder, marvel
- کردن - 1 to raise a clamor; to raise a turmoil 2 to work wonders, to work miracles

قیتک [qaitak] buckle, clasp ♦ جوراب - clasp on suspenders ◊ موی - hair clip

قیچی [qaychi] scissors ♦ آهن بری - *technical* metal snips or shears

قید [qayd][1] (*plural* قیود [qoyud]) 1 bonds, fetters; chains 2 confinement; detention; imprisonment; arrest 3 entry (on a list), note 4 safety position (of a gun, of a pistol)
- راواز کنید - Cock the hammer!
- کردن - 1 to imprison, to put into prison; to chain; to note 3 to squeeze
- این بوت در پایم است - *colloquial* These shoes pinch me.
- نفس کردن - to hold one's breath

قید [qahd][2] (*plural* قیود [qoyud]) *grammar* adverb

قیر [qir] 1 resin; tar; pitch 2 bitumen; asphalt
- کاغذ - roofing felt, tarred felt, tar paper

قیرپاش [qirpaash] (also- مو تر) asphalt paver

قیرریزی [qirrezi] asphalting, tarring

قیزه [qayza] bridle, halter

قیصر [qaisar] Caesar, emperor

قیف [qif] 1 funnel 2 crater, pit, hole

قیل [qil] *colloquial* 1 high ♦ بام - high roof 2 high *adverb*

قیل وقال [qiloqaal] 1 noise, cry, shout 2 gossip, talk

قیماغ [qaimaagh] (and) قیماق [qaimaaq] ghaymagh, cream

قیماغچای [gaimaaghchaay] tea with cream

قیمت [qimat] 1 price, cost ♦ از این چند است؟ - How much does this cost? ◊ هر به - شده no matter what it costs 2 dear, expensive ♦ بسیار - است It is very expensive!

قیمت بها [qimatbahaa] *colloquial* valuable, precious

قیمتدار [qimatdaar] 1 dear, expensive, valuable ♦ کتابهای - valuable books 2 important, significant, having great significance or meaning

قیمتی [qimati] 1 dearness, expensiveness 2 dear; valuable; expensive

قیمومت [qaimumat] (and) قیمومیت [qaimumiyat] 1 quardianship, wardship 2 protectorate

قیمه [qima] 1 chopped meat, minced meat; forcemeat, sausage meat 2 qima (dish made of chopped or minced meat)
- کردن - to chop, to mince, to cut up into small pieces (about meat)

قیود [qoyud] *plural of* قید [1,2]

ک
25th letter of the Dari Alphabet

کابلی [kaboli] 1 Kabul *adjective* 2.1 Kabulite, inhabitant of Kabul 2.2 (also - زبان) Kabuli (the colloquial language of Kabul), the Kabul dialect

قابلی [kaabeli] [qaabeli] کابلی

کابوس [kaabus] *literary* nightmare, terror, horror, something distressing, something unpleasant

کابینه [kaabina] cabinet (of ministers), council (of ministers) ♦ اعضای - members of the council, cabinet [of ministers]

کاپتالست [kaap (e) taalest] capitalist

کاپتالستی [kaapetaalesti] capitalistic, capitalist *adjective* ♦ ممالک کاپتالستی capitalistic states

کاپتالیزم [kaapetaalizm] capitalism

کاپی [kaapi]
• کردن - copy to copy

کاپی کاری [kapikaari] (and) کاپی نویسی [kapinawisi] making a copy, copying

کات [kaat]
• کردن - *colloquial cards* to cut (the pack)

کاتب [kaateb] 1 clerk 2 second secretary of an embassy *diplomatic*

کاتبی [kaatebi] 1 clerical work; work of a clerk 2 post of the second secretary of the embassy

کاتود [kaatod] *physics* cathode

کاج [kaaj]¹ (also - درخت) pine tree

کاج [kaaj]² loop or buttonhole in clothing (for fastening)

کاچی [kaachi] kachi (sweet, thin gruel made with flour)

کاخ [kaakh palace ♦ سفید - the White House

کادر [kaader] cadre, personnel; staff
• خارج – *military* non-table of organization; non-organic
• داخل – table of organization; organic, authorized

کار [kaar]¹ 1.1 work, labor; business; occupation, employment; pursuit ♦ جسمی - manual labor ◊ علمی - scientific work ◊ قدرت - capacity for work, fitness for work ◊ کار های تان چطور است؟ How are you getting along? 1.2 deed, act, action ♦ نیک - good deed ◊ خوبی کردی - You did a good deed. ◊ هنوزکاری نکردم - I never did any [such] thing. ◊ مراچه - (است)؟ But what is it to me? / What do I care? 1.3 operation; function; functioning 2 (second component of compound words with meanings "doing something" / "involved in something") ♦ جنایتکار criminal ◊ ورزشکار sportsman 3 to earn ♦ من از هر روز پنجاه افغانی - میکنم I earn 50 afghani a day.
• دادن - 1 to have an effect, to affect 2 to operate, to function ♦ این دستگاه خوب – میدهد This apparatus / equipment works fine.
• شدن - 1 to be made [of]; to be finished [with], to be trimmed [with] ♦ دیوارهای مسجد از سنگ مرمرکارشد The walls of the mosque were / are trimmed with marble. 2 to be worked over or through, to be worked out
• کردن - 1 to work, to be involved in a matter or business 2 to service, to maintain ♦ این ماشین را سه نفر - میکنند This machine is maintained by three people.
• گرفتن - to use, to make use [of] ♦ برای تنویر از چراغ ها - میگیریم We use lamps for illumination.
• از - اقتادن to go out of order, to malfunction; to go bad, to break
• از – انداختن 1 to disable, to put out of action 2 to stop, to switch off (an engine, etc.)
• به – انداختن 1 to put into operation, to put in motion 2 to hand over for operation
• به – رقتن to make use [of], to be used
• روی – آمدن to arise, to spring up, to appear
• روی – آوردن to bring to life, to create
• روی – بودن 1 to operate, to work, to function 2 to be in operation
• روی – بودن 2 ☞ زیر - بودن
• کسیرا ساختن - to be through with somebody; to be finished with somebody
• (چیزی) را – داشتن کسی *colloquial* 1 to have business with somebody 2 to need, to have need for something ♦ شیر برای شما - است؟ *colloquial* Do you need milk?

کار [kaar]² کاشتن [kastan] (and) *present tense stem* کشتن [kestan] 2 (second component of compound words with meanings of "sowing" / "cultivating") ♦ پخته کار cotton grower

کارآزمایی [kaaraazmaayi] 1 knowledge of [one's] business, experience; proficiency 2 test, trial; check, check-up (in business, in work)

کارآزموده [kaaraazmuda] 1 checked, tested 2 experienced, qualified

کارآمد [kaaraamad] necessary, needed; useful
• وزن -● net weight, payload

کاربر [kaarbor] 1 business *adjective*, efficient, business-like; clear, explanatory 2 decisive

کاربن [kaarbon] ☞ کاربون

کاربون [kaarbon] *chemistry* 1 carbon 2 graphite

کاربون پیپر [kaarbonpaypar] carbon paper

کاربون فیته [kaarbonfita] ribbon (for typewriter)

کاربونیک [kaarbonik] carbon carbonic *adjective*

کاربیتر [kaarbeetar] *technical* carburetor

کارت [kaart] 1 card 2 (business) card (also calling card)

کارتوس [kaartus] cartridge ♦ تفنگ - rifle cartridge

کارتوس دانی [kaartusdaani] bandoleer, cartridge belt

کارتوگرافی [kaartograafi] cartography

کارتون [kaarton] cardboard, cardboard box or carton 2 letter file 3 caricature, cartoon

کارته [kaarta] quarter, region, area (of a city)

کارخانه [kaarkhaana] *colloquial* 1 workshop, enterprise 2 shop 3 kitchen

کارد [kaard] knife ♦ قلبه - blade of a plow

کاردار [kaardaar] manager, steward; salesman, shop assistant

کاردان [kaardaan] knowing [one's] business; qualified; competent

کارروایی [kaarrawaayi] 1 conducting business; activity 2 actions, measures 3 conduct, behavior; acts, deeds

کارزار [kaarzaar] battle, combat, engagement

کارسازی [kaarsaazi] 1 arrangement (of matters), arranging (matters) 2 help, assistance; promotion, promoting 3 knack (for arranging matters); resourcefulness
• شدن - to be settled, to be arranged (about matters)
• کردن - 1 to put (somebody's) affairs in order 2 to help, to assist

کارشده [kaarshoda] used up, exhausted, used ♦ ریگ - used sand

کارشناس [kaarshenaas] specialist, expert
کارفرما [kaarfarmaa] 1 employer; owner of an enterprise, proprietor 2 manager
کارکشته [kaarkoshta] 1 experienced, worldly, wise 2 true; real, regular ♦ مانند دایه - like a true nurse or nanny
کارکن [kaarkon] 1 able-bodied, energetic; industrious, hard-working 2 collaborator; employee, worker ♦ کارکنان شعبه employees of section
کارگاه [kaargaah] 1 machine tool ♦ بافندگی weaving loom 2 workshop, shop ♦ ترمیم - repair shop 3 work place, work station
کارگذار [kaargozaar] 1 accomplishing; performing; executing, putting into practice, implementing 2 executive, executor; functionary
کارگر [kaargaar] 1 worker, laborer ♦ طبقه - working class 2.1 industrious, diligent, hard-working; businesslike ♦ این آدم خیلی - است This man is very diligent. 2.2 effective, having a useful effect
• شدن - to be effective, to have a positive result ♦ این دارو - شد This medicine took effect / had an effect.
کارگردان [kaargardaan] producer (in the cinema)
کارگزار [kaargozaar] ☞ کارگذار
کارنامه [kaarnaama] 1 exploit, feat; deed 2 deeds, acts, actions 3 story (of somebody's deeds)
کاروان [kaarwaan] caravan; train, column
کاروان سرای [kaarwaansaraay] caravansary, inn
کاروبار [kaarobaar] affairs, state of affairs
• کاروبار تان چطور است؟ How are things with you? (a question when greeting someone)
کاری [kaari] 1 energetic; businesslike ♦ این آدم هم کاری وهم باری است This man is a jack-of-all-trades. 2 effective; powerful (in influence); serious (in consequences)
• تیر -1 striking arrow 2 great sorrow, terrible bereavement
کاریدن [kaaridan] ☞ کاشتن
کاریز [kaareez] karez, subterranean irrigation canal
کاریگر [kaareegar] colloquial ☞ کارگر
کاسب [kaaseb] (plural کاسبان [kasebaan] (and) کسبه [kaasaba]) artisan, craftsman; factory hand, workman
کاسبی [kaasebi] 1 trade, craft 2 craft adjective, handmade
• کردن - to engage in crafts
کاست [kaast] diminution, decrease; subsidence
کاستن [kaastan] (present tense stem کا [kah]) to decrease (to be decreased), to diminish, to lessen (to be diminished, to br lessened), to reduce, to shorten (to be reduced, to be shortened)
کاسه [kaasa] 1 large cup, bowl; basin ♦ چینی - china bowl 2 resonator (of stringed musical instruments) 3 botany calyx, corolla
• سر - anatomy cranium
• چشم - anatomy eye socket
کاسه برگ [kaasabarg] botany sepal
کاش [kaash]
• ای کاش Oh, if only! / May I / he / etc.!
کاشتن [kaashtan] (present tense stem کار [kar]) 1 to sow 2 to till, to cultivate (ground)
کاشته [kaashta] 1 past participle کاشتن 2.1 sown; planted 2.2 tilled, cultivated
کاشف [kaashef] 1 discovering; exploring; investigating 2 explorer; investigator; discoverer

کاشی [kaashi] tiles; glazed tile; glazed brick
کاشی کاری [kaashikaari] trimming, finishing, decorating with tiles, glazed tiles, glazed-brick
کاشی گر [kaashigar] worker who manufactures tiles; a worker who glazes (tile or brick)
کاشین [kaashin] 1.1 ☞ کاشی 1.2 glazed plates and dishes
کاغذ [kaaghaz] paper
• تعمیراتی - (and) قیر - tarred felt, roofing felt, tar paper
کاغذ پیچ [kaaghazpeech] 1 paper roll 2 wrapped in paper, covered with paper
کاغذدانی [kaaghazdaani] (waste paper) basket
کاغذگیر [kaaghazgir] ☞ سنگکی
کاغذی [kaaghazi] (opposite of سنگکی [sangaki]) 1 paper adjective, of paper ♦ نوت - bank note 2 thin-barked, having a thin shell (usually about nuts)
کاغ کاغ [kaagh kaagh] cawing (of a crow)
کافتن [kaaftan] (present tense stem کاف [kaf]) ☞ کاوش کردن in کاوش entry
کافر [kaafer] 1.1 nonbeliever, infidel; apostate 1.2 Kafir, inhabitant of Nuristan 2 wicked, malicious, evil; fierce, ferocious; cruel; brutal
کافرستان [kaaferestan] historical Kafiristan, land of the Kafirs (now Nuristan)
کافری [kaaferi] Kafirs (nationality inhabiting Nuristan and Chitral)
کافور [kaafur] camphor
کافوری [kaafuri] 1 camphor adjective, camphoric 2 white, gray (about hair)
کافه [kaafa] (and) کافی [kaafi]¹ coffee
کافی [kaafi]² 1 sufficient, enough 2 sufficiently, it is enough ♦ بقدر - - to a sufficient degree
کافی [kaafee] cafe
کاک [kaak] cork
• کاغذ -• Whatman drawing paper
کاکا [kaakaa] 1 uncle (father's brother) 2 uncle (form of address to an elderly man)
کاکوتی [kaakoti] ☞ کاکوتی
کاکر [kaakar] (plural کاکران [kakaran]) 1 Kakars (tribe) 2 a Kakar
کاککش [kaakkash] corkscrew
کاکل [kaakol] 1 bang (of hair), forelock; curl, lock, ringlet 2 tuft, crest, hood (on a bird)
کاکوتی [kaakoti] botany mountain mint; thyme (an aromatic seasoning added to sour milk)
کاکه [kaaka] colloquial daredevil
کاگل [kaagel] ☞ کاه گل
کالا [kaalaa] 1 things, belongings; utensils 2 clothes; linens
کالابرانی [kaalaaboraani] ☞ رخت برانی
کالاشویی [kaalaashuyi] washing, laundering
کالبد [kaalbod] 1 body, figure (about a dead person or a sculpture) 2 form; pig, billet (casting)
کالج [kaalej] college
کالر [kaalar] collar
کالنی [kaalanáy] ☞ سالنامه
کاله [kaala] ☞ کالا
کام [kaam]¹ palate
کام [kaam]² 1 wish, desire, longing; bent, attraction, passion ♦ دل - [one's] heart's command 2 [one's] desire, the object of [one's] desires

235

ک

برداشتن • گرفتن - (and) - to attain [one's] desire (from somebody از); to satisfy [one's] passion
• به - خود رسیدن to attain [what one] desires, to find one's happiness
کامپیوتر [kampyutar] electronic computer
کامچن [kaamchan] sedan chair for carrying people
کامرا [kaamraa] ☞ کامره
کامران [kaamraan] 1 happy; succeeding, successful 2 *masculine proper name* Kamran
کامرانی [kaamraani] 1 enjoyment of life 2 success, happiness
• کردن - 1 to enjoy life 2 to succeed
کامره [kaamra] *technical* chamber
• سینما - motion picture camera
• عکاسی - camera
کامل [kaamel] 1.1 full; total, complete 1.2 exhaustive, comprehensive; finished 1.3 perfect, irreproachable 1.4 having attained perfection (in knowledge) 2 *masculine proper name* Kamel
• کردن - 1 to finish, to complete 2 to make perfect, to bring to perfection 3 to replenish; to reinforce; to complete; to man
کاملا [kaamelan] fully, completely; absolutely, perfectly; wholly, entirely; exclusively
کامه [kaama] comma
کامیاب [kaamyaab] 1 having achieved success; successful 2 having passed an examination
• برآمدن - (and) شدن - 1 to achieve success, to succeed 2 to pass an examination
کامیابی [kaamyaabi] 1 success, achievement, attainment, victory 2 passing an examination
کان [kaam] 1 mine, pit; shaft; mines; fields 2 beds, deposit 3 (also - مواد) ore 4 wellspring; depository, storehouse
کانال [kaanaal] 1 canal 2 *technical* channel ♦ - مخابره communications channel 3 tunnel (in mountains)
کانالیزاسیون [kaanaalizaasyun] sewerage system
کانج [kanj] *colloquial* walleyed, cross-eyed, slanting
کاندکتر [kaandaktar] conductor, bandleader
کاندنسر [kaandensar] *technical* condenser, capacitor
کاندید [kaandid] (*plural* کاندیدان [kaandidaan]) candidate, nominee (for public office)
• شدن - 1 to be a candidate (for public office) 2 to be an applicant or candidate (for entrance examinations), to be a participant (in competitive examinations)
کانسرت [kaansert] concert
کانسوننت [kaansonent] *linguistics* consonant, consonant [sound]
کانشکا [kaaneshkaa] *historical* Kanishka (Kushan ruler)
کانفرانس [kaanfarans] 1 lecture 2 conference ♦ - اطاق conference hall
کانکریت [kaankreet] concrete ♦ آهن دار - reinforced concrete
کانکریت ریزی [kaankreetreezi] (and) کانکریت کاری [kankretkari] concreting, concrete work
کان کن [kaankan] mining engineer, miner
کانکور [kaankur] competition ♦ امتحان کانکور - competitive examinations
کانگرس [kaangres] (and) کانگریس [kaangres] congress
کانون [kaanun]¹ nidus; focus, center ♦ زلزله - focus of an earthquake

کانون [kaanon]² kanoon (stringed musical instrument played by plucking, similar to a zither)
کانونشن [kaanwensaan] convention
کاوچوک [kaawchuk] caoutchouc, rubber
کاوش [kaawesh] 1 digging, excavation of ground 2 search, exploration (scientific) 3 excavations ♦ کاوش های علمی archeological excavations
• کردن - 1 to dig, to dig up 2 to carry on excavations 3 to explore, to conduct a search
کاونده [kaawenda] root crops
کاوه [kaawa] (also لیم کاری -) soldering iron ♦ برقی - electric soldering iron
کاویدن [kaawidan] to dig, to dig up, to dig out
کاه [kaah] 1 *present tense stem* کاستن 2 straw
کاه پر [kaahpor] stuffed with hay, stuffed with straw ♦ حیوان - stuffed animal
کاه خانه [kaahkhaana] place where clay and straw are mixed
کاه دان [kaahdaan] storehouse for straw; hayloft
• دزد نادان به - درآید *proverb* The inexperienced thief lands in the hayloft.
کاه ریزه [kaahreeza] wild safflower
کاه گل [kaahgel] adobe; coating for walls (made of straw and clay)
• کردن - to daub, to coat (walls)
کاهگل کاری [kaahgelkaari] plastering, daubing, coating (walls) with clay mixed with straw
کاهل [kaahel] 1 lazy, sluggish; slow, languid 2 inert
کاهلی [kaaheli] 1 laziness; sluggishness; languor 2 inertness
کاهنده [kaahenda]
• *technical* - تراسفارمر step-down transformer
کاهو [kaahu] lettuce salad
کاهیدن [kaahidan] ☞ کاستن
کایچی [kaaychi] rafters, trusses
کاین [kaayen]
• بودن - to be, to be located, to be situated
کاینات [kaayenaat] 1 cosmos, world, universe 2 essence, nature
کباب [kaabaab] kabob; roast meat (on a spit); shashlik
• کردن - 1 to make shashlik; to roast meat 2 to torture, to torment
• شدن - 1 to be roasted (about shashlik) 2 to be tortured, to be tormented
کبابی [kabaabi] 1 vendor of kabobs, vendor of shashlik 2 fit, suitable, or good for kabob, for shashlik
• گوشت – meat that is good for kabob, for shashlik
کبد [kobad] *anatomy* liver
کبر [kebr] pride, haughtiness, arrogance
کبک [kabk] partridge
• دری - mountain turkey (of pheasant family)
کبل [kabal] turf, sod
کبوتر [kabutar] pigeon, dove
کبود [kabud] gray ♦ قره قل - gray karakul ◊ نیلی - dark dapple-gray (about a horse's coat)
کبیر [kabir] great, large, big
کبیسه [kabisa] (also سال -) leap year
کبین [kabin] booth, cab ♦ پیلوت - pilot's cockpit, pilot's cabin
کپ [kap] *sport* cup (prize) ♦ کپ قهر مانی - championship cup
کپ [kop] *colloquial* hunched, bent; stooping ♦ پیرزن کپ - hunched-over old woman

کپتان [keptaan] captain (of a ship, of a sports team)

کپچه [kapcha] ☞ کفچه

کپرا [kapraa] ☞ کپره

کپړه [kapra] *colloquial* fabric, cloth, material

کپسول [kapsul] capsule

کپک [kopak] hunchback

کپه [kapa]
• کردن - *colloquial* to pour into the mouth (about powder, etc.)

کپه یی [kapayi] *colloquial* medicine (in powder form)

کتاب [ketab] (*plural* کتب [kotob]) book ♦ خطی - manuscript ◊ درس - textbook

کتابت [ketaabat] 1 writing 2 correspondence, business correspondence

کتابچه [ketaabcha] 1 notebook ♦ یادداشت - notebook 2 booklet, pamphlet

کتابخانه [ketaabkhaana] ☞ کتب خانه

کتابداری [ketaabdaari] library work

کتابفروشی [ketaabforoshi] 1 book trade 2 bookstore; row of book stalls (at a bazaar)

کتابی [kataabi] 1 book *adjective* 2 well-read, literate

کتاره [kataara] 1 railing; parapet 2 (small) fence ♦ چاه - framework around a well

کتان [kataan] 1 flax 2 linen ♦ تار - flaxen fiber; flaxen thread

کتانی [kataani] flaxen, linen *adjective*

کتب [kotob] *plural of* کتاب

کتب خانه [kotobkhana] 1 library; book respository 2 bookstore

کتبی [katbi] writing, written

کتره [katra] ambiguity; double entendre; hint
• گفتن - to speak in ambiguities, to use double entendres

کتک [kotak] *colloquial* stick, bludgeon, cudgel
• کالاشویی - battledore, paddle used to beat clothes during washing

کتلاک [katlaak] catalog

کتله [kotla] 1 mass, accumulation; gathering, crowd ♦ مردم - mass of people 2 mass *physics*
• یک - حماقت است He is an utter fool.

کته [katta] 1 large, big 2 base string

کته بیزی [kattabeezi]
• ایلک - coarse sieve

کته خرج [kattakharj] *colloquial* spendthrift, prodigal

کته سر [kattasar] *colloquial* leader, head, chief

کته کته [kattakatta] *colloquial* 1 very large, tremendous ♦ ماهی - large fish 2 rudely; impudently, insolently
• گپ - rude words, swearing
• گفتن - to scold, to scold rudely

کته گل [kattagol]
• قره قل - karakul in large curls

کته گوی [kattagoy] ribald man, quarreler, brawler

کتی [káti] with, together with ... *preposition*
• شما - with you

کثافت [kasaafat] 1 dirt, dirtiness 2 *physics* density, thickness 3 *technical* slag

کثرت [kasrat] 1 abundance, plenty, great number 2 frequency, state or quality of being repeated
• به - frequently; in large quantity or amount; abundantly

کثیر [kasir] 1 many; numerous 2 abundant, plentiful 3 frequent, frequently encountered

کثیف [kasif] 1 dirty; slovenly, untidy; soiled; polluted 2 dense, thick *physics*

کج [kaj] 1.1 crooked; curved, bent 1.2 erroneous, incorrect 2.1 crookedly, awry; slantwise, obliquely; aslant; at random; at a slant 2.2 erroneously, wrongly, incorrectly
• کج شدن 1 to bend *intransitive*, to stoop, to bow; to be warped 2 to become distorted, to change, to undergo change

کجا [koja] 1.1 (also - در) Where? 1.2 (also - به) [to] Where / Whither? ♦ میروی؟ - Where are you going? 1.3 از؟ From where? ♦ اینرا از – میدانی؟ 1.4 How do you know this? ♦ کجای اینجا – است؟ ◊ شما درد میکند؟ Where does it hurt you? 2 What place? ♦ است؟ How far? / As far as what place? What kind of place is that?

کجاوه [kajaawa] 1 seat (on the back of a camel) 2 side car (of a motorcycle)

کجاوه دار [kajaawadaar]
• موتر سیکل - motorcycle with a sidecar

کج بخت [kajbokht] unlucky

کج حساب [kajhesaab] *colloquial* dishonest (in trade, bargaining); cheating (in counting), cheating (in weighing)

کج حسابی [kajhesaabi] *colloquial* dishonesty, fraud, deception (in trade, bargaining); (an act or instance of) cheating (in counting), cheating (in weighing)

کج دارومریز [kajdaaromareez]
• کردن - *colloquial* to know how to maneuver; to shift, to dodge (in order to observe the rules of propriety)

کج رفتار [kajraftaar] 1 acting badly; ungentlemanly; or dishonorable 2 insidious, perfidious, deceptive, delusive ♦ چرخ - perfidious fate, ill fate

کج قلم [kajqalam] *colloquial* 1 ☞ کج حساب 2 pettifogger, bureaucrat, procrastinator

کجک [kajak]² *colloquial* a forelock that is out of place, ringlets of hair on [someone's] forehead

کجک [kajak]² iron hook (on the end of a goad used to drive an elephant)

کجکول [kajkol] cup for alms (used by a dervish or beggar)

کج گردشی [kajgardeshi] curve, bend, crook ♦ راه - bend or curve in a road

کجل [kajal] antimony (frequently with a touch of carbon black, used to tint the eyes)

کجل دان [kajoldaan] small silver box or case for antimony

کجلی [kajali] underlined or tinted with antimony, painted with antimony

کجی [kaji] 1 crookedness; winding; warping 2 incline, list 3 dishonesty, falsity, mendacity; duplicity, double-dealing

کجین [kajin] 1 silk combings 2 thick threads (for sewing or embroidering blankets)

کچاری [kachaari] *historical* residence of a governor or a district chief; governor's office, district headquarters

کچالو [kachaalu] potato

کچری [kechri] kechri (thick porridge or pudding made of rice, or lentils with gravy)

کچری قروت [kechri-qorut] kechri (in the shape of a mound with a depression on top for butter and melted qorut)

کچک [kochok] *colloquial* puppy; cub

کچکاسه [kachkaasa] scoop (for ladling off syrup when making sugar from sugar cane)

کچکک [kochokak] *anatomy* uvula

کچکول [kachkol] ☞ کجکول

کچل [kachal] *colloquial* 1 bowlegged, pigeon-toed 2 ☞ کل [kal]

کچوت [kachut] *colloquial* 1 low, base, mean 2 stingy, miserly, greedy, covetous

کخ [kekh] *children's speech* 1 naughty, bad 2 filth, dirt
• - کردن to kill, to do in

کدام [kodaam] 1 What kind [of]? 2 any kind [of], some 3 (with a negative predicate) no, none, no kind [of], any ♦ هنوز بکدام نتیجه ای نرسیده اند They have not yet arrived at any result.

کدخدا [kadkhodaa] 1 head of a household; head of a family 2 married man; bridegroom; fiance
• خانه مردم - *colloquial* taking liberties in somebody else's home; loving to play the master somewhere

کدخدایی [kadkhodaayi] marriage, matrimony

کدن [kadan] *colloquial* ☞ کردن

کدو [kadu] pumpkin

کدورت [kodurat] annoyance; trouble, grief, chagrin; offense, injury, wrong; sorrow

کدوگک [kadugak] *medicine* cupping glass

کده [kada] *colloquial* ☞ کرده

کر [kar] deaf

کراچی [karaachi] 1 cart, carriage, two-wheeled cart 2 wheelbarrow

کراچی ران [karaachiraan] (and) کراچی وان [karaciwan] driver, drayman

کراکتر [karaaktar] ☞ کرکتر

کراکش [karaakash] 1 pack (about a horse) *adjective* 2 driver, drayman

کرامت [karaamat] 1 miraculous power; miracle 2 generosity, favor, grace, mercy

کرانه [karaana] 1 edge, brim, brink, limit 2 ☞ کناره

کراه [keraah (and) keraay] *colloquial* ☞ کرایه

کراهت [karaahat] antipathy, aversion, repugnance, disgust

کراه شاهی [keraayshaahi] tax levied on inns, caravansaries, and shows for public services and amenities

کرایه [keraaya] 1 lease, rent; hire 2 (also - پول) rent, rental
• کرایه شاهی ☞ کراه شاهی
• - حمل ونقل freight, payment for shipment or transportation of cargo
• - به دادن to rent [out]; to hire out
• - کردن to hire; to rent; to charter
• چیزی را - دادن to pay for renting or for hiring something

کرایه دار [keraayadaar] leaseholder, lessee, tenant

کرایه کش [keraayakash] carrier, cabby, employed as a carrier or cabby

کرایه کشی [keraayakashi] carrier's trade
• - کردن to be occupied as a carrier, in the carrier's trade

کرایه نشین [keraayaneshin] tenant; lodger

کرایی [keraayi] rented, hired

کرایی [keraayi] frying pan

کرباس [karbaas] canvas, sackcloth, sacking; homespun cotton cloth

کرت [karat] *colloquial* time; once ♦ دو - twice

کرته [korta] shirt, Afghan long shirt

کرتی [korti] 1 jacket 2 tunic *military*

کرتی دامن [kortidaaman] woman's costume (consisting of skirt and jacket)

کرتی وار [kortiwaar] a length (of cloth) for a jacket

کرتی وپتلون [kortiwpatlun] man's suit

کرچ [kerch] saber, sword (officer's parade weapon, full dress weapon)

کرچ [kerech] *colloquial* crunch; gnashing or gritting (of teeth)
• کرچ کرچ کردن to crunch, to gnash or grit the teeth

کرچس [kerechas] ☞ کرچ [kerech]

کرخت [karakht] 1 numb, numbed 2 congealed, stiffened (from cold) 3 callous, unfeeling, cold ♦ وضع - cool treatment; cold relations ◊ اوباهمه مردم وضع – دارد He is cold (hardhearted) with everyone.
• ماندن - (and) شدن - *colloquial* 1 to become numb, to become stiff (about an arm, a leg, etc.) 2 to become numb (from cold) ♦ من از جنگ - مانده بودم I became numb from the cold 3 to become rigid, to freeze, to lose the ability to move (from fear, etc.) 4 to weaken, to become blunt (about pain)
• - مار *rarely* charmed snake, spellbound snake

کرد [kord] a built up section of a field, a plot (of land), a bed

کرد [kord] kurd

کردار [kerdaar] 1 act, action 2 conduct, behavior; manners

کردکی [kordaki] *colloquial* country, common people's ♦ - زبان country language, common people's language

کردگار [kerdagaar] creator, founder, originator

کردن [kardan] (*present tense stem* کن [kon]) 1 to do, to be occupied (with something) ♦ چه کنیم؟ What shall we do? 2 to do, to arrange, to accomplish, to perform (component of compound verbs) ♦ نیکی - to do good
• آب پاشی کردن to perform watering, to water, to irrigate

کرده [karda] 1 *past participle* کردن 2.1 *literary* work, creation 2.2 act; deed 2.3 (used to form the comparative degree of adjectives) ♦ ازگل - خوب است more beautiful than a flower
• از هیچ - باز چیزی بهتر است *proverb* Something is still better than nothing.

کرده [kerda] 1 good deed, boon 2 ☞ کردار

کرسمس [keresmas] Christmas

کرسی [korsi] 1 chair, armchair 2 seat (in a representative body) 3 base, pedestal (of a building)

کرشت [korosht] *colloquial* stiff, tough, hard, coarse (about cloth); astringent; dry

کرشمه [karashma] 1 winking 2 flirting
• - کردن 1 to wink, to make eyes (at someone) 2 to flirt

کرشنیل [koroshnil] crochet hook, knitting needle

کرفس [karafs] *botany* celery

کرک [kerk] *colloquial* 1 antipathy, hostility, enmity 2 contempt, scorn, disdain

کرک [kork] 1 underfur (of goats); goat down 2 cloth made of goat down

کرکتر [karaktar] character

کرم [karam]¹ 1 favor; grace, magnanimity, generosity 2 *masculine proper name* Karam

کرم [karam]² cabbage ♦ گلدار - cauliflower

کرم [kerm] worm; helminth, intestinal worm ♦ پیله - silkworm

کرمچ [kermech] tarpaulin, canvas

کرن [kren] ☞ کرین

کرنا(ی) [karnaa (y)] karnay, trumpet

کرنشافت [krenshaft] ☞ کرینشافت

کرنگ [korang] bay (about a horse's coat) ♦ نیلی - dark bay

کرنیل [karneel] *obscure* colonel

کرور [kror] kror, ten million, one hundred laks ☞ لک (one hundred thousand) ♦ سه - thirty million

کروزر [kruzar] cruiser

کروشنیل [korushnil] ☞ کرشنیل

کروکی [kroki] diagram; sketch; elementary sketch of a locality

کروم [krom] 1 *chemistry* chrome, chromium 2 a variety of leather

کرومیت کرومایت [kromit (and) kromayt] chromite, chrome iron ore

کروه [k (o) roh] koroh (a distance of about 3 kilometers)

کرویات [korawiyaat] *physiology* blood corpuscles ♦ خون سرخ - red blood corpuscles, erythrocytes ◊ خون سفید - white blood corpuscles, leukocytes

کره [kara] bracelet (on the arm)

کره [korra] ball, sphere ♦ زمین - the terrestrial globe

کره [korah] *colloquial* foal (of a horse or ass)

کری [kori] *colloquial* heel (of a shoe) ♦ بلند - high heel [of a shoe] ◊ پای - heel (of the foot)

کریدت [kreedet] credit

کریدتی [kreedeti]
● قرارداد - agreement, contract about granting credit

کریستال [kristal] crystal

کریله [kareela] karela (a bitter vegetable)

کریم [kreem] cream, paste ♦ دندان - toothpaste

کریم [karim] 1.1 magnanimous, gracious; kind; merciful; charitable 1.2 generous 2 *masculine proper name* Karim

کریملین [kreemlin] Kremlin

کرین [kreen] *technical* crane ♦ موتر - tow truck, crane truck

کرینشافت [kreenshaaft] *technical* crankshaft

کریه [karih] 1 disgusting, detestable, repulsive, infamous, foul, vile, loathsome, sickening 2 dirty, untidy

کژدم [kazhdom] scorpion

کس [kas] (*plural* کسان [kasaan]) 1 person ♦ کسی someone, somebody ◊ کسیکه ••• the person who…; the one who… ◊ هرکس each [person], everyone; any [person], anyone ◊ هیچ کس nobody, no one 2 relative, a near one

کساد [kasaad] 1 decline, depression, stagnation (usually in trade) 2 being in a state of decline (about trade)

کسالت [kasaalat (and) kesaalat] 1 indisposition, lethargy, feeling bad 2 weakness, feebleness, languor, sluggishness, weariness, fatigue

کسان [kasaan] *plural of* کس 2

کسب [kasb] 1 acquistion, getting, procuring; 2 trade, occupation, business
● معلومات - obtaining information; acquiring knowledge
● کردن - to acquire, to get ◊ اهمیت کردن - to acquire importance ◊ معلومات کردن - to acquire knowledge; to obtain information

کسبگر [kasbgar] artisan, craftsman

کسبه [kasaba] *plural of* کاسب

کسبی [kasbi] ☞ کسبگر

کسر [káser (*plural* کسور [kosur] (and) کسورات [kosuraat]) 1 diminishing, diminution, decrease lessening, reduction, subtraction 2 *mathematical* fraction ♦ اعشاری - decimal, decimal fraction ◊ (ساده) عادی - vulgar fraction, common fraction 3 lack, shortage; deficit 4 *medicine* fracture
● خفیف - crack, split
● شدن - 1 to diminish *intransitive*, to decrease, to lessen; to be reduced, to sink *intransitive*, to abate, to fall 2 to be subtracted, to be deducted
● کردن - *transitive* 1 to reduce, to diminish, to drop 2 to deduct, to levy; to subtract

کسره [kasra] kasra (the name of the diacritical mark -, which signifies the short vowel "e")

کسری [kasri] *mathematical* fractional ♦ عدد - fractgion, fractional number

کسل [kasal] 1.1 unhealthy, sickly, being indisposed, ill, sick 1.2 languid, sluggish, weary, tired 2 languidly, sluggishly, wearily ♦ گلم مینهاد - He was walking sluggishly, unhurriedly.
● کردن - *transitive* to tire; to bother, to pester, to vex, to annoy (somebody) (را)

کس مخر [kasmakhar] *colloquial* not finding demand, not being purchased by anyone

کسور [kosur] (and) کسورات [kosuraat] *plural of* کسر

کسوف [kosuf] eclipse of the sun

کش [kash] 1 *present tense stem* کشیدن 2.1 pulling, stretching 2.2 inhaling, drawing (while smoking) 3 sharpness, severity, tension (in relations) ♦ کش و مخالفت conflict 3 (second component of compound words) ♦ غمکش unfortunate creature, poor devil
● دل کش winning [one's] heart, charming, fascinating
● کش دادن to pull, to stretch
● کش کردن 1 to draw, to drag 2 ☞ کش دادن 3 to attract 4 *colloquial* to delay purposely, to interfere (in accomplishing something), to impede (the accomplishment of something) 5 *colloquial* to treat somebody sharply, sternly; to find fault [with] (با)

کش [kesh] Kesh! (cry with which to drive away birds, chickens)

کش [kosh] *present tense stem* کشتن [koshtan]

کشاد [koshaad] 1.1 spacious; wide, broad; biggish 1.2 vast 2 success, good luck; happiness

کشادن [koshaadan] to open

کشاده [koshaada] 1 *past participle* کشادن 2 open; wide, broad; free

کشاده دست [koshaadadast] generous

کشاده روی [koshaadaroy] affable, friendly, amiable; open-hearted

کشاف [kashshaaf] 1 scout, explorer, discoverer 2 boy scout

کشاکش [kashaakash] ☞ کشمکش

کشال [kashaal] 1.1 long, extensive, lengthy 1.2 protracted; prolonged 2 at length, at a leisurely pace

کشاله [kashaala] *colloquial* protracted controversy, conflict; quarrel

کشانیدن [kashaanidan] 1 to pull, to drag 2 to lay out (a route); to lay (an electrical transmission line, etc.)
● به طرف - to draw, to lure, to entice, to attract (to oneself)

کشت [kesht] 1 sowing 2 cultivation, tillage (of the land)

ک

کردن - 1 to sow 2 to cultivate, to till (the land)
کشت [kosht] murder, bloodshed ♦ وخون - slaughter, carnage
کشتار [koshtaar] 1 slaughter (of livestock) 2 slaughter, bloody battle, carnage, massacre
کشتزار [keshtzaar] sowed field, planted field; cornfield; tilled land
کشتگر [keshtgar] farmer, tiller, plowman
کشتگری [keshtgari] farming
• کردن - to be occupied in farming, to farm
کشتمندی [keshtmandi] sowing; plowing; tillage, husbandry
• کردن - to sow, to cultivate (a field)
کشتن [koshtan] (present tense stem کش [kosh]) 1 to kill, to slay, to destroy 2 to suppress, to put down; to stifle, to smother (a feeling, a sensation) 3 to slake (lime)
کشتن [keshtan] (present tense stem کار [kaar]) ☞ کاشتن
کشتوکار [keshtokaar] field work, sowing
کشته [keshta]¹ 1 past participle کشتن [keshtan] 2 area under grain crops, cornfield
کشته [keshta]² dried apricots
کشته [koshta] 1 past participle کشتن [koshtan] 2 (plural کشتگان [koshtagaan]) killed, slain 3.1 slaked (about lime) 3.2 colloquial dying from love
• کسی بودن - to die of love for somebody
کشتی [keshti] vessel, ship ♦ بادبانی - sailing vessel ◊ بخاری - steamship
کشتی [koshti] wrestling (sport)
- دادن to train, to teach wrestling
• گرفتن - to wrestle, to fight
کشتی بان [keshtibaan] (and) کشتی وان [keshtiwaan] 1 master of a vessel, boatman 2 helmsman, pilot
کشتی رانی [kashtiraani] navigation, ship-handling
کشتی گیر [koshtigir] wrestler, a participant in the sport of wrestling
کشش [kashesh] 1 technical traction ♦ قوه - tractive force 2 pull, tension 3 attraction 4 attractiveness
کشف [kashf] 1 discovery, uncovering; exposure 2 exploration; investigation; study 3 reconnaissance
• کردن - 1 to discover, to expose, to bring to light 2 to find, to detect; to open; to reconnoiter 3 to explore, to investigate
کشفیات [kashfiyat] 1 search, investigation, reconnaissance 2 discoveries, explorations
کشک [keshek] guard, watch
• دادن - to track, to shadow; to be on the watch [for]
• کردن - to stand guard, to guard
کشکچی [keshekchi] guard, sentry, watchman
کشکلک [keshkelak]
• کردن - to bathe, to wallow in dust (about a chicken)
کشمش [keshmesh] keshmesh, raisins
کشمکش [kashmakash] 1 quarrel, fight, skirmish; melee 2 confusion, disorder ♦ خانه - domestic squabbles
کشمیره [kashmira] woolen cloth
کشنده [koshenda] 1 present participle کشتن [koshtan] 2 killing, murderous, fatal
کشور [keshwar] country; state, power ♦ بزرگ - a great power ◊ کشورهای رو به پیشرفته the developed countries ◊ کشورهای انکشاف the developing countries
کشوگیر [koshogir] fight; brawl, scuffle
کشیدگی [kashidagi] tension, tense situation

کشیدن [kashidan] (present tense stem کش [kash]) 1 to pull out, to extract, to take, to get 2 to drive out, to turn out, to throw out ♦ من او را از خانه کشیدم I threw him out of the house 3 (component of compound words)
• انتظار - to wait
• زحمت – to toil, to labor
• سگرت – to smoke
• خط - to draw a line
• روغن – to squeeze out oil
• لباس – to remove clothing
کشیده اندام [kashidaandam] 1 tall 2 slender
کشیک [kesheek] ☞ کشک [kesheek]
کعبه [ka'ba] the Kaaba (sanctuary in Mecca)
کف [kaf]¹ (also کف دست) palm (of the hand) ♦ کف آستین cuff ◊ کف بادی bottom of a basket
• کف پای colloquial foot
• کف وکالر (stiff) collar and cuffs of a shirt
• به کف گرفتن to take into [one's] hand, to grasp with the hand
• سر به کف دست گرفتن colloquial to go headlong into some matter, to dash to meet danger
کف [kaf]² lather, foam ♦ کف صابون soap lather
• زدن to wash with soap, to rub or cover with soap, to soap
کف [kof]
• کف کردن colloquial to blow (on something), to breathe (on something)
کفار [koffaar] plural of کافر
کفالت [kafaalet] deputizing; execution of duties, discharge of duties
کفایت [kefaayat] 1 sufficiency, adequacy 2 qualification; ability
• کردن - to be sufficient, to suffice, to be enough
کفتار [kaftaar] hyena
کفتان [keftaan] colloquial 1 captain 2 class monitor
کفتر [kaftaar] ☞ کبوتر
کفچه [kafcha] 1 scoop, dipper, ladle 2 measure 3 (also - مار) ☞ کفچه مار
کفچه مار [kafchamaar] cobra
کف خورک [kafkhorak] gull
کفر [kofr] 1 unbelief; atheism, godlessness 2 blasphemy; profanity
کفران [kofraan] (also نعمت -) ingratitude
کفش [kafsh] footwear, shoes, (native) shoes
کفشکن [kafshkan] place in the home where shoes are removed; entrance hall, anteroom
کفک [kafak] scum (on soup or broth)
کف کف [kaf kaf] chapped, cracked
• شدن - to be covered with cracks, to be chapped
کفگیر [kafgir] (and) کف لیز [kafleez] ladle, scoop (for thick food)
کف مال [kafmaal]
• کردن - to rub, to massage, to knead (with the hand)
کفن [kafan] shroud
کفن دزد [kafandozd] 1 grave robber 2 fleecer, flayer
کفه [kafa] pan (of a scale)
کفیدن [kafidan] 1 to chap, to crack, to split, to break, to burst 2 to unravel, to tear (about cloth)

کفیل [kafil] 1 executing the duties, discharging the duties 2 deputy ♦ وزارت - deputy minister

کل [kal] 1 bald, balding ♦ سر کل bald head ◊ proverb سر کل از شانه فارغ است A bald head has no need of a comb. 2 scabby, mangy, with scab or mange on the head ♦ سر کل کلاه مخمل proverb [He / she has] a mangy head, but a velvet hat to make up for it. (said about an unworthy man who is lucky)
• کل شدن to go bald
• کل کردن 1 to cause balding 2 to shave

کل [kol (I)] all; every, everyone ♦ کل مردم all people, all the people

کلاس [kelaas] 1 rarely class (in school) 2 class (category)

کلاسیکی [kelaasiki] 1 classical; pertaining to the classics 2 excellent, first-class

کلاگک [kolaagak] technical head; tip, point

کلال [kolaal] potter

کلالی [kolaali] 1 potter's shop 2 pottery business, pottery trade ♦ چرخ - potter's wheel

کلام [kalaam] grammar 1 speech 2 combination of words; phrase ♦ اجزای - parts of speech

کلان [kalaan] 1 large, big, enormous, huge ♦ اطاق - large room 2 elder, senior ♦ برادر - older brother ◊ پدر - granddad ◊ مادر - grandma

کلانتر [kalaantar] head (of a district); elder (of a block, of a street)

کلان سال [kalaansaal] 1 adult, grown-up; senior in age, older 2 elderly

کلانشوندگان [kalaanshawendagaan] elders, leaders ♦ قوم - elders of a tribe

کلان صفت [kalaansefat] worthy (about a man); possessing great virtues

کلان کار [kalaankaar] putting on airs, vain

کلان کاری [kalaankaari] airs and graces, vanity; affectation

کلاوه [kalaawa] skein (of thread)

کلاوه پیچ [kalawapeech] reel

کلاه [kolaah] military headdress; hat; cap; cap ♦ فولادی - helmet

کلاهگک [kolaahgak] ☞ کلاگک

کلب [klab] club ♦ عسکری - officers' club ◊ مطبوعاتی - press club

کلپ [kelep] paper clip; snap fastener

کلپ [klap] ☞ کلپ

کلتور [kaltur] culture ♦ وزارت اطلاعات و کلتور Ministry of Information and Culture

کلتوری [kalturi] pertaining to culture, cultural ♦ روابط - cultural ties

کلجو [kaljaw] 1 husked barley 2 oats

کلچ [k(a)lach] technical clutch, coupling

کلچر [kalchar] rarely ☞ کلتور

کلچه [kolcha] 1 pastry; sweet roll 2 (numerative in counting certain piece goods with meanings of "piece" / "cake" / "slice", "head") ♦ پنج – صابون five cakes of soap ◊ دو – پنیر two heads of cheese

کلچه یی [kolchayi]
• پیاز - onions

کلخوز [kolxoz (and) kalxoz] kolkhoz (collective farm)

کلخوزی [kolxozi (and) kalxozi] 1 kolkhoz (collective farm) adjective 2 kolkhoz member, member of a collective farm, collective farmer

کلدارا [kaldaara] ☞ کله دار

کلدانی [kaldani] historical 1.1 a Chaldean, the Chaldeans 1.2 an Assyrian 2.1 Chaldean 2.2 Assyrian

کلسیم [kalsiyam] chemistry calcium ♦ هاید راکساید - calcium hydroxide, lime
• سلفیت - gypsum

کلسیوم [kalsiyom] ☞ کلسیم

کلفت [koloft] 1 coarse, crude, unrefined, inelegant 2 thick, heavy, fat; compact, dense

کلکین [kelkin] window

کلکینچه [kelkincha] 1 small window, ventilation window, casement 2 hatch 3 porthole

کلم [kalam] ☞ کرم [karam]

کلمه [kalema] (plural کلمات [kalemaat]) 1 word ♦ grammar ربط - conjunction ◊ ترکیب کلمات word-building ◊ به - word for word, literally verbatim 2 speech 3 religion (also اسلام -) symbol of faith, credo
• گفتن - to utter the Moslem symbol of faith
• کلمهء دو رگه hybrid
• کلمهء مرکب compound word
• کلمهء مشتق derivative word

کلمه بندی [kalemabandi] word combination, combination of words

کلنگ [kolang]¹ 1 pick, hoe 2 cooking piece, firing hammer (of a gun)

کلنگ [kolang]² crane (bird)

کلنیک [klenik] ☞ کلینیک

کلوخ [kolukh] clod, lump of dirt

کلوخی [kolukhi] made of lumps of earth; clay adjective

کلور [klor] chemistry chlorine

کلوراید [kloraayd] chemistry chloride ♦ هایدروجن - hydrochloric acid

کلوله [kolula] clod; lump; small ball, bead; round loaf ♦ نخ - ball of thread
• کردن (ساختن) - 1 to roll small balls (of bread) 2 to fashion a lump, to fashion a round loaf

کله [kalla] 1 skull, cranium 2 head

کله به کله شدن [kalabakalashudan] colloquial to knock heads

کله پریده [kallaparida] 1 scatterbrained, brainless 2 blockhead, idiot

کله پز [kallapaz] vendor of boiled sheep's heads and feet

کله جنبانک [kallajonbaanak] colloquial not having one's own opinion, agreeing with everyone

کله دار [kalladaar] colloquial 1 having a head on [one's] shoulders, intelligent; sensible 2 (also روپیه -) kalladar (an Indian rupee which was in circulation during the colonial period)

کله شخ [kallashakh] colloquial 1 stubborn, obstinate, willful 2 petty tyrant, willful and stupid person

کله گی [kallagi] head adjective ♦ تسمه - part of the harness worn on a horse's head

کله منار [kallamenaar] historical a pyramid of skulls of opponents killed in battle

کله و پاچه [kallawpaacha] head and feet (of a cow, of a sheep, etc.)
• شوربای - soup made out of heads and feet (seasoned with greens and vegetables)

کله ونگ [kallawang] colloquial utterly absorbed in a matter, utterly absorbed in a conversation; very busy

کلی [kali] 1 mange; scab 2 baldness 3 bald patch, bald spot

کلی [keli] *colloquial* ☞ کلید

کلی [kolli] rinsing, gargling (of the mouth, of the throat)
- کردن – to rinse, to gargle (the mouth, the throat)

کلیات [kolliyaat] 1 complete collection of works (of some author) 2 *plural* of کلیت

کلیات [kolliyaat] (*plural* کلیات [kolliyaat]) general conclusion, overall total (of something)

کلید [kalid] key

کلیرنگ [klireng] *finance* clearing
- اسعار – currency subject to exchange

کلیسا [kalisaa] Christian church

کلینر [kelinar] chauffeur's assistant

کلیگک [keligak]
- شدن – to become dumb; to be paralyzed ♦ زبانش شد – His tongue became dumb. / His tongue was paralyzed.

کلینیک [klinik] clinic

کلیه [kolya] *anatomy* kidney

کلیه [kolliya] 1 all ♦ اشخاص – all people, all the people 2 ☞ کلیت

کم [kam] 1.1 little *adverb*, a little, some; slightly ♦ کم از کم minimally, at least, minimum ◊ کم چیزی a little less [than], almost, nearly 2 rarely, infrequently ♦ او کم پیش من میاید He rarely comes to see me. 2 small *adjective*, little *adjective*, not large; insignificant ♦ کم درآمد small income 3 (first component of compound words with meanings "little-" / "not-")
- کم آب 1 shallow, dry; with little water 2 not juicy (about fruit)
- کم آمدن 1 to fall (in somebody's) eyes (پیش کسی) 2 to abase oneself, to grovel, to stoop [to]
- کم شدن 1 to diminish *intransitive*, to decrease *intransitive*, to grow short, to decline, to contract 2 to be deducted, to be subtracted
- کم کردن 1 to diminish, to decrease, to shorten, to reduce *transitive* 2 to deduct, to subtract *transitive*
- کم ما و کرم شما *proverb* Our modest gift -- your magnanimity. (You are welcome to all we have.)

کم آب [kamaab] 1 shallow, dry 2 not juicy (about fruit)

کم آبی [kamaabi] shoal, shortage of water

کمابیش [kamaabish] more or less, to a certain degree

کم استعمال [kameste'maal] little used, rarely used

کم اصل [kamásel] 1 non-pedigree, non-thoroughbred, not of pure blood (about animals) 2 ignoble, unworthy, worthless

کمال [kamaal] (*plural* کمالات [kamaalaat]) 1.1 perfection; completeness ♦ صاحب – having achieved perfection 1.2 *masculine proper name* Kamal 2.1 perfect; complete; the highest, the utmost 2.2 gifted, talented
- با (به) – میل 1 with great desire, with pleasure

کمالات [kamaalaat] *plural of* کمال 1

کمان [kamaan] 1 bow (the weapon) 2 arc 3 arch; vault ♦ رستم - rainbow

کمانچه [kamaancha] *music* 1 kamancha (type of violin, fiddle) 2 bow, fiddlestick

کم انکشاف [kamenkeshaaf] undeveloped, underdeveloped ♦ ممالک – underdeveloped countries

کمانه [kamaana] 1 arc 2 bend, curve (of a river)

کمانی [kamaani] spring

کمایی [kamaayi]
- کردن – to get, to obtain, to acquire; to earn

کمایگر [kamaayigar] ☞ پیداگر

کم بخت [kambakht] unhappy, unlucky; unfortunate

کمبر [kambar] narrow (about cloth, etc.)

کم بضاعت [kambezaaat] indigent, needy; insolvent, bankrupt

کمبغل [kambaghal] *colloquial* 1 poor, needy, indigent 2 a poor man

کمبود [kambud] 1.1 shortage, deficit 1.2 incomplete set 2 lacking, absent, missing

کمبودی [kambudi] ☞ کمبود 1

کم بین [kambin] seeing poorly, weak (about eyes)

کمپ [kamp] camp, tent camp, bivouac

کمپاس [kampaas] calipers

کمپریسر [kampreesar] (and) کمپریسور [kampreesor] compressor

کمپل [kampal] wool blanket; rug

کمپوندر [kampaundar] (and) کمپودر [kampudar] pharmacist; apothecary

کم پیدا [kampaydaa] rare

کمپیر [kampeer] old woman

کمپیرک [kampeerak] little old lady

کمپینگ [kamping] 1 campsite, tent camp 2 camp life

کم تجربه [kamtajreba] insufficiently experienced, inexperienced

کم جایداد [kamjaaydad] land-starved, land-hungry

کم جرأت [kamjor'at] shy, timid

کمحال [kamhaal] weak, pale, not having regained one's strength (after an illness)

کم حوصله [kamhawsela] languid, apathetic

کم خرج [kamkharj] limited in funds; not rich, not wealthy

کم خور [kamkhor] (and) کم خوراک [kamkhoraak] 1 eating little; underfed; malnourished 2 moderate in eating, abstemious in eating

کمر [kamar] 1 belt, girdle; loins; waist
- بستن – to decide (on something), to make up one's mind (about something), to intend (to do something), to prepare oneself (to carry out some job or work), to get ready (to carry out some job or work)
- کسی را شکستاندن – to shatter, to subdue, to plunge somebody into sorrow

کمر [kamar] 2 spur of a mountain, slope, incline

کمربسته [kamarbasta] 1 girded 2 having set out [for] 3 ready (to offer one's services) 4 *colloquial* unmarried (man or woman)

کمربند [kamarband] girdle, sash; belt ♦ محافظه – safety belt

کمرچین [kamarchin] gathered at the waist ♦ پیراهن – shirt with gathers at the waist

کمردار [kamardaar] 1 *tailoring* detachable ♦ لباس – two-piece dress 2 *colloquial* powerful, strong (about horse, etc.)

کمردراز [kamardaraaz]
- پیراهن – dress with elongated waist

کمرشکن [kamarshekan] 1 shattering, crushing 2 ruinous

کمر کیسه [kamarkisa] bag with powder (worn at the waist)

کمر گل [kamargol] buckle (on a belt)

کم رنگ [kamrang] (and) کم رنگه [kamranga] 1 pale, wan, dim, dull, faded 2 feeble, weak (about tea)

کمروی [kamroy] shy, bashful

کمرویی [kamroyi] shyness, bashfulness
کمره [kamra] 1 ☞ کامره 2 room; hotel room
کمسومول [komshomol] komsomol (Communist Youth League)
کمشنر [kameshenar] commissar, commissioner
• عالی - *historical* high commissioner (among English frontier troops in India)
کم طاقت [kamtaaqat] lacking endurance, weak; not possessing persistence and perseverance
کم ظرف [kamzarf] 1 cowardly, fainthearted, timid 2 petty creature
کمک [komak] 1 help, aid, assistance, support, encouragement ♦ کمک های اولیه first aid 2 confirmation, corroboration, reinforcement 3 grant, allowance
کم کم [kamkam] little by little, gradually
کمکنی [kamkoni] decrease, reduction; shortening, curtailment
کمکی [komaki] auxiliary, subsidiary ♦ - فعل *grammar* auxiliary verb
کم گوشت [kamgusht] lean, spare, skinny, gaunt
کم مایه [kammaaya] insolvent, bankrupt, not possessing enough capital
کم مصرف [kammasraf] economical, requiring minimal expenditures
کمند [kamand] 1 lasso, rope with a loop 2 horse tether
کم نظیر [kamnazir] rare, matchless, incomparable
کم وبیش [kamobeesh] (and) کم وزیاد [kamoziyaad] more or less
کمود [kamod] commode, toilet bowl
کم وکسر [kamkáser] 1 lack of, shortage 2 *colloquial* defect, flaw
کمونست [komunest] 1 a communist 2 communistic, communist *adjective* ♦ - حزب Communist Party
کمونستی [komunesti] communistic, communist *adjective* ♦ - جامعه communistic society
کمونیزم [komunizm] (and) کمونیسم [komunism] communism
کمی [kami]¹ quantitative ♦ - تغییرات *philosophical* quantitative changes
کمی [kami]² 1 diminution, lessening, decrease 2 lack of, shortage 3 pinching, jamming, constraint
• - نکردن 1 to spare no effort, not to miss the opportunity 2 to do everything possible
کمیاب [kamyaab] rare, rarely encountered
کمیابی [kamyaabi] rarity, inaccessibility (of something)
کمیت [kamiyat] quantity ♦ - وکیفیت *philosophical* quantity and quality
کمیته [komita] 1 committee 2 commission
کمیدان [komaydaan] *obscure* 1 commander 2 major
کمیدی [komeedi] comedy ♦ - فلم motion picture comedy
کمیدین [komeedyan] comedian, comic actor
کمیسار [komisaar] commissar ♦ - سرحدی border commissar, frontier commissar
کمیساریت [komisaaryat] commissariat ♦ - سرحدی officer's post on border
کمیسیون [komisyun] commission
کمیشن [kamishan] 1 *commerce* commission, commission operation 2 commissions (collections)
کمیشن کار [kamishankaar] broker, one who works on commission
کمیک [komik] comic, comical

کمین [kamin] ambush
کن [kan] *present tense stem* کندن
کن [kon] *present tense stem* کردن
کنار [kenaar] 1.1 ☞ کناره 1.2 shore, coast, bank 1.3 embrace 2.1 (also- در) by, near, at *denominative preposition* ♦ - در دریا by [the bank of] the river ◊ - راه در by [the side of] the road 2 - از by, close to, near
• در - گرفتن to embrace, to clasp in one's arms
کناره [kenaara] 1 edge, side; outskirts 2 end, border
• - گرفتن to resign, to retire
کناره جویی [kenaarajuyi] 1 reluctance to participate (in something), aspiration to remain aside 2 seclusion, solitariness; reticence, reserve
کناره گیری [kenaaragiri] self-dismissal, resignation, retirement
• - کردن 1 to avoid; to shun; to stand aside 2 to resign, to retire
کناری [kanaari] canary (bird)
کناری [kenaari] braid, (gold) lace
کنال [kanaal] canal ♦ سویز -Suez Canal
کنایت [kenaayat] (and) کنایه [kenaaya] 1 hint, allusion, hidden meaning 2 allegory
• - گفتن to hint, to allude, to speak in allusions; to make an allegory
کنتاکت [kontaakt] *technical* contact
کنترول [kontrol] control, monitoring, supervision
• - کردن 1 to control, to monitor, to check 2 to supervise, to watch [over]
• تحت - گرفتن to take under [one's] control or supervision, to monitor, to check
کنج [konj] corner; nook
کنجاره [konjaara] oilcake, cotton cake
کنجد [konjed] sesame
کنجک [konjak] *technical* (metal) corner brace, angle iron ♦ دروازه - door corner brace
کنجکاوی [konjkawi] curiosity
کند [kond] blunt, dull (*literally* and *figuratively*)
کندعقل [kondáqel] (and) کندفهم [kondfahm] dull; narrow; narrowminded; stupid
کندک [kandak] *obscure* battalion ♦ استحکام - sapper battalion
کندکمشر [kandakmésher] *obscure* battalion commander; major
کندن [kandan] (*present tense stem* کن [kan]) 1 to dig, to dig up or out 2 to tear off, to rip off, to strip off (skin, an envelope) 3 to tear out, to pull out 4 *colloquial* to bite (about a snake, etc.)
• از کسی چیزی - *colloquial* to get something out of somebody
کندنسر [kondensar] *technical* condenser
کندن کاری [kandankaari] digging, earth work, ground work ♦ تهداب - digging a pit for a foundation
کندو [kandaw] 1.1 gully, washout (a place eroded or washed away by water) 2 excavation; breach, gap (in a wall) 2 chipped; pierced; breached; washed away, eroded (by water)
کندو [kandu] clay or wooden vessel for storing grain

ک

کنده [kanda] 1 *past participle* کندن 2.1 ravine; hollow, depression 2 hole; pit, hollow, cavity, pothole
کنده [konda] block, stump ♦ چوب - log
کنده سوار [kondasowaar] *colloquial* witch (*literally*, riding or flying on a log)
کنده کار [kandakaar] engraver (on wood and stone); etcher
کنده کاری [kandakaari] 1 carving, engraving 2 profession of an engraver or of an etcher
کندی [kondi] 1 bluntness, dullness 2 slowness 3 sluggishness, inertness
کنسول [konsul] consul
کنسولگری [konsulgari] 1 consulate 2 post of consul
کنف [kanaf] ¹ hemp (*hibiscus cannabinus*)
کنف [kanaf] ² (*plural* اکناف [aknaf]) *literary* edge, side; outskirts outlying districts
کنفکشنری [kanfekshanari] 1 confectionery (shop) 2 confectionery (goods)
کنکتینگراد [kanektingraad] *technical* crank mechanism, connecting rod
کنکور [konkur] competition ♦ امتحانات - competitive examinations
کنگره [kangora] (and) کنگوره [kangura] merlon (of a fortress wall)
کنگینه [kangina] earthenware crockery (for prolonged storage of grapes)
کننده [konanda] (second component of compound words with meaning "doing (something)") ♦ تولید کننده producer
کنون [konun] now, nowadays ♦ تا - up to now
کنونی [konuni] present, contemporary, modern, present-day
کنیز [kaniz] 1 servant girl 2 *obscure* slave girl
کنیزک [kanizak] (and) کنیزه [kaniza] ☞ کنیز 1
کنین [konayn] cinchona [tree or shrub], quinine
کنیه [koniya] koniya (nickname formed from the name of a father or son), patrimonial name ♦ ابو علی Abu-Ali (*literally*, father of Ali)
کو [ku] *colloquial* ☞ کجا
کواسه [kawaasa] great-grandson; great-granddaughter
کواکب [kawaakeb] *plural of* کوکب
کوایل [kowaayel] *technical* ignition coil
کوب [kob] *present tense stem* کوفتن (and) کوبیدن
کوبه [koba] wooden beetle or beater (tool of a cotton scutcher)
  ● از زیر - برآمدن to go through the school of hard knocks; to experience much
کوبیدن [kobidan] *technical* 1 to beat, to strike, to hit, to knock 2 to smash, to break up, to pulverize, to pound 3 to drive in, to hammer in (a nail) 4 to thresh, to thrash 5 to forge
کوپان [kopaan] hump (of a camel)
کوپراتیف [koparaatif] a cooperative
کوپره [kopra] coconut; kernel of the coconut, copra
کوت [kot] ¹ *colloquial* 1.1 heap, pile ♦ خاک - heap of earth 2 guns, rifles (placed on the ground unstacked and fastened together) 2 much, a large quantity, amount (of something)
کوت [kot] ² 1 jacket, coat 2 overcoat
کوتاه [kutaah] 1.1 short ♦ راه - short journey 1.2 short, concise, brief; laconic, condensed 2 briefly, laconically, concisely ♦ بگویید - Speak concisely!
کوتاه اندیش [kotaahandeesh] careless, unwise, imprudent

کوتاه بین [kutaahbin] 1 shortsighted, nearsighted, myopic 2 improvident, not sagacious
کوتاه قد [kutaahqad (d)] undersized, short
کوتاه مدت [kutaahmoddat] of short duration, momentary, short-term
کوتاه نظر [kutaahnazar] near, not far off, short, limited, with narrow outlook, narrow-minded
کوتاهی [kutaahi] 1 trifle; brevity, conciseness 2 shortage 3 dereliction; negligence
  ● - کردن 1 to leave (something) unfinished 2 to commit negligence
کوت بند [kotband] (hanging) tab (for clothes)
کوتره [kotara] 1 wholesale *adjective* 2 wholesale *adverb*
کوتل [kotal] pass
کوتوال [kotwaal] *obscure* chief of city police, kotwal
کوتوالی [kotwaali] *obscure* police department
کوت ودامن [kotodaaman] (woman's) suit
کوته [kota] 1 room 2 house with a flat roof; hut, shack
کوته [kuta (h)] ☞ کوتاه
کوتی [koti] house, little house, villa
  ● - ستاره (name of summer residence of Habibullah Khan in Bektut) (Paghman)
کوچ [koch] roaming; migration, transmigration
  ● - دادن to migrate, to transmigrate, to move (to a new place of residence)
  ● - کردن to roam from place to place; to migrate, to transmigrate
کوچک [kuchek] little; small
کوچ کشی [kochkashi] migration, transmigration, move (to a new place of residence)
کوچگی [kuchagi] 1 neighbor living on the same street 2 street *adjective*
کوچ نشین [kochneshin] nomad
کوچه بندی [kochabandi] covered street (ending with a gate)
کوچه گشت [kochagasht] *colloquial* somebody who loafs about the streets, idler
  ● زن – wanton woman
کوچی [kochi] 1 nomadic; roaming, wandering ♦ طایفه - nomadic tribe 2 nomad
کوخه [kokhxa] *colloquial* cough
کود [kud] fertilizer ♦ کیمیاوی - chemical fertilizers
کودتا [kudetaa] plot, conspiracy; revolution, coup
کودک [kudak] child; baby, infant
کودکستان [kudakestaan] kindergarten
کودی [kawdi] kawdi, shells (used as money)
کودی چور [kawdichur] 1 cemetery beggar (usually a lad who snatches money distributed on the day of a burial or funeral feast) (☞ کودی) 2 *colloquial* greedy, greedily pouncing (upon something)
کور [kur] blind, unseeing
  ● - خود بینای مردم *proverb* He is blind to his own shortcomings, but he can see those of others.
  ● - شدن to go blind, to lose [one's] vision
  ● - کردن *colloquial* 1 to blind 2 to finish knitting or crocheting (by closing stitches)
کوربقه [kurbaqa] toad
کوردیپلوماتیک [kordiplomaatik] diplomatic corps
کورس [kurs] 1 courses ♦ لسان روسی - courses in the Russian language 2 *military* course, direction

کورکورانه [kurkuraana] 1 blind; reckless ♦ اطاعت - blind obedience 2 blindly, without reasoning; in the blind, by touch

کورکی [kuraki] hard, tough (about a nut) ♦ چارمغز - a hard walnut

کورگره [kurgera] *colloquial* hard knot (that is difficult to untangle)

کورمار [kurmaar] grass snake

کورموش [kurmush] mole

کوره [kura] stove, furnace; fire chamber; blast furnace ♦ اتمی - atomic reactor ◊ آهنگری - forge
• از – برآمدن - to go through fire and water, to become tempered

کوری [kori] heel (of a shoe) ♦ پای - heel (of a foot) ◊ بوت بدون shoes without a heel

کوری [kuri] blindness

کوزه [kuza] earthenware jug with a long neck
(and) - دولاب cup or bucket of a water wheel (for lifting water)

کوزه‌گر [kuzagar] potter

کوسه [kosa] *colloquial* (also کوسه ریش) man with a scanty beard, beardless man

کوش [kawsh] *colloquial* ☞ کفش

کوش [kosh] *present tense stem* کوشیدن

کوشا [kosha] striving, being zealous
• بودن - to endeavor, to strive

کوشان [kushan] *historical* the Kushan rulers
• کوشان شاهان [kushaanshaahaan] the period of the Kushan shahs, the epoch of the Kushan shahs - عصر

کوشانی [kushaani] *historical* Kushan *adjective*

کوشش [koshesh] endeavor; effort; zeal; diligence; striving
• کردن - 1 to endeavor, to try; to strive [for] 2 to try, to make attempts

کوششگر [kósheshgar] industrious, diligent

کوششی [kosheshi] ☞ کوشا

کوشنده [koshenda] ☞ کوشا

کوشیدن [koshidan] (کوش in entry) ☞ کوشش کردن

کوفت [koft] 1 blow 2 injury

کوفتن [koftan] (*present tense stem* کوب [kob]) ☞ کوبیدن

کوفته [kofta] 1 *past participle* کوفتن 2 pounded, tenderized (about meat) 3 meatballs, croquettes

کوک [kawk] *colloquial* ☞ کبک

کوک [kok] ¹ 1 winding mechanism, winding up (a watch, etc.) 2 tuning (a musical instrument) 3 cocking (a cocking piece)
• کردن - *military* 1 to wind (a watch, etc.) 2 to tune (a musical instrument) 3 to cock (a cocking piece)

کوک [kok] ² *medicine* 1 quilting; basting, tacking 2 large stitch, stitch 3 suture
• زدن - *medicine* 1 to tack, to baste; to sew hastily 2 to apply a suture

کوکب [kawkab] (*plural* کواکب [kawaakeb]) star; luminary, heavenly body

کوکره [kokra] *medicine* trachoma

کوکس [koks] coke

کوکو [koko] (and) کوکوگک [kokogak] *children's speech* little bird, birdie

کوکه [kuka] tack, small nail ♦ خار - shoe nail
• کردن - to nail; to line with nails; to resole [shoes]; to upholster

کوکه کاری [kukakaari] upholstering work

کوکی [koki] winding, cranking (about a mechanism)

کول [kol] 1 lake 2 artificial reservoir; pond

کولبار [kolbaar] (and) کولوار [kolwaar] bag, knapsack, shoulder bag (of a dervish)

کولت [kolt] (also - تفنگچه) Colt revolver

کولرا [kol (e)raa] cholera

کولن [kolon] colon

کولی [kuli] *colloquial* ill with leprosy, leprous; a leper

کوماندو [komaando] commando detachment

کومباین [kombaayn] combine

کومک [komak] ☞ کمک

کومه [koma] cheek, cheeks
• کردن - *colloquial* to grow heavy about the face, to become stout

کون [kawn] *obscure* 1 the world, the universe 2 being; existence

کون [kun] 1 anus 2 the posterior, the buttocks

کونه [kuna] *colloquial* ☞ کهنه

کونه کتل [kunakatal] *colloquial* old clothes, rags

کوه [koh] mountain; mountains ♦ سلیمان - Sulaiman mountains
• هفت - سیاه در میان *colloquial* God forbid that this should happen! (*literally*, Let it [remain] beyond seven impossible mountains.)

کوهان [kohaan] hump (of a camel, of a buffalo, of a yak)

کوهان‌دار [kohaandaar] humpbacked, with a hump (about a camel, buffalo, yak)

کوهبند [kohband] mountain, mountainous *adjective* ♦ منطقه - mountainous region

کوهپیمایی [kohpaymaayi] mountaineering, mountain climbing

کوهستان [kohestaan] mountain country; highlands; mountainous terrain 2 Kuhestan or Kohistan (region)

کوهستانی [kohestaani] 1 mountain *adjective*, mountainous 2 mountaineer (native or inhabitant)

کوه قاف [koheqaaf] legendary mountains of Kaf (which supposedly girdle the earth. According to legend, the simorgh bird lives in these mountains.)

کوه‌گردی [kohgardi] mountaineering, mountain climbing; walking in the mountains (as a form of sport)

کوه‌نشین [kohneshin] mountain inhabitant, mountaineer ♦ مردم - mountain people, mountaineers

کوه‌نورد [kohnaward] mountain climber, mountaineer

کوهی [kohi] 1 mountain *adjective*, mountainous ♦ مملکت - mountain country 2 wild, growing in the mountains ♦ ناک – wild pear

کویل [kweel] bobbin, coil ♦ برق - induction coil

کویه [kuya] moth

که [ke] I *pronoun*, who ♦ بر ای (از) که؟ For whom? / To whom? ◊ از که شنیدید؟ From whom did you hear [it]?

که [ke] *conjunction* (introduces various subordinate clauses) 1 which ♦ زمینی که بالای آن خانه آبادمینمایید خوب است The lot on which you are building a home is fine 1.2 because, since ♦ به اسباب برق دست زده نشودکه باعث مرگ میگر دد One must not touch electrical equipment with one's hands because [it]

245

can lead to death. **1.3** when ♦ در روز های قدیم که برق موجودنبود صندلی رواج زیاد داشت In former times, when there was no electricity, braziers were in great demand. **2** (becomes part of compound conjunctions) ♦ تاکه ◊ ۰۰۰ تاجاییکه so…that ♦ ۰۰۰ تا until ◊ ۰۰۰ چراکه because) **3** ◊ ۰۰۰ به نحوی که thus ♦ (introduces direct speech) ♦ گفت که نمی شناسمش He said: "I don't know him!"

کَه [kah] ☞ کاه

کَهالی [kahaali] **1** laziness **2** inertness, passivity
• کردن - to loaf, to be idle, to spend time in idleness

کَهَر [kahar] light chesnut (color); bay (about a horse)

کَهرُبا [kohrobaa] amber

کَهکَشان [kahkashaan] astronomy
• (also راه) the Milky Way

کُهَن [kohan] ancient, bygone; old, olden, antique

کُهنه [kohna] **1** old; decrepit, ramshackle **2** ancient, antique, olden

کُهنه چاک [kohnachak] experienced, old fox, old hand

کُهنه خیال [kohnakhiyaal] conservative, commonplace; outmoded, old-fashioned

کُهنه سال [kohnasaal] **1** elderly, old (man) **2** ancient, old, olden, antique

کُهنه فروش [kohnaforosh] *colloquial* vendor of secondhand clothing

کُهنه کار [kohnakaar] **1** experienced, worldly-wise **2** having acquired skill or experience (in something)

کُهنه و کَتَل [kohnaivakatal] old things, old stuff; old clothes

کی [kay] When? / At what time?

کیبل [keebal] **1** cable ♦ تیلفون - telephone cable **2** rope, line, cable ♦ کیبل فولادی steel cable

کیپنک [keepanak] shepherd's quilted jacket (pulled on over the head)

کیر [kir] male sex organ, penis

کیرکیرک [kirkirak] kingfisher

کیس [kays] Kays (legendary forefather of the Afghans)

کیسه [kisa] **1** tobacco pouch; bag, purse ♦ پشتی - knapsack **2** (also حمام -) mitten (for massaging the body)
• کردن - to massage, to rub with a bath mitten

کیسه مال [kisamaal] *colloquial* female bathhouse attendant (who massages with a mitten)

کیش [keesh] ¹ **1** cotton blanket; rug (in which men wrap themselves when it is cold) **2** silk fabric with designs or patterns

کیش [keesh] ² **1** faith, religion; cult **2** *literary* custom

کیف [kayf] **1** intoxication **2** enjoyment; pleasure **3** quality, property; virtue

کیفر [kayfar] retribution, punishment

کیفیت [kayfiyat] **1** quality **2** circumstances of a matter; essence of a matter; condition, state
• گفتن - to state the essence of a matter, to tell everything as it was

کیک [kayk] flea

کیک [keek] cake, raisin cake

کیلو [kilo] kilo, kilogram

کیلوگرام [kilograam] (and) کیلوکرم [kilogram] ☞ کیلو

کیلومتر [kilométer] kilometer

کیلووات [kilowaat] kilowatt

کیله [keela] banana; banana tree

کیلی [kili] *slang* ☞ کلید

کیمیا [kimyaa] chemistry ♦ عضوی - organic chemistry ◊ غیر عضوی - inorganic chemistry

کیمیادان [kimyaadaan] chemist

کیمیاگر [kimyaagar] alchemist

کیمیاگری [kimyaagari] alchemy

کیمیاوی [kimyaawi] chemical ♦ کیمیایی [kimyaayi] (and) تجزیه - chemical analysis

کینه [kina] spite; hatred

کیهان [kayhaan] the world, universe, cosmos

کیهان نورد [kayhaannaward] cosmonaut, astronaut

کیهانی [kayhaani] world *adjective*; cosmic, space *adjective* ♦ فضای - the cosmos, space

گ
26th letter of the Dari alphabet

گادر [gaadar] beam, girder; truss ♦ سقف - floor beam, ceiling beam

گادی [gaadi] **1** cart **2** carriage; phaeton ♦ تانکه - open carriage

گادی بان [gaadibaan] coachman, drayman, carter

گادی رو [gaadiraw] (also سرک -) cart road

گادی گک [gaadigak] children's carriage

گادی وان [gaadiwan] coachman, drayman, carter

گاراج [gaaraaj] garage (for motor vehicles)

گارد [gaard] guard ♦ احترام - guard of honor, honor guard ♦ شاهی - *historical* royal guard

گاز [gaaz] ¹ **1** rocking, swinging, oscillation, tossing **2** a swing **3** *colloquial* suspended baby cradle
• انداختن - to hang a swing
• خوردن - to ride on a swing, to swing on a swing

گاز [gaaz] ² (*plural* گازات [gaazat]) gas ♦ طبیعی - natural gas

گازر [gaazer] carrot, carrots

گازرگاه [gaazargaah]
• شریف - gazargah (mausoleum of Sheikh A. Ansari close to Herat and a burial place for saints that has been known since the 11th century)

گاف [gaaf] (also فارسی -) name of the letter گ

گالس [gaales] suspenders, braces ♦ جراب - garters for socks, for stockings

گام [gaam] step, stride
• برداشتن - to step, to stride; to walk
• نهادن - to step, to enter

گاو [gaaw] bull; cow; ox

گاودوشه [gaawdosha] milk pail

گاوزبان [gaawzabaan] bugloss (herb), oxtongue

گاوک [gaawak] snail

گاوگم [gaawgom]
• *colloquial* شام - late hour; twilight; evening dusk

گاومیش [gaawmeesh] buffalo

گاه [gaah] **1** time **2** *rarely* place (usually in compound words)
• گاه ۰۰۰ گاه - now … now …, sometimes … sometimes …
• آتش گاه شعله ور و گاه نیمه جانمیسوخت The bonfire sometimes burned with bright flames and sometimes barely glimmered.

گاه گاه [gaahgaah] sometimes, at times, from time to time

گاه وقت [gaahwaqt] now and then, sometimes, from time to time

گاهی [gaahee] sometimes, at times, from time to time
گاهیکه [gaahee-ke] when, while *conjunction*
گپ [gap] word; speech; talk, conversation
- گپ خام 1 thoughtless words, rash words, hasty words 2 empty talk, meaningless talk
- گپ راه serious words, serious talk
- گپ مفت nonsense, rot, rubbish
- گپ تمام شد The conversation is finished! / The deed is done!
- چه گپ است؟ What's the matter? / What happened?
- گپ زدن to talk, to converse
- گپ ساختن *colloquial* to smear, to slander
- سر گپ آمدن 1 to begin to speak, to start talking (about a child) 2 to get to the essence (of a matter), to get to the main thing
گپ ساز [gapsaaz] *colloquial* slanderer, gossip
گپ شنو [gapshenaw] *colloquial* obedient, dutiful
گپ گیرک [gapgirak] *colloquial* talebearer; informer
گپوک [gapok] 1 talkative, loquacious 2 windbag, chatterbox
گت [gat] *colloquial* ☞ گد
گچ [gach] lime; gypsum; alabaster ♦ گچ مالی plaster
گچ مالی [gachmaali] 1 coating with gypsum, with alabaster 2 *colloquial* plastering
گد [gad] 1 mixed 2 having flowed together (about a river)
- گد شدن 1 to be mixed 2 to flow together; to discharge [into] (about a river)
گدا [gadaa] beggar
گداختن [godaakhtan] (*present tense stem* گداز [godaz]) to melt, to fuse (*transitive* and *intransitive*)
گداز [godaaz] 1 *present tense stem* گداختن 2 smelting, melting, fusing ♦ آهن - melting of a metal
گدام [godaam] storehouse, warehouse ♦ تجارتی - trading base
- کردن - to store; to keep at a storehouse or warehouse
گدامدار [godaamdaar] manager of a storehouse or warehouse
گدایش [godaayesh] *colloquial* craving of a pregnant woman for spicy food
گدایگر [gadaaygar] beggar
گدایی [gadaayi] beggarliness, begging
- کردن - to beg, to go begging
گدر [godar] *colloquial* ☞ گذر 2.2, 2.3
گدود [gadowad] *colloquial* confused, tangled, muddled
گده [gada] 1 bunch; sheaf; bundle 2 skein (of wool, of yarn)
گدی [godi] doll
- بازی - to play with dolls
گدی پران [godiparaan] kite
گدیگک [godigak] (weaving) shuttle
گذار [gozaar] 1 *present tense stem* گذاردن (and) ☞ گذر 2.2
گذاردن [gozaardan] ☞ گذاشتن
گذاره [gozaara] 1 manners, approach (to people) 2 ☞ گذران 2.2
- کردن (با) - to treat (somebody)
گذاشتن [gozaashtan] (*present tense stem* گذار) 1 to place, to put 2 to leave, to abandon; to give up, to leave off 3 to give the opportunity, to permit; to allow
گذر [gozar] 1 *present tense stem* گذشتن 2.1 passage, pass, passageway; thoroughfare 2.2 crossing, ford 2.3 alley
گذران [gozaraan] 1 passing ♦ جهان - transient world, transitory world 2.1 conduct, behavior ♦ شیوه - mode of conduct, manners 2.2 means of subsistence or livelihood; life, living; existence, subsistence ♦ احمد خوب است - Ahmad lives well.
- داشتن - to treat (somebody)
- کردن - 1 to earn the means of subsistence, to earn a livelihood 2 ☞ داشتن -
گذراندن [gozaraandan] 1 to spend (time, a holiday, etc.) 2 to transport, to convey, to ferry (از)
گذشت [gozasht] 1 expiration, passing ♦ بعد از - یک ماه at the end of the month, after the end of the month 2 passing, marching ♦ عسکری - passing of troops, military parade 3 condescending, indulging 4 condescension, indulgence
گذشتاندن [gozashtaandan] 1 ☞ گذراندن 2 to suffer, to endure (an illness) ♦ باهم - to spend together (time, life) 3 to conduct, to lead off, to draw off, to drain ♦ آب - water run-off, water outlet
گذشتگان [gozashtagaan] ancestors, forefathers
گذشتن [gozashtan] (*present tense stem* گذر [gozar]) 1 to pass, to elapse, to fly (about time, events, etc.) 2 to cross [on foot or in a vehicle] (via something) (از) 3 to waive (something از); to let have; to yield; to sacrifice (از)
گذشته [gozashta] 1 *past participle* گذشتن 2 last, past 3 the past
- در - in the past, formerly, previously
- از - besides, except, apart from *compound conjunction*
گر [gar] (suffix forming nouns of agency) ♦ ریخته گر founder, caster, smelter
گر [gor] raw sugar
گراری [geraari] gear, cogwheel
گراف [geraaf] graph; diagram; curve (of growth of something) ♦ کاغذ - graph paper
گرافون [graafon] ☞ گرامافون
گرام [graam] gram
گرامافون [graamaafon] phonograph
گرامر [graamar] grammar
گرامی [geraami] dear, respected ♦ قارئین - Dear readers!
گران [geraan] 1 dear, expensive, valuable 2 heavy ♦ گرز - heavy club or cudgel
گرانبها [geraanbahaa] dear, expensive, valuable, precious
گرانجان [geraanjaan] depressed, sad, downcast
گرانجانی [geraanjaani] depressed state; state of being sad or downcast
گرانگ [geraang] *colloquial* heavy, weighty
گربه [gorba] *rarely* cat
گرچه [garche] ☞ اگرچه
گرزندوی [garzenduy] 1 traveler 2 tourist
گرد [gard] dust
گرد [gerd] 1 round 2 (also در, به -) around, round *denominative preposition*
- آمدن - to gather [together] in a circle
- آوردن - to gather, to unite
گرداب [gerdaab] whirlpool, abyss
گرداگرد [gerdaagerd] round, around, on all sides
گردان [gardaan] 1 rotation; revolution 2 repetition (of a lesson) 3 declension; conjugation *grammar*
- کردن - 1 to repeat, to learn (a lesson) by heart 2 to decline; to conjugate
گرداندن [gardaandan] 1.1 to revolve, to rotate 1.2 to swing, to turn 1.3 to change, to alter, to convert 2 (component of

247

گ

compound verbs) (synonym of verb کردن)
- • روشن - to elucidate, to shed light on, to explain
گردآورنده [gerdaawarenda] compiler (of a collection of stories); collector
گرد باد [gardbaad] wind with dust, dust storm
گردش [gardesh] 1 rotation, revolution, spinning; circulation (around something) 2 walking, taking a walk
- • کردن - 1 to rotate, to revolve, to spin; to circulate (around something) 2 to walk, to go for a walk, to stroll
گردن [gardan] neck
- • کشیدن - to behave obstinately, not to submit, not to be subordinate
- • ماندن - colloquial to submit, to obey
- • از – انداختن to get off, to get away (with something), to decline all responsibility
- • به - کسی افتادن to shift to somebody's shoulders, to place on somebody's shoulders (said of work, concern, etc.)
- • به – گرفتن to take on oneself; to set to (something)
- • گردنتان بشکنه May you break your neck!
گردن بلندی [gardanbelandi] pride; haughtiness
گردن بند [gardanband] 1 necklace 2 collar
گردن پتی [gardanpati] colloquial humility, shyness, timidity
گردوخاک [gardokhaak] dust; dirt; earth
گردونواح [gerdonawaah] environs; nearby regions
گرده [gerda] circle, disk, disc ◆ نان - flatcake
گرده [gorda] kidney; kidneys
گرده درد [gordadard]
- • از خنده - شدن colloquial to laugh until one's sides ache
گردیدن [gardidan] 1.1 to revolve, to rotate, to turn, to spin, to whirl 1.2 to roam, to wander, to stroll 2 (component of compound verbs) (synonym of verb شدن)
- • آزاد – to be freed, to be liberated, to become free
گرسنگی [gorosnagi] hunger; starvation
گرسنه [gorosna] hungry; starving
گرفت [gereft] 1 taking; seizure, capture 2 colloquial misfortune, trouble
گرفتار [gereftaar] 1 captured, seized, caught 2 very busy 3 colloquial enamored
- • شدن - 1 to be captured, to be caught 2 to be very busy 3 colloquial to fall in love
گرفتاری [gereftaari] 1 catching, detention, arrest 2 being busy 3 colloquial amorousness, love
گرفتم [geráftam] let us assume, let us suppose
گرفتن [gereftan] 1 to take, to collect; to take away 2 to catch, to seize, to grasp ◆ بگیرش که نگیردت colloquial Grab him before he catches you. 3 to get, to obtain, to receive ◆ پس - to take back, to return (to oneself) 4 colloquial to close up, to patch up, to repair; to sew, to mend ◆ درزهای دیوار را میگیرد He is patching up the cracks in the wall.
- • درپیش – راه خانه را to select (a path, a way, a course) ◆ درپیش گرفت He set out for home.
گرفته [gerefta] 1 past participle گرفتن 2.1 gloomy, somber; depressed, despondent, saddened 2.2 hidden (about the sun) ◆ آفتاب گرفته شد There is an eclipse.
گرفته گی [gereftagi] sadness, melancholy; bad mood
گرگ [garg] 1 itch, scab 2 mange
گرگ [gorg] wolf
گرم [garm] 1 warm, hot; torrid ◆ آب - hot water ◊ بحث heated argument 2 busy, lively ◆ بازار - lively trade

- • آمدن - 1 to get excited, to become excited 2 to flare up, to be flushed
- • آوردن - 1 to excite, to make excited 2 to anger, to tease (somebody)
- • کردن - 1 to warm, to heat 2 to enliven (a conversation)
- • باکسی گرم گرفتن to become very good friends, to become very close with someone
- • صبت - fascinated with [a] conversation
گرما [garmaa] heat, the hot season
گرماگرم [garmaagarm] at once, right now; immediately
- • ... - at the height (of something)
گرمجوشی [garmjoshi] zeal, fervor, enthusiasm
گرمسیر [garmseer] 1 torrid countries; the subtropics 2 tropical, with a torrid climate
گرمی [garmi] 1.1 heat, warmth 1.2 ardor, fervor 1.3 height (of passion), animation 2 با (and) - به - warmly, amicably, affably
- • خوردن - colloquial to get angry, "to blow up," to get angry without cause
گرنگ [gerang] colloquial heavy (about something)
گرو [geraw] 1 guarantee deposit, pledge; pawn 2 deposited, being in pawn
- • دادن - to give as a deposit
گروپ [gorup]¹ 1 tube, bulb ◆ برق - electric-light bulb ◊ رادیو - radio tube
گروپ [gorup]² group, team, section
گروپ دار [gorupdaar] tube; electron tube adjective ◆ جنریتر - electron tube generator, valve oscillator
گروپی [gorupi] group adjective ◆ رقص - group dance
گرونج [garwanj] wooden tables or shelves (for products at a food storehouse)
گروه [goroh] 1 group, detachment 2 crowd, throng 3 party
گروه گروه [gorohgoroh] in groups, in a body; in a crowd
گروی [gerawi] deposited, pledged, mortgage adjective, mortgaged
گره [gera] 1 knot 2 technical cramp iron, bracket, brace
- • بستن (زدن) - to tie a knot
- • بر ابروان – انداختن to knit one's brows, to frown, to knit one's brows sternly or sullenly
گری [gari] colloquial hour, small segment of time
- • سات وگری ☞ ساعت و -
گری [geri] present tense stem گریستن
گریال [garyaal] bronze disc attached to a tripod (for beating time); gong, bell
گریان [geriyaan] 1 whining 2 colloquial crying, weeping
- • کردن - to cry, to weep, to sob
گریبان [gereebaan] collar
- • دست بگریبان هم انداختن to fight, to grapple in a fight; to quarrel [with]
- • چاک کردن - to abandon oneself to despair (by tearing the collar of one's clothing)
گریختاندن [goreekhtaandan] 1 to put (somebody) to flight, to drive away 2 to convey (something) as contraband, to smuggle
گریختن [goreekhtan] (present tense stem گریز [gorez]) 1 to run away, to escape, to flee 2 to shun, to avoid
گریز [goreez] 1 present tense stem گریختن 2.1 flight, escape 2.2 evasion; digression; avoidance

248

گ

- کردن - to run away, to escape
- قوه گریز از مرکز centrifugal force

گریزان [goreezan] avoiding, shunning; evading ♦ از دربار و رسمیات – بود He avoided the court and official ceremonies.

گریزپای [goreezpaay] shy, avoiding; shunning

گریزی [goreezi] 1 contraband noun 2 contraband adjective ♦ - مال contraband goods

گریس [gris] grease ♦ گریسپمپ grease pump

گریستن [garistan] (present tense stem گری [gari]) to weep, to cry ♦ زارزار to sob bitterly, to sob violently

گریسکاری [griskaari] technical greasing, oiling, lubrication

گریوان [gereewaan] colloquial ☞ گریبان

گریه gerya weeping, crying, sobbing
- کردن - to weep, to cry
- (and) به – آوردن / انداختن to drive to tears; to make cry
- خون – کردن colloquial to cry bloody tears

گز [gaz] gaz (measure of length, approx. a meter) ♦ گزشاه shah's gaz (about 1.066 meters) ◊ گز شرعی ell (measure of length)

گزاره [gozaara]¹ life; living conditions, means of subsistence ♦ سخت است - جاییکه قند وقروت یک نرخ است proverb Where sugar and qorut (dried sour milk pellets) cost the same, life is hard.
- (ازراه) - کردن to live, to exist (on something)

گزاره [gozaara]² grammar predicate

گزباب [gazbaab] colloquial fabrics, textiles (literally, measured by the gaz)

گز ☞ گز

گزر [gozar] ☞ گذر 2

گزران [gozaraan] ☞ گذران

گزشتاندن [gozashtaandan] ☞ گذشتاندن

گزلک [gazalak] colloquial throw noun
- کردن - to throw, to fling, to hurl, to toss (something)

گزمه [gazma] patrol
- گشتن - colloquial to patrol, to guard (at night)

گزند [gazand] 1 misfortune, trouble ♦ چشم - the evil eye 2 harm, damage

گزوار [gazwaar] factory

گزیدگی [gazidagi] bite, sting; place of a bite or of a sting

گزیدن [gazidan] to bite, to sting

گزیدن [gozidan] (present tense stem گزین [gozin]) 1 to choose, to select; to pick out 2 to prefer (somebody or something) (را)

گستاخ [gostaakh] bold; impudent, impertinent, insolent

گستاخی [gostaakhi] boldness, impudence, insolence, impertinence

گستتنر [gestetnar] hectograph; rotary press
- کردن - to print, to duplicate on a hectograph

گستراندن [gostaraandan] ☞ گستردن

گستردن [gostardan] 1 to spread 2 to stretch, to propagate

گسترش [gostaresh] 1 spreading 2 propagating, unrolling, unfolding ♦ گستردن (بخشیدن)- دادن ☞
- یافتن - 1 to stretch intransitive 2 to be propagated; to unfold intransitive

گسستن [gosastan] 1 to tear 2 to cease; to annul; to abolish; to cancel

گسل [gosel] present tense stem گسیختن

گسیختن [gosikhtan] (present tense stem گسل [gosel]) 1 to tear intransitive 2 to cease intransitive; to be annulled; to be abolished; to be canceled

گشادن [goshadan] ☞ کشادن

گشت [gasht] 1 walking, taking a walk 2 conversion, change 3 colloquial time

گشتاندن [gashtaandan] 1 ☞ گردانیدن 2 to walk, to take for a walk

گشتک [gashtak] gatherings (arranged in turn by friends, usually in the winter)

گشتن [gashtan] (present tense stem گرد [gard]) ☞ گردیدن

گشتوگذار [gashtogozaar] colloquial 1 walk, stroll; walking, roaming 2 turning, spinning, rotation (in some medium)

گشنه [goshna] colloquial ☞ گرسنه

گشنه چشم [goshnachashm] greedy, avid, envious, grasping

گشنیز [gashniz] botany coriander seed, cilantro

گفت [goft] word; words ♦ به – او by his words, according to his words
- او به - من نمیکند He doesn't listen to me.

گفتار [goftaar] 1 speech, conversation, talk ♦ زبان colloquial language ◊ ملا برو به کردارش نه - به proverb Listen to what the mullah says, but don't do what he does. 2 colloquial arguing, altercation, argument

گفتگو [goftogo] 1 talk, conversation, interview 2 talks, negotiations
- کردن - 1 to talk 2 to conduct talks or negotiations

گفتن [goftan] (present tense stem گو(ی) [go(y)]) to talk, to say, to tell

گفتنی [goftani] that which must or may be said, to express in words ♦ گفتنی های زیاد دارم I have a few things to say / to tell about.

گفته [gofta] 1 past participle ☞ گفتن 2 ☞ گفت

گل [gel] 1 clay ♦ گل سرشویی clay for washing the head (compressed into a stone) ◊ گل سفید chalk ◊ گل سیل very pure loess / alluvial clay (used in dried form as a children's powder) 2 mud
- گل کردن to coat with clay

گل [gol]¹ 1 flower ♦ گل انار flower of the pomegranate ◊ گل سر decoration for women (in the form of a flower) 2 snuff (on a candle, on a wick) 3 pattern, design; lock, curl (of karakul) 4 (گل آتش) hot coals, embers 5 (also چشم -) walleye, leucoma ♦ گل افتادن colloquial to appear (about a leucoma on the eye)
- گل چیدن to gather flowers
- گل دادن to bloom, to blossom, to flourish, to break out into blossom
- گل زدن 1 to spoil, to rot, to grow moldy or musty (about fruit, etc.) 2 to place a brand [on], to brand (livestock)
- گل شکفتاندن colloquial to create a squabble, to inflame a matter
- گل کردن 1 ☞ گل دادن 2 to become apparent, to show 3 to erase (what has been written)
- گل گرفتن colloquial to make a happy choice, to hit the nail on the head
- گل نگفتن colloquial not to dare to speak (about something)
- گل بی خار good person, inoffensive person
- گل کمر بند belt buckle

249

گل [gol]²
• گل کردن 1 to switch off (a light) 2 *technical* to throttle down, to stop (an engine, etc.)

گل [gol]³ *sport* ☞ گول [gol]

گلاب [golaab] (also - گل) rose ♦ عرق - rose oil

گلابک بافی [golaabakbaafi] knitting with a design, knitting with little flowers, with clusters, or with bunches

گلابی [golaabi] rose-colored, of the color of the rose

گلاس [gelaas] glass; goblet; wine glass

گل آلود [gelaalud] 1 dirty, muddy, stained 2 turbid ♦ آب - turbid water

گل اندام [golandaam] 1 delicate, graceful 2 *feminine proper name* Golandam

گلباغ [golghaag] Golbagh or Gulbagh (suburb of Kabul)

گلبرگ [golbarg] petal

گلبید [golbeed] ☞ سرخ بید

گلپر [gelpor] ☞ گل آلود

گلچین [golchin] gathering flowers
• کردن - to compile a collection of poetry

گلخانه [golkhaana] hothouse, greenhouse

گلخن [golkhan] furnace (in a bathhouse)

گلخنچی [golkhanchi] furnace man in a bathhouse

گل دار [goldaar] 1 flowery, figured, patterned (about cloth or fabric) ♦ جوراب - delicate stockings, mesh stockings 2 *botany* flowering ♦ نباتات - flowering plants

گل دان [goldaan] flower pot

گل دانی [goldaani] vase for flowers

گلدوزی [goldozi] 1 embroidery 2 figured embroidery

گلزار [golzaar] 1 flower garden 2 flower bed

گلساز [golsaaz] master at making paper flowers

گلستان [golestaan] 1 rose garden; flower garden 2 Golestan or Gulistan (name of a work by Sa'di or Saadi)

گل سر [golsar] (and) گلسرک [golsarak] brambling, bramble finch

گل سنگ [golsang] lichen (on a stone)

گلشن [golshan] 1 flower garden, rose garden 2 laces 3 guipure [type of lace]

گل قند [golqand] 1 jam made of rose petals 2 candied rose petals *medicine*

گلکار [gelkaar] stonemason; bricklayer; plasterer

گل کار [golkaar] 1 flower grower 2 master at painting designs or figures

گلکاری [gelkaari] construction work (masonry or bricklaying, plastering)

گل کاری [golkaari] 1 flower growing 2 painting of designs or figures (on walls)

گل کرم [gol (e)karam] cauliflower

گلگچ [golgach] gypsum with an admixture of hay or cane (used as a building material)

گلگل [galgal] construction putty

گلگلی [golgoli] colored, gaily colored; multicolored (about fabric)

گلگون [golgun] 1 red, scarlet, pink; rosy 2 *poetic* like a rose

گلم [gelem] *colloquial* ☞ گلیم
• *colloquial* انداختن - to grieve; to mourn (for somebody)

گل ماله [gelmaala] *construction* trowel

گلمالی [gelmaali] plastering

گل ماهی [golmaahi] trout

گلموره [golmora] *colloquial endearment* little flower (about a beautiful child)

گل میخ [golmeekh] 1 nail with a large head 2 spike, bolt

گل میخی [golmeekhi] silver ornament in the form of a tack (on women's sleeves)

گلو [golu] throat, larynx, gullet ♦ گلویش خشک شد His throat is / was dry. ◊ گلویش پر (فشرده) میشد He was choked by his tears.

گلوبند [goluband] 1 neckerchief 2 necklace

گل وخشت [gelokhesht] *colloquial* nature; properties; virtues (of person)

گلو گرفتگی [golugereftagi] lump in the throat; spasms

گلولای [gelolaay] soft mud (in a road)

گلوله [golula] 1 ☞ کلوله 2 bullet; projectile, shell

گلوله باری [golulabaari] firing, fire

گلون [golun] ☞ گلو
• *colloquial* از - افتادن to have shouted for a long time; to hurt one's voice ♦ گلونش ششنه His throat became sore. / He lost his voice.

گلون بند [golunband] ☞ گلو بند

گله [gela] reproach, rebuke; blame, censure; complaint
• از چله چه - *proverb* What's the use of complaining about winter's cold?

گله [gal (I)a] 1 herd; herd of horses 2 flock (of birds)

گله [gola] *colloquial* ☞ گلوله 2

گله بان [gal (l)abaan] horse herder, herdsman; shepherd

گله داری [gal (l)adaari] breeding cattle, cattle-breeding horses
♦ اسپ - horse breeding

گلی [goli] rosy (about apples)

گلیم [gelim] rug without pile, reversible rug

گلین [gelin] clay *adjective*; earthen, made of earth

گم [gom]
• گم شدن to be lost, to get lost, to be missing, to disappear
• گم کردن 1 to lose 2 to hide, to conceal
• گمشو Away with you! / Make yourself scarce!

گمار [gomaar] *present tense stem* گماشتن

گماشتن [gomaashtan] (*present tense stem* گمار [gomar]) appoint (to a post, etc.); to authorize; to empower

گماشته [gomaashta] 1 *past participle* گماشتن 2 authorized agent or representative; agent

گمان [gomaan] 1 supposition, assumption; opinion; thought, idea ♦ به گمانم in my opinion 2 suspicion; doubt
• گمان - 1 to think, to suppose, to assume 2 to suspect (somebody بالای)

گمبز [gombaz] (and) گمبزی [gombazi] ☞ گنبد

گمراه [gomraah] 1 mistaken; good-for-nothing 2 heretic
• ساختن - to lead into error, to delude

گمراهی [gomraahi] 1 error, delusion 2 heresy

گمرک [gomrok] (*plural* گمرکات [gomrokaat]) customshouse

گمرک والا [gomrokwaalaa] customs employee

گمرکی [gomroki] customs ♦ محصول - customs duties

گمنام [gomnaam] unknown; anonymous

گناه [gonaah] 1 blame; fault, offense 2 sin, crime
• کردن - 1 to commit an offense 2 to commit a crime

گناهکار [gonaahkaar] 1 sinner, culprit 2 criminal

گمبد [gombad] cupola, dome, vault, canopy

گنج [ganj] 1 hoard, buried treasure, treasure 2 *colloquial* cup for alms (used by dervish)

گنجاندن [gonjaandan] (and) گنجانیدن [gonjaanidan] to stow, to place, to put (into something)

گنجایش [gonjayesh] capacity

گنجشک [gonjeshk] 1 sparrow 2 little bird, birdie

گنجیدن [gonjidan] 1 to have room for, to hold, to accommodate, to house 2 to contain (within itself)

گنجینه [ganjina] treasure house, depository

گند [gand] 1 embroidered front or bust (of a shirt, of a dress) 2 skirting of clay (along the edge of a millstone)

گند [gand] stinking, putrid, fetid

گند [gond] 1 group, subdivision (of a tribe) 2 circle, company, crowd, associates ♦ این آدم از - ما نیست This man is not from our crowd.

گندم [gandom] wheat
- گندم سیاه ☞ سیاه ●

گندم سیاه [gandomsiyah] rye

گندمی [gandomi] of the color of wheat; dark-complexioned

گندنه [gandana] leek

گنده [ganda] 1 dirty 2 stinking, putrid, fetid 3 foul, rotten, bad, tainted

گنده [gonda] thick, large; coarse

گندهارا [gandhaaraa] historical Gandhara

گندگی [gandagi] ☞ گندیدگی ●

گندیدگی [gandidagi] 1 depravity, rottenness 2 stink, stench; dirt, filth

گندیدن [gandidan] to rot, to decompose, to decay, to go bad, to spoil, to become foul

گنگ [gong] dumb, mute

گنگس [gangs] deafened; stunned; unconscious
- سرم - است ● My head is spinning. / I am dizzy.

گنگه [gonga] 1 deaf mute; mute 2 colloquial stutterer, stammerer

گنه [gonah] ☞ گناه ●

گنگی [gongi] dumbness, muteness

گو [gaw] ☞ گاو ●

گو [go] 1 present tense stem گفتن 2 (second component of compound words with meaning "speaking" / "talking") ♦ دروغگو liar

گوارا [gowaaraa] digestible; pleasant, pleasing, agreeable
- برخود – کردن ● to take on

گواره [gawaara] colloquial ☞ گهواره ●

گواه [gawaah] witness, eyewitness

گواهی [gawaahi] evidence, testimony
- دادن ● to testify, to give testimony, to confirm as a witness

گوتک [gotak] technical reel, spool; drum (for cable, etc.); pulley; block (i.e., pulley block)

گودال [godaal] 1 hole 2 hollow

گودی [gawdi] depth

گودی [godi] ☞ گدی ●

گور [gor] grave
- نه - دارد ونه کفن ● proverb He has neither grave nor shroud. (He is as poor as a church mouse.)
- کردن - ● 1 to bury, to inter (somebody) 2 to bury (something)
- در - رنگ ● abusive May you grow sickly!

گورستان [gorestaan] cemetery, graveyard

گورکن [gorkan] 1 gravedigger 2 grave robber

گورمشتی [gormoshti] colloquial a powerful blow with the fist, punch
- زدن ● to strike with the first, to punch, to give a punch

گاورنر [gawernar] governor

گوروان [gorwaan] cemetery watchman

گوره خر [gorakhar] 1 Asiatic wild ass, onager, kiang 2 zebra

گوزن [gawazn] deer, reindeer; maral, Siberian stag

گوساله [gusaala] calf, heifer ♦ گوشت veal
- دومادره ● a calf that nurses from two females (about somebody)

گوساله سرک [gusaalasarak] mole cricket (insect)

گوسبد [gawsabad] colloquial large wicker basket

گوسپند [gospand] ☞ گوسفند ●

گوسفند [gosfand] ram, sheep ♦ گوشت - mutton

گوسفندمرگی [gosfandmargi] an epizootic of sheep

گوش [gosh] ear; ears
- به- خود شنیدن ● to hear (something) with one's own ears
- به - فیل خواب شدن ● proverb to fall asleep in an elephant's ear (i.e., to manifest extreme carelessness)
- دادن ● to listen, to lend an ear
- دادن ☞ کردن - ●
- دادن 1 ☞ گرفتن - ● 2 colloquial to overhear, to eavesdrop
- پر کردن - ● to slander, to smear
- تو دادن ● colloquial to tell (somebody) off; to scold, to give a dressing down
- 1 - گرفتن ☞ فرادادن ●
- کش کردن - ● to pull by the ears
- لم کردن ● to prick up the ears (about a dog, about a horse, etc.)
- در – گرفتن ● to memorize
- به کری زدن - ● to pretend to be ignorant, to pretend to be an ignoramus

گوش با آواز [gosh-ba-aawaaz] having pricked up the ears, having prepared oneself (to listen to an order)

گوش پوشک [goshposhak] cap; cap with ear flaps

گوشت [gusht] 1 meat ♦ اسپ – horsemeat ◊ بز - goat meat ◊ سرخی - flesh (meat without bones) 2 pulp (of fruit)
- از ناخن جدایی نداره ● proverb You can't separate the fingernail from the finger.
- خر و دندان سگ - ● proverb You need a dog's teeth to eat donkey meat.
- آوردن - ● to heal, to skin over (about a wound or injury)
- باختن - ● to grow thin, to become emaciated (about animals)
- به سر - آمدن ● colloquial to grow fat (about animals)
- خوک - ● May I eat pork! (said when someone promises to do something)
- وناخن - ● [Like] finger and fingernail! (said about closely associated people)

گوشت خور [goshtkhor] predatory (about birds, i.e., birds of prey)

گوشت آلود [goshtaalud] fleshy, meaty, full, plump (about a face)

گوش خراش [goshkharaash] heartrending, deafening (about a cry or shout)

گوش خزک [goshkhazak] centipede

گوشکانی [goshakaani]
- کردن • - to entrust a secret [to], to whisper into (somebody's) ear
گوشکی [goshaki] earflap; earflaps; headphones
- تیلفون • - telephone receiver
گوشمالی [goshmaali] dressing down, scolding
گوشواره [goshwaara] earring; earrings
گوش وگلون [goshogalun]
- داکتر • - otolaryngologist
گوشه [gosha] 1 corner, angle ♦ اطاق - corner of a room part of a room 2 nook, secluded nook, cozy nook
گوشه نشین [goshaneshin] recluse, hermit
گوشه وکنار [goshawakenaar]
- از - کشور • - from all corners of the country
گوگادی [gawgaadi] cart to which oxen are harnessed
گوگرد [gugerd] chemistry 1 sulfur ♦ تیزاب - sulfuric acid 2 matches
گاوگم [gawgom] ☞ گاوگم
گول [gol] sport goal
- زدن • - to score a goal
گول [gul]¹ round ♦ سوهان - round file
گول [gul]² 1 fraud, swindle, cheating 2 colloquial blockhead, dullard, dunce
- خوردن • - to be swindled, to be cheated, to be misled
- زدن • - to swindle, to cheat, to mislead
گولایی [gulaayi] bend, curve (in a road)
گول کیپر [golkipar] sport goalkeeper
گوله [gul (I) a] colloquial ☞ گلوله
گوله باروت [gul (I)abaarut] colloquial ammunition; cartridges
گومرگی [gawmargi] foot-and-mouth disease
گوناگون [gunaagun] different, diverse, various; heterogeneous
گونه [guna] cheekbone ♦ گونه های برجسته - prominent cheekbones
گونی [guni] bag, sack (of burlap)
گونیا [gunyaa] technical 1 set square, try square 2 protractor
گوهر [gawhar] 1 precious stone, semiprecious stone 2 pearl, pearls 3 nature, essence 4 glint, glitter (of a saber)
گو(ی) [goy] ☞ گو [go]
گویا (and) گویان [goyaa] (and) [goyaan] speaking, talking, conversing
گوینده [goyenda] 1 storyteller, narrator, talker 2 announcer 3 author, poet
گهر [gohar] ☞ گوهر
گهواره [gahwaara] cradle
گیاه [giya (h)] plant, grass
گیاه شناس [giyaahshenaas] botanist
گیبی [geebi] wide trousers with gathers (tapering toward the bottom)
گیت [geet] bolt (of a rifle)
گیتی [giti] world, universe
گیچ [gich]¹ 1 experiencing dizziness, stupefied 2 having fainted or swooned
- سرم – میرود • - I am dizzy. / My head is spinning.
گیچ [gich]² technical probe ♦ نری - thread gauge, screw pitch gauge
گیر [gir]¹ present tense stem گرفتن 2 difficulty, embarrassment
- افتادن • - 1 to get to, to find oneself, to get into [a mess] 2 to be caught

- آوردن • - to catch, to trap
- افتادن • - 2 colloquial 1 ☞ شدن • - to land in a difficult situation, to get into a difficult situation
- آوردن • - کردن • -
- ماندن • - to be delayed (because of something)
گیر [gir]² technical gear, speed ♦ اول - first gear ◊ عقب - reverse gear
- انداختن • - to engage the transmission, to put (a car) in gear
گیرا [giraa]¹ 1 prehensile, tenacious, grasping 2 snaring, catching 3 alluring, fascinating, captivating; gripping
گیرا [giraa]² 1 clip (for the hair) 2 technical vice 3 technical clamp; screw clamp, C clamp; ferrule
گیر بکس [girbaks] technical gear box, transmission
گیرودار [girodaar] 1 melee, skirmish 2 confusion; embarrassment; fuss, bustle
گیر وگرفت [girogereft] round-up, mass arrests
گیره [gira] 1 latch, bolt [of door]; catch 2 rim, collar, yoke (fastening, strengthening a pan or other copper vessel) 3 ☞ گیرا 1.1
گیس [gays] gas ♦ ولدینگ - technical gas welding
گیسو [gisu] (plural گیسوان [gisowaan]) 1 tress, braid 2 long hair of a woman; locks (of hair)
گیلاس [gilaas]¹ cherry, cherries; cherry tree
گیلاس [gilaas]² ☞ گلاس 1.1

ل
27th letter of the Dari alphabet

لا [laa] layer, stratum; fold ♦ یک لا - in one layer, single
لا [laa] (negative prefix "without-" / "not-" / "non-" in words of Arabic origin) ♦ لاعلاج - incurable
لااقل [laaaqal] at least
لاله [laailaa(h)] religion abbreviation of لا اله الا الله "There is no God but Allah." (Moslem symbol of faith)
لاانتها [laaentehaa] infinite, boundless, eternal, endless
لابد [laabod] certainly, without fail
لابراتوار [laabraatwaar] laboratory
لابلا [laabalaa] 1 multilayered, formed in several layers, built in several layers 2 in layers; in several rows
لات [laat] 1 obscure colloquial lord, mister 2 historical Lord MacNaghten (head of an English military mission in Afghanistan in the 19th century)
لاتری [laatari] lottery, raffle
لاتی [laati] colloquial contemptuous Anglomaniac
لاتین [laatin]
- زبان • - Latin language
لاجرم [laajaram] 1 against one's will, by compulsion 2 consequently
لاجستری [laajestari] colloquial ☞ راجستری
لاجورد [laajward] lazurite, lapis lazuli, azure stone [semiprecious stone]
لاجوردی [laajwardi] 1 azure, sky blue 2 made of lazurite
لاچار [laachar] ☞ ناچار
لاحقه [laaheqa] grammar affix
لاحول [laahawl] abbreviation of لاحول ولاقوة الاباالله
- شیطان را - کردن • - to exorcise an evil spirit, to drive away the devil (before beginning some matter or undertaking)

لاحول ولاقوه [laahawlawalaaqow-wa] God, save [me] from the evil spirit. (said before the start of some undertaking)

لادار [laadaar] layered, laminated, foliated, stratified, having a layered structure ♦ چوب - veneer, plywood

لادرک [laadarak] vanished, missing, lacking, absent

لارد [laard] lord

لاری [laari] (also - موتر) lorry, truck

لازر [laazar] *technical* laser ♦ اشعه - laser beam

لازم [laazem] 1 needed, necessary ♦ میرود که ... it is necessary that ... 2 *grammar* intransitive (about a verb) - شدن ☞ - آمدن
• داشتن - to need, to be in need, to have a need (for something را)
• دانستن (and) دیدن - to consider [it] necessary

لازم الاجراء [laazemolejra] to be carried out without fail

لازمه [laazema] ☞ لازم 1 (*plural* لوازمات [lawaazem] (and) [lawaazemaat]) necessary thing, necessity, object article; belonging

لارمی [laazemi] 1 ☞ لازم 2 mandatory, compulsory; urgent, pressing

لاستیک [laastik] *rarely* elastic

لاش [laash] [1] precipice; sheer slope of a mountain

لاش [laash] [2] 1 dead body, corpse 2 carcass (of an animal)

لاشتیک [laashtik] *colloquial* ☞ لاستیک

لاشه [laasha] *colloquial* weak, sickly; puny (about an animal); "dead" (about an emaciated, broken-down horse or person)

لاعلاج [laa'elaaj] incurable

لاغر [laaghar] emaciated; lean, thin

لاغراندام [laagharandaam] lean, spare

لاف [laaf]
• زدن - to brag, to boast

لافزنی [laafzani] boasting, bragging

لافوک [laafok] *colloquial* boaster, braggart

لافیدن [laafidan] ☞ لاف زدن in entry لاف

لاقید [laaqayd] unbridled, unrestrained, undisciplined

لاک [laak] 1 varnish, lacquer 2 sealing wax
• ومهر کردن - to seal with wax

لاکموسی [laakmusi] litmus ♦ کاغذ - litmus paper

لاکن [laaken] ☞ لیکن

لاکی [laaki] 1 covered with lacquer or varnish 2 of the color of sealing wax; dark red

لال [laal] 1 mute man 2 stutterer

لال [laal] ☞ لعل

لالا [laalaa] 1 older brother 2 tutor; child's attendant, nanny; servant 3 uncle (form of address)

لالتین [laalteen] lantern (with a candle)

لالتین بازی [laalteenbaazi] dance with lanterns

لاله [laala] [1] 1 tulip 2 poppy

لاله [laala] [2] ☞ لالا 2

لاله زار [laalazaar] 1 a meadow strewn with tulips or with poppies 2 flower garden with tulips or poppies, flower bed with tulips or poppies

لاله سر [laalasar] red-legged pochard, duck

لالی [laali] 1 stuttering 2 muteness

لام [laam] name of the letter ل

لامحدود [laamahdud] unlimited, boundless, infinite

لامذهب [laamazhab] 1 atheist, heretic 2 atheistic, impious, godless

لامزروع [laamazru'] untilled, long-fallow, unused (about land)

لامسه [laamesa] touch

لاممکن [laamomken] impossible, unfeasible

لاندی [laandi] singed and dried carcass of a sheep (which is roasted whole over a fire)

لانه [laana] 1 nest 2 burrow, hole; lair; den

لاوا [laawaa] lava

لاوبالی [laawbaali] *colloquial* idle; shallow; good-for-nothing (about a person)

لاهوت [laahut]
• علم - theology

لای [laay] [1] 1 watery mud sludge; silt; slime, ooze 2 sediment, deposit

لای [laay] [2] ☞ لا

لایتجزی [laayatajazzaa] (and) لایتجزا • 1 indivisible, undecomposable 2 inseparable

لایتر [laaytar] lighter
• ولدنگ - *technical* igniter (for autogenous welding equipment)

لایحه [laayeha] (*plural* لوایح [lawaayeh]) project, plan

لایزار [laayzaar] impassable mud; swamp, marsh

لایسنس [laaysans] 1 license, permit 2 (also - دریور) driver's license

لایق [laayeq] 1 able, capable; making normal progress, passing (about a pupil) 2 worth, deserving

لایموت [laayamut] immortal, undying (epithet of Allah)

لاین [laayn] ☞ لین

لاینقطع [laayanqáte'] 1 continuous, uninterrupted 2 continuously

لایی [laayi] 1 packing stuffing, suitable to be used for stuffing or packing *adjective* 2 stuffing, packing *noun*

لب [lab] 1.1 lips, mouth ♦ لعل لب *poetic* red lips 1.2 brim, edge ♦ لب کاسه - brim or lip of a cup 1.3 shore, bank ♦ لب دریا bank of a river 2 لب by, near, at the brink (of something) *denominative preposition* ♦ لب جوی by an irrigation ditch, by a brook or stream ◊ لب سرک by [the edge of] a road لب به لب ☞ لبالب
• لب تر کردن *colloquial* to just barely taste (something); to just wet the lips
• لب خشک *colloquial* indigent, poor, beggarly
• لب خشک رفتن to go away with nothing, to get nothing for one's pains

لباس [lebaas] (*plural* البسه [albesa]) clothes, clothing ♦ ملی - national dress, native dress
• پوشیدن - to get dressed, to put on clothes
• کشیدن - to undress, to take off [one's] clothes

لباسی [lebaasi] *colloquial* artificial, imitation; for show; feigned, pretended; sham; false; dummy, counterfeit, forged

لبالب [labaalab] full to the brim; overcrowded, overfilled

لبریز [labreez] overfilled, spilling over the edge
• شدن - to spill over the edge, to overflow

لب سرین [labserin] lipstick

لبلبو [lablabu] beet

لب نی [labnay] mouthpiece; cigarette holder, cigar holder

لبنیات [labniyaat] dairy products
- فارم – ● dairy farm

لبی [labi] *grammar* labial (about sound)

لبی دندانی [labi-dandaani] *colloquial* labiodental (about sound)

لپ [lap] handful

لپ لپ [laplap]
- گریه کردن – *colloquial* to shed floods of tears

لت [lat] beating
- لت خوردن ● to be beaten, to be subjected to a beating
- زدن – ● to whip, to beat (cream, etc.)
- کردن ● **1** to beat, to inflict a beating **2** to beat off, to soften by beating

لت و پت [latopat] *colloquial* shabby, threadbare (about clothing)

لته [lata] *colloquial* rags
- از – کشیدن ● to filter, to strain

لته اشتک [lataoshtok] [baby] diaper

لجاجت [lajaajat] malicious obstinacy, stubbornness
- کردن – to be obstinate, to be stubborn

لجوج [lajuj] obstinate, stubborn, uncompromising

لجوک [lajok] *colloquial* ☞ لجوج

لچ [loch] naked, bare

لچر [lachar] *colloquial* **1** mean, base, foul, nasty, bad **2** impudent, insolent, impertinent, stubborn, too persistent

لحاظ [lehaaz] **1** view, opinion, point of view ♦ – از این from this point of view, therefore **2** consideration, respect
- به – کسی ● taking someone into consideration, out of respect for somebody
- کردن – ● to show consideration, to show respect (for somebody را); to take (somebody را) into consideration

لحاف [lehaaf] quilt, quilted blanket

لحظه [lahza] instant, moment

لحن [lahn] (*plural* الحان [alhaan]) **1** tone, intonation **2** *grammar* (*also* آهنگ و –) intonation (of a sentence)

لحیم [lahim] ☞ لیم

لحیم کاری [lahimkaari] ☞ لیم کاری

لخت [lakht] piece; part, portion; fraction, particle ♦ یک – a little, a small amount, a small quantity

لخته [lakhta] clot ♦ خون – clot of blood ◊ شد – خون The blood thickened / clotted. / The blood curdled.

لخچیدن [lakhchidan] *colloquial* ☞ لغزیدن

لخشان [lakhshaan] ☞ لغزان

لخشیدن [lakhshidan] ☞ لغزیدن

لخم [lokhm] meat without bones, flesh

لذا [lezaa] therefore, for this reason

لذت [lazzat] delight, enjoyment, pleasure, joy
- بردن – ● to take pleasure or delight [in], to obtain pleasure (از)

لذیذ [laziz] **1** tasty; savory; dainty **2** sweet, pleasant, pleasing

لر [lar] precipitous, steep ♦ ساحل لر steep bank
- لر کردن ● to crumble, to cave in, to fall, to fall in (about a wall)

لرز [larz] **1** *present tense stem* لرزیدن **2.1** shivering; fever; chill **2.2** quiver; quivering; shudder

لرزاندن [larzaandan] to set to shivering, to set to shuddering, to shake

لرزانک [larzaanak] *colloquial* unsteady, shaky, rickety; bumpy ♦ پل – rickety footbridge

لرزش [larzesh] vibration, trembling; shivering; quivering

لرزه [larza] trembling; shivering; quivering

لرزیدن [larzidan] *intransitive* to tremble; to shiver; to shake

لزوم [lozum] necessity, need, want ♦ بصورت – in case of necessity, if necessary ◊ دروقت – in time of need, when needed

لزومیت [lozumiyat] necessity, need, want

لسان [lesaan] (*plural* السنه [alsena]) tongue, language (in various meanings)

لسانی [lesaani] **1** linguistic **2** oral, verbal

لسانیت [lesaaniyat] philology ♦ و – ادبیات literature and philology

لست [lest] **1** list ♦ نفر – list of those invited, guest list **2** register **3** *colloquial* griddle

لشکر [lashkar] *obscure* army

لشکرگاه [lashkargaah] camp; general headquarters (of an army)

لشم [laashem] **1** soft and slippery **2** slippery; two-faced, duplicitous

لشمی [lashmi] *colloquial* duplicity, double-dealing

لطافت [lataafat] **1** elegance, refinement, grace **2** tenderness, softness **3** pleasantness, agreeableness; prettiness, comeliness

لطایف [lataayef] *plural of* لطیفه

لطف [lotf] (*plural* الطاف [altaaf]) courtesy, kindness, favor; goodness, liking, inclination
- کردن – to show favor, to show courtesy or kindness; to manifest a liking [for], to show an inclination, to regard with favor

لطفاً [lótfan] **1** graciously, politely **2** would you be so kind as, please (when expressing a request)

لطیف [latif] **1.1** tender, loving; fine; delicate **1.2** pleasant, agreeable, nice, sweet, dear ♦ جنس – the fair sex **2** *masculine proper name* Latif

لطیفه [latifa] (*plural* لطایف [lataayef]) **1.1** anecdote; funny story, amusing story, joke **1.2** *feminine proper name* Latifa **2** ☞ لطیف

لعاب [loaab (and) laaab] **1** mucus **2** (*also* دهن–) saliva **3** enamel, glaze

لعابی [loaabi] **1** covered with glaze; enameled **2** mucous membrane
- التهاب – معده inflammation of the mucous lining of the stomach, gastritis

لعل [la'l] **1** ruby; sapphire ♦ بیازی – amethyst **2** *masculine proper name* Lal
- هم – بدست آید و هم یار نرنجد *proverb* [You] will get a ruby and [your] friend will not be resentful. (The wolves are full and the sheep are whole.)

لعلی [la'li] of a ruby color, red, scarlet

لعنت [la'nat] curse, damnation, malediction
- فرستادن – to send damnations
- کردن (را،به) گفتن – to curse, to damn

لعنتی [la'nati] cursed, damned

لغات [loghaat] **1** *plural of* لغت [lojat] **2** glossary

لغامک [laghaamak] *medicine* lip infection

لغت [laghat] *colloquial* ☞ لگد
- خوردن– *colloquial* **1** to receive a kick **2** to suffer damage

ل

لغت [loghat] (*plural* لغات [lojaat]) 1 word ♦ کتاب - dictionary 2 language, dialect

لغت شناسی [loghatshenaasi] lexicology

لغتک [laghatak] not [to be able] to stand still (from anxiety); to tap [one's] feet (from impatience)

لغت کوب [laghatkub] 1 crushed, trampled 2 trampled down, tamped, packed
- کردن • 1 to trample down, to trample, to crush, to stamp [on] 2 to tamp, to pound

لغت نامه [loghatnaama] dictionary

لغزان [laghzaan] 1 sliding 2 slippery

لغزاندن [laghzaandan] to make slip, to make slide, to pull, to drag
- خود را • to brace oneself (in position when lying or sitting)

لغزش [laghzesh] 1 slip, sliding 2 mistake, error, blunder, slip

لغزیدگی [laghzidagi] *geology* landslide

لغزیدن [laghzidan] to slide; to slip

لغمه [loghma] slice, piece (of food)

لغو [laghw (and) laghwa] annulment, cancellation; abolition, abolishment

لغویات [laghwiyaat] *colloquial* empty words, nonsense, absurdity

لف [lof]
- کردن• to swallow, to devour ♦ ملخ همه را لف کرد - The locust destroyed everything.

لفافه [lafaafa] 1 cover, jacket 2 envelope, letter

لفت [left] 1 elevator 2 hoist

لفظ [lafz] الفاظ [alfaaz] *plural*
1 word, expression 2 speech 3 pronunciation

لفظی [lafzi] 1 oral, verbal 2 verbatim, word for word, literal (about translation)

لقان [laqaan] ☞ لقک [laqak]

لقب [laqab] (*plural* القاب [alqaab]) 1 title 2 nickname

لق چشم [loqchashm] lobster-eyed, goggle-eyed

لقک [laqak] *colloquial* 1 shaken, stirred 2 attached haphazardly, not fastened

لق لق [laqlaq] *colloquial* lapping (i.e., drinking with the tongue)
- به - سگ دریا مردار نمیشود • *proverb* One dog won't defile the whole river.

لق لق [loqloq] protruding, bulging, opened wide (about eyes)
- چشم را – کشیدن • to open one's eyes wide

لقمه [loqma] ☞ لغمه

لک [lak] one hundred thousand ♦ دو لک - two hundred thousand

لک [lok] thick ♦ اون لک - thick wool (in theads) ◊ برنج لک coarse-grained rice, large-grained rice

لکچر [lakchar] lecture
- ایراد کردن • to lecture, to give a lecture

لک لک [laklak] stork; crane

لکه [laka] spot; mark

لکه دار [lakadaar] 1 spotted, stained; blotchy 2 spotty, dappled

لگد [lagad] 1 a blow with the foot, a kick 2 recoil (of a gun)
- (زدن)کردن • 1 to kick *intransitive* 2 to kick *transitive*
- گاو پایش را – نکرده • *colloquial* He hasn't been kicked by a cow yet. (He has not yet experienced grief.)

لگن [lagan] 1 copper basin 2 *anatomy* (also خاصره-) pelvis

لگنچه [lagancha] small basin ♦ حمام - small basin that women take with them to a bathhouse

للمی [lalmi] not requiring irrigation

للمی کاری [lalmikaari] farming without (requiring) irrigation

للو [lalo] 1 cradle song, lullaby 2 *children's speech* bye-bye
- کردن • 1 to lull (a child) 2 *children's speech* to go bye-bye; to fall asleep

لم [lam] *colloquial* inclining, leaning, resting (against something)
- لم دادن • to sit (or) lie sprawled out
- شدن • to stoop, to bend over

لمبر [lambar] *colloquial* number

لمبرپلیت [lambarpalet] *colloquial* license plate (of an automobile)

لمبه [lamba] flame

لمبیدن [lombidan] to go to ruins, to fall to the ground, to fall in, to fall

لمپه [lampa] lamp

لمحه [lamha] instant, moment

لمس [lams] 1 touching, feeling 2 (sense of) touch
- کردن • to touch, to feel

لمیدن [lamidan] ☞ لم دادن in entry لم

لنده [londa] *colloquial* lover, fornicator

لنده غر [londaghar] *colloquial* rake (a person); idler, lazybones, good-for-nothing

لنگ [lang] a lame man or boy
- کردن • to limp

لنگ [long] loincloth (usually for a bathhouse)

لنگان [langaan] 1 limping, hobbling 2 with a limp, by hobbling

لنگر [langar] 1 anchor 2 [balancing] pole of a ropewalker 3 weight (of a clock) 4 weight, authority
- انداختن • to cast anchor (*literally* and *figuratively*)

لنگر خانه [langarkhaana] charity kitchen (for distribution of food as a form of charity)

لنگرگاه [langargaah] anchorage; port; harbor

لنگی [longi] turban

لنگیدن [langidan] to limp, to hobble

لوازم [lawaazem] (and) لوازمات [lawaazemaat] 1 *plural of* لازمه 2 inventory; property; equipment
- مدیر – • manager

لوایح [lawaayeh] *plural of* لایحه

لوبیا [lobiyaa] 1 kidney bean 2 string beans

لوته [lota] 1 small jug, small pitcher 2 (china) mug

لوجستیک [lojestik] ☞ لوژستیک

لوح [lawh] (*plural* الواح [alwaah]) board, small board (for writing)

لوحه [lawha] 1 strip, lath, slat; small board 2 plate, tablet 3 [name] plate
- تقسیمات • - *technical* graduated seale

لوحه سنگ [lawhasang] gravestone, tombstone

لودسپکر [laudspekar] loudspeaker

لوده [lawda] *colloquial* blockhead; dunderhead

لوزه [lawza] *anatomy* tonsil

لوزی [lawzi] 1 *mathematical* rhombus 2 almond-shaped

لوزستیک [lozestik] *military* rear services or logistics

لوطی [luti] *colloquial* 1 reveller, dashing follow, daredevil 2 cheat, swindler, old fox 3 dissolute man

لوکات [lokaat (and) lawkaat] *botany* Japanese medlar, loquat [tree or shrub]

لوکس [luks] deluxe, first-class ♦ هوتل - deluxe hotel

لول [lol] *colloquial* rolling (on the ground)
- خوردن - to roll; to be rolled up *intransitive*
- دادن - to roll; to roll (on the ground) *transitive*

لوله [lola] **1** bundle; roll **2** scroll **3** *anatomy* tract (intestinal tract)

لوله کباب [lolakabaab] rolled meat

لوله کشی [lolakashi] pipe laying

لون [lawn] *plural* الوان [alwan]) color, coloration

لوی درستیز [loyderstiz] *military* chief of the main staff

لویه جرگه [loyajerga] the Great Meeting, the Great Jirga, the Great Council of Elders ☞ جرگه

لهجه [lahja] **1** dialect **2** pronunciation, accent

لهذا [lehazaa] therefore, in consequence of

لیاقت [liyaaqaat] **1** aptitude, ability, talent
- تعلیمی – (also صنفی-) aptitude for progress or advancement, promotability
- عدم - **1** inability, incapacity **2** lack of qualification or skill
- کار – **1** aptitude for work, skill, qualification **2** virtue, merit **3** *proper name* Liyaqat

لیتراف کریدت [litaraafkredet] *finance* letter of credit

لیتی [leti] *colloquial* sweet, watery dish made of flour, butter, and sugar (prepared for women after childbirth)

لیدر [lidar] **1** leader **2** (also طیاره-) leading aircraft

لیدرشیپ [lidarship] leadership; leadership work, management

لیره [lira] lira; pound, pound sterling

لیسانس [lisaans] diploma (about completion of a higher educational institution)

لیسانسه [lisaansa] **1** student engaged in work on a degree **2** having a diploma from a higher educational institution

لیسه [lisa] secondary school; high school

لیسیدن [lisidan] to lick, to lick all over

لیکن [likan] but; however; nevertheless

لیل [layl] *literary* night

لیلام [lilaam] auction
- شدن - to be sold at auction
- کردن - to sell by auction

لیلام چی [lilaamchi] auctioneer

لیلامی [lilaami] **1** sold by auction **2** discounted or reduced in price, not new, used (about something)

لیلی [layli] **1** night *adjective* **2** *feminine proper name* Layli

لیلیتر [lilitar] *technical* ☞ ردیتر

لیلیه [layliya] **1** night, evening *adjective* **2.1** dormitory **2.2** boarding school, school boarding house

لیم [lim] **1** soldering, brazing **2** solder ♦ سخت - hard solder, brazing solder, brazing alloy ◊ نرم - soft solder
- شدن - to be soldered, to be brazed
- کردن - to solder, to braze, to weld

لیم کاری [limkaari] soldering work

لیمو [limu] lemon

لیمویی [limuyi] lemon yellow, the color of lemon

لین [layn] line ♦ تیلفونی - telephone line ◊ هوایی - airline

لین دوانی [layndawaani] **1** laying a line (a telephone line) **2** wires, wiring ♦ برق - electrical wiring

لین من [laynmen] *rarely* lineman

لینینی [leeneni] **1** Leninist *adjective* **2** a Leninist

لینینیزم [leenenizem] Leninism

م
28th letter of the Dari alphabet

م *abbrevation of* مسیحی Christian, AD (in date) ♦ ۱۴۱۲م 1412 AD

ما [maa] **1** *plural* مایان [maayaan] we **2** (as an attribute in an ezafah construction) our, ours ♦ مماکت ما our country ◊ اولاد ما our children **3** (in combination with the از, replaces the possessive ما) ♦ از ما ◊ خانه از ما our home

ما [maa] *colloquial* ☞ ماه

مابت [maabat] *colloquial* ☞ محبت

مابعد [maaba'd] **1** continuation (of something) **2** next, following, subsequent

مابین [maabayn] - (also در-) **1** in, inside [of] ♦ آب - in water ◊ باغ - in the garden **2** between, among ♦ مردم - among people

مابینی [maabayni] **1** middle, central **2** intermediate ♦ میدان - هوایی *military* intermediate airfield

مات [maat] **1.1** dumbfounded, stricken **1.2** conquered, defeated, vanquished, destroyed **2** *chess* mate, checkmate
- کردن - **1** to amaze, to strike dumb, to strike **2** to destroy, to smash up, to annihilate **3** to checkmate

ماتحت [maataht] **1** located (or) situated below **2** lower; subordinate

ماتریالیزم [maateryaalizm] (and) ماتریالیسم [maateryaalism] materialism

ماتقدم [maataqaddam] previous, former

ماتکه [maatka] *cards* queen
- قره - **1** queen of spades **2** "witch" (a card game)

ماتم [maatam] mourning; mourning for a deceased
- بودن(شدن) - to be in mourning; to observe mourning (for a deceased)

ماتم دیده [maatamdida] (and) ماتم زده [maatamzada] being in mourning; grieving (over the deceased)

ماتو [maataw] *colloquial* ☞ مهتاب

ماجرا [maajaraa] **1** event; incident **2** adventure

ماجراجو(ی) [maajaraajo (y)] **1** adventure; seeker of adventures **2** adventurous

ماجراجویی [maajaraajoyi] adventurism

ماجرایی [maajaraayi] *colloquial* intriguer, plotter, seditionary

ماچ [maach] *colloquial* a kiss
- کردن - to kiss

ماچه [maacha] female (animal, i.e., bitch or female dog, female donkey)

ماحول [maahawl] **1** surroundings, environment **2** neighboring, nearby ♦ تپه های - nearby hills

مأخذ [ma'xaz] **1** source (of information, rumors, etc.); primary source **2** origin, beginning

ماخوذ [ma'xuz] **1** borrowed, taken (on loan) **2** extracted **3** grasped, caught

مادر [maadar] mother ♦ مهربانم- My dear mother!
- مادرکلان ☞ کلان
- مادرآل ☞ آل

مادرآل [maadar (e)aal] witch, old witch

مادراندر [maadarandar] stepmother

مادربیزار [maadarbeezaar]
- وپدرآزار- *colloquial* gotten out of hand, good-for-nothing (about a son); hooligan

256

مادرخوانده [maadarkhaanda] foster mother

مادرکلان [maadarkalaan] grandmother

مادگی [maadagi] ☞ ماده گی

مادون [maadun] ☞ ماتحت

ماده [maada] 1 female 2 (first component of compound words with meaning of "female") ♦ ماده سگ bitch, female dog ◊ ماده گاو cow

ماده [maadda (plural مواد [maawaad (d)])] 1 material, stuff, matter, substance 2 *philosophical* matter 3 article, clause (of a treaty) 4 *physics* mass, matter

ماده سگ [maadasag] bitch, female dog

ماده گاو [maadagaaw] cow

ماده گی [maadagi] 1 buttonhole 2 staple, fastener (for a door bolt) ♦ - و نری staple and bolt, (door) bolt

مادی [maaddi] 1 material *adjective* ♦ - مصارف material expenditures 2 *philosophical* materialist

مادیات [maaddiyaat] *plural of* مادیت

مادیان [maadiyaan] mare; young mare, filly

مادیت [maaddiyat (plural مادیات [maaddiyaat]) 1 materiality, material nature 2 philosophical materialism

مار [maar] snake, serpant ♦ آبی - grass snake ◊ عینکی - cobra ♦ او را مار زد *colloquial* A snake bit him. ♦ - آستین a snake sheltered in one's bosom; an enemy in one's own home

مارپیچ [maarpeech] 1.1 winding, sinuous; twisted 1.2 spiral *adjective* 1.3 serpentine ♦ راه - winding or meandering road 2 a spiral

مارتول [maartul] large hammer for crushing rocks

مارچ [maarch] March

مارچوبه [maarchuba] asparagus

مارش [maarsh] *military* 1 march, marching 2 advance, forward movement; campaign ♦ مارش مارش Double time march!

مارک [maark] mark (monetary unit); factory mark, trademark

مارکسیزم [maarksizem] Marxism

مارکسیست [maarksist] Marxist *noun*

مارکسیستی [maarksisti] Marxist *adjective*

مارکیت [maarkeet] market; row of stalls (in a market)

مارگیر [maargir] 1 snake-catcher; snake charmer 2 *colloquial* cheat, swindler

مارماهی [maarmaahi] eel

مازدیگر [maazdigar] *colloquial* ☞ نماز دیگر in entry نماز

ماست [maast] yogurt; varenets (boiled sour milk)

ماستر [maastar] 1 teacher 2 master

ماستری [maastari]
● دوره- course leading to a master's degree
● دیپلوم — master's diploma, master's degree

ماسکه [maaska] *military* 1 mask 2 (also گاز-) gas mask

ماش [maash] mash (a variety of lentil), vetch

ماشاالله [maashaa'(a)llaah] 1 Bravo! / Well done! 2 God preserve him!

ماشام [maashaam] *colloquial* ☞ نماز شام in entry نماز

ماش و برنج [maashoberenj] gray, grayish (about color) ♦ ریش - beard with streaks of gray, graying beard

ماشوره [maashura] spool, bobbin

ماشه [maasha] trigger (of a gun)

ماشین [maashin] 1 machine, mechanism ♦ خیاطی - sewing machine ◊ ریش - razor (electrical or mechanical) ◊ گوشت - meat chopper, meat grinder 2 engine, motor ♦ موتر - automobile engine 3 plant; machine tool, machine, lathe ♦ برمه - 1 drilling lathe 2 drilling machine

ماشینخانه [maashinkhaana] *rarely* plant; factory; enterprise

ماشیندار [maashindaar] machine gun ♦ دستی - light machine gun ◊ تفنگچه - automatic weapon

ماشینری [maashineri] *rarely* equipment, machinery

ماشینکار [maashinkaar] 1 mechanic 2 machine operator; motor mechanic

ماشینگن [maashingan] ☞ ماشیندار

ماشینی [maashini] 1 machine *adjective*; mechanized 2 factory, factory-made

ماضی [maazi] 1 past, last 2 *grammar* past tense ♦ استمراری - iterative past tense; imperfective past tense ◊ مطاق - simple past tense, preterite past tense

ماضیه [maaziya] ☞ ماضی 2
● در اعصار - *literary* in past centuries, in past epochs

مافوق [maafawq] 1.1 senior (in rank), higher, superior 1.2 upper 2 over, above ♦ انتظار - beyond [all] expectation

مافوق صوت [maafawqesawt] supersonic ♦ طیاره - supersonic aircraft

مافیها [maafihaa]
● دنیا و - the whole world (*literally*, the world and everything in it)

ماقبل [maaqábel] previous, former ♦ ماقبل تاریخ prehistoric

ماکو [maaku] shuttle (of weaving machine)

ماکولات [maakulaat] food products, victuals, provisions

ماکیان [maakiyaan] 1 hen, chicken; brood hen 2 domestic brood hen (rearing fledglings)

مال [maal] (plural اموال [amwaal]) 1.1 property, belongings 1.2 goods 1.3 livestock 2 *rarely* (as the first part of an ezafeh word combination signifies "belonging to somebody") ♦ کیست؟ - Whose is this?
● مردم - 1 another's, somebody else's (about something) 2 somebody else's property or belongings

مال التجاره [maalottejaara] goods, object of trade or commerce

مالامال [maalaamaal] 1 full to the brim, overfilled; overcrowded 2 abundant, plentiful

مالته [maalta] orange, orange tree; oranges

مالدار [maaldaar] 1 well-to-do, rich, wealthy 2.1 owner of cattle; cattle breeder 2.2 rich man

مالداری [maaldaari] 1 cattle breeding, raising livestock 2 wealth, riches

مالش [maalech] 1 friction, rubbing 2 rubbing, massage; polishing 3 milling, fulling (of thick felt)

مالک [maalek] 1 owner, proprietor ♦ خانه - homeowner 2 landowner, landlord ♦ مالکان petty landowners

مالکانه [maalekaana] 1.1 landowner *adjective*, landowner's ♦ حاصلات - ground rent 1.2 proprietary 2 landowner's share, landlord's share (of a harvest); assessment; quitrent

مالکیت [maalekiyat] 1 ownership, proprietorship; possession, holding 2 property ♦ خصوصی - private property

مال مردم خور [maalemardomkhor] 1 appropriating somebody else's property 2 fleecer, extortioner

مال و آل [maaloaal] *colloquial* property, belongings; all [one's] property

ماله [maala] 1 heavy wooden board drawn by oxen (to bury seeds in soil after sowing) 2 putty knife

مالی [maali] 1 property *adjective* 2 financial, fiscal; monetary ♦ سال - fiscal year
مالیات [maaliyaat] *plural of* مالیه
● سیستم ـ و محصولات tax system
مالیاتی [maaliyaati] 1 tax *adjective*, taxation, fiscal 2 *agriculture* tax obligation, tax assessment
مالیه [maaliya] (*plural* مالیات [maaliyat]) 1 tax, duty, assessment ♦ رعیتی - tax on peasant's land 2 financial department 3 treasury, finances ♦ وزارت - Ministry of Finance 4 excise tax
مالیه ده [maaliyadeh] taxpayer
ماما [maamaa] uncle (mother's brother)
ماماجی [maamaaji] *regional form of courtesy* 1 little uncle, dear uncle (term of endearment for one's uncle) 2 uncle, little uncle (general form of address to an adult or older person)
ماماخیل [maamaakheel] relatives on the mother's side of the family
ماملە [maamela] *colloquial* ☞ معاملە
مأمن [ma'man] shelter, refuge
مأمور [ma'mur] 1.1 authorized empowered 1.2 sent (officially, on some mission) 2 employee; office worker; professional worker; official, functionary, bureaucrat ♦ پولیس - policeman
● - کردن 1 to authorize, to empower, to send (officially) 2 to appoint
مأموریت [ma'muriyat] 1 errand, mission 2 job, post 3 appointment (to a post) 4 (*also* پولیس-) police department
مأمون [ma'mun] 1 secured, guaranteed; conserved, preserved 2 safe (about a road)
ماندگی [mandagi] 1 tiredness, weariness, fatigue 2 *regional* indisposition
● انداختن – *colloquial* 1 ill health 2 to take a breath, to take a short rest
ماندن [mandan] (*present tense stem* مان [man] (and) بان [ban]) 1 to put down, to lay down; to put, to place, to set ♦ چوکی) بان (را اینجا بمان Put the chair here! 2.1 to leave, to let go 2.2 to let [one's] hair grow long; to grow a beard 3 to abandon, to stop, to cease, to discontinue (doing something) ♦ - از کار نمانید Don't stop working! 4 to permit, to allow 5 to remain, to stay, to continue to be located (somewhere) 6 to be like, to look like, to resemble
● - دیر to keep for a long time, not to spoil (about fruit)
● نمان Stop [him / her / it]! / Hold [him, etc.]! / Catch [him]!
مانده [maanda] 1 tired, fatigued, jaded, worn out, exhausted 2 *regional* ill, sick, unhealthy, sickly
● - نباشی *colloquial* Well done! Congratulations! (greeting on the occasion of the completion of some matter or return from a trip)
مانع [maane] (*plural* موانع [manwaane']) 1 obstacle, hindrance 2 hampering, preventing, hindering
مانند [maanand (and) maanend] 1 resembling, like, similiar [to] *adjective* 2 like *adverb / preposition*
مانوره [maanawra] 1 maneuver, ruse, trick, clever move 2 *military* maneuvers
مأنوس [ma'nus] 1 habitual, usual 2 accustomed, assimilated, acclimated 3 intimate, close, friendly

ماوراء [maawaraa'] 1.1 on the other side [of], across, beyond *denominative preposition* ♦ کوه - beyond the mountain 2 over, above 2 located on the other side (of something)
ماوراءالنهر [maawaraannahr] *historical* Transoxiana (ancient name of area between the Amu-Dar'ya and Syr-Dar'ya Rivers)
ماورای بحار [maawaraayebehaar] overseas *adjective*
ماورای بنفش [maaweraayebanafsh] ultraviolet
ماورای حمره [maaweraayehomra] infrared
ماه [maah] 1 moon ♦ تابان - shining moon (epithet of sweetheart) 2 month
● کم نما - like a new moon, stranger (about someone who rarely appears somewhere)
ماهانه [maahaana] 1 monthly *adjective* 2 every month, monthly, each month 3 monthly salary
ماهتاب [maahtaab] ☞ مهتاب
ماهتوی [maahtawi] a tiny room with a small window in it, a garret
ماهر [maaher] 1 skillful, deft, dexterous, able, capable 2 knowing one's business well
ماه رو(ی) [maahro (y)] 1 moon-faced, beautiful 2 *feminine proper name* Mahro(y)
ماهنامه [maahnaama] monthly magazine, monthly
ماهوار [maahwaar] (and) ماه وار [maahwaara] 1 ☞ ماهانه 2 (*also* - عادت) menses, menstruation
ماه و روز [maahoroz]
● سر - *colloquial* in the last month of pregnancy
ماهی [maahi] fish ♦ خالدار - trout
● گرفتن - to fish, to catch a fish
ماهیپر [maahipar] mahipar (a waterfall in the Garu Gorge on the Kabul River)
ماهی پشت [maahiposht] convex, oval *adjective*
ماهیت [maahiyat] 1 main point, essence 2 nature, property; character
ماهی تاوه [maahitaawa] large frying pan (for fish)
ماهیگک [maahigak] 1 calf (of the leg) 2 muscle of the forearm
ماهی گیر [maahigir] fisherman, angler
ماهی گیری [maahigiri] fishing (as a sport or industry)
● - کردن to fish, to catch fish; to be engaged in (the business of) fishing
مایحتاج [maayahtaaj] everything necessary; necessities
مایع [maaye] 1 liquid, fluid *adjective* ♦ جسم - *physics* a liquid, a fluid 2 (*plural* مایعات [maaye'aat]) liquid, fluid *noun*
مایعوی [maaye'wi] hydraulic, liquid, fluid *adjective* ♦ جمپن - hydraulic shock absorber
مایل [maayel] 1 stooped, bent; rickety, ramshackle; inclined, sloping, slanting 2 desiring, wishing [for] (something); inclined (toward something); striving, aspiring; craving (for something)
● بودن - to want, to wish, to desire; to be inclined (to do something)
● سبز به سیاه - dark green
مایملک [maayamlak] *literary* property, belongings; fortune
مایندر [maayendar] *colloquial* ☞ مادراندر
مایو [maayo] 1 bathing suit, swimming suit 2 trunks, swimming trunks
مأیوس [maa'yus] having despaired; discouraged, disheartened, dispirited; having lost hope

مآیوسی [maa'yusi] despair; hopelessness; disappointment

مایه [maaya] 1 essence; foundation, base, basis (of something) 2 root, source; original cause 3 ferment, leaven, yeast 4 *rarely* fortune, capital
- کردن - to ferment, to leaven

مباح [mobaah] *religion* 1 permitted, permissible 2 legal (from the point of view of the sharia)

مباحثه [mobaahesa] 1 discussion 2 arguing, argument
- کردن - 1 to discuss, to carry on a discussion 2 to argue

مبادا [mabaadaa] May it not be so! / I hope it isn't ... / I hope it doesn't ... (etc.)

مبادرت [mobaaderat] access; approach (to something); undertaking; initiative
- کردن - to set about, to proceed [to do something], to begin, to start (به)

مبادله [mobaadela] exchange, barter, mutual exchange ♦ اجناس - barter ◊ افکار - exchange of opinions

مبادی [mabaadi] *plural of* مبدأ

مبارز [mobaarez] 1 champion (of something), fighter (for something) 2 fighting, militant

مبارزه [mobaareza] fight struggle ♦ انتخاباتی - election campaign ◊ طبقاتی - class struggle

مبارک [mobaarak] blessed; happy
- عید شما – باشد May your holiday be happy! / I wish you a happy holiday!

مبارک باد [mobaarakbaad] 1 I congratulate [you]! / Congratulations! 2 ☞ مبارک بادی
- گفتن - 1 to congratulate; to wish happiness or good fortune 2 to bless, to give one's blessing [to]

مبارک بادی [mobaarakbaadi] 1 congratulations; good wishes 2 blessing

مبالغ [mabaalegh] *plural of* مبلغ

مبالغه [mobaalegha] exaggeration, hyperbole
- کردن - to exaggerate

مبانی [mabaani] *plural of* مبنا

مبتدا [mobtadaa] 1 beginning; foundation, basis; essence 2 *grammar* subject

مبتدی [mobtadi] 1.1 initial, first 1.2 beginning, starting 2.1 novice; pupil, apprentice, learner 2.2 founder

مبتذل [mobtazal] 1 banal, commonplace; hackneyed, trite 2 trivial, commonplace; vulgar

مبتکر [mobtaker] 1 initiator, pioneer, trailblazer ♦ شاعر - poet-innovator 2 having initiative, taking initiative, full of initiative

مبتلا [mobtalaa]
- شدن- to be seized, gripped, or consumed (by something); to undergo, to be subject [to], to be stricken (به)

مبحث [mabhas] 1 subject, topic, theme 2 problem, subject of discussion

مبدأ [mabda'] (*plural* مبادی [mabadi]) 1 beginning, starting point 2 principle, base, basis, foundation

مبدل [mobaddal]
- شدن- to be converted [into], to turn [into]; to be changed [into], to change [into]
- کردن - to convert, to turn; to change

مبذول [mabzul]
- داشتن - 1 to give, to make a present [of], to grant, to bestow, to confer 2 to show (attention); to display (effort)

مبرم [mobram] urgent, imperative, pressing ♦ پرابلم های مبرم - pressing problems

مبسوط [mabsut] thorough, detailed; extensive, vast

مبصر [mobasser] commentator, reviewer (of the press)

مبایل [moblaayl] *technical* (automobile) oil, motor oil

مبلغ [mablagh] (*plural* مبالغ [mabaalej]) sum (of money)

مبلغ [moballegh] 1 preacher ♦ مذهبی - missionary 2 propagandist

مبنا [mabnaa] (*plural* مبانی [mabaani]) foundation, basis, base

مبنی [mabni]
- بر -based (on something)

مبهم [mobham] 1 vague, obscure, indefinite 2 doubtful, questionable, dubious

مبیض [mobayyez] *literary* copyist who makes a clean copy, typist who makes a clean copy

مت [mat] silt, slime, mud, ooze

متابعت [motaaba'at] following (somebody), adherence (to somebody or something) ♦ ازچیزی - به following, imitating (somebody)
- کردن - to follow (somebody از), to imitate (somebody از)

متأثر [mota'asser] 1 being under a strong impression 2 grieved, pained, sad, downcast; moved, touched 3 subjected to an influence

متأخر [mota'axxer] 1.1 latest (in relation to time), new 1.2 contemporary, modern ♦ شاعر - modern poet, contemporary poet 2 (*plural* متأخرین [mota'axxerin]) modern man, a man of our times

متارکه [motaareka] 1 stopping, ceasing, abandoning 2 (*also* جنگ-) armistice, truce

متأسفانه [motaassefaana] unfortunately

متاع [mataa'] (*plural* امتعه [amte'a]) 1 goods, wares 2 thing, article

متانت [mataanat] 1 hardness, solidity; steadfastness; staunchness, inflexibility 2 steadiness, stability, durability

متأهل [motaahhel] married (about a man), family (about a man) *adjective*

متبلور [motabalwar (and) motabalwer] crystallized

متتبع [motatabbe'] investigating, inquiring, searching; inquisitive

متجاوز [motajaawez] 1 aggressor 2.1 aggressive 2.2 exceeding the bounds, overstepping the limits 3 از - over, above, beyond *compound preposition* ♦ از ده روز - more than 10 days

متجدد [motajadded] progressive, advanced, leading

متجسس [motajasses] 1 investigating, inquiring, searching 2 inquisitive ♦ نگاه - inquisitive glance

متحد [mottahed] 1 united ♦ موسسه ملل - Organization of the United Nations 2 ally
- شدن - to unite *intransitive*
- کردن - to unite, to join *transitive*

متحده [mottaheda] ☞ متحد
- اضلاع - امریکا - United States of America

متحرک [motaharrek] 1 moving, traveling 2 *grammar* vowelized, having a vowel sound (about a letter)

متحصن [motahassen] 1 having taken refuge in a shelter 2 *obscure* having ensconced oneself in a fortress
- شدن - to take refuge in a shelter

متحمل [motahammel] 1 experiencing, undergoing, enduring, bearing (something) 2 bearing, carrying (e.g., responsibility)
- شدن • 1 to experience, to undergo, to endure 2 to bear, to carry (e.g., responsiblity)

متحیر [motahayyer] amazed, dumbfounded; to be stricken, staggered, or startled
- شدن • to be amazed, to be dumbfounded, to be astonished

متخاصم [motakhaasem] hostile, warring ♦ طبقات - the warring classes

متخصص [motakhasses] specialist; expert

متداول [motadaawel] common, generally used, prevalent, widespread

متدرج [motadarrej] gradual

متدرجاً [motadarrejan] gradually

متذکر [motazakker]
- شدن • to remind; to indicate, to point out; to mention, to refer [to]

متر [matar] green peas

متر [méter] 1 meter stick (measuring stick one meter long); tape measure 2 meter (unit of length) ♦ مربع - cubic meter

مترادف [motaraadef] 1.1 located in one rank, file, or series 1.2 equivalent, synonymous 2 (also- کلمه) synonym

مترانه باب [metraanabaab] 1 goods measured or sold by the meter 2 textiles, dry goods

مترجم [motarjem] translator, interpreter, dragoman

مردد [motaradded] 1 indecisive, undecided, vacillating, hesitant 2 variable

مترصد [motarassed] 1 observing, watching lying in wait 2 military observer

مترقی [motaraqqi] 1 progressing, developing 2 increasing, rising, growing (about a price)

مترو [metro] subway

متروک [matruk] 1 left, abandoned, deserted; forgotten 2 antiquated, obsolete, having gone out of use

متروکات [matrukaat] legacy, inheritance; property, things left as an inheritance

متزلزل [motazalzel] 1 trembling, shivering, shaking 2 shaken; undermined
- کردن • to shake; to undermine (the foundations of something) transitive

متساوی [motasaawi] equal, same, identical

متسلسل [motasalsel] 1 continuous, uninterrupted (about an action) 2 continuous, unbroken; united, joint

متشابه [motashaabe (h)] 1 like, analogous, similar 2.1 grammar homonym 2.2 homograph

متشبث [motashabbes]
- شدن • to resort (to something به); to undertake (something به)

متشکر [motashakker] thankful, grateful
- بودن • to thank; to be grateful

متشکل [motashakkel] 1 consisting (of something از), formed, composed (of something از) 2 component ♦ اجزای - component parts
- شدن • to be formed, to be molded, to be put together, to be compiled, to be made up [of] (از)

متشادف [motashadef] ☞ مصادف

متصادم [motashadem]
- شدن • 1 to collide [with], to dash [against], to run [into] 2 to coincide

متصرف [motasarref] 1 seizing, capturing 2 possessing
- بودن • to possess (something)
- شدن • to seize, to take, to capture

متصرفات [motasarrefaat] ownership, possession

متصل [mottasel] 1.1 adjoining, bordering, abutting, adjacent, contiguous 1.2 close, neighboring 1.3 continuous, unbroken, uninterrupted 2.1 together 2.2 continuously, constantly 3 near, close to, by denominative preposition ♦ خانه - near the house, close by the house

متصوف [motasawwef] 1 related to sufism 2 a sufi, a mystic

متضاد [motazaad (d)] 1.1 opposite (in quality, in characteristics); contrasting 1.2 antagonistic 2 grammar antonym

متضمن [motazammen] containing within itself, including
- بودن • to contain within itself, to include in itself

متعاقب [mota'aaqeb] 1 immediately following, following, subsequent 2 after, following denominative preposition

متعجب [mota'ajjeb] astonishing, surprising, amazing
- شدن • to be astonished, to be surprised, to be amazed

متعدد [motaaddad] numerous

متعدی [motaadi] 1 attacking, encroaching, infringing 2 grammar transitive, causative (about a verb) 3 infectious, contagious

متعصب [motaasseb] 1.1 fanatical, fanatic 1.2 obstinate, stubborn 2 a fanatic; a wild fanatic

متعلق [motaalleq] (plural متعلقین [mota'alleqin]) 1.1 belonging [to] 1.2 relating (to something), referring (to something), connected, linked (with something) 1.3 depending, dependent 2 member of a family, member of a household
- بودن • 1 to belong [to](به) 2 to pertain [to], to bear a relation [to](به) 3 to depend [on](به)

متعلقات [motaalleqaat] 1 belongings, appurtenances, accessories 2 minor chapters (of a book); appendices

متعلقه [motaalleqa] ☞ متعلق 1
- و دیگر مسایل - به آن • and other matters connected with this
- و متفرقه • everything that has a direct or indirect relation (to a given subject or matter)

متعلم [motaallem] (plural متعلمین [motaallemin]) pupil; student

متعلمات [mota'allemaat] plural of متعلمه

متعلمه [motaallema] (plural متعلمات [motaallemat]) schoolgirl, female pupil, female student

متعهد [motaahhed] 1 pledged, obligated; having concluded an agreement, contract, or treaty 2 contractor, supplier
- شدن • to pledge oneself, to commit oneself, to conclude an agreement, a contract, or a treaty

متعهدین [motaahhedayn] diplomatic
- طرفین - • both contracting parties

متفرق [motafarreq] 1 differing, different 2 diverse, various, other 3 scattered

متفرقه [motafarreqa] 1 ☞ متفرق 2 all sorts of things
- خرج - • other expenditures

متفق [mottafeq] 1.1 agreeable, concordant, in agreement [with], unanimous 1.2 allied, united, unified, having entered into a union or alliance 2 ally

- شدن ‏- **1** to agree, to come to an agreement **2** to unite [with]

متفقاً [mottafeqan] in accord, according to, unanimously; together, in concert

متفقین [mottafeqin] *plural of* **2** متفق

متفکر [motafakker] **1** thinking **2** thinker

متقابل [motaqaabel] **1** opposite **2** reciprocal, mutual ♦ تأثیر ‏- mutual influence, reciprocal influence

متقارب [motaqaareb] *literary* motaqareb (a poetic meter usually used in epic poetry)

متقاعد [motaqaaed] **1** being on pension, retired **2.1** veteran **2.2** pensioner
- شدن ‏- to go on pension, to retire

متقدم [motaqaddem] **1** preceding, previous, former **2** old, bygone, ancient, antique

متقدمین [motaqaddemin] poets of the past, classics (i.e., the authors, not their works)

متکبر [motakabber] haughty, arrogant, overbearing

متکلم [motakallem] **1** speaking, talking **2.1** collocutor, interlocutor; orator, speaker **2.2** *grammar* first person of a verb

متکی [mottaki]
- بودن(شدن) ‏- to lean [on], to rest [on]; to be guided [by]; to be based [on], to be founded [on] (بربه)

متل [matal] ☞ مثل [masal]

متمایل [motamaayel] **1** having a tendency, tending (toward something) **2** inclined, disposed (toward something)

متمدن [motamadden] cultural, cultured, civilized

متمرکز [motamarkez] concentrated
- شدن ‏- to be concentrated

متمم [motammem] **1** supplementing; complementing; concluding, completing **2.1** *grammar* object **2.2** epilogue; enclosure, appendix, supplement

متمول [motamawwel] **1** well-to-do, prosperous **2** rich man

متن [máten] (*plural* متون [motun]) text (of a book, of a manuscript)

متناسب [motanaaseb] proportional; symmetrical; proportionate, commensurate

متناوب [motanaaweb] alternating, variable ♦ جریان برق ‏- *technical* alternating current

متنفر [motanaffer] having a loathing or an aversion [for], having a hatred [for]
- بودن(شدن) ‏- to have an aversion or a loathing [for]; to hate, to detest, to abhor (از)

متوازی [motawaazi] parallel ♦ خط ‏- parallel line

متوجه [motawajjeh]
- بودن- to be directed, to be addressed (to somebody)
- (به) شدن ‏- **1** to turn [one's] attention [to]; to turn one's eyes [to](به طرف) **2** to notice, to see
- کردن ‏– **1** to direct (somebody's) attention [to], to attract (somebody's) attention (به) **2** to direct, to send, to address [to] **3** to fix (attention) [on]

متوسط [motawasset] **1** mean, average, middle **2** mediocre, ordinary, commonplace

متوسل [motawassel]
- شدن ‏- to resort (to something), to have recourse (to something)

متوطن [motawatten] **1** having settled [in]; dwelling [in], inhabiting **2** native inhabitant, aboriginal

متوقف [motawaqqef]
- شدن ‏- to stop, to come to a stop; to stay too long, to linger [on]; to cease
- کردن ‏- to stop, to bring to a stop; to detain, to delay; to put an end to, to break off

متولد [motawalled] having been born, having come into being
- شدن ‏- to be born, to appear on earth, to be brought into the world

متولی [motawalli] **1** supervisor, guardian (of a waqf, i.e., real estate given or bequeathed to a mosque, or a sacred place) **2** executor (of a will)

متون [motun] **1** *plural of* متن **2** monumental works of written literature **3** (*also-* درس) course in textual criticism (at Kabul University)

متهکل [motahakkel] *geology* subjected to erosion; washed away, eroded (by water); weathered, eroded [by wind]

متهم [mottaham] **1** accused, the accused **2** suspected, a suspect
- کردن ‏- **1** to accuse **2** to suspect

متیقن [motayaqqen] assured, sure, confident, convinced, confirmed

متین [matin] **1** staunch, steadfast **2** durable, strong, firm **3** weighty, solid, sturdy

مثال [mesaal] **1** example **2** *literary* as, like *adverb*; like *adjective*

مثانه [masaana] *anatomy* urinary bladder

مثبت [mosbat] **1.1** positive **1.2** *literary* proven; confirmed **2** *mathematical* plus (positive magnitude)

مثقال [mesqal] mesqal (measure of weight equal to 4.6 grams and 1/24 of a hord) ☞ خورد

مثل [masal] (*plural* امثال [amsal]) saying; proverb
- مشهور است که ۰۰۰ ‏- as the proverb says …

مثل [mésel] (*also-* به) like, as *adverb*
- اینکه ‏- **1** as if **2** just as *compound conjunction*

مثلاً [masalan] for example

مثلث [mosallas]¹ **1** triangle **2.1** triangular **2.2** triple

مثلث [mosallas]² *literary* mosallas (poetry constructed on the base of a three-line stanza with a rhyming scheme of aaa, bba, cca)

مثلثات [mosallasaat] trigonometry

مثنوی [masnawi] *literary* masnawi (genre of verse characterized by pairs of rhyming lines: aa, bb, cc, etc.)

مجادله [mojaadala] **1** fight, struggle **2** argument, conflict
- کردن ‏- **1** to fight, to struggle [with / against / for] **2** to argue, to dispute; to have a conflict

مجاز [mojaaz] **1** having the right **2** permitted, authorized

مجاز [mejaz] *colloquial* ☞ مزاج

- مجازش گشت He flared up. / He flew into a rage. / He became furious.

مجازات [mojaazaat] punishment, penalty ♦ ومکافات ‏- punishments and rewards

مجازی [majaazi] figurative, metaphorical, allegorical

مجال [majaal] **1** opportunity, chance **2** strength, ability
- دادن ‏- to give an opportunity, to give a chance, to promote, to further

مجالس [majaales] *plural of* مجلس

مجامع [majaame'] *plural of* مجمع

مجانی [majaani] 1 free, free (of charge) *adjective* 2 free of charge, gratis, for nothing *adverb*

مجاور [mojaawer] 1 neighboring; adjacent; contiguous 2 mojawer (person who guards the tomb of a saint)

مجاورت [mojaawerat] 1 neighborhood, vicinity; contiguity ♦ - در in the environs; in the neighborhood or vicinity 2 protection of holy places (by those living in the vicinity)

مجاهد [mojaahed] 1 zealot, champion 2 fighter for [one's] faith or belief

مجاهدت [mojaahedat] (and) مجاهده [mojaaheda] 1 endeavor, fervor, ardor; zeal 2 fighting or struggle for [one's] faith or belief

مجبور [majbur] forced, compelled
- بودن - to be forced, to be compelled
- کردن - to force, to compel, to make [someone do something]

مجبوریت [majburiyat] necessity, compulsion

مجدد [mojaddad] renewed, resumed; repeated
- برقراری(استقرار) - restoration, renewal, rehabilitation

مجدداً [mojaddadan] anew, afresh; again

مجرا [majraa] riverbed; channel; canal

مجرد [mojarrad] 1.1 solitary, lone; isolated 1.2 single, unmarried [man] 1.3 absolute
- به - as soon as, at once *conjunction*

مجرم [mojrem] 1 guilty, criminal 2 a criminal

مجروح [majruh] injured, wounded

مجسم [mojassam] incarnate, personified, materialized

مجسمه [mojassama] 1 statue; monument, memorial; sculpture 2 incarnation, embodiment, personification

مجسمه ساز [mojassamasaaz] sculptor

مجلد [mojallad] 1 bound 2 a book in a binding, a volume

مجلس [majles] (*plural* مجالس [majaales]) 1 session, meeting ♦ عمومی - general meeting 2 company (of guests), society 3 party, soiree, evening ♦ شعر - party with reading of poetry 4 parliament, majles

مجلسین [majlesayn] (dual number of مجلس) both houses of parliment)

مجلل [mojallal] splendid, magnificent; solemn; festive

مجله [majalla] magazine

مجمع [majma'] (*plural* مجامع [majaame']) 1 meeting; assembly ♦ عمومی ملل متحد - U.N. General Assembly 2 gathering, crowd (of people)

مجموعاً [majmu'an] as a whole, on the whole, altogether, in sum, in all

مجموعه [majmu'a] 1 collection (of literary works) 2 collection
- مسکوکات - coin collection

مجمه [majma] 1 copper tray 2 (hawker's) tray

مجنون [majnun] (*plural* مجانین [majaanin]) 1 mad, insane, madly affectionate 2.1 madman 2.2 *masculine proper name* Majnun

مجنون بید [majnunbeed] weeping willow

مجهز [majahhaz] 1 outfitted, equipped; armed (with something) 2 prepared, ready
- کردن - 1 to outfit, to equip 2 to arm

مجهول [majhul] 1.1 unknown, unfamiliar 1.2 *grammar* passive (about a verb) 2.1 passive voice 2.2 *mathematical* the unknown, the unknown quantity ♦ واو - historically long vowel "o" ◊ یای - historically long vowel "e"

مچ [moch]
- مچ خوردن *colloquial* to have a sprained ankle (about a foot) ♦ پایم مچ خورد I sprained my ankle.

محاذ [mahaaz (and) mohaaz] (*plural* محاذات [mahazat]) front ♦ متحد - united front

محاربوی [mohaarebawi] *military* combat ♦ قابلیت - combat capability

محاربه [mohaareba] fight, combat, battle
- کردن - to wage combat, to do battle, to fight

محاسب [mohaaseb] 1 accountant; bookkeeper 2 cost accountant

محاسبه [mohaaseba] 1 calculation, counting ♦ شعبه - bookkeeping department 2 auditing accounts; bookkeeping
- کردن - to count, to calculate; to audit accounts

محاصره [mohaasera] siege, blockade, encirclement

محاط [mohaat] 1 surrounded, engirdled 2 fenced in, enclosed

محافظ [mohaafez] watchman, guard ♦ مکتب - school guard 2 keeper, custodian, protector

محافظت [mohaafezat] (and) محافظه [mohaafeza] guarding, protection, defense
- کردن - 1 to guard, to protect; to defend 2 to keep, to preserve

محافظه کار [mohaafezakaar] 1 a conservative (member of a conservative party or group) 2 consevative, outmoded, old-fashioned

محافل [mahaafel] *plural of* محفل
- حاکمه - ruling circles

محاکمه [mohaakama] court (of law), justice, judicial process
- کردن - to try a court case, to judge

محال [mohaal] impossible, incredible, inconceivable

محاوره [mohaawara] 1 talk, conversation; oral speech 2 dialect; popular speech, common parlance
- کردن - to talk [with / to], to speak [with / to], to converse

محبت [mohabbat] 1 love, affection, attachment 2 caress, endearment, kindness 3 *feminine proper name* Mohabbat
- کردن - 1 to feel love 2 to show tenderness, to show kindness (to somebody به، را)

محبس [mahbas] jail, prison

محبوب [mahbub] beloved, sweetheart

محبوبیت [mahbubiyat]
- داشتن - to be loved [by], to have the sympathy [of], to be liked [by]

محبوس [mahbus] prisoner, convict

محتاج [mohtaaj] needy, indigent, poor
- کسی بودن - to need somebody

محتاجی [mohtaaji] need, poverty, indigence

محترم [mohtaram] respected, esteemed

محتسب [mohtaseb] 1 mohtaseb (a person who watches over the observance of the morals and customs of the sharia) 2 overseer of a bazaar

محتکر [mohtaker] speculator, profiteer

محتوی [mohtawi] 1 containing, including 2 contents
- نقاشی - subject matter of a painting
- بودن - to contain, to include within itself

محتویات [mohtawiyaat] *plural of* محتوی 2

محجوب [mahjub] 1 covered with a veil or with a shawl (about a woman) 2 bashful, shy

محدود [mahdud] limited, restricted
- کردن - 1 to limit, to restrict 2 to localize (a war)

محراب [mehraab] 1 mehrab (niche in an inner wall of a mosque that indicates the direction of Mecca) 2 altar
- ومنبر - (emblem of coat of arms of Afghanistan)

محرر [moharrer] 1 author, writer 2 newspaper worker 3 editor

محرقه [mohreqa] (also- مرض) typhus

محرک [moharrek] 1 motive, incentive, stimulus 2 instigator, pioneer, trailblazer; initiator

محرم [mahram]¹ 1 close relative (whom one cannot marry according to the sharia) 2 close friend (or) trusted servant (who has access to the wife's part of the house) 3 husband

محرم [mahram]² secret, confidential *adjective* ♦ سند - secret document ◊ اشد - top secret *adjective*

محرم [moharram] muharram (first month of the Moslem lunar year)

محرمانه [mahramaana] 1 secret *adjective*, covert, clandestine 2 secretly, covertly, clandestinely

محروق [mahruq] burning

محروقات ☞ مواد -

محروقات [mahruqaat] fuel oil; fuel; combustibles, inflammables, fuels

محروم [mahrum] 1 devoid [of], not possessing (something) 2 unfortunate
- شدن - to be devoid, to be deprived (of something از)
- کردن - to deprive, to take away (something از)

محسوس [mahsus] 1 perceptible 2 palpable, tangible, noticeable, appreciable
- کردن - to sense, to feel

محشر [mahshar] 1 *religion* gathering place of mankind on the day of judgement 2 bustle, turmoil

محصل [mohassel] 1 pupil, student 2 tax collector

محصول [mahsul] (*plural* محصولات [mahsulaat]) 1 harvest, yield, crop 2 product, duty, tax

محصولات [mahsulaat] (*plural of* محصول) 1 produce, output production 2 income, tax revenues

محض [mahz] 1 absolute, perfect 2 only; merely, just
- برای ۰۰۰ - exclusively for …, only for …

محضر [mahzar] 1 presence (somewhere) ♦ در - عام in everyone's presence, in public 2 meeting 3 place for meetings, meeting place; place of business, office

محفل [mahfel] (*plural* محافل [mahafel]) 1 circle (of society), section (of society) 2 meeting, gathering 3 party, evening party

محفوظ [mahfuz] 1.1 kept, protected 1.2 retained (in memory), remembered 2 *masculine proper name* Mahfuz

- داشتن - to keep, to protect
- ماندن - to remain in safekeeping

محقر [mohaqqar] pitiful; insignificant, worthless; contemptible, despicable

محقق [mohaqqeq] investigator

محک [mahak(k)] 1 touchstone 2 criterion, measure, yardstick, standard

محکم [mahkam] 1.1 strong, durable, solid 2 steady, staunch, stable, firm, steadfast 2 firmly, solidly
- شدن - to persist; to manifest persistence; to resist, to oppose
- کردن - to strengthen, to consolidate
- گرفتن - 1 to hold, to retain, to hold back 2 to hold firmly, to adhere firmly (to something), not to budge, not to deviate (from something)

محکم بندی [mahkambandi] obstruction, obstacle, bar, barrier

محکمه [mahkama] court, tribunal

محکوم [mahkum] 1 convicted, condemned, sentenced 2 dependent [on], subject [to]; under the yoke [of]
- کردن - to condemn, to sentence (to something به)

محکومیت [mahkumiyat] 1 conviction, condemnation 2 submission; dependence

محل [mahal(l)] (*plural* محال [mahal(l)]) 1 place, locality 2 point
- قوماندہ - *military* command post

محلول [mahlul] 1 solution 2 dissolved

محله [mahalla] quarter, section (of a city)

محلی [mahalli] local

محمدزی [mohammadzi] Mohammedzai (a branch of the Durrani clan)

محنت [mehnat] 1 labor, work 2 efforts, endeavors 3 difficulties; burdens; trials, ordeals

محو [mahiw (a)] 1 destruction, annihilation, liquidation, elimination 2 disappearance
- کردن - 1 to destroy, to annihilate, to liquidate, to eliminate 2 to rub out, to erase (something written)

محور [mehwar] 1 axis ♦ زمین - earth's axis 2 *technical* axle, shaft

محول [mohawwal] 1 entrusted [with], charged [with] commissioned [to] 2 invested [with], trusted [with]
- کردن - to charge [with], to entrust [with] (به); to commission [with], to trust [with] (به)

محوله [mohawala] 1 *commerce* bill of lading 2 ☞ محول 1

محیط [mohit] 1 environment, surroundings ♦ حفاظت - زیست environmental protection 2 situation, atmosphere ♦ - دوستانه friendly situation, friendly surroundings

مخابرات [mokhaaberaat] *plural of* مخابره

مخابره [mokhaabera] (*plural* مخابرات [mokhaaberaat]) 1 communications ♦ بی سیم - wireless communications 2 communication, report
- کردن - to transmit (by telegraph, etc.), to communicate (by telegraph, etc.)

مخارج [makhaarej] expenditures, outlays; expenses

مخازن [makhaazen] *plural of* مخزن

مخاصم [mokhaasem] 1 enemy, foe 2 hostile, inimical

مخاصمت [mokhaasamat] enmity, hostility, animosity, antagonism
- کردن - to quarrel [with], to be antagonistic [toward]

مخاطب [mokhaatab] 1 the one referred to; addressee 2 *grammar* the second person (of a verb)

مخالف [mokhaalef] 1.1 opposite 1.2 opposed; contrary 1.3 dissenting, nonconcurring, objecting 2 opponent, enemy, adversary 3 against, despite *denominative preposition* ♦ آرزوی من - despite my wishes
- بودن - 1 to be in dissent, to be against, to contradict (با) 2 to come out against (با)

مخالفت [mokhaalefat] 1 counteraction, resistance 2 opposition 3 objection, contradiction
- کردن - 1 to exert counteraction, to resist 2 to object, to contradict

مخبر [mokhber] 1 reporter, correspondent 2 agent; informant, informer

مختار [mokhtaar] 1.1 plenipotentiary ♦ وزیر - *diplomatic* vizier moxtar, minister plenipotentiary 1.2 independent (in actions) 2 *masculine proper name* Moxtar

مخترع [moxtare'] inventor

مختصر [mokhtasar] 1.1 short, brief; condensed, compressed; concise 1.2 small, insignificant 2.1 (also - بطور) briefly, concisely, in brief, in short 2.2 a little, some

مختلط [mokhtalat] 1 mixed, joint; composite ♦ شرکت - joint stock company 2 *grammar* complex, compound (about a sentence)

مختلف [mokhtalef] 1 different diverse, various 2 differing [in], unlike, dissimilar, disparate

مختوم [makhtum] 1 sealed 2 finished, completed 3 *grammar* ending in …, having the ending …

مخدر [mokhadder] (and) مخدره [mokhaddera] narcotic ♦ مواد - narcotics

مخدرات [mokhaddaraat] narcotics

مخرج [makhraj] 1 place of egress, exit, outlet, way out 2 source, root 3 *mathematical* denominator

مخزن [makhzan] (*plural* مخازن [makhaazen]) 1 storehouse; warehouse, depot ♦ آب - reservoir 2 vessel; tank 3 treasury, depository

مخصوص [makhsus] 1 particular, specific 2 special 3 peculiar (to something), inherent
- کردن - to earmark (for something), to set aside (for something)

مخصوصاً [makhsúsan] especially, in particular

مخفف [mokhaffaf] 1 facilitated, eased, lightened 2 reduced, decreased, abbreviated contracted

مخفف نویسی [mokhaffafnawisi] 1 cursive writing 2 stenography; shorthand

مخفی [makhfi] 1 secret; covert, clandestine 2 illegal

مخلص [mokhles] 1 faithful, devoted; sincere 2.1 sincere friend 2.2 *masculine proper name* Moxles

مخلوط [makhlut] 1 mixed, intermingled; shuffled 2 mixture, solution

مخلوق [makhluq] (*plural* مخلوقات [makhluqat]) 1 created 2 creation, creature, being

مخمس [mokhammas] 1 *literary* moxammas (pentastich with a single rhyme) 2 *mathematical* pentagon ♦ منظم - regular pentagon

مخمل [makhmal] velvet

مخمور [makhmur] *literary* 1 intoxicated, drunk 2 languid, languorous (about eyes)

مد [mad (d)] 1 prolongation; drawling, slowness [of speech]; duration, length, extent 2 maddah (name of the long mark over the letter alef) 3 sea tide
- مد نظر داشتن to keep in mind
- مد نظر گرفتن to take into account

مداخل [madaakhel] *plural of* مدخل

مداخلت [modaakhelat] (and) مداخله [modaakhela] (*plural* مداخلات [modaakhelaat]) 1 interference 2 incursion, invasion, intrusion, encroachment, intervention 3 relation, connection
- کردن - 1 to interfere, to meddle 2 to intervene, to perpetrate an intervention

مدار [madaar] 1 center of rotation, pivot, fulcrum, axis 2 *astronomy* orbit 3 *geography* tropic (e.g., Tropic of Cancer) 4 *colloquial* chance; opportune moment, convenient moment

مدارس [madaares] *plural of* مدرسه

مدارک [madaarek] *plural of* مدرک

مداری [madaari]¹ orbital

مداری [madaari]² *colloquial* conjurer, juggler 2 cheat, swindler

مدافع [modaafe'] 1 protecting, defending 2 protector, defender ♦ وکیل - *law* defender, counsel for the defense; lawyer, barrister, solicitor

مدافعت [modaafe'at] (and) مدافعه [modaafe'a] defense, protection ♦ هوایی - antiaircraft defense
- کردن - to defend, to protect (را از)

مدام [modaam] always, constantly

مداوم [modaawem] constant, permanent, invariable

مداومت [modaawamat] 1 constancy, permanence, invariability 2 duration, length; eternity

مدبرانه [modabberaana] reasonable, sensible, judicious, wise; circumspect, wary; businesslike, efficient ♦ سیاست - wise policy

مدت [moddat] interval of time, period of time; term ♦ مدتی - some time, not long
- مدتیکه(در) while whereas; when, until *compound conjunction*

مدتها [moddathaa] 1 a long time 2 a long time ago, long ago, very long ago

مدح [madh] praise; laudation, eulogy
- خواندن(گفتن) - to praise, to extol; to eulogize

مدخل [madkhal] (*plural* مداخل [madakhel]) 1 entrance, place of entry 2 income, receipt, revenue

مدد [madad] help, support, assistance

مددخرج [madadkharch] (and) مددخرجی [madadkharchi] grant, allowance

مددگار [madadgaar] 1 assistant, ally 2 sponsor, patron

مددمعاش [madadma'aash] allowance, grant, scholarship

مدرس [modarres] teacher, instructor (usually of theology)

مدرسه [madrasa] (*plural* مدارس [madaares]) 1 school 2 madrasah, ecclesiastical school

مدرک [madrak] (*plural* مدارک [madaarek]) 1 document (serving as proof or evidence) 2 source, item of income

مدرن [modern] modern

مدعا [modda'aa] 1 claim, demand 2 subject of a (legal) suit, subject of a court case, claims 3 assertion, statement, allegation

مدعی [modda'i] 1 plaintiff, prosecutor 2 claimant

مدعى العموم [modda'ialomum] 1 (general) prosecutor 2 public prosecutor

مدفن [madfan] burial place; grave; tomb

مدفون [madfun] 1 buried (e.g., when dead) 2 buried (i.e., covered over with something)

مدقق [modaqqeq] 1 investigating, testing, checking, examining 2 investigator

مدل [model] model

مدل‌سازی [modelsaazi] *technical* molding, casting

مدلل [modallal] proven, proved; well-founded, valid, sound

مدم [madam] madam (Indian stringed musical instrument)

مدنی [madani] 1 civilized, cultured 2 urban, municipal, civil

مدنیت [madaniyat] civilization, culture

مدوجزر [maddojázer] ebb and flow, high and low tide

مدور [modawwar] round; ball-shaped, spherical

مدهش [modhesh] terrible, horrible, awful

مدهوش [modhush] 1 frightened; confused; perplexed 2 being unconscious 3 intoxicated, drunk

مدیحه [madiha] panegyric, ode

مدیر [modir] director; manager ♦ مکتب - school director ◊ روزنامه - newspaper editor ◊ لوازم - farm manager

مدیره [modira]
• هئیت- board of administration, board of directors, board, management 2 editorial staff, editors; editorial board

مدیریت [modiriyat] 1 office, administration, directorate; department 2 post of manager, post of director

مدینه [madina] 1 *literary* city 2 city of Medina

مذاق [mazaaq] 1 joke, jest, banter, mockery 2 merriment, mirth, hilarity, wit 3 taste, gustatory sense, sense of taste
• گفتن(کردن) - to joke, to jest

مذاکرات [mozaakarăt] 1 *plural of* مذاکره 2 negotiations, talks
• کردن - to negotiate, to carry on negotiations or talks

مذاکره [mozaakara] (*plural* مذاکرات [mozaakaraat]) discussion; debate; interview
• کردن - to discuss, to hold a discussion, debate, or talk

مذکر [mozakkar] 1 male, masculine, man's, men's 2 *grammar* masculine gender

مذکور [mazkur] above mentioned, aforementioned, aforesaid, the above

مذهب [mazhab] 1 religion, faith, belief, dogma 2 teaching, teachings, doctrine, tenet

مذهبی [mazhabi] 1 religious; pertaining to religion 2 pious, devout

مراتب [maraateb] 1.1 *plural of* مرتبه 1.2 circumstances, details
• به - significantly, by far; many times more, many times greater
• به سلسله - in accordance with the chain of command, through channels; in accordance with established procedure

مراجع [moraaje'] (*plural* مراجعین [moraje'in]) client; applicant, petitioner; patient

مراجعت [moraaje'at] 1 referring, appealing, making (a request) 2 ☞ مراجعه
• کردن - to appeal [to] (with a request, etc.), to make (a request, etc.)

مراجعه [moraaje'a] return
• کردن - to return *intransitive*

مراجعین [moraaje'in] clients, customers; applicants, petitioners

مراحل [maraahel] *plural of* مرحله

مراحم [maraahem] *plural of* مرحمت

مراد [moraad] 1 wish, desire; goal, aim, purpose 2 implied, meant, meaning, sense ♦ از این ۰۰۰ - this means ..., this implies that ... 3 *masculine proper name* Morad

مراسلات [moraaselaat] 1 *plural of* مراسله 2 sending of mail

مراسله [moraasela] letter, dispatch

مراسم [maraasem] 1 ceremony, rite 2 customs, traditions

مراعات [moraa'aat] 1 observance, fulfillment 2 attention, care, concern
• کردن - to observe, to fulfill, to keep, to adhere [to] (rules, etc.)

مراقب [moraaqeb] مراقبت کردن ☞ بودن(چیزی)کسی - in entry مراقبت

مراقبت [moraaqebat] 1 observation; care, charge 2 preservation, conservation; maintenance
• کردن - 1 to observe, to look [after]; to watch [over], to take care [of], to be guardian [of] 2 to keep, to save, to preserve

مراکز [maraakez] *plural of* مرکز

مرام [maraam] goal, aim, object, purpose; task; program

مرامنامه [maraamnaama] *political* program, platform

مراوده [moraawada] intercourse, contact, tie, bond; acquaintance, familiarity ♦ دوستی - friendly relations, friendship

مربا [morabbaa] jam

مربع [morabba'] 1 square ♦ متر - square meter 2 a square, a quadrangle, a tetragon

مربوط [marbut] 1 connected (with somebody or something), pertaining (to somebody or something) 2 appropriate ♦ مقامات - appropriate organs 3 subordinate, dependent

مربوطات [marbutaat] possessions (land, real estate); contiguous regions, contiguous areas

مربی [morabbi] *literary* teacher, tutor

مرتب [morattab] 1 put in order, regulated 2 regular, systematic, methodical
• کردن - 1 to put into order, to regulate 2 to work up, to develop, to compile (a document, plan, etc.)

مرتباً [moráttaban] one after another, in succession; regularly; systematically, methodically

مرتبان [martabaan] earthenware or china pot, jug (for jam, marinade, pickles, etc.)

مرتبه [martaba] 1 degree, rank 2 time ♦ پنج - five times

مرتجع [mortaje'] 1.1 reactionary *adjective* 1.2 resilient, elastic 2 a reactionary

مرتفع [mortafe'] 1 high; elevated, lofty ♦ سطح - a plateau 2 a height, a hill

مرتکب [mortakeb] 1 having attempted (a crime) 2 culprit, perpetrator
• شدن - to commit (a crime, a sin)

مرثیه [marsiya] 1 *literary* elegy 2 funeral speech 3 dirge

مرجان [marjaan] 1 coral 2 *masculine and feminine proper name* Marjan

مرچ [morch] pepper ♦ سرخ - red pepper ◊ سیاه - black pepper

مرچل [morchal] trench, emplacement, shelter, breastwork, rampart

م

مرحله [marhala] (*plural* مراحل [maraahel]) **1** stage, period **2** day's passage, day's march, stage span (between two stops or two stations)

مرحمت [marhamat] (*plural* مراحم [maraahem]) favor, grace, mercy, charity
- کردن - **1** to render a favor, to show mercy **2** to grant, to bestow, to make a present [of], to favor [with]

مرحوم [marhum] the late (about a deceased person) *adjective*, deceased *adjective*
- شدن - to die, to decease, to pass away

مرد [mard] **1.1** male; husband **1.2** man **2** noble, manly

مردار [mordaar] **1.1** dead (about animals) **1.2** foul, vile; unclean, impure **1.3** *colloquial* bad, nasty; infamous, villainous **2** carrion
- شدن - to die [about animals]
- کردن - *colloquial* **1** to soil, to dirty, to stain, to pollute **2** to defile, to profane **3** to do a vile thing (to somebody), to play a dirty trick (on somebody)

مردارخوار [mordaarkhaar] (and) مردار خور [mordaarkhor] **1** feeding on carrion **2.1** griffon-vulture, carrion vulture, buzzard **2.2** a person who disdains nothing for the sake of gain or profit

مردانگی [mardaanagi] **1** courage; valor **2** nobility, nobleness

مردانه [mardaana] **1** men's, for men **2** ☞ مردانه وار

مردانه وار [mardaanawaar] **1** manly; bold, courageous, daring **2** with fortitude, boldly, bravely, fearlessly

مردکار [mardekaar] **1** day laborer **2** unskilled worker

مردم [mardom] (and) مردمان [mardomaan] people; the people

مردم شناسی [mardomshenaasi] anthropology; ethnography

مردم فریبی [mardomfereebi] demagogy

مردم فهم [mardomfahm] comprehensible to all, popular

مردمک [mardomak] (also چشم -) pupil (of the eye)

مردن [mordan] (*present tense stem* میر [mir]) **1** to die **2** to go out, to die out (about a flame)

مردنی [mordani] **1** sickly, puny, emaciated **2** a sickly person, a puny person

مرده [morda] **1** dead, deceased **2** corpse, dead man, a deceased
- مرده مرده زنده شدن to recover (one's health) after a long illness
- با چشم - نگاه کردن to look with a vacant stare, to look absently
- باد - Down with! / Away with!
- ما با احمد - وزنده داریم *colloquial* Ahmad and I are inseparable unto death.

مرده دار [mordadaar]
- بودن - *colloquial* to have a deceased in one's home, to suffer the death of someone close

مرده دل [mordadel] unfeeling, callous, indifferent to everything; sad, dismal despondent

مرده شوی [mordashoy] one who bathes corpses
- کالای توارا – بره *abusive* May you drop dead! (*literally*, May your clothes be taken by the person who washes corpses!)

مردی [mardi] ☞ مردانگی

مرزا [merzaa] ☞ میرزا

مرسله [morsela] (also دستگاه -) (radio) transmitter

مرسوبات [marsubaat] *geology* deposit

مرشد [morshed] **1** murshid (spiritual teacher of murids) **2** head of a religious order

مرصع [morassa'] strewn with precious stones, decorated with jewels
- تاریخ – *Tarikh-i Morassa* (name of a history of the Afghans written by Afzal-Khan Kattak)

مرطوب [martub] damp, humid; moist

مرض [maraz] (*plural* امراض [amraz]) illness; disease, ailment ♦ ساری - infectious disease, contagious disease

مرغ [morgh] **1** bird ♦ خانگی - (and) خسک - poultry **2** chicken
- گوشت - fowl (i.e., the meat of a chicken); chicken meat

مرغابی [morghaabi] a duck

مرغانچه [morghaancha] chicken coop, hen house

مرغباز [morghbaaz] fancier of fighting birds

مرغ داری [morqdaari] raising poultry, poultry farming

مرغوب [marghub] pleasant, pleasing, attractive, alluring, nice, sweet

مرقع [moraqqa'] **1** album **2** memorandum book, notebook

مرکب [markab] riding animal (donkey, mule)
- تیز - اسپ استاده بهتر است *proverb* A fast donkey is better than a horse standing still.

مرکب [morakkab] **1** component *adjective*, constituent *adjective*, consisting (of something) (از) **2** compound ♦ کلمه - *grammar* compound word

مرکز [markaz] (*plural* مراکز [maraakez]) **1** center, middle, midst ♦ دایره - center of a circumference **2** chief city, capital **3** base, point ♦ ترمیماتی - repair base

مرکز گرمی [markazgarmi] **1** central heating plant [for several buildings or an area or district]; boiler room **2** central heating [for a home or one building] ♦ مرکز گریز [markazgoreez] centrifugal ♦ پمپ - *technical* centrifugal pump

مرکزی [markazi] central ♦ بانک - central bank

مرگ [marg] death; demise, decease ♦ طبیعی - natural death
- مرگ موش ☞ موش
- پشک کردن - to exaggerate a matter, "to make a mountain out of a molehill"

مرگامرگی [margaamargi] **1** large-scale deaths, plague, pestilence **2** epizootic *noun*

مرگ حال [marghaal] being in dying agony, being in agony of death

مرگ موش [margemush] arsenic

مرگامرگی [margomir] ☞ مرگ ومیر

مرمت [maram (m) at] repair, repairing, mending

مرمت کاری [maram (m)atkaari] repairs, maintenance, repair operations

مرمر [marmar] marble

مرمر [mormor] **1** creeps, shivers ♦ جانش - میکند He had the creeps / shivers all over his body. **2** *colloquial* a weak flame, a smoldering flame

مرمر کاری [marmarkaari] facing with marble, lining with marble

مرموز [marmuz] secret *adjective*, mysterious, enigmatic

مرمی [marmi] (*plural* مرمیات [marmiyaat]) shell, projectile, bullet

مرمیات [marmiyaat] ammunition; shells

مروارید [morwaarid] a pearl; pearls

مروت [morowwat] kindness, goodness, humaneness

266

مروج [morawwaj] (and) مروجه [morawwaja] widespread, generally accepted; in great demand, popular

مرور [morur] passing, passage (of time) ♦ به – زمان with the passage of time, in time

مرهم [marham] 1 ointment *medicine*, balsam, balm 2 plaster

مرهون [marhun] 1 mortgaged, pawned 2 obligated (to somebody for something); being in debt (to somebody)

مریخ [merikh] *astronomy* Mars

مرید [morid] *religion* murid (a disciple or pupil of a spiritual teacher, of a murshid)

مریض [mariz] ill, sick, unhealthy, sickly

مریضی [marizi] sickness, illness, ill health, indisposition

مزاج [mizaj] 1 nature 2 character, temperament, disposition, temper

مزاجی [mezaaji] *colloquial* capricious, whimsical

مزاح [mazaah] joke, prank; sneer, gibe ♦ – به for fun, in jest

مزاحم [mozahem] hindering, hampering, giving trouble [to]
• – شدن to hinder, to hamper; to give trouble [to]

مزار [mazaar] mazar, grave of a saint; place of pilgrimage

مزارع [mazaare'] *plural of* مزرعه

مزاق [mazaaq] *colloquial* ☞ مزاح

مزاقی [mazaaqi] *colloquial* joker, wag, jovial person

مزایا [mazaayaa] *plural of* مزیت

مزایده [mozaayeda] sale by auction, auction

مزبور [mazbur] [above-] mentioned

مزخرف [mozakhraf] 1.1 foolish, stupid, absurd 1.2 crude, coarse (about decoration or ornamentation) 2 nonsense, absurdity

مزد [mozd (and) mazd] 1 payment for labor; wages 2 compensation, bribe

مزدور [mazdur] 1 hired worker; day laborer; farmhand 2 unskilled workman

مزدورزن [mazdurzan] female worker, female farmhand

مزدوری [mazduri] 1 work for hire; work as a farmhand 2 unskilled labor 3 payment for labor (usually as a farmhand)

مزرعه [mazra'a] (*plural* مزارع [mazaare']) 1 planted field, cornfield 2 farm ♦ اشتراکی – collective farm

مزمن [mozmen] chronic ♦ مرض – chronic illness

مزه [maza] 1 taste, gustatory sense 2 interest; attractiveness ♦ این – ندارد This is devoid of interest. / This is pale. / This is colorless. / This is inexpressive. 3 pleasure

مزه دار [mazadaar] 1.1 tasty; palatable 1.2 interesting, attractive, alluring 2 *colloquial* thoroughly, magnificently ♦ اسد – لت خورد Asad was beaten soundly.

مزیت [maziyat] (*plural* مزایا [mazaayaa]) advantage, preference; merit, value, worth

مزید [mazid] 1 increased, supplemented ♦ انکشاف – further development ◊ معلومات – supplementary information 2 addition, supplement; increase, augmentation

مژده [mozhda] good news

مژگان [mezhgaan] *plural of* مژه 1

مژه [mezha (and) mazha] 1 eyelashes 2 *colloquial* fringe (on a shawl, etc.)

مس [mes] copper

مسابقه [mosaabeqa] 1 a competition; a contest 2 competition ♦ تسلیحات – arms race
• – کردن to compete

مساجد [masaajed] *plural of* مسجد

مساحت [masaahat] (and) مساحه [masaaha] 1 area, space 2 measurement, measuring, land-surveying
• – کردن to measure (area, land); to carry out land-surveying

مساعد [mosaa'ed] suitable, proper, appropriate; favorable, auspicious ♦ موقع را – دیدن to make use of favorable opportunity

مساعدت [mosaa'edat] favoring; promoting, furthering
• – کردن to promote, to further; to help, to assist

مساعی [masaa'i] effort, endeavor ♦ تشریک – interaction, cooperation

مسافر [mosaafer] 1 traveler, wayfarer 2 passenger

مسافرت [mosaaferat] journey, voyage; trip
• – کردن to journey, to voyage; to take a trip

مسافه [masaafa] distance, interval

مساکن [masaken] *plural of* مسکن

مساله [masaala] (*plural* مساله جات [masaalajaat]) 1 seasoning, condiment; spice 2 *colloquial* ☞ مصالح [masaala (h)]

مسأله [mas'ala] ☞ مسئله

مساوات [mosaawaat] equality, parity

مساوی [masaawi] 1.1 equal, parity *adjective* ♦ حقوق – equal rights 1.2 equivalent
• – به *mathematical* is equal [to] ♦ دو جمع دو – به چهار Two plus two equals four.

مسایل [masaayel] *plural of* مسئله

مست [mast] 1.1 intoxicated, not sober, drunk 1.2 excited 1.3 furious, violent, wild
• – شدن 1.1 to get drunk, to get intoxicated 1.2 to become furious or violent 2 *masculine proper name* Mast

مستاجر [mostaajer] leaseholder, lessee, tenant

مستاوه [mastaawa] soup with rice seasoned with sour milk

مستثنا [mostasnaa] (and) مستثنی 1 exceptional, special 2 exclusion, exception

مستحق [mostahaq (q)] having the right; deserving, worthy
• چیزی شدن – to obtain the right to something; to deserve something

مستحکم [mostahkam] strengthened, fortified; consolidated, intensified

مستخدم [mostakhdam] employee

مستر [mestar] mister (form of address to a foreigner)

مستری [mestari] master; technician; mechanic (who repairs machines)

مستری خانه [mestarikhaana] workshop

مستشار [mostashaar] adviser, consultant

مستشرق [mostashreq] orientalist

مستعجل [mosta'jel] 1 urgent; rush *adjective*; pressing 2 accelerated

مستعد [mosta'ed] 1 able, capable, talented 2 ready, prepared 3 prosperous, well-to-do

مستعمرات [mosta'maraat] *plural of* مستعمره

مستعمراتی [mosta'maraati] colonial

مستعمره [mosta'mara] (*plural* مستعمرات [mosta'maraat]) colony

مستعمل [mosta'mal] 1 utilized, used [for / as]; generally used, common 2 used, secondhand

مستغنی [mostaghni] not needy, well-to-do; rich, wealthy

مستفید [mostafid] obtaining use, extracting benefit, deriving benefit

267

مـ

- استفاده شدن - to get use [from], to get benefit [from] (از)
- انس شما بسیار شدیم *polite* We listened to your report with great interest.

مستقبل [mostaqbal] **1** future **2.1** the future **2.2** *grammar* (also - زمان) the future tense

مستقر [mostaqar (r)]
- شدن - to consolidate one's hold, to settle down (somewhere)

مستقل [mostaqel (l)] independent ♦ - دولت independent state ◊ - ریاست department, main directorate, main office

مستقیم [mostaqim] **1** straight ♦ - خط straight line **2** direct ♦ - جریان برق *electrical* direct current

مستلزم [mostalzem] demanding, requiring, stipulating
- چیزی بودن - to do something necessary, to demand something, to require something

مستملکات [mostamlakaat] *plural of* مستملکه
مستملکه [mostamlaka] colony

مستند [mostanad] **1.1** based (on something), well-grounded, valid, sound **2** confirmed by documents ♦ - فلم documentary film **2** foundation, support

مستوره [mastura] *obscure* chaste, modest (about a woman or girl)

مستوفی [mostawfi] *historical* mostawfi (manager of finances of a province)

مستوفیت [mostawfiyat] *historical* management of the finances of a province

مستوی [mostawi] even, flat, smooth (about a surface)

مستهلک [mostahlak] **1** consumed **2** *finance* amortized, liquidated, repaid (about a debt) **3** destroyed, obliterated, demolished

مستهلک [mostahlek] **1** consuming **2** consumer

مستی [masti] **1** intoxication **2** excitement, agitation **3** fury, rage

مسجد [masjed] (*plural* مساجد [masaajed]) mosque ♦ - جامع grand mosque

مسجع [mosajja'] rhymed; rhythmic, rhythmical ♦ - نثر rhymed prose

مسخره [moskhara] **1** fool, jester, clown **2** sneer, jibe, joke

مسخره باز [maskharabaaz] scoffer, mocker, joker

مسخره گی [maskharagi] buffoonery; clowning

مسدس [masaddas] **1** hexagon **2** *literary* masaddas (a stanza of six lines of verse with the same rhyme)

مسدود [masdud] **1** blocked, fenced in, enclosed; closed **2** stopped, halted
- کردن - **1** to bar, to block, to shut, to close **2** to stop, to halt, to put an end to *transitive*

مسرت [masarat] gladness, joy, merriment

مسرور [masrur] glad, joyous, joyful

مسطح [mosattah] smooth, even, flat

مسعود [mas'ud] **1** happy, blessed; lucky **2.1** masudi (a tribe) **2.2** *masculine proper name* Masud

مسقره [masqara] *colloquial* ☞ مسخره
- کردن -to consider (something) a trifling matter

مسکن [maskan] (*plural* مساکن [masaken]) dwelling, residence

مسکنت [maskanat] poverty, destitution

مسکن گزین [maskangozin]
- شدن - **1** to settle, to take up residence **2** to turn to a settled way of life (instead of a nomadic one)

مسکوک [maskuk] minted, coined, chased
مسکوکات [maskukaat] hard cash (coins), money
مسکون [maskun] inhabited, populated
مسکه [maska] butter
مسکین [meskin] **1.1** poor, unfortunate, miserable **1.2** humble **2** a beggar, a poor man
مسگر [mesgar] coppersmith
مسلح [mosallah] equipped with a weapon, armed
مسلحانه [mosallahaana] armed (about something) ♦ - قیام armed uprising, armed revolt
مسلخ [moslakh] slaughterhouse
مسلسل [mosalsal] **1** forming chain **2** successive, consecutive, continuous, systematic
مسلک [maslak] **1** trade; profession **2** *rarely* belief, conviction; world outlook, ideology
مسلکی [maslaki] vocational, special ♦ - تعلیمات vocational training
مسلم [mosallam] evident, obvious, manifest; unquestionable, undeniable, indisputable
مسلم [moslem] ☞ مسلمان
مسلمان [mosalmaan] a Moslem, a Mohammedan *noun*
مسلمانی [mosalmaani] **1** Islam, the Moslem faith **2** Moselem *adjective*
مسمات [mosammaat] *epistolary* the aforementioned (about a woman)
مسموم [masmum] poisoned, contaminated
مسمومیت [masmumiyat] state of being poisoned; state of contamination, state of pollution ♦ - ارضی - pollution of a locality
مسمی [mosammaa] called, named
- شدن - to be called, to be named
مسن [mosen (n)] elderly, getting on in years
مسند [masnad] **1** support, bearing, foundation, base **2** large pillow, cushion (for sitting) **3** *obscure* throne
مسند [mosnad] *grammar* predicate
مسند علیه [mosnadalayh] *grammar* subject
مسواک [meswak] **1** toothpick **2** wooden toothbrush
مسوده [mosawwada] **1** rough copy **2** draft
مسئول [mas'ul] **1** responsible ♦ - مقامات responsible agencies, responsible bodies **2** responsible person
مسئولیت [mas'uliyat] responsibility
- بدوش خود گرفتن - to take responsibility (on oneself)
مسهل [moshel] laxative
مسی [mesi] copper ♦ - ظروف copper vessel
مسیح [masih] (*and*) مسیحا [masihaa] messiah, Christ
مسیحی [masihi] **1** Christian *adjective* **2** a Christian
مسیر [masir] **1** direction, course, route ♦ - جریانات course of events **2** channel, bed (of a river)
مسین [mesin] ☞ مسی
مسله [masala] (*plural* مسایل [masaayel]) **1** question matter, problem **2** *mathematical* problem
مشابهت [moshaabahat] (*and*) مشابهه [mosabaha] likeness, resemblance, similarity; analogy
- داشتن - to bear a resemblance, to be alike (با)
مشاجره [moshaajara] argument, controversy, quarrel, conflict
مشاعره [moshaaera] moshaera, a contest of poets
مشام [mashaam] (sense of) smell
- به - رسیدن - to smell [of], to reek [of], to give off (a smell)
مشاور [moshaawer] adviser, consultant

268

مشاورت [moshaawarat] (and) مشاوره [moshaawara] conference, deliberation; consultation

مشاهده [moshaahada] 1 observation, contemplation 2 inspection, examination
- شدن - to be observed; to be encountered
- کردن - 1 to observe; to discover, to detect 2 to see
- به – پیوستن to be observed; to be noted, to be noticed, to be detected, to be discovered

مشاهیر [mashaahir] *literary* eminent people, celebrities

مشت [mosht] 1 fist 2 a blow with the fist, a punch 3 handful
- زدن - to hit with the fist
- کردن - to mix, to knead (dough, etc.)
- پر - *colloquial* weak, puny; sickly, thin and feeble
- بعد از جنگ - *colloquial* belated daring (*literally*, fists after the fight)
- او واز شد - *colloquial* His secret has been revealed. / He has been exposed / unmasked.

مشتبه [moshtabeh] 1 mistaken, incorrect 2 doubtful, suspicious

مشترک [moshtarak] 1 common, joint, combined 2 mixed

مشترک [moshtarek] 1 participant, accomplice 2 subscriber

مشترکاً [moshtarakan] jointly, all together

مشتری [moshtari]¹ client; buyer, purchaser; customer

مشتری [moshtari]² *astronomy* Jupiter

مشتعل [moshtagel]
- شدن -to catch fire, to blaze up

مشتق [moshtaq] 1 *grammar* derivative (about a word) 2 *geology chemistry* a derivative
- شدن - to be derived [from], to be formed [by] (از)

مشتقات [moshtaqaat] 1 *plural of* مشتق 2 *grammar* derivative words; derivatives

مشتمل [moshtamel] containing, containing within itself; consisting (of something)

مشت ومال [moshtomaal] massaging, kneading
- کردن - to rub, to knead, to massage

مشت وگریبان [moshtogereebaan] (and) مشت ویخن [moshtoyakhan] melee, brawl, fight, scuffle ♦ جنگ - hand-to-hand fight; combat, fighting

مشخص [moshakhxas] 1 definite, established 2 typical, characteristic; distinctive, notable, remarkable
- کردن - 1 to define, to establish 2 to pick out, to single out, to distinguish

مشخص [moshakhxes] *linguistics* diacritical (about marks)

مشخصات [moshakhxasaat] 1 indicators, indices 2 distinctive marks, distinguishing features

مشدد [moshaddad] 1 strengthened, reinforced, intensified 2 *linguistics* doubled, double (about consonants)

مشرب [mashrab] *literary* 1 character, disposition, temper 2 belief, conviction

مشرف [mosharraf]
- شدن -to be honored, to have the honor [of]

مشرق [mashreq] 1 east 2 rising (e.g., of the sun) 3 the East

مشروب [mashrub] (*plural* مشروبات [masrubat]) 1.1 suitable for drinking, potable, drinking ♦ آب - drinking water 1.2 watered, irrigated 2 beverage, drink

مشروط [mashrut] stipulated, specified
- شدن - to be stipulated, to make a reservation or stipulation

مشروع [mashru'] legal, permitted (by the sharia)

مشعل [mash'al] torch

مشغول [mashghul] occupied (with work, with a matter), engaged (in work, in a matter), involved (with work, with a matter)

مشق [mashq] exercise, training, training session ♦ وتمرین - training, training session

مشقت [mashaqqat] hard labor, work
- کردن - to labor, to perform very heavy work

مشک [mashk] wineskin ♦ آب بازی - air bladder for swimming

مشک [moshk] musk
- بگوید - آنست که خود ببوید نه که عطار *proverb* You judge musk by its odor, not by the words of the seller.

مشک بید [moshkbeed] Egyptian willow

مشکل [moshkel] 1 difficult, hard 2 ☞ مشکلی

مشکل کشا [moshkelkoshaa] solving difficulties, facilitating, easing, alleviating, helping (epithet of Allah)

مشکلی [moshkeli] difficulty, obstacle

مشکوک [mashkuk] suspicious, doubtful

مشکوله [mashkula] hot-water bottle

مشکی [moshki] 1 black (about a horse's coat) 2 a black horse

مشمول [mashmul] 1 included, listed (somewhere) 2 a participant (in a meeting, in a conference, etc.)

مشنگ [moshong] field pea

مشورت [mashwarat] advice, counsel; consultation
- کردن - to seek advice, to seek counsel, to consult (with somebody با)

مشورتی [mashwarati] deliberative, consultative, advisory

مشوش [moshaw (w) ash] agitated, disturbed, unsettled, harassed, anxious, uneasy

مشهود [mashhud] 1 visible, observable 2 evident, obvious; witnessed, certified

مشهور [mashhur] well-known, famous, celebrated

مشیر [moshir] *literary* adviser

مشین [mashin] ☞ ماشین

مشینری [mashinari] machinery; machines, apparatuses

مصاحبه [mosahaba] talk, conversation; interview
- کردن - to talk [to / with]

مصادر [masader] *plural of* مصدر

مصادف [mosadef] 1 coinciding 2 meeting, encountering
- شدن - 1 to coincide (with something با) 2 to encounter, to meet (with somebody با)

مصادمه [mosadema] 1 collision, blow 2 *military* skirmish

مصارف [masaref] *plural of* مصرف [masraf]

مصالح [masaleh] *plural of* مصلحت

مصالح [masala (h)] construction materials, building materials

مصایب [masayeb] *plural of* مصیبت

مصتر [mastar] mustard ♦ پلاستر - mustard plaster

مصحح [mosahheh] proofreader

مصدر [masdar] (*plural* مصادر [masaader]) 1 source, origin; root, cause, reason 2 *grammar* masdar, infinitive

مصراع [mesraa'] 1 hinge (of a door), shutter (of a door) 2 mesra (line of verse or poetry)

مصرف [masraf] (*plural* مصارف [masaref]) 1 expense, expenditure; expenses 2 consumption, use, spending, expending
- کردن - 1 to spend, to expend 2 to consume, to use
- کردن - به - رساندن 1 ☞

مصروف [masruf] busy, occupied, employed, loaded (with work)
• بودن - to be busy, to be employed

مصروفیت [masrufiyat] 1 employed, state of being busy, state of being loaded (with work, with matters) 2 occupation; business, duty responsibility

مصری [mesri] 1 Egyptian 2 an Egyptian

مصطلح [mostaleh] 1.1 idiomatic 1.2 used as a term 2.1 idiom 2.2 turn of speech

مصلا [mosallaa] an area outside a city for public praying

مصلحت [maslahat] (plural مصالح [masaaleh]) 1 good advice 2 wise decision 3 expediency, advisability, soundness, reasonability ♦ از - بعید است inadvisably, inexpediently, to no purpose

مصنوعات [masnu'aat] articles; manufactured goods, manufactured products, finished products

مصنوعی [masnu'i] artificial, man-made, made

مصوت [mosawwat] 1 ringing, clear, voiced (about a sound) 2 linguistics a vowel, a vowel sound ♦ مرکب - diphthong

مصور [mosawwar] 1 drawn, pictured, depicted, portrayed 2 illustrated

مصور [mosawwer] artist, painter

مصون [masun] protected, preserved; unharmed, safe
• ماندن - 1 to remain unharmed 2 to avoid, to evade (از), to get rid (of something)

مصونیت [masuniyat] 1 protection, state of being protected, state of being unharmed, state of being intact 2 inviolability, (diplomatic) immunity medicine immunity

مصیبت [mosibat] (plural مصایب [masaayeb]) misfortune, calamity, disaster

مصیبت زده [mosibatzada] stricken with misfortune, stricken by trouble, having suffered a calamity, having suffered a disaster

مضارع [mozaare'] grammar aorist, future imperfective tense of subjunctive mood

مضاف [mozaaf] 1 joined, appended, added (to something) 2 grammar the word being attributed (in an ezafeh construction)

مضاف الیه [mozaafalayh] grammar 1 attribute (in an ezafeh construction) 2 the object of the attribute

مضامین [mazaamin] plural of مضمون

مضایقه [mozaayeqa] 1 constraint, difficulty 2 need, shortage ♦ نکردن - not to stint, not to spare

مضحک [mozhek] amusing, funny

مضر [mozer (r)] harmful, injurious

مضطرب [moztareb] 1 agitated, disturbed, worked-up 2 unsettled, upset; grieved, saddened

مضمون [mazmun] 1 subject (of study), theme, topic 2 (educational) discipline 3 article; composition, work ♦ انتقادی - critical article

مطابق [motaabeq] 1 corresponding [to]; agreeing [with] 2 according to, in accordance with ... denominative preposition ♦ هدایت - in accordance with instructions, according to instructions

مطابقت [motabeqat] accordance, conformity, compliance, correspondence; coordination
• داشتن - to correspond [to / with], to conform [to], to coincide [with], to concur [with], to agree [with] (با) ♦

با آرزو مندی های مردم - دارد to satisfy the aspirations of the people

مطالب [mataaleb] plural of مطلب

مطالبه [motaalaba] demand; claim
• کردن - to demand

مطالعه [motaale'a] military 1 study, examination ♦ کشف و - reconnaissance, reconnoitering 2 reading
• کردن - 1 to study, to examine 2 to read, to be occupied (in reading books)

مطبخ [matbakh] kitchen ♦ سیار - military field kitchen

مطبعه [matba'a] printing shop, printing house

مطبوع [matbu'] printed; published

مطبوعات [matbu'aat] 1 the press 2 publications

مطبوعاتی [matbu'aati] publishing, pertaining to the press ♦ مصاحبه - (and) کنفرنس - press conference, news conference

مطرح [matrah]
• کردن - to examine, to discuss, to review, to consider

مطلب [matlab] (plural مطالب [mataaleb]) 1 meaning, sense, significance 2 goal, purpose, intention 3 advantage, interest

مطلب آشنا [matlabaashnaa] prudent, practical, economical

مطلب والا [matlabwaalaa] colloquial interested, concerned, mercenary

مطلع [matla'] literary initial couplet (of a poem)

مطلع [mottalle'] versed [in], conversant [with], informed; experienced [in]

مطلق [motlaq] absolute, complete ♦ اکثریت - absolute majority

مطلقاً [motlaqan] absolutely; completely, fully

مطلوب [matlub] required; desired ♦ نتیجه - sought for result, desired result

مطمئن [motma'en] calm, quiet; tranquil, serene

مطیع [moti'] humble; submissive, obedient, dutiful
• ساختن - to subordinate, to subdue, to subjugate

مظاهره [mozaahera] 1 demonstration 2 expression, manifestation
• کردن - 1 to go to a demonstration 2 to show, to demonstrate

مظفر [mozaffar] 1 triumphal, triumphant, victorious 2.1 conqueror; victor, winner 2.2 masculine proper name Mozaffar

مظلوم [mazlum] 1 depressed; oppressed 2 aggrieved, offended

مظلومیت [mazlumiyat] 1 depression 2 oppression; humbleness, humility

معابد [ma'aabed] plural of معبد

معابر [ma'aaber] plural of معبر

معادل [mo'aadel] 1 equal 2 ••• - conforming (to something), corresponding (to something)

معادله [mo'aadela] 1 equilibrium, balance 2 mathematical equation

معادن [ma'aaden] plural of معدن

معارف [ma'aarer] 1 plural of معرفت 2 enlightenment, education ♦ وزارت - Ministry of Education

معاش [ma'aash] 1 earnings, wages 2 means of existence, subsistence

معاشرت [mo'aasharat] 1 intercourse, contact, relation, connection 2 public life, public activities

معاصر [mo'aasher] 1 contemporary, modern 2 a contemporary

معاف [mo'aaf] 1 freed, relieved (of a tax, of a duty, of an obligation) 2 forgiven, absolved, pardoned
- کردن - 1 to free (from something) 2 to forgive, to pardon

معافی [mo'aafi] 1 freedom (from a tax, from a duty, from an obligation) 2 pardon, forgiveness, absolution

معافیت [mo'aaqebat] persecution, prosecution, punishment

معالجوی [mo'aalejawi] therapeutic, healing ♦ طب - healing medicine, curative medicine

معالجه [mo'aaleja] (medical) treatment
- کردن - to treat (medically)

معامله [mo'aamela] 1 transaction, operation (in banking, in commerce) ♦ تجرتی - commercial transaction 2 trade, commerce
- داشتن - to have business relations (with somebody با)
- کردن - to deal, to trade

معامله دار [mo'aameladaar] contractor

معانی [ma'aani] plural of معنی

معاوضه [mo'aaweza] 1 compensation, reimbursement ♦ نقدی - monetary compensation 2 substitution, replacement ♦ آواز - linguistics interchange of sounds

معاون [mo'aawen] 1 assistant, deputy 2 (also دریا-) tributary (of a river) ♦ فعل - grammar auxiliary verb

معاونت [mo'aawanat] assistance, help
- کردن - to assist, to render assistance, to help

معاهده [mo'aaheda] contract, treaty, pact, agreement

معایب [ma'aayeb] flaws, shortcomings, deficiencies, defects

معاینه [mo'aayena] 1 inspection, examination, check-up ♦ طبی - medical examination 2 medicine analysis
- کردن - 1 to examine, to inspect 2 to make an analysis, to analyze

معاینه خانه [mo'aayenaxaana] outpatient clinic, reception room, waiting room

معبد [ma'bad] (plural معابد [ma'aabed]) temple; place of worship; sanctuary

معبر [ma'bar] (plural معابر [ma'aaber] passage, passageway; crossing, ford; crossing (e.g., highway, railroad)

معتبر [mo'tabar] 1.1 correct, trustworthy, authentic 1.2 reliable, dependable 1.3 influential, authoritative 1.4 effective, operative (about an agreement) 2 masculine proper name Motabar

معتدل [mo'tadel] 1 moderate, temperate; average, middling 2 easy; soft

معتمد [mo'tamad] 1 enjoying trust, reliable 2 confidential agent

معجزه [mo'jeza] miracle, wonder, marvel

معدن [ma'dan] (plural معادن [ma'aadin]) 1 mine pit; layer, deposit 2 ore

معدنی [ma'dani] mineral adjective ♦ آب - mineral water

معدوم [ma'dum] destroyed; vanished
- شدن - to perish, to be destroyed

معده [me'da] anatomy stomach

معذرت [ma'zarat] apology; excuse; request for forgiveness
- خواستن - to appologize; to ask forgiveness

معذور [ma'zur] 1 excused, forgiven, pardoned 2 freed, exempt (from fulfilling something)

معرض [ma'raz]
- به(در) - فروش قرار دادن to put up for sale
- به(در) - نمایش گذاشتن to exhibit, to display, to demonstrate

معرفت [ma'refat] knowledge, erudition

معرفی [mo'arrefi]
- کردن - to acquaint, to introduce, to present; to recommend

معرکه [ma'reka] 1 field, scene of battle 2 battle; fight, combat; skirmish, melee

معروض [ma'ruz] 1 stated, set forth; presented 2 report, presentation
- داشتن - to state a request, to report, to communicate

معروف [ma'ruf] 1.1 well-known; famous, celebrated 1.2 grammar of the active voice (about a verb) 2 masculine proper name Maruf
- واو – long vowel "u"
- یای – long vowel "i"

معزول [ma'zul] 1 removed, suspended (from a post or position), displaced 2 deposed (about a monarch)

معشوق [ma'shuq] 1 beloved, sweetheart (female) 2 mistress

معصوم [ma'sum] 1 innocent, sinless 2 child, infant

معطر [mo'attar] fragrant, aromatic; scented

معطل [mo'attal] 1 delayed, postponed 2 unoccupied, free, vacant 3 expecting (something)
- شدن - to linger, to dally; to expect, to wait

معطلی [mo'attali] delay, dallying, waiting, expecting

معظم [mo'azzam] 1 great 2 respected, esteemed, highly revered, honored

معکوس [ma'kus] 1.1 reverse, opposite 1.2 overturned, turned inside out 1.3 reflected, repulsed 2 mathematical reciprocal

معلم [mo'allem] teacher; instructor (male)

معلمه [mo'allema] teacher, instructor (female)

معلمی [mo'allemi] 1 teaching 2 work of an instructor
- کردن - to be a teacher

معلوم [ma'lum] known, elucidate, cleared up, clear ♦ قرار - as is generally known
- شدن - 1 to be elucidated, to be cleared up 2 to turn out [to be], to be found, to prove [to be] 3 to appear

معلومات [ma'lumaat] knowledge; information ♦ گرفتن - to look up (in a dictionary); to obtain information

معلومدار [ma'lumdar] naturally, of course

معما [mo'ammaa] riddle, rebus

معمار [me'mar] builder, construction worker

معمولی [ma'muli] ordinary; plain ♦ پیراهن - everyday dress, everyday clothing

معنا [ma'naa] ☞ معنی

معنوی [ma'nawi] 1 moral, spiritual 2 semantic

معنی [ma'naa (and) ma'ni] (plural معانی [ma'aani]) sense, meaning

معه [ma'a] with, together with denominative preposition ♦ لشکر - with troops

معهذا [ma'hazaa] at the same time; nevertheless

معیار [me'yaar] 1 measure; norm 2 standard, model, pattern

معیاری [me'yaari] 1 model adjective 2 standard adjective, normative ♦ زبان - literary language; standard language

معیشت [ma'ishat] 1 means of existence, means of livelihood 2 life, existence

معین [moin] assistant, deputy ♦ وزارت - deputy minister, assistant minister

معیوب [ma'yub] 1.1 damaged, injured, spoiled 2 crippled, maimed ♦ شخص - a man with a physical defect or deformity, a cripple, an invalid 2 a cripple, an invalid

مغتنم [moghtanam]
- شمردن • 1 to seize an opportunity 2 to value

مغرب [maghreb] 1 setting of the sun, sunset 2 west (the direction) 3 the West 4 Maghrib (region in Africa)

مغرور [maghrur] haughty; conceited; arrogant

مغز [maghz] 1 brain 2 kernel, seed (of fruit) 3 interior, core, pith (of something)
- خوردن • (and) سر خوردن- to rack [one's] brain (over something), to agonize (about something)

مغزی [maghzi] 1 edging, finish, trim 2 piping

مغل [moghol] historical 1 a Mogul 2 Mogul adjective, of or pertaining to a Mogul or the Moguls

مغلوب [maghlub] conquered, vanquished
- کردن • to conquer, to vanquish

مغلیان [mogholiyaan] historical the Moguls

مغموم [maghmum] sad, melancholy, grieved

مغول [maghol] 1 a Mongol, a Mongolian 2 ☞ مغل

مفاد [mafaad] use, benefit advantage, interest

مفاصل [mafaasel] plural of مفصل

مفاهمه [mofaahema] mutual understanding; arrangement, understanding, agreement

مفت [moft] 1 free (of charge) adjective 2.1 gratis, free of charge, for nothing adverb 2.2 easily, without labor

مفت خور [moftkhor] parasite, sponger, idler

مفتش [mofattesh] inspector; investigator (of a case); auditor

مفتی [mofti] mufti, chief judge (who pronounces judgements on issues of Moslem law)

مفخرت [mafkharat] 1 an object of pride or of glory 2 glory, honor

مفرد [mofrad] 1 single, solitary, separate, individual 2 grammar singular, singular number

مفردات [mofradaat] 1 elements, components 2 articles, items, sections (of a document) ♦ پروگرام - provisions of a program

مفسر [mofasser] commentator, reviewer

مفصل [mafsal] (plural مفاصل [mafaasel]) 1 anatomy joint, articulation ♦ زانو - knee joint ◊ قطنی - sacrum 2 technical hinge, joint, articulation

مفصل [mofassal] 1 detailed 2 in detail

مفصل دار [mafsaldaar] 1 jointed, articulated, segmented 2 technical jointed, hinged, articulated

مفعول [maf'ul] grammar object of an action, object of a verb
- اسم ◊ direct object - مستقیم (and) ♦ بیواسطه - passive participle

مفکوره [mafkura] idea; thought ♦ عام - public opinion

مفلر [maflar] scarf, muffler

مفلس [mofles] 1 bankrupt, broke; indigent 2 a bankrupt, a poor man
- خوشحال • colloquial a carefree man, a man who is merry without reason

مفهوم [mafhum] 1 purport, content, substance 2 concept, idea, notion

مفید [mofid] useful; advantageous

مقابل [moqaabel] 1.1 opposite ♦ طرف - the opposite side 1.2 comparable; equivalent 2.1 (also - در) opposite denominative preposition 2 in return for, in exchange for ♦ پول - (در) for money, in exchange for money 3 in respect [to], with respect [to] ♦ در-او in respect to him

مقابله [maqaabala] 1 resistance; opposition; confrontation 2 comparison
- کردن • 1 to resist; to oppose to fight 2 to compare

مقاصد [maqaased] (plural مقاطعه [moqaate'a]) 1 cessation of relations; boycott 2 contract, agreement to a contract ♦ - بطور by contract, by the job ◊ کار - piecework

مقاله [maqaala] 1 article, report 2 speech; word; phrase, sentence

مقام [maqaam] (plural مقامات [maqamat]) 1 place, point 2 position, status, post, rank 3 organ, body, department ♦ دولتی - state organs

مقامات [maqaamaat] plural of مقام 3

مقاوم [moqaawem] steadfast (against something); durable, solid, strong ♦ حرارت - technical heat-resistant, fireproof

مقاومت [moqaawemat] 1 resistance, opposition ♦ دفاعی - medicine resistance, protective function 2 persistence, stableness

مقایسه [moqaayesa] comparison, collation
- کردن • to compare, to collate

مقبره [maqbara] grave, tomb, mausoleum

مقبول [maqbul] 1 handsome, beautiful; likable, attractive 2 acceptable, suitable

مقبولی [maqbuli] (and) مقبولیت [maqbuliyat] 1 likableness, attractiveness 2 acceptability, fitness, suitability

مقتدر [moqtader] powerful, mighty, influential

مقتضیات [moqtaziyaat] needs, requirements
- زمان • the requirements of time

مقتول [maqtul] murdered, killed

مقدار [meqdaar] 1 quantity, amount; measure 2 dose (e.g., of medicine)

مقدرات [moqaddaraat] predetermination, predestination

مقدس [moqaddas] holy, sacred ♦ وظیفه - sacred duty

مقدم [maqdam] arrival, coming ♦ - خیر Welcome!

مقدم [moqaddam] 1 going ahead, taking precedence 2 older, more ancient; previous, former
- به • before ♦ به ظهور اسلام - before the emergence of Islam
- بودن • to precede (به)

مقدمات [moqaddamaat] 1 plural of مقدمه [moqaddama] 2 preparatory measures, preparation

مقدمه [moqaddama] (plural مقدمات [moqaddamaat]) 1 introduce, preface; preamble ♦ بر علم زبان -introduction to the study of language 2 prerequisite

مقدمه [moqaddema] battle

مقدور [maqdur] possible, feasible, practicable, not beyond one's powers or abilities

مقر [maqar (r)] headquarters; residence ♦ شاهی - shah's residence

مقرر [moqarrar] 1 established 2 fixed, set, appointed
- کردن • 1 to establish, to determine, to define 2 to fix, to set, to appoint

مقررات [moqarraraat] provisions; resolutions, decisions

مقرری [moqarrari] 1 appointment 2 establishment, fixing, setting, determination, definition 3 salary, wages, pay

مقصد [maqsad] (plural مقاصد [maqaased]) 1 goal, purpose 2 point of a statement, implied meaning ♦ چیست؟ - What does he / do you have in mind?

مقصر [moqasser] 1 guilty 2 culprit, the guilty person

مقلوب [maqlub] 1 changed, overturned 2 distorted, falsified, counterfeited, forged 3 grammar inverted

272

مقناطیس [maqnaatis] magnet ♦ برقی - electromagnet
مقناطیسی [maqnaatisi] magnetic
مقوا [maqawwaa] 1 cardboard 2 folder 3 cardboard cover (of a book)
مقوله [maqula] 1 expression, saying, aphorism, adage, maxim 2 phrase 3 quotation
مقیاس [meqyaas] 1 scale, scope 2 dimension, size
مقیم [moqim] residing, living, abiding, being [at]
• بودن - to be located (somewhere), to reside, to live
مکاتب [makaateb] *plural of* مکتب
مکاتبه [makaateba] correspondence
مکاتیب [makaatib] *plural of* مکتوب
مکالمه [mokaalema] talk, conversation
• کردن - to talk, to converse, to conduct an interview
مکان [makaan] (*plural* اماکن [amaaken]) 1 place; abode, residence; dwelling 2 *colloquial* latrine, lavatory, toilet
مکتب [maktab] (*plural* مکاتب [makaateb]) 1 school; educational institution ♦ ابتدایی - primary school, elementary school ◊ عالی - higher educational institution (college) ◊ لیلیه - boarding school 2 maktab (primary ecclesiastical school) 3 school, trend
مکتب گریز [maktabgoreez] (*also* شاگرد) truant (from school)
مکتبی [maktabi] 1 school *adjective* 2 schoolboy
مکتشف [maktashef] 1 prospector 2 explorer 3 an inquisitive man
مکتوب [maktub] (*plural* مکاتیب [makaatib]) 1 a letter, note, message, epistle 2 written
مکث [maks] pause; delay, stop
مکثفه [maksafa] condenser, capacitor
مکرر [mokarrar] 1 repeated 2 ☞ مکرراً
مکرراً [mokárraran] repeatedly
مکروب [mekrob] microbe; bacterium
مکروه [makruh] offensive, vile, nasty, disgusting, repulsive
مکسچر [mekschar] mixture; medicine
مکسور [maksur] 1 broken 2 *linguistics* having the vowel point kasra (-)
مکشوف [makshuf] discovered, revealed, uncovered; prospected; located, known
مکعب [moka'ab] 1 cubic ♦ متر - cubic meter 2 *mathematical* cube
مکلف [mokallaf] obliged (to do or carry out something)
• کردن - 1 to oblige, to charge 2 to appoint, to put (to work), to hire
مکلفیت [mokallafiyat] duty, responsibility; obligation
مکمل [mokammal] 1 concluded, completed, finished 2 whole, full ♦ یک روز - the whole day, an entire day
مکیدن [makidan] 1 to suck, to suck out 2 to suck in, to drink in, to absorb
مگر [magar] 1 but, however *conjunction* 2 except [for], with the exception [of]
• اینکه ... - unless, perhaps ..., if only ...
مگس [magas] fly (insect)
• هرکاسه - *colloquial* pushy man, ubiquitous man
مگس پران [magasparaan] device to brush away flies
ملا [mollaa] 1 mullah 2 *obscure* teacher (at a rural school) 3 a literate man, a scholar
ملابنویس [mollaabenwis] *colloquial* an illiterate man, an uneducated man

ملاحظه [molaahaza] 1 examination, scrutiny, study 2 opinion, observation 3 rendering attention, rendering respect
ملاریا [malaariyaa] malaria
ملازم [molaazem] 1 servant (who is in somebody's retinue) 2 attendant 3 employee
ملازمت [molaazemat] 1 being in a retinue, attending 2 services, facilities 3 service
ملاق [malaaq] 1 doing a somersault, somersaults 2 *aviation* loop
• خوردن (زدن) - *colloquial* 1 to somersault 2 to fly upside down; to fall down (from somewhere) 3 to do a loop
• پس یک پیسه صد – زدن to be ready to hang oneself for a kopeck
ملاقات [molaaqaat] meeting, appointment, rendezvous
• کردن - to meet *intransitive*
ملاقی [malaaqi] casement window, small window (for ventilation)
ملاک [mallaak] landowner, landlord
ملاگک [mollaagak] lark (bird)
ملامت [malaamat] rebuke, reproach, blame, censure
• کردن - to rebuke, to reproach, to blame, to censure, to condemn
ملایک [malaayek] *plural of* ملک [malak]
ملایم [molaayem] 1 soft, delicate, tender 2 affectionate, gentle 3 temperate, moderate, mild ♦ آب - moderately warm water
ملایمت [molaayemat] 1 softness, tenderness 2 affectionateness, gentleness 3 moderateness, temperance (e.g., of a climate)
ملت [mellat] (*plural* ملل [melal]) nation, people
ملتفت [moltafet]
• شدن - 1 to note; to turn [one's] attention [to] 2 to comprehend, to realize
ملح [melh] (*plural* املاح [amlaah]) *chemistry* salt
ملحق [molhaq] 1 joined, connected (to something) 2 dependent 3 adjoining, adjacent, contiguous
• کردن - 1 to connect, to join, to add, to increase 2 to subordinate, to make dependent
ملحم [malham] ointment; balsam, balm
ملخ [malakh] locust
ملخک [malakhak] 1 grasshopper; cicada 2 (*also* ساعت -) watch hand, clock hand
ملعون [mal'un] damned; cursed
ملک [malak] (*plural* ملایک [malaayek]) angel
ملک [malek] (*plural* ملکان [malekaan]) 1 malek, elder (of village), head of a family 2 (*plural* ملوک [moluk]) czar, prince
ملک [melk (and) molk]¹ (*plural* املاک [amlak]) land (owned by somebody), property, real estate
ملک [molk]² *colloquial* 1 state, country 2 territory, district, province 3 estate, landed property
ملکدار [molkdaar] landowner; owner of a plot of land
ملکه [malaka] 1 quick-wittedness, comprehension 2 habit, practice; experience
ملکه [maleka] czarina, queen
ملکی [molki] 1 civilian; civil ♦ لباس - civilian clothes 2 administrative
ملکیت [melkiyat] property; possession

ملل [melal] *plural of* ملت
- مؤسسه – متفق United Nations Organization of the United Nations

ملم [malam] *colloquial* ☞ ملحم
- دل - darling child, beloved child

ململ [malmal] muslin, gauze, cheesecloth

ملنگ [malang] 1 malang, a dervish who goes begging 2 *masculine proper name* Malang

ملوک [moluk] *plural of* ملک [malek]

ملوک الطوایف [molukottawaayef] feudal lords

ملوک الطوایفی [molukottawaayefi] 1 feudal 2.1 feudalism 2.2 feudal division

ملوکانه [molukaana]
- *obscure* - ذات sire, your majesty, his majesty

ملی [melli] national; people's ♦ شورای - national council
- کردن - to nationalize

ملی [moli] 1 horseradish 2 radish

ملیارد [melyaard] billion, milliard

ملیت [melliyat] 1 nationality 2 national feelings

ملی تراش [molitaraash] (large) grater for radishes

ملیمتر [meliméter] millimeter

ملیون [melliyun] *political* 1 nationalists 2 fighters of the people's front; forces of national liberation

ملیون [melyun] million

ممالک [mamaalek] *plural of* مملکت

ممانعت [momaana'at] prohibition; preventing, hindering, creation of obstacles
- کردن - to forbid, to prohibit, to prevent, to hinder, to hamper, to impede, to interfere [with]

ممتاز [momtaaz] 1 choice, picked, excellent 2 selected, privileged

ممثل [momassel] 1 actor, (performing) artist 2 one who expresses (feelings, moods)

ممد [momed (d)] helping, assisting ♦ کتب – درسی training aids, school supplies

ممسک [momsek] 1 stingy, greedy 2 a miser, a skinflint

ممکن [momken] possible, probable, likely ♦ است - possibly, perhaps

مملکت [mamlakat] (*plural* ممالک [mamaalek]) country, state

مملو [mamlo] full, filled

مملوک [mamluk] 1 being in the possession [of], belonging [to] 2.1 serf, slave 2.2 *historical* mameluke

ممنوع [mamnu'] forbidden
- کردن - to forbid, to prohibit

ممیز [momayyez] 1 distinguishing, discriminating, differentiating, delimiting 2 point (in decimal fractions, represented by a comma)

ممیزه [momayyeza] distinction, difference, peculiarity

من [man]¹ 1 I 2 (in an ezafeh construction serves as an attribute) ♦ کتاب من my book 3 (in combination with the preposition, corresponds to the possessive pronoun) mine ♦ این خانه از من است This house is mine.

من [man]² man, maund (measure of weight that differs in different regions) ♦ سیر - کابل Kabul man, Kabul maund (equal to 8 sers or 56.5 kg)

منابع [manaabe'] *plural of* منبع
- طبیعی - natural resources

منار [monaar (and) menaar (and) monara] مناره 1 minaret 2 tower

منازعه [monaaze'a] argument, controversy; discord, strife; lawsuit

منازل [manaazel] *plural of* منزل

مناسب [monaaseb] 1 corresponding, suitable, appropriate, convenient, opportune 2 proper, becoming, decent

مناسبات [monaasebaat] *plural of* مناسبت - دوستانه
- friendly relations

مناسبت [monaasebat] (*plural* مناسبات [monaasebaat]) 1 tie, bond, relation 2 accordance, conformity, compliance

مناطق [manaateq] *plural of* منطقه

مناظره [monaazara] argument, controversy, dispute, debate

منافع [manaafe'] *plural of* منفعت

مناقشه [manaaqesha] 1 discord strife, conflict 2 fight, struggle
- کردن - to quarrel; to be in conflict [with]

مناقصه [monaaqesa] bids for delivery (of something), competing for a contract

منبت کاری [monabbatkaari] 1 relief modeling 2 inlaying; mosaic work

ممبر [membar] mimbar (pulpit in a mosque)

منبع [manba'] (*plural* منابع [manaabe']) spring; source; origin
- موثق - reliable source

منت [mennat] (*plural* منن [menan]) 1 favor; kindness 2 thankfulness, gratitude, thanks
- داشتن - to be thankful, to be indebted [to] (از)
- کشیدن - to please, to oblige, to try to win (somebody's) favor
- گذاشتن - to consider (somebody) indebted to oneself; to allude to a favor done, to allude to a good deed performed (بر)

منتخب [montakhab] 1 selected, chosen, elected 2 picked

منتخبات [montakhabaat] selected works (of some author)

منت دار [mennatdaar] grateful, thankful

منت داری [mennatdaari] gratitude, thankfulness, thanks

منتر [mantar] 1 magic; conjuration 2 *colloquial* fraud, deception, cheating, trickery

منتروالا [mantarwaalaa] snake charmer

منتشر [montasher] 1 issued, published, made public, promulgated 2 disseminated, distributed

منتظر [montazer] awaiting, expecting
- بودن - to wait, to expect

منت گذار [mennatgozar] demanding gratitude (from somebody), considering oneself (somebody's) benefactor

منتها [montahaa] (and منتهی) 1 end, limit, edge, brim 2 extreme, maximum, utmost 3 extremely, very

منج [monj] 1 fiber of palm leaves (from which rope is made) 2 kenaf, ambary

منجر [monjar (r)] ended, concluded, completed
- شدن - to be ended, to be concluded, to be completed (به)

منجم [monajjem] 1 astrologer 2 astronomer

منجمد [monjamed] frozen; congealed; hardened ♦ بحر – شمالی Arctic Ocean

منجیله [manjeela] (wicker) stand or support for a jug
- زدن - to coil up (about a snake)

منحرف [monharef] 1 having lost (one's way); having strayed 2 apostate, recreant, renegade
- شدن - to deviate, to digress

منحصر [monhaser] 1 pertaining exclusively (to somebody or to something) 2 monopolistic, being in the exclusive

possession [of]
- به بودن - to come (to something)

منحنی [monhani] 1 curved; bent; crooked 2 (also خط -) *mathematical* a curve

مندانو [mandaanu] a hand churn made of wood

مندرج [mondarej] included; inscribed; inserted ♦ فهرست مندرجات contents, table of contents (of a book)

مندوی [mandawi] food market, commercial row (in Kabul)

منزل [manzel] (*plural* منازل [manazel]) 1 stop, halt; station 2 stage, span, crossing, march, passage; interval, distance 3 *military* range; distance 4 floor, story (of a building)

منزلت [menzelat] 1 degree; rank, class; position, state, status 2 quality, value

منزلگاه [manzelgaah] stopping place; inn, carvansary

منزله [manzela] (at the end of compound words) –story / -step- / -stage ♦ سه منزله three-step, three-stage ◊ دو منزله two-story (about a building)

منسلک [monsalek] 1 strung (on thread) 2 connected, joined ♦ ممالک غیر - nonaligned nations, nonaligned countries

منسوب [mansub] 1 pertaining, referring, belonging (to something), numbered (among something) 2 a relation, a relative

منسوج [mansuj] (*plural* منسوجات [mansujat]) 1 spun; woven 2 cloth, fabric, material, textiles, textile ♦ پشمی - woolen fabrics

منسوجات [mansujaat] *plural of* منسوج 2

منشأ [mansha'] source; beginning; original cause; origin

منشور [manshur] 1 regulations, statutes; charter; manifesto 2 published, printed

منشی [monshi] 1 secretary 2 scribe; clerk

منصب [mansab] post, job; rank grade; title

منصبدار [mansabdaar] 1 officer 2 official, functionary

منصوب [mansub] appointed to a post, appointed to a job

منطق [manteq] 1 (also علم -) logic 2 logical thought, logical thinking 3 *literary* discourse; talk, conversation

منطقه [mentaqa] (*plural* مناطق [manaateq]) zone, region; district, province ♦ بارد - cold belt, frigid zone ◊ معتدله - temperate zone

منطقوی [mentaqawi] zonal; regional

منطقی [menteqi] logical

منظره [manzara] 1 view; landscape; panorama 2 sight; picture

منظم [monazzam] 1 adjusted, put right; put in good order 2 systematic, regular

منظور [manzur] adopted, affirmed, confirmed, sanctioned, approved

منظوری [manzuri] affirmation, confirmation; approval; sanction - کردن

منظومه [manzuma] 1 poem; rhyme 2 system; net, network ♦ شمسی - solar system

منع [man' (and) mána] ban; prohibition; preventing
- کردن - 1 to ban, to suppress, to prohibit 2 to hold back

منعقد [mon'aqed] 1 convoked, convened, held (about a conference, a meeting, etc.) 2 concluded (about a treaty, contract, agreement)

منفجر [monfajer]
- کردن - to blow up, to blast

منفجره [monfajera] explosive ♦ مواد - explosives

منفذ [manfaz] 1 point of penetration; opening, aperture, orifice; slit, slot, gap; manhole 2 (also هوا -) air hole, air vent 3 *anatomy* pore

منفعت [manfa'at] (*plural* منافع [manaafe']) 1 use 2 advantage, benefit, gain, profit 3 interest

منفک [monfak (k)] separated, detached; torn away, estranged, alienated

منفی [manfi] negative ♦ جواب - a negative answer ◊ فعل - *grammar* a verb in negative form

منقار [menqaar] beak, bill
- زدن - to peck

منقبض [monqabez] shrunk, contracted
- شدن - to shrink, to contract (in volume)

منقل [manqal] brazier, manqhal (with hot coals) ♦ برقی - electric heater

منقله [manqala] protractor

منقوش [manqush] decorated with painting; decorated with designs

منقوله [manqula] 1 mobile, movable 2 movable property, personal property

منکر نکیر [monker-nakeer] *religion* Monker and Naker (the names of two angels who supposedly interrogate the souls of the dead about their lives and faith)

منگ [mang] 1 *colloquial* stupefied, stunned, dazed
- شدن - to be stupefied, to be stunned, to be dazed

منگ [mang] 2 scale, scum

منگنیز [manganiz] manganese

منگول [mongol] 1 Mongolian *adjective* 2 a Mongol, Mongolian

منوط [manut] depending [on], stipulated [by]
- بودن - to depend

منهدم [monhadem] demolished, wrecked; destroyed

منیار [manyaar] frost, hoarfrost

مو [mu] ☞ موی

مواجب [mawaajeb] 1 *plural of* موجب 2 remuneration; fee

مواجه [mowaajeh]
- شدن - 1 to turn (one's face toward something) 2 to collide [with]; to meet [with], to encounter

مواجهه [mowaajeha] 1 face-to-face meeting 2 opposition (of planets)

مواد [mawaad (d)] *plural of* ماده [maadda]
- ارتزاقی - foodstuffs, provisions
- خام - raw material, raw materials
- سوخت - fuel oil, fuel

موارد [mawaared] *plural of* مورد

موازنه [mowaazana] 1 equilibrium; balancing, equilibration 2 balance ♦ تأدیات - balance of payment

مواشی [mawaashi] cattle; livestock

مواصلات [mowaasalaat] *plural of* مواصلت
- هوایی - airlines

مواصلاتی [mowaasalaati] 1 communication *adjective* ♦ خطوط - lines of communication 2 transport *adjective*

مواصلت [mowaasalat] (and) مواصله [mowaasala] (*plural* مواصلات [mowaasalaat]) 1 communication, communications 2 *literary* ☞ وصال

مواضع [mawaaze'] *plural of* موضع

275

م

موافق [mowaafeq] 1 agreeable, conforming [to], in agreement [with] 2 supporter, adherent, like-minded person, confederate
• ‑ بودن 1 to agree [with], to consent [to] 2 to conform [to], to correspond [to], to suit (با)
موافقت [mowaafaqat] 1 consent (to something), permission, authorization 2 agreement, arrangement, understanding
• ‑ کردن to agree (with somebody or something), to concur (with somebody or something), to give consent (to something)
موافقت نامه [mowaafaqatnaama] agreement, understanding, contract, treaty
موافقه [mowaafaqa] ☞ موافقت
مواقع [mawaaqe'] plural of موقع
موانع [mawaane'] plural of مانع
• ‑ طبیعی natural obstacles
موباف [mubaaf] ☞ موی باف
موبد [mobad] Mobed (Zoroastrian priest)
موبل [mobaal] furniture
موبل سازی [mobalsaazi] manufacture of furniture
موبلایل [moblaayl] motor oil
موت [mawt] literary death, destruction
موتر [motar] 1 automobile, motor vehicle ♦ تیزرفتار ‑ passenger car ◊ سرویس ‑ bus, motorbus ◊ لاری ‑ truck, lorry 2 ☞ موتور
موتربوت [motarbot] motorboat
موترخانه [motarkhaana] garage; motor pool
موتران [motarraan] chauffeur, driver (of a motor vehicle)
موترانی [motarraani] driving an automobile ♦ مکتب ‑ driving school, school for drivers
موتررو [motarraw] (also سرک ‑) motor road, highway
موترسایکل [motarsaaykal] motorcycle
موتر سایکل سوار [motarsaaykalsawaar] (and) موتر سایکلست [motarsaaykalest] motorcyclist
موتروان [motarwaan] chauffeur, driver (of a motor vehicle)
موتروان باشی [motarwaanbaashi] manager of a garage
موتور [motor] motor, engine ♦ برقی ‑ electric motor, electric engine
موتوریزه [motoriza] motorized
مؤثر [moasser] 1 effective 2 impressive
موثق [mowassaq] trustworthy
موج [mawj] (plural امواج [amwaaj]) wave ♦ دریا ‑ sea wave ◊ صوتی ‑ sound wave
• ‑ زدن (خوردن) to be rough, to be choppy, to be agitated (about a water surface), to move in waves, to lap
موجب [mawjeb] (plural مواجب [mawaajeb]) cause, reason; motive; precondition, prerequisite
• به ‑ according [to], in accordance with ... denominative preposition
• ‑ شدن to cause (something); to serve as the reason, as the occasion (of something)
موجدار [mawjdaar] 1 wavy, undulating 2 choppy, rough (about a water surface) 3 iridescent (about color)
موجود [mawjud] (plural موجودات [mawjudat]) 1.1 present, being present 1.2 on hand, ready 1.3 present [time] ♦ وقت ‑ the present 2.1 living being, creature 2.2 masculine proper name Mawjud

موجودات [mawjudat] 1 plural of موجود 2 everything real, everything existing
موجودی [mawjudi] 1 composition, contents; aggregate quantity, aggregate amount, aggregate number 2 presence, availability; available supply (of something)
موجودیت [mawjudiyat] 1 existence, availability, being 2 reality, objectivity 3 ☞ موجودی
موچی [mochi] 1 shoemaker cobbler 2 currier, tanner
مود [mod] mode, fashion, style, vogue
• از – افتادن to go out of style, to grow out of date, to grow old-fashioned
مؤدب [moaddab] well-bred, civil, courteous
مودت [mawaddat] literary friendliness; cordiality, friendly feelings
مودرن [modern] contemporary, modern
مودل [model] model, mock-up, dummy
مؤذن [moazzen] muezzin
مور [mur] 1 caterpillar (pest) 2 ☞ مورچه
• درخانه ‑ شبنمی طوفان است proverb In the house of an ant, even dew is a flood.
مورچانه [murchaana] colloquial rust (on metal)
مورچل [murchaal] ☞ مرچل [morchal]
مورچه [murcha] 1 ant, termite 2 ☞ مورچانه
مورچه خانه [murchakhaana] anthill
مورچه سواره [murchasawaara] (type of large ant with long legs)
مورخ [mowarrakh] dated, marked (with some number)
مورخ [mowarrekh] 1 historian 2 chronicler, annalist
مورد [mawred] (plural موارد [mawaared]) 1.1 case, circumstance 1.2 object ♦ احترام – respected ◊ نیاز ‑ needed, necessary
• در ‑ concerning, relative to, in relation to denominative preposition ♦ در این مسئله ‑ concerning this question
• چیزی قرار دادن ‑ to subject to something, to make the object of something
مورس [mors]
• ‑ الفبای Morse alphabet
مورفولوژی [morfoloji] (and) مورفولوژی [morfolozhi] morphology
مورفیم [morfeem] linguistics morpheme
• مورفیمهای آزاد Free Morpheme
• مورفیمهای بسته Bound Morpheme
مورفیم شناسی [morfeemshenaasi] morphology
مورم [morom] botany myrtle (a plant whose leaves are ignited by the evil eye)
موروث [mawrus] (and) موروثی [mawrusi] inherited, hereditary
مورملخ [muromalakh]
• ‑ است colloquial like in an anthill, real disorder
موره [mora] colloquial ☞ مهره
موریانه [muryaana] colloquial ☞ مورچانه
موریانه خور [muryaanakhor] colloquial eaten away by rust
موزون [mawzun] 1 rhythmic, rhythmical, measured 2 proportional, proportionate
موزه [maaza] boot; boots
موزیک [muzik] 1 ☞ موسیقی 2 orchestra
موزیم [muziam] museum
مؤسس [moasses] founder; initiator

276

مؤسسه [moassesa] institution, establishment; enterprise; organization ♦ دولتی - state institution
موسم [mawsem] season, time of the year
موسمی [mawsemi] seasonal ♦ باد - monsoon ◊ بارانهای - seasonal rains
موسوم [mawsum] called, named (به)
موسیچه [musicha] small turtledove
• گشتن - colloquial to become emaciated, to waste away
موسیقی [musiqi] music ♦ آلات - musical instruments ◊ دسته - orchestra
موسیقی نواز [musiqinawaaz] musician
موش [mush] mouse ♦ دشتی - field mouse
• شدن وبه غار درآمدن - colloquial to disappear as if swallowed by the earth
موش خرما [mush (e) xormaa] weasel
موشخورک [mushkhorak] kite (bird)
موشک [mushak] colloquial wick lamp
موشکاف [mushekaaf] ☞ موی شکاف
موشکش [mushkosh]
• تفنگ - small-caliber rifle
موصوف [mausuf] 1.1 above-mentioned 1.2 described, mentioned, noted 2 grammar (also - اسم) substantive
• کردن - 1 to describe, to characterize 2 to eulogize, to extol
موضع [mawze'] (plural مواضع [mawaaze']) 1 place, position, location 2 military position ♦ آتش - firing position
موظف [mowazzaf] 1.1 obliged, indebted 1.2 appointed; on duty ♦ پولیس - policeman on duty 2 an official, a functionary
• کردن - to appoint; to oblige
موعد [maw'ed] deadline, appointed time
موعود [maw'ud] 1 promised 2 appointed, agreed, fixed
موفق [mowaffaq] successful
• شدن - to achieve success, to have success ♦ شدم I succeeded.
موفقیت [mowaffaqiyat] success, good luck, achievement, attainment ♦ با - successfully
• به – رسیدن to achieve success
موقت [mowaqqat] temporary ♦ بطور - temporarily
موقتی [mowaqqati] ☞ موقت
موقر [mowaqqar] 1 respected, honorable 2 reliable; sedate
موقع [mauqe'] (plural مواقع [mawaaqe']) 1 time 2 place, location, position 3 chance, opportunity, convenient moment
• یافتن - to find the opportunity, to seize the opportunity
موقع شناس [mauqe' shenaas] 1 calculating, resourceful, knowing how to adapt oneself 2 opportunist
موقع شناسی [mawqeshenaasi] the ability to adapt oneself, the ability to pick the appropriate moment
موقعیت [mauqe'iyat] 1 position 2 location
موقف [mauqef] 1 position, point of view 2 position, location, place 3 stop, station; parking place
مولا [mawlaa] 1 god, the lord ♦ یا - O, creator! / O, God! 2 master, boss, owner
مولانا [mawlaanaa] mawlana, our master (form of address to Moslem scholars and theologians)
مولد [mowalled] 1 performing, making, producing, engendering, giving rise [to] ♦ ماشین - برق generator 2 producer, manufacturer

موّلده [mowalleda] ☞ مولد 1
• دستگاه های - production enterprises
مؤلف [mo'allef] author; writer
مؤلفه [mo'allafa] 1 composed, compiled 2 composition, work
مولوی [mawlawi] 1 mawlawi, a learned man; teacher 2 mawlawi, monlavi (honorary nickname of Jalal-ud-Din Rumi-Balkhi)
مولی [muli] ☞ ملی [moli]
موم [mom] wax ♦ شاتی(شهدی) - natural wax
• شدن - colloquial 1 to soften intransitive, to grow soft, to melt intransitive 2 to relent, to soften, to yield to persuasion
• کسی را – ساختن colloquial to mollify, to persuade somebody
موم جامه [momjaama] 1 oilcloth 2 wax paper
موم روغن [momrawghan] ointment made of wax and oil (for application on boils or abscesses)
مؤمن [mo'men] 1 true believer; Moslem 2 feminine and masculine proper name Momen
مومند [momand] Momands (a tribe)
مومیا [momiya] 1 mummy 2 mumia (mountain balsam; resin-like substance)
مومیایی [momiyaayi] embalmed
مؤنث [moannas] 1 of the feminine gender 2 (also -جنس) the feminine gender
موهوم [mawhum] superstition, prejudice
موی [muy] 1 hair; hairs 2 bristle, hair (of an animal)
• به - بند ماندن proverb to stumble over a hair (i.e., to suffer failure because of some trifle)
• - از خمیر جدا کردن proverb to pick small hairs out of the dough (to be very precise, to carry out some matter scrupulously)
• - و روی کندن colloquial to tear one's hair and beard (from grief)
موی باف [muybaaf] ribbon or cord for braiding the hair (with tassel on the end)
موی بر [muybar] compound for eliminating hair from the body
موی چینک [muychinak] tweezers for plucking out hairs
مویز [mawiz] large black currants; large seedless raisins
موی شکاف [muyshekaaf] scrupulous, meticulous
مویک [muyak] 1 tassel 2 crack (in glass or porcelain)
• شدن - to crack (about glass, about porcelain)
مه [ma]¹ colloquial ☞ من
مه [ma]² colloquial
• مه Here! / Take [it]!
مه [mah] ☞ ماه
مهاجر [mohaajer] emigrant, refugee
مهاجرت [mohaajerat] emigration
• کردن - to emigrate
مهاجم [mohaajem] 1 assaulting, attacking 2 aggressor
مهارت [mahaarat] mastery, skill, proficiency, craftsmanship
مهاراجه [mahaaraja] maharaja
مهتاب [mahtaab] 1 moon 2 moonlight
مهتر [mehtar] 1 head, chief 2 groom, stable man
مهتمم [mohtamem] 1 manager, administrator 2 trustee, guardian

م

مهر [mahr] wedding gift (money and part of his property granted by the groom to the bride at the wedding)
مهر [mehr] ¹ 1 love 2 kindness
مهر [mehr] ² *literary* sun, luminary, heavenly body
مهر [mohr] seal, stamp ♦ انگشت - fingerprint
• کردن - to apply a seal, to apply a stamp
مهربان [mehrbaan] 1 kind, good, loving ♦ - مادر loving mother 2 amiable, polite, civil, courteous
مهربانی [mehrbaani] 1 kindness, goodness; favor, liking 2 courtesy, civility
• کردن - 1 to show friendliness, to show favor, to show liking 2 to show mercy, to show courtesy, to show kindness
• کنید - 1 would you be so kind (as to … - when making a request 2 Please!
مهره [mohra] 1 beads, a bead 2 cockleshell 3 (also کمر -) vertebra
مهره دوزی [mohradozi] embroidery with beads
مهلت [mohlat] 1 postponement 2 delay 3 respite; leisure
مهلک [mohlek] 1 pernicious, destructive; dangerous 2 shattering, crushing
مهم [mohem (m)] important, significant, serious
مهمان [mehmaan] guest
مهمان خانه [mehmaankhaana] room for guests, reception room, living room
مهماندار [mehmaandaar] 1 host (receiving guests) 2 person appointed to meet and escort official guests of a government
مهمانداری [mehmaandaari] 1 entertainment of guests, entertaining guests, reception of guests, receiving guests 2 ☞ مهمان نوازی
مهمان نوازی [mehmaannawaazi] hospitality
مهمانی [mehmaani] 1 reception; banquet 2 being a guest
• رفتن - to pay a visit
مهمل [mohmal] empty, senseless, foolish, absurd
مهمند [mohmand] Momands (a tribe)
مهمیز [mahmeez] spur; spurs
مهندس [mohandes] 1 land surveyor 2 geometer, geometrician
مهیا [mohayyaa] ready, prepared
• کردن - to ready, to prepare; to found, to establish, to create
مهین [mahin] fine, delicate; tender
می [may] ¹ wine
می [may] ² may
میاشت [miyaasht]
• سره - Society of the Red Crescent (i.e., Red Cross in Afghanistan)
میان [miyaan] 1.1 middle; interior, inner part (of something) 1.2 *rarely* waist 2.1 (also - در) inside, within, in, between *denominative preposition* 2 among ♦ مردم-(در) among the people
• دو سنگ آرد شدن - *proverb* to be ground between two stones (i.e., to get into a hopeless situation)
• از - out of, from within
• به - آمدن to appear, to occur, to spring up, to arise
• به – آوردن to create, to accomplish; to advance (a question), to put forward, to raise (a question)
میانجی [miyaanji] mediator, negotiator; arbiter, arbitrator
میانجی گری [miyaanjigari] arbitration

میان وند [miyaanwand] *grammar* infix
میانه [miyaana] average, middling, moderate
میانه حال [miyaanahaal] of average quality, of middling quality, mediocre; moderate
میانه قد [miyaanaqad] of average height
میتر [mitar] 1 counter, meter ♦ برق - electric meter 2 speedometer (of an automobile)
میتود [meetod] method
میجر [meejar] *obscure* major
میجرجنرال [meejarjanraal] *obscure* major general
میخ [meekh *technical* 1 nail ♦ پرچین - rivet 2 peg, stake, picket ♦ چوبی - wooden pegs
میخانیک [meekhaanik] 1 mechanic 2 mechanics
میخانیکی [meekhaaniki] mechanical ♦ انسان - robot
میخچه [meekhcha] ornament (worn in the nose)
میخزین [meekhzin] arsenal; weapons depot, weapons storehouse
میخک [meekhak] 1 (also - گل) clove 2 ☞ میخچه
میخکش [meekhkash] nail puller claw
میخکوب [meekhkob] 1 nailed up, fastened with nails, studded with nails 2 hammer, beetle (wooden hammer)
میخی [meekhi]
• خط - cuneiform writing
میدان [maydaan] (*plural* میادین [mayaadin]) 1 court (e.g., basketball court); area, square; field ♦ محاربه - field of combat, battlefield ◊ هوایی - airfield 2 field of activity; walk of life, pursuits
• دادن - to give a chance, to afford an opportunity
• کشیدن - to get ready and to rear back (for momentum before a jump)
• رابردن - to win a pot, to win a hand (in a card game)
• به – ماندن to be left without protector or without a patron; to find oneself in need
• مرد – a champion, a hero
میده [mayda] small, little; crushed, ground, pulverized ♦ پول- small change
• کردن - 1 to crush, to pulverize, to pound, to crumble, to grind 2 to change (money) 3 to thresh
میده باران [maydabaaraan] drizzle, light rain
میده بیز [maydabeez] (also - غربال) fine sieve
میده سال [maydasaal] *colloquial* young
میده فروش [maydaforosh] retailer; haberdasher; grocer
میده گی [maydagi] 1 trifle 2 crumbs ♦ نان - bread crumbs
میر [mir] ¹ *present tense stem* مردن
میر [mir] ² 1 mir (form of address to a sayyid) 2 leader, head, chief (of a tribe)
میراب [mirab] 1 mirab (person in charge of distributing water during irrigation) 2 *masculine proper name* Mirab
میراث [miraas] 1 inheritance ♦ حق - succession, right of inheritance 2 legacy, heritage
میراثی [miraasi] hereditary; inherited
میراو [miraw] *colloquial* ☞ میراب
میربان [meerbaan] ☞ مهربان
میرزا [mirzaa] 1 mirza, prince 2 clerk, secretary
میرمن [mirman] 1 Mrs. (form of address) 2 woman, lady
میز [meez] table ♦ کار - work table; work bench
میزان [mizaan] 1 measure; measuring, measurement; quantity, amount 2 *astronomy* Libra (constellation) 3 Mizan (seventh

month of the Afghan solar year; corresponds to September-October)

میزان الحرارت [mizaanolharaarat] (and) میزان الحراره [mizaanolharaara] thermometer

میزبان [meezbaan] host (who receives guests); hospitable host

میسر [moyassar] accessible; possible, practicable, feasible
- شدن - to be possible, to be feasible; to be provided for, to provide oneself with
- کردن - to make possible, to make feasible; to provide for

میش [meesh] sheep

میشه [meesha] sheepskin

میشی [meeshi]
- چشمان - large brown eyes, large hazel eyes

میعاد [mi'aad] date, period; date of execution, deadline ♦ حبس - date of conclusion, deadline

میکروب [mikrob] microbe; bacterium

میکروسکوپ [mikroskop] microscope

میکروفون [mikrofon] microphone

میل [mayl] 1 wish, desire, aspiration 2 inclination, bent [for]
- داشتن - 1 to desire, to wish [for], to want 2 to have an inclination [for]

میل [mil] ¹ 1.1 rod, bar, pin; shaft ♦ یونیورسال - technical cardan shaft, propeller shaft 1.2 probe, needle 1.3 (also تفنگ -) barrel of a gun 2 (numerative in counting guns or weapons) ♦ دو – تفنگ two guns, two rifles
- کردن - colloquial to rear (about horse)

میل [mil] ² mile (1.6 km) ♦ دریایی - nautical mile

میلاد [milaad] 1 birth 2 religion Christmas
- قبل از - B.C.
- بعد از - A.D.

میلادی [milaadi] of the Christian era, A.D. (about the system of chronology)

میلان [maylan] 1 inclination bent [for]; tendency 2 desire, wish 3 list, bank

میلک [milak] technical rod, pin prong; spindle ♦ پستون - wrist pin, gudgeon pin

میله [mela] holiday; folk festival, fete; picnic, outing in the countryside, stroll in the country

میله [mila] ☞ میل

میم [mim] name of the letter

مین [min] mine

مینا [maynaa] myna, Indian starling

مینار [minaar] 1 minaret 2 tower

مین گذاری [mingozari] mine-laying

مینی ژوپ [minizhup] miniskirt

میوه [meewa] fruit ♦ باغ - fruit orchard ◊ خشک - dried fruits ◊ ودانه - fruit juice; fruit drink ◊ درخت - fruit tree ◊ آب - Eastern delights (raisins, fruits, roasted nuts)
- دادن - to give fruit, to bear fruit

میوه باب [meewabaab] fruits and berries, fruits

میوه دار [meewadaar] 1 fruitful, fruit-bearing 2 fruit (about a tree) adjective

میوه دانی [meewadaani] dish (or) vase for fruit

میوه فروش [meewaforosh] fruit vendor

میهن [mihan] homeland, native land

مین [mayin] ☞ مهین
- برنج - (variety of rice with oblong grains, for pilaf)

ن
29th letter of the Dari alphabet

ن [na] 1 no, not negative verbal prefix ♦ گپ نزن Don't talk! 2 ☞ نا

نا [naa] (noun and adjectival prefix indicating the lack of some characteristic or quality) ♦ نا امن unsafe

ناآباد [naaaabaad] unassimilated, unprocessed, crude, raw, untreated, unfinished ♦ زمین - uncultivated land, virgin land

ناآرام [naaaaraam] 1 uneasy, troubled ♦ دریای - [the] restless sea ◊ طفل - restless child 2 ☞ ناامن
- بودن - to be upset, to be disturbed, to be worried ♦ مادرش از خطر او بود [His] mother was worried about him.

ناآرامی [naaaaraami] 1 uneasy state, restless state, anxiety, uneasiness (of a child); agitation (of the sea) ♦ قلبی - emotional anxiety 2 riot, disturbance, disorders

نااصل [naaásel] 1 not genuine 2 ignoble, base 3 not thoroughbred, not pedigreed, not of pure blood (about an animal)

ناامن [naaámn] unsafe, uneasy, restless ♦ راه - unsafe road ◊ شهر - a restless city, city in which there are disorders

ناامنی [naaamni] 1 alarming situation, alarming condition, alarming state 2 disorders

ناامید [naaomeed] 1 having lost hope, having despaired 2 disappointed, disillusioned
- ساختن - 1 to plunge [somebody] into despair, to discourage, to dishearten 2 to disappoint (از)

ناامیدی [naaomeedi] 1 hopelessness, despair 2 disappointment

ناانسان [naaensaan] 1 ill-bred unmannerly, rude, coarse 2 cruel, inhuman, brutal

نااهل [naaahl] with a poor character, unsociable, quarrelsome

ناباب [naabaab] 1 unpleasant, disagreeable 2 out of use, unfashionable

ناباشمی [naabaashami]
- سر گرفتن - colloquial to show intractability, to be obstinate, to persist [in]; to brawl, to make a row

نابجا(ی) [naabajaa (y)] 1 out of place, inappropriate 2 inappropriately, inopportunely

نابسامان [naabasaamaan] unsettled ♦ زندگی - [an] unsettled life

نابسامانی [naabasaamaani] 1 disorder, unsettled state, state of disorder; neediness, precariousness (e.g., of life) 2 disorder (e.g., about affairs), discord, dissension; confusion

نابغه [naabegha] (plural نوابغ [nawaabeq]) genius, a genius, man of genius

نابلد [naabalad] 1 unfamiliar (with something); not having made oneself familiar (e.g., with a matter) 2 strange, foreign, alien, unfamiliar ♦ محیط - unfamiliar surroundings

نابود [naabud]
- شدن - 1 to disappear, to vanish, to perish, to be killed 2 to be destroyed, to be annihilated
- کردن - to ruin, to destroy, to do away [with], to annihilate

نابودی [naabudi] 1 disappearance, destruction, ruin, downfall 2 nonexistence, death

نابینا [naabinaa] blind, sightless ♦ آدم - blind man

نابینایی [naabinaayi] literary blindness

ناپاک [naapaak] 1 unclean, dirty ♦ دستهای - dirty hands 2 defiled, profaned, unclean, foul, vile 3 unscrupulous,

279

amoral, immoral ♦ آدم - dishonorable man, ungentlemanly man

ناپایدار [naapaaydaar] 1 unstable, unsteady, not strong, not durable, fragile 2 short-lived 3 inconstant, unreliable, untrustworthy ♦ یار - inconstant friend ◊ روزگار - fickle fate

ناپدید [naapadid]
- شد - to disappear from view, to vanish ♦ آفتاب پشت کوه – شد The sun disappeared behind the mountain.

ناپسند [naapesand] (and) ناپسندیده [napesandida] not deserving approval; unseemly, unbecoming

ناپیدا [naapaydaa] invisible; hidden, concealed, secret; vanished ♦ دنیاهای - invisible worlds

ناتراش و ناخراش [naataraashonaakharaash] colloquial 1 clumsy, awkward; thickset 2 uncouth, unpolished, ill-bred, unmannerly

ناترس [naatars] daring, bold, audacious; desperate; clashing

ناتوان [naatawaan] 1 weak, feeble, powerless, impotent ♦ پیرو است He is old and feeble. 2 colloquial poor, indigent

ناتوانی [naatawaani] 1 impotence, weakness, feebleness 2 colloquial poverty, need

ناجنس [naajens] 1.1 of low quality, of poor quality ♦ مال - low-quality goods 2 non-thoroughbred, not pedigreed 3 of low birth 2 a degenerate, a black sheep (figuratively)

ناجو [naaju] (also - درخت) cedar of Lebanon

ناجوان [naaj(a)waan] colloquial 1 fainthearted; cowardly 2 scoundrel, villain, rascal

ناجور [naajor] sick, ailing, unhealthy
- به نان خوردن جور است به کار کردن proverb Always ready to eat and drink, but soon unhealthy when work begins.

ناجوری [naajori] 1 illness, ailment, ill health, indisposition 2 colloquial sickly, puny

ناچار [naachaar] 1.1 forced, dictated by necessity 1.2 being in a desperate situation 2.1 (also - به) by compulsion, by necessity, necessarily 2 inevitably, of necessity
- شدن(بودن) - to be forced, to be compelled (to do something)
- ساختن(کردن) - to put in a desperate situation, to compel (به) ♦ آنها را به تسلیمی ساختند They were forced to surrender.

ناچاری [naachaari] 1 compulsion, desperation, hopelessness, need 2 (also - از) against one's will; because of need ♦ اواز ناچاری اسپ خود را فروخت He sold his horse because of need.

ناچیز [naachiz] insignificant; paltry ♦ پول - paltry sum of money ◊ خدمت - small favor

ناحق [naahaqq] 1.1 unjust; unfair 1.2 unjustified, unwarranted, undeserved 2 (also – به) بناحق ☞
- خون - innocently spilled blood

ناحیه [naahiya] (plural نواحی [nawaahi]) 1 region, area (of a city); district 2 territory, land, region ♦ سر سبز و شاداب - green, blooming locale
- گرمسیر - warm region, region with mild weather
- از ··· in respect [to], from the point of view [of] denominative preposition

ناخدا [naakhodaa] 1 atheist, not God-fearing 2 monster, villain, scoundrel

ناخراش و ناتراش [naakharaashonaataraash] ☞ ناتراش و ناخراش

ناخلف [naakhalaf]
- فرزند - a son who is not worthy of his parents

ناخن [naakhon] nail (e.g., on finger)
- از گوشت جدایی ندارد - proverb The nail adheres firmly to the flesh.
- کردن - to play, to strum (a stringed musical instrument)
- گرفتن - colloquial 1 to cut [one's] nails, to trim [one's] nails 2 ☞ ناخنک زدن (in entryناخنک)
- ناخنش بند شد (and) چسپید
- ناخنش He caught on. / He settled. (somewhere)

ناخنک [naakhonak] 1 small nail (e.g., on a finger), small claw 2 music pick 3 technical tenon, lug; bushing
- زدن - 1 (ب) to touch, to touch with the hands 2 to scratch, to scratch with [one's] nails 3 to make slits on rolled flatcakes before baking them

ناخن گیر [naakhongir] clippers (for fingernails)

ناخوان [naakhaan] not able to read, illiterate

ناخواه [naax(w)aah]
- خواه و - against [one's] will; willy-nilly

ناخوش [naakhosh] rarely ill, unhealthy, sickly

ناخوشی [naakhoshi] rarely illness, ailment

ناخون [naakhun] ☞ ناخن

نادار [naadaar] poor, indigent

ناداری [naadaari] poverty, lack of means

نادان [naadaan] 1 ignorant, unwise 2 ignoramus

نادانی [naadaani] 1 ignorance, lack of knowledge 2 foolishness, stupidity ♦ به - (and) - ازروی through ignorance, through stupidity

نادر [naader] 1.1 rare, rarely encountered 1.2 unique, matchless, peerless, incomparable 2 masculine proper name Nader

نادره [naadera] (plural نوادر [nawaader]) 1 rare phenomenon, uncommon thing; a wonder 2 ☞ نادر 3 feminine proper name Nadera

نادیده [naadida] 1 not having seen (something), inexperienced ♦ آدم - inexperienced man, a man who hasn't seen anything 2 not seeing, not looking, unmindful heedless 3 colloquial having plunged into power, having fallen greedily upon riches, nouveau riche
- را خدا زور ندهد - proverb God doesn't give a butting cow horns.

نار [naar]¹ ☞ انار

نار [naar]² stem, stalk; sprout, shoot ♦ گندم - stalk of wheat

نار [naar]³ colloquial ☞ نهر

ناراحت [naaraahat] 1 restless, uneasy; agitated, perturbed 2 experiencing discomfort, experiencing awkwardness
- بودن - 1 to worry, to be worried, to be anxious, to be uneasy, to be agitated, to be upset 2 to experience discomfort, to experience awkwardness; to be not quite oneself ♦ اوسخت – بود He was not quite himself.
- کردن - 1 to worry, to disturb, to agitate, to excite, to upset transitive 2 to create discomfort; to hinder, to hamper; to intereferee (ار)

ناراحتی [naaraahati] 1 anxiety, uneasiness, agitation 2 awkwardness; confusion; embarrassment

ناراستی [naaraasti] fraud, deception, sham, pretense, falsity ♦ - به by deception, treacherously, perfidiously

ناراض [naaraaz] dissatisfied, dissenting
- بودن(شدن) - 1 to be dissatisfied, to be angry [with] (از) 2 to disagree, not to approve
- کردن - to anger, to make angry, to irritate, to annoy

نارام [naaraam] colloquial ☞ ناآرام

نارس [naaras] 1 immature, unripe, green ♦ سیب - green apple 2 not ready, unready, new (about wine)

نارسا [naarasaa] literary 1 incomplete, insufficient, inadequate 2 immature, imperfect ♦ دلایل - unconvincing reasons, unconvincing arguments ◊ عقل - immature mind, immature intellect

نارسایی [naarasaayi] 1 inadequacy; imperfection; immaturity ♦ فکر - immaturity of thought 2 incomplete work; blemish, flaw ♦ لغزشها و نارساییها sins and omissions

نارضا [naarezaa (and) naarazaa] ☞ ناراض

نارضایت [naarezaayat] 1 dissatisfaction, dissent 2 anger, ire, vexation, annoyance, irritation, discontent

نارگل [naargol] 1 blossom of pomegranate 2 feminine proper name Nargol

نارنج [naarenj] bitter orange, wild orange, wild orange tree; narenj

نارنجی [naarenji] orange, orange-colored adjective

ناروا [naarawaa] impermissible, inadmissible, intolerable; unseemly ♦ کار - an unseemly matter
• گفتن - to speak unseemly words, to express oneself in an unseemly manner
• آدم – colloquial a wicked person, a ruthless person; an offender

ناری [naari] (and) ناریه [naariya]
• اسلحه - a firearm

ناریال [naariyaal] 1 (also- درخت) coconut palm 2 coconut

ناز [naaz] 1 (also - و کرشمه and - و عشوه) coquetry, mincing ways 2 whims, caprices (of a sweetheart, of a child, etc.) 3 sweet bliss, endearment ♦ در - و نعمت in bliss and clover
• دادن - 1 to indulge, to coddle, to spoil, to pamper 2 to caress, to pet, to try to persuade (e.g., crying child)
• کردن - to flirt, to mince; to be capricious
• ناز بردار داری کن که - proverb Be capricious while there is somebody who will put up with your caprices! 2 ☞ - دادن
• کسی را بر ناز داشتن - to endure somebody's caprices, to put up with somebody's caprices; to humor somebody, to indulge somebody
• نیاز ☞ نازونیاز

نازا [naazaa] 1 (a women who is) incapable of child-bearing, an infertile woman, a sterile woman, a barren woman 2 barren, dry (about a female animal)

نازبردار [naazbardaar] patiently putting up with (somebody's) caprices or whims; treating tenderly; pleasing (somebody)

نازبرداری [naazbaardaari] indulgence toward (somebody's) caprices or whims, indulgence, connivance, complaisance (toward somebody)

نازبو(ی) [naazbo (y)] botany basil

نازپرور [naazparwar] (and) نازپرورد [naazparward] literary 1 delicate, effeminate; spoiled 2 a mollycoddle, an effeminate man; a pet, a favorite

نازدانه [naazdaana] favorite, only, sole, beloved, darling

نازک [naazok] 1.1 fine, thin, elegant; delicate; fragile ♦ اندام - slender waist ◊ پوست - delicate skin ◊ تکه - delicate fabric, fine fabric, light fabric 2 ticklish, delicate ♦ مسئله a delicate question 2 colloquial darling, sweetheart, beloved (female)
♦ بیا – من - Come, my darling! (from a song)
• دل – داشتن - to be sensitive, to be touchy, to cry for any reason
• احمد روی – دارد colloquial Ahmad is very bashful, he is easily embarrassed.

نازکچه [naazokcha] nazokcha (a variety of karakul)

نازک خیال [naazokkhiyaal] possessing a sharp wit; wise, sage; shrewd, astute

نازک دانه [naazokadaana] colloquial ☞ نازدانه

نازکی [naazoki] 1 fineness, subtlety; fragility, frailness, refinement, elegance 2 delicacy, tact, ticklishness (of a question, etc.) ♦ این سخن - There is a subtle meaning in these words.

نازل [naazel] 1 low, reduced (about a price) 2 literary descending, granted, sent down
• شدن - 1 to be reduced, to be lowered (about a price) 2 literary to descend, to be sent down

نازنین [naazanin] 1.1 delicate, refined, elegant, charming, delightful 1.2 beautiful, attractive 1.3 nice, dear ♦ فرزند - dear son, dear child 2.1 darling, beloved 2.2 darling, sweetheart (female) ♦ من - my darling!

نازوردار [naazwardaar] ☞ نازبردار

نازونخره [naazonakhra] coquetry, playfulness

نازونیاز [naazoniyaaz] endearments (of lovers); amorous murmurings, playful conversation

نازی [naazi] 1 a Nazi 2 Nazi adjective

نازیدن [naazidan] 1 to be proud [of], to take pride [in], to pride oneself [on] ♦ او به زور خود می نازد (به) He takes pride in his strength. 2 ☞ ناز کردن in entry ناز

نازیزم [naazizem] Naziism

ناس [naas]¹ nas, snuff, chewing tobacco

ناس [naas]² colloquial ☞ نحس

ناسپاس [naasepaas] ungrateful, not responding with gratitude (for a favor, etc.)

ناسزا [naasazaa] ☞ ناروا
• گفتن- to swear, to curse, to express oneself indecently or unbecomingly

ناسکه [naasakka] step ♦ برادر - stepbrother

ناسور [naasur] 1 (also- زخم) a wound that does not heal for a long time, a chronic wound 2 fistula, ulcer, abscess

ناسیونالست [naasiunaalest] a nationalist

ناشاد [naashaad] 1 bored, melancholy; discontented, dissatisfied 2 colloquial unlucky, luckless, unfortunate ♦ شوی - abusive May you never have good luck! / May you never be happy!

ناشتا [naashtaa] breakfast, a morning snack

ناشتایی [naashtaayi] food for newlyweds (sent by the parents of the bride on the morning after the wedding)

ناشد [naashod] (and) ناشدنی [naashodani] impossible, unrealizable ♦ این کار – است This matter is not feasible.

ناشر [naasher] 1 publishing; issuing; disseminating, propagating 2 publisher
• ناشر افکار - اندیشه ها

ناشر افکار [naasher (e) afkaar] 1 organ (printed publication) 2 spokesman

ناسپاس [naashokor] ☞ ناسپاس

ناشکری [naashokri] 1 ingratitude 2 dissatisfaction, grumbling
• کردن - 1 to be ungrateful 2 to grumble

ناشناس [naashenaas] 1.1 unknown, unfamiliar ♦ صدای - an unfamiliar voice 2 ignorant, not conversant [with] stranger, alien

281

ناشناسی [naashenaasi] ignorance, lack of information

ناشی [naashi] ¹ 1 inexperienced, unskillful 2 a novice (in some matter)

ناشی [naashi] ²
- از - *literary* appearing, arising; occurring, happening
- از چیزی بودن - *literary* to appear, to arise; to happen, to take place, to occur

ناصح [naaseh] (*plural* نصاح [nossaah] نصحا (and) [nosaha]) *literary* adviser; tutor; mentor

ناصر [naaser] 1 *literary* assistant, defender (usually about God) ♦ خدا حافظ وناصرت باشد May God protect you and help you! 2 *masculine proper name* Naser

ناصری [naaseri] 1 Naseri (an Afghan tribe) 2 *biblical* a Nazarene

ناصواب [naasawaab] 1 bad, improper, unseemly 2 unreasonable, unwise (about an act, about speech)

ناطق [naateq] 1.1 talking, endowed with the gift of speech ♦ طوطی - talking parrot 1.2 provided with sound, sound (about film) 2 (*plural* ناطقین [nateqin]) orator, speaker, lecturer

ناطقه [naateqa] 1 ☞ ناطق [naateq]1 2 (also- قوه) the gift of eloquence, the ability to speak

ناظر [naazer] 1 overseeing, supervising, superintending (something) 2.1 (also جایداد -) manager, steward (e.g., of an estate) 2.2 overseer; watchman

ناظم [naazem] poet, composer of verses

ناعلاج [naaelaaj] 1 forced; inevitable, unescapable 2 by compulsion, against one's will
- کسی را ساختن - to put somebody in a desperate position, to compel (somebody) to do something

ناعم [naa'em] soft
- حیوانات - mollusks

ناغه [naagha] *colloquial* absent; having exceeded (something)

ناف [naaf] navel; umbilical cord
- کردن - to cut the umbilical cord

نافذ [naafez] 1 having force, effective 2 penetrating; moving, sincere, heartfelt ♦ نگاه - a sincere view

نافرمان [naafarmaan] 1 disobedient; obstinate, refractory ♦ بچه - a disobedient boy 2 insubordinate, unruly ♦ گل - snapdragon (flower)

نافرمانی [naafarmaani] disobedience, insubordination

نافه [naafa] 1 musk gland of the musk deer 2 musk 3 (also گل -) stamen

نافهم [naafahm] 1 not understanding, unreasonable 2 unwise, stupid

نافهمی [naafahmi] 1 lack of understanding, incomprehension, irresponsibleness 2 misunderstanding; mistake ♦ از روی - because of a misunderstanding

نافی [naafi] *literary* 1 denying (something) 2 negative
- چیزی بودن - 1 to deny (something) 2 to annul, to cancel, to rescind (something)

ناق [naaq] *colloquial* ☞ ناحق

ناقابل [naaqaabel] 1 incapable, incompetent; unfit, useless; unsuitable, inappropriate 2 (first component of set expressions with meanings of "not subject to something"/ "not yielding to something," etc.) ♦ ناقابل فهم incomprehensible, inscrutable

ناقابل انکار [naaqaabeleenkaar] unquestionable, undeniable, irrefutable, indisputable, immutable

ناقابل فهم [naaqaabelefahm] incomprehensible, inscrutable

ناقرار [naaqaraar] ☞ بی قرار

ناقص [naaqes] 1 incomplete, inadequate ♦ جمله - *grammar* incomplete sentence ◊ فعل - *grammar* defective verb 2 with a flaw, defective 3 out of order, spoiled

ناقص عقل [naaqesáql] silly, foolish, imbecile

ناقض [naaqez] *literary* violating (an agreement, a treaty, etc.), contradicting (something)

ناقل [naaqel] 1 storyteller, narrator 2 *physics* conductor 3 carrier (of microbes); vector (of disease) ♦ ناقلین امراض vectors of diseases

ناق وبناق [naaqobanaaq] *colloquial* 1 for no reason at all, without cause, without motive, without reason 2 ☞ بناحق

ناقوس [naaqus] *literary* bell ♦ کلیسا - church bell

ناک [naak] pear (fruit) ♦ اوی - (winter variety of pears)

ناک [naak] *adjectival suffix*
- نمناک humid, moist, damp

ناکاره [naakaara] (also ویکاره -) *colloquial* 1 not knowing how to do anything, good-for-nothing 2 a good-for-nothing (person)

ناکام [naakaam] 1 unfortunate, unlucky 2 backward (about a pupil); failing (in an examination)
- شدن (ماندن) - 1 to fail, to suffer a failure 2 to fail (in examinations)

ناکامی [naakaami] 1 misfortune, an unhappy lot 2 failure, setback, reverse; failure (e.g., in examinations) 3 failure (of a pupil)

ناکس [naakas] 1 low, base, contemptible, despicable (about a person) 2 a scoundrel, a villain

ناکشته [naakeshta]
- را درو کردن - *proverb* to reap what hasn't been sown (to make up tales about somebody)

ناگاه [naagaah] unexpectedly, all of a sudden, suddenly

ناگزیر [naagozir] *literary* 1 inevitably, of necessity, unavoidably 2 by compulsion, against one's will; willy-nilly

ناگوار [nogowaar] unpleasant, disagreeable, causing annoyance, causing vexation ♦ حادثه - unpleasant incident

ناگاهان [nagahan] ☞ ناگاه

نال [naal] *colloquial* ☞ نعل

نالایق [naalaayeq] 1 unworthy, unseemly 2 incapable, incompetent; unfit, useless

نالت [naalat] *colloquial* ☞ لعنت

نالش [naalesh] 1 moan, groan, moaning, groaning; weeping, crying 2 whining, whimpering, complaining
- کردن - 1 to moan, to groan; to cry, to weep 2 to whine, to whimper, to complain (از)

ناله [naala] moan, groan; howl; cry, wail, crying, weeping
- کردن - ☞ نالیدن

نالی [naali] wooden sandals

نالیدن [naalidan] 1 to moan, to groan; to cry, to weep; to whine; to whimper 2 to complain (about somebody or something از دست ; از)

نالین [naalin] (and) نالینچه [naalincha] mattress

نام [naam] 1.1 name, appellation ♦ نیک - good name, good reputation 2 fame, reputation
- رستم به از رستم - *proverb* [He has] a great name, but he's not much to look at.
- به — 1 in the name [of] ♦ خدا (به) - for God's sake; by God

ن

2 under the guise [of], under pretense [of] ♦ به – میانجی as a mediator, as an intermediary
- نام وننگ ☞ وننگ
- (از،را) - to call by name, to name
- (بالای) - ماندن to name to give name [to]
- ماندن to leave fond از خود - ماندن (and) از خود - نیک ماندن memories about oneself
- به - کسی بودن colloquial to be engaged to someone (about a girl)
- نام شو ☞ شب
نامبارک [naamobaarak] not promising good, not promising joy; unfortunate, unhappy
نامبرده [naamborda] named, above-mentioned
نامحرم [naamahram] 1 another's, strange, outside (for a family) 2 not having access to the females' part of a house
نامدار [naamdaar] 1 famous, celebrated, renowned 2 eminent, distinguished
نامراد [naamoraad] not having achieved what one desires, unhappy
- شدن - to die young
نامرد [naamard] 1.1 ignoble, base, dishonorable, ungentlemanly 1.2 cowardly, craven 2.1 a coward 2.2 a cad
نامردی [naamardi] 1 dishonor; dishonorableness 2 cowardice
- کردن - 1 to act like a cad 2 to show cowardice
- مردی را بگی - جایی نمیره colloquial Pursue the truth and a lie won't escape anywhere!
نامرئی [naamar'i] invisible ♦ - اشعه invisible rays
نامزاد [naamzaad] 1 betrothed, engaged 2 fiancé, betrothed, groom; fiancée, bride
- شدن - to be betrothed, to be promised in marriage
نامزادبازی [naamzaadbaazi] meetings of the groom and bride before the wedding
نامزادی [naamzaadi] betrothal, engagement
نامزد [naamzad] 1 candidate, pretender, claimant, aspirant ♦ نامزد ☞ - candidate for president 2 ریاست جمهور
- شدن - 1 to be nominated (as a candidate) 2 ☞ نامزد شدن in entry کردن
- نامزد - to nominate, to propose as a candidate
نامزدی [naamzadi] 1 nomination as a candidate 2 ☞ نامزادی
نامشو [naameshaw] password
نامعقول [naama'qul] unwise, absurd ♦ کار - an unwise act; dumb trick
ناملایم [naamolaayem] 1 hard, strict, stern, severe 2 sharp, harsh, rough, rude ♦ پیشامد - rude treatment
ناملایمات [naamolaayemaat] adversities; difficulties
ناممکن [naamomken] impossible; impracticable, unfeasible
نام نویسی [naamnawisi] recording by name; registration
- کردن - to record, to write down, to register
نام نهاد [naamnehaad] so-called ♦ سیاست - so-called policy
ناموَر [naamwar] literary ☞ نامدار
ناموس [naamus] 1 female honor, chastity 2 good name, reputation
- طبیعت - law of nature
نام ونَنگ [naamonang] honor, reputation
نامه [naama] 1 letter, message, epistle 2 rarely newspaper, magazine, periodical 3 obscure book, work
نامه رسان [naamarasaan] postman, letter carrier
نامه نگار [naamanegaar] correspondent

نامی [naami] ☞ نامدار
- او دزد - است He is a well-known swindler / cheat.
نامی [naamee] someone by the name [of] (used after a proper name) ♦ کریم - someone by the name of Kerim
نامیدن [naamidan] to call, to name
نان [naan] 1 food; dinner, meal ♦ چاشت – dinner ◊ صبح - breakfast 2 (also خشک -) bread; flatcake ♦ تندوری - (and) تنوری - a homemade flatcake ◊ خاصه - a homemade flatcake (with holes made by fingernails) ◊ روغنی - rich flatcakes ◊ سنگکی - flatcakes baked on hearth stone
- نانت گرم باشد وآبت سرد colloquial May your dinner be warm and your water cold! (a good wish)
- نان وپیاز ☞ نان وپیاز
- دادن - 1 to feed, to give subsistence 2 to entertain, to receive (guests)
- به - خواستن to invite, to invite to dinner
- بیغیرتی خوردن - colloquial to strive to live at somebody else's expense
- نانش (در) روغن افتاده است colloquial 1 He began to earn a lot. 2 He lived in clover.
نانا [naanaa] (child's talk) bread
نان بایی [naanbaayi] ☞ نان وایی
نان پزی [naanpazi] baking of bread
نان خور [naankhor] colloquial 1 dependent, member of the family 2 an epicure, a good judge of food
- کسی بودن - 1 to be somebody's dependent 2 to be hired in somebody's service
نان دان [naandaan] (and) ناندانی [naandaani] breadbasket, bread plate
نان ده [naandeh] 1 generous, hospitable 2.1 a hospitable person 2.2 a breadwinner
نانوای [naanwaay] 1 baker 2 vendor of bread, vendor of flatcakes
نانوایی [naanwaayi] 1 bread baking 2 a bakery; a shop where they sell flatcakes
نان وپیاز [naanopiyaaz]
- پیشانی واز - You are welcome to all we have.
نان ونمک [naanonamak] bread and salt; hospitality
- شدن - to maintain an acquaintanceship (with somebody), to be acquainted (with somebody)
ناوخت [naawakht] (and) ناوقت [naawaqt] 1 late adjective, tardy 2 late adverb, not on time ♦ چرا - آمدی؟ Why did you arrive late?
ناول [naawel] novel, story; short story
ناولست [naawelest] novelist
ناوه [naawa] 1 gutter, trough, chute (for draining off water) 2 rarely channel for draining water, aqueduct 3 valley, oasis (amidst mountains)
ناودان [nawadan] ☞ ناوه 1
نایاب [naayaab] 1 difficult to find, scarce, in short supply 2 rare, unique
نایب [naayeb] deputy; assistant ♦ رئیس - deputy chairman; vice-president
نایب الحکومگی [naayebolhokumagi] 1 general governorship; province 2 post of governor-general
نایب الحکومه [naayebolhokuma] 1 governor-general 2 historical vicegerent of an emir in a province
نایب السلطنت [naayebossaltanat] 1 viceroy 2 regent
نایتروجن [naaytrojan] nitrogen

283

ن

نایل [naayel]
- (شدن) آمدن - to obtain, to attain, to achieve; to be honored [with], to be awarded (به)

نبات [nabaat] ¹ (*plural* نباتات [nabaataat]) a plant; greens, vegetables

نبات [nabaat] ² nabat, granulated sugar

نباتات [nabaataat] *plural of* نبات
- خودرو - wild plants
- باغ – botanical garden
- تربیه – plant-growing

نبات شناسی [nabaatshenaasi] botany

نباتی [nabaati] vegetable ♦ تیل - vegetable oil

نبرد [nabard] battle

نبض [nabz] pulse ♦ تیز - rapid pulse
- دیدن - to check the pulse, to take the pulse ♦ داکتر او را دید - The doctor checked his pulse.

نبوغ [nobugh] genius; talent

نبی [nabi] (*plural* انبیاء [anbiyaa]) 1 *literary* prophet, envoy 2 *masculine proper name* Nabi

نبیره [nabera] grandson; granddaughter

نت [nat] nut ♦ نت شش رخ - hexagonal nut

نتایج [nataayej] *plural of* نتیجه

نتی [nati] a ring worn in the nostril

نتیجه [natija] (*plural* نتایج [nataayej]) 1 result, consequence 2 conclusion 3 *medicine* analysis ♦ ادرار - analysis of the urine, urinalysis

نثار [nesaar]
- کردن - 1 to strew (flowers, money, etc., before somebody as a sign of respect) 2 to shower (a bride with money or flowers on her wedding day) ♦ بالای او گل نثار میکنند - They are showering her with flowers. 3 to distribute, to dispense (money during a holiday) 4 to sacrifice, to make an offering

نثر [náser] prose, work of prose ♦ بدیعی - literary prose

نثرنویس [nasrnawis] prosaist, prose writer

نجابت [najaabat] 1 eminence, nobility 2 decency

نجات [nejaat] escape; salvation, deliverance
- دادن - to save, to rescue, to deliver [from]
- یافتن - to be saved, to be rescued, to be delivered [from]

نجات بخش [nejaatbakhsh] rescue, lifesaving; liberation ♦ نهضت - liberation movement

نجار [najjaar] carpenter; joiner

نجارک [naj(j)aarak] woodpecker

نجاری [najjaari] carpentry; joiner's work ♦ مصنوعات - joiner's work, joinery

نجاست [najaasat] 1 uncleanness 2 garbage, sewage; excrement

نجباء [nojabaa] aristocrats

نجس [najes] 1 unclean, impure, dirty, foul 2 profaned, befouled, defiled, stained, sullied

نجم [nájem] *literary* star; planet; heavenly body

نجوم [nojum] 1 astrology 2 astronomy

نجومی [nojumi] 1 astrological 2 astronomical

نجیب [najib] 1.1 noble 1.2 honest, decent 2 *masculine proper name* Najib

نجیب زاده [najibzaada] aristocrat; a noble, nobleman

نحس [nahs] presaging evil, ominous, sinister, ill-boding, ill-starred, ill-fated ♦ روز - an ill-fated day ◊ طالع - evil fate

نحو [nahw] ¹ syntax

نحو [nahw] ² *literary* manner, means ♦ به – خوب - well, in the best manner ◊ به نحوی که... - in such a manner that…; so that…

نحوست [nohusat] 1 evil fate 2 evil sign, bad sign

نخ [nakh] 1 thread; string; cord, twine 2 cotton yarn, threads
- نخ تابیدن - to spin threads, to twist threads
- نخ رشتن - to spin yarn

نخات [nakhaat] (also که -) *colloquial* 1 It cannot be!; hardly ♦ که شما این را گفته باشید - It cannot be that you said that! / You cannot have said that! ◊ که بیاید - He will hardly arrive! 2 I hope… doesn't or won't… ♦ که بیفته - I hope he doesn't fall!

نخاس [nakhaas] market for trading cattle

نخاع [noxaa'] *anatomy* spinal cord

نخت [nakht] *colloquial* ☞ نقد
- کردن - to gain (from the sale of something), to make a gain

نخت وتیار [nakhtotiyaar] *colloquial* having at one's service, having available; accessible, available; ready

نخچ [nakhch] *colloquial* ☞ نقش

نخچه [nakhcha] *colloquial* ☞ نقشه

نخره [nakhra] *colloquial* 1 coquetry 2 simulation, pretense, sham
- کردن - 1 to flirt 2 to pretend [to be], to feign

نخرهیی [nakhrayi] *colloquial* 1 coquettish; mincing 2 pretender, sham; poser; affected person

نخریسی [nakhreesi] manufacture of cotton yarn, cotton-spinning

نخسان [nokhsaan] *colloquial* ☞ نقصان
- کردن - to have a miscarriage

نخسانی [nokhsaani] *colloquial* prematurely born baby

نخست [nokhost] at first, firstly, first *adverb*

نخست وزیر [nokhostwazir] Prime Minister

نخستین [nokhostin] first *adjective* ♦ روز - the first day ◊ درس - first lesson

نخسه [nokhsa] *colloquial from* نسخه ²

نخل [nákhel] *botany* 1 date-palm tree 2 palm tree

نخت [nakhot] *colloquial* ☞ نخود

نخوت [nakhwat] arrogance, haughtiness, swagger, self-conceit

نخود [nakhod] 1 pea, peas ♦ چل - hard pea, hard peas ◊ شور - pickled peas 2 naxod (old unit of weight equal to ½ a mesqal or 0.19 grams)
- پس سیاه راهی کردن - *colloquial* 1 to get rid (of somebody) in a fraudulent manner, to send (somebody) on his way 2 to destroy, to ravage, to ruin utterly

نخودی [nakhodi] yellowish-brown; pea-colored

نخورده [nakhorda]
- ونبرده درد گرده گرفته - *proverb* Even though I didn't eat the shashlik, my stomach still hurt.

نخ وسوزن [nakhosuzan] *colloquial* 1 women's finery; "threads and needles" 2 *ironic* bride's dowry

نخی [nakhi] cotton *adjective* ♦ تکه - cotton cloth, cotton fabric

نخیر [nakhair] no *particle*

ندا [nedaa] exclamation, cry; call
- آهنگ ● *grammar* intonation of an exclamation
- آهنگ افتاده ● Falling Tone
- آهنگ خیزان ● Rising tone
- آهنگ موازی ● Sing-song

نداف [naddaaf] cotton scutcher

ندافی [naddaafi] 1 scutching, combing or carding of cotton 2 place where they comb or card and sell cotton

ندامت [nadaamat] *literary* repentance, regret
- وپشیمانی کردن ● to repent, to be remorseful, to regret strongly

ندانسته [nadaanesta] 1 not knowing, not being aware [of] 2 accidentally, inadvertantly, by chance

ندایی [nedaayi]
- جمله ● *grammar* exclamatory sentence
- حالت ● *grammar* vocative case

ندرت [nodrat]
- به ندرت ☞ به ● ●

ندیم [nadim] *literary* 1 close friend, confidant 2 a person in attendance (to a shah), a favorite, a minion

نذر [názer] 1 vow, promise 2 alms, gift (in keeping with a vow); donation (for charitable causes) ♦ زیارت - alms dispensed at a cemetery (for a prayer to the deceased) ◊ - نان bread, alms (given in keeping with a vow)
- دادن ● to give alms (in keeping with a vow); to donate (for charitable causes)
- کردن (گرفتن) به ● to make a vow
- زیارت ادا کردن ● to dispense alms at somebody's grave

نذرونیاز [nazroniyaaz] alms, donation (in favor of the poor)

نذری [nazri] 1 promised in a vow; devoted (to God) 2 donated (for charitable purposes)

نر [nar] 1.1 male 1.2 man; husband 2 (first component of compound words with the meaning of names of male animals) ♦ نرگاو bull

نراد [narraad] *colloquial* a sly person, a cheat, a swindler; a rogue, a rascal

نرانه [narana] *colloquial* ☞ مردانه

نرتوت [nartut] a variety of mulberry (with a grainy berry)

نرخ [nerkh] 1 price; valuation, statutory price ♦ بازار - market price ◊ مستقل -fixed price 2 *economics* rate of exchange ♦ بین المللی روبل شوروی - the international rate of exchange of the Soviet ruble
- نرخ کار ☞ کار ●

نرخر [narkhar] male donkey

نرخ کار [nerkhekaar] 1 rate (of pay or cost) for manpower 2 schedule of changes (for types of work)

نرخ نامه [nerkhnaama] 1 schedule of rates (e.g., postal) 2 price list

نرد [nard] backgammon (a game consisting of dice and a board with pieces) ♦ دانه - a piece (in a game of backgammon)

نرس [nars] 1 nurse 2 practical nurse; medical attendant

نرسری [narsari] nursery, hotbed

نرسنگ [narseng] the work of a nurse, nursing; caring for a sick person ♦ مکتب - school for medical attendants

نرکله [narkalla] *colloquial* Well done! / A real man!

نرگاو [nargaaw] bull

نرگس [narges] narcissus, daffodil
- شهلا ● 1 narcissus, daffodil with a black core 2 *poetic* eyes of a sweetheart

نرم [narm] 1 soft, delicate ♦ - باد a soft breeze 2 loose, friable, soft ♦ - خاک loose soil 3 mild in nature, gentle, meek
- کردن ● 1 to make soft, to soften 2 to calm, to pacify, to placate, to prevail [upon], to tame, to subdue 3 to alleviate, to lessen (pain, etc.)
- باکسی – گرفتن ● *colloquial* to treat somebody gently, to treat somebody leniently

نرمبر [narmbor] *colloquial* acting on the sly; secretly, crafty (about a person)

نرمدل [narmdel] good, kind, softhearted

نرمش [narmesh] 1 gentleness (of treatment) 2 flexibility, suppleness, pliability, pliancy, plasticity

نرمش پذیری [narmeshpaziri] flexibility (of policy)

نرم نرم [narmnarm] (and) نرمک نرمک [narmaknarmak] *colloquial* 1 softly, delicately 2 gently, quietly

نرمه [narma]
- گوش ● - ear lobe
- بینی ● - nostril

نرمی [narmi] 1 softness, delicateness 2 looseness, friability (e.g., of soil) 3 mildness of character, gentleness, meekness ♦ - به softly, gently, delicately; affectionately

نره [nar (r)a] 1 ☞ نر 2 having grown a hard stem, stalk (of some vegetables on which a calyx with seeds is formed) ♦ پیاز - onion stalk
- کردن ● - to form stalks, to go to stalk (about onions, etc.)

نری [nari]¹ 1 male sex, belonging to the male sex 2 manliness; bravery, valor 3 bolt, bar
- هم - وهم غری ● *proverb* blaming someone else for one's own fault
- ● – وماده گی ☞

نری [nari]² *technical* thread, threading ♦ هموار - fretwork ◊ پل - screw tap, tap borer (tool for making threads in the nuts, etc.)

نری تاب [naritaab] *technical* tap wrench

نرینه [narina] of the male sex, male, masculine

نری وماده گی [nariwmaadagi] bar with a loop, bolt with a bracket; (door) bolt

نزاع [nezaa'] *literary* argument, controversy; quarrel; conflict

نزاکت [nazaakat] 1 tenderness, delicacy 2 courteousness, tact 3 *masculine proper name* Nazakat

نزد [nazd] (also - در) 1 near, close to; at; by *denominative preposition* ♦ الماری - near the cupboard 1.2 for (somebody); in somebody's eyes, in somebody's opinion ♦ او ◊ پول - من مهم نیست For me it's not money that's important. پدرم خیلی عزیز بود He was very dear to my father. 2 (also - به) to (somebody's) [house] ♦ رفیق خود آمدم - I arrived at my friend's [house] 3 ٠٠٠ : ♦ از - ارباب بیست سیر گندم از He borrowed 20 sers of wheat from the landlord.

نزدیک [nazdik] 1.1 near (in time) *adjective* ♦ - درآینده in the near future 1.2 near, nearby, neighboring 1.3 close (about a friend, about a relative) 2 near, close, near at hand, hereabouts *adverb*
- از -● from a close distance, nearby, close by
- ● *denominative preposition* 1 ☞ نزد 2 shortly [before], not long [before], before ♦ چاشت - about noon

ن

- شدن • - to approach, to come nearer [to], to come up [to], to drive up [to]
- بود (که) • - almost, nearly

نزدیکان [nazdikaan] 1 relatives ♦ آن جوان از - ما است This young man is our relative. 2 retainers, persons in attendance

نزدیک بین [nazdikbin] 1 nearsighted 2 shortsighted

نزدیک ها [nazdikhaa] 1 near, close to, next to, beside *denominative preposition* ♦ شهر - near the town or city 2 shortly before, not long before, before ♦ غروب - [right] before sunset

نزدیکی [nazdiki] 1.1 close location, neighborhood, vicinity 1.2 closeness, intimacy
- در - • near, next to *denominative preposition* ♦ کابل – near Kabul
- درین - • 1 hereabouts 2 soon, shortly after 3 recently, the other day

نزدیکها [nazdikihaa] ☞ نزدیکها

نزول [nozul] 1 reduction, drop, fall (of prices) 2 depositing (of sediment)
- کردن • - *religion* to be sent down (from heaven) (about the Koran)
- اجلال کردن (فرمودن) • - to deign to come, to deign to stop [at] (about a high-ranking person)

نژاد [nezhaad] 1 family, tribe 2 race 3 birth, parentage, descent

نژادی [nezhadi] 1 pertaining to [one's] birth, parentage, or descent 2 racial ♦ تبعیض نژادی racial discrimination

نساء [nasaa] (*plural* نسوان [neswaan]) 1 *literary* woman 2 *feminine proper name* Nesa

نساجی [nassaazhi] weaving, textile manufacturing ♦ فابریکه - textile factory

نساخ [nassaakh] copier (of manuscripts); calligrapher

نسایی [nesaayi] female, women's ♦ امراض - women's diseases ◊ داکتر - gynecologist

نسب [nasab] (*plural* انساب [ansab]) parentage, descent, genealogy
- اصل و نسب ☞ اصل •

نسبت [nesbat] 1.1 relation, connection, affiliation (with something, to something) 1.2 ties of relationship, ties of blood, relationship, kinship ♦ مادری - relationship through the mother (i.e., the mother's side of the family) 1.3 *mathematical* proportion 2.1 for *denominative preposition* ♦ حفظ صحت - for the preservation of health 2.2 (also - به) in comparison [with] ♦ سال گذشته به in comparison with last year 2.3 because [of], in connection [with], on the occasion [of] *conjunction* ♦ مریضی – به because of illness
- به - ☞ به •
- دادن - • 1 to concern, to have to do [with], to ascribe [to] (به) 2 to compare, to make an analogy
- داشتن - • 1 to bear a relation [to], to have a tie [with] (با) 2 to be related [to] (با)
- ی - • *grammar* (suffix of relative adjectives)

نسبتاً [nesbatan] relatively, comparatively

نسبتی [nesbati] relative, comparative ♦ اندازه - comparative dimensions ◊ صفت - *grammar* relative adjective

نسب نامه [nasabnaama] genealogical tree, genealogy

نسبی [nesbi] ☞ نسبتی

نسبیت [nesbiyat] *mathematical physics* ♦ نظریه - (and) انشتاین • - Einstein's theory of relativity

نسترن [nastaran] 1 white dog rose, white sweetbriar, white eglantine 2 *feminine proper name* Nastaran

نستعلیق [nasta'liq] (also - خط) nastaliq (a type of calligraphic handwriting)

نسج [nasj] (*plural* انساج [ansaaj]) *biology* tissue

نسخ [naskh] neskhi (kind of handwriting and type)

نسخ [nasakh] *historical* punishment (in which a man's hand, ear, or nose was cut off)
- کردن • - to punish, to subject (somebody) to a disgraceful execution

نسخچی [nasakhchi] *historical* executioner (who subjected a guilty person to a humiliating punishment) ☞ نسخ

نسخه [noskha]¹ (also - خطی) (also - قلمی) manuscript; copy ♦ قلمی دیوان - manuscript of a divan 2 copy (in counting books) ♦ دو – کتاب two copies of a book

نسخه [noskha]² prescription (for medicine); prescription (of a physician)

نسخه برداری [noskhabardaari] copying, making copies ♦ کاغذ – carbon paper

نسک [nask] lentil

نسق [nasaq] 1 ☞ نسخ 2 *obscure* order, system; arrangement

نسقچی [nasaqchi] ☞ نسخچی

نسل [násel] 1 generation, posterity, offspring ♦ نسلهای بعدی future generations ◊ به - (and) بعد - from generation to generation 2 race, breed, species, genus ♦ خالص - pure breed 3 breed, issue
- گرفتن • - to breed (e.g., livestock), to obtain offspring

نسل به نسل [naslbanasl] from generation to generation

نسلگیری [naselgiri] 1 breeding (of livestock), obtaining offspring 2 raising purebred animals
- شدن • - to breed (about livestock)

نسلی [nasli] 1 ancestral; patrimonial; hereditary 2 pedigree (about livestock)

نسوار [naswar] naswar, nas (chewing tobacco)

نسواری [naswaari] 1 brown; of the color of tobacco 2 man who uses nas (chewing tobacco)

نسوان [neswaan] *plural of* نساء
- انجمن – • women's society

نسیان [nasyaan] oblivion ♦ درطاق – ماندن to bury in oblivion

نسیب [nasib] *literary* nasib (lyrical introduction to a qasida)

نسیم [nasim] 1 light wind, whiff, puff, zephyr 2 *masculine proper name* Nasim

نسیه [nasya] 1 credit, granting of credit 2 (also - به) on credit

نشاط [nashaat] merriment, mirth, gaiety, rejoicing

نشان [nashaan] 1 ☞ نشاند 2 medal, decoration, order; badge 3 emblem, arms, coat of arms ♦ دولتی افغانستان - state emblem of Afghanistan, national emblem of Afghanistan 4 ☞ نشانه 2, 3
- دادن - • 1 to show, to indicate 2 to give an order (decoration), to award an order (decoration) (به)
- گرفتن - • to aim, to take aim
- میدهمت - • *colloquial* I'll show you! (a threat)

نشانچی [neshaanchi] marksman; sniper

نشاندادن [neshaandaad] show, demonstration ♦ فلم - نشانداد (and) motion picture show, show of motion pictures

286

نشان دادن [neshaandaadan] ☞ in entry نشان
نشانچی [neshaandast] ☞ نشاندست
نشاندن [neshaandan] 1 to make sit down, to seat, to ask to sit down 2 to plant, to transplant (trees)
نشانزن [nashaanzan] *military* gun layer
نشانگاه [neshaangaah] *military* [gun] sight ♦ ترتیبات - sighting mechanism, rear sight
نشانه [neshaana] 1 sign; symbol, index, indicator ♦ - نکره *grammar* indicator of indefiniteness 2 target 3 front sight (on a gun barrel)
• زدن - to hit the target
• نشانهء اضافت Possessive marker
• نشانهء افزایش Incremental marker
• نشانهء افزایش Attributive marker, in adjective
نشانی [neshaani] 1 mark, sign; token 2 (also دست-) remembrance, gift of remembrance, souvenir ♦ این تفنگ - پدرم است [My] father left this gun to me as a keepsake. 3 *colloquial* gift, present (sent by a bridegroom, fiancé to the home of the bride, fiancée) 4 ☞ آدرس 5 bookmark
• دادن - 1 to give signs (of something), to indicate signs (of something) 2 to give (somebody's) address 3 to leave as a keepsake, to make a present of
• کردن - to place a mark, to mark, to designate
نشایسته [neshaayesta] starch
نشر [náser] 1 publication ♦ اول - first edition 2 dissemination (of ideas, etc.) 3 transmission, relaying, broadcast ♦ اخبار - broadcast of the news (over the radio)
• کردن - 1 to issue, to publish 2 to transmit, to relay, to broadcast 3 to disseminate, to emit (rays, beams) 4 to absorb ink (about paper) ♦ این کاغذ رنگ – میکند This paper absorbs ink.
نشراتی [nasharaati]
• اورگان - organ, organ of the press
• ستیشن – radio station
• مؤسسه – publishing house
نشره [nashra] *regional* church service or public prayer arranged in honor of the birth of a boy (with the invitation of guests and entertainment)
نشریات [nashriyaat] *plural of* نشریه
نشریه [nashriya] (*plural* نشریات [nashriyaat]) publication; issue ♦ نشریات متناوب periodic publications, periodicals
نشست [neshast] 1 landing (of an airplane) 2 settling (of a building)
نشستن [neshastan] (*present tense stem* نشین [nesin]) 1 to sit; to sit down (روی بر) 2 to live, to be housed, to reside (در) ♦ این خانه تابستانها می نشست He lived in this house in the summer. 3 to crumble, to cave in, to settle (about a structive)
• فرو – 1 to subside, to cease, to fade away (about pain) 2 to abate (about noise) 3 to die out (about anger, about a fire) ♦ همه را با یک – باخت He lost everything at one sitting.
نشست و برخاست [neshastobarkhaast] (*and*) نشست و برخاست [neshastobarkhaast] intercourse, contact, acquaintance
• داشتن - to get acquainted [with], to associate [with] (ب)
نشنیده [nashnida]
• گرفتن - not to listen, to disregard, not to pay heed to, not to pay attention [to]
نشوونما [nashwonomaa (y)] (ی) growth; growth (of trees, of plants)

نشه [nesha (and) nasha] 1 intoxication, unconsciousness 2 rapture, ecstasy, delight, enjoyment 3 narcotic
• کردن - to get drunk; to smoke to one's heart's content; to be intoxicated
• به - کسی خار زدن *colloquial* to divert from a pleasant pursuit
نشه یی [neshayi] 1 drinker; smoker 2 drug addict
نشیب [nesheb] slope, descent; inclination
نشیبی [nesheebi] 1 incline, declivity, pitch 2 slope; sloping hill 3 low place, depression, low-lying terrain
نشیمن [nesheeman]
• عمارت - dwelling *noun*
نشین [neshin] 1 *present tense stem* نشستن 2 (second component of compound words with meaning "living (somewhere)" / "inhabitant") ♦ صحرانشین inhabitant of the steppe, nomad
نشئت [nash'at]
• کردن - 1 *literary* to arise, to spring up, to come [from] 2 to grow, to appear (از)
نصاب [nesaab] 1 quorum ♦ عدم - lack of a quorum 2 established norm, limit, quota ♦ تعلیمی - educational program 3 taxable minimum of property
نصارا [nasaaraa] *plural of* نصرانی
نصایح [nasaayeh] *plural of* نصیحت
نصب [nasb] 1 installation (of something); fastening (something to something); hoisting (e.g., a banner) 2 appointment (e.g., to a post)
• کردن - 1 to install, to fasten; to hoist 2 to appoint (to a post)
نصبالعین [nasbol'ayn] goal, mission, task ♦ صحیح - the right purpose
• خود قرار دادن - to set a goal for oneself
نصرانی [nasraani] (*plural* نصارا [nasaaraa]) *literary* 1 Christian *adjective* 2 a Christian
نصف [nesf] half ♦ روز - half a day
• نصف کره ☞ کره -
نصف النهار [nesfonnahar] meridian
نصف کره [nesfekor (r) a] earth's hemisphere ♦ شمالی - northern hemisphere
نصفه کار [nesfakaar] tenant-sharecropper
نصفه کاری [nesfakaari] leasing of land for sharecropping or for half the crop, sharecropping
نصوار [naswaar] 1 (also بینی - (and) دماغ -) naswar, nas, snuff 2 (also دهن -) chewing tobacco
نصواری [naswari] 1.1 a person who uses naswar or nas (☞ نصوار) 1.2 a vendor of naswar 2 greenish-brown; of the color of tobacco
نصیب [nasib] lot, destiny, fate
• کسی شدن - to fall to someone's lot
نصیحت [nasihat] (*plural* نصایح [nasayeh]) directions, admonition, advice, counsel
• کردن - to admonish, to advise (به)
نطاق [nattaaq] 1 speaker, lecturer, orator 2 representative (making some kind of declaration) 3 (radio) announcer
نطفه [notfa] 1 seed, sperm 2 embryo; fetus 3 descendant; offspring
نطق [notq] 1 speech, address 2 (also - استعداد) gift of eloquence, speech
• کردن - to speak, to make a speech

نظار [nozzaar] *plural of* ناظر[^1]
- هیئت – **1** inspection committee, auditing commission **2** supervisory council (of a society)

نظارت [nazaarat] observation; supervision, monitoring
- کردن - to observe; to monitor
- (ازر برر بالای)

نظاره [nazaara]
- کردن - to look, to look [at]; to gaze [at]

نظافت [nazaafat] cleanness, neatness, tidiness

نظام [nezaam] **1** structure, order, system ♦ اقتصادی - economic structure ◊ حکومتی - state system **2** *military* formation; daily detail

نظامنامه [nezaamnaama] **1** military regulations **2** *historical* code, code of laws

نظایر [nazaayer] *plural of* نظیره

نظر [nazer] (*plural* انظار [anzaar]) **1** look, glance, gaze ♦ به - اول at first glance **2** opinion, point of view ♦ به نظرم in my opinion, in my view **3** *masculine proper name* Nazar
- به - in view [of], taking into account; depending on *denominative preposition* ♦ به احتیاجات مردم - depending on the needs of the people
- از - from the point of view [of], in relation [to], with respect [to]
- (زیر) تحت **1** under the care [of], under the control [of], under the supervision [of]; under the leadership [of] **2** under the editorship [of]
- انداختن - to cast a glance, to glance [at], to look [at]; to look (به)
- شدن - *colloquial* to be subjected to the evil eye, to undergo damage
- کردن - *colloquial* to bewitch (with the evil eye)
- از – گذراندن to take in with a glance, to run one's eyes [over]
- به – آمدن to seem, to appear
- به - خوردن to be noticed, to be striking (i.e., to be especially noticeable)
- به – نامدن *colloquial* not to be taken into account, not to be considered
- به – ناوردن *colloquial* not to take into account, not to consider
- در - بودن to be foreseen, to be provided for, to be taken into consideration
- در – گرفتن to foresee, to provide for, to take into consideration
- از - دور داشتن to lose sight [of]; to ignore
- از – کسی افتادن to lose somebody's favor, to lose somebody's attention
- به - قدر دیدن to value, to appreciate, to respect, to esteem, to consider, to recognize (را)
- تحت (زیر) – گرفتن **1** to take under [one's] command, to take under [one's] guidance **2** to establish control [over], to establish supervision [of] (را)

نظربند [nazarband] being under the supervision [of]
- کردن - **1** to take under supervision **2** to take under house arrest

نظر کرده [nazarkarda] *colloquial* **1** charmed; invulnerable **2** saved by God, guarded by God

نظری [nazari] theoretical ♦ درس - theoretical studies

نظریه [nazariya] (*plural* نظریات [nazariyat]) **1** theory; **2** view, opinion

نظم [názem][^1] order, routine
نظم [názem][^2] poetry, verses

نعره [na'ra] loud cry, shout, yell, howl, wail; exclamation
- کشیدن (زدن) - to cry loudly, to shout, to yell, to cry, to wail; to scream out, to call out

نعش [na'sh] body, corpse

نعل [na'l (and) naal] **1** (horse) shoe **2** tap (on a heel)
- کردن - to shoe (a horse)
- و(به) - میخ زدن *colloquial* to run with the hare and hunt with the hounds
- حق – a percentage of the winnings (to benefit the owner of a gambling house)

نعلبکی [na'lbaki] saucer

نعلبند [na'lband] blacksmith, farrier

نعلبندی [na'lbandi] shoeing (horses)

نعمت [ne'mat] **1** abundance, plenty, prosperity, the good things of life **2** gift, favor

نعنا [na'naa] *botany* mint

نغمه [naghma] melody; motif; tune

نغمه سرا(ی) [naghmasaraa(y)] **1** singer-musician **2** singing, song (about birds)

نفاذ [nefaaz]
- شرف - یافتن *epistolary* to obtain effect, to be carried out (about a law, an order, etc.)

نفاق [nefaq] dissension, discord, strife

نفت [neft] oil, petroleum
- نفت باب ☞ محصولات -

نفت باب [neftbaab] oil products

نفت بر [neftbar] (*also* موتر) tank truck (for oil, for kerosene)

نفر [nefar] **1** man, person **2** servant, attendant **3** (collectively) people, personnel, group ♦ دیگر - کجا است؟ Where are the rest of the workers? **4** (numerative in counting people and camels) ♦ برای هر - از اهالی per capita
- نفر خدمت ☞ خدمت -

نفرت [nafrat] aversion/repugnance, hatred/detestation, antipathy
- داشتن - to have an aversion [for]/to loathe, to hate/to detest (از)

نفرت آمیز [nafrataameez] expressing aversion or repugnance, expressing hatred ♦ نگاه - contemptuous look, scornful look

نفرت انگیز [nafratangeez] nasty, offensive, repulsive, evoking aversion

نفر خدمت [nafarkhedmat] *military* batman, officer's orderly

نفره [nafara] (forms an adjective with a number) ♦ پنج نفره rated for five, five-place

نفری [nafari] **1** people; company, society **2** personnel, staff ♦ پولیس - policemen ◊ طیاره - *military* crew of an aircraft **3** the men, the enlisted men

نفرین [nafrin] *literary* swearing, bad language, abuse, defamation, curse

نفس [nafas] (*plural* انفاس [anfas]) breathing, respiration, deep breath, sigh ♦ آخرین - last breath ◊ نفسهای کوتاه rapid breathing
- بایک – **1** at one go, in a flash **2** without respite
- نفسک زدن ☞ کشیدن in entry
- زدن - ☞
- کشیدن - to breathe

288

- گرفتن • - to recover one's breath, to take a breath, to take a short rest
- از افتیدن (ماندن) • *colloquial* to breathe heavily and gasp (from tiredness, etc.)
- نفسش بند شد - to take breath ♦ کردن راست • His breath was taken away. / It took his breath away.
- نفسم سوخت • *colloquial* I was breathing heavily. / I was panting. / I was out of breath.

نفس [nafs] *plural* انفس [anfos]) 1 soul, inner life (of man) ♦ - پاکی spiritual purity, purity of soul 2 essence, main point ♦ به خود - in its essence 3 carnal needs and desires (of man) ♦ - بد 1 greed, avidity 2 carnality 3 passion ♦ او بنده - خود است He is a slave to his passions.
- خود را کشتن - • 1 to keep oneself in check 2 to mortify one's flesh

نفسانی [nafsani] *colloquial* 1 insatiable; voracious, gluttonous 2 carnivorous

نفس تنگی [nafastangi] asthma; short wind, short breath

نفسک [nafasak]
- زدن • *colloquial* - to breathe heavily and rapidly, to hardly take a breath

نفع [náf' (and) náfa] 1 use, benefit, advantage, gain, profit 2 profit, gain ♦ خالص - net profit
- به ••• • 1 in the interests (of somebody or something) 2 to the benefit (of somebody or something)
- داشتن • - to have a benefit; to obtain profit

نفع دوست [naf'dost] money-grubber, miser, skinflint

نفقه [nafaqa] 1 expenditures to support a family; means of subsistence 2 alimony

نفل [náfel] *religion* prayer (said in addition to the five prayers established by the Koran)

نفوذ [nofuz] 1 penetration; intrusion, inculcation, implantation 2 authority, weight 3 force, effectiveness (of a law); influence ♦ تحت - under the influence [of] 4 *grammar* government
- غیر قابل • impermeable, impervious, impenetrable, tight; hermetic
- داشتن • - to enjoy influence, to carry weight
- کردن • (در) - to penetrate, to pass (through something), to be inculcated, to be implanted

نفوس [nofus] inhabitants, population

نفوس شماری [nofusshomaari] census of the population

نفی [nafy] *literary* denial, negation; rejection, repudiation; - ادات

نفیس [nafis] beautiful, elegant, of fine work ♦ صنایع - the fine arts

نق [neq]
- نق زدن • *colloquial* 1 to whimper, to snivel, to whine 2 to beg, to pester (with requests)

نقاب [neqaab] 1 mask 2 guise 3 visor (of a helmet)
- برداشتن • - 1 to remove a mask 2 *figuratively* to cast off a guise

نقاد [naqqaad] 1 critic 2 *obscure* assayer

نقاش [naqqaash] artist, painter, graphic artist

نقاشی [naqqaashi] a painting, a drawing ♦ نمایشگاه - an exhibition of paintings or of works of art

نقاط [noqaat] *plural of* نقطه 2
- نظامی • - military objectives

نقب [náqeb] ¹ underground passage, tunnel
- کردن • - 1 to dig a tunnel 2 to make an underground passage, to undermine (also *figuratively*)

نقب [náqeb] ² mine

نقب پران [naqeb paraan] 1.1 blasting *adjective*; mine, mining *adjective* 1.2 sapper (about troops) *adjective* 2 a miner, a sapper

نقب زن [naqebzan] 1 a thief who makes an underground passage 2 a miner

نقد [náqed] ¹ 1 on hand (about money) 2 (also پول -) cash
- نقداً ☞ به - •
- کردن • - to convert into money, to realize (goods)

نقد [naqed] ² *literary* critical analysis, criticism ♦ آثار - book review (section of criticism in magazines)

نقداً [náqdan] [payment] with cash, for cash

نقدی [naqdi] cash ♦ تحویل دار - cashier

نقره [noqra] silver ♦ مصنوعات - articles made of silver

نقره کار [noqrakaar] decorated with silver, inlaid with silver

نقره یی [noqrayi] (and) نقره ئین [noqrayin] silver, made of silver

نقش [naqsh] ¹ 1 drawing *noun*, picture; pattern, design 2 impression, imprint ♦ پای - footprint
- نقش ونگار ☞ - ونگار •
- شدن • - 1 to be drawn 2 to leave an impression 3 to be engraved (upon the memory)

نقش [naqsh] ² role ♦ در ••• – in the role (of somebody or something)
- بازی کردن (and) ایفا کردن - • to play the role [of], to act the role [of]

نقش ونگار [naqshonegaar] patterns, designs, painting; decorative pattern, decorative design

نقشه [naqsha] 1 plan, map; sketch ♦ اراضی - site plan ◊ عمارت - drawing of a building, design of a building 2 layout, design, scheme 3 project, plan
- شدن • - to be drawn, to be put on a plan; to be designed, to be planned
- کردن • - to plot on a map; to compile a plan, to compile a drawing
- کشیدن • - to plan, to design

نقشه کش [naqshakash] 1 draftsman; cartographer 2 planner 3 designer

نقشه کشی [naqshakashi] 1 cartography; drawing 2 planning; designing ♦ دفتر - design bureau 3 layout ♦ عمودی - profile layout, side elevation

نقص [noqs] (*plural* نواقص [nawaqes]) 1 lack, shortage, deficiency 2 damage, loss 3 fault, malfunction, defect
- رساندن • (به) - to inflict damage, to inflict loss
- کردن • - to suffer a loss

نقصان [noqsaan] damage, detriment; loss, losses

نقض [naqz] *literary* 1 violation (of a vow, of an oath, of a law) 2 annulment, cancellation; dissolution, abrogation (of a treaty, a contract, etc.)

نقط [noqat] *plural of* نقطه

نقطه [noqta] (*plural* نقط [noqat]) 1 period (punctuation mark) ♦ چند - dots, ellipsis ◊ دو - colon 2 (*plural* نقاط [noqaat]) point
- مسکونی • - settlement, populated area

نقطه نظر [noqteynazar] point of view ♦ از اقتصاد – in an economic sense, in respect to economics

نقل [náqel] 1 carrying over, transference; shift, displacement 2 story, tale, account, narration, narrative; broadcast 3 copy; copying 4 *colloquial* crib (i.e., device for cheating)
- نقل قول ☞ قول •
- برداشتن - to make a copy •
- دادن - to transfer •
- کردن - 1 to tell, to narrate, to recount, to retell 2 *colloquial* to answer by means of a crib (i.e., to cheat)

نقل [nóq'l] noqol (candied fruits, nuts, almonds) ♦ بادامی - almonds in sugar
- محفل - 1 the life of the party, a charming man 2 wag, joker, a funny person, a funny chap •

نقلاً [náqlan] 1 literally, verbatim; word for word 2 according to tales, according to stories

نقل قول [naqleqawl] quotation ♦ مستقیم - *grammar* direct speech ◊ غیر مستقیم - *grammar* indirect speech

نقلیه [naqliya] 1 (also وسایل) means of transport 2 *military* train (not necessarily a railroad train), transportation units 3 transportation expenses, freight

نقیض [naqiz] 1 contradicting (something); opposite, contrary, opposed 2 *linguistics* antonym

نکات [nokaat] *plural of* نکته 1

نکاح [nekaah] wedding, marriage, matrimony ♦ عقد - marriage agreement, conjugal union
- بستن - to perform a marriage ceremony •
- کردن - 1 to marry, to contract matrimony [with], to join in marriage [with] (را) 2 [about a man] to marry (somebody را); to marry off (to somebody با) •

نکاح نامه [nekaahnaama] 1 marriage contract 2 marriage certificate

نکتایی [nektaayi] necktie

نکته [nokta] (*plural* نکات [nokaat]) 1 subtle thought, witty saying 2 circumstance, moment; consideration, reason ♦ نکات نازک ticklish circumstances, delicate circumstances

نکته گیر [noktagir] 1 carping; critic 2 pedant

نکره [nakara] *grammar* indefinite ♦ نشانه - (and) یای - indefinite article, "ya of indefiniteness" ◊ اسم - indefinite noun (with the indefinite article)

نکل [nekel] nickel

نکل کاری [nekelkaari] nickel-plating

نکهت [nakhat] ☞ نگهت

نگار [negaar]¹ 1 *present tense stem* نگاشتن 2 second component of compound words with meaning "writing" ♦ نامه نگار correspondent

نگار [negaar]² *literary* idol; sweetheart (female)

نگارش [negaaresh] writing; style ♦ اصول - style manual

نگاشتن [negashtan] (*present tense stem* نگار [negaar]) ☞ نوشتن

نگاه [negaah] 1 look, gaze 2 survey; sketch, essay ♦ نگاهی به ادبیات معاصر survey of modern literature
- انداختن - to cast a glance [at], to take in at a glance •
- اجمالی انداختن (به) - to make a brief survey (of something) •
- داشتن - 1 to hold, to support (something in some position) 2 to retain; to delay, to hold back, to keep [from] •
- کردن - 1 to take care [of], to keep, to preserve 2 to keep, to maintain (animals, birds, etc.) 3 to look [after] •

نگاهبان [negaahbaan] watchman, guard

نگاهبانی [negaahbaani] guarding protection, safeguarding
- کردن - to guard, to keep watch [over] •

نگاهداری [negaahdaari] 1 preserving, saving 2 care

نگاهداشت [negaahdaasht] ☞ نگهداشت

نگر [negar] *present tense stem* نگریستن

نگران [neg(a)raan] 1 watching [over], supervising (somebody or something) 2 maintaining order, observer ♦ صنف - 1 classroom supervisor; classroom instructor 2 classroom monitor

نگرانی [neg(a)raani] observing, maintaining (order), monitoring ♦ تحت - under the supervision [of], under the leadership [of]

نگریستن [negaristan] to look [at], to gaze [at] (را،به)

نگه [negah] ☞ نگاه
- داشتن - 1 to keep, to maintain (in safety, intact, in purity, in neatness, in cleanliness) ♦ خانه باید پاک نگهداشته شود The home should be kept in cleanliness. 2 to hold back, to stop 3 to preserve, to protect [from] (از) 4 to keep, to breed (birds, animals) •

نگهبان [negahbaan] ☞ نگاهبان

نگهت [naghat] *literary* aroma, fragrance

نگهداری [negahdaari] ☞ نگاهداری

نگهداشت [negahdaasht] 1 keeping, custody, storage, maintaining in safekeeping; handling or use (of something), care ♦ اصول - حسن - proper storage ◊ instructions for the care (of something) 2 keeping, breeding (of domestic animals, birds)

نگهداشتن [negahdaashtan] ☞ نگه داشتن in entry نگه

نگین [negin] (and) نگینه [negina] precious stone (mounted in a ring)

نل [nal] 1 pipe ♦ نل بخاری chimney 2 pipeline ♦ نل پطرول gasoline line 3 tube

نل آب [naleaab] water pipe, water supply line

نلبند [nalband] *technical* pipe sleeve

نلپیچ [nalpeech] tube of water pipe or of a hookah

نل دوان [naldawaan] 1 pipe layer 2 pipe fitter; plumber

نل دوانی [naldawaani] 1 laying water pipes 2 installation of a plumbing system

نم [nam] 1 moisture, dampness 2 wet, moist, damp
- نم کشیدن - to become damp, to become wet ♦ دیوار نم کشیده است The wall became damp. •

نماز [namaaz] namaz, prayer
- نماز پیشین ☞ پیشین •
- نماز دیگر ☞ عصر (and) دیگر •
- خواندن - to say a prayer, to pray •

نماز پیشین [namaaz (e) peshin] 1.1 midday prayer 1.2 noon, midday 2 at noon

نماز دیگر [namaaz(e)digar] 1 prayer said after midday (before sunset) 2 in the afternoon

نمازی [namaazi] *colloquial* 1 clean, pure, cleaned (of dirt or filth) 2 authoritative, deserving of faith or confidence ♦ حرف او – نیست One can't believe his words.

نما(ی) [nomaa(y)] 1 *present tense stem* نمودن 2 (also خرجی -) outward appearance, exterior, appearance, looks

نمایان [nomaayaan] 1 visible, distinguishable, discernible 2 striking, noticeable

نمایش [nomaayesh] 1 demonstration, show 2 performance, play (i.e., on the stage) 3 showing (of a motion picture); scene (of a play)
- دادن - 1 to show, to demonstrate 2 to give a performance •

نمایشگاه [nomaayeshgaah] exhibition

نمایشنامه [nomaayeshnaama] play (i.e., in a theater)

290

نمایندگی [nomaayendagi] **1** duties of a representative (of something or somebody) ♦ به -... on the instructions [of], on behalf [of], in the name [of] **2** representation
• تجارتی - commercial representation, commercial representatives, trade representation, trade representatives
• کردن - **1** to represent (somebody), to act in the name (of somebody) (از) **2** to witness something (از)

نماینده [nomaayenda] representative, delegate, authorized agent

نمبر [nambar] ☞ نمره

نمد [namad] thick felt, felting
• مالیدن - to mill felt

نمدمال [namadmal] felter, fuller

نمره [nomra] **1** number ♦ خانه - house number **2** grade, mark (on a test)
• اول نمره ☞ اول

نمک [namak] **1** salt ♦ طعام - salt, table salt **2** essence, point (of a story) **3** fascination, charm (of a personality), zest
• انداختن - to put salt (on food به)
• زدن- (را) to salt
• پاشیدن - به زخم کسی to rub salt in somebody's wounds

نمک پرورده [namakparwarda] **1** reared, brought up (by somebody) **2** foster child

نمک حرام [namakharaam] **1** returning evil for good; treacherous **2** traitor, scoundrel, villain

نمک حلال [namakhalaal] **1** grateful, remembering hospitality **2** faithful, devoted, staunch

نمک خور [namakkhor] **1** enjoying hospitality **2** ☞ نمک پرورد

نمک دان [namakdaan] (and) نمک دانی [namakdaani] salt cellar, saltshaker
• جاییکه نمک خوری - مشکن! *proverb* Don't smash the saltshaker where you have tasted the salt. (Don't spit in the well.)

نمکسار [namaksaar] salt marsh

نمکی [namaki] **1** salt, salty, salted **2** likable, charming

نمو [nomo] growing, growth to grow
• کردن - to grow up, to grow out of; to develop

نمود [nomud] **1** appearance, view, exterior ♦ پیش روی - front view **2** scene ♦ نمودی از زندگی مردم scene from the people's life, scene from popular life
• بخود گرفتن - to show, to become apparent, to take shape, to acquire visible features

نمودار [nomudaar] **1** apparent, visible **2** manifestation, evidence [of]; indicator
• از چیزی – بودن to be a manifestation of something, to attest to something

نمودن [nomudan (and) namudan] (*present tense stem* نما(ی) [noma(y)]) **1** to seem; to look [to look new] ♦ این امر به نزد ما طبیعی می‌نماید This [matter] seems natural to us. **2** component of compound words ♦ کوشش نمودن to try, to endeavor, to exert effort

نمون [nomun] second component of compound words with meanings "indicating" / "showing" ♦ راه نمون guide

نمونوی [nomunawi] taken as a standard; model *adjective*

نمونه [nomuna] **1** model, sample, standard, example ♦ برای نمونه as a sample, as an example **2** specimen, sample, standard **3** *colloquial* type (about a person) (can also have a contemptuous or pejorative connotation)

نندارتون [nendaartun] exhibition

ننگ [nang] **1** shame ♦ ازکار ننگ نیست to toil without shame **2** honor, dignity
• ننگ و ناموس ☞ و ناموس
• داشتن - to be ashamed, to consider (something) shameful for oneself (از)
• کردن - to refuse (something) out of pride; to be ashamed to accept (something from somebody)

ننگ و ناموس [nanganaamus] honor, reputation, good name

ننگین [nangin] shameful, disgraceful ♦ حادثه ننگین disgraceful event, shame, disgrace

ننه [nana] *colloquial* **1** mama, mommy **2** grandmother, grandma

ننی [nenee] *endearment children's speech* doll, dolly (about a child, nickname)

نو [naw] **1.1** new (not secondhand) ♦ بوت نو new shoes **1.2** new, fresh, the latest, recent ♦ ماه نو new moon **2** recently, just, just now ♦ ایشان نو آمدند They just arrived. / They arrived just now.
• سرازنو anew; again
• کردن نو *colloquial* to try fresh fruit for the first time (in the spring)

نوا [nawaa]¹ **1** voice, sound **2** tune, melody; motif

نوا [nawaa]² *rarely* fortune, means of subsistence
• به نوایی رسیدن to achieve prosperity, to be well-to-do

نوابغ [nawaabegh] *plural of* نابغه

نواحی [nawaahi] *plural of* ناحیه **1**

نواختن [nawaakhtan] (*present tense stem* نواز [nawaz]) **1** to play (a musical instrument) **2** *colloquial* to deal a blow [to], to hit, to slap ♦ یک چوب نواختش He hit him with a stick.

نوادر [nawaader] *plural of* نادره

نوار [nawaar] **1** braid; cord, string, lace **2** film, tape (of a tape recorder)
• بروی - ثبت کردن to record on tape
• نور - strip of light, band of light

نواز [nawaaz] *present tense stem* نواختن

نوازش [nawaazesh] caress, endearment, kindness; cordiality
• کردن - to treat affectionately (را); to show much kindness [to]; to caress, to pet, to stroke

نوازنده [nawaazenda] musician

نواسه [nawaasa] grandson; granddaughter

نوبانه [nawbaana] *abusive / abbreviation of* نوبماند May you not wear out your clothes! (a wish for a quick death)

نوبت [nawbat (and) nobat] **1** period (of time), interval **2** turn ♦ به - in turn, by turns **3** a bout (of fever), an attack (of fever) **4** intermittent fever

نو بدولت رسیده [nawbadawlatrasida] nouveau riche; upstart, parvenu

نوبه [nawba (and) noba] ☞ نوبت

نوت [not]¹ currency bill, banknote

نوت [not]² note; footnote
• کردن(گرفتن) - to make notes; to make an abstract, summary, or synopsis

نوت [not]³ *music* note

نوجوان [nawjawaan] **1** very young, quite youthful **2** youth, young man; a juvenile

نوحه [nawha] crying for the deceased, lamentation
• کردن - to cry, to lament (for the deceased)

نوحه گر [nawhagar] weeper, mourner (male and female)

نوحه گری [nawhagari] mourning (for the deceased), lamenting (for the deceased)

نوخانه [nawkhaana] *colloquial* a newlywed (man)

نوخط [nawkhaat] with fuzz above the lips, with sprouting whiskers

نود [nawad] ninety

نوده [nawda] a young sprout, shoot, sprig (of a tree)

نور [nur] light, beams of light ♦ آفتاب - beams of the sun, sunlight

نور چشم [nurechashm] 1 dear, darling, beloved 2 a dear child, a dear son, the light of one's eyes

نورد [naward] (and) نوردان [nawardaan] a roller (in a weaving loom), weaving beam

نورس [nawras] (and) نورسیده [nawraside] 1 just ripened, fresh (about fruit) 2 youthful, just grown-up ♦ دختر - a young girl

نورمال [normaal] 1 normal, usual 2 normally, usually

نوروز [nawroz] 1 New Year's Day, Nawroz (March 21 according to the Western calendar) ♦ عید - the New Year's holiday 2 *masculine proper name* Nawroz

نورونمک [nuronamak] charm, fascination, zest

نوزاد [nawzaad] just born, newborn

نوزده [nuzdah] nineteen

نوش [nosh] 1 sweet drink; honey, nectar 2 pleasure, enjoyment, delight
• هرجاکه - است نیش است *proverb* Where there is enjoyment there also is poison.
• جان -! You're welcome! / To [your] heart's content!
• جان کنید -! Enjoy yourself! / Drink / Eat to [your] heart's content!

نوشادر [nawshaader] ammonium chloride, sal ammoniac

نوشتن [naweshtan] (*present tense stem* نویس [nawis]) to write

نوشته [nawesh ta] 1 *past participle* نوشتن 2 writing
• کردن - to write

نوشکن [nawshekan]
• اراضی - newly-plowed virgin land

نوش و نعمت [noshone'mat] viands, various eats and drinks

نوشیدن [noshidan] to drink, to partake (of a beverage)

نوشیر [nawshir] 1 nursing (about a woman) 2 newly calved (about a cow)

نوع [naw'] (and) náwa] (*plural* انواع [anwa']) 1 sort, kind; category ♦ قوای مسلح – arm or branch of service ◊ در خود - in his, its way 2 *biology* genus 3 manner, way
• چه نوع؟ 1 What kind [of]? / Of what kind? 2 How? / In what way or manner?
• بشر - the human race, humanity

نوعیت [naw'iyat] 1 categorial affiliation, variety 2 specific character, specificity

نوک [nok] point, spike, pointed end, sharp tip ♦ قلم - tip of a pen
• افتو *colloquial* the first ray of the sun; sunrise

نوکار [nawkar] novice (in some matter), a beginner

نوکر [nawkar (and) nokar] 1 servant 2 serviceman

نوکری [nawkari (and) nokari] 1 post of servant 2 service, work (in an establishment) 3 *colloquial* military service
• کردن - to serve (including in military service)
• به - رفتن to go to work

نوکریوال [nokariwaal] on duty, duty *adjective* ♦ داکتر - doctor on duty ◊ نفر - *military* man on duty

نوکیسه [nawkisa] ☞ نوبدولت رسیده

نول [nol] (bird's) bill, beak
• زدن - to peck with the beak, to peck

نوله [nola] spout (of a teapot, of a watering can)

نومبر [nowambár] November

نومید [nawmeed] ☞ ناامید

نون [nun] name of the letter ن

نوید [nawid] good news, glad tidings

نویس [nawis] *present tense stem* نوشتن

نویسندگی [nawisendagi] authoring, writing; literary work

نویسنده [nawisenda] 1 knowing how to write ♦ خواننده و - literate 2 writer, author

نه [na] 1.1 no/not *negative particle* ♦ نه آنقدر زیاد not too much, not to that degree 1.2 ☞ نـ 1 2.1: نه...نه... neither... nor *compound conjunction* 2.2 نه تنها...بلکه... not only …, but even…

نه [neh] *present tense stem* نهادن

نه [noh] nine

نهاد [nehaad] 1 nature (of men) 2 *grammar* subject

نهادن [nehaadan] (*present tense stem* نه) to put; to place

نهار [nahaar] 1 on an empty stomach ♦ این دوا را میخورند This medicine is taken on an empty stomach. 2 (regional) hungry, not having eaten since morning ♦ من - استم I haven't eaten since morning. 3 ☞ نهاری

نهاری [nahaari (and) naari] morning meal, breakfast

نهال [nehaal (and) niyaal] young sapling, seedling
• شاندن - to plant trees

نهال شانی [nehaalshaani] planting of trees, planting of seedlings, transplanting of seedlings

نهایت [nehaayat] 1 extreme degree, limit ♦ با - خوش with great joy 2 very, extremely ♦ ضرور است - It is extremely necessary.

نهایی [nehaayi] 1 maximum, extreme 2 final

نهر [nahr] (*plural* انهار [anhaar]) large irrigation ditch; little river, rivulet

نهصد [nohsad] nine hundred

نهضت [nahzat] movement (as a social activity), political trend ♦ کارگری - workers' movement

نهفتن [nohoftan] to hide, to hide oneself, to conceal, to conceal oneself

نهنگ [nehang] whale

نی [nee] no, not *negative particle* ♦ گرسنه استی یانی؟ Are you hungry or not?
• نی تنها...بلکه... not only…, but even…

نی [nay] 1 cane, rush, reed ♦ نی چلم mouthpiece of a water pipe ◊ نی قلم reed pen 2 pipe (made from reed)
• نی زدن to play a reed pipe

نیابت [niyaabat] substitution [in an office or post], deputizing
• سلطنت – 1 regency; 2 vicegerency

نیاز [niyaaz] 1 need, want 2 request, entreaty, supplication 3 vow, promise, pledge 4 *masculine proper name* Niyaz
• نیاز کردن to ask, to request, to beg, to entreat (از)

نیاز مند [niyaazmand] needing (something); asking or begging for (something) ♦ نیاز مندان the poor, the needy

نیاز مندی [niyaazmandi] need, poverty

نیاکان [niyaakaan] grandfathers, great-grandfathers; ancestors, forefathers

نیایش [niyaayesh] *literary* entreaty, supplication
• کردن - to entreat God (for something); to pray (to God)

292

نیت [niyat] 1 will, desire 2 intention, design ♦ بد - evil intent
• بد قضای سر - proverb [He] who contemplates evil will be punished by fate.
• به… - for the purpose [of], with the intention [of]
• داشتن(کردن) - to intend, to contemplate

نیچه [naycha] 1 thin reed; a small pipe / fife, a small tube 2 (also تار) textiles bobbin 3 (also قلم - (and) خودکار -) writing cartridge, refill of a ballpoint pen 4 pinfeather (of a bird)
• زدن - colloquial to pop out, to sprout (about the feathers of a fledgling)

نیرنگ [nayrang] ruse, subterfuge, trick, stunt, swindle, fraud
• زدن - to use cunning, to cheat, to swindle; to trick

نیرنگباز [nayrangbaaz] a cunning person, a cheat, a swindler; a trickster

نیرو [nayro] 1 strength, force, energy; power, might 2 military force; army ♦ نیروی هوایی air force, air forces

نیرومند [nayromand] strong, powerful

نیز [niz] also, as well, too

نیزه [nayza] 1 lance, pike, spear 2 nayza (measure of length equal to the length of a lance or spear)
• او که از سر گذشت چه یک - چه صد - proverb If water rises higher than [one's] head, it's all the same whether it's by one nayza or a hundred.
• زدن - to lance, to spear

نیست [neest] opposite of هست، است does not exist, is not available, is not on hand ♦ اوبه خانه - He is not at home.
• ونابود کردن - (and) کرد - to destroy, to ruin, to annihilate

نیستی [neesti] 1 nonexistence 2 death, ruin, wreck, downfall, destruction 3 (also ناداری و -) need, poverty, indigence

نیش [neesh] 1 sting (of a bee, of a snake) 2 point, thorn ♦ سوزن - point of a needle 3 incisors (of man); fangs, tusks (of an animal)
• زدن - 1 to sting, to bite, to stab, to prick 2 to sprout, to spring (about seeds) 3 to cut, to erupt (about teeth) 4 to taunt, to tease

نیشتر [neeshtar] lancet, scalpel
• زدن - to dissect, to cut (with a lancet, with a scalpel)

نیشخند [neshkhand] venomous smile; sneer

نیشدار [neshdaar] caustic, biting; venomous (about words)

نیشکر [nayshakar] sugar cane

نیک [neek] 1 good, kind; kindly, happy ♦ کار - good deed 2 very good, as it should be ♦ درست - quite correctly, magnificently, perfectly

نیک اختر [neekakhtar] happy, lucky, successful

نیک اندیش [neekandeesh] ☞ نیک خواه

نیک بختی [neekbakhti] ☞ خوشبختی

نیک خواه [neekkhaah] 1 benevolent, well-wishing 2 a well-wisher; a benevolent person

نیکخو(ی) [neekxo(y)] 1 well-behaved; respectable 2 good, kind, of good character

نیکار [nikar] 1 shorts; trunks 2 obscure trousers, pants (narrow at the bottom)

نیکل [neekel] ☞ نکل

نیک نام [neeknaam] known for one's honesty, respected

نیکنامی [neeknaami] good name, good reputation

نیکو [neeko] 1.1 ☞ نیک 1.2 beautiful, handsome 2 nice, well
• گفتی - You said [it] well.

نیکوکار [neekokaar] 1.1 virtuous, of irreproachable conduct 1.2 doing good 2 a virtuous person or man

نیکوکاری [neekokaari] 1 virtue, decency 2 good deed; boon

نیکویی [neekoyi] 1.1 ☞ نیکی 1.2 beauty

نیک همجواری [neekhamjawaari] (and) نیک همسایگی [neekhamsaayagi] good-neighborliness, neighborly relations

نیکی [neeki] blessing, good; good deed, boon
• کردن - to do good
• به - یاد کردن - to think kindly, to speak kindly [of somebody]

نیل [nil] 1 indigo, blue paint dye 2 blue, bluing

نیلوفر [nilofar] 1 water lily 2 lotus

نیلون [naylon] nylon ♦ جراب - nylon stockings

نیلی [nili] dark blue, bright blue, of the color of indigo

نیم [nim] 1 half ♦ نان - half a loaf of bread, half a flatcake ◊ دو - two and a half ◊ بعد از دو - سال in two-and-a-half years ◊ نیم in half 2 (first component of compound words with meanings "half-" / "semi-"/ "under-"/ "incompletely") ♦ نیم رس semi-ripe ◊ نیم کاره unfinished, uncompleted

نیم بند [nimband]
• تخم - fried eggs

نیم تنه [nimtana] outer jacket (woman's); jacket; lined vest, padded vest

نیم جان [nimjaan] half-alive, barely alive

نیم جو [nimjaw] coarsely ground, crushed in large pieces

نیم جوش [nimjosh]
• کردن - to boil lightly, not to allow to be boiled soft (rice)
• تخم – poached egg

نیم چاشت [nimchaasht] the time before noon (ten to eleven o'clock)

نیمچه [nimcha] 1 ☞ نیم 2 colloquial juvenile; half-educated person 3 (first component of compound words with meaning "not having achieved perfection" (in something) / "a person of shallow learning") نیمچه ملا a mullah of shallow learning, a half-learned mullah

نیم خواب [nimkhaab] sleepy, half-asleep
• بودن - to be half asleep, to be not quite awake

نیم خورده [nimkhorda] ☞ پس خورده
• نخورد شیر - سگ - proverb It is not fit for a lion to feed on the leavings of dogs.

نیم خیز [nimkheez]
• شدن - to stand up, to rise (for a greeting, etc.)

نیم دایره [nimdaaira] semicircle, semi-circumference

نیم دم [nimdam] ☞ نیم جان

نیم راه [nimraah] half of journey, the middle of a journey
• رفیق – fair-weather friend, unreliable comrade

نیم راهی [nimraahi (and) nimraayi]
• کردن - 1 to take a shortcut 2 to return after going halfway

نیم رس [nimras] half-ripe, unripened ♦ زردآلوی - an unripened apricot

نیم روز [nimroz] 1 midday, noon 2 obscure south 3 historical Nimroz (ancient name of Seistan or Sistan)

نیم رویه [nimroya] colloquial half-turned, from the side ♦ عکس - photograph in profile

نیم سری [nimsari] colloquial headache, migraine

نیم سوخته [nimsokhta] charred remains (of something) ♦ چوب - charred log; smoldering brand
• او ـ چوب واری است colloquial He is just like a charred brand (about an emaciated man).
نیم قطر [nimqótor] radius
نیم کاره [nimkaara] unfinished, uncompleted, incomplete
نیم کاسه [nimkaasa] small basin, small tureen ☞ کاسه
• زیر این کاسه ـ است colloquial There is something behind that. / There is some kind of dirty trick here.
نیم گول [nimgul] (also - سوهان) technical half-round file
نیمه [nima] 1 ☞ نیم 1 2 colloquial not full, half-full ♦ این بوطل ـ است This bottle is [only] half full.
نیمه جان [nimajaan] 1 ☞ نیم جان 2 barely, just barely, scarcely, hardly ♦ آتش میان اجاق ـ میسوخت The fire in the hearth was just barely burning.
نیمه خیالی [nimakhiyaali] half-mythical, half-imaginary, semi-fictitious
نیمه شب [nimashab](and) نیمه شو [nimashaw] 1 midnight 2 around midnight, at midnight
نیمه گی [nimagi] in two, half and half, in half, in halves
• ـ کردن to divide in two, to divide half and half; to cut into two parts, to cut into two halves
نی نواز [naynawaaz] 1 piper, one who plays a pipe, one who plays a reed pipe 2 playing a pipe, playing a reed pipe
نیی [nayi] reed, rush, made from reed or rush adjective ♦ قلم ـ reed pen, pen made from reed

و
30th letter of the Dari alphabet

و [wa, o (and) w]¹ 1 and conjunction ♦ آمد وگفت He came and said 2 but ♦ احمد رفت و من نرفتم Ahmad left, but I didn't.
• وغیره and so forth, and so on, etcetera
• مه وتو colloquial you and I
و [o (and) no]² (linking vowel in compound words and expressions) ♦ آب و هوا climate
وا [waa] ☞ وای
• وا به جانت colloquial You'd better watch out [for me]! / You'd better beware of me!
وابستگان [waabastagaan] plural of وابسته
وابستگی [waabastagi] 1 tie, bond, connection, relation; dependence 2 kinship, relationship, kindred relationships
وابسته [waabasta] (plural وابستگان [waabastagaan]) 1 adherent, follower; advocate, supporter 2 a relative
• ـ بودن to be tied [to], to be connected [with], to depend [on] (به)
واپس [waapas] back, backwards
• ـ آمدن to return, to go back, to come back
وات [waat] electrical watt
واترپمپ [waatarpamp] water pump
واجب [waajeb] 1 mandatory, compulsory, necessary 2.1 (plural واجبات [waajebaat]) duty, responsibility 2.2 religious instructions
واجبی [wajebi] 1 mandatory, compulsory, indispensable 2 necessary, due
• ـ است without fail; it is the custom, as one is supposed to
واحد [waahed] 1.1 unit ♦ اداری - administrative unit ◊ پولی - monetary unit ◊ قیاسی - unit of measurement 1.2 (also - نظامی) military subunit, military unit 2 united, unified; whole, entire, aggregate total, overall
واخ [waakh Oh! / Eh! interjection
وادار [waadaar] present tense stem واداشتن
• واداشتن ☞ - ساختن
واداشتن [waadaashtan] (present tense stem وادار [wadar]) 1 to impel, to compel 2 to hold, to not let go, to keep from, to stop
واده [waada] colloquial ☞ وعده
وادی [waadi] river valley; oasis ♦ هلمند - Helmand River valley
وار [waar] suffix forming 1 words with the meaning of "likeness" / "resemblance" ♦ فهرست وار like a list, like a copy 2 words with meaning of "length" (of cloth, etc.) ♦ یک کرتی وار one coat length
وار [waar]
• ـ کردن colloquial to throw, to hurl, to toss
وارث [waares] heir
وارثی [waaresi] inheritance; legacy
وارخطا [waarkhataa] 1.1 confused, perplexed, embarrassed 1.2 agitated, perturbed, alarmed 2 in confusion; in embarrassment; in fright; in panic ♦ اطفال - دویدند The children fled in panic.
• ـ کردن to throw into confusion; to confuse, to disturb, to embarrass; to frighten, to scare
وارخطایی [waarkhataayi] confusion, perplexity; embarrassment
وارد [waared] 1 incoming; arriving; forthcoming 2 inflicted [by], caused [by] ♦ آوردن - to inflict; to cause
• ـ شدن to enter; to arrive; to be forthcoming, to be received
• ـ کردن to import
واردات [waaredaat] 1 an import 2 imported goods
وارداتی [waaredaati] import, imported ♦ اشیای - imports, articles of import
وارده [waareda] 1 ☞ وارد 2 (also مکتوب های) office incoming correspondence
• ـ گرفتن to register incoming documents, to log incoming documents
وارستگی [waarastagi] deliverance, salvation
وارستن [waarastan] literary to be delivered [from], to be freed
وارسی [waarasi] control, monitoring, check, inspection
واره [waara] colloquial benefit, gain, profit (in trade)
واره دار [waaradaar] colloquial advantageous, profitable (in trade)
واری [waaree] postposition 1 like, as adverb ♦ ما ـ درس بخوان Study as we do! / Learn as we do! 2 similar, like adjective ♦ طفل ما ـ like our son
واز [waaz] 1 open; opened 2 opened (about a bud) 3 unsealed, opened (about a package); undone
• ـ کردن 1 to open 2 to unseal, to open (a package, etc.) 3 to let out, to unravel (e.g., laces)
واسطه [waaseta] (plural وسایط [wasaayet]) 1 means, tool 2 medication, patronage
• به ـ by means [of], with the aid [of]; owing to denominative preposition
• ـ داشتن enjoy the patronage [of], to have a "hand," to have a [helping] "hand"

و

- شدن • - to mediate, to be a mediator
- سلام مرا به مادرتان - شوید • Please give [my] regards to your mother!

واسکت [waaskat] 1 men's vest (worn under a jacket) 2 sleeveless jacket, sleeveless blouse 3 underbodice, brassiere

واسوخت [waasokht]
- شدن • - colloquial 1 not to be fully satisfied or content (with something) 2 to remain half hungry 3 not to have [enough] time to see enough (of somebody)

واشل [waashal] technical washer; gasket ♦ رابری - rubber washer, gasket

واصل [waasel] to arrive, to come [in], to be received (about correspondence, etc.)

واصله [waasela]
- اسناد - • incoming documents; documents received

واضح [waazeh] 1 evident, obvious, clear 2 clear-cut, definite
- ♦ مطلب بیخی - است • The question is perfectly clear.

واعظ [waa'ez] 1 one who delivers sermons, a preacher 2 tutor, teacher

وافر [waafer] 1 abundant plentiful; rich 2 large

واقع [waaqe'] 1 happening, occurring 2 found, located, settled, set, placed (somewhere) 3 actual, real ♦ جهان - objective world
- بودن • - to be located, to be found, to be settled, to settle (somewhere)
- شدن • - 1 to happen, to occur 2 to turn out [to be], to prove [to be]
- مؤثر شدن • to prove to be effective, to have an effect

واقعاً [waaqean] actually, really, in fact ♦ این درست نیست - But that's really not so.

واقعات [waaqe'aat] plural of واقعه

واقعه [waaqe'a] 1 (plural واقعات [waaqe'aat]) fact, case, occurrence 2 (plural وقایع [waqaaye']) event, incident, accident ♦ محل - scene of an accident or incident

واقعی [waaqe'i] 1.1 real genuine, actual, true ♦ این کار - است This is a fact. 1.2 philosophical opposite of خیالی real, objectively existing 2 (also - به) really, in fact

واقعیت [waaqe'iyat] actuality, reality; actual state of affairs
- باید این-را بپذیرید که ۰۰۰ • You must acknowledge the fact that …

واقف [waaqef] knowing, versed [in], experienced [in]; informed
- بودن • - to know, to be informed, to be in the know

واکسین [waaksin] vaccine ♦ کولرا - (anti-) cholera vaccine ◊ - تطبیق vaccination

واگذار [waagozaar] present tense stem واگذاشتن
- شدن • - to be placed at (somebody's) disposal, to come under (somebody's) disposal
- کردن - ☞ • واگذاشتن

واگذاشتن [waagozaashtan] (present tense stem واگذار [waagozaar]) to give back, to give up, to leave (at somebody's disposal), to grant

وال [waal] technical valve

والا [waalaa] colloquial (suffix of noun of agency) ♦ شیروالا milk vendor, milkman ◊ خروالا donkey owner

والا [waaellaa] if not, then …; otherwise conjunction

والاحضرت [waalaahazrat] his highness

والاقدر [waalaaqadr] and والاشأن [waalaashan] (and) obscure highly esteemed (when addressing persons of high rank)

والده [waaleda] polite mother, mama

والدین [waaledayn] parents, father and mother

وال ساکت [waalsaaket] electrical socket, receptacle, wall socket

والسلام [waassalaam] And that's it! / And that's all! / And that's the end of it! / And that's the end of the matter!

والله [waallaa (h)] Really and truly! / I swear to God! interjection

والی [waali] ruler of a district, governor-general

والیبال [waalibaal] volleyball

وامانده [waamaanda] colloquial 1 left without supervision (e.g., about a child) 2 unfortunate, helpless, having gotten into a desperate situation

وان [waan] suffix of a noun of agency ♦ موتروان driver, chauffeur

وانمود [waanomud]
- کردن • - to depict, to portray (something); to pretend [to], to feign

واو [waaw] name of the letter و
- مجهول • - the sound "obreve" in the vowel system of the Dari language

واوا [waawaa] 1 ☞ واه in entry واه 2 children's speech something good; a good thing

واوایی [waawaayi] 2 ☞ واوا
- چه کالای - پوشیدی • ironic Oh, how dressed up you are!

واول [waawaal] vowel sound, vowel phoneme ♦ عطف - grammar a linking vowel (in compound words)

واه [waah] (and) واه واه Oh! That's what I like! / That's more like it! / Well done! (in expressing approval, in expressing delight) interjection ♦ واه واه چه مقبول است Oh, how beautiful!

وای [waay] interjection O! / Oh! / Oh, woe! ♦ برای خدا - Oh, help! ◊ به حال آنها - Woe is me! ◊ به حال من - I'll show them!

وایلون [waaylon] ☞ ویلون

وبا(ه) [wabaa (h)] epidemic, pestilence, plague, epidemic diseases

وتیره [watira] literary method, manner ♦ به این - thus / in this manner, so

وسایق [wasaayeq] plural of وثیقه

وثیقه [wasiqa] (plural وثایق [wasaayeq]) official paper; document; certificate
- بدون- • unofficial, uncertified

وجد [wajd] 1 delight, rapture 2 religion ecstasy, exaltation

وجدان [wejdaan] conscience

وجوب [wojub] philosophical opposite of امکان necessity

وجود [wojud] 1 being, existence 2 presence 3 body, organism ♦ انسان - human organism ◊ He بخار در تمام وجودش دیده میشود - has a rash over his entire body. 4 individual, person
- داشتن • to take place, to occur, to be
- به-آمدن • to appear, to arise
- با-آنکه (اینکه) • despite the fact that …

وجوه [wojuh] plural of وجهه [wájha]
- گرامری • grammatical categories

وجهه [wájha] (plural وجوه [wojuh]) 1 side, aspect 2 sum of money 3 manner, mode, way ♦ به-احسن in the best (possible)

و

manner 4 *grammar* mood

• رفته- ٭ invariable form of verb with the ending " "
• وصفی-

وحدانیت [wahdaaniyat] 1 singleness, soleness (of God) 2 monism

وحدت [wahdat] unity, wholeness ٭ فکر- harmony of ideas / identity of ideas ◊ ملی- national unity

• -ی ٭ *grammar* auxiliary formant "e" (expressing indefiniteness)

وحش [wahsh] wild animal, beast
• باغ-٭ zoo, zoological park

وحشت [wahshat] 1 great fear, terror, horror 2 savagery, wildness

• افتادن-به 1 to be horrified, to be terrified 2 to become wild

وحشت آور [wahshataawar] inspiring terror, frightful, dreadful, terrible ٭ فریاد- terrible howl, terrible wail

وحشت زده [wahshatzada] 1 extremely frightened, terror-stricken 2 in panic, in terror

وحشتناک [wahshatnaak] ☞ وحشت آور

وحشی [wahshi] 1.1 wild, savage 1.2 unsociable 2 a savage, a barbarian

وحشیگری [wahshigari] 1 wildness, barbarity 2 brutality, atrocity, cruelty

وحی [wahy] *religion* revelation granted by God

وخامت [wakhaamat]
• اوضاع- tenseness (of a situation); danger, threat, menace

وخت [wakht] ☞ وقت

وخم [wákhem] escheat
• از سرت- بانه ٭ *abusive* May you die without heirs!

وخیم [wakhim] strained, tense, serious ٭ عاقبت- serious consequences

وداع [wedaa'] parting, farewell, leave-taking
• کردن- (با) to part, to take leave [of one another], to say goodbye, to bid farewell

ودان [wadaan] (*also* -آهنگری) large forge hammer, sledgehammer

ودیعه [wadi'a] 1 guarantee, security (deposit), pledge, pawn 2 deposit

ور [war] *adjectival suffix* ٭ نام ور distinguished, eminent, well-known

وراثت [weraasat] 1 inheritance 2 legacy, heritage

ورد [werd]
• زبان بودن- to be on [one's] lips all the time, to repeat oneself

وردار [wardaar] *present tense stem*

ورداشت [wardaasht] ☞ برداشت

ورداشتن [wardaashtan] (*present tense stem* وردار [wardaar]) ☞ برداشتن

وردک [wardak] Wardak (name of an Afghan tribe)

ورزش [warzesh] sports, exercises, gymnastics ٭ بدنی- physical culture

ورزشی [warzeshi] sports *adjective*, athletic ٭ مسابقه- sports competition, athletic competition

ورزیدن [warzidan] *rarely* (component of compound verbal combinations) ٭ استفاده- to make use [of], to use

ورزیده [warzida] 1 experienced 2 trained, conditioned, hardened

ورشکست [warshekast] having failed, bankrupt

ورشکستن [warshekastan] to fail, to go bankrupt; to be ruined, to ruin oneself

ورق [waraq] (*plural* اوراق [awraq]) 1 sheet (of paper) 2 page (of a book) 3 ☞ ورقه 4 hunk, chunk ٭ گوشت- یک slice of meat

• (زدن) گرداندن- to leaf (through), to turn (a page)

ورقه [waraqa] paper, document, certificate ٭ رخصتی- pass ◊ هویت- identification card

ورکشاپ [warkshap] 1 shop, workshop ٭ ترمیم موتر- automobile repair shop 2 plant, factory

ورم [waram] 1 tumor; swelling, edema 2 abscess, boil

ورود [worud] 1 coming, arrival; entrance, entry 2 receipt (of something), delivery

وریب [wreeb (and) wrib] 1 slanting, canted, sloped 2 flared ٭ دامن- flared skirt

ورید [warid] *anatomy* 1 vein 2 jugular vein
• داخل-٭ intravenously

وزارت [wazaarat] ministry ٭ خارجه- Ministry of Foreign Affairs

وزراء [wozaraa] *plural of* وزیر

وزن [wazen] 1 (*plural* اوزان [awzaan]) weight, heaviness ٭ با- مخصوص- net weight ◊ خالص- gross weight ◊ بارجامه- specific weight, specific gravity 2 weight, significance, importance; authority; prestige 3 rhythm, time ٭ شعر- rhythm of a verse, meter (of a verse) 4 (the order of vowelizations in a word)

• داشتن- 1 to weigh 2 to have weight, to have authority or prestige
• کردن- to weigh (on scales)

وزنین [waznin] 1 heavy 2 weighty, solid

وزیدن [wazidan] to blow [in / into], to blow (about the wind)

وزیر [wazir] (*plural* وزرا [wazaraa]) 1 minister ٭ خارجه- Minister of Foreign Affairs 2 *historical* vizier 3 *chess* queen

وزیری [waziri] Waziri (Afghan tribe)

وزین [wazin] ☞ وزنین
• اثر-٭ a significant work [e.g., of literature], an original work

وساطت [wasaatat] 1 mediation 2 intercession ٭ با- with the mediation [of]; with the intercession [of]

وسایط [wasaayet] *plural of* واسطه 1.1
• نقلیه- means of transport, means of transportation

وسایل [wasaayel] *plural of* وسیله
• تولید- means of production
• به خود- by one's own resources

وسط [wasat] 1 middle *noun*, middle part; center 2 average, middling, mediocre

وسطی [wasati] middle *adjective*, medium *adjective*; intermediate

وسطی [wostaa]
• آنگشت-٭ middle finger
• شرق وسطی Middle East
• قرون-٭ Middle Ages

وسعت [wos'at] 1 wide open space or expanse; extensiveness ٭ دشت- the vastness of the steppe 2 width, breadth, scope, range

• دادن-٭ to enlarge, to widen, to expand, to develop; to spread, to disseminate, to propagate

وسعت نظر [wos'atnazar] possessing a broad horizon, possessing a broad mental outlook

وسمه [wasma] wasma, black hair-dye
- کردن ‏ - to color with wasma, to color with black hair-dye (eyebrows, hair)

وسواس [waswaas] 1 anxiety, nervous state 2 doubt, misgiving, apprehension

وسوسه [waswasa] 1 fixed idea; obsession 2 ☞ وسواس

وسیله [wasila] (*plural* وسایل [wasayel]) means, method of communication, support
- پیدا کردن ‏ - 1 to find means 2 to help, to support

وصال [wesaal] 1 meeting, rendezvous, date (with a beloved) 2 *religion* decease, demise, death

وصف [wasf] (*plural* اوصاف [awsaaf]) 1 property, characteristic, quality, trait 2 description, testimonial, reference 3 praising, praise
- کردن ‏ - 1 to describe, to characterize 2 to extol, to eulogize, to praise

وصفی [wasfi] 1 descriptive 2 *grammar* determinative, determinant
- فعل ‏ impersonal form of verb (translated by participle or gerund)

وصل [wásel] 1 joining, junction, merging 2 fastening, tying together, binding together
- کردن ‏ - to join, to connect, to unite; to bind, to tie together, to fasten

وصلت [waslat] 1 joining, meeting (of lovers) 2 relationship, relationship by marriage
- کردن ‏ - 1 to marry 2 to become in-laws, to become relatives

وصله [wasla] 1 rag, shred, scrap 2 patch 3 *grammar* wasla (diacritical mark)

وصول [wosul] 1 arrival 2 receipt (e.g., of money)
- کردن ‏ - to be received

وصی [wasi] *literary* 1 executor (of a will) 2 guardian, trustee

وصیت [wasiyat] 1 (last) will, testament 2 behest, legacy, precept
- کردن ‏ - to bequeath, to leave by will or testament

وضاحت [wazaahat] clarity, lucidity, clearness; definiteness

وضع [waz' (and) wáza] 1 introduction, establishment (e.g., of a law, of a custom) 2 (*plural* اوضاع [awzaa]) situation, condition, state, status ♦ مادی ‏ - financial position 3 conduct, behavior; manner, manners ♦ این آدم خوبی دارد ‏ - That / this man has a pleasant manner.
- کردن ‏ - 1 to introduce, to establish (a law, a custom) 2 to calculate, to deduct, to subtract
- حمل ‏ - delivery of a child, childbirth

وضعیت [waz'iyat] 1 state, status, condition; situation ♦ اراضی ‏ - relief of the terrain 2 *sports, military* stance, standing position, position

وضو [wazu (and) wozu] ablution before prayer
- کردن ‏ - to perform the rite of ablution, to perform the ceremony of ablution

وطن [watan] 1 homeland, fatherland 2 (*plural* اوطان [awtaan]) native land, place of birth

وطن پرست [watanparast] ☞ وطن دوست

وطن پرستی [watanparasti] ☞ وطن دوستی

وطن دار [watandaar] compatriot; fellow countryman / fellow townsman; fellow citizen

وطن دوست [watandost] patriot

وطن دوستی [watandosti] patriotism

وطنی [watani] 1 local, indigenous, native; home, domestic ♦ منسوجات ‏ - fabrics of domestic production 2 fellow countryman, fellow townsman; compatriot ♦ جنگ ‏ - war for the homeland, patriotic war

وظایف [wazaayef] *plural of* وظیفه

وظیفه [wazifa] (*plural* وظایف [wazaayef]) 1 duty, responsibility ♦ عسکری ‏ - military duty 2 service, work, job 3 task, function, purpose ♦ دستوری ‏ - grammatical function 4 daily prayer ♦ او هر روز یک ساعت میکند ‏ - He prays for an hour every day. 5 pension, allowance; dole (to the needy)
- خود دانستن ‏ - to consider (something) one's duty
- اجرای کردن ‏ - to carry out one's responsibilities, to serve
- داخل بودن ‏ - to be on duty; to serve

وظیفه دار [wazifadaar] 1 official, official in charge 2 ☞ وظیفه شناس

وظیفه شناس [wazifashenaas] conscientious, responsible; endowed with a sense of duty

وظیفه شناسی [wazifashenaasi] conscientiousness, responsibility; sense of duty

وعا [we'aa] (*plural* اوعیه [awiya]) *anatomy* blood vessel; capillary

وعده [wa'da (and) waada] 1 time, period 2 promise, [one's] given word ♦ و وعید ‏ - promises and threats 3 compact, agreement, contract, appointment 4 (*also* دیدار -) prearranged time, appointed hour; appointment, rendezvous
- دادن ‏ - to promise
- کردن ‏ - 1 to arrange (with somebody to do something) 2 to set a time, to set a deadline

وعده دار [wa'dadaar]
- من از امروز ‏ - هستم ‏ - I have a date / rendezvous / appointment today.

وعظ [wa'z] sermon
- کردن ‏ - to deliver a sermon, to preach

وفا [wafaa] faithfulness, fidelity, loyalty, devotion, constancy
- کردن ‏ - to be faithful, to be loyal, not to change
- به وعده خود کردن ‏ - to keep [one's] word, to fulfill a promise

وفات [wafaat] 1 death, decease, demise 2 (*plural* وفیات [wafiyaat]) fatal incident

وفادار [wafaadaar] faithful, loyal, true, devoted; constant

وفاداری [wafaadaari] faithfulness, loyalty, fidelity, devotion
- کردن ‏ - to keep faith, to remain faithful, to be constant, not to change

وفرت [wafrat] abundance, plenty ♦ آب ‏ - abundance of water ♦ به ‏ - abundantly, in abundance, in a great number

وفیات [wafiyaat] 1 *plural of* وفات 2 mortality, death rate ♦ نسبت ‏ - average mortality, average death rate

وقار [waqaar (and) weqaar] importance, pomposity; staidness, sedateness ♦ با ‏ - pompously; gravely, staidly, sedately; with dignity

وقایع [waqaaye'] *plural of* واقعه 2

وقایوی [weqaayawi] precautionary, protective; preventive, prophylactic 2 ‏ - طب ‏ preventive medicine

وقایه [weqaaya] 1 preventive measures (in medicine), prophylaxis 2 spine (of a book)
- کردن ‏ - to conduct a preventive inspection, to perform prophylaxis

وقت [waqt] 1 (plural اوقات [awqaat]) time; interval of time ♦ بسیار - پیش ◊ long ago, long since ◊ به - کم within a short time ◊ یگان - sometime 2 در - سر in good time, opportunely, in time ◊ colloquial early ♦ زلمی - از خواب می خیزد Zalmay wakes up early.
- وقتیکه ☞ وقتی که ...
- از آن - که ... since the time when..., since the time that..., ever since...
- من یگان - به هرات میروم I will go to Herat sometime.
وقتاًفوقتاً [waqtanfawaqtan] from time to time; at times
وقتیکه [waqteeke] while; when
وقف [waqf] (plural اوقاف [awqaaf]) 1 waqf, waqof (real estate given or bequeathed for the benefit of a mosque) 2 ownership or possession of real estate (under certain conditions)
- کردن ● 1 to bequeath (an estate, etc.) as a waqof 2 to dedicate (something to somebody)
وقف نامه [waqfnaama] deed to property donated to a mosque
وقفه [waqfa] 1 stop, delay 2 break, intermission, pause 3 grammar dash 4 stagnation, depression, slump, recession ♦ فعالیت اقتصادی - a recession in economics
وقوع [woqu'] 1 appearance, onset, coming 2 accomplishment (of an action, etc.) ♦ زمان - حادثه - event, fact, case ◊ grammar tense of action (of a verb) 3 arrangement, order (of movement) ♦ ترتیب - کلمات درجمله order of words in a sentence
وقوف [woquf] conversance; knowledge, understanding
وکالت [wakaalat] 1 deputation; representation 2 powers
- دادن ● to confer powers [on]
- به - انتخاب شدن ● to be elected a deputy
وکالت نامه [wakaalatnaama] document about authority, about powers; warrant, power of attorney
وکلا [wokalaa] plural of وکیل
وکیل [wakil] (plural وکلا [wokalaa]) 1 deputy (of a town council, of a parliament, of a majles) 2 confidential agent, authorized agent, representative 3 lawyer ♦ مدافع - (law) counsel for the defense
وگرنه [wagarná] but if not, then ...; otherwise
ولا [welaa] literary territory, district
ولادت [walaadat] birth, delivery, childbirth ♦ طبیعی - natural childbirth
- کردن ● to give birth [to], to bring into the world
ولادی [walaadi] pertaining to birth or to delivery, pertaining to childbirth; maternity, labor ♦ پولی کلنیک - maternity home, lying-in hospital
ولانس [walaans] chemistry valence
ولایات [welayat] plural of ولایت
ولایات [welaayaat] (plural ولایت [welaayat]) 1 welayat, province, district; state ♦ کابل - Kabul Province 2 governorship
ولایت [walaayat] 1 literary mystical merging with the deity (through self-resignation); holiness 2 clairvoyance
ولتاژ [woltaazh] electrical voltage ♦ تغذیه - power supply voltage
ولچک [wolchak] ☞ اولچک
ولد [walad] (plural اولاد [awlaad]) infant, child, baby; son
ولدنگ [weldeng] technical welding ♦ برقی - electric welding
ولدنگ کاری [weldengkaari] technical welding, welding work, welding operations

ولس [wolos (and) olos] people, population inhabitants ♦ این - قشلاق the inhabitants of this village
ولسی [wolosi (and) olosi] people's, popular
- ولسی جرگه ☞ جرگه
ولسی جرگه [wolosi-jerga] People's Council, popular council (lower house)
ولکتون [walaktun] kindergarten
ولوله [walwala] noise, hubbub, din, racket, uproar; turmoil, commotion
- انداختن ● to raise an uproar, to make a din, to make commotion
ولی [wali] (plural اولیا [awliya]) 1 esteemed person; saint 2 patron, guardian 3 masculine proper name Wali
ولی [wale] but, however conjunction
ولیعهد [waliahd] crown prince
ولیکن [walikan] literary but, however conjunction
ولی نعمت [waline'mat] 1 benefactor 2 master
وند [wand] grammar affix
ونگ ونگ [wangwang]
- کردن ● colloquial to whimper, to snivel (about a child)
وهم [wahm] (plural اوهام [awhaam]) 1 apprehension, anxiety; doubt 2 whim, caprice; fantasy, fancy
وی [way] he; she
ویران [wayraan (and) weeraan] 1 destroyed, demolished, razed; ruined, devastated, wasted 2 uninhabited, deserted, abandoned
ویران کار [wayraankaar] 1 destroyer, ravager 2 vendor of spare parts, vendor of scrap metal ♦ دکان - spare parts store
ویرانه [wayraana] 1 debris, ruins 2 an uninhabited place, a deserted or abandoned place
ویرانی [wayraani] 1 devastation, destruction ruin 2 state of being uninhabited, of being deserted
ویرگول [wergul] (and) ویرگیول [weergiul] comma
ویش [weesh] wesh (periodic reallotment of land among Afghan tribes)
ویلا [wilaa] villa
ویلون [waylon] violin, fiddle

ه
31st letter of the Dari alphabet

ه abbreviation of هجرت ♦ درسال ۱۰۰۱ ه in the year 1001 of the hegira
[-a] suffix of nouns, adjectives and participles ♦ خنده laughter ◊ رنگه colored ◊ بسته locked
ها [haa]¹ (also هوز های) name of the letter ه
- زینه [zina] ♦ های خاموش the silent "h"
ها [haa]² particle colloquial 1 Yes! / Good! / All right! / Okay! 2 Look out! / Be careful! / Beware! 3 (question) Eh?
ها [haa] plural suffix ♦ بچه ها children, lads, boys, fellows
هادی [haadi] 1 spiritual father, leader 2 leader, instructor; tutor, mentor, teacher
هارس پاور [haarspaawar] physics horsepower
هارمونیم [haarmuniyam] (and) هارمونیه [haarmuniya] accordion
هارن [haaran] 1 bugle, horn 2 automobile horn, siren
- کردن ● to hoot, to honk, to blow [a horn or siren], to signal
هاضمه [haazema]
- جهاز - digestive tract

298

هان [haan] *colloquial* **1** Of course! But what about …? / How in the world? **2** So, let's see now …
هاوان [haawaan] mortar ♦ خفیف - light mortar
هاونگ [haawang] mortar (and pestle)
هایدروجن [haaydrojan] hydrogen ♦ بم - hydrogen bomb ◊ کلوراید - hydrochloric acid
هایدروسفیر [haaydrosfeer] hydrosphere
های و هوی [haayohuy] (and) های هوی [haayhuy] noise, din, hubbub, racket; bustle, turmoil
های های [haayhaay] loud weeping, howls, groaning, moaning
هجا [heja] syllable ♦ حروف - alphabet
هجایی [hejaayi] **1** syllabic **2** consisting of syllables ♦ سه - trisyllabic (about a word)
هجران [hejraan] *literary* separation
هجرت [hejraat] **1** migration, emigration **2** *historical* the hegira (the flight of Mohammed from Mecca to Medina on 16 July 622 - the beginning of the Moslem system of chronology)
♦ کردن - to move, to migrate, to emigrate
هجری [hejri] numbered on the basis of the hegira (the Moslem system of chronology)
هجو [hajw] satire, ridiculing
هجوم [hojum] **1** attack; assault **2** attack (of locusts)
♦ آوردن - **1** to make an attack, to storm, to assault **2** to rush in a body (toward somewhere), to swoop down [on]
هجومی [hojumi] attacking ♦ قوای هوایی - attack aviation
هجویه [hajwiya] accusatory poem; epigram; lampoon
هجی [heji]
♦ کردن - **1** to read by syllables, to read by pronouncing each syllable distinctly **2** to read letter by letter
هدایت [hedaayat] guide, manual, instructions
♦ کردن - to guide, to give instructions
هدایت نامه [hedaayatnaama] instructions, directions, directive
هدر [hadar]
♦ به - رفتن to prove to be in vain, to perish for naught
هدف [hadaf] (*plural* اهداف [ahdaaf]) **1** goal, purpose **2** target
هدیه [hadiya] gift, present
♦ کردن - to make a present [of], to give [as a gift]
هذا [hazaa] *literary* this ♦ درسنه - [in] that year
هذیان [hazyaan] **1** delirium, fever **2** ravings
هر [har] any, every, each ◊ هر آنکه anyone who ◊ هرجا (and) هرکجا everywhere, anywhere; no matter where ◊ هرچه anything that, anything which ◊ هردفعه every time, each time ◊ هریک از شما each of us
♦ هرچه باداباد What will be, will be!
هراتی [heraati] **1** Herat *adjective*, of Herat ♦ لهجه - the Herat dialect **2** an inhabitant or native of Herat
هراس [heraas] fear, fright, dread
هرجایی [harjaayi] **1** tramp, vagrant; lazybones, good-for-nothing loafer ♦ زن - woman of loose morals, prostitute **2** unprincipled, unscrupulous; inconstant
هرج و مرج [harajomaaraj] **1** confusion, muddle, chaos **2** disorders, riots, disturbance
هرچند [harchand] **1** though; despite the fact that … **2** ☞ هرقدر

هردم خیال [hardamkhiyaal] *colloquial* whimsical; capricious; unbalanced
هرنگه [harranga] every, every possible, all sorts and kinds [of]; all colors and hues
هرزه [harza] foolishness, nonsense
هرزه گرد [harzagard] idler; slovenly person, featherbrain
هرقدر(که) [harqadar (ke)] as much as …, no matter how … *compound conjunction*
هرکاره [harkaara] **1** courier, messenger; peddler, hawker **2** efficient person, adroit person; jack of all trades
هرکس [harkas] each person, every person
هرگاه [hargaah] never
هرگز [hargez] **1** when **2** if
هروقت(که) [harwaqt (ke)] when; every time that, every time when
هروی [herawi] ☞ هراتی **1**
هزارداستان [hazaardaastaan] (*also* - بلبل) *poetic* nightingale
هزاره [hazara] Hazara, the Hazaras (name of a people in Afghanistan)
هژده [hazhda] eighteen
هست [hast] **1** to be, is, exist, **2** life, being, existence
♦ کردن - to create
هستوبود [hastobud] ☞ هستی **2**
هستوی [hastawi] ☞ هسته یی
هسته [hasta] **1** *physics biology* nucleus ♦ اتوم - atomic nucleus **2** kernel, essence, crux, basis (of something), foundation (of something)
هسته یی [hastayi] *physics* nuclear ♦ بم - nuclear bomb
هستی [hasti] **1** being, existence **2** property, belongings
هشت [hasht] eight
هشتاد [hashtaad] eighty
هشتصد [hashtsad] eight hundred
هشتن [heshtan] (*present tense stem* هل [hel]) **1** to leave, to let go **2** to permit, to authorize, to allow
هضم [házem] **1** digestion **2** (in various meanings) assimilation
♦ کردن - to digest, to assimilate
هفت [haft] seven
هفتاد [haftaad] seventy
هفت اقلیم [hafteqlim] *poetic* the whole world, the entire earth; the universe
هفتالی [haftaali] *historical* **1** Ephthalite *adjective* **2** an Ephthalite
هفت پوست [haftpost] a deep boil, a furuncle
هفتصد [haftsad] seven hundred
هفت لا [haftlaa] puff, made of puff paste ♦ نان - flatcakes made of puff paste
هفت میوه [haftmeewa] haftmewa (a traditional holiday food made of several kinds of raisins, roasted peas, and nuts)
هفته [hafta] week
هفته بارانک [haftabaaraanak] (and) هفته بارش [haftabaaresh] *colloquial* incessant spring rain
هفته گی [haftagi] **1** ☞ هفته وار **2** weekly pay of an apprentice in a shop or store
هفته وار [haftawaar] weekly ♦ جریده - weekly newspaper, a weekly (i.e., a publication)
هفت هیکل [hafthaykal] seven prayers (copied from the Koran and used as an amulet)
هفده [hafda] seventeen

هکذا [hakazaa] thus, so, in that way; in the same way or manner

هکک [hekak] hiccuping, hiccup
- زدن - to hiccup

هک وپک [hakopak] *colloquial* 1 dumbfounded, stunned 2 having lost one's head, crazed

هل [hel] *present tense stem* هشتن

هلاک [halaak]
- شدن - 1 to lose one's life, to perish; to be killed 2 *colloquial* to exert oneself to the utmost, to overstrain oneself, to strain oneself (on the job, at work)
- کردن - to ruin; to destroy; to kill

هلاکت [halaakat] 1 destruction, wreck, downfall, ruin, ruination; death 2 calamity, disaster, catastrophe

هلال [helaal] new moon; crescent (moon); half-moon

هلالین [helaalayn] quotation marks

هله [hala] (and) هله هله [hala-hala] *colloquial* Giddap! / Off with you! / Begone! / Go ahead! / Move out!

هلیکوپتر [helikoptar] helicopter

هم [ham]¹ 1 and, and also *conjunction* ♦ تو هم او را ندیدی؟ And you [also] didn't see him? / You didn't see him either?
- هم ... هم - both ... and
- هم دهل میزند هم سرنای *colloquial* [He] both beats the drum and plays the lute. (Run with the hare and hunt with the hounds.) (about someone who tries to please opposing sides) 2 and; but; (particles used to indicate contrast or opposition) ♦ پدرش هم باغبان بود But his father was a gardener.

هم [ham]²
- با هم together; with each other, with one another; between themselves *reciprocal pronoun*
- بهم ☞ به هم
- به هم آمدن *intransitive* to close, to shut (about eyes)

هم [ham] 1 (word-building prefix meaning "fellow-", "like-") ♦ هم وطن fellow-countryman ◊ همفکر like-minded person 2 intensifying prefix ♦ همان the very same

هما [homaa] ☞ همای

همان [hamaan] the same; the very same (person or thing) ♦ همان چیز است - [It is] the same thing.

هم آهنگ [hamaahang] 1 consonant [with], in harmony [with]; harmonious 2 unanimous, solid

هم آهنگی [hamaahangi] 1 consonance; harmony; agreement coordination ♦ به - in unison with... 2 unanimity, solidarity

همای [homaay] *mythology* a bird that brings happiness and good luck

همایون [homaayun] *literary* happy, blissful

همایونی [homaayuni] royal, imperial, most august (in the title of a monarch) ♦ ذات - most august person, monarch, sovereign

هم بازی [hambaazi] 1 partner (in a game, in a sport) 2 partnership

همباق [hambaaq] ☞ امباق

همت [hemmat] 1 valor, courage 2 fervor, zeal 3 *masculine proper name* Hemmat
- کمر بستن - to toil selflessly (for the good of something), to fight valiantly (for something)

همجنس [hamjens] 1 fellow-tribesman, kinsman 2.1 of the same race, breed, species, kind, etc. 2.2 of the same grade or sort, of the same quality

همجوار [hamjawaar] neighboring; contiguous

همجواری [hamjawaari] neighborhood, vicinity ♦ حسن - good neighborliness, neighborly relations

هم چشم [hamchashm] 1 equal, not conceding (anything to anybody) 2 rival

همچشمی [hamchashmi] rivalry; competition

همچو(ن) [hamcho (n)] (and) همچه [hamche] such, this kind of, like, similar, of the same kind ♦ در - موارد in such cases, in similar cases

همدرد [hamdard] 1 sympathetic; empathetic 2 friend; consoler, comforter

همدردی [hamdardi] sympathy; empathy ♦ اظهار - expression of condolence

همدست [hamdast] accomplice, partner, confederate ♦ آنها با یک دیگر - میباشند They are all (in something) together.

همدیگر [hamdigar]
- با - one with another, with each other, together
- روبروی - against each other, face to face, vis-a-vis

همراز [hamraaz] *poetic* close friend; confidant, keeper of secrets

همراه [hamraah] (and) همرای [hamraay] 1 companion, fellow traveler 2 escorting (somebody) 3.1 (also - با) with; together with; jointly with *denominative preposition* ♦ او صحبت داشتم - I had a talk with him. ◊ ما چه کار داری؟ - What business do you have with us? 3.2 with, by means [of], with the aid [of] *denominative preposition* ♦ قاشق - with a spoon
- داشتن - to carry with oneself; to have on one's self; to be accompanied (by something) ♦ نسیم بهار عطر گل - دارد The spring breeze carries with itself the scent of flowers.

همرنگ [hamrang] identical, of the same kind or type; similar

همزمان [hamzamaan] synchronous, simultaneous

همزه [hamza] hamza (the mark ء which signifies a glottal stop in words of Arabic root)

همساز [hamsaaz] friend, comrade; assistant, helpmate; like-minded person, companion-in-arms, brother-in-arms

همسال [hamsaal] a coeval, someone of the same age [as somebody else]

همسایه [hamsaaya] 1 neighbor ♦ دربدیوار - close neighbor 2 *historical* sharecropper (who works land close to the halting place of a nomadic tribe)

همسبق [hamsabaq] ☞ همصنف

همسر [hamsar] wife

همسری [hamsari]
- کردن - to strive to be equal (to somebody); to claim to be equal (to somebody)

همسن [hamsen (n)] ☞ همسال

همشیره [hamshira] 1 foster sister 2 sister (form of address for women)

همصنف [hamsenf] school friend, schoolmate, classmate

هم عصر [hamasr] 1 contemporary modern 2 a contemporary

همفکر [hamfékr] 1 sharing (somebody's views); solidarity [with] 2 like-minded person

همکار [hamkaar] collaborator, fellow worker; colleague

همکاری [hamkaari] joint work, collaboration

همگذر [hamgozar] a neighbor living on the same street

همگی [hamagi] ☞ همه گی

همنشین [hamneshin] associate, partner, friend; companion

همنشینی [hamneshini] friendly company, social intercourse, amicable relations

هموار [hamwar] 1 even, smooth; flat ♦ راه - smooth path 2 even, smooth; uniform
- کردن - 1 to make even, to make smooth, to smooth, to level; to smooth out, to smooth over 2 to spread, to lay
- (برای) راه - کردن to prepare soil (for something)
- بر خود – داشتن to take on oneself, to go to … (some kind of difficulty, etc.)

هم وطن [hamwatan] compatriot; fellow countryman, fellow townsman

همه [haama] 1 the whole; entire, whole 2 all ♦ شاگردان - all students ◊ مردم - all people 3 each, every ♦ سال - every year

همه جا [hamajaa] everywhere

همه کاره [hamakaara] knowing how to do everything, master of all trades; a hard worker

همه گی [hamagi] 1 everything; in total, in the aggregate 2 all ♦ مهمانها - رفتند All the guests left.

همهمه [hamhama] noise, talk
- انداختن - to make a racket, to cause talk

همیانی [hamyaani] a small bag for money

همیش [hameesh] (and) همیشه [hameesha] always, constantly; eternally, perpetually, everlastingly

همیل [hameel] ☞ امیل

همین [hamin] the same, the very same; it is precisely this one ♦ دیروز - just yesterday, only yesterday

همینطور [hamintawr] in the same manner, in just this way, just so ♦ باید باشد - It should be thus!

همینکه [haminke] as soon as, no sooner than … conjunction

هندسه [handasa] (also علم) geometry

هندل [handal] ☞ اندل

هندو [hendu] Hindu

هندوستانی [hendustaani] 1 Indian adjective 2 Indian noun

هندوسوزان [hendusozaan] place of cremation of the dead among the Hindus

هندی [hendi] (plural هنگ [honud]) 1.1 Indian adjective 1.2 an Indian 2 (also زبان -) the Hindi language

هنر [honar] 1 art, artistic trade or profession ♦ اهل - painters; artists 2 skillfulness, ability, skill, mastery craftsmanship 3 talent

هنرمند [honarmand] 1 artist; painter; art figure 2.1 able, skillful, clever (about somebody) 2.2 talented

هنری [honari] pertaining to art, artistic ♦ هیئت - a delegation of art figures

هنگاف [hangaaf] ☞ انگاف

هنگام [hangaam] time, period of time

هنگامه [hangaama] 1 noisy assemblage, a crowd 2 noise, hubbub, stir, hullaballoo; bustle, turmoil 3 skirmish, encounter, conflict, clash

هنگامیکه [hangaamee-ke] while; when conjunction

هنود [honud] plural of هندی 2.1

هنوز [hanuz] still, yet, for the present ♦ تا - up to now, for the present, for the time being

هوا [hawaa]¹ 1 air ♦ تازه - fresh air 2 weather ♦ خراب - bad weather 3 desire, wish, aspiration ♦ وطن - a desire to see [one's] native land, a yearning for [one's] native land
- وهوس - 1 passion 2 whim, caprice 4 arrogance, conceit, self-importance
- خوردن - to breathe fresh air, to be in the open (air), to be out of doors
- دادن - to air; to set out in the sun
- (به) رفتن - colloquial to die for nothing
- گرفتن - colloquial 1 to be aired out, to be ventilated 2 to get puffed up, to give oneself airs
- هوای اتاق رابدل کردن to air out a room, to ventilate a room
- واری است colloquial He is weak and emaciated (literally, [Only his] soul is holding [him] together).

هوا [hawaa]² tune, motif, melody

هواباز [hawaabaaz] pilot, aviator

هوابازی [hawaabaazi] aviation, flying, aeronautics, piloting ♦ میدان - civil aviation ◊ ملکی - airfield

هواخواه [hawaakhaah] 1 supporter, partisan, adherent, follower 2 disposed (in favor of somebody), loving (somebody)

هواخوری [hawaakhori] walk, stroll (in the fresh air)

هوادار [hawaadaar] having enough air (about a room or premises), spacious, roomy

هوارسیده گی [hawaarasidagi] colloquial a cold, grippe, flu, influenza

هواشناسی [hawaashenaasi] meteorology

هواکش [hawaakash] 1 casement window, ventilating pane 2 air vent

هوایی [hawaayi] 1 adjective air, aviation ♦ پوسته - airmail ◊ ترافیک - air communications ◊ قوای - air force, aviation 2 light, empty, frivolous

هوتک [hotak] (and) هوتکی [hotaki] Hotaki (Ghilzai tribe)

هودج [hawdaj] saddle on an elephant (in the form of an arm chair with a canopy)

هوز [hawwaz] (the second group of letters according to the Abjad (☞ ابجد), including ه و ز)
- های - name of the letter "ه"

هوس [hawas] strong desire, bent, inclination; passion
- کردن - to desire strongly, to crave, to lust [for]

هوسانه [hawasaana] a favorite dish, a favorite food (prepared, for example, for a sick person)

هوس رانی [hawasraani] dissoluteness, licentiousness, indulgence in one's passions

هوش [hosh] 1 mind, reason, intellect 2 understanding 3 ability to feel, consciousness
- هوش و گوش ☞ و گوش -
- کردن - 1 to beware, to be careful, cautious 2 to guard, to keep watch [over]
- به آمدن to come to one's senses, to regain consciousness
- به - آوردن to bring (somebody) to [his, her, their] senses (literally and figuratively)
- رفتن - 1 to lose consciousness 2 to be badly shaken

هوش پرک [hoshparak] colloquial confused, perplexed; agitated

هوش و گوش [hoshogosh]
- هوش و - گرفتن to listen carefully; to concentrate [on] ♦ گوشش طرف بازی است He is engrossed in the game.

هوشیار [hoshyaar] 1 possessing a clear mind 2 vigilant, watchful, circumspect, wary 3 sober

هوشیاری [hoshyaari] 1 clarity of mind, sense, prudence 2 vigilance, circumspection, discretion 3 soberness, sobriety, temperance

ی

هویت [howiyat] individuality, identity ♦ این شخص معلوم نیست - This person's identity has not been established. ◊ ورقه - identity card, identification card

هویدا [howaydaa] literary 1 clear, obvious, evident 2 ascertained, established
• ساختن - to make obvious; to clear up, to ascertain

هی [hay] Hey! (in urging on an animal)
• کردن 1 - to urge on (a horse); to drive (a vehicle) 2 to drive, to drive away

هیجان [hayajaan] 1 agitation, excitement ♦ عصبی - nervous excitement 2 alarm, anxiety, uneasiness

هیچ [heech] 1 none, no kind of, no … whatever ♦ شک نیست که ••• - There is no doubt whatever that … ◊ به دول - by no means 2 nothing, anything ♦ ندیدم - I didn't see anything. ◊ از - کرده بهتر است [It's] better than nothing.
• بر - sports a draw, a tie

هیچکس [heechkas] nobody
هیچوقت [hechwaaqt] never
هیچ یک [hechyak] not one, none, no kind of; nobody
هیزم [heezom] firewood
هیزم کش [heezomkash] 1 laying in and selling firewood 2 stoker, furnace man
• دوزخ - colloquial gossip, scandalmonger, slanderer

هیکل [haykal] 1 sculpture, statue 2 figure, figurine, statuette
هیکل تراش [haykaltaraash] scupltor
هیکل تراشی [haykaltaraashi] (and) هیکل سازی [haykalsaazi] carving out of stone (figures of people and animals); sculpture, sculpturing

هیل [heel] botany cardamom
هیلیوم and هیلیم [heeliyam] chemistry helium
هیهات [hayhaat] literary Alas! Woe is me! interjection ♦ که ایام جوانی طی شد - Alas, the days of youth are over!
هی هی [hay-hay] interjection Hey-hey! / Oh-oh! / There-there! (in expressing regret or pity)
• کردن 1 - to pity, to be sorry [for]; to lament 2 to drive, to urge on
• به پاده ونظر به گاو خود - colloquial To pasture the [whole] herd, but watch over [only] your own cow.

هینت [hay'at] 1 staff membership, board ♦ رئیسه – presidium ◊ وزیران - cabinet of ministers 2 organ, body, apparatus ♦ مقننه - legislative body 3 team, crew, party ♦ اطفائیه - fire-fighting team

ی
32nd letter of the Dari alphabet

یا [yaa]¹ 1 name of the letter ی and the sounds designated by it ♦ یای معروف "i" 2 ◊ یای مجهول historically long vowel "e" ♦ name of a number of grammatical and word-building formants ♦ یای مصدری the indefinite article ◊ یای تنکیر suffix of abstract nouns ◊ یای نسبت suffix of relative adjectives

یا [yaa]² conjunction or ♦ یا •••, either … or …
• یا تخت است یا تابوت - proverb Either the throne or the grave. (Either all or nothing.)

یا [yaa]³ interjection Oh! ♦ یا خدا Oh God! / Oh Lord!
یاالله [yaallaa (h)] interjection Now then! / Come! / Let's! ♦ برداریم - Let's get, going!

یاب [yaab] present tense stem یافتن

یابو [yaabu] pack horse, draft or draught horse
یابیدن [yaabidan] ☞ یافتن
یاد [yaad] memory; recollection
• دادن 1 - to teach, to instruct, to train 2 colloquial to prompt, to put (somebody) up to do (something)
• داشتن 1 - to keep in memory, to remember 2 to know how [to], to be able [to] ♦ دارد موتررانی راخوب - He knows how to drive a vehicle well.
• شدن 1 - to be mentioned, to be referred [to], to be noted 2 to be named
• کردن 1 - to mention, to remember, to recall
• به نیکی - کردن to think kindly [of somebody], to speak well [of somebody] 2 colloquial to honor with a gift, to present (something) (as a remembrance, as a sign of respect) ♦ یادت مه کنم سیرت خدا کنه My deed is to honor you, but God will satiate you. (said upon presenting a gift) 3 to memorize, to learn by heart 4 to call, to name (something-somehow)
• گرفتن - to learn, to master
• از بردن - to forget
• به بودن - to be remembered, to be kept in memory ♦ پوره به یادم است که ••• I well remember that …

یادآور [yaadaawar]
• شدن - to mention, to note; to remind (از,را)
یادآوری [yaadaawari] reminder, reminding ♦ ••• میشود که - epistolary We remind [you], that …; we direct your attention to the fact that …

یادبود [yaadbud]
• به - memories of somebody, in memory of somebody
• روز - day of remembrance, day dedicated to somebody or something
• محفل - memorial meeting

یادداشت [yaaddaasht] 1 note, record, entry ♦ کتابچه - notebook 2 note, memorandum
• کردن - to take notes, to note, to jot down, to record

یادداشته ها [yaaddaashthaa] memoirs
یاددهانی [yaaddehaani]
• کردن - to remind (somebody of somebody or something) (از)

یادگار [yaadgaar] 1 memory (of something) 2 memorial 3 gift of remembrance, souvenir
یادوبود [yaadobud] ☞ یادبود
یار [yaar] 1 friend, comrade ♦ جانی – bosom friend ◊ و یاور - friend and helpmate 2 dear one, sweetheart, beloved (female) 3 lover (male) 4 masculine proper name Yar
• چهار - historical the first four caliphs-the successors of Mohammed
• زنده صحبت باقی - colloquial If we live, we'll meet.

یاری [yaari] 1 help, support 2 friendship, attachment, affection
• کردن - to help, to aid, to assist
• بخت به من - کرد Fate was good to me.

یازده [yaazda] eleven
یازنه [yaazna] sister's husband, brother-in-law
یأس [ya's] despair, woe, sorrow, desperation
یأس آور [ya'sawar] (and) یأس انگیز [ya'sangeez] full of despair, sorrowful ♦ خاطره - a sad recollection, a sad memory
یاسمن [yaasaman] lilac; jasmine

ی

یاسین [yaasin] yasin (one of the chapters of the Koran that is usually read over the sick and dying)

یاغستان [yaaghestan] *historical* Yaghestan (one of the names of a belt of independent Afghan tribes between Afghanistan and British India)

یاغی [yaaghi] 1 rebel, insurgent, mutineer, rioter 2.1 rebellious, insurgent, mutinous 2.2 stubborn, obstinate (e.g., about a horse)
- شدن - to stir up a riot, to stir up a rebellion or revolt, to rebel (against somebody)

یاف - [yaaf] *colloquial present tense stem* یافتن
- می یافیم we obtain; we find

یافتن [yaaftan] (*present tense stem* یاب [yaab] and *colloquial* یاف [yaaf]) 1 to find 2 to obtain, to receive, to get

یاقوت [yaaqut] ruby; sapphire; garnet

یال [yaal] 1 mane (of a horse) 2 withers, nape of the neck

یالان [yaalaan] cape, cloak; overcoat without sleeves ♦ - کوتاه pelerine cape

یاور [yaawar] 1 adjutant, aide-de-camp, aide 2 assistant, accomplice

یاوه [yaawa] nonsense, rubbish
- گفتن - to chatter pointlessly, to talk nonsense

یتیم [yatim] orphan; fatherless child

یخ [yakh] 1.1 ice 1.2 cold, frost 2 cold, icy, ice; very cold *adjective*
- یخ بستن to freeze, to be covered with ice
- یخ شدن to get cold, to become cool, to cool down ♦ هوا یخ شد It has gotten colder.
- یخ کردن 1 to freeze, to feel cold, to suffer from the cold, to shiver ♦ دست وپایش یخ کرد His hands and feet are stiff / numb from the cold. 2 to cool off, to cool
- دل خود را یخ کردن to satisfy one's passion (or feeling of revenge); to unburden one's soul

یخ آب [yakhaab] (and *colloquial* یخ او [yakhaw]) 1 water with ice 2 the last spring watering of root crops (before they are dug out of the garden)

یخبندی [yakhbandi] freezing (of lakes, of streams); freeze-up, complete freezing

یخچال [yakhchaal] 1 ice house, ice box (in the mountains); *geology* glacier ♦ دوره - glacial epoch, ice age 2 refrigerator

یخدان [yakhdaan] 1 hole for storing ice (to be sold) 2 a large trunk (bound with iron)

یخمالک [yakhmaalak] sliding on ice, skating (on ice)
- زدن - to skate (on ice)

یخمن [yakhman] *botany* mountain cherry or cherries; mountain bushes (with small red edible berries)

یخن [yakhan] collar (of a shirt, of a dress) ♦ گرد - round collar
- به - شدن *colloquial* to grapple (with somebody), to come to blows in a fight, to get into hand to hand fighting
- کسی را بدست کسی دادن to get somebody reprimanded, to place (somebody) in an unpleasant situation

یخن کنده [yakhankanda] *colloquial* cutthroat, ruffian; riff-raff; rabble

یخنی [yakhni] 1 meat broth ♦ گوشت - boiled meat 2 sauce, gravy, dressing (for meat, for pilaf)

یخه [yakha] ☞ یخن [yakhan]

ید [yad] *literary* 1 hand 2 power, might, strength
- ید طلا داشتن to be master (in some matter or business); to wield (some skill or trade) skillfully

یرغمل [yarghamal] hostage

یزدان [yazdaan] *literary* God, the Lord

یشت [yasht] the Yashts (of the Avesta, the scriptural work of Zoroastrian religion)

یعنی [ya'nee] that is; in other words

یغما [yaghmaa] 1 robbery, pillage, plundering 2 booty, spoils, loot

یقین [yaqin] 1 true, right, undeniable 2 confidence, certitude, conviction, persuasion
- داشتن - to have confidence, to know precisely

یک [yak] 1 unit, one ♦ یک فیصد one percent ◊ یک یک one by one 2 one, some, a certain ♦ یک روز some day, once 3 the same, identical, one and the same ♦ یک چیز است [it's] one and the same ◊ یک رقم of one kind, of one sort
- یکنیم ☞ یک(و)نیم
- یک تیر و دو فاخته (To kill) two birds with one arrow (stone).
- یک جو *colloquial* a little bit
- یک دم one second or instant, for just a second or instant ♦ یک دم آرام باش Calm down (even) for just an instant!
- یک عمر all [one's] life

یک انداز [yakandaaz] 1 whole, unbroken, continuous, entire ♦ قالین - a rug (that covers the entire floor of a room) 2 wholly, as a whole, in complete form

یکایک [yakaayak] one after the other; thoroughly, in detail ♦ سرگذشت خود را - به من گفت He told me in detail about everything that had happened to him.

یکباره [yakbaara] 1 at once; at one go, at a stretch 2 suddenly, all of a sudden

یک برابر [yakbaraabar] equal; identical; equivalent ♦ اول حمل روز وشب - میشود At the beginning of the month of Hamal the days become equal to the nights.

یک بردو [yakbardu]
- ساختن - to increase twofold, to double

یک بره [yakbara] *colloquial* single (about fabric or cloth); of one width, of the same width

یک بغله [yakbaghala] heeled over, listed; fallen to one side
- شدن - to list, to heel over, to be on one side, to slip down

یک پای گاو [yakpaaygaaw] *obscure* measure of land area equal to half a qolba ☞ قلبه

یک پهلو [yakpahlu] *colloquial* straightforward, frank, truthful, sincere

یکتا [yaktaa] 1 one and only; unique, exceptional 2 one item, one piece

یگانه پرستی [yaktaaparasti] ☞ یکتا پرستی

یکجای [yakjay]
- شدن - 1 to gather together; to unite 2 to flow together, to merge (about rivers, etc.)

یک جایی [yakjaayi] 1 together; as a whole, on the whole 2 at once, all at once ♦ تنخواه دو ماهه خود را - گرفته بود He received two months' salary all at once 3 in full, in total, as a whole
- آستین - raglan sleve

یک چند [yakchand] 1 a certain amount or quantity, some 2 a little; somewhat

یک خاشه [yakkhaasha] *colloquial* very little, a little bit

303

ی

یکدانه [yakdaana] 1 only, sole 2 the only one of its kind, matchless, peerless 3 (also بافت -) a stitch without increase (in knitting)

یک دست [yakdast] 1.1 accomplice, confederate, like-minded person 2.1 uniform, similar, of the same quality; made by the same master 2.2 ☞ یک انداز 1

یک دل [yakdel] unanimous, solid

یکدیگر [yakdigar] ☞ همدیگر

یکرنگ [yakrang] 1 identical 2 monotone; one-color; plain, unfigured (about cloth or fabric) 3 ☞ یکپهلو

یکرویه [yakroya]
• تخم - fried eggs

یکسان [yaksaan] 1 identical, equal; uniform 2 identically, in equal measure; uniformly
• کردن - to make uniform, to unify

یک سر [yaksar] at once, right away, without delay

یکشنبه [yakjambe] Sunday

یک طرفه [yaktarafa] 1 one-sided, unilateral 2 unilaterally
• کردن - to decide finally; to settle (a matter, a problem)

یک لا [yaklaa] 1 single (about cloth or fabric) 2 colloquial emaciated, gaunt, lean

یک لخت [yaklokht] 1 whole; unbroken; not detached ♦ - پیراهن one-piece dress 2 wholly, as a whole; in whole form, in one piece
• و بی تکه - colloquial frankly, openly, not hiding anything

یک لنگه [yaklenga] colloquial 1 one-legged, hobbling on one leg 2 solitary, single; helpless, feeble; deserted; orphaned

یک مشت [yakmosht] colloquial handful, a small quantity or amount

یک مشتپر [yakmoshtepar] colloquial 1 weak, feeble, sickly, puny, thin and feeble 2 having aged very much, having become decrepit

یک موی [yakmoy] (with the negative) not a drop, not at all, not in the least, not a bit ♦ - فرق ندارد does not differ by a single drop

یکنفس [yaknafas] at once; at one go, at a stretch; at one stroke

یک نیم [yaknim] one and a half ♦ ساعت - one and a half hours ◊ صد - one hundred and fifty

یکه [yakka] 1 one, sole 2.1 one-horse (carriage) 2.2 *cards* ace

یکه دانه [yakadaana] premises, room with one window ☞ ارسی

یکه راست [yakarast] directly, at once, right away

یکه یکه [yakka-yakka] colloquial ☞ یکه یکه

یگان [yagaan] some, some kind of, a kind of, one ♦ چیز - something, anything ◊ کسی - somebody, anybody ◊ وقت - some time, some day, ever

یگانگی [yagaanagi] 1 unity 2 community, relationship, kinship 3 uniqueness, exclusiveness

یگانه [yagaana] one, sole, only ♦ فرزند - only son

یگانه پرستی [yagaanaparasti] monotheism

یله [yala] ☞ ایله [ela]

یله سر [yalasar] 1 released (to freedom), set free 2 left without care or without supervision, orphaned

یله گرد [yalagard] colloquial 1 an idler, a lounger; a homeless waif ♦ پشک - stray cat 2 tramp, vagrant, dissolute man

یله گردی [yalagardi] roaming idly; loafing

ینگه [yanga] wife of one's brother, sister-in-law

یوچی [yuchi] historical Yueh-Chih or Yuechi (ancient people)

یورانیم [yuraaniam] chemistry uranium

یورش [yuresh] raid, foray; attack

یوز [yuz] (also یوزپلنگ) cheetah, hunting leopard

یوزباشی [yuzbaashi] obscure commander of a hundred men

یوسفزی [yusofzay] Yusofzai (a group of tribes)

یوغ [yugh] 1 yoke (in harness of oxen) 2 figurative yoke ♦ زیر کسی آمدن - to fall under somebody's yoke

یوم [yawm] (plural ایام [ayaam]) day

یومیه [yawmiya] 1 day; daily 2 ordinary, commonplace adjective

یونانی [yunaani] Greek adjective, Hellenic ♦ طب - Eastern medicine

یونیورستی [yuniwersity] university

یهودی [yahudi] 1 Jewish, Hebrew, Judaic 2 Jew, Hebrew, Israelite

ییلاق [yaylaaq] summer place (among nomads)